D1162720

ENGLISH

COMMUNICATION SKILLS IN THE NEW MILLENNIUM

LEVEL I

J.A. Senn
Carol Ann Skinner

BARRETT KENDALL PUBLISHING
AUSTIN, TEXAS

Project Manager
Sandra Stucker Blevins

Editorial Director
Sandra Mangurian

Editorial Staff
Marianne Murphy
Kim Choi
Marlene Greil
Donna Laughlin
Susan Sandoval
Vicki Tyler
Catherine Foy
Michelle Quijano
Elizabeth Wenning
Cheryl Duksta
Margaret Rickard

Production Directors
Gene Allen
Pun Nio

Photo Research and Permissions
Laurie O'Meara

Art and Design
Pun Nio
Leslie Kell
Rhonda Warwick

Production
Bethany Powell
Isabel Garza
Rhonda Warwick

Cover
Leslie Kell Designs
Pun Nio
Images © Photodiscs, Inc.

Editorial and Production Services
Book Builders, Inc.
Gryphon Graphics
Inkwell Publishing Solutions, Inc.
NETS

Barrett Kendall Publishing has made every effort to locate the copyright holders for the images and text used in this book and to make full acknowledgement for their use. Omissions brought to our attention will be corrected in a subsequent edition.

Printed in the United States of America.

ISBN 1-58079-110-7 2 3 4 5 6 7 RRD 06 05 04 03 02 01

Senior Consultants

Tommy Boley, Ph.D.
Director of English Education
The University of Texas at El Paso
El Paso, TX

Deborah Cooper, M.Ed.
Coordinating Director of PK-12 Curriculum
Charlotte-Mecklenburg Public Schools
Charlotte, NC

Susan Marie Harrington, Ph.D.
Associate Professor of English, Director of Writing, Director of Placement and Assessment, and Adjunct Assistant Professor of Women's Studies
Indiana University-Purdue University, Indianapolis
Indianapolis, IN

Carol Pope, Ed.D.
Associate Professor of Curriculum and Instruction
North Carolina State University
Raleigh, NC

Rebecca Rickly, Ph.D.
Department of English
Texas Tech University
Lubbock, TX

John Simmons, Ph.D.
Professor of English Education and Reading
Florida State University
Tallahassee, FL

John Trimble, Ph.D.
University Distinguished Teaching Professor of English
The University of Texas
Austin, TX

Contributing Writers

Jeannie Ball

Grace Bultman

Richard Cohen

Elizabeth Egan-Rivera

Laurie Hopkins Etzel

Bobbi Fagone

Lesli Favor

Nancy-Jo Hereford

Susan Maxey

Linda Mazumdar

Elizabeth McGuire

Shannon Murphy

Carole Osterink

Michael Raymond

Duncan Searl

Jocelyn Sigue

Lorraine Sintetos

James Strickler

Diane Zahler

Kathy Zahler

Critical Readers

Alan Altimont
St. Edwards University,
Austin, TX

Larry Arnhold
Deer Park High School,
Houston, TX

Kerry Benson
Santa Fe Public School,
Santa Fe, NM

Elaine Blanco
Gaither High School,
Lutz, FL

Peter Bond
Randolph School,
Huntsville, AL

Christina M. Brandenburg
Rancho Cotate
High School,
Rohnert Park, CA

Paulette Cwidak
John Adams High
School, South Bend, IN

Jean Ann Davis
Miami Trace High
School, Washington
Courthouse, OH

Terri Dobbins
Churchill High School,
San Antonio, TX

Susan Drury
Springwood High
School, Houston, TX

David Dunbar
Masters School,
Dobbs Ferry, NY

Chuck Fanara
Brebeuf Preparatory,
Indianapolis, IN

Jason Farr
Anderson High School,
Austin, TX

Marilyn Gail
Judson High School,
San Antonio, TX

Gary Gorsuch
Berea High School,
Berea, OH

Monica Gorsuch
MidPark Sr. High School,
Cleveland, OH

Donna Harrington
Churchill High School,
San Antonio, TX

Janis Hoffman
John Adams High
School, South Bend, IN

Norma Hoffman
John Adams High
School, South Bend, IN

David Kidd
Norfolk Academy,
Norfolk, VA

Kate Knopp
Masters School,
Dobbs Ferry, NY

Suzanne Kuehl
Lewis-Palmer High
School, Monument, CO

Michelle Lindner
Milken Community High
School, Los Angeles, CA

Stephanie Lipkowitzs
Albuquerque Academy,
Albuquerque, NM

Sarah Mfon
Hubbard High School,
Chicago, IL

Linda Martin
Valley Torah,
North Hollywood, CA

Lisa Meyer
Lincoln High School,
Tallahassee, FL

Karla Miller
Durango High School,
Durango, CO

Stacy Miller
Santa Fe High School,
Santa Fe, NM

Eddie Norton
Oviedo High School,
Oviedo, FL

Diana Perrin
Johnson High School,
Huntsville, AL

William Petroff
R. Nelson Snider High
School, Ft. Wayne, IN

Linda Polk
Deer Park High School,
Houston, TX

Lila Rissman
Suwanne Middle School,
Live Oak, FL

Carmen Stallard
Twin Springs High
School, Nickelsville, VA

Jeanette Taylor
Rye Cove High School,
Duffield, VA

Eric Temple
Crystal Springs Uplands
School, Hillsborough, CA

Sherry Weatherly
Denton High School,
Denton, TX

Exploring Writer's Craft

CHAPTER 1 Using Your Writing Process

CHAPTER 2 Developing Your Writing Style

CHAPTER 4 Writing Other Kinds of Paragraphs

CHAPTER 5 Writing Effective Compositions

Achieving Writer's Purpose

CHAPTER 6 Personal Writing: Self-Expression and Reflection

Chapter 7 Using Description: Observation

Chapter 8 Creative Writing: Stories, Plays, and Poems

Chapter 9 Writing to Inform and Explain

Chapter 10 Writing to Persuade

Chapter 11 Writing About Literature

Applying Communication Skills

Chapter 12 Research Reports

CHAPTER 13 Letters and Applications

CHAPTER 14 Speeches, Presentations, and Discussions

Communication Resource

Chapter 15 Vocabulary

Chapter 16 Reference Skills

Grammar

CHAPTER 1 The Sentence

CHAPTER 2 Nouns and Pronouns

CHAPTER 3 Verbs

CHAPTER 4 Adjectives and Adverbs

CHAPTER 5 Other Parts of Speech

CHAPTER 6 Complements

Chapter 7 Phrases

Chapter 8 Clauses

Chapter 9 Sentence Fragments and Run-ons

Usage

Chapter 10 Using Verbs

Chapter 11 Using Pronouns

Chapter 12 Subject and Verb Agreement

CHAPTER 13 Using Adjectives and Adverbs

Mechanics

CHAPTER 14 Capital Letters

CHAPTER 15 End Marks and Commas

CHAPTER 16 Italics and Quotation Marks

CHAPTER 17 Other Punctuation

Spelling

Chapter 18 Spelling

Study and Test-Taking Skills Resource

COMPOSITION

CHAPTER 1

Using Your Writing Process

At the beginning of a writing project, you are faced with a challenge. You want to create something you can be proud of, and you want to engage the interest of others. You may hope for inspiration to help you start and to keep the words flowing. While inspiration helps, it is not something you can always rely on. That is where your writing process comes in. Your writing process includes the strategies you use to generate ideas, develop a draft, organize and refine the draft, and find an effective way to share your work.

In the past you have probably experienced how the process of writing does not always proceed in a straight line. Because writing is a creative process, writers usually move freely back and forth between the stages. As a writer you can shift from one stage to another or shift the order. As you become more familiar and comfortable with the writing process, you will find that you can adapt it to your unique way of thinking and writing.

Reading with a Writer's Eye

In "Straw into Gold," Sandra Cisneros writes how her family experiences and ethnic heritage as a Mexican American shaped her voice as a writer. As you read, notice how Cisneros uses the people and events in her neighborhood as inspiration for her writing. After reading the autobiographical account, think about how people and events at home and in your neighborhood could serve as inspiration.

Straw into Gold

The Metamorphosis of the Everyday

Sandra Cisneros

When I was living in an artists' colony in the south of France, some fellow Latin-Americans who taught at the university in Aix-en-Provence[1] invited me to share a home-cooked meal with them. I had been living abroad almost a year then on an NEA[2] grant, subsisting mainly on French bread and lentils while in France so that my money could last longer. So when the invitation to dinner arrived, I accepted without hesitation. Especially since they had promised Mexican food.

What I didn't realize when they made this invitation was that I was supposed to be involved in preparing this meal. I guess they assumed I knew how to cook Mexican food because I was Mexican. They wanted specifically tortillas, though I'd never made a tortilla in my life.

It's true I had witnessed my mother rolling the little armies of dough into perfect circles, but my mother's family is from Guanajuato,[3] *provinciales*,[4] country folk. They only know how to make flour tortillas. My father's family, on the other hand, is *chilango*,[5] from Mexico City. We ate corn tortillas but we didn't make them. Someone was sent to the corner tortilleria to buy some. I'd never seen anybody make corn tortillas. Ever.

Well, somehow my Latino hosts had gotten a hold of a packet of corn flour, and this is what they tossed my way with orders to produce tortillas. *Asi como sea*. Any ol' way, they said and went back to their cooking.

---

[1] **Aix-en-Provence** (āk′säN-prō väns′): City in southeastern France.

[2] **NEA:** National Endowment for the Arts.

[3] **Guanajuato** (gōō ä nō hwä′tō): State in central Mexico.

[4] ***provinciales*** (prō vēn sē äl′ās): "Country folk." (Spanish)

[5] ***chilango*** (chē län′gō): "City folk." (Spanish)

Why did I feel like the woman in the fairy tale who was locked in a room and ordered to spin straw into gold? I had the same sick feeling when I was required to write my critical essay for my MFA[6] exam—the only piece of noncreative writing necessary in order to get my graduate degree. How was I to start? There were rules involved here, unlike writing a poem or story, which I did intuitively. There was a step-by-step process needed and I had better know it. I felt as if making tortillas, or writing a critical paper for that matter, were tasks so impossible I wanted to break down into tears.

Somehow though, I managed to make those tortillas—crooked and burnt, but edible nonetheless. My hosts were absolutely ignorant when it came to Mexican food; they thought my tortillas were delicious. (I'm glad my mama wasn't there.) Thinking back and looking at that photograph documenting the three of us consuming those lopsided circles I am amazed. Just as I am amazed I could finish my MFA exam (lopsided and crooked, but finished all the same). Didn't think I could do it. But I did.

I've managed to do a lot of things in my life I didn't think I was capable of and which many others didn't think me capable of either.

Especially because I am a woman, a Latina, an only daughter in a family of six men. My father would've liked to have seen me married long ago. In our culture, men and women don't leave their father's house except by way of marriage. I crossed my father's threshold with nothing carrying me but my own two feet. A woman whom no one came for and no one chased away.

To make matters worse, I had left before any of my six brothers had ventured away from home. I had broken a terrible taboo. Somehow, looking back at photos of myself as a child, I wonder if I was aware of having begun already my own quiet war.

I like to think that somehow my family, my Mexicanness, my poverty all had something to do with shaping me into a writer. I like to think my parents were preparing me all along for my life as an artist even though they didn't know it. From my father I

---

[6] **MFA:** Master of Fine Arts.

inherited a love of wandering. He was born in Mexico City but as a young man he traveled to the U.S. vagabonding. He eventually was drafted and thus became a citizen. Some of the stories he has told about his months in the U.S. with little or no English surface in my stories in *The House on Mango Street* as well as others I have in mind to write in the future. From him I inherited a sappy heart. (He still cries when he watches the Mexican soaps—especially if they deal with children who have forsaken their parents.)

My mother was born like me—in Chicago but of Mexican decent. It would be her tough, streetwise voice that would haunt all of my stories and poems. An amazing woman who loves to draw and to read books and can sing an opera. A smart cookie.

When I was a little girl we traveled to Mexico City so much I thought my grandparents' house on La Fortuna, Number 12, was home. It was the only constant in our nomadic ramblings from one Chicago flat to another. The house on Destiny Street, Number 12, in the colonia Tepeyac,[7] would be perhaps the only home I knew, and that nostalgia for a home would be a theme that would obsess me.

My brothers also figured greatly in my art. Especially the oldest two; I grew up in their shadows. Henry, the second oldest and my favorite, appears often in poems I have written and in stories which at times only borrow his nickname, Kiki. He played a major role in my childhood. We were bunkbed mates. We were co-conspirators. We were pals. Until my oldest brother came back from studying in Mexico and left me odd-woman-out for always.

What would my teachers say if they knew I was a writer? Who would've guessed it? I wasn't a very bright student. I didn't much like school because we moved so much and I was always new and funny-looking. In my fifth-grade report card, I have nothing but an avalanche of C's and D's, but I don't remember being that stupid. I was good at art and I read plenty of library books and Kiki laughed at all my jokes. At home I was fine, but at school I never opened my mouth except when the teacher called on me, the first time I'd speak all day.

---

[7] **colonia Tepeyac** (kō lō′nē ä tā pā′äk): District of Mexico City.

When I think how I see myself, it would have to be at age eleven. I know I'm thirty-two on the outside, but inside I'm eleven. I'm the girl in the picture with skinny arms and a crumpled shirt and crooked hair. I didn't like school because all they saw was the outside me. School was lots of rules and sitting with your hands folded and being very afraid all the time. I liked looking out the window and thinking. I liked staring at the girl across the way writing her name over and over again in red ink. I wondered why the boy with the dirty collar in front of me didn't have a mama who took better care of him.

I think my mama and papa did the best they could to keep us warm and clean and never hungry. We had birthday and graduation parties and things like that, but there was another hunger that had to be fed. There was a hunger I didn't even have a name for. Was this when I began writing?

In 1966 we moved into a house, a real one, our first real home. This meant we didn't have to change schools and be the new kids on the block every couple of years. We could make friends and not be afraid we'd have to say good-bye to them and start all over. My brothers and the flock of boys they brought home would become important characters eventually for my stories—Louie and his cousins. Meme Ortiz and his dog with two names, one in English and one in Spanish.

My mother flourished in her own home. She took books out of the library and taught herself to garden, producing flowers so envied we had to put a lock on the gate to keep out the midnight flower thieves. My mother is still gardening to this day.

This was the period of my life, that slippery age when you are both child and woman and neither, I was to record in *The House on Mango Street*. I was still shy. I was a girl who couldn't come out of her shell.

How was I to know I would be recording and documenting the women who sat their sadness on an elbow and stared out a window? It would be the city streets of Chicago I would later record, but from a child's eyes.

I've done all kinds of things I didn't think I could do since then. I've gone to a prestigious university, studied with famous writers, and taken away an MFA degree. I've taught poetry in the schools in Illinois and Texas. I've gotten an NEA grant and run away with it as far as my courage could take me. I've seen the bleached and bitter mountains of the Peloponnesus.[8] I've lived on a Greek Island. I've been to Venice[9] twice. In Rapallo, I met Ilona once and forever and took her sad heart with me across the south of France and into Spain.

I've lived in Yugoslavia. I've been to the famous Nice[10] flower market behind the opera house. I've lived in a village in the pre-Alps[11] and witnessed the daily parade of promenaders.

I've moved since Europe to the strange and wonderful land of Texas, land of polaroid-blue skies and big bugs. I met a mayor with my last name. I met famous Chicana/o artists and writers and *politicos*.[12]

Texas is another chapter in my life. It brought with it the Dobie-Paisano Fellowship, a six-month residency on a 265-acre ranch. But most important Texas brought Mexico back to me.

Sitting at my favorite people-watching spot, the snaky Woolworth's counter across the street from the Alamo,[13] I can't think of anything else I'd rather be than a writer. I've traveled and lectured from Cape Cod to San Francisco, to Spain, Yugoslavia, Greece, Mexico, France, Italy, and finally today to Seguin, Texas. Along the way there is straw for the taking. With a little imagination, it can be spun into gold.

---

[8] **Peloponnesus** (pĕl′ə-pə nē′səs): A peninsula forming the southwestern part of the Greek mainland.

[9] **Venice** (ven′is): Seaport in northern Italy.

[10] **Nice** (nēs): Seaport and resort in southeastern France.

[11] **pre-Alps:** Foothills of the Alps, a mountain range in south-central Europe.

[12] ***politicos*** (pō lē′tē cōs): Politicians. (Spanish)

[13] **the Alamo** (ăl′ə-mō′): Mission in San Antonio, Texas, that was the scene of a famous battle between Texans and Mexican troops in 1836.

Thinking as a Writer

Analyzing a Writer's Process

- Make a list of the people and places that contributed to Cisneros's ability to write. How did her insight into her own life affect her development as a writer?
- Add to the list the places and events that have helped Cisneros develop as a writer. Which people, places, events, and things from your life would you use for inspiration?

Interpreting a Writer's Vision

Viewing Cisneros describes the places in which she lived that provided her with a vision of the world.

- Look at the photograph of an outdoor market below. What details do you notice—the people, the physical environment, the actions taking place? Which details capture your imagination?

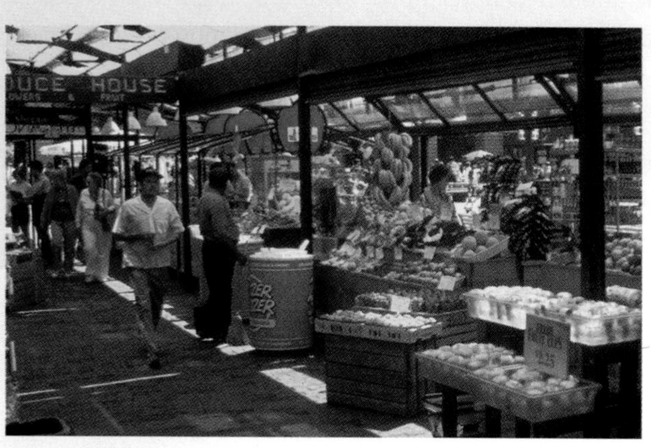

Analyzing a Writer's Tone

Oral Expression Cisneros's relationships with her family members and cultural experiences as a Mexican American woman contribute to the nostalgic tone in her writing.

- How do you think her experiences and relationships could have been reflected differently in her tone? Think about the people and events in your life. What different tones might you use in portraying them in your writing?

Refining Your Writing Process

"Reading maketh a full man; conference a ready man; and writing an exact man," said the English philosopher Francis Bacon in 1625 in *Of Studies*. To communicate well, you must be able to write well. The stronger your writing skills, the better you will be able to complete writing assignments in school or in a future job. While no two writers will go through the exact same steps in putting thoughts into written language, there is a general process that you can use to develop ideas and communicate them effectively.

Your **writing process** is the recursive series of stages that you proceed through when developing your ideas and discovering the best way to express them.

The word *recursive* indicates that, as a writer, you may often move back and forth among the stages of the writing process, depending on the specific needs of your work, rather than simply proceeding from the first stage straight through to the last. This is because writing is a creative process. As a writer you can shift from one stage to another or change the order of the stages you follow. For example, you may choose to revise your writing as you draft it or edit your writing as you revise it. Each stage has its own distinct characteristics. The diagram on the following page illustrates and describes these stages and shows the relationship between them. As you review the diagram, think about the stages you go through when you create a piece of writing.

You will notice this icon throughout this book as you work through the stages of writing various essays. It will remind you to save your work in a convenient place so you can return to it and continue to work on it, or use it later for inspiration. You may wish to use a folder or a pocket in your binder to store your work. If you usually work on a computer, you will probably want to create a folder on your hard drive, along with some kind of backup copy on a removable storage disk. Use whatever storage system is most convenient for you.

Process of Writing

The following diagram illustrates the stages writers go through as they create. Notice that the diagram loops back and forth. This looping shows how you often move back and forth among various stages of writing instead of going step-by-step from beginning to end. You can go back to any stage at any point until you are satisfied with the quality of your writing.

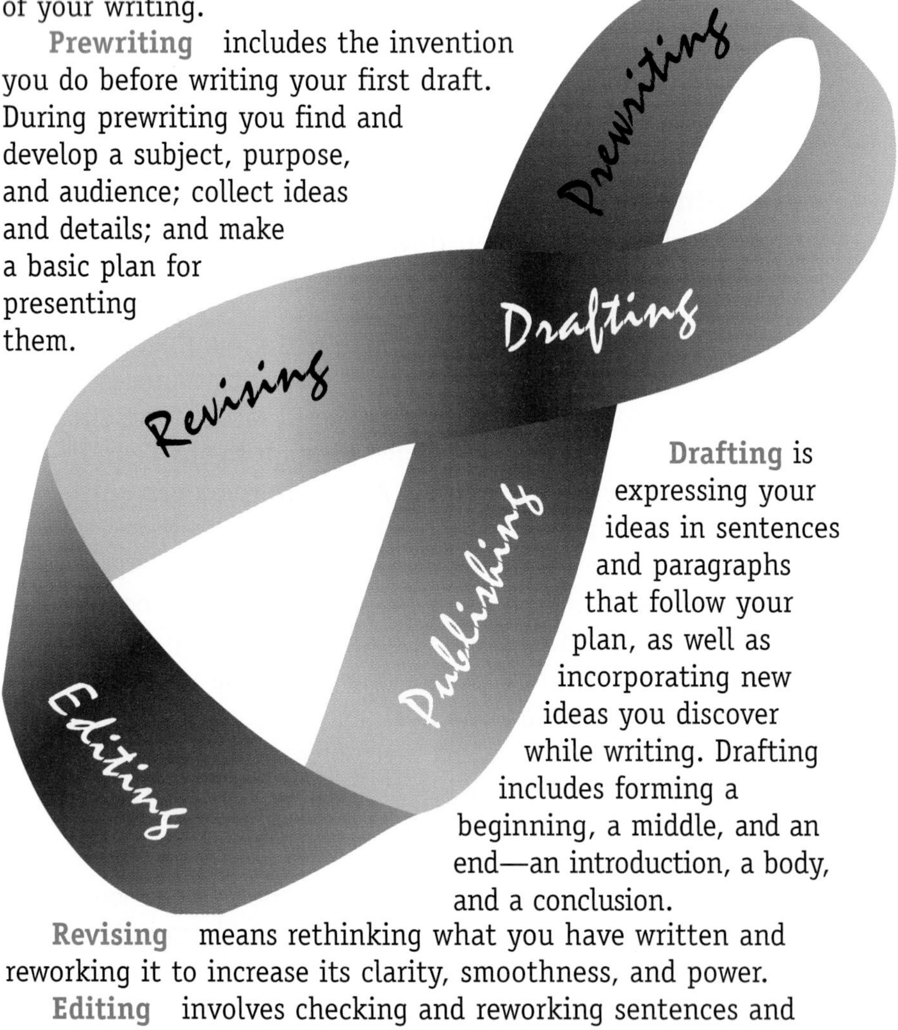

Prewriting includes the invention you do before writing your first draft. During prewriting you find and develop a subject, purpose, and audience; collect ideas and details; and make a basic plan for presenting them.

Prewriting

Drafting

Revising

Publishing

Editing

Drafting is expressing your ideas in sentences and paragraphs that follow your plan, as well as incorporating new ideas you discover while writing. Drafting includes forming a beginning, a middle, and an end—an introduction, a body, and a conclusion.

Revising means rethinking what you have written and reworking it to increase its clarity, smoothness, and power.

Editing involves checking and reworking sentences and sentence structure. It also includes looking for and correcting errors in grammar, usage, spelling, and mechanics, and proofreading your final version before making it public.

Publishing is sharing your work with an interested audience.

Your Writer's Portfolio

As you begin your writing, think of yourself as an apprentice learning a craft. Ideally, with each new essay you write, you come a step closer to developing your own composing processes. A good way to track your progress is to keep a **portfolio**—a collection of your work that represents various types of writing and your progress in them.

PORTFOLIO

This icon is a reminder to place your work in your writing portfolio. Be sure to date each piece you add so you will later have an accurate chronological record of your work. You will also be reminded in the chapter-closing checklists to consider including in your portfolio, the essay you have been working on, but the choice is always yours.

As you work through the writing assignments in your class, you will be asked to do many kinds of writing—sharing a story from your life, writing a poem, proposing a solution to a social problem, describing a scene from nature, researching a complex topic, writing a letter, and much more. Collecting these essays along the way can demonstrate the range of your growing skills as a writer.

You may be asked to write evaluations of your progress as a writer throughout the year; you should include these in your portfolio. This will help you examine both your successes as a writer and the areas of your work that could be improved. At the term's end, you may be asked to write a "cover letter" in which you summarize your portfolio's contents, explain why you included each piece, and evaluate your overall progress, strengths, and weaknesses.

On occasion, you will be asked to take "Time Out to Reflect." Use your written reflections to think about what you have learned, what you want to learn, and how you can continue to grow as a writer.

On the following page are a few guidelines for including work in your portfolio. Throughout the year look at the work you have kept in your portfolio and notice how your writing skills have developed over time.

Guidelines for Including Work in Your Portfolio

- Date each piece of writing so that you can see where it fits into your progress.
- Write a brief note to yourself about why you included each piece—what you believe it shows about you as a writer.
- Include unfinished works if they demonstrate something meaningful about you as a writer.

Something usually happens to trigger the act of writing. This "something" can range from a required homework assignment to the need to capture a memorable image in verse. All the thinking and planning that take place from this moment to the moment you start to write is called **prewriting.**

Prewriting strategies that you can apply to your own writing appear on the following pages. The purpose of these strategies is to help you generate ideas for a piece of writing. As you work through these pages, keep a writing folder in which you can put all your prewriting ideas.

Strategies for Finding a Subject

Finding a good subject—one that holds genuine interest for you and your readers—is an important first step in prewriting. Subjects come from many sources. You may discover good ideas for subjects through your reading, for example, or through your own experiences. The following strategies will help you identify possible subjects.

Taking an Inventory of Your Interests All the writing you ever do will take its subject matter from your own interests, experiences, and knowledge and its character from your imagination. Therefore, a good way to start thinking about possible subjects is to think about your life. Try the technique of self-interview. Ask yourself questions and write your answers.

Practice Your Skills

Finding a Writing Subject

Use the following prompts to take a personal interest inventory. Write as many items as you can think of for each one.

1. If I had a band, the music we'd play would be . . .
2. I am especially proud of my accomplishments in . . .
3. The hardest thing I ever had to do is . . .
4. Friends who have influenced me include . . .
5. A public figure I really respect is . . .
6. My advice to someone younger would be . . .
7. In ten years' time, I'd like to be . . .

Freewriting Another strategy for discovering possible subjects for writing is freewriting. This strategy can help you bring your thoughts to the surface. **Freewriting** means writing freely about ideas as they come into your mind, without stopping. Because the work you produce by freewriting is for your eyes only, you need not worry about making mistakes. Just write—and keep writing—whatever is on your mind. If you can't think of anything, choose a nearby object. Start by describing the object and then free associate—write down whatever that object or its description brings to mind. Go wherever your thoughts lead you. The following is an example of how you can use freewriting to get ideas about subject matter.

Model: Freewriting from Scratch

I'm sitting here in my English class wondering what to write about. I'm supposed to keep an open mind, but it's not happening that way. I feel like I have to come up with a good idea. OK, so here I am in school, working hard. But I like school. I've always done well when I applied myself. School might be an interesting topic.

As the writer wrote whatever came to mind, one idea—high school—began to emerge out of the muddle. Freewriting brought to mind a subject to write about.

Another student found herself writing about some creative ideas for a career.

Model: Freewriting with a Focus

I'm supposed to write about what I'd like to have as a career when I get older. I'm trying to keep my mind open but I can't think of anything. Maybe I'll do this when I get home. Lucky for me today's game was canceled because of the rain. What our school needs is a domed stadium. I know that sounds crazy. But you know, maybe that's what I can write about. Maybe I can design stadiums. I'm good at art and math. And I like playing sports. Being an architect, designing stadiums and arenas, would be a combination of all three.

Practice Your Skills

Freewriting from Scratch

For five minutes, freewrite by jotting down everything that passes through your mind. Without stopping to think, keep your pen or pencil moving. After five minutes, stop and read what you have written. Underline any ideas you think are interesting.

Freewriting with a Focus

Freewrite again for five minutes; this time, however, write about one of the subjects you underlined. Ask yourself which of these two kinds of freewriting worked better for you.

Keeping a Journal Keeping a journal is another strategy you can use to help you find a subject. A journal is a daily notebook in which you record your thoughts, feelings, and observations. Because you use your journal to write about subjects that interest you, it becomes an excellent source of writing ideas. Be sure to write in your journal every day and to date each entry. You can also use your journal in other ways to get writing ideas.

In this book you will usually find a journal-writing activity in every chapter. These activities will help you improve your fluency and discover subjects for your writing. The activities, however, are only suggestions.

Journals can record frustration:

> April 21, 1897
>
> Father took Nessa and me for a walk along the Parade to the Steine or some place of that kind—near the Pagoda at the other end of Brighton—I regret to say that various circumstances conspiring to irritate me, I broke my umbrella in half. . . .
>
> —*Virginia Woolf*
> *author*

They can record reflections:

> June 1837
>
> I look forward to the event which it seems is likely to occur soon, with calmness and quietness. I am not alarmed at it, and yet I do not suppose myself quite equal to all; I trust, however, that with good-will, honesty and courage I shall not, at all events, fail.
>
> —*Queen Victoria*
> *from her diaries*

They can record flashes of inspiration:

> October 15, 1914
>
> Two weeks of good work; full insight into my situation occasionally.
>
> —*Franz Kafka*
> *author*

It is important to choose a notebook you enjoy writing in and to date each entry. You are always free to write about whatever *you* want in your journal. You may write about whatever is on your mind, or you may help yourself to the prompts offered in this book.

Practice Your Skills

Writing in Your Journal

Look through old magazines for images that evoke a strong reaction in you. In your journal, freewrite everything that comes to mind as you look at those images.

Keeping a Response Log Your journal is a good place to record your responses and reactions to books, stories, poems, plays, and other works of literature. You might set aside a section of your journal as your **Response Log**. Here are some ways you can record your responses.

Exploring Literature for Writing Ideas

Fiction, Poetry, and Drama

- Write about the piece of literature itself, or write a script for television or film. Explore plot, character, setting, or some other aspect of the medium.
- Write about the theme, or central message, of a story, poem, or play. For example, a story about a quest for the truth may give you ideas for writing about the importance of trust in relationships. '
- Write about some trait of a character in a story or play. For instance, a character who envies others may give you ideas for writing about the problems envy can cause.
- Write about some aspect of the work that you really enjoyed.

You can learn more about literary analysis on pages C482–C513.

Nonfiction

- Decide whether you agree or disagree with a newspaper editorial or letter to an editor.
- Look through newspapers and magazines to find issues that you could explore.
- Use a biography or autobiography you have read as a basis for a writing project.

Practice Your Skills

Responding to Reading

Create a tabbed section in your journal called a Response Log. Then find a newspaper or magazine article that interests you, or use "Straw into Gold." Search for three possible subjects to write about. List the subjects in your Response Log.

Keeping a Learning Log A **Learning Log** is a section of your journal set aside for ideas and information about subjects that interest you. A Learning Log helps you to keep track of your interests, and to identify what you already know about a subject and what you want to find out. Your entry may look like this:

Model: Learning Log Entry

I know I've always liked being around the ocean. Swimming, surfing, dolphin watching, checking the tides. I know you can be a lifeguard and be at the ocean all summer, but I wonder what other jobs you can have at the ocean. Would I have to study oceanography or could I learn on the job? How can I find answers to these questions?

Practice Your Skills

Learning More About a Subject

Create another new section in your journal, this one labeled Learning Log. (Once again, attach a tab about three-fourths of the way through your journal, a little lower on the page than you placed the Response Log tab.) Think of some subject you know a bit about but would like to know more about. Write a Learning Log entry identifying what you already know, what else you would still like to find out, and where you could find additional information.

…g a Personalized Editing Checklist

A …lized **Editing Checklist** is a section of your journal …you can keep a list of errors that you frequently make in …writing—misspellings, usage mistakes, grammar and …anical errors, and the like. When you edit your writing, …should refer to this checklist.

…can learn more about the Personalized Editing Checklist on page C45.

PRACTICE YOUR SKILLS

Keeping Track of Errors

Create another section in your journal called Personalized Editing Checklist. Add to it as you work on the writing assignments in this book.

COMPUTER TIP

If you keep your **journal** on your computer, you can organize your documents in a way that works best for you. For instance, you can create a single document or a folder containing four separate documents (one for personal entries, one for your Response Log, one for your Learning Log, and one for your Personalized Editing Checklist) or folders within a main folder.

Choosing and Limiting a Subject

How can you use the prewriting work you have done so far—exploring your interests, freewriting, reading literature, and journal writing—to find a good subject? One good way is …review everything you have written to see if any ideas or …ts appear more than once. Ideas that come up often in …ing probably mean the most to you, which is an …haracteristic of a good writing subject. Following

are guidelines for choosing a good subject. Remember, though, that the most important guideline is your genuine interest in exploring a subject more fully in writing.

Guidelines for Choosing a Subject

- Choose a subject that genuinely interests and engages you and your readers.
- Choose a subject that you know well or can research in a reasonable amount of time.

Limiting a Subject When you choose a subject, you will often start with a general topic, such as "sports" or "current events." Your next step, therefore, is to narrow, or limit, your subject. By limiting your subject, you are making it specific enough to cover completely in the amount of space you have for writing. To limit your subject, use one or a combination of the following strategies.

Guidelines for Limiting a Subject

- Limit your subject to one person or one example that represents the subject.
- Limit your subject to a specific time or place.
- Limit your subject to a specific event.
- Limit your subject to a specific condition, purpose, or procedure.

In the model on the following page, notice how the student writer limited the subject of her essay on the differences between high school and middle school. Having started out with the subject of "school," which is too broad a subject to cover in a short essay, she ended up with the limited subject of "differences between middle school and high school." Later, when developing her subject, she could limit it even more by deciding to write about only two or three aspects of high school that are different from middle school.

GENERAL SUBJECT:
school

MORE LIMITED:
high school

LIMITED SUBJECT:
differences between middle and high school

Practice Your Skills

Limiting a Subject

For each broad subject, write two limited subjects. Then, for each limited subject, write one subject that is even more limited.

Example:

General	cats
Limited Subjects	cats I have known, cats in history
More Limited	my cat Frodo, cats in ancient Egypt

1. games
2. film actors
3. forms of transportation
4. ...ls
6. television talk shows
7. spectator sports
8. music styles
9. money
10. reptiles

Across the Media: Purposes of Media Forms

In newspapers and newsmagazines, publishers are usually careful to make clear the different types of writing they include. For example, news stories have certain familiar features, including headlines, internal heads, and often photos. Readers assume that these stories are carefully researched and accurately reported. Editorials, in contrast, are clearly marked as such, often containing a picture of the author to stress that these ideas are one person's point of view. Advertisements are also easy to spot. Sometimes, though, the advertiser tries to make the ad look like a news story, hoping the reader will think that the information in the ad is as reliable as that in a news story. Publishers usually write "Advertisement," often in a small type size, at the top of the page so that readers will not be completely fooled. Some people call this type of advertisement an *advertorial,* a mix of advertising and editorial.

On the Internet, the distinctions among the different types of writing are far less clear. Banner ads are easy enough to spot, but something that looks like a news story or a fact-filled informational piece could be nothing more than an advertisement.

Distinguishing among the various purposes of writing on the Internet requires a critical eye. Before giving too much credence to information you find on the Internet, ask yourself, *Who wrote this, and when did they write it?* High-quality information will pass this test with flying colors.

Media Activity

Do some critical surfing on the Internet. Choose a topic likely to have informative as well as commercially slanted sites, such as "weight loss" or "skin care," and browse through three or four of these sites. Find and save a solid, trustworthy piece of informational writing and a piece of writing that is really an advertisement. Write a few sentences that explain how you could tell the difference between them. Discuss your findings with your classmates.

Considering Your Occasion, Audience, and Purpose

Often your writing has a specific purpose, such as completing a school assignment or writing a letter to the editor of a newspaper. At the same time, every piece of writing has a general purpose. **Purpose** is your reason for writing or speaking. For example, the purpose of your school assignment may be to explain something; the purpose of your letter to the editor may be to persuade readers. Whatever your purpose may be, it is important to define it clearly before you begin writing. In successful communication, the purpose of your message is appropriate to both the occasion that prompts it and the audience who will receive it. The following chart lists the most common purposes and the forms they may take, although writing purpose can take almost any form in the hands of a creative writer.

WRITING PURPOSES	POSSIBLE FORMS
Informative to **explain** or **inform**; to focus on your subject matter and audience	**Factual writing** scientific essay, research paper, business letter, summary, descriptive essay, historical narrative, news story
Creative (literary) to **create**; to focus on making imaginative use of language and ideas	**Entertaining writing** short story, novel, play, poem, dialogue
Persuasive to **persuade**; to focus on changing your readers' minds or getting them to act in a certain way	**Convincing writing** letter to the editor, persuasive essay, movie or book review, critical essay (literary analysis), advertisement
Self-expressive to **express** and **reflect** on your thoughts and feelings	**Personal writing** journal entry, personal narrative, reflective essay, personal letter

Sometimes writing purposes overlap. For example, you can give people information and express your thoughts at the same time. You can write informatively about a place you have visited and persuade your audience to visit that place. Being clear about your purpose is important because it will affect many of the writing decisions you make.

Occasion is your motivation for composing—the factor that prompts or forces you, as a writer, to decide on your process for communicating. In other words, do you put a message in writing, or do you prepare a speech? Suppose you are applying to a college, which involves writing an essay. In this case, filling out the application is the occasion for writing.

Occasion usually can be stated well using one of the following sentences.

- I feel a need to write for my own satisfaction.
- I have been asked to write this by [name a person].
- I want to write an entry for [name a publication].
- I want to enter a writing contest.

As you plan your writing, you also need to remember the **audience** you will be addressing, or who will be reading your work. What are their interests and concerns? How can you best communicate to this particular audience? For example, if you were writing a description of some place you had visited, you would present details in a different way for an eight-year-old than for someone your own age.

Audience Profile Questions

- Who will be reading my work?
- How old are they? Are they adults? teenagers? children?
- What do I want the audience to know about my subject?
- What background do they have in the subject?
- What interests and opinions are they apt to have? Are there any words or terms I should define for them?

Practice Your Skills

Writing for Different Audiences

Write two paragraphs that describe an important event of the last fifty years, such as Martin Luther King Jr.'s "I Have a Dream" speech. Address your first paragraph to a third-grade student. Address the second paragraph to an adult.

Writing Tip

Make sure the **purpose** of your message is appropriate to the **occasion** that prompts it and the **audience** who will receive it.

Developing Your Voice and Tone

Sometimes writing is described as giving voice to your thoughts. Part of a writer's growth involves the discovery of his or her distinctive voice and the ability to adapt that voice appropriately to different situations. **Voice** is an important part of writing style that has to do with word choice as well as the particular sound and rhythm of those choices.

Your voice can and should be affected by your subject, occasion, audience, and purpose. In speaking you probably use a different voice when speaking to your teacher than when speaking to a friend. Similar differences in voice can be applied to your writing. In your **journal** you might use one voice when you are in a good mood and another when you are feeling irritable, one voice when recording a private hope and another when responding to a short story. Whether in writing or in speaking, your voice reflects these differences.

Do not confuse voice with tone. **Tone** is the feeling or attitude that a narrator conveys in a piece of writing. For example, when you write, your tone may be reflective, sad, or sympathetic.

You can learn more about tone on pages C230 and C266–C268.

PRACTICE YOUR SKILLS

Recognizing a Writer's Voice and Tone

1. Reread aloud the passage by Sandra Cisneros on pages C5–C6 in which she describes her early school experiences. Try to match your expression with the feeling contained in Cisneros's words. Listen to your speaking voice as you read the passage. Choose the word below that for you best expresses Cisneros's writing voice. Write a sentence explaining your choice.

a. anxious
b. amused
c. brash
d. mechanical

2. Using the same method, reread aloud the paragraph that begins "Why did I feel like the woman in the fairy tale . . ." (page C4) Choose the word that for you best expresses Cisneros's voice in this passage. Then write a sentence that explains your choice.

a. nostalgic
b. sad
c. affectionate
d. proud

At any time during your writing process, reading your work aloud to yourself will help you hear your own writing voice and determine whether it sounds the way you want it to sound. When you hear yourself read your own writing aloud, the work becomes a slightly different piece, and you will detect features that you could miss in a silent reading. In this way you can also determine whether your writing voice conveys the appropriate tone.

Writing Tip

To evaluate your written **voice** and **tone**, read your work aloud.

Strategies for Developing a Subject

After you have chosen and limited a subject and determined your purpose, audience, and occasion, you can flesh out your ideas with supporting details. **Supporting details** are the facts, examples, incidents, reasons, or other specific points that back up your ideas. Following are some strategies for developing supporting details.

Observing Observation is essential for developing supporting details—especially if you are describing a person, a place, or an object. **Observing** involves taking in sensory details—sights, sounds, tastes, feelings, and smells. Although your brain automatically records and interprets sensory input, observing as a skill requires both awareness and practice. Without paying attention, you may not notice all the details that describe a scene.

Suppose you were writing a description of a city street in the rain. Your senses determine that it is raining because of the sound and feel of rain and the sight of open umbrellas. Observing more closely, however, you may notice less obvious details, such as the small rapids formed by water rushing along the gutters, the hollow sound of water dropping into a storm drain, and the rainbow-colored reflections of streetlights on the wet pavement.

Techniques for Observing

- Be aware of why you are observing. Keep your purpose in mind as you decide what and how to observe.
- Use your senses: look, listen, smell, touch, and taste.
- Use your mind. Think about what your observations mean.
- Observe from different viewpoints: near and far, above and below, and inside and out.
- Sketch your subject. Make a drawing of what you observe.

It is important to know how to collect and organize the information you get from observing. Taking notes using note cards or computer files is a good way to keep information in a way that is easy to arrange and rearrange when drafting. The following note card shows how a student took notes on "Straw into Gold."

SUMMARIES OF MAIN IDEA:

YOUR NOTES RECORD THE WRITER'S MAIN MESSAGE AND FACTS.

Sandra Cisneros
Mexican American
Sandra Cisneros talks about how she found her
identity and started writing. She talks about her
career as a writer and her early education.

You can learn more about observing on pages C308 and C310.

Practice Your Skills

Observing

Use the preceding guidelines to observe the scene in the photograph below. Place yourself in the scene so you can use all your senses. Then record ten or more details that you could use to describe the scene, including ones that may not be obvious at first.

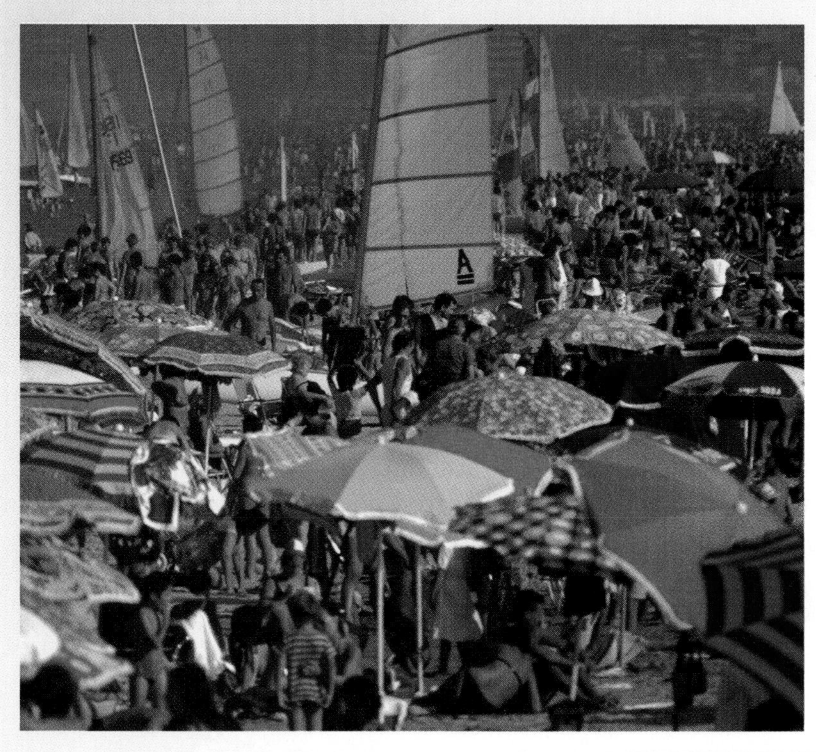

Brainstorming for Details Brainstorming is another good way to discover details for an essay once you have chosen and limited your subject. In **brainstorming** your goal is to work with a partner or a group of classmates and freely list all ideas related to your subject as they occur to you. The guidelines on the next page will help you brainstorm.

Guidelines for Brainstorming

- Set a time limit, such as 15 minutes.
- Write the subject on a piece of paper and assign one group member to be the recorder. If your group meets frequently, take turns recording ideas.
- Start brainstorming for supporting details, such as facts, reasons, and examples. Since you can eliminate irrelevant ideas later, record any and all ideas.
- Build on the ideas of other group members. Add to those ideas or modify them to improve them.
- Avoid criticizing the ideas of other group members.

You can learn more about cooperative learning on pages C614–C615.

When you have finished brainstorming, you should get a copy of all the supporting details from the group recorder. Then, from the group list, select the details that are most appropriate for your own essay.

Following is part of a brainstorming list made by a small group of students on the subject of the differences between middle school and high school. The students wrote the subject at the top of a sheet of paper and then jotted down whatever came to mind about that subject.

Model: Brainstorming List

Differences Between Middle School and High School

—lots of homework (more papers and projects)
—big building (actually three buildings)
—crowded parking lot (looking forward to getting learner's permit)
—nice gym (brand-new basketball court)
—crowded halls (still getting lost!)
—lots of new people (miss friends)
—new teachers
—separate study halls

Practice Your Skills

Brainstorming for Details

With a group, brainstorm for ideas on the subject of status symbols, such as brand-name sneakers, jeans, or cars. Follow the preceding guidelines.

Clustering Another strategy for developing supporting details is clustering. **Clustering** is a visual brainstorming technique that lets you both record and group your ideas. A cluster looks something like a wheel. At the hub, or center, you write your limited subject. Each idea or detail you think of to develop your subject is connected to the hub like a spoke in a wheel. Sometimes supporting ideas become new hubs with spokes of their own. The student who was writing about the differences between middle school and high school created the following cluster.

Model: Clustering

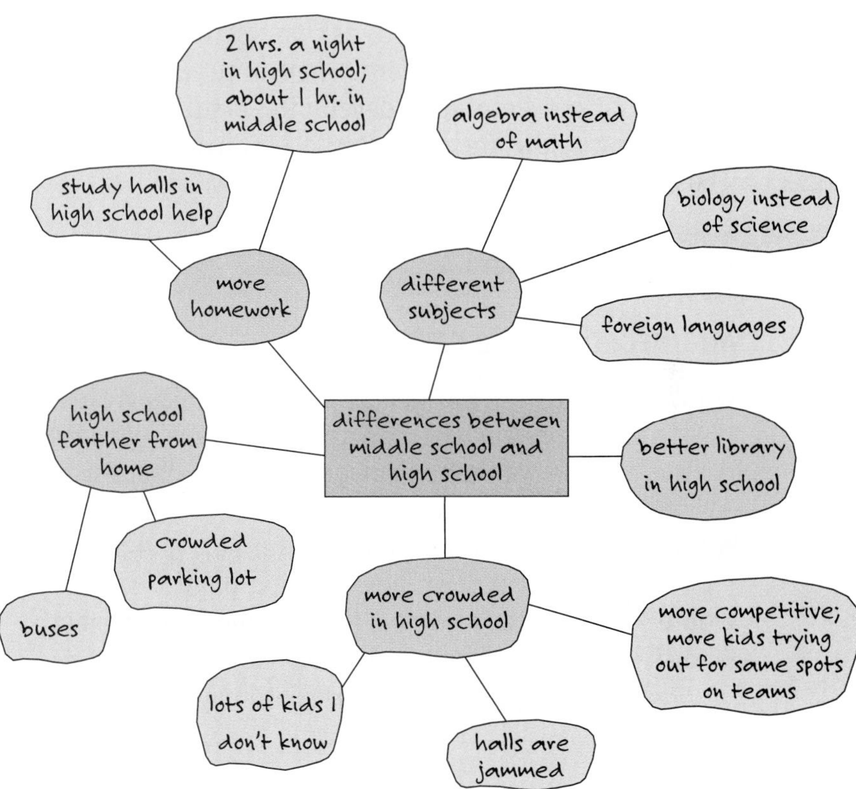

After clustering, the student further limited the subject to three aspects of high school that are different from middle school. This subject was suitable for the student's purpose (to inform) and audience (students).

PRACTICE YOUR SKILLS

Clustering

Using the brainstorming notes you developed earlier on status symbols, create a cluster like the preceding one. If you prefer, you may create a cluster on one of the following subjects.

1. music of the 1990s
2. influence of technology
3. movie ratings
4. public education
5. stress on teenagers in today's society

Inquiring Another good way to generate the supporting details you need to develop your subject is to ask yourself questions. Questions that begin *who, what, where, when, why,* and *how* can produce answers that are helpful in developing a subject. The following model shows how one writer used inquiring to develop details on the subject "an unforgettable cast party."

MODEL: Inquiring to Develop Supporting Details

AN UNFORGETTABLE CAST PARTY

Who?	All the cast members from the play *West Side Story* and the directors, the stage manager, the wardrobe manager, the stage hands, and the set builders
What?	Celebration of a successful play and a chance to wind down after closing night
Where?	Director's home—Mr. Jennings's apartment
When?	After we had struck the set following our final performance last Saturday night

How?	Brought CDs, snacks, and soft drinks—also gifts of appreciation for Mr. Jennings and the stage manager
Why?	Traditional to have a cast party after a school play. "Unforgettable" party because we worked so hard and long at the play. After spending so much time together, we all felt especially close, like a family. Felt like a reward for all of our hard work.

Use **clustering** and **inquiring** to generate supporting details.

Practice Your Skills

Inquiring

Practice the strategy of inquiring by using it to develop details on two of the following subjects. To write answers, follow the form of the student model that starts on the preceding page.

1. a memorable trip
2. a lucky break
3. a foolish mistake
4. a hard lesson
5. a big responsibility
6. a wise decision
7. a dangerous encounter
8. a welcome surprise
9. a good investment
10. foolish behavior

Classifying

When freewriting, clustering, or brainstorming, you generate ideas freely as you think of them. Then, to organize those ideas, you must group them into meaningful categories. When you group your ideas, you will be using a thinking skill called classifying. **Classifying** is a process of grouping items into classes, or categories. The following chart, for example, compares equipment for English-style and Western-style horseback riding. Notice that details are classified under two categories of equipment: Saddle and Bridle.

HORSEBACK RIDING EQUIPMENT

	English Style	Western Style
Saddle	flatter, lighter, small saddle pad, short stirrups	higher back, horn, saddle blanket, long stirrups
Bridle	snaffle or double bit single or double reins	curb bit single pair of reins

While classifying, you may add categories as needed to group new details. In the above chart, for example, you could add the category "Other Equipment" to classify any new details about horseback riding equipment—such as spurs, crops, and lariats—that do not fit logically under the existing categories.

THINKING PRACTICE

Create categories to classify details about one of the following subject comparisons or one of your own. Then make a classification chart like the one above.

1. the similarities between ice hockey and field hockey
2. the pros and cons of bringing or buying school lunches
3. the benefits and drawbacks of summer and winter

Strategies for Organizing Details

Prewriting strategies such as freewriting, brainstorming, inquiring, observing, and clustering allow you to free your thoughts as you search for subjects and details for your essay. Once you have collected those details, you need to organize them in a clear, logical order. The following strategies will help you do just that.

Focusing Your Subject Before you arrange your ideas logically, you should decide on a focus, or main idea, for your essay. To think of a main idea, look over your notes and ask yourself what you want to say about your limited subject. Next think again about your purpose. Being aware of why you are writing helps you select the most appropriate main idea for your composition. For the composition on differences between middle school and high school, for example, the student who made the cluster on page C29 wrote three possible main ideas, which are listed below.

Model: Possible Main Ideas

- Of the differences between middle school and high school, three have had the greatest effect on me.
- Because of the differences between middle school and high school, I have sometimes felt lost in high school.
- The differences between middle school and high school are all for the best.

The student chose the first idea as the focus because it seemed most meaningful and because it suited the writing purpose (to inform) and the audience (students).

Guidelines for Deciding on a Focus

- Look over your details. Can you draw meaningful generalizations from some or all of the details? If so, the generalization could be the focus of your writing.
- Choose a main idea that intrigues you.
- Choose a main idea that suits your purpose and audience.

Classifying Your Details When you carefully look over your supporting details, you will often see that they fall naturally into groups, or categories. For example, if you are explaining good study habits, you might create categories such as advance preparation and time management. As you classify, you may find that some details don't fit into any category and may eventually have to be discarded.

The writer who chose to write about the differences between middle school and high school decided to group her details into three categories: (1) different subjects, (2) more homework, and (3) crowded feeling. By presenting her ideas in logical groups, she will help readers understand what she is trying to say.

Ordering Your Details Once you have classified your details, you need to place them in an order that will best achieve your purpose and also make the most sense to your reader. The following chart will help you determine the appropriate method of organization for your writing.

WAYS TO ORGANIZE DETAILS

Types of Order	Definition	Examples
Chronological	the order in which events occur	story, explanation, history, biography, drama
Spatial	location or physical arrangement	description (top to bottom, near to far, left to right, etc.)
Order of Importance	degree of importance, size, or interest	persuasive writing, description, evaluation, explanation
Logical	logical progression, one detail growing out of another	classification, definition, comparison and contrast

The student writing about differences between middle school and high school made the following list of organized details. Notice that the list includes only those details from the cluster on page C29 that relate to the main idea, and that the details are listed in order of importance. The student used this list as a guide when writing the first draft.

MODEL: Ordering Details

Focus (Main Idea): Of the differences between middle school and high school, three have had the greatest effect on me.

Order of Ideas	Reasons
1. Different subjects —math versus algebra —science versus biology —foreign languages	Good to start with because the course schedule is the first you see of high school
2. More homework —1 hour versus 2 hours —study halls	Next in importance and follows logically from above
3. Crowded feeling —halls jammed —kids I don't know —competition	Save for last as the most important difference; makes my point that you have to get used to high school

Organizing Details

Explain which method of organization you would use to organize the details for each of the following subjects. Write *chronological, spatial,* or *order of importance* for each item.

1. an explanation of what to pack for a camping trip

2. a description of your school building

3. an account of your first day in high school

4. a story about the first time you used the subway or the bus

5. a comparison between cable and network television

When you are satisfied that you have some good ideas to work with and a logical organization, you can test your plan by writing a first draft. Unlike your prewriting notes, which are for your eyes only, your first draft should be targeted for your audience. Therefore the language you use should be appropriate to the subject and the occasion. At this stage you should be paying attention to voice and tone, and to expressing your ideas in complete sentences. Use these strategies for drafting as a guide:

Strategies for Drafting

- Write an introduction that will capture the reader's interest and express your main idea.
- After you write your introduction, use your organized prewriting notes as a guide. Feel free to depart from those notes, however, when a good idea occurs to you.
- Write fairly quickly without worrying about spelling or phrasing. You will have the opportunity to go back and fix your writing when you revise.
- Stop frequently and read what you have written. This practice will help you move logically from one thought to the next as you draft.
- Return to the prewriting stage whenever you find that you need to clarify your thinking. You can always stop and freewrite, brainstorm, or cluster to collect more ideas.
- Write a conclusion that drives home the main point of the essay.

Following is a draft written on the subject of three differences between middle school and high school. Notice that the first and last paragraphs serve as an introduction and conclusion, which are essential to an effective essay. Also notice that the draft follows the order of ideas that was planned in the student model on page C35. Last, notice that while drafting, the student writer made several mistakes in spelling, grammar, and punctuation. These mistakes will be corrected at a later stage in the writing process.

Model: First Draft

High school was a real surprise for me. I knew it would be different from middle school, but not this different. There were three things especially that made me realize that high school would never be the same.

One difference you notice write away from middle School is the courses you take. In middle school for example you take science and and math. In high school the courses are definately more avanced. In highschool you take Biology in stead of science and Algebra insteadof math. High school offers also foriegn languages which some middle schools don't, I'm taking spanish.

You also find you have more homework in high school. I find I have twice as much homework in high school. In middle school I used to spend about an hour every week night doing homework. Now that I'm in high school I spend about two hours a night and sometimes even week ends. It does help that high schools have longer study hall periods. In study halls you can get some of your work do during school hours. There should be some way to keep things quieter in study halls at least some of the time.

High school is also much more crowded than middle school. The halls are jammed with students, and I dont even know alot of them. You sometimes feel lost. The other thing about so many students is that high school has a pretty competative atmosphere. There are more kids trying out for the same spots on sports teams, or in other groups. The added competition is a plus because it keeps you on you toes you really have to do your best at all times.

I guess I'm getting used to the idea that high school is a hole new experience. There are alot of diffrences between middle school and high school and these are only three of them. Such differences can be unsettling at first but you will find that they all have a strong plus side too.

Drafting a Title You may think of a good title at any stage in the writing process. Whenever you come up with a title, however, consider carefully whether it will get your readers' attention. The title should also be appropriate to your subject, purpose, and audience.

Guidelines for Choosing a Title

- Choose a title that identifies your subject or relates to your subject focus.
- Choose a title that is appropriate for your purpose and audience.
- Choose a title that will capture the reader's interest.

Practice Your Skills

Drafting a Title

Read over the draft about high school and write three possible titles for that essay.

COMPUTER TIP

One of the more important steps in using a word processor is to save your work often. Power outages can happen at any time. Get in the habit of using the Save command whenever you pause in your writing.

File Edit View Insert Format
New... ⌘N
Open... ⌘O
Open Web Page...
Close ⌘W
Save ⌘S
Save As...

Revising

Writing Process

Revising means "seeing again." When writers revise, they stand back from their work and look at it again with the eyes of someone reading it for the first time. The heaviest revising is usually done after a first draft is completed, but until you are completely satisfied with your revision, you may write a second, third, or even fourth draft. If you compose your draft on a word processor, the task of revising will be easier.

Before starting to revise your essay, put it away for a few days if you can. Then come back to it with a fresh eye and evaluate it as objectively as possible. Try reading it aloud to see how it sounds. Ask a classmate to read it and make suggestions. Revise your work as often as needed to convey your thoughts clearly and effectively.

Revising on Your Own

After evaluating your draft, you are ready to revise, paying particular attention to the problems you identified. The following strategies will help you rework your draft until you are satisfied that it is the best it can be.

Adding Ideas Look over your draft. Have you included all aspects of the subject? Are your ideas interesting to you, and will they be interesting to your audience? Are they fresh, original ideas, rather than ones that people have heard over and over? Does the essay satisfy its purpose? Have you explored the subject in depth? Is the language appropriate to the subject and occasion? If your answer to any of these questions is *no,* then you need to make changes or think of new ideas by freewriting about the subject or talking about it with others.

Adding Details and Information As you reread your essay, ask yourself the following questions. Does it seem fully developed? Are your ideas fully supported? If not, you probably need to add more details and information. Use one of the prewriting strategies to come up with additional lively, supporting details.

Rearranging Check the organization of your words, sentences, and ideas. Does one idea lead logically into another? If not, rearrange and reorganize your sentences or paragraphs so that the reader can easily follow your train of thought.

Deleting Unnecessary Words or Details If you have included any details in your draft that do not really relate to your limited subject and main idea, delete, or remove, them. Also delete any extra or unneeded words and repetitive sentences.

Substituting Words and Sentences Reread your draft once more. If any part of it might confuse the reader, think of a clearer way to express the same idea. For any word or phrase that may sound dull and boring, substitute a more interesting, original way to say the same thing. In addition, vary the structure and length of sentences to keep them from sounding monotonous.

Revising challenges you to look at the content and style of your work. Using a checklist can help you determine what you need to do to improve your draft. In addition, you may want to ask a classmate to use the checklist as a guide when reviewing your work. You will find evaluation checklists in various chapters throughout this book to guide you through the revision stage for different types of writing. The general checklist below will help you keep track of revisions you have made and identify revisions you still need to make.

Evaluation Checklist for Revising

- ✓ Did you clearly state your main idea? *(page C33)*
- ✓ Does your essay have a strong introduction, body, and conclusion? *(page C36)*
- ✓ Did you support your main idea with enough details? *(pages C25–C31)*
- ✓ Do your details show instead of merely telling what you want to say? *(page C39)*
- ✓ Did you present your ideas in a logical order? *(pages C34–C35)*
- ✓ Do any of your sentences stray from the main idea? *(pages C38–C40)*
- ✓ Are your ideas clearly explained? *(page C39)*
- ✓ Are your words specific? *(page C39)*
- ✓ Are any words or ideas repeated unnecessarily? *(page C39)*
- ✓ Are your sentences varied and smoothly connected? *(page C40)*
- ✓ Is the purpose of your essay clear? *(pages C22–C23)*
- ✓ Is your writing suited to your audience? *(page C23)*
- ✓ Is your title effective? *(page C38)*

PRACTICE YOUR SKILLS

Studying a Revision

Study the following unedited portion of a revised draft on three differences between high school and middle school. Compare the revised draft with the first draft on page C37. Then, based on your comparison of the drafts, write answers to the following questions.

Although
High school was a real suprise for me. I knew it would
a change   Three
be ~~different~~ from middle school, ~~but not this different.~~ ~~There~~
differences   suprised me the most and
~~were three things~~ especially ~~that~~ made me realize that high
                    a whole new experience.
school would ~~never~~ be ~~the same.~~

                                I
One difference ~~you~~ notice write away, ~~from middle School~~
                I am taking, which   I
is the courses ~~you take.~~ In middle school for example ~~you~~
took courses called
~~take~~ science and and math. ~~In high school the courses~~ are
                                             I
definately more avanced. In highschool ~~you~~ take Biology
in stead of science and Algebra insteadof math. High
          more subjects than middle school, including
school offers also foriegn languages. ~~which some middle~~
I find that all the new courses make the subjects more interesting.
~~schools don't, I'm taking spanish~~.

1. In the revision, which detail was deleted?
2. Which idea was out of place?
3. Point out two places where additional information or new details were added.
4. Point out three places where sentences were rearranged.
5. Point out two places where a weak statement was replaced by a stronger one.
6. Make one suggestion for further revision of this portion of the draft.

Revising Through Conferencing

At some point during the revising stage, you may wish to have a conference about your writing. **Conferencing** is meeting with somebody else for the purpose of sharing information and ideas or identifying and solving problems. Arranging a conference is as simple as inviting a reader—a friend, relative, classmate, or teacher—to tell you honestly what he or she thinks about your work. Ask for comments about what your reader likes in your writing and also for specific suggestions about what could be improved. Afterward, analyze the comments and suggestions, and use those that you think will improve your draft. In addition, you should be prepared to provide feedback to your reader on his or her writing.

Peer Conferencing Sometimes you might form a small group with three or four other students and read one another's essays. Then take turns offering praise for what each person has done well in addition to any suggestions for improvement.

Guidelines for Conferencing

Guidelines for the Writer

- List some questions for your classmate. What aspects of your essay most concern you?
- Try to be grateful for your critic's candor rather than being upset or defensive. Keep in mind that the criticism you are getting is well intended.

Guidelines for the Critic

- Read your partner's work carefully. What does the writer promise to do in this essay?
- Point out strengths as well as weaknesses. Start your comments by saying something positive like, "Your opening really captured my interest."
- Be specific. Refer to a specific word, sentence, or section of the essay when you comment.
- Be sensitive to your partner's feelings. Phrase your criticisms as questions. You might say, "Do you think your details might be stronger if . . . ?"

Practice Your Skills

Revising and Conferencing

Pair up with a partner. Using the strategies on the preceding page and the Evaluation Checklist for Revising on page C40, review the following draft about fifties fashions, and then make revisions. Using the Guidelines for Conferencing on the previous page, look at each other's revisions. Check to see if there are any areas in which you could make improvements that either of you may have left uncorrected.

Fifties Fashions

As in every era, the 1950s had its own distinctive fashion code for teenagers. The uniform was unmistakable and easy to spot. The fashionable teenage girl of the fifties wore her hair in a high pony tail, often with a scarf or kerchief around the rubber band that held it in place. Matching sweater sets were popular too. These included a pullover and a cardigan in a matching color. The fifties girl also usually wore her hair with bangs. Boys in the fifties often wore their hair greased back, with a wave or two in front. For skirts, the big item was a wide circular skirt made out of felt, often with a poodle dog embroidered or appliquéd on the front. It was considered very "cool" to wear a sweater clip connecting the two sides of the cardigan, rather than buttoning the sweater. On her feet, the same girl usually wore bobby socks and two-tone saddle shoes. Shoes for boys were sharply pointed. If you ever stage a fifties theme party, you will know just how to dress. From head to toe, most teenagers dressed in the uniform of the 1950s. Unlike teenagers of today, the great majority of teenagers in the 1950s adopted a dress code that seemed to vary little from school to school and from region to region.

During the prewriting, drafting, and revising stages, you have concentrated your efforts on the content and form of your work. While you may have tried to follow rules for correct spelling, punctuation, capitalization, grammar, and usage along the way, your focus has remained primarily on presenting your ideas clearly and refining your words. Once you are satisfied with the substance and structure of your draft, you can begin to polish your work by correcting mechanical errors.

Strategies for Editing

Errors in spelling, usage, punctuation, grammar, and capitalization can muddle your writing and seriously jeopardize your credibility. A piece of writing is not finished until you have checked it for these errors. An editing checklist and proofreading symbols will help you find and correct them.

Using an Editing Checklist Just as commercial pilots use a preflight checklist, good writers often use an editing checklist to help them avoid forgetting things. The best way to use such a list is to go over your paper several times, each time looking for a different kind of problem. For instance, you might look for spelling errors in one reading and comma errors in the next. You might also want to read your essay backward, word by word. You will find that you are able to spot many errors that you might otherwise miss. The following checklist will help you guard against some common errors.

Editing Checklist

- ✓ Are your sentences free of errors in grammar and usage?
- ✓ Did you spell each word correctly?
- ✓ Did you use capital letters where needed?
- ✓ Did you punctuate each sentence correctly?
- ✓ Did you indent paragraphs as needed and leave proper margins on each side of the paper?

Using a Manual of Style As you edit, you may wish to consult one of the following style guides or handbooks to review rules for grammar, usage, and mechanics.

- *APA Publication Manual of the American Psychological Association.* 4th ed. Washington, DC: American Psychological Association, 1994.
- *The Chicago Manual of Style: The Essential Guide for Writers, Editors, and Publishers.* 14th ed., Chicago: University of Chicago Press, 1993.
- *MLA Handbook for Writers of Research Papers.* 5th ed. New York: Modern Language Association of America, 1999.

Creating a Personalized Editing Checklist You may want to reserve an eight-page section at the end of your **journal** to use as a Personalized Editing Checklist. Write one of the following headings on every other page: *Grammar, Usage, Spelling*, and *Mechanics* (capitalization and punctuation). Use these pages to record your errors. See the index in this book to find the pages on which each problem is addressed. Write the page numbers in your **journal** next to the error, with examples of the corrected problem. Add to this checklist and refer to it each time you edit an essay.

Proofreading During the revising stage, you may become so familiar with your essay that you skip over mistakes. Proofreading during the editing stage gives you the distance to help you see mistakes that you missed earlier. **Proofreading** means carefully rereading your work and marking corrections in grammar, usage, spelling, and mechanics. Following are techniques that may help make proofreading easier.

Proofreading Techniques

- Focus on one line at a time.
- Exchange essays with a partner and check each other's work.
- Read your essay backward, word by word.
- Read your essay aloud, very slowly.
- Use a dictionary for spelling and a handbook for grammar, usage, and mechanics.

Proofreading symbols are convenient shorthand notations that writers frequently use to make corrections and indicate changes during the editing stage. Commonly used proofreading symbols are shown below.

Proofreading Symbols

Symbol	Meaning	Example
^	insert	We ^went on^ ~~completed~~ an ^eventful^ journey.
^,	insert comma	Meg enjoys hiking, skiing^, and skating.
⊙	insert period	Gary took the bus to Atlanta⊙
~~	delete	Refer ~~back~~ to your notes.
¶	new paragraph	¶Finally Balboa saw the Pacific.
no ¶	no paragraph	no ¶The dachshund trotted away.
....	let it stand	I appreciated her ~~sincere~~ honesty.
#	add space	She will be allright in a moment.
⁀	close up	The airplane waited on the run way.
∿	transpose	They only have two dollars left.
≡	capital letter	We later moved to the south.
/	lowercase letter	His favorite subject was Science.
(sp)	spell out	I ate 2 oranges.
∨" ∨"	insert quotes	"I hope you can join us," said my brother.
=	insert hyphen	I attended a school related event.
∨'	insert apostrophe	The ravenous dog ate the cats food.
⟲	move copy	I usually on Fridays go to the movies.

Prewriting Workshop
Drafting Workshop
Revising Workshop
Editing Workshop
Publishing Workshop

Sentences

Language is your way of communicating with others. Communication in writing, however, can break down if the sentences are filled with errors. For this reason, editing is an important stage in the writing process.

When you edit you pull together, or integrate, everything you know about usage, mechanics, and other language skills. As you review different language skills in each composition chapter, write them in your Personalized Editing Checklist, where you can refer to them when you edit. At the end of the composition section, you will see that you have covered every major language skill in this book.

Sentence Fragments

When editing, you might begin with subjects and verbs, which are the foundation of all sentences. Without a subject and a verb, you have no sentence. Instead you have a **sentence fragment**—only part of a sentence. Therefore, always check for any missing subjects or verbs.

SENTENCE FRAGMENT	In high school, courses like science and math. (The verb is missing. You do not know what is being said about the courses.)
SENTENCE	In high school, courses about science and math include biology and algebra.

Subject and Verb Agreement

Once you know that each of your sentences has a subject and a verb, your next step is to check to see if the subject and verb in each sentence agree in number. **Number** refers to whether the subject and verb are singular (one) or plural (more than one). To agree, both the subject and the verb must be either singular or plural. In the following examples, the subject is underlined once and the verb is underlined twice. Notice how they agree in number.

SINGULAR SUBJECT AND VERB	The study hall was quiet.
PLURAL SUBJECT AND VERB	The study halls were quiet.

Words Interrupting a Subject and a Verb

Subject and verb agreement is seldom a problem when the subject and verb are side by side. Sometimes, though, words separate the subject from the verb. When this happens you may easily make a mistake by having the verb agree with a nearby word rather than with the subject.

AGREEMENT ERROR	The halls at the high school is jammed with students. (The verb must agree with the subject *halls,* not with *high school.*)
CORRECT AGREEMENT	The halls at the high school are jammed with students. (The plural verb *are* now agrees with the plural subject *halls.*)

Editing Checklist

- ✔ Are there any sentence fragments?
- ✔ Do the subjects and verbs in each sentence agree in number?
- ✔ Does the verb agree with the subject in each sentence, despite any interrupting words?

In the following student model, notice how proofreading symbols were used to edit a portion of the revised draft of "Making a Transition to High School."

MODEL: Edited Draft

Although I knew it would be a change from middle school, high school was a real suprise for me. Three differences especially suprised me the most and made me realize that high school would be a whole new experience.

One difference I notice write away is the courses I am taking which are definately more avanced. In middle school for example I took courses called science and and math In high school I take Biology in stead of science and Algebra insteadof math. High school offers also more subjects than middle school, including foriegn languages I find that all the new courses make the subjects more interesting.

PRACTICE YOUR SKILLS

Editing a Draft

Using the proofreading symbols on page C46 and the *Editing Checklists* on the previous page and on page C44, edit the remaining section of the essay on the differences between middle school and high school. Make sure you check for errors in spelling, punctuation, capitalization, grammar, and usage.

You also find you have more homework in high school. I find I have twice as much homework in high school. In middle school I used to spend about an hour every week night doing homework. Now that I'm in high school I spend about two hours a night and sometimes even week ends. It does help that high schools have longer study hall periods. In study halls you can get some of your work do during school hours. There should be some way to keep things quieter in study halls at least some of the time.

High school is also much more crowded than middle school. The halls are jammed with students, and I dont even know alot of them. You sometimes feel lost. The other thing about so many students is that high school has a pretty competative atmosphere. There are more kids trying out for the same spots on sports teams, or in other groups. The added competition is a plus because it keeps you on you toes you really have to do your best at all times.

I guess I'm getting used to the idea that high school is a hole new experience. There are alot of diffrences between middle school and high school and these are only three of them. Such differences can be unsettling at first but you will find that they all have a strong plus side too.

Publishing

Writing Process

Sometimes you write just for yourself to express your thoughts and feelings, as when you write in your **journal** or diary. Often, however, you will be sharing your writing in final form with an audience, or making it "public."

This final stage of the writing process is called **publishing.** The form in which you publish may vary—it could be anything from writing a letter to a friend or family member to publishing an illustrated book.

Neat presentation is essential for making your work appear inviting to read. Following are some choices for publishing your writing.

Ways to Publish Your Writing

In School

- Read your work aloud to a small group in your class.
- Display your final draft on a bulletin board in your classroom or school library.
- Read your work aloud to your class or present it in the form of a radio program or videotape.
- Create a class library and media center to which you submit your work. This library and media center should have a collection of folders or files devoted to different types of student writing and media presentations.
- Create a class anthology to which every student contributes one piece. Use electronic technology to design a small publication. Share your anthology with other classes.
- Submit your work to your school literary magazine, newspaper, or yearbook.

Outside School

- Submit your written work to a newspaper or magazine.
- Share your work with a professional interested in the subject.
- Present your work to an appropriate community group.
- Send a video based on your written work to a local cable television station.
- Enter your work in a local, state, or national writing contest.

Using Standard Manuscript Form

The appearance of your essay may be almost as important as its content. A marked-up paper with inconsistent margins is difficult to read. A neat, legible paper, however, makes a positive impression on your reader. When you are using a word-processing program to prepare your final draft, it is important to know how to lay out the page and how to choose a typeface and type size. Use the following guidelines for standard manuscript form to help you prepare your final draft. The model on page C53 shows how the writer used these guidelines to prepare her final draft on the differences between middle school and high school.

Standard Manuscript Form

- Use standard-sized 8½-by-11-inch white paper. Use one side of the paper only.
- If handwriting, use black or blue ink. If using a word-processing program or typing, use a black ink cartridge or black typewriter ribbon and double-space the lines.
- Leave a 1.25-inch margin at the left and right. The left margin must be even. The right margin should be as even as possible.
- Put your name, the course title, the name of your teacher, and the date in the upper right-hand corner of the first page. Follow your teacher's specific guidelines for headings and margins.
- Center the title of your essay two lines below the date. Do not underline or put quotation marks around your title.
- If using a word-processing program or typing, skip four lines between the title and the first paragraph. If handwriting, skip two lines.
- If using a word-processing program or typing, indent the first line of each paragraph five spaces. If handwriting, indent the first line of each paragraph 1 inch.
- Leave a 1-inch margin at the bottom of all pages.
- Starting on page 2, number each page in the upper right-hand corner. Begin the first line 1 inch from the top. Word-processing programs allow you to insert page numbers.

Time Out to Reflect

After working through the five stages of the writing process, ask yourself how closely this process matches your previous experiences as a writer. What might account for any differences between the writing process as described in this chapter and the writing process as you have previously experienced it? What stage do you feel you need to work on? How might you do that?

1 INCH

Sandra Diorio
English: Mr. Lee
September 15, 2000

2 LINES

Making a Transition to High School

4 LINES

Although I knew it would be a change from middle school, high school was a real surprise to me. Three differences especially surprised me the most and made me realize that high school would be a whole new experience.

1.25 INCHES

One difference I noticed right away is the courses I am taking, which are definitely more advanced. In middle school, for example, I took courses called science and math, while in high school I take biology instead of science and algebra instead of math. High school also offers more subjects than middle school, including foreign languages. I find that all the new courses make the subjects more interesting.

Another surprise was the amount of

1.25 INCHES

homework. I find I have twice as much homework in high school. In middle school I spent about an hour every weeknight doing homework, but now I spend about two hours a day, sometimes even on weekends. Longer study hall periods, however, help me to get some of my homework done during school hours. Although the homework takes longer

1 INCH

1 INCH

2

and is harder than before, I usually feel like I'm accomplishing things.

When I discovered I was having trouble concentrating in study hall, I realized how much more crowded high school is compared to middle school. The halls are jammed with students, many of whom I don't even know. With so many students, high school has a more competitive atmosphere. Many kids are trying out for the same spots on sport teams, for example. The added competition does have a positive side, however. It keeps me sharp.

1.25 INCHES

I'm getting used to the idea that high school is a whole new experience. Although the differences between middle school and high school unsettled me at first, I find they all have a strong plus side. The changes, such as the different courses, more homework, and a bigger crowd, become less surprising every day.

1.25 INCHES

Writing Process Checklist

Remember that a writing process is recursive—you can move back and forth among the stages of the process to achieve your purpose. The numbers in parentheses refer to pages where you can get help with your writing.

PREWRITING

- Find a subject to write about by taking an inventory of your interests, freewriting, exploring the Internet, keeping a journal, and reading and thinking about literature. *(pages C12–C17)*
- Choose and limit a subject. *(pages C18–C20)*
- Consider your purpose, audience, and occasion. Be aware of the voice you choose. *(pages C22–C24)*
- Develop your subject by observing, brainstorming for details, clustering, and inquiring. *(pages C25–C31)*
- Organize your material by focusing your subject, classifying your details, and ordering your details. *(pages C33–C35)*

DRAFTING

- Write a first draft and choose a title. *(pages C36–C38)*

REVISING

- Revise your draft by adding ideas, adding details and information, rearranging, deleting needless words and ideas, and substituting words and sentences. *(pages C38-C40)*
- Use the **Evaluation Checklist for Revising** as a reminder and guide. *(page C40)*
- Use conferencing to help you revise your draft. *(page C42)*
- Revise your draft as often as needed. Repeat some of the prewriting and drafting strategies if necessary.

EDITING

- Use the editing checklists to look for errors in grammar, usage, spelling, capitalization, and punctuation. *(pages C44 and C48)*
- Use proofreading symbols to correct errors. *(page C46)*

PUBLISHING

- Follow standard manuscript form and make a neat final copy of your work. Then find an appropriate way to share your work with others. *(pages C51–C54)*

CHAPTER 2

Developing Your Writing Style

If you are like most people who are skilled in a particular activity, you've gotten better and better at it because you do it often. Most likely, you've noticed that the better you get at doing something, the more you like it. You've also probably become aware that over time you have added your own touches and variations in carrying out the activity.

Suppose you have a knack for mixing and matching your clothes in ways that your friends admire. You may have some natural ability, but you probably also learned your unique style by experimenting with ways to combine the elements of line, color, shape, and texture with the design principles of pattern, unity, and variety.

The same can be true for writing. As you experiment with different approaches to composing, you'll continue to develop your writing style, which can be as distinctive as you are!

Reading with a Writer's Eye

A great writer's style grabs the reader's attention with vivid words and varied, uncluttered sentences. After you read the following excerpt from the autobiography of Maya Angelou, select a paragraph or two to read aloud. You will become more aware of the author's rhythm and of the surprising ways in which she describes her own experiences.

FROM

I KNOW WHY the Caged Bird Sings

Maya Angelou

For nearly a year, I sopped around the house, the Store, the school and the church, like an old biscuit, dirty and inedible. Then I met, or rather got to know, the lady who threw me my first life line.

Mrs. Bertha Flowers was the aristocrat of Black Stamps. She had the grace of control to appear warm in the coldest weather, and on the Arkansas summer days it seemed she had a private breeze which swirled around, cooling her. She was thin without the taut look of wiry people, and her printed voile[1] dresses and flowered hats were as right for her as denim overalls for a farmer. She was our side's answer to the richest white woman in town.

Her skin was a rich black that would have peeled like a plum if snagged, but then no one would have thought of getting close enough to Mrs. Flowers to ruffle her dress, let alone snag her skin. She didn't encourage familiarity. She wore gloves too.

I don't think I ever saw Mrs. Flowers laugh, but she smiled often. A slow widening of her thin black lips to show even, small white teeth, then the slow effortless closing. When she chose to smile on me, I always wanted to thank her. The action was so graceful and inclusively benign.

She was one of the few gentlewomen I have ever known, and has remained throughout my life the measure of what a human being can be. . . .

One summer afternoon, sweet-milk fresh in my memory, she stopped at the Store to buy provisions. Another Negro woman of her health and age would have been expected to carry the paper

---

[1] **voile** (vöil): Light, thin fabric (French).

sacks home in one hand, but Momma said, "Sister Flowers, I'll send Bailey up to your house with these things."

She smiled that slow dragging smile, "Thank you, Mrs. Henderson. I'd prefer Marguerite,[2] though." My name was beautiful when she said it. "I've been meaning to talk to her, anyway." . . .

She said, without turning her head, to me, "I hear you're doing very good school work, Marguerite, but that it's all written. The teachers report that they have trouble getting you to talk in class." We passed the triangular farm on our left and the path widened to allow us to walk together. I hung back in the separate unasked and unanswerable questions.

"Come and walk along with me, Marguerite." I couldn't have refused even if I wanted to. She pronounced my name so nicely. Or more correctly, she spoke each word with such clarity that I was certain a foreigner who didn't understand English could have understood her.

"Now no one is going to make you talk—possibly no one can. But bear in mind, language is man's way of communicating with his fellow man and it is language alone which separates him from the lower animals." That was a totally new idea to me, and I would need time to think about it.

"Your grandmother says you read a lot. Every chance you get. That's good, but not good enough. Words mean more than what is set down on paper. It takes the human voice to infuse them with the shades of deeper meaning."

I memorized the part about the human voice infusing words. It seemed so valid and poetic. She said she was going to give me some books and that I not only must read them, I must read them aloud. She suggested that I try to make a sentence sound in as many different ways as possible . . . .

The sweet scent of vanilla had met us as she opened the door.

---

[2] **Marguerite:** Maya Angelou was named Marguerite Johnson at birth.

"I made tea cookies this morning. You see, I had planned to invite you for cookies and lemonade so we could have this little chat. The lemonade is in the icebox." . . .

They were flat round wafers, slightly browned on the edges and butter-yellow in the center. With the cold lemonade they were sufficient for childhood's lifelong diet. Remembering my manners, I took nice little lady-like bites off the edges. She said she had made them expressly for me and that she had a few in the kitchen that I could take home to my brother. So I jammed one whole cake in my mouth and the rough crumbs scratched the insides of my jaws, and if I hadn't had to swallow, it would have been a dream come true.

As I ate she began the first of what we later called "my lessons in living." She said that I must always be intolerant of ignorance but understanding of illiteracy. That some people, unable to go to school, were more educated and even more intelligent than college professors. She encouraged me to listen carefully to what country people called mother wit. That in those homely sayings was couched the collective wisdom of generations.

When I finished the cookies she brushed off the table and brought a thick, small book from the bookcase. I had read *A Tale of Two Cities*[3] and found it up to my standards as a romantic novel. She opened the first page and I heard poetry for the first time in my life.

"It was the best of times and the worst of times . . ."[3] Her voice slid in and curved down through and over the words. She was nearly singing. I wanted to look at the pages. Were they the same that I had read? Or were there notes, music, lined on the pages, as in a hymn book? Her sounds began cascading gently. I knew from listening to a thousand preachers that she was nearing the end of her reading, and I hadn't really heard, heard to understand, a single word.

---

[3] ***A Tale of Two Cities*:** Novel by Charles Dickens.

[4] **"It was . . . times":** First sentence of *A Tale of Two Cities*.

"How do you like that?"

It occurred to me that she expected a response. The sweet vanilla flavor was still on my tongue and her reading was a wonder in my ears. I had to speak.

I said, "Yes, ma'am." It was the least I could do, but it was the most also.

"There's one more thing. Take this book of poems and memorize one for me. Next time you pay me a visit, I want you to recite."

I have tried often to search behind the sophistication of years for the enchantment I so easily found in those gifts. The essence escapes but its aura remains. To be allowed, no, invited, into the private lives of strangers, and to share their joys and fears, was a chance to exchange the Southern bitter wormwood[5] for a cup of mead[6] with Beowulf[7] or a hot cup of tea and milk with Oliver Twist.[8] When I said aloud, "It is a far, far better thing that I do, than I have ever done . . ."[9] tears of love filled my eyes at my selflessness.

On that first day, I ran down the hill and into the road (few cars ever came along it) and had the good sense to stop running before I reached the Store.

I was liked, and what a difference it made. I was respected not as Mrs. Henderson's grandchild or Bailey's sister but for just being Marguerite Johnson.

Childhood's logic never asks to be proved (all conclusions are absolute). I didn't question why Mrs. Flowers had singled me out for attention, nor did it occur to me that Momma might have asked her to give me a little talking to. All I cared about was that she had made tea cookies for *me* and read to *me* from her favorite book. It was enough to prove that she liked me.

---

[5] **wormwood:** Something bitter.

[6] **mead:** Drink of the Middle Ages made from honey.

[7] **Beowulf:** Hero of an Old English epic poem.

[8] **Oliver Twist:** Hero of a novel by Charles Dickens.

[9] **"It is. . . done":** Line in *A Tale of Two Cities*, spoken by a character who dies so that another may live.

Thinking as a Writer

Discovering the Elements of Style

The two main elements of a writer's style are the words he or she chooses and the way those words are put together in sentences. These elements will result in a great variety of styles that depend on individual choice, the purpose of the writing, and the intended audience.

- What was Maya Angelou's purpose in writing her autobiography?
- How would you characterize Angelou's writing?

Analyzing Individual Styles

Oral Expression

In the autobiography, Mrs. Flowers tells Maya Angelou that reading out loud gives a whole new meaning to a book or essay. Reading aloud is also a valuable tool to help you improve your own writing.

- Form a small group with two or three classmates. Read aloud the passage on the next page from *I Know Why the Caged Bird Sings.* How does the language that Maya Angelou uses in describing Mrs. Flowers affect how you read the passage? How does it affect how you picture Mrs. Flowers? As a group, choose another passage to read aloud, thinking again about the words Maya Angelou uses. How does her word choice affect how your group reads and interprets the passage?
- With a group of classmates, select one paragraph from the excerpt from Maya Angelou's autobiography that you find memorable. Then take turns reading the selection aloud. What do you discover about different people's ways of speaking? How is your reading affected by Angelou's writing style?
- Would Angelou's style be different if she were relating the same incidents in a speech or expressing them in an audio or video recording? Explain your response, using examples from her autobiography.

Her skin was a rich black that would have peeled like a plum if snagged, but then no one would have thought of getting close enough to Mrs. Flowers to ruffle her dress, let alone snag her skin. She didn't encourage familiarity. She wore gloves too.

Assessing Visual Styles

Viewing John Biggers, the artist of this painting, has selected people of Africa and African Americans as subjects of his drawings for more than fifty years. Maya Angelou commented that "John Biggers . . . leads us through his expression into the discovery of ourselves at our most intimate level. His pen and pencil and brush take us without faltering into the individual personal world where each of us lives privately."

- Explain what you think Maya Angelou means by her comments. Analyze Biggers' use of the elements of art (line, shape, form, space, color, texture) and the principles of design (balance, emphasis, proportion, pattern, rhythm, unity, variety) to support your interpretation of Angelou's statement.

John Biggers, *Three Quilters (Quilting Party)*, 1952. Conté crayon, 30 by 40 inches. Dallas Museum of Art.

Developing Your Stylistic Skills

The American writer E. B. White wrote, "The main thing I try to do is write as clearly as I can. Because I have the greatest respect for the reader, . . . the least I can do is make it as easy as possible for him to find out what I'm trying to say. . . ." White, who is considered one of the finest American stylists of this century, developed his writing style by pursuing this seemingly simple goal. Yet writing clearly is far from simple, in part because you first have to figure out exactly what you are trying to say. As you develop your writing style, you may find it helpful to set one basic goal, as E. B. White did. Writing as clearly as you can with your audience in mind may seem like a modest goal, yet figuring out what you are trying to say and then saying it clearly can be a challenge. You may, in fact, discover your writing style in the process of trying to communicate clearly.

Your writing **style** is the distinctive way you express yourself through the words you choose and the way you shape your sentences.

Your Writer's Journal

Freewrite for a few minutes about people who have influenced you. Then choose one person who stands out in your memory. Jot down words that describe this person—both external and internal traits. Throughout the week, continue noting vivid words that remind you of others who have influenced or impressed you—including some you may never have met. Soon you'll have a wealth of vivid language to draw from in your future writing.

Choosing Vivid Words

Writers look for ways to make their writing shine. One way to do this is by choosing words and expressions that express what you mean specifically.

Summer burned the canals dry. Summer moved like a flame upon the meadows. In the empty Earth settlement, the painted houses flaked and peeled. Rubber tires upon which children had swung in back yards hung suspended like stopped clock pendulums in the blazing air.

—*Ray Bradbury,* "Dark They Were and Golden Eyed"

Specific Words

Specific words help readers visualize what they read. For example, the following examples describe the same item on a restaurant menu. The first example uses general words that leave only a vague impression. The second uses specific words that whet the appetite.

GENERAL Cooked meat covered with a good sauce, served with tasty potatoes and cooked fresh vegetables

SPECIFIC Barbecued spareribs smothered in a tangy sauce, served with sizzling French-fried potatoes and crisp steamed broccoli

General words may mean different things to different people, but specific words appeal to the senses through the reader's imagination. Compare the following general and specific words.

GENERAL AND SPECIFIC WORDS

	General	Specific	More Specific
NOUNS	meat	pork	spareribs
	clothes	pants	blue jeans
ADJECTIVES	uneasy	nervous	jittery
	thin	delicate	fragile
VERBS	went	walked	strolled
	saw	watched	examined
ADVERBS	happily	gleefully	exuberantly
	soon	promptly	now

PRACTICE YOUR SKILLS

Revising Specific Words

Revise the following composition by replacing each underlined word or words with more vivid, specific language. The first sentence has been done for you as an example.

After the Movies

Kathy's dad took us out for **(1)** dessert after the movie. While we were eating, we **(2)** talked about the movie. Kathy thought the acting was convincing, but the story was **(3)** weak. I thought the scenes with the Martians were **(4)** good. The chase scenes were comical because the four-legged Martians **(5)** walked oddly. Kathy's dad thought the special effects were **(6)** poor. He **(7)** laughed during one scene when you could see the strings that were attached to the spaceship. Before leaving the **(8)** place where we were having dessert, each of us gave the movie a grade. Kathy and her dad gave it a D+, but I gave the movie an **(9)** excellent grade. Later that night I dreamed that little green **(10)** creatures helped me finish my algebra homework.

Figurative Language

You can create vivid pictures in your readers' minds not only by using specific words, but also by using figurative language. The two most common types of **figurative language** are similes and metaphors.

Newspapers

How do writers find ways to keep their stories lively and fresh? One way is to search for fresh synonyms for tired words. Another is to add powerful descriptive words. Here is an example from sports journalism.

The Chicago Bears were leading the Green Bay Packers in the first game since Bears legend Walter "Sweetness" Payton passed away. Green Bay was poised for a game-winning field goal. Here's how two *Chicago Tribune* writers described what happened.

With a nod to Payton for the assist, [Bryan] Robinson capitalized on a low snap by the Packers and blocked what would have been a game-winning field goal by Ryan Longwell as time expired to preserve a 14–13 victory. . . .

"I have just one word," said running back James Allen. "It's sweet. Sweetness."

It will be Walter's Game forever now that the Bears have won it, the 159th rendering of pro football's most storied border war. This is, of course, absurd in any real, touchable sense. It was Bryan Robinson's and not Walter Payton's hand that blocked the dead certain Packer field goal at the end. . . .

Was it Payton who raised Robinson up to block that kick, the first blocked kick of Robinson's career?

"Walter Payton picked me up in the air," insisted Robinson. "I can't jump that high."

There is some language that is the same in both pieces. *Field goal* and *blocked kick* mean something specific and cannot easily be replaced by synonyms. But there is plenty of variety for the many other actions and reactions that happen on the field.

Media Activity

Imagine you work at the rewrite desk of a newspaper. Rewrite the opening sentence of each story above. Keep the meaning the same, but rewrite using synonyms and fresh descriptions.

Similes and Metaphors These figures of speech stimulate the reader's imagination by expressing a similarity between two things that are essentially different.

Similes state a comparison by using the words *like* or *as.* **Metaphors**, however, imply a comparison by simply saying that one thing *is* another.

SIMILE	Her skin was a rich black that would have peeled **like a plum** if snagged. . . .
METAPHOR	To be allowed, no, invited, into the private lives of strangers, and to share their joys and fears, was **a chance to exchange the Southern bitter worm wood for a cup of mead with Beowulf or a hot cup of tea and milk with Oliver Twist.**

A woman's skin and the skin of a plum are different things, of course. Maya Angelou suggests that Mrs. Flowers had skin as plump and smooth, and as richly hued, as a plum. By evoking the image of a peeling plum, the author also conveys a sense of how vulnerable to harm that smooth skin might be.

A human life is not like a drink, but the metaphor suggests that to enter the private world of Mrs. Flowers and the literary England of the eighth and nineteenth centuries is sweet nourishment for Marguerite.

PRACTICE YOUR SKILLS

Identifying Similes and Metaphors

Write *simile* or *metaphor* to identify each underlined figure of speech in the following sentences.

1. My brother's room <u>is a federal disaster area</u>.
2. With crashing cymbals and booming drums, the symphony was <u>like a thunderstorm</u>.
3. Good friends revolve around Keisha <u>as the planets revolve around the sun</u>.

4. Hope went through me like a faint breeze over a lake.

–Antoine de Saint-Exupéry

5. The coach growled when his players quit too soon.
6. Her secret was as dark as her eyes.
7. Hermit crabs, like frantic children, scamper on the bottom sand.

–John Steinbeck

8. All the strength went out of me, and I toppled forward like an undermined tower.

–Mark Twain

9. Memories poured from every corner of the old house.
10. The black bat, night, has flown.

–Alfred, Lord Tennyson

Create clear and vivid images by using **specific words** and **figurative language.**

Clichés Some comparisons that were once clever and striking have become dull with overuse. Such worn-out expressions are called **clichés**. If you find yourself using a simile or metaphor that you have heard before, replace it with a fresh comparison or with specific words.

CLICHÉ	knocked me over with a feather
SPECIFIC WORDS	completely surprised me; made me weak with amazement
CLICHÉ	make a mountain out of a molehill
SPECIFIC WORDS	exaggerate unnecessarily; needlessly make things more difficult
CLICHÉ	as cool as a cucumber
SPECIFIC WORDS	relaxed; nonchalant

FRESH COMPARISONS	as calm as a blind man in the dark; as self-possessed as a snail

PRACTICE YOUR SKILLS

Revising to Eliminate Clichés

Revise the following personal narrative by replacing each underlined cliché with a fresh simile or metaphor, or with specific words.

Tryouts

Everyone told me the tryouts for the school play would be **(1)** as easy as A, B, C, but when I saw how many juniors and seniors were trying out, I felt **(2)** like a duck out of water. By the time I was called to read my lines, I was **(3)** shaking like a leaf, and my throat was **(4)** as dry as a desert. Somehow I managed to **(5)** spit out the first few lines. Then suddenly my voice became **(6)** a squeaky, old hinge. Mercifully the director stopped me and told me **(7)** to start from scratch. This time I was **(8)** as steady as a rock and my voice was **(9)** as clear as a bell. When the cast list was announced the next day at school, **(10)** it was music to my ears.

Creating Sentence Variety

Good writing flows with the natural, varied rhythms of speech. As you read the passage by Ernest Hemingway on page C71, notice how the varied rhythm of his sentences contributes to the pleasure of reading the paragraph.

Developing Vivid Comparisons

When you write a simile or a metaphor, you are using a thinking skill called comparing. When you **compare**, you tell how two things are similar. Thinking of a fresh comparison to use in a simile or metaphor, however, is sometimes difficult to do. The following chart illustrates a thinking strategy that will help you develop vivid comparisons.

Qualities of a Strawberry	Things with Similar Qualities
plump	a marshmallow, a baby's cheek
juicy	a watermelon, an orange
red	a ruby, a clown's nose
rough	a cat's tongue; cornmeal

To create a comparison chart, first think about what you want to describe. Then make a list of its most important qualities. Next to each quality list some other things that have the same quality. Stretch your imagination and avoid overused comparisons like *red as a rose.* Once you have a list of comparisons, you can select the best one for your simile or metaphor.

SIMILE Red, ripe strawberries gleamed under the shadowy leaves **like unmined rubies in a gem field.**

THINKING PRACTICE

Use the thinking strategy described above to help you write a fresh simile or metaphor for each of the following items.

1. waves hitting rocks
2. a ferris wheel at night
3. a stubbornly determined child going up stairs

> Before it was really light he had his baits out and was drifting with the current. One bait was down forty fathoms. The second was at seventy-five and the third and fourth were down in the blue water at one hundred and one hundred and twenty-five fathoms.
>
> —*Ernest Hemingway,* The Old Man and the Sea

Sentence-Combining Strategies

To appreciate how important rhythm is in writing, try reading a paragraph that consists only of a string of short sentences. Too many short sentences in a row make the writing choppy and difficult to read. When you revise your writing, you can improve the flow of short sentences by combining them to make longer, varied ones. The following sentence-combining strategies show you how.

Combining Sentences with Phrases One way to combine short sentences is to express some of the information in a phrase. The following examples show how to combine sentences using three kinds of phrases.

A. Handlers can usually train dogs. Training is in basic obedience. Training takes about eight weeks.

Handlers can usually train dogs **in basic obedience in about eight weeks.** (prepositional phrases)

B. Handlers and dogs work together. This strengthens the bond between pet and master.

Handlers and dogs work together, **strengthening the bond between pet and master.** (participial phrase)

C. A training collar helps the handler correct the dog. It is the handler's most important tool.

A training collar, **the handler's most important tool**, helps correct the dog. (appositive phrase)

Practice Your Skills

Combining Sentences with Phrases

Using the examples on page C71, combine each pair of sentences. The letter in parentheses indicates which example to use. Remember to insert commas where needed.

1. Tim Gallwey wrote a book. He wrote about becoming a winner. (A: prepositional phrase)
2. His book captured great attention. His book is *The Inner Game of Tennis.* (C: appositive phrase)
3. Gallwey identifies an "inner game." This is a game between the player's actions and his or her thoughts and feelings. (B: participial phrase)
4. The inner game influences the play between opponents. The inner game tests a player's confidence and powers of concentration. (B: participial phrase)
5. Playing the inner game well brings rewards. The rewards are in concentration. The rewards are in relaxation. The rewards are in success in the game. (A: prepositional phrase)
6. Each player plays two roles that determine his or her skill. These are the director and the doer. (C: appositive phrase)
7. The director is the inner player. The director gives the doer such instructions as, "OK, hit the next volley high." (B: participial phrase)
8. In good players the director and the doer interact. They interact in harmony. (A: prepositional phrase)
9. In weaker players, the doer can become frustrated. The doer tries too hard and fails. (B: participial phrase)
10. Mastering the inner game has value. The value is in life as well as in tennis. (A: prepositional phrase)

Combining Sentences by Coordinating Another way to smooth out short, choppy sentences is to link ideas of equal importance with a coordinating conjunction.

COORDINATING CONJUNCTIONS						
and	but	for	nor	or	so	yet

The following sentences about dog training show how to combine sentences with coordinating conjunctions.

A. Kindness is also important. Praise is important, too.

Kindness and **praise** are also important. (compound subject)

B. Soon your dog will heel on command. Soon your dog will sit on command.

Soon your dog **will heel** and **sit** on command. (compound verb)

C. The dog should be confined before each session. The place of confinement should be comfortable.

The dog should be confined before each session, but **the place of confinement should be comfortable.** (compound sentence)

PRACTICE YOUR SKILLS

Combining Sentences by Coordinating

Combine each pair of sentences, using the model identified in parentheses following each pair. Add punctuation as needed.

1. F. M. Alexander, who lived in the 1800s, acted. He also gave speeches. (B: compound verb)
2. In the 1880s he suddenly lost his voice. His career ground to a halt. (C: compound sentence)

3. He visited doctors. None of them could help him. (C: compound sentence)

4. He had little choice but to help himself. He had no medical training. (C: compound sentence)

5. He began observing in the mirror his efforts to speak. He saw something odd about his movements. (B: compound verb)

6. His head moved when he tried to talk. His neck also moved. (A: compound subject)

7. These movements affected his posture. His posture in turn affected his speech. (C: compound sentence)

8. He kept up his observations. He eventually cured himself by relaxing his head and neck. (B: compound verb)

9. Alexander's method became a classic treatment. It is still used to help people solve some medical problems through better posture. (B: compound verb)

10. The treatment stresses simple, everyday exercises, such as walking. Anyone can do them. (C: compound sentence)

Combining Sentences by Subordinating If the ideas in two short sentences are of unequal importance, you can combine them by subordinating. To subordinate, express the less important idea in an adjective clause that begins with a relative pronoun or in an adverb clause that begins with a subordinating conjunction. The pronouns and conjunctions below are often used to begin clauses.

FOR ADJECTIVE CLAUSES		FOR ADVERB CLAUSES	
Relative Pronouns		**Subordinating Conjunctions**	
who	which	after	unless
whom	that	although	until
whose		because	whenever

The following example sentences about dog training show how to combine sentences by creating adjective or adverb clauses.

A. Mother dogs use a barking sound to get their pups to obey. The barking sound resembles the word *out.*

Mother dogs use a barking sound, **which resembles the word *out,*** to get their pups to obey. (adjective clause)

B. Handlers can also use this sound. Dogs have a long memory of their mothers' stern corrections.

Handlers can also use this sound **because dogs have a long memory of their mothers' stern corrections.** (adverb clause)

Practice Your Skills

Combining Sentences

Combine each pair of sentences, using the method indicated in brackets following each pair. Refer to the examples on pages C71 and C73 and to those above. Add punctuation as needed.

On the Trail

(1) We wanted to do something different on our vacation. We chose backpacking in the wilderness. (compound sentence) **(2)** We walked the entire distance. We had packs on our backs. (prepositional phrases) **(3)** I could carry my own pack. It weighed 50 pounds. (adverb clause) **(4)** The trail was steep and hazardous. It had been a logging road. (adjective clause) **(5)** At one point we came to a lookout tower. It was in good condition. (adjective clause) **(6)** I climbed the tower. I strapped my camera around my neck. (participial phrase) **(7)** Fog had covered the valley. I could barely see. (compound sentence) **(8)** In the distance a river came down from the mountains. It flowed east. (compound verb) **(9)** A footpath followed the river. An old railroad track followed the river. (compound subject) **(10)** That foggy view has stayed in my memory to this day. It was a highlight of the vacation. (appositive phrase)

Varying Sentence Beginnings

The most natural way to begin a sentence is with the subject. If too many sentences begin in the same way, however, even a gripping story will sound dull. The following examples show how Hal Borland varied the beginnings of his sentences in his novel *When the Legends Die*.

SUBJECT	**The boy** caught trout in the pool and watched for his friend, the bear.
ADVERB	**Reluctantly** the boy fastened the collar on the bear cub.
PHRASE	**For days** he watched them. (prepositional phrase)
	Driving with one hand, he headed for home. (participial phrase)
CLAUSE	**If he rode the horse with its own rhythm,** he could ride every horse in the herd. (adverb clause)

When you revise, vary the rhythm of your writing by starting your sentences in a variety of ways.

PRACTICE YOUR SKILLS

Varying Sentence Beginnings

Vary the beginning of each of the following sentences by using the openers suggested in parentheses.

1. The universe, stretching endlessly beyond the reaches of our imagination, holds many mysteries. (participial phrase)
2. There are 100 billion stars in just our own galaxy, the Milky Way. (prepositional phrase and appositive phrase)
3. However, only the nearest and brightest stars are visible when we gaze into the vast sea of stars. (adverb clause)
4. We can see fewer than 3,000 stars on a clear night. (prepositional phrase)

5. The Milky Way would look like a giant fried egg if we could look down on it. (adverb clause)
6. Our galaxy, bulging in the middle, spans 10,000 light-years at the center. (participial phrase)
7. Orbiting stars in the outer part of the galaxy form graceful spiral arms. (prepositional phrases)
8. One spiral arm extending through the constellations Perseus and Cassiopeia reaches out 7,000 light-years from the sun. (participial phrase)
9. Our solar system travels 250 miles per second, although we do not feel the motion. (adverb clause)
10. One complete orbit around the galaxy nevertheless takes 250 million years. (adverb)

Varying Sentence Structure

Another way to achieve a natural sound and rhythm in your writing is to vary the structure of your sentences. In the following example, Marjorie Kinnan Rawlings describes a part of her stay near a North Carolina orphanage. Notice how she uses a variety of sentence structures to create a flowing rhythm.

SIMPLE
COMPLEX
COMPOUND-COMPLEX
COMPLEX
COMPOUND-COMPLEX

At daylight I was half wakened by the sound of chopping. Again it was so even in texture that I went back to sleep. When I left my bed in the cool morning, the boy had come and gone, and a stack of kindling was neat against the cabin wall. He came again after school in the afternoon and worked until it was time to return to the orphanage. His name was Jerry; he was twelve years old, and he had been at the orphanage since he was four.

—*Marjorie Kinnan Rawlings,* "A Mother in Manville"

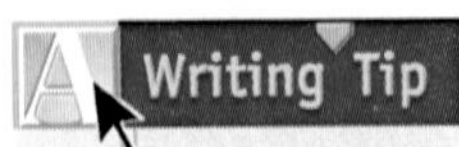

When you revise, create a natural rhythm by **varying** the beginning, length, and structure of your sentences.

Practice Your Skills

Revising for Sentence Variety

The following paragraph contains only simple sentences. Create a variety of simple, compound, complex, and compound-complex sentences by combining the sentences according to the structure indicated in parentheses. Use commas where needed.

Handwriting Analysis

(1) Handwriting analysis is not an exact science. Police often seek the opinion of a handwriting expert in cases of forgery. **(complex)** **(2)** The handwriting in question is placed under a microscope. A known piece of handwriting is placed beside it. **(compound)** **(3)** The handwriting expert analyzes the two samples. The expert does this by comparing significant details. These details include the dots above *i*'s, the crosses through *t*'s, the angle of the pen, and the beginnings and ends of pen strokes. **(simple)** **(4)** Experts sometimes contradict each other's analyses. Many people doubt the reliability of handwriting analysis. **(complex)** **(5)** Doubts persist. Courts allow handwriting experts to testify. Juries are often persuaded by the testimony of these experts. **(compound-complex)** **(6)**

Time Out to Reflect

As you learn more ways to improve your writing style, take a moment to think about other kinds of writing that may improve as a result. Is your writing for other subjects getting a better response?

Describing the treats Mrs. Flowers prepares for her, Maya Angelou writes, "They were flat round wafers, slightly browned on the edges and butter-yellow in the center. With the cold lemonade they were sufficient for childhood's lifelong diet. . . . I jammed one whole cake in my mouth and the rough crumbs scratched the insides of my jaws. . . ." These sentences would not make much of an impact without specific nouns like *wafers, edges, diet, crumbs, insides,* and *jaws*. Learning to use specific nouns is a valuable tool in bringing your written ideas to life.

Capitalization of Proper Nouns

One way to make nouns more specific is to substitute proper nouns for common nouns. A **common noun** is any person, place, or thing. A **proper noun** is a particular person, place, or thing. Remember that proper nouns always begin with a capital letter.

Common Nouns	After leaving the **city,** we boarded the **spaceship** for another **planet.**
Proper Nouns	After leaving **Philadelphia,** we boarded ***Unisurf*** **for Venus.**

Punctuation with Possessive Nouns

With a few exceptions, to show ownership or possession, a singular noun must end with *'s*. To form the possessive of a plural noun, however, do one of two things: add only an apostrophe to a plural noun that ends in *s* or add *'s* to a plural noun that does not end in *s*.

Singular Possessive	The **spaceship's** cabin is comfortable, but **Venus's** climate is not.
Plural Possessive	The **adults'** spacesuits were blue, but the **children's** spacesuits were green.

Punctuation with a Series of Nouns

Three or more nouns in a row are confusing to read if they are not separated by commas.

INCORRECT	The alien had three heads seven arms and only one leg.
CORRECT	The alien had three heads, seven arms, and only one leg.

Spelling the Plurals of Nouns

Simply add an *s* to form the plural of most nouns. The endings of a few nouns must be changed, however, before you add an *s*. For example, if a word ends in a consonant and a *y*, you must change the *y* to *i* and add *es*.

SINGULAR	The **baby** in the space **capsule** slept peacefully.
PLURAL	The **babies** in the space **capsules** slept peacefully. (*Baby* ends in a consonant and *y*; change *y* to *i* and add *es.)*
SINGULAR	Everyone was busy the **day** before the spaceship took off.
PLURAL	Everyone was busy the **days** before the spaceship took off.(**Day** ends in a vowel and *y*; add *s*)

Editing Checklist

- ✔ Are proper nouns capitalized?
- ✔ Are apostrophes used correctly with possessive nouns?
- ✔ Do commas separate words in a series?
- ✔ Are plural nouns spelled correctly?

Writing Concise Sentences

Compact cars go farther on a gallon of gasoline than do huge gas-guzzlers. In the same way, concise sentences deliver more meaning from each word than do repetitive, wordy sentences.

Create **concise** sentences by expressing your meaning in as few words as possible.

Rambling Sentences

A sentence that rambles on too long is dull and hard to understand. In the following description, too many ideas are strung together in one sentence.

RAMBLING — The buzz saw screams as you watch the tree come up the conveyor belt, and as the tree hits the saw, chips fly left and right, and when it reaches the end of the saw, the log folds over into two slabs.

When you revise, eliminate rambling sentences by separating the ideas into a variety of short and long sentences.

REVISED — The buzz saw screams as you watch the tree come up the conveyor belt. As the tree hits the saw, chips fly left and right. When it reaches the end of the saw, the log folds over into two slabs.

PRACTICE YOUR SKILLS

Revising Rambling Sentences

Revise the following paragraph by breaking up the rambling sentence. Use capital letters and punctuation where needed.

Winchester House

Winchester House is the name of a huge, rambling mansion in San José, California, that was built by Sarah Winchester, who was heir to the Winchester fortune and who believed that she would go on living as long as she was adding to the house, which has 160 rooms, 200 doors, and 47 fireplaces.

Redundancy

Unnecessary repetition is called **redundancy**. In a redundant sentence, the same idea is expressed more than once with no new or different shades of meaning.

REDUNDANT	The **hungry** wolf ate **ravenously.**
CONCISE	The wolf ate **ravenously.**
REDUNDANT	The **hot, steamy** asphalt shimmered.
CONCISE	The **steamy** asphalt shimmered.

PRACTICE YOUR SKILLS

Revising to Eliminate Redundancy

Revise each of the following sentences by eliminating the redundancy.

1. Do you have a spare pencil that you are not using?

2. Friday is the final deadline for the report.

3. Each and every member of the class must help.

4. Can you keep this secret confidential?

5. I can begin to get started on the project now.

Wordiness

The use of words and expressions that add nothing to the meaning of a sentence is called **wordiness**. Like redundancy, wordiness is tiresome and distracting to a reader.

Empty Expressions One way to avoid wordiness is to rid your sentences of empty expressions. Notice how the revisions for conciseness improve the following sentences.

WORDY	I can't go to the movies **due to the fact that** I have my guitar lesson tonight.
CONCISE	I can't go to the movies **because** I have my guitar lesson tonight.
WORDY	**There are** dozens of games **that** resemble checkers.
CONCISE	Dozens of games resemble checkers.

EMPTY EXPRESSIONS	
the thing that	due to the fact that
on account of	the reason that
what I want is	the thing/fact is that
in my opinion	there is/are/was/were
It is/was	what I mean is that
it seems as if	I believe/feel/think that

PRACTICE YOUR SKILLS

Eliminating Empty Expressions

Revise each of the following sentences by eliminating the empty expressions. If necessary, replace empty expressions with more precise language.

EXAMPLE	The thing that I enjoy is skiing.
POSSIBLE ANSWER	I enjoy skiing.

1. We canceled the game due to the fact that it rained.

2. The reason that I called is to ask if you need help.

3. Because of the fact that he was sick, his report is late.

4. The thing that I really hate is getting up early.

5. There are some places in the river that are dangerous.

Wordy Phrases and Clauses Another way to avoid wordiness is to shorten wordy phrases and clauses. In many cases a phrase can be reduced to a single word.

Wordy	Archaeologists found ancient tools **made of stone.** (participial phrase)
Concise	Archaeologists found ancient **stone** tools. (adjective)
Wordy	Elana spoke to the shy horse **in a gentle tone.** (prepositional phrase)
Concise	Elana spoke **gently** to the shy horse. (adverb)
Wordy	**To be tardy** is often a sign of laziness. (infinitive phrase)
Concise	**Tardiness** is often a sign of laziness. (noun)

Similarly, a clause can be reduced to a phrase or even to a single word.

Wordy	People **who are in show business** lead a hectic life of rehearsals and performances. (clause)
Concise	People **in show business** lead a hectic life of rehearsals and performances. (prepositional phrase)
Wordy	In Yosemite, **which is a national park in California,** cars are forbidden past a certain point. (clause)
Concise	In Yosemite, **a national park in California,** cars are forbidden past a certain point. (appositive phrase)
Wordy	Climates **that are dry** are good for people with allergy problems. (clause)
Concise	**Dry** climates are good for people with allergy problems. (adjective)

Practice Your Skills

Revising Wordy Phrases and Clauses

Revise each of the following sentences by shortening the underlined wordy phrase or clause.

1. Misha likes chicken <u>cooked with barbecue sauce</u>.
2. Students <u>who are trying out for band</u> should come to school on Saturday morning.
3. An exchange student <u>who came to our neighborhood from France</u> lives with our neighbors.
4. Tamara, <u>who is an accident victim</u>, competed in the marathon in a wheelchair.
5. Games <u>that are in good condition</u> will be accepted for the charity drive.
6. Luis organized his bookshelf <u>in a neat way</u>.
7. The motel had a pool <u>that was heated</u>.

Applying Revision Techniques

Revise the following paragraph to eliminate the problems indicated in parentheses.

Up in the Air

(1) Some people do not like going into skyscrapers. Being so high up makes them feel sick as a dog. (cliché, short and choppy sentences) **(2)**The fact is that acrophobiacs, who are people with a fear of heights, may even suddenly lose their balance and fall. (empty expression, wordy clause) **(3)** The tallest skyscrapers are the most frightening, since the top of one of these buildings can sway as much as three feet in the wind, and on a windy day, people who are riding in the elevator can hear it hitting the sides of the shaft. (rambling sentence, wordy clause) **(4)** Because of the fact that skyscrapers sway and move, some people feel airsick when they are on the upper floors. (empty expression, redundancy)

Your Writing Style Checklist

Style is created through the careful drafting of sentences and words. Use the following checklist to review some of the many ways you can develop your writing style. The numbers in parentheses refer to pages where you can get help with your writing.

CHOOSING VIVID WORDS

- Use specific nouns, verbs, adjectives, and adverbs to make your writing clear and vivid. *(pages C63–C64)*
- Use figurative language, such as similes, metaphors, personification, and onomatopoeia; to create strong mental images. *(pages C65–C68)*
- Avoid clichés. *(pages C68–C69)*

CREATING SENTENCE VARIETY

- Vary the length and structure of sentences by combining short, choppy sentences into longer ones that read more smoothly. *(pages C71–C75)*
- Use the techniques of coordination and subordination to add variety and clarify ideas. *(pages C73–C75)*
- Vary sentence beginnings to avoid monotony. *(page C76)*
- Vary your sentence structure. Strive for a mixture of the four basic sentence types: simple, compound, complex, and compound-complex. *(pages C77–C78)*

WRITING CONCISE SENTENCES

- Keep your sentences concise by eliminating rambling sentences, redundancy, wordiness, empty expressions, and inflated language. *(pages C81–C84)*

Connection Collection

Representing in Different Ways

From Visuals . . .

. . . to Print

Imagine you work for your school newspaper and write a brief description of the skier shown in the picture. Without using wordy phrases or clichés, try to match your writing style to the picture.

From Print . . .

When Homer McCracken leaned into the pitch thrown by Joey Strikezone, there was a hush in the air. As the bat and ball connected, cheers from the crowd shook the whole stadium. Homer McCracken would once again stride around the bases in triumph. . . .

— *The Battersville Times*

. . . to Visuals

Draw a picture, or do research to find a photograph of someone who matches the description of what Homer McCracken is doing in the newspaper clipping. Try to match your photo to the writing style of *The Battersville Times.*

- **Which strategies can be used for creating both written and visual representations? Which strategies apply to one, not both? Which type of representation is more effective?**
- **Draw a conclusion, and write briefly about the differences between written ideas and visual representations.**

Writing in Everyday Life

Informal E-mail

Last April you won third prize in the Megabucks Clearinghouse Sweepstakes. Your prize is a free vacation. However, the destination seems strange—a remote Atlantic island called Sula Sula. It is late November when your plane lands at the tiny airport. Just before you settle into one of the two restaurants for dinner, you decide to write to a friend back home.

Write an E-mail to your friend describing every detail of what you have seen so far. What specific words, similes, or metaphors will keep your friend's interest? Although an E-mail message can be informal, avoid clichés in structuring your sentences.

What strategies did you use to compose a vivid and effective E-mail to your friend?

You can find information on writing an E-mail in A Writer's Guide to Using the Internet, pages C724–C767.

Writing in the Workplace

Descriptive Note

You have recently been promoted in your job at WZAP, a local television station. Your new task is to recommend four classic programs for the station's Saturday morning cartoon lineup.

Write a descriptive note to Mr. Zapster, the president of WZAP. In the note, list your favorite Saturday morning shows. Explain in concise terms what you like about each program. Vary your sentence beginnings, and avoid redundancy. Try to make the writing style of your note vivid and clear so Mr. Zapster can see an image of each show in his mind.

What strategies did you use to describe your favorite shows to Mr. Zapster?

Assess Your Learning

You started *The Groove Gazette* as a music newsletter. Now it is a Website with glossy features. Your old review of *Head 2 Paradise* by the Blister Sisters has resurfaced, but the writing style needs work before you can reprint it.

Revise the album review shown below. Choose specific words, vary your sentences, and replace clichés with figurative language. Eliminate wordiness and redundancy to create a logical flow. Use transitions to combine sentences and create coherence for your readers.

The Blister Sisters' **Head 4 Paradise** is like the pot of gold at the end of the rainbow. In collaborating on this album, the Sisters really worked together. Due to the fact that a record was not made by them since **Porcupine Love**, I feared that the Blisters might sound rusty, but I was relieved to hear an album tailor-made for all the fans who follow their music. **Head 4 Paradise** has a slow song. It is called "Chalkboard Blues." It is a sad song that made me feel pensive. The mellow new sound is a breath of fresh air.

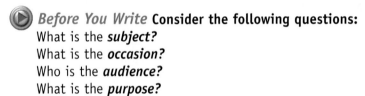

Before You Write **Consider the following questions:**
What is the ***subject?***
What is the ***occasion?***
Who is the ***audience?***
What is the ***purpose?***

After You Write **Evaluate your work using the following criteria:**

- Is your writing style appropriate for the audience of music fans?
- Have you used special words to create clear, vivid images?
- Have you avoided using jargon?
- Have you combined short, choppy sentences, using phrases and conjunctions?
- Have you eliminated wordy phrases, unnecessary clauses, and rambling sentences?
- Have you added similes or metaphors to appeal to your reader's imagination?
- Have you used correct grammar, spelling, and punctuation?

Write briefly on how well you did. Point out your strengths and areas for improvement.

CHAPTER 3

Writing Informative Paragraphs

In this chapter you will explore how to write informative paragraphs. Informative writing explains or informs. The subjects of informative paragraphs can range widely, from simple, everyday things to the great puzzles of nature. For instance, you might use informative writing in a science report on tornadoes. In presenting the causes and effects of a tornado, you are using informative writing to communicate facts. To tell how a tornado forms and what people should do during a tornado, you are using informative writing to explain. You can apply the skills of writing informative paragraphs to any topic you want to write about.

In "The Life and Death of a Western Gladiator," you will discover how one writer effectively uses informative writing. In the selection, Finney writes both to inform and to explain. The selection demonstrates effectively how captivating informative writing can be.

Reading with a Writer's Eye

In "The Life and Death of a Western Gladiator," Charles G. Finney explains the life cycle of a desert rattlesnake. As you read this informative article, pay attention to what you are learning about the diamondback rattler. Look for paragraphs that inform by telling what the snake looks like, what it eats, who its enemies are, and generally how it survives. Finally, pay attention to Finney's unusual and exciting way of writing about the rattlesnake.

FROM

The Life and Death of a Western Gladiator

Charles G. Finney

He was born on a summer morning in the shady mouth of a cave. Three others were born with him, another male and two females. Each was about five inches long and slimmer than a lead pencil.

Their mother left them a few hours after they were born. A day after that his brother and sisters left him also. He was all alone. Nobody cared whether he lived or died. His tiny brain was very dull. He had no arms or legs. His skin was delicate. Nearly everything that walked on the ground or burrowed in it, that flew in the air or swam in the water or climbed trees was his enemy. But he didn't know that. He knew nothing at all. He was aware of his own existence, and that was the sum of his knowledge.

The direct rays of the sun could, in a short time, kill him. If the temperature dropped too low he would freeze. Without food he would starve. Without moisture he would die of dehydration. If a man or a horse stepped on him he would be crushed. If anything chased him he could run neither very far nor very fast.

Thus it was at the hour of his birth. Thus it would be, with modifications, all his life.

But against these drawbacks he had certain qualifications that fitted him to be a competitive creature of this world and equipped him for its warfare. He could exist a long time without food or water. His very smallness at birth protected him when he most needed protection. Instinct provided him with what he lacked in experience. In order to eat he first had to kill, and he was eminently adapted for killing. In sacs in his jaws he secreted a virulent[1] poison. To inject that poison he had two fangs, hollow and pointed. Without that poison and those fangs he would have been among the most helpless creatures on earth. With them he was among the deadliest.

He was, of course, a baby rattlesnake, a desert diamondback, named *Crotalus atrox* by the herpetologists[2] Baird and Girard and so listed in the *Catalogue of North American Reptiles* in its issue of 1853. He was grayish brown in color, with a series of large, dark, diamond-shaped blotches on his back. His tail was white with five black crossbands. It had a button on the end of it.

Little Crotalus lay in the dust in the mouth of his cave. Some of his kinfolk lay there too. It was their home. That particular tribe of rattlers had lived there for scores of years.

The cave had never been seen by a white man.

Sometimes as many as two hundred rattlers occupied the den. Sometimes the numbers shrunk to as few as forty or fifty.

The tribe members did nothing at all for each other except breed. They hunted singly; they never shared food. They derived some automatic degree of safety from their numbers, but their actions were never concerted toward using their numbers to any end. If any enemy attacked one of them, the others did nothing about it.

Young Crotalus's brother was the first of the litter to go out into the world and the first to die. He achieved a distance of fifty feet from the den when a Sonoran racer, four feet long and hungry, came upon him. The little rattler, despite his poison fangs, was a tidbit. The racer, long skilled in such arts, snatched him up by the head and swallowed him down. Powerful digestive juices in the racer's stomach did the rest. Then the racer, appetite whetted, prowled around until it found one of Crotalus's little sisters. She went the way of the brother.

---

[1] **virulent** (vîr′yə lənt): Extremely malignant.

[2] **herpetologists** (hûr′pĭ tŏl′ə gĭsts): Researchers who study reptiles.

Nemesis[3] of the second sister was a chaparral cock. This cuckoo, or road runner as it is called, found the baby amid some rocks, uttered a cry of delight, scissored it by the neck, shook it until it was almost lifeless, banged and pounded it upon a rock until life had indeed left it, and then gulped it down.

Crotalus, somnolent[4] in a cranny of the cave's mouth, neither knew nor cared. Even if he had, there was nothing he could have done about it.

On the fourth day of his life he decided to go out into the world himself. He rippled forth uncertainly, the transverse[5] plates on his belly serving him as legs.

He could see things well enough within his limited range, but a five-inch-long snake can command no great field of vision. He had an excellent sense of smell. But, having no ears, he was stone deaf. On the other hand, he had a pit, a deep pock mark between eye and nostril. Unique, this organ was sensitive to animal heat. In pitch blackness, Crotalus, by means of the heat messages recorded in his pit, could tell whether another animal was near and could also judge its size. . . .

The single button on his tail could not, of course, yet rattle. Crotalus wouldn't be able to rattle until that button had grown into three segments. Then he would be able to buzz.

He had a wonderful tongue. It looked like an exposed nerve and was probably exactly that. It was weird, and Crotalus thrust it in and out as he traveled. It told him things that neither his eyes nor his nose nor his pit told him.

Snake fashion, Crotalus went forth, not knowing where he was going, for he had never been anywhere before. Hunger was probably his prime mover.[6] In order to satisfy that hunger, he had to find something smaller than himself and kill it.

He came upon a baby lizard sitting in the sand. Eyes, nose, pit, and tongue told Crotalus it was there. Instinct told him

---

[3] **nemesis** (nĕm′ ĭ sĭs): A victorious rival, from the name of a Greek goddess.

[4] **somnolent** (sŏm′ nə lənt): Drowsy.

[5] **transverse** (trăns vûrs′): Crosswise.

[6] **prime mover:** The source of motion.

what it was and what to do. Crotalus gave a tiny one-inch strike and bit the lizard. His poison killed it. He took it by the head and swallowed it. Thus was his first meal.

During his first two years, Crotalus grew rapidly. He attained a length of two feet; his tail had five rattles on it and its button. He rarely bothered with lizards any more, preferring baby rabbits, chipmunks, and roundtailed ground squirrels. Because of his slow locomotion,[7] he could not run down these agile little things. He had to contrive[8] instead to be where they were when they would pass. Then he struck swiftly, injected his poison, and ate them after they died.

At two he was formidable.[9] He had grown past the stage where a racer or a road runner could safely tackle him. He had grown to the size where other desert dwellers—coyotes, foxes, coatis, wildcats—knew it was better to leave him alone. . . .

He had not experienced death for the simple reason that there had never been an opportunity for anything bigger and stronger than himself to kill him. Now, at two, because he was so formidable, that opportunity became more and more unlikely.

He grew more slowly in the years following his initial spurt. At the age of twelve he was five feet long. Few of the other rattlers in his den were older or larger than he.

He had a castanet[10] of fourteen segments. It had been broken off occasionally in the past, but with each new molting a new segment appeared.

His first skin-shedding back in his babyhood had been a bewildering experience. He did not know what was happening. His eyes clouded over until he could not see. His skin thickened and dried until it cracked in places. His pit and his nostrils ceased to function. There was only one thing to do and that was to get out of that skin.

---

[7] **locomotion:** Way of moving from place to place.

[8] **contrive** (kən trīv′): To plan with cleverness; scheme.

[9] **formidable** (fôr′ mĭ də bəl): Arousing fear; inspiring awe.

[10] **castanet** (kăs′ tə nĕt′): A hand-held musical instrument that makes a clicking sound.

Crotalus managed it by nosing against the bark of a shrub until he forced the old skin down over his head, bunching it like the rolled top of a stocking around his neck. Then he pushed around among rocks and sticks and branches, literally crawling out of his skin by slow degrees. Wriggling free at last, he looked like a brand-new snake. His skin was bright and satiny, his eyes and nostrils were clear, his pit sang with sensation.

For the rest of his life he was to molt three or four times a year. Each time he did it he felt as if he had been born again.

At twelve he was a magnificent reptile. Not a single scar defaced his rippling symmetry.[11] He was diabolically beautiful, and he was deadly poison.

His venom was his only weapon, for he had no power of constriction. Yellowish in color, his poison was odorless and tasteless. It was a highly complex mixture of proteins, each in itself direly toxic. His venom worked on the blood. The more poison he injected with a bite, the more dangerous the wound. The pain rendered by his bite was instantaneous, and the shock accompanying it was profound. Swelling began immediately, to be followed by a ghastly oozing. Injected directly into a large vein, his poison brought death quickly, for the victim died when it reached his heart.

At the age of twenty, Crotalus was the oldest and largest rattler in his den. He was six feet long and weighed thirteen pounds. His whole world was only about a mile in radius. He had fixed places where he avoided the sun when it was hot and he was away from his cave. He knew his hunting grounds thoroughly, every game trail, every animal burrow.

He was a fine old machine, perfectly adapted to his surroundings, accustomed to a life of leisure and comfort. He dominated his little world.

The mighty seasonal rhythms of the desert were as vast pulsations, and the lives of the rattlesnakes were attuned to

---

[11] **symmetry** (sĭm′ ĭ-trē): Balance in size and shape; correspondence of parts.

them. Spring sun beat down, spring rains fell, and, as the plants of the desert ended their winter hibernations, so did the vipers in their lair. The plants opened forth and budded; the den "opened" too, and the snakes crawled forth. The plants fertilized each other, and new plants were born. The snakes bred, and new snakes were produced. The desert was repopulated.

In the autumn the plants began to close; in the same fashion the snake den began to close. The reptiles returned to it, lay like lingering blossoms about its entrance for a while, then disappeared within it when winter came. There they slept until summoned forth by a new spring.

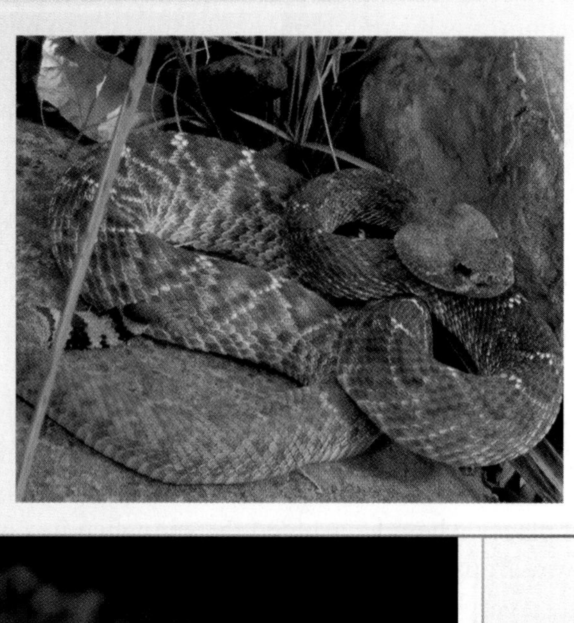

Thinking as a Writer

Evaluating Types of Informative Writing

"The Life and Death of a Western Gladiator" both informs and explains by providing a variety of details about a diamondback rattlesnake. If a friend were to ask you about this desert rattlesnake, you might write a paragraph that informs by detailing several unique features of this creature, or you might decide to compose a paragraph that explains by elaborating on a process related to one of those features.

- Which paragraphs in Finney's article would make good models for a paragraph that informs? For a paragraph that explains? Explain why you chose those particular models. What other types of information or explanations might Finney have included?

Acquiring Information from Images

Viewing

- Look closely at the two images on the previous page of the diamondback rattlesnake. Work in small groups and discuss the information each image conveys about the diamondback. Recalling details from "The Life and Death of a Western Gladiator," each group member should sketch an image that conveys something else about the snake. Share your drawings and discuss the information or explanations they convey.

Improvising an Oral Presentation

Oral Expression

- Imagine you are an expert on the desert diamondback rattlesnake. You have been invited to address a group of teenagers planning to take a trip into the desert. What do these campers need to know about the diamondback rattlesnake? Using information from Finney's article, improvise what you might say. Then, working with a partner or in a small group, listen to each other's presentations. Critique the presentations for the amount, usefulness, and accuracy of the information given.

Developing Your Skills of Writing Paragraphs

No matter what your purpose for writing, you create a composition by forming a series of paragraphs. Each paragraph is made up of sentences. While each sentence expresses a complete thought, a paragraph *develops* a thought. Before you learn the specific characteristics of informative paragraphs, you will identify what makes up a paragraph and how to write a good one.

A **paragraph** is a group of related sentences that present and develop one main idea.

Paragraph Structure

In a good paragraph, every sentence plays a role. Notice the role of each sentence in the paragraph that follows from "The Life and Death of a Western Gladiator."

Model: Paragraph Structure

Topic Sentence: states the main idea

Supporting Sentences: develop the main idea

Concluding Sentence: has a strong ending

His venom was his only weapon, for he had no power of constriction. Yellowish in color, his poison was odorless and tasteless. It was a highly complex mixture of proteins, each in itself direly toxic. His venom worked on the blood. The more poison he injected with a bite, the more dangerous the wound. The pain rendered by his bite was instantaneous, and the shock accompanying it was profound. Swelling began immediately, to be followed by a ghastly oozing. Injected directly into a large vein, his poison brought death quickly, for the victim died when it reached his heart.

Paragraph structure varies. While the model paragraph begins with a topic sentence and ends with a concluding sentence, you may construct a paragraph differently. For example, you may express your main idea in two sentences rather than in one topic sentence. While the topic sentence appears at the beginning of the model, you may express your main idea in the middle of the paragraph or at the end. Also, your paragraph may not need a concluding sentence if you end with your topic sentence or if your paragraph is part of a longer composition. In a one-paragraph composition, however, you must make clear the main idea, whatever paragraph structure you choose.

Guidelines for a One-Paragraph Composition

- Make your main idea clear.
- Develop your main idea fully.
- Provide a strong ending.

You may accomplish these three goals by including a clear topic sentence, a body of supporting sentences, and an effective concluding sentence in your paragraph.

Topic Sentence

Wherever your topic sentence appears—as the first sentence in the paragraph, the last sentence, or any one of the middle sentences—it serves the same purpose.

A **topic sentence** states the main idea of the paragraph.

Because it states the main idea, a topic sentence is usually more general than the sentences that develop that idea. At the same time, the topic sentence is specific enough to be developed adequately in one paragraph.

Features of a Topic Sentence

A topic sentence

- states the main idea.
- focuses the limited subject to one main point that can be adequately covered in the paragraph.
- is more general than the sentences that develop it.

MODEL: Topic Sentence

The Heavy Task of Fighting Fires

TOPIC SENTENCE

Fighting a major fire takes tremendous strength and endurance. The protective clothing that a fire fighter wears into a burning building will weigh more than 20 pounds. To protect himself from the smoke, the fire fighter will usually wear an oxygen tank and mask. These self-contained breathing units may weigh as much as 50 pounds. The weight of the hose and other tools that the fire fighter carries will raise the total weight to more than 100 pounds.

—*Walter Brown/Norman Anderson,* Fires

As the following example shows, the topic sentence in the model is general enough to cover all the details yet specific enough to develop adequately in one paragraph.

TOO GENERAL	Fire fighting is hard work.
SPECIFIC ENOUGH	Fighting a major fire takes tremendous strength and endurance.

PRACTICE YOUR SKILLS

Evaluating Topic Sentences

Write the letter of the topic sentence that is specific enough to be covered adequately in a single paragraph.

1. a. Bats use sonar to locate prey.

b. Bats are complex animals.

2. a. Many medical discoveries were made by accident.

b. There have been some interesting discoveries.

3. a. Folk songs are part of life.

b. Folk songs reveal a country's values.

4. a. Many people like camping.

b. Pitching a tent is easy if you follow directions.

5. a. Dolphins are generally friendly to humans.

b. Dolphins are amazing creatures.

Writing Topic Sentences

For each general statement below, write a topic sentence that is specific enough to be developed adequately in a single paragraph.

6. Life can be difficult at times.

7. Good health is important.

8. Holidays are nice.

9. Movies today are very exciting.

10. Dinner should be eaten in peace.

Supporting Sentences

A topic sentence on an interesting subject will usually prompt readers to ask questions as they read. Supporting sentences answer those questions and form the body of the paragraph.

Supporting sentences explain the topic sentence by giving specific details, facts, examples, or reasons.

The following topic sentence begins a paragraph about Robert Peary's successful return from the North Pole.

Model: Topic Sentence

On the sixth of September, 1909, the gallant little *Roosevelt* steamed into Indian Harbor, Labrador, and from the wireless tower on top of a cliff two messages flashed out.

Readers will naturally wonder, What were the two messages? The supporting sentences answer that question.

Model: Supporting Sentences

The first was to Peary's anxiously waiting wife, more eager, if the truth be known, to hear of her husband's safety than of the discovery of the Pole. This message read: "Have made good at last. I have the Pole. Am well. Love." The second one was to his country, for which he had sacrificed so much. It read: "Stars and Stripes nailed to the North Pole. Peary."

–*Marie Peary Stafford,* Discoverer of the North Pole

When you write supporting sentences, think of the questions readers might ask and then answer those questions.

Practice Your Skills

Writing Supporting Sentences

Write three sentences that would support each item.

1. Styles of dress may reveal people's personalities.

2. Life without a computer seems impossible.

3. Old photographs can help you understand history.

Concluding Sentence

A paragraph often needs a concluding sentence to summarize the ideas presented in the paragraph.

A **concluding sentence** recalls the main idea and adds a strong ending to a paragraph.

Strategies for Ending a Paragraph

- Restate the main idea using different words.
- Summarize the paragraph.
- Add an insight about the main idea.
- Express how you feel about the subject.

Model: Strong Concluding Sentence

An All-Around Player

Although Babe Ruth is best remembered for his home runs, he was also a great pitcher. In 1916, he led the American League in lowest earned-run percentage. He won 23 games that year, including 9 shutouts. The next year he won 24. Until 1961, Ruth held the record for pitching scoreless innings in the World Series. Ruth's impressive pitching statistics show that he was more than a great hitter.

Concluding Sentence

Practice Your Skills

Writing Concluding Sentences

Write three more sentences that could each provide a strong conclusion to the paragraph about Babe Ruth.

Paragraph Development

A topic sentence is like a baseball score. It gives the general idea without the specifics of how the game developed. Readers, like sports fans, want to know the details. They want to see the idea developed play by play.

Methods of Development

You can use a variety of methods to develop a topic sentence.

Strategies for Developing Your Main Idea

- Give descriptive details.
- Give facts, examples, or reasons.
- Relate an incident.
- Make a comparison or draw a contrast.
- Give directions or explain the steps in a process.

Practice Your Skills

Recognizing Method of Development

Decide which method of development is used in the following paragraph. Indicate your answer by writing *descriptive details, facts or examples, reasons,* or *steps in a process.*

Taking the Plunge

Most experts agree that swimming is the healthiest form of vigorous exercise. Because water offers so little resistance, swimmers are unlikely to experience the muscle strain associated with land sports such as jogging and tennis. Yet swimming strengthens many areas of the body—arms, legs, torso, and neck. Most important, if done regularly, it is strenuous enough to condition the heart and lungs. See your doctor before starting any new exercise program, but don't be surprised if he or she tells you to go jump in a lake!

Adequate Development

Insufficiently developed writing makes readers quickly lose interest. Even an interesting idea loses merit if not backed up with sufficient information. The supporting sentences in a paragraph develop the main idea with specific details. These specific details can take the form of facts or examples, reasons, incidents, or descriptive images. Regardless of the form, supporting details must be numerous and specific enough to make the main idea clear, convincing, and interesting. This is called **adequate development**.

Writing Tip

Use specific details and information to achieve **adequate development** of your main idea.

The following paragraph provides such ample specific details that readers can clearly picture the subject.

Childhood Treasures

Aunt Sally's cabinet of art supplies was like a toy chest to me. The top shelf, beyond my reach, had an endless supply of paper. There was stiff, brilliant-white paper for watercolors, blank newsprint for charcoals, glossy paper, dull paper, tracing paper. On the second shelf sat oozing tubes of bright-colored oils, bottles of the blackest ink, and cartons of chalk in sunrise shades of pastels. The third shelf—my favorite—held the damp lumps of gray clay, waiting to be shaped into creatures only my aunt and I would recognize. On the bottom shelves were brushes and rags for cleaning up. Despite the thorough cleanups Aunt Sally insisted on, that cabinet was a paradise of play for me on countless Sunday afternoons.

PRACTICE YOUR SKILLS

Recognizing Adequate Development

List all the details in "Childhood Treasures" that provide adequate development.

Unity

In developing a paragraph fully, avoid straying from the main idea, which can confuse the reader. In a well-developed paragraph, all the supporting sentences relate directly to the main idea expressed in the topic sentence. This quality of a well-written paragraph is called **unity**.

Achieve **unity** by deleting sentences that do not relate directly to the paragraph's main idea.

In the following example, sentences that detract from the unity of the paragraph are underlined.

MODEL: A Paragraph Lacking Unity

Candlelight

Candles, which go back to prehistoric times, were a chief source of light for 2,000 years. The first candle may have been discovered by accident when a piece of wood or cord fell into a pool of lighted fat. In ancient times crude candles were made from fats wrapped in husks or moss. <u>Early people also used torches.</u> Later a wick was placed inside a candle mold, and melted wax was poured into the mold. Candles could be used to carry light from place to place and could be stored indefinitely. <u>The first lamps used a dish of oil and a wick.</u>

Although the underlined sentences relate to the general subject, they do not relate directly to the specific main idea expressed in the topic sentence.

PRACTICE YOUR SKILLS

Checking for Unity

Write the two sentences that destroy the paragraph's unity.

The First Cheap Car

Henry Ford was not the first person to build a car, but he was the first to figure out how to make cars cheaply. His assembly-line methods resulted in huge savings and changed the car from a luxury to a necessity. The mass-produced Model T sold for about $400, a price the average wage earner could afford. Ford sold over 15 million cars from 1908 to 1927. Ford reduced the workday for his employees from nine to eight hours. He set the minimum wage at $5 a day. By building a cheap, easy-to-operate car, Ford changed the nation.

Coherence

In a coherent paragraph, each idea follows logically and smoothly from one to the next.

Achieve **coherence** by presenting ideas in logical order and by using transitions.

The following chart lists some methods of organization and transitions you can use to write coherent paragraphs.

METHODS OF ORGANIZATION			
Chronological Order			
Method used with events or stories to tell what happened first, second, third, and so on. Also used to explain a sequence of steps in a process.			
TRANSITIONS	first	later	finally
	before	next	by evening
Spatial Order			
Method used in descriptions to show how objects are related in location.			
TRANSITIONS	beside	left	at the top
	beyond	north	in front of
Order of Importance, Interest, or Degree			
Method often used in paragraphs that describe, persuade, or explain. Presents ideas in order of importance, interest, or size.			
TRANSITIONS	first	moreover	more important
	finally	in addition	most important

You can find more information about transitions on pages C138–C139.

Practice Your Skills

Identifying Method of Organization

Write *chronological, spatial,* or *order of importance, interest, or degree* to identify the method of organization used in "Childhood Treasures" on page C105.

Time Out to Reflect

As you work to improve your skills for developing topic, supporting, and concluding sentences, what have you learned about your writing? What are your strengths and weaknesses? On what areas do you notice yourself spending more time? In what areas do you feel confident? Do you have a talent for writing strong conclusions, but find that your supporting sentences lack some necessary details? Take some time to note any errors in your writing and jot down strategies for correcting them in the future. Record your thoughts in the Learning Log section of your **journal.**

Process of Writing an Informative Paragraph

Better to understand a little than to misunderstand a lot.

—Anonymous

Informative, or explanatory, writing is the most common and practical of the four types of writing. In writing an informative paragraph, your goal is always to help your readers to understand something. Any time your purpose is to *explain* or to *inform*, you will be using informative writing.

Informative writing explains or informs.

Your Writer's Journal

Explore different topics for informative writing in your journal. You might list topics inspired by Finney's article, such as desert animals, the environment, and plant life; or you might jot down subjects that interest you—for example, computers or video games. Also note things you're good at—such as navigating the Internet—which you can explain to others. Try to add a new entry every day. You may decide to use these topics or ideas later in your writing.

The subjects of informative paragraphs can range widely, from simple information and processes to the great themes and puzzles of the universe. You probably have written many informative paragraphs that explain how to do something or how something works, or that inform by providing facts or ideas about a topic. You use informative paragraphs in business letters, in reports, and in answers to essay questions. Chances are you can think of many instances when you write to explain or to inform.

The following models show the two main purposes of informative paragraphs.

MODEL: Paragraph to Explain

Orphans from the Wild

A small baby [mammal] that has no hair or whose eyes are not yet open may be picked up in your bare hands. Gently slide your fingers under the baby, scoop it up, and cradle it in your palms. Most babies, particularly very small ones, will enjoy the warmth of your hands. Adjust your fingers to fit snugly around the baby, so it can absorb the maximum warmth from your fingers, but not so snugly that it can't shift its position. The tiny, hairless baby will become quiet almost at once and will soon drop off to sleep.

—*William J. Weber,* Wild Orphan Babies

MODEL: Paragraph to Inform

Food for Thought

Dr. Wolfgang Koehler did a great many experiments with chimpanzees in which he found that they were able to solve very difficult problems. In one experiment he hung some bananas from the ceiling of a cage. He then placed some boxes around the cage. The chimps stacked the boxes like blocks and got their bananas. Next he placed the bananas outside the cage and gave the chimps two sticks that were not long enough to reach. The chimps fitted the two sticks together and got their bananas. One animal, who could not reach a banana hanging from the ceiling of his cage, took the scientist by the hand, placed him just under the banana and climbed up on his shoulders. Apparently the animal was quite capable of reasoning a solution. It did not need to learn through trial and error.

—*Gloria Kirshner,* From Instinct to Intelligence

When writing an informative paragraph, you already know your writing purpose: to explain or inform. Your first goal during prewriting, then, is to think of subjects suitable for that purpose. As you move through the prewriting stage, remember to keep your purpose clearly in mind. Pay particular attention to the strategies, guidelines, and models that relate most directly to your purpose.

Discovering Subjects to Write About

Subjects for informative paragraphs will present themselves naturally throughout your life as a writer. In order to prepare yourself for those opportunities, however, you will need to seek out subjects that can help you develop your skills. The following strategies will help you think of possible subjects for an informative paragraph. Use the ones that work best for you.

Strategies for Thinking of Subjects

- Look through your **journal**, particularly your Learning Log, for ideas you could explain.
- Think about books or magazine articles you have read lately on subjects of special interest to you.
- Think about an interesting television show or movie you have seen lately.
- Try to recall a conversation you had recently that made you stop and think.
- Browse through the library or media center.
- Think about what interests you in your other classes.
- Talk to friends and family members to find out what they would like to know more about.
- Start freewriting to see what is on your mind.
- Brainstorm with a partner or in a group for ideas.

Communicate Your Ideas

PREWRITING *Subjects of Interest*

Find at least five subjects for writing an informative paragraph and list them. Look back at your **journal** for ideas, or use other suggestions in the strategies on page C111. You might also choose to list subjects related to nature, the environment, and conservation. Save your notes for later use.

SAVE YOUR WORK

Choosing a Subject

After you have thought of several possible subjects, the next step is to choose one of them. The following guidelines will help you make that choice.

Choosing a Subject for an Informative Paragraph

- Choose a subject that interests you.
- Choose a subject that will interest your audience.
- Choose a subject you know well enough or can learn enough about to explain accurately.

Knowledge is the basis of all informative writing. While some examples of this purpose of writing come from firsthand experience and observation, others require research—reading books and magazines, searching the Internet, and talking with experts. Before choosing a subject for an informative paragraph, determine what you know about it by writing answers to the following questions.

Exploratory Questions

- What do I already know about the subject?
- Do I know enough to explain it thoroughly to others? If not, what else do I need to know?
- Where can I find that information?

PRACTICE YOUR SKILLS

Identifying Types of Subjects

List five subjects you could write about from firsthand experience. Then list five subjects you would need to research. Label the first list "Experience" and the second "Research."

Communicate Your Ideas

PREWRITING *Subject for an Informative Paragraph*

Review the possible subjects for an informative paragraph you listed previously. Jot down what you know about each subject. Label subjects you know about from firsthand experience with "Experience." Label subjects you need to learn more about with "Research." Decide on a subject that best follows the guidelines of Choosing a Subject for an Informative Paragraph on the previous page. Save your notes for later use.

Limiting a Subject

After you have chosen a subject, the next step is to limit it so that you can treat your subject thoroughly in one paragraph. The following chart gives examples of how general subjects may be limited and then limited even further.

LIMITING A SUBJECT

General	Limited	More Limited
computers	programs	word processing
science fiction	movie monsters	Godzilla
Texas history	famous heroes	Davy Crockett
sports	basketball	fouls
school	high school	high school sports
nature	trees	hemlock forests

After you decide on a more limited subject, focus your thoughts by expressing the main idea in a phrase. Then write a sentence that contains your main idea.

Model: Focusing a Limited Subject

LIMITED SUBJECT	basketball fouls
FOCUS	why players sometimes commit fouls on purpose
MAIN IDEA	A good basketball player knows when to foul on purpose.

Writing Tip

Limit your subject so that it can be covered adequately in one paragraph.

Practice Your Skills

Limiting Subjects

Make three columns and label them "General Subject," "Limited Subject," and "More Limited Subject." Then list and limit each of the following general subjects by completing the columns.

1. music
2. bicycles
3. vitamins
4. careers
5. dogs
6. deserts
7. fire fighting
8. mass media

Focusing Limited Subjects

Choose five "More Limited Subjects" from the preceding activity and write a phrase that focuses your thoughts for each one. Then, using that phrase, write a sentence that expresses your main idea.

PREWRITING *Focused Subject*

Limit the subject you chose for your informative paragraph. After you write a phrase that focuses your thoughts about the subject, work the phrase into a complete sentence that expresses your main idea. Save your work for later use.

Determining Your Audience

Early in the planning stage, you should also think about your **audience**—the people who will read your paragraph. Asking yourself the following questions about your readers will help you determine their interests, needs, and attitudes.

Audience Profile Questions

- What do my readers already know about my subject? What else might they need to know or want to know?
- What are my readers' attitudes toward my subject? If they differ from mine, how can I address those differences?
- Why are my readers reading my writing? How can I address their needs?

When thinking about your readers' attitudes, consider how their past experiences with your subject might color their views. For example, if you are writing about football—the great love of your life—keep in mind that not all of your readers will share your enthusiasm. Some may even dislike the game.

When considering your audience, also ask yourself why they will be reading your work. For example, your classmates may read to learn more about an interesting subject. If you are writing for your teacher, keep in mind that often his or her reason for reading is to evaluate what you know and how well you express that knowledge.

Communicate Your Ideas

PREWRITING *Audience Profile*

Review the sentence you wrote that expresses your main idea. Determine who your audience will be. Then think about what your audience knows about your topic or wants to know and what your purpose is for writing your paragraph. Using the questions on the previous page, write a brief audience profile. Add other notes that will help you in writing for this audience. Save your work for later use.

Developing Supporting Details

Without strong supporting details, the main idea of your paragraph will not be clear to your audience. To support your main idea in an informative paragraph, use one of the following types of supporting details or a combination of them.

You can learn more about supporting details on pages C25–C31.

TYPES OF SUPPORTING DETAILS		
facts	incidents	steps or stages
examples	causes	directions
reasons	effects	characteristics
parts	differences	similarities

When choosing what type of supporting details to use, you should first consider your main idea and the questions a reader may have about the subject.

List **details** that suit the main idea of your paragraph and that explain the subject clearly.

For a paragraph explaining *why* basketball players sometimes commit fouls on purpose, for example, you would list *reasons* as supporting details. This type of detail would be most suitable for developing your main idea and for answering readers' likely questions.

The focus of your subject, stated as your main idea, often offers a clue to the types of details you should use. In the first model below, for example, the focus calls for *facts* about the heart. In the second model, the focus calls for *examples* of whale spouts.

Model: Facts as Supporting Details

Limited Subject the heart

Focus how hard the human heart works

Facts

- beats between 60 and 80 times per minute
- pumps a little more than 5 quarts of blood each minute
- in an average lifetime, beats 3 billion times
- work done by heart over a lifetime is equivalent to lifting 70 pounds every minute of your life

Model: Examples as Supporting Details

Limited Subject whale spouts

Focus different spouts of the great whales

Examples

- blue whale—high and narrow
- gray whale—low and bushy
- right whale—V-shaped, like a heart
- sperm whale—blown sharply forward

Inquiring One way to generate a list of details for an informative paragraph is to think of questions your readers may have and to brainstorm a list of answers. Your list may include a combination of different types of supporting details, such as facts and examples. Although you may not use all your details in your paragraph, you should list as many as you can.

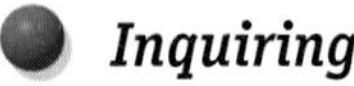PRACTICE YOUR SKILLS

Inquiring

For each of the following focused subjects, write at least three questions readers may ask about it. Then write one type of supporting detail from the list on page C116 that would be appropriate for answering each question.

EXAMPLE School spirit at your school

POSSIBLE QUESTIONS
- How is school spirit shown at games? (give examples)
- How is school spirit shown by club members? (relate incidents)
- What does school spirit mean in your school? (describe characteristics)

1. the importance of good nutrition
2. student clubs at your school
3. the benefits of learning to type
4. how to pack for a camping trip
5. comparing and contrasting volleyball and tennis

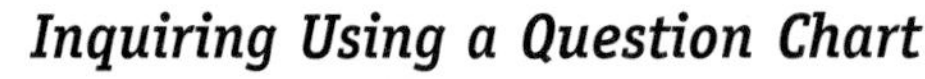*Inquiring Using a Question Chart*

Using the chart on the next page, add at least one more example of each kind of question. Then write one type of supporting detail from the list on page C116 that would be appropriate for answering each of the questions.

SUBJECT: Desert Diamondback Rattlesnake		
	QUESTIONS	**SUPPORTING DETAILS**
WHAT?	What does a diamondback rattlesnake look like?	
WHERE?	Where does a diamondback rattlesnake live?	
WHEN?	When is a rattlesnake the most dangerous?	
WHY?	Why does a rattlesnake shed its skin?	
HOW?	How does a rattlesnake capture its prey?	

Communicate Your Ideas

PREWRITING *Inquiry, Supporting Details*

Review your main idea and audience profile for your informative paragraph. Develop details to support the main idea. One way to begin is by writing a list of questions your readers might have about the subject and freewriting a list of answers. For questions that you cannot answer based on your own knowledge or experience, look in appropriate reference books or on the Internet for accurate, useful information. Jot down any information you think you may need to draft your paragraph. Next evaluate your information. When you are sure you have enough supporting details to develop your subject fully, save your notes for later use.

You can learn more about doing research on pages C527–C537 and in A Writer's Guide to Using the Internet, pages C724–C767.

Writing Is Thinking

Analyzing

To think of supporting details for a paragraph that gives directions, begin by analyzing the process or task you want to explain. **Analyzing** means breaking down a whole into its parts to see how the parts fit together to form the whole.

Suppose your focused subject is *planning a costume party*. To analyze the planning, break the planning process down into its different parts. Brainstorm a list of all the steps you can think of for planning a party. Then number the steps in the order in which they should be carried out. The result will be a chart like this.

SUBJECT: PLANNING A COSTUME PARTY

Brainstormed Steps	Best Order of Steps
make guest list	**1.** get permission
put up decorations	**2.** make guest list
get permission	**3.** send invitations
get costume	**4.** plan music and games
send invitations	**5.** get costume
prepare food	**6.** shop for food and drinks
plan music and games	**7.** put up decorations
shop for food and drinks	**8.** prepare food and drinks

THINKING PRACTICE

Choose one of the following subjects or use one of your own. Make a chart similar to the one above to help you analyze the steps required to accomplish the task.

1. how to organize a car wash
2. how to make the world's best pizza
3. how to make wise consumer choices when buying clothes

Classifying Supporting Details

After listing details about your subject, classify them to find the best way to develop your paragraph. When you **classify**, you group details into categories. The following examples show different ways to explain a main idea and classify the supporting details.

You can learn more about classifying on page C32.

1. MAIN IDEA Whales' spouts vary in size and shape.
DETAILS **Classify** information according to facts about whales' spouts and examples of how they vary.
METHOD OF DEVELOPMENT Facts and examples

2. MAIN IDEA Locating whales is a complex process.
DETAILS **Classify** information according to steps in the process of locating whales.
METHOD OF DEVELOPMENT Steps in a process

3. MAIN IDEA After locating a pod of whales, whale watchers must approach cautiously.
DETAILS **Classify** information about approaching whales in a set of directions.
METHOD OF DEVELOPMENT A set of directions

4. MAIN IDEA The right whale was the most widely hunted during the nineteenth century.
DETAILS **Classify** information according to characteristics of the right whale.
METHOD OF DEVELOPMENT Definition

5. MAIN IDEA The bottlenose dolphin and killer whale can be trained to perform, but the dolphin is more adaptable to captivity.
DETAILS **Classify** information according to similarities and differences between dolphins and killer whales in captivity.
METHOD OF DEVELOPMENT Comparison/contrast

6. MAIN IDEA Early mariners' reports about narwhals were like myths about unicorns.
DETAILS **Classify** information according to similar characteristics of unicorns and narwhals.
METHOD OF DEVELOPMENT Analogy

7. MAIN IDEA Whales have bodies that are especially adapted to living in the sea.

DETAILS **Classify** information according to the different parts of a whale's body.

METHOD OF DEVELOPMENT Analysis

8. MAIN IDEA Because of commercial whaling practices in the early twentieth century, the number of whales dropped dramatically.

DETAILS **Classify** information into causes (whaling practices) and effects (drop in the number of whales).

METHOD OF DEVELOPMENT Causes and effects

9. MAIN IDEA There are two main types of whales.

DETAILS **Classify** information according to the two main types.

METHOD OF DEVELOPMENT Grouping into types

The following model shows how a writer classified details about types of whales by making a chart.

MODEL: Charting to Classify Details

MAIN IDEA There are two main types of whales.

Two Types of Whales

	Baleen Whales	Toothed Whales
DETAILS	• have slats (baleen) instead of teeth • slats grow from upper jaw • strains food out of seawater	• use teeth to catch food • eat fish, squid, small sea mammals • swallow food whole
EXAMPLES	blue whale, right whale, humpback, bowhead	sperm whale, killer whale, narwhal, dolphin

Notice how the writer converted details and examples into sentences that make up the body of the paragraph.

Two Types of Whales

BODY OF THE PARAGRAPH

The two main types of whales are baleen whales and toothed whales. Baleen whales have slats that grow from their upper jaws instead of teeth. These slats, called baleen, strain food out of seawater. Whales that get their food this way include the blue whale, the right whale, the humpback, and the bowhead. Toothed whales, on the other hand—such as the sperm whale, killer whale, narwhal, and dolphin—use their teeth to catch food. They eat fish, squid, and small sea mammals, which they swallow whole. The main difference between baleen whales and toothed whales, therefore, is the way they get food.

PRACTICE YOUR SKILLS

Identifying Methods of Development

Using the models on pages C121–C122 for guidance, write the best method of development for each of the following main ideas.

1. Athens and Sparta were both founded by Greek tribes but developed strikingly different ways of life.
2. Spartans valued harsh self-discipline in many ways.
3. Ancient Greek armies consisted of two main parts.
4. The Greek phalanx was a fearsome fighting force.
5. Because of political reforms in 594 B.C., Athens became a democracy.
6. Voting in ancient Athens was a simple process.
7. The Greeks made lasting contributions to architecture.
8. Constructing a plaster model of Greek columns is fun to do if you know how.

9. Greek theaters presented several types of drama.
10. The presentation of Greek plays was like the competition of athletes in the ancient Olympics.

Classifying Details

Think of details for an informative paragraph on one of the following main ideas. Decide the best method of development and classify your details in a chart like the one on page C122.

11. Our school offers several types of extracurricular activities.
12. Our school is active in intramural sports.
13. You can reach school in a shorter time by taking this shortcut.
14. Both small schools and large ones have advantages.
15. Poor attitudes can lead to poor grades.
16. Good study habits and test-taking skills will lead to academic success.

Communicate Your Ideas

PREWRITING *Classification of Details*

Review the supporting details you developed for your informative paragraph. Classify the details by using one of the methods on pages C121–C122. Remember to use your main idea to help you decide the best method of development. Save all your work for later use.

Arranging Details in Logical Order

After you have listed and classified your supporting details, you need to arrange your ideas in a logical, understandable order. Arranging your details in a logical order will help make your explanation clear to readers. When organizing details for an informative paragraph, use one of the following strategies.

Strategies for Organizing Details

- Arrange details in order of importance, interest, size, or degree.
- Arrange details in sequential, or step-by-step, order.
- Arrange details in chronological, or time, order.
- Arrange details in spatial, or place-to-place, order.

You can learn more about organizing details on pages C33–C35.

When you arrange details in order of importance, you arrange them either from **least to most** or from **most to least** important. In the following paragraph, the main supporting details are underlined. You will see that the writer used facts and examples to develop the main idea that dogs that aid the blind must be trained to overcome some basic fears. Notice that the writer chose to organize those facts and examples in order from the least to the most important.

MODEL: Order of Importance

Training a Seeing-Eye Dog

Dogs who will aid the blind must be trained to overcome some basic fears. To learn how to keep calm in a crowd, the dogs are taken to playgrounds when students are leaving school. The dogs are sharply corrected if they get excited in all the bustle. To overcome any fear of loud noises, they must hold still while blanks are fired above their heads. Sometimes they are even trained on an airport runway. Especially important is overcoming a fear of heights, for the day may come when a dog will have to lead its master down a fire escape. A well-trained dog is more than a pair of eyes; it can also be a lifesaver.

For an explanation in which you give directions or tell the steps in a process, sequential order is most commonly used. **Sequential order** arranges details in the order in which they take place or are done. The details in the following paragraph, for example, explain a training sequence.

MODEL: Sequential Order

Rope Jumping for Tennis Players

There are very few exercises that really help a tennis player get in shape and stay there. One form of exercise that I strongly urge on a player is to skip rope. It is wonderful for the wind and legs. If it is to do you any good at all, it must be done systematically, and not just now and again. Start slowly for your first week or so. Jump a normal "two-foot" skip, not over ten times without resting, but repeat five separate tens and, if possible, do it morning and evening. Take the ten up to twenty after two days, then in a week to fifty. Once you can do that, begin to vary the type of skipping. Skip ten times on one foot, then ten times on the other. Add a fifty at just double your normal speed. Once that is all mastered, simply take ten minutes in the evening and skip hard, any way you want and at any speed. Let your own intelligence direct you to what gives you the best results. Remember always that stamina is one of the deciding factors in all long, closely contested tennis matches, so work to attain the peak of physical conditioning when you need it most.

—*Bill Tilden,* How to Play Better Tennis

Some subjects call for details to be arranged in chronological or spatial order. **Chronological order** is time order. It places events in the order in which they occurred over time. Chronological order may be appropriate, for example, when you want to explain the causes and effects of an event.

Spatial order, on the other hand, arranges details according to their location—for example, from near to far, from top to bottom, or from east to west. Spatial order may be appropriate when you want to explain the parts of a whole, such as the different departments of a department store.

The models on the following page demonstrate the use of chronological and spatial order.

Model: Chronological Order

Cracking an Ancient Code

Although the Rosetta Stone was discovered in 1799, the ancient Egyptian hieroglyphics written on it remained a mystery for 20 more years. The first person to try cracking the code was Silvestre de Sacy. He managed to figure out that some signs referred to proper names, but the rest stumped him. He turned his work over to a Swedish expert, David Akerblad, who made a little more progress. Then Sir Thomas Young, an Englishman, went to work on the code. He discovered that some of the signs stood for sounds as well as ideas. The real honor of cracking the Rosetta code belongs to Jean François Champollion. After years of careful study, he had his first breakthrough in 1821. The puzzle pieces then began to fall swiftly into place. Others may have paved the way, but Champollion deserves the credit for discovering a 1,500-year-old secret.

Model: Spatial Order

A Formidable Mountain Barrier

The Sierra Nevada is a chain of peaks 400 miles long, longer than any one range of the American Rockies. The range stretches from Tehachapi Pass in the south nearly to Lassen Peak in the north where the Sierra block disappears beneath sheets of younger volcanic rocks. The Sierra's western flank rises gradually from one of the world's richest agricultural areas, the great Central Valley, while to the east the mountains rise in a magnificent abrupt escarpment to soar 7,000 to 10,000 feet above the arid basin of the Owens Valley. With not a single river passing through the range, the Sierra forms a formidable mountain barrier.

—*Fred Beckey,* Mountains of North America

Practice Your Skills

Arranging Details in Logical Order

Read each of the following subjects and main ideas for informative paragraphs. Then arrange the details in a logical order. Indicate how you ordered the details by writing *sequential order, chronological order, spatial order, order of importance, order of interest,* or *order of size or degree.*

1. Focused Subject: calories burned per hour

Main Idea: In every hour you spend in any form of exercise, you burn calories.

Details:
- roller skating—330 calories
- cleaning your room—70 calories
- running (10 mph)—900 calories
- bicycling (5 mph)—200 calories
- sitting and thinking—5 calories
- touch football—400 calories
- walking—110 calories

Method of Development: facts and examples

2. Focused Subject: getting a driver's license

Main Idea: To get a driver's license, it is best to follow certain steps.

Details:
- study manual
- when permit issued, practice
- take road test to get license
- get driver's manual
- get driver's permit by taking eye test and written test

Method of Development: steps in a process

3. Focused Subject: muscles helped by swimming the front crawl

Main Idea: Swimming the front crawl is beneficial for developing certain muscles.

Details	• leg muscles in kicking • arm and chest muscles in reaching • waist and lower back in side-to-side motion • neck in breathing motion
Method of Development	examples, analysis

4. | | |
|---|---|
| Focused Subject | famous volcanic eruptions |
| Main Idea | Of volcanic eruptions during the twentieth century, five became the most famous. |
| Details | • Mount Pelée—1902
• Mount St. Helens—1980
• Mount Agung—1963
• Mount Kilauea—1990
• Mount Katmai—1912 |
| Method of Development | facts |

5. | | |
|---|---|
| Focused Subject | the supply of fresh water |
| Main Idea | The world's supply of fresh water comes from several different sources. |
| Details | • ground water—22 percent of total
• Arctic ice cap, glaciers—8 percent
• atmosphere—less than 1 percent
• Antarctic ice cap—70 percent |
| Method of Development | facts, analysis |

Communicate Your Ideas

PREWRITING ***Logical Order of Details***

Review the details you classified in the practice activity on page C124. Then make a chart that shows the most logical arrangement for ordering your ideas and identify the method of organization you used. Save your work.

After prewriting, you are ready for the next stage of the writing process—the first draft. Although the first draft need not be polished, it should contain all of the elements of a paragraph. Remember, these elements include a topic sentence, supporting sentences, and a concluding sentence.

As you move through the drafting stage, remember to keep your purpose for writing clearly in mind—to explain or inform. Pay particular attention to the strategies and models that relate most directly to your purpose.

You may wish to review paragraph structure on pages C98–C103.

Drafting the Topic Sentence

When you are ready to write a topic sentence, you will refer back to your prewriting notes; these include your focused subject and an organized list of details. Keep in mind that a topic sentence should clearly express the main idea of your paragraph and bind together all the supporting details.

The following examples show how a student developed a topic sentence for a paragraph about whales.

Model: Developing a Topic Sentence

Main Idea	The spouts of the great whales have different shapes.
Details (Examples)	• blue whale—high and narrow • gray whale—low and bushy • right whale—V-shaped, like a heart • sperm whale—blown sharply forward
Topic Sentence	Some whale spouts are low plumes, while others shoot high into the air.

This first attempt at writing a topic sentence, however, does not bind together all the details. Notice how the following revised topic sentence is general enough to cover the V-shaped spout of the right whale and the angled spout of the sperm whale, as well as the low and high spouts of the blue and gray whales.

REVISED TOPIC SENTENCE — Whale watchers can tell one kind of great whale from another by the shape of its spout.

PRACTICE YOUR SKILLS

Drafting a Topic Sentence

Read the following prewriting notes for an informative paragraph. Then write two possible topic sentences.

FOCUSED SUBJECT — things to do in national parks

DETAILS
- hiking
- canoeing
- observing wildlife
- photographing
- rock climbing
- swimming

Drafting the Body

When you are satisfied with your topic sentence, you should write the body of the paragraph. The **body** is made up of the supporting sentences that contain your details. These details support the main idea expressed in your topic sentence. Begin by writing a complete sentence to express information about your first supporting detail. Then use the following strategies to help you draft the body of your paragraph.

Strategies for Drafting the Body

- Work fairly quickly without worrying about mistakes.
- Follow the order of details you developed in your prewriting notes.
- Pause occasionally to read over what you have written. This will help you keep track of the flow of your ideas.
- Add transitional words and phrases where necessary to make one sentence lead smoothly to the next.

In the following model, the notes about whales on page C130 were converted into complete sentences to form the body of a paragraph. Notice that the first draft of the body contains some transitional words and phrases to tie the sentences together. Other transitions can be added during the revising stage.

Model: First Draft of an Informative Paragraph

Topic Sentence	Whale watchers can tell one kind of great whale from another by the shape of its spout.
Body	For example, the blue whale has a high, narrow spout. The spout of the gray whale is low and bushy. The right whale has a V-shaped spout. The sperm whale can also be identified by its spout, which is blown forward at a sharp angle.

Practice Your Skills

Drafting the Body of a Paragraph

Using the following prewriting notes, draft the topic sentence and body of an informative paragraph. Notice that the details are arranged in the order of *most to least in size.*

Main Idea: Although dinosaurs were huge in size, they lacked intelligence.

Details:
- Brontosaurus—70 feet long, 40 tons, apricot-sized brain
- Tyrannosaurus—50 feet long, 10 tons, smaller brain than Brontosaurus
- Stegosaurus—10 tons, walnut-sized brain (smallest); first to become extinct

Drafting a Concluding Sentence

To write a concluding sentence, reread your paragraph. Then, use one or more of the following strategies to add a conclusion.

Strategies for Writing a Concluding Sentence

- Restate the main idea in different words.
- Summarize the paragraph, emphasizing key ideas or terms.
- Evaluate the information given in the supporting details.
- Add an insight that shows some new understanding of the main idea.

Read the following examples of concluding sentences for the paragraph about the whale spouts. Any one of them would make an effective ending. Which would you choose? Why?

MODEL: Drafting the Concluding Sentence

These differences in spouts help whale watchers tell one type of great whale from another. (restates the main idea)

Narrow or angled, V-shaped or bushy, the spouts of the great whales can be clearly identified. (summarizes)

Although recognizing whale spouts takes practice, this method works well as a way for observers to tell one kind of whale from another. (evaluates the details)

Because whales are underwater most of the time, whale watchers at the water's surface rely on the shape of the spout to tell what kind of whale they are watching. (adds an insight)

PRACTICE YOUR SKILLS

Concluding a Paragraph

Write four possible concluding sentences for the paragraph about dinosaurs that you wrote in the previous practice activity. Identify each concluding sentence as *restating main idea, summarizing, evaluating details,* or *adding an insight.*

Communicate Your Ideas

DRAFTING *Topic Sentence, Body, Concluding Sentence*

Oral Expression

Form a small discussion group with your classmates. Using only your prewriting notes for your paragraph, explain your ideas orally to the group. As you listen to others' explanations, note any questions you have about the subject and make a comment that will help each writer create a first draft. Then draft your own paragraph. When you write the body, remember to use the list or chart you developed for ordering the details in the most logical way. Save your draft for revising.

COMPUTER TIP

In an informative paragraph, information, such as facts, data, and other supporting details, can be presented in words or through visuals like charts and diagrams. You might use a chart or diagram to clarify details in the text or as the primary means of communicating certain information. To create a neat, easy-to-read, easy-to-revise chart, click on the Table icon or on Table in the top menu.

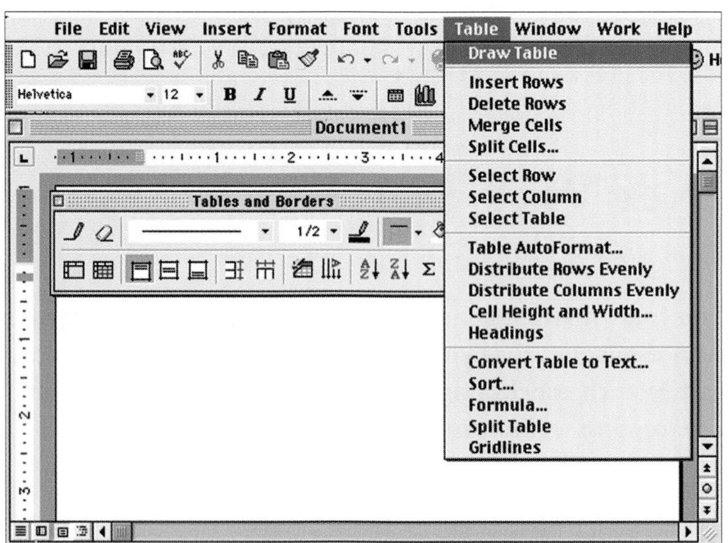

Nightly News, Newsmagazines, Documentaries

"I saw it on TV—it must be true." There certainly are reliable information sources on television. Understanding the different ways in which information is presented in this visual medium will help you evaluate what you hear and see. It may also help you become a better writer as you try to capture in your writing what television can do so easily: show pictures. A good way to begin is to compare and contrast a news story in three visual information forms: the nightly news, television newsmagazines, and documentaries. The chart below shows the characteristics that make each of these unique.

Nightly News	Newsmagazines	Documentaries
very brief (two to three minutes)	usually twenty-minute segments	fifty minutes or longer
introduction by anchor	introduction by anchor	dramatic visual before introduction
brief videotape shots	lengthy videos	carefully crafted
brief interview or quote from person involved	lengthy interviews/ multiple quotes and sources	multiple quotes and sources, real-life conversations
editing to stay within time limit, balanced presentation	editing with much concern for effect and balance	editing to enhance overall effect—music and voiceover added
closing by anchor	closing by anchor	stands alone, conclusion strong
can be made on day news happens	requires preparation time (weeks at least)	requires longest preparation time

Media Activity

For practice, view each of these visual media. Then describe how each type might present a major news event. Write a paragraph for each medium telling what the story might be like, giving special attention to how the length of each type might affect the quality and balance of the coverage. Then write another paragraph explaining how you might improve your writing by using some of the techniques used in these media.

During the revising stage, look for ways to improve your first draft. As you revise, read your paragraph with a fresh eye, as if you were reading it for the first time. Remember to keep your purpose for writing in mind—to explain or to inform. Use the strategies, word choices, and models that relate most directly to your purpose.

Checking for Adequate Development

When you reread your draft, evaluate the effectiveness of your supporting details. Do you have enough specific facts, examples, or directions to explain your subject fully?

Achieve **adequate development** by adding any specific information the reader will need to understand your subject.

You may wish to review the information about adequate development on pages C104–C105.

Practice Your Skills

Revising for Adequate Development

Using a dictionary, find additional details to improve the development of the paragraph below. Then revise the paragraph.

All in a Name

People's names have sometimes become the words for familiar items. One example is the Earl of Sandwich, who supposedly invented the hand-held, stuffed bread that we call the *sandwich*. Another example is *maverick*. Still another example is the *Ferris wheel. Sousaphone* also comes from a name. Such words give people's names a permanent place in the English language.

Checking for Unity

A paragraph has unity when all the sentences in the paragraph support the topic sentence. A paragraph with unity is easy to follow because it keeps the reader's attention on the main idea. In the following paragraph, which lacks unity, the sentences that stray from the subject are underlined. In revising, these sentences would be deleted.

You may wish to review the information about unity on pages C105–C106.

MODEL: Revising for Unity

The Real McCoy

Elijah McCoy became famous as the inventor of an oiling system for machines. Granville T. Woods was another black inventor. In the 1870s, the factory owners had to turn off all their machines before oiling them. McCoy's system, developed in 1872, allowed the machines to be oiled while they were still running, saving time and money for the factory owners. McCoy also held patents for an "Ironing Table" and a "Lawn Sprinkler." McCoy applied his system to steam engines, including those on locomotives, and to the air brakes on trains. His system was so much better than others' that when people bought new machinery, they always asked, "Is this the real McCoy?" To this day, people use that expression to mean "the real thing."

Writing Tip

Achieve **unity** in a paragraph by eliminating any sentences that stray from the main idea.

PRACTICE YOUR SKILLS

Revising for Unity

The following paragraph about dreaming lacks unity. Write the three sentences that should be deleted because they do not support the topic sentence.

Busy Nights

Sleeping is for rest, but parts of your body remain active when you dream. For centuries people have wondered about the meaning of dreams. In the dream state, your closed eyes dart around rapidly, following the action of your dream. Sleep expert Dr. Dement did many experiments to learn about dreams. Your brain waves are also as active as when you are awake. Your breathing is sometimes faster, and your heart rate increases. If people are awakened each time they enter the dream state, they will make up for lost dream time the next night. Although your large muscles are limp and relaxed, your eyes, brain, and breathing system get little rest when you dream.

Checking for Coherence

Coherence is the quality of writing that acts like a glue to bond each sentence to the one before and after it. As a result of such bonds, a paragraph becomes a coherent whole that easily makes sense to the reader. The information that follows explains several strategies that will help you achieve coherence in informative paragraphs.

You can find more information about coherence on page C107.

Using Transitions When writing a first draft, you may not always make clear, smooth connections between your sentences. Therefore, during the revising stage, you need to add transitional words and phrases to connect your ideas. The chart on the next page lists commonly used transitions, including general ones for development, that relate to particular ways of ordering information.

You can learn more about ordering information on pages C34–C35.

COMMONLY USED TRANSITIONS			
Order of Importance	**Chronological Order**	**Spatial Order**	**General Transitions**
even more	after	above	also
finally	as soon as	ahead	besides
first	at first	behind	despite
more important	at last	below	for example
most	first, second	beneath	however
one reason	later	inside	in addition
to begin with	meanwhile	outside	while

Practice Your Skills

Revising for Coherence

Revise the following paragraph, adding transitional words and phrases where needed.

Days of Our Lives

Although the calendar we use today is the most accurate one yet devised, it has many irregularities. We have two different types of years: common years and leap years. The number of days in each month varies. April and June have 30 days. May and July have 31 and February 28 and 29. Many holidays fall on a different day each year, which causes considerable confusion. The calendar we use today has been keeping time successfully for more than 400 years.

Rearranging, Repeating, and Substituting During the revising stage, you may need to rearrange the sentences so all of your ideas follow in a logical order. Aside from using transitions, you can also give your paragraph coherence by occasionally repeating a key word or by replacing a key word with a pronoun, a synonym, or a substitute expression. In a paragraph about bats, for example, instead of always using the word *bats*, you could substitute *creatures*, *animals*, and *mammals*. As you read the following paragraph, notice the nouns and pronouns in **boldface** that refer to the key word, *tree*.

Model: Using Repetition and Substitution for Coherence

Death of a Tree

For a great **tree** death comes as a gradual transformation. **Its** vitality ebbs slowly. Even when life has abandoned **it** entirely **it** remains a **majestic thing**. On some hilltop a dead **tree** may dominate the landscape for miles around. Alone among living things **it** retains **its** character and dignity after death. Plants wither; animals disintegrate. But a dead **tree** may be as arresting, as filled with personality, in death as **it** is in life. Even in **its** final moments, when the **massive trunk** lies prone and **it** has moldered into a ridge covered with mosses and fungi, **it** arrives at a fitting and noble end. **It** enriches and refreshes the earth. Later, as part of other green and growing things, **it** rises again.

—*Edwin Way Teale,* Dune Boy

Other substitutes for the key word *tree* might include references to particular kinds of trees as examples of the main idea, such as an *old oak* or a *fallen birch*. The paragraph "Death of a Tree" illustrates all of the strategies in the list below.

Strategies for Achieving Coherence

- Organize your ideas logically.
- Use transitional words and phrases.
- Occasionally repeat key words.
- Use synonyms or alternative expressions in place of key words.
- Use pronouns in place of key words.

Checking Sentence Construction and Word Choice

When you are satisfied that your paragraph is well structured, adequately developed, and clearly organized, you should look for ways to improve your sentence constructions and choice of words. As you revise your sentences, consider adding, deleting, substituting, and rearranging words. Refer to the following checklist.

You can learn more about revising sentences on page C40.

Evaluation Checklist for Revising

Checking Your Paragraph

✓ Do you have a clear topic sentence? *(pages C130–C131)*

✓ Is your paragraph adequately developed? *(page C136)*

✓ Does your paragraph have unity? *(page C137)*

✓ Does your paragraph have coherence? Did you use transitional words and phrases? *(pages C138–C140)*

✓ Do you have a strong concluding sentence? *(pages C132–C133)*

Checking Your Sentences

✓ Do your sentences have variety?

✓ Did you combine sentences that go together?

✓ Did you avoid rambling sentences?

✓ Did you trim away any unnecessary repetition?

Checking Your Words

✓ Did you choose specific words?

✓ Did you use descriptive words that bring your subject to life?

Practice Your Skills

Analyzing a Revision

Study the following revised draft of the paragraph about whales on page C132. After referring to the checklist above, explain why each change was made.

Whale Watching

Whale watchers can tell one kind of great whale from another by the shape of its spout. For example, the blue whale has a high, narrow spout, while the spout of the gray whale is a low and bushy plume. The right whale, on the other hand, has a V-shaped spout that looks like a heart to whale watchers. The sperm whale can also be identified by its unusual spout, which is blown forward at a sharp angle. Although recognizing whale spouts takes practice, this method works well as a way for observers to tell one kind of whale from another.

Communicate Your Ideas

REVISING *Adequate Development, Unity, Coherence*

Evaluate your draft for adequate development, unity, and coherence. Revise your paragraph, drawing on what you have learned about each quality of writing. Use the Evaluation Checklist for Revising on page C141 for guidance as well. Consider the strategies of adding, deleting, substituting, and rearranging words to improve your writing. After you revise, read your paragraph aloud to check if your explanation sounds logical and clear. Then save your work for later use.

Editing

Writing Process

As you revised your informative paragraph, you considered ways to make it clear and logical. Now you are ready to edit your paragraph by checking your grammar, usage, mechanics, and spelling.

Prewriting Workshop
Drafting Workshop
Revising Workshop
Editing Workshop
Publishing Workshop

Verbs

This cuckoo, or road runner as it is called, found the baby amid some rocks, uttered a cry of delight, scissored it by the neck, shook it until it was almost lifeless, banged and pounded it upon a rock until life had indeed left it, and then gulped it down.

In this excerpt from "The Life and Death of a Western Gladiator," all of the underlined words are verbs; they tell what the cuckoo did to the baby snake. Colorful verbs, such as *scissored* and *gulped*, let the reader imagine the scene clearly and vividly. Because of their power to bring events to life, verbs are important in all writing.

Tenses of Verbs

The verbs in "The Life and Death of a Western Gladiator" are written in the *past tense*—to show that the action has already taken place (for example: *crawled*). Two other tenses are *present* (*crawls*) and *future* (*will crawl*). When you edit your writing, always check that you have used the same tense throughout or that necessary shifts in tense are clear. Accidental shifts in tense can confuse the reader about the order of events or about the relationship between events in a sentence.

Confusing Tense Shift	When Crotalus **left** the cave, a rabbit **hops** in front of him. (shifts from the past tense to the present tense)
Consistency in Tense	When Crotalus **left** the cave, a rabbit **hopped** in front of him. (Both verbs are in the past tense.)

Principal Parts of Verbs

The tenses are formed from the principal parts of the verb—the *present*, the *present participle*, the *past*, and the *past participle*. The present tense is usually formed by adding *-s* or *-es* to the present while the present participle is usually formed by adding *-ing*. The past tense and the past participle of most verbs are formed by adding *-d* or *-ed* to the present.

PRESENT	As friction increases, the rope **frays**.
PRESENT PARTICIPLE	The **fraying** rope lost its ability to bear weight. The rope **was fraying** continually.
PAST	The rope gradually **frayed** beyond repair.
PAST PARTICIPLE	The **frayed** rope finally broke and had to be replaced. This type of rope **has frayed** repeatedly in the past.

Irregular Verbs

Some verbs do not form the past tense and past participle in the usual way. For example, the principal parts of the irregular verb *leave* are *leaves, leaving, left,* and *have left*.

Editing Checklist

- ✔ Have you used the correct tense for each verb?
- ✔ Are there any accidental shifts in tense?
- ✔ Have you used the correct principal parts of verbs for each tense?

Communicate Your Ideas

EDITING *Verb Tense*

Edit your revised paragraph, using the **Editing Workshop** on the previous page for guidance in using the correct tense and principal parts of verbs. Referring to the Editing Checklist on the previous page for general guidance, read your paragraph several times, looking for different kinds of errors each time. As you carefully reread your paragraph, refer to your Personalized Editing Checklist to make sure you are not repeating errors you have made in the past.

Adequate Development, Unity, and Coherence

As you edit your paragraph, you may see places where you need to reorganize sentences and add, substitute, or delete words. Remember that you can return to the revision stage to continue to improve the development, unity, and coherence of your paragraph. Save your paragraph in your portfolio.

PORTFOLIO

Time Out to Reflect

Use this informative paragraph as a measure of your growth as a writer. Date your final copy. Compare it to any examples of informative writing that you have done previously or that you will do in the future. Look for areas of improvement in your writing as well as weaknesses to focus on in your next piece of informative writing. Record your self-assessment in the Learning Log section of your **journal**.

Process of Writing an Informative Paragraph

Remember that the writing process is recursive—you can move back and forth among the stages of the process to achieve your purpose. For example, during editing you may wish to return to the revising stage to add details that have occurred to you while editing. The numbers in parentheses refer to pages where you can get help with your writing.

PREWRITING

- Use the Strategies for Thinking of Subjects to think of possible subjects for a paragraph that explains or informs. (*page C111*)
- Determine your audience and analyze their knowledge, attitudes, needs, and interests. *(page C115)*
- Determine what you know or can learn about the subjects to explain accurately, and then choose a subject that interests you and will interest your audience. *(page C112)*
- Limit and focus your subject. *(pages C113–C114)*
- List and classify your supporting details to determine the best way to develop your paragraph. *(pages C116–C123)*
- Arrange your details in logical order. *(pages C124–C129)*

DRAFTING

- Write a topic sentence that clearly expresses the main idea of your paragraph. (*pages C130–C131)*
- Draft the supporting sentences in the body of your paragraph. *(pages C131–C132)*
- Add a concluding sentence that restates the main idea, summarizes the paragraph, evaluates the information, or adds an insight. *(pages C132–C133)*

REVISING

- Using the Evaluation Checklist for Revising, check paragraph structure, development, unity, coherence, and word choices. *(pages C136–C141)*

EDITING

- Using the Editing Checklist, check your grammar, usage, mechanics, and spelling. *(page C144)*

PUBLISHING

- Prepare a neat final copy and present it to a reader. *(pages C50–C54)*

A Writer Writes

An Explanation of a Behavior

Purpose: **to explain a behavior or characteristic**

Audience: **younger students**

Prewriting

Brainstorm or browse through your science book or other books on nature to discover an interesting behavior or characteristic of a plant or animal. For example, you might explain how oysters form pearls or why some flowers close their petals at night. When you have three or four good ideas, choose the one that interests you the most. After you list the details you already know about your subject, find additional details in a science book or on the Internet. Then choose an appropriate method of development and arrange all of your details in a logical order.

Drafting

Using your prewriting notes, draft your paragraph. To keep your ideas clear as you write, pause occasionally to read aloud what you have written.

Revising

Check your draft for adequate development, unity, and coherence. Then, using the checklist on page C141 as a guide, revise your draft. You may also want to read your paragraph to a classmate to find out if you have left any questions unanswered.

Editing

Use the **Editing Checklist** on page C144 to correct any errors in your writing. You may also wish to refer to the Personalized Editing Checklist in your **journal.**

Publishing

Prepare a final copy of your paragraph and present it with those of your classmates to a class of younger students.

Connection Collection

Representing in Different Ways

From Print . . .

. . . to Visuals

Use this selection from Patty Sue's menu to draw a picture or take a photograph of an entrée that fits the menu description. You may also find a photo in a book, a magazine, or on the Internet. Be sure the picture contains the same information as the written statement.

12 Bank Street

Patty Sue's Catering is committed to using only the freshest ingredients in our entrées. Look for our special Vegetarian Items, or ask about our hearty Meat Dishes. We look forward to catering your next party!

Patty Sue Thymeleaf

From Visuals . . .

. . . to Print

The photograph above shows other items that Patty Sue's Catering might offer. Write a menu description for her customers based on the photograph. Be as detailed and informative as you can.

- **Which strategies can be used for creating both written and visual representations? Which strategies apply to one, not both? Which type of representation is more effective?**
- **Draw a conclusion, and write briefly about the differences between written ideas and visual representations.**

Writing in the Workplace

Business Note

At Sandy's Sandwich Shop, your special recipe for the Triple Decker Tower has become the most popular sandwich on the menu. Thrilled by the increase in sales, your manager gives you a week off. Before you leave for your vacation, your manager asks you to write down your secret recipe so the entire staff can make the Triple Decker Tower while you are gone.

Write a note to your manager explaining how to make the Triple Decker Tower sandwich. Arrange the details involved in making the sandwich in a logical order by placing them in sequence.

What strategies did you use to explain the process?

Writing for Oral Communication

Story of an Invention

You have just completed the final model for the Bike Blender, a bicycle that allows you to make fruit shakes while you pedal. WLAB, the local radio station for inventors, wants to interview you about it. They have asked you to relate the story of where you were and what you were doing when you came up with the idea for the Bike Blender.

Write a story relating all the events leading up to your discovery of the Bike Blender. Use transitions to organize the steps in chronological order. Consider the radio audience's knowledge and attitude as you write. You may read your story aloud to your classmates or friends to see if it flows in a logical manner.

What strategies did you use to relate your story to your listeners?

Assess Your Learning

Matilda Armstrong, the principal of Whistling Pines High School, is creating an orientation brochure for next year's freshman class. The brochure will include photographs of the school and its students, as well as five personal statements that she will select from entries submitted by your freshman class. Ms. Armstrong has asked each student in your class to write a paragraph about one aspect of going to school at Whistling Pines. She will choose entries about academic life, sports and athletic events, as well as extracurricular activities.

- **Write a paragraph to inform the new students about an aspect of high school you find enjoyable. Be sure to choose a subject that is appropriate to your audience, that is, Ms. Armstrong, the students, and their families.**
- **Write a topic sentence that is clear and develop it fully. Revise your supporting sentences and concluding sentence so they flow together in a logical way and relate back to the topic sentence. Use facts and specific details to support your ideas.**

Before You Write **Consider the following questions:**
What is the ***subject?***
What is the ***occasion?***
Who is the ***audience?***
What is the ***purpose?***

After You Write **Evaluate your work using the following criteria:**

- Does your paragraph for the brochure have a strong topic sentence?
- Have you used supporting sentences that expand on the topic sentence by giving specific details, facts, examples, or reasons?
- Have you presented your information in a clear and organized way?
- Have you checked your paragraph structure for unity and coherence?
- Have you revised your paragraph to add transitions between ideas?

Write briefly on how well you did. Point out your strengths and areas for improvement.

A Writer's Guide to Presenting Information

The world is bursting with information. There is so much to absorb that you may at times find yourself overwhelmed by it all. Whether it is nutrition information on a cereal box, directions to your school, or an article in a magazine about your favorite band, information comes at you in a barrage from all directions.

The most basic function of writing is to convey information. In fact, when you have information you want to convey to others, often writing is the best means to organize and present it clearly. It is helpful to choose the organizational model and method of development best suited to what you want to write.

Information can be categorized in several ways, depending on its type. If, for example, you need to explain how to assemble a piece of furniture, you would write a how-to paragraph. A how-it-works paragraph might explain how data is sent over the Internet, while a cause-and-effect paragraph might explain what makes your heart beat faster when you exercise. You could write a compare-and-contrast paragraph to compare one kind of tree to another, but a definition paragraph to tell what a cyborg is. This guide offers you information that will help you decide how best to gather and present the information you want to convey.

How-to Paragraphs

A process is a sequence of steps by which something is made or done. There are several kinds of processes; one common type is the how-to process. Use this kind of paragraph to describe the sequence of steps in the process of making or doing something.

A **how-to paragraph** gives step-by-step instructions for doing or making something.

Generally these paragraphs describe simple tasks or processes that almost anyone could do. No matter what process you write about, your goal is to provide a clear and simple explanation for your readers. The following is an example of a how-to paragraph.

MODEL: How-to Paragraph

Interviewing an Expert

To conduct a successful interview with an expert for a school report, there are several important steps to follow. First contact the person. Explain who you are and what your purpose is in seeking an interview. Then arrange a date and time to meet or speak by telephone. Find out how much time the expert will have to talk, so you can determine the number of questions you can ask. Next prepare for the interview by learning as much as you can about both the expert's background and the topic you want to discuss. Make a list of questions, and arrange them chronologically or in order of importance. If you will be recording the interview, test your equipment in advance to make sure it is working properly. On the day of the interview, be on time. Follow your list of questions to be sure you get the information you need. Stick to the agreed-on schedule. End the interview by thanking the person for talking with you. By remembering these steps, you will help make the interview a more pleasant and productive experience for both you and the expert.

Writing a How-to Paragraph

The following activities will help you write your own how-to paragraph that explains how to do something.

Prewriting

Brainstorm for ideas of things you know how to do, such as playing an instrument or a sport, doing a search on the Web, or planting a garden. Freewrite for a few minutes, thinking of as many subjects as you can. Then go over your list and look for those subjects that you are most comfortable explaining to others. Choose the one you want to write about. Limit the subject so that you can adequately cover it in one paragraph. (For example, *how to play baseball* is too broad, but *how to bat* could be handled in one paragraph.) Think about who your audience for this subject would be. Then write a list of steps you will need to include in your explanation. Put the steps in order, from the first to the last, to complete the process you are explaining.

Drafting

Using your list of steps, draft your paragraph. Begin with a topic sentence that will prepare readers for your subject. Explain the steps clearly in the order in which they must be followed. Be sure to tell your readers everything they need to know to complete the process you are describing. Use transition or time order words and phrases to help connect the steps smoothly. Finish with a concluding sentence.

Revising

Read over your paragraph. Are all of the steps included? Are they in the correct order? Does your paragraph have a strong beginning and ending? Revise your paragraph using these questions as guidelines. Then check whether the how-to process is clear by sharing the paragraph with a test reader. Use the reader's comments and the Evaluation Checklist for Revising on page C40 to continue revising your paragraph. Then save your paragraph in your writing folder in case you want to polish it to share with someone later.

SAVE YOUR WORK

How-It-Works Paragraphs

When you are describing how something forms, happens, or is put together, you are explaining the stages in a process or an operation. The information is usually arranged in chronological order.

A **how-it-works paragraph** describes how something happens, forms, or is put together.

This type of paragraph explains a technical or abstract process, rather than something readers could do themselves, as in a how-to paragraph. A how-it-works paragraph follows chronological order and resembles narrative writing. The following is an example of a how-it-works paragraph.

MODEL: How-It-Works Paragraph

Twister!

When cold air meets hot air near Earth's surface, watch out! That is the perfect condition for a tornado to form. Here's what happens. Cold air is heavier than hot air, so it flows under the warmer air. The lighter hot air rises quickly and, as it does, it spins around and spreads out, creating a twisting funnel of air. (That's why tornadoes are often called *twisters*.) The small part of the funnel touches the ground, while the large part reaches into storm clouds in the sky. The air around a tornado all moves toward the funnel, feeding a roaring, spinning wind that can reach up to 300 miles an hour, the fastest wind on Earth. Meanwhile, storm winds push the funnel along the ground. Most tornadoes occur during April, May, and June, when Earth's surface is warming but cold air can still sweep in to disturb it. And what a disturbance a powerful tornado can be!

Writing a How-It-Works Paragraph

The following activities will help you write a paragraph that explains how something happens or works.

Prewriting

Brainstorm for subjects to write about. You might choose a science subject, such as how a hurricane forms, how the heart works, or how photosynthesis occurs. You might choose a topic related to an interest you have, such as how a car runs or how an electric guitar makes sounds. Freewrite for a few minutes, thinking of as many subjects as you can. Then go over your list and look for subjects that you know the most about or that interest you most. If a topic is too broad, limit the subject so that you can adequately cover it in one paragraph. Think about who your audience for this subject would be. Then write what you know about the subject. Gather information to check your knowledge for accuracy and to fill in missing details. Then order the information in a logical way. Most likely you will use chronological order to explain what happens first, next, and so on in the process of explaining how something works.

Drafting

Using the details you have gathered and ordered, draft your paragraph. Begin with a topic sentence that will capture your readers' attention and prepare them for what follows. Explain the stages clearly and logically, using transition words to help your paragraph flow smoothly. Finish with a strong concluding sentence.

Revising

Read over your paragraph. Are all of the stages included? Are they in the correct order? Does your paragraph have a strong beginning and ending? Use these questions to guide you in revising your paragraph. You may need to go back to the prewriting stage to gather more information on the subject to fill in stages that are missing or not clear. Share your how-it-works paragraph with a test reader to see if the information is clearly presented. Use the reader's comments and the **Evaluation Checklist for Revising** on page C40 to continue revising your paragraph. When you are satisfied with it, save your paragraph in your writing folder in case you want to polish it to share with someone later.

Compare-and-Contrast Paragraphs

To understand a concept, you might find it helpful to compare it to another that is similar or contrast it with one that is dissimilar. A compare-and-contrast paragraph is a good way to do that.

A **compare-and-contrast paragraph** examines the similarities and differences between two subjects.

This type of paragraph will help you interpret, understand, and explain two related subjects or events (such as a film and a book on the same topic). One way to do this is to explain all the characteristics of Subject A and then, in the same order, all the characteristics of Subject B. Another way is to take the characteristics one at a time, describing them alternately as they appear in Subject A and then in Subject B until all the characteristics are covered. The following paragraph is an example of the first approach.

Model: Compare-and-Contrast Paragraph

Pet Personalities

If cats and dogs are different, so are cat owners and dog owners. Granted, both types of owners are alike in their willingness to share their homes with a furry creature. But that is where the similarities seem to end. Cat owners are independent people. They admire their feline companions for their solitary ways and secretly long to be as aloof and indifferent to the world as their "purrfect" pets. Dog owners, on the other hand, are open, friendly, and as comfortable being part of a pack as their canine pals. They value the loyalty, trust, and eagerness to please that their good-natured hounds display. Of course, just as there are sociable cats and unfriendly dogs, there are exceptions among cat people and dog people, too. For the most part, however, if you want to get a snapshot of someone's personality, ask whether the person has or prefers a cat or a dog.

Writing a Compare-and-Contrast Paragraph

The following activities will help you write a paragraph that compares a concept or object to another that is similar and/or contrasts it with one that is dissimilar.

Prewriting

Choose a topic to write about. The paragraph may be part of a class assignment; for instance, you might compare international explorers for a history report or two types of organisms for a science investigation. For other ideas of subjects to write about, think about your own interests. You might compare types of media, such as a movie and a television show; or musicians, such as two rap artists. When you have a list of ideas, review it and choose your subjects. Decide who your audience will be. Then brainstorm for what you know about the similarities and differences between the two subjects. Gather information to check your knowledge for accuracy and to fill in supporting details. Then order the information in a logical way.

Drafting

Using the information you have organized, draft your paragraph. Write a topic sentence that explains the main idea of your paragraph. Follow with supporting sentences that detail how the two subjects are alike and different. You may wish to write about all the differences first and then all the similarities—or vice versa. Or you may choose to write about one difference and one similarity, then another difference and similarity, and so on. Finish with a conclusion that ends your paragraph in an interesting way.

Revising

Read over your paragraph. Be sure the main idea is clearly stated and the supporting sentences explain how the subjects are similar and different. If necessary, go back to the prewriting stage to gather more information to provide stronger details that show similarities and differences between the subjects. You might ask a reader to check your paragraph for unity, clarity, and coherence. Use the reader's comments and the **Evaluation Checklist for Revising** on page C40 to continue revising your paragraph. When you are satisfied with it, save it in your writing folder.

Cause-and-Effect Paragraphs

When your informative subject requires you to explain *why* something happened, very often the best type of writing to use is a cause-and-effect paragraph.

A **cause-and-effect** paragraph explains why actions or situations (causes) produce certain results (effects).

A simple cause-and-effect paragraph deals with a single cause, such as an icy sidewalk, and a single effect, such as a fall. A more complex paragraph describes a series of causes and effects, each one dependent on the one before, dubbed appropriately a chain of events. Here is an example of a cause-and-effect paragraph.

Model: Cause-and-Effect Paragraph

The Secret Oath

Rutherford B. Hayes is the only U.S. president ever to be secretly sworn into office before his public inauguration. Here's the story behind this little-known event in American history. In the election of 1876, Hayes lost the popular vote to his opponent, Samuel Tilden. But neither candidate won a majority of the electoral votes because there were votes, mainly from southern states, that were in dispute. Hayes promised to end Reconstruction and remove all federal troops from the South if the southern states would cast their votes for him. They agreed, and Hayes then won the electoral vote. However, Tilden's supporters were so angry at what they thought was a stolen election that there was fear they would riot to prevent Hayes's inauguration. So three days before the ceremony at the Capitol, Hayes took the oath of office in the Red Room of the White House, with the outgoing president, Ulysses S. Grant, as witness. Today, President Hayes's official portrait hangs in the Red Room, where his presidency secretly began.

Writing a Cause-and-Effect Paragraph

The following activities will help you write a paragraph that explains why something happened or happens.

Prewriting

Choose a topic to write about. To help you narrow down the many possibilities, you might start by thinking of results (effects) that you could research for causes. For instance, why are dinosaurs extinct? Why did England's Queen Elizabeth I never marry? Why do most fast-food restaurants sell hamburgers? Freewrite as many subjects as you can. Then choose the one that you know something about or are most interested in. Think about who your audience would be. You might begin by identifying the effect and then listing causes you know. Gather information to check your knowledge for accuracy and to add details, such as additional causes you are not aware of. Then order the information in the way that makes the most sense. For example, you might explain multiple causes in the order they occurred or list them by order of importance; or you might start instead with the effect and explain what caused it or start with the cause(s) and build to the effect.

Drafting

Using the information you have gathered and ordered, draft your paragraph. Begin with a topic sentence that will capture your readers' attention and prepare them for what will follow. You may want to include the effect at the beginning of the paragraph or at the end. Explain the actions or situations that have led to this result.

Revising

Read over your paragraph. Look for ways to revise it to make the cause-and-effect relationship clearer. You may need to go back to the prewriting stage to gather more information on the subject so that you can better explain a particular cause or effect. Also ask a test reader to check your paragraph for unity, clarity, and coherence. Use the reader's comments and the **Evaluation Checklist for Revising** on page C40 to continue revising your paragraph. When you are satisfied with it, save your paragraph in your writing folder in case you want to polish it to share with someone later.

Definition Paragraphs

One of the most basic functions of informative writing is to explain what something means. If you suspect your audience may be unfamiliar with a term you are using, or if a concept you are discussing might be misinterpreted, use a definition paragraph to explain the meaning of the term or concept.

A **definition paragraph** explains the nature and characteristics of a word, object, concept, or phenomenon.

The paragraph below is an example of a definition for an abstract concept.

Models: Definition Paragraph

Democracy

Democracy is a form of government in which the people being governed play an active role. The concept originated in ancient Greece, where an elite group of educated citizens helped make laws. Roman imperial rule ended this early attempt, and it was not until the Middle Ages that kings began to appoint representatives to petition them on behalf of their subjects. Later it was argued that a natural contract existed between ruler and ruled. If the contract were broken by the ruler, the ruled could take power. In Great Britain and especially in the United States, the idea of democracy was more fully developed to expand the freedoms to which people are entitled. Today, limits on governmental power, participation by representation, and individual rights are the hallmarks of contemporary Western democracy.

Writing a Definition Paragraph

The following activities will help you write a paragraph that explains or defines a word, a concept, an object, or a phenomenon.

Prewriting

Choose a word, object, concept, or phenomenon to explain in a definition paragraph. A class assignment might inspire ideas. For example, you might explain free enterprise for history class or Impressionism for art. Or focus on your own interests by perhaps defining a style of music or fashion. When you have a list of subjects that you could define by describing their characteristics—either from your own knowledge or through research—then choose the one you want to write about. Remember to identify your audience, such as a teacher, peers, or younger students. Then begin by brainstorming for what you know about the nature and characteristics of your subject. Gather information as needed to check your knowledge for accuracy and to fill in supporting details. Then order the details in a logical way.

Drafting

Using the information you have organized, draft your paragraph. Write a topic sentence that explains the main idea of your paragraph. Follow with supporting sentences that explain and define your subject. Finish with a concluding sentence that wraps up the paragraph.

Revising

Read over your paragraph. Be sure the main idea is clearly stated and that the supporting sentences help to define the subject you are writing about. If necessary, go back to the prewriting stage to gather stronger details to explain the nature and characteristics of the subject. You might ask a reader to check your paragraph for unity, clarity, and coherence. Use the reader's comments and the **Evaluation Checklist for Revising** on page C40 to continue revising your paragraph. When you are satisfied with it, save your work in your writing folder in case you decide to polish it to share with someone later. You may also want to consider compiling your paragraph with those of your classmates into a class dictionary.

Your Checklist for Presenting Information

When you are writing to inform, you will probably find that the information you want to express falls into one of the categories below. Use the following checklist to review some of the guidelines for developing the information in each category. The numbers in parentheses refer to pages where you can get additional help with your writing.

HOW TO

- The process should be clear. *(page C154)*
- Give step-by-step instructions. *(page C154)*

HOW IT WORKS

- Your paragraph should have a clear beginning, middle, and end. *(page C156)*
- Always describe a process clearly. *(page C156)*

COMPARE AND CONTRAST

- Clearly identify two subjects. *(page C158)*
- Discuss the two subjects in the same order in which they were presented. *(page C158)*

CAUSE AND EFFECT

- Place your causes and effects in the correct order. *(page C160)*
- Your tone should be appropriate to the subject. *(page C160)*

DEFINITION

- Your topic should be sufficiently narrow. *(page C162)*
- Make sure your facts are correct and accurate. *(page C162)*

CHAPTER 4

Writing Other Kinds of Paragraphs

In Chapter 3 you explored paragraphs that explain or inform. In this chapter you will explore other kinds of paragraphs: narrative paragraphs, descriptive paragraphs, and persuasive paragraphs. Narrative writing tells a real or an imaginary story, while descriptive writing vividly depicts a person, object, or scene. Persuasive writing expresses an opinion and tries to persuade others, using facts and reasons.

Whatever your writing purpose is, you may decide to use narrative, descriptive, or persuasive writing, or a combination of them. In *A Flag at the Pole*, the purpose is to express thoughts and feelings. To achieve this purpose, the author writes both narrative and descriptive paragraphs—telling a story and describing the setting. If you were writing about the dangers of drugs, on the other hand, you might include descriptive and persuasive paragraphs to help achieve your purpose of explaining and informing. In this chapter you will write different kinds of paragraphs for a variety of purposes.

Reading with a Writer's Eye

In *A Flag at the Pole,* Paxton Davis reconstructs the unsuccessful expedition of the British explorer Robert Falcon Scott to be the first to reach the South Pole. As you read the excerpt from *A Flag at the Pole,* imagine yourself in Scott's situation. Notice, too, how the writer uses narrative and descriptive paragraphs to create an exciting piece of writing.

From

A Flag at the Pole

Paxton Davis

It was the first of November before we set out, too late, too late. And almost from the start there were difficulties. The motorized sledges, by which I'd set such store and from which I'd hoped for so much, proved worthless. The horses, despite Oates's miraculous ministrations,[1] faltered and fell. We'd brought too few dogs and handled them poorly. The weather had an unseasonable edge, gray and cutting and with temperatures too low too soon, when in fact it should have been the very mildest time of the year. The wind on the Great Ice Barrier was the worst any of us had ever encountered, so sharp and unrelieved as to be all but unendurable; and, men and beasts alike stuck, bogged, we lost a crucial week waiting for a chance to go forward, decreasing day by day the food and fuel we'd need later on. And always, at the back of my mind, perhaps at the back of the minds of all sixteen of us, lurked the terrible suspicion that Amundsen might by now be ahead. . . . Despite my fear of failure, or maybe because of it, I stirred myself to a heartier show of cheer and confidence than ever, giving encouragement here, a smile of approval there, applauding Wilson's cooking, Bowers's determination to keep up his measurements and records, Oates's soldierly stoicism, Evans's cleverness with gear; and thus I stirred them all, when, it now appears, the wiser course might have been to turn back.

Yet we didn't and we continued, under my leadership, Day and Hooper turning back at the end of November, Meares and Dimitri and the dog teams at the end of the Ice Barrier, while those remaining, I and eleven more, made our way up the

[1] **ministrations:** Efforts to help.

Beardmore Glacier, nearly seven thousand feet high, the hardest task of the journey. Scurvy was beginning to show itself, frostbite was endemic,[2] the bad weather was worsening; and just before Christmas, at Upper Glacier Depot, I sent back Atkinson, Wright, Cherry-Garrard and Keohane. And I and the four Happy Few, the Band of Brothers—Wilson *(the finest character I ever met)*, Bowers *(a positive treasure, absolutely trustworthy and prodigiously[3] energetic)*, Oates *(a delightfully humorous cheery old pessimist)* and Petty Officer Evans *(a giant worker with a really remarkable headpiece[4])*—were left to face the Pole, now one hundred and seventy miles away.

Already well past the moment at which, according to our own exacting calculation, chances for success were greatest, we met the bleakest terrain, the harshest and most nearly impassable snow, the coarsest winds, the ugliest falls in temperature any of us could have imagined; and in a burst of self-indulgence I let myself confess to the journal the misery we all five felt: *This is an awful place.*

Yet no foreboding, however melancholy, could have readied me for the disappointment when it came, too weak a word perhaps, for to my journal at that instant I burst forth: *The worst has happened.* No more than a dozen miles from the Pole, Bowers's sharp eye picked up way ahead a dark speck that he, that we all, at first believed must be a shadow along the snow, a trick of the light, but which, as foot after foot between us fell away, we had to admit, tears freezing along our eyelids and cheeks, could be nothing less than a deliberately moulded mound of snow, topped by a flag, a black flag.

Amundsen's black flag—nothing less, nothing other—and then as the gray day darkened, the signs of Amundsen's priority continued to mount: dog tracks, ski tracks, sledge tracks, footprints, all of them leading, as my own instruments were

---

[2] **endemic:** Widespread within a group.

[3] **prodigiously:** To an extraordinary degree.

[4] **headpiece:** Intelligence.

leading, toward the Pole; which next day, dreaming no longer, not even of it, we reached. Amundsen had pitched his tent there, a tidy affair supported by a single bamboo, Norse flag above, skis upstanding alongside, sextants and spare supplies inside, leaving a courteously deferential[5] note asking me, should I survive instead of himself, to pass on a second note, attached to King Haakon[6] . . . which I shall, if I can, if I live.

It was only a pretense of cheer and sportsmanship and courage with which I turned toward the haggard, fallen faces of my companions and, with smiles and gestures and words that mocked my emptiness, demanded their spirit. But it worked. So we spent the rest of the day sighting and measuring, allowing ourselves only an instant's rest for a bit of food, and then, at my urging too, we placed the camera on its tripod, lined up before it, myself standing in the center, Oates and Evans on either side, Bowers and Wilson seated in the snow before us, the Union Jack behind, and, Bowers pulling the cable, took our own picture. Someday, I suppose, if our bodies are found, the negative will be developed, the photograph printed. I hope it will not show the depth of the defeat. I asked them to smile.

Will it show we knew ourselves doomed? For though the likelihood of our dying was at that moment a thought still unspoken, to my journal, to myself, I admitted my apprehension: *Now for the run home and a desperate struggle. I wonder if we can do it.* As, a day or two later: *I'm afraid we are in for a bad pull.* And, a day after that: *Things beginning to look a little serious.* It would be, as all of us knew, an eight-hundred-mile job of it, sledge-hauling the entire way, temperatures falling rapidly, winds rising, snow surface at its most unpredictably dangerous, and without—what we'd had most of the way out—the support of a party larger than five

---

[5] **deferential:** Showing respect.

[6] **King Haakon:** The king of Norway in 1911, in whose name Amundsen explored Antarctica.

tired men who'd just stared into the refuse[7] of their own shattered dreams. *I don't like the look of it.* Evans and Oates were suffering from spreading frostbite, Wilson from snow blindness; and though Bowers continued strong and energetic and I was myself, despite my seniority in age, unaware of serious physical decline, I saw what lay ahead for us both in the faces of our three weakening companions. Still—food dwindling and mysteriously short at the depots, fuel running low as our pace fell—we went on. I scarcely knew how, often lagging behind the mileage I'd calculated we must make to beat the winter. But then, approaching the decent of the Glacier, Evans and I fell into crevasses, Evans's second such spill; and afterward, though to that point the strongest of us all, Evans grew increasingly dull and confused, his cuts and wounds reopening, eyes glazed, needing more and more the help that till then he'd been able to give the rest. We got him down the Glacier, but by then he could no longer assist at night with the tent. But at last, hanging back farther and farther, the poor sick fellow collapsed altogether. Then, we others helplessly watching, he fell into a coma and died.

The first to go, as I myself shall be the last. So at length, now down to four, and Oates noticeably failing, we set forth again, following our own tracks when we could find them, taking bearing and sighting always, weather continuing to worsen. . . .

Well, worse was, temperatures now down to thirty or more below zero; fuel at the depots less and less than we'd expected; food thinning; Wilson in agony from his eyes; all of us frost-bitten; daily mileage falling critically. Then, stricken at having to do so, Oates showed us his feet.

We had no choice, of course, but to urge Oates on, gangrene notwithstanding, and by insisting he ride one of the sledges, we perhaps reduced a little the terrible pain his toes

---

[7] **refuse** (rĕ'fyüs) *n.*: Leavings; rubbish.

must have been giving him. But that meant both a heavier load and one fewer to haul it; and though Oates went on without complaint, soldier to the end, his withering face and empty eyes told us everything.

He tried to, though; we all did; and if the rest of us could see Oates was dying, unable any longer to walk, taking more and more time in the morning to get into his boots and thus costing us more and more time on the march, he did so without complaint, struggling always to summon some sort of smile to his face.

Yet in the end, moral strength, which we'd all shown, was not quite enough; for not even Oates's supreme courage could heal the corruption of gangrenous frostbite. And at last, admitting both his inability to go on and his recognition that his decay was slowing fatally the progress of his companions, the Soldier, we'd come to call him, begged us to leave him behind, in his sleeping bag. But we couldn't do that, we *couldn't.* And the next morning, after a prolonged battle with his boots, he stood suddenly and said, "I am just going outside and may be some time." When he failed to return we staggered into the snow ourselves but of course he was gone; no trace of him remained. Only the seemingly endless snow remained. Snow will always remain.

Oh, another desperate day into the wind, and another, a few miles; but by then there was little to choose between the three of us left. Bowers, perhaps, was in the best condition, though badly frostbitten. Wilson was nearly blind, and his hands and feet useless. As for myself, I mixed a small spoonful of curry with my melted pemmican,[8] got violent indigestion, lay awake all night in pain, saw my bad foot turn black. Well, no matter; no doubt by then nothing could have held off the inevitable.

Which now, at last, came. Each day, for days, Wilson and Bowers readied themselves for the final march on One Ton

---

[8] **pemmican:** Lean dried meats.

Depot, now only eleven miles ahead. Each day the blizzard stopped them from leaving the tent. And the fuel gave out. And the last of the food went. And the blizzard continued.

And then they died, Wilson and Bowers, quietly, without a murmur of regret, sleeping away in their sleeping bags so slowly that even I, surviving them, could not say with certainty which had gone first; though from the occasional rise and fall of their chests I believed, as I wanted to, that Wilson was last, clinging, noble heart, to life, to me, to Scott, for as long as he could. So finally, except for the howl of the wind, there was only . . . silence.

Silence; yet knowing I must keep my courage high, I wrote, to the sounds of their expiring breaths: *I do not think we can hope for any better things now. We shall stick it out to the end, but we are getting weaker, of course, and the end cannot be far.*

But that was days ago, I myself scarcely know how many, and in my stiffened hands the journal and the pencil seem almost mute; so I try for a coda and write: *It seems a pity, but I do not think I can write more.* Yet I can, after all, and sign my name: *R. Scott.*

Perhaps at that I dozed; perhaps not. One task remains. I raise myself, lean across and close their sleeping bags above the faces of my beloved companions. I have strength for nothing more—except, if it is given me, to *know.*

. . . Snow, then: it will be snow; we are all of us flakes of snow, blown willy-nilly[9] through the eternal night.

The bodies of Robert Scott and two of his companions were found in November 1912. They died of cold and exhaustion while returning from the Pole. Also found was the diary Scott had kept until the end—the basis of this story.

---

[9] **willy-nilly:** Randomly, without choice.

Thinking as a Writer

Narration Evaluating Effectiveness of Storytelling

"A Flag at the Pole" is a fictional account about real people and true events. Using information in Scott's diary and writing from Scott's point of view, the author tries to re-create what the explorer actually experienced.

- Imagine that you are in a writers' group with the author Paxton Davis. He wants feedback from the group on how effective his writing is. Did Davis accomplish his purpose? What details in the story support your evaluation? Is there anything you as a writer might have done differently? If so, what?

Description Describing People and Objects in a Setting

Viewing This photograph shows Scott's team at the South Pole.

- Work in a group of three or four. Ask one member of the group to close his or her book. The other members should then describe the photograph—both the people and the objects in the setting—in as much detail as possible. The person who was listening to the description should then draw a sketch of what he or she thinks the picture looks like based on the oral descriptions given by the other members of the group.

- Compare the sketch to the photograph. How effective were you in giving the sketcher a complete and vivid description of the people, objects, and setting? What additional details might you have included?

PERSUASION Convincing Your Audience

Oral Expression

When people reach the extremes, they often need to summon more courage and strength than most can imagine. At times when people are on the verge of giving up, the words from a strong leader can make all the difference. Recall this passage from "A Flag at the Pole" *(page C167)*:

> It was only a pretense of cheer and sportsmanship and courage with which I turned toward the haggard, fallen faces of my companions and, with smiles and gestures and words that mocked my emptiness, demanded their spirit. But it worked. . . .

- Imagine that you are Robert Scott, needing to persuade Oates to continue on. Under these circumstances, what kinds of arguments might be strong enough to overcome pain and fear, to "demand his spirit"?
- Improvise what you might say to Oates to urge him onward. Then with a partner or in a small group, listen to each other's speeches. Which words and arguments hit the mark? Which fail to persuade?

Developing the Skills of Narration

Any time your purpose in writing is to tell *what happened,* you will be writing a narrative. Learning how to write a narrative paragraph will help you develop the skills for any kind of narrative writing.

Narrative writing tells a real or imaginary story.

Your Writer's Journal

Keep track of the happenings in your life by writing about them in your journal. At the end of each day, record anything that happened to you that would make a good story. Jot down ideas that will help you flesh out your happenings. What started things rolling? Then what happened? *Then* what happened? How did it all work out in the end? You might use these occurrences later in your writing.

Narrative Paragraph Structure

The following chart shows the function of each part of a narrative paragraph. Make sure the narrative paragraphs you write have all three parts.

Structure of a Narrative Paragraph

- The **topic sentence** makes a general statement about the story, captures attention, or sets the scene.
- The **supporting sentences** tell the story, event by event, of how the problem or situation developed, what happened at its height, and how it was resolved.
- The **concluding sentence** summarizes the story or makes a point about its meaning.

The following narrative paragraph, based on a true story, tells the story event by event. Notice how the topic sentence introduces the main character and captures attention by making readers wonder why July 17, 1972, was a day to remember. The supporting sentences give specific details that tell about the problem or crisis faced by the main character. The concluding sentence summarizes the story by concisely restating how the main character solved a potentially fatal problem.

MODEL: Narrative Paragraph

Rescue!

TOPIC SENTENCE — For thirteen-year-old Karen Edwards, July 17, 1972, became a day to remember. SUPPORTING SENTENCES — She was resting on the side of a motel pool in Duncansville, Pennsylvania, when she saw a young boy struggling in the deep end. Then she saw the boy's father dive in after him and not come up. While others stood by, Karen jumped in and towed the drowning boy to the side. Tired but not waiting to rest, she went back for the father, who was floating face down. As she dragged him to the side, he began struggling, his waving arms splashing water in Karen's eyes. Her chest heaving, she finally made it to the side of the pool, and in a few minutes father, son, and Karen were all well. CONCLUDING SENTENCE — Karen's quick thinking and heroic effort had saved two lives.

–L. B. Taylor, Jr., Rescue!

Like this rescue story, most stories are about some conflict or problem. The topic sentence introduces the subject and prepares the reader for what will happen. The supporting sentences then tell how the problem developed, what happened at its height (the climax), and how it was resolved. In telling the story, the supporting sentences answer the questions *who, what, where, why, when,* or *how.* The concluding sentence summarizes the meaning or outcome of the story.

Practice Your Skills

Writing Topic Sentences

Write three different topic sentences for each of the following subjects for narrative paragraphs. One topic sentence should make a general statement, one should capture attention, and one should set the scene.

1. going to the orthodontist to get braces
2. spotting a tornado in the distance
3. having a narrow escape from danger
4. being lost
5. helping someone in need

Communicate Your Ideas

PREWRITING *Topic Sentences*

Look over the happenings you recorded in your **journal**. Choose the one you would most like to turn into a narrative paragraph. Brainstorm, freewrite, or cluster to think of all the elements that will be contained in your paragraph. Write a topic sentence for your paragraph. Save your work for later use.

SAVE YOUR WORK

Chronological Order and Transitions

Because a story has a beginning, a middle, and an end, the most logical organization for a narrative paragraph is chronological order. In a paragraph organized chronologically, transitions help the reader see how the events are related according to the passage of time.

In **chronological order** (time order), events are arranged in the order in which they happened.

The following chart lists a variety of transitions that you may find useful when arranging details chronologically.

TRANSITIONS FOR CHRONOLOGICAL ORDER			
after	during	afterward	immediately
before	at last	finally	after a while
later	at noon	just as	in December
next	first	meanwhile	last night
when	second	suddenly	the next day
while	until	on Monday	by evening
then	early	as soon as	throughout the day

In the following paragraph, the transitions that show the passage of time are in **bold** type. Notice that the story begins one morning and ends the following morning.

MODEL: Chronological Order and Transitions

Thirst

I never thought I would prefer a glass of water to birthday cake, but that's what happened **when I had my tonsils out.** It was **the morning before** I turned 14. I woke up in the recovery room, thinking only of WATER. **Then** a nurse wheeled me to my room, where my mother was waiting. She told us that all I could have was chipped ice, and definitely no water. **Immediately** I asked my mother for a cup of ice, but it melted so slowly that my thirst wasn't quenched. **Throughout the long afternoon,** I dozed in thirsty misery, waking only to get more ice and see my mother patiently reading a book. **At dinnertime** my mother left for 15 minutes, and I **finally** saw my chance to get a good gulp of water. The ice in the pitcher had melted, and **just as** I was pouring a glass of cold, wonderful water, a nurse came in and whisked it away. I was **still** miserable **the next morning until** I heard some voices singing "Happy Birthday" and saw my mom and the nurse enter my room.

They had a big pitcher of water with a bright red ribbon around it. That water tasted better than any birthday cake **before or since.**

Practice Your Skills

Using Chronological Order

Use the following list of events to write a narrative paragraph. First write the events in chronological order, using complete sentences. Then add transitions that show how the events are related in time. Underline each transition.

- teacher told me I should try out for all-state chorus
- couldn't find my good-luck pin to wear to tryouts
- teacher rehearsed me for two weeks before tryouts
- got a letter a few days later saying I had made it
- ran downstairs to show my father
- heard something crack under my running feet
- looked down and saw my pin—smashed
- sang "The Star-Spangled Banner" at audition, wishing I had my pin
- miss the pin but glad to learn success doesn't depend on good-luck charm

Using a Time Line

A good way to keep track of the events in your paragraph is to create a time line. Copy and finish this time line, using events from "A Flag at the Pole."

explorers set out | *lost week because of storm* | *Day and Hooper turn back*

November 1 ——————————— *end of November*

Communicate Your Ideas

PREWRITING, DRAFTING *Chronological Order*

Return to the work you did in your **journal** on a happening in your life. Arrange your supporting details in chronological order. Use a **time line** to help you order the events if you like. Then write a draft of your narrative paragraph. Be sure to add transitions to show the passing of time. Save your work for later use.

Point of View

In narrative writing, the person telling the story is called the narrator. The narrator can tell the story from one of two points of view. If the narrator participates in the story and uses such personal pronouns as *I, we, our,* and *us,* the story is being told in a **first person narrative**. The narrator tells his or her own thoughts, feelings, actions, and observations.

MODELS: First Person Narrative

In **my** younger and more vulnerable years, **my** father gave **me** some advice that **I**'ve been turning over in **my** mind ever since.

—*F. Scott Fitzgerald,* The Great Gatsby

We marched across the stage; **our** diplomas were **ours**; **our** parents filed out; to the strains of a march on the school organ **we** trailed to the hall. **I** unbuttoned **my** brown suit coat, stuffed the diploma in **my** pocket, and sidled out of the group and upstairs.

—*William Stafford,* The Osage Orange Tree

If, however, the narrator stands back from the action and tells what happened to others, the story is called a **third person narrative**. A third person narrative contains pronouns such as *he, she*, and *they*.

MODEL: Third Person Narrative

Just then the hyena stopped whimpering in the night and started to make a strange, human, almost crying sound. **The woman** heard it and stirred uneasily. **She** did not wake.

—*Ernest Hemingway,* "The Snows of Kilimanjaro"

As you plan your narrative paragraph, decide which point of view would be better for your story and then use it consistently.

Writing Tip

If you are a character in a story, use **first person point of view**. If your story is about others, use **third person point of view**.

PRACTICE YOUR SKILLS

Recognizing Point of View

Determine the point of view of each of the following excerpts. Indicate your answer by writing *first person* or *third person.*

1. The sled started with a bound, and they flew on through the dusk, gathering smoothness and speed as they went, with the hollow night opening out below them and the air singing by like an organ.

—*Edith Wharton,* Ethan Frome

2. Before Roger Chillingworth could answer, they heard the clear, wild laughter of a young child's voice, proceeding from the adjacent burial-ground.

—*Nathaniel Hawthorne,* The Scarlet Letter

3. There was no shame in his face. He ran like a rabbit.

—*Stephen Crane,* The Red Badge of Courage

4. If that staid old house near the green at Richmond should ever come to be haunted when I am dead, it will be haunted, surely, by my ghost.

—*Charles Dickens,* Great Expectations

5. She was shown into the breakfast-parlour, where all but Jane were assembled, and where her appearance created a great deal of surprise.

—*Jane Austen,* Pride and Prejudice

6. I went back to the Devon School not long ago, and found it looking oddly newer than when I was a student there fifteen years before.

—*John Knowles,* A Separate Peace

7. In this manner we journeyed for about two hours, and the sun was setting when we entered a region infinitely more dreary than any yet seen.

—*Edgar Allan Poe,* "Hop-Frog"

8. On the battlements of their castle at Camelot, during an interval of peace between two Gaelic Wars, the young king of England was standing with his tutor, looking across the purple wastes of evening.

—*T. H. White,* The Once and Future King

Communicate Your Ideas

REVISING *Point of View*

Look over the narrative paragraph that you've been working on. Most likely you wrote from the first person point of view. As an experiment, try rewriting your paragraph from the third person point of view. Save your paragraphs; you may wish to revise and polish them later.

Process of Writing a Narrative Paragraph

"In any story," wrote Malcolm Cowley, "there are three elements: persons, situations, and the fact that in the end something has changed. If nothing has changed, it isn't a story." As you look for ideas for narrative paragraphs, think back to times when something has changed. Then develop the persons, the situation, and the change in the story.

Writing a First Person Narrative Paragraph

Prewriting

The "firsts" in your life are good subjects for narrative paragraphs because they represent a change or turning point, however modest. Think back to times when you did or experienced something for the first time. These may include your first date, your first dance, your first movie, your first time on stage, your first broken heart.

- Through brainstorming, freewriting, or clustering, list all the firsts in your life that you can recall.
- Choose the one idea that would make the most interesting narrative.
- Develop a list of details, using the technique of inquiring to answer the questions *who, why, what, when, where,* and *how.*
- Arrange your ideas in chronological order. Use a **time-line** if you wish.

Oral Expression Share your ideas with three or four other students. Without using your notes, take turns telling your story to the rest of the group. Then ask your listeners to offer comments about any strong or weak points in your narrative. Make some notes about these comments.

Drafting

Use the notes from your journal, your writing folder, and comments from your writing group to make a first draft of your narrative.

Revising Conferencing

Exchange papers with a classmate. Comment on your partner's work, noting what might be added, deleted, rearranged, or substituted. Use your reader's comments and Process of Writing a Narrative Paragraph on the next page to revise your work.

PORTFOLIO

Writing a Third Person Narrative Paragraph

Every family has its own stories. These are often repeated at family gatherings as relatives share memories. Think of a relative or ancestor you find particularly interesting. What incident in that person's life has become part of your family's lore? Write that story in a third person narrative paragraph. Use Process of Writing a Narrative Paragraph as a guide. Then tape-record your story and play it for family members.

PORTFOLIO

Writing a Narrative Paragraph of Your Choice

Write a paragraph about a funny or serious incident that happened while you were with a friend or group of friends. Decide whether it would be more effective to tell about the event from the first person or third person point of view. If you like, try writing a version from each point of view. Use Process of Writing a Narrative Paragraph for help. Share your paragraph or paragraphs with the friends with whom you had the experience.

PORTFOLIO

Process of Writing a Narrative Paragraph

Remember that the writing process is recursive—you can move back and forth among the stages of the process to suit your needs as a writer. For example, after you finish drafting, you may decide to revisit your prewriting notes to see if there is another detail or idea that you might want to add to your draft.

PREWRITING

- Using various strategies for thinking of subjects, scan your memory for experiences and events that would make a good story. Then choose one and limit it. *(pages C12–C20)*
- Consider your purpose and audience. *(pages C22–C24)*
- Think back to the first incident that sets the story in motion. Then list all the events in the story, including details of time and place. *(pages C25–C31)*
- After arranging your notes in chronological order, delete any details that you decide not to use. *(pages C175–C177)*

DRAFTING

- Write a topic sentence that makes a general statement about the story, captures attention, or sets the scene. *(pages C173–C175)*
- Use your prewriting notes to tell the story from beginning to end—the conflict that developed, the climax or turning point, and the resolution. *(pages C173–C175)*
- Add a concluding sentence that summarizes the story or makes a point about its meaning. *(pages C173–C175)*

REVISING

- Does your paragraph have all the elements listed in the checklist for narrative paragraphs? *(page C173)*
- Should you add anything to strengthen development? *(page C39)*
- Should you delete anything to strengthen unity? *(page C39)*
- Should you rearrange anything to strengthen coherence? *(page C39)*
- Do your sentences have variety? *(pages C71–C78)*
- Did you avoid rambling sentences? *(pages C81–C85)*
- Can you substitute any vivid, specific words for general ones? *(pages C63–C68)*

EDITING

- Using the **Editing Checklists**, check your grammar, usage, spelling, and mechanics. *(pages C44 and C198)*

PUBLISHING

- Is your handwriting clear or your typing clean?
- Prepare a neat final copy and publish it in one of the ways suggested on page C51.

Developing the Skills of Description

Any time your writing purpose is to give someone a picture of something that they can "see" in their minds, you will be writing a description. Learning how to write a descriptive paragraph will help you develop the skills for any kind of descriptive writing.

Descriptive writing creates a vivid picture in words of a person, an object, or a scene.

Your Writer's Journal

Keep track of any sensory impressions you experience by writing about them in your journal. At the end of each day, record any impressions you may have of an unusual place, person, or object. You may be able to use these impressions later in your descriptive writing.

Descriptive Paragraph Structure

Like a narrative paragraph, a descriptive paragraph has three main parts. The following chart shows the function of each part of a descriptive paragraph.

Structure of a Descriptive Paragraph

- The **topic sentence** introduces the subject, often suggesting an overall impression of the subject.
- The **supporting sentences** supply details that bring the subject to life.
- The **concluding sentence** summarizes the overall impression of the subject.

In the following descriptive paragraph, American novelist Willa Cather describes strangely shaped desert trees. As you read the paragraph, notice how the topic sentence, the supporting sentences, and the concluding sentence—the three main elements in the paragraph—each serve a descriptive purpose.

MODEL: Descriptive Paragraph

Twisted Shapes

TOPIC SENTENCE

SUPPORTING SENTENCES

CONCLUDING SENTENCE

Beside the river was a grove of tall, naked cottonwoods . . . so large that they seemed to belong to a bygone age. They grew far apart, and their strange twisted shapes must have come about from the ceaseless winds that bent them to the east and scoured them with sand, and from the fact that they lived with very little water—the river was nearly dry here for most of the year. The trees rose out of the ground at a slant, and forty or fifty feet above the earth all these white, dry trunks changed their direction, grew back over their base line. . . . High up in the forks, or at the end of a preposterous length of twisted bough, would burst a faint bouquet of delicate green leaves. . . . The grove looked like a winter wood of giant trees, with clusters of mistletoe growing among the bare boughs.

–*Willa Cather,* Death Comes for the Archbishop

Notice that Willa Cather's topic sentence suggests an overall impression of the grove. Through the use of the words *tall* and *naked* and the phrases "so large" and "bygone age," the writer conveys to readers that the cottonwoods make a strange sight. The supporting sentences call on readers' imaginations and senses to picture these trees, detail by detail. Finally, the concluding sentence frames the picture by summarizing the scene in a simile that reinforces the odd, unusual, strange overall impression of the description.

Practice Your Skills

Writing Topic Sentences

For each of the following subjects, write two topic sentences for a descriptive paragraph. In one topic sentence, suggest a positive overall feeling about the subject; in the other, suggest an overall negative feeling.

Example	an old house in the woods
Positive Impression	The graceful old house, nestled in a grove of young pines, welcomed travelers to the meadow beyond.
Negative Impression	The shabby old house, hidden as if abandoned in a menacing stand of pines, discouraged trespassers.

1. a stray dog

2. nightfall on the beach

3. a city park on a Sunday

4. a new acquaintance

Communicate Your Ideas

PREWRITING *Topic Sentences*

Look over the sensory impressions you recorded in your **journal**. Choose the one that you think would make the best subject for a descriptive paragraph. Then write a topic sentence that expresses the overall impression that you want to convey. Save your work for later use.

Specific Details and Sensory Words

At the core of every good descriptive paragraph is one main impression. This impression may be scary, peaceful, barren, lush, chilly, warm, comical, sad, or it may suggest any other feeling or mood. The overall impression comes to life when you use your supporting details to *show* the subject rather than merely to *tell* about it. When you *show* readers—by using specific details and sensory words—you make them see, hear, smell, taste, and feel the impression you are creating.

Use **specific details** and **sensory words** to bring your description to life.

Notice how the word choices in the following paragraph create an overall impression of cool comfort.

MODEL: Specific Details and Sensory Words

Harbored for the Night

In the breeze-cooled cabin of the *Jodi-Lee*, daylight seems ages ago. Outside, the dark, cool waters splash in whispers against the hull in an ageless rhythm. Creaking ropes and mellow clangs of other boats blend in the harbor hush. The musty smell of wet wood is carried by the breeze. All around the harbor, the damp night air cools away the sunburns of the day. In the *Jodi-Lee*, the moon is a comforting night-light.

This chart shows how the writer used specific details and sensory words to create an overall impression of cool comfort.

SPECIFIC DETAILS	SENSORY WORDS
cabin of the *Jodi-Lee*	breeze-cooled
water against hull	dark, cool, splash, whispers, rhythm
ropes and other boats	creaking, clangs, hush
wet wood	musty
night air, sunburns	damp, cools
moon	night-light

Comparison and Contrast

In "Twisted Shapes" on page C185, the concluding sentence contains a **simile** that compares the cottonwood grove to a wintertime forest with mistletoe. Similarly the concluding sentence of "Harbored for the Night" on page C187 presents a **metaphor**, comparing the moon to a night-light. A comparison in which you give human qualities to an animal, object, or idea—as if it were a person—is called **personification**. "The waves danced ashore," for example, personifies water. A metaphor, a simile, or a personification—figurative language—adds richness to a description by suggesting a striking, fresh comparison.

Direct comparisons and contrasts also enhance descriptive writing. For example, you could enhance a description of a calm sea by directly comparing it with some other thing that shares the same qualities. Your description might also be strengthened by means of contrasting it with a stormy sea. Whether you use figurative language or comparison and contrast, remember to avoid clichés.

Simile	As wary as a panther behind a screen of bamboo, she quickly sought an opening among the tall players.
Metaphor	His mustache was a small black bird poised for flight; his beard, its nest.
Personification	After the quake the shivering building fought for control, failed to collect its wits, and promptly collapsed.
Comparison	The lava flow had the consistency of old-fashioned custard, crusted on top and smoothly thick below.
Contrast	Unlike the uniform ranks of doorways in the nearby housing tract, the cottages on Poole's Lane had cheerfully haphazard shapes.

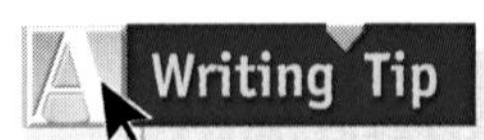

Use **figurative language** or **comparison and contrast** to enrich your description.

You can learn more about figurative language on pages C65, C67, and C68.

Practice Your Skills

Recognizing Details and Sensory Words

After reading the following paragraph, make a chart like the one on page C187. Begin by making two columns, labeled *Specific Details* and *Sensory Words*. Then fill in the columns with words from the paragraph. Include at least five items in each column.

The Aftermath

The sky was already beginning to get light by the time the fire had been reduced to smoldering ashes. The crowd of curious onlookers had mostly dispersed, and the remaining homeless had been swept away by local charity groups. The shrunken, black skeleton of the building looked defeated as it loomed over the awakening city and contrasted with the brightening sky. The dirty fire fighters collected near the still shiny engine and, after wiping the soot off their faces and hands, drove away. Finally all was silent, and the orange arms of the sun reached greedily, grabbing and pulling at invisible handholds in the pinkish sky.

Recognizing Comparisons

Identify and write four comparisons that appear in "The Aftermath." For each comparison explain what two things the writer compares and what quality those things have in common.

Communicate Your Ideas

PREWRITING *Details, Sensory Words, and Comparisons*

 Review the subject you chose for your descriptive paragraph. Then use brainstorming and clustering to generate specific details, sensory words, and comparisons that will help you describe that subject vividly. Keep in mind the overall impression of the subject that you decided on. Save your notes for later use. 

Spatial Order and Transitions

Often the most natural way to organize a descriptive paragraph is to use spatial order. Transitions are used to tell how details are located in space.

In **spatial order** details are arranged according to their location. Transitions make clear the spatial relationships among details.

The following chart shows several ways to organize details in different spatial order. Also listed are some transitions that are used with each method of organization.

TRANSITIONS FOR SPATIAL ORDER

Spatial Order	Transitions
near to far (or reverse)	north, south, east, west, beyond, around, in the distance, close by, farther, across, behind
top to bottom (or reverse)	higher, lower, above, below, at the top (bottom)
side to side	at the left (right), in the middle, next to, beside, at one end, at the other end, to the east (west, north, south)
inside to outside (or reverse)	within, in the center, on the outside, at the edge

When you describe a scene, you might use near-to-far order to guide readers from the foreground of the scene to the background, or you might use side-to-side order to show the panorama of a scene from left to right. In the following paragraph, the details are arranged spatially from side to side. The transitions in **bold** type make clear the location of each item.

MODEL: Side-to-Side Spatial Order and Transitions

Depending on how you look at it, we live in a wildflower garden or a weed patch. Our dooryard extends **from** the big old barn **on one side to** the vegetable garden **on the other, from** the home pasture **in the back to** the country road and the riverbank **in front**. I keep the grass **around** the house mowed, in season, for lawn. The garden has a fence only theoretically rabbit- and woodchuck-proof; that fence is thickly twined with vines, and catbirds and cardinals nest **there**. Half a dozen old apple trees are huge bouquets, loud with bees, **in the backyard** each May.

–*Hal Borland,* The Countryman's Flowers

PRACTICE YOUR SKILLS

Identifying Types of Spatial Order

Identify the type of spatial order used in each of the following paragraphs by writing *near to far, top to bottom, side to side, inside to outside,* or the reverse of any of these.

1. A Writer's Study

The study was a catastrophe. On the floor was a layer of typed pages, and near the desk chair, books lay opened flat. On the chair was an empty glass, resting in a bowl which looked as if it had held tomato soup. The desk lamp lit the countless pages of the writer's work and assorted writing tools. The shelves above the desk held books positioned at every imaginable angle. Crowning the mess was a stack of newspapers on top of the bookcase. The scene lacked only the writer, who clearly had gone out for air.

2. New Bicycle

Luis's new bike was a beauty, so beautiful in fact that I forgot for a moment to envy him. The gracefully thin front wheel was attached to the frame with two sparkling chrome wheel locks. The handlebar turned downward in racing style and was wrapped in red tape that matched the fire red of the frame. The gear levers were chrome and the seat was soft leather. In the center of the rear wheel was the source of speed—the five black gears and the chrome derailleur. Proud and smug, Luis watched my long gaze, but I was too filled with awe to care.

3. London at Night

The view from the balcony of the Royal Festival Hall could have been photographed for a travel guide. The navy blue tinge of the night sky made the luminous backdrop for the stars. On the far side of the Thames River, seemingly just below the deep blue sky, several old buildings stood like huge guards, positioned shoulder to shoulder to protect the river. An orangish light, which must have come from the lights placed on the buildings' lawns, illuminated them. The river itself was black and untraveled. All tourist boats were docked. Along the near riverbank, a lamplit, concrete walk was filled with people in fancy evening dresses and a few teenagers in blue jeans. Farther from the river on the near bank stood the modern performing arts complex from which others like myself enjoyed the view of London.

4. The Big Game

The most important game of the year was almost under way. José Magarolas of our team crouched at center court, waiting to jump against Tech's big man. Positioned so that the tips of their sneakers nearly touched the white arc of the jump circle, our forwards, Jimmy Jones and Don Fox, stood against Tech's forwards. All four pairs of eyes already looked up into the space where the ball would soon be tossed. Outside the jump circle, behind one pair of forwards, Blake Roberts and a Tech guard of equal height readied themselves. Ken Wan, our captain, and Tech's other guard jogged to their positions at opposite ends of the court, still farther outside the center circle. The lights of the scoreboard showed only "Home 00, Visitor 00." Leaping and shouting along the edges of the court, cheerleaders for both teams stirred the crowd. From every seat around the court, in a multitude of red and green hues, Central and Tech fans screamed their delight that the championship game was about to begin.

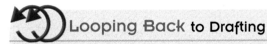

Communicate Your Ideas

DRAFTING, REVISING *Spatial Order*

Return to the ideas you generated for a descriptive paragraph. Choose the best order for your details and write your first draft. Remember to include transitions to make clear the relationship among your details. Then revise your draft, using **Process of Writing a Descriptive Paragraph** on page C199 as a guide. Save your paragraph; you may wish to edit and polish it later.

Looping Back to Drafting

Media Description

Instead of writing your description as a descriptive paragraph, use your ideas to turn your description into a piece for one of the media examined on page C194. For example, you may want to create a description suitable for a newsmagazine or for a radio broadcast. If the medium you choose includes visuals, suggest possible pictures you could include to help your description be even more effective.

IN THE MEDIA

Across the Media: News Stories

How do the different communications media—television, newsmagazines, radio, and the Internet—use description in news stories? Answer that question by tracking the same news story in all the media. As a class select a story from this week's headlines. Divide into five teams, one for each of the media named above. Then follow these steps.

- Make sure everyone understands that the goal is to look for how description is used in news stories in each medium. How is description presented—in words or pictures? If it is in words, is the writing full and vivid or sketchy? What is expressed in words and with pictures? How are words and pictures used to support each other? What differences and similarities are there in all the forms?
- Create a checklist for each team member to record his or her findings.

  - ❑ How long is the story?
  - ❑ What verbal descriptions are used, if any?
  - ❑ What visual descriptions are used?
  - ❑ How effective are the descriptions?

- Assign work to each team member. If you are on the television team, for example, you might have each team member watch a different channel.
- Decide how your group will report its findings to the class. You may decide to have each team member make an individual presentation or to give one team report.

Finally, discuss the following questions: What are the descriptive strengths of each of the various media? What does each medium do well descriptively, and what does each do poorly or not at all? Which medium presents the most powerful descriptions?

Process of Writing a Descriptive Paragraph

Develop the habit of switching on your senses to experience and appreciate your surroundings. Everywhere you turn there is something worth describing in writing. Readers enjoy letting a writer's words work on them and engage their imaginations to recreate a scene.

Writing a Paragraph That Describes a Setting

Prewriting

Popular television shows often make viewers feel as familiar with the details of the show's setting as they are with their own living rooms. Describe the set of one of your favorite television shows, following Process of Writing a Descriptive Paragraph on page C199.

- Begin by listing several television shows you know well. For each one, note the main setting in which the action takes place. For example, if the show is a family comedy, much of the action probably takes place in a living room.
- Choose the setting you know best and would most enjoy re-creating in words. Jot down all the details you remember about the set. If possible, include details that appeal to all five senses.
- Look over your notes and decide which type of spatial order would be best for your description.

Drafting

Use your prewriting notes to write your first draft.

Revising Conferencing

Share your draft with a classmate. Ask your partner what you could add to make the description even more vivid. Then use your partner's comments, your own evaluation, and Process of Writing a Descriptive Paragraph on page C199 to revise your first draft.

Editing

Using the checklist in the Editing Workshop, edit your descriptive paragraph and/or media descriptions. (You may also want to use the guidelines in Process of Writing a Descriptive Paragraph on page C199.) Ask a classmate to illustrate what you described. If the illustration generally resembles what you imagined as you wrote, you will know that you have written an effective description.

PORTFOLIO

Writing a Paragraph That Describes a Character

Picture each of the following situations. Choose one and create a character in that situation to describe. Describe the character, including his or her appearance, thoughts, and actions in the situation. Be especially careful to avoid stereotypes. Refer to Process of Writing a Descriptive Paragraph on page C199 to write, revise, and edit your paragraph.

1. a new teacher teaching for the first time
2. a veteran preparing to march in a parade
3. a candidate running for office
4. a law enforcement officer directing traffic
5. an athlete training for a contest

PORTFOLIO

Time Out to Reflect

You can use this descriptive writing as a measurement of your growth as a writer. Put a date on your paper. Then, in a month or so, compare it to other writing you are doing to see how you have improved.

Prewriting Workshop
Drafting Workshop
Revising Workshop
Editing Workshop
Publishing Workshop

Adjectives

As you read the excerpt from *A Flag at the Pole,* you probably began to feel cold in response to the story's vivid details.

> Already well past the moment at which, according to our own exacting calculation, chances for success were greatest, we met the bleakest terrain, the harshest and most nearly impassable snow, the coarsest winds, the ugliest falls in temperature. . . .

The underlined words in this passage are adjectives: words that describe nouns and pronouns. If you omit all of the adjectives, you will see how much color and exactness they add to the description.

Comparison of Adjectives

Adjectives are often used to make a comparison. To compare two people or things, add *–er* to most adjectives that have one or two syllables and add *more* to adjectives with three or more syllables.

ONE OR TWO SYLLABLES	Their bread was **staler** than it had been the week before.
THREE OR MORE SYLLABLES	Dogs were **more beneficial** than horses to Scott and his men.

When you compare three or more people or things, add *–est* to most adjectives with one or two syllables and add *most* to any adjective with three or more syllables.

ONE OR TWO SYLLABLES	They suffered from the **harshest** snow of the whole trip.

THREE OR MORE SYLLABLES	Seeing Amundsen's flag was the **most miserable** part of the trip so far.

Punctuation with Adjectives

When you use two adjectives before a noun, often you must separate them with a comma. Sometimes, however, a comma is not needed. To decide, read the sentence as if the two adjectives were joined by *and*. If this wording sounds right, or natural, then you do need a comma between the two adjectives.

COMMA NOT NEEDED	They felt the **cold Arctic** winds on their faces.
COMMA NEEDED	They felt the **cold, coarse** winds on their faces.

Editing Checklist

- ✔ Have you used the correct form when writing comparisons with adjectives?
- ✔ Have you correctly punctuated two adjectives before a noun?

Process of Writing a Descriptive Paragraph

Remember that the writing process is recursive—you can move back and forth among the stages of the process to accomplish your writing goal.

PREWRITING

- Using various strategies for thinking of subjects, scan your memory of persons, objects, or scenes to describe. Then choose one and limit it. *(pages C12–C20)*
- Determine your audience by asking yourself questions about your readers. *(page C23)*
- Form an overall impression of your subject—either positive or negative. Then list all the specific details and sensory impressions you could include to convey that overall feeling. *(pages C25–C31)*
- After you arrange your details in spatial order, delete any that do not support the overall impression. *(page C190)*

DRAFTING

- Write a topic sentence that introduces your subject and suggests your overall impression of it. *(pages C184–C185)*
- Use your prewriting notes to write supporting sentences that reveal the details one by one. *(pages C184–C185)*
- Add a concluding sentence that summarizes the overall impression of the subject. *(pages C184–C185)*

REVISING

- Does your paragraph have all the elements listed in the checklist for descriptive paragraphs? *(page C184)*
- Should you add anything to strengthen development? *(page C39)*
- Should you delete anything to strengthen coherence? *(page C39)*
- Should you delete anything to strengthen unity? *(page C39)*
- Should you rearrange anything to strengthen coherence? *(page C39)*
- Do your sentences have variety? *(pages C71–C78)*
- Did you avoid rambling sentences? *(pages C81–C85)*
- Can you substitute any vivid, specific words for general ones? *(pages C63–C68)*

EDITING

- Using the Editing Checklists, check your grammar, usage, spelling, and mechanics. *(page C44 and C198)*

PUBLISHING

- Prepare a neat final copy and publish it in one of the ways suggested on page C51.

Developing the Skills of Persuasion

Whenever you are defending or disagreeing with a viewpoint or an action, you are using your skills of persuasion. Learning how to write a persuasive paragraph will help you develop the skills for any kind of persuasive writing.

Persuasive writing states an opinion and uses facts, examples, and reasons to convince readers.

Your Writer's Journal

Use your journal to record any disagreements, conflicts, or strong opinions that surfaced during the day. Try to write every day. You may want to use some of these ideas later in your persuasive writing.

Persuasive Paragraph Structure

Like narrative and descriptive paragraphs, persuasive paragraphs have three main parts. The following chart shows the function of each part. Use the parts any time you write a persuasive paragraph.

Structure of a Persuasive Paragraph

- The **topic sentence** states an opinion on a subject.
- The **supporting sentences** use facts, examples, and reasons to back up the opinion.
- The **concluding sentence** makes a final appeal to readers.

The following model shows how each sentence in a persuasive paragraph functions. Notice how facts back up the opinion.

MODEL: Persuasive Paragraph

TOPIC SENTENCE Although the United States Air Force has dismissed reports of UFOs, there is so much evidence that UFOs exist that we should take them seriously.

SUPPORTING SENTENCES More than 12,000 sightings have been reported to various organizations and authorities. Many of these reports were made by pilots, engineers, air-traffic controllers, and other reliable people. According to a Gallup poll, five million Americans believe they have sighted UFOs, and some have even taken photographs.

CONCLUDING SENTENCE The great number of sightings warrants an open mind on the subject of UFOs.

Writing Topic Sentences

Write a topic sentence for a persuasive paragraph on each of the following subjects. Each topic sentence should state an opinion.

1. television commercials
2. fast food
3. the legal driving age
4. computers in schools
5. school awards ceremonies
6. animal rights
7. team selection in sports
8. field trips
9. part-time jobs for students
10. elections of class officers

Communicate Your Ideas

PREWRITING *Topic Sentences*

Look over the ideas you have been recording in your **journal**. Choose one of them, or another idea about which you have a strong opinion, to develop as a subject for a persuasive paragraph. Remember that the idea must have some controversy about it, or there would be no need to be persuasive. Then write a topic sentence that clearly states your opinion. Save your work for later use. SAVE YOUR WORK

Facts and Opinions

The opinion you present in a persuasive paragraph will often conflict with readers' opinions. Therefore, to win readers over to your viewpoint, you must present a convincing argument. Because facts, real-life examples, and clear reasons are convincing, they are your most important tools. Few readers will argue with facts—statements that can be proven to be true.

Writing Tip

As you develop your persuasive paragraph, use **facts and examples** to convince your reader. Do not use **opinions** to support your argument.

PRACTICE YOUR SKILLS

Distinguishing Facts and Opinions

For each of the following statements, write *F* if it states a fact or *O* if it states an opinion. Then, for each factual statement, write an opinion about it.

EXAMPLE Advertising often appeals to the emotions.

POSSIBLE ANSWER *F*—Consumers should buy products for their usefulness and quality, not for the emotional appeal of their advertising.

1. Fighting in sports such as hockey should be outlawed.
2. The U.S. Constitution contains a Bill of Rights.
3. Not all students want to go on to college.
4. Citizens who are at least eighteen years old can vote.
5. Touring bikes are better than racing bikes.
6. Playing a violin requires more skill than playing the piano.
7. Computers create as many problems as they solve.
8. Alaska is the northernmost state in the United States.

Communicate Your Ideas

PREWRITING *Facts and Opinions*

Reread your original topic sentence which expresses your opinion. Use brainstorming or clustering to develop a list of facts, examples, and reasons you could use to support your opinion. If necessary, gather additional information from a library or media center, or discuss the subject with others. Save all your notes for later use.

Order of Importance and Transitions

When you arrange your evidence in a logical order, you may find that order of importance often works best. It is the most common way to organize facts, examples, and reasons in a persuasive paragraph. Saving the most important or most convincing evidence for last is a common strategy.

In **order of importance**, supporting evidence is arranged in the order of least to most (or most to least) important. Transitions show the relationships between ideas.

TRANSITIONS FOR ORDER OF IMPORTANCE		
also	for this reason	moreover
another	furthermore	more important
besides	in addition	most important
finally	in the first place	similarly
first	likewise	to begin with

In the following model, the transitions are printed in **bold** type. Notice that the facts and examples that support the argument are presented in order from the least to the most important.

MODEL: Order of Importance and Transitions

Saving Our History

Although some people support tearing down old buildings, cities should restore them instead. **In the first place,** cities gain a sense of pride when neglected buildings are restored by skillful workers. The work of restoring old landmarks **also** provides many needed jobs. When buildings are improved, **moreover**, the value of property goes up. Seeing the rebuilt homes, other people want to buy and rebuild. **Most important,** restored buildings save a city's history and give people a sense of their roots. A salvaged city is salvaged history.

PRACTICE YOUR SKILLS

Using Transitions

Revise the following paragraph by adding transitions where needed to show order of importance.

Buckling Up

Drivers should always wear their seat belts. Buckling up is a reminder to drive carefully. With seat belts fastened, drivers are more aware of the potential danger of accidents. Drivers wearing seat belts set a good example, and passengers will follow their lead. Wearing seat belts saves lives and reduces the chances of serious injury. The National Safety Council estimates that wearing seat belts would save more than 14,000 lives in the United States each year. A five-second buckle-up could mean the difference between life and death.

Communicate Your Ideas

PREWRITING, DRAFTING *Transitions*

Review the facts, examples, and reasons you listed to support your opinion. Then make a simple chart that shows how your details can be arranged in the most logical order. Using your chart as a guide, write the first draft of your persuasive paragraph. Remember to add transitions where needed. Save your work for later use.

COMPUTER TIP

You can use different styles to highlight some of your most important ideas. Notice how the *italic* type in this sentence requires the reader to pay more attention to the word *never*.

EFFECTIVE: First of all, children should be taught that violence in schools is *never* tolerated.

Avoid overdoing italics, though. If you use them too often, they lose their effect.

OVERUSED: *First* of all, children should be *taught* that violence in schools is *never* tolerated.

Most word processing programs have a toolbar that shows different options for text styles: bold, italic, small capital letters, and different color text. First highlight the text you want to emphasize. Then select the appropriate icon from the toolbar.

B *I* U A Aa

Persuasive Language

If you present your opinions in reasonable language, your audience will probably keep an open mind about what you have to say. If you use insulting, exaggerated, or overly emotional language, however, readers will not take you seriously.

Model: Persuasive Language

Exaggerated	The best suspense story ever written is by Edgar Allan Poe.
Precise	"The Fall of the House of Usher" shows that Edgar Allan Poe was a master of suspense.
Loaded	Driving a car in the city is really stupid.
Reasonable	Using public transportation is preferable to driving a car in the city.

Use **precise, reasonable language** that is not exaggerated or loaded with emotion.

Practice Your Skills

Using Reasonable Language

Rewrite each of the following sentences, replacing exaggerations and loaded words with reasonable language.

1. People who ride bicycles without wearing a helmet should have their heads examined.
2. The most stupendous, all-around greatest sport is baseball.

3. Rock is the only music worth playing.
4. Study-hall classes are zoos.
5. Professional wrestling is a joke.
6. Only movies with special effects are exciting.
7. Movies based on books are terrible.
8. The computer is the most awesome invention.
9. Dress codes are absolutely ridiculous.
10. People who spend hours on the Internet need to get a life.

Communicate Your Ideas

REVISING *Reasonable Language and Alternative Arguments*

Check the draft you wrote to make sure you have used reasonable language. Also be sure to consider alternative arguments that you might be able to use to persuade your audience. Writing Is Thinking on page C208 can help you do that. Then revise your paragraph using Process of Writing a Persuasive Paragraph on page C211. Save your paragraph; you may wish to edit and polish it later. 

Time Out to Reflect

Read or listen to as many of your classmates' persuasive paragraphs as time and circumstances allow. Then, with your classmates, decide what makes one persuasive paragraph better than another. Develop a list of five criteria, or traits, a good persuasive paragraph should have, and write them in the Learning Log section of your **journal**. Evaluate the paragraph you wrote against the criteria you have come up with. Does your paragraph need further work to meet the criteria? If so, continue revising. If not, then use the guidelines in Process of Writing a Persuasive Paragraph on page C211 to edit your work.

Writing Is Thinking

Evaluating Alternative Arguments

When you write to persuade, you are trying to change readers' minds. To do so, you need to recognize the different positions that your readers may take on an issue. The more you understand these positions, the better you can develop an effective argument that will reach more members of your audience. For example, suppose you want to write a speech opposing the use of pesticides on food crops. The audience profile chart below shows alternative arguments you might develop, depending on your readers' concerns.

AUDIENCE PROFILE CHART

	Positions on the Issue	Alternative Arguments
City Dwellers	• indifferent; uninformed	• People should be concerned.
	• fearful of effects of pesticides; want them banned	• Pesticides should be classified and harmful ones banned.
Farmers	• concern about possible ill effects on health	• Research is needed to assess ill effects of pesticides.
	• fearful that banning pesticides may lead to crop damage from insects	• New ways must be found to protect crops and control insects.

THINKING PRACTICE

Suppose you want to give a speech to persuade a group to raise money to improve local schools. Make an audience profile chart for each audience below.

1. parents
2. local business people
3. people without school-age children

Process of Writing a Persuasive Paragraph

With practice, you can become a forceful persuader. The skills you develop writing persuasive paragraphs will help you stretch your reasoning powers.

Writing a Persuasive Paragraph to Change Behavior

Prewriting

Imagine that you have been asked to write a paragraph for your local newspaper, persuading people to bring their old newspapers, glass bottles, and metal cans to a new recycling center instead of discarding them.

- Brainstorm or freewrite to develop a list of reasons why citizens should take the trouble to recycle their household waste.
- Use a library or media center to find out where your city or town dumps its trash and why a recycling center is a good idea. For more information call the mayor's office or the town hall.
- After gathering the necessary information, organize your details in the order you wish to present them.

Drafting

As you write, be sure to state your opinion clearly to provide sufficient evidence to persuade your readers.

Revising Conferencing

Exchange papers with a classmate. Explain why you would or would not be persuaded by what you read and make suggestions for improving your partner's argument. Then use your partner's comments, your own evaluation, and Process of Writing a Persuasive Paragraph on page C211 to revise your work. PORTFOLIO

Looping Back to Prewriting, Drafting, Revising

Appealing to Readers' Emotions

In addition to appealing to reason, writers of persuasion sometimes appeal to their readers' emotions. Advertising especially uses emotional appeals, hoping to reach people by stirring strong feelings in them. Design an advertisement for your town's recycling center that appeals to emotions. Your ad should include a picture—either taken from a magazine or drawn by you—and a paragraph about why people should recycle. Through freewriting or brainstorming, decide what aspects of trash and recycling carry emotional impact. Make the picture represent one or more of these aspects. In the paragraph that goes with the picture, use more emotional appeals, setting aside appeals to reason for now.

Combining Reason and Emotion

Look over your original recycling paragraph in light of the advertisement you designed. Are there any appeals to emotion that you could work into your original paragraph to add strength? Too much emotion may put your readers off, but some emotion will add force to your appeal. Revise your original paragraph to include a few well-chosen appeals to emotion.

Writing a Persuasive Paragraph to Convince

Write a persuasive paragraph on one of the following subjects or another one of your choice. Use Process of Writing a Persuasive Paragraph on the next page as a guide.

1. wheelchair access in your community
2. a dangerous intersection
3. physical education as a required subject
4. the availability of bicycle lanes
5. vocational school as an educational alternative

PORTFOLIO

Process of Writing a Persuasive Paragraph

Remember that the writing process is recursive—you can move back and forth among the stages of the process to achieve your purpose. For example, after revising, you may wish to return to the drafting stage and try a different approach to your subject.

PREWRITING

- Using various strategies for thinking of subjects, explore your opinions on a variety of subjects. Then choose one opinion you feel strongly about and limit it. *(pages C12–C20)*
- Determine your audience by asking yourself questions about your readers' opinions. *(page C23)*
- Gather whatever information you need to persuade people that your opinion is worthwhile. As you gather evidence, also note opposing views. *(page C203)*
- Arrange your ideas in a logical order. *(pages C203–C204)*

DRAFTING

- Write a topic sentence that states your opinion. *(pages C200–C201)*
- Use your prewriting notes to provide facts, examples, and reasons that support your opinion. *(pages C200–C201)*
- Add a concluding sentence that makes a final appeal to your readers. *(pages C200–C201)*

REVISING

- Does your paragraph have all the elements listed in the checklist for persuasive paragraphs? *(page C200)*
- Should you add anything to strengthen development? *(page C39)*
- Should you delete anything to strengthen unity? *(page C39)*
- Should you rearrange anything to strengthen coherence? *(page C39)*
- Do your sentences have variety? *(pages C71–C78)*
- Do you use precise, reasonable language? *(page C206)*

EDITING

- Using the **Editing Checklists**, check your grammar, usage, mechanics, and spelling. *(pages C44 and C198)*

PUBLISHING

- Prepare a neat final copy and present it to a reader. *(pages C52–C53)*

A News Story

Many subjects can be developed in a number of different ways. Using the same general subject, for example, you can write a narrative, descriptive, or persuasive paragraph.

Narrative

Purpose: to tell a story about an imaginary discovery

Audience: newspaper readers

Recall stories about the adventures of European explorers during the Age of Discovery. Then refer to the guidelines on page C183 to write a fictional narrative about the discovery of an imaginary new land.

Descriptive

Purpose: to describe an imaginary land

Audience: newspaper readers

Review the fictional narrative you wrote. Then decide on an overall impression of the newly discovered land that you wish to convey and brainstorm a list of specific details and sensory impressions. Using the guidelines on page C199, write a paragraph in which you describe the new land.

Persuasive

Purpose: to persuade people to support or oppose an imaginary exploration

Audience: newspaper readers

Following the guidelines on page C211, write a paragraph in which you urge people to support or oppose the exploration for oil and ores in the new land.

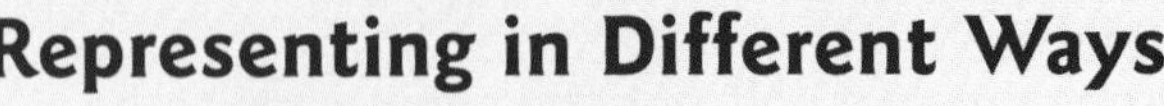

Connection Collection

Representing in Different Ways

From Print . . .

. . . to Visuals

Create a bar graph from the print information to the right that shows the average amount of snack food consumed per person each year, and the number of sick days each person used. To show the information more clearly, shade the bars with different colors: one for food consumption and another for sick days.

4393 Tempe Street
Northampton, MA 01060
August 15, 2000

Ms. Candy Caniro
The Sweet Sweets Company
8822 Main Street
Northampton, MA 01060

Dear Ms Caniro:

I am writing on behalf of my colleagues at Sweet Sweets who would like management to construct a small lunchroom to serve hot and wholesome food. The vending machines in the employee lounge sell only pre-packaged snack foods, soda, and hard candy.

We believe better food will improve the health and productivity of all of the employees. The number of sick days has steadily increased in the last three years: two years ago, each employee used four sick days; last year, five sick days; and this year, eight sick days. The consumption of snack food by employees has also been on the rise: two years ago, each employee consumed a total of 100 pounds of candy and snack food; last year, each employee consumed 130 pounds; and this year, 150 pounds. We believe that healthier lunches will lead to healthier bodies and healthier minds—and a more productive workforce too!

Please consider our request.

Sincerely,

Anita Gomez

Anita Gomez

From Visuals . . .

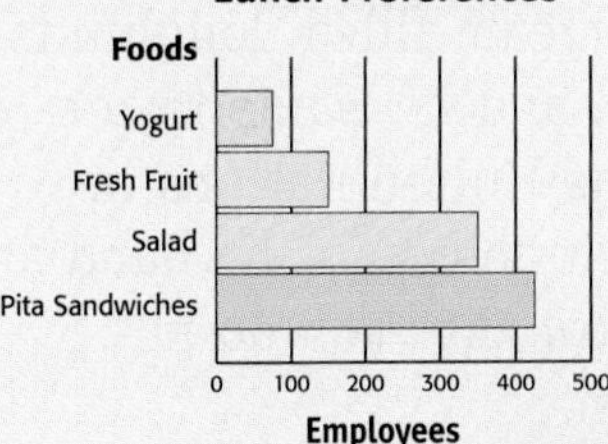

. . . to Print

The bar graph above illustrates the lunch preferences of 500 Sweet Sweets employees. Based on the graph, write a letter to the company suggesting foods they should offer in the new lunchroom.

- **Which strategies can be used for creating both written and visual representations? Which strategies apply to one, not both? Which type of representation is more effective?**
- **Draw a conclusion, and write briefly about the differences between written ideas and visual representations.**

Writing for Oral Communication

Narrative Oral History

Your aunt's eyes light up when you tell her that you want to be a history major when you go to college. "Well, that is just great," she says, "because I was wondering who would write the speech for this year's family reunion."

Write a narrative speech about three generations in your family's history. Begin the history with your grandparents—how they met and started a family together, and how the family has grown since then. Include a topic sentence to make a general statement about your story, to capture your audience's attention, and to set the scene. Include supporting sentences to tell the story, event by event. Include a concluding sentence to summarize the story and make a point about its meaning. Organize your paragraphs chronologically.

What strategies did you use to tell your family history to your relatives?

You can find information on making oral presentations on pages C596–C601.

Writing in the Workplace

Persuasive Business Letter

Your job as production manager at the Take-a-Bite Doughnut Shack is getting more stressful. Your zero-fat, ice cream-filled doughnuts have been discovered by a famous diplomat, and he wants to present them to a World Food Convention at the United Nations in two days. So far, you have been making each doughnut by hand at your small family-run business, and you know that you do not have the equipment to fill such a large order.

Write a persuasive letter to your suppliers asking for help and supplies. Avoid highly charged language. State your problem and idea clearly. Give facts and opinions explaining why this loan is good for business.

What strategies did you use to convince your suppliers?

You can find information on persuasive writing on pages C447–C464.

Assess Your Learning

The National Science Association is holding a competition to design the house of the future. You have many innovative ideas about what the house should be able to do and what it should look like. To present these ideas, you want to create some high-quality images to go with your description, and you have a friend who is very skilled at using a new computer graphics program. Before she can begin, you must give her a detailed description of the house.

- **Write a letter to your friend telling her what she needs to know to complete the drawings. Consider the following questions: What material will be used to build the house? How big will it be? What kind of rooms will it have?**
- **Create a vivid picture of your subject that readers can "see" in their minds. Use specific details and sensory words to bring your description to life. Include a topic sentence in each paragraph that introduces the subject and suggests an overall impression of the subject. Include supporting sentences in each paragraph to supply details that bring the subject to life. Include a concluding sentence in each paragraph to summarize the overall impression of the subject.**

Before You Write **Consider the following questions:**
What is the ***subject?***
What is the ***occasion?***
Who is the ***audience?***
What is the ***purpose?***

After You Write **Evaluate your work using the following criteria:**

- Have you used specific details and sensory words to bring your description to life?
- Have you included topic sentences in your paragraphs that introduce the subject and suggest an overall impression of the subject?
- Have you included supporting sentences in each paragraph to supply details that bring the subject to life?
- Have you included concluding sentences in each paragraph to summarize the overall impression of the subject?

Write briefly on how well you did. Point out your strengths and areas for improvement.

CHAPTER 5

Writing Effective Compositions

Effective communication in writing often involves more than a single paragraph. On many subjects, you need to write several paragraphs to fully develop your main idea and communicate what you want to say. In short, you need to write a composition.

The composition is one of the most flexible and familiar pieces of writing. You can use the composition form for a variety of purposes: to explain or inform, to create, to persuade, and to express your thoughts and feelings.

Most likely you have already had the experience of writing compositions in school for English, history, science, or other classes. In this chapter you will refine your skills for writing effective compositions.

Reading with a Writer's Eye

In the following selection from *When Heaven and Earth Changed Places*, Le Ly Hayslip describes the significance of rice in Vietnam. As you read this short composition, consider the details the author provides to support her thesis. Could she have developed the main idea as effectively in one paragraph? Why or why not?

FROM

WHEN HEAVEN AND EARTH CHANGED PLACES

Le Ly Hayslip

Although we grew many crops around Ky La—sweet potatoes, peanuts, cinnamon, and taro—the most important by far was rice. Yet for all its long history as the staff of life in our country, rice was a fickle provider. First, the spot of ground on which the rice was thrown had to be just right for the seed to sprout. Then, it had to be protected from birds and animals who needed food as much as we did. As a child, I spent many hours with the other kids in Ky La acting like human scarecrows—making noise and waving our arms—just to keep the raven-like *se-se* birds away from our future supper . . .

When the seeds had grown into stalks, we would pull them up—*nho ma*—and replant them in the paddies—the place where the rice matured and our crop eventually would be harvested.

After the hard crust had been turned and the clods broken up with mallets to the size of gravel, we had to wet it down with water conveyed from nearby ponds or rivers. Once the field had been flooded, it was left to soak for several days, after which our buffalo-powered plow could finish the job. In order to accept the seedling rice, however, the ground had to be *bua ruong*—even softer than the richest soil we used to grow vegetables. We knew the texture was right when a handful of watery mud would ooze through our fingers like soup.

Transplanting the rice stalks from their "nursery" to the field was primarily women's work. Although we labored as fast as we could, this chore involved bending over for hours in knee-deep, muddy water. No matter how practiced we were, the constant search for a foothold in the sucking mud made the tedious work exhausting. Still, there was no other way to transplant the seedlings properly; and that sensual contact between our hands and feet, the baby rice, and the wet, receptive earth, is one of the things that preserved and heightened our connection with the land . . .

Beginning in March, and again in August, we would bring the mature rice in from the fields and process it for use during the rest of the year. In March, when the ground was dry, we cut the rice very close to the soil—*cat lua*—to keep the plant alive.

In August, when the ground was wet, we cut the plant halfway up—*ca gat*—which made the job much easier.

The separation of stalk and rice was done outside in a special smooth area beside our house. Because the rice was freshly cut, it had to dry in the sun for several days. At this stage, we called it *phoi lua*—not-yet rice. The actual separation was done by our water buffalo, which walked in lazy circles over a heap of cuttings until the rice fell easily from the stalks. We gathered the stalks, tied them in bundles, and used them to fix roofs or to kindle our fires. The good, light-colored rice, called *lua chet*, was separated from the bad, dark-colored rice—*lua lep*—and taken home for further processing.

Once the brown rice grains were out of their shells, we shook them in wide baskets, tossing them slightly into the air so that the wind could carry off the husks. When finished, the rice was now ready to go inside where it became "floor rice" and was pounded in a bowl to crack the layer of bran that contained the sweet white kernel. When we swirled the cracked rice in a woven colander, the bran fell through the holes and was collected to feed the pigs. The broken rice that remained with the good kernels was called *tam* rice, and although it was fit to eat, it was not very good and we used it as chicken feed (when the harvest was good) or collected it and shared it with beggars when the harvest was bad.

We always blamed crop failures on ourselves—we had not worked hard enough or, if there was no other explanation, we had failed to adequately honor our ancestors. Our solution was to pray more and sacrifice more and eventually things always got better. Crops ruined by soldiers were another matter. We knew prayer was useless because soldiers were human beings, too, and the god of nature meant for them to work out their own karma[1] just like us.

In any event, the journey from seedling to rice bowl was long and laborious and because each grain was a symbol of life, we never wasted any of it. Good rice was considered god's gemstone—*hot ngoc troi*—and was cared for accordingly on pain of divine punishment. Even today a peasant seeing lightning will crouch under the table and look for lost grains in order to escape the next bolt. And parents must never strike children, no matter how naughty they've been, while the child is eating rice, for that would interrupt the sacred communion between rice-eater and rice-maker. Like my brothers and sisters, I learned quickly the advantages of chewing my dinner slowly.

---

[1] **karma** (kär′mə) *n.*: Fate.

Thinking as a Writer

Analyzing the Effectiveness of a Composition

When Heaven and Earth Changed Places is a detailed description of rice and its significance for a town in Vietnam.

- Imagine that Le Ly Hayslip has asked you to give her feedback on her composition. Was she effective in making her readers understand the process of cultivating rice and its importance? What details in the composition support your evaluation? Would you have included any additional information? If so, what?

Evaluating Language

Oral Expression

Throughout her composition, Le Ly Hayslip includes Vietnamese terms pertaining to the cultivation of rice.

- Form a small group with two or three of your classmates, and take turns reading aloud the sentences in *When Heaven and Earth Changed Places* that contain words or phrases in Vietnamese. If a student in your class speaks Vietnamese, ask him or her to read aloud. Why do you think the writer decided to include these words and phrases? What do they contribute to the overall composition?

Acquiring Information from a Photograph

Viewing

- Study carefully this photograph of a mature Vietnamese rice plant. What can you learn from the photograph that you did not learn from Le Ly Hayslip's descriptions?

The Power of Composing

In your lifetime you will read and write thousands of compositions. The power of the composition form stems from the fact that it can be used to explore any subject. However, for a composition to be truly effective—to interest, inform, excite, or even infuriate the reader—it must be well written, with a clearly stated introduction, vivid details that develop the main idea, and a memorable ending. When those elements are in place, a composition can have the staying power of the finest works of poetry, fiction, and drama.

Uses of Composition Writing

The following examples demonstrate the range of subjects that compositions may cover and the variety of writers who produce them.

- **A famous television reporter writes an article** critical of sensational tabloid news programs for a magazine published for journalists.
- **A contributor to an Internet site on Native American art posts an explanation** of the significance of the totem pole.
- **A former First Lady delivers a speech** to a group of designers about redecorating the White House.
- **For an elective class on "future studies," high school students write predictions** about what they think life will be like in fifty years.
- **An actor prepares a character study** for a class on dramatic technique.
- **A published novelist writes an essay** on writing effectively for a college English textbook.

Developing Your Composition Writing Skills

An effective composition has a tone that immediately signals the writer's purpose and view of the subject. Contemporary writer Ellen Bryant Voigt describes tone in a composition as "what the dog registers when you talk to him sternly or playfully—the form of the emotion behind or within the words. It's also what can allow an obscenity to pass for an endearment, or a term of affection to become suddenly an insult." So, too, an effective composition can caress readers or hit them hard like a slap in the face; it can tickle or teach, inspire or annoy.

A **composition** presents and develops one main idea in three or more paragraphs.

Your Writer's Journal

In your journal, make entries on subjects that you would like to write about in a short composition. Remember that a composition can be about any topic, so jot down any and all subjects that interest you. For instance, you may include subjects that you can explain or describe, or topics you can provide information on or want to share your feelings about. Return to your journal to make an entry whenever an idea strikes you. In this way, you'll compile a substantial list of subjects that you might use later in your writing.

Structure of a Composition

A composition has three main parts—an introduction, a body, and a conclusion. As the following chart shows, these three parts of a composition parallel the three-part structure of a paragraph.

PARAGRAPH STRUCTURE	COMPOSITION STRUCTURE
Introduction	
topic sentence that introduces the subject and expresses the main idea	introductory paragraph that introduces the subject and expresses the main idea in a thesis statement
Body	
supporting sentences	supporting paragraphs
Conclusion	
concluding sentence	concluding paragraph

As you read the following composition, notice how the three-part structure introduces the thesis statement and works to present the subject.

MODEL: Composition

Cat Lovers, Dog Lovers

INTRODUCTION

One controversy in this highly controversial era is that between those who love only cats and those who love only dogs. "I love dogs, but I can't stand cats" is a statement I often hear; or "I hate dogs, but I adore cats." I stand firmly on my belief that both dogs and cats give richness to life, and both have been invaluable to humankind down the ages.

THESIS STATEMENT

PARAGRAPHS OF THE BODY

Historians agree that dogs moved into humans' orbit in primitive days when they helped hunt, warned of the approach of enemies, and fought off marauding wildlife. In return, bones and scraps were tossed to them, and they shared the warmth of the first fires. Gradually they became part of the family clan.

As for cats, it was cats who saved Egypt from starvation during a period when rats demolished the grain supplies. Cats were imported from Abyssinia and became so valuable that they moved into palaces. At one time a man who injured a cat had his eyebrows shaved off. When the cats died, they were embalmed and were put in the tombs of the Pharaohs along with jewels, garments, and stores of food to help masters in their journey to the land of the gods. There was even a cat goddess, and a good many bas-reliefs picture her.

CONCLUSION

So far as service to humankind goes, I do not see why we should discriminate between dogs and cats. Both have walked the long roads of history with humankind. As for me, I do not feel a house is well-furnished without both dogs and cats, preferably at least two of each. I am sorry for people who limit their lives by excluding either. I was fortunate to grow up with kittens and puppies and wish every child could have that experience.

—Gladys Taber, Country Chronicle

PRACTICE YOUR SKILLS

Analyzing a Composition

Write answers to the following questions about "Cat Lovers, Dog Lovers." If necessary, reread all or part of the composition.

1. What is the main idea that the author expresses in the introduction?
2. How does each paragraph of the body relate to the thesis statement?
3. What is the conclusion?
4. How does the conclusion relate to the main idea in the introduction?

Communicate Your Ideas

PREWRITING *Subject*

Review your **journal** notes for possible subjects for a composition, and then choose the one that you would like to write about most. Use clustering to explore the topic. Save your notes for later use.

Introduction of a Composition

Like the topic sentence of a paragraph, the introduction of a composition prepares the reader for what will follow. When you write a short composition, you can usually complete the introduction in one paragraph.

Functions of the Introduction

- It introduces the subject of your composition.
- It states or implies your purpose for writing.
- It presents the main idea of your composition in a thesis statement.
- It establishes your tone.
- It captures your readers' interest.

The introduction of "Cat Lovers, Dog Lovers" performs these functions very well. It introduces the subject—the controversy between cat lovers and dog lovers—and establishes a serious tone. The thesis statement then presents the main idea that both cats and dogs have been important to people throughout history. The writer's purpose, clearly implied in the introduction, is to persuade the reader that people should love both dogs and cats. With strongly worded, eye-catching quotes, the introduction also captures the reader's attention.

Thesis Statement

The thesis statement is usually a single sentence. It may appear anywhere in the first paragraph, although it often has the strongest impact when it is the first or the last sentence.

The **thesis statement** states the main idea and makes the purpose of the composition clear.

In the following examples, each thesis statement is underlined. The implied purpose of each model is, in order, to inform, to express thoughts and feelings, and to persuade.

Models: Thesis Statements

<u>The name "Indian Summer" has no valid relationship to the Indians that I can discover.</u> There was no such season on the Indian calendar, which reckoned time by the moon and not the weather. The moons were named for the weather or for the seasonal occupation, but I can find no Indian Summer moon.

–*Hal Borland,* An American Year

<u>My coming to America in 1979 was not very pleasant.</u> When I was twelve, my parents had to leave my homeland, Vietnam. We lived near My Tho all my years and I did not want to leave, but they said we must. My two sisters were younger, four and seven, and they did not know what it meant to leave. My mother said that we must not tell any of our friends, that our going was a secret. It was hard for me to think I would never see my home or some of my family again. Some of my story I tell here I remember well, but some is not clear and is from stories my family tells.

–*Hieu Huynh,* "Coming to America"

Nowhere is modern thinking more muddled than over the question of whether it is proper to debate moral issues. Many argue it is not, saying it is wrong to make "value judgments." This view is shallow. If such judgments were wrong, then ethics, philosophy, and theology would be unacceptable in a college curriculum—an idea that is obviously silly. As the following cases illustrate, it is impossible to avoid making value judgments.

—*Vincent Ryan Ruggiero,* "Debating Moral Questions"

Practice Your Skills

Identifying Thesis Statements

Read each of the following introductory paragraphs and write the thesis statement. Then below each thesis statement, identify the purpose for writing that is stated or implied. Indicate the purpose by writing *to express thoughts and feelings, to explain or inform,* or *to persuade.*

1. The difference between "a place in the country" and a farm is chiefly a matter of livestock. It is in New England, anyway. You can own 200 acres, you can pick your own apples, you can buy a small tractor—and you're still just a suburbanite with an unusually large lot. But put one cow in your pasture, raise a couple of sheep, even buy a pig, and instantly your place becomes a farm.

—*Noel Perrin,* "Raising Sheep"

2. Running is the sport of the people. If it is not the largest participant sport already in terms of numbers, it no doubt is in terms of time devoted to it. It requires little in the way of skills or money, and no particular body type or age or location. It doesn't discriminate. Even at competitive levels it thrives on friendship. Where has it been all this time?

—*Robert E. Burger,* Jogger's Catalogue

3. Analysts have had their go at humor, and I have read some of this interpretive literature, but without being greatly instructed. Humor can be dissected, as a frog can, but the thing dies in the process and the innards are discouraging to any but the pure scientific mind.

—*E. B. White,* "Some Remarks on Humor"

Writing a Thesis Statement

For each of the following subjects, write a thesis statement. Base each one on the ideas and information provided.

1. SUBJECT Brasília

IDEAS AND INFORMATION
- became capital of Brazil in 1960
- was built from scratch in Brazil's interior to open up the frontier to settlers
- has buildings with unique, modern design
- is a source of national pride
- is isolated from older cities on coast
- has problems: overpopulation, poverty

2. SUBJECT savings accounts

IDEAS AND INFORMATION
- Anyone can open one by making a deposit.
- Each deposit is added to the balance.
- Deposits and withdrawals are recorded in a passbook.
- Banks pay interest on the balance.
- When interest is compounded daily, interest is paid on the interest and added to the balance.
- Banks may pay higher interest rates on an account that keeps a high minimum balance.

Communicate Your Ideas

PREWRITING ***Thesis Statement***

Draw conclusions from your notes about the subject of your composition. After making a list of conclusions, choose one to be the main idea of your composition. Then write the main idea in the form of a complete sentence. The main idea will be expressed in your thesis statement when you draft your introduction. Save your notes for later use.

Drawing Conclusions

Before you write a thesis statement, you should first draw conclusions about your subject. When you **draw a conclusion,** you make a reasoned judgment based on all the information you have. The following list shows how Le Ly Hayslip provided details about the process of growing rice, and then drew a conclusion about its significance.

INFORMATION:
- Rice seedlings had to be protected from birds that would eat them.
- The young stalks were pulled up and transplanted by hand into the wet, muddy ground.
- The good rice, called "floor rice," was pounded in a bowl to release the sweet white kernels.

CONCLUSION: ". . . the journey from seedling to rice bowl was long and laborious . . ."

THINKING PRACTICE

Analyze the information given below and write three possible conclusions you could draw from it.

SUBJECT: the Louisiana Purchase of 1803

INFORMATION:
- Napoleon unexpectedly offered French territory in North America for sale
- purchase price only $15 million
- Jefferson almost passed up the opportunity because he thought the Constitution did not give a president the right to buy land.
- purchase doubled the size of the U.S.
- provided valuable waterways and natural resources

Tone

Your tone in writing is like your tone of voice when you speak. That is, the way you express yourself reveals your attitudes—positive, negative, or neutral—toward a subject.

Tone is the writer's attitude toward subject and audience.

Your word choices and sentence constructions should make clear to readers what they should expect and how they should interpret what you say. Your tone should suit your subject, purpose, and audience.

In "Cat Lovers, Dog Lovers," the tone is serious, persuasive, and enthusiastic, while the selection from *When Heaven and Earth Changed Places* has a more personal tone.

Writing Tip

Choose a **tone** that is appropriate for your subject, writing purpose, and audience.

Practice Your Skills

Recognizing Tone

Write two or more adjectives that describe the tone of the following introductory paragraph.

> Industry blasted the ore out of the earth and Ontonagon developed under the settling dirt. The ore held out for ten years; then the blasting stopped. Production closed and big industry moved on, leaving behind a loading platform and four empty Northern Iron freight cars. The townspeople stayed on; they had nowhere to go or couldn't summon up the interest to leave. They opened five-and-dime stores, hardware, and live bait shops. Some worked in the paper mill by the tracks; others joined the logging crews.
>
> –*Kristen King Bibler,* "Ontonagon"

Capturing the Reader's Interest

You can capture your readers' interest in many ways. For example, in her introduction to "Cat Lovers, Dog Lovers," Gladys Taber uses two eye-catching quotations. In the excerpt from *When Heaven and Earth Changed Places*, Le Ly Hayslip provides both an unexpected image of rice (as "fickle") and a vivid description of herself and other children as "human scarecrows" protecting their "future supper." Below are several strategies for starting an introduction.

Strategies for Capturing the Reader's Interest

- Start with an interesting quotation.
- Start with a question.
- Present an unusual or little-known fact.
- Present an idea or image that is unexpected.
- Cite a statistic that is alarming or amusing.
- Lead in with a line of dialogue from a conversation.
- Give an example or illustration of the main idea.
- Relate an incident or personal experience.

Practice Your Skills

Analyzing an Introduction

Briefly explain how the following introduction captures the reader's interest.

Merely as an observer of natural phenomena, I am fascinated by my own personal appearance. This does not mean that I am pleased with it, mind you, or that I can even tolerate it. I simply have a morbid interest in it.

–*Robert Benchley,* "My Face"

Capturing Interest

The following chart shows how Le Ly Hayslip might have developed different ways to capture her readers' interest. Copy and complete it using information from the selection.

Main Idea: Importance of Rice in Vietnamese Culture	
Quotation	
Question	
Unusual or Little-known Fact	Sweet potatoes, peanuts, cinnamon, and taro are also grown in Vietnam.
Unexpected Idea or Image	Rice is a "fickle" provider.
Alarming or Amusing Statistic	
Dialogue from a Conversation	
Example or Illustration of a Main Idea	
Personal Incident or Experience	Children acted as "human scarecrows" to the keep the birds away from the newly planted rice.

Communicate Your Ideas

DRAFTING *Introduction*

Draft the introductory paragraph of your composition, using the chart on page C225 and the strategies on page C231 for guidance. You may also want to use a chart like the one above. When you are satisfied that the thesis statement clearly expresses the main idea, experiment with placing it at the beginning or end of the introduction. Save the version of the introduction that you like best for later use.

COMPUTER TIP

If you are using a computer and word-processing program to draft your composition, you can use the Save As function to save more than one version of your work. Save your original draft with its own title. Then, after you have revised your composition, go to File and select Save As and give the revised version a new name. If you find that some of the revisions you have made don't work as well as your original material, you still have a complete copy of your original draft.

Body of a Composition

Following the introduction, the body of a composition explains the thesis statement by developing the main idea in supporting paragraphs. A composition body, therefore, is much like the body of a paragraph.

PARAGRAPH BODY	COMPOSITION BODY
The body consists of **sentences** that support **the topic sentence.**	The body consists of **paragraphs** that support the **thesis statement.**
All the sentences relate to the **main idea** expressed in the topic sentence.	All the paragraphs relate to the **main idea** expressed in the thesis statement. At the same time, each paragraph has a topic sentence, a body, and a conclusion of its own.
Each sentence develops a **supporting detail** that supports the main idea.	Each paragraph develops a **supporting idea** that supports the main idea. At the same time, each supporting idea contains **supporting details.**

Supporting Paragraphs

The information in the body of your composition may come from your own experience and observations or from research. Wherever it comes from, the information proves or supports your thesis by serving as the supporting paragraphs in the body of your composition.

The **supporting paragraphs** of a composition develop the thesis statement with specific details.

The topic sentence of each supporting paragraph supports the thesis statement of the composition. The sentences in each paragraph then develop that paragraph's topic sentence by giving supporting details. As you read the following model, notice how each paragraph of the body develops the main idea that is expressed in the thesis statement. Also notice how each paragraph has its own structure, with a topic sentence and a body of supporting sentences.

Model: Supporting Paragraphs

The Anza-Borrego Desert

INTRODUCTION

We approach the Anza-Borrego Desert in southern California from the west, driving through lush, velvety green mountains, forested and thriving with life. Suddenly, as we leave the mountains behind us, the landscape takes on the character of a planet long ago deserted of all life. In the Anza-Borrego Desert, every detail for miles around adds to the sense of desolation.

THESIS STATEMENT

TOPIC SENTENCE OF THE FIRST PARAGRAPH IN THE BODY

In such a setting, our eyes search in vain for a sign of the life we saw thriving on the other side of the mountains. The barren, sandy land is mostly flat, but craggy hills, worn into strange shapes by the wind-driven sand, lurch up from the desert floor in scattered patterns. Cacti contorted into menacing human shapes cast gray shadows over the sand and scraggly desert grasses. Colors are faded; the sand is a dull beige or a bleached-out white. Only the leathery green of the cacti and

TOPIC SENTENCE OF THE SECOND PARAGRAPH IN THE BODY

the blue of the cloudless sky serve as reminders that the bright colors of life even exist.

Not only is the sight of the desert desolate, but sounds too seem weirdly nonexistent. There are no sounds of natural life, no calling birds or rustling leaves. There are also no sounds of human life, no whir of cars down the hot asphalt road that seems forgotten. So complete is the silence of the desolate area that we speak in the whispers of an unbelieving awe.

The body of this model can be presented in a simple outline that shows how the main idea of each paragraph supports the thesis statement of the whole composition.

THESIS STATEMENT: In the Anza-Borrego Desert, every detail for miles around added to a sense of desolation.

I. Our eyes searched in vain for a sign of the life we saw thriving on the other side of the mountain.

II. Not only did the sight of the desert seem desolate, but sounds too seemed weirdly nonexistent.

PRACTICE YOUR SKILLS

Listing Supporting Ideas

For each of the following thesis statements, list at least two supporting ideas that could be developed into two supporting paragraphs for the body of a composition. After you write each supporting idea, add at least two details you could use to develop that paragraph.

EXAMPLE: Hobbies can lead to money-making ventures.

Possible Answers:

I. Some hobbies produce salable goods.

- Gardeners can sell their vegetables.
- Knitters can sell their sweaters.
- Jewelry makers can sell their creations.

II. Some hobbies involve salable services.

- Photographers can take pictures at weddings.
- Musicians can perform at dances.
- Mechanics can fix cars.

1. Going to the country is my idea of a perfect outing.
2. Holidays have important meanings in American life.
3. Everyone should have a hero—someone they can look up to and emulate.
4. The neighborhood I live in could use some improvements.
5. Our state played an important role in United States history.
6. Doing volunteer work is a good way to learn new job skills.

Communicate Your Ideas

DRAFTING *Body*

Review your notes and the introduction to your composition. List all the ideas you will use to support your thesis statement. Under each idea, group the details you will use to support it. As you work, arrange your notes in a simple outline like the one on page C235. Then, using the outline as a guide, write the body of the composition by developing each supporting idea and related details into a separate paragraph with its own topic sentence. Save your draft for later use.

Reworking Introduction and Adding Supporting Ideas

After conferencing with a partner, you may need to rework your introduction to create a more clearly worded thesis statement that identifies the main idea of your composition. Use the Functions of the Introduction on page C225 for guidance. You may also need to do more research to find ideas and details to develop stronger supporting paragraphs.

Unity, Coherence, and Clarity

Like a paragraph, a composition should keep to the subject, move smoothly from one idea to the next in a logical order, and make sense to the reader. These three qualities of a composition are called unity, coherence, and clarity.

Unity A composition has **unity** if none of the ideas wanders off the subject. Every sentence in each paragraph of the body should develop the main idea expressed in the paragraph's topic sentence. At the same time, every paragraph in the composition should develop the thesis statement.

In the body of "The Anza-Borrego Desert" on pages C234–C235, for example, the paragraphs develop the details of sight and sound that are needed to support the thesis statement. The topic of the first supporting paragraph is the sights of the desert, and the topic of the second supporting paragraph is the sounds of the desert. The composition has unity because both paragraphs develop the thesis and neither paragraph contains any details that are not related to the topic sentence. For example, there is no paragraph about weather in the desert, and the paragraph about desert sounds does not contain details about desert colors.

You can find more information on unity on page C105.

Coherence A composition has **coherence** if the ideas follow in logical order and if transitions are used to connect those ideas.

In the body of "The Anza-Borrego Desert," for example, the first supporting paragraph describes only the sights that give the impression that the desert lacks signs of life, while the second supporting paragraph describes only the sounds that give that impression. Transitional words and phrases connect all the supporting details within each paragraph. At the same time, a transition between the two supporting paragraphs is provided by the sentence that begins, "Not only is the sight of the desert desolate, but also . . ." If the composition mixed up the sights and sounds and lacked transition between the paragraphs, then it would not have coherence.

You can find more information on coherence on page C107.

Clarity A composition has **clarity** if the meaning of the paragraphs, sentences, and words is clear. One way you can achieve clarity is by writing sentences that are not wordy or rambling. You can also add clarity to your paragraphs by making sure they are adequately developed. Using specific words and precise images also helps you make your writing clear.

In the introduction of "The Anza-Borrego Desert," the writer's negative attitude toward the unfamiliar desert is obvious. In the body, crisp sentences and specific details make the meaning clear. In the sentence "There are no sounds of natural life, no calling birds or rustling leaves," the specific examples "calling birds" and "rustling leaves" add clarity to the meaning of "sounds of natural life."

You can find more information on clarity and adequate development on pages C104, C416, and C419–C420.

Practice Your Skills

Analyzing the Body of a Composition

Reread the introduction and the body of the composition "Cat Lovers, Dog Lovers" on pages C223–C224. Then develop an outline that shows the relationships between the thesis statement and the supporting paragraphs. Follow the model of an outline on page C235. When you have finished, think about how your outline illustrates the unity and coherence of the composition.

Across the Media: Representing Culture

When you read the model paragraph by the Vietnamese student writer Hieu Huynh on page C226, what images came to mind? If you are not Vietnamese yourself, chances are that your mental images were a compilation of pictures you saw and stories you heard on TV about Vietnam. Visual media, especially television, leave powerful, lasting impressions. Unfortunately, those media-based impressions are never the complete story. A culture is far too rich and complex to capture in a few images, however strong.

Take a few minutes to make a list of mental images you have of Vietnam and the Vietnamese people. Draw a composite picture summarizing those images. How did you acquire each image? Was it through a film, a TV show, a book? Was it a firsthand experience? What associations can you make to recent historical events, ways of earning a living, or styles of clothing and architecture? To what parts of the Vietnamese culture do you have few, if any, associations? Finally, to help fill in some of the gaps in your cultural impression, spend some time browsing through this site on the Internet:

http://www.destinationvietnam.com/aboutvn/culture/aboutvn.culture.htm

Be sure to visit the art gallery as well:

http://www.destinationvietnam.com/cyclo/cyclo.htm

Scholars spend a lifetime learning about a culture and never learn all there is to know. The brief browsing you do on the Internet is still only a scratch on the surface of this rich culture, but it may well lead to a much richer picture of this culture than the one you had before browsing.

Media Activity

Write a three-paragraph composition comparing your original impression of Vietnamese culture to the one you have after having done some research.

Conclusion of a Composition

In the conclusion of a composition, you should summarize your supporting ideas and recall the main idea that is expressed in your thesis statement. As in the conclusion of a paragraph, you may also want to add an insight in the concluding paragraph of a composition. This concluding paragraph may be long or short, but it should end with a memorable sentence—the clincher. As the last sentence in your composition, the clincher sentence should leave as strong an impression as does the opening line of your introduction.

Remember that the **concluding paragraph** completes the composition and reinforces the main idea.

The paragraph below is the conclusion to the model composition about the Anza-Borrego Desert. Notice how it reinforces the main idea stated in the introduction: "In the Anza-Borrego Desert, every detail for miles around adds to the sense of desolation."

Model: Conclusion

As if to make up for the emptiness all around, our imaginations fill with fears and threats. What seems to be the hiss of some venomous snake turns out to be the gentle fizz of the just-opened soft drink. What we thought was a permanently ruined car that would leave us stranded forever has cooled down and starts up easily. Not until we cross the mountains once again do our thoughts turn from snakes and sunstrokes to the everyday worries of ordinary life.

Clincher Statement

The clincher sentence in this paragraph captures the reader's attention by referring to snakes and sunstrokes. These references leave a memorable impression because readers can imagine the relief the travelers must have felt as they drove out of the desert.

Practice Your Skills

Writing a Clincher Sentence

Write a clincher for the following concluding paragraph.

Despite their fearsome looks and formidable sting, mud wasps are gentle creatures. Their lives are devoted to collecting balls of wet earth for their intricate constructions. You can observe them at work whenever the hot sun begins to bake a rain puddle. While gathering mud, a wasp will barely notice an observer. Tread carefully, however. . . .

Communicate Your Ideas

DRAFTING, REVISING *Conclusion, Unity, Coherence, Clarity*

Write a strong conclusion to the introduction and body of your composition. As you write the conclusion, remember to refer back to your main idea. End your composition with a good clincher sentence. Add a title.

You can get more information on writing a title on page C38.

Revise your composition by checking to be sure the introduction, body, and conclusion have unity, coherence, and clarity. Then refer to the **Evaluation Checklist for Revising** on page C40 to revise your writing further. Save your work for later use.

Standard English

Even when the subject of your composition is personal, it is still considered formal writing. For your composition to be truly effective, you should choose standard English usage.

among, between *Among* is used to refer to three or more people or things. *Between* is used to refer to two people or things.

AMONG	The cast discussed the show **among** themselves.
BETWEEN	**Between** TV and radio, I prefer TV for getting the news.

fewer, less *Fewer* is plural and refers to things that can be counted. *Less* is singular and refers to quantities and qualities that cannot be counted.

FEWER	This fall TV had **fewer** new programs.
LESS	I watched **less** television this month.

double negative Words such as *but* (when it means "only"), *hardly*, *never*, *no*, *none*, *no one*, *nobody*, *not*, *nothing*, *nowhere*, *only*, *barely*, and *scarcely* are all negatives. Do not use two negatives to express one negative meaning.

NONSTANDARD	I do**n't hardly** know why I watch so much TV.
STANDARD	I do**n't** know why I watch so much TV.
STANDARD	I **hardly** know why I watch so much TV.

Editing Checklist

✓ Is your composition written in standard English?
✓ Have you avoided words and phrases used only in informal English?
✓ Have you avoided the use of the double negative?

Communicate Your Ideas

EDITING

Edit your revised draft by using the following as guides. Use the **Editing Workshop** and the **Editing Checklist** on page C44 to help you check for grammar, standard English usage, spelling, capitalization, punctuation, and proper usage of words. You may find it helpful to read through your composition several times, looking for different kinds of errors each time. When you are completely satisfied with your composition, save it in your writing folder.

Communicate Your Ideas

PUBLISHING

Produce a neat final draft of your composition using the correct manuscript form on page C52. Then, with your teacher's permission, share your writing with a classmate. Use this time to comment on each other's work. You can find ideas for publishing your work on page C51. Place a copy of your composition in your portfolio. **PORTFOLIO**

Time Out to Reflect

In what ways have your skills in writing an effective composition improved as a result of your work in this chapter? If you have written a composition earlier in the year, take it out and read it over again. How does it differ from the writing you just completed? What did you do better in your most recent work? Is there anything you did better before? What would you like to improve in your next composition? Record your answers in the Learning Log section of your **journal**.

Process of Writing an Effective Composition

Remember that the writing process is recursive—you can move back and forth among the stages of the process to achieve your purpose. For example, during editing you may wish to return to the revising stage to add details that have occurred to you while editing. The numbers in parentheses refer to pages where you can get help with your writing.

PREWRITING

- List possible subjects and choose one. *(pages C12–C19)*
- After you consider your purpose and audience, limit and focus your subject. *(pages C19–C23)*
- Make a list of supporting details. *(pages C25–C31)*
- Organize your details into a simple outline. *(page C235)*

DRAFTING

- Write a thesis statement. *(pages C226–C228)*
- Draft an introduction that includes your thesis statement and captures the reader's interest. *(pages C225–C231)*
- Using your outline as a guide, draft the paragraphs for the body of your composition. *(pages C233–C238)*
- Use transitions to connect your supporting paragraphs. *(page C238)*
- Add a concluding paragraph. *(pages C240–C241)*
- Add a title. *(page C38)*

REVISING

- Check your composition for unity, coherence, and clarity. *(pages C237–C238)*
- Check your paragraphs for adequate development. *(page C104)*
- Check your paragraphs for varied sentences and vivid, precise words. *(pages C71–C78 and C63–C69)*

EDITING

- Use the **Editing Checklist** on pages C44 and C242 and the proofreading symbols on page C46 to correct errors in grammar, usage, spelling, and mechanics.

PUBLISHING

- Publish your polished final draft. *(pages C50–C51)*

A Writer Writes

A Composition About Cultural Identity

Purpose: to inform others about an aspect of your own culture

Audience: your classmates and teacher

In the selection from *When Heaven and Earth Changed Places,* Le Ly Hayslip explains the significance of rice, both as a source of food and as a symbol of life in Vietnamese culture. Think about an aspect of your own culture that you want to share with peers through an illustrated composition. For your illustrated composition, you may use actual photographs, pictures from magazines or other sources, or your own drawings.

Prewriting

Use freewriting and clustering to decide on a subject that reflects your culture. Perhaps you will write about the foods, clothing, or customs of your culture. Write a thesis statement that conveys the main idea of your composition and makes your purpose clear. Then search for images or make your own drawings to represent ideas and details that support the main idea. Organize your ideas and supporting details into a simple outline. Include details conveyed through each image, and indicate where you will position the images in your composition. You may want to choose an image for each paragraph—one for the introduction, one for each supporting paragraph, and one for the conclusion. Try to capture your reader's interest in the introduction. To generate ideas, you may want to use a chart like the one on page C232.

Drafting

Write the introduction, body, and conclusion of your composition. The introduction should include your main idea in a clearly worded thesis statement. Remember, the thesis statement has the strongest impact when it is in the first or last sentence. Each paragraph of the body should support the main idea expressed in the thesis statement. As you write, keep in mind the images you will use. Your written words and images should clearly relate, with images showing details that are explained or described in the text. The conclusion should reinforce the main idea and wrap up the composition in a memorable way. Give your illustrated composition a title.

Revising

Read over your first draft and check it for unity, coherence, and clarity. Use the **Evaluation Checklist for Revising** on page C40 for guidance in revising your draft.

Editing

Check your revised draft for errors in grammar, usage, spelling, capitalization, and punctuation using the **Editing Checklist** on page C44.

Publishing

Make a neat final copy of your composition. Then arrange the images and text to create a logical flow from introduction to conclusion. You might actually cut and paste the text and images onto a large sheet of paper or posterboard. You also may want to add captions to clarify the ideas expressed in each photo or illustration. When you are satisfied with the look and organization of your illustrated composition, share it with classmates. You might read it aloud, explaining the images as you read, or display your composition in a place where they can read it on their own. You can find more ideas for publishing your work on page C51.

Representing in Different Ways

From Print . . .

. . . to Visuals

Based on the information given in Maude Mars's letter, create a line graph to show the declining percentages of high school students enrolled in art courses.

6000 Forbes Avenue
Pittsburgh, PA 15216
April 1, 2002

Sheldon Belvedere
Sculpt and Paint Studios
325 Fifth Avenue
Pittsburgh, PA 15220

Dear Mr. Belvedere,

Did you know that in the past five years, the number of students who take art courses in high school has rapidly declined? In 1998, 75 percent of students took art courses. In 1999, it had dropped to 30 percent; in 2000 25 percent. In 2001, an astonishingly low 17 percent of the students were taking art courses!

This May, I am compiling a book about art studies for teenagers. Because of your expertise in the field, I would like you to contribute a short essay explaining why it is important and beneficial for students to take art courses. Please let me know if you are interested in completing the essay for me.

Thank you!

Maude Mars

Maude Mars

From Visuals . . .

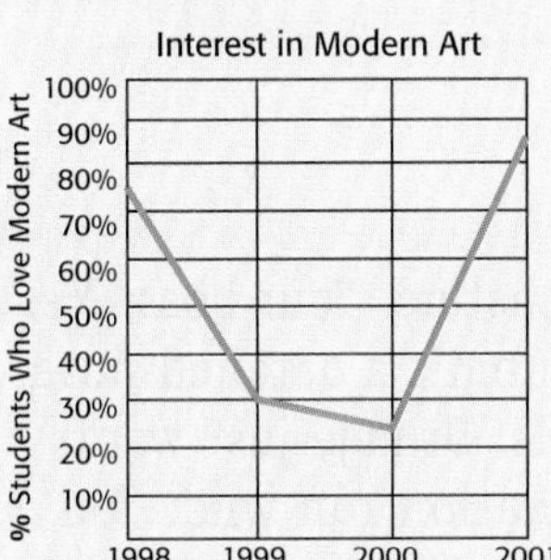

. . . to Print

Using the line graph above, write a letter to the director of the Modern Art Museum persuading him that enough students are interested in modern art to support an after-school art program.

- **Which strategies can be used for creating both written and visual representations? Which strategies apply to one, not both? Which type of representation is more effective?**
- **Draw a conclusion and write briefly about the differences between written ideas and visual representations.**

Writing in Everyday Life

E-Mail to an Internet Friend

You have a new Internet friend named Quig. Quig lives in a small rural area in Outer Mongolia and has never visited America. He would like to know more about what it is like to live in your city or town.

Write an E-mail message to Quig describing your city or town and what it is like to live there. Describe the sights, sounds, even smells and tastes of your town. Remember to write a topic sentence, supporting sentences, and a concluding sentence. Also remember to include specific words and precise images.

What strategies did you use to describe your city or town to your friend?

You can find information on writing E-mail in A Writer's Guide to Using the Internet, *pages C724–C767.*

Writing in the Workplace

Note to the Boss

You work at a company that designs roller coasters. Your boss, Ms. Drudge, has asked everyone on the staff to submit a detailed note for a brand-new kind of coaster. Right now Ms. Drudge just wants rough ideas, so you are free to let you imagination run wild. You can use tunnels and loops, laser lights, or any other features.

Write a note to Ms. Drudge explaining why the company should build your fantasy coaster. Be sure to include specific details and effective transitions. Check your paragraphs for unity, coherence, and clarity.

What strategies did you use to describe a ride on the roller coaster to Ms. Drudge?

Assess Your Learning

Cavity Masters, Inc., the world's most popular candy company, is holding a contest. The winner will receive a larger-than-life statue of himself or herself made entirely of chocolate. In order to win, you have to write an essay of 200 to 300 words, explaining the experience of eating chocolate to someone who has never seen, smelled, touched, or tasted it. Then you must mail the essay to the Cavity Masters, Inc. home office.

- **Write an essay explaining the experience of eating chocolate to someone who has never seen, smelled, touched, or tasted it.**
- **Use a lighthearted tone in your essay. Include a topic sentence, supporting sentences, and a concluding sentence in each paragraph. You really want to win the chocolate statue, so be sure you develop drafts before you craft the finished product. Use vivid and descriptive words to create a complete description of the smell, sight, and taste of chocolate.**

Before You Write **Consider the following questions:**
What is the ***subject?***
What is the ***occasion?***
Who is the ***audience?***
What is the ***purpose?***

After You Write **Evaluate your work using the following criteria:**

- Is the introduction to the essay clearly stated and interesting? Have you provided a clearly stated thesis statement?
- Are the meanings of the words, sentences, and paragraphs in your essay clear?
- Does every sentence in each paragraph of the body develop your main idea?
- Have you used vivid and descriptive words to create a complete and evocative description of the smell, sight, and taste?
- Have you used connective devices so that your thinking moves in a logical progression?
- Have you revised by adding, elaborating, deleting, combining, and rearranging text?

Write briefly on how well you did. Point out your strengths and areas for improvement.

CHAPTER 6

Personal Writing: Self-Expression and Reflection

Every day you experience many different events. Some of those events have little meaning or impact on your life. Others are significant—even life-changing. You may often share your thoughts and feelings about important happenings in your everyday life in conversation with friends and family. When you write about an event in your life and tell how it affected you, you are writing a personal narrative. The process of writing a personal narrative may require some reflection as you reconstruct what happened and determine the meaning it has for you. As you reflect, you may be surprised by what you discover about yourself.

Reading other people's personal narratives is a good way to gain insights about how to use words to relate an event, set a tone, and express and reflect on your own thoughts and feelings. No doubt you have read examples of personal narratives, such as autobiographies, letters, and diary entries. A powerfully written personal narrative can touch your heart, stir up angry feelings in you, or motivate you to take action in the world. It can also inspire you to write your own real-life story.

Reading with a Writer's Eye

Barrio Boy is the real-life account of a pivotal time in Ernesto Galarza's youth—when his family moved from the *barrio* into a new house they had purchased in a neighborhood of "Americans." As you read this personal narrative, think about how Galarza's own future opportunities and goals were greatly expanded by this significant change. On a second reading, notice the specific details Galarza includes to help you envision this time and place in his life.

FROM

BARRIO BOY

Ernesto Galarza

To make room for a growing family it was decided that we should move, and a house was found in Oak Park, on the far side of town where the open country began. The men raised the first installment for the bungalow on Seventh Avenue even after Mrs. Dodson explained that if we did not keep up the monthly payments we would lose the deposit as well as the house.

The real estate broker brought the sale contract to the apartment one evening. Myself included, we sat around the table in the living room, the gringo[1] explaining at great length the small print of the document in a torrent of words none of us could make out. Now and then he would pause and throw in the only word he knew in Spanish: "Sabe?"[2] The men nodded slightly as if they had understood. Doña[3] Henriqueta was holding firmly to the purse which contained the down payment, watching the broker's face, not listening to his words. She had only one question. Turning to me she said: "Ask him how long it will take to pay all of it." I translated, shocked by the answer: "Twenty years." There was a long pause around the table, broken by my stepfather: "What do you say?" Around the table the heads nodded agreement. The broker passed his fountain pen to him. He signed the contract and after him Gustavo and

---

[1] **gringo** (grēn′gō): An English-speaking foreigner, especially from North America.

[2] **Sabe?** (sä′bā): You know?

[3] **Doña** (dō′nyä): Respectful term of address, used before women's first names.

José. Doña Henriqueta opened the purse and counted out the greenbacks. The broker pocketed the money, gave us a copy of the document, and left.

The last thing I did when we moved out of 418L was to dig a hole in the corner of the backyard for a tall carton of Quaker Oats cereal, full to the brim with the marbles I had won playing for keeps around the *barrio*.[4] I tamped the earth over my buried treasure and laid a curse on whoever removed it without my permission.

Our new bungalow had five rooms, and porches front and back. In the way of furniture, what friends did not lend or Mrs. Dodson gave us we bought in the secondhand shops. The only new item was an elegant gas range, with a high oven and long, slender legs finished in enamel. Like the house, we would be paying for it in installments.

It was a sunny, airy spot, with a family orchard to one side and a vacant lot on the other. Back of us there was a pasture. With chicken wire we fenced the back yard, turned over the soil, and planted our first vegetable garden and fruit trees. José and I built a palatial[5] rabbit hutch of laths and two-by-fours he gathered day by day on the waterfront. A single row of geraniums and carnations separated the vegetable garden from the house. From the vacant lots and pastures around us my mother gathered herbs and weeds which she dried and boiled the way she had in the pueblo.[6] A thick green fluid she distilled from the mallow that grew wild around us was bottled and used as a hair lotion. On every side our windows looked out on family orchards, platinum stretches of wild oats and quiet lanes, shady and unpaved.

---

[4] **barrio** (bä′rē ō′): District of a large town or city.

[5] **palatial** (pə lā′shəl): Of or suitable for a palace.

[6] **pueblo** (pwĕb′lō): Village.

We could not have moved to a neighborhood less like the *barrio*. All the families around us were Americans. The grumpy retired farmer next door viewed us with alarm and never gave us the time of day, but the Harrisons across the street were cordial. Mr. Harrison loaned us his tools, and Roy, just my age but twice my weight, teamed up with me at once for an exchange of visits to his mother's kitchen and ours. I astounded him with my Mexican rice, and Mrs. Harrison baked my first waffle. Roy and I also found a common bond in the matter of sisters. He had an older one and by now I had two younger ones. It was a question between us whether they were worse as little nuisances or as big bosses. The answer didn't make much difference but it was a relief to have another man to talk with.

Some Sundays we walked to Joyland, an amusement park where my mother sat on a bench to watch the children play on the lawn and I begged as many rides as I could on the roller coaster, which we called in elegant Spanish "The Russian Mountain." José liked best the free vaudeville because of the chorus girls who danced out from the stage on a platform and kicked their heels over his head.

Since Roy had a bicycle and could get away from his sister by pedaling off on long journeys, I persuaded my family to match my savings for a used one. Together we pushed beyond the boundaries of Oak Park miles out, nearly to Perkins and the Slough House. It was open country, where we could lean our wheels against a fence post and walk endlessly through carpets of golden poppies and blue lupin. With a bike I was able to sign on as a carrier of the *Sacramento Bee*, learning in due course the art of slapping folded newspapers against people's porches instead of into the bushes or on their roofs. Roy and I also became assistants to a neighbor who operated a bakery in his basement, taking our pay partly in dimes and partly in broken cookies for our families.

For the three men of the household as well as for me the bicycle became the most important means for earning a living. Oak Park was miles away from the usual places where they worked and they pedaled off, in good weather and bad, in the early morning. It was a case of saving carfare.

I transferred to the Bret Harte School, a gingerbread two-story building in which there was a notable absence of Japanese, Filipinos, Koreans, Italians, and the other nationalities of the Lincoln School. It was at Bret Harte that I learned how an English sentence could be cut up on the blackboard and the pieces placed on different lines connected by what the teacher called a diagram. The idea of operating on a sentence and rearranging its members as a skeleton of verbs, modifiers, subject, and prepositions set me off diagramming whatever I read, in Spanish and English. Spiderwebs, my mother called them, when I tried to teach her the art.

My bilingual library had grown with some copies of old magazines from Mexico, a used speller Gustavo had bought for me in Stockton, and the novels my mother discarded when she had read them. Blackstone was still the anchor of my collection and I now had a paperback dictionary called *El inglés sin maestro*.[7] By this time there was no problem of translating or interpreting for the family I could not tackle with confidence.

It was Gustavo, in fact, who began to give my books a vague significance. He pointed out to me that with diagrams and dictionaries I could have a choice of becoming a lawyer or

---

[7] ***El inglés sin maestro*** (ĕl ēn glās′ sēn mä ās′trō): *English without a Teacher.*

a doctor or an engineer or a professor. These, he said, were far better careers than growing up to be a *camello*,[8] as he and José always would be. *Camellos*, I knew well enough, was what the *chicanos*[9] called themselves as the worker on every job who did the dirtiest work. And to give our home the professional touch he felt I should be acquiring, he had a telephone installed.

It came to the rest of us as a surprise. The company man arrived one day with our name and address on a card, a metal tool box and a stand-up telephone wound with a cord. It was connected and set on the counter between the dining room and the parlor. There the black marvel sat until we were gathered for dinner that evening. It was clearly explained by Gustavo that the instrument was to provide me a quick means of reaching the important people I knew at the Y.M.C.A., the boy's band, or the various public offices where I interpreted for *chicanos* in distress. Sooner or later some of our friends in the *barrio* would also have telephones and we could talk with them.

"Call somebody," my mother urged me.

With the whole family watching I tried to think of some important person I could ring for a professional conversation. A name wouldn't come. I felt miserable and hardly like a budding engineer or lawyer or doctor or professor.

Gustavo understood my predicament and let me stew in it a moment. Then he said: "Mrs. Dodson." My pride saved by this ingenious suggestion, I thumbed through the directory, lifted the earpiece from the hook, and calmly asked central for the number. My sisters, one sitting on the floor and the other in my mother's arms, never looked less significant, but they, too, had their turn saying hello to the patient Señora[10] Dodson on the other end of the line.

---

[8] **camello** (kä mā′yō): Camel.

[9] **chicanos** (chĭ kä′nōs): Mexican Americans.

[10] **Señora** (sān yôr′ə): Mrs.

Thinking as a Writer

Evaluating the Effectiveness of Storytelling

Imagine you are in a writers' group with Ernesto Galarza. He wants feedback on how effective his writing is.

- Did Galarza accomplish his purpose? What details in the story support your evaluation? Is there anything you as a writer might have done differently? If so, what?

Picturing a Setting

Viewing

Using details is an important part of writing a personal narrative. In *Barrio Boy,* Galarza describes his family's new home in Oak Park. His description includes the layout of the house and the yard where the family planted their first vegetable garden and fruit trees.

- Visualize as many of these details as possible and use them to draw a picture of Galarza's garden. Your aim should be to draw a clear, vivid picture.
- After you have finished, share your drawing with your classmates and critique one another's representations. How do the details that other students chose to represent compare to those that you focused on in your drawing?

Improvising a Personal Introduction

Oral Expression

Galarza describes his experiences in transferring to a new school. Imagine he is a new student in your school. It is his first day, and he has just introduced himself by sharing details from his personal narrative.

- Improvise an introduction in which you tell something about yourself, and acknowledge and respond to details he has shared about his family, new home, and interests. In a small group, listen to one another's introductions. Critique each one using the following questions: What words would help Galarza feel welcome? What details about yourself have you provided that could keep the conversation going? How could you be friendlier and more informative?

The Power of Personal Writing

You have read one example of a personal narrative. In it the author shares his experiences and emotions with the reader. His aim is to invite you into his life for a brief time and help you understand a significant period in it. Although every person's life is unique, many human experiences and emotions are universal. A personal narrative has the power to touch readers deeply when they can identify with the experience or emotion the author describes.

Uses of Personal Writing

We encounter many examples of personal narratives, and we use personal narratives in different ways. Here are just a few examples.

- **A sports star writes an autobiography,** telling about the opportunities her career in soccer has afforded to her.
- **Musicians reflect on the music they listened to while growing up** and the singers who influenced their own work for a magazine article.
- **An archaeology student working in Nepal writes letters to friends,** including stories about the foods she has tasted, the people she has met, the temples she has visited, and the customs she has experienced.
- **Teenagers share stories about some of their worst experiences with drugs** and reveal the lessons they have learned from recovery on a popular talk show.

Process of Writing a Personal Narrative

"Great thoughts come from the heart," wrote Luc de Clapiers, an eighteenth-century French writer. He might have been referring to the art of writing a personal narrative. When you write about experiences in your own life, your thoughts should come from the heart; that is, you should write about an experience that is meaningful to you. If you write about an event that seems unimportant to you, it will seem unimportant to your readers as well, while an account of a significant event will capture your reader's interest.

A **personal narrative** expresses the writer's personal point of view on a subject drawn from the writer's own experience.

Your Writer's Journal

In your journal, jot down experiences in your life that have special meaning for you. Start by brainstorming particularly vivid memories. Also record more recent experiences at school and at home that stand out as important or unique. Reflect on each experience you identify, and write a sentence explaining its significance. In this way, you will compile a list of subjects you can use later in your writing.

Prewriting

Writing Process

During prewriting, your mind should be free to roam through your memories and reflect on experiences you have had. As you think freely, you will discover ideas that you might develop into subjects of personal narratives. For example, you may recall an important conversation, a surprise, a disappointment, an observation that affected you deeply, or a decision that had fateful consequences. In the following excerpt from her autobiography, Jamaica Kincaid recalls how she learned her personal history as a child.

MODEL: Subject of a Personal Narrative

> From time to time, my mother would fix on a certain place in our house and give it a good cleaning. If I was at home when she happened to do this, I was at her side, as usual. When she did this with the trunk, it was a tremendous pleasure, for after she had removed all the things from the trunk, and aired them out, and changed the camphor balls, and then refolded the things and put them back in their places in the trunk, as she held each thing in her hand she would tell me a story about myself. Sometimes I knew the story first hand, for I could remember the incident quite well; sometimes what she told me had happened when I was too young to know anything; and sometimes it happened before I was even born. Whichever way, I knew exactly what she would say, for I had heard it so many times before, but I never got tired of it.
>
> –*Jamaica Kincaid,* Annie John

Drawing on Personal Experience

When you write from personal experience, narrative subjects may sometimes seem inexhaustible. At other times, however, you may need to stir your memories and emotions. To think of subjects for a personal narrative, look through your **journal** entries and use freewriting, inquiring, or brainstorming to stimulate your thinking. You may also find the following sources helpful in jogging your memory.

IDEA SOURCES FOR SUBJECTS OF PERSONAL NARRATIVES	
letters	family stories
photographs	favorite things
souvenirs or mementos	albums or scrapbooks

Communicate Your Ideas

PREWRITING *Subject Related to Personal Experience*

Use your **journal** and the suggestions on page C259 to create a list of ten possible subjects. Then narrow the choice to five and think back on the details surrounding each experience. Choose the one subject you recall most clearly and that is most meaningful to you. Save your subject idea for your personal narrative.

SAVE YOUR WORK

Exploring the Meaning of an Experience

American novelist John Irving wrote, "Every writer uses what experience he or she has. It's the translating, though, that makes the difference." In this context *translating* means "finding meaning in an experience." That insight could be the main idea of a personal narrative. The expression of your main idea then serves the same function as the thesis statement in other kinds of writing.

Model: Expressing the Meaning of an Experience

As she told me the stories, I sometimes sat at her side, leaning against her, or I would crouch on my knees behind her back and lean over her shoulder. As I did this, I would occasionally sniff at her neck, or behind her ears, or at her hair. She smelled sometimes of onions, sometimes of sage, sometimes of roses, sometimes of bay leaf. At times I would no longer hear what it was she was saying; I just liked to look at her mouth as it opened and closed over words, or as she laughed. How terrible it must be for all the people who had no one to love them so and no one whom they loved so, I thought.

—*Jamaica Kincaid,* Annie John

As Kincaid makes clear, her experience taught her the importance of loving and being loved. This insight is the main idea of her narrative.

Interpreting Experience

Think about an event in your life that seems important to you now. Why is it important? What is the meaning of this event for you? Such questions may be hard to answer because when you are experiencing events, it is often difficult to stand back from them to see their significance. Only after some time has passed can you gauge their meaning. When you reexamine an experience to interpret its meaning, you might begin by completing a checklist like the one below.

CHECKLIST FOR INTERPRETING EXPERIENCE

Experience: I unexpectedly received an award in sixth grade for showing the greatest improvement.

This experience is important to me now because it
- ☐ helped me see something in a new way.
- ☐ changed the way I felt about someone.
- ☑ changed the way I felt about myself.

I will always remember this experience because it
- ☐ strongly affected my emotions.
- ☐ gave me new knowledge or understanding.
- ☑ had important consequences.

This experience is worth writing about because
- ☑ it will be familiar to many readers.
- ☐ it is unique or extraordinary.
- ☐ writing will help me to understand it better.

Interpretation: This event boosted my self-confidence. It was the first time I realized I might amount to something. I became a better student because of it.

THINKING PRACTICE

Think of any memorable experience and interpret it by developing a checklist like the preceding one.

Communicate Your Ideas

PREWRITING *Meaning of Experience*

Review the subject of your personal narrative. Think deeply about it. Make a checklist like the one on page C261 to help you interpret this experience. In a sentence or two, write what this experience means to you—what makes it important. Save your work for later use.

Considering Purpose and Audience

When you have decided on a subject and its meaning for your personal narrative, you need to think about your writing purpose and your audience. Personal narratives are usually written to express thoughts and feelings in a way that will interest readers and win their appreciation. To accomplish this purpose, however, you may include different kinds of paragraphs to combine the overall purpose with specific aims.

You can learn more about other kinds of paragraphs on pages C173–C212.

PURPOSE IN PERSONAL WRITING

OVERALL PURPOSE: to express thoughts and feelings about participating in an outdoor survival program

Specific Aims	Kinds of Paragraphs
to explain why I felt ashamed	informative
to tell a funny story	narrative
to help readers see the mountain I climbed	descriptive

Considering Your Audience It is just as important to consider your audience as it is to decide on your purpose and goals. You should take into account the interests and knowledge of your readers so you can make sure they will understand your purpose and meaning. Whether you write for friends, classmates, or wider audiences, your audience will partly determine the kinds of details you select to include in your narrative.

Determine your **purpose** and **audience** when writing a personal narrative to help ensure that you capture and hold your readers' interest.

Communicate Your Ideas

PREWRITING *Purpose and Audience*

Reread the interpretation of your subject for your personal narrative. You may want to continue refining your interpretation. Then make notes on your purpose in writing this personal narrative and the type of paragraphs you might use. Also identify who your audience will be. Save your work for later use.

Developing and Selecting Details

When you write a personal narrative, you want your readers to understand the event, experience it with you, and share your feelings about it. For this sharing to occur, you must give your readers ample details—*showing* the event rather than just *telling*—to bring your experience to life. **Descriptive details** help readers visualize the experience you describe. **Sensory details** engage all the senses of your readers and vividly convey your ideas, making your audience see, hear, smell, and feel the impression that you are trying to create. **Background details** provide a context so your readers can understand what is happening.

The following guidelines will help you choose the details to include in your personal narrative.

Guidelines for Selecting Details

- Choose details that develop your main idea.
- Choose details that are appropriate for your purpose.
- Choose details that are appropriate for your audience.
- Use factual details to provide background information.
- Use vivid descriptive and sensory details to bring your experience to life.

Practice Your Skills

Identifying Different Types of Details

Reread parts of *Barrio Boy* on pages C251–C255 and find details the author uses to make his experience real to you. List five examples under each category of details identified in the above guidelines.

Communicate Your Ideas

PREWRITING *Different Types of Details*

Brainstorm for details on the subject of your personal narrative. Use the guidelines above to help you select different types of details. List background details that will give readers a clear understanding of the time and place of your experience and descriptive and sensory details that will help them live the experience with you as they read. Save your work.

Organizing Details

After you select your details, group them into categories and decide on an appropriate order. Each category becomes the basis of a supporting paragraph. The following examples show common ways of organizing details in personal narratives.

You can find more information on types of order on pages C34–C35 and C107.

ORGANIZING DETAILS	
Kind of Details	**Type of Order**
events in a story, narrated beginning to end	chronological order
descriptive details to help readers visualize a person, object, or scene	spatial order
background details and details explaining the meaning of an experience	order of importance or interest
sensory details and details leading up to an impression or interpretation of an experience	developmental order

Practice Your Skills

 *Identifying Types of Order*

Study paragraphs 4, 5, and 9 in *Barrio Boy* on pages C251–C255. Identify the type of order used in each paragraph by writing *spatial*, *order of importance*, or *developmental*.

Communicate Your Ideas

PREWRITING *Order of Details*

Review the list of details you made for your personal narrative. Organize those details by grouping them into categories. Then decide how to arrange the groupings, drawing on what you have learned about types of order. Determine which organization best suits your narrative—chronological, spatial, or developmental order, or order of importance. Save your work for later use.

Writing the first draft of your personal narrative is a matter of transforming the information in your groupings of details into sentences and paragraphs. As you write, keep in mind that personal writing is less formal than other kinds of writing. Unlike informative writing, for example, a personal narrative is written from the first person point of view and does not have a formal thesis statement. Like all compositions, however, a personal narrative should have a clear main idea, an attention-getting introduction, a well-organized body, and a strong conclusion.

Drafting the Introduction

In a personal narrative, the introduction lets readers know what they are about to hear, who you are, and how you feel about your subject. The introduction should also interest readers enough so that they want to continue reading about your experience.

The introduction of a personal narrative

- makes clear the subject, purpose, and main idea of the personal narrative.
- sets the tone to reveal the writer's point of view.
- captures the readers' interest.

You can find more information on writing introductions on page C225.

Creating a Tone The **tone** of a personal narrative reveals the writer's attitudes toward the subject and the audience. The words and expressions you use give readers clues to your intentions. In setting the tone of a personal narrative, therefore, you need to decide how you want readers to feel. Do you want them to laugh, cry, to feel nostalgic or reflective? You also have to decide if you want them to feel sympathetic toward you and the insight you gained through your experience.

The following models show how a writer experimented with four different tones in introducing the same subject. Keep in mind, however, that once you choose a tone, you should maintain it throughout your entire personal narrative.

Models: Tone

My Guitar and I

Sympathetic

Life in a big family can be hectic. Someone is always playing with the dog, usually riling him up to a fever pitch of barking and jumping. Someone else is always watching television, and in the same room two people might be listening to two different radio stations. When I need an escape, I go up to the roof of our apartment building and play my guitar. I lose the rest of the world when I play the guitar, but I find myself.

Humorous

It was four o'clock on a humid afternoon and the household was in an uproar. J.C. was riling up the dog, which had reached a fever pitch of hysterical barking. My sisters in the next room were each listening to a different rock station on their radios, and Gramps had raised the volume on the television set to compensate for all the noise. Amidst the nerve-racking roar of sports fans, the brain-numbing basses of the two rock numbers, and the dog's pandemonium, I grabbed my guitar and headed for the roof. Peace at last, peace at last, peace at last!

Angry

Life in a big family does not have to be hectic if only everyone would be considerate of one another's basic needs. This is not the case at my house, where the rule seems to be everyone for oneself. People don't think twice about making the dog bark, turning up the television, or playing their music too loud—often all at the same time.

I can take it only for so long before I have to escape to the roof with my guitar. If it weren't for my guitar, there would be far more arguments at my house about peace and quiet.

REFLECTIVE

I remember the time I first left my hectic family behind and escaped to the roof to play my guitar. It had been a humid afternoon, and everyone seemed to be in a contrary mood—even the dog. The result was more noise than I could stand. The dog was barking, my sisters were listening to two different radio stations, and my grandfather had turned up the volume on the television set to hear the ball game. I can still sense the sudden relief I felt as my guitar and I let our first gentle chords float down from the quiet rooftop.

PRACTICE YOUR SKILLS

Analyzing Tone

Reread each of the four models of tone in personal narrative writing. Decide which tone you would choose for this subject if you were the writer. Write an explanation stating the reasons for your choice of tone.

Determining Tone

A cluster diagram can be helpful in generating words, phrases, or entire sentences that set a desired tone. In *Barrio Boy,* the writer's tone is one of optimism toward his family and his own growing confidence and accomplishments. Copy and complete the cluster diagram on the next page with words, phrases, and sentences from *Barrio Boy* that best communicate this optimistic tone.

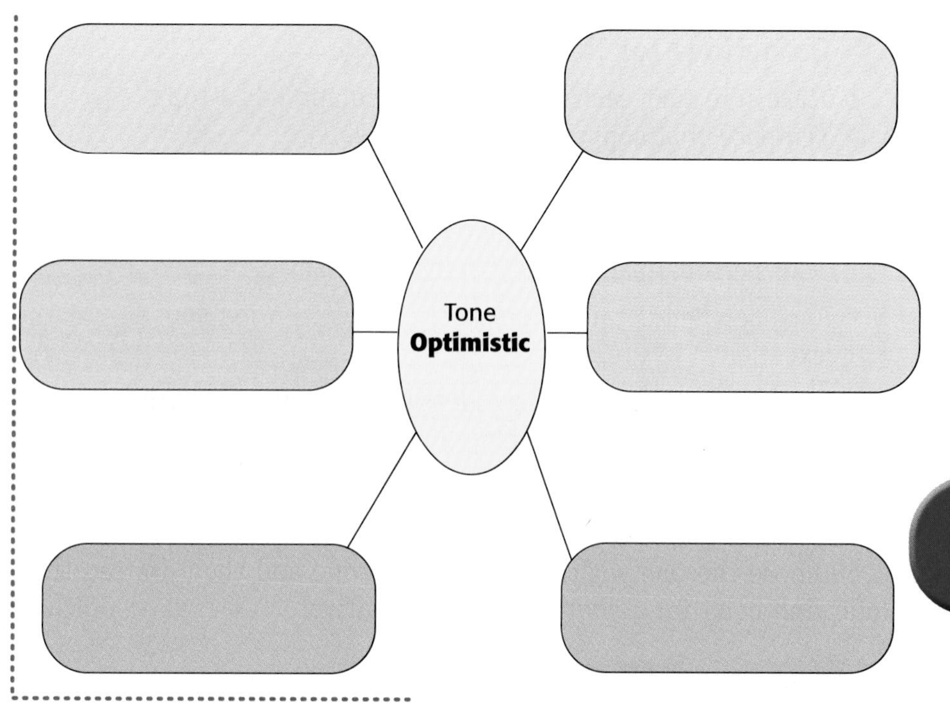

Communicate Your Ideas

DRAFTING *Introduction and Tone*

Draft an introduction for your personal narrative, following the guidelines on page C266. You may want to experiment with different tones by trying different words and expressions to describe the same person, place, or event in your introduction. If you like, create several **cluster diagrams** to help you. Save your work.

Drafting the Body

After you have introduced the subject and set a tone appropriate for your purpose, you are ready to draft the body of your personal narrative. Use the groupings that you arranged to convert the details of your experience into paragraphs. As you write, make your interpretation of your experience clear and use vivid, well-organized details to hold your readers' attention.

Guidelines for Drafting the Body

- Make sure that each supporting paragraph has a topic sentence that supports the main idea.
- Write your ideas and details in logical order.
- Use transitions between sentences and paragraphs to give your personal narrative coherence.
- Include vivid details and sensory words to bring your experience to life.
- As you write, add any new ideas and details you discover, if they will help you develop your main idea.

The writer who wrote the introductions on pages C267 and C268 chose the one with a sympathetic tone and then drafted the following body for a short personal narrative.

Model: Body of a Personal Narrative

My escape to the rooftop always works for me because I am listening only to my sounds for a change. As I sing along with my guitar, I can hear my own voice—however weak it may be. If I finger the wrong strings or frets, then at least they are my mistakes. Whatever mistakes I make, my music always sounds good to me, because when I concentrate on playing the right notes and chords, the rest of the world seems far away.

The greatest value of escaping with my guitar, however, is the chance it gives me to express my feelings. The tunes I play depend on my mood. Sometimes I play simple, quiet ballads or sad, bluesy refrains. Other times I strum loud sets, joyous or angry, until my fingertips sting. After each session on the roof with my guitar, I feel as if I have had a good long talk with an understanding friend.

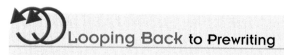

Communicate Your Ideas

DRAFTING *Body*

Choose the introduction you like best for your personal narrative. Then, keeping the same tone, draft the body of your narrative, following the guidelines on the previous page. Be sure to include the most effective details from your prewriting notes. Save your work for later use.

Looping Back to Prewriting

Details

As you draft the body of your personal narrative, it may be helpful to talk to others who are familiar with your subject or, even better, have experienced it with you. Use their recollections to help you identify additional background, descriptive, and sensory details to include in your draft.

Drafting the Conclusion

The conclusion of your personal narrative should emphasize the meaning of your experience. You might give your readers a sense of completion and make your last sentence as memorable as your first. You might also end your personal narrative in any of the following ways or a combination of them.

Ways to End a Personal Narrative

- Summarize the body.
- Restate the main idea in new words.
- Add an insight that shows a new or deeper understanding of the experience.
- Add a striking new detail or memorable image.
- Refer back to ideas in the introduction to bring your personal narrative full circle.
- Appeal to the readers' emotions.

The following conclusion ends the personal narrative that was entitled "My Guitar and I." This conclusion refers back to the introduction on page C267 and restates the main idea.

MODEL: Conclusion of a Personal Narrative

By the time I come down from the roof, the television does not seem so loud anymore, and the dog seems like his old self again. I even smile when I hear my sisters' noisy radios. Although I have come back to reality, I am glad to know that my guitar is there for me the next time I need to escape.

PRACTICE YOUR SKILLS

Analyzing a Conclusion

Reread the concluding paragraphs of *Barrio Boy* on page C255. Using the suggestions on page C271, identify the techniques Galarza uses to end his personal narrative. Then write responses to these questions, using examples from the narrative: What makes this an effective conclusion? How does the author reinforce the significance of leaving the barrio for himself and his family?

Communicate Your Ideas

DRAFTING *Conclusion*

Reread the introduction and body of your personal narrative. Using the ideas in Ways to End a Personal Narrative on the preceding page, draft at least two different approaches to a conclusion. Also think of three or four possible titles for your personal narrative. Then choose the conclusion and title that work best with the rest of your narrative. You may want to set aside your writing for a day or two to be able to make that choice with a fresher eye. Save your work for later use.

Newsmagazines

A 19-year-old wins a multimillion dollar lottery. Despite his winnings, however, his life begins to fall apart. He no longer seeks a career. His friends treat him differently. This story is reported on a television newsmagazine, featuring interviews with the winner, his friends, and his family. There is a dramatic reenactment of an emotional scene with his destitute grandmother.

On another newsmagazine, a story is presented about a report showing that a high percentage of lottery-ticket buyers are from the low-income group and that some in this group spend as much money on tickets as they do on groceries. Critics of the report say that in many states the money raised by lotteries goes back into low-income areas, often to help support schools. The story contains interviews with lottery-ticket purchasers, authors of the study, lottery officials, and elected representatives.

Where is the line between news and entertainment? When is a personal story the appropriate subject of a respectable newsmagazine? How each story is handled will really answer those questions. It may also help to consider the following: A personal story is news if it is one example of many others like it, and it touches on a matter that can be acted upon in the public arena (changing the law, for example).

Media Activity

Few stories are completely news or completely entertainment. To learn to see the distinctions, watch a story as it is covered on a television newsmagazine this week. Are the camera angles noteworthy? Is there any music? How does the way the shots are edited convey meaning? Then rate the story on a scale of 1 to 10, 1 being pure entertainment and 10 being a pure news story. Write a paragraph explaining your rating.

Once you have turned the raw materials of your personal perceptions and reflections into a rough draft, you can turn to the important task of revision. Revising a personal narrative involves attention to three important points.

- Have you developed your personal narrative in sufficient detail?
- Have you made your ideas and feelings clear?
- Have you maintained a consistent tone?

Checking for Adequate Development

Part of the success in writing a personal narrative comes in making the reader clearly see and hear what you want to share. Therefore, you should check to make sure you have included enough specific supporting details to give substance to your ideas. The following strategies will help.

STRATEGIES FOR REVISING FOR ADEQUATE DEVELOPMENT	
Events	Close your eyes and slowly visualize the experience you are writing about. Write down the details as you "see" them in your mind's eye.
People	Visualize each person you are writing about. Start by visualizing the head and face of each person and slowly move down to the feet. Write down details as you "see" them.
Place	Visualize the place you are describing. Start at the left of the setting and visualize slowly to the right. Also visualize from the foreground to the background.
Feelings	Imagine yourself repeating the experience you are writing about. Focus on your thoughts and feelings as you relive the experience.

Appositive Phrases

Details that identify a person, place, or thing that may be unknown to your reader are important to the success of your narrative. As you revise, you can add informative details in the form of appositive phrases.

An **appositive phrase** is a group of words with no subject or verb that adds information about another word in the sentence, usually a person, place, or thing. In the following sentence from *Barrio Boy*, for example, readers would not know who the Harrisons are without the appositive phrase. Notice that the appositive phrase is set off by commas.

Appositive Phrase	The Harrisons, **the people across the street,** were cordial to us.

Combining Sentences with Appositive Phrases

Often you can make your writing more concise by using an appositive phrase to combine two sentences.

Two Sentences	I transferred to Bret Harte School. It was a gingerbread two-story building.
Combined Sentence	I transferred to Bret Harte School, **a gingerbread two-story building.**

Two Sentences	The telephone was a communications tool. It would connect me with important people.
Combined Sentence	The telephone, **a communications tool,** would connect me with important people.

Communicate Your Ideas

REVISING *Adequate Development*

Return to the first draft of your personal narrative and revise it. Check for adequate development, using the strategies on page C274 for guidance. Use the **Revising Workshop** on page C275 to help you add appositive phrases that will provide clarifying details for readers or link sentences. Save your work for later use. 

Checking for Unity, Coherence, and Clarity

After you have developed your ideas adequately, check for unity, coherence, and clarity. Look for places where you can add transitions to help your writing flow smoothly. The following checklist will help you identify other areas for improvement.

Evaluation Checklist for Revising

✓ Does your introduction capture the readers' interest? If not, can you make a stronger beginning? *(page C225)*

✓ Are there any parts of your personal narrative where your readers' attention might wander? How can you add interest to them? *(pages C262–C264)*

✓ Does your feeling about your subject come through? If not, how can you convey your feeling more clearly? *(page C266)*

✓ Does your ending give readers a sense of completion? If not, how might you make it more effective? *(page C271)*

Communicate Your Ideas

REVISING *Unity, Coherence, and Clarity*

Continue revising your personal narrative. Be sure to check for unity, coherence, and clarity. Save your work for later use. 

COMPUTER TIP

If you are using a word-processing program to write your personal narrative, you can use the *I* button on the formatting toolbar to italicize words, thereby attaching visual emphasis and emotion to those words. As you revise, highlight a word or phrase you want to emphasize, and then change the style to italics accordingly.

Editing

Writing Process

As you revised your personal narrative, you looked for ways to help your reader clearly see and hear what you wanted to share. You also checked for adequate development, clarity, and consistency of tone. Now you are ready to edit, or polish, your writing.

Communicate Your Ideas

EDITING

You may want to share your personal narrative with classmates, friends, or family members. Then edit your essay, considering listeners' comments. Read your writing several times, checking for a different language convention each time. As you carefully reread your personal narrative, refer to your Personalized Editing Checklist in your **journal**. Save your work for later use.

Time Out to Reflect

How have your editing skills progressed? Compare the edited version of your personal narrative with the edited version of a piece of writing you did earlier in the year. Can you see ways to strengthen your writing that you did not see at the time? Make notes in your Learning Log of your areas of improvement and strategies that will help you continue to develop your editing capabilities.

Publishing

Writing Process

You may decide to complete the writing process by sharing your writing with someone who was part of your experience or may have an interest in it.

Communicate Your Ideas

PUBLISHING

Identify one or more individuals with whom you would like to share your experience. Think back to the prewriting stage and the audience you had in mind. You may wish to tape-record your personal narrative and present it as a surprise to a friend or relative who was part of your experience. You can find more ideas for publishing your work on page C51.

PORTFOLIO

Process of Writing a Personal Narrative

Remember that the writing process is recursive—you can move back and forth among the stages to achieve your purpose and address your audience. For example, during editing you may wish to return to the revising stage to add details that have occurred to you while editing.

PREWRITING

- Search your memory for personal experiences and insights to share with readers. *(page C259)*
- Choose one subject that interests you most and interpret its meaning. *(pages C260–C261)*
- Decide on your specific purpose in writing, your main idea, and your audience. *(page C262)*
- List background details of time and place and vivid descriptive and sensory details. *(pages C263–C264)*
- Group your details and organize them in logical order. *(pages C264–C265)*

DRAFTING

- Introduce your subject in a way that captures the reader's interest and sets the tone of the personal narrative. *(pages C266–C269)*
- Build the body of your personal narrative, using the most effective details for accomplishing your purpose. *(pages C269–C271)*
- Add a conclusion that clearly expresses the idea or feeling you want to convey. *(pages C271–C272)*
- Choose a title that is consistent with the tone of your personal narrative. *(page C38)*

REVISING

- Revise your personal narrative for adequate development. *(page C274)*
- Revise your personal narrative for unity, coherence, and clarity. *(pages C105–C107 and C276)*

EDITING

- Use your Personalized Editing Checklist in your **journal** to polish your grammar, usage, spelling, and mechanics. *(page C45)*

PUBLISHING

- Make a neat final copy of your personal narrative and share it with an interested audience. *(pages C50–C52)*

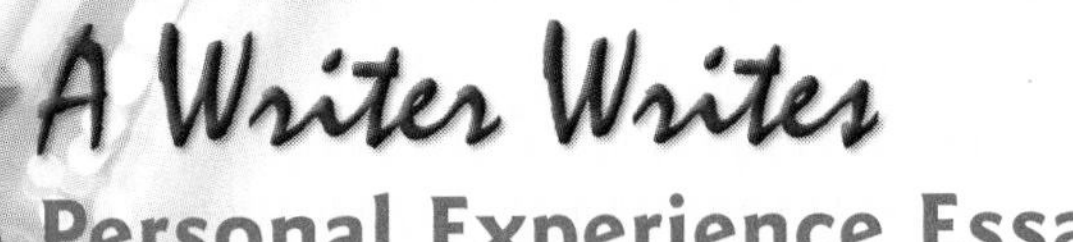

A Personal Experience Essay

Purpose: to express thoughts and feelings about a family relationship or friendship

Audience: your classmates and teacher

Prewriting

Sometimes an extended family member or friend offers special understanding. Decide on a particularly meaningful relationship in your past. Use freewriting, inquiring, or clustering to recall details of the relationship, the person with whom you shared it, and the context in which it became meaningful.

Drafting

Write an introduction that states or suggests your main idea, a body of supporting details, and a conclusion.

Revising

Have you included enough details to develop your main idea sufficiently? Is your tone consistent from beginning to end? Will you hold your readers' attention to the end? Make any necessary revisions and add transitions that will help your narrative flow smoothly.

Editing

Use the Editing Checklist on page C44 to polish your work.

Publishing

Photocopy or print out copies of your corrected narrative so that all your classmates can read it.

Connection Collection

Representing in Different Ways

From Print . . .

. . . to Visuals

Create a bar graph from the memo on the right to represent the number of people in attendance at the Rockville Circus from 1995 through 1999.

To: Sam Ringmaster
From: Mayor Wallace

Dear Mr. Ringmaster:

I am dismayed at the decline in attendance at your circus. Here are the numbers from my recent report. In 1995, there were 5,200 total attendees. In 1996, there were 4,300. In 1997, 4,000. In 1998, 3,100. And in 1999, 2,500. If this trend continues, the city can no longer give you money.

From Visuals . . .

Percentage of Public Who Enjoyed the Circus

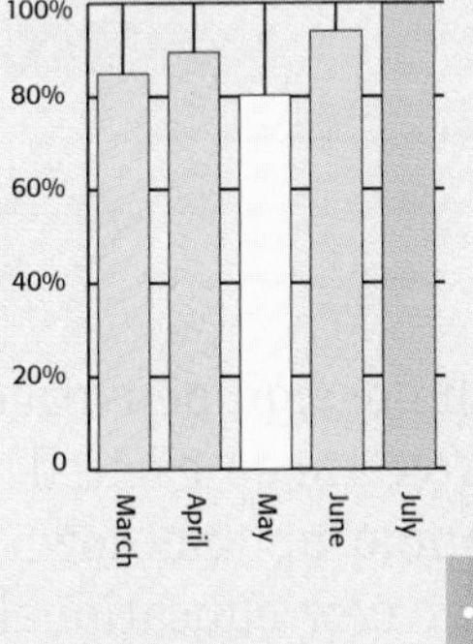

. . . to Print

Write a letter to Max Francis, president of the Rockville Bank, requesting a loan to help the circus advertise. In your letter to him, use the information about public opinion in the bar graph. Include personal experiences and details about the circus to interest Mr. Francis and convince him to give you the loan.

- **Which strategies can be used for creating both written and visual representations? Which strategies apply to one, not both? Which type of representation is more effective?**
- **Draw a conclusion and write briefly about the differences between written ideas and visual representations.**

Writing in Everyday Life

Narrative Friendly Letter

Your cousin lives on a llama farm in a town with one stoplight. You are a city-dweller who rarely sets foot on grass. Your mother has invited your cousin to spend the summer with your family. In every picture you've ever seen of her, your cousin has been wearing rubber boots and a straw hat. You are worried that she might not fit into life in the big city.

Write a friendly letter to your cousin preparing her for city life. Describe your daily routine and facts about city life of which she might be unaware. Use as much detail as possible to give your cousin an idea of what to expect.

What strategies did you use to help your cousin imagine where she'll be living?

You can find information on writing friendly letters on pages C577–C578 and C586.

Writing in the Workplace

Journal Entry

You have recently been promoted to head of the design department at the video game company where you work. You are so excited that you can barely restrain yourself from jumping up and down on your desk and shouting out all of your ideas for new educational video games.

Write a journal entry that describes your feelings about receiving your big promotion. Also describe your plans for the new award-winning educational video games you want to design. Use vivid details, and be sure to arrange them in a logical and coherent order.

What strategies did you use to describe your feelings about your promotion?

You can find information on writing journal entries on pages C14–C15.

Assess Your Learning

Have you ever been so excited that you screamed and jumped for joy? Most people have experienced such excitement, but not all people handle it the same way.

- **Write a short essay addressed to your classmates describing a time when you were excited at a gathering of family, classmates, or friends, at a sporting competition, or at a public event. What happened? What did you see, hear, or feel? What did you do?**
- **In trying to explain the situation, be sure that your details convey the tone you want. Use chronological order, spatial order, or order of importance to organize your details.**

Before You Write **Consider the following questions:**
What is the ***situation?***
What is the ***occasion?***
Who is the ***audience?***
What is the ***purpose?***

After You Write **Evaluate your work using the following criteria:**

- Does the introduction capture the reader's interest?
- Is the interest held until the end? How can you add to the reader's interest?
- Have your feelings about the incident come through clearly? How can you clarify it further?
- Does the conclusion give a striking detail or memorable image? If not, how can it be made more effective?
- Have you organized your ideas to ensure coherence, logical progression, and support for your ideas?
- Have you written in a style and voice appropriate to audience and purpose?
- Have you written in complete sentences, varying the types, and have you appropriately punctuated clauses?

Write briefly on how well you did. Point out your strengths and areas for improvement.

CHAPTER 7

Using Description: Observation

"All of us are watchers—of television, of time clocks, of traffic on the freeway—but few are observers," wrote Peter Leschak. "Everyone is looking, but not many are seeing."

What is the difference between looking and seeing? One way to understand the difference is to separate the simple visual act of looking from the more complex mental act of making sense out of what you see. Observing with your eyes—in fact, with all of your senses—means little unless your mind is switched on and busy interpreting what you observe.

Writing descriptions sharpens your ability to observe. When you write descriptively, you draw from your memory of observations to paint a picture that is both vivid and multifaceted.

Reading with a Writer's Eye

Few people observe as well as writer Annie Dillard. As you read the following selection about an encounter with a weasel, think about times you have brushed up against an animal or some other nonhuman part of nature. Also try to see how Dillard observes with both her eyes and her mind.

FROM *Teaching a Stone to Talk*

Living Like Weasels

Annie Dillard

A weasel is wild. Who knows what he thinks? He sleeps in his underground den, his tail draped over his nose. Sometimes he lives in his den for two days without leaving. Outside, he stalks rabbits, mice, muskrats, and birds, killing more bodies than he can eat warm, and often dragging the carcasses home. Obedient to instinct, he bites his prey at the neck, either splitting the jugular vein at the throat or crunching the brain at the base of the skull, and he does not let go. One naturalist refused to kill a weasel who was socketed into his hand deeply as a rattlesnake. The man could in no way pry the tiny weasel off, and he had to walk half a mile to water, the weasel dangling from his palm, and soak him off like a stubborn label.

And once, says Ernest Thompson Seton—once, a man shot an eagle out of the sky. He examined the eagle and found the dry skull of a weasel fixed by the jaws to his throat. The supposition is that the eagle had pounced on the weasel and the weasel swiveled and bit as instinct taught him, tooth to neck, and nearly won. I would like to have seen that eagle from the air a few weeks or months before he was shot: was the whole weasel still attached to his feathered throat, a fur pendant? Or did the eagle eat what he could reach, gutting the living weasel with his talons before his breast, bending his beak, cleaning the beautiful airborne bones?

I have been reading about weasels because I saw one last week. I startled a weasel who startled me, and we exchanged a long glance.

Near my house in Virginia is a pond—Hollins Pond. It covers two acres of bottomland near Tinker Creek with six inches of water and six thousand lily pads. There is a fifty-five mph highway at one end of the pond, and a nesting pair of wood ducks at the other. Under every bush is a muskrat hole or a beer can. The far end is an alternating series of fields and woods, fields and woods, threaded everywhere with motorcycle tracks—in whose bare clay wild turtles lay eggs.

One evening last week at sunset, I walked to the pond and sat on a downed log near the shore. I was watching the lily pads at my feet tremble and part over the thrusting path of a carp. A yellow warbler appeared to my right and flew behind me. It caught my eye; I swiveled around—and the next instant, inexplicably, I was looking down at a weasel, who was looking up at me.

Weasel! I'd never seen one wild before. He was ten inches long, thin as a curve, a muscled ribbon, brown as fruitwood, soft-furred, alert. His face was fierce, small and pointed as a lizard's; he would have made a good arrowhead. There was just a dot of chin, maybe two brown hairs' worth, and then the pure white fur began that spread down his underside. He had two black eyes I did not see, any more than you see a window.

The weasel was stunned into stillness as he was emerging from beneath an enormous shaggy wildrose bush four feet away. I was stunned into stillness, twisted backward on the tree trunk. Our eyes locked, and someone threw away the key.

Our look was as if two lovers, or deadly enemies, met unexpectedly on an overgrown path when each had been thinking of something else: a clearing blow to the gut. It was also a bright blow to the brain, or a sudden beating of brains, with all the charge and intimate grate of rubbed balloons. It emptied our lungs. It felled the forest, moved the fields, and drained the pond; the world dismantled and tumbled into that black hole of eyes. If you and I looked at each other that way, our skulls would split and drop to our shoulders. But we don't. We keep our skulls.

He disappeared. This was only last week, and already I don't remember what shattered the enchantment. I think I blinked, I think I retrieved my brain from the weasel's brain, and tried to memorize what I was seeing, and the weasel felt the yank of separation, the careening splashdown into real life and the urgent current of instinct. He vanished under the wild rose. I waited motionless, my mind suddenly full of data and my spirit with pleadings, but he didn't return.

Please do not tell me about "approach-avoidance conflicts." I tell you I've been in that weasel's brain for sixty seconds, and he was in mine. Brains are private places, muttering through unique and secret tapes—but the weasel and I both plugged into another tape simultaneously, for a sweet and shocking time. Can I help it if it was a blank?

What goes on in his brain the rest of the time? What does a weasel think about? He won't say. His journal is tracks in clay, a spray of feathers, mouse blood and bone: uncollected, unconnected, loose-leaf, and blown.

I would like to learn, or remember, how to live. I come to Hollins Pond not so much to learn how to live as, frankly, to forget about it. That is, I don't think I can learn from a wild animal how to live in particular—shall I suck warm blood, hold my tail high, walk with my footprints precisely over the prints of my hands?—but I might learn something of mindlessness, something of the purity of living in the physical senses and the dignity of living without bias or motive. The weasel lives in necessity and we live in choice, hating necessity and dying at the last ignobly in its talons. I would like to live as I should, as the weasel lives as he should. And I suspect that for me the way is like the weasel's: open to time and death painlessly, noticing everything, remembering nothing, choosing the given with a fierce and pointed will.

I missed my chance. I should have gone for the throat. I should have lunged for that streak of white under the weasel's chin and held on, held on through mud and into the wild rose, held on for a dearer life. We could live under the wild rose wild as weasels, mute and uncomprehending. I could very calmly go wild. I could live two days in the den, curled, leaning on mouse fur, sniffing bird bones, blinking, licking, breathing musk, my hair tangled in the roots of grasses. Down is a good place to go, where the mind is single. Down is out, out of your ever-loving mind and back to your careless senses. I remember muteness as a prolonged and giddy fast, where every moment is a feast of utterance received. Time and events are merely poured, unremarked, and ingested directly, like blood pulsed into my gut through a jugular vein. Could two live that way? Could two live under the wild rose, and explore by the pond, so that the smooth mind of each is as everywhere present to the other, and as received and as unchallenged, as falling snow?

We could, you know. We can live any way we want. People take vows of poverty, chastity, and obedience—even of silence—by choice. The thing is to stalk your calling in a certain skilled and supple way, to locate the most tender and live spot and plug into that pulse. This is yielding, not fighting. A weasel doesn't "attack" anything; a weasel lives as he's meant to, yielding at every moment to the perfect freedom of single necessity.

I think it would be well, and proper, and obedient, and pure, to grasp your one necessity and not let it go, to dangle from it limp wherever it takes you. Then even death, where you're going no matter how you live, cannot you part. Seize it and let it seize you up aloft even, till your eyes burn out and drop; let your musky flesh fall off in shreds, and let your very bones unhinge and scatter, loosened over fields, over fields and woods, lightly, thoughtless, from any height at all, from as high as eagles.

Thinking as a Writer

Evaluating Description

- In a sentence or two, summarize what Dillard actually sees with her eyes. List at least six details Dillard records in her weasel encounter. In another sentence or two, summarize what Dillard sees with her mind—that is, the sense she makes out of the experience. What does her encounter with a weasel mean to her?

Describing from Memory

Oral Expression

- Work with a partner. Talk to each other about a memorable scene with many sights, sounds, smells, feelings, or tastes. Some possibilities include an amusement park, a concert, a restaurant, or a party. Spend about three to five minutes talking about your scene. Tape-record your description or ask your partner to take notes while you talk.
- After each of you has had a turn, look over the notes or listen to the recordings. How effective were your descriptions? Did you use any unusual words, or were most of them ordinary? Did you use any words—like *awesome* or *cool*—that may have lost some of their power through overuse? What did you especially like about your description? What would you improve upon if you were to produce a written version?

Looking and Seeing

Viewing

- Study the photograph on the next page. Describe what you observe, incorporating sentences like "The birds seem to be flying over sand or snow." Be as thorough as you can in recapturing what you observe.
- Decide how the details you have noticed contribute to an overall feeling. Is this a comforting, peaceful photograph, or is it ominous, filled with frightening shadows and perplexing mysteries? Use details from the photograph to back up your interpretation.

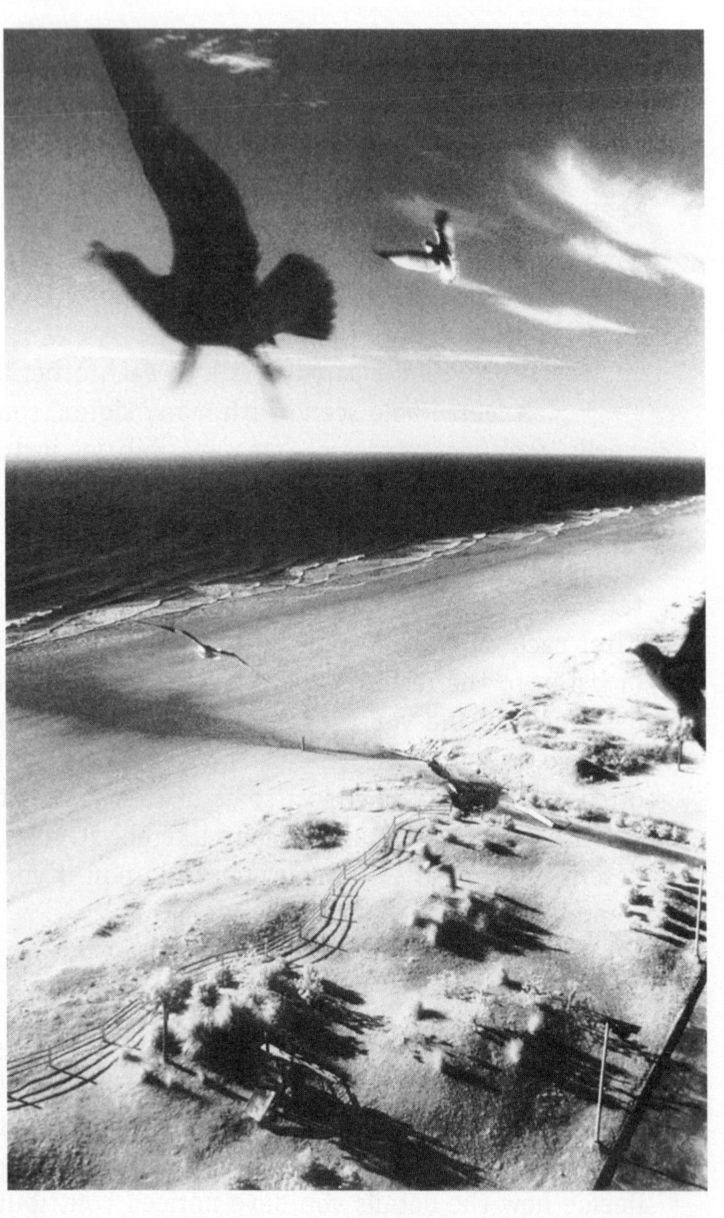

Jane Tuckerman. *Untitled (aerial view of shore),*
The Kate and Hall J. Peterson Fund.

The Power of Description

One way to appreciate the power of description is to read something without it. How much can you picture in the following "Deep Thought" by Jack Handey, a creation of satirist Al Franken?

> The memories of my family outings are still a source of strength to me. I remember we'd all pile into the car—I forget what kind it was—and drive and drive. I'm not sure where we'd go, but I think there were some trees there. The smell of something strong was in the air as we played whatever sport we played. I remember a bigger, older guy we called "Dad." We'd eat some stuff or not, and then I think we went home. I guess some things never leave you.
>
> *–Jack Handey*

Uses of Description

Such fuzzy describing shows, by contrast, what a gift clear description can be. Think of how important accurate, vivid descriptions are in each of the cases listed below.

- **A research scientist documents the appearance** of a cell as part of an experiment to find a cure for a serious illness.
- **A travel writer describes the sights and sounds** of a foreign city.
- **A fiction writer sets the scene** and creates lifelike characters.
- **A nature writer records the activities** of animals in the wild.

Refining Your Skills of Description

Baseball coach Yogi Berra is known, in part, for his charmingly confused language mistakes. He noted, in his typical style, that "you can observe a lot just by watching." An even better way, though, is to develop your observations into a thoughtful essay.

When you write to help readers visualize an object, a scene, or a person, you are writing a description. Using colorful words and careful organization can make your readers see, hear, smell, taste, and feel what you are describing—what you *observed*. This response in readers is the goal of descriptive writing.

Descriptive writing creates a vivid picture in words of a person, an object, or a scene by stimulating the reader's senses.

Your Writer's Journal

Annie Dillard said about her meeting with the weasel: "Our eyes locked, and someone threw away the key." What do you think she means?

Have you had an encounter with an animal that seemed to create such a bond? Was it a deep, long-lasting relationship, like that between pet and person? Was it a fleeting but heartstopping connection like the one between Dillard and the weasel? Was it a real animal or an animal in your dreams?

Freewrite, brainstorm, or cluster—get your ideas flowing in your journal about such times. Try to include as many descriptive details as you remember from one such event. Also try to draw meaning from the experience. Why do you remember it? What did it mean to you?

 Descriptive Essay Structure

Like the descriptive paragraph *(pages C184–C186),* the descriptive essay has three main parts.

Structure of a Descriptive Essay

- The **introduction** captures attention, introduces the subject, and often suggests an overall impression of the subject.
- The **body of supporting paragraphs** presents details, especially sensory details, that bring the subject to life.
- The **conclusion** reinforces the overall impression and gives the essay a feeling of closure.

In the following description, Joanna Greenfield—like Annie Dillard—describes a close encounter with an animal. As you read, notice that this encounter is both physical and emotional—a deadly flesh-and-blood bond.

Model: Descriptive Essay

Hyena

Spotted hyenas are the sharks of the savanna, super-predators and astounding recyclers of garbage. They hunt in large, giggling groups, running alongside their prey and eating chunks of its flesh until it slows down through loss of blood, or shock, or sheer hopelessness, and then the hyenas grab for the stomach and pull the animal to a halt with its own entrails or let it stumble into the loops and whorls of its own body. They eat the prey whole and cough back, like owls, the indigestible parts, such as hair and hooves.

Efa had been taken from his parents as a cub because his mother rejected him. Also, he was a cross between a North African and an Israeli striped hyena, and nobody wanted him to confuse the gene pool further by mating. He was a beautiful animal. A mane trickled down sloped shoulders like a froth of leftover baby hair; he looked strangely helpless, as if weighed down by the tangled strands, and his back rounded to a dispirited slump. Even though he had a hyena's posture, he was like a German shepherd, a little dirty, but graceful, and so strong he didn't seem to have any muscles. His stripes twisted a bit at the ends and shimmered over the coat like feathers at rest. With his bat face and massed shoulders, he would have been at home in the sky, poised in a great leap, or swooping for prey. But here he was given aged meat, and he often left even that to rot before he ate it.

He had been, they said, an adorable cub, crying "*Maaaaaa!*" to Shlomi, the gentlest of the workers and the one who reared him, and he followed Shlomi everywhere. Then he grew too big to run loose, and he started biting at people, so they put him in a corral—a square of desert surrounded by an electrified fence with a large water basin perched in the center.

Efa was bored and lonely. He flipped the basin over every day, attacking it as if it were prey. When we fed him in the morning, there was nowhere to put his water. He knocked over everything, so we had no choice: we had to put him in a holding cage outside his corral while we built a concrete pool that he couldn't move. This was worse. Locked in a cage, he rebelled. He refused to eat, and every box we gave him for shade was torn to pieces. After a few days, I walked by and saw him standing defiant in the cage, his shade box in splinters and his water overturned again. "*Maaaaaaaa! Mmaaaaa!*" he croaked at me. I made a note to return and water him when I'd finished with the others.

I stopped to talk to the leopard.

"You're so beautiful."

She purred, and rubbed against the mesh. The men said you could stroke her like a house cat when she was in these moods. I wanted to touch her, a leopard from the oases of Israel's last deserts, but I stayed away, in case she changed her mind, and squatted out of reach to talk to her. I didn't want to force her to defend herself.

It might have been the attention I gave the leopard, but Efa was in a frenzy of "*Mmmaaaaaaaa*"s when I returned to his cage. He crouched like a baby, begging for something. I filled a water tray and unlatched the door that opened into a corridor running between the cage and the corral, then I closed it. If only I'd just squirted the hose into the cage, but instead I unlatched the cage door and bent over to put the dish down, talking to him. The mind, I found, is strange. It shut off during the attack, while my body continued to act, without thought or even sight. I don't remember him sinking his teeth into my arm, though I heard a little grating noise as his teeth chewed into the bone.

Everything was black and slow and exploding in my stomach. Vision returned gradually, like an ancient black-and-white television pulling dots and flashes to the center for a picture. I saw at a remove the hyena inside my right arm, and my other arm banging him on the head. My body, in the absence of a mind, had decided that this was the best thing to do. And scream. Scream in a thin angry hysteria that didn't sound like me. Where was everyone? My mind was so calm and remote that I frightened myself, but my stomach twisted. I hit harder, remembering the others he'd nipped. He'd always let go.

Efa blinked and surged back, jerking me forward. I stumbled out of my sandals into the sand, thinking, with fresh anxiety, I'll burn my feet. I tried to kick him between the legs, but it was awkward, and he was pulling me down by the arm, down and back into the cage. When I came back from Africa the first time, I took a class in self-defense so I'd feel safer with all the soldiers, guerrilla warriors, and policemen when I returned. I remembered the move I'd vowed to use on any attacker: a stab and grab at the jugular, to snap it inside the skin. But the hyena has callused skin on its throat, thick and rough, like eczema. I lost hope and felt the slowness of this death to be the worst insult. Hyenas don't kill fast, and I could end up in the sand watching my entrails get pulled through a cut in my stomach and eaten like spaghetti, with tugs and jerks. I started to get mad, an unfamiliar feeling creeping in to add an acid burn to the chill of my stomach. Another removal from myself. I never let myself get mad. I want peace. I tried to pinch his nostrils so he'd let go of my arm to breathe, but he shook his head, pulling me deeper into the cage.

I think it was then that he took out the first piece from my arm and swallowed it without breathing, because a terror of movement settled in me at that moment and lasted for months. He moved up the arm, and all the time those black, blank eyes evaluated me, like a shark's, calm and almost friendly. By this time, my right arm was a mangled mess of flesh, pushed-out globs of fat, and flashes of bone two inches long, but my slow TV mind, watching, saw it as whole, just trapped in the hyena's mouth, in a tug-of-war like the one I used to play with my dogs—only it was my arm now instead of a sock. It didn't hurt. It never did.

The hyena looked up at me with those indescribable eyes and surged back again, nearly pulling me onto his face. I remembered self-defense class and the first lesson: "Poke the cockroach in the eyes." All the women had squealed, except me. "Ooooh, I could never do that." Ha, I'd thought. Anyone who wants to kill me has no right to live. I'd poke him in the eyes.

I looked at those eyes with my fingers poised to jab. It was for my family and my friends that I stuck my fingers in his eyes. I just wanted to stop watching myself get eaten, either be dead and at peace or be gone, but other lives were connected to mine. I'm not sure if I did more than touch them gently before he let go and whipped past me to cower against the door to the outside, the Negev desert.

Events like this teach you yourself. We all think we know what we would do, hero or coward, strong or weak. I expected strength, and the memory of my tinwhistle scream curdles my blood, but I am proud of the stupid thing I did next. He cowered and whimpered and essentially apologized, still with those blank unmoving eyes, and I stood still for a second. My arm felt light and shrunken, as if half of it were gone, but I didn't look. From the corridor, I had a choice of two doors: the one through which I'd entered, leading back to the desert, and the one opening onto the corral. I didn't think I could bend over him and unlatch the door to the desert. He'd just reach up and clamp onto my stomach. And I didn't want to open the door to the corral, or he'd drag me in and be able to attack the men if they ever came to help me. My body, still in control, made the good hand grab the bad elbow, and I beat him with my own arm, as if I had ripped it free to use as a club. "No!" I shouted. "No, no!" Lo lo lo, in Hebrew. I might even have said "Bad boy," but I hope not. It was the beating that damaged my hand permanently. I must have hit him hard enough to crush a ligament, because there is a lump on my hand to this day, five years later, but he didn't even blink. He came around behind me and grabbed my right leg, and again there was no pain—just the feeling that he and I were playing tug-of-war with my body—but I was afraid to pull too hard on the leg. He pulled the leg up, stretching me out in a line from the door, where I clung with the good hand to the mesh, like a dancer at the barre. It felt almost good, as if the whole thing were nearer to being over. In three moves I didn't feel, he took out most of the calf.

I opened the door to the desert and he ran out, with a quick shove that staggered me. I couldn't move the right leg, just crutched myself along on it into the Negev. He waited for me. The cold in my stomach was stabbing my breath away. The hyena and I were bonded now. Even if someone did come to help, there was still something left to finish between us. I was marked—his. I saw, in color, that he was going to knock me over, and I thought, in black-and-white, No, don't, you'll hurt my leg, I should keep it still.

A workman stood by a shed uphill, leaning on a tool in the sand. He watched me walk toward the office, with the hyena ahead and looking back at me. He was the only spectator I noticed, though I was told later, in the hospital, that some tourists, there to see the animals, were screaming for help, and three—or was it five?—soldiers had had their machine guns aimed at us throughout the whole thing. Israeli soldiers carry their arms everywhere when they're in uniform; but they must have been afraid to shoot. I don't know. Stories get told afterward. I didn't see anyone except the workman, looking on impassively, and the leopard, pacing inside her fence, roaring a little, with the peace of her heat gone as suddenly as it had appeared.

–*Joanna Greenfield,* Hyena

PRACTICE YOUR SKILLS

Analyzing Descriptive Writing

Answer the following questions that relate to the description of the human-animal encounter in "Hyena."

1. What overall impression is suggested in the introduction of this essay?
2. What sentences or phrases contribute to that overall impression?
3. Write five details from the body of supporting paragraphs that call on the sense of sight.
4. Write three details from the body of supporting paragraphs that call on the sense of touch.
5. Write five details from the body of supporting paragraphs that call on the sense of hearing.
6. Find two examples in which the writer uses a comparison to make a point.
7. How would you describe the organizational pattern of this essay? What is the underlying logic connecting one paragraph to the next?
8. Read the conclusion carefully. What reason might the writer have had to end with a sentence about a workman and a leopard watching what took place?

Specific Details and Sensory Words

A main impression is at the core of good descriptive writing. This overall impression—no matter what it is—comes to life when you use your supporting details to *show* the subject rather than simply *tell* about it. When you *show* readers, chances are you are using strong specific details and words that appeal to the senses. You are making your readers see, hear, smell, and feel the impression you are creating. These are the flesh and blood of descriptive writing.

Use **specific details** and **sensory words** to bring your description to life.

Writer Barry Lopez is especially good at painting word pictures. In the following selection, he describes a wolf moving through the northern woods.

Model: Sensory Details

He moves along now at the edge of a clearing. The wind coming down-valley surrounds him with a river of odors, as if he were a migrating salmon. He can smell ptarmigan and deer droppings. He can smell willow and spruce and the fading sweetness of fireweed. Above, he sees a hawk circling, and farther south, lower on the horizon, a flock of sharp-tailed sparrows going east. He senses through his pads with each step the dryness of the moss beneath his feet, and the ridges of old tracks, some his own. He hears the sound his feet make. He hears the occasional movement of deer mice and voles. Summer food.

Toward dusk he is standing by a creek, lapping the cool water, when a wolf howls—a long wail that quickly reaches pitch and then tapers, with several harmonies, long moments to a tremolo. He recognizes his sister. He waits a few moments, then, throwing his head back and closing his eyes, he howls. The howl is shorter and it changes pitch twice in the beginning, very quickly. There is no answer.

–*Barry Lopez,* Of Wolves and Men

One reason this passage is so richly descriptive is that Lopez is really painting two pictures. First he recreates the wolf's experience from the wolf's point of view. Then Lopez presents the wolf from the perspective of an imaginary human observer. The most important reason this description succeeds so well, however, is the writer's generous use of specific details and sensory words.

SPECIFIC SENSORY DETAILS	
Sights	edge of a clearing, hawk circling, flock of sharp-tailed sparrows
Sounds	his own footsteps, occasional movement of deer mice and voles, howl of other wolf with its distinctive sound, his own shorter howl with its own distinctive changes of pitch
Smells	ptarmigan and deer droppings; willow, spruce, and fireweed
Taste	cool water
Feelings	wind, dryness of moss and ridges of old tracks through pads of his feet, throwing head back, closing eyes

Figurative Language

Many writers rely on imaginative comparisons to help pump life into their descriptions. These can be either similes or metaphors, or just general comparisons. Here are a few examples from selections you have already read.

Metaphor	The wind coming down-valley surrounds him with **a river of odors**. . . . (The wind is compared to a river.)
Simile and Metaphor	He was ten inches long, **thin as a curve, a muscled ribbon**, brown as fruitwood, soft-furred, alert. (The weasel's thinness is compared to a curve with the word *as* signaling the simile; weasel is also said metaphorically to be a ribbon.)
General Comparison	They eat the prey whole and cough back, like owls, the indigestible parts, such as hair and hooves. (The hyenas' eating habits are compared to those of owls.)

Practice Your Skills

Identifying Specific Details

The next two paragraphs continue Lopez's description of the wolf. Read them carefully, and then answer the questions.

The female is a mile away and she trots off obliquely through the trees. The other wolf stands listening, laps water again, then he too departs, moving quickly, quietly through the trees, away from the trail he had been on. In a few minutes the two wolves meet. They approach each other briskly, almost formally, tails erect and moving somewhat as deer move. When they come together they make high squeaking noises and encircle each other, rubbing and pushing, poking their noses into each other's neck fur, backing away to stretch, chasing each other for a few steps, then standing quietly together, one putting a head over the other's back. And then they are gone, down a vague trail, the female first. After a few hundred yards they begin, simultaneously, to wag their tails.

In the days to follow, they will meet another wolf from the pack, a second female, younger by a year, and the three of them will kill a caribou. They will travel together ten or twenty miles a day, through the country where they live, eating and sleeping, birthing, playing with sticks, chasing ravens, growing old, barking at bears, scent-marking trails, killing moose, and staring at the way water in a creek breaks around their legs and flows on.

1. Compare the use of specific details and sensory details in this passage and in the previous passage. Which is richer in detail? Explain your answer.

2. Why do you think Lopez wrote such a long sentence about the wolves' first meeting? What effect does it have?

3. The final sentence contains a long list of things the wolves do. Which of these activities is the most specific? Why do you think Lopez places that detail where it is?

Developing Details Using a Sensory Diagram

To help you develop specific details, you can try the technique of diagraming a general idea. Here's how a **sensory diagram** might look on the following general idea:

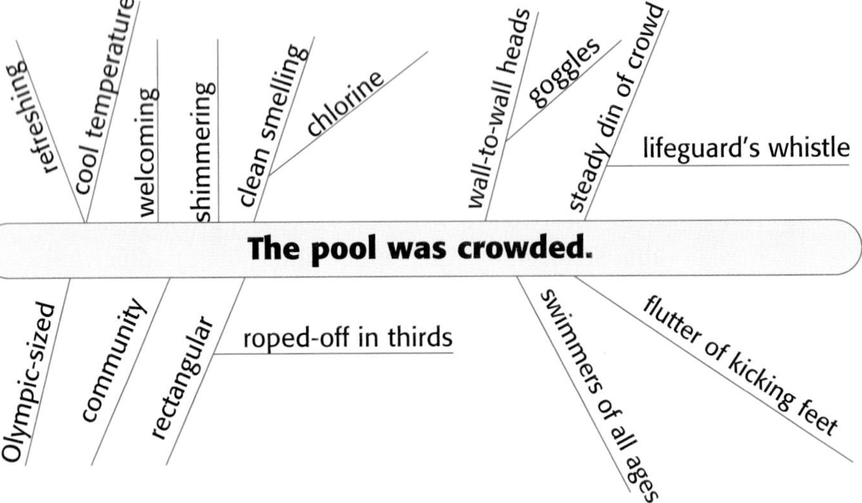

Create a sensory diagram of your own, using the following idea:

The street was bustling.

Understanding Figurative Language

Read the following passage from a description of an eclipse of the sun. Write a few sentences explaining the comparison John Updike, the author, is making. Try "translating" the imaginative language into everyday descriptive language.

The eclipse was to be over 90 percent in our latitude and the newspapers and television had been warning us not to look at it. I looked up, a split second Prometheus, and looked away. The bitten silhouette of the sun lingered redly on my retinas. The day was half-cloudy, and my impression had been of the sun struggling, amid a furious huddle of black and silver clouds, with an enemy too dreadful to be seen, with an eater as ghostly and hungry as time.

Process of Writing a Description

There *are* some purely descriptive essays—those whose purpose is to describe a subject as completely as possible. More often, though, writers use description in the service of some other writing purpose: to enrich a story they are narrating, to add interest and life to an explanation, to give heart and soul to an argument. Writing a description will give you the skills you need for enriching any essay you write.

Some people think of writing as a product: a sentence, a paragraph, an essay. Yet writing is a process, a tool. Even though the term *prewriting* suggests an activity that takes place *before* writing starts, you should do your prewriting work *in writing.* Often you cannot really focus your thoughts until you put your ideas on paper.

Choosing a Subject

If you look back over the longer selections included in this chapter, you can see that the subjects the writers chose had a lot in common. The most obvious is that the writers all wrote about animals. Yet an even more important common thread is the great personal significance of the subjects. To Dillard, locking eyes with a weasel taught a profound life lesson. To Greenwood, locking flesh with a hyena put her face to face with her own animal instincts and the possibility of her own death.

A good subject for a description does not have to be about one of life's mysteries, but it does have to have real meaning to you if it is to be any good.

The following guidelines can help you choose the best subject for your description.

Guidelines for Choosing a Subject

- Choose a subject that matters to *you*. Your interest will carry over to the reader.
- Choose a subject that you can develop with descriptive details such as sensory words and figurative language.
- Choose a subject you know well enough to describe better than anyone else you know.

Identifying Your Audience

A naturalist writing for other naturalists would use scientific language and concepts that might not be familiar to the general reading public. A reader who does not know your school would need more background for a description of your campus than would a fellow student. Readers who do not know much about hyenas or weasels need some factual information to get a clear understanding. The following questions can help you shape your ideas for a specific audience.

Questions for Analyzing an Audience

- What does my audience already know about my subject?
- What background information, if any, do I need to provide to make the description more meaningful?
- What attitude does my audience have toward my subject?
- Do I want to reinforce that attitude or try to change it?

Practice Your Skills

Identifying Audience

Identify four possible audiences for each of the following descriptive subjects.

EXAMPLE a poorly maintained and littered beach

ANSWER sanitation district officials, environmentalists, surfers, beach-goers

1. a weed patch

2. a school playground

3. a car repair shop

4. an orchestra rehearsal

5. a skyscraper

Communicate Your Ideas

PREWRITING *Subject and Audience*

Look over your **journal** for ideas for a description. Follow the suggestions on pages C12–C17 for thinking of subjects. Then use the guidelines on the previous page to choose the best subject from among those you have listed. Decide who your audience will be. Write answers to the questions on the previous page to help you target your writing effectively. Brainstorm, freewrite, cluster, or write down ideas in other ways for people, places, objects, and scenes or events that have genuine meaning to you. Look over your **journal** for ideas as well. Save your work in your writing folder for later use.

SAVE YOUR WORK

Developing an Overall Impression

If you tried to record every detail about your subject, the resulting writing would be a meaningless overload. Readers depend on writers to filter out the details they do not need to know so they can focus on what is important. To know what is important, you need to develop the overall impression you want to convey. What is the general feeling you have about your subject? You need to have a clear sense of your overall impression in order to develop your work successfully.

The overall impression Dillard wants to convey about the weasel is a fierce but positive one—that it lived according to its nature, and that it pursued its nature and its living single-mindedly. Although she does not state this position in a thesis statement at the beginning of the essay, she does provide factual examples that make this point by way of introducing her subject. In a similar way, Greenfield's overall impression of the hyena is one of ferociousness, so she begins her description with facts about the hyena that lay out the terrifying landscape of an encounter with such an animal.

Writing Tip

Filter your **details** and develop your **overall impression** to make your writing meaningful for a reader.

PRACTICE YOUR SKILLS

Determining Overall Impressions

1. What overall impression does Barry Lopez create in his description of the wolves? *(page C299)*

2. Explain your answer to question 1 with examples from Lopez's writing.

Communicate Your Ideas

PREWRITING *Overall Impression*

Look over your work on a descriptive subject. What overall impression do you want your essay to make? Positive? Negative? Scary? Soothing? Joyous? Try to pin down the impression with as precise an adjective as possible. Then save your work in your writing folder for later use.

Product Packaging

The jolly faces of elves, a sports hero making a slam dunk, a fresh, ripe strawberry—all of these images appear or have appeared on cereal boxes to help create a quick overall impression. Designers of product packaging work hard to choose an image that will appeal to potential buyers—an image that conveys a message. What message does the product on the left convey?

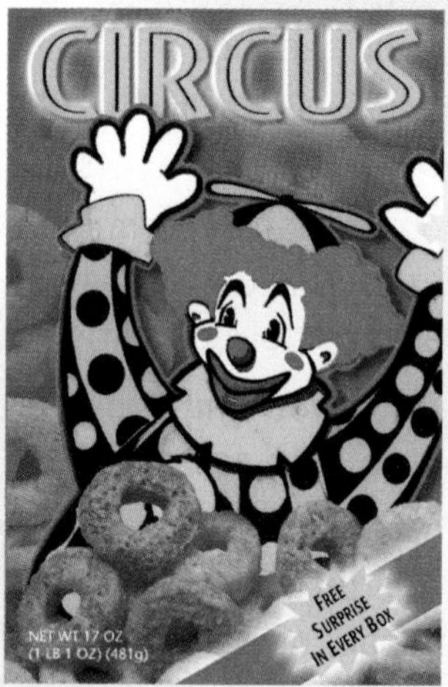

Even if a busy shopper does not take the time to note the words about a free surprise, the colorful pieces of cereal suggest a kid-friendly cereal. Also the smiling clown says, as if shouting from the shelf, "Children love this cereal."

What messages—overall impressions—does the packaging design of the product on the right convey? Explain your thinking.

Media Activity

Try designing a package for a cereal product you know well. What is the main message you want to convey? What specific images and designs can you use to convey that image quickly? Describe the front of your box. Also draw a sketch and share it with your class.

Developing a Description

With your overall impression in mind, you can begin to flesh out the details you will use to develop your description. Consider your audience as well. With both of these in mind, use the strategies below for developing descriptive details.

Strategies for Developing a Description

- Use your memory and direct observation, if appropriate, to list the sights, sounds, smells, tastes, and feelings you associate with your subject. Making a chart like the one on page C300 may help.
- Brainstorm for a list of imaginative comparisons you might make to help readers understand your description. These could be metaphors or similes or other types of comparisons.
- Gather any factual details and information you might need to provide background for your readers or to help set the stage for your overall impression.
- If you are describing a scene, draw a picture or a map so you can clearly see the relationship of one part of the subject to another.
- Apply your filter: remember to test each detail against your desired overall impression to make sure it adds rather than detracts.

PRACTICE YOUR SKILLS

Filtering Details

Look at the following list of details for a description about a cabin in the woods. Write the ones that do not fit the overall impression. Explain why you think they do not fit.

OVERALL IMPRESSION: comforting, inviting, safe, warm

Details:

- long drive on cold night to get there
- in northern Michigan
- stepped out of the car to blast of cold clean air
- starry, moonless night
- fingers and toes felt frozen
- stepped inside cabin and out of wind
- soon had fire going in fireplace
- good smell of burning hardwood
- musty odor in bathroom
- pictures on walls of fishing scenes
- old upholstery—tears on arms of chairs
- rustic wood floors
- made hot chocolate
- had to wash out the pans because of dust
- warm afghan draped across the couch
- snow began to fall
- poor lock on door—wouldn't really stay shut

Communicate Your Ideas

PREWRITING *Development of Details*

Use the strategies on the previous page to help you develop the supporting details for your description. When you have a good collection of factual details, sensory details, and imaginative comparisons, apply your writer's filter to them to be sure they support your overall impression. Delete any details that detract from your main impression. Save your work for later use.

Writing Is Thinking

Observing

A movie camera simply takes in images and places them on the film. This is an example of **objective observation**: observing facts, without opinion or perspective.

Most of the time, however, our observations are colored by our feelings and beliefs. In a hot, crowded lobby, the only details we notice are those that reinforce our discomfort. This is **subjective observation**.

Henry David Thoreau, an American author and philosopher, pointed out that there really is no such thing as purely objective observation. We are always filtering what we see through our human prejudices and opinions. He writes, ". . . what the writer . . . has to report is simply some human experience."

Nonetheless, there may be some things about your subject that you can observe objectively. The following chart shows both objective and subjective observations Annie Dillard made about her weasel soulmate.

OBJECTIVE DETAILS	SUBJECTIVE DETAILS
size	quality of eyes
shape	alertness
colors	fierceness

If you compare the details, you can see that the objective ones can be verified by some tangible measure. The subjective details have no proof, but they are the details that make Dillard's essay as descriptive as it is.

THINKING PRACTICE

Make a chart like the one above to record objective and subjective observations of an object in nature. Compare your work to that of other students.

Organizing a Description

How you organize your description depends on your writing aim and the nature of your details. The chart below shows some good possibilities.

WRITING AIM	KINDS OF DETAILS	TYPE OF ORDER
to **describe** a person, place, object, or scene	sensory details	spatial *(pages C126–C127)*
to **recreate** an event	sensory details, events	chronological *(pages C126–C127)*
to **explain** a process or how something works	sensory and factual details, steps in a process, how parts work together	sequential *(pages C125–C126)*
to **persuade**	sensory and factual details, examples, reasons	order of importance *(page C125)*
to **reflect**	sensory and factual details, interpretations	order of importance *(page C125)*

PRACTICE YOUR SKILLS

Organizing Descriptive Details

Review the details describing the feeling inside the warm cabin in the woods on pages C308–C309. Decide on a suitable organizational pattern for them and make a rough outline showing the order in which you would present them. Then write a sentence or two explaining your choice.

Communicate Your Ideas

PREWRITING ***Organization of Details***

Look over your details for your description. Then use the chart on page C311 to help you choose an appropriate order in which to present your supporting points. Make an outline to help you as you draft, and save it in your writing folder for later use.

Drafting

Writing Process

If you have taken your prewriting work seriously, by now most of the hard work of writing your description is over. During the drafting stage, concentrate on the flow of your ideas, always thinking about your reader. Keep the following points in mind as you draft your description.

Tips for Drafting a Description

- Experiment with interest-catching introductions. (Review the selections in this chapter for ideas.)
- Suggest your overall impression early in your writing to frame your description for readers.
- Follow your outline when drafting the body of your description, but feel free to make improvements as they occur to you.
- Use fresh, vivid, descriptive words that appeal to the senses as you write.
- Remember to use transitions appropriate to the type of order you have chosen *(pages C107 and C138)* to help your reader get smoothly from one point to the next.
- Look for a strong way to end your description and consider referring back to an idea in your introduction to tie together the writing.

Communicate Your Ideas

DRAFTING *Observations*

Draft your description, using the preceding tips. Make sure your description is clear and your ideas flow. Save your work for later use.

Revising

Writing Process

"You always feel when you look it straight in the eye," wrote Canadian artist Emily Carr, "that you could have put more into it, could have let yourself go and dug harder." Look your description "straight in the eye" as you begin the revising stage. Where could you have "put more into it"? Where could you have "dug harder"?

Time Out to Reflect

How do you feel about revising your work? If you're like many writers, it's something you would rather not bother doing. Once the idea hits paper, it seems hard to change. Can you give yourself advice on how to get past any resistance to revising? Write freely in the Learning Log section of your **journal** to explore your attitudes toward revising. Then write about two or three revisions you have made in recent papers that really seemed to make a difference.

Practice Your Skills

Revising for Specific Language

Reread "Deep Thought" on page C291. Revise it so that you have included a generous supply of sensory words and details to replace the generalities. Use details from your own life to make the revisions. Share your revisions with your class. The resulting paragraphs will be less funny but more descriptive.

Prewriting Workshop
Drafting Workshop
Revising Workshop
Editing Workshop
Publishing Workshop

Adjectives

In her description of an encounter with a weasel, Annie Dillard artfully paints a vivid word picture. A writer's careful choice and varied use of adjectives can help readers really see what is being described.

Position of Adjectives

Adjectives can modify different nouns or pronouns, or they can modify the same noun.

DIFFERENT NOUNS	"I would like to have seen that eagle from the air a **few** weeks or months before he was shot: was the **whole** weasel still attached to his **feathered** throat, a **fur** pendant?"
SAME NOUN	"Or did the eagle eat what he could reach, gutting the living weasel with his talons before his breast, bending his beak, cleaning the **beautiful airborne** bones?"

Usually an adjective comes in front of the noun it modifies. However, a good writer varies the position of nouns; sometimes an adjective follows a noun or a linking verb.

BEFORE A NOUN	"The man could in no way pry the tiny weasel off, and he had to walk half a mile to water, the weasel dangling from his palm, and soak him off like a **stubborn** label."
AFTER A NOUN	The weasel, **stunned**, stood and watched Dillard.
AFTER A LINKING VERB	"A weasel is **wild**."

Communicate Your Ideas

REVISING *Specific Language*

Use the **Evaluation Checklist For Revising** to revise your description. When you are reasonably satisfied that you can answer *yes* to all the questions on the checklist, divide into small groups and share your paper with classmates. Make any further revisions you feel appropriate based on your peers' comments. Save your work. 

Evaluation Checklist for Revising

Checking Your Introduction

✓ Does your introduction capture the reader's attention? *(page C293)*

✓ Does your introduction suggest an overall impression of your subject? *(pages C305–C306)*

✓ Does your introduction set the right tone for your subject and audience? *(pages C305–C306)*

✓ Does your introduction provide enough background information for your audience? *(page C304)*

Checking Your Body Paragraphs

✓ Have you supported your overall impression with appropriate details? *(pages C305–C306)*

✓ Did you include well-chosen sensory words and details and avoid generalities? *(pages C298–C300)*

✓ Is each paragraph within the body well developed, with a clear main idea and supporting details? *(pages C233–C235)*

✓ Did you use comparisons and figurative language effectively? *(page C300)*

✓ Did you move logically from one paragraph to the next in a clear organization and with helpful transitions? *(pages C107 and C138)*

Checking Your Conclusion

- ✓ Does your conclusion reinforce the overall impression you are trying to make? *(page C305)*
- ✓ Do you refer back to your introduction to give a sense of completion? *(pages C240–C241)*
- ✓ Did you end with a memorable phrase or image that might linger in the reader's mind? *(pages C240–C241)*

Checking Your Words and Sentences

- ✓ Are your words specific and lively, stimulating all the senses? *(page C298)*
- ✓ Are your sentences varied? *(pages C76–C77)*
- ✓ Have you used adjectives to bring your description alive for readers? *(page C197)*
- ✓ Have you varied the placement of adjectives for variety? *(page C314)*

COMPUTER TIP

If you are working on a word-processing program, you can easily find synonyms when revising your description by using your program's thesaurus.

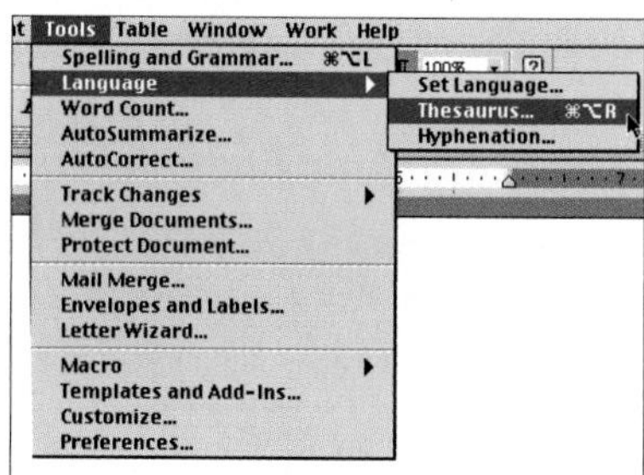

Editing

Writing Process

Remember that writing is a process that loops back and forth. In other words, if you are editing your work and suddenly think of another detail you would like to include, take the time to work it in. Being a tough critic of your own work will help your writing improve dramatically.

Communicate Your Ideas

EDITING

When you are happy with your latest revision, spend some time polishing it. During the editing stage, carefully go over your essay, looking for any errors. Be sure to consult your Personalized Editing Checklist to avoid repeating errors you are prone to make. Save your work for later use.

Publishing

Writing Process

An act of communication is incomplete unless it reaches a receiver. Be sure to make your writing available to interested readers. Some possibilities for a descriptive essay include:

- a class anthology of descriptive pieces, accompanied by illustrations;
- an E-mail to a friend who may have been part of the experience you describe;
- a bulletin board display with accompanying illustrations;
- a submission to a magazine or other periodical that publishes student writing.

Communicate Your Ideas

PUBLISHING

Prepare a neat final copy of your edited description. Then use one of the ideas above, or any other idea you may have for sharing it.

PORTFOLIO

Process of Writing Descriptive Essays

Remember that writing is a recursive process. At any point in the process, you may get a new idea that you wish to include in your description. It is important to be open to these new ideas, even as you write your draft and revise.

PREWRITING

- Use brainstorming, freewriting, clustering, and any other techniques that work for you in order to choose a subject. *(pages C12–C19)*
- Select a subject that matters or means something to you. *(page C304)*
- Identify your writing purpose and intended audience. *(pages C22–C24)*
- Determine the overall impression you intend to convey through your description of the subject. *(pages C305–C306)*
- Filter details according to how much they contribute to the overall impression. *(pages C305–C306)*
- Make a plan for writing your description. *(page C311)*

DRAFTING

- Draft an introduction that will catch readers' attention. Suggest your purpose and your desired overall impression early on in your essay. *(page C312)*
- Refer to your outline when drafting the body of your essay. *(page C235)*
- Use transitions to help your ideas and words flow logically from one to the next. *(pages C107 and C138)*
- Provide a strong concluding paragraph that refers back to the overall impression and ties your essay together. *(page C240)*
- Add a title. *(page C38)*

REVISING

- Use all of the senses to engage the reader. *(page C300)*
- Make sure your word choices are vivid and specific. *(pages C298–C300)*
- Use peer conferencing to get feedback on your essay and to hear suggestions for improvement. *(page C42)*
- Revise for adequate development, logical progression, coherence, and emphasis. *(pages C104–C107)*
- Use the **Evaluation Checklist for Revising**. *(pages C315–C316)*

EDITING

- Use the **Editing Checklist** and your Personalized Editing Checklist to eliminate errors in grammar, usage, spelling, and mechanics. *(page C44)*

PUBLISHING

- Make a neat final copy of your essay using standard manuscript form. *(page C52)*
- Search for ways to reach your audience in print, on-line, or orally. *(page C317)*

A Writer Writes

A Description of a Problem

Purpose: to record accurately and forcefully the outward signs of a problem that needs fixing

Audience: fellow citizens and elected officials who could make a difference

Prewriting

In 1890, Jacob Riis published a book called *How the Other Half Lives: Studies Among the Tenements of New York*. His book, and others written about the same time by writers called *muckrakers*, exposed conditions so serious that reforms soon followed. Here is a selection from Riis's book, describing the once handsome houses packed with poor families.

> This one, with its shabby front and poorly patched roof, what glowing firesides, what happy children may it once have owned? Heavy feet, too often with unsteady step . . . have worn away the brown-stone steps since; the broken columns at the door have rotted away at the base. Of the handsome cornice barely a trace is left. Dirt and desolation reign in the wide hallway, and danger lurks on the stairs. Rough pine boards fence off the roomy fire-places—where coal is bought by the pail at the rate of twelve dollars a ton these have no place. The arched gateway leads no longer to a shady bower on the banks of the rushing stream, inviting to day-dreams with its gentle repose, but to a dark and nameless alley, shut in by high brick walls, cheerless as the lives of those they shelter.

For this descriptive essay, identify places or conditions with which you are familiar that call out for improvement—a littered schoolyard, an abandoned building, your room, the

state of your garage, even your desk. You need not propose the solution in this paper; just describe it so vividly that people will recognize that *something* needs to be done.

Once you have settled on a subject, brainstorm, freewrite, and/or cluster to develop vivid supporting details. The overall impression is no doubt negative, since you have chosen a problem area. Be sure your details support that impression.

After you have collected details that appeal to all the senses, group them into categories and choose an order in which to present them.

Drafting

Write the first draft of your description. Strive for an introduction that captures attention and shows the reader your opinion in no uncertain terms. Use vivid, specific language to develop your supporting paragraphs, and be sure to connect your ideas with appropriate and clear transitions. Add a strong ending that leaves an afterglow in the reader's mind.

Revising

Use the **Evaluation Checklist for Revising** on pages C315–C316 to revise your descriptive essay. Share it with a reader who may be able to help you improve your work.

Editing

Use the checklists on page C44 to edit your description.

Publishing

Prepare a neat copy, using headings if appropriate and adding illustrations. Share your description with someone else who knows your subject, and brainstorm a few ideas about how the problem might be solved.

Connection Collection

Representing in Different Ways

From Print . . .

. . . to Visuals

Draw a series of frames from a film illustrating the construction of a skyscraper, using the information from the film treatment on the right.

Treatment

Nothing stands in the empty lot except some small, scrubby pine trees and a dotting of orange poppies. The construction work begins. Men and women wearing helmets arrive early in the morning with cranes and steam shovels. Machines unearth the trees and flowers and start digging the deep foundation. In short time the steel support beams stand in place like a strange behemoth skeleton. The edifice grows and grows. First there are three stories, then six, then sixteen. Workers install mirrored windows that reflect the two- and three-story buildings, which the new skyscraper now dwarfs. Landscapers arrive and plant new trees. Slowly the earth around the skyscraper grows green again.

From Visuals . . .

. . . to Print

The storyboard above shows Artie's trip down the Grand Canyon. Based on these scenes, write a treatment for the opening of a short documentary video.

- **Which strategies can be used for creating both written and visual representations? Which strategies apply to one, not both? Which type of representation is more effective?**
- **Draw a conclusion, and write briefly about the differences between written ideas and visual representations.**

Writing in Everyday Life

Descriptive Letter

You are on vacation in Hawaii and are spending the day scuba diving. Unfortunately you accidentally knock your camera overboard while you are putting on your fins and goggles. Once you are underwater, you are amazed by the color of the water and the amount and variety of marine life that you see, and you regret not having your camera to take photographs.

Write a letter describing your experience to your friend Gina, who lives in Kansas and has never gone swimming in the ocean. Paint a written picture for her, including descriptions of what you saw, what it felt like to be underwater with the fish, and your excitement at being there. Try using similes and metaphors in your description.

What strategies did you use to describe your experience to your friend?

You can find information on writing friendly letters on pages C577–C578 and C586.

Writing for Oral Communication

Descriptive Phone Call

All of your friends have tickets to a hip-hop concert at the local civic center tonight featuring Heavy Kevy. You could not get a ticket. As you are walking home, a stretch limousine pulls up next to you. The back window rolls down and suddenly you are face to face with Heavy Kevy, giving him directions to the civic center. When you get home, you are eager to call your friends to tell them about your experience.

Improvise a telephone conversation with your best friend describing the experience of meeting Heavy Kevy. Be sure to use colorful words that will make your best friend see, hear, smell, and feel what you are describing.

What strategies did you use to describe your encounter with Heavy Kevy to your friends?

You can find information on informal conversations on pages C613–C614.

Assess Your Learning

Your English teacher has decided to write a travel book describing interesting places to visit during summer vacation. She has asked you and everyone else in your class to contribute an article. In the articles she wants the descriptions of the terrain, weather, and the architecture of places to be so vivid that the people who read the book will feel as though they have been there.

- **Write an article describing the most amazing place you have ever visited. The place you choose to write about does not have to be an exotic, far-away location—it can be a place in or near your hometown. You can make anyplace sound interesting with vivid descriptions!**
- **Choose a location you know well enough to describe better than anyone else. In describing location, be sure to include specific details and vivid sensory words to bring your description to life. Also use figurative language and comparisons to add color and vividness to your description. Be sure to create an overall impression with your description.**

Before You Write **Consider the following questions:**
What is the ***subject?***
What is the ***occasion?***
Who is the ***audience?***
What is the ***purpose?***

After You Write **Evaluate your work using the following criteria:**

- Have you identified an audience?
- Have you written in a voice and style that is appropriate to your audience and your purpose?
- Have you used specific details and vivid sensory words to bring your description to life?
- Have you included similes and metaphors to add color and depth to your descriptions?
- Have you filtered and organized details to create an overall impression?
- Have you revised for specific language?

Write briefly on how well you did. Point out your strengths and areas for improvement.

CHAPTER 8

Creative Writing: Stories, Plays, and Poems

Life and creative writing mirror each other in many ways. Creative writing, like life, stirs characters up with conflicts that they must face. In creative writing, however, the author organizes and presents how the characters deal with their conflicts, using just the right words.

Creative writing invents characters, events, and images to use in such literary forms as stories, plays, and poems. Each of these literary forms contains a unique structure that communicates elements of a story in different ways. For example, feelings are expressed through the dialogue and action of characters in a play; adjectives in a poem can express feelings just as powerfully. Understanding the inner workings of each literary form in relation to the story that is being told is the first step toward learning how to write an effective story. If you understand how the structure of each literary form enhances what you want to express or vice versa, then you are ready to write a story with great impact.

Reading with a Writer's Eye

In the following article from *The New York Times,* Arthur Miller writes about the play as a literary form. First read the article to familiarize yourself with its content. Then, as you read it again, think about whether you agree or disagree with each of Arthur Miller's assertions about the play as a literary form and why. If you were writing this article, what would you add that you think would be of interest about plays?

The Past and Its Power

WHY I WROTE *THE PRICE*

Arthur Miller

The sources of a play are both obvious and mysterious. "The Price" is first of all about a group of people recollected, as it were, in tranquillity. The central figures, the New York cop Victor Franz and his elder brother, Walter, are not precise portraits of people I knew long, long ago, but close enough, and Gregory Solomon, the old furniture dealer, is as close as I could get to reproducing a dealer's Russian-Yiddish accent that still tickles me whenever I hear it in memory.

First, the bare bones of the play's story: the Great Crash of 1929 left Victor and Walter to care for their widowed father, who had been ruined in the stock market collapse and was helpless to cope with life. While Victor, loyal to the father, dropped out of college to earn a living for them both and ended up on the police force, Walter went on to become a wealthy surgeon.

The play begins decades later on the attic floor of the decrepit[1] brownstone where the cop and his father had lived, surrounded by piles of furniture from their old apartment that the father had clung to. Now the building, owned by the father's brother, is to be torn down, so the furniture must be sold.

The conflict of how to divide the proceeds cuts open

---

[1] **decrepit** (dĭ krĕp′ĭt): Worn out, broken down by old age.

the long-buried lives of both men, as well as that of Victor's wife, Esther, and reveals the choices each has made and the price each has paid. Through it all weaves the antic 90-year-old furniture dealer Gregory Solomon, who is yards ahead of them as he tries to shepherd them away from the abyss[2] toward which he knows they are heading.

Behind the play—almost any play—are more or less secret responses to other works of the time, and these may emerge as disguised imitation or as outright rejection of the dominating forms of the hour. "The Price" was written in 1967, and since nobody is going to care anymore, it may as well be admitted that in some part it was a reaction to two big events that had come to overshadow all others in that decade. One was the seemingly permanent and morally agonizing Vietnam War, the other a surge of avant-garde plays that to one or another degree fit the absurd styles. I was moved to write a play that might confront and confound[3] both.

I enjoyed watching some of the absurd plays—my first theater experiences were with vaudeville in the 20's, after all, and absurdist comics like Bert Williams and Willie Howard, with their delicious proto-shaggy-dog stories and skits, were favorites. More, for a while in the 30's our own William Saroyan, who with all his failings was an authentic American inventor of a domestic absurdist[4] attitude, had held the stage. One would not soon forget his Time magazine subscription salesman reading—not without passion—the entire page-long list of names of Time's reporters, editors, sub-editors, fact checkers, department heads and dozens of lesser employees, to a pair of Ozark hillbillies dressed in their rags, seated on their rotting porch and listening with rapt incomprehension.

But the 60's was a time when a play with recognizable characters, a beginning, middle and end was routinely condemned as "well made" or

---

[2] **abyss** (ə bĭs′): A yawning gulf.

[3] **confound** (kən found′): To cause to become confused.

[4] **absurdist:** Believing that human beings exist in a meaningless, irrational universe.

ludicrously old-fashioned. (That plays with no characters, beginning or end were not called "badly made" was inevitable when the detonation of despised rules in all things was a requisite for recognition as modern. That beginnings, middles and ends might not be mere rules but a replication of the rise and fall of human life did not frequently come up.)

Often against my will, however, I found myself enjoying the new abstract theater; for one thing, it was moving us closer to a state of dream, and for dreams I had nothing but respect. But as the dying continued in Vietnam with no adequate resistance to it in the country, the theater, so it seemed to me, risked trivialization by failing to confront the bleeding, at least in a way that could reach most people. In its way, "Hair" had done so by offering a laid-back lifestyle opposed to the aggressive military-corporate one. But one had to feel the absence—not only in the theater but everywhere—of any interest in what had surely given birth to Vietnam, namely its roots in the past.

Indeed, the very idea of an operating continuity between past and present in any human behavior was démodé[5] and close to a laughably old-fashioned irrelevancy. My impression, in fact, was that playwrights were either uninterested in or incapable of presenting antecedent material altogether. Like the movies, plays seemed to exist entirely in the now; characters had either no past or none that could somehow be directing present actions. It was as though the culture had decreed amnesia as the ultimate mark of reality.

As the corpses piled up, it became cruelly impolite if not unpatriotic to suggest the obvious, that we were fighting the past; our rigid anti-Communist theology, born of another time two decades earlier, made it a sin to consider Vietnamese Reds as nationalists rather than Moscow's and Beijing's yapping dogs. We were fighting in a state of forgetfulness, quite

[5] **démodé** (dā′ mō dā′): No longer in fashion.

as though we had not aborted a national election in Vietnam and divided the country into separate halves when it became clear that Ho Chi Minh would be the overwhelming favorite for the presidency. This was the reality on the ground, but unfortunately it had to be recalled in order to matter. And so 50,000 Americans, not to mention millions of Vietnamese, paid with their lives to support a myth and a bellicose[6] denial.

As always, it was the young who paid. I was 53 in 1968, and if the war would cost me nothing materially, it wore away at the confidence that in the end Reason had to return lest all be lost. I was not sure of that anymore. Reason itself had become unaesthetic, something art must at any cost avoid.

"The Price" grew out of a need to reconfirm the power of the past, the seedbed of current reality, and the way to possibly reaffirm cause and effect in an insane world. It seemed to me that if, through the mists of denial, the bow of the ancient ship of reality could emerge, the spectacle might once again hold some beauty for an audience. If the play does not utter the word Vietnam, it speaks to a spirit of unearthing the real that seemed to have very nearly gone from our lives.

Which is not to deny that the primary force driving "The Price" was a tangle of memories of people. Still, these things move together, idea feeding characters and characters deepening idea.

Nineteen sixty-eight, when the play is set, was already nearly 40 years since the Great Crash, the onset of the transformed America of the Depression decade. It was then that the people in this play had made the choices whose consequences they had now to confront. The 30's had been a time when we learned the fear of doom and had stopped being kids for a while; the time, in short, when, as I once noted about the era, the birds came home to roost and the past became present. And that Depression cataclysm,[7]

---

[6] **bellicose** (bĕl′ ĭ kōs): Warlike.

[7] **cataclysm** (kăt′ ə klĭz′ əm): A violent upheaval that causes great destruction.

incidentally, seemed to teach that life indeed had beginnings, middles and a consequential end.

Plays leave a wake behind them as they pass into history, with odd objects bobbing about in it. Many of these, in the case of "The Price," are oddly funny for such a serious work. I had just finished writing it and with my wife, Inge Morath, went to the Caribbean for a week's vacation. Hurrying onto the beach in our first hour there, we noticed a man standing ankle-deep in the water, dressed in shorts and a wide-brimmed plantation hat, who looked a lot like Mel Brooks. In fact, he *was* Mel Brooks. After a few minutes' chat I asked if there was any fishing here. "Oh, God, yes," he said, "yesterday there was one came in right there," and he pointed a yard away in the shallow water. "Must have been three feet long. He was dead. But he may be over there today," he added, pointing down the beach.

He wanted to know if I was writing and I said we were casting a new play called "The Price," and he asked what it was about. "Well," I said, "there are these two brothers . . . "

"Stop, I'm crying!" he yelled, frightening all the Protestants lying on the beach.

Then there was the letter from the Turkish translator, who assured me that he had made only one change in the text. At the very end, he wrote, after the two brothers nearly come to blows and part forever, unreconciled and angry, there follows a quiet, rather elegiac[8] moment with the old furniture dealer, the cop and his wife.

Just as they are leaving the state, the translator explained, he had to bring back the elder brother, Walter, to fall tearfully into the cop's arms. This, because the audience would fear that *the actors themselves* would have had to have a vendetta that could only end in a killing if they parted as unreconciled as the script required. And so, out of the depths, rose the Turkish past. . . .

[8] **elegiac** (ĕl′ ə jī′ ək): Involving mourning or sorrow for that which is irrecoverably lost.

Thinking as a Writer

Evaluating an Author's Motivation

Arthur Miller writes that his perception of 1960s culture—particularly the war in Vietnam and absurdist plays—influenced his writing of *The Price*.

- If Miller had lived in another time and place, how might that background have affected his choice of subject matter?
- Would he have written a different play if the war had never happened? What might be different if he were writing the play today?

Describing a Setting

Viewing

Settings provide a framework for the story. They help create the overall mood and impression of a piece. A vivid description of a place, a description of a time when a story takes place, or an actual physical representation such as a set on a stage conveys this information.

- Look at the photograph that accompanies this article and examine the setting in it. Think of words or phrases that describe the setting and share them with a partner or other members of your group. What impressions do these words bring to mind?

Understanding Characterization

Oral Expression

- With a partner, give a reading before a small group of the dialogue between Arthur Miller and Mel Brooks on the previous page. Improvise the lines that are not given directly.
- How do the words on the page translate into speech? What vocal tricks help make the exchange entertaining?

Power of Creative Writing

Stories, plays, and poems provide an opportunity for writers to express perceptions and points of view that they might not be able to express otherwise. They enable people to think about old issues in new ways. They give "voice" to new ideas and the unexplored.

Uses of Creative Writing

Here are just some of the forms in which the creative power of stories, plays, and poems can be found in the real world.

- **People read stories for entertainment** in magazines and books, and online, and see stories performed in movies and on television.
- **People write poems in journals** to express their deepest feelings and to think about their problems.
- **Parents and child care workers read stories to children** to help them go to sleep.
- **Theater groups present plays** in community centers and senior centers.
- **Campers tell one another scary stories.**
- **Older people tell young people stories** about the histories of their families or communities.

Writing a Short Story

Your purpose in writing a short story is to create a piece of fiction that will entertain your reader. In the process you will be using both your narrative skills and your descriptive skills to express yourself. In a short story, you tell what happens to a character or characters who try to resolve a conflict or problem. As the narrative unfolds, you describe the characters, places, events, and objects in order to give the reader a clear picture of what happens.

You can learn more about narrative and descriptive writing on pages C173–C199 and pages C284–C323.

A **short story** is a fictional account of characters resolving a conflict or situation.

The following short story was written by Ernest Hemingway. Read the story once for pleasure. As you read it for the second time, think about how the characters relate to one another. Think, too, about each character's role in resolving the central problem or conflict of the story.

A Day's Wait

He came into the room to shut the windows while we were still in bed and I saw he looked ill. He was shivering, his face was white, and he walked slowly as though it ached to move.

"What's the matter, Schatz?"

"I've got a headache."

"You better go back to bed."

"No. I'm all right."

"You go to bed. I'll see you when I'm dressed."

But when I came downstairs he was dressed, sitting by the fire, looking a very sick and miserable boy of nine years. When I put my hand on his forehead I knew he had a fever.

"You go up to bed," I said, "you're sick."

"I'm all right," he said.

When the doctor came he took the boy's temperature.

"What is it?" I asked him.

"One hundred and two."

Downstairs, the doctor left three different medicines in different colored capsules with instructions for giving them. One was to bring down the fever, another a purgative, the third to overcome an acid condition. The germs of influenza can only exist in an acid condition, he explained. He seemed to know all about influenza and said there was nothing to worry about if the fever did not go above one hundred and four degrees. This was a light epidemic of flu and there was no danger if you avoided pneumonia.

Back in the room I wrote the boy's temperature down and made a note of the time to give the various capsules.

"Do you want me to read to you?"

"All right. If you want to," said the boy. His face was very white and there were dark areas under his eyes. He lay very still in the bed and seemed very detached from what was going on.

I read aloud from Howard Pyle's *Book of Pirates;* but I could see he was not following what I was reading.

"How do you feel, Schatz?" I asked him.

"Just the same, so far," he said.

I sat at the foot of the bed and read to myself while I waited for it to be time to give another capsule. It would have been natural for him to go to sleep, but when I looked up he was looking at the foot of the bed, looking very strangely.

"Why don't you try to go to sleep? I'll wake you up for the medicine."

"I'd rather stay awake."

After a while he said to me, "You don't have to stay in here with me, Papa, if it bothers you."

"It doesn't bother me."

"No, I mean you don't have to stay if it's going to bother you."

I thought perhaps he was a little light-headed and giving him prescribed capsules at eleven o'clock I went out for a while.

It was a bright, cold day, the ground covered with a sleet that had frozen so that it seemed as if all the bare trees, the bushes, the cut brush and all the grass and the bare ground had been varnished with ice. I took the young Irish setter for a little walk up the road and along a frozen creek, but it was difficult to stand or walk on the glassy surface and the red dog slipped and slithered and I fell twice, hard, once dropping my gun and having it slide away over the ice.

We flushed a covey of quail under a high clay bank with overhanging brush and I killed two as they went out of sight over the top of the bank. Some of the covey lit in trees, but most of them scattered into brush piles and it was necessary to jump on the ice-coated mounds of brush several times before they would flush. Coming out while you were poised unsteadily on the icy, spongy brush they made difficult shooting and I killed two, missed five, and started back pleased to have found a covey close to the house and happy there were so many left to find on another day.

At the house they said the boy had refused to let anyone come into the room.

"You can't come in," he said. "You mustn't get what I have."

I went up to him and found him in exactly the position I had left him, white-faced, but with the tops of his cheeks flushed by fever, staring still, as he had stared, at the foot of the bed.

I took his temperature.

"What is it?"

"Something like a hundred," I said. It was one hundred and two and four tenths.

"It was a hundred and two," he said.

"Who said so?"

"The doctor."

"Your temperature is all right," I said. "It's nothing to worry about."

"I don't worry," he said, "but I can't keep from thinking."

"Don't think," I said. "Just take it easy."

"I'm taking it easy," he said and looked straight ahead. He was evidently holding tight onto himself about something.

"Take this with water."

"Do you think it will do any good?"

"Of course it will."

I sat down and opened the *Pirate* book and commenced to read, but I could see he was not following, so I stopped.

"About what time do you think I'm going to die?" he asked.

"What?"

"About how long will it be before I die?"

"You aren't going to die. What's the matter with you?"

"Oh, yes, I am. I heard him say a hundred and two."

"People don't die with a fever of one hundred and two. That's a silly way to talk."

"I know they do. At school in France the boys told me you can't live with forty-four degrees. I've got a hundred and two."

He had been waiting to die all day, ever since nine o'clock in the morning.

"You poor Schatz," I said. "Poor old Schatz. It's like miles and kilometers. You aren't going to die. That's a different thermometer. On that thermometer thirty-seven is normal. On this kind it's ninety-eight."

"Are you sure?"

"Absolutely," I said. "It's like miles and kilometers. You know, like how many kilometers we make when we do seventy miles in the car?"

"Oh," he said.

But his gaze at the foot of the bed relaxed slowly. The hold over himself relaxed too, finally, and the next day it was very slack and he cried very easily at little things that were of no importance.

Your Writer's Journal

In "A Day's Wait," Ernest Hemingway tells a touching story about a boy who believes for an entire day that he is about to die. How effectively does Hemingway portray the characters of the narrator and Schatz? In your journal, note your responses to the story. Then use those responses to collect thoughts about similar situations you may have heard of or witnessed. Note your thoughts and ideas over the course of a week. After a week, reread your journal entries and think about how you might use your imagination to turn some of your ideas into short stories. In the margin next to your ideas, add an imaginative twist or turn to add creative angles to seemingly ordinary situations.

Elements of a Short Story

All short stories have three main sections: a beginning, a middle, and an end. Usually in the beginning of a story, the writer provides all the necessary background information that readers will need to understand and to enjoy the story. For example, readers will find out where the story takes place, who the main characters are, and what problem, or conflict, the main character has to solve or overcome. The middle of the story then develops the plot; that is, the writer relates—usually chronologically—what happens to the characters as a result of the conflict and how the characters react to those events. The ending of the story tells the outcome or shows how the central conflict is resolved.

For information about how the elements of a short story contribute to its meaning, turn to pages C481–C500.

Plot and Central Conflict

The **plot**—the sequence of events leading to the outcome or point of the story—is the story's core. The plot tells what happens as the characters meet and struggle to resolve a **central conflict**. This conflict can come from within a character, such as a conflict of conscience; between characters, such as a conflict between friends; or between characters and the outside world, such as a struggle against the forces of nature. The plot usually begins with an event that triggers the central conflict. Once the central conflict is revealed, the plot develops more quickly, bringing the story to a **climax**, or high point. After resolving the conflict (or explaining why it remains unresolved), the story ends.

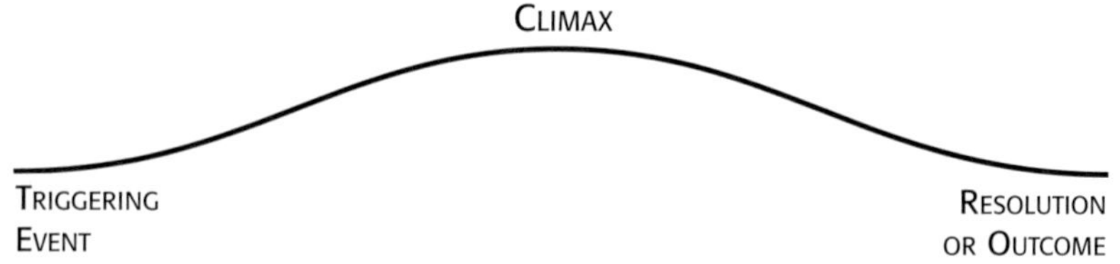

Characters

Most short stories focus on one main character who has or faces the conflict, or on two main characters whose relationship is often the source of the conflict. The other characters in the story—the minor, or supporting, characters—either help or hinder the main character in resolving the crisis. In the best short stories, **characters** are colorful, authentic, and memorable to readers in some way. Authors develop characters through narration, description, and dialogue.

Setting

The **setting** of a story is the environment in which the action takes place. It is like the backdrop of scenery and the props on a stage set. The setting also includes the time during which the story occurs.

One of the functions of a setting is to create a **mood**—the overall feeling that the story conveys. The mood of the setting might reflect the story's theme. A neglected park at dusk, for instance, might make a tale of suspense more suspenseful. An author might also plan settings that either match or contrast with the main character's mood. For example, a confused character might be lost at sea in a dense fog or might wander around in a perfectly ordered formal garden.

Narrator

The person who tells a story is the **narrator**. Readers see the events of a story through the eyes of the narrator, or from the narrator's **point of view**. The following chart describes the different points of view from which a story can be told.

POINT OF VIEW	NARRATOR'S ROLE IN THE STORY
FIRST-PERSON	Participant in the action; relates the events as he or she sees them; uses pronouns such as *I, me, we, us,* and *our*
THIRD-PERSON OBJECTIVE	Does not participate in the action; relates the words and actions of characters but not thoughts or feelings; uses pronouns such as *he, she, they, him, her,* and *them*
THIRD-PERSON OMNISCIENT ("ALL-KNOWING")	Does not participate in the action; relates the thoughts and feelings of all the characters as well as their words and actions

Each point of view has certain advantages. For example, the third-person objective narrator can relate two events happening simultaneously in different places. The omniscient narrator can relate not only simultaneous events but also all the characters' thoughts and feelings; that is, the inner life of the characters as well as the outer action. In the excerpt below, the narrator reports the characters' thoughts and feelings.

MODEL: Third-Person Omniscient Point of View

Neither [Mr. nor Mrs. Delahanty] wanted, in the midst of their sorrow for the good man whose life was ending, to enter into any discussion of Cress [their daughter]. What was the matter with Cress? What happened to her since she went away to college? She, who had been open and loving? And who now lived inside a world so absolutely fitted to her own size and shape that she felt any intrusion, even that of the death of her own grandfather, to be an unmerited invasion of her privacy. . . .

—*Jessamyn West,* Sixteen

Theme

Most short stories have a **theme,** or main idea, of some kind, such as the healing power of love, the rewards of showing courage, or the wastefulness of despair. The outcome of the story may then imply some lesson or moral about the theme, or it may affirm some meaningful observation or conclusion about life. However, some short stories aim chiefly to surprise or entertain readers rather than to give a message.

Practice Your Skills

Understanding Short Story Elements

Write answers to the following questions about *A Day's Wait* on pages C332–C335.

1. What is the plot of the story? Briefly outline the main events.
2. What is the central conflict? Briefly describe it.
3. Who are all the characters in the story? Which one is the main character and how do you know that?
4. What is the setting? Describe it in a few sentences.
5. From what point of view is the story told? How do you think that point of view affects the story?
6. What do you think the theme of the story is? Express the theme in a few sentences in your own words.

Author Kurt Vonnegut once compared writing fiction to making a movie, saying, "All sorts of accidental things will happen after you've set up the cameras. . . . You set the story in motion, and as you're watching this thing begin, all these opportunities will show up. Keeping your mind open to opportunities will help you imagine your story." Unless you think through the basic elements of your story, however, it may remain only as bits of "footage." For this reason your prewriting work should include building a plot.

Building a Plot

Many of your best ideas for a plot will come from your own experiences and observations, while others will come from your imagination. The following strategies may stimulate your thinking about plot ideas.

Strategies for Thinking of a Plot

- Brainstorm for a list of story ideas based on conflicts you have experienced or observed firsthand. Then use clustering or inquiring to develop plot details. For each conflict you think of, identify the triggering event and describe the resolution or outcome.
- Scan newspaper headlines and news items for an event you could build into a fictional story. Some items might suggest a comic or a tragic tale, for example, or might report a discovery or a mystery that you could explore in fiction.
- Think of conflicts or events in history—including your family history and local history—that might be interesting to develop in fiction writing.
- Observe people and events in your life. Sometimes even small events or snatches of conversation will suggest a conflict on which to build a plot. An incident that you noticed in a mall, for example, could become the basis of a story.

Once you have a story idea and a conflict, you can build the plot around it. A plot usually unfolds from the event that triggers the conflict to the event that resolves it. Therefore, you will need to arrange the details of your plot so that they naturally unfold as the story progresses. The following chart shows some steps for developing a plot, along with examples.

Strategies for Developing a Plot

1. Introduce the event or circumstance that triggers the action. Include descriptive details about the triggering event, making the source of the conflict clear.

From Within a Character	• the desire to change one's circumstances
From The Outside World	• the receipt of a letter or phone call • an accident

2. Develop details describing the nature of the conflict.

Conflict with Self	• one's conscience
Conflict with Others	• friend or family members • enemies or strangers
Conflict with Nature	• severe weather conditions • disease or disability

3. Develop details about the obstacles the characters will struggle against or overcome to resolve the central conflict.

Within a Character	• fears or other emotions
In the Outside World	• other characters • trials of nature

4. Develop details about how the main character might overcome the obstacles.

By the Character	• strength of character • perseverance
Through Outside Events	• luck or chance • new knowledge or understanding

5. Develop details about how the conflict will be resolved and how the story will end.

OBSTACLES OVERCOME	• new wisdom • success or satisfaction
OBSTACLES NOT OVERCOME	• acceptance of shortcomings • decision to try again

PRACTICE YOUR SKILLS

Developing Plots for Stories

Using the chart that starts on the previous page, briefly describe a possible plot based on each of the following triggering events.

1. A boy loses his wallet, which contains money he has saved to buy his mother a birthday present.
2. After some students have climbed a mountain, they realize that it will be dark before they can get down.
3. A girl discovers that her friend has been untruthful.
4. A man starts getting strange messages on the computer he is working on.
5. Two friends discuss dropping out of school.

Communicate Your Ideas

PREWRITING *Idea, Plot, and Conflict*

Using Strategies for Thinking of a Plot on page C340, generate possible plots for a short story. After you choose one plot, refer to Strategies for Developing a Plot on pages C341–C342 and make a chart or diagram to show how your plot might unfold around a central conflict. Imagining possibilities freely is the basis of all creative writing. When you are satisfied that you have some good ideas for a plot, save your notes in your writing folder. SAVE YOUR WORK

Sketching Characters

Readers usually enjoy and remember stories that have interesting, believable characters. As you plan your story, you should visualize the characters that will appear in it. You could, for example, write a brief sketch of each one by brainstorming for details such as the character's name, age, physical appearance, voice, mannerisms, background, and personality traits.

The more completely you visualize your characters, the more independent they can become in your imagination. Many fiction writers report that the characters themselves seem to come alive during writing, directing the plot and dictating the dialogue. In a sense, therefore, visualizing your characters gives them life. Notice how the following writer uses details that allow you to visualize the character.

MODEL: Characterization

> In the smallest of these huts lived old Berl, a man in his eighties . . . Old Berl was one of the Jews who had been driven from their villages in Russia and had settled in Poland. In Lentshin, they mocked the mistakes he made while praying aloud. He spoke with a sharp "r." He was short, broad-shouldered, and had a small white beard, and summer and winter he wore a sheepskin hat, a padded cotton jacket, and stout boots. He walked slowly, shuffling his feet. He had a half acre of field, a cow, a goat, and chickens.
>
> —*Isaac Bashevis Singer,* The Son from America

PRACTICE YOUR SKILLS

Sketching Characters

Imagine characters for each of the following scenes from short stories. Then write brief sketches of the characters you invented.

1. two men fishing from the end of a pier

2. two students doing their homework together

To help you develop characters, learn to be a careful observer. Focus on details of how people move and stand, how they sound, and how they look and dress. Make notes in your **journal** for use later. You can also create a cluster of details to help you. Your objective is to use such details to develop characters.

MODEL: Character Cluster

Character

- Name
- Age
- Family history
- Occupation and interests
- Physical characteristics
- Speech
- Mannerisms, expressions, habits
- Behavior toward others
- Attitude toward self
- Reactions of others to character
- Strengths
- Weaknesses

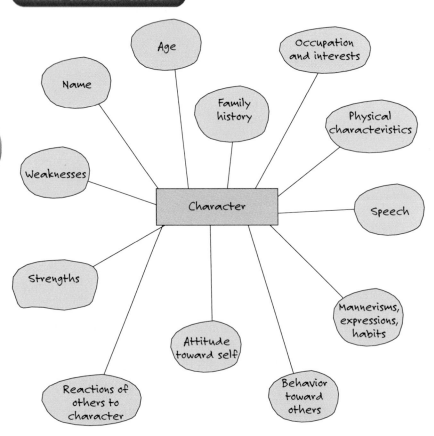

Communicate Your Ideas

PREWRITING *Characters*

After visualizing the characters that will appear in your story, write a brief character sketch of each one. Make a character cluster if you wish. Save your work. 

Imagining

To create characters and events, fiction writers often use **imagining**—visualizing and feeling what it would be like to be a character and to experience an imaginary event. If you take time for imagining as you plan, later you will more easily find the right words to express yourself when you draft your story. The following passages from "A Day's Wait" on pages C332–C335 are evidence of the author's imagining.

IMAGINING CHART

FOCUS FOR IMAGINING: Schatz's experience of his illness

Results of Imagining	Written Expression
in pain	"He was shivering, his face was white, and he walked slowly as though it ached to move." "He lay very still in the bed and seemed very detached from what was going on."
worrying about something he cannot discuss	"It would have been natural for him to go to sleep, but when I looked up he was looking at the foot of the bed, looking very strangely." "He was evidently holding tight onto himself about something."
realizing he is not dying	"He had been waiting to die all day, ever since nine o'clock in the morning."

THINKING PRACTICE

For ten minutes, use imagining to visualize the conversation in which Schatz's French classmates tell him that people die when their body temperature reaches forty-four degrees. Describe to your classmates what you "saw" and "heard" during your imagining.

Creating a Setting

When you have your plot and characters in mind, you can more fully visualize the main setting of your story, because the setting may mirror the feelings of the main character. By relating the setting to the central conflict and to the characters' feelings, you can create the mood you want for your story. In a sketch of your setting, you might note details you could use to describe the indoor or outdoor location where the action of the story takes place. For example, you might visualize objects, dimensions, terrain, the time of day, the weather, or the season of the year. Notice how the following description of a setting creates a suspenseful mood.

For more information about descriptive writing, turn to pages C284–C323.

MODEL: Details of a Setting

At the most remote end of the crypt there appeared another . . . Its walls had been lined with human remains, piled to the vault overhead, in the fashion of the great catacombs of Paris. . . . From the fourth side the bones had been thrown down . . . forming at one point a mound of some size. Within the wall thus exposed by the displacing of the bones, we perceived a still interior crypt or recess, in depth about four feet, in width three, in height six or seven.

–*Edgar Allan Poe,* "The Cask of Amontillado"

Sketching Settings

Choose three of the following imaginary situations. Then write a brief sketch of an appropriate setting for each one.

1. An exasperated Inspector Jylika finally finds the murder weapon in a woodchuck hole.
2. While waiting, fifteen-year-old Cara suddenly feels insignificant and small.

3. Humming with satisfaction, old Mrs. Santos arranges flowers for the church.
4. Hunched tensely in concentration, a small boy enters the world of his action figures.
5. Drained of energy, Michael sinks to the ground.

Communicate Your Ideas

PREWRITING *Setting*

Determine the mood you want to convey in your short story and imagine an appropriate setting in detail. After writing a sketch of the setting in the form of a summary or list of details, save it in your writing folder.

Choosing a Point of View

As you learned on page C338, you can choose among three different points of view for telling your stories: first-person, third-person objective, and third-person omniscient. If you are writing a story with a narrator who is a participant, the first-person point of view is probably the most natural. If the narrator is writing about other characters and is not a participant in the story, use third-person objective or omniscient. Use the same point of view throughout your story.

Practice Your Skills

Writing from Different Points of View

The following portion of a narrative is written from a first-person point of view. Rewrite it from either the third-person objective or the third-person omniscient point of view.

We might have drowned if it hadn't been for Rhonda. She rooted us out of bed just in time to get from our bunk beds to the big old willow. How Rhonda knew there was a wall of water rolling down the valley, I'll never know. Craig, who always said that even pet pigs belong in a pen, had put Rhonda out after I was asleep. I don't know what Craig has against pigs, but for once I was glad he'd acted behind my back. It was Rhonda's frantic efforts to get back in that saved us.

Writing Tip

Plot, characters, setting, point of view, and other story elements should all fit together so that the reader believes in the story and finds meaning in it.

Communicate Your Ideas

PREWRITING *Point of View*

Review your prewriting notes for the story that you have been developing. Imagine how your story would read if it were told from the point of view of your main character and from that of each of the other characters. Next, imagine how your story would sound if it were told from the first-person, the third-person objective, and the third-person omniscient points of view. Finally, choose the best point of view for your story, make a note of your decision, and save it in your writing folder.

Ordering Events

When you have developed the central conflict, plot, characters, and setting, and have chosen the narrator's point of view, you are almost ready to begin drafting. First, however, you should visualize all the events you want to include in your story and arrange them in chronological order. You may later decide to deviate from this order. For instance, you could start your story at the end and then go back to the beginning, or you could start in the middle and remember back to the beginning in a **flashback** before ending your story. Whatever order you decide to use when you draft, you will find it helpful to have a chronological list of all the events you plan to include.

Practice Your Skills

Ordering Events in a Story

List the events of "A Day's Wait" in the order in which they are written. Are there any flashbacks in the story, or is its order chronological?

Using a Story Map to Understand Sequence of Events

A story map is a useful tool in helping you track the order of events in the story as well as to understand their relation to the entire story. Make a copy of the story map below and fill it in to help you track the sequence of events.

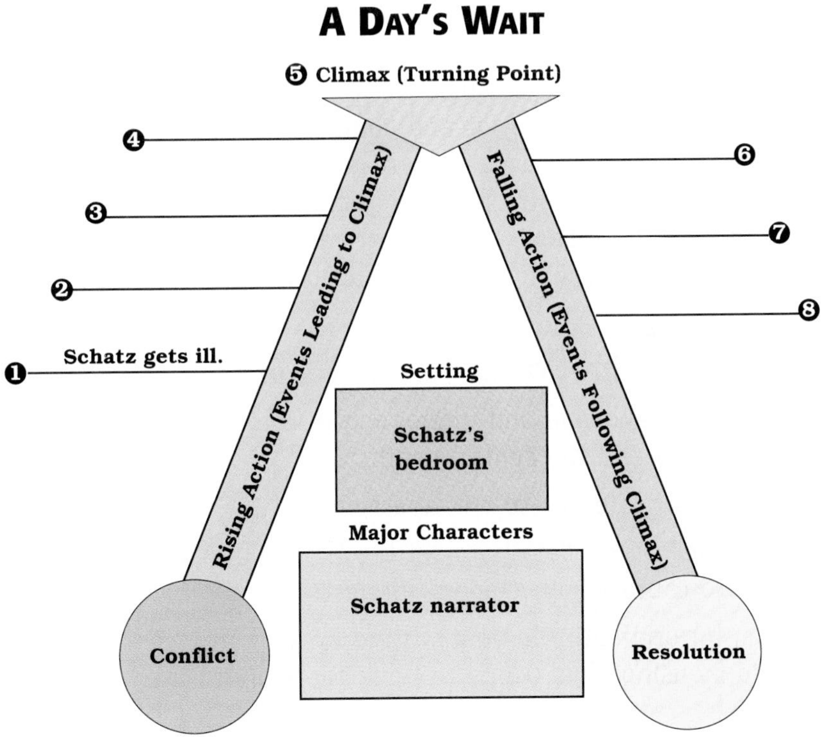

A Day's Wait

❺ Climax (Turning Point)

❹

❸

❷

❶ Schatz gets ill.

Rising Action (Events Leading to Climax)

Falling Action (Events Following Climax)

❻

❼

❽

Setting

Schatz's bedroom

Major Characters

Schatz narrator

Conflict

Resolution

Communicate Your Ideas

PREWRITING *Order of Events*

After you list all the events you plan to include in your story, arrange them in chronological order. As you study your list, think of other possible ways to order the events that would make sense to readers and would capture their interest. Then save your organized list of events and your ideas for other possible ways to order them in your writing folder to use when drafting your story.

Drafting

Writing Process

As you write your story, keep in mind your reasons for writing and your audience. While the purpose of all creative writing is to create, you may have particular writing goals. For example, you may want your readers to laugh or cry, or you may want them to identify with your main character. To achieve these purposes, you have available a variety of types of writing. For instance, you can use narrative writing to advance the plot. You can use descriptive writing to create the settings and characters' appearances *(pages C284–C323)*. Informative writing allows you to explain background information about the plot or characters *(pages C90–C145)*. In addition to these basic types of writing, you can use the following strategies, which are specific to fiction writing.

Strategies for Drafting a Short Story

- Use vivid language and interesting details to introduce the characters and the central conflict.
- Use sensory details to create a mood.
- Use background details to set the time and place of the story and to capture your readers' interest.
- Aim for originality in your writing by avoiding stereotypes and by using vivid words to bring the story to life.

- Start the plot early in the story by introducing the triggering event.
- Reveal the characters and unfold the plot through a combination of description; narration, or action; and dialogue.
- Maintain a clear and consistent point of view.
- Include only those events that have a direct bearing on the plot and the central conflict. Connect the events in your story by showing how each event in the plot relates naturally and logically to the central conflict.
- Use chronological order and transitions to show the passing of time and to build up tension.
- End your story in a way that makes the outcome clear and that leaves a strong emotional impression on your readers.

Using Dialogue

In many cases you can use dialogue to develop your characters and to advance your plot. The following examples from "A Day's Wait" show how the author used dialogue for a variety of purposes.

Model: Using Dialogue

To Present the Central Conflict

When the doctor came he took the boy's temperature.

"What is it?" I asked him.

"One hundred and two."

To Reveal Thoughts

After a while he said to me, "You don't have to stay in here with me, Papa, if it bothers you."

"It doesn't bother me."

"No, I mean you don't have to stay if it's going to bother you."

I thought perhaps he was a little light-headed and giving him prescribed capsules at eleven o'clock I went out for a while.

To Advance the Plot

"You can't come in," he said. "You mustn't get what I have."

I went up to him and found him in exactly the position I had left him, white-faced, but with the tops of his cheeks flushed by fever, staring still, as he had stared, at the foot of the bed.

I took his temperature.

"What is it?"

"Something like a hundred," I said. It was one hundred and two and four tenths.

"It was a hundred and two," he said.

"Who said so?"

"The doctor."

"Your temperature is all right," I said. "It's nothing to worry about."

"I don't worry," he said, "but I can't keep from thinking."

"Don't think," I said. "Just take it easy."

To Express the Climax

"About what time do you think I'm going to die?" he asked.

"What?"

"About how long will it be before I die?"

"You aren't going to die. What's the matter with you?"

"Oh, yes, I am. I heard him say a hundred and two."

"People don't die with a fever of one hundred and two. That's a silly way to talk."

"I know they do. At school in France the boys told me you can't live with forty-four degrees. I've got a hundred and two."

To Express the Resolution

"You poor Schatz," I said. "Poor old Schatz. It's like miles and kilometers. You aren't going to die. That's a different thermometer. On that thermometer thirty-seven is normal. On this kind it's ninety-eight."

"Are you sure?"

"Absolutely," I said. "It's like miles and kilometers. You know, like how many kilometers we make when we do seventy miles in the car?"

"Oh," he said.

Practice Your Skills

Writing Dialogue

Imagine each of the following situations. Then select one of the situations or another of your choice and write a dialogue about 12 lines long between the characters. You may want to review the correct form for writing dialogue on the preceding pages.

1. A stranger asks for directions to the police station.
2. A hurried shopper seeks help from a salesclerk.
3. A student has a conference with his or her advisor.
4. Two teenagers discuss someone else's problem.
5. Two friends argue over what movie to see.

Communicate Your Ideas

DRAFTING *Conferencing*

After you review all your prewriting notes, write the first draft of the short story you have been developing. Use the Strategies for Drafting a Short Story on pages C350–C351, but as you write, let your imagination roam freely. Add fresh details and new ideas as you think of them. If you get stuck, skip that part and continue writing another part that you have visualized more fully. Although you should try to get all the way to the end of your story, you may go back and work on any part of it at any time. Use peer conferencing to test your ideas or to get help with trouble spots. Keep writing until you have a workable first draft. Save your work.

Many fiction writers report that they often keep only the few best parts of a first draft and drop all the rest. When you revise, therefore, be ready to give up ideas or details that weaken your short story or that rob it of life. Look especially for ways of strengthening your plot, enhancing your descriptions, and sharpening your characterizations.

Revising Strategies for Short Stories

Strengthening the Plot

- Add background details and transitions to ensure adequate development and coherence.
- Delete any plot details that do not relate to the central conflict and its resolution.
- Check for clarity to ensure that readers will understand the story's meaning, point, or theme.

Enhancing Descriptions

- Add or substitute sensory details to enliven descriptions of characters, settings, and actions.
- Use imaging to visualize your descriptions again so you can improve them.
- Enrich your descriptions by using figurative language.

Sharpening Characterizations

- Add or eliminate details to sharpen the characterization of your main character.
- Look for ways to reveal characters and their motivations through dialogue and action.
- Rewrite dialogue until it sounds as natural as real-life conversations.

After you have applied the revising strategies above, review the structure and content of your story. The following checklist will help you remember the basic points to look for as you revise your short story.

Evaluation Checklist for Revising

✓ Does the beginning of your story describe the setting, capture the readers' attention, introduce characters, and include the triggering event? *(pages C336–C346)*

✓ Does the middle develop the plot by making the central conflict clear and by including events that are directly related to that conflict? *(pages C336–C337* and *C340–C341)*

✓ Are events in the plot arranged in chronological order or in an order that makes the chronology of events clear? *(pages C348–C349)*

✓ Does the story build until the action reaches a climax? *(pages C336–C337)*

✓ Did you use dialogue and description to bring your characters to life? *(pages C350–C353)*

✓ Does the ending show how the conflict was resolved and bring the story to a close? *(pages C336–C337)*

✓ Did you choose an appropriate point of view and stick to it throughout the story? *(pages C338 and C347–C348)*

✓ Does the story have a theme or express your reasons for writing it? Does it accomplish your specific purpose for creative writing? *(page C339)*

Practice Your Skills

Sharpening Characterization

Add, eliminate, and rearrange details in the following passage to sharpen the characterization and to enhance the description. Provide transitions as you write.

She sat in the tree with her journal. She had black hair and was not unpretty. She wore a blouse and jeans. She was barefoot. From her serious expression, you could see she had something important to write about. She liked hiking and playing the flute.

Communicate Your Ideas

REVISING

Revise your story using the **Revising Strategies for Short Stories** on page C354 and the checklist on page C355. Then save it for editing.

COMPUTER TIP

Use the global search-and-replace function of your word-processing software if you decide to change the name of a character or place as you revise. Pull down the Edit menu, and click Replace. Do this for words, phrases, or even punctuation marks that you want to change throughout an entire story.

Edit View Insert Fo
Can't Undo ⌘Z
Can't Repeat ⌘Y
Cut ⌘X
Copy ⌘C
Paste ⌘V
Paste Special...
Paste as Hyperlink
Clear
Select All ⌘A
Find... ⌘F
Replace... ⌘H
Go To... ⌘G
Links...
Object
Publishing

Editing

Writing Process

Once you have drafted your short story and revised it to your satisfaction, you are ready to edit it. In the editing stage, you correct your writing so that it shows accurate spelling, punctuation, and capitalization, as well as control over grammatical elements such as subject-verb agreement, pronoun-antecedent agreement, verb forms, and parallelism.

You may become so familiar with your work that you miss errors. Putting your writing aside long enough to give you some distance will help you see mistakes. You may want to use the checklist on page C358 as you edit your work.

Prewriting Workshop
Drafting Workshop
Revising Workshop
Editing Workshop
Publishing Workshop

Pronouns

To write strong dialogue, you need to choose the appropriate pronouns. A **pronoun** is a word that takes the place of a noun. Pronouns have different cases, or forms, for different uses. **Nominative case** pronouns are used as subjects and predicate nominatives; they include *I, you, he, she, it, we,* and *they*. **Objective case** pronouns are used as objects; they include *me, you, her, it, us,* and *them*. **Possessive case** pronouns indicate possession or ownership. They include *my, mine, your, yours, his, her, hers, its, our, ours, their,* and *theirs*.

Nominative Case	**I** can't work after school and play football too.
Objective Case	I don't want **him** to be like me!
Possessive Case	It's **my** job. It's **my** responsibility!

Standard and Nonstandard Speech

Keep in mind that in real life, people do not always speak grammatically—they do not always speak standard English. In order to make dialogue realistic, playwrights often write nonstandard English on purpose. For example, a nonstandard sentence may use the objective case of a pronoun instead of the nominative case.

Standard	**Your mama and I** worked that out between us.
Nonstandard	**Me and your mama** worked that out between us.

In writing formal papers, such as reports for school, always write standard English. In writing dialogue, write the way your characters would really speak.

To write dialogue clearly, you will need to understand how to use quotation marks correctly.

Quotation Marks with Dialogue

When writing dialogue, use quotation marks to enclose a person's exact words. Put the opening quotation marks before the first word a person says and the closing quotation marks after the last word.

> He said, **"**No, I'm a stranger here.**"**

Capitalization and Indentation with Dialogue

Begin each sentence of a direct quotation with a capital letter. Also begin a new paragraph each time the speaker changes, using indentation to show that the speaker has changed.

> "I'll introduce you to people. I know everybody."
>
> "Everybody?" he asked.

Commas and End Marks with Dialogue

Use a comma to separate a direct quotation from the speaker tag—the words that identify the speaker—for example, *she said* or *he replied*. If the speaker tag comes at the end of the sentence, place the comma inside the closing quotation marks. If the quotation ends the sentence, place the end marks inside the closing quotation marks.

> "Well, almost everybody**,**" she admitted modestly.
>
> He said, "I think I'm going to be glad I know you**.**"

Editing Checklist

✔ Have you used the correct case of each pronoun?

✔ Have you correctly punctuated, capitalized, and indented all dialogue?

Communicate Your Ideas

EDITING

Use the preceding checklist and the one on page C48 to edit your story. Make sure you have punctuated, capitalized, and indented all dialogue correctly. When you are pleased enough with your story that you are eager to have others read it, write a final copy.

Publishing

Writing Process

After editing your work, prepare a neat final draft to share with your intended audience. Your audience might include classmates, family, friends, and other readers interested in your subject.

Communicate Your Ideas

PUBLISHING

After writing a title page and possibly illustrating your story, publish it by giving it to your teacher and classmates to read. Consider making your story available to a wider audience through your school newspaper or literary journal.

PORTFOLIO

Writing a Play

The main difference between plays and other kinds of writing is that plays are written to be performed, not just read. In a play, the story is told through the use of dialogue and the actions of the characters.

A **play** is a piece of writing intended to be performed on a stage by actors.

In the following scene from Arthur Miller's *The Price*, a husband and wife discuss the idea of asking his brother for help. As you read the scene, think about your responses to the following questions: Why should the content in this play be performed and not just read? What makes this play a success or failure and why?

The Price

Esther: I don't want to be a pest—but I think there could be some money here, Vic.

He is silent.

You're going to raise that with him, aren't you?

Victor, *with a formed decision:* I've been thinking about it. He's got a right to his half, why should he give up anything?

Esther: I thought you'd decided to put it to him?

Victor: I've changed my mind. I don't really feel he owes me anything, I can't put on an act.

Esther: But how many Cadillacs can he drive?

Victor: That's why he's got Cadillacs. People who love money don't give it away.

Esther: I don't know why you keep putting it like charity. There's such a thing as a moral debt. Vic, you made his whole career possible. What law said that only he could study medicine—?

Victor: Esther, please—let's not get back on that, will you?

Esther: I'm not back on anything—you were even the better student. That's a real debt, and he ought to be made to face it. He could never have finished medical school if you hadn't taken care of Pop. I mean we ought to start talking the way people talk! There could be some real money here.

Victor: I doubt that. There are no antiques or—

Esther: Just because it's ours why must it be worthless?

Victor: Now what's that for?

Esther: Because that's the way we think! We do!

Victor, *sharply:* The man won't even come to the phone, how am I going to—?

Esther: Then you write him a letter, bang on his door. This *belongs* to you!

Victor, *surprised, seeing how deadly earnest she is:* What are you so excited about?

Esther: Well, for one thing it might help you make up your mind to take your retirement.

A slight pause.

Victor, *rather secretively, unwillingly:* It's not the money been stopping me.

Esther: Then what is it?

He is silent.

I just thought that with a little cushion you could take a month or two until something occurs to you that you want to do.

Victor: It's all I think about right now, I don't have to quit to think.

Esther: But nothing seems to come of it.

Victor: Is it that easy? I'm going to be fifty. You don't just start a whole new career. I don't understand why it's so urgent all of a sudden.

Esther—*laughs:* All of a sudden! It's all I've been talking about since you became eligible—I've been saying the same thing for three years!

Victor: Well, it's not three years—

Esther: It'll be three years in March! It's *three years*. If you'd gone back to school then you'd almost have your Master's by now; you might have had a chance to get into something you'd love to do. Isn't that true? Why can't you make a move?

Victor—*pause. He is almost ashamed:* I'll tell you the truth. I'm not sure the whole thing wasn't a little unreal. I'd be fifty-three, fifty-four by the time I could start doing anything.

Esther: But you always knew that.

Victor: It's different when you're right on top of it. I'm not sure it makes any sense now.

Esther, *moving away, the despair in her voice:* Well . . . this is exactly what I tried to tell you a thousand times. It makes the same sense it ever made. But you might have twenty more years, and that's still a long time. Could do a lot of interesting things in that time. *Slight pause.* You're so young, Vic.

Victor: I am?

Esther: Sure! I'm not, but you are. God, all the girls goggle at you, what do you want?

Victor—*laughs emptily:* It's hard to discuss it, Es, because I don't understand it.

Esther: Well, why not talk about what you don't understand? Why do you expect yourself to be an authority?

Victor: Well, one of us is got to stay afloat, kid.

Esther: You want me to pretend everything is great? I'm bewildered and I'm going to act bewildered! I*t flies out as though long suppressed:* I've asked you fifty times to write a letter to Walter—

Victor, *like a repeated story:* What's this with Walter again? What's Walter going to—?

Esther: He is an important scientist, and that hospital's building a whole new research division. I saw it in the paper, it's his hospital.

Victor: Esther, the man hasn't called me in sixteen years.

Esther: But neither have you called him!

He looks at her in surprise.

Well, you haven't. That's also a fact.

Victor, *as though the idea were new and incredible:* What would I call him for?

Esther: Because, he's your brother, he's influential, and he could help—Yes, that's how people do, Vic! Those articles he wrote had a real idealism, there was a genuine human quality. I mean people do change, you know.

Victor, *turning away:* I'm sorry, I don't need Walter.

Your Writer's Journal

In this scene from *The Price,* Victor and Esther discuss his unwillingness to go back to college to get a graduate degree. In your journal record the exchanges that reveal the most information about the characters or their situation. Think about a conversation you have taken part in or witnessed recently. Put yourself in the scene so it comes alive in your mind and you almost see and hear what is going on. Ask yourself whether a stranger listening in would have understood all that was happening. Note in your journal several such conversations that you can remember. You may be able to use such notes later as a source of ideas for a dramatic scene.

Finding Ideas for a Play

Like stories and novels, plays are based upon conflict. A conflict can occur between two or more people: To find possible subjects for a play scene, think about conflicts you have seen and heard—or just heard of. They may come from your own life, the lives of people you know, or your imagination. Freewrite about some of them in your **journal.** Visualize them in all their drama. Use other prewriting techniques that you like, too, such as clustering or self-questioning.

PRACTICE YOUR SKILLS

Finding Ideas for a Scene in a Play

Freewrite a response to each question below. Elaborate with details. Save your work.

1. What is the most dramatic conflict that you have lived through, witnessed, or heard about?
2. What events in the news or in history have made you feel most strongly?
3. Who are the most interesting two or three people you know, and why? What might happen if they clashed?
4. How would you change if, in a few years, you lived through a major event such as war, serious illness, or falling in love?
5. What might you be like if you had grown up in a different family or a different place?
6. What would be the most surprising thing that could happen to you today? How would you respond? How would it change you?

Characters

As in stories and novels, characters are the basis of plays. In plays, the characters are brought to life by actors, real people who move and talk and have individual gestures and tones of voice. Each actor shapes a role in his or her own special way, but the character must be vividly brought out by the playwright's words.

PRACTICE YOUR SKILLS

Sketching Characters

Return to your answer to Question 3 in the previous activity. For each of the people you named, write a character sketch. Each sketch should be a paragraph describing the important facts

and details about the person. An actor preparing to play the role of the character should be able to learn a lot from the sketch. You may want to copy and complete the herringbone diagram below onto a sheet of paper to help you develop your character.

Characters

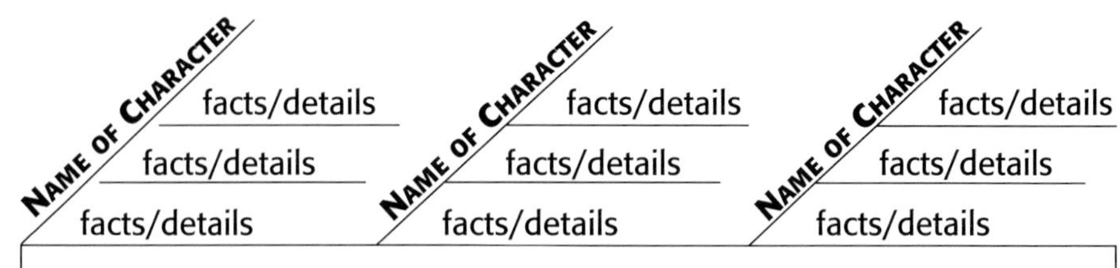

Setting

Novels, stories, and movies can wander from setting to setting: the action might be on Earth one minute and on Mars the next. In contrast, most plays remain within a very limited setting. It may be one room. That is the simplest of settings, for it requires no changes of scenery. If a play contains more than one setting—such as several rooms within a house, or the apartments of two different characters—the scenery must be changed, usually between acts. One of the playwright's first jobs is to visualize an interesting, dramatic setting that can be shown physically on a stage.

PRACTICE YOUR SKILLS

Visualizing Settings

Make a list of five or six places in your community that might make good settings for stage plays. For each location, state briefly your reason for thinking it would make a good stage setting. Be sure your settings are specific enough to be physically shown on a stage. For example, "school" is not a specific setting, because an entire school cannot be shown onstage at one time. "The gym" is specific enough to be shown in that way.

Dialogue

Because plays consist of live action, and because one of the things that makes human life interesting is talk, most plays contain a lot of **dialogue**—that is, the words spoken by the characters. Dialogue is the medium in which the action in most plays transpires; it expresses emotion and conveys meaning. It is through dialogue, in fact, that the audience is informed of the dramatic situation and its background.

As in a story, the dialogue in a play should seem real. Each character should have his or her own personal way of speaking. In addition, the dialogue in plays needs to deliver information to the audience. Keep in mind that the audience watching a play is not reading any descriptions or any background information. Everything that the audience learns about the characters must be conveyed through action and dialogue. For example, if a character returned home injured from a war five years before the play began, some character at some point is probably going to say something like, "Well, it's been five years since Jill came home from that war with her arm in a cast." The need to express information and characterization at the same time makes the dialogue in plays particularly rich in content.

PRACTICE YOUR SKILLS

Writing Dialogue

Write a conversation between a teenager and his or her parent in which the two characters disagree about the teen's goals. Set the conversation in a community like your own, and have the characters be people from a background similar to yours. Write at least two separate speeches for each character. Write only the dialogue; do not include descriptions. Save your work.

Stage Directions

Playwrights usually supply some directions for the reader (and the actor and director) about how the characters speak and move. These are called **stage directions**. They are usually found in italic print. Most modern playwrights like to keep their stage directions short. They feel that the dialogue itself should convey most of what the audience learns about the characters. For example, if the character's words are angry, it should not be necessary to add a stage direction, *Angrily.* Stage directions are necessary at times, however. For instance, they state which characters are entering or exiting. They also express meaningful actions, such as *He stands slouched over, and Troy shoves him on his shoulder.* They may even say when a character falls down dead! At the beginning of a play, there is usually a brief description of the set; when a new character appears, there is usually a brief physical description of the character, perhaps including how the character is dressed. **Props**—short for *properties,* or physical objects that appear on stage—are also mentioned in stage directions.

Practice Your Skills

Writing Stage Directions

Return to the parent-teen dialogue you wrote, and add at least two stage directions. Make sure that they express aspects of the characters' speech or actions that the dialogue does not already express.

Communicate Your Ideas

SCENE FROM A PLAY

Write a dramatic scene. It can be on any subject you choose. Use the suggestions on subjects, characters, setting, dialogue, and stage directions to help you craft your scene. Write a first draft, and then read it aloud to a friend to make sure the dialogue sounds real. Then revise, thinking about how to strengthen your dialogue and how to make the action more vivid and believable. Make a final copy, using the same play script format as in the scene from *The Price*. You might even want to gather a group of classmates or friends and give a live or videotaped performance of your scene.

Across the Media: Evaluating Artistic Performances

Some literary works—even nondramatic ones—cannot be fully appreciated until they are performed. This process can in fact help both the performer and the audience understand the work more fully. Books on tape, poetry and short story readings on the radio, and literary television shows attract faithful listeners and viewers.

How can you tell if such an artistic performance is effective? Here are some of the criteria that may help you evaluate artistic performances.

Criteria for Evaluating Artistic Performances

1. Does the performance move you?
2. Does the performance make confusing parts clearer?
3. Are the performers confident and well prepared?
4. Did the performers establish eye contact and use effective body language?
5. Do the performers use vocal variety to express the work's underlying meanings?
6. Does the performance use the stage effectively, with variety of pacing and use of space?
7. For example, are camera angles, lighting, editing, and music used effectively? How do they contribute to the overall effect?

Media Activity

Use the criteria above to evaluate the following:

- The poem "On the Pulse of the Morning" by Maya Angelou, read at President Clinton's first-term inauguration in 1993 available at: http://virtual.park.uga.edu/~erochest/eng101/texts/angelou.html Practice reading it aloud and take turns performing it for the class.
- An audio recording of this work read by Angelou. (The last stanza is online as an audio file at: http://ucaswww.mcm.uc.edu/worldfest/about.html #audio.)
- A video presentation of a literary work.

Writing a Poem

"Poetry is the art of understanding what it is to be alive," wrote Archibald MacLeish. Even before writing was invented, poets sang or chanted the deepest feelings of humanity, and people listened. Poetry is a way of using language that gets the most out of each word and syllable.

Poetry is a writing form that expresses powerful feelings through sound, images, and other imaginative uses of language.

Feel how much is expressed in so few words as you read this poem written by Walt Whitman. Think about how these feelings would be expressed in a play or a short story.

When I Heard The Learn'd Astronomer

When I heard the learn'd astronomer,
When the proofs, the figures, were ranged in columns
before me,
When I was shown the charts and diagrams, to add,
divide, and measure them,
When I sitting heard the astronomer where he
lectured with much applause in the lecture-room,
How soon unaccountable I became tired and sick,
Till rising and gliding out I wander'd off by myself,
In the mystical moist night-air, and from time to time,
Look'd up in perfect silence at the stars.

Your Writer's Journal

Look through the journal entries you have made in this course, and make a new entry that lists the ideas, experiences, descriptions, or individual words and phrases that seem to you to be the most powerful. You will be able to use this entry as a starting point when you search for a subject for a poem.

Finding Ideas for Poems

Poetry is the form of writing that depends most upon the emotions of the writer. In choosing a subject for a poem, the important thing is to find something that moves you. It may move you to joy, to sadness, to anger, to laughter, or to any other emotional response. One good way to discover the emotionally powerful ideas that are already within you is to make an Idea Chart like the one below. List general subject areas on the left side of the chart. Write down some specific examples on the right-hand side. You can explore those examples further by additional brainstorming, freewriting, clustering, or questioning.

IDEA CHART

Events	getting an A; buying shoes; playing trumpet
Scenes	an empty schoolyard at night; a crowded beach; a sailboat skimming the waves
Sensations	the sound of a subway train; the taste of hot peppers; the sight of sunset

Practice Your Skills

Charting to Find Ideas for a Poem

Create an idea chart using the following general topics as the left-hand entries. Think of at least five examples for each topic. Save your work.

1. growing up
2. emotions
3. places
4. hopes and dreams
5. imaginary worlds

Freewriting to Find Ideas for a Poem

Select one of the specific examples you wrote in your Idea Chart, and freewrite about it for two to five minutes. Save your work.

Using Sound Devices

How words sound is extremely important in poetry. Not only can the sounds of the words be beautiful in themselves, but they can make beautiful connections among ideas in a poem. Through a hard-to-define verbal magic, the sounds of the words can highlight the poem's meaning and affect how the reader feels.

Poets use certain sound devices to please the ear and to stir the emotions. Use some of these devices when you write a poem.

SOUND DEVICES	
ONOMATOPOEIA	Use of words whose sounds suggest their meaning hum, splash, whistle, hoot, murmur, fizz
ALLITERATION	Repetition of a consonant sound or sounds at the beginning of a series of words **B**aa, **B**aa, **b**lack sheep
CONSONANCE	Repetition of a consonant sound or sounds, used with different vowel sounds, usually in the middle or at the end of words the pa**tt**er of li**tt**le fee**t**
ASSONANCE	Repetition of a vowel sound within words the b**o**wling ball r**o**lled **o**ver and **o**ver

Repetition Repetition of an entire word or phrase

> O **Captain**! my **captain**! **rise up** and hear the bells;
> **Rise up**—**for you** the flag is flung—**for you** the bugle trills
>
> —*Walt Whitman,* "Oh Captain! My Captain!"

Rhyme Repetition of accented syllables with the same vowel and consonant sounds

> The woods are lovely, dark, and **deep,**
> But I have promises to **keep,**
> And miles to go before I **sleep**
>
> —*Robert Frost,* "Stopping by Woods on a Snowy Evening"

Rhythm and Meter

Almost all poems have **rhythm**—a sense of flow produced by the rise and fall of accented and unaccented syllables. In many poems, the rhythm is a specific beat called a **meter**. The accented and unaccented syllables of metered poetry follow a regular, countable pattern like the beats of a piece of music. In the lines below, the accented syllables are marked with ′ and unaccented syllables are marked with ˘. Read the lines and notice the strong, regular rhythm.

> Týger, týger, búrning bríght,
> Ín the fórests óf the nígh́t:
> Whát immórtal hánd or eýe
> Could fráme thy féarful sýmmetry?
>
> —*William Blake,* "The Tyger"

Poetry without meter is called **free verse**. Poems in free verse have rhythm, but not a regular, patterned beat. "When I Heard the Learn'd Astronomer" is free verse like most of Walt Whitman's poems. Its rhythm comes from repetition, variation, and the natural flow of speech.

The Loon on Oak-Head Pond

cries for three days, in the gray mist.
cries for the north it hopes it can find.

plunges, and comes up with a slapping pickerel.
blinks its red eye.

cries again.

you come every afternoon, and wait to hear it.
you sit a long time, quiet, under the thick pines,
in the silence that follows.

as though it were your own twilight.
as though it were your own vanishing song.

–Mary Oliver

Practice Your Skills

Developing Sound Devices

Write a series of statements on the subject Life at School, as follows. Your statements may be either in prose or in verse, but they must contain the listed sound devices.

1. a statement containing rhyme
2. a statement containing alliteration
3. a statement containing assonance
4. a statement using a strong rhythm
5. a statement using onomatopoeia

Using Figurative Language

Good readers see mental pictures of the things they read about, and good poets help them by using **figurative language** that is vivid and imaginative. The following chart illustrates the major kinds of figurative language.

FIGURATIVE LANGUAGE

Imagery use of visual details or details that appeal to other senses

Cold and raw the north wind blows
Bleak in the morning early.
All the hills are covered with snow
And winter's now come fairly.

—Nursery Rhyme

Simile comparison using the words *like* or *as*

My love is like a red, red rose

—*Robert Burns,* "My Love is Like a Red, Red Rose"

Metaphor implied comparison that does not use *like* or *as*

Life is a broken-winged bird
That cannot fly.

—*Langston Hughes,* "Dreams"

Personification use of human qualities to describe something non-human

Because I could not stop for Death—
He kindly stopped for me—

—*Emily Dickinson,* "Because I Could Not Stop for Death"

Hyperbole use of extreme exaggeration or overstatement

And fired the shot heard 'round the world.

—*Ralph Waldo Emerson,* "Concord Hymn"

Oxymoron use of opposite or contradictory terms such as *living death, black snow, happy to be sad*

Symbol use of an object or action to stand for another, as William Blake's tiger is a symbol of nature's untamed natural destructiveness

Tyger, tyger, burning bright,
In the forests of the night:
What immortal hand or eye
Could frame thy fearful symmetry?

—*William Blake,* "The Tyger"

Practice Your Skills

Developing Figurative Language for Poems

Return to the subject of Life at School, which you wrote about in the previous activity. Now write statements (in prose or verse) as follows.

1. a statement using imagery
2. a statement using a simile
3. a statement using a metaphor
4. a statement using personification
5. a statement using hyperbole
6. a statement that includes an oxymoron
7. an explanation of how some object in school is a symbol for some idea or quality

Choosing a Form

As you have seen, a poem can take the form of rhymed or unrhymed verse; it can be metered or free verse. Sometimes, a poet knows the form of a poem before writing a word; at other times, a poem may go through major changes of form at different stages of the writing process. The form of a poem should fit its subject, mood, and tone. For example, if your subject is a snake slithering quickly through the grass, you might choose the form of free verse in short lines to create a lively, dashing rhythm. In contrast, if your subject is the tragedy of world hunger, you might choose to write longer lines in a strong, solemn meter. If you are writing a comic poem, you might use bouncy, simple rhymes; if you are expressing deep, sincere feeling, you might omit rhyme. At times, you might find yourself writing a poem in a certain form simply because it feels right, without being able to explain exactly why.

If you choose to write in rhyme, you will need to use a **rhyme scheme**—a regular pattern of rhyming. A poem's rhyme scheme can be shown by letters of the alphabet. Each rhyming sound gets its own letter.

a It was many and many a year ago,
b In a kingdom by the sea,
a That a maiden there lived whom you may know
b By the name of Annabel Lee;
c And this maiden she lived with no other thought
b Than to love and be loved by me.

—*Edgar Allan Poe,* "Annabel Lee"

The six lines from "Annabel Lee," above, make up one stanza of that long poem. A **stanza** is a group of lines that the poet decides to set together. A space should be left between stanzas; sometimes, stanzas are numbered. There are some specific kinds of stanzas in English, such as the **quatrain** (four lines). You do not need to choose stanzas of a specific length, but if you do, you should be consistent.

Communicate Your Ideas

POEM

Write a poem on a subject of your own choice. It may be inspired by your **journal** entries or another source. Use the suggestions on pages C371 and C374 and your notes from practice activities to develop sound devices and figurative language. Choose a form for your poem—decide whether it will be rhymed or not, and metered or free verse. After writing a first draft, obtaining feedback from your peers, and rereading it yourself, make any changes you feel would improve it, including changes of form. Read the final draft aloud to interested classmates or friends. Gather your poem, with others by your classmates, into a class anthology.

Time Out to Reflect

You have had opportunities to write a story, play scene, and poem in this chapter. Which form do you prefer working in and why? How has your experience in writing a story, a play, and a poem changed since you read this chapter? Which skills do want to practice more?

A Writer Writes

A "Why" Story

Purpose: **to entertain**

Audience: **your classmates**

Prewriting

Use your imagination to create a "why" story that explains the origin of a phenomenon of nature, such as thunder and lightning or the changing of the seasons. A "why" story explains how and why such a phenomenon came into being—and usually does so in an unexpected and imaginative way.

Throughout history people have made up "why" stories. The Greeks and Romans created stories about gods to explain every important process of nature, such as the rising and setting of the sun. The Native Americans of the southeastern United States told a "why" story to explain the origins of Spanish moss. According to the story, a young Native American mother and her two children were caught by surprise in a hurricane that sent floodwaters rising. To escape drowning, the mother climbed the nearest tree, carrying her babies. After the storm, the air turned sharply colder and the mother feared that she and her children would die from the cold. Despite the cold, however, they slept. When they awoke, they were wrapped in a furry gray blanket, which had kept them warm and saved their lives. According to the story, a loving spirit of nature had provided this blanket—Spanish moss, which has hung on trees throughout the South ever since.

Plan your "why" story by looking through your **journal** and brainstorming for any wonders of nature that you find intriguing. After choosing one, plan the plot of your story, including a central conflict, a triggering event, a climax, and a resolution.

After planning the plot, sketch your characters, establish your setting, and decide on the point of view.

Drafting

Using your prewriting work, draft a version of your "why" story. Follow a chronological order to unfold the plot from its triggering event to its resolution. Unlike the simple summary of the story about Spanish moss, take the time during drafting to fully develop your story. Add details that bring the characters and setting to life. Use dialogue, description, and narration.

Revising

Read your story aloud, listening particularly for the natural sound of the dialogue. Then use the **Evaluation Checklist for Revising** on page C355 to revise your draft.

Editing

Use the **Editing Checklist** on page C358 to go over your final draft, looking for mistakes.

Publishing

After preparing a neat final copy, add it to a classroom anthology of "why" stories. Consider illustrating your story and putting a copy on file in the library.

Process of Writing Stories, Plays, and Poems

Remember that you can move back and forth among the stages of the writing process to achieve your purpose.

Writing a Short Story

PREWRITING

- Choose a conflict and a theme. *(pages C336–C339)*
- Sketch all the characters for your story. *(page C343)*
- Choose a point of view for your story. *(page C347)*
- Match the setting of your story to the action, mood, and characters' feelings. *(page C337)*
- Plan a plot with a high point and resolution. *(pages C336–C337)*
- Use chronological order except for flashbacks. *(pages C348–C349)*
- Build and develop the plot. *(pages C340–C342)*

DRAFTING

- Draft a beginning that interests the reader and introduces the setting, the main character, and the conflict. *(pages C336–C346)*
- Use transitions, dialogue, and descriptive details. *(pages C350–C351)*
- Draft an ending that resolves the conflict and completes the action of the plot. *(page C337)*

REVISING

- Revise plot, characterization, and style. *(pages C354–C355)*
- Use the **Evaluation Checklist for Revising** to improve your story. *(page C355)*

EDITING

- Use the **Editing Checklist** *(page C358)* to check your story for errors in grammar, usage, spelling, and mechanics.
- Punctuate, capitalize, and indent dialogue. *(pages C357–C358)*

PUBLISHING

- Prepare a final copy and publish your work. *(page C359)*

Writing a Play

- Develop characters who are involved in dramatic conflicts. *(pages C364–C365)*
- Select a stage-specific setting. *(page C365)*
- Use dialogue to convey emotion and information. *(page C366)*
- Use stage directions at appropriate moments. *(pages C366–C367)*

Writing a Poem

- Use sound devices in your poem. *(pages C371–C372)*
- Use figurative language. *(pages C373–C374)*
- Write rhymed verse or free verse. *(pages C372–C373)*

Connection Collection

Representing in Different Ways

From Print . . .

"The Boy in the Butter": Scene 12

A Boy is taking his chimpanzee friend Bobo for a walk in the country. Along the way, Bobo sees a large banana tree loaded with fruit and slips off his leash. He grabs a bunch of bananas from the tree and scampers away. The Boy follows a trail of banana peels until he comes to an ice cream factory.

. . . to Visuals

Draw a storyboard for a cartoon that shows four separate panels from "The Boy in the Butter."

From Visuals . . .

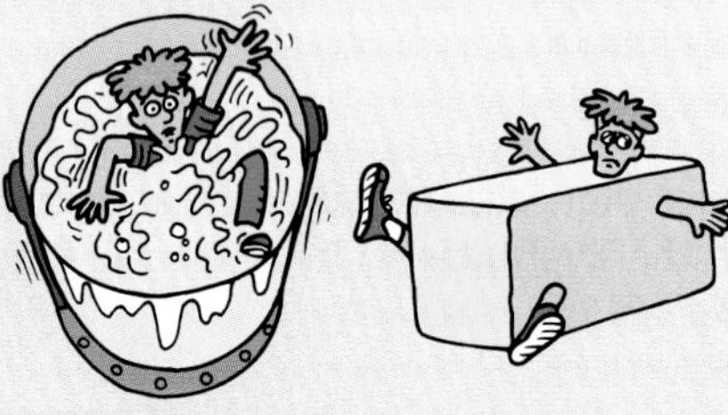

. . . to Print

You have just finished creating a cartoon version of "The Boy in the Butter," a story written by your sister, who is a famous author. She likes the cartoon so much that she has asked you to write a sequel! She has given you the four above storyboard panels. Decide how the boy gets from slipping on the banana peel to the block of butter, and write a brief story for your sister. Pay special attention to specific details and vivid sensory language in your story.

- **Which strategies can be used for creating both written and visual representations? Which strategies apply to one, not both? Which type of representation is more effective?**
- **Draw a conclusion, and write briefly about the differences between written ideas and visual representations.**

Writing in Everyday Life

Poem About a Place

Your friend is creating a new poetry magazine called *Places with Faces* that will feature work by famous poets about places they fondly remember from their childhood. Your friend does not know any famous poets, so she asks you to write the first poem of the inaugural issue.

Write a poem, 15 to 20 lines long, for your friend's magazine. Vividly describe a special place from your childhood and how you felt when you were there. Use examples of the different types of sound devices and figurative language you have learned: simile, alliteration, consonance, assonance, onomatopoeia, rhyme, repetition, and metaphor.

What strategies did you use to describe the place in your poem?

You can find information on writing poetry on pages C369–C376.

Writing in Academic Areas

Humorous Poem

On Friday afternoons you volunteer as a teacher's assistant for a class of sixth graders. The students are currently studying poetry. Their teacher, Mrs. Quatrain, has noticed that you have quite a knack for writing poems yourself and has asked you to compose a humorous poem for the students.

Write a poem, 15 to 20 lines long, for the students to examine. To help them learn about poetic devices, Mrs. Quatrain has asked that you include at least three of the following in the poem: a simile, metaphor, oxymoron, personification, or hyperbole.

What strategies did you use to make the poem humorous and instructive for the students?

You can find information on writing poetry on pages C369–C376.

Writing in the Workplace

Narrative E-mail

This morning you were ten minutes late for work. When you arrived, the boss's secretary was not happy, and he vowed he would report your lateness. You have a good reason for being late, but you admit it is very hard to believe. You decide to write an E-mail to your boss to explain your reason.

Write an E-mail to your boss explaining why you were late for work. Use the narrative form, with first-person point of view. Keep the events of your story ordered in a concise and chronological manner. Try to include strong and vivid physical and sensory details that will make your boss believe your story.

What strategies did you use to explain to your boss why you were late?

You can find information on writing E-mails in A Writer's Guide to Using the Internet, *pages C724–C767.*

Writing for Oral Communication

Dramatic Scene

You work for WACT, a public radio station devoted to producing radio dramas. Your boss has finally given you a chance to write a short dramatic scene to be performed during the ten minutes of free airtime before the 3 A.M. news. Your boss gives you only one requirement for the scene—it has to be exciting enough to keep the late-night audience awake!

Write a lively scene for a radio drama that will be performed by two or three actors. During the prewriting stage, consider the setting and make character sketches. Then perform the scene with other members of your class.

What strategies did you use to write your play scene?

You can find information on writing plays on pages C360–C367.

Assess Your Learning

Congratulations! You have been chosen to submit an entry for a book of short stories that will be published next year about the life experiences of contemporary American high-school students. Although all the entries will be very short pieces of fiction—no more than 1,000 words long—the editors want you to base the stories on your own experience.

- **Write a short story about an extremely important moment in your life. Use the third-person point of view.**
- **Spend time prewriting before you begin your story. Include important and vivid details, but strive to be concise within the length limits the editors have set. Use background details to set the time and place of the story and to capture your reader's interest. Be sure the story has a beginning, middle, and end. Decide what conflict was at the center of your important moment, and try to resolve this conflict by the end of the story.**

Before You Write **Consider the following questions:**
What is the ***subject?***
What is the ***occasion?***
Who is the ***audience?***
What is the ***purpose?***

After You Write **Evaluate your work, using the following criteria:**

- Have you used vivid language and interesting details to introduce the characters and the central conflict?
- Have you used background details to set the time and place of the story and to capture your readers' interest?
- Have you written the story in the third-person and does this point of view stay clear and consistent throughout the story?
- Have you ended your story in a way that makes the outcome clear and leaves a strong emotional impression on your readers?
- Have you proofread your story for spelling, capitalization, and punctuation errors?

Write briefly on how well you did. Point out your strengths and areas for improvement.

CHAPTER 9

Writing to Inform and Explain

Whenever you write a letter, a postcard, an E-mail message, a journal entry, or a report in which you provide information on a subject—from what you did last night to an assignment for school—you are using informative writing skills. Examples of informative writing are everywhere—in newspapers, magazines, books, manuals, and reports; in television news and documentary programs; in news and information programming on radio; and on Websites.

You rely on informative writing in your everyday life: to obtain information you need, to obtain information that interests you, and to communicate information that you want to share.

This chapter will help you develop strategies for sharing your understanding—of the world and the way it works—with others.

Reading with a Writer's Eye

In "Mercury, Gemini, and Saturn," Joy Hakim tracks the early history of the United States space program that led to the first moon landing. As you read this article, pay attention to what you are learning about the early days of space travel. Notice how Hakim has narrowed the broad subject of space exploration to a time period that can be covered in a short article.

FROM

MERCURY, GEMINI, AND SATURN

Joy Hakim

Some 4 billion years ago, a small planet hurtled onto Earth and sent exploding pieces into the atmosphere. Those objects circled the earth, collided, collected, and became the moon. The earth and the moon eventually settled into a gravitational balance about 239,000 miles apart, with the moon orbiting Earth and its pull influencing the oceans' tides.

It was a long time before earthlings appeared; when they did, they watched the moon and the cycles of its appearance, and they planted crops when the moon seemed to tell them to do it. They told stories of the moon, and dreamed by its bright, reflected light. So it was not surprising, when we actually pushed ourselves off the surface of the earth, that the moon was where we wanted to go.

It was an outrageous idea, to expect to leave the earth's atmosphere and make it to that distant globe, especially in the very century that people had first learned to fly.

We might not have tried it at all if it hadn't been for Russia. When the Russians sent a vehicle into space—called *Sputnik*—we couldn't quite believe it. We Americans had the idea that we were better than others. It was a kind of national arrogance. We aren't better or smarter than other people. (What we have is a terrific idea—for free government—that is the envy of a lot of other nations and has helped most of us pursue happiness.)

But scientific achievement? We have to work as hard as anyone else to make and do things. Russia's *Sputnik* got us energized. We didn't want our communist foes to take over space.

Then, in April 1961, the Russians sent a man rocketing into space. His name was Yuri Gagarin,[1] and he had a boyish grin and a lot of courage. When he came back to earth he landed in a field where he startled a cow and two farm workers. "Have you come from outer space?" stammered Anya Takhtarova to the man in the orange flight suit. "Yes. Would you believe it, I certainly have," said cosmonaut Gagarin.

The United States had a space agency, NASA (the National Aeronautics and Space Administration), and a space program—but we were behind the Russians, and we couldn't stand that idea.

President John F. Kennedy made a speech announcing our intention to put a man on the moon "before the decade is out." We were off on a space race.

What would life be like in space? On the earth, it is the pull of gravity that keeps your legs on the ground. But when there is zero gravity—as in space—there is no pull. You float around. You have no weight. If you eat a cookie in space, the crumbs float. If you want to sleep in a bed, you have to be strapped down. Other things have to be considered. Normal breathing is impossible in the vacuum of space; a spacecraft or spacesuit has to be equipped with its own atmosphere.

A trip to the moon would be a voyage like the one that Columbus made. No one knew where it might lead. Would we create colonies in space? Would we mine the moon's resources? Would we put factories in space and return the earth to its gardenlike heritage? Would we explore other galaxies? Would we meet other beings out there?

This moon trip became the will of a nation. It took the talent of thousands of brains, it took the lives of some astronauts (who were killed in explosive misfires), and it cost $25.5 billion, which came from the earnings of America's citizens.

---

[1] Yuri Gagarin: Russian astronaut (1934–1968).

The first step toward the moon was a flight into space. Alan B. Shepard was squeezed into a spacesuit in a space capsule just big enough to hold him. This was the *Mercury* project, named for the swift messenger of the ancient Roman gods. (The craft was called *Freedom 7*). . . .

Next came *Gemini*, named for twin stars. They were two-man flights intended to test rendezvous (meeting) and docking techniques. *Gemini* met a target vehicle, named *Agena*; the spacecraft touched noses and clamped themselves together. The *Gemini* astronauts walked outside the capsule—into outer space—but with a cord that firmly tied them to their vehicle.

The Gemini spacecraft was a big improvement over Mercury. It was bigger and could be steered by the astronauts.

On the morning of July 16, 1969, five months before President Kennedy's deadline of the end of the decade (Richard Nixon was now president), the sun was bright and the skies were clear at Cape Canaveral on Florida's east coast. Some 8,000 people were packed into a special viewing area; others jammed nearby roads and beaches. Photographers in TV helicopters flew overhead taking pictures of the crowds and of the good-luck messages written in beach sand.

Nearby, three men sat strapped elbow to elbow inside a narrow capsule on top of a rocket that stood as tall as a 30-story building. Neil Armstrong, a civilian pilot, was in the left seat. Some said he was the nation's best jet test pilot. Armstrong had the personality of a cowboy-movie hero: cool. Edwin E. Aldrin sat in the middle. Everyone called him by his school nickname, Buzz. Buzz Aldrin was an air force colonel with a big brain. Some of his scientific ideas had gone into this mission. Michael Collins, another air force officer and test pilot, was to pilot the command ship, which would orbit the moon while the other two men descended to the lunar surface in the landing vehicle.

The rocket—named *Saturn*—belched fire and its own billowing clouds, lifted off, and seemed to rise slowly. But that was an illusion; after two and a half minutes *Saturn* was 41 miles above Earth. It was traveling at 5,400 mph (miles per hour) when its first stage fell away. (How fast can an automobile go? How about a commercial jet?)

The next stage took the astronauts 110 miles above Earth, carrying them at 14,000 mph, and was jettisoned (dropped away). The third stage got them to 17,400 mph; they were now weightless and orbiting the earth. It was 17 minutes after liftoff. After they had circled the globe twice, the third-stage engine fired the ship away from Earth's orbit. "It was beautiful," said Armstrong. He was cruising toward the moon. It would take three days to get there.

(Three days was the time it took Thomas Jefferson to make the 90-mile trip, in a horse-drawn carriage, from his plantation at Monticello to his plantation at Poplar Forest.)

Everyone on Earth went on this trip. Television took us into space and then put us on the rocky, craggy, pockmarked moon. When two men stepped out of the landing vehicle, we were there—all the peoples of the earth. It was an American spaceship, but it was a world event.

Neil Armstrong stepped onto the moon's crunchy soil and said, "One small step for man, one giant leap for mankind." It was an understatement. The man in the moon was now real, and we were standing with him.

The view from the moon was of one Earth—it was not one of small, separate nations. Perhaps the next bold journey would be one that the united nations of the earth would take together.

Thinking as a Writer

Evaluating Quantity and Quality of Information

"Mercury, Gemini, and Saturn" informs by providing a variety of details about the U.S. effort to land a crewed space vehicle on the moon in the 1960s.

- Imagine you are writing a report on the major activities of the U.S. space program in that same decade. Your first source is Joy Hakim's article. Do you have enough information or do you need to seek out other sources? Decide why or why not, using details from the article to support your thinking.
- Then sort the information in the article by importance. Which details are critical to understanding the effort to land a person on the moon? Which details add fascinating information that clarifies a point or makes an event more interesting and vivid?

Capturing a Reader's Attention

Oral Expression

- Imagine you are a volunteer tutor in a sixth-grade classroom. The class is learning about the effort to land on the moon. One student you are tutoring tells you that "all this space stuff is boring." Choose a paragraph or passage from the selection that you think would make the sixth grader see how interesting and exciting the study of space exploration can be.
- With a partner, read aloud what you have chosen. Discuss each other's choices. Do you both agree that what you've read is an exciting, vivid way to present information? Do you both agree that your selected reading would appeal to a sixth grader?

Acquiring Information from a Photograph

Viewing Work in a small group of three or four students. Study the photograph below, which was taken during the first moon landing in 1969. Freewrite to find information that can be acquired from the photograph. Then, as a group, think of a caption for the photo that summarizes the most important information communicated.

The Power of Informative Writing

You have read one example of an informative essay—a piece of writing that informs on a particular subject. You may read many other examples of informative writing every day.

Uses of Informative Writing

The following examples show informative writing at work. They demonstrate a few of the many ways that people depend on informative writing.

- **A high school student gives an oral report** on the history of the National Aeronautics and Space Administration (NASA).
- **A newspaper sportswriter reviews the highlights** of a local team's championship season.
- **A club secretary uses notes** from the last meeting to write the minutes, a record of what happened and what was decided.
- **A health and beauty magazine publishes a feature** on the 20 best foods and the 20 worst foods for your body.
- **A television writer creates a script** for a documentary on the behavior of gorillas in the wild.
- **A NASA employee updates the agency's Website** with text, photographs, and video clips that summarize activities and outcomes from the latest space mission.

Process of Writing an Informative Essay

"It is better to know some of the questions than all of the answers," said James Thurber. For an informative writer, that is good advice to remember. In writing an essay that informs, you first need to ask some important questions—such as what your audience needs and wants to know about a subject. If you know the right questions to ask, you can find the answers that will make your informative essay interesting and instructive to your readers.

An **informative essay** presents information or offers an explanation.

Your Writer's Journal

In your journal, keep track of subjects that interest you. For example, you might want to know more about what you watched in a documentary on television or read in a magazine. For each topic, make a journal entry about what you learned and what new questions you have. In this way, you'll compile a list of subjects that you might use later for your writing.

Prewriting

Writing Process

The prewriting stage of the writing process helps you discover possible subjects for an informative essay, develop your ideas, and shape those ideas into an organized plan. Planning and writing an informative essay on a subject that interests you can lead you to new knowledge and understanding.

Discovering and Choosing a Subject

Subjects for informative essays may come from your own interests and knowledge or from your reading or research. The first step in discovering subjects for informative essays is to identify those subjects that you already know about from your own experiences. For example, through an activity, hobby, or job, you may have learned enough about a favorite sport, a software game, or baby-sitting to write about one of those subjects.

Strategies for Finding Subjects for Informative Essays

- Brainstorm or freewrite to list subjects that you know well enough to explain.
- Ask yourself questions about your interests and skills.
- Review your **journal** entries to find possible subjects that are suitable for explaining or informing.
- Skim books, newspapers, and magazines for subjects that interest you.
- Read your notes from courses in other subject areas to find possible subjects.
- View television documentaries or educational television programs to discover subjects that you would like to explore in writing.
- Search for interesting contemporary topics on the Internet.

After you think of a number of possible subjects, the next step is to choose one. Choose a subject that you know enough about to explain or can learn about through reading or research. The subject you choose should also be one that you will enjoy writing about and your audience will enjoy reading.

Determining Your Audience

Sometimes your choice of a subject will depend in part on who will be reading your essay. A classmate, a teacher, and a school newspaper editor, for example, may prefer to read about quite different subjects. At other times, however, you will be able to choose both your subject and the audience you wish to write for. For example, you may decide to write an essay about synthesizers for an audience of musicians and others who are interested in electronic keyboards.

Whether you choose a subject to suit your audience or choose an audience for the subject you want to write about, you will need to take into account the interests, knowledge, opinions, and needs of your audience.

You can learn more about analyzing an audience on pages C22–C23.

Communicate Your Ideas

PREWRITING *Subjects*

List ten possible subjects for an informative essay. For ideas, look back at your **journal** and use other suggestions in the strategies on the previous page. Then review your list and choose one subject as the topic of your informative essay. Write a brief explanation about why you think this subject is a good one and what audience you would write for. Save your work for later use.

SAVE YOUR WORK

Limiting and Focusing a Subject

Many informative subjects—such as the subject of space exploration—may be too broad to be developed adequately in a short essay. Therefore, after you choose a subject, you usually need to narrow, or limit, it. To limit a subject, think of specific aspects or examples of it. If your new subjects are still too broad, continue the process of limiting by thinking of specific aspects or examples of your narrower subjects. The example on the next page shows how a writer might limit the subject of space exploration to arrive at subjects suitable for a short essay.

Subject: Space Exploration

Limited Subjects	More Specific Subjects
early space flights	moon probes
firsts in space	first moon landing
Soviet achievements	*Sputnik*
space flight projects	*Skylab*
space encounters	*Vega*'s encounter with Halley's Comet

After you have limited a subject, your next step is to find a focus for your thoughts. One way to find a focus is to make a preliminary survey of your subject by reading about it in a reference book or searching the Internet. Another way is to brainstorm general questions you could ask about the subject, based on what you know about it.

For example, if you chose moon probes as your limited subject, you might decide to focus on the adventures of *Surveyor I* as an example of an early moon probe, or you might focus on the question of what new facts scientists learned from moon probes before the astronauts' first moon landing.

Strategies for Focusing a Subject

- Focus on a specific event or incident.
- Focus on a specific time and place.
- Focus on one example that best represents your subject.
- Focus on one person or group that represents your subject.

The example on the next page shows how a limited subject may have more than one possible focus.

LIMITED SUBJECT: *Sputnik*

POSSIBLE SUBJECT FOCUSES	
	• how *Sputnik* started a space race between the United States and the Soviet Union
	• the story of Laika, first dog in space on *Sputnik II*
	• the effect of *Sputnik* on education in the United States
	• how *Sputnik II* differed from *Lunik I*—the first missile to reach the moon
	• why putting an object into orbit for the first time was so difficult

PRACTICE YOUR SKILLS

Limiting and Focusing a Subject

Limit each of the following general subjects. Then write two phrases that can serve as a focus for each limited subject.

1. astronomy
2. planets
3. weather
4. space movies
5. geography
6. Mars landing

Communicate Your Ideas

PREWRITING *Focused Subject*

Review the subject you chose for your informative essay. Then make a list of limited subjects. Continue to limit your subjects until each one is narrow enough to be developed adequately in a short essay. Use reference materials, if necessary, to find ideas. After you choose one limited subject, think of ways to focus it, using the strategies on page C395. Then save your focused subjects.

COMPUTER TIP

If you have an Internet connection, you can use a search engine to help you limit a subject. Go to your favorite search engine site, or start with one of the following:

www.yahoo.com	www.metacrawler.com
www.excite.com	www.hotbot.com

Follow the screen directions to enter your subject. Then review the matches for topics that limit the subject. You might do searches of those more limited subjects too. Bookmark sites with useful information to return to later, when you are ready to research your subject in detail.

Gathering Information

Once you have a focused subject, you should then gather more information that will help you explain it clearly to your reader in an essay of three or more paragraphs. Use brainstorming, freewriting, clustering, inquiring, or researching to explore your subject and find details that will help you to inform others about it.

Collect as much information as possible so that you will be able to choose the details that will best explain your subject. Your list may include any of the types of details shown in the box below. Remember that the type of detail often indicates the best method of development for your paragraphs.

You can learn more about gathering information on page C393 and about methods of development on pages C39–C40.

TYPES OF DETAILS USED IN INFORMATIVE ESSAYS		
facts and examples	analogies	similarities
reasons	incidents	differences
steps in a process	definitions	causes and effects

The following prewriting notes, list facts and examples for an essay about firsts in space exploration. As you read the notes, notice that the information is not yet arranged in any logical order.

MODEL: Gathering Information

SUBJECT FOCUS	firsts in space exploration
FACTS AND EXAMPLES AS DETAILS	• Alan Shepard first American in space—1961 • 1969—first crewed moon landing (U.S.) • June 1965—first American space walk • first space walk (USSR, March 1965) • Yuri Gagarin first Soviet in space—1961 • 1963—first Soviet woman in space • *Explorer I*—first U.S. satellite (1958) • *Sputnik*—first satellite (USSR, 1957)

PRACTICE YOUR SKILLS

Identifying Types of Details

Read the following sentences from *Mercury, Gemini, and Saturn*. Use the chart on page C397 to identify the types of details the writer has used.

1. The moon trip became the will of the nation.
2. Armstrong had the personality of a cowboy movie hero: cool.
3. Some 4 billion years ago, a small planet hurtled onto Earth and sent exploding pieces into the atmosphere.
4. On the earth, it is the pull of the gravity that keeps your legs on the ground.
5. A trip to the moon would be a voyage like the one Columbus made.
6. They told stories of the moon, and dreamed by its bright, reflected light. So it was not surprising, when we actually

pushed ourselves off the surface of the earth, that the moon was where we wanted to go.

7. Other things have to be considered. Normal breathing is impossible in the vacuum of space; a spacecraft or spacesuit has to be equipped with its own atmosphere.
8. [I]n April 1961, the Russians sent a man rocketing into space.
9. When there is zero gravity—as in space—there is no pull.

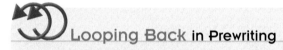

Communicate Your Ideas

PREWRITING *Information Gathering*

Review the limited subject that you chose for your informative essay. Choose one focus for your subject and then gather information on this topic. Use reference books and other sources, including the Internet. Refer to the chart Types of Details Used in Informative Essays on page C397 for guidance as you do research on your subject. Save your work for later use.

Looping Back in Prewriting

Limiting and Focusing a Subject

If the resources available to you lack detailed information about the focus you chose for your limited subject, go back to your list of focus ideas and choose a different one. Your goal is to gather enough supporting details to develop a short informative essay.

Developing a Working Thesis

As you gather information, a main idea for your essay will begin to emerge. At this point you should express this emerging main idea as a **working thesis**—a preliminary statement of what you think the main idea will be. For example, as you look over the details on page C398 about firsts in space exploration, you see that the United States achieved many firsts. Therefore, you could write the following thesis.

Working Thesis	The United States achieved many firsts in the development of its space program.

This working thesis would guide you in selecting information to use in your essay. That is, you would select details from the list only about firsts in the United States space program. You would not, however, use the information that refers to the Soviet space program. If you wanted to include information about achievements in space by both the United States and the Soviet Union, you could broaden your working thesis.

Working Thesis	The United States and the Soviet Union both achieved firsts in space exploration.

As you can see, a list of details can lead to several different theses. As you gather and think about information, you may wish to modify your working thesis. You may find the following steps helpful in developing a working thesis.

Steps for Developing a Working Thesis

- Look over the information you have gathered.
- Express the main idea you plan to convey.
- Select the details you will use to support your main idea.
- Check that the working thesis takes into account all of the information you selected to include in your essay.

Writing Tip

Think of a **working thesis** as a place to start in identifying the main idea of your informative essay. You can revise a working thesis as many times as needed to include new details that will make your essay more interesting and informative.

PRACTICE YOUR SKILLS

Developing a Working Thesis

Study the following details and cross out any items that would not help you to explain the focused subject. Then use the remaining items to develop a working thesis for an essay.

SUBJECT the effects of *Sputnik* on education in the United States

INFORMATION

- *Sputnik*—first artificial satellite, launched by the Soviets in 1957
- caused Americans to worry that the Soviets were more advanced in science education
- news media reported "crisis in education"
- Congress voted National Defense Education Act in 1958
- government spent $1 billion to teach science in the schools

Communicate Your Ideas

PREWRITING *Working Thesis*

Review the information that you gathered on your essay subject. Using the Steps for Developing a Working Thesis on the previous page, develop a working thesis for your informative essay. Then select relevant ideas and details from your research notes and list them. Then, if necessary, find more information or discard information that does not relate to your thesis. You may need to revise your working thesis to be able to include more of the information you have. Save your working thesis and list of relevant supporting details for later use.

Writing Is Thinking

Evaluating Information for Relevance

To decide which ideas and details to include in an essay, evaluate the information for **relevance** by asking yourself the following questions: Is it appropriate for my purpose in writing? Does it relate directly to my working thesis? Will it help me support or prove my thesis? Study the following prewriting notes. Which ideas and information, do you think, lack relevance to the given thesis?

	THESIS STATEMENT	The chambered shell of the nautilus has long fascinated marine biologists.
1.	SUPPORTING IDEA	The nautilus is a marine mollusk.
	DETAILS	• soft-shelled sea animal • lives in warm waters of South Pacific
2.	SUPPORTING IDEA	The nautilus grows a unique shell with many chambers.
	DETAILS	• adds chambers as it grows • moves into new chamber and closes old one
3.	SUPPORTING IDEA	Oliver Wendell Holmes was inspired to write a poem about the nautilus.

The first idea and its details are relevant because they describe the subject. The second idea and details are also clearly relevant because they are about the shell of the nautilus. The third idea, however, is not directly relevant.

THINKING PRACTICE

Explain why item 3 above is not directly relevant. Then refine the thesis statement to make this item relevant to an essay about the nautilus.

Organizing Your Essay

In planning an informative essay, you will usually be handling a great deal of information, so you will have to organize the information by developing an outline. Before you start an outline, you should group your information into categories and then arrange those categories in a logical order.

Grouping Information into Categories

A **category** is a group, or class, of related pieces of information. In the list of firsts in space exploration on page C398, for instance, the information could be grouped into two categories: the United States space program and the Soviet space program.

To group information, write your categories at the top of a sheet of paper, listing information under the appropriate column. The following examples show how an astronaut might have categorized some of the information viewing Earth from space.

MODEL: Classifying Details

CATEGORY 1 **Geography seen from space**	CATEGORY 2 **Signs of civilization**
• Antarctic ice flows	• Great Wall of China
• Ganges River	• irrigated land
• Caribbean Sea	• airports
• mountain ranges	• city lights at night
• "boot" of Italy	• oil slicks
• Sahara desert	• piers in large harbors

PRACTICE YOUR SKILLS

Grouping Details

Using the article "Mercury, Gemini, and Saturn," group the following list of details under each of the two categories.

1. *Gemini* missions in space

2. *Saturn* moon mission

two-man flights   first space walks   test docking techniques

three-man crew	three stages	cord tied astronauts
three-day voyage	July 16, 1969	to capsule

Creating Categories

Study the following groups of details from "Mercury, Gemini, and Saturn" to determine what they have in common. Write a word or phrase that creates a specific category name for each group.

3. *Sputnik*
Freedom 7
Agena

4. ocean tides
cycles
reflected light

5. space shuttle
space capsule
landing vehicle

6. Yuri Gagarin
Alan Shepard
Neil Armstrong

Communicate Your Ideas

PREWRITING *Categories and Details*

Organize the list of supporting details for your informative essay. First group related details together. Then develop categories and arrange your groups of details under those categories. These groupings of ideas and information will later form the supporting paragraphs of your essay. Save your work for later use.

Arranging Categories in Logical Order Once you have grouped your information into categories, you should then arrange those categories in the order in which you want to include them in your essay. The type you choose will depend partly on your subject and partly on your thesis. For example, the thesis that radioactivity is more common in nature than most people think lends itself to an organization based on order of importance or developmental order. The thesis that radioactivity was an important discovery in the history of science, on the other hand, suggests chronological order. The following chart uses some commonly used types of logical order. The examples show how Joy Hakim arranged information in "Mercury, Gemini, and Saturn."

TYPES OF ORDER	
CHRONOLOGICAL ORDER	Information is presented in the order in which it occurred.
EXAMPLE	**first** lifting off, **then** orbiting the Earth, **finally** reaching the moon
SPATIAL ORDER	Information is given according to location.
EXAMPLE	41 miles **above** Earth; 110 miles **above** Earth; 239,000 miles **to** the moon.
ORDER OF IMPORTANCE	Information is given in order of importance, interest, size, or degree.
EXAMPLE	*Mercury* space capsule, *Gemini* spacecraft, *Saturn* rocket **(increase in size and speed)**
DEVELOPMENTAL ORDER	Information of equal importance is arranged to lead up to a conclusion.
EXAMPLE	moon trip united Americans; view from space is of one Earth—space exploration has the potential to unite nations **(conclusion)**
COMPARISON/CONTRAST	Information is arranged to point out similarities and differences.
EXAMPLE	Astronauts reached moon by spacecraft in three days—the same amount of time required for Thomas Jefferson to make a 90-mile trip in a horse-drawn carriage. **(comparison)**

Practice Your Skills

Ordering Details in a Category

Review the list of details on page C398 on firsts in space exploration. Select the details that belong under the category of firsts in the American space program. Then decide on a type of order for those details, and arrange them accordingly. Explain your reasoning for the type of order you choose.

Ordering Categories

Review the two categories of details in the practice activity *Grouping Details* on pages C403–C404. Order those categories for an essay on space exploration. First decide how you would order them chronologically, and explain your reasoning. Then choose a different type of order, arrange the categories, and explain your reasoning.

Organizing Comparison and Contrast If you have chosen to compare and contrast two subjects in your essay, you have two ways to organize your information. One way is to write first about one subject and then about the other subject. For example, if you were comparing *Mercury* flights (subject A) to *Gemini* flights (subject B), you would first write all your information about subject A (*Mercury* flights). Then you would write all your information about subject B (*Gemini* flights). For convenience this is called the **AABB pattern** of comparison and contrast.

You could use the *AABB* pattern within a paragraph by discussing subject *A* in the first half of the paragraph and subject *B* in the second half. As an alternative, you could use the *AABB* pattern in two paragraphs by discussing subject *A* in the first paragraph and subject *B* in the second one. The following portion of an essay shows how the *AABB* pattern works.

MODEL: AABB Pattern of Organization

Conflict Between the North and the South

As Americans pushed westward during the early 1800s, conflict grew between the North (subject *A*) and the South (subject *B*). Since the nation's early days, the northern and southern parts of the United States had followed different ways of life. Each section wanted to extend its own way of life to the western lands.

(A)The North had a diversified economy with both farms and industry. **(A)Northern farmers** raised a variety of crops that fed the thriving northern cities. **(A)Mills and factories in the North** competed with Great Britain in making cloth, shoes, iron, and machinery. For both its farms and factories, **(A)the North** depended on free workers. Such workers could move from place to place to meet the needs of industry. They could also be laid off when business slumped.

(B)The South depended on just a few cash crops, mainly cotton. To raise cotton, **(B)planters in the South** needed a large labor force year-round. They relied on slave labor. **(B)Southerners** traded their cotton for manufactured goods from Europe, especially from Great Britain. **(B)The South** had little industry of its own.

In the second paragraph above, the writer makes several points about the economy of subject *A*—the North. In the third paragraph, the writer turns to subject *B*—the South—and presents several ways in which the economy of the South was different from that of the North.

The second way to organize comparison and contrast is called the ABAB pattern. As you might expect, in the **ABAB pattern**, first you compare both subject *A* and subject *B* in terms of one similarity or difference. Then, you compare both of them in terms of another similarity or difference. The following continuation of the essay on the conflict that led to the Civil War switches to the ABAB pattern.

MODEL: ABAB Pattern of Organization

The economic differences between the two sections soon led to political conflicts. The worst conflicts arose over slavery. **(A)Many people in the North** considered slavery morally wrong. They wanted laws that would outlaw slavery in the new western territories. Some wanted to abolish slavery altogether. **(B)Most white Southerners, on the other hand,** believed slavery was necessary for their economy. They wanted laws to protect slavery in the West so that they could raise cotton on the fertile soil there.

(A)Northerners had great political power in the national government. **(B)Southerners** feared the North's rising industrial power and growing population. Soon, they reasoned, the North would completely dominate the federal government. The election of 1860 seemed to confirm their worst fears. Abraham Lincoln, a Northern candidate who opposed the spread of slavery, was elected president.

In this passage the writer discusses the differences between the North and the South regarding attitudes toward slavery. Then the writer discusses differences between the North and the South regarding political power at the federal level.

PRACTICE YOUR SKILLS

Organizing Comparison and Contrast

For three of the following pairs of subjects, list similarities and differences. Use reference materials if necessary. Then organize your information according to the AABB or the ABAB pattern.

1. microscope/telescope
2. pinball machine/video game
3. typewriter/computer
4. television/motion pictures

5. tape/compact disc
6. dogs/cats
7. volleyball/table tennis
8. science fiction/fantasy
9. silver/gold
10. credit card/cash

Using a Venn Diagram to Compare and Contrast

Copy and complete the following Venn diagram by comparing and contrasting swimming and jumping rope. List the similarities in the area where the two circles overlap. Then organize your information according to the AABB or the ABAB pattern.

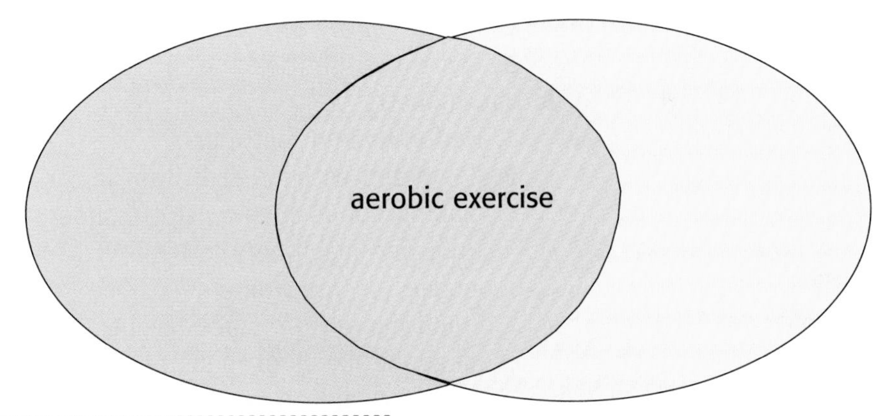

Communicate Your Ideas

PREWRITING *Order of Details and Categories*

Review the categories of details you have created for your informative essay. Order the details in each category, using an ordering scheme from **Types of Order** on page C405. Then decide on a type of order for the categories, and arrange them accordingly. Save your work for later use.

Making an Outline

When you select and group details, you probably write simple outlines to keep track of your decisions. You might number the points you want to make, for example. By developing an even more detailed outline, you can plan the whole body of your essay. The first two supporting paragraphs of the essay on page C407 were written from the following outline.

Model: Making an Outline

Working Thesis	Conflict grew as Northerners and Southerners followed different ways of life.
Main Topic:	**I.** The way of life in the North
Subtopic	**A.** Had a diversified economy
Supporting Points	**1.** Had farms and industry **2.** Had a variety of crops **3.** Fed thriving cities
Subtopic	**B.** Had industry
Supporting Points	**1.** Had mills and factories **2.** Competed with Great Britain in making goods such as cloth, shoes, iron, and machinery
Subtopic	**C.** Depended on free workers
Supporting Points	**1.** Could move from place to place to meet the needs of industry **2.** Could be laid off when business slumped
Main Topic:	**II.** The way of life in the South
Subtopic	**A.** Depended on a few cash crops
Supporting Points	**1.** Grew mainly cotton **2.** Needed a large labor force year-round **3.** Depended on slave labor
Subtopic	**B.** Depended on trade with Europe
Supporting Points	**1.** Traded cotton for manufactured goods **2.** Traded mainly with Great Britain **3.** Had little industry of its own

Notice that when you write a formal outline for the body of your essay, you use Roman numerals for each idea that supports your thesis. Each idea becomes the **main topic** of a supporting paragraph. You then use capital letters for each category of information that comes under a topic. Then, under each subtopic, you use Arabic numerals to list the *supporting points* or details. When you draft the body of your essay, the information below each Roman numeral in the outline will form a separate paragraph.

Guidelines for Making an Outline

- Use Roman numerals for topics.
- Use capital letters for subtopics and indent them under the topic. If you use subtopics, always include at least two of them.
- Use Arabic numerals for supporting points and indent them under the subtopic. If you use supporting points, include at least two of them.
- Use lowercase letters for any other details and indent them under the supporting point to which they refer. If you use supporting details, include at least two of them.

Model: Outline Form

I. (Main topic)
  A. (Subtopic)
    1. (Supporting point)
    2. (Supporting point)
      a. (Detail)
      b. (Detail)
  B. (Subtopic)
    1. (Supporting point)
      a. (Detail)
      b. (Detail)
    2. (Supporting point)
II. (Main topic)
  Etc.

Practice Your Skills

Making an Outline

Outline the third and fourth supporting paragraphs of "Conflict Between the North and the South" on page C408. These paragraphs—Roman numerals III and IV of the outline for the essay body—are about political conflicts between Northerners and Southerners before the Civil War.

Communicate Your Ideas

PREWRITING *Outline*

Review your working thesis, and review the way you grouped and classified your ideas and information for your essay. After you decide what your topics, subtopics, and supporting points will be, organize them in a logical order. Then follow the guidelines on page C411 to write an outline of the body of your essay. Rework your outline until you are satisfied with the content, order of information, and form. Save your outline for later use.

During the drafting stage of the writing process, you will use your prewriting notes and outline to write an introduction, a body, and a conclusion. Before you draft your introduction, however, you should refine your working thesis into a thesis statement.

Writing a Thesis Statement

The thesis statement, which expresses your main idea, should appear somewhere in the introduction of the essay. Thesis statements are often most effective when they appear at the beginning or at the end of the introduction.

The thesis statement makes the main idea of the essay clear to readers.

In an informative essay, the most important feature of a thesis statement is that it accurately covers all of the information you include in the essay. The following guidelines suggest the steps you should take to refine your working thesis into an effective thesis statement.

Drafting a Thesis Statement

- Look over your outline and revise your working thesis so that it covers all of your main topics.
- Express your working thesis in a complete sentence.
- Check your thesis statement for clarity; use peer conferencing to check that the thesis is clearly stated.
- Look over all your information again to make sure it is relevant to the thesis statement.
- Continue to refine your thesis statement as you take into account any changes you make in the main idea or in the information you include.

Drafting the Introduction

In an informative essay, the introduction has several functions other than stating the thesis. For example, in the introduction, you also set the tone of your essay and capture the reader's interest. Because the purpose of writing an informative essay is to inform or explain, a candid, matter-of-fact tone is usually appropriate. The following are common ways to attract the reader's attention in an informative essay.

Writing Introductions for Informative Essays

- Tell about an incident that shows how you became interested in your subject.
- Give some background information.
- Cite an example that illustrates your thesis.

- Cite a startling statistic about the subject.
- Define or describe the subject.
- Quote an expert on the subject.

The model below presents an introduction for the essay on pages C407–C408 about conflicts between the North and the South that led to the Civil War. Notice how this introduction introduces the subject, captures interest, and sets the tone. Also the main idea is clearly expressed in a refined thesis statement.

MODEL: Introduction of an Informative Essay

As Americans pushed westward during the early 1800s, conflict grew between the North and the South. The main reason for this conflict was the contrast between the different ways of life that had developed in the North and the South ever since colonial times. As each section tried to extend its own way of life to the new western lands, those different ways of life began to threaten the nation's unity. By the 1860s, differences between the ways of life in the North and the South had brought the nation to the brink of war.

REFINED THESIS STATEMENT

Communicate Your Ideas

DRAFTING *Thesis and Introduction Statement*

Review all your previous notes for your essay. Then refine your working thesis statement. Experiment with placing your thesis statement at the beginning and at the end of the introduction. Then choose the introduction that you like best and save it for use later.

Across the Media: Writing Strategies

Recognizing the power of visuals on television can remind you to incorporate strong description into your writing. Understanding how other media present information can help you improve your informative writing.

Techniques for grabbing a reader's attention are especially useful to study. A newspaper story usually begins with the whole story summarized in the first sentence, for example. The rest of the story supplies the details, but the reader is drawn in by knowing the outcome. A newsmagazine, in contrast, might begin with a paragraph setting the scene, and then take time leading up to the outcome.

Media Activity

Skim through a newspaper until you find a headline that interests you. Read the first few paragraphs. Then scan the table of contents of a newsmagazine until you find an article in which you are interested. Read only the first few paragraphs. Finally, surf the Internet until you find a Website that interests you. Read only the first screenful of text.

For each introduction, ask yourself the following questions:

- Does the introduction grab my attention? Why or why not?
- What method did the writer use to get my attention?
- What is the implied or stated thesis statement? If it is stated, where is it placed in the introduction?

Finally, in your Learning Log, sum up what you have learned about writing introductions to informative essays from the three pieces you examined from other media.

Drafting the Body

When you draft the body of your informative essay, you should follow your outline. Each main topic, with some or all of the subtopics and supporting points, will become at least one paragraph. If you have a number of supporting details, you may need two or more paragraphs to cover each topic adequately. Make sure to include enough detail to help support your ideas.

On page C225 you can learn more about the relationship of an introduction to the essay.

Guidelines for Adequately Developing an Essay

- Include enough supporting ideas to develop your thesis statement fully.
- Leave no question unanswered that you would expect readers to ask.
- Include enough information to present each topic and subtopic fully.
- Use specific details and precise language to present each piece of information fully.

As you draft the body of your informative essay from your outline, connect your words, sentences, and paragraphs with transitions to make the essay read smoothly and to give it unity, coherence, and clarity.

You can learn more about making transitions on pages C107 and C138–C139. Check pages C33–C40 for guidance on achieving unity, coherence, clarity, and adequate development.

Strategies for Achieving Coherence

- Use transitional words and phrases.
- Repeat a key word from an earlier sentence.
- Use synonyms for key words from earlier sentences.
- Use a pronoun in place of a word used earlier.

PRACTICE YOUR SKILLS

Writing an Outline

Convert the following outline into a short introduction and body of an essay. As you write, refer to the Guidelines for Adequately Developing an Essay and the Strategies for Achieving Coherence on the preceding page.

THESIS STATEMENT The launching of the satellite *Sputnik* by the Soviets caused a revolution in American education.

I. *Sputnik* launch was a worldwide sensation
   A. Launched by Soviets in October 1957
   B. First artificial Earth satellite

II. *Sputnik's* success troubled Americans
   A. In 1959, Americans and Soviets were rivals
   B. Americans feared Soviets were ahead in science and education
   C. Magazines began to publish articles about a "crisis in education"

III. United States government responded by funding education
   A. Congress voted National Defense Education Act
      1. In 1958, after December 1957 launch of American Vanguard Rocket failed
      2. $1 billion to teach more science in public schools
   B. School improvements included modern science labs, science fairs, and teacher training in sciences

Communicate Your Ideas

DRAFTING *Body*

Working from the outline you developed, draft the paragraphs for the body of your informative essay. Save your work for use later.

Drafting the Conclusion

An informative essay is not complete without a conclusion. The concluding paragraph sums up your information and reinforces your thesis. You might also add an interesting detail from your notes that you did not previously include.

You can learn more about the conclusion of an essay on page C240.

Strategies for Writing a Conclusion

- Summarize the body of the essay.
- Restate the thesis in new words.
- Draw a conclusion based on the body of the essay.
- Add an insight about the thesis.
- Write a memorable clincher sentence.

The following paragraph concludes the essay on pages C407–C408 about conflicts that led to the Civil War in the United States. Notice that the conclusion adds interesting details about the start of the Civil War and also restates the thesis in a memorable clincher sentence.

MODEL: Conclusion of an Informative Essay

After Lincoln's election, 11 southern states made the fateful decision to withdraw from the United States. They established a separate nation called the Confederate States of America. On April 12, 1861, Confederate guns opened fire on Fort Sumter, a fort in South Carolina held by soldiers of the federal government. This event marked the beginning of the Civil War—a tragic clash between Americans following different ways of life.

CLINCHER SENTENCE

Drafting a Title To complete your first draft, you need to think of an appropriate title. A good title suggests the main idea of your essay and captures the attention of your audience.

Communicate Your Ideas

DRAFTING *Conclusion*

Reread the introduction and body of your essay. Then draft a strong concluding paragraph with a final clincher sentence. Write two or three possible titles for your essay. Choose the best one and save your draft for use later. 

Revising

Writing Process

The purpose of revising is to make your final draft as clear and readable as possible. If time allows, put away your draft for a day or two so you can revise it with a fresh eye. Also read your draft aloud to notice parts that need improvement. A peer reader can also tell you whether your explanations are clear.

Checking for Unity, Coherence, and Clarity

In revising, as in drafting, you should be alert for ways to improve the unity, coherence, and clarity of your essay. The following questions will help you to check for these qualities.

Checking for Unity, Coherence, and Clarity

Checking for Unity

- ✓ Does each idea and each piece of information relate to the subject?
- ✓ Does every paragraph support the thesis statement?
- ✓ Does every sentence in each paragraph support its topic sentence?

Checking for Coherence

- ✓ Did you follow a logical order of ideas or topics?
- ✓ Did you follow a logical order of supporting points or details?

- ✓ Did you use transitions to connect the introduction, body, and conclusion?
- ✓ Did you use transitions between paragraphs?
- ✓ Did you use transitions between sentences within each paragraph?

Checking for Clarity

- ✓ Does each word express clearly and precisely what you want to say?
- ✓ Does the introduction make your subject, purpose, tone, and thesis clear to readers?
- ✓ Does the body clearly support the thesis and lead to the conclusion?
- ✓ Does the conclusion make clear to readers how the body supports the thesis?

Communicate Your Ideas

REVISING *Unity, Coherence, Clarity*

Revise your draft, using Checking for Unity, Coherence, and Clarity and the Evaluation Checklist for Revising on the following page for guidance. Save your revised draft for later use.

Time Out to Reflect

Compare your process of revising on this piece of informative writing with the way you revised your writing earlier in the year. In what ways have you improved your writing? What strategies have helped you do a better job of revising, such as setting a draft aside for a few days? Record your responses in your Learning Log.

A general revision checklist also helps you keep track of all the points you should check when you revise. As you use the following checklist, read through your essay several times, focusing on a different point each time.

Evaluation Checklist for Revising

Checking Your Essay

- ✓ Do you have a strong introduction? *(pages C413–C414)*
- ✓ Does your thesis statement make your main idea and purpose clear? *(pages C412–C413)*
- ✓ Do you have enough details to support your thesis fully? *(page C416)*
- ✓ Does your essay have unity? *(page C419)*
- ✓ Does the topic sentence of each paragraph relate directly to the thesis? *(page C416)*
- ✓ Does your essay have coherence? *(page C419)*
- ✓ Does your essay have clarity? *(page C420)*
- ✓ Does your essay have a strong conclusion? *(page C418)*
- ✓ Did you add an interesting and appropriate title? *(page C418)*

Checking Your Paragraphs

- ✓ Does each paragraph have a topic sentence? *(page C411)*
- ✓ Does each paragraph have adequate development? *(page C416)*
- ✓ Does each paragraph have the qualities of unity, coherence, and clarity? *(pages C419–C420)*

Checking Your Sentences and Words

- ✓ Did you vary your sentences and sentence beginnings? *(pages C71–C78)*
- ✓ Are your sentences concise? *(pages C81–C85)*
- ✓ Did you use words that are specific and precise? *(page C64)*
- ✓ Did you use vivid words? *(page C63)*

As you revised your informative essay, you looked for ways to be sure it is clear, unified, and coherent. Now you are ready to edit your essay by checking for errors in grammar, spelling, capitalization, and punctuation.

Communicate Your Ideas

EDITING

Use the checklists on pages C44 and C424 to edit your informative essay. You will edit most effectively if you read through your paper several times, looking for different kinds of errors each time.

COMPUTER TIP

As you edit your informative essay, you may want to use the Spelling and Grammar Check features on your word processing software to help you. Simply pull down the Tools menu and select Spelling and Grammar. Be careful, however, not to assume the suggestions made by this feature are correct or complete. For example, the Spell Check feature will tell you if a word you have used is not in the application's dictionary. What it cannot correct includes homophones, such as *to* for *too,* or another typographical error that might result in an existing word, such as *ham* for *him*. You must proofread carefully yourself for such errors.

File Edit View Insert Format
New... ⌘N
Open... ⌘O
Open Web Page...
Close ⌘W
Save ⌘S
Save As...

The Grammar Check feature will alert you to incorrect grammar, usage, and mechanics, but again the software is limited to the rules that it knows and can apply. Review each suggested change carefully. If what you wrote is grammatically correct, then leave it. In other words, these features can only help you edit your writing; they cannot edit for you.

Prewriting Workshop
Drafting Workshop
Revising Workshop
Editing Workshop
Publishing Workshop

Prepositional Phrases

Prepositional phrases can help a writer describe even the indescribable, as shown in Joy Hakim's remarks in her essay "Mercury, Gemini, and Saturn."

> Some 4 billion years ago, a small planet hurtled **onto Earth** and sent exploding pieces **into the atmosphere**. Those objects circled the earth, collided, collected, and became the moon. The earth and the moon eventually settled **into a gravitational balance about 239,000 miles apart**, with the moon orbiting Earth and its pull influencing the oceans' tides.

Hakim's use of prepositional phrases helps the reader imagine the magnificence of the moon's formation.

Prepositional Phrases

A **prepositional phrase** is a group of words that has no subject or verb and that modifies, or describes, other words in a sentence. It is useful for adding important words in the sentence. In the following examples, each prepositional phrase adds information by answering a question.

WHERE?	**From space shuttle height**, we couldn't see the entire globe. (From *where* couldn't they see?)
WHEN?	The lightning ignites the clouds **at night.** (*When* does lightning ignite the clouds?)
HOW?	The land was obscured **by a huge dust storm.** (*How* was the land obscured?)
WHAT KIND?	Patches **of pollution-damaged trees** dotted the European forest. (*What kind* of patches dotted the forests?)

Punctuation with Prepositional Phrases

When a long prepositional phrase comes at the beginning of a sentence, you should put a comma after it.

LONG INTRODUCTORY PREPOSITIONAL PHRASE	**In her well-researched article on the brave and bold American space program**, Joy Hakim uses facts, examples, definitions, and incidents.

Combining Sentences with Prepositional Phrases

As the following examples show, you can use prepositional phrases to combine two short sentences into one sentence.

SEPARATE SENTENCES	Bolts of lightning are diffused by the clouds. The lightning bolts burst into balls of light.
COMBINED SENTENCE	Bolts of lightning are diffused by the clouds **into bursting balls of light**.
SEPARATE SENTENCES	They told stories of the moon. They dreamed by its bright, reflected light.
COMBINED SENTENCES	They told stories of the moon and dreamed **by its bright, reflected light**.

Editing Checklist

- ✔ Have you used prepositional phrases to incorporate additional information into a sentence?
- ✔ Are all prepositional phrases punctuated correctly?
- ✔ Could you use prepositional phrases to combine any sentences?

Complete the writing process by sharing your informative essay with someone who you think might have an interest in reading it.

Communicate Your Ideas

PUBLISHING

Prepare a neat final draft of your informative essay, using the manuscript form on pages C52–C54. Then think back to the prewriting stage and the audience you had in mind to identify an individual who might be interested in the information you present. Share your work with a member of that audience—a teacher, fellow student, family member, or another interested person.

PORTFOLIO

Process of Writing an Informative Essay

Remember that the writing process is recursive—you can move back and forth among the stages of the process to achieve your purpose. For example, during editing you may wish to return to the revising stage to add details that have occurred to you while editing. The numbers in parentheses refer to pages where you can get help with your writing.

PREWRITING

- Find subjects by drawing on your experience and reading. *(page C393)*
- Choose and limit your subject. *(pages C394–C396)*
- Focus your ideas by asking yourself questions about your subject, purpose, and audience. *(pages C393–C394)*
- Gather information and develop a list of supporting ideas. *(pages C397–C398)*
- Develop a working thesis. *(pages C399–C400)*
- Group together, categorize, and order your ideas and information. *(pages C403–C408)*
- Make an outline. *(pages C410–C411)*

DRAFTING

- Write an introduction that includes your refined thesis statement. *(pages C412–C414)*
- Use your outline as you write the paragraphs of the body. *(page C416)*
- Use transitions to connect your ideas. *(page C416)*
- Add a concluding paragraph. *(page C418)*
- Add a title that will capture your reader's interest. *(page C418)*

REVISING

- Check for unity, coherence, and clarity. *(pages C419–C420)*
- Refer to the **Evaluation Checklist for Revising**. *(page C421)*

EDITING

- Refer to the **Editing Checklist** to check your prepositional phrases. *(page C424)*

PUBLISHING

- Publish a neat final copy of your essay in standard manuscript form. *(page C452)*

A Writer Writes

A Science Article

Purpose: to explain an aspect of outer space that would interest and enlighten children

Audience: students in the fourth or fifth grade

Prewriting

Look through print and nonprint resources for fascinating information about space and use the strategy of brainstorming to generate more ideas. For example, you may want to find out how heat from the sun can travel 93,000,000 miles to Earth and still be warm when it gets there. On the other hand, you may want to know, for instance, what would be required before people could colonize the planet Mars.

After choosing and limiting a subject, brainstorm for all the facts you already know about that subject. Then find any additional information you need, using the Internet and/or science reference materials. Based on the information you gather, develop a working thesis, group your ideas, and arrange them in a logical order. Then develop an outline from your notes.

Drafting

Keeping in mind your purpose and audience, refine your thesis and work your thesis statement into an introduction. Then draft the body of your essay and the conclusion. Be sure to add a title that will captivate your young audience.

Revising

Read your essay aloud to find places where you can improve your wording or flow of ideas. Also use the guidelines on page C421 to make changes that will improve the quality and

style of your writing. Before you edit, also read your work for unity, coherence, and clarity.

Editing

Use the **Editing Checklists** on pages C44 and C424 to polish your work.

Publishing

After you make a neat, error-free final copy, submit your essay to a fourth- or fifth-grade teacher to read to his or her students or to give to the students to read on their own. You can check the effectiveness of your explanation by finding out what questions the students have about it.

Connection Collection

Representing in Different Ways

From Print . . .

Dear Horatio,

Thanks for your card informing me about your decision to get a new pet. Personally, I think goldfish make great pets. They are quiet and independent creatures. Unlike a pet dog or cat, goldfish can be left alone for hours without receiving any attention; and, unlike a pet shark, they won't cost an arm and a leg to feed! Goldfish, however, do not make good traveling companions. It is almost impossible to walk with them in the park, and they never seem interested in what you have to say. They are not very receptive to learning tricks either.

I hope this makes your decision easier.

Sincerely,

Julie

Horatio Milano
435 Highway Pass
El Cerrito, CA 94740

From Visuals . . .

A Pet Monkey

PROS	CONS
Greatly amusing	Requires natural habitat
Very intelligent	Requires professional care
	Requires constant attention
	Can be very noisy
	Very active
	Extremely curious

. . . to Visuals

Using the information in the postcard above, create a chart of the pros and cons of having a pet goldfish.

. . . to Print

Your grandmother thinks she wants a pet monkey to keep her company. Using the information in the above chart, write a letter to your grandmother informing her of the pros and cons of owning a pet monkey. Be sure to organize your ideas in a logical order and to clearly support the choice you think is best.

- **Which strategies can be used for creating both written and visual representations? Which strategies apply to one, not both? Which type of representation is more effective?**
- **Draw a conclusion and write briefly about the differences between written ideas and visual representations.**

Writing in Everyday Life

Informative E-mail

You are trying to make plans to go to Chilly Thrills Amusement Park. A couple of your friends think that flying through the air on fast rides is a dangerous way to spend the afternoon. They say they are especially frightened of riding the Icy Road Roller Coaster that they have seen advertised on television.

Write an E-mail to your friends informing them about the safety precautions amusement parks take to make roller coasters safe. Be sure to outline your ideas first so that your friends get an organized, well-developed picture of how safe the roller coasters are.

What strategies did you use to explain the safety of roller coasters to your friends?

You can find information on writing E-mails in A Writer's Guide to Using the Internet, *pages C724–C767.*

Writing in the Workplace

Informative Note

You have just been hired by Virtually Fun, a video-game company that produces educational games. Your boss wants you to help develop a new game that will appeal to people who are fans of both classical music and skateboarding.

Write a note to your boss informing her of the features that make video games fun. Suggest ways to apply the features to the video game that incorporates both skateboarding and classical music. Be sure to arrange the information in your note in developmental order.

What strategies did you use to write your note to your boss?

Assess Your Learning

The editor of the school newspaper has just discovered that your principal plans to renovate the cafeteria this summer. Your assignment is to write an article that will represent the voice of the students by informing the faculty of how the students would like the new cafeteria to be designed.

- **Write an article for the school newspaper informing the faculty about what kind of cafeteria the students would like. Write about what kind of furniture and what type of food you think the student body would prefer.**
- **Use your prewriting notes to create an outline. Be sure to draft a strong thesis statement and an introduction that gives the reader appropriate background information. Organize the information in the body of your article in spatial order. Use specific details and precise language to present each piece of information fully.**

Before You Write **Consider the following questions:**
What is the ***subject?***
What is the ***occasion?***
Who is the ***audience?***
What is the ***purpose?***

After You Write **Evaluate your work using the following criteria:**
- Have you used your prewriting notes to create an outline?
- Does the thesis statement express the main idea clearly?
- Do you have a strong introduction that sets the tone clearly?
- Have you organized your ideas in spatial order?
- Have you used transitions to connect the introduction, body, and conclusion?
- Does the body of your story clearly support the thesis and lead to a conclusion?
- Have you written in a voice and style appropriate to your audience and purpose?

Write briefly on how well you did. Point out your strengths and areas for improvement.

CHAPTER 10

Writing to Persuade

No doubt you have had the experience of reading something that had an effect on you, such as a tragedy or injustice, a moving story, or a disturbing article. Persuasive writing, by its very nature, is meant to stir you strongly. The subject of a persuasive article is always controversial. Persuasive writing is an attempt to convince the reader to adopt a particular point of view.

Throughout history, persuasive writing has been used positively—to uncover injustice or topple tyrants, and negatively—to incite prejudice or justify war. Whether it relates to world events and politics, literature, or communication on a personal level, persuasive writing can have dramatic and powerful results.

Reading with a Writer's Eye

Sometimes the news media will present both sides of a controversy as a "point/counterpoint." You are about to read two opposing views on a controversial question. Read both opinions as if you are an editor or the director of a television news show. Decide whether you would print or broadcast these opinions. What persuasive tools have these writers used? How effectively have they conveyed their opinions?

ARE NATIVE AMERICAN Team Nicknames Offensive?

Gary Kimble and Bob DiBiasio

At the Association on American Indian Affairs, we support any Native American community that finds certain nicknames, logos, or portrayals of Native American people to be offensive. We support its right to express its pain, to go out and protest, and to work to try to get a nickname changed.

A lot of the sentiment among Native Americans today has to do with their concern over other people's appropriation of Indian spiritual activities. Some non-Indian people are trying to create the idea that they have secret knowledge of the Indians. They disguise their own beliefs and theories as Indian beliefs. New Age gurus, for instance, pass themselves off as Indian medicine men. Native Americans' dissatisfaction with such practices is the foundation for the protest against names and logos in sports. One controversy energizes the other.

Any kind of portrayal of Native Americans that isn't respectful bothers me. Too many times, we're portrayed as hostile and criminal, as some kind of blood-thirsty savages. Or we're *noble* savages, nobler than other people because supposedly we're closer to nature. Both portrayals are stereotypes. Anytime you turn people into symbols and move away from reality, that's bad.

A lot of people are offended by caricatures such as the one the Cleveland Indians use for their logo. When you do a caricature, you're dealing with someone's identity, and that puts you on thin ice. Even the name makes you wonder. They wouldn't call themselves the "Cleveland White People" or the "Cleveland Black People." What would happen if a soccer team in South Africa wanted to name itself the "Johannesburg White People"?

A name such as "Redskins"[1] causes concern because certain tribes feel the term is a holdover from the days when there was a bounty on American Indians. Suzanne Harjo, a Cheyenne, has written that "redskin" was a designation used by bounty hunters: Instead of bringing in the whole Indian, the hunters would just bring in the hide. They'd get paid the same for it, and it was less cumbersome than carrying around the whole body.

Not all the relationships between sports and Native Americans are bad. When Joe Robbie was the owner of the Miami Dolphins, for example, his major philanthropy work involved American Indians. Few people know he was one of the best friends our people ever had. I also recognize the danger in becoming too politically correct. I wouldn't want to see things get to the point where we can't ever enjoy ourselves or create a fun atmosphere. The tomahawk chop[2] doesn't bother me that much, and a name such as "Braves"[3] is fairly neutral.

However, there has to be some kind of balance struck, to make sure that no particular group is demeaned or damaged. And many Native Americans today believe that some of the teams they see in sports haven't found that balance.

Gary N. Kimble, a Native American, was formerly executive director of the Association on American Indian Affairs in Sisseton, South Dakota. Currently, he is commissioner for the Administration for Native Americans in the Department of Health and Human Services, Washington, D.C.

[1] **"Redskins":** Name of a football team based in Washington, D.C., the Washington Redskins.
[2] **tomahawk chop:** Popular way for fans to root for the baseball team the Atlanta Braves.
[3] **"Braves":** Name of a baseball team based in Atlanta, the Atlanta Braves.

NO

Our organization is very aware of the sensitivities involved in this issue, and we have gone to great lengths to respect those sensitivities. In no way do we intend to demean any group, especially one as proud as Native Americans.

Any discussion of the Cleveland Indians' name and the team logo, Chief Wahoo, must begin with a history lesson. Not many people realize the origin of "Indians," but there is a historical significance to how the Cleveland franchise got its name.

From 1901 to 1914, Cleveland's entry in the American League utilized three different names: Blues, Bronchos, and Naps—the last of which honored the legendary Nap Lajoie. Upon Lajoie's retirement in 1914, the officials of the Cleveland team determined a new name was in order for the following season. They turned to a local newspaper and ran a contest. The winning entry, Indians, was selected in honor of Louis Francis Sockalexis, a Penobscot Indian who was the first Native American to play professional baseball. *(Sockalexis played from 1897 to 1899 for the Cleveland Spiders of the National League.)*

Newspaper accounts at the time reported that the name Indians was chosen as "a testament to the game's first American Indian." Today, 79 years later, we're proud to acknowledge and foster the legacy of Sockalexis. That's why you don't see us animating or humanizing our logo in any way; it's simply a caricature that has enjoyed decades of fan appeal in the Northeast Ohio area. The name and logo received public support in the form of a recent "Save the Chief" campaign. We also go to great lengths to avoid any use of tomahawks, tepees, or warriors on horseback—Indian motifs that are questionable, at best.

There is an inconsistency among Native American groups as to what they think on this matter. The team name is one issue, the logo is a separate issue, and the combination of the name and the logo is yet another issue. All three elements elicit different reactions, but many Native Americans in the Northeast Ohio area have an appreciation for our understanding of their sensitivity. They consider our name to be an honoring of both their culture and the memory of Sockalexis.

Our view of this issue doesn't get a lot of publicity in the media, but we don't belabor it because we're comfortable with our position. Once you have an understanding of the historical significance of why we are named the Indians and understand the organization's conscious efforts to present that issue, we believe it becomes a matter of individual perception.

When someone looks at our name and logo, he or she thinks of Cleveland Indians baseball, and the great moments in the team's history. They don't think of Native American people; they just think of Bob Feller,[4] Al Rosen,[5] Larry Doby,[6] and Sam McDowell.[7]

Bob DiBiasio is Vice President of Public Relations for the Cleveland Indians.

[4] **Bob Feller:** Cleveland Indians pitcher elected to the Baseball Hall of Fame in 1962; pitched no-hit games during the 1940, 1946, and 1951 seasons.

[5] **Al Rosen:** Cleveland Indians player who received the Most Valuable Player Award in 1953.

[6] **Larry Doby:** Cleveland Indians player elected to the Baseball Hall of Fame in 1998; first African American player in the American League.

[7] **Sam McDowell:** Star Cleveland Indians pitcher in the 1960s.

Thinking as a Writer

Evaluating Persuasive Evidence

How persuasively did Gary Kimble and Bob DiBiasio present their arguments?

- Summarize Kimble's main point in one sentence. Then identify the evidence Kimble used to support that point. Do the same for DiBiasio's piece. Is each writer's supporting evidence effective? Is one writer more persuasive than the other? If so, why?

Representing Ideas Through Images

Viewing

- In a small group, identify any new arguments that could be applied to Kimble's or DiBiasio's position on the Cleveland Indians' team logo. Then look at other sports teams. How do logos and nicknames create an identity for a team?

Evaluating Persuasive Tone

Oral Expression

- Work with a partner. One of you read aloud Kimble's opinion and the other read aloud DiBiasio's. Each reader should use appropriate emphasis and expression to reflect the tone of the writing. Is the tone of each the same? If not, what words would you use to describe Kimble's tone? DiBiasio's tone? Is each writer's tone effective for persuading the audience to his point of view? Why or why not?

The Power of Persuasion

You have read two examples of persuasive writing on the same subject. As these examples demonstrate, persuasive writing states an opinion and then provides facts, reasons, and examples to support it. The writer's aim is to persuade readers to agree with his or her particular point of view.

Uses of Persuasion

All of the following examples show ways people in different positions and professions use persuasive writing to influence others' views and, ultimately, their actions and opinions.

- **The editor of the school newspaper writes an editorial** speaking out against a proposal that students be required to wear uniforms.
- **A candidate for state senator hands out a pamphlet** explaining her qualifications for office and why she is a better choice than her opponent.
- **A charity sends a letter** detailing the plight of poor children overseas and asking for donations to help.
- **An outraged sports writer pens a column** calling for the dismissal of an underperforming team's coach.
- **The president gives a speech** asking people to work harder and save more money to create "a stronger America."

Refining Your Skills of Persuasion

Contemporary writer Francine Prose advises young writers to "keep your eyes open, see clearly, think about what you see, ask yourself what it means." For a persuasive writer, Prose's points are important to remember. Good persuasive writing is a response to real life—to events, problems, and questions in the here and now that people are dealing with and caring about. The world around you is sure to provide you with a host of issues on which to take a stand. Good persuasive writing requires thought, reflection, and often research. Only then can you develop a powerful opinion supported by the solid evidence that is key to convincing your readers.

A **persuasive essay** states an opinion on a subject and uses facts, reasons, and examples to convince readers.

Your Writer's Journal

In your journal, make entries on issues about which you feel strongly. They might be issues you learn about in school, read about in books or magazines, watch on television, or view when on the Internet. They may be things that happen to you—while playing a sport, for example—that become issues you care about. For each subject, write a sentence that states your opinion, and then write a sentence that explains an opposing view. Save your work for later use.

Persuasive Essay Structure

Like all essays, a persuasive essay has three main parts: an introduction, a body, and a conclusion. The following chart shows how each part helps develop an argument.

Structure of a Persuasive Essay

- The **introduction** captures the reader's attention, presents the issue, and expresses the writer's opinion in a thesis statement.
- The **body of supporting paragraphs** presents reasons, facts, examples, and expert opinions to back up the writer's opinions.
- The **conclusion** presents a summary or strong conclusive evidence—logically drawn from the argument—that drives home the writer's opinions.

The writer of the following persuasive essay argues for a fresh attitude toward competition in one of the most popular pastimes: sports. As you read the essay, notice how each part develops the writer's viewpoint.

MODEL: Persuasive Essay

New Games

INTRODUCTION: CAPTURES ATTENTION AND PROVIDES BACKGROUND

Can you recognize yourself in the following scene? On a cold winter day, students—glad finally to be in the gym for physical education—prepare to play a game of volleyball. Eagerness turns to anxiety, though, when they are told to choose sides. The team captains call on the best players first, and within a few minutes, the remaining players are feeling left out and inadequate. As the choosing continues, the last few players are feeling very small indeed. Nobody seems to want them, and maybe even worse, everyone *knows* nobody wants them. When the game gets underway, the last-chosen play timidly, afraid to confirm their reputation. Even strong players become frustrated if the points start stacking up against them. Too often, the competitive nature of sports and games interferes with the learning and pleasure that they

THESIS STATEMENT

could be providing. Enjoyable, relaxing alternatives to competitive sports should be the rule rather than the exception in physical education.

First Body Paragraph: ADDRESSES OPPOSING VIEWS; OFFERS EXPERT EVIDENCE

Some people argue that without competition athletes would not perform at their very best. In fact, competition sometimes has the opposite effect. Tennis pro Tim Gallwey believes that a key part of success in any sport is conquering "such obstacles as lapses in concentration, nervousness, self-doubt, and self-condemnation." For the dedicated athlete, competition may help enhance the ability to overcome these inner obstacles. However, for the vast majority of students in physical education, the team-choosing, score-keeping scene described would only make the obstacles all the more insurmountable. Remove the competition, however, and students are free to experiment, make mistakes, and—by so doing—improve their skills in a sport.

Second Body Paragraph: PROVIDES ADDITIONAL REASONS

Besides sometimes getting in the way of improving in a sport, competition can also reduce other positive side effects of play. When winning becomes more important than playing, pleasure may give way to frustration. The joy that comes from a relaxed body at play is out of reach if players are only reaching for another notch on the scoreboard. Also, as players face off against an imagined enemy, their muscles could become tense, increasing the risk of injury. Finally, sports help young people learn social skills. If competition and winning are stressed, the skills learned might help shape an isolated, aggressive, self-centered outlook. Less competition might foster cooperation and trust.

Third Body Paragraph: OFFERS ALTERNATIVE

Instead of competitive sports, physical education programs should incorporate "New Games" activities. These made-up games have three basic rules, which are reflected in the motto of the "New Games" Association. The rules are "Play hard, play fair, nobody gets hurt."

FOURTH BODY PARAGRAPH:
ELABORATES ON ALTERNATIVE WITH CLEAR EXAMPLE

One of the games suggested in the "New Games" Association's guidebook is "infinity volleyball." According to the guide, "The object of this game is to keep the ball on the volley indefinitely. In general, the normal rules of volleyball apply, except that no specified number of players is required. As in regular volleyball, one team may hit the ball no more than three times before sending it over the net. Players of both teams chant aloud the number of times the ball has been volleyed. Both teams share the final score. For average players, any score over 50 is very good; 100 or more is phenomenal."

CONCLUSION:
DRIVES HOME THE MAIN POINT

"New Games," or other innovative approaches to sports that steer clear of competition, can help restore the kind of joy young people should have when they get together to play. And, along the way, the players are more likely to develop confidence in their physical abilities. When the outer obstacle of competition is removed, students can begin to master their inner obstacles and at the same time enjoy their time in the gym or on the playing field. Everyone is always chosen first; everyone is a winner.

PRACTICE YOUR SKILLS

Analyzing a Persuasive Essay

Write answers to the following questions.

1. In your own words, state the opinion that the writer of the "New Games" essay is expressing in the thesis statement.
2. What method does the writer use in the introduction to capture the reader's attention?
3. List four reasons given by the writer to back up the opinion that competitive sports may have undesirable effects.

4. How does the reference to Tim Gallwey add strength to the writer's argument?
5. Why do you think the writer includes information about the "New Games" Association?
6. Explain three specific ways in which the conclusion refers back to other parts of the essay.
7. Where does the writer use descriptive and/or narrative writing? What persuasive purpose does it serve?
8. In what specific ways does the writer address the concerns of readers who might disagree with the thesis?
9. Reread the introduction. To what audience is this essay addressed? Do you think the writing and ideas are effective for this audience? Explain your answer.
10. Does this essay succeed in persuading you that noncompetitive sports should be the rule in physical education programs? Why or why not?

Facts and Opinions

Stories in the front section of a newspaper report the news as it happened—simply presenting the facts. Facts are statements that can be proved. The editorial page presents opinions based on facts. Opinions are beliefs or judgments that can be supported but not proved.

A **fact** is a statement that can be proved.

An **opinion** is a belief or judgment that cannot be proved.

Facts and opinions are presented together in persuasive essays. The thesis statement is an opinion—the author's judgment on a subject of controversy. The body of the essay backs up the thesis statement with facts and supporting examples.

There are several ways to test whether a statement is a fact or an opinion. First, ask yourself, "Can I prove this statement through my own experience and observation?"

FACT Some physical education programs stress competitive sports.

(Your own school may do this.)

Another test of a fact is to ask, "Can I prove this statement by referring to accepted authorities and experts?"

FACT Muscle tension increases the risk of injury during sports.

(You might suspect this yourself, but to know for sure you could ask a sports doctor.)

Use your own experiences and observations as well as reliable authorities to verify **facts**.

Opinions, unlike facts, can never be proved. They are judgment calls, personal likes or dislikes, and interpretations that vary from person to person. Consider these opinions.

Movies are **more satisfying** on a big screen than on TV.

Competition **should be** downplayed in school sports.

The following words often signal opinions.

OPINION WORDS		
should	good, better, best	probably
ought	bad, worse, worst	might
can	beautiful	perhaps
may	terrible	maybe

Opinions gain strength when they are supported by factual evidence, logical arguments, or both.

UNSUPPORTED OPINION	Volleyball is more fun than soccer. (There are no supporting facts available.)
SUPPORTED OPINION	Noncompetitive volleyball may teach positive social skills. (Experts in sports and society can offer supporting facts.)

Support your **opinions** with convincing **facts** and with evidence from real life as well as from knowledgeable experts and authorities.

PRACTICE YOUR SKILLS

Identifying Facts and Opinions

Write *fact* or *opinion* for each of the following statements.

1. Games are an age-old way of passing time.

2. Michael Jordan is the greatest basketball player ever.

3. Chess clubs are popular activities in school.

4. Made-for-TV movies are inferior to theatrical releases.

5. Video games are engaging and educational.

Supporting Opinions

Write one fact that could be used as evidence to support each of the following opinions. Use the library or media center as needed.

6. Only touch football should be allowed in schools.

7. Watching too much TV is bad for the mind and body.

8. Playing games is a good way to develop thinking skills.

Generalizing

When you write a persuasive essay, you often use the thinking skill of generalizing. When you **generalize**, you form an overall rule or principle based on specific details or facts. For example, suppose you know three excellent musicians who are also good in math. You might form a generalization about the positive effects that music lessons have on students' math abilities.

You need to be careful, however, that your generalizations are sound, not hasty. Do *all* students who take music lessons excel in math? Probably not. Be sure to state your generalization so that it covers all possible exceptions. Qualifying words such as *some, many,* or *most* can limit your generalization so that it leaves room for the exceptions.

Check your generalizations by trying to list possible exceptions. Then revise your generalizations with qualifying words.

REVISING A GENERALIZATION

Generalization	Hobbies are just a way to pass time.
Exceptions	My uncle's childhood hobby of building model airplanes led to a profession as an aeronautical engineer. My sister's love of computer games got her interested in programming.
Revised Generalizations	*Some* hobbies are just ways to pass time.

THINKING PRACTICE

Make a chart like the one above to test and revise a generalization on each of the following topics.

1. physical activities versus quiet games as recreation
2. shopping as a pastime
3. belonging to clubs

Process of Writing a Persuasive Essay

In a persuasive essay, your goal is to win your readers over to your point of view—and sometimes to convince them to take an action that you recommend. To do this effectively in a persuasive essay, you need to build a convincing, logical argument and present it in a convincing and powerful way. The strategies that follow will help you accomplish your purpose effectively.

Prewriting

Writing Process

Thinking your subject through carefully and marshaling the best possible evidence are the surest ways to develop a good argument. If you take your time during prewriting, you will be able to anticipate your opponents' reactions and be ready for them.

Choosing a Subject

The two most important aspects of a good persuasive subject are (1) that the subject is genuinely controversial and (2) that you feel strongly about it. Brainstorm a list of possible subjects about which you can say, "I believe," while some other people would say, "I don't believe." Use brainstorming, freewriting, clustering, or other strategies in narrowing your list of possible subjects. Then use the following guidelines to choose one.

Guidelines for Choosing a Persuasive Essay Subject

- Choose a subject involving a local or national issue that is important to you.
- Choose a subject involving an issue on which people hold very different opinions.

- Choose a subject you can support with examples, reasons, and facts from your own experience or from other reliable sources.
- Choose a subject for which there is an audience whose beliefs or behavior you would like to influence.

Practice Your Skills

Choosing a Persuasive Subject

Explain why each following statement would or would not make a good subject for a persuasive essay.

1. Every child needs loving parents.
2. Pro athletes are paid too much money.
3. There is never a good reason to go to war.
4. The United States is a world leader.
5. A city is a great place to live.

Identifying Your Audience

Just as you take aim before shooting an arrow at a target, you need to identify your target audience when writing a persuasive essay. Readers who initially disagree with your viewpoint will mentally try to block your ideas. The following questions will help you understand your readers.

Questions for Analyzing an Audience

- What does my audience already know about my subject?
- What is my audience's point of view about my subject? Do they already agree or disagree with my position?
- What are the chances of changing the opinions and behavior of my audience?
- Are there any sensitive issues I should be aware of?

Practice Your Skills

Identifying Your Audience

Suppose you wanted to start a chess club at school. Decide whether each of the following statements would be more persuasive to *students* or to the *principal.* If you think they hold equal importance to both audiences, write *both.*

1. A parent has offered to organize and supervise the club.
2. Small dues would pay for all the expenses of the club.
3. Chess is lots of fun. Speed chess is even thrilling.
4. The school's prestige would rise with a winning team.
5. The club would provide a chance to make new friends.
6. There are plenty of rooms available after school.
7. Players would be grouped according to ability, so even beginners could compete at their own level.
8. Playing chess keeps the brain agile and alert.
9. The cost of running the club would be low because equipment is not expensive.
10. Playing chess is a good way to develop strategic skills.
11. Students who play chess after school are less likely to get into trouble.
12. Students who win national chess championships can win cash prizes.

Communicate Your Ideas

PREWRITING *Subject and Audience*

Review your **journal** notes for possible subjects for your persuasive essay. Use the guidelines on pages C447–C448 to make a final choice. Then use the questions on the previous page to help you analyze your audience. Place a check mark beside your choice in your **journal**, and save your paper in your writing folder for use later.

SAVE YOUR WORK

IN THE MEDIA

Presentations in Public Forums

How does a newspaper decide to write an editorial? In many cases, the idea comes from an interested citizen or group. For example, say a citizens' group wants affordable health care. The group will present its arguments to the editors of a local newspaper. The editors, however, could decide to do an editorial supporting the opposing point of view.

Virtually all of the persuading that leads up to a newspaper editorial is oral. For practice in making strong oral presentations of your arguments, complete the following activities. Work in three groups of eight to ten.

First decide on an issue to address—anything students in your school are talking about. Have one of the three groups be the editorial board, another present the issue, and the third present the opposing side.

Carefully think through the best way to divide up your points and express them as effectively as possible. Decide who will be the best speaker to make each point. Be sure all group members understand and practice the plan.

The editorial board must evaluate the presentations, using the following questions.

Questions for Evaluating Public Presentations

- How impressive was each group?
- What really hit home in what they were saying? What fell flat?
- How strong was their evidence and other supporting information?
- How effective were they in using eye contact, posture, and in varying the pitch and tone of their voices?

Put these evaluations in writing. Then collaborate on preparing a brief editorial. Choose one person to present that editorial to the class as effectively as possible.

The other groups should now evaluate the editorial board using the questions above. Discuss what the class learned from the experience.

Developing a Thesis Statement

Once you have chosen your subject and identified your audience, you can begin to develop your **thesis statement**—a statement that clearly and strongly expresses the viewpoint you will be arguing for in your essay. A strong thesis statement expresses a supportable opinion, not just a simple preference. Often a thesis statement will take the form of a recommendation for action.

Simple Preference	Horseback riding is a better pastime than watching television. (unsuitable)
Supportable Opinion	Although horseback riding is a pleasurable pastime, it should not be enjoyed at the expense of the horses' well-being.
Call for Action	Until the care of the horses at Sunset Ridge Stables improves, riders should avoid doing business there.

The guidelines that follow will help you develop your thesis statement.

Guidelines for Developing a Thesis Statement

- Choose a debatable opinion—one that has two sides.
- State the thesis simply in one sentence.
- Avoid hasty generalizations by limiting your statement.
- Give a supportable opinion or a recommendation for action.
- As you gather information, keep revising your thesis statement so that it covers all your evidence.

If you find that you cannot develop a thesis statement according to these guidelines, do not hesitate to try again on a different topic or to rethink your viewpoint.

Practice Your Skills

Choosing a Suitable Thesis Statement

Write whether each of the following statements would be *suitable* or *unsuitable* as a thesis statement for a persuasive essay. Use the preceding guidelines to evaluate each statement.

1. Gardening is the best way to learn about nature.
2. Citizens who enjoy gardening should rally together to convince the city to establish community gardens.
3. Nothing relaxes me as much as listening to music.
4. Cars should not be allowed into any of our national parks.
5. The government should limit auto traffic in national parks to help preserve wildlife habitat and air quality.

Communicate Your Ideas

PREWRITING *Thesis Statement*

Review the subject you chose for your persuasive essay and the audience you have in mind. Use the guidelines on the previous page to write a clear thesis statement. Save your work for later use.

Developing an Argument

In some ways, writing a persuasive essay is like gathering facts and evidence for a courtroom trial. After you have defined your thesis, you need to build a sound case to convince your jury of readers. In addition to listing all the pros—facts, reasons, examples, and expert opinions that support your view—you should also be prepared to answer your opponents by anticipating the cons—the evidence used to oppose your position. Unlike a trial lawyer, however, you are free to go back and revise your position before presenting your final case. The following guidelines will help you develop your argument.

Guidelines for Developing an Argument

- List pros and cons in separate columns in your prewriting notes. Be prepared to address any opposing views
- Use facts and examples to support your opinions.
- If those with an opposing view have a good point, admit it. Then show why the point is not enough to sway your opinion. Such an admission is called **conceding a point,** and it will strengthen your credibility.
- Use polite and reasonable language rather than words that show bias or overcharged emotions.
- Refer to well-respected experts and authorities in the field who agree with your position.

Practice Your Skills

Listing Pros and Cons

For each of the following thesis statements, list three facts, examples, incidents, or expert opinions that support the thesis (pros) and three that oppose it (cons). Save your work.

1. Instead of spending free time in self-centered pastimes, people should devote their energies to worthy causes.
2. The most valuable pastimes are those that a whole family can share together.
3. Movie studios should try to make more high-quality movies even if they never become box office blockbusters.
4. American companies should match the policies of companies in some other countries by providing much longer paid vacations for employees.

Supporting or Contradicting an Argument

A **decision chart** can help you identify the pros and cons of your argument. Use it to organize your ideas or as a check to make sure you have enough information to support your position.

Copy the decision chart shown here. In the center circle, write your thesis statement. Use the boxes to cite facts, examples, and expert views that either support or contradict your argument.

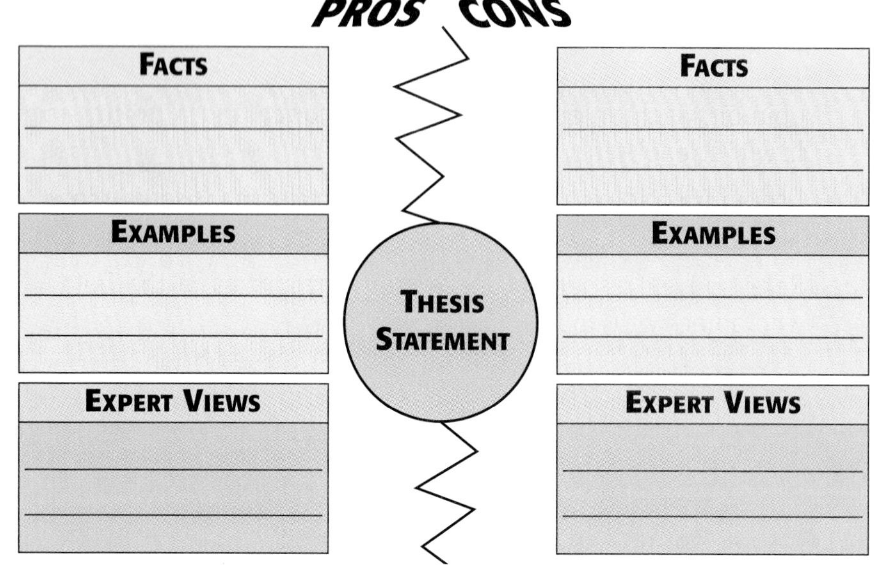

Organizing an Argument

Presenting your evidence in a well-organized way will strengthen your position. Perhaps the most common pattern for persuasive compositions is **order of importance**—starting with the least important point and building up to the most important. Saving your best point for last will help your readers remember your most convincing evidence.

To help you readers follow your organizational pattern, remember to use transitional words and phrases. The transitions that follow are very useful when you are conceding a point or showing contrasting viewpoints.

TRANSITIONS FOR PERSUASIVE WRITING		
although	instead	on the other hand
admittedly	nevertheless	still
however	nonetheless	while it is true that

Practice Your Skills

Organizing Persuasive Evidence

Choose one of the thesis statements from the previous practice activity and decide which side of the issue you wish to support.

1. Revise the thesis statement, if necessary, to state your view.
2. Review the supporting evidence you prepared in the previous activity. Then list, in the order of least to most important, the three points that support your position. Leave two blank lines under each point.
3. Assign each point a Roman numeral as in an outline.
4. Add at least two new supporting points under each Roman numeral. Your outline should look like this.

I. (Least important point)
   A. (Supporting point)
   B. (Supporting point)
II. (More important point)
   A. (Supporting point)
   B. (Supporting point)
III. (Most important point)
   A. (Supporting point)
   B. (Supporting point)

Communicate Your Ideas

PREWRITING *Organization of Evidence*

Review the thesis statement you wrote for your persuasive essay. Use the guidelines on page C453 to help you gather, organize, and evaluate evidence for your essay. Then organize your evidence, using a **decision chart** like the one on the previous page and an outline like the one above. Save your work for later use.

Your outline will guide you as you draft your persuasive essay. You may notice that certain sections of your essay need additional supporting details to be convincing. Make notes in the margin to remember these locations. Rethink your thesis if your draft is not developing as you had hoped.

Pay special attention to the introduction. You may want to begin with an incident or example to show the importance of the issue. Many writers save their thesis statement for the end of the introduction.

When drafting the body, follow your outline ideas unless you see a better way to organize. Write one full paragraph for each of your main supporting points. At appropriate spots, address your opponents' possible differing viewpoints. To achieve a smooth flow, use transitional words and phrases.

You may wish to review transitions on pages C138–C139.

In your conclusion, combine your ideas in a compelling and memorable summary. Restate your recommendations for action, if you are including any. Then add a title that will engage the interest of your audience.

Using Persuasive Language

Overly emotional language weakens your arguments. Powerful, well-chosen words strengthen your case. Use strong but direct words.

EMOTIONAL LANGUAGE	The **slave-driving** owners of the **sickeningly run-down** stables **deserve the same treatment** they give their animals.
FORCEFUL LANGUAGE	The **unsympathetic** owners of the **poorly kept** stables should begin to consider the animals' welfare.

Symbols

Often, especially in advertising, a message will be conveyed through the use of a symbol. Consider the following advertisement.

The purpose of this ad is to represent a feeling and attitude through the use of a visual symbol and then to attach that feeling to the product. The symbol is the eagle in flight, bringing to mind feelings of unlimited freedom and strength. The ad is designed to make you think of the bank's services as so complete that you will be free of down-to-earth concerns. Obviously, unexamined symbolic analogies are as unreliable as other false analogies.

Media Activity

Imagine that you, too, are designing an advertisement for a bank. You have been told to use a visual symbol to help customers associate the bank with solidity, stability, and endurance. You have also been asked to think of a name for the bank. Design an ad that uses a visual symbol, and explain your symbolic analogy in a paragraph.

Communicate Your Ideas

DRAFTING *Persuasive Language*

Write a first draft of your persuasive essay that includes an introduction, a body of well-organized arguments, and a powerful concluding summary. Use strong, yet sincere, persuasive language. Save your work for later use.

Revising

Writing Process

Before you can revise your draft, you need to evaluate it for appropriateness of organization, content, and style.

Checking for Unity, Coherence, and Clarity

You can revise your work on your own by studying it carefully for flaws in unity, coherence, and clarity. When considering unity, ask yourself, "Have I stuck faithfully to my intended subject? Do all of my supporting points relate directly to my thesis statement? Did I include any unnecessary information that might distract my readers?"

When checking for coherence, carefully review your organizational pattern. Did it follow a logical order? Does one idea flow smoothly and logically to the next? Did you include clear and ample transitions?

When evaluating your essay for clarity, check to make sure there is no possibility that your points could be misunderstood. Replace vague language with forceful, specific words. Make sure all terms are clearly defined within the context of your subject. Fully explain any reasons or examples that fail to support your thesis clearly. Erase from your mind all that you already know about your subject and imagine that you are a reader who is completely unfamiliar with the issues of your argument. Will the pros and cons be clear to such a reader?

COMPUTER TIP

You can use **boldface** or *italic* type to accentuate persuasive words in your essay. Use the tool bar to select the style you want.

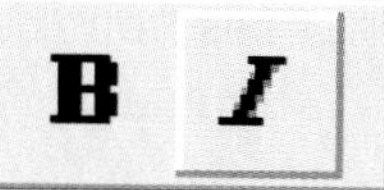

Communicate Your Ideas

REVISING ***Unity, Coherence, and Clarity***
Conferencing

Exchange drafts with a classmate. Ask your partner whether your points are clearly organized and whether your words are convincing. Consider your classmate's comments, your own evaluation, and the following checklist to guide you in strengthening your essay. Save your work for later use.

Evaluation Checklist for Revising

Checking Your Introduction

- ✓ Does the thesis statement present your opinion powerfully? *(page C451)*
- ✓ Will your introduction convince the readers that your topic is important? *(page C456)*
- ✓ Is the language you use both persuasive and objective? *(page C456)*

Checking Your Body Paragraphs

- ✓ Does each paragraph have a topic sentence? *(pages C99–C100)*
- ✓ Have you supported your main points with facts, real-life examples, and expert opinions? *(pages C443–C445)*
- ✓ Have you developed your arguments well and organized them in the most logical way? *(pages C452–C454)*
- ✓ Have you addressed opposing views honestly and effectively? *(page C453)*
- ✓ Have you achieved unity, coherence, and clarity? *(page C458)*

Checking Your Conclusion

✓ Does your conclusion draw your ideas together in a forceful summary? *(page C456)*

✓ Did you include a recommendation for action if appropriate to your thesis? *(page C456)*

Checking Your Words and Sentences

✓ Are your sentences varied? *(pages C71–C78)*

✓ Did you avoid biased, emotionally charged words? *(page C456)*

Editing

Writing Process

After you have revised your essay, edit it for errors in sentence structure, spelling, grammar, capitalization, and punctuation. Use the Editing Workshop and checklist on pages C461–C462 as sources for guidance. You may want to share your work with classmates or family members for additional feedback.

Communicate Your Ideas

EDITING *Sentence Fragments and Run-on Sentences*

Edit your revised draft. Use the Editing Checklist on page C462 to check for sentence fragments and run-ons. Also be sure to check for spelling, capitalization, punctuation, and other errors in grammar. Read through your essay several times, looking for different kinds of errors each time. When you are satisfied, save your essay in your writing folder.

Prewriting Workshop
Drafting Workshop
Revising Workshop
Editing Workshop
Publishing Workshop

Sentence Fragments and Run-on Sentences

"They don't want this. MORE MICE." So wrote the distributor of the animated short *The Skeleton Dance*, an early work by Walt Disney that did not feature mice. In asking the cartoonist to add mice, the distributor relied on capital letters for emphasis and did not even write a complete sentence to express his most important point.

No doubt Walt Disney understood. In more formal writing, however, incomplete sentences can be misunderstood and are usually not appropriate. In your persuasive essay, make sure your sentences are complete.

Sentence Fragments

A **sentence fragment** is a group of words that does not express a complete thought. A common type of fragment is a phrase that has neither a subject nor a verb.

Sentence Fragments	
	Settling back in my seat
	In the dark of a theater
	To share the experience

One way to detect a fragment is to read aloud. When you finish reading most fragments, your voice will still be pitched high, as if you were expecting more information.

Sentences	
	Settling back in my seat, **I lose myself in the larger-than-life screen**.
	In the dark of a theater, **nothing stands between me and the images on the screen**.
	To share the experience, **nothing beats being part of an appreciative movie audience.**

Run-on Sentences

Another common writing mistake is a **run-on sentence.** This mistake happens when one sentence literally runs into another sentence. To correct a run-on sentence, you need to separate the two sentences—with a period and a capital letter, with a comma and a conjunction, or with a semicolon.

Run-on Sentence	Disney's first feature-length cartoon was *Snow White* audiences loved it.
Corrected Sentences	Disney's first feature-length cartoon was *Snow White*. **A**udiences loved it.
	Disney's first feature-length cartoon was *Snow White*, **and** audiences loved it.
	Disney's first feature length cartoon was *Snow White*; audiences loved it.

Another way to correct a run-on sentence is to make one of the sentences a subordinate clause.

Corrected Sentences	**When Disney made *Snow White,* the studio's first feature-length cartoon,** audiences loved it.
	Audiences loved it **when Disney made *Snow White,*** the studio's first feature-length film.

Editing Checklist

✔ Are there any sentence fragments?
✔ Are there any run-on sentences?
✔ Did you use commas and semicolons correctly?
✔ Did you use the correct capitalization and punctuation for complete sentences?

Part of the satisfaction of persuasive writing is that you might make a difference in the world—even if you change just one person's point of view—through what you write.

Communicate Your Ideas

PUBLISHING

Complete the writing process by sharing your essay with a reader who has an interest in the subject. If appropriate, you may wish to submit your essay to your school or local newspaper.

PORTFOLIO

Time Out to Reflect

If you wrote a persuasive essay earlier in the year, use it as a basis for comparison with the persuasive essay you just completed. How have your persuasive writing skills deepened? In writing your persuasive essay(s), which techniques did you find especially effective? Why? What would you like to improve in writing your next persuasive essay? Record your responses in the Learning Log section of your **journal**.

Process of Writing a Persuasive Essay

As you move through the various stages of the writing process, remember that you can move back and forth among them in an effort to produce your best work. For example, you may return to the revising stage to add important details that occurred to you during the editing stage.

PREWRITING

- Use brainstorming, freewriting, or clustering to identify issues about which you have strong opinions. *(page C447)*
- Choose one subject, and identify the audience you want to persuade. Write a thesis statement that accurately and powerfully presents your opinion. *(pages C447–C451)*
- Brainstorm a list of supporting ideas. *(pages C27–C28)*
- Develop a strong argument by supporting the thesis with facts and examples. *(pages C452–C453)*
- Organize the details of your argument in an outline in order of importance. *(pages C454–C455)*

DRAFTING

- Write an introduction that includes your thesis statement. *(pages C225–C227)*
- Use your outline to write the body. *(pages C234–C235)*
- Use transitional words to link your thoughts. *(pages C237–C238)*
- Add a concluding paragraph and a title. *(page C240)*

REVISING

- Avoid highly charged, emotional language. *(page C456)*
- Revise your essay after peer conferencing and incorporate worthwhile suggestions. *(page C42)*
- Revise your essay for unity, coherence, and clarity. *(page C458)*

EDITING

- Use the Editing Checklists to check your grammar, usage, mechanics, and spelling. *(pages C44 and C462)*

PUBLISHING

- Make a neat final copy of your essay in standard manuscript form and share your persuasive essay with readers. *(page C463)*

A Writer Writes

A Persuasive Essay

Purpose: to persuade adults in authority to regulate video games in some way or to oppose regulation

Audience: lawmakers or video game producers

The growth in the video game industry, which earns billions of dollars a year in the United States alone, has raised challenging questions about how young people spend much of their free time. Of special concern to many is the violence in many popular video games, the goals of which are to score as many "fatalities" as possible. As the technology has improved, the graphics on the screen have become more and more realistic. Sometimes disturbing images flash across the screen as players try to outmaneuver their electronic enemies.

Should this violence be regulated? Should violent video games be banned altogether? If violence in video games should be regulated, what are some appropriate ways to do so? Should studies be undertaken to determine the possible relationship between the violence in video games and violence in real life? Are the violent video games potentially harmful, or are they a safe and useful way for young people to spend time and "blow off steam"?

Prewriting

Before you decide your position on this issue, read some newspaper and magazine articles. Talk to your friends and anyone else who might have a worthwhile insight. Then form your opinion. Decide whether you want to address lawmakers or video game manufacturers. Draft a thesis statement.

Continue to gather information until you have a sound set of facts, reasons, and examples to support

your thesis. You may need to revise your thesis statement to reflect what you have learned. Then outline an organizational plan for your editorial.

Drafting

As you begin your draft, consider ways to capture your readers' interest and attention in the introduction. Also include your clearly worded thesis statement in your introduction. In the body of your essay, follow your outline and use logical reasoning to develop your supporting points. As you draft your conclusion, try to draw your ideas together in a strong summary. Restate your recommendation for action or nonaction clearly and forcefully.

Revising

If possible, put your essay away for a few days so that you can come back to it with a fresh, objective view. Use the **Evaluation Checklist for Revising** on pages C459–C460 to guide you in making your essay as strong as it can be.

Editing

Polish your persuasive essay with the help of the checklists on pages C44 and C462.

Publishing

After making a neat final draft, write a letter to accompany it to its intended audience. In your letter, explain why you wrote the essay. Send the letter and essay to your intended audience.

Connection Collection

Representing in Different Ways

From Print . . .

27 Olympia Drive
Bourne, TX 78006
October 1, 2000

Mr. U. R. Money
Deep Pockets Investors
101 Insider Street
Cashville, KY 40160

Dear Mr. Money:

The Internet is the wave of the future, and our company, Solvent Internet Technologies, is riding that wave! We build servers that allow people all over the world to access the Internet. Our company's stock value rose from $12 per share in 1998, to $20 per share in 1999, to over $36 per share in 2000. Purchasing stock in our company can bring a huge return on your investment. Please contact me for further information regarding this exciting investment opportunity.

Yours truly,

Jimmy Stock

Jimmy Stock
Vice President of
Investor Development

. . . to Visuals

Create a line graph based on the information in the letter above. The graph should illustrate the value of Solvent Internet Technologies' stock between 1998 and 2000.

From Visuals . . .

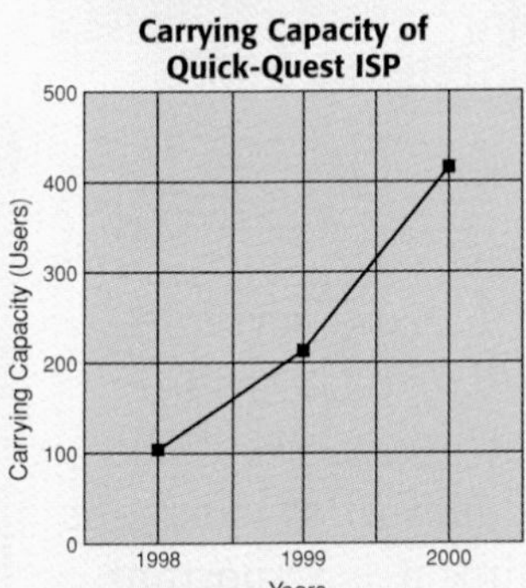

. . . to Print

The graph above illustrates that the carrying capacity of Quick-Quest ISP has quadrupled over the past three years. Write a letter to convince a friend that Quick-Quest ISP is the best Internet service provider in town.

- **Which strategies can be used for creating both written and visual representations? Which strategies apply to one, not both? Which type of representation is more effective?**
- **Draw a conclusion and write briefly about the differences between written ideas and visual representations.**

Writing for Oral Communication

Persuasive Oral Presentation

You have a summer job working for the street division of Rockin' Robots Incorporated. While setting up your demonstration table in the park, you meet someone who may be interested in buying a Rockin' Robot. You want to explain why buying a robot from your company will help your potential customer to conduct business and personal affairs efficiently.

Prepare and deliver an oral presentation persuading the person you meet in the park that buying a Rockin' Robot will improve the quality of his or her life. Offer a thesis and use examples to support it. Remember to use transitions for persuasive writing and a voice appropriate to your audience. Deliver your proposal to classmates or family members who will listen as the potential customer.

What strategies did you use to persuade the person in the park?

You can find information on oral presentations on pages C596–C603.

Writing in the Workplace

Persuasive Business Letter

You are a site supervisor for Interstellar Building Manufacturers—a firm that constructs hotels on the planet Mars. The spaceship flight between Earth and Mars takes three months each way. The food on the flight is horrendous, and the poor quality of cuisine is clearly demoralizing for the employees. You think it is important to persuade your boss that serving better-quality food is a good business decision. The employees are not eating well, and when they arrive on Mars, they are too tired and weak to work well.

Write a letter to your boss persuading him that serving tastier food will increase worker productivity. Be sure to use polite and reasonable language. Also be sure to provide examples that support your opinion.

What strategies did you use to persuade your boss?

You can find information on writing business letters on pages C579–C588.

Assess Your Learning

You play guitar and write songs for a rock-and-roll band called The Garbage Gurus. Your manager just received a letter from your record company, Recycled Records. The letter says that some executives at Recycled Records are unhappy with certain songs from your latest recording session. Specifically they do not like the song "My Record Company Stinks" and do not want it included on The Garbage Gurus' next CD. This is your favorite song from the session, and you also really believe it will be a big seller.

- **Write a letter to Recycled Records explaining why "My Record Company Stinks" should be included on your next album.**
- **Be sure to present both sides of the issue, acknowledging opposing views. Use facts and examples to support your position. Make sure your letter has an introduction, supporting details, and a conclusion. Also make sure you are using a voice appropriate to your audience.**

Before You Write **Consider the following questions:**
What is the ***subject?***
What is the ***occasion?***
Who is the ***audience?***
What is the ***purpose?***

After You Write **Evaluate your work using the following criteria:**

- Have you presented both sides of the issue and acknowledged opposing views?
- Does your persuasive letter include an introduction, supporting points, and a conclusion?
- Have you supported your main thesis statement with facts and examples?
- Have you organized your ideas in writing to ensure coherence, logical progression, and support for ideas?
- Did you use transitions for persuasive writing such as *although*, *on the other hand*, *nevertheless,* and *however*?
- Have you checked for grammatical, spelling, and punctuation errors that might weaken your authority in the eyes of the audience?

Write briefly on how well you did. Point out your strengths and areas for improvement.

CHAPTER 11

Writing About Literature

"That was the scariest movie I've ever seen!"

"I hated that book. It was completely unrealistic."

"I like their music, but their lyrics are the best."

Almost everybody has a response after seeing a movie, reading a book, or attending a concert. Works of literature are meant to have an effect. Sometimes the effect is a fizzle, and sometimes it's volcanic—powerful enough to change someone's life.

When you respond to a work of literature by writing about it, you can develop a greater appreciation for the craft of the writer. You can also enhance your own critical and imaginative abilities as a reader and writer.

Reading with a Writer's Eye

In the following story, "Say It with Flowers," the main character, Teruo, faces a dilemma. He can do the right thing, which may prove costly, or he can change or lower his standards. As you read, look for the standards that form the basis of Teruo's decision. On a second reading, notice how the author, Toshio Mori, builds the character's internal conflict and guides him to a decision.

FROM *Yokohama, California*

SAY IT WITH FLOWERS

Toshio Mori

He was a queer one to come to the shop and ask Mr. Sasaki for a job, but at the time I kept my mouth shut. There was something about this young man's appearance which I could not altogether harmonize with a job as a clerk in a flower shop. I was a delivery boy for Mr. Sasaki then. I had seen clerks come and go, and although they were of various sorts of temperaments and conducts, all of them had the technique of waiting on the customers or acquired one eventually. You could never tell about a new one, however, and to be on the safe side I said nothing and watched our boss readily take on this young man. Anyhow we were glad to have an extra hand because the busy season was coming around.

Mr. Sasaki undoubtedly remembered last year's rush when Tommy, Mr. Sasaki and I had to do everything and had our hands tied behind our backs from having so many things to do at one time. He wanted to be ready this time. "Another clerk and we'll be all set for any kind of business," he used to tell us. When Teruo came around looking for a job, he got it, and Morning-Glory Flower Shop was all set for the year as far as our boss was concerned.

When Teruo reported for work the following morning Mr. Sasaki left him in Tommy's hands. Tommy had been our number one clerk for a long time.

"Tommy, teach him all you can," Mr. Sasaki said. "Teruo's going to be with us from now on."

"Sure," Tommy said.

"Tommy's a good florist. You watch and listen to him," the boss told the young man.

"All right, Mr. Sasaki," the young man said. He turned to us and said, "My name is Teruo." We shook hands.

We got to know one another pretty well after that. He was a quiet fellow with very little words for anybody, but his smile disarmed a person. We soon learned that he knew nothing about the florist business. He could identify a rose when he saw one, and gardenias and carnations too; but other flowers and materials were new to him.

"You fellows teach me something about this business and I'll be grateful. I want to start from the bottom," Teruo said.

Tommy and I nodded. We were pretty sure by then he was all right. Tommy eagerly went about showing Teruo the florist game. Every morning for several days Tommy repeated the prices of the flowers for him. He told Teruo what to do on telephone orders; how to keep the greens fresh; how to make bouquets, corsages, and sprays. "You need a little more time to learn how to make big funeral pieces," Tommy said. "That'll come later."

In a couple of weeks Teruo was just as good a clerk as we had had in a long time. He was curious almost to a fault, and was a glutton for work. It was about this time our boss decided to move ahead his yearly business trip to Seattle. Undoubtedly he was satisfied with Teruo, and he knew we could get along without him for a while. He went off and left Tommy in full charge.

During Mr. Sasaki's absence I was often in the shop helping Tommy and Teruo with the customers and the orders. One day Teruo learned that I once worked in the nursery and had experience in flower-growing.

"How do you tell when a flower is fresh or old?" he asked me. "I can't tell one from the other. All I do is follow your instructions and sell the ones you tell me to sell first, but I can't tell one from the other."

I laughed. "You don't need to know that, Teruo," I told him. "When the customers ask you whether the flowers are fresh, say yes firmly. 'Our flowers are always fresh, madam.'"

Teruo picked up a vase of carnations. "These flowers came in four or five days ago, didn't they?" he asked me.

"You're right. Five days ago," I said.

"How long will they keep if a customer bought them today?" Teruo asked.

"I guess in this weather they'll hold a day or two," I said.

"Then they're old," Teruo almost gasped. "Why, we have fresh ones that last a week or so in the shop."

"Sure, Teruo. And why should you worry about that?" Tommy said. "You talk right to the customers and they'll believe you. 'Our flowers are always fresh? You bet they are! Just came in a little while ago from the market.'"

Teruo looked at us calmly, "That's a hard thing to say when you know it isn't true."

"You've got to get it over with sooner or later," I told him. "Everybody has to do it. You too, unless you want to lose your job."

"I don't think I can say it convincingly again," Teruo said. "I must've said yes forty times already when I didn't know any better. It'll be harder next time."

"You've said it forty times already so why can't you say yes forty million times more? What's the difference? Remember, Teruo, it's your business to live," Tommy said.

"I don't like it," Teruo said.

"Do we like it? Do you think we're any different from you?" Tommy asked Teruo. "You're just a green kid. You don't know any better so I don't get sore, but you got to play the game when you're in it. You understand, don't you?"

Teruo nodded. For a moment he stood and looked curiously at us for the first time, and then went away to water the potted plants.

In the ensuing weeks we watched Teruo develop into a slick salesclerk but for one thing. If a customer forgot to ask about the condition of the flowers Teruo did splendidly. But if someone should mention about the freshness of the flowers he wilted right in front of the customers. Sometimes he would splutter. He would stand gaping speechless on other occasions without a comeback. Sometimes, looking embarrassedly at us, he would take the customers to the fresh flowers in the rear and complete the sales.

"Don't do that anymore, Teruo," Tommy warned him one afternoon after watching him repeatedly sell the fresh ones. "You know we got plenty of the old stuff in the front. We can't throw all that stuff away. First thing you know the boss'll start losing money and we'll all be thrown out."

"I wish I could sell like you," Teruo said. "Whenever they ask me, 'Is it fresh?' 'How long will it keep?' I lose all sense about selling the stuff, and begin to think of the difference between the fresh and the old stuff. Then the trouble begins."

"Remember, the boss has to run the shop so he can keep it going," Tommy told him. "When he returns next week you better not let him see you touch the fresh flowers in the rear."

On the day Mr. Sasaki came back to the shop we saw something unusual. For the first time I watched Teruo sell some old stuff to a customer. I heard the man plainly ask him if the flowers would keep good, and very clearly I heard Teruo reply, "Yes, sir. These flowers'll keep good." I looked at Tommy, and he winked back. When Teruo came back to make it into a bouquet he looked as if he had a snail in his mouth. Mr. Sasaki came back to the rear and watched him make the bouquet. When Teruo went up front to complete the sale Mr. Sasaki looked at Tommy and nodded approvingly.

When I went out to the truck to make my last delivery for the day Teruo followed me. "Gee, I feel rotten," he said to me. "Those flowers I sold to the people, they won't last longer than tomorrow. I feel lousy. I'm lousy. The people'll get to know my word pretty soon."

"Forget it," I said. "Quit worrying. What's the matter with you?"

"I'm lousy," he said, and went back to the store.

Then one early morning the inevitable happened. While Teruo was selling the fresh flowers in the back to a customer Mr. Sasaki came in quietly and watched the transaction. The boss didn't say anything at the time. All day Teruo looked sick. He didn't know whether to explain to the boss or shut up.

While Teruo was out to lunch Mr. Sasaki called us aside. "How long has this been going on?" he asked us. He was pretty sore.

"He's been doing it off and on. We told him to quit it," Tommy, said. "He says he feels rotten selling old flowers."

"Old flowers!" snorted Mr. Sasaki. "I'll tell him plenty when he comes back. Old flowers! Maybe you can call them old at the wholesale market but they're not old in a flower shop."

"He feels guilty fooling the customers," Tommy explained.

The boss laughed impatiently. "That's no reason for a businessman."

When Teruo came back he knew what was up. He looked at us for a moment and then went about cleaning the stems of the old flowers.

"Teruo," Mr. Sasaki called.

Teruo approached us as if steeled for an attack.

"You've been selling fresh flowers and leaving the old ones go to waste. I can't afford that, Teruo," Mr. Sasaki said. "Why don't you do as you're told? We all sell the flowers in the front.

I tell you they're not old in a flower shop. Why can't you sell them?"

"I don't like it, Mr. Sasaki," Teruo said. "When the people ask me if they're fresh I hate to answer. I feel rotten after selling the old ones."

"Look here, Teruo," Mr. Sasaki said. "I don't want to fire you. You're a good boy, and I know you need a job, but you've got to be a good clerk here or you're going out. Do you get me?"

"I get you," Teruo said.

In the morning we were all at the shop early. I had an eight o'clock delivery, and the others had to rush with a big funeral order. Teruo was there early. "Hello," he greeted us cheerfully as we came in. He was unusually highspirited, and I couldn't account for it. He was there before us and had already filled out the eight o'clock package for me. He was almost through with the funeral frame, padding it with wet moss and covering it all over with brake fern, when Tommy came in. When Mr. Sasaki arrived, Teruo waved his hand and cheerfully went about gathering the flowers for the funeral piece. As he flitted here and there he seemed as if he had forgotten our presence, even the boss. He looked at each vase, sized up the flowers, and then cocked his head at the next one. He did this with great deliberation, as if he were the boss and the last word in the shop. That was all right, but when a customer soon came in, he swiftly attended him as if he owned all the flowers in the world. When the man asked Teruo if he was getting fresh flowers Teruo without batting an eye escorted the customer into the rear and eventually showed and sold the fresh ones. He did it with so much grace, dignity and swiftness that we stood around like his stooges. However, Mr. Sasaki went on with his work as if nothing had happened.

Along toward noon Teruo attended his second customer. He fairly ran to greet an old lady who wanted a cheap bouquet around fifty cents for a dinner table. This time he not only went back to the rear for the fresh ones but added three or four extras. To make it more irritating for the boss, who was watching every move, Teruo used an extra lot of maidenhair because the old lady was appreciative of his art of making bouquets. Tommy and I watched the boss fuming inside of his office.

When the old lady went out of the shop Mr. Sasaki came out furious. "You're a blockhead. You have no business sense. What are you doing here?" he said to Teruo. "Are you crazy?"

Teruo looked cheerful. "I'm not crazy, Mr. Sasaki," he said. "And I'm not dumb. I just like to do it that way, that's all."

The boss turned to Tommy and me. "That boy's a sap," he said. "He's got no head."

Teruo laughed and walked off to the front with a broom. Mr. Sasaki shook his head. "What's the matter with him? I can't understand him," he said.

While the boss was out to lunch Teruo went on a mad spree. He waited on three customers at one time, ignoring our presence. It was amazing how he did it. He hurriedly took one customer's order and had him write a birthday greeting for it; jumped to the second customer's side and persuaded her to buy Columbia roses because they were the freshest of the lot. She wanted them delivered so he jotted it down on the sales book, and leaped to the third customer.

"I want to buy that orchid in the window," she stated without deliberation.

"Do you have to have orchid, madam?" Teruo asked the lady.

"No," she said. "But I want something nice for tonight's ball, and I think the orchid will match my dress. Why do you ask?"

"If I were you I wouldn't buy that orchid," he told her. "It won't keep. I could sell it to you and make a profit but I don't want to do that and spoil your evening. Come to the back, madam, and I'll show you some of the nicest gardenias in the market today. We call them Belmont and they're fresh today."

He came to the rear with the lady. We watched him pick out three of the biggest gardenias and make them into a corsage. When the lady went out with her package a little boy about eleven years old came in and wanted a twenty-five-cent bouquet for his mother's birthday. Teruo waited on the boy. He was out in the front, and we saw him pick out a dozen of the two-dollar-a-dozen roses and give them to the kid.

Tommy nudged me. "If he was the boss he couldn't do those things," he said.

"In the first place," I said, "I don't think he could be a boss."

"What do you think?" Tommy said. "Is he crazy? Is he trying to get himself fired?"

"I don't know," I said.

When Mr. Sasaki returned, Teruo was waiting on another customer, a young lady.

"Did Teruo eat yet?" Mr. Sasaki asked Tommy.

"No, he won't go. He says he's not hungry today," Tommy said.

We watched Teruo talking to the young lady. The boss shook his head. Then it came. Teruo came back to the rear and picked out a dozen of the very fresh white roses and took them out to the lady.

"Aren't they lovely?" we heard her exclaim.

We watched him come back, take down a box, place several maidenhairs and asparagus, place the roses neatly inside, sprinkle a few drops, and then give it to her. We watched him thank her, and we noticed her smile and thanks. The girl walked out.

Mr. Sasaki ran excitedly to the front. "Teruo! She forgot to pay!"

Teruo stopped the boss on the way out. "Wait, Mr. Sasaki," he said. "I gave it to her."

"What!" the boss cried indignantly.

"She came in just to look around and see the flowers. She likes pretty roses. Don't you think she's wonderful?"

"What's the matter with you?" the boss said. "Are you crazy? What did she buy?"

"Nothing, I tell you," Teruo said. "I gave it to her because she admired it, and she's pretty enough to deserve beautiful things, and I liked her."

"You're fired! Get out!" Mr. Sasaki spluttered. "Don't come back to the store again."

"And I gave her fresh ones too," Teruo said.

Mr. Sasaki rolled out several bills from his pocketbook. "Here's your wages for this week. Now, get out," he said.

"I don't want it," Teruo said. "You keep it and buy some more flowers."

"Here, take it. Get out," Mr. Sasaki said.

Teruo took the bills and rang up the cash register. "All right, I'll go now. I feel fine. I'm happy. Thanks to you." He waved his hand to Mr. Sasaki. "No hard feelings."

On the way out Teruo remembered our presence. He looked back. "Good-bye, Good luck," he said cheerfully to Tommy and me. He walked out of the shop with his shoulders straight, head high, and whistling. He did not come back to see us again.

Thinking as a Writer

Analyzing the Use of a Narrator

Think about the narrator—the "I"—in "Say It with Flowers."

- What kind of person do you think he is? Cite evidence in the story that supports your opinion.
- Why do you think the writer chose to have this character tell the story? How would the story's effect be similar or different if Teruo were the narrator?

Interpreting Character Motivation and Conflict

Oral Expression

- In a small group, role-play a meeting with Teruo, Mr. Sasaki, and a business counselor who wants to help the two men resolve their conflict. Mr. Sasaki can state reasons for his dissatisfaction with Teruo. Teruo can offer explanations for his behavior. The business counselor should work to help each character understand—not necessarily agree with—the other's point of view. The outcome of the session may be a parting of the ways or a new understanding of how the boss and employee might work things out.

Judging the Effectiveness of a Logo

Viewing

The logo below is one that Mr. Sasaki might use to advertise his flower shop.

- What message does the logo convey? Which words express Mr. Sasaki's business philosophy? Which words describe Teruo's approach to selling flowers?

Morning-Glory
Flower Shop
"Fresh flowers that
touch the heart!"
FAST, FRIENDLY SERVICE

The Power of Literary Analysis

Literature plays an important role in our individual lives and in the "life" of our society. It is a powerful means of expressing common experiences and emotions and universal truths. By analyzing literature, we often come to better understand ourselves and the world we live in.

Uses of Literary Analysis

Written and oral responses to literature take many different forms. Here are some examples you may have read, heard, or experienced.

- **A television movie critic reviews a new film** and analyzes character development, imagery, and dialogue.
- **A child presents her first oral report** on a book she has read, explaining what the story was about and why she liked it.
- **A reporter discusses a poem that was recited at a presidential inauguration,** commenting on what he thinks the poem means and how it appropriately commemorates the event.
- **An Internet company encourages users to post online reviews of books and movies** to guide other shoppers and boost sales.
- **A book group ponders new ideas** as the members share their personal responses to a new novel.

Process of Writing a Literary Analysis

Writing about a literary work helps you digest and appreciate it. Vladimir Nabokov described the process this way:

> Literature, real literature, must not be gulped down . . . Literature must be taken and broken into bits, pulled apart, squashed. . . . [T]hen, and only then, its rare flavor will be appreciated . . . and the broken and crushed parts will come together again in your mind.

This process enables a reader to respond to a work of literature—to write a literary analysis.

A **literary analysis** presents an interpretation of a work of literature and supports that interpretation with appropriate responses, details, and quotations.

Your Writer's Journal

In your journal, write the titles of, and your responses to, various pieces of literature that you read in school and on your own. Also pay attention to the quality of writing in the scripts for your favorite television programs. Jot down the titles of the shows, and describe what you like about the dialogue, characters, or themes. Do the same for the screenplays of movies you rent or see in a theater. In this way, you will begin to become aware of some common features among all literary forms—features you might focus on in a literary analysis.

"Say It with Flowers" is a literary work of the type known as the short story. Other literary forms—**genres**—include novels, poems, and plays. These genres have the following characteristics.

Characteristics of Literary Genres

Short Story	A short work of narrative fiction. The story often occurs within a short period of time and involves few characters and settings. Readers rely mainly on the writer's descriptions and on dialogue to understand the plot, characters, setting, and theme.
Novel	A long work of narrative fiction with a plot that is unfolded by the actions, speech, and thoughts of the characters. Like most short stories, a novel presents a central conflict and its resolution or outcome.
Poem	A form of writing that presents images using condensed, vivid language that is chosen for the way it sounds as well as for its meaning. Characteristics commonly include the use of meter, rhyme, and figurative language.
Play	A work written for dramatic performance on the stage. Like a short story, a play usually tells a story that revolves around the resolution of a central conflict. The audience relies on dialogue, stage sets, and action to understand the setting, plot, characters, and theme.

Prewriting

Writing Process

Reading is more than appreciating the "rare flavor" of a literary work. Like writing, reading is a creative process. As a reader, you help create the meaning of a literary work. Because each reader brings personal meanings to a work, a story, poem, or play affects different readers in different ways, and no work has a single, correct meaning. Instead, the meaning grows out of the relationship between the writer's words and each reader's response. That response comes from several sources. Reading is a process of interpretation within an acceptable range.

Sources of a Reader's Response to Literature

- Individual characteristics—such as age, sex, and personality
- Cultural or ethnic origins, attitudes, and customs
- Personal opinions, beliefs, and values
- Life experiences and general knowledge
- Knowledge of literature and literary genres
- Knowledge of the historical and cultural context of a work
- Reading and language skills

All of these sources combine to affect your response to anything you read. Who you are, where you live, and what your life has been like so far, for example, may enable you to identify with a character, situation, or feeling in a work. When you identify with characters, you put yourself in their shoes; you see what they see and feel what they feel. The more closely you can identify with characters, the more enjoyment and meaning you will usually find in reading and writing about a literary work.

Responding from Personal Experience

One of the reasons you may enjoy reading and writing about a particular work is the pleasure you get from recalling your own past. A story, play, or poem will often trigger memories of your feelings and experiences. You use these memories to identify closely with characters.

In the process of identifying, you may recall times in your life when you were in similar situations and how you felt at those times. For example, if you identify with Teruo in "Say It with Flowers," you may remember a time in your life when you were in conflict with others over behaviors that you felt were wrong. This type of memory may give the story a deeper meaning for you. The following strategies will help you explore your personal responses to a literary work.

Personal Response Strategies

1. In your **journal,** freewrite answers to the following questions.
   - **a.** Which character do you identify with most closely? Why? Do other characters remind you of people you know? If so, how?
   - **b.** How does the work make you feel? Why?
   - **c.** If you were a character in the work, would you have behaved differently? What behaviors in the story puzzle you?
   - **d.** What experiences from your own life came to your mind as you read this work? How did you feel about those experiences?
2. Write a personal response statement in which you summarize what the work means to you.
3. In small discussion groups, share your responses to the work. As you listen to your classmates' reactions, refine your ideas about the work. Afterward write freely about how, if at all, your ideas about the work have changed.

Practice Your Skills

Responding from Personal Experience

Complete the following activity in your journal.

1. Based on your first reading of "Say It with Flowers," write answers to the questions in the Personal Response Strategies above.
2. Reread the story up to the last paragraph on page C473, and stop to write your reactions. What do you think of the characters? What do you think of Teruo's approach to learning his job? When you first read the story, what did you think was going to happen next?

3. Continue rereading, this time stopping before the last paragraph on page C475. Again write your reactions. Have your feelings about any of the characters changed? What does Teruo mean by saying, "I'm lousy"? What is he trying to do when he defies his boss? Did your predictions about the ending change at this point? Why or why not?
4. Finish rereading the story, and write whether your predictions were accurate. Then write freely about any memories you had from your own life as you read the story. Conclude by writing a personal response statement that explains what this story means to you.

Communicate Your Ideas

PREWRITING *Personal Response*

Reread "A Day's Wait" *(pages C332–C335)* by Ernest Hemingway, and write a personal response statement about this short story. Explain how you feel about the characters and what the story means to you. Save your work for later use.

SAVE YOUR WORK

Responding from Literary Knowledge

As a reader, you not only respond to each work on the basis of your past experience and background, but you also apply your knowledge of other stories, poems, or plays that you have read. Through reading, you develop a deeper understanding of the characteristics that distinguish each genre. This knowledge helps you interpret a work and appreciate a writer's skill. When you respond to literature on the basis of your literary knowledge, you analyze its **elements**.

The following chart describes the three main elements of literature—fiction, poetry, and drama. Because drama has most of the same elements as other works of fiction, the elements listed under "drama" show only how reading a dramatic work differs from reading other kinds of fiction.

ELEMENTS OF LITERATURE

FICTION

Plot	the events in a story that lead to a **climax** (high point) and to an outcome that resolves a central conflict
Setting	when and where the story takes place
Characters	the people in the story who advance the plot through their thoughts and actions
Dialogue	conversations among characters that reveal their personalities, actions, and **motivations**, or reasons for behaving as they do
Tone	the writer's attitude toward her or his characters
Point of View	the "voice" telling the story—first person *(I)* or third person *(he, she,* or *they)*
Theme	main idea or message of the story

POETRY

Persona	the person whose "voice" is saying the poem, revealing the character the poet is assuming
Meter	the rhythm of stressed and unstressed syllables in each line of the poem
Rhyme Scheme	the pattern of rhymed sounds, usually at the ends of lines
Sound Devices	techniques for playing with sounds to create certain effects, such as **alliteration** and **onomatopoeia**
Figures of Speech	imaginative language, such as **similes** and **metaphors**, which create images by making comparisons
Shape	the way a poem looks on the printed page, which may contribute to the underlying meaning of the poet's thoughts and feelings
Theme	the overall feeling or underlying meaning of the poem, which expresses the poet's thoughts and feelings

DRAMA	
SETTING	the time and place of the action; lighting and the stage sets, as described in the stage directions
CHARACTERS	people who participate in the action of the play
PLOT	the story of the play divided into acts and scenes and developed through the characters' words and actions
THEME	the meaning of a play, revealed through the setting and the characters' words and actions

How Literary Elements Contribute to Meaning The elements of each genre contribute to the meaning of a work. The following list of questions can help you explore the meaning of a poem, a play, a short story, or a novel.

Questions for Finding Meaning in Fiction

Plot

- What is the impact of each main event in the development of the plot? How does each event affect the main characters?
- What details in the plot reveal the narrator's attitude toward the central conflict? What do the climax and the ending reveal about the theme?

Setting

- How does the setting contribute to the mood of the story? How do details of the setting help define the characters?
- What details of the setting are most important in the development of the plot? How do details relate to the theme?

Characters

- How do the characters relate to their setting?
- How does each character contribute to the development of the plot? How do the details of characterization reveal personalities?
- What does the dialogue reveal about the characters' personalities and motivations? How does the point of view of

the story affect the characterizations? What does the point of view contribute to the theme?

Theme

- What passages and details in the story best express the main theme? What other story elements contribute to the meaning?
- How does the author communicate the theme through the development of setting, characters, and plot? What else have you read that has a similar theme?

Questions for Finding Meaning in Poetry

- What is the poet's persona? How does the persona relate to the subject, mood, and theme of the poem?
- How does the meter affect the rhythm of the poem? How does that rhythm express the mood?
- How does the rhyme scheme affect the expression of thoughts and feelings?
- If the poet uses sound devices like alliteration and onomatopoeia, what sounds do you hear in the poem? What images do those sound devices create in your mind?
- What images do the figures of speech create? What feelings do those images suggest?
- How does the shape of the poem relate to the subject, mood, or theme?
- What effect does the poem have on you? How does the poem achieve its effect? What meaning does the poem have for you?
- What feeling, theme, or message does the poem express?
- What specific word choices are memorable and effective?

Questions for Finding Meaning in Drama

- What details of setting and character do the stage directions emphasize? How do those details contribute to the impact of the play?

- What are the key relationships among the characters? How do those relationships reveal the central conflict? What changes in the relationships help resolve the conflict?
- How does the dialogue advance the plot? What plot developments occur with each change of act and scene?
- What subject and theme does the play treat? What in the play has meaning for you?

Evaluating a Literary Work Analyzing the elements in a story or a poem helps you make judgments about the work. However, because there are many different standards of evaluation, your personal judgment will not always agree with the judgments of literary critics, historians, biographers, teachers, and classmates. You may find it helpful to know the criteria by which any great work of literature, or classic, is usually judged. **Classics** are literary works that withstand the test of time and appeal to readers from generation to generation and from century to century. When you evaluate a literary work, consider the following characteristics.

Some Characteristics of Great Literature

- Explores great themes in human nature and the human experience that many people can identify with—such as growing up, family life, personal struggles, or war
- Expresses universal values—such as truth or hope—to which people from many different backgrounds and cultures can relate
- Conveys a timeless message that remains true for many generations of readers
- Presents vivid impressions of characters, settings, and situations that many generations of readers can treasure

Not all works of literature, of course, are classics. You may discover a contemporary story about which you wish to write a literary analysis. Some of the characteristics listed above may apply to a new work you have read. Whether or not a literary work you are reading is regarded as a classic, you can apply other standards of evaluation. When you are making judgments about a work, ask yourself the following questions.

Questions for Evaluating Literature

- How inventive and original is the work?
- How vividly and believably are the characters, settings, dialogue, actions, and feelings portrayed? In fiction, how well structured is the plot? Is there a satisfying resolution of the central conflict?
- How strongly did you react to the work? Did you identify with a character, situation, or feeling? Did the work touch your memories and emotions?
- Did the work have meaning for you? What do you think you will remember about it in the future?

Practice Your Skills

Responding from Literary Knowledge

Express your opinions about "Say It with Flowers" on pages C471–C479 by answering the following questions.

1. What are the three most important events in the plot and what is the importance of each one? How do the events relate to the central conflict in the story?
2. Why does Teruo behave the way he does when he is working at the flower shop? Do his actions change much from the beginning of the story to the end? Explain how and why his actions do or do not change.
3. How do the other characters react to Teruo's actions? Do their opinions of him change? On what grounds do they conclude that Teruo would not succeed in business?
4. What details in the setting bring the story to life?
5. What is the theme of the story—that is, what thought or message does the story convey?
6. From what point of view is the story told? Who is the "I"?
7. How would the story have changed if it were told from Teruo's point of view?

Communicate Your Ideas

PREWRITING *Literary Knowledge*

Write a response to "A Day's Wait" *(pages C332–C335)* that uses your literary knowledge. Describe the characters, setting, plot, point of view, and theme. Save your work for later use.

Choosing and Limiting a Subject

As you respond to a work by using both your personal experience and your literary knowledge, you will develop some definite ideas about the meaning of the work. Your understanding will then become the basis for choosing a subject for a literary analysis.

Unless your teacher has assigned you a specific subject for a literary analysis, you will have a wide choice of possible subjects. When choosing a subject, jot down your initial responses to the work. Then narrow your choice by asking yourself the following questions.

Questions for Choosing a Subject

- What elements of the work would you like to understand better? What parts of the work puzzle you?
- What parts of the work do you find especially moving? Why?
- What images and details made a strong impression on you? What do they contribute to the overall work?
- With which character do you identify the most? Why?
- How do the characters relate to one another? How do their relationships affect the plot?
- What feeling, meaning, or message does the work convey to you? What insight or understanding have you gained?

Writing Is Thinking

Making Inferences

Making inferences, or **inferring**, means filling in the gaps in your knowledge on the basis of what you already know. The following chart shows you how to make inferences about a character from appearance, behavior, and speech.

CHARACTER CHART

Question: In "Say It with Flowers," why does Teruo give away flowers?

Type of Clue	Clue
Description of Character	Teruo's appearance did not "harmonize with a job as a clerk in a flower shop"; he was "a quiet fellow with very little words for anybody, but his smile disarmed a person."
Statements About Character's Actions	He added extra flowers "because the old lady was appreciative of his art of making bouquets"; gave roses to a child with 25 cents to spend for his mother's birthday; gave a dozen roses to a pretty girl.
Character's Own Words	"I just like to do it that way, that's all." "I gave it to her because she admired it, and she's pretty enough to deserve beautiful things, and I liked her."

Logical inferences about Teruo's motives based on these clues:

In giving away flowers, Teruo bases his decisions on personal values of honesty and generosity. He gives away flowers to people he thinks deserve them. His actions represent his decision not to compromise his values, even if it means getting fired.

THINKING PRACTICE

Make a chart like the one above to help you infer an answer to this question: In "Say It with Flowers," how does the narrator feel about Teruo?

Synthesizing Personal and Literary Responses Another strategy for choosing a subject is to **synthesize**, or combine, your personal responses with responses based on your literary knowledge. For example, in discussing or writing about "Say It with Flowers," you may have expressed disapproval of dishonest business practices. Perhaps you once had an unpleasant experience as a consumer in which you were a victim of dishonesty. To synthesize that personal reaction with a literary response, you might discuss the central conflict in the story, which relates to the issue of dishonesty in business. By synthesizing your personal and literary responses in this way, you can best focus your thoughts for a literary analysis.

Finding a Subject Focus Whichever strategy you use for choosing a subject, check to make sure the subject is focused on a specific aspect of the work. Ask yourself, "What do I want to say about my subject?" When you can clearly answer that question in a phrase or sentence, you have suitably focused your subject.

MODEL: Focusing a Subject

GENERAL SUBJECT	The character Teruo
LIMITED SUBJECT	Teruo's response to the central conflict
QUESTION	What do you want to say about Teruo's impact on the central conflict in the story?
POSSIBLE ANSWER	Teruo's refusal to compromise his high principles does not necessarily mean that he would not be successful in business.
FOCUSED SUBJECT	Qualities Teruo has that would contribute to his success in business

Practice Your Skills

Choosing and Limiting a Subject

For each of the following literary elements, think of a possible subject for a literary analysis of "Say It with Flowers." Then limit each subject by expressing it in a phrase or a sentence.

1. character
2. point of view
3. plot
4. theme
5. setting
6. tone
7. dialogue
8. conflict

Communicate Your Ideas

PREWRITING *Limited and Focused Subject*

Review your personal and literary responses to "A Day's Wait." Using the Questions for Choosing a Subject on page C492, list ideas for a literary analysis of this short story. Choose one idea and limit it to a specific aspect of the work. Then write a phrase or sentence that expresses your focus. Save your work for later use.

Developing a Thesis

When you clearly focus your subject, you will discover the thesis, or main idea, for your literary analysis. By expressing your main idea in a complete sentence, you will have a working thesis statement on which to build. Your specific purpose in writing a literary analysis is to prove that your thesis, or interpretation, is true. Your **thesis** is a proposition that you must defend by presenting evidence that will convince the reader that your interpretation is valid. The example on the next page shows the thesis statement for the focused subject from the previous page. Notice that the thesis statement is carefully worded. In a literary analysis, a thesis statement should be specific enough to be proven conclusively.

Model: Thesis Statement

Focused Subject	Qualities Teruo has that would contribute to his success in business
Working Thesis	Despite his experience in Mr. Sasaki's shop, Teruo has qualities that would make him successful in business without having to compromise his high principles.

Practice Your Skills

Writing a Working Thesis Statement

Write one working thesis statement for each of the following focused subjects from "Say It with Flowers."

1. the mood created by descriptions of the setting
2. how the characters in the story are affected by their jobs
3. how the other characters respond to Teruo

Communicate Your Ideas

REVISING *Unity, Coherence, and Clarity*
Conferencing

Review the focused subject for your literary analysis of "A Day's Wait." Identify the main idea of your focused subject, and then use it to develop a thesis statement for your essay. Write your thesis statement in a complete sentence.

Read your thesis statement to a partner. Ask your partner to offer comments about any strong or weak points in your thesis statement. Discuss ways to clarify the thesis statement. Save your work for later use.

Looping Back in Prewriting

Revised Focused Subject

After conferencing with a partner, you may decide that you want to rethink your choice of subject. Feel free to review "A Day's Wait" and make another choice.

Gathering Evidence

To prove the truth of your thesis, you must supply the reader of your literary analysis with evidence. You automatically gather evidence when you read, whether you are aware of it or not. Each detail fits into a pattern of ideas that you develop as you read. This pattern of ideas leaves you with an overall impression of a work and leads you to your thesis.

After you have stated your thesis, however, you should reread the work and look for specific details that will help you prove it. The kinds of details you will use include specific examples of dialogue, action, imagery, and characters' thoughts.

Model: Kinds of Evidence in Literature

Background Details	We were glad to have an extra hand [in the flower shop] because the busy season was coming around.
Descriptive Details	Teruo came back to the rear and picked out a dozen of the very fresh white roses.
Narrative Details	He told Teruo what to do on telephone orders; how to keep the greens fresh; how to make bouquets, corsages, and sprays.
Dialogue	Teruo looked at us calmly. "That's a hard thing to say when you know it isn't true." "You've got to get over it sooner or later," I told him.
Action	He hurriedly took one customer's order and . . . jumped to the second customer's side and persuaded her to buy Columbia roses. . . .

To develop a list of supporting details, skim the work from start to finish, looking for any elements that will directly contribute to proving your thesis. As you skim, jot down each supporting detail you find—either on a note card or on a separate sheet of paper.

Writing Tip

Even if you are not sure a story detail supports your **thesis**, note it on a card or a sheet of paper. You can always discard it later if you decide it is not relevant.

The following models show how a writer gathered evidence on commentary cards to support the proposition that Teruo has qualities that would help him succeed in business. Notice that each card has a page reference for easily locating the passage used. In addition, each card includes a brief note reminding the writer of why that detail helps support the thesis.

MODEL: Gathering Evidence

Text Portions	Commentary Cards
We soon learned that he knew nothing about the florist business. He could identify a rose when he saw one . . . but other flowers and materials were new to him. "You fellows teach me something about this business and I'll be grateful. I want to start from the bottom," Teruo said.	1.a "knew nothing about the florist business," "flowers and materials were new to him" (narrator) "You fellows teach me something about this business and I'll be grateful. I want to start from the bottom." (Teruo, p. C472) 1.b—shows that Teruo is willing to learn and to work his way up
In a couple of weeks Teruo was just as good a clerk as we had had in a long time. He was curious almost to a fault, and was a glutton for work.	2. Became a good clerk in two weeks, "was curious almost to a fault, and was a glutton for work" (narrator, p. C472) —shows that Teruo is a fast learner and a hard worker

When I went out to the truck . . . Teruo followed me. "Gee, I feel rotten," he said to me. "Those flowers I sold to the people, they won't last longer than tomorrow. I feel lousy. I'm lousy. The people'll get to know my word pretty soon."

3. "I feel rotten" [for selling old flowers], "I'm lousy. The people'll get to know my word pretty soon." (Teruo, p. C475)
—shows that Teruo has integrity, cares about customers, and cares about his reputation

"You've been selling fresh flowers and leaving the old ones go to waste. . . ." Mr. Sasaki said. "Why don't you do as you're told? We all sell the flowers in the front. . . . Why can't you sell them?"

"I don't like it, Mr. Sasaki," Teruo said. "When the people ask me if they're fresh I hate to answer. I feel rotten after selling the old ones."

4.a "Why don't you do as you're told?" (Mr. Sasaki, p. C475) "I don't like it. . . . When the people ask me if they're fresh I hate to answer. I feel rotten after selling the old ones." (Teruo, p. C476)

4.b —shows that Teruo cares about customers, values honesty, and does not easily obey orders that go against his moral principles

Teruo was there early. "Hello," he greeted us cheerfully as we came in. . . . He was there before us and had already filled out the eight o'clock package. . . . When Mr. Sasaki arrived, Teruo waved his hand and cheerfully went about gathering the flowers. . . . As he flitted here and there he seemed as if he had forgotten our presence. . . .

5.a "Teruo was there early," "greeted us cheerfully," "had already filled out the eight o'clock package," "cheerfully went about gathering the flowers," "flitted here and there" (narrator, p. C476)

5.b —shows that Teruo is prompt, cheerful, and industrious

He looked at each vase, sized up the flowers, and then cocked his head at the next one. He did this with great deliberation, as if he were the boss and the last word in the shop. . . . [W]hen a customer soon came in, he swiftly attended him as if he owned all the flowers in the world. . . .

6.a Worked "with great deliberation, as if he were the boss and the last word in the shop," "swiftly attended [a customer] as if he owned all the flowers in the world" (narrator, p. C476)

He [sold the fresh flowers] with so much grace, dignity and swiftness . . .

. . . Mr. Sasaki came out furious. "You're a blockhead. You have no business sense. . . ."

Tommy nudged me. "If he was the boss he couldn't do those things," he said.

"In the first place," I said, "I don't think he could be a boss."

6.b "[worked with] grace, dignity, and swiftness" (narrator, p. C476) —shows that Teruo can take charge and is self-confident and efficient

7.a "You have no business sense." (Mr. Sasaki, p. C477) "If he was the boss he couldn't do those things [give away flowers]." (Tommy, p. C478) "I don't think he could be a boss." (narrator, p. C478)

7.b —shows that the others don't understand that Teruo has what it takes to succeed in business. As a boss, Teruo could give up some profits in exchange for customer goodwill and could insist on selling only quality products.

PRACTICE YOUR SKILLS

Using an Arch Diagram to Evaluate Evidence

Copy and complete the arch diagram below. Provide details from "Say It with Flowers" to support this thesis: *Teruo has qualities that will enable him to succeed in business*. When you have completed the diagram, evaluate it. Do you have enough evidence to support the main idea?

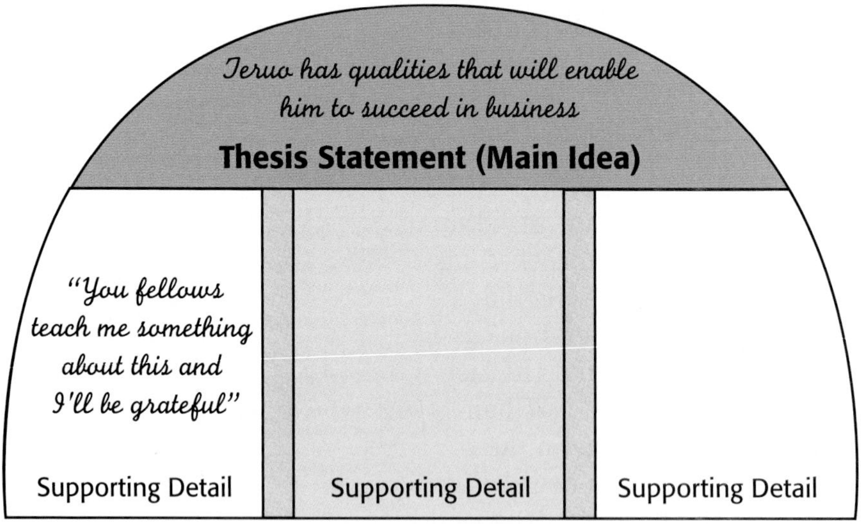

Teruo has qualities that will enable him to succeed in business

Thesis Statement (Main Idea)

"You fellows teach me something about this and I'll be grateful"		
Supporting Detail	Supporting Detail	Supporting Detail

Communicate Your Ideas

PREWRITING *Evidence*

Gather evidence on commentary cards to support the thesis statement you wrote for your literary analysis of "A Day's Wait." You may wish to use an arch diagram to evaluate your evidence. Save your work for later use.

Organizing Details into an Outline

For your literary analysis, you should group your details into categories. Then you can arrange your ideas and information in a logical order. You might arrange your details in the order in which they appear in the work.

The following chart shows examples of how different types of order may be appropriate for proving different kinds of theses.

ORDERING EVIDENCE

Kind of Thesis	Type of Order
To show how a character or elements of a plot change or develop over time	Chronological order *(page C405)*
To show similarities and differences between characters or to compare two different works of literature	Comparison/contrast, using the AABB or the ABAB pattern of development *(pages C406–C408)*
To analyze a character's motivation or to explain the significance of the setting	Order of importance or cause and effect *(pages C405 and C122)*
To draw conclusions about the theme	Developmental order *(page C405)*

IN THE MEDIA

Photography

In the same way that literary elements communicate meaning, the visual arts such as photography also have elements that convey meaning. A photograph can and should be "read." Look at the photograph below. What overall feeling or message does it convey to you?

To most viewers, this picture conveys strength, speed, solidity, cleanliness. The following analysis shows how each element contributes to the overall effect.

Shape	Curves, anchored by rectangles signifying stability and strength, are enhanced by silver tubes.
Line	Lines formed by the silver tubing lend a sense of motion and speed.
Color	Blue sky makes the beige cylinder look like adobe; silver adds flash.
Texture	Hard concrete, smooth steel, and rough wall surface create a clean, rich look.

Media Activity

In a part of your community where industry is present, take some photographs that convey messages beyond just the subject of the picture. Strive for interesting and meaningful lines, shapes, colors, and textures as you frame your shot. Then choose one photo and make a chart that tells how each element contributes to the overall effect and message.

As you order your **evidence**, check to be sure each detail directly supports your **thesis**. Set aside **commentary cards** with details that you decide are not relevant.

After you decide how to organize your ideas and evidence, you should make a list, chart, or outline to use as a guide for writing your literary analysis. When outlining, you may use either an informal outline—a simple listing, in order, of the points you wish to cover—or a formal outline like the one on page C235.

Following is a simple outline for a literary analysis about "Say It with Flowers." Notice that the writer included ideas for the introduction and the conclusion. Also, because the details have equal importance in proving the thesis, the writer placed them in developmental order. In developmental order, information is arranged to lead up to a conclusion.

Model: Outline

Introduction

Background details about Teruo's experience

Thesis statement: Despite his experience in Mr. Sasaki's shop, Teruo has qualities that would help him succeed in business without having to compromise his high principles.

Body

Qualities Teruo has for success in business:

I. Willingness to learn and to work hard (commentary cards 1, 2, and 5)

II. Positive attitude and the ability to take charge (commentary cards 5 and 6)

III. Honesty and integrity (commentary cards 3 and 4)

Conclusion

Why the other characters thought that Teruo could not succeed in business (commentary card 7)

How my evidence shows that they were wrong

Communicate Your Ideas

PREWRITING ***Outline***

Review the evidence that supports the thesis statement for your literary analysis of "A Day's Wait." Decide on an appropriate order for your supporting details and create an outline as a plan for your composition. Save your work for later use.

Drafting

Writing Process

When you are ready to draft your literary analysis, you may find the following guidelines helpful.

Guidelines for Drafting a Literary Analysis

- In the introduction identify the title and author of the work you are discussing and include your thesis statement.
- In the body of your literary analysis, include clearly organized supporting details, using transitions to show how one detail relates to another. Using quotation marks, include direct quotations from the work wherever they strengthen your thesis points.
- In the conclusion reinforce the main idea of your literary analysis by explaining how the details that you included prove your thesis.
- Add an interesting, appropriate title that suggests the focus of your literary analysis.

The following model was written from the outline on page C503 and the commentary cards on pages C498–C500. Notice how the model, which has already been revised and edited, follows the guidelines above.

TITLE: IDENTIFIES FOCUS

Teruo in Business

INTRODUCTION: IDENTIFIES AUTHOR AND PURPOSE

In the story "Say It with Flowers," author Toshio Mori explores the potential conflict between succeeding in business and preserving one's integrity. For Teruo, the eager young clerk in the flower shop, preserving his integrity means selling only the freshest flowers. He even gives flowers away to customers. For his actions he earns the scorn of his co-workers and of his boss, Mr. Sasaki, who eventually fires him. Like them, readers might conclude that Teruo would be a failure in business unless he learns to "play the game." Despite his experience in Mr. Sasaki's shop, however, Teruo has many qualities that would help him succeed in business without having to compromise his high principles.

THESIS STATEMENT

DETAILS IN THE FIRST SUPPORTING PARAGRAPH

When Teruo first comes to work at the shop, he asks his co-workers to teach him about the florist business. "You fellows teach me something about this business and I'll be grateful. I want to start from the bottom," he explains, implying that he might someday like to run his own flower shop. In only two weeks, Teruo becomes a good clerk who is "curious almost to a fault" and "a glutton for work." This behavior shows that Teruo is willing to learn and to work his way up. He is also a fast learner and a hard worker. These are all qualities that are needed for success in business.

DETAILS IN THE SECOND SUPPORTING PARAGRAPH

Teruo has positive attitudes that would contribute to any person's success in business. Descriptions of his work in the Morning-Glory Flower Shop, for example, show that he is prompt, conscientious, cheerful, and industrious. In addition, he works "with great deliberation, as if he were the boss and the last word in the shop." He swiftly attends to customers "as if he owned all the flowers in the world." His coworkers are awed by his "grace, dignity, and swiftness" as he works. These observations show that Teruo can take charge and can use his initiative. He is clearly self-confident and efficient in his work.

Third Supporting Paragraph

When Teruo is forced to go against his principles by lying and selling flowers that are not fresh, he says, "I feel rotten. . . . I'm lousy. The people'll get to know my word pretty soon." Even after Mr. Sasaki confronts him and tells him to do as he's told, Teruo insists, "When the people ask me if they're fresh I hate to answer. I feel rotten after selling the old ones." This quote shows that Teruo values his honesty and integrity—qualities that certainly contribute to success in business. He cares about his customers and about his reputation. He risks losing his job rather than going against his moral values.

Conclusion

The other characters in the story do not understand that Teruo has what it takes to succeed in business. "You have no business sense," Mr. Sasaki accuses. "If he was the boss he couldn't do those things," Tommy says. "I don't think he could be a boss," the narrator replies. As a boss, however, Teruo could choose to give up some of his profits in exchange for customer goodwill, more customers, and more business. He could insist on selling only the best quality products and still afford to be generous toward his customers. When viewed in this way, everything about Teruo's character suggests that he could become a successful businessman—without compromising his high principles.

DRAFTING *Literary Analysis*

Using the **Guidelines for Drafting a Literary Analysis** on page C504 and your outline from the writing activity on page C504, write a first draft of your literary analysis of "A Day's Wait." Remember to stop every now and then and read over what you have written to keep your ideas on track. Save your draft for revising later. 

Looping Back to Prewriting

Additional Evidence

If you have difficulty drafting your literary analysis, you may not have enough evidence to support your thesis statement. Go back to "A Day's Wait" *(pages C332–C335)* and look for evidence you may have missed. Check pages C497–C500 for reminders on gathering evidence. Review your commentary cards or create additional cards to support your proposition.

When you finish your first draft, stop and think about the process you have just completed. Compare this essay with other writing you have done. Is it getting easier for you to put your thoughts down on paper? In what areas has your confidence increased? What is still difficult for you about writing a first draft? What might help you in overcoming these writing stumbling blocks? Jot down your reflections in the Learning Log section of your **journal.**

After completing your first draft, set it aside for a day or two so that you can return to it with a critical eye. You may want to share your literary analysis with a peer reader. Using your partner's comments and the following checklist, you should then revise your essay.

Evaluation Checklist for Revising

Checking Your Essay

✓ Do you have a strong introduction that identifies the author and the work you will discuss? *(page C504)*

✓ Does your introduction contain a clearly worded thesis statement? *(pages C495–C496)*

✓ Does the body of your essay provide ample details from the work to support your thesis? *(pages C497–C501)*

✓ Did you use quotations from the work to strengthen your points? *(page C504)*

✓ Does your conclusion summarize the details in the body and reinforce your thesis statement? *(page C504)*

✓ Does your whole essay have unity, coherence, and clarity? *(pages C237–C238)*

✓ Did you add an interesting, appropriate title that suggests the focus of your essay? *(page C504)*

Checking Your Paragraphs

✓ Does each paragraph have a topic sentence? *(page C223)*

✓ Does each paragraph have unity, adequate development, coherence, and clarity? *(pages C105–C108)*

Checking Your Sentences and Words

✓ Are your sentences varied and concise? *(pages C69–C77)*

✓ Did you use vivid, precise words? *(pages C63–C65)*

Verbal Phrases

"Tommy and I watched the boss fuming inside of his office." The words *fuming inside of his office* in this sentence from "Say It with Flowers" form a phrase. Like all phrases, it lacks a subject and a verb. Because this phrase begins with a verb form—*fuming*—it is called a **verbal phrase.**

There are three kinds of verbal phrases: participial phrases, gerund phrases, and infinitive phrases. *Fuming inside of his office* is a participial phrase.

Participial Phrases

A **participle** is a verb form that is used as an adjective to describe nouns and pronouns. Present participles end in *–ing*, and past participles end in *–ed, –n, –t,* and *–en*. In the following sentences, you can see how participial phrases can not only add liveliness to the writing but also provide variety to your sentence structure.

Participial Phrases	**Ignoring us**, Teruo waited on customers. We watched Teruo **talking to the young lady**.

Punctuation with Participial Phrases

In the first example above, a comma follows an introductory participial phrase. Commas also enclose a **nonessential participial phrase**—one that can be removed without changing the meaning of the rest of the sentence.

Nonessential Participial Phrase	Sometimes, **looking embarrassedly at us,** he would sell the fresh flowers first. (Commas are needed because removing the phrase does not change the meaning of the sentence.)

ESSENTIAL PARTICIPIAL PHRASE	We watched Teruo **talking to the young lady.** (Comma is not needed because removing the phrase *talking to the young lady* changes the meaning. The phrase is essential because the idea is incomplete if it is removed.)

Combining Sentences with Participial Phrases

You can eliminate choppiness in your writing by using participial phrases to combine sentences. Combining sentences also helps to show the relationship between ideas.

TWO SENTENCES	I was often in the shop. I helped Tommy and Teruo with the customers and the orders.
COMBINED	I was often in the shop, **helping Tommy and Teruo with the customers and the orders.**
TWO SENTENCES	I sat in the back. I could watch Teruo.
COMBINED	**Sitting in the back,** I could watch Teruo.
TWO SENTENCES	Tommy and I watched the boss. He was fuming.
COMBINED	Tommy and I watched the boss **fuming in his office.**

Communicate Your Ideas

REVISING *Participial Phrases*

Using the Evaluation Checklist for Revising and the Revising Workshop, revise the draft of your literary analysis of "A Day's Wait." Pay particular attention to participial phrases. Use them to show connections between ideas and make your writing flow smoothly. Save your revised draft to edit later.

COMPUTER TIP

As you revise your literary analysis, you may need to rearrange sentences or whole paragraphs. If you are revising your writing on a computer, the Cut and Paste commands make it fast and easy to move around blocks of text. You can find those commands on the pull-down menu under Edit. You can also use the Cut and Paste icons on the Toolbar. Look for scissors for Cut and a clipboard with text for Paste.

Editing

Writing Process

Now you are ready to polish your literary analysis to give it authority with your audience. As you carefully reread your essay, refer to your Personalized Editing Checklist to make sure you are not repeating errors you have made before. Asking others to help you identify errors is another good way to work.

Communicate Your Ideas

EDITING

Read aloud your literary analysis of "A Day's Wait." Listen especially for any verbal phrases. Then use the Revising Workshop on page C509 for guidance on when and where to use commas with participial phrases. Read through your literary analysis several times, looking for different kinds of errors each time. When you are completely satisfied, save the work in your writing folder. 

Publishing

Writing Process

Complete the writing process by connecting your literary analysis with a reader who would have an interest in it. You might want to submit your essay to the school literary magazine. If your school has an Intranet, you might consider publishing your essay as a Web page.

Communicate Your Ideas

PUBLISHING

Produce a neat and presentable final draft of your literary analysis of "A Day's Wait," using the correct manuscript form shown on page C52. Share it with a teacher, fellow student, family member, or someone else who would be interested in reading it. You can find more ideas for publishing your work on page C51. **PORTFOLIO**

Process of Writing a Literary Analysis

Remember that the writing process is recursive—you can move back and forth among the stages of the process to achieve your purpose. For example, during editing you may wish to return to the revising stage to add details that have occurred to you while editing. The numbers in parentheses refer to pages where you can get help with your writing.

PREWRITING

- Read the literary work carefully, and respond to it from both personal experience and literary knowledge. *(pages C483–C491)*
- By synthesizing your personal and literary responses, choose and limit a subject for your literary analysis. *(pages C492–C494)*
- Think of a subject focus, and shape it into a statement of your thesis. *(pages C494–C496)*
- Skim the work again, looking for details to use as evidence to support your thesis. On a separate sheet of paper or card, note each detail, its page reference, and its significance. *(pages C497–C500)*
- Organize your ideas and supporting details into an outline. *(pages C501–C503)*

DRAFTING

- In the introduction identify the title and author of the work you are discussing and include your thesis statement. *(page C504)*
- In the body include supporting details, using transitions to show how one detail relates to another. Using quotation marks, include direct quotations from the work wherever they strengthen your thesis points. *(page C504)*
- In the conclusion reinforce the main idea by explaining how the details that you included prove your thesis. *(page C504)*
- Add a title that suggests the focus of your literary analysis. *(page C504)*

REVISING

- After conferencing, use the **Evaluation Checklist for Revising** on page C508 to revise your literary analysis.

EDITING

- Use the **Editing Checklist** to check your grammar, spelling, usage, and mechanics. *(page C44)*

PUBLISHING

- Prepare a neat final copy of your work and publish it in one of the ways listed on page C51.

A Literary Analysis of a Poem

Purpose: **to explain your response to a poem**

Audience: **peer readers**

Prewriting

A literary analysis can be about any form of literature, such as a poem, play, novel, or short story. You have written a literary analysis of a short story. Now you can use what you have learned to write analyses of literary works of other genres. For instance, you might choose to analyze "When I Heard the Learn'd Astronomer" by Walt Whitman on page C369, or another poem that is a favorite of yours.

Once you have chosen a poem to analyze, read it over a few times to become familiar with it. Then record your personal reactions to the poem. Using the information from Elements of Literature on pages C487–C488 and Questions for Finding Meaning in Poetry on page C489, respond to the poem on the basis of your literary knowledge. Use the strategy of synthesizing to combine your personal responses with responses based on your literary knowledge. Next choose, limit, and focus a subject related to your personal literary response to the poem. After you write a thesis statement, use commentary cards to gather evidence that supports your thesis. Then arrange your supporting details in logical order in an outline.

Drafting

Using your outline and prewriting notes for guidance, draft your literary analysis about the poem you have chosen. You may want to review the guidelines on page C504 before you begin to write.

Revising Conferencing

Exchange drafts with a partner. Then answer the following questions about your partner's literary analysis.

- Is the thesis statement clear?
- Are there adequate and compelling examples from the poem, including quotations of words or lines? Do these details all support the thesis?
- Does the literary analysis contain a clear introduction, body, and conclusion?
- Does the essay have unity, coherence, and clarity?
- Is the title interesting and appropriate? Does it suggest the focus of the literary analysis?

After you evaluate your partner's responses to your literary analysis, use the comments you agree with and the Evaluation Checklist for Revising on page C508 to revise your essay.

Editing

Use the Editing Checklist on page C44 as a guide to editing your literary analysis.

Publishing

Make a neat final copy of your literary analysis, using the manuscript form on page C51. Share it with classmates. If you have chosen the Whitman poem and your classmates have also analyzed it, form a discussion group and compare responses, looking for similarities and differences.

Representing in Different Ways

From Visuals . . .

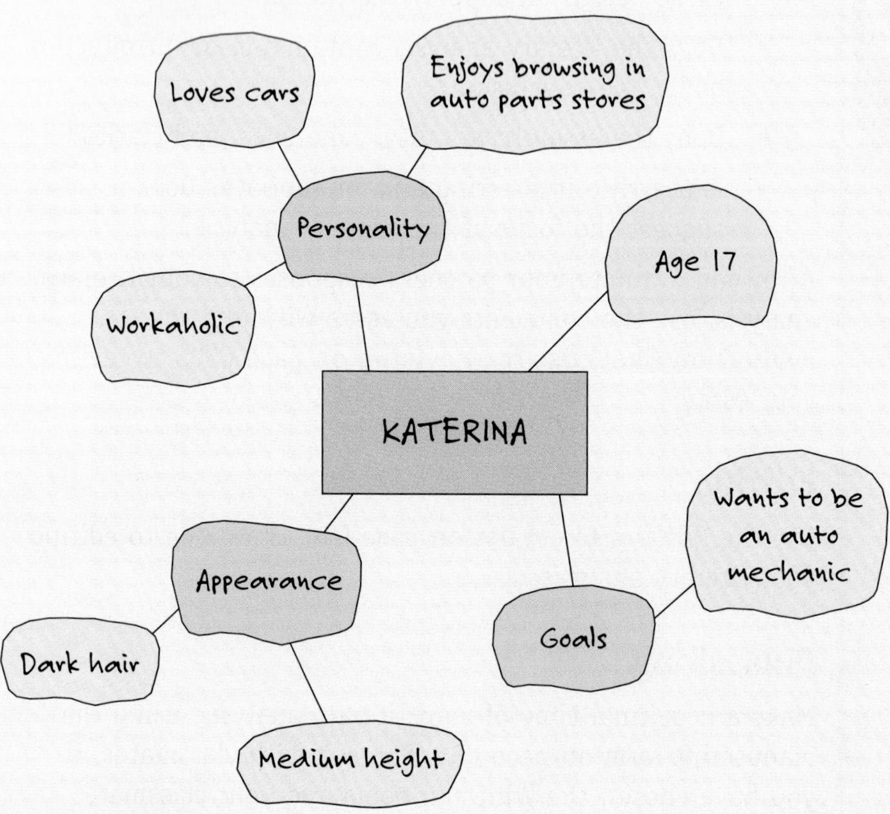

. . . to Print

Use the prewriting web above to write a short character description of Katerina. Use your imagination to elaborate on her appearance, personality, and goals as shown in the web.

From Print . . .

Passage from "Any Other Day"

It was one week before the holidays, and the aisles were jammed with shopping carts. Katerina was working behind the Customer Service counter, doing her best to remain polite. She wished more people would say please and thank you. After all, it was the holiday season.

Outside the automatic doors, Katerina saw the parking lot darkening in the twilight. Tonight, she would rent a movie, go home, make a bowl of popcorn, and watch the movie from beginning to end. She had earned it. If she fell asleep in front of the television, her mom would cover her with a quilt and let her sleep peacefully on the couch.

It was 8:50—ten minutes until the store closed. Katerina was tidying up her work space when she heard a voice. "Not another customer," she thought to herself. She looked up to see a man standing in front of her. He was holding a shopping bag.

"Are you Katerina Persakova?" he asked.

"Yes," she said. She had never seen the man before.

"Well, Katerina Persakova," he said calmly, "you have won a million dollars."

. . . to Visuals

Using a web, break down the elements of the story passage on the right into the following categories: Character and Actions, Setting Description, Time Sequence, and Turn of Events.

- **Which strategies can be used for creating both written and visual representations? Which strategies apply to one, not both? Which type of representation is more effective?**
- **Draw a conclusion, and write briefly about the differences between written ideas and visual representations.**

Writing in the Workplace

Analytical Oral Presentation

You are applying for a job at a detective agency. During your interview you are told that they need somebody disguised as a poet to stake out a local coffee shop. To get the job you have to undergo a series of physical and personality tests, all of which you pass with flying colors. The final test, however, is the most challenging—they want you to analyze a poem.

Prepare an oral presentation analyzing the meaning of your favorite poem. What images do the figures of speech in the poem create? What feelings do those images suggest? What effect did the poem have on you? What meaning does the poem have for you? Be sure that you support your analysis with quotes from the poem.

What strategies did you use to analyze the poem?

You can find information on oral presentations on pages C596–C603.

Writing for Oral Communication

Analytical Phone Message

You and your best friend are huge fans of comedy films. Every Friday night you two go to the Megaplex 50 to see the latest comedy. This Friday, however, you go to the Megaplex alone because your friend has to proofread her brother's research report on the health benefits of laughter. The movie is the greatest comedy you have ever seen. After the movie you try to call your friend to tell her, but you have to leave a message on her answering machine because she does not pick up the phone.

Prepare a phone message for your best friend analyzing your favorite comedy film. Describe how the setting of the comedy contributes to the tone or mood of the story. Practice delivering your phone message to classmates or family members.

What strategies did you use to analyze the movie for your friend?

Assess Your Learning

The Awesome Art Review is inviting readers to submit reviews of books, plays, and films for a writing competition. Winning reviews will be printed in a special issue highlighting the best readers' essays from all over the country, and winning authors will have statues of themselves erected in their town squares. Submitted reviews must focus on works that teach people something worth learning.

- **Choose a novel, play, or short story that you think can inspire people to learn something valuable about life. Write a review in which you analyze the work in terms of its value to the reader/viewer.**
- **Use quotes, scenes, and specific lines from the work to support your thesis of the work's importance. Be sure to include appropriate information to support your ideas. Organize your content logically. Proofread your review for appropriateness of organization, content, style, and conventions.**

Before You Write **Consider the following questions:**
What is the ***subject?***
What is the ***occasion?***
Who is the ***audience?***
What is the ***purpose?***

After You Write **Evaluate your work using the following criteria:**

- Who is your audience? Have you clearly communicated in a voice that is geared to the reader?
- Is your content organized logically? Have you included appropriate information to support your ideas? Do your ideas hold together throughout the paper?
- Have you refined your draft? Have you revised your paper for content and style?
- Have you revised your draft by elaborating, deleting, combining, and rearranging text?
- Does your writing voice show a sense of individuality?
- Have you successfully connected the work's content to your ideas about its importance?

Write briefly on how well you did. Point out your strengths and areas for improvement.

CHAPTER 12

Research Reports

You have probably heard the statement, "Write about what you know." Poets, novelists, and playwrights might agree with that advice, but in writing research reports you are often called upon to write about topics of which you may have little personal knowledge or experience. Regardless of how much you already know about your subject, knowing how to gather interesting and accurate information is important. The very nature of writing a research report involves exploring a subject by gathering information from a variety of sources.

Much of the information you read in newspapers, magazines, nonfiction books, and on the Internet, as well as much of what you watch on the news or in documentaries, is research reporting. No doubt you have already written research reports, or research papers, in some of your classes in school. This chapter will help you to develop your ability to gather and convey information on any subject.

Reading with a Writer's Eye

As you read "Rancho Buena Vista," think about traditions and folklore—how they start, how they persist, and how they affect people's lives. You might also remember some of the traditions and stories in your own family, in your community, or at school. As a writer, think about the information that Fermina Guerra includes in the story to bring it to life. Consider the strategies she uses to hold your attention.

FROM *Texas Stomping Ground* by J. Frank Dobie

RANCHO Buena Vista

Fermina Guerra

In the northeastern part of Webb County, fifty miles from Laredo[1] and twenty-one miles from Encinal, lies the Buena Vista Ranch. It is not large as ranches go, only about three thousand acres; but it has its share in the traditions of the ranch country. . . .

The traditions pertaining to Buena Vista that have been told over and over among the children and grandchildren of Florencio Guerra and his wife, Josefa Flores, are the kind of traditions to be heard all up and down the Border Country.[2]

Some of them, perhaps a majority of them, treat of actual happenings, and are folklore only in that they are traditional and that they are hardly important enough for history. The stories are of Indians, floods, captives, sheepherders, buried treasure, violent death, happenings when the bishop came or the wool went to town. When a fire burns on a winter night or when it is raining and the water in Becerra Creek is high, people at Buena Vista tell and hear these traditions of the land.

Ever-present in the minds of ranch people is the question of water. The foremost topic of conversation among them is the condition of the range, the prospect of rain, the water of the tanks. This part of the country has never found good well water

[1] **Laredo:** City in Texas.

[2] **Border Country:** Lands bordering the Rio Grande.

to pump up with windmills, and tanks are depended on for stock water.

In the old days there were no tanks. The cattle watered at the two or three creeks in the country. In time of drouth[3] they were driven the eighteen miles to the Nueces River. There was never trouble over water rights. Through the years these ranchmen kept the peace among themselves; the struggle with Nature occupied their chief energies. The first fence went up in 1891. Don Florencio's son, Donato, used to go out of his way before and after school to watch the fence-building operations being carried on by the Callaghan Ranch hands, who were erecting a fence between Buena Vista Ranch and theirs.

Three times in the history of Buena Vista Ranch, La Becerra Creek has been half a mile wide—in 1878, 1903, and 1937. Of course, the oldest flood is the most romantic. Don Justo and his wife were still living then, old and set in their ways. Their ranch house was of mesquite poles and adobe, thatched with grass and set on the very banks of La Becerra Creek.

One day it started to rain; torrents poured down. As the creek began to rise and there was no abatement[4] of the downpour, the other members of the family grew frightened. Not Don Justo. He had seen rain before; nothing ever came of it. But the rain poured all night and a second day; the creek continued to rise.

Now it was up to the corral, adjoining the house. No matter; it would go down presently. A second night, and a third day, the rain continued pouring. At dusk of the third day, the water began to enter the house. A young matron, wife of Don Carmen, holding her child in her arms, told her husband to take her to higher ground. She feared remaining in the house another night with that constantly rising water. Gladly enough, he complied.

---

[3] **drouth** (variation on the word *drought*): Long spell with no water.

[4] **abatement:** Reduction in degree or intensity.

Before leaving, he begged his aged father and mother to accompany him, but they laughed. "You will get all wet for nothing," they said. "We have a roof over our heads. What if there is a little water in the house?"

But the young mother set out for the hill to the east. Before she reached it, she was obliged to swim to save herself and child, her husband aiding her. The rain was still pouring so hard that they got lost in the brush, but they went on eastward.

Eventually they found themselves on a well-known hill. Don Florencio's ranch was just a mile to the northwest. The mother asked her husband to go down there and ask for some dry clothing for the baby, as the night was cold and it was still raining hard. Willingly enough, Don Carmen set out.

On reaching the house, he told Don Florencio what had happened at the upper ranch. Hurriedly the latter saddled his best horse and set out to see what he could do to persuade his parents to leave their house and take to the hills. The water was not so high at Buena Vista, though it was at the door of the main house.

About daybreak, he reached the shore opposite his parents' ranch. There was a raging torrent between him and them. From afar off, barely to be seen among the treetops, he could discern the roof of the house and two people perched on it. He could hardly hear their feeble cries, so great was the distance.

Like most ranchmen of his time, Don Florencio could not swim. He depended upon his horse to carry him across streams. This task his present mount refused to perform. Time after time he forced the animal into the water, only to have it turn back. At length he returned to his own ranch for a fresh mount. This horse, too, refused to venture out into the flood. So Florencio was forced to flounder at the edge of the current and watch those faraway forms, fearing to see them disappear from sight. But towards evening, the waters began to recede, and the next day he was able to go out and rescue the exhausted old people from their predicament.

The flood of 1903 was unusual in that no rain accompanied it. One hot, sunny morning Don Florencio noticed what appeared to be a cloud of mist rising rapidly from the bushes south of the house along the creek. It was coming fast, with a rushing sound. Suddenly he realized that a wall of water, far wider than the creek banks, was bearing down upon him. One of his laborers was down the creek bed driving some goats to higher ground. Racing his horse, he hurried to get within calling distance of the man, Carlos. The laborer saw Don Florencio and heard his call, but not realizing that the danger was so close, went leisurely on with his work. Suddenly the turbulent water was upon him, and he was borne along with it as it swirled among the bushes. Fortunately, after his first fright, he was able to collect his wits sufficiently to grasp at an overhanging limb and so save his life.

The flood of 1937 was more prosaic;[5] the creek itself did no particular damage, but the water destroyed all but three tanks in a radius of twenty miles and left the range worse off than before the rain.

Such is the life of the ranchmen of Southwest Texas; drouth and flood; too much water or not enough; then, now, and always.

[5] **prosaic** (prō zā′ ĭk): Ordinary.

Thinking as a Writer

Evaluating Research Techniques

- How might Fermina Guerra have approached doing research pertaining to the traditions of Buena Vista? What information in the story might she have obtained by interviewing or talking to people? What information might she have needed to verify, using other sources? Explain.

Critiquing Interview Questions

Oral Expression

- Imagine you are going to interview a local rancher for a report on how ranching has changed over time. Develop a set of questions you would ask, and read your questions aloud to a group of classmates. Ask them to critique the appropriateness of your questions.

Analyzing an Image for Information

Viewing

- Study the photograph below. What information does it present? What does it tell you about a rancher's life? How might this same information be presented in a print medium? Is one way of presenting information better than another? Explain.

The Power of Research Reports

Writing that is the product of well-documented research is one of the most effective means of presenting information. A strong report—with the potential to influence the viewpoints, decisions, and actions of those who read it—is always made up of accurate and compelling facts and opinions from reliable experts and other sources.

Uses of Research Reports

People in many professions and occupations use research reports to communicate and acquire information or to recommend and justify a particular course of action. Here are just a few examples.

- **A report by the U.S. Surgeon General on the dangers of secondhand smoke is used to create laws** regulating smoking in public places.
- **An educator advocating year-round schooling presents a report** on the educational benefits of shorter vacation periods to justify his argument.
- **A NASA report on the challenges and opportunities for future space exploration is released on the Internet** to build grass-roots support for new space initiatives.
- **A presidential commission studying environmental concerns issues a report** identifying key problems and proposals for the next decade.
- **A business executive prepares a marketing report** that includes information on the buying patterns of 20– to 30–year-olds.

Process of Writing Research Reports

Both in school and in many workplaces, you will need to be able to do research and state your findings in a written report. Often in your studies you will write about subjects that are not part of your personal experiences and knowledge. The essay that you write based on your findings will be in the form of a research report, or research paper.

A **research report** is an essay based on information drawn from sources such as books, periodicals, the media, and interviews with experts.

Because the main purpose of a research report is to explain or inform, you will use the skills and techniques of informative writing. You will also draw upon the skills involved in using the library or media center, as well as the Internet, to find the information you need for your report.

You can learn how to search for accurate, up-to-date information in A Writer's Guide to Using the Internet *(pages C724–C767).*

Your Writer's Journal

In your journal write about traditions that you have followed or observed. Use freewriting to develop a list of traditions that are important to you, your family, or your community. Write about the role you think traditions play in modern society. You may also want to do research on the origins of particular traditions in your own or another culture. For each tradition list information that can give you a head start in doing research, such as the names of experts, titles and authors of books and articles on the subject, and addresses of related Websites.

One challenge in writing a research paper is keeping track of the information you collect from several different sources. The first step, therefore, is to gather the supplies you will need to organize your research. These supplies usually include a notebook, a folder with pockets, and index cards. With these materials in hand, you will be better prepared to begin your research. The next step is to choose a subject that is limited enough to allow you to cover it adequately in your research report.

Choosing and Limiting a Research Subject

Sometimes teachers assign research subjects or list alternatives for you to choose among. Often, however, the choice of a subject is left entirely to you. You may already have thought of several subjects you want to know more about. You may also find the following suggestions helpful when you begin searching for a good subject.

Finding Ideas for Research Reports

- Using the online or traditional card catalog, find a section in the library or media center that interests you. Then walk up and down the aisles, looking for book titles that catch your eye.
- Skim through magazines and other periodicals, in print or online.
- Skim through any volume of an encyclopedia, in print or on CD-ROM.
- Ask your potential readers what they would like to know more about.
- Check the assignments in your other courses to see if any of them require a research paper.
- Do a keyword search and browse Websites that interest you for report subjects.
- Watch documentary television programs or videos that might contain report topics.

After you have listed five to ten possible subjects for a research paper, choose one for which the following statements hold true.

Choosing a Suitable Research Subject

- I would like to know more about this subject.
- My audience would like to know more about this subject.
- This subject is appropriate for my purpose; that is, I can explain it well in a short research report of three to five pages.
- I can find enough information on this subject by using resources such as those in the library or media center and through other sources, such as interviewing or searching on the Internet.

Once you have chosen a subject, the next step is to limit it. One way to limit a subject is to break it down into its different aspects or elements. Suppose, for example, that you decided to write a report on the movie *The Wizard of Oz*. Realizing that this subject is too broad for a short research paper, you might then list the following aspects of the movie as possible limited subjects.

SUBJECT	*The Wizard of Oz*	
LIMITED SUBJECTS	the story	the cast
	the music	the special effects
	the sets	the costumes

Limit a subject for a research paper by listing elements, or aspects, of the subject and by selecting one of them to research.

Practice Your Skills

Limiting Research Subjects

Decide which of the following subjects are suitable for a research paper of three to five pages and which ones are too broad. Answer each item by writing *limited enough* or *too broad.* Then, using reference materials if necessary, limit each subject that is too broad by listing three aspects that could serve as limited subjects.

1. the history of Mexico
2. types of helicopters
3. the movie *Star Wars*
4. how Mars was surveyed
5. the brain
6. World War II
7. the life cycle of a tarantula
8. how sandstone forms
9. the main duties of a senator
10. basic moves in the merengue

Communicate Your Ideas

PREWRITING *Limited Subject*

After you reread your **journal** entries about traditions, apply the suggestions on page C528 to find ideas for a research subject. For example, you could find the section in the library that contains books about traditions and read the titles or look through a few of the books. Explore all kinds of traditions and their origins and meanings—from the celebration of Mardi Gras to graduation week at your school. Once you have a list of at least five possible subjects, use the criteria on the previous page to help you select one subject. Then limit it by listing as many aspects or elements of that subject as you can. When you have finished, save your notes for later use. SAVE YOUR WORK

Gathering Information

After you have limited your subject, decide what you already know about it. Then, on the basis of what you already know, pose questions about what more you would like to find out. These questions will serve as a guide for gathering more information. By summarizing your questions into one general research question, you can focus your efforts and thoughts. The chart below shows how this questioning process works.

LIMITED SUBJECT	special effects in *The Wizard of Oz*
FOCUS QUESTIONS	**POSSIBLE ANSWERS**
WHAT DO I ALREADY KNOW ABOUT THESE SPECIAL EFFECTS?	• I saw the movie. • I remember the tornado, the flying monkeys, and the melting witch. • I saw a program on how the special effects for another movie were made.
WHAT MORE DO I WANT TO FIND OUT?	• What other special effects are in *The Wizard of Oz?* • How were the tornado, flying monkeys, melting witch, and other special effects created? • Which effects were easiest to make? Which were the hardest and costliest? • What is the background of the movie: when was it made, who created the special effects, etc.? • How do the special effects in *The Wizard of Oz* compare with those in that other movie?
GENERAL RESEARCH QUESTION	• How were the special effects in *The Wizard of Oz* created?

With your research questions clearly in mind, you can begin gathering the information you need to answer them. As you find answers, be alert for possible main ideas that you could use as the thesis of your research paper.

You can learn more about developing a thesis on pages C399–C400.

Use the following guidelines to gather the information you need to answer your research questions.

Guidelines for Gathering Information

- Consult a general reference work, such as an encyclopedia, in print or on CD-ROM, to find an overview of your subject, some references to other resources on that subject, and cross-references to related topics.
- Use the online card catalog to do a keyword search in the library or media center, or use the subject cards in the traditional card catalog to find more books on your subject.
- Consult the *Readers' Guide to Periodical Literature* and a news index, such as *Facts on File*, in print or online, to find magazine and newspaper articles on your subject.
- Use an Internet search engine to find Websites related to your limited subject. Remember, not all Websites contain accurate and reliable information. As you gather information for your report, take time to think about who created the site and for what purpose, and how that might affect the credibility of the information you find there. (A Writer's Guide to Using the Internet on pages C724–C767 will help you to search efficiently for useful, reliable Websites.)
- Make a list of all your sources. For each book, video, or CD-ROM, write the author, title, copyright year, publisher's name and location, and call number (if available). For each periodical, include the date (month, day, and year), the volume, the issue number, and the pages. For each Website, include the exact address, the site author, and the date accessed.
- Assign each source on your list a number that you can use to refer to that source in your notes.

The following is a list of sources for the report on the special effects in *The Wizard of Oz*.

Model: List of Sources

Books

Down the Yellow Brick Road by Doug McClelland, 1976, Pyramid Books, New York, 791.437 W792M (1)

The Making of The Wizard of Oz by Aljean Harmetz, 1977, Alfred A. Knopf, New York 791.437 W792H (2)

Magazines

Newsweek, August 21, 1939, pp. 23–24 (3)

Senior Scholastic, September 18, 1939, p. 32 (4)

Good Housekeeping, August 1939, pp. 40+ (5)

Newspapers

The New York Times, February 5, 1939, Section IX, page 5, column 6 (6)

The New York Times, July 11, 1939, page 28, column 4 (7)

Internet

Review of "The Wizard of Oz" by Tim Docks in "The 100 Best Movies Ever Made." *Movieline Magazine,* December 1995. <*http://www.filmsite.org* > *1999.*

"Baum, L. Frank," Compton's Encyclopedia online, 1997. < *http://www.optonline.net/plweb-cgi*> September 13, 1999.

COMPUTER TIP

If you plan to prepare your report on the computer, you may want to record your list of sources in the Notepad feature. You will also want to be sure to keep a hard copy of your list of sources in your writing folder.

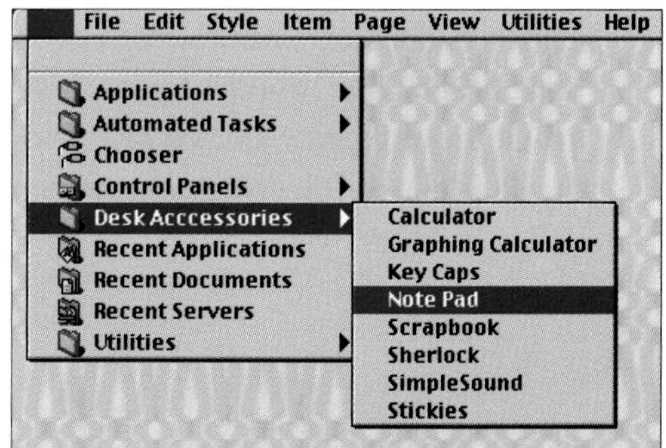

When researching a subject from the past, such as the 1939 movie *The Wizard of Oz*, you may want to locate primary sources from that period, such as statements by the actors or director at the time of filming or comments by reviewers when the film was originally released. You might find such direct, firsthand information in magazines and newspapers of the time. Remember, you need to distinguish between direct statements and opinions or comments derived from those original statements. These resources, as well as books listed as out-of-print in an online resource, can often be found in a library or media center collection on microfilm.

Practice Your Skills

Gathering Information Using a KWL Chart

Copy and complete a KWL chart like the one below for three of the following subjects. Use at least one print and one online source to find information on the subject.

SUBJECT:		
What do I **know** about the subject?	What do I **want** to learn about the subject?	What have I **learned** about the subject?

Determining Sources for Information

Make charts like the one above for posing research questions using three of the subjects below. Then use the library or media center to list four sources for each of the subjects you chose. At least one of the sources for each subject should be a magazine article from a print source and one from an online source. Follow the Guidelines for Gathering Information on page C532.

1. blues singers
2. dieting fads
3. zoo habitats
4. professional football
5. noise pollution
6. computer graphics
7. musical instruments
8. movie special effects
9. endangered animals
10. uses of laser light

Communicate Your Ideas

PREWRITING *Information Sources*

Review your earlier notes on traditions. For your limited subject for a report on a tradition, use a **KWL chart** to generate a list of facts you already know and a list of questions you would like to answer through your research. After you pose a basic research question, use the library or media center to find five sources on your subject, including at least one magazine article and one online source. Then follow the **Guidelines for Gathering Information** on page C532. Save all of your notes for later use.

Looping Back to Prewriting

Revised Topic

If you have difficulty finding sources on your limited subject, you may need to choose a different topic. Return to the list of aspects, or elements, of the subject that you made earlier. Choose a different aspect as the limited subject of your report. Continue this process until you find a limited subject that you can research adequately with the sources at your disposal.

Taking Notes and Summarizing

After you have developed a list of print and online sources, gather the books and periodicals together and bring them, along with printouts of any online source materials, to the place you plan to work. Then skim each source, looking for the information you need for your research report. With books, you will find the tables of contents and the indexes especially helpful in your search. Once you have located the relevant portion of a reliable source, take a note card and, in the upper right-hand corner of the card, write the identifying number you gave that source. This number should appear on each note card you use for that source.

(Remember, you should always evaluate the quality of your sources. Watch for information that is outdated, biased, inaccurate, or unreliable.) Keep the following goals in mind as you read the source and begin taking notes.

When you **summarize**, you write information in a condensed, concise form, touching only on the main ideas. To record direct quotations, you copy the words exactly and enclose them in quotation marks. Always write the name of the person who made the statement you are quoting and the page number where you found the statement in the source. The example below shows the form for quotations and summaries.

QUOTATION	"Three times in the history of Buena Vista Ranch, La Becerra Creek has been a half mile wide—in 1878, 1903, and 1937." (Fermina Guerra, p. C522)
SUMMARY	La Becerra Creek flooded in 1878, 1903, and 1937.

The excerpt on the following page is from page 244 of the book *The Making of the Wizard of Oz*. The note card that follows the excerpt shows how this information can be summarized.

MODEL: Taking Notes from a Source

Basically, what Gillespie [the special-effects director] knew about tornados in 1938 was that "we couldn't go to Kansas and wait for a tornado to come down and pick up a house." Everything beyond that was an experiment. . . . "I was a pilot for many years and had an airplane of my own. The wind sock they used in airports in the old days to show the direction of the wind has a shape a little bit like a tornado and the wind blows through it. I started from that. We cast a cone out of thin rubber. We were going to whirl the rubber cone and rotate it. But tornados are called twisters and the rubber cone didn't twist. So that was rather an expensive thing down the drain. We finally wound up by building a sort of giant wind sock out of muslin." The giant thirty-five-foot muslin tornado was—technically—a miniature.

–*Aljean Harmetz,* The Making of the Wizard of Oz

Sample Note Card

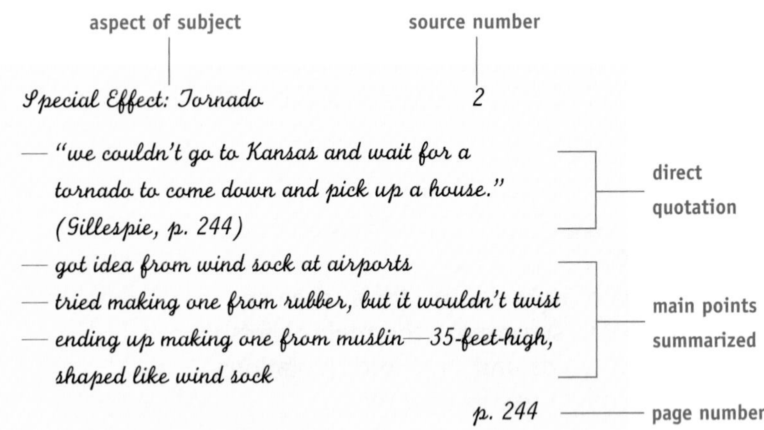

aspect of subject
source number
Special Effect: Tornado
2
— "we couldn't go to Kansas and wait for a
tornado to come down and pick up a house."
(Gillespie, p. 244)
— got idea from wind sock at airports
— tried making one from rubber, but it wouldn't twist
— ending up making one from muslin—35-feet-high,
shaped like wind sock
p. 244
direct
quotation
main points
summarized
page number

COMPUTER TIP

On most software programs, you can save the information from your source cards in a convenient place by using the Notepad feature on your computer.

PRACTICE YOUR SKILLS

Taking Notes and Summarizing

The excerpt below is from page 165 of *The Making of Star Trek–The Motion Picture.* Assume the book is your third source and make a note card for the following excerpt.

Alex's most spectacular effects were prepared in connection with [the movie's] only exterior set built at Paramount—the planet Vulcan. Location scenes had already been shot at Yellowstone [National Park], and it was up to Alex to find a way of duplicating the swirling pools of milky steam with a look of authenticity. Both dry ice and steam machines were used. . . . To match the appearance of the swirling pools of water in the real Yellowstone, Alex used evaporated milk and white poster paint, mixed with water and poured into the set's pools. The pressure of the steam caused just the proper amount of movement in the pale white whirlpools and eddies duplicated in this enormous outdoor set.

—*Gene Roddenberry,* The Making of Star Trek—The Motion Picture

Writing Tip

The goals of **note-taking** for a research report are to summarize the main points in your own words and to record quotations that you might use in your report.

Communicate Your Ideas

PREWRITING *Notes*

Follow the model for note-taking above to gather information from your sources for your report on traditions. Keep all your note cards together in your writing folder.

Developing a Thesis

During your research you will likely discover what you want to say about your subject. Consequently, after you have gathered information and have taken notes from many sources, your next step is to pull together your ideas and information to form a working thesis. A **working thesis** is a statement that expresses a possible main idea for your research paper. In a research paper, as in a critical essay, you may frame your thesis as a statement that you intend to prove is true. You then give the information you researched as evidence to support your thesis.

Keep in mind that you may change your working thesis as you continue to develop your research report. When organizing your notes to write a first draft, you may even think of new ideas that lead you to change your thesis and do additional research. You may modify your working thesis at any stage in the process of planning, drafting, and revising your report.

To create your working thesis, think about what you have discovered about your subject. For instance, the writer of the research report on The *Wizard of Oz* gathered information about how the special effects in that film were made. One example was how the filmmakers used a 35-foot wind sock to create the impression of a tornado. From this and similar examples, the writer concluded that the special-effects creators had used great ingenuity. A working thesis based on this conclusion was easy to write.

MODEL: Working Thesis

LIMITED SUBJECT	special effects in *The Wizard of Oz*
WORKING THESIS STATEMENT	Much wizardry went into creating the special effects in *The Wizard of Oz*.

Communicate Your Ideas

PREWRITING *Working Thesis*

Using all your notes for your research report on traditions, develop three or four possible theses. Select the one you like best as the working thesis of your report. Save your notes for later use.

Organizing Your Notes

As you take notes, you will begin to notice closely related ideas that could be grouped together into a single category. Building a system of categories is the first step in organizing your notes into an outline.

To create meaningful categories, review the information in your note cards, looking for ideas that are closely related. Then think of a category that would cover each group of related ideas. Once you have determined your categories, you can easily sort through your notes and clip together all the cards that belong in each category.

If some of your notes do not fit into any of the categories, clip them together separately for possible use in your introduction or conclusion. After you have arranged your categories in a logical order, wrap the whole bundle of note cards together with a rubber band to prevent losses or mix-ups.

The writer of the research report on the special effects in *The Wizard Oz* initially sorted the notes into the following categories.

Category 1	general information: cost, year of release, quotations from reviews, name of special-effects director
Category 2	the tornado
Category 3	the melting witch
Category 4	Glinda's arrival in the glass bubble
Category 5	the flying monkeys
Category 6	the horse-of-a-different-color
Category 7	the crystal ball
Category 8	the lifting and dropping of the house

After reviewing all of the information in the eight categories, the writer decided to combine some categories to create a smaller number of them to serve as main topics in an outline. For example, the special effects in categories 3, 4, 7, and 8 had something in common; they were all simple tricks that were easy to achieve.

The following revised organization consists of only four categories, which are broad enough to cover all the information.

Category 1	general information
Category 2	hardest effect to achieve—tornado
Category 3	simple tricks—house being picked up and dropped, crystal ball, glass bubble, melting witch
Category 4	tricks that should have been simple but proved difficult—flying monkeys, horse-of-a-different-color

Based on these categories, the writer chose to arrange the information in order of importance. For a memorable effect, the writer decided to place the more interesting information at both the beginning and the end of the report.

Group your notes into three to five main categories that are broad enough to include all your information.

Classifying Information

Think of three main categories into which the following tourist attractions could be grouped for a research report on "Tourist Attractions in San Diego." Then under each category write the letters of the attractions that fit into the category. Save your work for the next practice activity.

a. Point Loma, historic lighthouse
b. Wild Animal Park
c. Old Town, historic mission
d. ocean
e. San Diego Zoo
f. nearby mountains
g. Sea World aquarium
h. palm trees
i. nearby desert
j. *Star of India*, historic ship

Communicate Your Ideas

PREWRITING *Organization of Information*

Classify the information for your report about a tradition by developing three to five broad categories that cover all of your notes. After you organize your categories in a logical order, arrange your note cards and keep them banded together in your writing folder. Save your notes for later use.

Synthesizing

Often in your research projects, you will need to **synthesize**, or merge together, information from different kinds of sources. The following diagram shows the steps you can take to synthesize information.

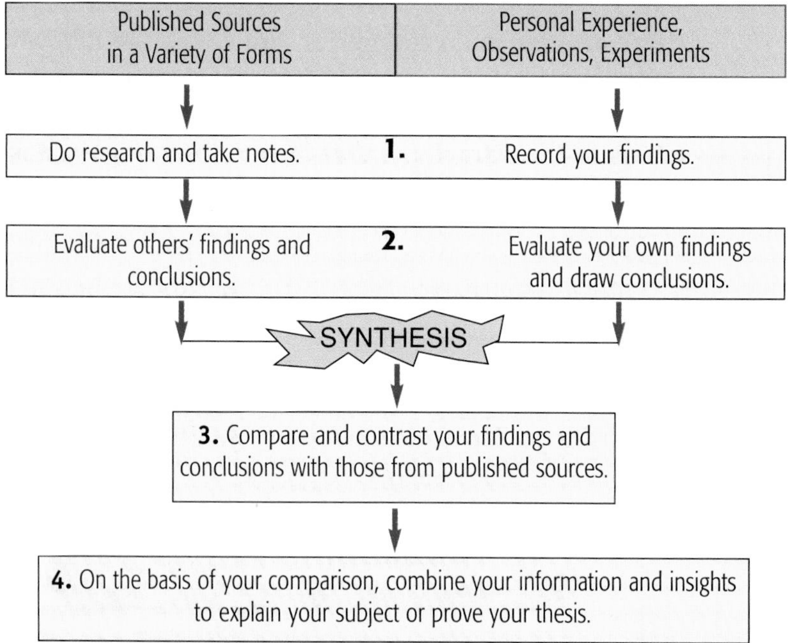
SYNTHESIZING INFORMATION FROM DIFFERENT SOURCES
Published Sources in a Variety of Forms
Personal Experience, Observations, Experiments
Do research and take notes.
1.
Record your findings.
Evaluate others' findings and conclusions.
2.
Evaluate your own findings and draw conclusions.
SYNTHESIS
3. Compare and contrast your findings and conclusions with those from published sources.
4. On the basis of your comparison, combine your information and insights to explain your subject or prove your thesis.

THINKING PRACTICE

Choose one of the research questions below. Then write a two-page report synthesizing information from both published sources and personal study.

1. What environmental problems concern young people?
2. How intelligent are ants?
3. What factors contribute to creating a safe community?

Outlining

The final step in the prewriting stage is to develop an outline as a guide to drafting. Your outline will be based on the categories and the order of categories that you have already created for your notes. In your outline each main category becomes a **main topic** with a Roman numeral, as in the outline of the main topics for the body of the report on special effects in *The Wizard of Oz*.

Model: Topic Outline for the Body of a Research Report

SUBJECT	Special Effects in *The Wizard of Oz*
MAIN TOPICS	**I.** Hardest special effect: tornado
	II. Simple tricks
	III. Simple tricks made difficult by unexpected problems

When you are satisfied with the organization of your main topics, study the information in your note cards again and add **subtopics** with capital letters under the Roman numerals. Then add **supporting points** with numbers under the subtopics and if necessary to cover all the facts you gathered, add **supporting details** with lowercase letters under each point.

MAIN TOPIC	**I.** Hardest special effect: tornado
SUBTOPIC	**A.** First attempt
SUPPORTING POINTS	**1.** Cost and materials
	2. Why it failed
SUBTOPIC	**B.** Attempt that succeeded
SUPPORTING POINTS	**1.** Cost and materials
	2. How it moved
	3. Related effects
SUPPORTING DETAILS	**a.** Storm clouds
	b. Dark sky

Convert your note-card categories into the **main topics** of an outline. Then use your notes to add **subtopics, supporting points,** and additional **details** to the outline.

Use this outline as a model when you outline a research report.

MODEL: Expanded Outline for the Body of a Research Report

MAIN TOPIC	**I.** Hardest special effect: tornado
SUBTOPIC	**A.** First attempt
SUPPORTING POINTS	**1.** Cost and materials **2.** Why it failed
SUBTOPIC	**B.** Attempt that succeeded
SUPPORTING POINTS	**1.** Cost and materials **2.** How it moved **3.** Related effects
SUPPORTING DETAILS	**a.** Storm clouds **b.** Dark sky
MAIN TOPIC	**II.** Simple tricks **A.** House's lifting and dropping **B.** Crystal ball **C.** Glinda's glass bubble
MAIN TOPIC	**III.** Simple tricks made difficult by unexpected problems **A.** Flying monkeys **1.** Technique **2.** Problems **B.** Horse-of-a-different-color **1.** Technique **2.** Problems **a.** Objection of ASPCA **b.** Horses' licking off colored gelatin

Practice Your Skills

Outlining

Outline the information about tourist attractions in San Diego from the practice activity on page C541. Show three main topics with at least three subtopics under each one.

Communicate Your Ideas

PREWRITING *Outline*

Review your categories and notes on traditions and write an outline for the body of the report. Save your outline for drafting.

Drafting

Writing Process

Your main goal in writing the first draft is to use your thesis statement, outline, and notes to write a well-structured report.

Like an essay, a research report has three main parts: an introduction, a body, and a conclusion. In addition, a research report usually contains some form of references—such as parenthetical citations or footnotes—and a works cited page that, like a bibliography, lists all the sources you used. The following chart shows the function of each part of a report.

STRUCTURE OF A RESEARCH REPORT	
Parts	**Purpose**
TITLE	• suggests the subject of the research report
INTRODUCTION	• captures the readers' attention • provides necessary background information related to the subject • contains the thesis statement

Body	• supports the thesis statement • has paragraphs that each cover one topic or subtopic
Conclusion	• brings the research to a close, often by restating the thesis in different words
Citations	• give credit to other authors for their words and ideas
Works Cited	• lists all the sources that you have cited in the research report • appears at the end of the research report

Notice that in the structure of a research report, the introduction makes your thesis clear to readers. As you draft your introduction, therefore, you should refine your working thesis into an appropriate thesis statement.

Guidelines for Refining a Thesis Statement

- Make the thesis statement specific enough so the main point of your research report is clear to the readers.
- Make the thesis statement general enough to include all the main topics in your outline.

Practice Your Skills

Refining Thesis Statements

Rewrite each thesis statement to include all the main topics in the outline.

1. Some lifesaving techniques are simple enough for anyone to learn.

I. Heimlich maneuver

II. Cardiopulmonary resuscitation (CPR)

III. Techniques only doctors should use

2. Dogs are beneficial to their owners' lives.

I. Lower blood pressure in owner

II. Feeling of being needed

III. Experiments letting prisoners have birds and hamsters

3. The Constitution of the United States grew out of the Articles of Confederation.

I. Summary of Articles of Confederation

II. Changes from Articles to Constitution

III. Constitution as model for other countries

Using Sources

As you consult your note cards for the details you will need to draft the body of your research paper, think of ways to work your source materials smoothly into your own writing. The following tips may help you.

Tips for Using Sources

- Use a quotation to finish a sentence you have started.
- Quote a whole sentence. If you omit words from a quoted sentence, indicate the omission with an ellipsis (. . .).
- Quote only a few words as part of a sentence.
- Paraphrase information from a source. When you paraphrase, reword the text, in your own words. When you summarize on note cards, you are often paraphrasing.

Model: Paraphrasing

Original Source "To match the appearance of the swirling pools of water in the real Yellowstone, Alex used evaporated milk and white poster paint, mixed with water and poured into the set's pools. The pressure of the steam caused just the proper amount of movement in the pale white whirlpools and eddies duplicated in this enormous outdoor set."

Paraphrase With condensed milk, paint, and steam, Alex made a model of a Yellowstone hot spring.

Practice Your Skills

Using Sources

The following paragraph is an explanation of how fire fighters classify fires into four groups. Read the explanation carefully. Then use it as a source for completing the following paragraph.

Classifying Fires

Fire fighters classify fires into four groups. Class A fires are those in which such things as wood or paper are burning. These fires can usually be put out with water. Class B fires are caused by burning liquids, such as gasoline, oil, or alcohol. Putting water on fires of this type usually results in spreading the fire, since the fuel will float on the water. Only carbon dioxide or dry chemical extinguishers can be safely used on these fires. The same type of chemicals can be used on Class C fires. These are caused by electrical wires or equipment that becomes overheated. If the current is still on, the person trying to put out the fire might be electrocuted if he put water onto the blaze. Class D fires are those rare ones in which certain metals burn. These special chemical fires require specific types of chemicals to put out the fires.

—Walter R. Brown, Billye W. Cutchen, and Norman D. Anderson, Catastrophes

1. Write a sentence about Class B fires that ends with a quotation.

2. Write three sentences about Class C fires, making one of the sentences a direct quotation from the source.

3. Write a sentence about fires that includes only a few words that are quoted from the source.

4. Write a sentence paraphrasing the information about Class D fires.

Paraphrasing

Write a sentence paraphrasing the following passage.

> Class B fires are caused by burning liquids, such as gasoline, oil, or alcohol. Putting water on fires of this type usually results in spreading the fire, since the fuel will float on the water. Only carbon dioxide or dry chemical extinguishers can be safely used on these fires.

Studying a Model Draft of a Research Report

The following passage is the final draft of the research report on special effects in *The Wizard of Oz*. As you read it, notice how it follows both the Structure of a Research Report on pages C545–C546 and the outline on page C544. You will also see how the writer added transitions—such as *although*, *instead*, *first*, and *meanwhile*—to connect the parts of the outline into coherent paragraphs.

As you read, notice how the writer incorporated source material, with quotes and paraphrases worked into the sentences and paragraphs. You will see that sources are cited in parentheses in the body of the report. The writer chose this method of citing sources, called **parenthetical citation**, instead of using footnotes at the bottom of each page. A parenthetical citation briefly identifies the source and page number within each sentence in which the source of information must be credited. When you finish reading the model report, you will learn more about citing sources.

Model: Draft of a Research Report

Title

The Wizardry of Oz

Introduction

The Wizard of Oz was released in 1939 after two years in production at a cost of three million dollars. One motion picture reviewer remarked that "the wizards of Hollywood have turned on their magic full force in the making of this film" (Rev. of The Wizard of Oz 32). The "magic" referred to the movie's special effects, such as the "realistically contrived cyclone" praised by

Newsweek ("The Fabulous Land of Oz" 23). Other reviewers raved about the Good Witch's arriving in a golden bubble, the Wicked Witch's skywriting and her later melting away to nothing, the monkeys' flying, the trees' talking, and the horse's changing colors. The movie won an Oscar in 1939 for these creative effects by special effects director A. Arnold (Buddy) Gillespie.

THESIS STATEMENT

Although these effects looked effortlessly magical, much real wizardry went into creating the special effects in The Wizard of Oz.

FIRST PARAGRAPH IN BODY
(ROMAN NUMERAL I IN OUTLINE)

The most challenging effect was the twister. Gillespie knew he "couldn't go to Kansas and wait for a tornado to come down and pick up a house" (Harmetz 244). Instead he got an idea from watching cone-shaped wind socks used at airports to indicate wind direction. First he made a similar cone out of rubber at a cost of $8,000; but when the rubber did not twist properly, he had to start over. After several experiments he built a 35-foot miniature cyclone out of muslin. He attached it to a machine that moved along a track and blew a dusty substance through the model twister to create a dust cloud. The $12,000 machine moved and twisted the muslin cone in a convincing way. Meanwhile a worker perched above the machine made huge clouds of yellowish-black smoke from carbon and sulfur. In front of the cameras, glass panels covered with gray cotton gave the tornado scene a dark, menacing quality on film and at the same time hid all the machinery (Harmetz 247–48).

SECOND PARAGRAPH IN BODY
(ROMAN NUMERAL II IN OUTLINE)

A much simpler effect was the illusion that the cyclone lifted Dorothy's house off the ground. Gillespie's crew filmed a three-foot-high model of the house falling onto a floor painted like the sky. Then the film was simply run in reverse. The crystal ball in the witch's castle was also a simple trick. It was a big glass bowl placed over a small screen. Film shot earlier was projected onto the screen, giving the illusion of real images appearing in the crystal ball. Another simple effect was the glass bubble that transports Glinda into Munchkinland. Gillespie's crew first filmed a silver ball, "just like a Christmas tree ornament, only bigger," by moving the camera closer and closer, making the ball seem to grow larger (Harmetz 254–55). Then, by layering the films, they added the scene of Munchkinland and Billie Burke, the actress playing Glinda.

Third Paragraph in Body
(ROMAN NUMERAL III IN OUTLINE)

Some effects that should have been simple became complicated because of unexpected problems. The flying monkeys, for example, were models suspended from a trolley, attached by 2,200 piano wires that moved them and their wings (McClelland 92). The wires kept breaking, however, which forced the crew to reshoot the scene repeatedly. Another problem was the horse-of-a-different-color, the creature that keeps changing hues. Six matching white horses were used for the trick photography—each colored a different shade. When the crew proposed to paint the horses to achieve the desired effect, however, the American Society for the Prevention of Cruelty to Animals protested. As a creative solution, the horses were "painted" with colored gelatin, but the crew had to work fast because the horses kept licking it off (McClelland 92–3)!

Conclusion

While the cyclone was the most difficult effect, the melting disappearance of the Wicked Witch was the simplest of all. "As for how I melted," said Margaret Hamilton, the actress playing the witch, "I went down through the floor on an elevator . . . leaving some fizzling dry ice and my floor length costume" (McClelland 96–7). While the demise of the Wicked Witch was truly effortless, the other tricks and illusions in The Wizard of Oz required both effort and skill. Every bit of "magic," from the cyclone to the electric tail wagger in the Cowardly Lion's costume (Hall 137), was created by Gillespie's wizards of special effects. The enduring story and all of these technological achievements have made the film a frequent item on several lists of "best films" ever made (Dirks 1995).

Works Cited

Dirks, Tim. Rev. of The Wizard of Oz, dir. Victor Fleming, in "The 100 Best Movies Ever Made." Movieline Magazine December, 1995. 8 November 2001 <http://www.filmsite.org>

"The Fabulous Land of Oz: Dream World via Cyclonic Ride Recreated in Technicolor." Newsweek 21 Aug. 1939: 23–4.

Hall, Jane. "The Wizard of Oz." Good Housekeeping Aug. 1939: 40–1+.

Harmetz, Aljean. The Making of The Wizard of Oz. New York: Alfred A. Knopf, 1977.

McClelland, Doug. Down the Yellow Brick Road: The Making of The Wizard of Oz. New York: Pyramid Books, 1976.

Rev. of The Wizard of Oz, dir. Victor Fleming. Senior Scholastic 18 Sept. 1939: 32–33.

Communicate Your Ideas

DRAFTING *Citations*

Following your outline, write a first draft of your report on traditions. Be sure your thesis statement achieves the goals outlined on page C538. Add a parenthetical citation each time you include a quotation or an idea that is not your own. Simply identify the source and page number in parentheses, as in the model. As long as you know which source you mean, you can rewrite each citation in the proper form if necessary when you revise your draft. Save your draft for later use.

COMPUTER TIP

Sometimes you may find that the presentation of information is better suited to a visual format than to text. If you are using a computer, you can create diagrams that will convey information in a clearer, more concise way than text does. You can also scan photos and artwork—even download them from the Internet—and incorporate visual images into your paper. You can find more information on incorporating visual images into your reports in A Writer's Guide to Electronic Publishing on pages C700–C723.

Citing Sources

Laws protect authors, illustrators, photographers, and publishers whose materials have been copyrighted. Using another person's words, pictures, or ideas without giving proper credit is called **plagiarism,** a serious offense. Whenever you use source materials, therefore, you must give credit to the authors—even if you only paraphrase. You have already taken steps to avoid plagiarism by taking notes in your own words and by recording the author, the page number, and the exact words of any quotation you plan to use. The chief methods of citing sources are parenthetical citations, as you have seen, and footnotes or endnotes.

Parenthetical Citations The following guidelines and examples will help you use parenthetical citations correctly. Keep in mind that the citations in parentheses are intentionally brief. Their purpose is to provide the reader with only enough information to identify the source of the material you have borrowed. Readers then refer to the works cited page at the end of your report for complete information about each source.

Book by One Author	Give author's last name and a page reference: (Harmetz 244).
Book by Two or More Authors	Give both authors' names and a page reference: (Morella and Epstein 27).
Article	Give author's last name and a page reference: (Hall 40).
Article; Author Unnamed	Give shortened form of title of article and page reference: ("The Fabulous Land of Oz" 24).
Article in a Reference Work; Author Unnamed	Give title (full or shortened) and page number, unless title is entered alphabetically in an encyclopedia: ("Special Effects").
Article from an Online Database with a Print Version	Give title (full or shortened) and page number if author is unnamed. ("Munchkins Aplenty" 16). If author is named, give name and page, paragraph, or screen number.
Online Material That Has No Print Version	Give name of the author, if available, and page numbers. If no author is given, give title of material and page numbers. No page number is needed if reference is to a single page from an encyclopedia ("Baum, L. Frank").

Parenthetical citations should be placed as close to the words or ideas being credited as possible. To avoid interrupting the flow of the sentence, place them at the end of a phrase, a clause, or a sentence. If a parenthetical citation falls at the end of a sentence, place it before the period. If you are using quotation marks, the citation goes after the closing quotation mark but before the period.

Footnotes and Endnotes If your teacher directs you to use footnotes or endnotes instead of parenthetical citations, you will use a different form. For either footnotes or endnotes, you put a small numeral halfway above the line immediately after the borrowed material. This numeral is called a **superscript**. It refers readers to a note at the bottom, or foot, of the page. Your teacher will tell you whether to number your notes consecutively throughout your report or to begin the first note on each page with the numeral *1.* Endnotes are the same as footnotes, except that they are listed at the end of the paper.

General Reference Works	[1]Frederick J. Hoffman, "L. Frank Baum," World Book Encyclopedia, 1998 ed.
Books by One Author	[2]Aljean Harmetz, The Making of *The Wizard of Oz* (New York: Alfred A. Knopf, 1977) 244.
Books by Two or More Authors	[3]Joe Morella and Edward Epstein, The Films and Career of Judy Garland (New York: Citadel Press, 1969) 34.
Articles in Magazines	[4]Jane Hall, "The Wizard of Oz," Good Housekeeping, Aug. 1939: 137.
Articles in Newspapers	[5]Frank S. Nugent, "A Critic's Adventure in Wonderland," New York Times 5 Feb. 1939, sec. 9: 5.
Article from an Online Database with a Print Version	[6]Dirks, Tim. Review, "The Wizard of Oz" in "The 100 Best Movies Ever Made." Movieline Magazine Dec. 1995. 9 November 2001 <http://www.filmsite.org>.
Online Material with No Print Version	[7]"Baum, L. Frank" Compton's Encyclopedia 13 Sept. 1999 <http://www.optonline.net/plweb-cgi>.

Whenever you cite a work that you previously cited in full, you can use a shortened form of footnote for all repeated references to that work.

First Reference	[2]Aljean Harmetz, The Making of *The Wizard of Oz* (New York: Alfred A. Knopf, 1977) 244.
Later Reference	[6]Harmetz 247.

COMPUTER TIP

If you use a word-processing program to draft your research report, you can create footnotes with the footnote feature. From the pull-down menu under Insert, choose Footnote.

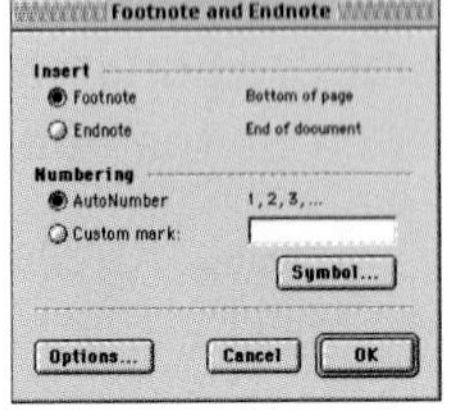

Works-Cited Page The sources you cited in your research paper should be listed on a works cited page at the end of the report. In the research report on *The Wizard of Oz*, for example, the writer added a works-cited page to give a complete list of references for the parenthetical citations in the report *(page C552)*.

> A **works-cited page** is an alphabetical listing of sources cited in a research report.

On a works-cited page, sources are listed alphabetically by the author's last name or by the title if no author is given. Page numbers are given for articles but usually not for books. The following examples show the correct form for works-cited entries. In each example note the order of information, the indentation, and the punctuation. When citing online sources, always give the date you accessed the site before the Web address.

General Reference Works	Hoffmann, Frederick J. "L. Frank Baum." World Book Encyclopedia. 1998 ed.
Books by One Author	Harmetz, Aljean. The Making of *The Wizard of Oz*. New York: Alfred A. Knopf, 1977.
Books by Two or More Authors	Morella, Joe, and Edward Epstein. Judy: The Films and Career of Judy Garland. New York: Citadel Press, 1969.
Articles, Author Named	Hall, Jane. "The Wizard of Oz." Good Housekeeping Aug. 1939: 40–1+
Articles Author Unnamed	"The Fabulous Land of Oz: Dream World via Cyclonic Ride Recreated in Technicolor." Newsweek 21 Aug. 1939: 23–4.

ARTICLES IN NEWSPAPERS	Nugent, Frank S. "A Critic's Adventure in Wonderland." The New York Times 5 Feb. 1939, sec. 9: 5.
REVIEWS	Rev. of The Wizard of Oz, dir. Victor Fleming. Senior Scholastic 18 Sept. 1939: 32–33.
ARTICLE FROM AN ONLINE DATABASE WITH PRINT VERSION	Dirks, Tim. Rev. of The Wizard of Oz, dir. Victor Fleming, in "The 100 Best Movies Ever Made." Movieline Magazine December, 1995. 15 Sept. 1999 <http://www.filmsite.org>.
ARTICLE FROM AN ONLINE DATABASE THAT HAS NO PRINT EQUIVALENT	"Baum, L. Frank" Compton's Encyclopedia Online. 1997. 13 Sept. 1999 <http://www.optionline.net/plweb-cgi>.

Sometimes your teacher may ask you to include a works-consulted page—often called a bibliography—on which you include all the works you consulted but did not necessarily cite in your research report. A works-consulted page or bibliography uses the same form as the works-cited page.

Preparing a Works-Cited Page

The following sources for a research report on Titan (Saturn's largest moon) do not have the correct form for a works-cited page. Following the examples, rewrite each entry correctly and place it in the correct order. Save your work for the next practice activity.

Randall Black. Science Digest, "Blimp on Titan," Aug. 1983, 14–15.

Ridpath, Ian, "The Living Void," Encyclopedia of Space Travel and Astronomy, 1979, 112–113.

Isaac Asimov, The Universe: From Flat Earth to Quasar Avon Books, New York, 1966, 38.

"Titan's Sea," Omni, by Patrick Moore July 1983: 28–31.

New York Times: "The Gases of Titan," June 21, 1983, sec. 4, pp. 2–4.

The Cassini Mission, jpl.nasa.gov/cassini/mission/probe.html

Using Parenthetical Citations

Write a parenthetical citation for each of the following references to the works cited page about Titan that you prepared in the previous practice activity.

EXAMPLE	Information from the article by Patrick Moore in Omni magazine
ANSWER	(Moore 28)

1. A quotation from the article in *Science Digest*

2. A fact from the book by Isaac Asimov called The Universe: From Flat Earth to Quasar

3. A reference to information in the article in The New York Times

4. A quote from "The Living Void" article in the Encyclopedia of Space Travel and Astronomy

Communicate Your Ideas

DRAFTING *Parenthetical Citations, Works Cited Page*

After you review what you have learned about citing sources correctly, reread the first draft of your report on a tradition and write the parenthetical citations in the proper form. Then prepare a works cited page to add at the end of your report. If you have a source that does not fit one of the categories described above, refer to the *MLA Handbook for Writers of Research Papers* for information on how to cite the source correctly. Save your completed draft for revising.

Drafting your research report is like stitching together a quilt. You join the various pieces of information you have collected through your research. Your time and effort are rewarded when you have the finished product in your hands, at which point you can stand back from it and check to make sure you have no missed stitches or wrong patterns. Two qualities of a research paper are especially important to check for—adequate development and accuracy.

Checking for Adequate Development

As you read over your draft, check the development of your main ideas. Did you use sufficient supporting details to back up your thesis? Have you adequately covered all the main points on your outline? Have you consulted enough sources to write authoritatively about your subject? If your answer to any of these questions is *no*, consider doing additional research to improve the content of your report.

Checking for Accuracy

Check for accuracy in your use of sources by examining all the quotes in your report. Have you accurately represented each source? Have you quoted any source out of context, thus distorting the author's real meaning? Have you used enough different sources so that you are not relying too heavily on one viewpoint? The more accurate and balanced your report is, the greater will be its power to explain or inform.

Conferencing to Revise

A second opinion is valuable when you are preparing the final draft of your research report. If possible, ask a reader to review and critique your work. Specifically, ask your reviewer to summarize in his or her own words the main idea of your report and to point out any words, sentences, or paragraphs that seem unclear. Then, as you revise, take into account the reader's specific comments and suggestions. If your reviewer cannot summarize your main idea, you may need to make your focus or thesis more clear. The following checklist will help you in the revising stage.

Evaluation Checklist for Revising

- ✓ Does your research report include an introduction with a thesis statement? *(page C545)*
- ✓ Does the body adequately develop and support the thesis statement and main points? *(pages C543–C546)*
- ✓ Is your research report accurate and balanced?
- ✓ Does your research report and the paragraphs within it have unity, coherence, and clarity? *(pages C458–C459)*
- ✓ Are your sentences concise and your words precise? *(page C298)*
- ✓ Did you use and cite sources correctly? *(pages C547 and C553–C556)*
- ✓ Did you add a suitable conclusion? *(page C546)*
- ✓ Did you include a works-cited page? *(pages C556–C558)*
- ✓ Did you add an appropriate title? *(page C545)*
- ✓ Did you follow standard manuscript form? *(pages C51–C52)*

Communicate Your Ideas

REVISING *Adequate Development, Accuracy, Clauses*

Evaluate your report and do more research if necessary to develop your ideas. Be sure you check the accuracy of any information you obtain from searching the Internet. Then, using the **Evaluation Checklist for Revising** revise your report. Try to use variety in your sentence structure so your writing will hold your reader's interest.

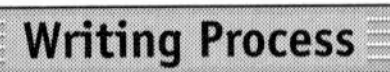

Editing

Writing Process

You are now ready to find and correct any errors in your work. You have worked hard on your paper, and you do not want any errors to distract your audience from what you have to say.

Clauses

As you revise your report, you can use clauses to vary your sentences and add interest to your writing. A **clause** is a group of words that has a subject and a verb. In the following example, the clause in bold type is a **subordinate clause**. It cannot stand alone as a complete sentence. It is attached to an **independent clause**, which can stand alone as a sentence.

CLAUSE **As the creek began to rise**, the other members of the family grew frightened.

There are two types of subordinate clauses: adverb clauses and adjective clauses.

Adverb Clauses

An **adverb clause** is a subordinate clause that acts as a single adverb, usually describing a verb. You can vary your sentences by beginning some of them with an adverb clause.

ADVERB CLAUSES **As the rain continued**, the creek rose higher.
(The clause tells when the action of the verb *rose* took place.)

The horse swam **as if its life depended on it**.
(The clause tells how the action of the verb *swam* took place.)

Adjective Clauses

An **adjective clause** is a subordinate clause that acts as a single adjective, describing a noun or a pronoun.

ADJECTIVE CLAUSES	He watched the workers **who were erecting a fence.** (The clause describes *workers*.)
	The flood of 1903, **which was not caused by rain**, was the most severe. (The clause describes *flood*.)

Punctuation with Clauses

Always place a comma after an introductory adverb clause. Also use commas to separate a **nonessential adjective clause** from the rest of the sentence. A nonessential adjective clause can be removed without changing the meaning of the sentence.

NONESSENTIAL CLAUSE	The wall of water, **which was far wider than the creek banks**, bore down upon him. (The clause is nonessential because the sentence makes sense without it.)

Combining Sentences with Clauses

With an understanding of clauses, you can combine short, choppy sentences to form more interesting sentences that read smoothly.

TWO SENTENCES	The sun rose. He reached his home.
COMBINED	**As the sun rose**, he reached his home.
TWO SENTENCES	He watched the torrent. It raged before him.
COMBINED	He watched the torrent **that raged before him.**

Editing Checklist

✔ Are all clauses punctuated correctly?

✔ Did you use subordinate clauses to combine any sentences?

Communicate Your Ideas

EDITING

Check your work for grammar, usage, mechanics and spelling. As you edit your research report, refer to your Personalized Editing Checklist. A classmate or family member may be able to help you identify errors. Save your work. 

Publishing

Writing Process

The final draft of your report should be a useful document—something that you can refer to later as a basis for future work, and something that your readers can use as a reference.

Communicate Your Ideas

PUBLISHING

Produce a final draft of your research report. Share it with a teacher, a classmate, or family member. Place a copy of your report in your portfolio.

PORTFOLIO

Time Out to Reflect

Think about the process you used in writing your research paper. What resources did you find useful? How will you go about finding new resources in the future?

Documentaries

Video and film documentaries are images, interviews, and narration woven together to present a powerful research report. Their subjects may range from boys who dream of being star basketball players to the unseen life of bugs. Some documentaries have helped bring about positive changes. A documentary highlighting the poor living conditions of migrant farm workers might spur change. Others may tell a moving true-life story.

Making a full-scale documentary is expensive and time-consuming. Yet anyone with a critical mind, an observant eye, a good team to work with, and access to video recording and editing tools can create a short documentary. The following activities will guide you. Work in groups of about six students each.

Begin by Viewing

As a first step, view as many documentaries as you can, either from the library or on television. As you watch, think about the following:

- Who made the documentary and why?
- What is the intended audience?
- What messages are stated directly and which are implied?
- What might the effect be on its audience?
- What effect did it have on you?

When group members have seen at least two documentaries, compare responses. Make a list of features common to the best. Write up this list and save it for later use.

Develop and Research the Concept

As a group, choose a concept for your documentary. Keep in mind that you will need to have access to places and people you want to capture on film. For example, does anyone you know work in a hospital emergency room? at your favorite restaurant? Will your documentary be strictly informational, or will it be critical or praising? Summarize your concept in a paragraph. Then you can begin your research. Whom do you need to interview? Keep good notes as each team member gathers information. Assign each group member a job, such as writer, director, or editor. Draw upon each person's special skills in assigning roles.

Creating a Three-Minute Documentary

Use A Writer's Guide to Electronic Publishing *(pages C700–C723)* as you follow the process sketched out below.

- Prepare a **treatment** in which you organize your ideas and identify people to interview and live-action or background footage to shoot. Bear in mind that three minutes is a very short time.
- Record your video footage, including live interviews, background and live-action shots. Take more footage than you think you'll need. Remember, you can edit out all but the best. Keep "log sheets" to record everything you have shot. Also take any still photographs that may be needed and record any additional sounds.
- View everything you have shot with a critical eye. Do you have what you need to flesh out your concept? If not, shoot what you need.
- Using your treatment as a guide, do a **rough edit** of your footage. Once you see your shots in place, make sure they are ordered the way you want. Go back to your list of features that good documentaries share. Reshoot and re-edit as necessary.
- Make a **final cut** that clarifies and enhances the message of your documentary.
- Determine what else you may need to weave the shots together and make your points effectively. Music? Narration? Titles? Add these elements.

Showing Your Video

Share your documentary with your class and ask for feedback. Meet with your group after the showing and discuss those responses. Also discuss what you learned in the process and what you would do differently to improve your next documentary.

Process of Writing a Research Report

Remember that the writing process is recursive—that is, you can move back and forth among the stages of the process to achieve your purpose. For example, you may want to return to the revising stage to add new details that occurred to you while editing. The numbers in parentheses refer to pages where you can get help with your writing.

PREWRITING

- Use a variety of strategies to discover ideas to write about that require research. *(page C528)*
- Make a list of possible subjects for a research report. Then choose one and limit it. *(pages C528–C530)*
- Develop research questions about the limited subject. *(page C531)*
- Gather information and take notes. *(pages C532–C536)*
- Develop a working thesis. *(pages C538–C539)*
- Organize your notes into categories and create an outline for your report. *(pages C539–C544)*

DRAFTING

- Include your refined thesis statement in the introduction and then write the body and conclusion. *(pages C545–C546)*
- Avoid plagiarism by using and citing sources carefully. *(pages C547–C549 and C553–C559)*
- Prepare the citations and a works-cited page. *(pages C556–C557)*
- Add an interesting, informative title. *(page C545)*

REVISING

- Check your research report for adequate development and accuracy. *(page C559)*
- Use the **Evaluation Checklist for Revising** to revise your report. *(page C560)*

EDITING

- Check your work for proper grammar, usage, spelling, and mechanics? *(page C44)*

PUBLISHING

- Make a neat final copy of your work and share it with an interested reader, or look for other ways to publish your report. *(page C51)*

A Writer Writes

An I-Search Paper on a Cultural Tradition

Purpose: to inform and explain a cultural tradition

Audience: your teacher and classmates

An I-Search paper is a research report on a topic that is of personal interest to you. Conducting an I-Search can be an adventure, as you track down sources of information and interview experts to answer your questions. In an I-Search paper, you still need to identify sources and document them, but the tone of your writing is personal. You can write in the first person, using *I* to describe your experiences gathering information.

Prewriting

Choose a cultural tradition that interests you. It may be a custom practiced in your community or in another country. Once you have chosen your topic, take it to a group of classmates and ask if they can help you by providing names, addresses, phone numbers of experts, and other tips.

Find experts or authorities and ask them where to locate the most useful resources—books, newspapers, films, tapes, or other experts on your topic. Look at or listen to this information and these ideas, taking notes on what may be useful to you.

Test the statements of experts against those of other experts. Do they seem to uphold each other's statements?

Consult both firsthand sources (people you talk with directly as well as events you observe on you own) and secondhand sources (books, magazines, newspapers, Websites, or people who tell you about what they have observed). Remember, experts are persons who know a great deal about something. A new student at your school may be the best

authority on the customs of another region in the U. S. or another country.

Drafting

A good way to organize your paper is simply to tell what you did in your I-Search, in the order that everything happened. You might divide your report into four parts: what you knew (and did not know) about the custom you chose; why you chose that custom; how you went about the search; what you learned (or did not learn) about the custom.

Revising

When you have finished your first draft, check your report for adequate development, unity, coherence, and accuracy, using the Evaluation Checklist for Revising on page C560. Then look for ways to improve your language, words, sentences, and paragraphs to capture your reader's interest.

Editing

Be sure you have used the proper forms and punctuation for all your citations. Review the examples on pages C553–C555 if necessary. Then using the Editing Checklists on page C44 and C562, check your paper for errors in sentence structure, grammar, usage, and spelling.

Publishing

Make a neat final copy of your report to share with your teacher, classmates, and family members.

Connection Collection

Representing in Different Ways

From Print . . .

To: Sales Managers
From: Lorne Rogerson, CEO
Date: 04/07/00
Subject: Pinchy's phrases

This holiday season we hope to repeat the success of last season's smash hit, Icky the Glob, which broke all of our previous sales records. This year's new product is Pinchy the Chimp, a cuddly and impish plush toy with opposable thumbs and toes.

Pinchy the Chimp will come with a voice chip capable of repeating several phrases. We have tested these phrases before an audience of five-year-olds and determined the percentage that enjoyed the following phrases: "Come here, I want to pinch you!"—95%; "Pinchy loves you!"—75%; "Pinchy wants bananas!"—70%; "Pinchy wants to play!"—65%; "Pinchy is scared and lonely!"—12%; "Pinchy wants to go back to his mommy in the jungle!"—4%.

We would love your suggestions on additional phrases for Pinchy, or ideas you may have for making this toy our most successful ever.

Thank you.

. . . to Visuals

Using the information in the letter, draw a bar graph that charts the popularity of Pinchy's phrases. Mark the horizontal axis "Phrases" and the vertical axis "Popularity." Use different colors to represent each phrase.

From Visuals . . .

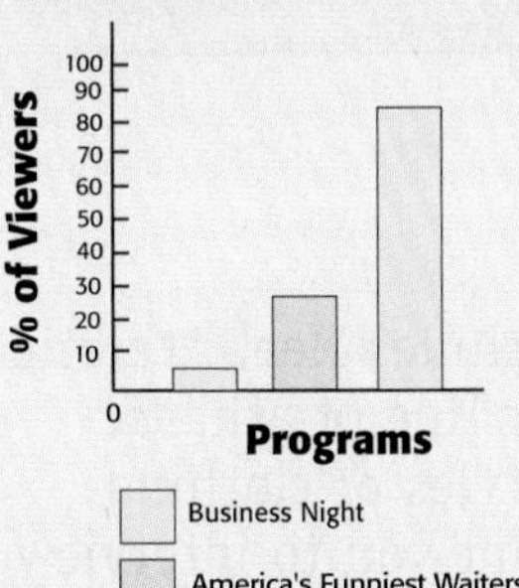

. . . to Print

You are a sales manager with Amalgamated Toys. Write a letter to your CEO based on the information in the bar graph, which shows television programs and their popularity with the target audience of Amalgamated Toys. Suggest which program Amalgamated should sponsor.

- **Which strategies can be used for creating both written and visual representations? Which strategies apply to one, not both? Which type of representation is more effective?**
- **Draw a conclusion, and write briefly about the differences between written ideas and visual representations.**

Writing in the Workplace

Writing a Business Report

You work for Pave the World, Inc., a company dedicated to making remote areas of the planet accessible to wheeled vehicles. You have just been asked by your boss to prepare a report on the profitability of paving the Florida Everglades. You think the plan is a horrible idea and that it will result in an environmental disaster.

Write a brief report for Pave the World. Begin with a thesis that states your position. Support your thesis with facts and specific details that you have learned through your research. Remember that your purpose is to persuade your boss to agree with your viewpoint. Conclude your report by restating your thesis in different words or by recommending a plan of action for the company.

What strategies did you use to write your thesis and persuade your boss?

You can find information on writing a thesis on pages C399–C400 and C538–C539.

Writing for Oral Communication

Interviewing for Information

You have been hired as a style consultant for Achilles Heel Athletic Footwear Corporation. They plan to create a new line of athletic clothing and have asked you to find out what styles of clothing would sell well in your area. To do this, they want you to interview the trendsetters in your community about what kind of clothing they think would become popular.

Prepare five interview questions that you could ask these stylish members of your community to help your company design fashionable athletic clothing. Then conduct an oral interview with three members of your class. Make sure your information is relevant to your topic, and have your subjects critique your questions for their appropriateness to the topic.

What strategies did you use to conduct an effective interview?

Assess Your Learning

You are working as a legislative aide to a newly elected member of Congress. As part of her campaign agenda, the congress-woman promised to "protect the environment," but she did not provide any specific details about what needs to be done. Your job is to help her establish a list of priorities and to choose one for a full report.

- **Write a list of possible topics for a report about protecting the environment. You might consider the protection of a river, mountains, or park land in your area. When you have finished your list, choose the topic that interests you most and do some research about what kinds of environmental problems affect the place. Take notes and compare your sources of evidence. Then develop a thesis for your report. Choose facts and ideas that support your thesis and use an outline or graphic organizer to order this information.**
- **One way to begin a research report is to start with an introductory paragraph that gives background information and ends with your thesis. Develop your report by using facts and examples you gathered in your research. End your report with a strong conclusion so that the congresswoman knows why the issue is important.**

Before You Write **Consider the following questions:**
What is the **subject?**
What is the **occasion?**
Who is the **audience?**
What is the **purpose?**

After You Write **Evaluate your work using the following criteria:**

- Does the title clearly present the topic?
- Does your introduction capture the reader's attention and provide necessary background for the environmental topic?
- Does the body of your report include paragraphs that each cover one topic or subtopic?
- Does the conclusion bring the research report to a close and restate your thesis about the environment in different words?
- Did you use proper format for citations of your sources in the body of the report and in the list of works cited?

Write briefly on how well you did. Point out your strengths and areas for improvement.

CHAPTER 13

Letters and Applications

In some kinds of writing, you need to think carefully about your purpose. When writing letters or filling out applications the purpose is clear from the start.

When you write a letter, you know to whom you are writing—and why. Whether you are inviting a friend to party, ordering something from a catalog, or registering a complaint to a company, you shape your letter to suit your purpose and the letter's recipient.

In this chapter, you will learn the correct form for friendly letters and business letters. You will also practice filling out applications for employment—another very practical form of writing to help you accomplish a specific purpose. In all cases, you will practice writing clearly and concisely because you want your readers to know exactly what you mean.

Reading with a Writer's Eye

The letter that follows was written by a young widowed mother who moved to Wyoming early in the 20th century. She and her daughter, Jerrine, plan to homestead on their own land in summer. Read the letter once to capture the essence of the writer's tale. As you reread, pay attention to the various uses of descriptive and informative writing and how these tools are adapted to the letter-writing form.

FROM

Letters of A Woman Homesteader

Burnt Fork, Wyoming
April 18, 1909

Dear Mrs. Coney,

Are you thinking I am lost, like the Babes in the Wood? Well, I am not and I'm sure the robins would have the time of their lives getting leaves to cover me out here. I am way up close to the Forest Reserve of Utah, within half a mile of the line, sixty miles from the railroad. I was twenty-four hours on the train and two days on the stage, and oh, those two days! The snow was just beginning to melt and the mud was about the worst I ever heard of.

The first stage we tackled was just about as rickety as it could be and I had to sit with the driver, who was a Mormon and so handsome that I was not a bit offended . . . especially when he told me that he was a widower Mormon. But, of course, as I had no chaperone I looked very fierce (not that that was very difficult with the wind and mud as allies) and told him my actual opinion of Mormons in general and particular.

Meantime my new employer, Mr. Stewart, sat upon a stack of baggage and was dreadfully concerned about something he calls his "Tookie," but I am unable to tell you what that is. The road, being so muddy, was full of ruts and the stage acted as if it had the hiccoughs and made us all talk as though we were affected in the same way. . . . Every time the stage struck a rock or a rut Mr. Stewart would "hoot," until I began to wish we would come to a hollow tree or a hole in the ground so he could go in with the rest of the owls.

At last we "arriv," and everything is just lovely for me. I have a very, very comfortable situation and Mr. Stewart is absolutely no trouble, for as soon as he has his meals, he retires to his room and plays on his bagpipe, only he calls it his "bugpeep." It is "The Campbells are Coming," without variations, at intervals all day long and from seven till eleven at night. Sometimes I wish they would make haste and get here.

There is a saddle horse especially for me and a little shotgun with which I am to kill sage chickens. We are between two trout streams, so you can think of me as being happy when the snow is through melting and the water gets clear. We have the finest flock of Plymouth Rocks and get so many nice eggs. It sure seems fine to have all the cream I want after my town experiences. Jerrine is making good use of all the good things we are having. She rides the pony to water every day.

I have not filed on my land yet because the snow is fifteen feet deep on it, and I think I would rather see what I am getting, so will wait until summer. They have just three seasons here, winter and July and August. We are to plant our garden the last of May. When it is so I can get around I will see about land and find out all I can and tell you.

I think this letter is about to reach thirty-secondly, so I will send you sincerest love and quit tiring you. Please write me when you have time.

Sincerely yours,
Elinore Rupert

Thinking as a Writer

Evaluating a Friendly Letter

- What is the purpose of the letter? What does the writer express to her reader?
- What specific facts do we learn about the writer?
- How would you describe the feeling of the letter? Give a specific example to support your answer.

Hearing the Writer's Voice

Oral Expression

- Read the letter aloud. What is the tone of the letter? Is it serious or carefree, happy or brooding?
- What is the rhythm and tempo of the letter? Does the writer use short, businesslike sentences or relaxed, casual sentences that are more conversational?
- What do the words chosen tell you about the writer, and the time and place she was writing?

Studying an Illustration

Viewing

- Though it looks like a painting, this is a photograph. Examine it carefully. Compare and contrast the scene it depicts with the imagery in the letter you have just read. Which elements do both the writer and the painter use in their compositions? Which elements work in one medium but not the other?

Developing Your Everyday Writing Skills

The purpose of letters and applications is to make contact in a positive and clear way. Maybe you want the recipient to write back, send you information, or interview you for a job. For each purpose, there is a correct format for your letter, which is demonstrated in this chapter.

 Writing Friendly Letters

Some friendly letters are written between friends or relatives to share news and keep in touch. Others serve such special purposes as offering or responding to invitations, expressing congratulations or sorrow, or thanking. The following model shows the correct form for a friendly letter.

Each part of a friendly letter is explained in the chart below.

PARTS OF A FRIENDLY LETTER	
Heading	The heading includes your full address with the ZIP code. Use the two-letter abbreviation for your state. Always include the date after your address.
Salutation	The salutation is your friendly greeting and is followed by a comma. Capitalize the first word and any proper nouns.
Body	In the body of your friendly letter, include your conversational message. Indent the first line of each paragraph.
Closing	End your letter with a brief personal closing, followed by a comma. Capitalize the first word of the closing.
Signature	Your signature should be handwritten below the closing, even if the rest of the letter is typed.

MODEL: Friendly Letter

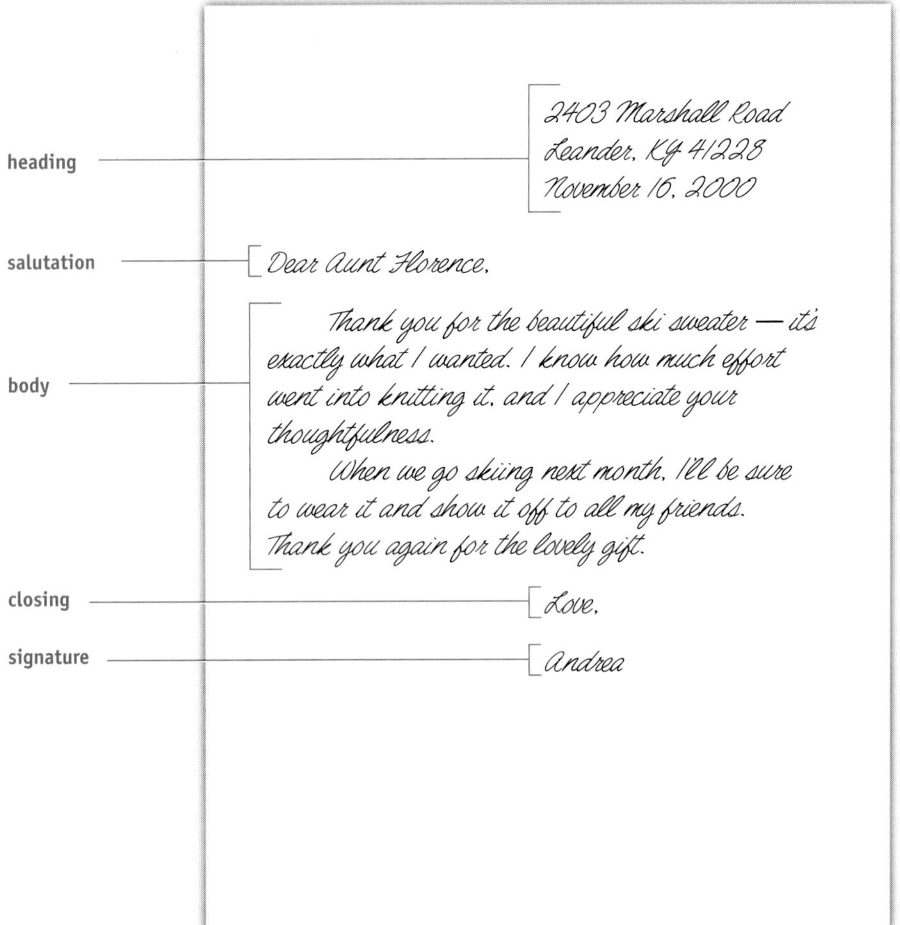
heading

2403 Marshall Road
Leander, KY 41228
November 16, 2000

salutation

Dear Aunt Florence,

body

Thank you for the beautiful ski sweater — it's exactly what I wanted. I know how much effort went into knitting it, and I appreciate your thoughtfulness.

When we go skiing next month, I'll be sure to wear it and show it off to all my friends. Thank you again for the lovely gift.

closing

Love,

signature

Andrea

The envelope for a friendly letter may be handwritten. It should contain the same information as that on the envelope of a business letter as shown on the next page. Be sure both addresses—yours and your recipient's—are clear and complete.

Writing Business Letters

Most of the business letters you will write call for some action on the part of the recipient. You may write to request information or to order merchandise. To make sure busy companies understand your point, keep your letter simple and direct.

You may wish to write a draft of your main message to make sure you have included all necessary information. Then you can prepare a neat final version that follows the correct form for a business letter.

Because a business letter is more formal than a friendly letter, it requires a more precise form. One of the most common forms is called **modified block form**. The heading, closing, and signature are positioned at the right, and the paragraphs are indented. The examples in this chapter follow this form.

A few simple guidelines will help your letter be as neat as possible. When writing a business letter, use standard white paper, 8½-by-11 in size. Whenever possible, type or word process your letters, leaving margins at least 1 inch wide.

Make a copy of your business letters in case you do not receive a reply in a reasonable amount of time and need to follow up by writing a second letter. If you are using a computer, be sure to save an electronic copy of your letters. If not, use a copying machine.

Business Envelope

If you use a word-processing program or a typewriter to write your business letter, do the same for the envelope. Place your name and address in the upper left-hand corner. The receiver's address is centered on the envelope. Use the postal abbreviations for the state and include the ZIP code.

Model: Business Envelope

Robert Tessler
1411 Vista Drive
Oakland, CA 94611 — your name and address

Customer Service Department
Silvertone Tapes, Inc.
352 Rosemont Avenue
Olympia, WA 98502 — recipient's address

PARTS OF A BUSINESS LETTER	
Heading	The heading of a business letter is the same as the heading of a friendly letter. Include your full address, including two-letter state abbreviation and the full ZIP code, and, on the line below, the date.
Inside Address	A business letter includes a second address, called the inside address. Start the inside address one line below the heading. Write the name of the person who will receive the letter if you know it. Use *Mr.*, *Mrs.*, *Ms.*, or *Dr.* If the person has a business title, such as Manager or Personnel Director, write it on the next line. Write the receiver's address, using the two-letter state abbreviation and the full ZIP code.
Salutation	Start the salutation, or greeting, one line below the inside address. Use *Sir or Madam* if you do not know exactly who will read your letter. Otherwise, use the person's last name preceded by *Mr.*, *Ms.*, *Mrs.*, *Dr.* or other title. Use a colon after the salutation.
Body	One line below the salutation, begin the body or main message of your letter. Single-space each paragraph, skip a line between paragraphs, and indent each new paragraph. If you enclose anything with your letter, such as a check, money order, or returned merchandise, mention this clearly and specifically.
Closing	In a business letter, use a formal closing such as *Sincerely, Sincerely yours, Very truly yours,* or *Yours truly*. Start the closing one line below the body. Line up the closing with the left-hand edge of the heading. Capitalize only the first letter and use a comma at the end of the closing.
Signature	In the signature of a business letter, your name appears twice. First type it—or print it if your letter is handwritten—four or five lines below the closing. Then sign your name in the space between the closing and your typed name. Use your full formal name but do not refer to yourself as *Mr.* or *Ms.*

When you are writing a business letter, always make sure it is clearly written, has a neat appearance, and follows the correct form, as in the sample that follows.

Model: Business Letter

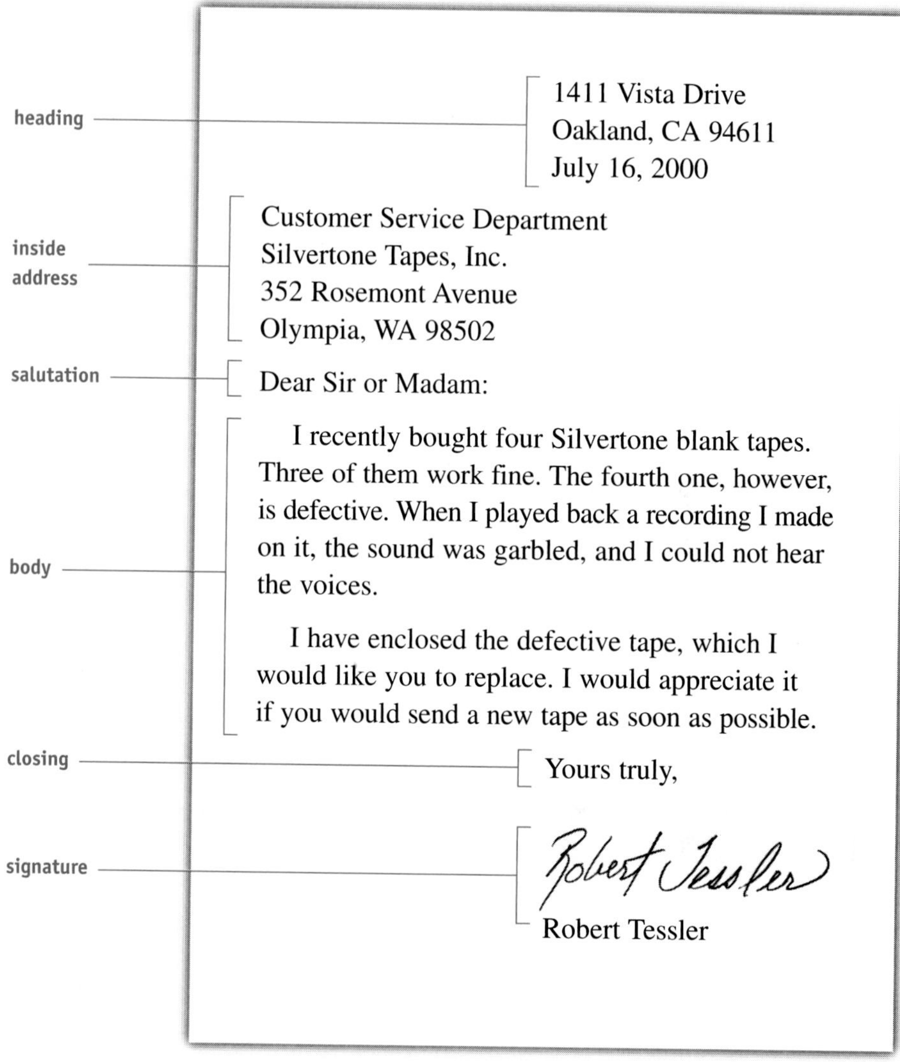

1411 Vista Drive
Oakland, CA 94611
July 16, 2000

Customer Service Department
Silvertone Tapes, Inc.
352 Rosemont Avenue
Olympia, WA 98502

Dear Sir or Madam:

I recently bought four Silvertone blank tapes. Three of them work fine. The fourth one, however, is defective. When I played back a recording I made on it, the sound was garbled, and I could not hear the voices.

I have enclosed the defective tape, which I would like you to replace. I would appreciate it if you would send a new tape as soon as possible.

Yours truly,

Robert Tessler

Robert Tessler

Letters of Request

When writing a letter of request, be as specific as possible about the information you want and state your request politely. *Please* and *thank you* are essential. Notice how the form of a business letter is used to request information.

Model: Letter of Request

3412 Falcon Road
Mobile, AL 36619
May 29, 2000

Dr. Alan Morley
Membership Director
National Science Club
8880 Wilton Drive
Cooperstown, NY 13326

Dear Dr. Morley:

I learned about the National Science Club in a magazine, and I am eager to know more about it. Please send me information about activities the club sponsors, rules for membership, and annual dues. If a membership application is required, please send me the necessary form.

I would also be interested in learning whether there is a local chapter somewhere in the Mobile area. Thank you for your assistance.

Sincerely,
Carla Rodriguez
Carla Rodriguez

Prewriting Workshop
Drafting Workshop
Revising Workshop
Editing Workshop
Publishing Workshop

Commas and Capitalization

Commas

When you write the date in the heading of a letter, use a comma to separate the month and day from the year.

March 11, 2000

Always use commas to separate parts of an address on the same line (the city from the state, for example). Do not use a comma to separate the state from the zip code.

455 Wilmington Drive, Apartment 2-C
Bozeman, MT 59715

Capitalization

Capitalize the names of all streets, cities, states, and months.

2119 **S**pring **S**treet
Skokie, **IL** 60025
October 24, 1992

Capitalize the first word of your salutation, as well as all names and titles.

Dear **M**r. **S**addlebrook:

Capitalize the first word only of the closing, and your name.

Sincerely yours,
Shelley **G**arfield

Editing Checklist

✔ Are commas used correctly in the heading and address?
✔ Are all names and titles capitalized?

Order Letters

A business letter to order merchandise should give complete information, including the description, size, order number, price, and quantity of the items. If you enclose payment for your order, the letter should state the amount enclosed.

Model: Order Letter

142 Harper Drive
Buffalo Gap, TX 79508
November 11, 2000

Capital Music Store
6554 Northwest Highway
Austin, TX 78756

Dear Sir or Madam:

Please send me the following items from your 2000 catalog:

1 Starlite music notebook, size 8½" by 11", Order #267-C	$ 3.95
1 music stand, Olympia model, order #383-F	$39.95
Shipping and handling	$ 8.50
TOTAL	$52.40

I have enclosed a money order for $52.40 to cover the cost of the merchandise, plus shipping and handling.

Sincerely yours,
Raymond Stevenson
Raymond Stevenson

Letters of Complaint

If you have a complaint about a product, express yourself courteously in a letter to the company. The following letter uses a polite but firm tone, which is appropriate for a letter of complaint.

Model: Letter of Complaint

313 Lavender Way
Millville, PA 17846
September 30, 2000

Subscription Department
Stars and Sky Magazine
36 Parkway Drive
Evanston, IL 60201

Dear Sir or Madam:

On August 4, I mailed an order form and a check for $19.95 to cover the cost of receiving your magazine for one year. Two weeks later I received a card indicating that my first issue would arrive by September 1. My check was cashed on August 21. So far I have not received a magazine.

Please look into this and notify me what is being done to resolve this problem as soon as possible.

Thank you for your cooperation.

Very truly yours,
Michael Chin
Michael Chin

Writing Different Kinds of Letters

Writing Friendly Letters

With a Specific Purpose

Choose one of the following purposes for writing a friendly letter. Write the letter to a friend or relative. Make sure that your completed letter uses the correct form.

1. Inviting someone to a surprise party
2. Congratulating someone on earning an award
3. Thanking a friend's parent after a weekend visit at their house
4. Expressing sympathy for someone who broke a leg
5. Declining an invitation to a Halloween party

To Relate a Personal Experience

Using Elinore Rupert's letter as a model (pages C573–C575), draft a letter to a friend or relative telling about something going on in your life. To encourage an answer, end your letter with questions for the person who will receive it.

Writing Business Letters

To Request Information Use the following information to write a letter of request. Be sure that you clearly state the information being requested.

HEADING: 364 Willow Street, Hainesburg, New Jersey 07832, January 10, 2001

INSIDE ADDRESS: Ms. Sandra Hanson, Quality Computer, Inc., 1167 Sequoia Boulevard, Belmont, California 94002

REQUEST: Arna Silverstein is shopping for a personal computer. She has heard that the Vectronic7000 has all the features that she requires. She is writing to request a brochure and the current price of this computer.

To Place an Order

Use the following information to write an order letter. Be sure the information is shown clearly, as in the model on page C584.

ADDRESS: Order Department, The Cycle City, 4212 Emerson Street, Emporia, Kansas 66801

MERCHANDISE: 2 rolls of Ace 1/2 inch handlebar tape, Item #33, $3.00 each; 4 Nite-Glow reflectors, Item #48, $5.95 each; $3.00 for shipping and handling

To Make a Complaint

Rewrite the following body of a letter of com-plaint, revising the tone so that it is polite but firm.

I can't understand how anyone can be so careless! I ordered a kit for building a bird feeder (kit #BF-34) from your fall catalog, and you sent me a kit that doesn't include instructions. How do you expect a person to figure out how to put it together? I demand my money back or a set of instructions, immediately.

IN THE MEDIA

Open Letter

Nearly everyone agrees that no one may open a letter addressed to someone else. But anyone may read an **open letter**—a publicly printed and widely distributed document that is an expression of opinion intended to persuade both the addressee(s) and the public. Here is an example, published on the Internet (**http://www.marswest.org/NSSLetter.html**) and signed by former astronauts and NASA experts, as well as hundreds of supporters.

An Open Letter to the President and Leaders of Congress
From the National Space Society (NSS)

Thirty-five years ago John F. Kennedy clearly established the United States as the world technology leader by sending the human race to the Moon. Now this country lives off the memories of past accomplishments.

Late last year, serious evidence of past life on Mars was unveiled. This may be one of the single most important discoveries of this century. Robotic probes are a useful follow-up to this find, but only human hands, human eyes, and human minds operating on the Red Planet can fully uncover the secrets Mars offers. What better time to recommit NASA to its fundamental mission—pioneering the space frontier?

Therefore, we, the undersigned, urge our nation's leaders to call immediately for NASA to plan and implement a human mission to Mars that will be the beginning of a sustained program of human exploration and eventual settlement of the Red Planet.

The United States and its friends have the ability to make such a program happen. We have the opportunity to open a New World to humanity, one full of wonders yet to be discovered and history yet to be made. It is time for the United States to lead human exploration of space yet again.

Media Activity

Write an open letter to someone who can make a difference on an issue you care about. You may work alone or with a group. When you have finished, design a Web page on which to present your open letter.

You can learn more about creating Web pages in **A Writer's Guide to Using the Internet** *(pages C724–C767).*

Completing a Job Application

When you apply for a job, you may be asked to fill out an application form. Application forms vary, but most of them ask for similar kinds of information. You may wish to prepare your information ahead of time so that you will be ready to complete the form when you apply for a job. The following is a list of items that most likely will be required to complete a job application form.

Information Often Requested on Job Applications

- the current date
- your complete name, address, and telephone number
- your date and place of birth
- your Social Security number
- names and addresses of schools you have attended and dates of attendance
- any special courses or advanced degrees
- names and addresses of employers for whom you have worked and the dates you were employed
- any part-time, summer, and volunteer jobs
- names and addresses of references (Obtain permission beforehand from each person you intend to list as a reference.)

When you fill out a job application, use the following guidelines.

Guidelines for Completing a Job Application

- Print all information neatly, accurately, and completely.
- Do not leave blanks. If a section does not apply to you, write *N/A* ("Not Applicable").
- List schools attended and work experience in order, giving the most recent first.
- If you mail the application form, include a brief cover letter, stating the job for which you are applying. The cover letter should follow the correct form for a business letter as shown on page C581.

Model: A Completed Job Application

Barton's Department Store

APPLICATION FOR EMPLOYMENT

PERSONAL INFORMATION (Please print)

Name Last *Samuels* First *Paula* Middle *Jane* Social Security/Social Insurance Number *181-78-0945* Birth Date (M/D/Y) *11/15/85*

Other names you are known by ______ Are you less than 18 years of age? Yes ✓ No ___ (Barton's is required to comply with federal, state, or provincial law.)

U.S. Applicant Only: Are you legally eligible for employment in the U.S.? Yes ✓ No ___ (proof of U.S. citizenship or immigration status will be required if hired for a position in the U.S.)

Have you been convicted of a felony in the last seven (7) years? Yes ___ No ✓
If Yes, list convictions that are a matter of public record (arrests are not convictions). A conviction will not necessarily disqualify you for employment.

Present Address Street *414 Broad St.* City *Garfield* State/Province *Pennsylvania* Zip Code/Postal Code *19015*

Permanent Address Street *same* City State/Province Zip Code/Postal Code

Phone Number Daytime Evening *(555) 874-3198* Referred By

EMPLOYMENT DESIRED (If you are applying for a retail hourly position, please keep in mind that the availability of hours may vary.)

Position Location/Department Salary Desired Date You Can Start

	Sunday	Monday	Tuesday	Wednesday	Thursday	Friday	Saturday
Specify hours available for each day of the week	*Any*	*4p.m.–8p.m.*	*4p.m.–8p.m.*	*4p.m.–8p.m.*	*4p.m.–8p.m.*	*4p.m.–8p.m.*	*Any*

Are you able to work overtime? *no*

Have you ever worked for Barton's Department Store? ______ If yes, when? *no* Which store/department? ______

EDUCATION

	Name and Address of School	Circle Last Years Completed	Did You Graduate?	Subjects Studied and Degrees Received
High School	*Wilson High School*	1 2 3 4	Y (N)	*in first year*
College		1 2 3 4	Y N	*N/A*
Post College		1 2 3 4	Y N	*N/A*
Trade, Business, or Correspondence School		1 2 3 4	Y N	*N/A*

List skills relevant to the position applied for *can run a cash register; computer experience*

SKILLS *For Office/Administrative positions only* Typing WPM: ______ 10-Key: ☐ Yes ☐ No

Computer Proficiency: ☐ Word for Windows ☐ Excel ☐ Others: ______

Have you ever visited a Barton's Department Store? Where? Describe your experience. *I went to the Barton's in Pittsburgh and was impressed by the selection of merchandise and the courtesy of the sales associates.*

What do you like about clothing? *I like to look nice and feel that I have a good fashion sense. I am good at helping people.*

Why would you like to work for Barton's Department Store? *It would be a convenient after-school location. I like working with people.*

Describe a specific situation where you have provided excellent customer service in your most recent position. Why was this effective? *When I worked at a bookstore I called around to all of our branches until I found a hard-to-find copy of a book a customer was looking for.*

FORMER EMPLOYERS

Date (M/D/Y): 11/15/01

List below current and last three employers, starting with most recent one first. Please include any non-paid volunteer experience which is related to the job for which you are applying.

#	From / To	Current Employer (Name and Address–Type of Business)	Salary or Hourly	Position	Reason for Leaving
1.	From: 10/10/01 To: 11/01/01	Della's Soup Kitchen 5 Gale Road, Garfield	Starting $4.25 Ending $4.75 If hourly, average # of hours per week 8 hrs.	Waitress	to gain more work experience
	Duties Performed: serving soup; clearing; setting tables				
	Supervisor's Name: Della Nathan	Phone Number: (555) 330-1234	May We Contact? yes		
2.	From: 6/5/01 To: 8/10/01	Reese's Candy Shop 55 Marsh Street, Garfield	Starting $4.00 Ending $4.00 If hourly, average # of hours per week 5 hrs.	Cashier	lack of hours
	Duties Performed: working the register, opening the store				
	Supervisor's Name: Dana Reese	Phone Number: (555) 774-2350	May We Contact?: yes		
3.	From: 12/7/00 To: 5/1/01	Garfield Grocery 125 Main Street, Garfield	Starting $5.75 Ending $6.25 If hourly, average # of hours per week	Cashier	insufficient wages
	Duties Performed: working the register, straightening shelves, sweeping				
	Supervisor's Name: Lovey Gaber	Phone Number: (555) 525-3725	May We Contact?: yes		

REFERENCES Give below the names of three professional references, whom you have known for at least one year.

Name	Address & Phone Number	Profession	Years Acquainted How Do You Know This Person?
1. Carl Smith	14 Main Street, Garfield (555) 705-2319	Principal	3, at school
2. Jane Bart	211 Main Street, Garfield (555) 858-2672	Manager	5, friend
3. Michael Reese	45 Dorand Road, Garfield (555) 646-2792	Accountant	7, friend's father

Date 11/15/01 Signature Paula Samuels

WE ARE AN EQUAL OPPORTUNITY EMPLOYER COMMITTED TO HIRING A DIVERSE WORKFORCE.

Barton's Department Store

CHAPTER 14

Speeches, Presentations, and Discussions

Think about a time you listened to an accomplished and compelling speaker communicating ideas in unforgettable words delivered in such a way that the entire audience was moved to the depth of its being. Perhaps you have listened to a tape of Martin Luther King, Jr.'s powerful "I Have a Dream" speech given before two hundred and fifty thousand people in 1963. Perhaps you have heard a local politician delivering an eloquent speech about the importance of an environmental project such as recycling. The spoken word carries the speaker's thoughts directly to the audience, who publicly share the listening experience.

True communication occurs when a speaker presents his or her ideas in a clear, organized, and forceful way and the listeners are able to comprehend and respond to the speaker's message. In this chapter you will learn effective strategies for speaking and listening to help you become a better communicator.

Reading with a Writer's Eye

The following is an excerpt from a speech delivered by Antonia C. Novello, who in 1990 became the first Hispanic American woman to serve as United States Surgeon General. A native of Fajardo, Puerto Rico, Dr. Novello gave this speech in 1992 in Los Angeles. Imagine that you are listening to the speech at a public town hall meeting. Does the speech appeal to you? What feelings do you have about it?

FROM

ADDRESS TO A TOWN HALL AUDIENCE, LOS ANGELES, 1992

Antonia C. Novello

Good afternoon. I am delighted to be here in Los Angeles. It is a wonderful city, and I am honored to be here. It is a long way from the town center of Fajardo to Los Angeles, California.

I come here with two messages: first, that for most of us our health status is molded and shaped one decision at a time and, second, that women and minorities are threatened by a large number of serious health concerns, which we can only address one decision at a time. Unless we make every effort to provide the attention, recognition, respect, empathy and care necessary for each of our citizens, then we fail as policy makers and as a community.

I accepted the job as Surgeon General because our citizens must have the facts—as Cervantes said, we cannot "Mince the matter." I am dedicated to the proposition that we must give our people the health information they need to make vital health choices and decisions that will ripple out for years to come.

As Surgeon General of the U.S. Public Health Service, I serve as the Surgeon General for all the people of these United States. When I was appointed, I didn't focus on being a woman or a minority—although I realized that in terms of an appointment, each of these characteristics was symbolic.

In my efforts to protect our nation's health, I have spoken out especially about the dangers associated with illegal underage drinking, smoking, AIDS, and violence. What I have learned since taking on this task has alarmed me, but at the same time, it has also taught me that my efforts cannot let up.

I promised myself when I accepted this position that my job would not be complete until I truly felt that I had "touched" the young people of this country by teaching them what I knew. I believe that our kids are smart—perhaps smarter than we were at their age—and if we will give them honest and factual information and treat them with respect, they will make good decisions. I know that I'm *far from finished*, and I will continue to speak out about these issues whenever and wherever possible. But I am here today to enlist your help.

Gathering together in forums such as this accomplishes my first important goal—*we learn from one another, and education is our most valuable tool* to get us where we need to go.

One phrase I have continued to recite during my tenure as Surgeon General is that *our young people are our nation's most valuable resource*—I say it over and over again because I believe it myself so fervently. When we say we have hope for the future, what we are really saying is that we have hope for our children. The work we do now can ensure that our hope becomes a reality.

In the work that we do—as legislators, educators, business leaders, health care providers, and most importantly, *as parents*—our focus must be on our young people.

The America of today is far different from what it was when we were young. The challenges are different, the pressures greater, the poverty and despair more rampant, and the availability of drugs and alcohol more widespread. These things are tragic—and we must do everything we can to turn them around.

Thinking as a Writer

Matching the Message to the Audience

- To whom is this speech directed?
- Try to condense the speaker's main idea or message into a single, clearly expressed statement.
- What arguments and examples does Dr. Novello use to win over her audience?
- With what feelings does the last paragraph leave you?

Delivering the Speech

Oral Expression

- Take turns with a partner reading aloud and listening to parts of the speech. What special words or phrases does Dr. Novello use to appeal to her target audience?
- Try to match your style of reading to the tone and rhythm of the speech. Do you think the speech allows a distinct style to come through? How so?

Interpreting Nonverbal Appeals

Viewing

- Compare the two antismoking posters shown below. Which one do you think is more effective? How do these nonverbal persuasions add to or detract from the purpose of the oral speaker? To what emotions do these posters appeal? Explain your views.

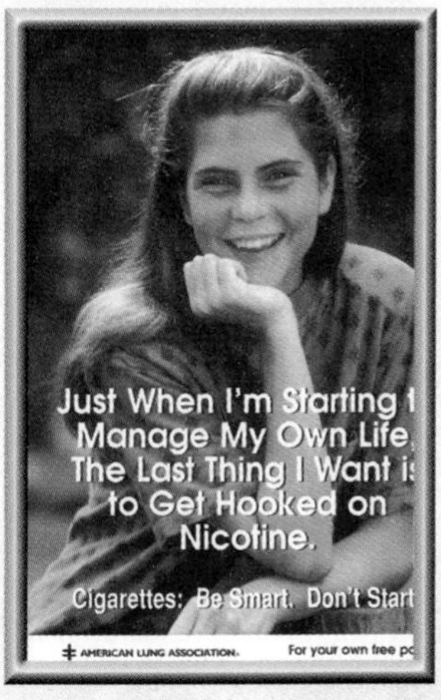

Developing Your Public Speaking and Presentation Skills

You have already read an example of a speech written for a specific purpose, to let young people know how the country's surgeon general plans to help them with health issues. This speech illustrates three of the most common purposes of a public speech—to inform, inspire, and persuade.

 Preparing Your Speech

In school, as well as in your future career, you may sometimes find yourself in a situation where you must give a formal speech. In school you may make a speech to a group of students, parents, or teachers. In your career, you may make a formal presentation to a group of coworkers at a small meeting or a large convention.

Knowing Your Audience and Purpose

Who is going to hear your speech? You may have an opportunity to speak formally to an audience made up of parents or voters, or you may be asked to speak informally to a group of your classmates. The following strategies will help you think about your audience and your purpose as you limit the subject of your speech.

Strategies for Considering Audience and Purpose

- Find out the interests of your audience. Then limit your subject to match your listeners' interests.
- Try to determine what your audience already knows about the subject you plan to talk about. Consider what your audience may expect to hear.
- Is your purpose to inform, to persuade, or to entertain?

You can learn more about specific purposes for written and oral essays on page C22.

The following examples illustrate three ways to limit the subject of skiing according to the purpose of your speech.

PURPOSES OF SPEECHES	
Purposes of Speech	**Example**
to inform	Explain the similarities and differences between downhill and cross-country skiing.
to persuade	Convince students to take up cross-country skiing.
to entertain	Tell about your experiences the first time you went downhill skiing.

Practice Your Skills

Identifying a Subject That Relates to a Purpose.

1. **Write an example of a subject for a speech the purpose of which is to inform.**
2. **Write an example of a subject for a speech the purpose of which is to persuade.**
3. **Write an example of a subject for a speech the purpose of which is to entertain.**

Choosing and Limiting a Subject

While thinking about choosing an interesting subject, you should limit and refine it. Limiting the subject enables you to present it fully for a given audience within a limited period of time. As a rule of thumb, it takes about as long to deliver a ten-minute speech as it does to read aloud slowly four pages of a typed, double-spaced, written composition. The strategies for choosing and limiting a subject for a speech are the same as the strategies you would use to choose and limit a subject for an essay.

You can learn more about choosing and limiting a subject on pages C18–C20.

Strategies for Choosing and Limiting a Subject

- Choose a subject that is of interest to you and to your intended audience.
- Choose a subject that you are very familiar with or can research thoroughly.
- Limit the subject by choosing one aspect of it. For example, for a ten-minute speech about the planet Mars, you could limit the subject to weather on Mars.

PRACTICE YOUR SKILLS

Determining a Subject

For each of the following items, write a subject for a speech. Share your ideas with the class.

1. personal experiences
2. experiences of others
3. current events or issues
4. past events or people
5. how to do something
6. how to make something
7. jobs or professions
8. school-related subjects
9. ideas for inventions
10. ideas about the future

Limiting a Subject

Limit each subject to be suitable for a ten-minute speech.

11. pollution
12. favorite holidays
13. country music
14. parental problems
15. the homeless
16. explorers
17. sports
18. my life goals
19. good health
20. music trends

Gathering and Organizing Information

After choosing and limiting your subject, you should begin to gather information. First, brainstorm with someone for any information you already know about your subject. *(pages C27–C28)* Think of knowledgeable people you might interview. Before interviewing, prepare the questions you will ask. Another excellent source is the library or media center, where you will find useful articles in encyclopedias, other reference works, and periodicals.

Taking Notes Take notes on note cards throughout your research. Note cards are best for recording ideas because the information can be easily organized later as you prepare to make an outline of your speech. Use a separate card to summarize each important idea, and include facts and examples to support the idea. Record accurately any quotations you plan to use. If you conduct an interview, take notes or use a tape recorder and then transfer the information to note cards. Your presentation should contain accurate and truthful information.

Collecting Audiovisual Aids Audiovisual aids, such as maps, pictures, slides, CDs, CD-ROMs, and tapes, will add to the impact of your speech. Decide which of your main points to enhance with the use of audiovisual aids, and gather or create these materials as you prepare your speech.

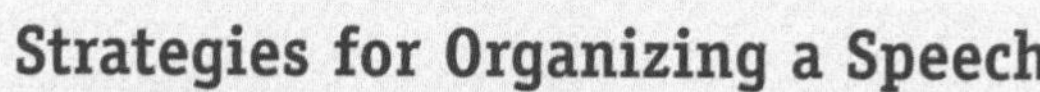

Strategies for Organizing a Speech

- Arrange your notes in the order in which you intend to present your information.
- Use the cards to make a detailed outline of your speech, and then draft an introduction.
- To catch the interest of your audience, begin your speech with an anecdote, an unusual fact, a question, or an interesting quotation. Be sure to include a thesis statement that makes clear the main point and the purpose of your speech.
- The body of your speech should include several ideas, with facts and examples to support each idea.
- Arrange the ideas in a logical order, and think of the transitions you will use.
- Choose valid evidence, proofs, or examples to support claims.
- Use appropriate and effective appeals to support points or claims.
- Write a conclusion for your speech that summarizes your important ideas. Try to leave your audience with a memorable sentence or phrase.

Gathering and Organizing Information

Choose and limit a subject for a ten-minute speech in which the purpose is to inform. Write what you know about the subject on note cards. Next, visit the library or media center and find information for four more note cards. Organize your cards and write a detailed outline of your speech.

COMPUTER TIP

You can create a folder to contain text, sound, and image files for a multimedia slide presentation. You can also store any material that you have gathered from the Internet and copy and paste information from these files directly into the slides of a multimedia presentation program.

Practicing Your Speech

Although you need to rehearse your speech, in most cases you should not attempt to write it out or to memorize it. Instead, use your outline, or convert your outline and note cards into cue cards. Cue cards help you remember your main points, your key words and phrases, and any quotations you plan to use in your speech.

Strategies for Practicing a Speech

- Practice in front of a long mirror so that you will be aware of your gestures, facial expressions, posture, and body language.
- Look around the room as if you were looking at your audience.
- Time your speech. If necessary, add or cut information.
- As you practice, use your cue cards and any audiovisual aids or props that are part of your speech.
- Practice over a period of several days. Your confidence will grow each time you practice.
- If you intend to use a microphone, practice your technique.

Revise your speech as you practice. You can do this by experimenting with your choice of words or adding and deleting information to make your main points clearer. You may find it helpful to practice your speech with a friend. Listeners' comments may help you revise and improve your speech.

Practice Your Skills

 *Practicing and Revising Your Speech*

Make cue cards for the speech you have been preparing. Then, using the strategies above, practice your speech before a relative, friend, or classmate. Use your listener's comments to make improvements, and then practice your revised speech.

Delivering Your Speech

If you have followed the strategies for preparing and rehearsing, you should feel confident when the time comes to stand up in front of your audience and deliver the speech. The following strategies will help you deliver an effective speech.

Strategies for Delivering a Speech

- Have ready all the materials you need, such as your outline or cue cards and audiovisual materials or props.
- Make sure that computer presentation equipment is assembled and running properly.
- Wait until your audience is quiet and settled.
- Relax and breathe deeply before you begin your introduction.
- Stand with your weight evenly divided between both feet. Avoid swaying back and forth.
- Look directly at the people in your audience, not over their heads. Try to make eye contact. Smile!
- Speak slowly, clearly, and loudly enough to be heard.
- Use good, clear diction.

- Use pitch and tone of voice to enhance communication of your message.
- Be aware of using correct grammar and well-formed sentences.
- Use informal, technical, or standard language appropriate to the purpose, audience, occasion, and subject.
- Use rhetorical strategies appropriate to the message, whether your purpose is to inform or to persuade.
- Use appropriate gestures and facial expressions to emphasize your main points.
- Remember to use your audiovisual aids, such as charts and overhead projection, making sure everyone in your audience can see them.
- After finishing your speech, take your seat without making comments to people in the audience.

COMPUTER TIP

From the View menu of your multimedia presentation application, choose Slide Show. Select the options that best suit your purposes. Run your slide show by advancing each slide by hand (pressing the Enter key on your keyboard), or set timings so that the slides advance automatically. Practice working with the slide show before you give your presentation.

Evaluating an Oral Presentation

The ability to evaluate and make judgments about an oral presentation will help you and your classmates improve your future speeches. The Oral Presentation Evaluation Form on the next page may be useful. When evaluating a classmate's speech, remember to be honest by making positive and helpful comments. Make your comments specific in order to help the speaker understand your suggestions. Then complete an assessment form for speeches presented by your classmates. Each speaker should collect and read the listeners' evaluations of his or her speech. Use listener feedback to evaluate the effectiveness of your speech and to help you set goals for future speeches.

ORAL PRESENTATION EVALUATION FORM

Subject: ______________________________

Speaker: ____________________ **Date:** ______________

Content

Were the subject and purpose appropriate for the audience?

Was the main point clear?

Were there enough details and examples?

Did all the ideas clearly relate to the subjects?

Was the length appropriate (not too long or too short?)

Organization

Did the speech begin with an interesting introduction?

Did the ideas in the body follow a logical order?

Were transitions used between ideas?

Did the conclusion summarize the main points?

Presentation

Did the speaker use a good choice of words?

Was the speech sufficiently loud and clear?

Was the rate appropriate (not too fast or too slow)?

Did the speaker make eye contact with the audience?

Did the speaker make effective use of pitch and tone of voice?

Did the speaker use gestures and pauses effectively?

Were audiovisual aids or other props used effectively?

Were cue cards or an outline used effectively?

Comments: ______________________________

PRACTICE YOUR SKILLS

Delivering and Evaluating Your Speech

Evaluate your performance with your classmates, using the Oral Presentation Evaluation Form. In addition, complete a form for speeches presented by your classmates. Use listeners' feedback to improve your your future speeches.

Developing Your Critical Listening Skills

Listening usually involves much more than simply hearing the words that are spoken. When listening to directions, a speech, or a lecture, you must comprehend, evaluate, organize, and remember the information. A good listener engages in critical, empathic, reflective, and appreciative listening. Skillful listening requires that you pay close attention to what you hear. When listening for information or ideas, you must be able to evaluate critically and reflect on what the speaker says. When you are listening to a persuasive speech, it is important that you evaluate the speaker's evidence as well as the organization and logic of the argument. By recording the information in an organized way, you will be able to remember the information for future reference. You can also assess the emotional tone of the speech by putting yourself in the speaker's place. **Empathic listening,** or listening with feeling, will help you recognize the misuse of illogical emotional appeals. Skills that you have practiced while learning how to prepare and present a speech will be invaluable to you as you work to develop and sharpen your critical listening skills.

Listening Appreciatively to Presentations and Performances

You may have occasion to attend a public reading or oral interpretation of any one of a variety of written forms, such as an essay, a report, a poem, a play, a chapter of a novel, or an excerpt from a memoir. **Oral interpretation** is the performance or expressive reading of a literary work. As a listener you must judge how successfully the performer has managed to express the intentions, style, and meaning of the work through use of verbal and nonverbal techniques. The following guidelines will help you listen appreciatively to oral presentations and performances.

Strategies for Listening Appreciatively

- Be alert to the expressive power of the dramatic pause.
- Observe the use of gestures, voices, and facial expressions to enhance the message.
- Listen for changes of volume, intonation, and pitch used to emphasize important ideas.
- Listen for rhymes, repeated words, and sounds.
- Listen for rhetorical strategies and other skillful uses of language.
- Take time to reflect upon the message and try to experience, with empathy, the thoughts and feelings being expressed.

PRACTICE YOUR SKILLS

Listening to Presentations and Performances

Perhaps your local bookstore hosts readings of original works of prose and poetry by well-known authors. A nearby theater group might be performing a dramatic work that you have read for school, such as *The Price.* You may also have occasion to attend original artistic performances by your peers. You will get the most out of the experience by preparing a listening strategy suited to the speaker's subject and purpose.

Prepare your own strategies for listening to and evaluating the following oral presentations. Identify what you would listen for in each case.

1. an actor reading a dramatic monologue from a play
2. a poet reading a collection of new poetry
3. a writer reading selections from a novel, essay, memoir, or short story
4. a classmate reading John F. Kennedy's inauguration speech
5. a celebrity delivering a speech on public health issues

Oral Interpretation

Choose a poem, short story, or dramatic scene to perform for your class. Instruct your classmates to take notes and analyze the effect of the following artistic elements.

1. character development
2. rhyme
3. imagery
4. oral language style
5. physical actions and gestures

Listening to Directions

When you are assigned a task, listen carefully to the instructions. Do not assume you know what to do or what the speaker will say. Then follow the strategies below for understanding directions.

Strategies for Listening to Directions

- Write down the directions as soon as the speaker gives them. You may not remember them as well as you think.
- Ask specific questions to clarify the directions.
- When you finish an assignment, briefly review the directions once more to make sure you have followed them correctly.

Practice Your Skills

Following Directions

Have paper and pencil ready. As your teacher reads you a set of directions, follow them carefully.

Evaluating the Effectiveness of Directions

To practice giving and following directions, think of a simple task that can be completed in the classroom, such as making a book cover out of a paper bag or putting new laces in a pair of

sneakers. Write step-by-step directions for completing the task. Read your directions to a classmate and have the classmate follow them using the strategies for Listening to Directions. Have your classmate repeat your instructions back to you. As the teacher reads you a set of instructions, follow them carefully. Check your work with a partner.

Listening for Information

When you listen to a speech or a lecture, pay close attention so that you can understand and evaluate what you hear. Listening for the purpose of learning requires extra concentration. You may find the following strategies helpful.

Strategies for Listening for Information

- Sit comfortably but stay alert. Try to focus on what the speaker is saying, without being distracted by people and noises.
- Determine the speaker's purpose, whether it is to inform, to persuade, or to entertain.
- Listen for verbal clues to identify the speaker's main ideas. Often, for example, a speaker emphasizes important points by using such phrases as *first, later, also consider, most importantly, remember that,* or *in conclusion.*
- Use your knowledge of language and develop your vocabulary to interpret accurately the speaker's message.
- Watch for nonverbal clues such as gestures, pauses, or changes in the speaking pace. Such clues often signal important points.
- Determine the speaker's point of view about the subject. For example, is the speaker expressing positive or negative attitudes or arguing for or against an issue?
- As you listen, note anything that seems confusing or unclear.
- Ask relevant questions to clarify understanding.
- Take notes to organize your thoughts and to help you remember details. Your notes provide a basis for further

discussion. You may also want to use your notes to outline your speech or write a summary of it. If the speech is a course lecture, notes will help you study for a test on the subject.

Listening and Taking Notes

Organize a classroom experiment. The following test will show how well you communicate, how well your audience listens, and the extent to which note taking helps. Prepare a short speech for the purpose of informing. Write a few key questions that you think your listeners should be able to answer after listening to your talk. Deliver the speech while one half of the class listens without taking notes and the other half of the class listens and takes notes. Instruct all the students to answer the questions you wrote.

Recognizing Propaganda

As a critical listener, you must evaluate the content or message of a speech and make judgments about what you hear. To make sound judgments about what you hear, you must be able to recognize propaganda devices, which people may use to mislead you.

The aim of propaganda is to get you to accept a point of view or to take some action. Rather than provide facts and examples as evidence, however, speakers who use **propaganda** distort or misrepresent information or disguise opinions as facts. Propaganda techniques also appeal to people's emotions by using emotional language, stereotypes, and exaggerations. By listening critically, you can learn to detect the following propaganda techniques.

Distinguishing Fact and Opinion

A **fact** is a statement that can be proved to be true or accurate. An **opinion** is a personal feeling or judgment about something. When opinions are stated as facts, misunderstanding or confusion often results for the listener. You can avoid confusion by listening critically to distinguish between facts and opinions.

FACT	I ate tacos for dinner last night.
OPINION	Tacos make the best meal.
FACT	Dogs are members of the canine family.
OPINION	Dogs make the most loving and intelligent pets.

PRACTICE YOUR SKILLS

Distinguishing Between Fact and Opinion

Label each of the following statements *F* for *fact* or *O* for *opinion.*

1. Charles Dickens wrote *Great Expectations.*
2. Dogs are more fun than cats.
3. The sun sets at 7:02 this evening.
4. My sister plays basketball on the high school team.
5. All roller-coaster rides are dangerous.
6. Dickens was the best writer of all time.
7. I had my first roller-coaster ride when I was five.
8. My brother should be captain of the basketball team.
9. A German shepherd is larger than a cocker spaniel.
10. Fall is the most beautiful season of the year.

Bandwagon Appeals

A **bandwagon appeal** is an invitation to do or think the same thing as everyone else. Advertisements that use bandwagon appeals often try to make consumers feel inferior if they do not conform. A political campaign may use bandwagon appeals to make voters feel useless if they do not vote on the winning side. Common slogans associated with this type of propaganda include *Get on board! Join the crowd! Everyone loves . . .* and *Don't be left out!*

> The with-it generation drinks Vita-Juice. If you don't drink Vita-Juice, you're not with it; you're out of it!

Testimonials

A **testimonial** is a statement, usually given by a famous person, that supports a product, a candidate, or a policy. A testimonial can be misleading because it suggests that a famous person's opinions must be right or that a product must be excellent if a celebrity endorses it.

> Hi! I'm Greg Husky, quarterback for the Longhorns. Since getting to each game on time is important, I depend on my Leopard convertible to get me there. If you need a dependable car the way I do, get yourself a Leopard.

Unproved Generalizations

A **generalization** is a conclusion that is based on many facts and examples. However, a generalization that is based on only one or two facts or examples is unsound or unproved. Unsound generalizations are misleading when they are used as if they were proven facts that apply to all cases. Unproved generalizations usually contain words such as *always, never, all,* or *none.*

UNPROVED GENERALIZATIONS	Television **always** makes children violent.
	Watching a movie is **never** as good as reading the book.
ACCURATE GENERALIZATIONS	**Some** children behave violently after watching violent programs on television.
	Watching a movie is **usually** not as satisfying as reading a book.

Glittering Generalities

A speaker may try to manipulate your feelings about a subject by using glittering generalities. Glittering generalities are words and phrases most people associate with virtue and goodness that are used to trick people into feeling positively about a subject. Words such as democracy, values, family, moral, motherhood, and education stir powerful feelings in the minds of most people. Like flashbulbs, they make it difficult to focus on anything other than the light itself. A speaker may try to manipulate your attitude toward a controversial idea by associating it with one of these dazzling virtue words. For example, the politician who says, "This law will keep the country safe for democracy" assumes that you have strong feelings about democracy and would do anything to preserve it.

The following guidelines, recommended by the Institute for Propaganda Analysis, will help you recognize a glittering generality.

Recognizing Glittering Generalities

- What does the virtue word really mean?
- Does the idea in question have a legitimate connection with the real meaning of the word?
- Is an idea that does not serve my best interests being "sold" to me through the mere use of an appealing name?
- What are the merits of the idea itself, when the virtue word is omitted?

PRACTICE YOUR SKILLS

Dimming a Glittering Generality

Analyze the following glittering generality by writing answers to the four questions above.

Because nothing is more corrosive to the moral fiber of our democracy than rock and roll, you should vote to close down Big Bopperooni's House of Rock.

Advertising

Unsound generalizations may occur most often in advertisements, which are often slanted toward emotion rather than reason. They can also contain misleading information. Look at the following example:

AREN'T WE ALL IN THE PURSUIT OF
American
POP
HAPPINESS?

Bandwagon: invites the viewer to do what everyone else is doing

Stereotype: attracts audiences who identify with the fantasy

Unsound generalization: based on only one or two details and contains the word *all*

Testimonial: an opinion stated by a celebrity who is endorsing a product, which could boost sales

Glittering generality: ties product to patriotic buzzword

Symbol: equates fresh, clean image of water with product

Work with a partner. Look for illustrated dramatic ads from a magazine or newspaper and take turns showing them and reading them aloud to the class. Listeners should identify opinions masquerading as facts, bandwagon appeals, unsupported generalizations, and other propaganda techniques.

Participating in Group Discussions

Group discussion is a way for you to share your ideas and learn from others. In both formal and informal group discussions, you communicate ideas, exchange opinions, solve problems, and reach decisions. Groups will often appoint a leader to focus the discussion and keep it on track. Such discussions are referred to as directed discussions.

Discussing ideas with your classmates plays an important role in the learning process. In the writing process, group brainstorming can help you in the prewriting stage—particularly in generating ideas for subjects. Peer conferencing can help you in the revising stage, when you are looking for ways to improve an essay. In addition, you may use discussion skills in practicing a speech or an oral report, or in preparing for a test.

Learning group discussion skills will help you to state your own ideas effectively and to listen carefully to others' ideas.

You can learn more about group discussion skills on page C28.

Strategies for Participating in Group Discussions

- Listen carefully and respond respectfully to others' views.
- Ask questions to make sure you understand others' views and information.
- State or express your own ideas clearly. Present examples or evidence to support your ideas.
- Keep in mind that everyone in the group should have an equal opportunity to speak.
- Make sure your contributions to the discussion are clear, constructive, and relevant to the subject.
- Formulate and provide effective verbal and nonverbal feedback.
- Try to help your group draw a conclusion or reach a consensus.

Directed Discussions

Sometimes the teacher will lead the discussion to make sure that it does not stray from the agenda. Sometimes a group appoints its own leader to focus the discussion and keep it on track. Such discussions are referred to as **directed discussions.** The leader, or moderator, of a directed discussion group has certain additional responsibilities. If you are chosen to lead a group discussion, use the following strategies for meeting these responsibilities.

Strategies for Discussion Leaders

- Introduce the topic, question, or problem. With the group's help, state the purpose or goal of the discussion.
- Keep the discussion on track to help the group reach agreement and accomplish its goals. Encourage everyone to participate.
- Make sure that everyone has equal opportunity and equal time to speak.
- Keep a record of the group's main points and decisions, or assign this task to a group member.
- At the end of the discussion, summarize the main points, and restate any conclusions or decisions the group reached.

PRACTICE YOUR SKILLS

Conducting a Directed Discussion

Form small groups for a directed discussion. Choose a subject related to school. Choose a leader and establish a goal. Take turns as discussion leader.

Cooperative Learning

A special kind of discussion group is the **cooperative learning** group, sometimes called a **task group**. In a cooperative learning **group,** you work with others to achieve a particular goal. Tasks connected with the goal are divided among members of the group. Then, with the help of a leader, members coordinate the results of their individual efforts. For example, members of a cooperative learning group in a social studies class may work together to prepare an oral presentation on Saudi Arabia. One member of the group may research the geography and economy of Saudi Arabia, another member may concentrate on the history and government of that country, and a third member may explore its religion and art.

In addition to performing a task, you might have a particular role in the group, such as acting as the group leader. Besides being a discussion leader, the leader of a cooperative learning group helps to coordinate the group's efforts. Every member of the group has an important role to play, and the success of the project depends on successful interaction among group members.

Strategies for Cooperative Learning

- Observe the Strategies for Participating in Group Discussions *(page C613)*.
- Participate in planning the project and assigning tasks.
- When you have been assigned a task, do not let your group down by coming to a meeting unprepared.
- Cooperate with others in the group to resolve conflicts, solve problems, reach conclusions, or make decisions.
- Help your group achieve its goals by taking your fair share of responsibility for the group's success.

PRACTICE YOUR SKILLS

Organizing a Cooperative Learning Group

Form groups of three to five and plan a presentation on deserts. Choose a leader. Follow the Strategies for Cooperative Learning above. Prepare an oral presentation and deliver it to the class. Remember to follow the steps for preparing and delivering an oral presentation.

Form a group to prepare a presentation on propaganda techniques. Decide how you will achieve this goal. Then assign tasks and choose a leader to help coordinate your efforts.

A Speaker Speaks

Oral Interpretation

Purpose: to form a group and perform a reading of a scene from *The Price*

Audience: classmates and members of the local community

Oral interpretation is the performance or expressive reading of a literary work. As a performer, you must understand the meaning of the work before you can convincingly express it to an audience. The oral interpreter conveys the meaning through expressive use of voice and gestures. When acting a speech from a dramatic work, for example, you must be able to convince your audience, through effective use of voice and body language, that you are the character. When reciting verse, you can employ pauses, changes of volume, and modulation of tone and pitch to emphasize important structural elements in the passage such as rhyme, imagery, and key words. Take advantage of the expressive power of punctuation and grammar. Aim for clear and convincing communication of meaning to your listeners.

Preparing

Form a small group and choose a scene from *The Price* to perform as a reading for your classmates. Sit in a circle and read through the scene. Look up unfamiliar words. Analyze the content and discuss the ideas that you think are most important in the scene. Identify repeated words and sounds, rhetorical strategies, and other features of the language that you wish to stress. Using the five *W*s and *H*, analyze the scene for an understanding of character, purpose, and situation.

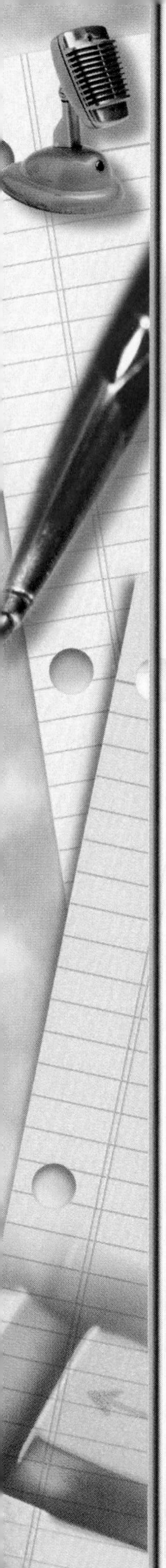

Who are you? **W**hat are you saying? **W**here are you saying it? **W**hy are you saying it? **W**hy and **h**ow are you saying it?

Prepare a written passage from the play. Include a brief introduction to the passage. Highlight the lines that you are going to perform. Mark key words that you want to emphasize through gestures, voices, or facial expressions.

Practicing

Rehearsing is revising. Every performance brings out different meanings in the text. When rehearsing, emphasize different words each time you read your part until you arrive at the interpretation that you think is best. Listen to the other characters as they speak, and respond to them as though you were conducting a real conversation. Dramatic performance is a dynamic group effort. Use the techniques that you have learned to assess your performance and that of your peers. Give praise where it is due and make constructive suggestions for improvement.

Performing

Perform the reading for your classmates. When you have finished, ask them to assess your performance. Use their feedback to determine whether you successfully conveyed the meaning of the scene. Record your performance and send a copy of your tape to the local radio station. Give a performance at an elder care center or at a day care center for children. Share with members of your community the riches you have found in literature.

Connection Collection

Representing in Different Ways

From Print . . .

To: Mason
From: Larry Bank, Pony Express Deliverers
Date: June 22, 2000
Subject: Delivery of package to Josephine Bowman

1. Leave Pony Express.
2. Take taxi ten miles east to corner of Turner and Adams.
3. Board city bus and ride five miles south to ferry station.
4. Take ferry 20 miles south to Saturn Island.
5. Ride company bicycle the final five miles east toward Island Street.
6. Deliver package to Mrs. Bowman, 2 Island Street.

Thanks.

. . . to Visuals

From the information given in Mr. Bank's memo, draw a pie chart demonstrating the different distances, 40 miles in all, which will be traveled via each method of transportation.

Connection Collection

From Visuals . . .

Mrs. Bowman's Jewel Collection

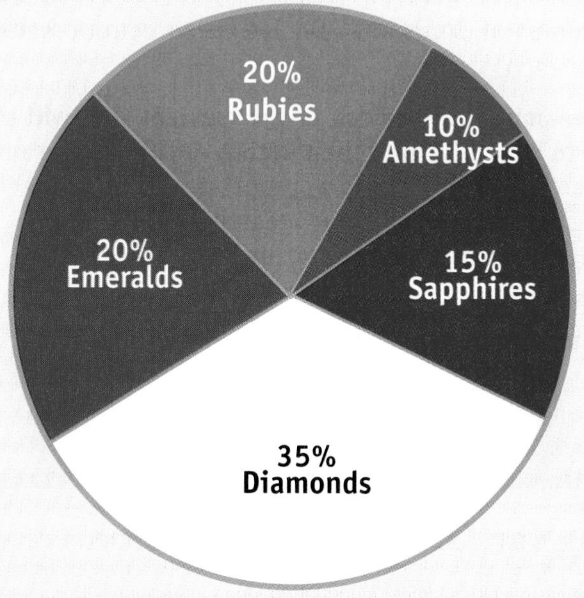

. . . to Print

Mrs. Bowman has decided to donate her jewels to the Big Rock Museum. Using the information in the pie chart, draft a speech for Mrs. Bowman to deliver to the museum trustees detailing her donation.

- **Which strategies can be used for creating both written and visual representations? Which strategies apply to one, not both? Which type of representation is more effective?**
- **Draw a conclusion and write briefly about the differences between written ideas and visual representations.**

Writing for Oral Communication

Persuasive Academic Speech

You are employed as a research assistant to Dr. Helmut Heimlich, a world-famous ornithologist at Collegiate University. Tomorrow, Dr. Heimlich must present a speech to the board of trustees. He wants to convince them to continue funding his groundbreaking research on the yellow-throated kingfisher, a rare species of bird found only in the swamps of Louisiana. Dr. Heimlich cannot write and present his own speech.

Prepare and give a speech to the trustees that will persuade them to award Dr. Heimlich with a million-dollar grant for further research. Provide appropriate visuals if necessary. Make sure you arrange your ideas in a logical order and use transitions that connect your ideas clearly.

What strategies did you use to persuade the trustees?

You can find information on persuasive speeches on pages C596–C603.

Writing for Oral Communication

Entertaining Narrative Speech

Next week you will be a contestant on the new game show *Crack That Grin*. The show, which is getting great ratings, consists of a group of stone-faced panelists who will not laugh or change expression. Contestants compete to tell stories that will make the panelists laugh; the winners take home cash prizes.

Prepare an entertaining and funny narrative speech for the stone-faced panelists on the show. Make certain you include vivid and humorous details in a logical, clear order that will make the panelists "crack grins" and allow you to win the money. Practice your speech on a friend or family member.

What strategies did you use to make your narrative speech entertaining?

Assess Your Learning

Your student council has elected you to present a speech to the entire school faculty. It has been argued recently that, with the construction of a new school gymnasium, your old gym should be demolished. You and your student peers have decided that instead it should be converted into a student activities center. It is your job to prepare a speech that convinces the faculty to keep the old gymnasium for this purpose.

▶ **Prepare the speech to give to the faculty. Think of useful, informative, and enjoyable activities that could result from the conversion of the gymnasium into a student center. Be sure to use a tone and presentation style that addresses your faculty audience. Remember to flavor your speech and support your arguments with personal experiences or the experiences of others. Consider any visual materials—slides, photographs, or video or sound clips—that you could use to make your points stronger.**

Before You Write **Consider the following questions:**
What is the ***subject?***
What is the ***occasion?***
Who is the ***audience?***
What is the ***purpose?***

After You Write **Evaluate your work using the following criteria:**

- Have you thought of an introduction that captures the listener's interest?
- Have you chosen evidence, proof, and examples to support your points?
- Does your speech about the school gymnasium flow smoothly between ideas and make logical transitions?
- Have you changed your tone, rhythm, and style of reading to address the faculty audience clearly and effectively?
- Does your conclusion summarize important points and leave the audience with a memorable sentence, phrase, or image?
- Have you remembered to speak slowly, use clear diction, relax and breathe deeply, and stand confidently when speaking?

Write briefly on how well you did. Point out your strengths and areas for improvement.

CHAPTER 15

Vocabulary

The saddest words of tongue or pen
Are those you didn't think of then.

—*Betty Phillipp*

How can you be sure that you think of the right word when the situation demands it? When you are engaged in an argument or debate, how do you think of words to answer you opponent's arguments? When you write a story, how do you think of the right words for your characters to say? Having a rich vocabulary will help you select the word that is most effective and precise in communication situations like these. In this chapter you will learn a variety of strategies for expanding your storehouse of words. First, though, you will see how English developed into a language that is both rich and varied.

Reading with a Writer's Eye

Political commentator William Safire is well known for his weekly column that traces words in current usage back to their earliest known roots. In the following article, Safire discusses the origins of the words *disgruntled, uncouth*, and *unkempt*. As you read, consider how much our language has changed in the past 1,500 years.

How to Be GRUNTLED, KEMPT and COUTH

William Safire

In wordplay you can sometimes get word understanding. Phrases like "If vegetarians eat vegetables, what do humanitarians eat?" and "Why do we put suits in a garment bag and put garments in a suitcase?" have been knocking about the Internet.

Such *double-entendres* can be funny. For example, two meanings of *funny* are the bases for the line "Is it true cannibals don't eat clowns because they taste funny?" Because *season* has several meanings, we can ask, "If it's tourist season, why can't we shoot them?"

These one-liners, spuriously attributed to the word players George Carlin and Steven Wright, neither of whom claims credit, cause us to take another look at what we're saying.

The word to be examined today is treated in a similarly thought-provoking phrase: "How come you don't ever hear about *gruntled* employees?"

Those of us in the scandal-mongering dodge rely heavily on "disgruntled former employees" for leaks, tips and other often-slanderous leads; in gratitude, we change their designation to the more upbeat *whistle-blower.* But they are surely in a state of disgruntlement, and the time has come to get to the bottom of the word.

It begins, as great armies and New England dessert makers do, with *grunts.* These are the short, deep, guttural sounds made by hogs, especially when eating. The word seeks to imitate the sound; a Roman farmer was probably responsible for the Latin *grunire,* "to grunt; to sound like a rooting pig or sickly cow."

Gruntle is what lexicographers call a frequentive, a verb that describes repeated or recurrent action. (Some call it "frequentative," but they need preventive, not preventative, medicine.) The frequentive of *wrest is wrestle;* of *prate, prattle;* of *spark, sparkle;* and the frequentive of *grunt* is *gruntle.*

The Oxford English Dictionary defines *gruntle* as "to grumble, murmur, complain," and cites a 1589 sermon by Robert Bruce: "It becomes us not to have our hearts here *gruntling* upon this earth."

Haynes Goddard of Cincinnati writes to suggest that the verb *disgruntle* means "to deprive of the opportunity to register dissatisfaction and complaint"—that is, to deny the release of a good, loud grunt, and thereby to make the would-be gruntler sullen. We don't know; the O.E.D. mysteriously lists *disgruntle* as appearing in 1682 and meaning "to put into sulky dissatisfaction or ill humor." You might think that if the old *gruntle* meant "complain," then *disgruntle* would mean "to stop from complaining," but language is not always logical.

However, thanks to a comic writer, *gruntled*—having died as obsolete—has indeed made it back into the dictionaries. P. G. Wodehouse, creator of Jeeves, wrote, in his 1938 "Code of the Woosters," "If not actually *disgruntled,* he was far from being gruntled." The O.E.D. and Merriam-Webster list that play on a word as a back-formation from *disgruntle,* and the word *gruntle* is born again—meaning "to put in a good humor."

Wodehouse has answered the comedic question. There are, indeed, gruntled employees. They're the ones with the soaring 401(k) accounts, and those fat kittens rarely blow their whistles to scandalmongers.

While we're at it, and to save each other mail, let's look at the humorous use of *couth* and *kempt,* wordplay on *uncouth* and *ill kempt*.

As the current [second] millennium began, *kempt* meant "combed." Such personal tidiness was not always taken to be a positive: "If a man have a *kempt* hed," John Wyclif warned young women in 1380, "thanne he is a leccherous man." (That same suspiciously slicked-down hair gave rise to the pejorative *city slicker.*) In the 16th century, kempt divided into *ill kempt* (slobs a girl could trust) and *well kempt,* as in James Joyce's *Ulysses:* "a well-kempt head, new-barbered" and still lecherous. Today, the seldom-used *kempt* is neutral, as if with hair hastily combed by the fingers.

Also a thousand years ago, *couth* meant "known, familiar" and *uncouth* was "unknown, foreign, strange" (as the admonition to young women later went, "uncouth, unkissed"). *Couth* faded out, but was back-formed and born again, thanks to Max Beerbohm in 1896. It was popularized in a funny line delivered by a shrewd dumb-blonde character, played by Judy Holliday in Garson Kanin's 1946 "Born Yesterday." When criticized by her overbearing lover as *uncouth,* she replied, "I'm every bit as *couth* as you are!" Thanks to the comic spirit of language, we still have *couth, kempt* and *gruntled.* Like a stand-up comedian on a sit-down strike, I am still working at 186,300 miles per second on the cosmological-linguistic question "So, what's the speed of dark?"

Thinking as a Writer

Exploring the History of Words

In his article, William Safire traces the origin, disappearance, and re-emergence of several English words. He does so in an authoritative yet humorous manner.

- What research tools do you suppose Safire used in writing this article? List the resources on language available at your school's media center in your **journal**.
- Brainstorm a list of words you like. Using the resources you found, choose one or two and write a paragraph for each word describing its history. Be sure to include in your paragraph any questions you have about the words for which you were not able to find any answers.

Hearing Changes in Language

Oral Expression

- Pair up with a classmate and look at the following excerpt from *Beowulf*. Try to read the excerpt aloud to each other.

> Hwæt. We Gardena in geardagum,
> þeodcyninga, þrym gefrunon,
> hu ðа æþelingas ellen fremedon.

- Now look at the translation and notice how much the spelling and vocabulary have changed. How has the language changed? Take turns reading the translation aloud as you would if you were reading it for an audience.

> Lo, praise of the prowess of people-kings
> of spear-armed Danes, in days long sped,
> we have heard, and what honor the athelings won!

Observing Changes in Language

Viewing

- Look closely at the two examples above. What similarities and differences can you find in the alphabet? Be specific, citing particular letters in both passages to support your thinking.

Understanding the Development of the English Language

From the Past to the Future

English is now the official language of several countries around the world, including Australia, the United States, Canada, and the Philippines. More than 300 million people throughout the world speak English as their native language. In order to understand how English developed, it is important to understand its heritage.

Old English

Our language began to develop more than 1,500 years ago, in about A.D. 450. During this period England was part of the Roman Empire, and Latin was its written language. At that time three Germanic tribes—the Angles, the Saxons, and the Jutes—invaded England from the shores of the North Sea. After conquering the Celts who lived there, they stayed and settled on the land. These tribes discarded the older Celtic and Roman cultures. Soon their language became the language of the land.

The language those Germanic tribes spoke is now called Old English, although to English-speaking people today it would sound like a foreign language. Nevertheless, some Old English words are still part of the language. They include common nouns and verbs: *man, child, house, mother, horse, knee, eat, sing, ride, drink*, and *sell*. They also include most modern numbers such as *one, five*, and *nine*; pronouns such as *you, he, they*, and *who*; the articles *a, an*, and *the*; and prepositions such as *at, by, in, under, around*, and *out*.

Middle English

Old English began its change into Middle English when William the Conqueror invaded England from northwestern France in 1066 and made French the official language. Although the royal court and the upper classes spoke French, the common people continued to speak Old English. Nevertheless, English might eventually have faded out if the parliament had not started to use it in 1392. By 1450,

Middle English, which included hundreds of French words, had evolved. At this time, Geoffrey Chaucer, a famous writer, wrote his works in Middle English.

MODEL: Middle English

The Knyghtes Tale

Heere bygynneth the Knyghtes Tale
Whilom, as olde stories tellen us,
Ther was a duc that highte Theseus;
Of Atthenes he was lord and governour,
And in his tyme swich a conquerour,
That gretter was ther noon under the sonne.

—Geoffrey Chaucer, The Canterbury Tales

Here is the same passage, translated more than five hundred years later into modern language.

MODEL: Modern Translation

The Knight's Tale

Here begins the Knight's Tale
Once on a time, as old tales tell to us,
There was a duke whose name was Theseus;
Of Athens he was lord and governor,
And in his time was such a conqueror,
That greater was there not beneath the sun.

—Geoffrey Chaucer, The Canterbury Tales

PRACTICE YOUR SKILLS

Analyzing Language

List ten similarities and differences you observe between the original Chaucer passage and the modern translation. Be specific, citing particular words and phrases. Next to each difference, write a statement, telling how the language has changed over time.

Modern English

Modern English started to evolve out of Middle English in the middle of the 1400s. During that time many writers and scholars borrowed words from Latin. In fact, it has been estimated that about half of the present words in modern English are from Latin. By the time Shakespeare was writing in the last half of the 1500s, English had become a versatile language that is understandable to modern speakers of English.

Read the following sonnet by William Shakespeare aloud. In comparison with Old or Middle English, notice how much closer this passage is to the English that you are used to speaking.

MODEL: Beginning of Modern English

Shall I compare thee to a summer's day?
Thou art more lovely and more temperate;
Rough winds do shake the darling buds of May,
And summer's lease hath all too short a date:
Sometime too hot the eye of heaven shines,
And often is his gold complexion dimm'd;
And every fair from fair sometime declines,
By chance or nature's changing course untrimm'd;
But thy eternal summer shall not fade,
Nor lose possession of that fair thou owest;
Nor shall Death brag thou wander'st in his shade,
When in eternal lines to time thou grow'st;
So long as men can breathe, or eyes can see,
So long lives this, and this gives life to thee.

—*William Shakespeare,* Sonnet XVIII

PRACTICE YOUR SKILLS

Analyzing Language

With a partner, describe how Shakespeare's language is different from Old English and the English you speak today. Be specific, citing particular words and phrases as needed. Summarize what you discover and report your findings to the class.

American English

The next phase in the history of the English language occurred when North America was settled. Separated from Europe, settlers began to develop a new kind of English, drawing on a variety of sources and influences. The language we, in America, know as English is truly a mosaic: it is a language that has been influenced by London merchants, Native American nations, enslaved Africans, Spanish and French colonists, and immigrants from many other nations. Many of the words we consider as "English" are, in fact, drawn from entirely different languages, and our language is all the richer because of it. How would anyone paddle river rapids without the Inuit word *kayak*? How boring Thanksgiving dinner would be without the West African word *yam*!

Notice the differences in language in the following models, which come from different periods in American history. The first model is from a letter written in 1776 by Abigail Adams. The letter is addressed to her husband, John Adams, prior to the writing of the Declaration of Independence. In her letter, she encourages her husband not to forget that women, too, are fighting for independence.

Model: Early American English

Tho we felicitate ourselves we sympathize with those who are trembling least the Lot of Boston should be theirs. But they cannot be in similar circumstances unless pusilanimity and cowardise should take possession of them. They have time and warning given them to see the Evil and shun it. —I long to hear that you have declared an independency—and by the way, in the Code of Laws which I suppose it will be necessary for you to make, I desire you would Remember the Ladies, and be more generous and favourable to them than your ancestors. Do not put such unlimited power into the hands of the Husbands. Remember, all Men would be tyrants if they could. If perticular care and attention is not paid to the Ladies, we are determined to foment a Rebelion, and will not hold ourselves bound by any Laws in which we have no voice, or Representation.

–*Abigail Adams,* from letter to husband, John Adams

The passage below is from Martin Luther King, Jr.'s famous "Letter from a Birmingham Jail." King wrote the letter after being jailed for "civil disobedience." The letter is addressed to prominent members of the clergy who have criticized his methods of pursuing racial equality. This letter was written in 1963, nearly 200 years after Adams' letter. Note how much the language has changed. Also note how much has stayed the same.

Model: Contemporary American English

You may well ask, "Why direct action? Why sit-ins, marches, etc.? Isn't negotiation a better path?" You are exactly right in your call for negotiation. Indeed, this is the purpose of direct action. Nonviolent direct action seeks to create such a crisis and establish such creative tension that a community that has constantly refused to negotiate is forced to confront the issue. It seeks so to dramatize the issue that it can no longer be ignored. I just referred to the creation of tension as a part of the work of the nonviolent resister. This may sound rather shocking. But I must confess that I am not afraid of the word tension. I have earnestly worked and preached against violent tension, but there is a type of constructive nonviolent tension that is necessary for growth. Just as Socrates felt that it was necessary to create a tension in the mind so that individuals could rise from the bondage of myths and half-truths to the unfettered realm of creative analysis and objective appraisal, we must see the need of having nonviolent gadflies to create the kind of tension in society that will help men to rise from the dark depths of prejudice and racism to the majestic heights of understanding and brotherhood. So the purpose of the direct action is to create a situation so crisis-packed that it will inevitably open the door to negotiation. We, therefore, concur with you in your call for negotiation.

—*Martin Luther King, Jr.*, "Letter from a Birmingham Jail"

Practice Your Skills

Analyzing Language

List ten of the similarities and differences you observe between the Adams letter and the King letter. Be specific, citing particular words and phrases. Next to each difference, write a statement telling how the language has changed over time.

Cultural Origins

Words are often influenced by many different cultures. Next time you're eating some french fries, think of the origins of the word *potato*. When Columbus landed, he was met by the Taino tribe, who called this tuber *batata*. The Quechua people, another group indigenous to South America, called it *papa*. In Spanish, the word is *patata*.

Next time you're at a cook-out, consider the word *barbecue* (or the word's cousin, *bar-b-q*). The Taino people used a four-legged stand made from sticks to cook and roast meat. This stand was called a *barbacoa*.

English in the New Millennium

English has become the dominant language in political diplomacy, science, technology, and trade. Every day new words are coined, and with every edition dictionaries grow thicker and thicker. Not only have different cultures influenced English, but computer technology has had a tremendous influence on the way we use English. No longer does *surf* apply only to the ocean; it now means "to skim television channels with the remote control," and it also means "to move quickly from one Web page to another on the Internet." No one can say with certainty exactly how English will change in the coming century, but one thing is bound to be true: English will continue to evolve as cultures come into closer and closer contact and as technology continues to influence the way people around the world speak and think.

Computer Language

The technology revolution has had an enormous impact on the way we use language. Many computer terms are words that have taken on new meanings. The word *mouse*, for example, no longer only means "a small, furry mammal"; it also means "a handheld computer device." Here are other examples:

Word	Original Meaning	New Meaning
crash	collide	computer failure
hang	suspend	freeze up
enter	go in	add data to computer memory

The technology revolution has also generated a considerable number of new terms: *hyperlink, online, log on, Internet,* and *Website.*

Your Writer's Journal

Build your vocabulary by writing in your journal any unfamiliar words that you read or hear. Look up new words in a dictionary. Pay particular attention to words that relate to diplomacy, science, technology, and trade. Then include a brief definition of each word and an example of its appropriate context or use. Whenever you are revising your work, look over your list and include in your writing as many new words as possible. Use your word list as a resource for choosing words that are vivid, appropriate, and precise.

Understanding the Varieties of English

Almost a million words make up the English language. Not all of these words are spoken exactly the same way by all English-speaking people. People in different countries and even different regions of the same country often have their own way of pronouncing certain words.

American Dialects

The different ways of speaking the same language are called **dialects**. In the United States, for example, New Englanders are said to speak with a twang and Southerners with a drawl.

American English varies among three main regional dialects: Eastern, Southern, and General American. Each of these dialects contains many subdialects. For instance, the Southern dialect includes distinctive subdialects spoken in Texas and Louisiana.

Dialects can be different from one another in vocabulary, pronunciation, and even grammar. In Columbus, Ohio, for instance, a *green pepper* may be called a *mango*, and in New York City, many local residents pronounce *birds* as *boids*. Although dialects vary across the country, none are so different that one group cannot understand another. In fact, dialects add color and richness to American English.

Standard American English

Dialects have appropriate uses in informal conversation and in creative writing. In a formal speech or informative writing, however, you should use standard English. **Standard English** is the formal English taught in school and used in newspapers, scholarly works, and many books.

Use **standard English** when writing for school and for a large general audience.

Practice Your Skills

Identifying Dialects

With a small group, discuss the dialect that is spoken in your region of the country. Brainstorm examples of the vocabulary, pronunciation, and grammar that characterize the dialect. For example, do speakers of the dialect say *sofa, lounge, davenport, couch,* or *settee*? Do they say *soda, pop,* or *tonic*? Is the dialect influenced by another language, such as Spanish? After you have developed a list of examples of the dialect, compare and contrast them with standard English. Make a chart, index, or dictionary of words to introduce your regional dialect to people from other parts of the country.

Idioms, Colloquialisms, Slang, and Jargon

Besides dialect, another source of the richness of English is found in its figurative language, such as idioms, colloquialisms, slang, and jargon. Because these types of expressions are informal, they are not usually appropriate in your writing.

Idioms

An **idiom** is a phrase or expression of a given group of people that has a meaning different than the literal translation of the words. Idioms do not often make sense when taken literally, yet they are quite meaningful to most people who speak a particular language.

> Elise was **beside herself with worry** (very concerned) because she had not heard from Barbara.

When Henry came home that night, he **looked like something the cat dragged in.** (didn't look very good)

Colloquialisms

A **colloquialism** is an informal phrase or colorful expression that is appropriate for conversation, but not for formal writing.

As soon as Dan and Luis met, **they hit it off.** (got along well together)

For dinner the Hendersons certainly **put out a spread.** (served a generous amount of food)

Slang

Slang consists of nonstandard English expressions that are developed and used by particular groups. Such expressions are highly colorful, exaggerated, and often humorous. Although most slang goes out of fashion quickly, a few slang expressions—such as those that follow—have become a permanent part of the language.

Simone earned ten **bucks** (dollars) by mowing the Henshaws' lawn.

Sitting and waiting for someone in an airport can be **a real drag.** (tiresome)

Jargon

Jargon is the specialized vocabulary that people within the same profession use to communicate precisely and efficiently with one another. Using jargon to communicate with other experts, such as in an article for a scientific journal, is appropriate. However, using jargon to communicate with a general audience can cause lack of understanding. The second sentence below would be much clearer to a general audience than the first sentence.

JARGON	There is no locality similar to a structure that is used exclusively for a permanent residential domicile and/or noncommercial purpose.
TRANSLATION	There is no place like home.

PRACTICE YOUR SKILLS

Using Appropriate Standard English

Substitute words or phrases in standard English for the underlined colloquialisms, idioms, jargon, and slang expressions in the following sentences.

1. The gymnastics coach told Midori to go all out in her next routine.
2. Some adventurous people go nuts over hang gliding.
3. You should get a load of Beth's car.
4. It can be difficult and time-consuming to score a part-time summer job.
5. Maria asked her little brother to stop bugging her while she tried to read.
6. I've got to motor through the rest of that book before tomorrow's test.
7. The explorers trying to scale Mount Everest have had a tough time of it.
8. Julia would jump at the chance to work for the newspaper during the summer.
9. The library has tons of books, articles, and pamphlets on that topic.
10. Are you going to see them off at the train station tomorrow afternoon?

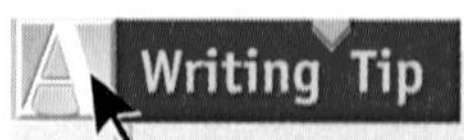

Idioms, colloquialisms, slang, and **jargon** can make your fiction and poetry convincing and lively. They are not, however, appropriate for formal writing such as you will do in school and work.

Clichés, Tired Words, Euphemisms, and Loaded Words

Sometimes certain words and phrases get used so often that they lose their precise meaning. Some expressions become so commonplace that they lose their originality and become tired. Be careful to avoid this kind of language in your writing and it will be more interesting to read.

Clichés

A **cliché** is an example of figurative language that has been so overused that it is no longer fresh or interesting to a reader. Many cliches are similes: *My stomach felt as if it was* ***tied in knots,*** or *Abner is* ***as strong as an ox.*** Some common clichés are listed below.

1. I would not touch that old ham sandwich **with a ten-foot pole.** (under any circumstances)
2. Mr. Hargroves has been **busy as a beaver** lately. (very busy)
3. Her voice was as **clear as a bell.** (clear and strong)
4. The way Harold has been acting, you would think he **had bats in his belfry.** (was emotionally disturbed)
5. As soon as **my head hit the pillow** I **was out like a light**, and I slept **like a baby.** (I lay down)(fell asleep)(peacefully)

Tired Words

A **tired word** is a word that has been so overused that it has been drained of meaning. Take, for example, the word *awesome*. This word literally means "inspiring a mixed emotion of reverence, respect, dread, and wonder inspired by authority, genius, great beauty, sublimity, or might." Now, through overuse, the word is used to mean "good," and it no longer conveys its original precise meaning.

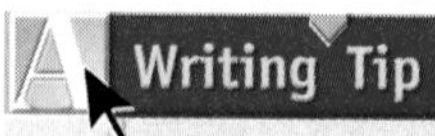

Avoid **clichés** and **tired words** and your writing will be fresher, more precise, and more interesting to read.

Euphemisms

A **euphemism** is a vague word or phrase that substitutes for something considered blunt or offensive. Euphemisms are polite, inoffensive terms that are used to conceal an unpleasant fact. The following chart displays some common euphemisms you can find almost every day in your newspaper.

EUPHEMISM	TRANSLATION
peace-keeper	soldier
let go	fired
street person	homeless person
preowned automobile	used car
downsized	laid off

Noted author George Orwell called such words "doublespeak," and he warned his readers to be aware of how easy it is to manipulate language to cover up ugly truths with euphemisms.

Loaded Words

Subjective words that are interjected into a seemingly objective report of an event are loaded words. These words are meant to emotionally sway the audience one way or another without the audience knowing it. You can find loaded words in advertisements, in political campaigns, and on television.

> The school committee meeting got off to **another slow** start, with the committee members arguing among themselves. **Finally** the board **settled down** to review the budget for the proposed school annex. **While the clock ticked,** the committee **still** could not come to a decision.

The writer of this news item is using loaded words to get across the point that he or she thinks the school committee is ineffectual; the writer's opinion has crept into the news story. Another writer may have seen the meeting differently. See if you can spot the loaded words in the following report.

> Once again, the school committee members tackled the monumental task of sorting out the budget for the proposed school annex. The ten members wrestled with the budget throughout the evening and adjourned, having made significant progress but not yet having brought the matter to a close.

Practice Your Skills

Identifying Clichés, Tired Words, Euphemisms, and Loaded Words

Write the clichés, tired words, euphemisms, and loaded words in the following sentences. Then rewrite each sentence, using vivid, specific language.

1. Our trip to the city was really neat, and we had a great time.

2. The custodial engineer will mop the cafeteria floor after the meal is finished.

3. Senator Smith delivered his usual longwinded speech to his small patch of supporters.
4. Harold was walking on eggshells when he entered the class late.
5. The storm ravaged the coastal states before veering north to menace the placid hilltowns and peaceful farms.
6. The football game was an emotional roller coaster.
7. Tina's new video game has some awesome graphics.
8. Nigel is not short; he is vertically challenged.
9. When the drama cast was announced today, it was music to my ears.
10. I forgot to save my work before my computer crashed, so I had to start from scratch.

Denotation and Connotation

All words convey a literal meaning, the direct, specific meaning found in a dictionary. Many words, however, also stir up emotions or suggest associations; this is called **connotation.** The words *trip* and *vacation*, for example, have similar denotations, but *vacation* has an extra level of meaning. Its connotation brings many feelings to mind: freedom from the usual routine, fun, relaxation, different surroundings.

Understanding connotations is important when you write because some words have similar denotations but opposite connotations.

Positive Connotation	The city was **bustling** with people during the holiday.
Negative Connotation	The city was **mobbed** with people during the holiday.

In these examples the words *bustling* and *mobbed* both mean "filled." *Bustling*, however, suggests a positive feeling of energy and excitement, while *mobbed* suggests a negative feeling of overcrowding, noise, and restricted movement. A word's connotation helps to stir readers' emotions. You can add to your writing by using words with rich connotations.

Practice Your Skills

Using Connotation to Add Meaning

Write the word in each of the following sentences that has the connotation given in brackets.

EXAMPLE Ellen is very (frank, blunt). [negative]

ANSWER blunt

1. Every October the old maple (paints, litters) the lawn with its falling leaves. [positive]
2. The girl ran (courageously, recklessly) into the flaming barn to save her colt. [positive]
3. We walked at a (leisurely, sluggish) pace. [negative]
4. The rabbit (scrambled, scampered) across the lawn. [positive]

Newspapers

How do writers find ways to keep their stories lively and fresh? One way is to search for fresh synonyms for tired words. Another is to add powerful descriptive words. Here is an example from sports journalism.

The Chicago Bears were leading the Green Bay Packers in the first game since Bears legend Walter "Sweetness" Payton passed away. Green Bay was poised for a game-winning field goal. Here's how two *Chicago Tribune* writers described what happened.

> With a nod to Payton for the assist, [Bryan] Robinson capitalized on a low snap by the Packers and blocked what would have been a game-winning field goal by Ryan Longwell as time expired to preserve a 14–13 victory. . . .
>
> "I have just one word," said running back James Allen. "It's sweet. Sweetness."

> It will be Walter's Game forever now that the Bears have won it, the 159th rendering of pro football's most storied border war. This is, of course, absurd in any real, touchable sense. It was Bryan Robinson's and not Walter Payton's hand that blocked the dead certain Packer field goal at the end. . . .
>
> Was it Payton who raised Robinson up to block that kick, the first blocked kick of Robinson's career?
>
> "Walter Payton picked me up in the air," insisted Robinson. "I can't jump that high."

There is some language that is the same in both pieces. *Field goal* and *blocked kick* mean something specific and cannot easily be replaced by synonyms. But there is plenty of variety for the many other actions and possibilities that happen on the field.

Media Activity

Imagine you work at the rewrite desk of a newspaper. Rewrite the opening sentence of each story above. Keep the meaning the same, but rewrite using synonyms and fresh descriptions.

Determining Word Meanings

Often you may hear or read words that are new to you. One way to learn their meanings is to look up the words in a dictionary. The remainder of this chapter shows you several other ways to discover and remember word meanings.

Context Clues

One of the best ways to learn the meaning of a word is through context clues. The **context** of a word is the sentence, the surrounding words, or the situation in which the word occurs. The following examples show the four most common kinds of context clues.

DEFINITION OR RESTATEMENT	During the storm, travelers took a detour because the *isthmus*, **a narrow strip of land connecting two larger landmasses,** was flooded. (The word *isthmus* is defined within the sentence.)
EXAMPLE	You may find a *fossil* here, perhaps **like the one in our science lab that has an imprint of a leaf.** (The word *fossil* is followed by an example that is known to readers or listeners.)
COMPARISON	The mayor said that tax *revenues*, **like personal income,** should be spent wisely. (The word *like* compares *revenues* to its synonym *income*.)
CONTRAST	*Contemporary* students learn more about computers **than did students a few years ago.** (A contrast is drawn between today's students [*contemporary* students] and students of the past.)

Practice Your Skills

Using Context Clues

Write the letter of the word or phrase that is closest in meaning to each underlined word. Then identify the type of context clue that helped you determine the meaning by writing *definition or restatement*, *example*, *comparison*, or *contrast*.

1. The team members gathered in a huddle but <u>dispersed</u> when the coach blew her whistle.

(A) cheered (B) scattered (C) exercised
(D) planned (E) answered

2. Because ferns, orchids, and bromeliads are <u>indigenous</u> to the tropics, they must be grown in hothouse conditions in the North.

(A) unknown (B) exotic (C) warlike
(D) unemployed (E) native

3. Louise Nevelson, a famous sculptor, <u>salvaged</u> useless scraps of metal and wood and transformed them into beautiful works of art.

(A) built (B) created (C) rescued
(D) destroyed (E) judged

4. Ms. Ord thought that the impatient <u>patron</u> should wait her turn, just like all the others in the grocery store.

(A) owner (B) speaker (C) prisoner
(D) customer (E) hypnotist

5. We were fascinated by the strange, large, green insect that was climbing up the wall, but Matthew seemed <u>oblivious</u> to it.

(A) devious (B) clear (C) unaware
(D) pale (E) superior

6. The dogwood in our garden is a <u>perennial</u> source of delight, beautiful at every season of the year.

(A) perfect (B) timid (C) slippery
(D) victorious (E) lasting

7. The politician accused his opponents of <u>contriving</u> to defeat his proposal.

(A) scheming (B) refusing (C) electing
(D) grieving (E) answering

8. The idea was <u>infamous</u>, a scheme that no fair or honest person could accept.

(A) disgraceful (B) unknown (C) childlike
(D) diseased (E) well-known

9. My <u>hypothesis</u>, the way I explain it, is that Shana made the phone call.

(A) mistake (B) theory (C) dream
(D) publicity (E) thanks

10. Her <u>graphic</u> description enabled readers to picture each object in detail.

(A) musical (B) vague (C) geometric
(D) vivid (E) exaggerated

11. National parkland cannot be <u>exploited</u> for resorts, industries, or other money-making projects.

(A) explored (B) defended (C) observed
(D) used (E) donated

12. Have an expert <u>appraise</u>, or estimate the worth of, a major purchase before you buy it.

(A) record (B) buy (C) evaluate
(D) announce (E) glorify

13. Winning the blue ribbon is her <u>incentive</u> to practice daily for the race.

(A) excuse (B) reward (C) payment
(D) idea (E) motivation

14. Heavy rain fell continuously for four days, ending the drought and <u>saturating</u> the soil.

(A) dissolving (B) soaking (C) drying
(D) planting (E) mixing

15. Although city streets are <u>congested</u> during the rush hour, traffic decreases between 6:00 P.M. and 7:00 A.M.

(A) clogged (B) deserted (C) paved
(D) wide (E) narrow

Prefixes, Suffixes, and Roots

Words in English often have Latin or Greek roots, prefixes, and suffixes. These word parts offer clues to help you unlock the meanings of words. A **root** is the part of a word that carries the basic meaning. A **prefix** is one or more syllables placed in front of the root to modify the meaning of the root or to form a new word. A **suffix** is one or more syllables placed after the root to change its part of speech or meaning.

In the following examples, notice how the meaning of each word part is related to the meaning of the word as a whole.

USING WORD PARTS TO DETERMINE MEANINGS

Word	Prefix	Root	Suffix
dissimilarity (state of being unlike)	dis– (not)	–similar– (alike)	–ity (state of)
independence (state of not relying)	in– (not)	–depend– (to rely)	–ence (state of)
intergalactic (relating to area between galaxies)	inter– (between)	–galaxy– (star system)	–ic (relating to)
transporter (one who carries across)	trans– (across)	–port– (to carry)	–er (one who)
resourceful (able to use ways and means again)	re– (again)	–source– (ways and means)	–ful (full of)

Because word meanings in any language often change over years of use, you might not always find a perfect match between words and the meanings of their Latin and Greek word parts. Even so, knowing prefixes, roots, and suffixes can help you figure out the meanings of thousands of words.

COMMON PREFIXES AND SUFFIXES		
Prefix	**Meaning**	**Example**
com–, con–	with, together	con + form = to become the same shape
dis–	not, lack of	dis + harmony = a lack of agreement
extra–	outside, beyond	extra + curricular = outside the regular school courses
in–, il–, im–	in, into, not	im + migrate = to come into a country, il + legal= not lawful
inter–	between, among	inter + state = among or between states
post–	after	post + date = to give a later date
re–	again	re + occur = to happen again
sub–	under	sub + standard = under the standard
trans–	across	trans + Atlantic = across the Atlantic
Suffix	**Meaning**	**Example**
–ance, –ence	state of	import + ance = state of being important
–er	one who, that	foreign + er = one who is foreign
–ful	full of	hope + ful = full of hope
–ic	relating to	atom + ic = relating to atoms

–ite	resident of	Milford + ite = resident of Milford
–ity	state of	active + ity = state of being active
–less	without, lack of	pain + less = without pain

Practice Your Skills

Understanding Prefixes and Suffixes

Write the prefix or the suffix that has the same meaning as the underlined word or words. Then write the complete word as it is defined after the equal sign.

Example under + marine = beneath the water
Answer sub — submarine

1. among + stellar = taking place among the stars
2. together + press = to squeeze together
3. depend + state of = the state of relying on someone or something for support
4. patriot + relating to = relating to love of country
5. across + plant = to lift from one place and to reset in another
6. not + similar = not like
7. actual + state of = state of being real
8. speech + without = without conversation
9. after + game = following a game
10. not + frequent = not often
11. again + examine = to inspect again
12. Brooklyn + resident = one who lives in Brooklyn
13. contend + one who = one who strives in a competition
14. meaning + full = full of meaning or purpose
15. solid + condition = state of being solid

Using Prefixes

Write the letter of the phrase that is closest in meaning to each word in capital letters. Use the prefixes as clues to meaning.

16. DISUNITY: (A) agreement with (B) agreement between (C) lack of agreement

17. INTERVENE: (A) come into (B) come together (C) come between

18. TRANSPOLAR: (A) extending across a polar region (B) moving out of a polar region (C) extending under a polar region

19. SUBMERGE: (A) put underwater (B) place together (C) float across

20. EXTRAORDINARY: (A) after what is usual (B) beyond what is usual (C) among what is usual

21. CONJUNCTION: (A) joining together (B) not joining (C) joining across

22. POSTPONE: (A) delay to a future time (B) move across a barrier (C) place under

23. IMPLODE: (A) fly across at a high speed (B) burst out of (C) collapse inward

24. REACTIVATE: (A) give energy again (B) be energetic with (C) take away energy

25. IMPARTIAL: (A) lacking parts (B) not favoring one side (C) after each part

Your Writer's Journal

Choose five words from your journal that contain one of the common prefixes or suffixes listed on pages C648–C649. Separate the words into their parts (prefix, root, suffix). Using the meanings from the charts of Common Prefixes and Common Suffixes, determine the meaning of each word.

Synonyms and Antonyms

A **synonym** is a word that has nearly the same meaning as another word. An **antonym**, on the other hand, is a word that means the opposite of another word. Knowing synonyms and antonyms of words can help you choose the best words when you write or speak.

SYNONYMS	affable : friendly	terminate : finish
ANTONYMS	affable : hostile	terminate : begin

Your dictionary contains information on synonyms and often explains the slight differences among the synonyms for a given word. A **thesaurus** is a kind of specialized dictionary for synonyms. It lists words and their synonyms alphabetically or provides an index of words for finding synonyms easily.

You can learn more about using a thesaurus and other specialized dictionaries on pages C685–C686.

PRACTICE YOUR SKILLS

Recognizing Synonyms

Write the letter of the word that is closest in meaning to the word in capital letters. Then check your answers in the dictionary.

1. ACUTE: (A) lovely (B) mountainous (C) sharp (D) prior (E) hasty

2. COMPREHEND: (A) write (B) bother (C) lose (D) collect (E) understand

3. COURIER: (A) spy (B) gentleman (C) pilot (D) employer (E) messenger

4. DEBRIS: (A) ruins (B) corruption (C) debt (D) poverty (E) confidence

5. EXASPERATE: (A) depart (B) irritate (C) increase (D) reduce (E) evaporate

6. EXEMPT: (A) perfect (B) empty (C) required (D) excused (E) important

7. GENTEEL: (A) real (B) selfish (C) polite (D) nonspecific (E) lifeless

8. INTEGRITY: (A) honesty (B) cleverness (C) wealth (D) annoyance (E) fame

9. KNOLL: (A) holiday (B) noise (C) mound (D) forest (E) merrymaker

10. LUDICROUS: (A) fortunate (B) questionable (C) laughable (D) happy (E) shy

11. MUTUAL: (A) active (B) changed (C) deep (D) shared (E) solitary

12. NARRATE: (A) tell (B) judge (C) notch (D) separate (E) believe

13. OBSOLETE: (A) outdated (B) lost (C) hidden (D) wrecked (E) reversed

14. OBSTRUCT: (A) teach (B) disagree (C) build (D) hinder (E) watch

15. PHENOMENAL: (A) lucky (B) remarkable (C) hasty (D) musical (E) unemotional

Recognizing Antonyms

Write the letter of the word that is most nearly opposite in meaning to the word in capital letters.

16. ABSTRACT: (A) hazy (B) total (C) honest (D) concrete (E) theoretical

17. ADJACENT: (A) distant (B) acceptable (C) vague (D) accidental (E) near

18. ADVERSE: (A) unreliable (B) favorable (C) clever (D) hostile (E) risky

19. BIZARRE: (A) crowded (B) familiar (C) odd (D) commercial (E) unreasonable

20. BREVITY: (A) briefness (B) wittiness (C) dullness (D) wordiness (E) slowness

21. COMPRESS: (A) expand (B) point (C) accuse (D) squeeze (E) impress

22. CRUCIAL: (A) unimportant (B) required (C) stern (D) unbelievable (E) refined

23. DISSIMILAR: (A) truthful (B) different (C) prompt (D) genuine (E) alike

24. ESSENTIAL: (A) unnecessary (B) secret (C) incorrect (D) tall (E) easy

25. EXEMPT: (A) taxed (B) dependent (C) excused (D) perfect (E) obligated

26. HACKNEYED: (A) thoughtful (B) overused (C) skilled (D) original (E) wide

27. IMPROVISE: (A) disprove (B) react (C) increase (D) plan (E) stop

28. INFAMOUS: (A) pleasant (B) untrustworthy (C) honorable (D) huge (E) shady

29. OBSTRUCT: (A) refuse (B) assist (C) improve (D) suggest (E) obtain

30. PHENOMENAL: (A) poisonous (B) brilliant (C) ordinary (D) pitiful (E) generous

Your Writer's Journal

Choose six words from the list in your journal. For three of the words find synonyms, and find antonyms for the other three. Be sure to list any synonym or antonym that helps you to understand the meaning of the unfamiliar word.

Analogies

One type of standardized test that calls upon your knowledge of synonyms and antonyms is analogies. **Analogies** ask you to identify relationships between pairs of words.

REMEDY : CURE : : (A) simple : fancy (B) wet : dry (C) lessen : reduce

To answer this test question, first identify the relationship between the two words in capital letters. In the test item on the previous page, the words are synonyms because *remedy* and *cure* have similar meanings. Then, from the possible answers, you need to find the other pair of words that has the same relationship as the words in capital letters. Choice *A* is not correct because the two words, *simple* and *fancy*, are antonyms, not synonyms. Choice *B* is not correct because those two words, *wet* and *dry*, are also antonyms. Choice C is the correct one because the two words, *lessen* and *reduce*, are synonyms.

Practice Your Skills

Recognizing Analogies

Write the letter of the word pair that has the same relationship as the word pair in capital letters. Then identify the type of relationship by writing *synonym* or *antonym*.

Example WILD : TAME
(A) sleepy : tired (B) empty : full
(C) loud : noisy

Answer B—antonyms

1. COLD : HOT : : (A) high : low (B) kind : gentle
(C) fast : quick

2. SLIM : THIN : : (A) young : old (B) open : closed
(C) careful : cautious

3. LATE : EARLY : : (A) round : circular (B) right : wrong
(C) distant : far

4. SOAR : GLIDE : : (A) raise : lower (B) watch : observe
(C) arrive : depart

5. REASON : LOGIC : : (A) courage : bravery
(B) fantasy : reality (C) joy : sorrow

6. VALID : LEGAL : : (A) certain : sure (B) tall : short
(C) rough : smooth

7. QUALIFIED : ELIGIBLE : : (A) hopeful : discouraged (B) fair : just (C) tidy : messy

8. FOREIGN : ALIEN : : (A) peaceful : calm (B) wet : dry (C) soft : hard

9. GENUINE : AUTHENTIC : : (A) real : imaginary (B) hungry : full (C) fortunate : lucky

10. WEAKNESS : STAMINA : : (A) box : carton (B) car : automobile (C) beginning : conclusion

11. COMPETITION : RIVALRY : : (A) safety : danger (B) cooperation : teamwork (C) top : bottom

12. CURE : REMEDY : : (A) cause : effect (B) guilt : innocence (C) value : worth

13. USEFUL : FUTILE : : (A) wicked : evil (B) true : false (C) prompt : punctual

14. THOUGHTFUL : PENSIVE : : (A) hazy : bright (B) necessary : essential (C) wide : narrow

15. DOUBTFUL : DUBIOUS : : (A) tart : sweet (B) alert : watchful (C) shiny : dull

Time Out to Reflect

In what ways have your vocabulary skills improved as a result of going through this chapter? Look back at an essay you wrote early in the year. How would the vocabulary differ if you were writing the essay now? What vocabulary skills do you need to work on the most? With which skills are you most comfortable? Record your thoughts in the Learning Log section of your **journal.**

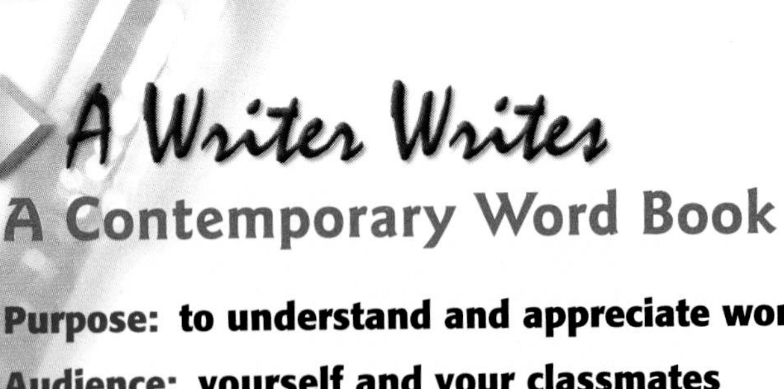

A Writer Writes

A Contemporary Word Book

Purpose: to understand and appreciate words

Audience: yourself and your classmates

Prewriting

William Safire's column *(pages C623–C625)* takes a single word and pursues the meaning of that word through several hundred years of history. The main tools he uses on his pursuit are the same tools available to you—the dictionary and the Internet.

Use your **journal** to list informal language you use when you write (idioms, colloquialisms, slang, jargon). After you have created your list, freewrite responses to the following questions.

- Where did you first hear the words?
- What do they mean to you? What do they mean to others?
- Are the words only appropriate for certain occasions, purposes, and audiences?
- Did the words (or phrases) once mean something different from their use today?

Try to refine your list to five words or phrases that you will spend time researching. Look up the words in the best dictionary you can find. (Safire uses the *Oxford English Dictionary* for his research.) Pay particular attention to the etymology of the words you are looking up. Are the words from Old English? from French? from Italian? Cross-reference your research with another good dictionary (as Safire does with *Merriam-Webster*). Also, do an Internet search on your words to see if there's additional information on their use in the past and/or present.

Drafting

Write a paragraph about each word or phrase you have chosen and explain what you have discovered. Organize your draft by discussing why you chose the word or phrase that you did, what it means to you, and where it comes from. Also explain where and when the word or phrase is appropriate to use, especially in your own writing. Conclude your vocabulary examination by explaining what you have learned from your language research.

Revising

Set your writing aside for a day or so. In the meantime, pay close attention to the words you see and hear in newspapers, magazines, or books you are reading for other classes during that time. Make a list of words that you find interesting. When you return to your writing, add those words that can improve your presentation and cut or replace words that you think are overused.

Editing

Be sure to allow enough time to put your paper aside for a while. It's easier to find mistakes after you've had a break and can see your work with a fresh perspective. Polish your work to give it authority.

Publishing

Consider the following ways to publish your work.

- Compile a class dictionary of contemporary words and phrases.
- Create a class Website to post the words and phrases, and encourage classmates in other grades to post their words and phrases.

CHAPTER 16

Reference Skills

If your brain were like a pre-programmed computer database, imagine how easy the writing process would be. You wouldn't need to do research or go to the library to seek information every time you had to complete a writing assignment. Since your brain isn't a computer, improving and applying your reference skills can make getting new information interesting and exciting.

Doing research and using references skills are a major part of the writing process. Some day you are likely to be asked to write a report about something you know little or nothing about. Or you may want to write a story that takes place on the Amazon, but you know almost nothing about this mighty river. In such instances you put your research and reference skills into play to investigate your topic. There are many ways to delve into the mysteries of a topic, including visiting the library and media center and exploring the Internet. Each resource helps you to explore the unknown and to make your writing accurate, informative, and meaningful.

Reading with a Writer's Eye

While reading a really interesting article about a faraway place or a recent discovery, you may have wondered how the author wrote about the subject so clearly. Was the author there? Most likely that person did something that you can do, too—research! As you read the following passages, think about all the information they provide and the various sources the author may have used to create such vivid accounts.

Buddhas and Dragons

Tranquil Buddhas[1] or fierce warriors: Artists in China, Japan, and India sculpted in stone, jade, ivory, or bronze. One of the most extraordinary works, a life-size army fashioned from clay, was ordered by the Chinese Emperor Qin[2] and buried with him in 209 B.C. Thousands of soldiers, bronze weapons drawn, stand guard over his tomb. Molded and modeled in separate pieces, fired at high temperatures, then assembled and painted in red, green, yellow, and purple, each soldier is different. Archaeologists have counted as many as eight different mustache styles!

Craftsmen buried the clay army in Emperor Qin's tomb and built booby traps with crossbows to kill looters. Then it became obvious that the workmen, familiar with the plans, would be able to rob the tomb. So, in absolute secrecy, the entrance to the tomb was walled up, imprisoning the workmen—not a single one escaped! Trees were planted so the tomb would look like a mountain.

Secrets in Bronze

The Chinese created many masterpieces, but their production methods were a jealously guarded secret. With a passion for hunting, they loved to fashion animals in bronze or jade: buffalo, bears, rhinoceroses, elephants, tigers. The strength and purity of jade made it a highly prized material. But because of the stone's hardness, it was so difficult to carve that craftsmen would sometimes spend years handling and examining a piece of stone before starting to carve.

---

[1] **Buddha** (bo͞o də): *n.* In the Buddhist religion, a person who has attained spiritual enlightenment; also an image of the religious figure, Gautama Buddha.

[2] **Emperor Qin** (chǐn): The First Emperor of China from 221 B.C. to 207 B.C. The Great Wall of China was built while he ruled.

Thinking as a Writer

Evaluating Information

- Identify three main topics that the author presents in the article on the art of sculpture.
- Think about how crucial the information is to presenting an interesting article. How does each detail add to the description? Do the details make the article come to life for you? If so, in what ways?

Discussing the Importance of Research

Oral Expression

The author most likely used a variety of sources to write this article, including history books and specialized encyclopedias on art and archaeology.

- Think about how this article might have been different if it had not been researched. What would the article lack?

Comparing Visual and Print Information

Viewing

In many references, including encyclopedias and Websites, photographs often reveal details and information that descriptions do not. Study this image of the terracotta warriors from the army in Emperor Qin's tomb.

- What details do you notice? What do you see in this image that you want to know more about? How do the descriptions in the article on sculpture help you understand the photograph?

Developing Your Researching Skills

"To furnish the means of acquiring knowledge is . . . the greatest benefit that can be conferred upon mankind," said John Quincy Adams, our sixth president. When he said these words in 1846, he was referring to the establishment of the national museum, the Smithsonian Institution. The Smithsonian—which is now an impressive network of sixteen museums in Washington, D.C., and nineteen branch libraries in five cities in North America—is one valuable resource for exploring all areas of history, culture, nature, and science. It even has its own Website where you can visit the libraries in cyberspace. Later in this chapter, you will learn how to access this site and others like it.

In "Buddhas and Dragons" and "Secrets in Bronze," you saw how researching and becoming familiar with a topic are essential for writing an interesting and well-crafted article. Applying your reference skills should be an enjoyable part of the writing process. The author of this article may have traveled to China to gather information, but it is more likely that he or she used reference skills to discover the stories behind these unusual works of Chinese art and sculpture. Here are some of the reference materials the author might have used.

- an **encyclopedia**, to learn about the Qin dynasty
- a **specialized encyclopedia**, to explore the techniques that artists use for working with jade
- a **nonfiction book** about Chinese history
- an **article from a periodical**, such as a magazine, that was specifically about the Chinese clay army
- an **Internet site** from a university, for up-to-date information about Chinese art and progress on the archaeological dig

Doing research and exploring a topic in depth is like solving a mystery. Reference materials provide the information you need to investigate your topic and answer your unsolved questions. Determining the right reference materials is the only way to find the information that will make your writing stand out. To gain knowledge, you need to do research, and to do good research you need to improve your reference skills. For all of your future research projects, solid reference skills will make your writing richer and broader.

Your Writer's Journal

Think about topics that you find fascinating but know very little about. List as many of these topics as you can in your writing journal. Each of these ideas can be used as a starting point for a nonfiction research report. As you come across new sources of information about these topics in reference materials, either in print or online, write them in your journal. Then, when you need a subject to write about, you can use one or more of these sources to get you started.

Using the Library or Media Center

The library or media center is the best place to begin researching, whatever your topic may be. This storehouse of knowledge and information includes printed media, such as books, newspapers, magazines, encyclopedias, and other forms of writing, and an ever-increasing variety of electronic or on-line resources, such as computer databases, CD-ROMs, and the Internet. Whenever you start a new research project, however, the most valuable resource may be the librarian or media specialist—the trained professional who can help you find the references that you need most.

Fiction

The books you find in this section may be inspired by factual information, but the stories that fill them are creations of the authors' imagination. In the fiction section of the library, the books are shelved alphabetically according to the authors' last names. Here are a few guidelines for locating these resources.

Guide for Finding Fiction

- Two-part names are alphabetized by the first part of the name. (**De** Soto. **O**'Connor, **Van** Buren)
- Names beginning with *Mc* and *St.* are usually alphabetized as if they began with *Mac* and *Saint.*
- Books by authors with the same last name are alphabetized first by last name, and then by first name.
- Books by the same author are alphabetized by the first important word in the title.

Nonfiction

Books in this section include factual information and document real events. These reference materials are perfect for finding in different subject areas.

More than a hundred years ago, an American librarian, Melvil Dewey, came up with a numerical system to categorize nonfiction books. Today his system, known as the **Dewey decimal system**, is used in most school libraries around the country. If you want to find a specific book on boa constrictors, for example, the book would have the same **call number**, or number and letter code, identifying it by subject and category, throughout the country. Books are then arranged on the shelves in numerical order. The following categories are included in the Dewey decimal system.

DEWEY DECIMAL SYSTEM	
000–099	General Works (reference books)
100–199	Philosophy (psychology, ethics)
200–299	Religion (bibles, theologies)
300–399	Social Sciences (law, education, economics)
400–499	Languages (dictionaries, grammars, language texts)
500–599	Science (mathematics, biology, chemistry)
600–699	Technology (engineering, business, health)
700–799	Fine Arts (painting, music, theater)
800–899	Literature (poetry, drama, essays)
900–999	History (biography, geography, travel)

Each general subject is then divided into smaller categories.

800–899 LITERATURE			
800–809	General	**850–859**	Italian
810–819	American	**860–869**	Spanish
820–829	English	**870–879**	Latin
830–839	German	**880–889**	Greek
840–849	French	**890–899**	Other

Because ten numbers and categories are not enough to cover the many books about American or French literature, one or more decimal numbers may also be used.

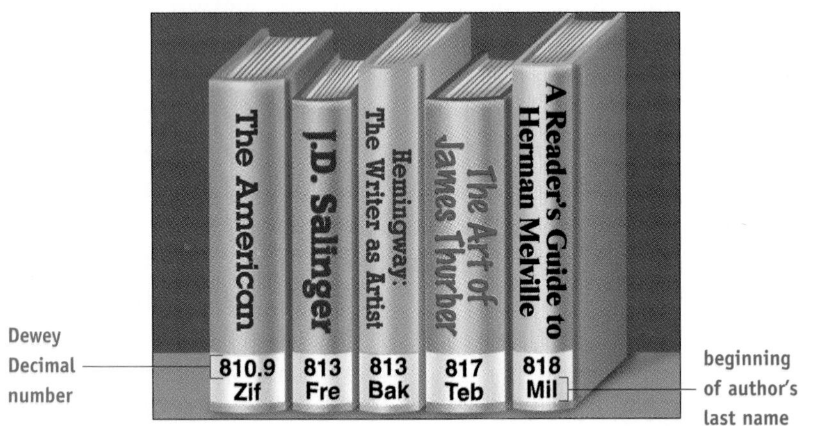

Biographies and Autobiographies

Biographies and autobiographies are usually in a separate section and are shelved in alphabetical order by the subject's last name rather than by the author's last name. Each book is labeled *B* for *biography* or 92 (a shortened form of the Dewey decimal classification of *920*), followed by the first letters of the subject's last name. A biography of George Washington, for example, is labeled on the spine of the book in one of the following ways.

BIOGRAPHY	B	92
BEGINNING OF SUBJECT'S LAST NAME	WAS	WAS

Practice Your Skills

Using the Dewey Decimal System

Using the chart on page C663, write the range of numbers and the general category for each of the following titles.

1. *The Joy of Music*
2. *All About Language*
3. *Basic Biology*
4. *The Making of a Surgeon*
5. *You and the Law*
6. *Chemistry Today*
7. *Trial by Jury*
8. *Shakespeare's Plays*
9. *To a Young Dancer*
10. *The European Middle Ages*

Types of Catalogs

The **traditional card catalog** is a cabinet of drawers filled with cards arranged in alphabetical order. Each drawer is labeled to show what part of the alphabet it contains. All books—fiction and nonfiction—have title and author cards. Nonfiction books, however, also have subject cards and sometimes cross-reference cards that tell you where additional information on the subject may be found.

All catalog cards give the same information: the book's title, author, and call number. They may also give publication facts, indicate the book's page count, and show whether it contains illustrations or diagrams.

In some libraries and media centers, however, the traditional card catalog has been replaced by the **online catalog**—a computerized version of the card catalog. Using the same categories as the traditional card catalog, you can locate information more quickly. While many libraries and media centers have computerized their traditional card catalogs, both cataloging systems are still used in most places.

Computer systems can vary from library to library, but generally the search methods are the same. The computer will present a list of items for each search request (by the author's last name, book title, or subject). Depending on how many references are provided, you may have to make more specific selections. If your book is available, the computer displays information about the book similar to that in the following example.

ONLINE CATALOG RECORD	
CALL NUM.	NCW (Dickens, C. Tale of Two Cities. Philadelphia, 1859)
AUTHOR	Dickens, Charles, 1812–1870
TITLE	A Tale of Two Cities/with illustrations by John M'Lenan.
IMPRINT	Philadelphia: T.B. Peterson, c1859.
LOCATION	Humanities–Gen. Research
EDITION	People's ed.
DESCRIPT.	415 p., [12] leaves of plates; ill. 19 cm.
SERIES	Dickens' works
SUBJECT	France–History–Revolution, 1789–1799–Fiction

Works may also be categorized by their Library of Congress call numbers, as in the preceding example.

To search the listings in an online catalog, you select a category—author, title, or subject—and enter the necessary commands. On some systems, you can also do a keyword search, just as you would on an Internet search engine. A keyword search can search the library's collections for both title and subject headings at the same time. If the book you are looking for is not listed or not available, the computer can tell you if it has been checked out and when it is due back. By using the Web to search other library databases, the media specialist can tell you if the book is available elsewhere.

You can use the **online catalog** in your library or media center to search for a book by subject, author, or title. In some databases, a keyword search can do this even more quickly by searching subject and title categories at the same time.

Catalog Entries

A card in the card catalog will tell you where to find a book, but it cannot tell you if the book has been checked out. If a book is not on the shelf where it should be, you need to ask the media specialist to help you locate it. Using the card catalog is a more time-consuming research method, but the cataloging system is still useful. Both computerized and traditional systems will give you the same information about a source, and both systems are equally precise. Most important, being familiar with the organization and categories of the card catalog will no doubt make you a better on-line researcher as well.

Each drawer in the card catalog is labeled to show what part of the alphabet it contains. Each nonfiction book has three cards listed in the following ways: by the author's last name, by the book's title, and by the subject.

Author Cards To find books by a particular author, look for the author's last name in the card catalog. To find books by Melvin Berger, for example, find *Berger* in the drawer marked *B*. Following is the author card for the book *Computers in Your Life* by Melvin Berger.

AUTHOR CARD

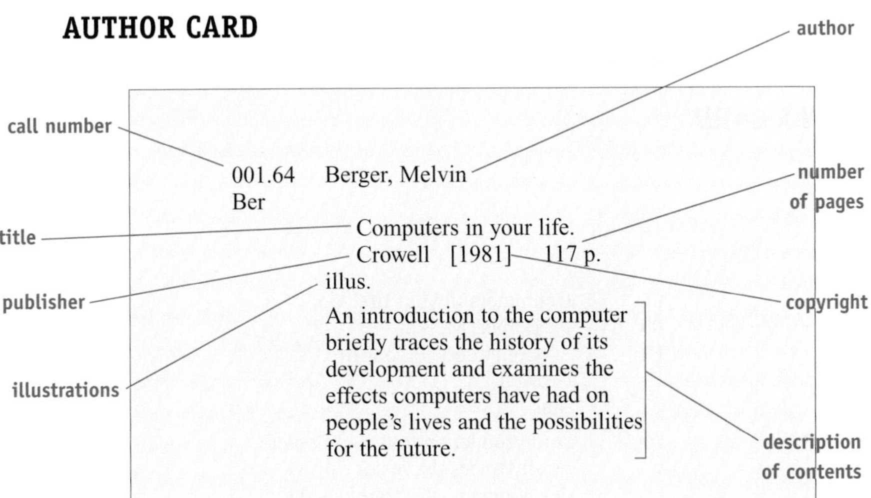

author
call number
001.64 Berger, Melvin
Ber
number of pages
title
Computers in your life.
Crowell [1981] 117 p.
illus.
publisher
copyright
An introduction to the computer briefly traces the history of its development and examines the effects computers have had on people's lives and the possibilities for the future.
illustrations
description of contents

If you search for this author's name in an online catalog, you might get a list of several authors with the same name. You would also get a list of several titles of books by each author with that name. From that list, you could select the title of the book that you want. You would see this information:

AUTHOR:	Berger, Melvin
TITLE:	Computers in your life/Melvin Berger.
EDITION:	1st ed.
PUBLISHED:	New York: Crowell, c1981.
DESCRIPTION:	117 p. : ill. ; 24 cm.
LC CALL NO.:	QA76.23.B47
DEWEY NO.:	001.64 19
ISBN:	0690041004
NOTES:	Includes index. Explains how computers work and discusses their increasing importance in more and more areas of day-to-day life.
SUBJECTS:	Computers—Juvenile literature. Electronic data processing—Juvenile literature. Computers. Data processing.
CONTROL NO.:	80002452/AC/r84

Title Cards When you know the title but not the author, you can find out if the library or media center has the book by looking up the title card. Title cards are alphabetized by the first word in the title, except for the words *A, An*, and *The*.

TITLE CARD

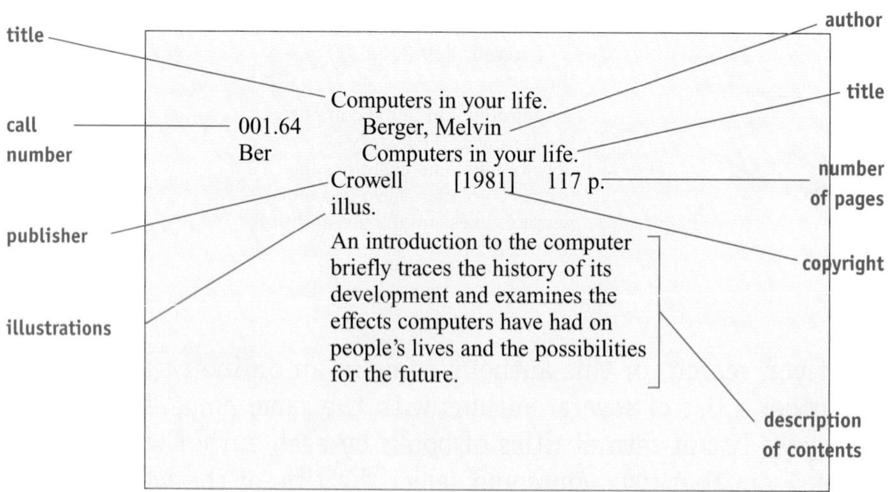

If you search for this book by title in an online catalog, you might get a list of several editions of the same book, especially if it was reprinted and updated after its first release. If you know the exact year that you want, you will see the following information for the 1981 edition. Notice that all of the information is the same, but in this search, the title is listed first.

TITLE:	Computers in your life/Melvin Berger.
AUTHOR:	Berger, Melvin
EDITION:	1st ed.
PUBLISHED:	New York: Crowell, c1981.
DESCRIPTION:	117 p. : ill. ; 24 cm.
LC CALL NO.:	QA76.23.B47
DEWEY NO.:	001.64 19
ISBN:	0690041004
NOTES:	Includes index. Explains how computers work and discusses their increasing importance in more and more areas of day-to-day life.
SUBJECTS:	Computers—Juvenile literature. Electronic data processing—Juvenile literature. Computers. Data processing.
CONTROL NO.:	80002452/AC/r84

Subject Cards When you want to gather information on a specific subject, you can use subject cards. For example, If you look up computers in the drawer that holds the *C*'s, you will find cards for all the books about computers that the library or media center has in its collection.

SUBJECT CARD

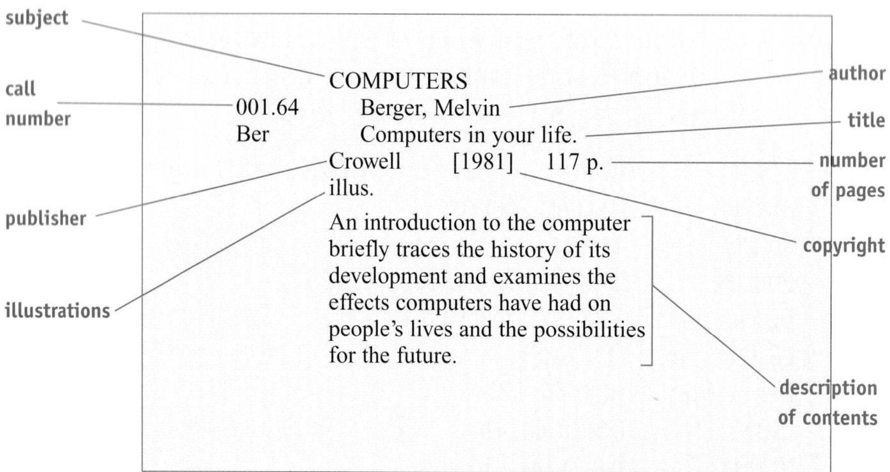

subject
call number
publisher
illustrations
COMPUTERS
001.64 Berger, Melvin
Ber Computers in your life.
Crowell [1981] 117 p.
illus.
An introduction to the computer briefly traces the history of its development and examines the effects computers have had on people's lives and the possibilities for the future.
author
title
number of pages
copyright
description of contents

Compare the catalog cards for subject, title, and author. Notice that the information on each card is the same. Different search routes will take you to the same information, and any one of these cards can help you find the book on the shelf.

Searching online by subject often produces more results than you actually need. The computer searches for keywords in the titles and descriptions of books simultaneously. If you search for books on the subject *computers*, as in the example above, you might get hundreds of titles. Limiting your search by year of publication or by more specific subject terms, such as *computer software* or *computer programming*, will focus your search and produce results that may be more relevant and useful. If you limit your search to *computers and juvenile literature*, for example, the title of Melvin Berger's book would be listed along with others. If you were to select that title, you would see the same information that appeared in the previous online entries.

AUTHOR:	Berger, Melvin
TITLE:	Computers in your life/Melvin Berger.
EDITION:	1st ed.
PUBLISHED:	New York: Crowell, c1981.
DESCRIPTION:	117 p. : ill. ; 24 cm.
LC CALL NO.:	QA76.23.B47
DEWEY NO.:	001.64 19

ISBN:	0690041004
NOTES:	Includes index.
	Explains how computers work and discusses their increasing importance in more and more areas of day-to-day life.
SUBJECTS:	Computers—Juvenile literature.
	Electronic data processing—Juvenile literature.
	Computers.
	Data processing.
CONTROL NO.:	80002452/AC/r84

Cross-Reference Cards While researching your topic by subject, you might come across cards in the card catalog that say *See* or *See also*. A *See* card tells you that the subject is listed under a different heading. A *See also* card lists other subjects you could look up for more information on your topic.

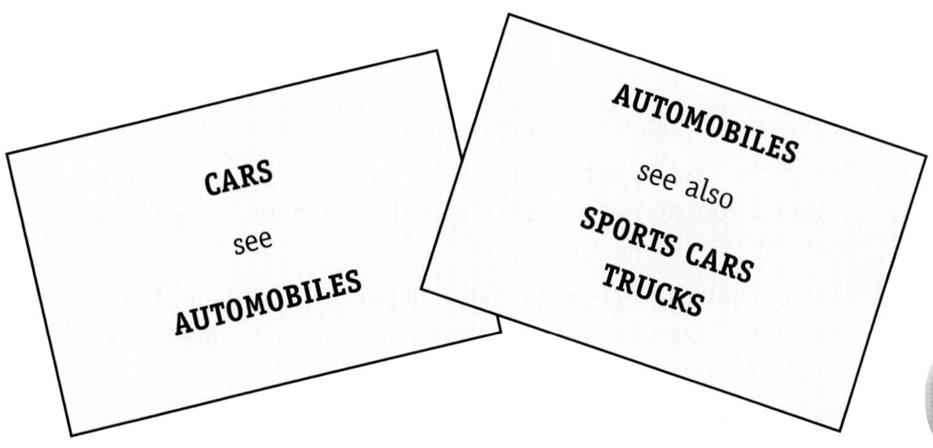

Online versions of *See* and *See also* cards appear as text notes in the search results. When you enter a large subject category such as *cars*, the database will list in alphabetical order several subcategories. Cross-references appear when other search words or phrases are recommended for a subcategory.

Num	Mark	SUBJECTS (1-12 of 274)	Entries 507 Found
1		**Cars -- see --**Cambridge Antiquarian Records Society	1
2	☐	Cars Accounting	1
3	☐	Cars And Car Building -- 3 Related Subjects	3
4	☐	Cars And Car Building	1
5		**Cars Antique -- see --**Antique And Classic Cars	1
6		**Cars Armored Tanks -- see --**Tanks Military Science	1
7		**Cars Automobiles -- see --**Automobiles	1
8	☐	Cars Broad Gage Railroads England West Country Drawings	1
9	☐	Cars Catalogs	3
10		**Cars Classic -- see --**Antique And Classic Cars	1
11	☐	Cars Coupling Automatic	1
12	☐	Cars Design And Construction	1

Strategies for Using a Traditional Card Catalog

- Think about the information you already have. Do you know the book's author? title? subject?
- Look for the book you want by finding the appropriate card.
- Read the card to determine if the book is likely to contain information that you need. Check the copyright to see how current the information is.
- In your **journal**, copy the call number, the title, and the name of the author (any information you don't already know) for each book you want to find.
- Use the call number located on the book's spine to find each book. The first line of the call number tells you in which section of the library or media center to look. Then find each book on a shelf by looking for its call number.

F or FIC	fiction section
B or 92	biography section
Dewey number	nonfiction section

Strategies for Using an Online Catalog

Think about what you already know that can limit your search. A title or author search will always give you more focused results than a subject search. If you are doing a subject search, find a way to limit the category, either by year or by subcategory.

Searching by Author's Name

- If the last name is common, type the author's complete last name followed by a comma and a space and the author's first initial or complete first name.
- Omit all accent marks and other punctuation in the author's name.
- For compound names, try variations in placement of the parts: **von neuwirth james** or **neuwirth james von**

Searching by Title

- If the title is long, type only the first few words. Omit capitalization, punctuation, accent marks, and the articles *a*, *an*, and *the*.

  red badge of cour (you need not include the full title)

  sun also rises (omit initial article words)

  red white and blue (omit punctuation)

- If you are unsure of the correct form of a word, try variations such as spelling out or inserting spaces between initials and abbreviations; entering numbers as words; using an ampersand (&) for *and*; spelling hyphenated words as one or two words.

Searching by Subject

- Omit commas, parentheses, and capitalization.
- Broad categories can be divided into subcategories to make your search more specific.
- If you don't know the correct subject heading, find at least one source relevant to your topic by doing a title or keyword search. Use one or more of the subject headings listed there for additional searches.

Searching by Keyword

- Searching with a single word, such as *computers*, will look for that word anywhere in the entry: in the title, author, subject, or descriptive notes.
- A phrase, such as *solar energy*, finds entries containing the words *solar* and *energy*. To search for solar energy as a phrase, type *solar and energy*, or *solar adj energy* (adj = adjacent).
- An open search will look anywhere in the entry for your word. You can limit your keyword searches to specific search fields—author, title, or subject—by checking the keyword menu and selecting the appropriate field.

COMPUTER TIP

You can also limit your search by using the Boolean search terms (*and, or, not*):

and searches for several terms anywhere in the same entry

or searches for any or all of the terms in the same entry

not searches for the first term and will match the words only if the second word is NOT in the same entry

Practice Your Skills

Locating Catalog Cards

Identify the type of card–author, title, or subject–you would use to find each item. Then write the first three letters that you would look under to find each item.

EXAMPLE: S. E. Hinton
ANSWER: Author—Hin

1. country music
2. Scott O'Dell
3. *A Single Light*
4. moons of Jupiter

5. John Le Carré
6. *A Tree Grows in Brooklyn*
7. forms of transportation
8. *The Double Planet*
9. 20th-century inventions
10. *The Milky Way*

Searching Online Catalogs

Write the category you would select for a search on the following items. Then write the words that you would enter to find each item.

11. the life and times of Roberto Clemente
12. the books of C. S. Lewis
13. the skills of snowboarding
14. the work of Jane Goodall
15. the country's best roller coasters
16. ancient Egypt
17. expeditions to the Polar regions
18. the way insects change and grow

Parts of a Book

Once you find several sources that you think may be useful for your project, you need to spend some time looking through them to see if they have information that you need. Finding this information is easier if you know how to use the parts of a book. Each part of a book gives you different types of information.

INFORMATION IN PARTS OF A BOOK	
Title Page	shows the full title, author's name, publisher, and place of publication
Copyright Page	gives the date of first publication and dates of any revised editions
Table of Contents	lists chapter or section titles in the book and their starting page numbers
Introduction	gives an overview of the author's ideas in each chapter and in relation to the work that other writers have done on the subject

Appendix	gives additional information on subjects in the book; charts, graphs, and maps are sometimes included
Glossary	lists, in alphabetical order, difficult or technical words found in the book and their definitions
Bibliography	lists sources that the author used in writing the book, including titles and publication information
Index	lists topics that are mentioned in the book and gives the page numbers where these topics can be found

Using Parts of a Book

Write the part of the book you would use to find each of the following items of information.

1. the year of publication
2. definition of a difficult or technical word
3. a specific topic or person mentioned in the book
4. the title and publication information for a source used by the author
5. the name and location of the publisher
6. a chart or graph with additional information
7. the title of a specific chapter
8. the author's explanation of the book's contents

Using Print and Nonprint Reference Materials

Along with fiction and nonfiction sections, most libraries or media centers have a separate area called a reference room. This room contains encyclopedias, dictionaries, atlases, almanacs, and reference books on specific subjects. Many libraries and media centers now have online versions of these print sources as well. The following chart indicates the kinds of reference works available in most libraries and media centers.

Print and Electronic References

- encyclopedias
- dictionaries
- atlases
- almanacs
- other specialized reference books
- online indexes to periodicals (including magazines and journals)
- online indexes to newspapers
- CD-ROM versions of specialized encyclopedias, dictionaries, and almanacs
- microfilm and microfiche files of periodicals and government documents
- computer terminals with access to the Internet and World Wide Web
- audio recordings and video documentaries

Readers' Guide to Periodical Literature

Magazines and journals are excellent sources for current information. These are called **periodicals**. An index called the *Readers' Guide to Periodical Literature* can help you find magazine and journal articles on almost any subject. The complete *Readers' Guide*—which indexes articles, stories, and poems published in more than 175 magazines—is issued in paperback form twice a month during most months. A quarterly issue comes out at the end of each year. Many libraries and media centers subscribe to the abridged *Readers' Guide*, which indexes about sixty magazines.

The volumes are arranged by year and can be accessed through an online database in the reference section. *The Readers' Guide* can also be found in print form in the library stacks. For example, if you want to know more about an event that happened in the 1960s, and you know the exact year, you can look up the event in the volume for that year and jot down reference information for several articles about the event. Articles indexed in the *Readers' Guide* are listed alphabetically by subject and author. Each entry, such as the one below, provides all the information you need to locate the articles you want.

To save space in the entry, abbreviations are used. For example, in this entry, the abbreviation *S* in the date stands for *September*. A list of abbreviations is provided at the front of every volume of the print version of the *Readers' Guide*. Once you know the name of the magazine or journal that you want, you will need to check the computer catalog to see if the library has the specific magazine or journal that you need.

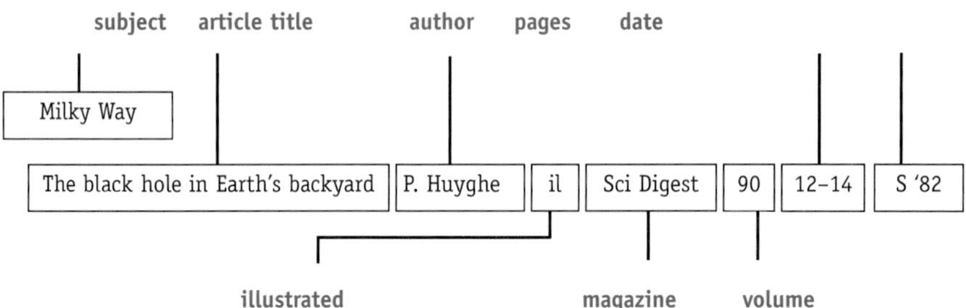

The *Readers' Guide* is also available online in most database indexes. In a way similar to that in the computer catalog above, searches can be done by author, title, or subject. If you entered the words *Milky Way* for a subject search, a list of entries would appear. For each entry, the following information will appear.

NUMBER:	BRGA98068824
AUTHOR:	Kraan-Korteweg, Renee C.; Lahav, O.
TITLE:	Galaxies Behind the Milky Way
SOURCE:	Scientific American v. 279 no. 4 (Oct. '98) pp. 50–7 bibl. il. STANDARD NO: 0036–8733 DATE: 1998 RECORD TYPE: art
CONTENTS:	feature article

ABSTRACT: Techniques developed by astronomers over the past few years allow visual access to the more than one-fifth of the Universe formerly blocked from view by dust and stars in the disk of the Milky Way. Without knowing what lies in this area, researchers cannot entirely map the matter in this corner of the cosmos, preventing them from resolving some of the most important unknowns in cosmology. To date astronomers have found, among other things, a new galaxy so close that it would dominate Earth's skies if it was not obscured by the disk, colossal galaxy clusters never before seen, and the core of the elusive Great Attractor.

SUBJECT: Galaxies, Milky Way

Whether you search in print or online, once you know the name of the magazine or journal you want, you will still need to check the computer catalog to see if the library or media center has the specific periodical that you need.

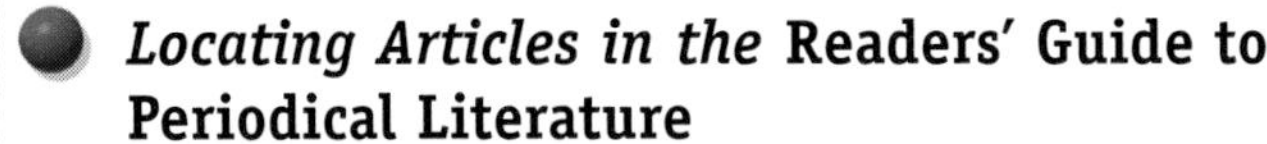

PRACTICE YOUR SKILLS

Locating Articles in the Readers' Guide to Periodical Literature

Using the *Readers' Guide*, list two recent articles on four of the following subjects. List the title of the article, the name of the magazine in which each article can be found, the publication date, and the pages on which the article can be found.

1. astronomy
2. gymnastics
3. journalism
4. law
5. youth
6. pollution
7. music
8. nuclear energy
9. marine biology
10. medical costs

Newspapers

Newspapers are valuable sources of current and historical information. The periodical reading room in the library or media center should have the most recent print issues of all the newspapers to which the library subscribes. To save space, most libraries transfer older issues of newspapers into photographic reproductions of print pages that are stored on rolls or sheets of film. These materials are located in another part of the library or media center and can be viewed on special projectors.

Searching online gives you a few more options for finding this information. If a particular newspaper is available, a title search in the computer catalog will tell you if it is located in the reading room or on microform. Newspapers on photographic film are assigned call numbers that are listed in the computer catalog. A title search may also show you a hyperlink with an Internet address for the newspaper's home page.

Most major newspapers now have their own Websites and electronic databases where you can view current issues and search for archived articles in past issues. By searching directly on the Web, you can also access databases that allow you to locate and search newspapers from every state in the United States and from most countries around the world.

Both of the following sites list hundreds of newspapers by location (country and state) and by subject (business, arts and entertainment, trade journals, or college papers). These databases send you to the home pages for specific major newspapers where you can search for articles.

THE INTERNET PUBLIC LIBRARY http://www.ipl.org/reading/news
NEWSPAPERS ONLINE! http://www.newspapers.com

News services allow you to search the databases of many newspapers, periodicals, and other documents at the same time for articles on specific subjects. Check with the media specialist to see if your library or media center subscribes to these news services.

LEXIS-NEXIS http://www.lexis-nexis.com/lncc
PROQUEST http://www.umi.com.au

Always read the guidelines carefully on the home page for each newspaper or news service. The most recent articles are usually available free of charge, but you may have to pay a fee to download and print a copy of an archived article.

Encyclopedias

An encyclopedia may be the first place to go when gathering information for a report. Encyclopedias provide basic information on just about every subject imaginable. Encyclopedias are usually not one book but a series of large volumes. The subjects are arranged in alphabetical order. Letters on the spine of each volume show which part of the alphabet that volume covers. A volume labeled *Nel–O*, for example, would have information about the North Pole, the octopus, and the Olympic Games. Guide words at the top of each page show you at a glance which entries are on that page.

Some encyclopedias have a comprehensive index, either as a separate volume or at the back of the last volume. This index will help you find out quickly if your subject is covered and under what headings it appears. If it is not covered, the index might refer you to other subjects. At the end of each encyclopedia entry, you might also find a listing of other, related topics. For example, after the article on *sky*, an encyclopedia might indicate "*See also:* Astronomy, Horizon, and Light."

Several general encyclopedias are also available on CD-ROM and online. These can be used to look up information just as you would with any other published encyclopedia.

CD-ROM: Encarta Encyclopedia
The World Book Multimedia Encyclopedia
Compton's Interactive Encyclopedia

ONLINE: http://www.encyclopedia.com

Specialized Encyclopedias

Specialized encyclopedias focus on a variety of specific subjects from auto racing to weaving. Because they concentrate on a specific subject, these encyclopedias provide more in-depth information than general encyclopedias do. Specialized encyclopedias can also be found in the reference section of the library or media center. Specialized encyclopedias online let you search for information by subject and connect to other Websites on your topic through hyperlinks. The online *Encyclopedia Smithsonian*, for example, covers topics in physical sciences, social sciences, and U.S. and natural history.

PRINT: *Encyclopedia of World Art*
The Sports Encyclopedia
The Encyclopedia for American Facts and Dates
The International Encyclopedia of the Social Sciences

ONLINE: Encyclopedia Smithsonian
http://www.si.edu/resource/faq/start.htm
The World eText Library
http://www.netlibrary.net/WorldReferenceE.html

Includes: *Arts and Leisure Encyclopedia, Techweb/Technology Encyclopedia*, and the *Britannica Internet Guide*

Biographical References

Information about famous historical figures is usually found in encyclopedias; for information about contemporary personalities or people who are well known in specialized fields, you may need to turn to other biographical references. General references such as *Who's Who* and *Who's Who in America*, now published each year, have biographical sketches on people in popular culture that are not always found in an encyclopedia. Other biographical references include important basic information, such as date of birth, education, occupation, and the person's accomplishments, and may have longer entries describing the person's life in more detail. Several online and CD-ROM resources, in particular, document the lives of women and African Americans in U.S. history, and some multimedia versions contains film clips and audio recordings of important historical events.

PRINT:	*Who's Who* and *Who's Who in America* *Current Biography* *Dictionary of American Biography* *Dictionary of National Biography* *Webster's Biographical Dictionary* *American Men and Women of Science*
MULTIMEDIA CD-ROM:	*Her Heritage: A Biographical Encyclopedia of Famous American Women*
ONLINE:	*Distinguished Women of Past and Present* **http://www.netsrq.com/** *Encyclopedia Britannica Guide to Black History* **http://www.blackhistory.eb.com/**

References About Literature

Quotations are wonderful devices to liven up reports and add weight to already factual information. The quotation from John Quincy Adams on page C661 was found in a book of famous quotations. This kind of reference book is often arranged by topic or by author. If you have a specific quotation in mind but can't remember all the words, an index of first lines and key words at the end of the book will lead you to the page where the full quotation can be found.

Other references about literature focus on actual stories or literary elements, including plot summaries, descriptions of characters, information about authors, or definitions of literary terms, such as imagery and plot. On CD-ROM, *The Columbia Granger's World of Poetry* tells you where to find specific poems indexed by subject, title, and first line; and the *Gale Literary Index* contains information about authors and their major works.

PRINT:	*Bartlett's Familiar Quotations* *The Oxford Dictionary of Quotations* *The Oxford Companion to American Literature* *The Reader's Encyclopedia*

CD-ROM: *Gale's Quotations: Who Said What?*
The Columbia Granger's World of Poetry
Gale Literary Index

ONLINE: Bartlett's *Familiar Quotations*
http://www.bartleby.com/99/

Atlases

An atlas is generally a book of maps, but you can often find much more information in one. An atlas usually contains information about the location of continents, countries, cities, mountains, lakes, and other geographical features and regions. Moreover, some atlases also have information about population, climate, natural resources, industries, and transportation. Historical atlases include maps of the world during different moments in history. Some online resources from the U.S. Geological Survey incorporate satellite imagery to let you examine the geography of the United States by state and by region.

PRINT: *Rand McNally International World Atlas*
The Times Concise Atlas of the World
The National Geographic Atlas of the World
Rand McNally Atlas of World History

ONLINE: U.S. Geological Survey
http://www.nationalatlas.gov/mapit.html

Almanacs

Almanacs, which are generally published each year, contain up-to-date facts and statistical information on topics related to population, weather, government, and business. If you want to know the batting averages of Hall of Fame baseball players, countries that suffered natural disasters last year, or the most popular films and television shows in any year, an almanac is a good place to look. Almanacs also provide historical facts and geographic information. Some, such as *The Old Farmer's Almanac,* focus on weather-related and seasonal information.

PRINT: *Information Please Almanac*
World Almanac and Book of Facts
Guiness Book of World Records

ONLINE: *The Old Farmer's Almanac*
http://www.almanac.com

Specialized Dictionaries

If you are doing research for a report on a specialized topic, you may come across an unusual word that you do not recognize. A specialized dictionary is a good resource for learning more about the word. These dictionaries provide information about specific fields of study, such as medicine, music, and computer science. Some online sites include dictionaries in several languages and excerpts from guidebooks on writing.

PRINT: *Harvard Dictionary of Music*
Concise Dictionary of American History
Webster's New Geographical Dictionary

ONLINE: English and foreign language dictionaries; and excerpts from *MLA Handbook for Writers of Research Papers*
http://www.dictionary.com
Strunk's *Elements of Style*
http://www.bartleby.com/141/index.html

Books of Synonyms

In all of the writing that you do, word choice and word usage are always important. Another type of dictionary, called a thesaurus, features synonyms (different words with the same meanings) and antonyms (words with opposite meanings). This resource is especially helpful if you are looking for a specific word or if you want to vary your word usage and build your vocabulary.

PRINT: *Roget's Thesaurus in Dictionary Form*
Webster's New Dictionary of Synonyms

Funk and Wagnall's Standard Handbook of Synonyms, Antonyms, & Prepositions

ONLINE: *Roget's Thesaurus*
http://www.thesaurus.com

PRACTICE YOUR SKILLS

Using Specialized References

Write one kind of reference book, other than a general encyclopedia, which would contain information about each of the following subjects.

1. famous Americans
2. records in sports
3. countries of Asia
4. Spanish phrases
5. synonyms for *run*
6. the source of a quotation
7. the location of the Andes
8. the life of Thurgood Marshall
9. dates of past hurricanes
10. twentieth-century art

Other Reference Materials

Most libraries and media centers have a variety of printed resources that are not found in bound forms such as books and magazines. They also have other nonprint resources such as audio recordings and video documentaries that often provide information that cannot be conveyed in print form.

Vertical Files Most libraries keep a collection of printed materials, including pamphlets, pictures, art prints, unpublished letters and papers, and government publications and catalogs. These materials are usually arranged alphabetically by subject and kept in a filing cabinet in the library called the **vertical file**.

Microforms Many libraries and media centers save storage space by storing some documents and back issues of periodicals on **microfilm** and **microfiche**—photographic reproductions of printed material that are stored on rolls or sheets of film. References stored on microforms usually include past issues of newspapers, magazines, journals, and other periodicals; government documents from state and federal agencies; and original, historic records and papers.

These rolls and sheets of film are stored in filing cabinets in another part of the library or media center and can be viewed easily on special projectors. Newspapers, for example, are arranged in file drawers alphabetically by keywords in their titles. The holdings for each newspaper are then filed chronologically by date. For example, if you want to know what happened in Dallas on the day you were born, you could go to the file cabinets and get the roll of film for *The Dallas Morning News* on that day in that year.

Audio, Video, CD-ROM Audiovisual materials and CD-ROMs, other valuable sources of information, are often available through your library or media center. Audiovisual materials may include recordings of interviews and speeches, and videotapes of documentaries and educational programs. If you cannot check out these materials to view in the classroom, listening and viewing equipment is usually available in the library. The CD-ROM format also makes it possible to include multimedia features like audio recordings and video clips on the disk itself. Many CD-ROMs also contain hyperlinks and Internet software that allow you to connect to Websites with more information about each subject. The CD-ROM collection of your library or media center may include specialized indexes and databases as well as references such as *Encarta* and *Compton's* encyclopedias and specialized dictionaries such as the complete *Oxford English Dictionary*. Check with the media specialist to see which resources are available in these forms.

IN THE MEDIA

Web Search

Have you ever tried to find information on the Internet using a search engine? Chances are good that you've gotten a message like this:

4,678,321 pages were found that match your search criteria.

How are you ever going to dig through all of those pages?

Researching on the Internet has been compared to being thirsty. When all you want is a drink of water, you get knocked over with the force of a firehose. To increase your chances of success, refine your searches.

Techniques for Web Searches

- Enclose your keywords in quotation marks.
- Put a **+** before a word or phrase that must appear; use a **–** before terms not needed.
- Use Boolean search techniques (named after English mathematician George Boole). For information on Boolean search techniques, point your browser to **http://adam.ac.uk/info/boolean.html**

Boolean search techniques will also help you if you are searching through an online public access catalog (OPAC), which is an electronic version of a library card catalog.

Media Activity

Take a few minutes the next time you are online to try these different search techniques. Write a paragraph explaining what you did and what results you got from the different techniques.

Developing Your Word-Search Skills

After you have gathered your references and compiled your notes, you need to organize all of this information into an interesting and well-written composition. Some of the most important elements of effective writing are proper spelling, word choice, and usage. The dictionary is your best resource if you need help in any of these areas.

Using the Dictionary

When you think of using a dictionary, you already know that it helps you define or spell words. That, of course, is a dictionary's main purpose. Yet there is so much more it can do! A dictionary also helps you pronounce words and explain how words can be used in a sentence. Many dictionaries also include some background on words and their history. In this section you will review the information available in a dictionary and learn how to use a dictionary effectively. Whether you are working with a print dictionary or an online version, the following information should make your word search easier.

Word Location

Like many references books, a dictionary is organized to help you quickly find the information you need. Two things will help you here.

Guide Words If you look at the top of a dictionary page, you will see two words; these are called **guide words.** They show you, with just a glance, the first and last words defined on that page. For example, if the guide words are *ooze • or*, the word *operate* would be among the words that appear on the page. The word *orbit* would not be there.

Alphabetical Order From beginning to end, the dictionary is a single, alphabetical list. From *aardvark* to *zygote*, and every word in between, you will find a wealth of information to aid in writing. Words beginning with the same letters are alphabetized by the next letter that is different, then the next, and so on. For example, *face* comes before *facet*. Compound words, abbreviations, prefixes, suffixes, and proper nouns also appear in alphabetical order.

Single Word	acrobatics
Hyphenated Compound	across-the-board
Two-word Compound	acute angle
Prefix	ad-
Abbreviation	AFL (American Federation of Labor)
Proper Noun	Alaska Standard Time
Suffix	-ally

Note: Compound words are alphabetized as if there were no space or hyphen between each word. Abbreviations are alphabetized letter by letter, not by the words they stand for.

Alphabetizing Words

Make six columns and number them 1 through 6. Then list each group of words to show how they would be alphabetized in a dictionary.

1. glaze, glow, glimpse, glimmer, glossy, glacier, glance, glisten, glamour

2. hiccup, hi-fi, hike, hickory, hilarious, hibernate, hide, high jump

3. beehive, bee tree, beeline, beetle-browed, beech, beetle, beet, bazaar

4. splint, splice, spirt, splinter, spirit, spicy, sphinx

5. precut, profile, prefill, prefire, prefile, preset, presale

6. tread, treason, tree farm, treaty, tree toad, tremor

Information in an Entry

All the information provided for each word is called an **entry.** Each entry usually provides the spelling, pronunciation, parts of speech, definitions, and the origins of the word.

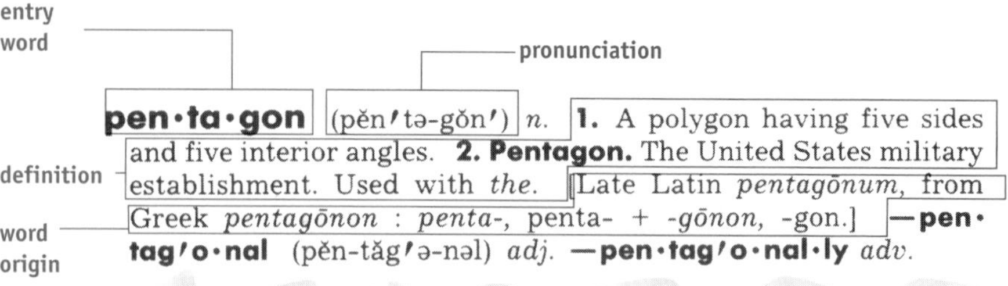

pen·ta·gon (pĕn′tə-gŏn′) *n.* **1.** A polygon having five sides and five interior angles. **2. Pentagon.** The United States military establishment. Used with *the.* [Late Latin *pentagōnum,* from Greek *pentagōnon* : *penta-,* penta- + *-gōnon,* -gon.] **—pen·tag′o·nal** (pĕn-tăg′ə-nəl) *adj.* **—pen·tag′o·nal·ly** *adv.*

Entry Word The entry word in **bold** type tells you (1) how to spell a word, (2) whether to capitalize it, and (3) where to divide it at the end of a line.

coun·sel·or also **coun·sel·lor** (koun′sə-lər, -slər) *n.* **1.** A person who gives counsel; an adviser. **2.** An attorney, especially a trial lawyer. See Synonyms at **lawyer. 3.** A person who supervises young people at a summer camp. See Usage Note at **council. —coun′se·lor·ship′** *n.*

First, in addition to showing the correct spelling of a word, an entry also shows any alternate spellings. The more common spelling, called the preferred spelling, is usually listed first.

chime[1] (chīm) *n.* **1.** An apparatus for striking a bell or set of bells to produce a musical sound. **2.** Often **chimes.** *Music.* A set of bells tuned to scale and used as an orchestral instrument. **3.** A single bell, as in the mechanism of a clock. **4.** The sound produced by or as if by a bell or bells. **5.** Agreement; accord: *a flawless chime of romance and reality.* **—chime** *v.* **chimed, chim·**

Plural nouns, comparatives and superlatives of adjectives, and principal parts of verbs are also given if these spellings are irregular.

chiv•al•ry (shĭv′əl-rē) *n., pl.* **-ries. 1.** The medieval system, principles, and customs of knighthood. **2. a.** The qualities idealized by knighthood, such as bravery, courtesy, honor, and gallantry toward women. **b.** A manifestation of any of these qualities. **3.** A group of knights or gallant gentlemen. [Middle English *chivalrie,* from Old French *chevalerie,* from *chevalier,* knight. See CHEVALIER.]

choose (cho͞oz) *v.* **chose** (chōz), **cho•sen** (chō′zən), **choos•ing, choos•es.** —*tr.* **1.** To select from a number of possible alternatives; decide on and pick out. **2. a.** To prefer above others: *chooses the supermarket over the neighborhood grocery store.* **b.** To determine or decide: *chose t*

chop•py[1] (chŏp′ē) *adj.* **-pi•er, -pi•est. 1.** Having many small waves: *choppy seas.* **2.** Marked by abrupt transitions; jerky: *choppy prose.* **—chop′pi•ly** *adv.* **—chop′pi•ness** *n.*

Second, the entry word is printed with a capital letter if it is capitalized. If it is capitalized only in certain uses, it will appear with a capital letter near the appropriate definition.

Milk•y Way (mĭl′kē) *n.* The galaxy containing the solar system, visible as a broad band of faint light in the night sky. [Middle English, translation of Latin *via lactea* : *via,* way + *lactea,* milky.]

jer•sey (jûr′zē) *n., pl.* **-seys. 1. a.** A soft, plain-knitted fabric used for clothing. **b.** A garment made of this fabric. **2.** A close-fitting knitted pullover shirt, jacket, or sweater. **3.** Often **Jersey.** Any of a breed of fawn-colored dairy cattle developed on the island of Jersey and producing milk that is rich in butterfat. [After JERSEY.]

Third, when writing, you sometimes need to divide a word at the end of a line. Because a word may be divided only between syllables, use a dictionary to check where each syllable ends.

sus • pense • ful   char • ac • ter   per • fec • tion

Practice Your Skills

Using a Dictionary for Editing

Write the following paragraph, using a dictionary to help you correct the errors in spelling and capitalization. Then underline each correction.

Starlit Skies

At night, thosands of stars appear accross the sky. Over the centurys, stargazers have observed that some stars form particular shapes. These star clusters are called constellations. Two of the most familar are ursa major, "great bear," and ursa minor, "little bear." Within these constellations are the big dipper, the little dipper, and the bright north star. Some constellations can be observed only durring certain seasons. Leo the Lion appears in Spring. During the winter, orion the Hunter is visable. At present, more than 80 constellations have been identifyed in the night sky.

Pronunciation To learn how to pronounce a word, look up the phonetic spelling of the word in the dictionary. The phonetic spelling directly follows the entry word, as in these examples.

clang (klăng)	**knack** (năk)
phone (fōn)	**clock** (klŏk)
quick (kwĭck)	**school** (sko͞ol)

A ***pronunciation* key** at the front of the dictionary shows what sound each phonetic symbol stands for. Most dictionaries also place an abbreviated pronunciation key at the bottom of every other page.

PARTIAL PRONUNCIATION KEY			
Symbols	**Examples**	**Symbols**	**Examples**
ă	p**a**t	oi	b**oy**
ā	p**ay**	ou	**ou**t
âr	**c**are	o͝o	t**oo**k
ä	f**a**ther	o͞o	b**oo**t
ĕ	p**e**t	ŭ	c**u**t
ē	b**e**	ûr	**ur**ge
ĭ	p**i**t	th	**th**in
ī	p**ie**	*th*	**th**is
îr	p**ier**	hw	**wh**ich
ŏ	p**o**t	zh	vi**s**ion
ō	t**oe**	ə	**a**bout, it**e**m
ô	p**aw**		

Stress marks: ′ (primary); ′ (secondary), as in dictionary (dĭk ′ shə nĕr ′ ē)

To learn to pronounce a word, compare the phonetic spelling to the symbols in the key. For example, the key shows that *zh* stands for the *s* sound in *vision*. The *s* in the following words is also pronounced *zh*.

pleas • ure (plĕzh′ ər) **treas • ure** (trĕzh′ ər)

In the pronunciation key above, marks over vowels indicate different vowel sounds. For example, the different sounds of the vowel *o* are represented in the following ways.

ŏ as in *pot* ō as in *toe* ô aw as in *paw*

These marks over the letter *o* are called **diacritical marks**. To find out how a vowel with a diacritical mark is pronounced, you refer to the pronunciation key:

odd (ŏd)	[*o* as in *pot*]
ode (ōde)	[*o* as in *toe*]
off (ôf)	[*aw* as in *paw*]

In some words, the vowels *a, e, i, o,* and *u* are pronounced *uh*, as in the second syllables of *item* and *broken*. Most dictionaries use a schwa (ə) to represent this sound in an unaccented syllable.

a • bout (ə bout′)
i • tem (ī′təm)
li • bel (lī′ bəl)

In many words, one syllable receives more emphasis than the other syllables in the word. An **accent mark** indicates a syllable that should be stressed.

lob • ster (lôb′ stər)
de • sign (di zīn′)

In *lobster,* the first syllable receives emphasis. In *design,* the second syllable should receive emphasis.

In longer words, where two syllables should be stressed, the syllable receiving more stress is marked with a **primary accent** (′). The less emphasized syllable is marked with a **secondary accent** (ˊ). In the example below, the third syllable receives the most stress in pronunciation.

primary accent

en • er • get • ic (enˊ ər jĕt′ ĭk)

secondary accent

Practice Your Skills

Marking Pronunciations

Using a dictionary, write the phonetic spelling of each word.

1. mocha
2. discus
3. nova
4. hedge
5. kiwi
6. kayak
7. hydrophobia
8. equestrian
9. jerboa
10. catamaran

Dividing Words into Syllables

Write the words above, showing the number of syllables in each word and where the words would break.

Definitions A dictionary is a handy reference for finding the meanings of a word. At the end of some entries, the dictionary will also list synonyms, or words that have similar definitions.

The following entry for the word *train* shows the information provided to make each meaning clear.

part of speech

numbered definition

example

part of speech

train (trān) *n.* **1.** *Abbr.* **tn.** A series of connected railroad cars pulled or pushed by one or more locomotives. **2.** A long line of moving people, animals, or vehicles. **3.** The personnel, vehicles, and equipment following and providing supplies and services to a combat unit. **4.** A part of a gown that trails behind the wearer. **5.** A staff of people following in attendance; a retinue. **6. a.** An orderly succession of related events or thoughts; a sequence. See Synonyms at **series. b.** A series of consequences wrought by an event; aftermath. **7.** A set of linked mechanical parts: *a train of gears.* **8.** A string of gunpowder that acts as a fuse for exploding a charge. **—train** *v.* **trained, train·ing, trains.** —*tr.* **1.** To coach in or accustom to a mode of behavior or performance. **2.** To make proficient with specialized instruction and practice. See Synonyms at **teach. 3.** To prepare physically, as with a regimen: *train athletes for track-and-field competition.* **4.** To cause (a plant or one's hair) to take a desired course or shape, as by manipulating. **5.** To focus on or aim at (a goal, mark, or target); direct. See Synonyms at **aim. 6.** To let drag behind; trail. —*intr.* **1.** To give or undergo a course of training: *trained daily for the*

In the entry for *train,* the abbreviations *n.* and *v.* show that *train* can be used as a noun or a verb. Dictionaries use the following abbreviations for the eight parts of speech.

n.	noun	*pron.*	pronoun	*prep.*	preposition
v.	verb	*adj.*	adjective	*conj.*	conjunction
		adv.	adverb	*interj.*	interjection

A dictionary also indicates the present usage of words by including such labels as *obsolete, informal, colloquial,* and *slang.* The abbreviation *obs.* in the entry below means that the word *buck*

OBSOLETE

buck·board (bŭk′bôrd′, -bōrd′) *n.* A four-wheeled open carriage with the seat or seats attached to a flexible board running between the front and rear axles. [Obsolete *buck,* body of a wagon (from Middle English *bouk,* belly, from Old English *būc*) + BOARD.]

is no longer used with this meaning. *Informal, colloquial* and *slang* indicates words that are used only in informal situations, as in the fifth definition of *rag* below.

informal

raft[1] (răft) *n.* **1.** A flat structure, typically made of planks, logs, or barrels, that floats on water and is used for transport or as a platform for swimmers. **2.** A flat-bottomed inflatable craft for floating or drifting on water: *shooting the rapids in a rubber raft.* —*v.* **raft·, raft·ed, raft·ing, rafts.** —*tr.* **1.** To convey on a raft. **2.** To make into a raft. —*intr.* To travel by raft. [Middle English, from Old Norse *raptr,* beam, rafter.]

raft[2] (răft) *n.* *Informal.* A great number, amount, or collection: *asked a raft of questions.* [Alteration of dialectal *raff,* rubbish, from Middle English *raf.* See RAFFISH.]

slang

rag[1] (răg) *n.* **1.a.** A scrap of cloth. **b.** A piece of cloth used for cleaning, washing, or dusting. **2. rags.** Threadbare or tattered clothing. **3.** Cloth converted to pulp for making paper. **4.** A scrap; a fragment. **5.** *Slang.* A newspaper, especially one specializing in sensationalism or gossip. **6.** The stringy central portion and membranous walls of a citrus fruit. [Middle English *ragge,* from Old English **ragg,* from Old No... **rögg,* wo... tuft o...

Practice Your Skills

Choosing the Appropriate Definition

Using the dictionary entry for *train* on the preceding page, write the number of the appropriate definition of train. Next to each number, write the appropriate part of speech—*noun* or *verb*.

1. A train of horses lead the parade.

2. I lost my train of thought during my speech.

3. Peter trained for two years to be an electrician.

4. Sara trained the horse's mane to curl.

5. The king tripped over the train of the queen's gown.

6. Julie trained her dog to jump two feet.

Finding the Meaning of a Word

Using a dictionary, write the definition that best fits the use of the underlined word in each sentence.

1. The plane gathered speed as it raced down the runway.
2. He gathered from the evidence that they were guilty.
3. I want to review my notes before the final exam.
4. The new movie received a disappointing review.
5. The track team jogged around the school grounds.
6. I jogged my memory to find the correct exam answer.

Finding Synonyms for Words

Using a dictionary, find at least two synonyms for each of the following words.

7. dialect
8. flock
9. like
10. mind
11. perform
12. polite
13. branch
14. frown
15. opposite
16. practice
17. excel
18. defeat

Time Out to Reflect

Think about the different reference sources that you explored in this chapter. Look back at the notes you made in your **journal** as you used each type of resource. Now that you have used both print and online versions of the same type of resources, think about how the different versions compare. Which dictionary version did you find easier to use? Which encyclopedia was better organized?

Assess Your Learning

Your school is preparing to broadcast a production on a local public access television show. Your principal, Mr. Skinner, has asked all students to research information about themselves. He wants you to find the meaning and derivation of your first and last names. He also wants you to find the city or town where you were born. All the information you learn will be included in your individual televised report.

- **Research to find the information that you will give in the program. Use your library or media center, and locate material about your name, birthplace, and birth date in resources such as encyclopedias, newspapers, CD-ROMs, and Internet sites. Determine the right reference materials to discover the most interesting and descriptive information about yourself so that your televised report will stand out. Then organize the information in a way that will fit the report.**

Before You Write **Consider the following questions:**
What is the ***subject?***
What is the ***occasion?***
Who is the ***audience?***
What is the ***purpose?***

After You Write **Evaluate your work using the following criteria:**

- Have you organized your ideas to ensure coherence and logical progression in your report?
- Have you used research materials such as encyclopedias, specialized encyclopedias, nonfiction books, articles from periodicals, or Internet sites to find information about your topics?
- Have you enlisted the help of your librarian or media specialist?
- Does the information from your research include material to make your report stand out and is your writing accurate, informative, and meaningful?
- Does the information you have researched show accurate spelling and correct use of conventions of punctuation and capitalization?

Write briefly on how well you did. Point out your strengths and areas for improvement.

A Writer's Guide to Electronic Publishing

Using the Internet, your local media center, plus E-mail and other research sources, you can gather an abundant amount of data to help you create a well-developed article or an up-to-date report. Once all your material is written and organized, the question you will want to ask yourself is, How can I publish my information?

Years ago, your options might have been limited to using text from a typewriter, photos and glue, construction paper and art materials. Today the world of electronic publishing has opened a world of options. Depending on the nature of your project, just some of the choices open to you include desktop publishing, audio and video recordings, and online publishing on the World Wide Web.

Each of these communication methods has unique advantages and drawbacks. Some media are more suitable to certain types of projects. For example, a visual topic, such as an article about bonsai trees, might be better expressed as a video. Reports with numerous facts, figures, and graphs might be better served in a document. An opinion poll in which many people are interviewed might lend itself well to an audio recording. And a subject that branches off into many different areas, such as a presentation about volunteer opportunities in your community, could be very effective as a Website.

Talk to your teacher to help you decide which publishing method is right for your project. Then let your imagination go and take advantage of all the creative possibilities electronic publishing has to offer.

Desktop Publishing

The computer is a powerful tool that gives you the ability to create everything from party invitations and banners to newsletters and illustrated reports. Many software programs deliver word-processing and graphic arts capabilities that once belonged only to professional printers and designers. Armed with the knowledge of how to operate your software, you simply need to add some sound research and a healthy helping of creativity to create an exciting paper.

Word-Processing Magic

The written word is the basis of almost every project. Using a standard word-processing program, such as Microsoft Word, makes all aspects of the writing process easier. Use a word-processing program to:

- create an outline;
- save multiple versions of your work;
- revise your manuscript;
- proof your spelling, grammar, and punctuation;
- produce a polished final draft document.

Fascinating Fonts

Once your written material is revised and proofed, it's fun to experiment with type as a way to enhance the content of your written message. Different styles of type are called **fonts** or **typefaces**. Most word-processing programs feature more than 30 different choices. You'll find them listed in the Format menu under Font.

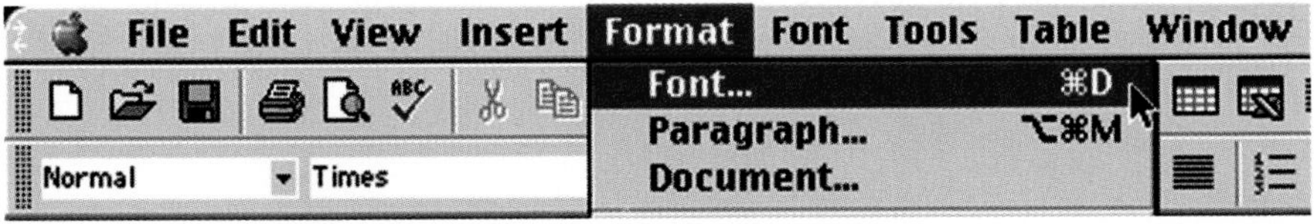

Or they may be located on the toolbar at the top left of your screen.

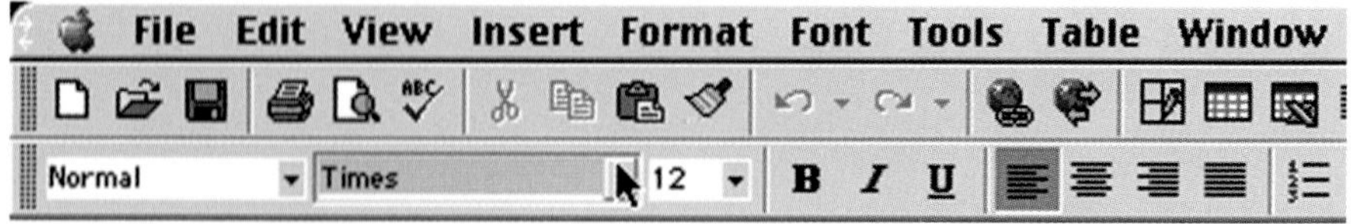

Although each typeface has its own distinguishing characteristics, most fonts fall into one of two categories: serif typefaces or sans serif typefaces. A serif is a small curve or line added to the end of some of the letter strokes. A typeface that includes these small added curves is called a **serif** typeface. A font without them is referred to as **sans serif,** or in other words, *without* serifs.

Times New Roman is a serif typeface.

Arial is a sans serif typeface.

In general, sans serif fonts have a sharp look and are better for shorter pieces of writing, such as headings and titles. Serif typefaces work well as body copy.

Of all the typefaces, whether serif or sans serif, which is best? In many cases, the answer depends on your project. Each font has a personality of its own and makes a different impression on the reader. For example:

This is French Script MT and might be fun to use in an invitation to a special birthday party.

This is Playbill and would look great on a poster advertising a melodrama by the Theatre Club.

This is Stencil and would be a great way to say "Top Secret" on a letter to a friend.

As fun as they are, these three typefaces are probably inappropriate for a school report or term paper. Specialized fonts are great for unique projects (posters, invitations, and personal correspondence) but less appropriate for writing assignments for school or business.

Since most school writing is considered formal, good font choices include Times New Roman, Arial, Helvetica, or Bookman Antiqua. These type styles are fairly plain and straightforward. They allow the reader to focus on the meaning of your words instead of being distracted by the way they appear on the page.

One last word about fonts: With so many to choose from, you may be tempted to include a dozen or so in your document. Be careful! Text **printed** *in* multiple fonts *can* be extremely *confusing* **to read**. The whole idea of different typefaces is to enhance and clarify your message, not the other way around!

A Sizable Choice

Another way to add emphasis to your writing is to adjust the size of the type. Type size is measured in points. One inch is equal to 72 points. Therefore, 72-point type would have letters that measure one inch high. To change the point size of your type, open the Format menu and click Font.

Or use the small number box on the toolbar at the top left side of your screen.

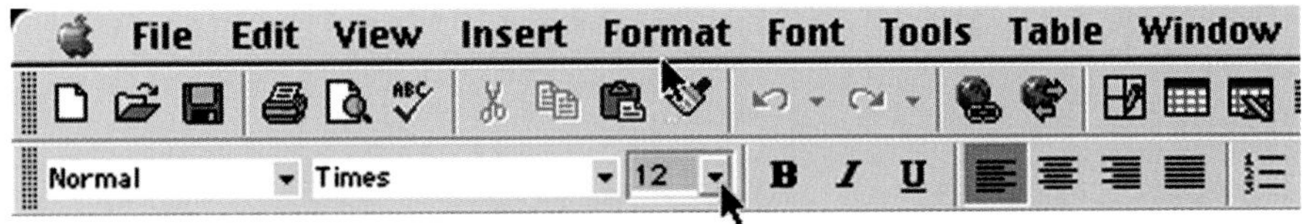

For most school and business writing projects, 10 or 12 points is the best size of type for the main body copy of your text. However, it's very effective to change the type size for titles, headings, and subheadings to give the reader a clear understanding of how your information is organized. For example, look how the type in the subheading "A Sizable Choice" is different from the rest of the type on this page, indicating the beginning of a new section.

Another way to add emphasis is to apply a style to the type, such as **bold**, *italics*, or underline. Styles are also found in the Format menu under Font.

Or look for them in the top center section of the toolbar on your screen abbreviated as **B** for bold, *I* for italics, and U for underline.

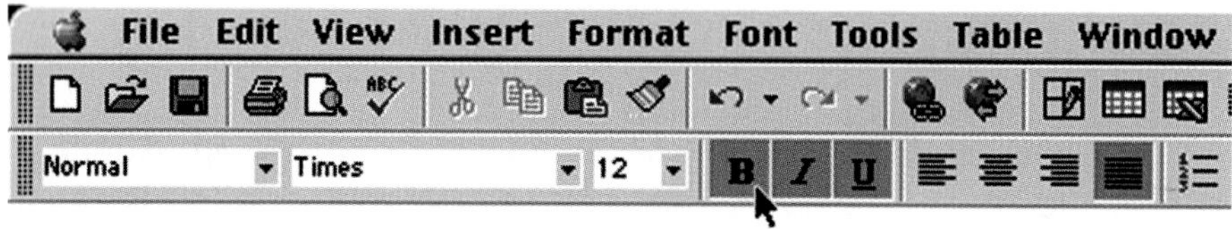

Here's one more suggestion—color. If you have access to a color printer, you may want to consider using colored type to set your heading apart from the rest of the body copy. Red, blue, or other dark colors work best. Avoid yellow or other light shades that might fade out and be difficult to read.

Like choosing fonts, the trick with applying type sizes, styles, and colors is to use them sparingly and consistently throughout your work. In other words, all the body copy should be in one style of type. All the headings should be in another, and so on. If you pepper your copy with too many fonts, type sizes, styles, and colors, your final product could end up looking more like a patchwork quilt than a polished report.

Layout Help from Your Computer

One way to organize the information in your document is to use one of the preset page layouts provided by your word-processing program. All you have to do is write your document using capital letters for main headings, and uppercase and lowercase letters for subheadings. Set the headings apart from the body copy with returns. Then open the Format menu and click the Autoformat heading. Your copy will probably look like the illustration at the top of the next page.

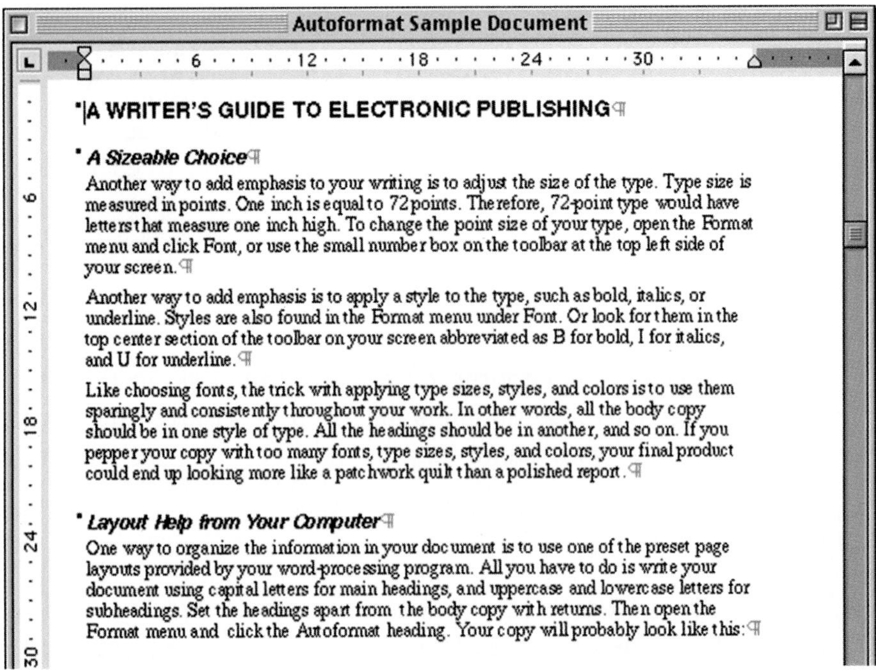
Autoformat Sample Document

A WRITER'S GUIDE TO ELECTRONIC PUBLISHING

A Sizeable Choice

Another way to add emphasis to your writing is to adjust the size of the type. Type size is measured in points. One inch is equal to 72 points. Therefore, 72-point type would have letters that measure one inch high. To change the point size of your type, open the Format menu and click Font, or use the small number box on the toolbar at the top left side of your screen.

Another way to add emphasis is to apply a style to the type, such as bold, italics, or underline. Styles are also found in the Format menu under Font. Or look for them in the top center section of the toolbar on your screen abbreviated as B for bold, I for italics, and U for underline.

Like choosing fonts, the trick with applying type sizes, styles, and colors is to use them sparingly and consistently throughout your work. In other words, all the body copy should be in one style of type. All the headings should be in another, and so on. If you pepper your copy with too many fonts, type sizes, styles, and colors, your final product could end up looking more like a patchwork quilt than a polished report.

Layout Help from Your Computer

One way to organize the information in your document is to use one of the preset page layouts provided by your word-processing program. All you have to do is write your document using capital letters for main headings, and uppercase and lowercase letters for subheadings. Set the headings apart from the body copy with returns. Then open the Format menu and click the Autoformat heading. Your copy will probably look like this:

This automatic, preset format is probably fine for most of the writing you do in school. You'll also find other options available in the File menu under Page Setup.

Document

Margins | Layout

Top: 1"
Bottom: 1"
Left: 1.25"
Right: 1.25"
Gutter: 0"

From edge
Header: 0.5"
Footer: 0.5"

Mirror margins

Preview

Apply to: Whole document

Default... | Page Setup... | Cancel | OK

Here you can change the margins and add headers, footers, and page numbers. **Headers** and **footers** are descriptive titles that automatically appear at the top or bottom of each page without having to retype them each time. For example, you may wish to add the title of your project and the date as a header or footer to each page.

Header
Project Title Here
Date Here

To insert a header or a footer, go to View and click on Header and Footer. Note that page numbers may also be inserted by way of the Insert option on your menu bar.

Let's Get Graphic

The old saying "A picture is worth a thousand words" is particularly true when it comes to spicing up papers and reports. Desktop publishing programs (such as Adobe PhotoDeluxe Home Edition, Macromedia FreeHand, Microsoft PhotoDraw, and Microsoft PowerPoint) give you the ability to include photographs, illustrations, and charts in your work that can express your ideas more clearly and succinctly than words alone.

The key to using graphics effectively is to make sure each one conveys a message of importance. Don't use them just for decoration. Be sure they add something meaningful, or you'll actually detract from your written message.

Drawings Many paint and draw programs allow you to create or **import** (bring in from another program) an illustration into your document. Drawings can help illustrate concepts that are difficult to describe, such as mechanical parts or procedures. Cartoons can also add a nice touch. If you use them sparingly, they can lighten up an otherwise dry, technical report.

Clip Art Another kind of drawing is called **clip art.** These simple, black-and-white or color line pictures are often included in desktop publishing or word-processing programs. Pre-drawn clip art usually is not suitable for illustrations, but it does work well as graphic icons that can help guide your reader through various parts of a long report.

For example, suppose you are writing a report on the top arts programs in the United States. You might choose the following clip art for each of the sections:

When you introduce the section of your report that deals with music, you might use the music icon at the large size pictured above. Then, in the headers of all the following sections that deal with music, you might use a smaller version of the icon that looks like this:

Music Trends

Using clip art as icons in this manner lets your readers know at a glance which part of the report they are reading.

Charts and Graphs If your project, or part of your project, deals with comparing numbers and statistics, one of the best ways to communicate this information is by using charts and graphs. Programs such as Microsoft PowerPoint allow you to create bar graphs, pie charts, and line graphs that can communicate fractions, figures, and comparative measurements much more powerfully than written descriptions.

Photographs When you flip quickly through a book or a magazine, what catches your eye? Probably photographs. Most of us are naturally curious and want to see what we are reading about. Photos are the perfect companions to written work. With the widespread availability of digital cameras and scanners, adding photos to your project is an easy and effective way to enhance your content.

Using a digital camera or a scanner, you can load photos directly into your computer. Another option is to shoot photographs with a regular camera, but when you have them developed, specify that they be returned to you as "pictures on disc," which you can open on your computer screen.

Photographic images are stored as bits of data in an electronic file. Once you have the photos in your computer, you can use a graphics program such as Adobe PhotoDeluxe Home Edition to manipulate the images in a variety of ways and create amazing visual effects. You can crop elements out of the photo, add special filters and colors, combine elements of two different pictures into one—the possibilities are endless.

After you have inserted the edited photo into your document, be careful when you print out your final draft. Standard printers often don't reproduce photographs well. You may want to take your document on disc to a professional printing company and have it printed out on a high-resolution printer to make sure you get the best quality.

Captions and Titles While it's true that a single photo can say a great deal, some pictures still need a little explanation in order to have the strongest impact on your reader. Whenever you include an illustration or photograph in a document, also include a simple caption or title for each image.

Add captions in a slightly smaller type size than the body copy and preferably in a sans serif typeface. Use the caption to add information that isn't immediately apparent in the photo. If there are people in the picture, tell readers who they are. If the photo features an odd-looking structure, explain what it is. Be smart with your captions. Don't tell the reader the obvious. Give him or her a reason to read your caption.

For example, suppose you are doing a report about Mt. Everest and you include a dramatic photo of its snowy peak.

WEAK CAPTION	The summit of Mt. Everest is very high and treacherous.
STRONG CAPTION	At its summit, Mt. Everest soars to 29,028 feet, making it the tallest mountain in the world.

Stand-Alone Graphics Occasionally you may include well-known graphics or logos in a story or report. These graphics convey powerful messages on their own and don't require captions. Examples of these logos or symbols include:

Nonprint Media—Audio and Video

The world we live in is becoming increasingly more multimedia-savvy. The power of the spoken word and the visual image is widely recognized for the impact it carries. Many businesses rely extensively on multimedia presentations to market their products or convey messages to consumers and employees. Exciting opportunities exist for people who can produce clear, concise messages in audio and visual formats.

Pre-Production—Put It on Paper First

Although the final presentation of your subject material may be an audiotape or a video, your project needs to begin on paper first. When you write down your ideas, you do four things:

- Organize your thoughts.
- Narrow your focus.
- Isolate the main messages.
- Identify possible production problems.

Grabbing a tape recorder or camcorder and then running off to record your project is a sure-fire way to create an unorganized mess. This helter-skelter collection of shots and sound bites probably takes hours longer to unravel and fix than if you had taken the time to plan your production in the first place. Resist the urge to jump right in! You'll be glad you did.

Concept Outline The first task in the writing process is a short, one-page document that describes the basic idea of the project. Ideally this should be three paragraphs—one paragraph each describing the beginning, the middle, and the end. Do not go forward until you have clearly identified these three important parts of your project.

Brief Next ask yourself, What is the purpose of this video or audiotape? Who is the audience? What is the result you hope to achieve when this group of people sees or hears your presentation? Do you want them to be informed about something? Motivated to do something? Emotionally moved in some way? Or excited about something? Write one to two pages that describe in detail the point of your project: how it will be used, who the intended audience is, and what you hope to achieve with the presentation.

Treatment The next phase of the writing process fleshes out the ideas you expressed in your outline and brief. The treatment is several pages long. It contains descriptions of the characters, dialogue, and settings, and describes the presentation scene by scene in order of how it will appear. Include in your treatment descriptions of the mood and the tone of your piece. Is it upbeat and whimsical, or dark and ominous? If your project is a video, set the stage by describing the overall look and feel of the production.

Script Once you've completed the first three steps, you are ready to go to script. The script is the blueprint for your production, similar to a blueprint for a house. Everything that is mentioned in the script is what will wind up in the audio recording or on the screen. Conversely, anything that is left out of the script will likely be overlooked and omitted from the final production. So write this document carefully.

For an audio recording, the script contains all narration, dialogue, music, and sound effects. For a videotape, it contains all of these elements plus descriptions of the characters, any sets, props, or costumes, plus all camera shots and movements, special visual effects, and onscreen titles or graphic elements. In short the audio script encompasses everything that is heard, and the video script covers everything that is seen and heard.

Storyboard Last, for video productions, it's also helpful to create storyboards—simple frame-by-frame sketches with explanatory notes jotted underneath—that paint a visual picture of what the video will look like from start to finish.

The final stages of pre-production include assembling all of the elements you will need before you begin recording your audiotape or shooting your video. Here's a general checklist.

Pre-Production Checklist

Audiotape Tasks

- ✓ Arrange for audio recording equipment
- ✓ Cast narrator/actors
- ✓ Find music (secure permission)
- ✓ Arrange for sound effects
- ✓ Set up recording schedule
- ✓ Coordinate all cast and crew
- ✓ Arrange for transportation if needed
- ✓ Rehearse all voice talent

Videotape Tasks

- ✓ Arrange for video equipment (including lighting and sound recording equipment)
- ✓ Cast narrator/host/actors
- ✓ Find music (secure permission)
- ✓ Arrange for sound/visual effects
- ✓ Set up shooting schedule
- ✓ Coordinate all cast and crew
- ✓ Arrange for transportation if needed
- ✓ Set up shooting locations (secure permission)
- ✓ Arrange for costumes, props, sets
- ✓ Arrange for make-up if needed
- ✓ Rehearse all on-camera talent

Video Production Schedule Tucked into the list of pre-production tasks is "Set up recording/shooting schedule." For videotaping, this means much more than just deciding what day and time you will begin shooting.

During the video production phase of your project, the idea is to shoot everything that your script calls for in the final production. Often the most efficient way to do this is what is called "out-of-sequence" filming. This means that, rather than shooting scenes sequentially (that is, in the order that they appear in the script), you shoot them in the order that is most convenient. Later you will edit them together in the correct order in post-production.

For example, your video might begin and end in the main character's office. Rather than shoot the first office scene, then move the cast and crew to the next location, then later at the end of the day return to the office, it might be easier to shoot both office scenes back-to-back. This will save a great deal of time and effort involved in moving people, lights, and props back and forth.

Lighting may be a factor in the order in which you shoot your scenes. For example, scenes 3, 4, and 7 may take place in the daytime, and scenes 1, 2, 5, and 6 may take place at night.

To accommodate all of these factors, you will need to plan your shooting schedule carefully. The difference between a smooth shoot day and chaos is a well thought-out shooting schedule.

Last, for video or audio recording, it's also a good idea to assemble your team for a pre-production meeting before you begin. This is your chance to read through the script together, go over time schedules, review responsibilities of each person involved, and answer any questions or discuss potential problems *before* you begin rolling tape. Pre-production meetings are well worth the time they take for reducing stress levels and headaches during production!

Production—We're Rolling!

At last, you've completed all your preparation. Now it's time to roll tape!

Audio Production The better the recording equipment, the higher-quality sound recording you will be able to achieve. The most convenient format for student audio recording is the audiocassette—a high-quality tape in a plastic case that you simply drop inside your cassette recorder.

The forerunner of the audiocassette was reel-to-reel tape, in which audiotape was threaded through a recording machine from one reel to another. This format is still used in some recording studios, although recording on CDs—compact discs—has become increasingly more common.

Most professional recording facilities record on **DAT**—digital audiotape. DAT provides the cleanest, highest-quality sound of all, but the equipment is still quite expensive and limited usually to professional recording situations.

If you are using an audiocassette recorder, use an external microphone rather than the built-in microphone on the tape recorder for best results. Other ways to enhance the quality of your production include the following:

- Select a high-quality, low-noise tape stock.
- Choose a quiet place to do your recording. Look for a quiet room with carpeting, soft furniture, and a door you can close firmly. Hang a sign outside the door that says "Quiet Please—Recording in Progress" so you will not be disturbed in the middle of your session.
- Do a voice check before you begin recording so you know whether the sound level on the recorder is set correctly.
- Lay the script pages out side-by-side to eliminate the rustling sound of turning pages.
- If music is part of your production, cue up the correct cut and practice turning it on and fading the volume up and down at the appropriate parts. Do a sound check on the music volume before you start. Do the same with any sound effects.

Video Production As with audio recording, there are a number of different formats to choose from for video recording. Some of the more common ones include those listed on the following page.

VHS	A full-sized tape machine that produces moderate quality video. The camera is large and heavy, and requires some skill to operate effectively.
VHSC	A compact version of the VHS model. The camera is easier to hold and use. You will need a special adapter to play the tape back on a standard VCR tape player.
Super VHS	A format that produces excellent picture and sound quality, but is very expensive to buy or rent. Super VHS cannot be played on a standard VCR tape machine.
Super VHSC	A compact version of Super VHS.
Video 8	A format sometimes referred to as a camcorder. The Video 8 shoots 8-millimeter videotape. It produces a good quality picture and high-fidelity sound. With special cable attachments, you can play the tape back through your VCR or television.
High 8	A compact and lightweight format. High 8 is substantially more expensive than Video 8, but the quality of sound and picture is excellent. High 8 video can be played back on a TV or VCR using special cable attachments.
Betacam	A professional standard video that delivers top-quality sound and picture. Most news crews shoot Betacam video. Betacam tape can only be played back on a Betacam tape deck.

Ideally you will have ironed out issues regarding shooting sequence when you wrote your production schedule back in the pre-production phase. This will leave you free during production to focus on your production values, your camera shots, and your actors' performances.

Production value is another way of describing the polish and professionalism of your finished project. There are many ways to increase the production value of your presentation. Some of the easiest include the following:

- Use a tripod to keep the camera steady. Nothing screams "Amateur!" louder than shaky, hand-held camera shots. If you can't get your hands on a tripod, lean against something sturdy, such as a tree or the side of a car, to keep your subjects from bouncing around in the frame.

- Use sufficient light. If your audience can't see what's happening, they will quickly lose interest in your show. The best way to light a subject is from one side at a 45-degree angle with the light shining in a downward direction. Supplement this with a slightly less powerful light from the other side and even from behind your subject to avoid unsightly shadows.
- Check your focus frequently. Don't wait until your entire production is nearly finished to check whether the shots are clear. Sometimes the manual focus on some cameras is more reliable than the auto-focus feature. Experiment with your camera using both methods *before* your shoot day to see which gives you the better result.
- Use an external microphone. The built-in microphone on the camera will only pick up sounds that are very close by. If you want to record sounds that are farther off, try using an external microphone that can plug into the video recorder. Poor sound quality can greatly diminish the production values of your video.

Next think about *how* you will shoot your video. One way to keep your production lively and interesting is to vary your camera shots. The next time you watch a television show or movie, keep a little notepad handy. Every time you notice a different camera move or cut, make a hash mark on your notepad. At the end of 15 minutes, count the hash marks. You may be amazed to find out how many shots were used!

To hold the interest of your audience, use a variety of camera shots, angles, and moves. Check your local library or media center for good books on camera techniques that describe when and how to use various shots—from long shots to close-ups, from low angles to overhead shots. As a rule, every time you change camera shots, change your angle slightly as well. This way, when the shots are edited together, you can avoid accidentally putting two nearly identical shots side-by-side, which creates an unnerving jarring motion called a "jump cut."

Do some research on framing techniques as well to make sure you frame your subjects properly and avoid cutting people's heads off on the screen. Also, try to learn about ways to move the camera in order to keep your audience interested.

For example, three common, but effective camera moves include panning, tracking, and zooming. **Panning** means moving the camera smoothly from one side of the scene to another. Panning works well in an establishing shot to help orient your audience to the setting where the action takes place.

Tracking means moving the camera from one place to another in a smooth action as well, but in tracking, the camera parallels the action, such as moving alongside a character as he or she walks down the street. It's called tracking because in professional filmmaking, the camera and the operator are rolled forward or backward on a small set of train tracks alongside the actor or actress.

Zooming means moving the camera forward or back, but zooming actually involves moving the lens, rather than the camera. By touching the zoom button, you can focus in on a small detail that you would like to emphasize, or you can pull back to reveal something in the background.

The important factor in any kind of camera move is to keep the action fluid and, in most cases, slow and steady. Also, use camera movement sparingly. You want to keep your audience eager and interested, not dizzy and sick!

Another good way to keep your presentation moving is to use frequent cuts. While the actual cuts will be done during post-production, you need to plan for them in production. Professional filmmakers use the word *coverage* for making sure they have ample choices for shots. You can create "coverage" for your production by planning shots such as the following:

Kinds of Video Shots

establishing shot	This shot sets up where the action of the story will take place. For example, if your story takes place inside an operating room, you might begin with an establishing shot of the outside of the hospital.

reaction shot	It's a good idea to get shots of all on-camera talent even if one person does not have any dialogue but is listening to, or reacting to, another character. This gives you the chance to break away from the character who is speaking to show how his or her words are affecting other people in the scene.
cutaway shot	The cutaway shot is a shot of something that is not included in the original scene, but is somehow related to it. Cutaways are used to connect two subjects. For example, the first shot may be of a person falling off a boat. The second shot could be a cutaway of a shark swimming deep below the water.

If you are adventurous, you may want to try some simple special effects. For instance, dry ice can create smoke effects. You can also have your actors freeze; then stop the camera, remove an object from the set, and restart the camera. This technique will make objects seem to disappear as if by magic. Other effects can be achieved using false backdrops, colored lights, and filters. Just use your imagination!

Post-Production—The Magic of Editing

Without access to a sound mixing board, it's difficult to do post-production on audio recordings. However, there's a vast amount of creative control you can have over your video project in post-production using your camera and your VCR.

Once all of your videotaping is complete, it's time to create the **final cut**—that is, your choice of the shots you wish to keep and the shots you wish to discard. The idea, of course, is to keep only your very best shots in the final production. Be choosy and select the footage with only the best composition, lighting, focus, and performance to tell your story.

There are three basic editing techniques:

in-camera editing	In this process you edit as you shoot. In other words, you need to shoot all your scenes in the correct sequence in the proper length that you want them to appear. This is the most difficult editing process because it leaves no margin for error.
insert editing	In insert editing you transfer all your footage to a new video. Then on your VCR you record over any scenes that you don't want with scenes that you do want in the final version.
assemble editing	This process involves electronically copying your shots from the original source tape in your camera onto a new blank tape, called the edited master, in the order that you want the shots to appear. This method provides the most creative control.

In the best scenario, it is ideal to have three machines at your disposal—the camera, a recording VCR for transferring images, and a post-production machine or computer program for adding effects. These effects might include a dissolve from one shot to another instead of an abrupt cut. A **dissolve** is the soft fading of one shot into another. Dissolves are useful when you wish to give the impression that time has passed between two scenes. A long, slow dissolve that comes up from black into a shot, or from a shot down to black, is called a **fade** and is used to open or close a show.

In addition to assembling the program, post-production is the time to add titles to the opening of your program and credits to the end of the show. Computer programs, such as Adobe Premiere, can help you do this. Some cameras are also equipped to generate titles. If you don't have any electronic means to produce titles, you can always mount your camera on a high tripod and focus it downward on well-lit pages of text and graphics placed on the floor. Then edit the text frames into the program.

Post-production is also the time to add voiceover narration and music. Voiceovers and background music should be recorded separately and then edited into the program on a separate sound track once the entire show is edited together. Video editing programs for your computer, such as Adobe Premiere, allow you to mix music and voices with your edited video. Some VCRs will allow you to add additional sound tracks as well.

After post-production editing, your video production is ready to present to your audience.

Publishing on the World Wide Web

The World Wide Web is an exciting part of the Internet where you can visit thousands of Websites, take part in online discussion groups, and communicate with other people all over the world via E-mail. You can also become a part of the exciting Web community by building and publishing a Website of your own.

Scoping Out Your Site

The Web is a unique medium with distinctive features that make it different from any other form of communication.
The Web offers

- universal access to everyone
- interactive communication
- the ability to use photos, illustrations, animation, sound, and video
- unlimited space
- unlimited branching capabilities
- the ability to link your site with other Websites

If you are going to publish on the Web, it makes sense to take advantage of all of these features. In other words, it's possible to take any written composition, save it in a format that can be displayed in a Web browser, upload it to a server, and leave it at that. Think about it, though: how interesting is it to look at a solid page of text on your computer screen?

Just like planning a video, you need to plan your Website. Don't just throw text and graphics together up on a screen. The idea is to make your site interesting enough that visitors will want to stay, explore, and come back to your site again—and that takes thought and planning.

Back to the Drawing Board

Again, you need to capture your thoughts and ideas on paper before you publish anything. Start with a one-page summary that states the purpose of your Website and the audience you hope to attract. Describe in a paragraph the look and feel you think your site will need in order to accomplish this purpose and hold your audience's attention.

Make a list of the content you plan to include in your Website. Don't forget to consider any graphics, animations, video, or sound you may want to include.

Next go on a World Wide Web field trip. Ask your friends and teachers for the URLs of their favorite Websites. (URL stands for Universal Resource Locator.) Visit these sites and bookmark the ones you like. Then ask yourself, "Do I like this site? Why or why not?" Determine which sites are visually appealing to you and why. Which sites are easy to navigate and why? Print out the pages you like best, and write notes on your reactions.

On the other hand, which sites are boring and why? Print out a few of these pages, and keep notes on how you feel about them. Chances are the sites you like best will have clean, easy-to-read layouts, be well written, contain visually stimulating graphic elements, and have intuitive **interfaces** that make it simple to find your way around.

One sure drawback in any Website is long, uninterrupted blocks of text. Scrolling through page after page of text is extremely boring. Plan to break up long passages of information into manageable sections. What will be the various sections of your site? Will there be separate sections for editorial content? news? humor? feedback? Which sections will be updated periodically and how often?

Pick up your drawing pencil and make a few rough sketches. How do you envision the "home" page of your site? What will the icons and buttons look like? Then give careful thought to how the pages will connect to each other, starting with the home page. Your plan for connecting the pages is called a **site map**.

Because the Web is an interactive medium, navigation is critical. Decide how users will get from one page to another. Will you put in a navigation bar across the top of the page or down the side? Will there be a top or home page at the beginning of each section?

Once you have planned the content, organized your material into sections, and designed your navigation system, you are ready to begin creating Web pages.

Planning Your Pages

In order to turn text into Web pages, you need to translate the text into a special language that Web browsers can read. This language code is called HTML—HyperText Markup Language. There are three methods available:

- You can use the Save As HTML feature in the File menu of most word-processing programs.
- You can import your text into a Web-building software program and add the code yourself if you know how.
- You can use a software program such as Adobe PageMill that does the work for you. Web-building software programs are referred to as WYSIWYG (pronounced "Wiz-E-Wig"), which stands for What You See Is What You Get.

Web-building software also allows you to create links to other Web pages using a simple process called **drag and drop.** Be sure to read the directions that come with your software package for complete instructions.

Putting It All Together

Writing for the Web is different from writing for print. The Web is a fast medium. It's about experiences, not study time, so write accordingly. Keep your messages succinct and to the point. Use short, punchy sentences. Break up your copy with clever subheads. Try not to exceed 500 to 600 words in any single article on any one page.

Compose your Web copy on a standard word-processing program. This will give you access to your formatting tools and spell-check features. Following the directions of your Web-building software, you can then import the completed text into the software program for placement on your Web page.

Next you will want to lay out your Web page and flow the text around some interesting graphics. Be sure to include blank space on the page as well. Blank space lets your page "breathe" and makes for a much more inviting experience.

You can use a variety of images on your Website including charts, graphs, photographs, clip art, and original illustrations. Collect graphics for the Web in exactly the same way you would get graphics for any desktop publishing project—scan in images, use a digital camera, or create your own graphics using a graphics software program.

It's also possible to add audio files and video files (referred to as QuickTime Video) to your Website. These are fun and interesting additions. However, there are two drawbacks—audio and video files are very time-consuming to prepare and take a long time for the user to load. Also, audio quality can be quite good on the Net, but full-motion video is still not at the broadcast-quality level most people have come to expect.

As an alternative to video, consider animated graphics. Animated graphics are much easier to create using graphics software programs. These programs also allow you to compress the animations so that they load much faster than video files and still run smoothly on screen.

If you would like to learn more about adding audio and video features, as well as graphics, to your Web pages, visit http://msc.pangea.org/tutorials/www/cap_5-eng.htm. For more information about adding other multimedia features, check out Plug-ins for Browsers at http://www.seidata.com/~city/reference/plugins/.

Going Live

Once all your pages are put together you are ready to go live on the World Wide Web, right? Not quite.

Before you upload your new Website, it's a good idea to test all your pages first, using common Web browsers such as Netscape Navigator or Microsoft Internet Explorer—browsers your visitors are likely to use. Open your pages on these browsers and look at them closely. Do the text and graphics appear the way you had designed them? Are all the page elements fitting neatly into the screen space, or do you need to tweak the copy or graphics a little to make them fit better?

Test all links on your page. Click on every page and be sure that it takes you to the site you originally intended. Click on all your navigation elements and buttons. Is everything working the way it's supposed to work? Make any corrections on your home or classroom computer before uploading your Website to a host server and going live to the world.

Your Web-building software program has built-in features that make uploading and adding files to your Website easy. In fact, some of this software is even available free on the Internet and is easy to download right onto your home or classroom computer.

For more information on how to build and launch your own Website, check the Web. You'll find some great tips at http://www.hotwired.com/webmonkey/kids.

This site even features a guided lesson plan called "Webmonkey for Kids" with step-by-step directions on how to create your own site. It also has information about useful software programs that schools and other educational institutions can download for free.

Here's one more shortcut to building a Website. If you or your school already has an Internet Service Provider (ISP), you may be entitled to a free Website as part of your service package. In fact, if you already have an E-mail address for correspondence, this address can be modified slightly and serve as the URL address of your Website. Call your ISP and ask about Website services included in your sign-up.

Finally, beware of small errors that can occur during the transmission of your Website material to the Web. As soon as you have finished uploading your Website, open your browser, enter the URL address, and take your new site out for a test drive. Click on all your navigational buttons, links, animations, or any other multimedia features. Check to make sure all the pages are there and everything looks the way you planned it.

Does everything check out? Great. Now all you have to do is send an E-mail to everyone you know and invite each person to visit your brand new Website!

A Writer's Guide to Using the Internet

The Internet is a global network of computers that are connected to one another with high-speed data lines and regular telephone lines. Anyone with a computer, a modem, and a telephone or cable line can be connected to it—just like you!

The idea of the Internet began in 1969 when a government agency called ARPA (Advanced Research Projects Agency) connected the computers of four universities together. They called this connection the ARPANET. It was used primarily to exchange research and educational information between scientists and engineers.

Gradually people outside the scientific community began to realize the potential of this tool. By 1980, the U.S. Department of Defense had created an early version of the Internet, and soon most universities and government agencies were using it too.

Up to this point, the information was not organized in any way. Imagine a library with thousands of books and no card catalog! The next challenge was to find a way to locate and access information quickly and efficiently. Over the next few years, several different search tools were proposed. The names of these systems included Archie, Jughead, and Veronica. If you haven't already guessed, these program names were inspired by the *Archie* comics.

One of the best search systems developed, and today the most widely used, is the World Wide Web. The Web is a network of computers *within* the Internet. This network is capable of delivering multimedia content—images, audio, video, and animation as well as text. Like the Internet, it comes over the same communication lines into personal computers worldwide, including yours!

How Does the Internet Work?

The Internet is made up of literally thousands of networks all linked together around the globe. Each network consists of a group of computers that are connected to one another to exchange information. If one of these computers or networks fails, the information simply bypasses the disabled system and takes another route through a different network. This rerouting is why the Internet is so valuable to agencies such as the U.S. Department of Defense.

No one "owns" the Internet, nor is it managed in a central place. No agency regulates or censors the information on the Internet. Anyone can publish information on the Internet as he or she wishes.

In fact, the Internet offers such a vast wealth of information and experiences that sometimes it is described as the *Information Superhighway*. So how do you "get on" this highway? It's easy. Once you have a computer, a modem, and a telephone or cable line, all you need is a connection to the Internet.

The Cyberspace Connection

A company called an Internet Service Provider (ISP) connects your computer to the Internet. Examples of ISPs that provide direct access are AT&T, Microsoft Network, Earthlink, MediaOne, and Netcom. You can also get on the Internet indirectly through companies such as America Online (AOL), Prodigy, and CompuServe.

ISPs charge a flat monthly fee for their service. Unlike the telephone company, once you pay the monthly ISP fee, there are no long-distance charges for sending or receiving information on the Internet—no matter where your information is coming from, or going to, around the world! Once you are connected to the Information Superhighway, all you have to do is learn how to navigate it.

Alphabet Soup—Making Sense of All Those Letters!

Like physical highways, the Information Superhighway has road signs that help you find your way around. These road signs are expressed in a series of letters that can seem confusing at first. You've already seen several different abbreviations so far—ARPA, ISP, AOL. How do you make sense out of all these letters? Relax. It's not as complicated as it looks.

Each specific group of information on the World Wide Web is called a **Website** and has its own unique address. Think of it as a separate street address of a house in your neighborhood. This address is called the URL, which stands for Uniform Resource Locator. It's a kind of shorthand for where the information is located on the Web.

Here's a typical URL: **http://www.bkschoolhouse.com.**

All addresses, or URLs, for the World Wide Web begin with **http://**. This stands for HyperText Transfer Protocol and is a programming description of how the information is exchanged.

The next three letters are easy—**www**—and they let you know you are on the World Wide Web. The next part of the URL—**bkschoolhouse**—is the name of the site you want to visit. The last three letters, in this case **com**, indicate that this Website is sponsored by a **com**mercial company. Here are other common endings of URLs you will find:

- "org" is short for organization, such as in http://www.ipl.org, which is the URL of the Website for the Internet Public Library.
- "edu" stands for education, as in the Web address for the Virtual Reference Desk, http://thorplus.lib.purdue.edu/reference/index.html, featuring online telephone books, dictionaries, and other reference guides.
- "gov" represents government-sponsored Websites, such as http://www.whitehouse.gov, the Website for the White House in Washington, D.C.

To get to a Website, you use an interface called a **browser.** Two popular browsers are Netscape Navigator and Microsoft Internet Explorer. A browser is like a blank form where you fill in the information you are looking for. If you know the URL of the Website you want to explore, all you have to do is type it in the field marked Location, click Enter on your keyboard, and wait for the information to be delivered to your computer screen.

There are many other ways to find information on the Web. We'll talk more about these methods later in this guide.

Basic Internet Terminology

Here are some of the most frequently used words you will hear associated with the Internet.

address The unique code given to information on the Internet. This may also refer to an E-mail address.

bookmark A tool that lets you store your favorite URL addresses, allowing you one-click access to your favorite Web pages without retyping the URL each time.

browser Application software that supplies a graphical interactive interface for searching, finding, viewing, and managing information on the Internet.

chat Real-time conferencing over the Internet.

cookies A general mechanism that some Websites use both to store and to retrieve information on the visitor's hard drive. Users have the option to refuse or accept cookies.

cyberspace The collective realm of computer-aided communication.

download The transfer of programs or data stored on a remote computer, usually from a server, to a storage device on your personal computer.

E-mail Electronic mail that can be sent all over the world from one computer to another. May also be short for Earth-mail because no paper (and no rainforest acreage) is involved.

FAQs The abbreviation for Frequently Asked Questions. This is usually a great resource to get information when visiting a new Website.

flaming	Using mean or abusive language in cyberspace. Flaming is considered to be in extremely poor taste and may be reported to your ISP.
FTP	The abbreviation for File Transfer Protocol. A method of transferring files to and from a computer connected to the Internet.
home page	The start-up page of a Website.
HTML	The abbreviation for HyperText Markup Language—a "tag" language used to create most Web pages, which your browser interprets to display those pages. Often the last set of letters found at the end of a Web address.
http	The abbreviation for HyperText Transfer Protocol. This is how documents are transferred from the Website or server to the browsers of individual personal computers.
ISP	The abbreviation for Internet Service Provider—a company that, for a fee, connects a user's computer to the Internet.
keyword	A simplified term that serves as subject reference when doing a search.
link	Short for Hyperlink. A link is a connection between one piece of information and another.
Net	Short for Internet.
netiquette	The responsible and considerate way for a user to conduct himself or herself on the Internet.
network	A system of interconnected computers.
online	To "be online" means to be connected to the Internet via a live modem connection.
plug-in	Free application that can be downloaded off the Internet to enhance your browser's capabilities.
real time	Information received and processed (or displayed) as it happens.
search engine	A computer program that locates documents based on keywords that the user enters.

server	A provider of resources, such as a file server.
site	A specific place on the Internet, usually a set of pages on the World Wide Web.
spam	Electronic junk mail.
surf	A casual reference to browsing on the Internet. To "surf the Web" means to spend time discovering and exploring new Websites.
upload	The transfer of programs or data from a storage device on your personal computer to another remote computer.
URL	The abbreviation for Uniform Resource Locator. This is the address for an Internet resource, such as a World Wide Web page. Each Web page has its own unique URL.
Website	A page of information or a collection of pages that is being electronically published from one of the computers in the World Wide Web.
WWW	The abbreviation for the World Wide Web. A network of computers within the Internet capable of delivering multimedia content (images, audio, video, and animation) as well as text over communication lines into personal computers all over the globe.

Why Use the Internet?

By the end of the 1990s, the Internet had experienced incredible growth. An estimated 196 million people were using the Internet worldwide, spending an average of 8.8 hours a week online. By 2003, this number is estimated to increase to more than 500 million people who will be surfing the Web. Why? What does the Internet offer that makes so many people want to go online? And what are the advantages of using the Internet for writers in particular?

The World at Your Fingertips

The answer is, the Internet offers an amazing amount of knowledge and experiences at the touch of your computer keyboard. For writers, it's a great way to get ideas and do in-depth research. You'll find thousands upon thousands of Websites offering a mind-boggling array of subjects. You can explore the Web as a way to jumpstart your creativity or tap into unlimited information.

The Internet also lets you communicate with experts that you might not otherwise have access to. In addition, you can connect with other people all over the world who have the same interests you do—maybe even find a new writing partner!

In short, the Internet is an invaluable tool for creating great writing. In the next section, we'll explore just some of the exciting advantages.

Just an E Away

One of the most popular features of the Internet is electronic mail, or E-mail for short. Unlike traditional mail (nicknamed "snail mail" by tech-savvy people), E-mail messages are practically instantaneous. It's so convenient that by 1999, 46 percent of Americans were sending or receiving E-mail every day.

E-mail is a fun and easy way to keep in touch with friends and relatives. You can send anything from a lengthy family newsletter to a quick question or "news flash." E-mail is also appropriate for formal correspondence, such as responding to a job opening and sending a résumé. In this case it's a good idea to follow up with hard copies in the traditional mail.

Have you ever teamed up with another student or a maybe a group of students in your class to work on a project together? With E-mail you can collaborate with other students in other states or even other countries. Many schools are taking advantage of E-mail to pair a class in say, San Jose, California, to work on a cooperative project with a class in New York City, or maybe one as far away as Sydney, Australia.

For writers, E-mail is an especially valuable tool. It's a great way to communicate with people who are experts in their fields. Many times well-known authorities, who are difficult to reach by phone or in person, will respond to questions and requests for information via E-mail. E-mail comes in particularly handy when the person you would like to communicate with lives in another part of the world. It eliminates the expense of long-distance phone calls and awkward problems due to different time zones.

An easy way to locate experts in a particular area is to visit Websites about that subject. Many times these Websites will list an E-mail address where you can send questions.

Another way writers can use E-mail is to gather information and make contacts. E-mail queries can be sent out to many people in a single click by simply adding multiple addresses to the same message. For example, suppose you are writing a paper about raising exotic birds. With one click you can send out an E-mail to 30 friends and associates that asks, "Do you know anyone who has an exotic bird?" Chances are at least a few of the people you ask will have one or two contacts they can provide—and think how much faster corresponding by E-mail is than making 30 phone calls!

You can learn more about sending E-mail on pages C738–C741.

Widening Your World

Your E-mail account also gives you access to **mailing lists**—discussion groups that use E-mail to exchange ideas. Subscribing to a mailing list is free and opens a floodgate of information about specific subjects that is sent directly to your E-mail box.

There are hundreds of lists to choose from, with topics ranging from animal rights to Olympic volleyball. Join a mailing list about the subject you are currently writing about, and it will net you dozens of messages about your topic every day. (Don't worry—you can always *un*subscribe at any time from these lists!)

A similar way to get information and contacts about a particular topic is through the Users Network, called Usenet for short. Usenet is the world's largest discussion forum, providing people with common interests the opportunity to talk to one another in smaller groups called **newsgroups.**

Like mailing lists, there are thousands of newsgroups you can join. Instead of receiving information via E-mail, newsgroups post articles and information on their sites. Subscribing to a newsgroup is like subscribing to a magazine. By visiting the newsgroup site, you can select which articles you wish to read. You can also reply to articles and discuss them with other people in the newsgroup to gather more ideas.

You can find out more about mailing lists and newsgroups on pages C742–C743.

 One **cautionary note** when surfing the Web:

- No matter how tempting, do not give out your name, address, telephone number, or school name to any site that may ask for this information.
- If you are interested in getting on a mailing list or joining a newsgroup, check with your teacher and/or your parents first.

Picture This

Whatever you write will probably have more impact if it is accompanied by some sort of visual. Many sites on the World Wide Web offer photos, illustrations, and clip art that can be downloaded and integrated into your work. Sometimes there are fees associated with this artwork, but many times it is free.

Another way to illustrate your writing is to take your own photos, turn them into electronic images, and integrate them into your work. One way to do this is to use a digital camera and download the images directly into your computer. If you don't have a digital camera, you can also take pictures using a regular camera. When you have the photos developed, ask the developer if you can have them returned to you either on disc or via E-mail.

Another option is to use a scanner, a device that looks somewhat like a copy machine. You place the photo on the glass, and the image is scanned into your computer.

Once you have an image in your computer, you can add it to a report or article in a number of ways—for example, on the cover page as a graphic or border design. There are even a number of photo-editing programs available that give you the ability to manipulate images in all sorts of creative ways.

Sometimes a graph or chart can help you illustrate your point more clearly than just text. Using a program such as Microsoft PowerPoint, you can create a myriad of graphs and tables that you can incorporate into your writing project for extra emphasis.

One of the best advantages of photos, charts, and artwork that are stored as electronic images is that you can also send them as E-mail attachments. Imagine—with a click of a button, you can:

- share photos of your last soccer game instantly with friends and relatives anywhere in the world;
- take your pen pals on a "virtual" tour of your home, school, or neighborhood;
- swap pictures and graphs with writing partners in other classrooms across the globe and double your resources.

Online Help

You're working on a paper for your Shakespeare class. You come across the phrase, "Thou craven rough-hewn maggot-pie" in the text. Huh? Find out all about how to make sport of someone using Shakespearean language at The Shakespearean Insult Server at http://www.alabanza.com/kabacoff/Inter-Links/sgi/bard.cgi.

This is only one of hundreds of Websites that can help you with specific subjects you are probably studying right now. These sites cover a variety of topics in English, history, math, science, foreign languages, and more. Here's just a sample of some of the sites waiting to help you.

- How to Be a Web Hound! (http://www.mcli.dist.maricopa.edu/webhound/index.html)
- The Guide to Grammar and Writing (http://webster.commnet.edu/HP/pages/darling/grammar.htm)
- The Math Forum—featuring interesting math challenges and the whimsical "Ask Dr. Math" (http://forum.swarthmore.edu/students)
- MapQuest—type in your starting point and destination and get exact mileage and directions (http://www.mapquest.com)
- The Guide to Experimental Science Projects (http://www.isd77.k12.mn.us/resources/cf/SciProjInter.html)

- The Human Languages Page—gateways to foreign-language resources on the Web (http://www.june29.com/HLP/)
- The Smithsonian Institution—featuring links to sites ranging from Aeronautics to Zoology (http://www.si.edu)
- The Perseus Project—*the* online resource for studying the ancient world (http://www.perseus.tufts.edu/)
- Education Index—a guide to useful educational Websites (http://www.educationindex.com/)
- Up Your Score—the underground guide to scoring well on the SAT (http://www.workmanweb.com/upyourscore/)
- My Homework Helpers/My Virtual Reference Desk (http://www.refdesk.com/homework.html)
- The Writing Center (http://researchpaper.com/writing.html)

The Internet also offers free programs and services that can be of use to writers. For example, sometimes valuable articles are available in a format called PDF, which stands for Portable Document Format. In order to view this kind of document, you must have software called the Adobe Acrobat Reader. You can download this software free of charge by visiting the Adobe Website at http://www.adobe.com.

Fun and Games

Many people enjoy the fun side of the Internet's personality. A vast number of Websites offer news, entertainment, online games, and adventures in shopping (often referred to as **e-commerce)**.

While these areas may not seem to be related to writing, if the topic you are working on crosses into the realm of news or the entertainment industry, a gold mine of material awaits you. Then again, maybe a quick game is just what you need to shake off a touch of writer's block!

Don't Believe Everything You Read

Wow, all this terrific information—just a click away. There's only one problem: Not all of it is credible or accurate.

When you check out a book from the library, a librarian or a committee of educators has already evaluated the book to make sure it's a reliable source of information, but remember, no one owns or regulates the Internet. Just because you read something online, doesn't mean it's true. How can you tell the difference? Here are a few guidelines on how to evaluate an online source.

- **Play the name game**
  First, find out who publishes the site. Does the URL end in ".com" (which means it's a commercial company)? If so, is it a large, reputable company, or one you've never heard of that might just be trying to sell you something? An educational site in which the URL ends in ".edu," such as a college or university, might be a more reliable choice. A site sponsored by a well-known organization (with a URL that ends in ".org"), such as the American Red Cross (http://www.crossnet.org), would also probably be a credible source.
- **Scope it out**
  Click around the site and get a feel for what it's like. Is the design clean and appealing? Is it easy to navigate the site and find information? Are the sections clearly labeled? Does the site accept advertising? If you think the site seems disjointed or disorganized, or you just have a negative opinion of it, listen to your instincts and move on to another one.
- **Says who?**
  Suppose you find an article on the Web that seems chock-full of great information. The next question you need to ask yourself is, Who is the author? Is the person an acknowledged expert on the subject? If you don't recognize the author's name, you can send a question to a newsgroup asking if anyone knows about the person. You can also do a search on the Web, using the author's name as the keyword, to get more information about him or her.

In some cases, an article won't list any author at all. If you don't find an author's name, be skeptical. A credible site clearly identifies its authors and usually lists the person's professional background and his or her credentials.

- **Is this old news?**
  If you are doing research on the Roman Empire, it's probably all right if the information wasn't posted yesterday. But if you're looking for information in quickly changing fields, such as science and politics, be sure to check the date of publication before you accept the data as true.
- **Ask around**
  Reliable Websites frequently provide E-mail addresses or links to authors and organizations connected to the content on the site. Send off a quick E-mail to one of these sources, tell them what you are writing, and ask them: Is this material accurate?

Perhaps the best way to find out if the information on any Website or the information in any article (signed or unsigned) is accurate is to check it against another source—and the best source is your local library or media center.

Internet + Media Center = Information Powerhouse!

Although the Internet is a limitless treasure chest of information, remember that it is not catalogued, so it can be tricky to locate the information you need, and sometimes that information is not reliable. The library is a well-organized storehouse of knowledge, but it has finite resources. If you use the Internet in *conjunction* with your local media center, you have everything you need to create well-researched articles, reports, and papers.

Use the Internet to

- get great ideas for topics to write about;
- gather information about your topic from companies, colleges and universities, and professional organizations;
- connect with people who are recognized experts in your field of interest;
- connect with other people who are interested in the same subject and who can provide you with information or put you in touch with other sources.

Use the Media Center to

- find additional sources of information either in print or online;
- get background information on your topic;
- cross-check the accuracy and credibility of online information and authors.

I Don't Own a Computer

You can still access the Internet even if you don't have your own computer. Many schools have computer labs that are open after school and on weekends. Some schools will even allow students to use these labs even though they are not enrolled at that particular school. Many libraries are also equipped with computers and Internet connections.

Consider taking a computer course after school or even attending a computer camp. You'll find information about these programs listed at the library, the YMCA, and in parenting magazines.

Last, maybe you have a friend or neighbor with a computer that you can use in exchange for a service you might provide, such as baby-sitting or yard work.

How to Communicate on the Internet

E-mail, mailing lists, and newsgroups are all great ways of exchanging information with other people on the Internet. Here's how to use these useful forms of communication, step-by-step.

Keep in Touch with E-mail

Any writer who has ever used E-mail in his or her work will agree that sending and receiving electronic messages is one of the most useful ways of gathering information and contacts for writing projects. It's fast, inexpensive, and fun!

Once you open your E-mail program, click on the command that says Compose Mail or New Message. This will open a new blank E-mail similar to the one pictured below. Next, fill in the blanks.

Type the person's E-mail address here. There is no central listing of E-mail addresses. If you don't have the person's address, the easiest way to get it is to call and ask the person for it. You can address an E-mail to one or several people, depending on the number of addresses you type in this space.

CC stands for *courtesy copy*. If you type additional E-mail addresses in this area, you can send a copy of the message to other people.

BCC stands for *blind courtesy copy*. By typing one or more E-mail addresses here, you can send a copy of the message to others without the original recipient knowing that other people have received the same message. Not all E-mail programs have this feature.

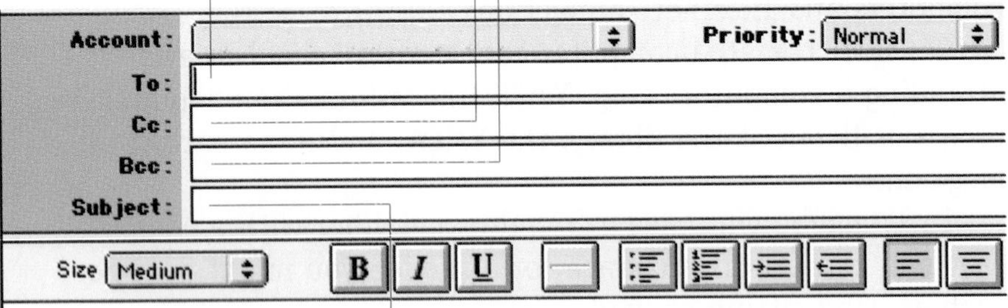

This is where you type your message.

This is called the subject line. Write a few brief words that best describe what your E-mail message is about.

Say It with Style

Like regular letters, E-mail can assume different tones and styles, depending on to whom you are writing. Usually informal E-mails, such as instant messages (IMs) to close friends, are light, brief, and to the point. In the case of more formal E-mails, such as a request for information from an expert or a museum, it's important to keep the following guidelines in mind.

- Make sure your message is clear and concise.
- Use proper grammar and punctuation.
- Check your spelling. (Some E-mail programs have their own spell-check function—use it!)
- Double-check the person's E-mail address to be sure you've typed it correctly.

Because E-mail is a fast medium designed for quick communication, E-mail users have developed a kind of shorthand that helps them write their messages even faster. Here are a few commonly used abbreviations that you may find in informal E-mail.

COMMON E-MAIL ABBREVIATIONS

BRB	be right back	BTW	by the way
FYI	for your information	F2F	face-to-face
HAND	Have a nice day	J/K	just kidding
IMHO	in my humble opinion	IOW	in other words
LOL	laughing out loud	L8R	later
OIC	Oh, I see	ROFL	rolling on the floor laughing
WU	What's up?		

IMHO, TBC RTTR ETU, FWIW!
(*Translation:* In my humble opinion, the best conversations are those that are easiest to understand, for what it's worth!)

Are you sending the E-mail to a friend or relative? If so, would you like to add a touch of fun? Then you may want to explore **emoticons** (also know as "smileys")—little faces turned sideways made out of keyboard symbols that you add to your messages to express how you feel about something.

EMOTICONS			
:)	happy	:(	sad
:-D	laughing	:`-(	crying
;-)	winking	:-}	smirking
:-0	shocked	:-/	skeptical
:-#	my lips are sealed	*<|:-)	Santa Claus
:s	confused	:<>	bored
8)	I'm wearing glasses	B)	I'm wearing sunglasses/shades

Attach a Little Something Extra

When you send E-mail, you can also send other information along with your message. These are called **attachments**. Depending on your E-mail program's capabilities, you can attach documents, photos, illustrations—even sound and video files. Click Attach, and then find and double-click on the document or file on your computer that you wish to send.

After you have composed your message and added any attachments you want to include, click the Send button. Presto! Your message arrives in the other person's mailbox seconds later, regardless of whether that person lives right next door or on the other side of the world. Because there is usually no charge to send E-mail, it's a great way to save money on postage and long-distance telephone calls.

Follow Up

It's important to note, however, that just because you have sent a message, you shouldn't automatically assume that the other person has received it. Internet Service Providers (ISPs) keep all messages that are sent until the recipient requests them. The person you sent your E-mail to might be away from his or her computer or may not check messages regularly.

Also, the Internet is still an imperfect science. From time to time, servers go down or other "hiccups" in electronic transmissions can occur, leaving your message stranded somewhere in cyberspace. If you don't get a reply in a reasonable amount of time, either resend your original E-mail message or call the person and let him or her know that your message is waiting.

You've Got Mail

When someone sends *you* an E-mail message, you have several options:

Reply:	Click Reply, and you can automatically send back a new message without having to retype the person's E-mail address. (Be sure you keep a copy of the sender's E-mail address in your Address Book for future use.)
Forward:	Suppose you receive a message that you would like to share with someone else. Click Forward, and you can send a copy of the message, plus include a few of your own comments, to another person.
Print:	In some instances, you may need to have a paper copy of the E-mail message. For example, if someone E-mails you directions to a party, click Print to take a hard copy of the instructions with you.
Store:	Do you want to keep a message to refer to later? Some E-mail programs allow you to create folders to organize stored messages.
Delete:	You can discard a message you no longer need just by clicking Delete. It's a good idea to throw messages away regularly to keep them from accumulating in your mailbox.

Care to Chat?

Another way to communicate online is Internet Relay Chat (IRC), or "chat rooms" for short. Chat rooms focus on a large variety of topics, so it's possible you'll be able to find a chat room where people are discussing the subject you are writing about.

"Chat" is similar to talking on the telephone except, instead of speaking, the people in the chat room type their responses back and forth to each other. As soon as you type your comment, it immediately appears on the computer screen of every person involved in the "conversation." There are also more advanced forms of chat available on the Net, such as 3-D chat and voice chat.

To participate in a chat room, you'll need to invent a nickname for yourself. This name helps to identify who is speaking, yet allows you to remain anonymous. Everyone uses a made-up name in chat rooms (like Zorro, Twinkle, Venus, or Elvis), so don't make the mistake of believing that people really are who their name says they are!

To get started, you will need a special program for your computer. Two sites that offer this program free of charge include mIRC program (http://huizen.dds.nl/~mirc/index.htm) and Global Chat (http://www.prospero.com/globalchat).

One last word about chat rooms: While they are a great way to meet and communicate with other people, the anonymous nature of a chat room can make people less inhibited than they might otherwise be in person. If you sense that one of the participants in your chat room is responding inappropriately, ask your parents or teacher to step in, or simply sign off.

Join the Group

Mailing lists and newsgroups are larger discussion forums that can help you get even more information about a specific subject.

Mailing Lists

To find a directory of available mailing lists, check out http://www.neosoft.com/internet/paml. If you find a mailing list that interests you and wish to subscribe to it, just send a message to the administrative address. You will start to receive messages from the mailing list within a few days.

Remember, mailing lists use E-mail to communicate, so be sure to check your E-mail often because once you subscribe to a list, it's possible to receive dozens of messages in a matter of days. In fact, it's a good idea to unsubscribe from mailing lists whenever you go on vacation. Otherwise, you might come home to a mailbox stuffed to overflowing with messages!

Another good idea is to read the messages in your new mailing list for a week or so before submitting a message of your own. This will give you a good idea of what has already been discussed so you can be considerate about resubmitting old information.

You can reply to a message any time you wish. However, it doesn't do anyone any good to respond by saying, "Yes, I agree." Get in the habit of replying to messages only when you have something important to add. Also, be sure to repeat the original question in your reply so that people understand which message you are responding to.

Be sure that you really want to belong to a mailing list before you subscribe. Unwanted E-mail can be a nuisance. Fortunately, if you change your mind, you can always unsubscribe to mailing lists at any time.

Newsgroups To join a newsgroup, check with your ISP. Service providers frequently list available topics under the heading "Newsgroups." Another way to find a newsgroup about a topic you want to research is to visit Deja News at http://www.dejanews.com on the World Wide Web.

Newsgroups are named with two or more words separated by a period. For example, there is a newsgroup named rec.sport.baseball.college. The first three letters—"rec"—defines the main subject, in this case *recreation*. Each word that follows—*sport, baseball,* and *college*—narrows the scope of the subject to an increasingly more specific area of interest.

As with mailing lists, you can always unsubscribe to newsgroups at any time.

Mind Your Manners!

As in any social setting, there are a few guidelines to follow when you are talking to people online—via E-mail, in a chat room, or in a newsgroup. This conduct is called **netiquette.** The following suggestions will help you be considerate of others in cyberspace.

E-mail and Chat

- Never use harsh or insulting language. This is called **flaming** and is considered rude. A continuing argument in which derogatory words are swapped back and forth is called a **flamewar**. Avoid this situation.

- Type your messages using uppercase and lowercase letters. WRITING IN ALL CAPITAL LETTERS IS DIFFICULT TO READ AND IS REFERRED TO AS "SHOUTING."
- Respect other people's ideas and work. Don't forward a message or attach documents written by someone else without first asking the author's permission.
- Don't send spam. **Spamming** refers to sending messages to entire lists of people in your address book, on mailing lists, or in newsgroups for the purpose of selling something.
- Respect other people's privacy. The Internet is an enormous public forum, so be careful what you write and post on the Internet that hundreds or thousands of people might see. Don't use the Internet to spread rumors or gossip.

Newgroups

- Read the articles in a newsgroup for 7 to 10 days before posting articles yourself. No one in a newsgroup wants to read the same article twice.
- Make sure the article you are proposing is appropriate to the subject of the newsgroup.
- If you are going to post an article, be sure you express the title clearly in the subject heading so readers will know what the article is about.
- Read the FAQ (Frequently Asked Questions) so you can avoid repeating a question that has already been discussed.

How to Do Research on the Internet

The Information Superhighway could be the best research partner you've ever had. It's fast, vast, and always available. But like any other highway, if you don't know your way around, it can also be confusing and frustrating. This is particularly true of the Internet because the sheer volume of information often can be intimidating.

In this section we'll explore ways to help you search the Web effectively. Be patient. It takes time to learn how to navigate the Net and zero in on the information you need. The best thing to do is practice early and often. Don't wait until the night before your term paper is due to learn how to do research on the Internet!

Getting Started

Just as there are several different ways to get to your home or school, there are many different ways to arrive at the information you're looking for on the Internet.

CD-ROM Encyclopedia One way to begin is not on the Web at all. You might want to start your search by using a CD-ROM encyclopedia. These CD-ROMs start with an Internet directory. Click the topic that is closest to your subject. This will link you to a site that's likely to be a good starting point. From there, you can link to other resources suggested in the site.

Search Page Another good way to get information is to use your browser's search page.

Search Tools There are several different free search services available that will help you find topics of interest by entering words and phrases that describe what you are searching for. Just some of these tools, sometimes referred to as **search engines,** include:

- AltaVista—http://www.altavista.com
- Excite—http://www.excite.com
- HotBot—http://www.hotbot.com
- InfoSeek—http://www.infoseek.com
- Lycos—http://www.lycos.com
- WebCrawler—http://www.webcrawler.com
- Yahoo!—http://www.yahoo.com

Search services usually list broad categories of subjects; they may also offer other features, such as "Random Links" or "Top 25 Sites," and customization options. Each one also has a search field. Type in a word or short phrase, called a **keyword**, which describes your area of interest. Then click Search or the Enter key on your keyboard. Seconds later a list of Websites known as "hits" will be displayed containing the word you specified in the search field. Scroll through the list and click the page you wish to view.

So far this sounds simple, doesn't it? The tricky part about doing a search on the Internet is that a single keyword may yield a hundred or more sites. You may also find many topics you don't need. For example, suppose you are writing a science paper about the planet Saturn. If you type the word *Saturn* into the search field, you'll turn up some articles about the planet, but you'll also get articles about NASA's Saturn rockets and Saturn, the automobile company.

Search Smart!

Listed below are a few pointers on how to narrow your search, save time, and search *smart* on the Net.

1. The keyword or words that you enter have a lot to do with the accuracy of your search. Focus your search by adding the word

and or the + sign followed by another descriptive word. For example, try Saturn again, but this time, add "Saturn + space." Adding a third word, "Saturn + space + rings," will narrow the field even more.

2. On the other hand, you can limit unwanted results by specifying information that you do *not* want the search engine to find. If you type "dolphins not football," you will get Websites about the animal that lives in the ocean rather than the football team that lives in Miami.
3. Specify geographical areas using the word "near" between keywords as in "islands near Florida." This lets you focus on specific regions.
4. To broaden your search, add the word "or" between keywords; for example, "sailboats or catamarans."
5. Help the search engine recognize familiar phrases by putting words that go together in quotes such as "Tom and Jerry" or "bacon and eggs."
6. Sometimes the site you come up with is in the ballpark of what you are searching for, but it is not exactly what you need. Skim the text quickly anyway. It may give you ideas for more accurate keywords. There might also be links listed to other sites that are just the right resource you need.
7. Try out different search engines. Each service uses slightly different methods of searching, so you may get different results using the same keywords.
8. Check the spelling of the keywords you are using. A misspelled word can send a search engine in the wrong direction. Also, be careful how you use capital letters. If you capitalize the word *Gold,* some search services will only bring up articles that include the word with a capital *G*.

Pick a Category

Another way to search for information is by using subject directories. Many of the search engines on the Web provide well-organized subject guides to a variety of handpicked Websites. On the next page, you can see what a sample subject-tree directory looks like on Yahoo! under the topic "Food Safety."

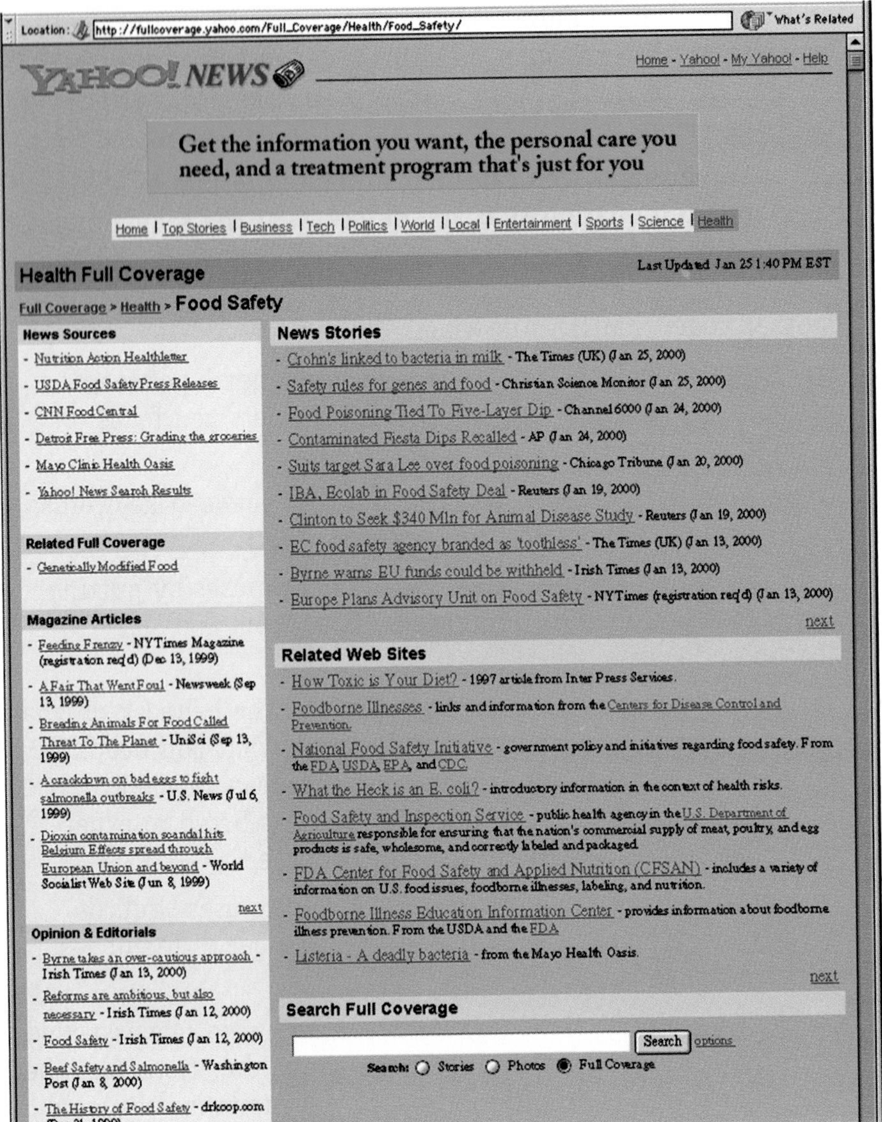

Saving a Site for Later

You may want to keep a list handy of favorite Websites or sites you are currently using in a project. This will save you time because you can just click on the name of the site in your list and return to that page without having to retype the URL.

Different browsers have different names for this feature. For example, Netscape calls it a **bookmark**, while Microsoft Internet Explorer calls it **favorites**.

Searching Out a Subject

Suppose you are writing a paper about the unique role computer-generated special effects play in today's blockbuster motion pictures. Here's an idea of one way to research this topic.

First, we'll select a search engine. We'll start with WebCrawler—at http://www.webcrawler.com. The first keywords we enter are "computer generated graphics." The search engine found these sites:

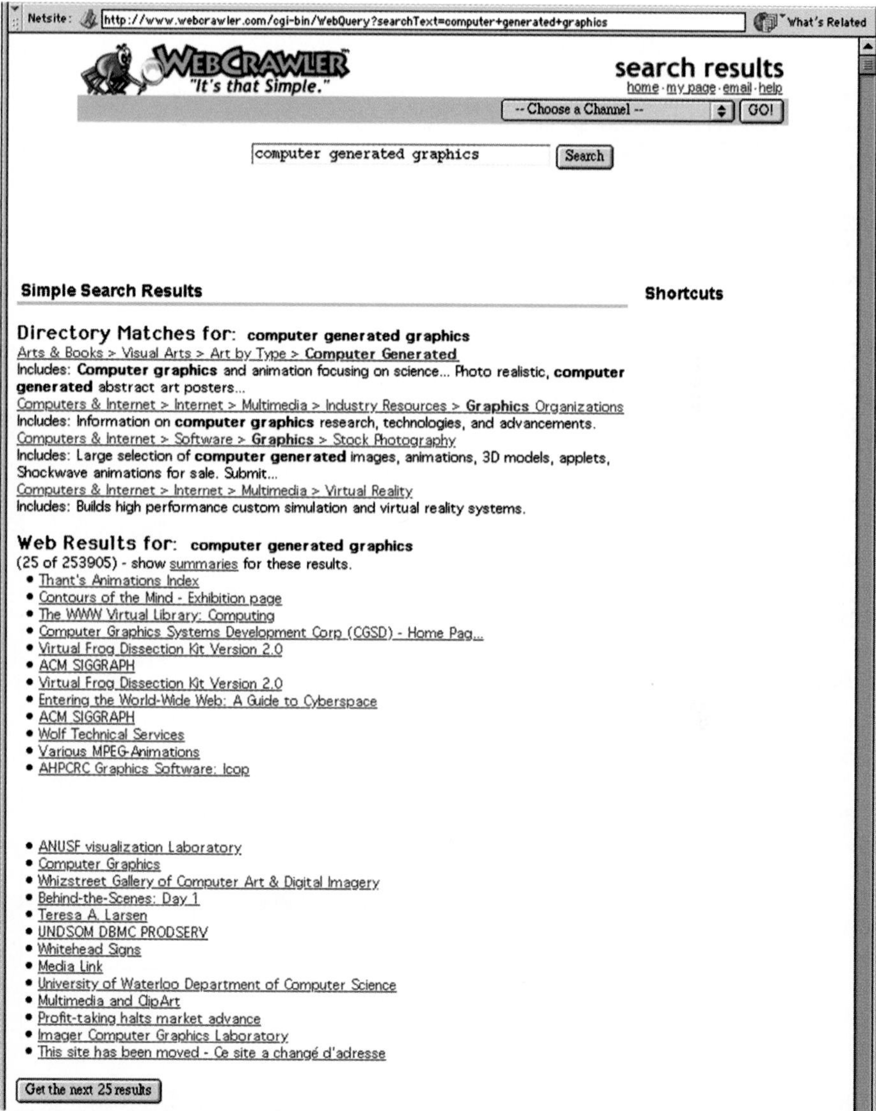

No good. Few sites on this list seem to mention special effects or computer graphics. Let's narrow the search. We'll try again, but this time we'll enter the keywords "computer generated effects + films." Now look at the list of topics:

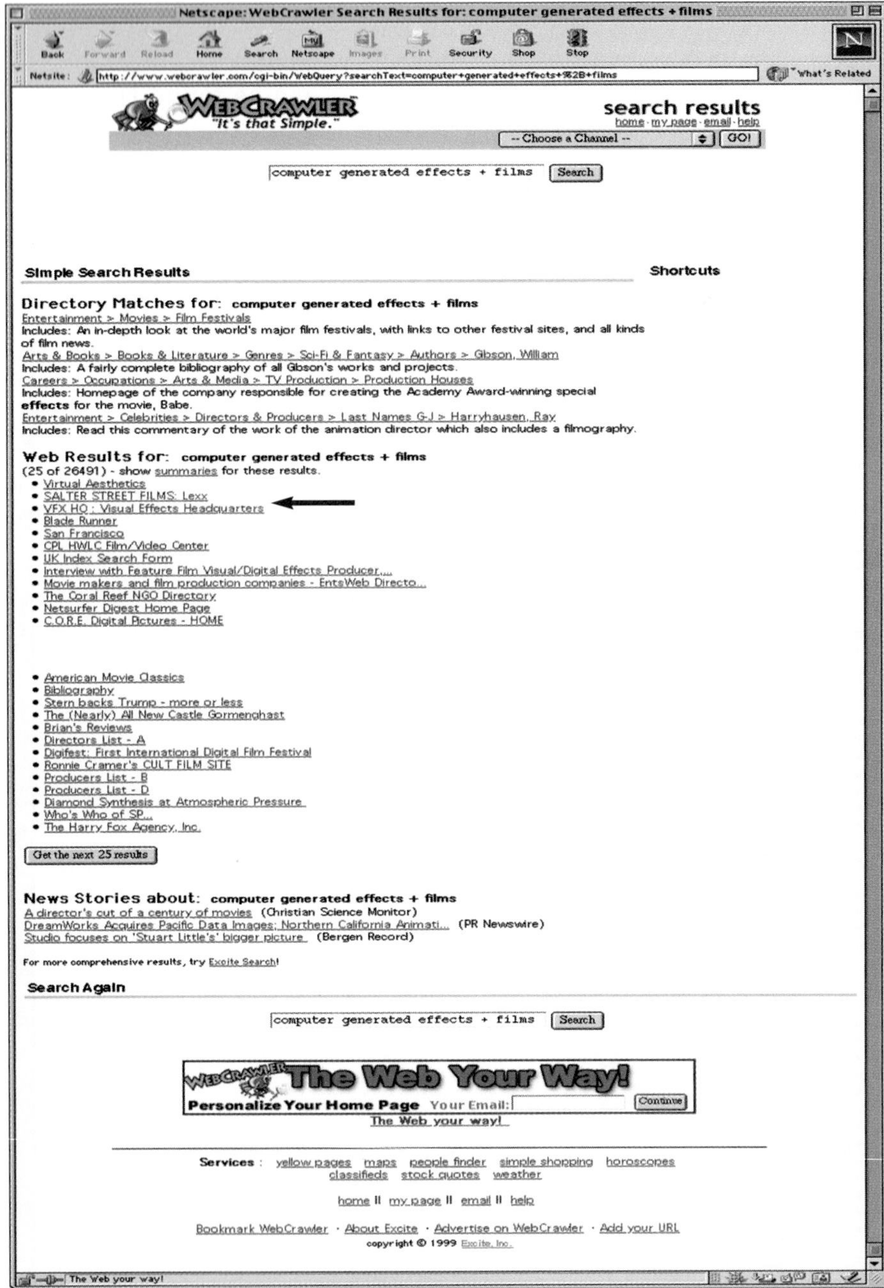

As you can see, there are many more choices to pick from. We'll click Visual Effects Headquarters Archive.

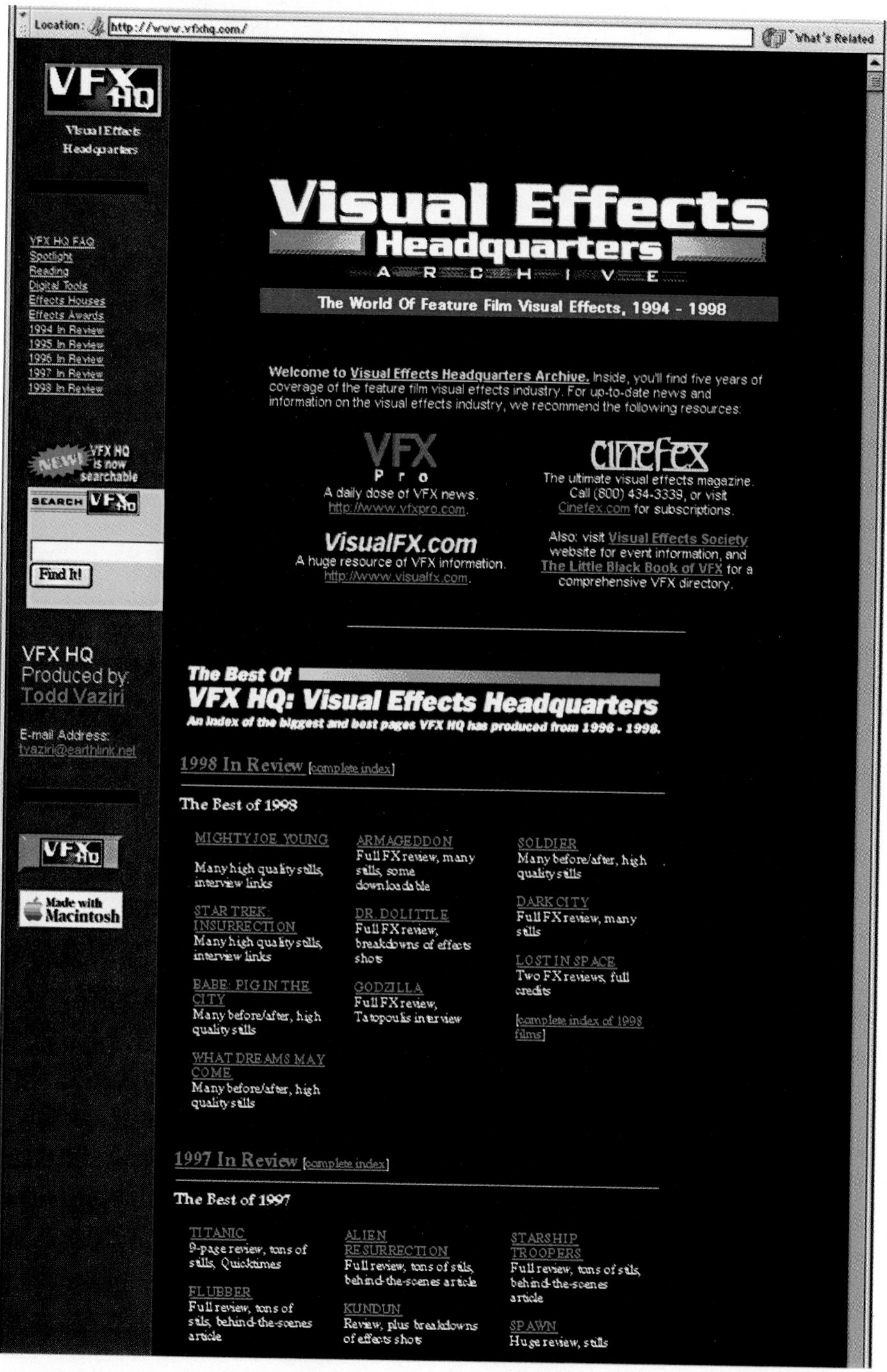

VFX HQ produced by Todd Vaziri . . . http://www.vfxhq.com . . . email tvaziri@earthlink.net.
All text Copyright ©Todd Vaziri, unless otherwise noted.

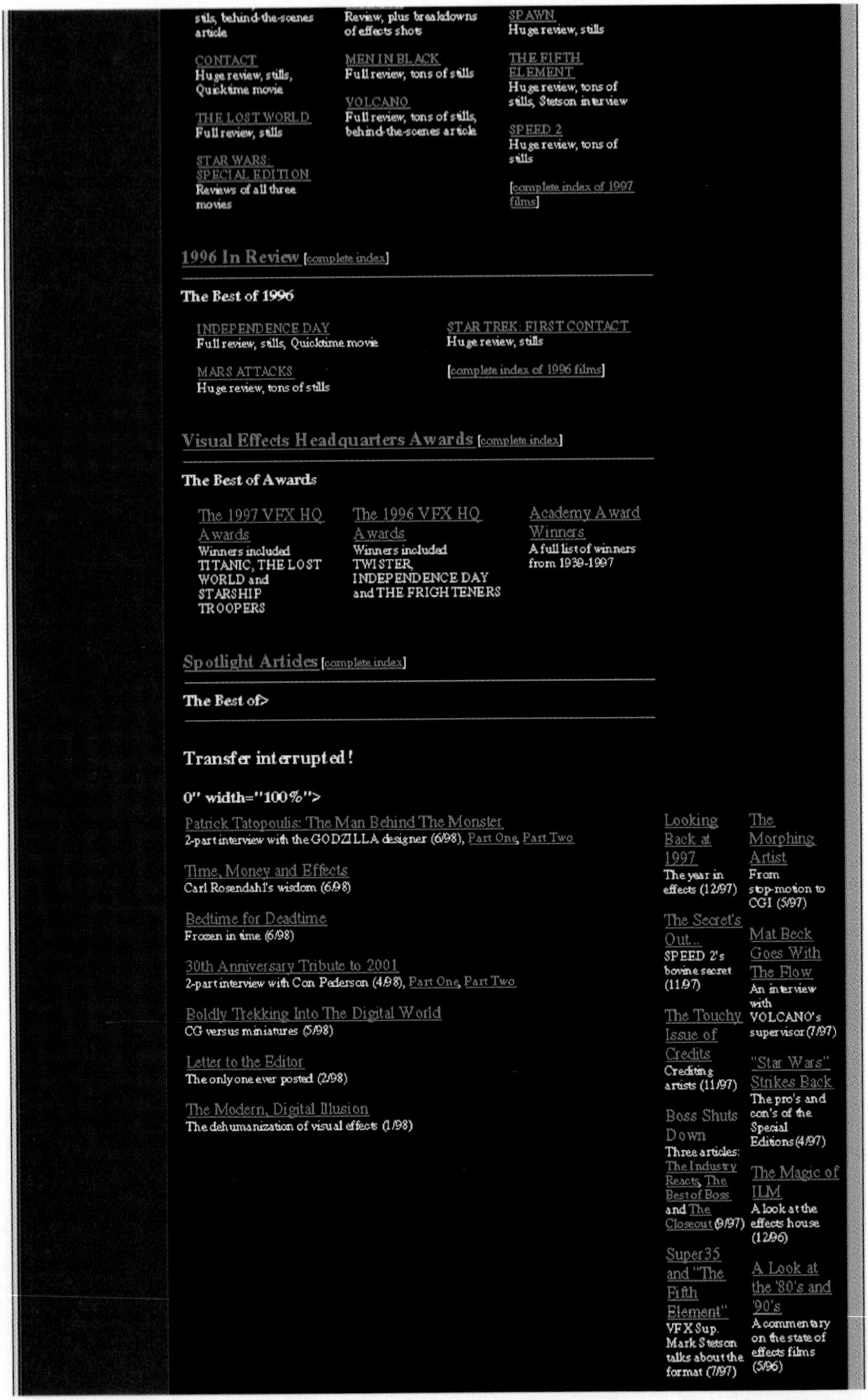

stills, behind-the-scenes article

CONTACT
Huge review, stills, Quicktime movie

THE LOST WORLD
Full review, stills

STAR WARS: SPECIAL EDITION
Reviews of all three movies

Review, plus breakdowns of effects shots

MEN IN BLACK
Full review, tons of stills

VOLCANO
Full review, tons of stills, behind-the-scenes article

SPAWN
Huge review, stills

THE FIFTH ELEMENT
Huge review, tons of stills, Stetson interview

SPEED 2
Huge review, tons of stills

[complete index of 1997 films]

1996 In Review [complete index]

The Best of 1996

INDEPENDENCE DAY
Full review, stills, Quicktime movie

MARS ATTACKS
Huge review, tons of stills

STAR TREK: FIRST CONTACT
Huge review, stills

[complete index of 1996 films]

Visual Effects Headquarters Awards [complete index]

The Best of Awards

The 1997 VFX HQ Awards
Winners included TITANIC, THE LOST WORLD and STARSHIP TROOPERS

The 1996 VFX HQ Awards
Winners included TWISTER, INDEPENDENCE DAY and THE FRIGHTENERS

Academy Award Winners
A full list of winners from 1939-1997

Spotlight Articles [complete index]

The Best of>

Transfer interrupted!

0" width="100%">

Patrick Tatopoulis: The Man Behind The Monster
2-part interview with the GODZILLA designer (6/98), Part One, Part Two

Time, Money and Effects
Carl Rosendahl's wisdom (6/98)

Bedtime for Deadtime
Frozen in time (6/98)

30th Anniversary Tribute to 2001
2-part interview with Con Pederson (4/98), Part One, Part Two

Boldly Trekking Into The Digital World
CG versus miniatures (5/98)

Letter to the Editor
The only one ever posted (2/98)

The Modern, Digital Illusion
The dehumanization of visual effects (1/98)

Looking Back at 1997
The year in effects (12/97)

The Secret's Out...
SPEED 2's bovine secret (11/97)

The Touchy Issue of Credits
Crediting artists (11/97)

Boss Shuts Down
Three articles: The Industry Reacts, The Best of Boss and The Closeout (9/97)

Super35 and "The Fifth Element"
VFX Sup. Mark Stetson talks about the format (7/97)

The Morphing Artist
From stop-motion to CGI (5/97)

Mat Beck Goes With The Flow
An interview with VOLCANO's supervisor (7/97)

"Star Wars" Strikes Back
The pro's and con's of the Special Editions (4/97)

The Magic of ILM
A look at the effects house (12/96)

A Look at the '80's and '90's
A commentary on the state of effects films (5/96)

VFX HQ produced by Todd Vaziri . . . http://www.vfxhq.com . . . email tvaziri@earthlink.net.

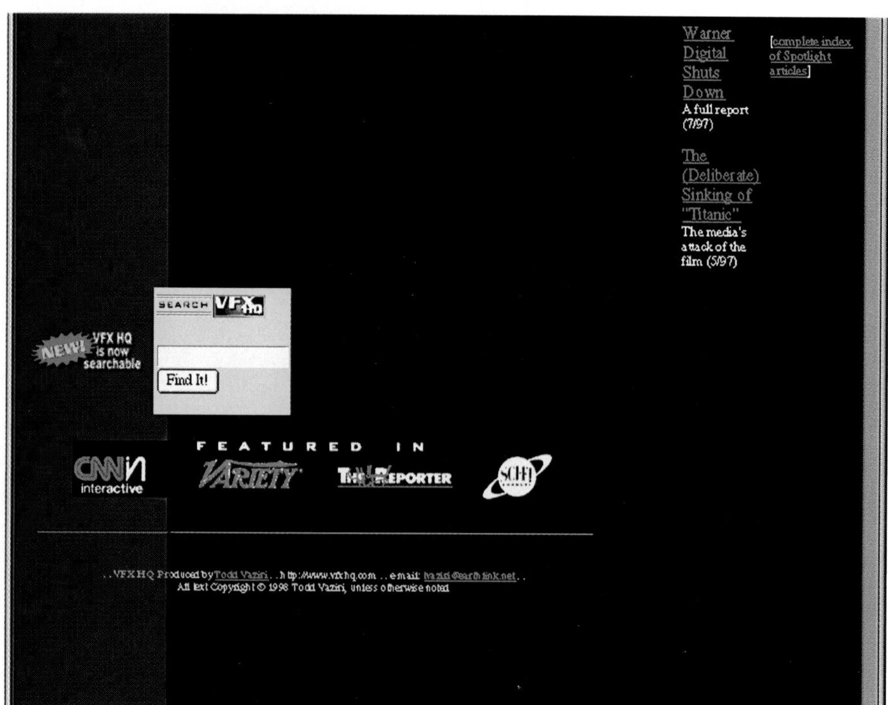

VFX HQ produced by Todd Vaziri . . . http://www.vfxhq.com . . . email tvaziri@earthlink.net.
All text Copyright ©Todd Vaziri, unless otherwise noted.

Wow—look at all these articles about computer-generated effects in well-known movies! Let's click "Babe, Pig in the City."

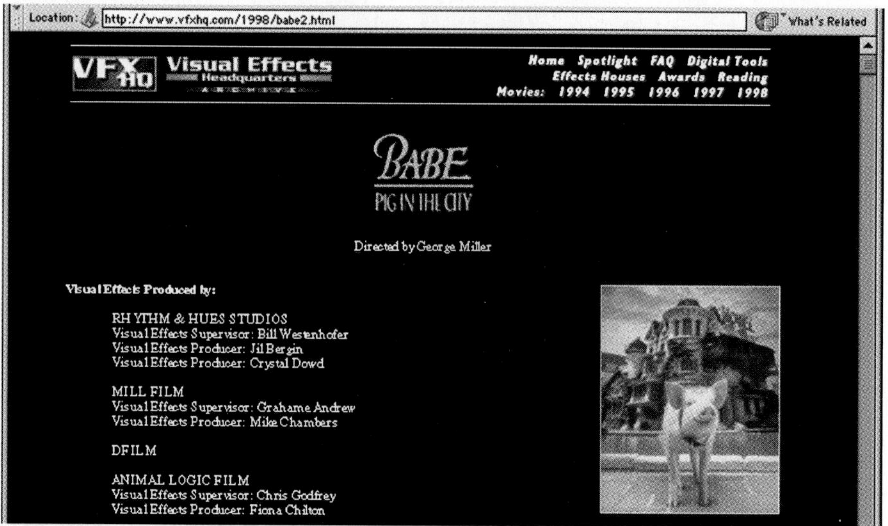

VFX HQ produced by Todd Vaziri . . . http://www.vfxhq.com . . . email tvaziri@earthlink.net.
All text Copyright ©Todd Vaziri, unless otherwise noted.

Animatronics by NEAL SCANLAN STUDIO

[credits not complete]

Even more talking animals are featured in BABE: PIG IN THE CITY, sequel to 1995's highly successful BABE. The original won an Academy Award for Best Visual Effects in 1995, and Mill Film, Rhythm & Hues, and Animal Logic contributed to the visual effects to the sequel.

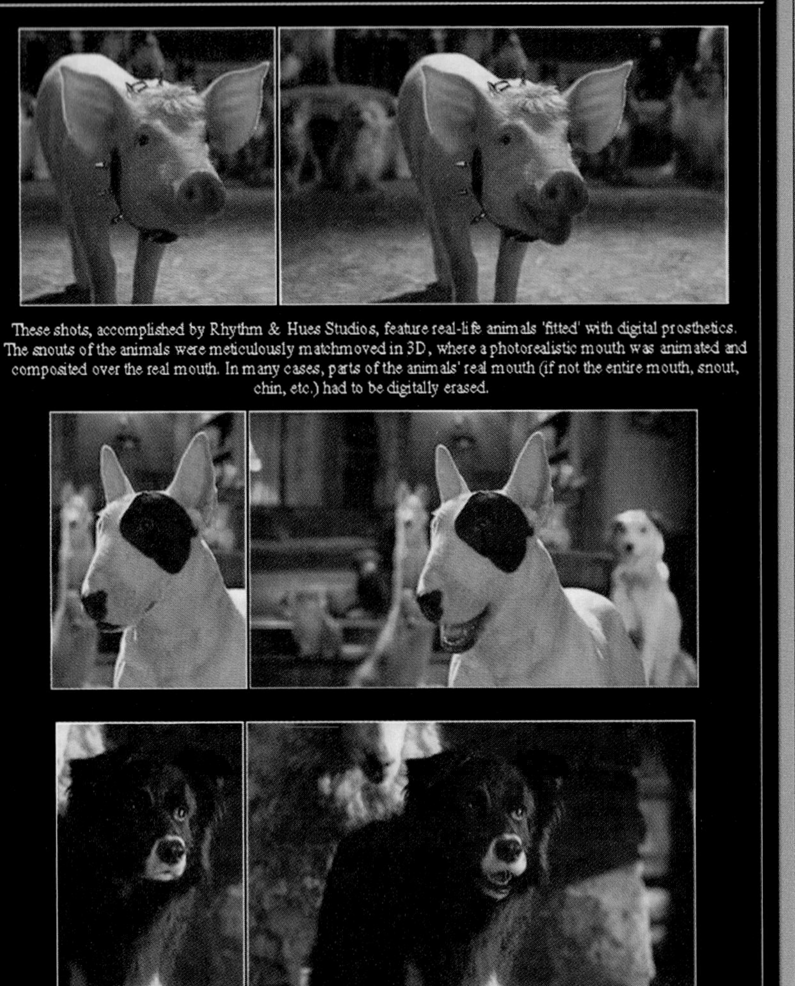

These shots, accomplished by Rhythm & Hues Studios, feature real-life animals 'fitted' with digital prosthetics. The snouts of the animals were meticulously matchmoved in 3D, where a photorealistic mouth was animated and composited over the real mouth. In many cases, parts of the animals' real mouth (if not the entire mouth, snout, chin, etc.) had to be digitally erased.

Official Web Site: http://www.babeinthecity.com

Back to the 1998 Menu

VFX HQ Visual Effects Headquarters

Home Spotlight FAQ Digital Tools
Effects Houses Awards Reading
Movies: 1994 1995 1996 1997 1998

. . VFX HQ Produced by Todd Vaziri . . http://www.vfxhq.com . . email tvaziri@earthlink.net . .

VFX HQ produced by Todd Vaziri . . . http://www.vfxhq.com . . . email tvaziri@earthlink.net.

There's some interesting information here about how they made the animals appear to speak using computer effects. We might also want to incorporate some of these fun pictures of the talking pig into our finished project. Again, more interesting information about how computer-generated effects contributed to the making of the film. For now, let's click the Back button and return to the Visual Effects Headquarters Archive to check out another film—*Godzilla*.

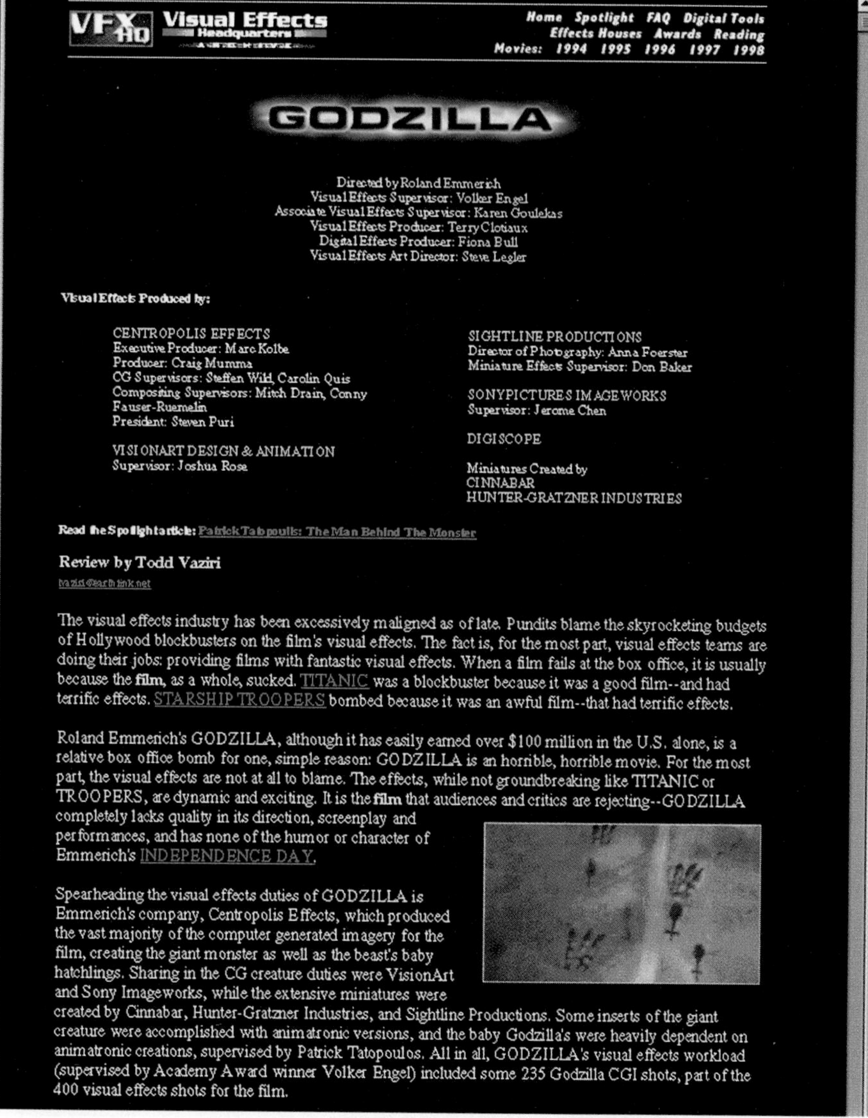

VFX HQ Visual Effects Headquarters

Home Spotlight FAQ Digital Tools
Effects Houses Awards Reading
Movies: 1994 1995 1996 1997 1998

GODZILLA

Directed by Roland Emmerich
Visual Effects Supervisor: Volker Engel
Associate Visual Effects Supervisor: Karen Goulekas
Visual Effects Producer: Terry Clotiaux
Digital Effects Producer: Fiona Bull
Visual Effects Art Director: Steve Legler

Visual Effects Produced by:

CENTROPOLIS EFFECTS
Executive Producer: Marc Kolbe
Producer: Craig Mumma
CG Supervisors: Steffen Wild, Carolin Quis
Compositing Supervisors: Mitch Drain, Conny Fauser-Ruemelin
President: Steven Puri

VISIONART DESIGN & ANIMATION
Supervisor: Joshua Rose

SIGHTLINE PRODUCTIONS
Director of Photography: Anna Foerster
Miniature Effects Supervisor: Don Baker

SONY PICTURES IMAGEWORKS
Supervisor: Jerome Chen

DIGISCOPE

Miniatures Created by
CINNABAR
HUNTER-GRATZNER INDUSTRIES

Read the Spotlight article: Patrick Tatopoulis: The Man Behind The Monster

Review by Todd Vaziri
tvaziri@earthlink.net

The visual effects industry has been excessively maligned as of late. Pundits blame the skyrocketing budgets of Hollywood blockbusters on the film's visual effects. The fact is, for the most part, visual effects teams are doing their jobs: providing films with fantastic visual effects. When a film fails at the box office, it is usually because the **film**, as a whole, sucked. TITANIC was a blockbuster because it was a good film--and had terrific effects. STARSHIP TROOPERS bombed because it was an awful film--that had terrific effects.

Roland Emmerich's GODZILLA, although it has easily earned over $100 million in the U.S. alone, is a relative box office bomb for one, simple reason: GODZILLA is an horrible, horrible movie. For the most part, the visual effects are not at all to blame. The effects, while not groundbreaking like TITANIC or TROOPERS, are dynamic and exciting. It is the **film** that audiences and critics are rejecting--GODZILLA completely lacks quality in its direction, screenplay and performances, and has none of the humor or character of Emmerich's INDEPENDENCE DAY.

Spearheading the visual effects duties of GODZILLA is Emmerich's company, Centropolis Effects, which produced the vast majority of the computer generated imagery for the film, creating the giant monster as well as the beast's baby hatchlings. Sharing in the CG creature duties were VisionArt and Sony Imageworks, while the extensive miniatures were created by Cinnabar, Hunter-Gratzner Industries, and Sightline Productions. Some inserts of the giant creature were accomplished with animatronic versions, and the baby Godzilla's were heavily dependent on animatronic creations, supervised by Patrick Tatopoulos. All in all, GODZILLA's visual effects workload (supervised by Academy Award winner Volker Engel) included some 235 Godzilla CGI shots, part of the 400 visual effects shots for the film.

VFX HQ produced by Todd Vaziri . . . http://www.vfxhq.com . . . email tvaziri@earthlink.net.

Much has been said and written about the incessant rain that obscures the giant creature in its New York setting. While the addition of rain to these night shots obscures some artifacts and allows artists to 'get away' with more, it also complicates the CG process, since the creature must appear to be rain-soaked in nearly every scene. Looking at the entire film, the most satisfying Godzilla shots are those where he is completely visible, in daylight, with the camera not moving. Godzilla's first appearance in a New York's harbor featured plenty of daylight (albiet overcast) shots of the giant monster--beginning with tight shots of his massive foot smashing cars, and ending with his dazzling confrontation with cameraman Hank Azaria, where Godzilla is fully revealed. Early shots of the sequence contained terrific matchmoving--the real camera and the CG camera were perfectly in synch--and the interaction between the CG creature and the real-life elements, like cars and people, was very convincing. Careful attention to shadows and extensive rotoscoping of foreground elements allowed these sequences to be successful, although the lack of motion blur on the creature frequently hurt CG shots.

The mutated lizard wanders its way through New York City. The CGI Godzilla was created by newly formed Centropolis Effects. Only a handful of shots of the title creature were completed with animatronic versions of the beast.

The subsequent full-body shots of Godzilla confronting Azaria are brilliant, especially because of the kinetic camera movement. The director was able to use as many dollys and cranes as he wanted, and the CG and compositing teams were able to place the creature realistically within the scene. The best shot of the sequence is a terrific rotational camera move around Azaria as Godzilla approaches his position. Once again, lighting and rotoscoping of these shots make them successful.

Less successful is the design and texture of Godzilla. A monster movie's main creature needs to have character--something inherent to the design of the beast that lends an idea as to its character, its emotions, its desires. TROOPERS' bugs, JURASSIC PARK's dinosaurs, even T2's T-1000 all have some visual characteristics that give us a glimpse of what drives them. Godzilla looks like a man in a lizard suit, plainly and simply. This is not only due to the design, but the choreography and direction of the Godzilla sequences. There seems to be no rhyme or reason to his movements; the audience subsequently cares very little about this creature.

Not to be forgotten are some of the film's non-lizard effects shots. The very best of which is the fantastic helicopter shot of the beached tanker found on the Panamanian coast. From the POV of a hovering helicopter, the camera rotates around the massive liner, perched on the sandy shores of the beach. The shot is incredible--the CG boat is perfectly lit and matchmoved into the scene, even with the bouncy nature of the helicopter-shot background plate. The subsequent bluescreen shot of Matthew Broderick staring at the clawprint on the hull of the ship is less successful, due to the widly varying contrast levels of that shot, relative to the rest of the sequence.

"...the compositing of the creature into the backgrounds make these effects shots look like... well... effects shots."

Speaking of helicopters, they're all over GODZILLA. Flying overhead, helicopter POVs, even in the distant background, there are dozens upon dozens of shots involving the compositing of CG and model helicopters

VFX HQ produced by Todd Vaziri . . . http://www.vfxhq.com . . . email tvaziri@earthlink.net.

into background plates. The most convincing shots are those where the camera is on the ground, slightly drifting to follow the path of the choppers. The most obvious are those where the helicopters fly only a few feet away from the camera, in situations where no real camera could possibly photograph the action. Overall, textures and lighting of the helicopters are quite realistic.

As these choppers pursue Godzilla through the streets of New York, the camera weaves down city streets. The CG creature and (mainly) CG helicopters were composited into background plates of miniature cityscapes, and although these shots are exciting, they do not look photorealistic. The lights from buildings' windows are far too bright and have an unnatural glow, and the compositing of the creature into the backgrounds make these effects shots look like... well... effects shots. The miniatures for the film, overall, are quite fantastic--the best of which appear in daylight shots, where miniature buildings are destroyed right and left with the accurate appearance of scale.

As revealed by a massive panning shot of the Madison Square Garden interior, Godzilla has laid hundreds of eggs. The reveal shot, realized with extensive miniatures, looks muddy and blurry, while subsequent shots of the Garden interior are much more successful. (An earlier version of this review incorrectly stated that a matte painting was used for the reveal shot. VFX HQ regrets the error.) The hatchlings were executed with a combination of animatronic and CG techniques, and the visual differences between them is obvious. Many of the CG baby shots seemed rushed--lighting, animation and compositing are sometimes brilliant, integrating the raptors--ahem, lizards into their background plates, and at other times awful, as if the CG elements were cut and pasted into plates without concern to shadows, reflections, or color levels. There are a ton of baby Godzilla shots, and only half of them achieve the realistic integration of CG element and background plate as such films as JURASSIC PARK and STARSHIP TROOPERS.

"It's too bad that director Emmerich and producer Dean Devlin couldn't have done a better job creating the non-effects shots."

The single best Godzilla sequence occurs after his 'resurrection'--his chase of our heroes, fleeing in a NYC cab, as Godzilla pursues them. Although one must suspend disbelief heavily for the sequence to work (as if big 'G' couldn't smash the cab with one swoop of his foot), the scene displays the best animation, lighting, and compositing of any other of the film. The Brooklyn Bridge sequence is perhaps more complicated than it has to be, with the bridge disintegrating around Godzilla, poles and supports flying all over the place. The eventual destruction of the beast isn't particularly interesting, with explosions obviously composited over and behind big 'G'.

The few effects' shortcomings aside, the effects teams did a terrific job on GODZILLA. It's just too bad that director Emmerich and producer Dean Devlin couldn't have done a better job creating the non-effects shots.

Check out **Cinefex 74**.
Official Web Site: http://www.godzilla.com
GODZILLA ©1998 Tri-Star Pictures

VFX HQ produced by Todd Vaziri . . . http://www.vfxhq.com . . . email tvaziri@earthlink.net.

One more time, let's go back to Visual Effects Headquarters Archive, but this time, we're going to scroll down to the bottom of the page. Here, they have links to more than a dozen articles about effects and the movie industry. Let's try "The Magic of ILM."

The Magic of ILM
By Todd Vaziri

If you've visited the Effects Houses section of the VFX HQ, you have seen over a dozen of the biggest names in visual effects. Every house listed creates great images for today's feature films. Although parity of the industry exists, there is a definitive leader of the pack: Lucas Digital's Industrial Light & Magic (ILM).

Effects technology has become much cheaper over the years, and the capital it takes to start a new company has slowly been shrinking. Software like Softimage is now available to the consumer market, and SGIs are becoming a bit more affordable. Also, the talent pool seems to be getting larger as universities train students on valuable animation software.

VFX HQ produced by Todd Vaziri . . . http://www.vfxhq.com . . . email tvaziri@earthlink.net.

Amidst all of the competition, ILM remains on top. They have the experience, the creativity, the tools, the history and the power to work on high profile shows and consistently perform well. The folks who built ILM pioneered the use of many techniques that are commonplace today. Think of how important CG imagery is in today's films. Where did feature film's use of CG begin? The most significant step in CG, in my opinion, was 1982's STAR TREK II: THE WRATH OF KHAN, whose dramatic Genesis simulation was an entirely computer generated sequence, the first of its kind. The group that worked on the sequence at ILM later separated from LucasArts and became a company called Pixar, whose TOY STORY represented yet another huge step in CG animation.

The Pixar example is just one of many arms of ILM's far-extending reach. Nearly every respected effects veteran is or was connected to ILM. The president of Sony Pictures Imageworks, Ken Ralston, spent almost two decades at ILM. Richard Edlund, who was integral to the effects of STAR WARS founded his own company, Boss Film Studios. Phil Tippett, the go-motion innovator, did the same and is currently running Tippett Studios. Digital Domain was founded by three men, all of which had serious relationships with ILM; James Cameron worked with ILM on THE ABYSS and T2, Stan Winston collaborated with them on JURASSIC PARK and T2, and Scott Ross was ILM's general manager.

The past ten years have been extraordinary for ILM in terms of the shows on which they've worked. (Never mind the fact that ILM provided effects for such blockbusters as E.T., RAIDERS OF THE LOST ARK, the STAR WARS trilogy, etc.) Since 1987, ILM has earned seven out of nine Academy Awards for visual effects. Just like other effects houses, ILM must prove its worth during the negotiations period--productions do not simply hand off their project to ILM blindly. Take TWISTER, for example. Director Jan DeBont and producer Steven Spielberg needed to be convinced that a CG tornado would work on film, or else the picture wouldn't have been made at all. The ILM test team was led by effects veteran Dennis Muren, and consisted of fx producer Kim Bromley, animator Dan Taylor, and CG artists Scott Frankel, Carol Hayden, Stewart Lew and Scott Frankel. The test was overwhelmingly successful--you may have even seen it. It was so fantastic, Warner Bros. attached it to the end of the teaser and trailer for the film.

The continuing power of ILM is also due to the snowball effect. ILM revolutionized effects in 1977, they get more high-profile, big-budget projects, ILM grows, the tools and resources expand, ILM gets more big-budget projects, ILM expands its talent, ILM gets another $80 million movie, etc.

ILM has brought about effects revolutions; techniques such as the morph and CG creation and animation were used effectively in their shows. They successfully graduated from the optical world to the digital world. Just look at the compositing in MISSION: IMPOSSIBLE and TWISTER. It is impeccable.

High profile, risky projects are nothing new to ILM. No matter what imagery is presented before them in a screenplay--not even if the technology isn't available yet--the effects house comes through with stunning results. A mysterious water tentacle? "We can do that (THE ABYSS)." Fully computer generated dinosaurs? "We can do that (JURASSIC PARK)." A chase scene with a virtual helicopter, a virtual train and a virtual tunnel? "We can do that (MISSION: IMPOSSIBLE)." They are constantly given the impossible and achieve it.

Owner George Lucas has crafted the company into an image factory. Easily the largest of all the effects houses, ILM is sometimes criticized for its 'assembly line' attitude in creating visual effects. No matter how ILM runs its business, they are at the top of their game.

The effects industry should be very proud of itself right now. Fantastic images are being created by the big companies, like ILM and Digital Domain, as well as other companies like Boss Film and Rhythm & Hues. But ILM is the heart of the industry--they are the most consistent effects house in terms of quality and quantity of images. The company is synonymous with special effects because of its rich history and continually expanding resources and talent.

Back to the Spotlight Main Menu

VFX HQ produced by Todd Vaziri . . . http://www.vfxhq.com . . . email tvaziri@earthlink.net.

This article is more about the history of the company, ILM, than it is about how computer-generated effects are used in movies. Let's drill down a little farther. Inside this article is some hot type on *Star Wars*. The *Star Wars* movies introduced some amazing advances in computer-generated effects. This might be a good place to investigate.

VFX HQ Visual Effects Headquarters

Home Spotlight FAQ Digital Tools
Effects Houses Awards Reading
Movies: 1994 1995 1996 1997 1998

SPECIAL THE STAR WARS TRILOGY EDITION

STAR WARS EPISODE IV

THE EMPIRE STRIKES BACK EPISODE V

RETURN OF THE JEDI EPISODE VI

The legendary effects films of the STAR WARS trilogy are being re-released in 1997, and George Lucas and Lucas Digital's Industrial Light & Magic have spent most of their efforts giving the original STAR WARS: A NEW HOPE an enormous face-lift. Fox invested $15 million into the restoration project, and ILM has been working on the Special Editions since the middle of 1994. Many original sequences, especially from Episode Four, have been reconstructed and produced with the latest in digital tools. Their goal was to give the STAR WARS trilogy a new life, consistent with the visual effects to which a new generation of film audiences are accustomed.

- STAR WARS: THE SPECIAL EDITION
- THE EMPIRE STRIKES BACK: THE SPECIAL EDITION
- RETURN OF THE JEDI: THE SPECIAL EDITION

Read the VFX HQ News Article: STAR WARS Strikes Back
Check out **Cinefex 69**.
Check out **American Cinematographer Feb. '97 and Apr. '97**.
Official Web Site: http://www.starwars.com

Back to the 1997 Menu

VFX HQ Visual Effects Headquarters

Home Spotlight FAQ Digital Tools
Effects Houses Awards Reading
Movies: 1994 1995 1996 1997 1998

..VFX HQ Produced by Todd Vaziri..http://www.vfxhq.com..email: tvaziri@earthlink.net..
All text Copyright © 1998 Todd Vaziri, unless otherwise noted.

VFX HQ produced by Todd Vaziri . . . http://www.vfxhq.com . . . email tvaziri@earthlink.net.
All text Copyright ©Todd Vaziri, unless otherwise noted.

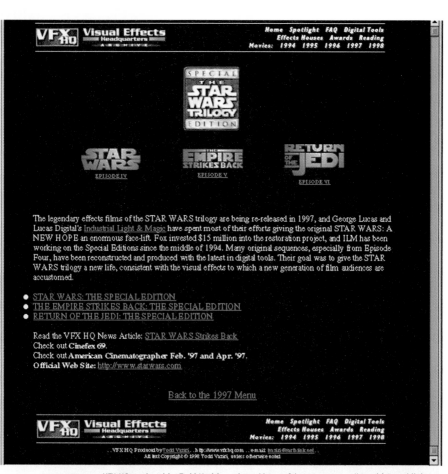

Again, still no specific information. Let's keep drilling. We'll click The Star Wars Trilogy: Special Edition.

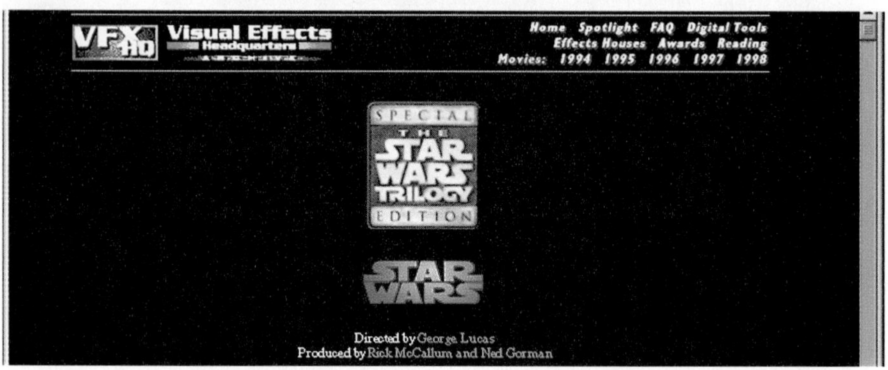

VFX HQ produced by Todd Vaziri . . . http://www.vfxhq.com . . . email tvaziri@earthlink.net.
All text Copyright ©Todd Vaziri, unless otherwise noted.

INDUSTRIAL LIGHT & MAGIC
Visual Effects Supervisors: Dave Carson, John Knoll, Steven Williams, Bruce Nicholson and Alex Seiden
Visual Effects Producer: Tom Kennedy
Visual Effects Consultant: Dennis Muren
CG Supervisors: Joe Letteri and John Berton

The impetus of the STAR WARS project was the desire to restore of the classic film for its 20th Anniversary. Lucas and Fox jumped at the chance to re-release all three films in grand fashion, adding and enhancing certain visual effects shots.

Certain effects shots from the film have been completely replaced using digital technology, while others use original photography as plates for brand new background and foreground elements. With a few exceptions, the new and enhanced shots fit seamlessly into the classic sci-fi flick.

The first of the brand new shots is a gorgeous establishing shot of R2D2 on Tatooine, just before the Jawas capture him. The shot begins on a stunning Tatooine sky at dusk, and tilts down to the lonely droid navigating the Tatooine surface.

In addition to the new R2 establishing shot, two more new 'replacement' establishing shots were made for Obi-Wan's home and Luke's moisture farm. The 1977 Obi-Wan establishing shot was an odd, nondescript, low angle of Luke's speeder parked outside a hut. This new shot is very wide and beautiful, featuring a lot of great colors and textures of the Tatooine surface. A slight zoom was added to the shot--if the artists had created a dolly-in instead of a zoom, the shot wouldn't have fit into the film. If you look carefully at the original film, there are very few dynamic camera movements, like cranes and dollys. The other establishing shot is an extended wide shot of Luke's farm. Using the original 1977 shot, the artists shrunk the footage, and added more sky, more of the Jawa's cruiser and more of Luke's farm in this breathtaking shot.

An isolated shot of the new CG Dewback and CG Stormtrooper. The background plate is a new shot, photographed in Yuma, AZ. Notice the slight highlight added to the trooper's helmet, consistent with the filters used back in 1977 for Tatooine scenes.

A CG Stormtrooper dismounts from a CG Dewback in this enhanced shot. The animation of the Trooper getting off the beast is phenomenal.

The first shot of the search sequence features real Stormtroopers and the synthetic Dewback and trooper in the background, along with an Imperial craft zooming across the sky.

Searching for the C3PO and R2D2, Imperial Stormtroopers use Dewbacks to help in the search. Originally, the scene consisted of a single shot of a Stormtrooper on an unmoving Dewback far in the distance--then the camera pans left to two troopers in the foreground. The sequence is now three shots long, with two brand new shots using newly shot Stormtrooper footage in Yuma, Arizona (the original photography took place in Tunisia). The two brand new shots feature fully computer generated Dewbacks with CG Stormtroopers riding them. The CG models look great, and the compositing of these two shots have the same 'look' as the original 1977 photography. The last shot is the 1977 pan, but instead of the immobile Dewback in the distance, we now see fully mobile CG Dewbacks and Stormtroopers. The CG elements and plate photography are perfectly married together.

A great new tigher shot of the Jawa's land cruiser is included in the Special Edition, replacing a very long, wide shot of the same cruiser.

Many of Luke's landspeeder shots (around 6 in all) have been 'fixed'--the orange optical blur underneath the floating speeder from the 1977 version has been erased and a new shadow was created.

VFX HQ produced by Todd Vaziri . . . http://www.vfxhq.com . . . email tvaziri@earthlink.net.

The enhanced landspeeder shots (4 in all) add the illusion of the floating craft.

This enhanced shot features a man walking a Ronto (frame left) and the elimination of the orange distortion pattern underneath the floating landspeeder.

A speeder-bike nearly hits a Ronto as its Jawa riders get flung off the beast in this all-new shot from the Mos Eisley sequence.

Luke, Obi-Wan Kenobi and the two droids then venture off to Mos Eisley, Tatooine's bustling spaceport. The new Mos Eisley sequences feature both completely brand new shots as well as many brilliant enhanced shots.

The first is a brand new wide shot of the spaceport--the view that Obi-Wan and the gang sees as Kenobi calls it "a wretched hive of scum and villany." Spacecraft can be seen zooming in and out of the port, and the buildings look a lot more dense in this great establishing shot.

The landspeeder zooms over the camera into the city in another replacement shot. Instead of a blank sandy surface, many tiny creatures are seen hanging around the city--the Mos Eisley equivalent of pigeons. The design is very cute and the animation is really nice as the landspeeder zooms overhead, although it was quite apparent that the effect was accomplished in post-production. The contrast levels seemed a bit too high--the animals didn't seem as if they were actually in front of the camera.

The hero shot of the sequence appears next, as a completely new shot begins on two fighting droids, follows the landspeeder with a pan right, and cranes up, dozens of feet above the ground, allowing the audience to see the large, bustling city for the first time. The animation of the two droids (one a human-like droid and the other a floating probe droid) is fanatstic and quite funny. Numerous CG elements made up the shots, along with many digital matte paintings and miniatures. Although the shot technically and aesthetically brilliant, it simply does not fit into STAR WARS. The establishing crane shot is a standard in many films, but the 1977 version of STAR WARS had very little camera movement.

The hero shot of the sequence appears next, as a completely new shot begins on two fighting droids, follows the landspeeder with a pan right, and cranes up, dozens of feet above the ground, allowing the audience to see the large, bustling city for the first time. The animation of the two droids (one a human-like droid and the other a floating probe droid) is fanatstic and quite funny. Numerous CG elements made up the shots, along with many digital matte paintings and miniatures. Although the shot technically and aesthetically brilliant, it simply does not fit into STAR WARS. The establishing crane shot is a standard in many films, but the 1977 version of STAR WARS had very little camera movement.

Another five shots follow (some brand new, some enhanced), and many include new, thirty foot tall creatures, called Rontos. The animation and models of these CG models look fantastic, and compositing of these shots integrated them into the plate photography. If the Ronto's shape looks familiar, it should--it's actually a altered version of the CG model created for JURASSIC PARK's Brontosaurus, hence the name Ronto. In a few other shots outside the cantina, CG Rontos and Dewbacks, along with the floating Imperial droids are featured in the backgrounds of original 1977 photography. The match-moving and rotoscoping of these shots are **fantastic**--the shadows created for the floating droid are right on the money and are completely integrated into the 1977 shot.

The CG Stormtrooper makes another appearance in an enhanced shot--the Stormtrooper dismounts from the Dewback in some of the best humanoid CG animation I've ever seen.

Jabba the Hutt makes a cameo in STAR WARS in this newly restored sequence.

One of the biggest new scenes is the restored conversation between Han Solo and Jabba the Hutt. Originally shot with a human actor as Jabba, CG Supervisor Joe Letteri and animator Steve "Spaz" Williams replaced him with a fully CG Jabba slug, as he appeared in RETURN OF THE JEDI. This Jabba can slithers and squirms his way to Han, and has a discussion with Solo in the 5 shot sequence. Small alterations to Harrison Ford's movements were made to accomplish a seamless (and sometimes very funny) encounter between the human and the CG creature. A new feature to the sequence is Boba Fett--an actor in costume performed in front of a bluescreen in order to integrate the bounty hunter into the sequence. One problem I have with the new Jabba sequence is Jabba's eyes. The bright orange eyes of the puppet Jabba in JEDI are realized in the new shots as glossy, desaturated bulbs. Also, Jabba is far too expressive in this chapter of the STAR WARS saga, which betrays the way Jabba appears in RETURN OF THE JEDI.

An exclusive side-by-side comparison of the 1977 production footage and the newly enhanced shot including a computer generated Jabba. Careful erasure of the original actor as well as extensive rotoscoping and animation of Solo add to the realism of the sequence.

As the Falcon takes off from Mos Eisley, one brand new shot shows a CG Falcon rising from Bay 94, and an enhanced wide shot of the Falcon zooming into the air features a new, dynamic aerial move. As the Falcon tries to escape the Death Star's tractor beam, new, accurate camera shake animation was added to the interior shots.

A new explosion was shot for Alderaan's destruction, and features a colorful shockwave, very similar to ILM's shockwave created for STAR TREK VI. The Death Star's explosion was enhanced with this shockwave, as well.

A terrific enhanced shot was created for Han Solo's furious attack on a group of Stormtroopers. In the original shot, eight Stormtroopers turn around and fire on Solo. In the hilarious enhanced shot, an entire legion of Stormtroopers appear in the background.

In this incredible composite, the Rebel base exterior has been enhanced, giving the huge structure a new, rougher exterior.

No new model photography was used for space sequences for the Special Edition of STAR WARS--all spacecraft were created as CG models. Textures were scanned directly off of the original miniature models created in the late '70's, however. CG representations of the Millennium Falcon, the X- and Y-Wing fighters, as well as TIE Fighters will appear onscreen.

Intending to keep the pacing of the original film intact, the effects artists crafted each new space shot (around 30) to be the same frame length as the original shot. The choreography of the shots in question was enhanced--the new CG craft afford the animators a greater range of movement than the motion-control shot models. Instead of a limited three dimensional space for which the camera and the model to interact (due to stage size, model and camera rigging, etc.), the virtual camera and virtual model have infinite possibilities in terms of distance and perspective. New, exciting dynamics have been created to **enhance** the sequences' drama, not alter them.

VFX HQ produced by Todd Vaziri . . . http://www.vfxhq.com . . . email tvaziri@earthlink.net.

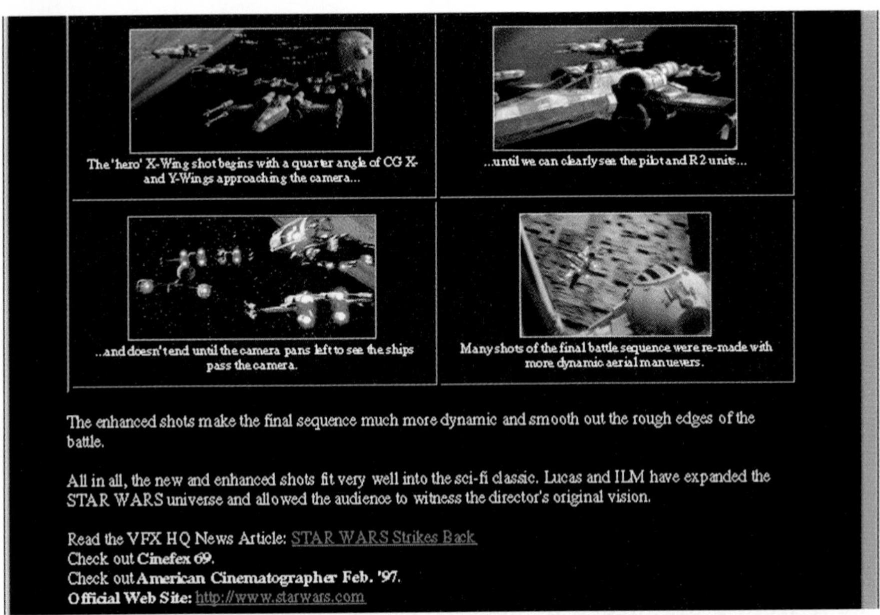
The 'hero' X-Wing shot begins with a quarter angle of CG X- and Y-Wings approaching the camera...

...until we can clearly see the pilot and R2 units...

...and doesn't end until the camera pans left to see the ships pass the camera.

Many shots of the final battle sequence were re-made with more dynamic aerial manuevers.

The enhanced shots make the final sequence much more dynamic and smooth out the rough edges of the battle.

All in all, the new and enhanced shots fit very well into the sci-fi classic. Lucas and ILM have expanded the STAR WARS universe and allowed the audience to witness the director's original vision.

Read the VFX HQ News Article: STAR WARS Strikes Back
Check out **Cinefex 69**.
Check out **American Cinematographer Feb. '97**.
Official Web Site: http://www.starwars.com

Here's the payoff! This article talks about how several years after the original *Star Wars* film was completed, advanced computer-graphic effects enhanced the Special Edition version of the film.

The Visual Effects Headquarters Archive produced a wealth of articles for our project. We could spend much longer on this one site alone. For now, let's set a bookmark here and go back to the Webcrawler site listing one more time.

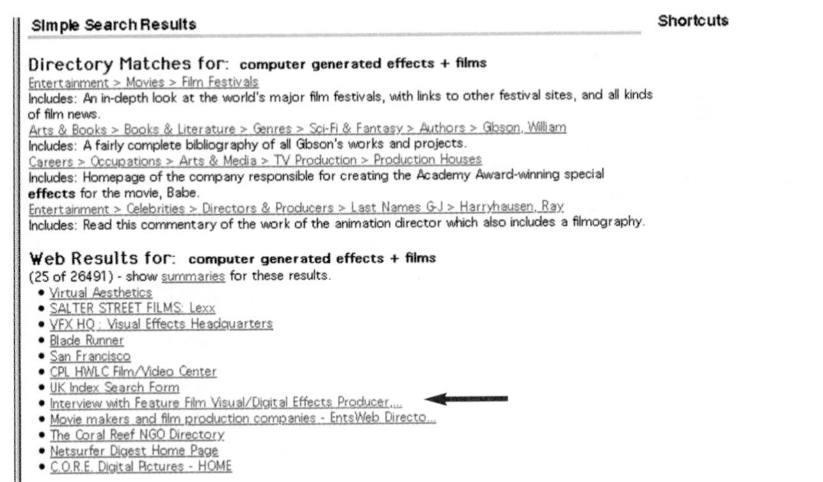
Simple Search Results **Shortcuts**

Directory Matches for: **computer generated effects + films**
Entertainment > Movies > Film Festivals
Includes: An in-depth look at the world's major film festivals, with links to other festival sites, and all kinds of film news.
Arts & Books > Books & Literature > Genres > Sci-Fi & Fantasy > Authors > Gibson, William
Includes: A fairly complete bibliography of all Gibson's works and projects.
Careers > Occupations > Arts & Media > TV Production > Production Houses
Includes: Homepage of the company responsible for creating the Academy Award-winning special **effects** for the movie, Babe.
Entertainment > Celebrities > Directors & Producers > Last Names G-J > Harryhausen, Ray
Includes: Read this commentary of the work of the animation director which also includes a filmography.

Web Results for: **computer generated effects + films**
(25 of 26491) - show summaries for these results.
- Virtual Aesthetics
- SALTER STREET FILMS: Lexx
- VFX HQ : Visual Effects Headquarters
- Blade Runner
- San Francisco
- CPL HWLC Film/Video Center
- UK Index Search Form
- Interview with Feature Film Visual/Digital Effects Producer....
- Movie makers and film production companies - EntsWeb Directo...
- The Coral Reef NGO Directory
- Netsurfer Digest Home Page
- C.O.R.E. Digital Pictures - HOME

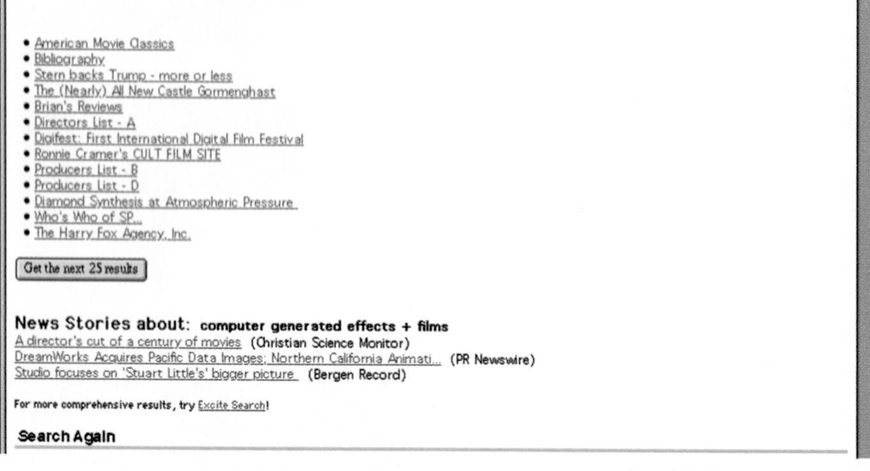
- American Movie Classics
- Bibliography
- Stern backs Trump - more or less
- The (Nearly) All New Castle Gormenghast
- Brian's Reviews
- Directors List - A
- Digifest: First International Digital Film Festival
- Ronnie Cramer's CULT FILM SITE
- Producers List - B
- Producers List - D
- Diamond Synthesis at Atmospheric Pressure
- Who's Who of SP...
- The Harry Fox Agency, Inc.

Get the next 25 results

News Stories about: computer generated effects + films
A director's cut of a century of movies (Christian Science Monitor)
DreamWorks Acquires Pacific Data Images; Northern California Animati... (PR Newswire)
Studio focuses on 'Stuart Little's' bigger picture (Bergen Record)

For more comprehensive results, try Excite Search!

Search Again

Here we find another article about computerized effects, but this one is from a producer's perspective.

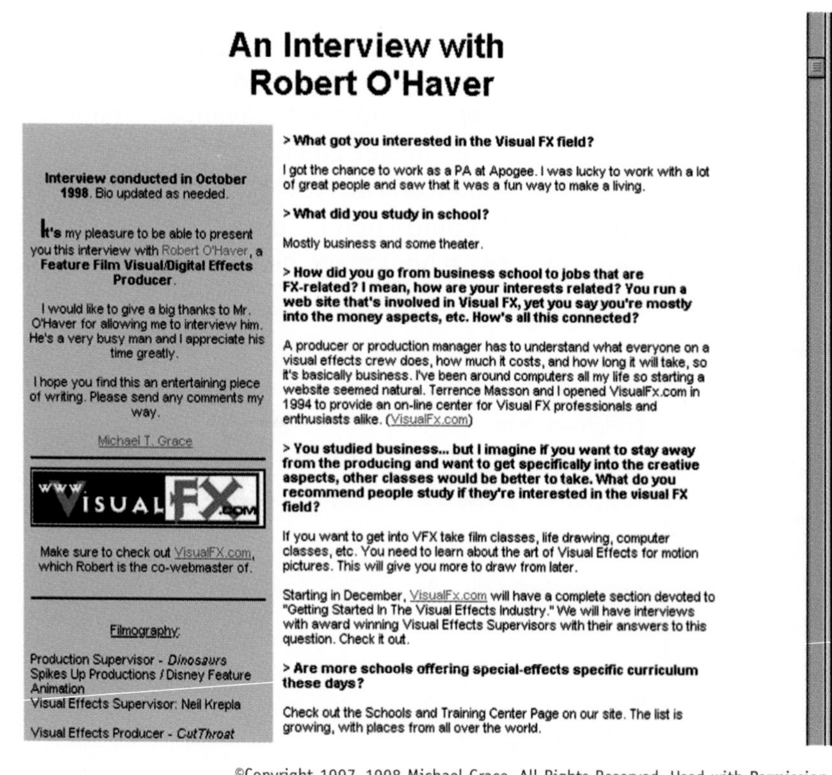
The Reel Site

An Interview with Robert O'Haver

Interview conducted in October 1998. Bio updated as needed.

It's my pleasure to be able to present you this interview with Robert O'Haver, a **Feature Film Visual/Digital Effects Producer**.

I would like to give a big thanks to Mr. O'Haver for allowing me to interview him. He's a very busy man and I appreciate his time greatly.

I hope you find this an entertaining piece of writing. Please send any comments my way.

Michael T. Grace

Make sure to check out VisualFX.com, which Robert is the co-webmaster of.

Filmography:

Production Supervisor - *Dinosaurs*
Spikes Up Productions / Disney Feature Animation
Visual Effects Supervisor: Neil Krepla

Visual Effects Producer - *CutThroat*

> What got you interested in the Visual FX field?

I got the chance to work as a PA at Apogee. I was lucky to work with a lot of great people and saw that it was a fun way to make a living.

> What did you study in school?

Mostly business and some theater.

> How did you go from business school to jobs that are FX-related? I mean, how are your interests related? You run a web site that's involved in Visual FX, yet you say you're mostly into the money aspects, etc. How's all this connected?

A producer or production manager has to understand what everyone on a visual effects crew does, how much it costs, and how long it will take, so it's basically business. I've been around computers all my life so starting a website seemed natural. Terrence Masson and I opened VisualFx.com in 1994 to provide an on-line center for Visual FX professionals and enthusiasts alike. (VisualFx.com)

> You studied business... but I imagine if you want to stay away from the producing and want to get specifically into the creative aspects, other classes would be better to take. What do you recommend people study if they're interested in the visual FX field?

If you want to get into VFX take film classes, life drawing, computer classes, etc. You need to learn about the art of Visual Effects for motion pictures. This will give you more to draw from later.

Starting in December, VisualFx.com will have a complete section devoted to "Getting Started In The Visual Effects Industry." We will have interviews with award winning Visual Effects Supervisors with their answers to this question. Check it out.

> Are more schools offering special-effects specific curriculum these days?

Check out the Schools and Training Center Page on our site. The list is growing, with places from all over the world.

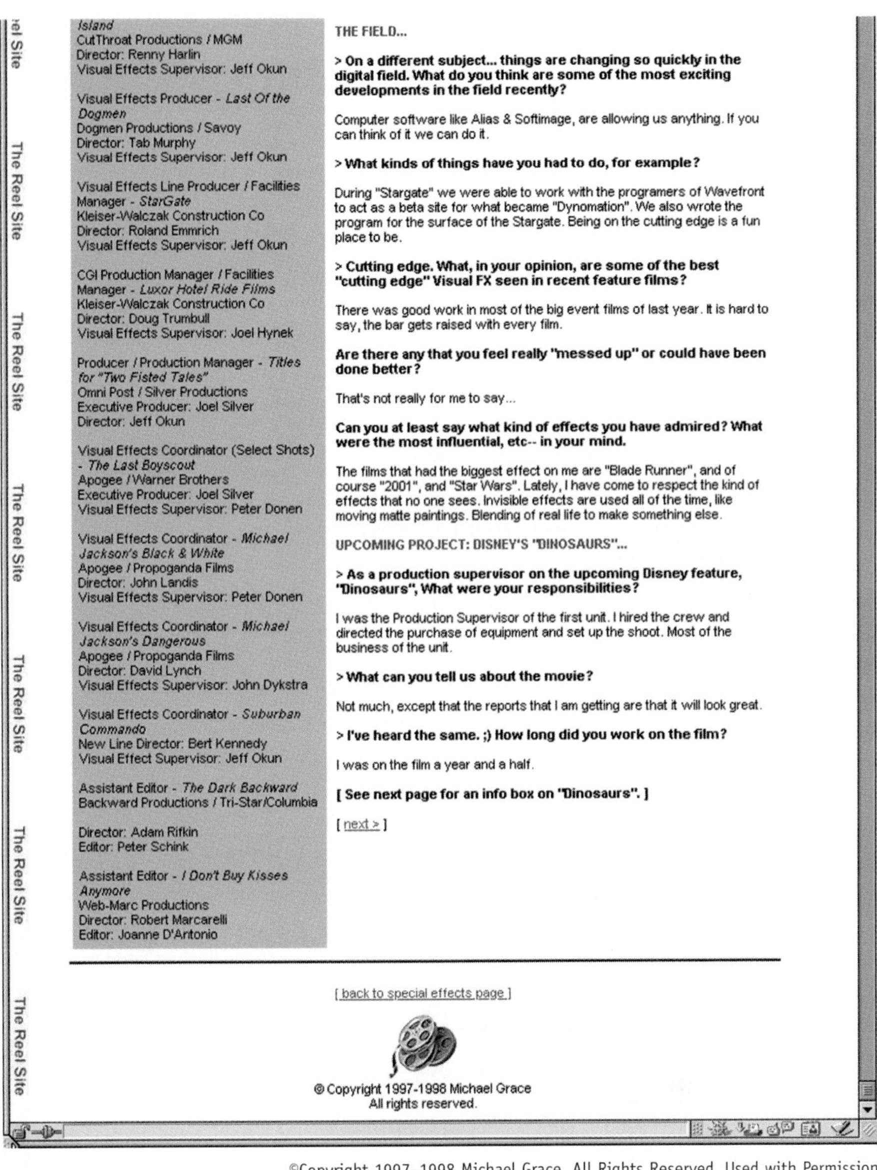

Island
CutThroat Productions / MGM
Director: Renny Harlin
Visual Effects Supervisor: Jeff Okun

Visual Effects Producer - *Last Of the Dogmen*
Dogmen Productions / Savoy
Director: Tab Murphy
Visual Effects Supervisor: Jeff Okun

Visual Effects Line Producer / Facilities Manager - *StarGate*
Kleiser-Walczak Construction Co
Director: Roland Emmrich
Visual Effects Supervisor: Jeff Okun

CGI Production Manager / Facilities Manager - *Luxor Hotel Ride Films*
Kleiser-Walczak Construction Co
Director: Doug Trumbull
Visual Effects Supervisor: Joel Hynek

Producer / Production Manager - *Titles for "Two Fisted Tales"*
Omni Post / Silver Productions
Executive Producer: Joel Silver
Director: Jeff Okun

Visual Effects Coordinator (Select Shots) - *The Last Boyscout*
Apogee / Warner Brothers
Executive Producer: Joel Silver
Visual Effects Supervisor: Peter Donen

Visual Effects Coordinator - *Michael Jackson's Black & White*
Apogee / Propoganda Films
Director: John Landis
Visual Effects Supervisor: Peter Donen

Visual Effects Coordinator - *Michael Jackson's Dangerous*
Apogee / Propoganda Films
Director: David Lynch
Visual Effects Supervisor: John Dykstra

Visual Effects Coordinator - *Suburban Commando*
New Line Director: Bert Kennedy
Visual Effect Supervisor: Jeff Okun

Assistant Editor - *The Dark Backward*
Backward Productions / Tri-Star/Columbia

Director: Adam Rifkin
Editor: Peter Schink

Assistant Editor - *I Don't Buy Kisses Anymore*
Web-Marc Productions
Director: Robert Marcarelli
Editor: Joanne D'Antonio

THE FIELD...

> On a different subject... things are changing so quickly in the digital field. What do you think are some of the most exciting developments in the field recently?

Computer software like Alias & Softimage, are allowing us anything. If you can think of it we can do it.

> What kinds of things have you had to do, for example?

During "Stargate" we were able to work with the programers of Wavefront to act as a beta site for what became "Dynomation". We also wrote the program for the surface of the Stargate. Being on the cutting edge is a fun place to be.

> Cutting edge. What, in your opinion, are some of the best "cutting edge" Visual FX seen in recent feature films?

There was good work in most of the big event films of last year. It is hard to say, the bar gets raised with every film.

Are there any that you feel really "messed up" or could have been done better?

That's not really for me to say...

Can you at least say what kind of effects you have admired? What were the most influential, etc-- in your mind.

The films that had the biggest effect on me are "Blade Runner", and of course "2001", and "Star Wars". Lately, I have come to respect the kind of effects that no one sees. Invisible effects are used all of the time, like moving matte paintings. Blending of real life to make something else.

UPCOMING PROJECT: DISNEY'S "DINOSAURS"...

> As a production supervisor on the upcoming Disney feature, "Dinosaurs", What were your responsibilities?

I was the Production Supervisor of the first unit. I hired the crew and directed the purchase of equipment and set up the shoot. Most of the business of the unit.

> What can you tell us about the movie?

Not much, except that the reports that I am getting are that it will look great.

> I've heard the same. ;) How long did you work on the film?

I was on the film a year and a half.

[See next page for an info box on "Dinosaurs".]

[next >]

[back to special effects page]

© Copyright 1997-1998 Michael Grace
All rights reserved.

The keywords "computer generated effects + films" seemed to work well. Let's try our search again, using the Lycos search engine this time. We'll also narrow our search even further by adding the word *visual*, so our keywords will be "computer generated visual effects + films." Here's the list the service retrieved.

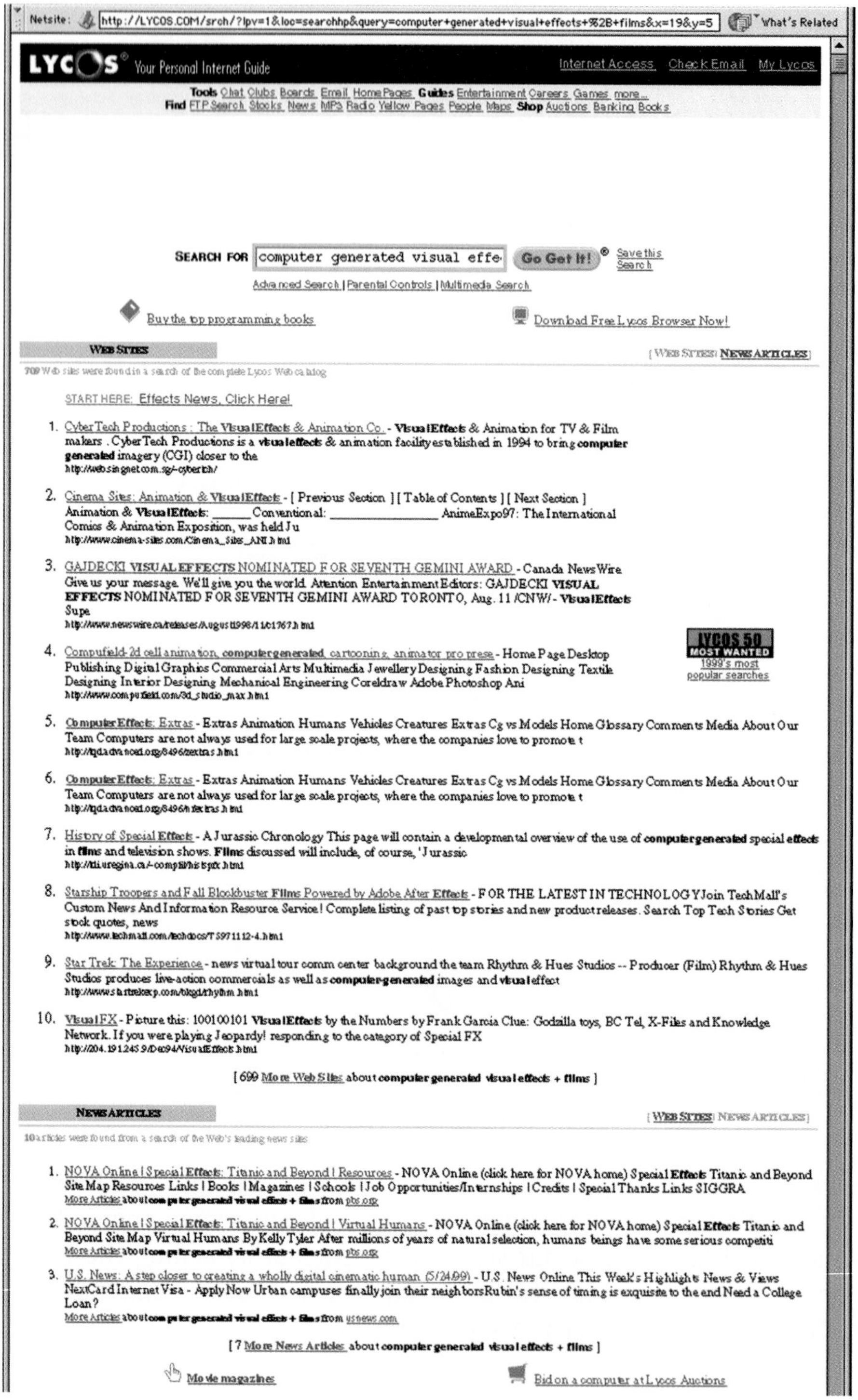

Netsite: http://LYCOS.COM/srch/?lpv=1&loc=searchhp&query=computer+generated+visual+effects+%2B+films&x=19&y=5 What's Related

LYCOS® Your Personal Internet Guide Internet Access Check Email My Lycos

Tools Chat Clubs Boards Email HomePages Guides Entertainment Careers Games more...
Find FTP Search Stocks News MP3 Radio Yellow Pages People Maps Shop Auctions Banking Books

SEARCH FOR computer generated visual effe Go Get It! Save this Search

Advanced Search | Parental Controls | Multimedia Search

Buy the top programming books Download Free Lycos Browser Now!

WEB SITES [WEB SITES | NEWS ARTICLES]

709 Web sites were found in a search of the complete Lycos Web catalog

START HERE: Effects News, Click Here!

1. CyberTech Productions : The VisualEffects & Animation Co. - **VisualEffects** & Animation for TV & Film makers . CyberTech Productions is a **visualeffects** & animation facility established in 1994 to bring **computer generated** imagery (CGI) closer to the
http://websingnet.com.sg/~cybertch/

2. Cinema Sites: Animation & VisualEffects - [Previous Section] [Table of Contents] [Next Section] Animation & **VisualEffects**: ______ Conventional: ________________ AnimeExpo97: The International Comics & Animation Exposition, was held Ju
http://www.cinema-sites.com/Cinema_Sites_ANI.html

3. GAJDECKI **VISUAL EFFECTS** NOMINATED FOR SEVENTH GEMINI AWARD - Canada NewsWire Give us your message. We'll give you the world. Attention Entertainment Editors: GAJDECKI **VISUAL EFFECTS** NOMINATED FOR SEVENTH GEMINI AWARD TORONTO, Aug. 11 /CNW/ - **VisualEffects** Supe
http://www.newswire.ca/releases/August1998/11/c1767.html

4. Compufield- 2d cell animation, **computergenerated**, cartooning, animator pro prese - Home Page Desktop Publishing Digital Graphics Commercial Arts Multimedia Jewellery Designing Fashion Designing Textile Designing Interior Designing Mechanical Engineering Coreldraw Adobe Photoshop Ani
http://www.compufield.com/3d_studio_max.html

LYCOS 50 MOST WANTED 1999's most popular searches

5. **ComputerEffects**: Extras - Extras Animation Humans Vehicles Creatures Extras Cg vs Models Home Glossary Comments Media About Our Team Computers are not always used for large scale projects, where the companies love to promote t
http://tqd.advanced.org/8496/extras.html

6. **ComputerEffects**: Extras - Extras Animation Humans Vehicles Creatures Extras Cg vs Models Home Glossary Comments Media About Our Team Computers are not always used for large scale projects, where the companies love to promote t
http://tqd.advanced.org/8496/n/extras.html

7. History of Special **Effects** - A Jurassic Chronology This page will contain a developmental overview of the use of **computergenerated** special **effects** in **films** and television shows. **Films** discussed will include, of course, 'Jurassic
http://tdi.uregina.ca/~compsh/histsfx.html

8. Starship Troopers and Fall Blockbuster **Films** Powered by Adobe After **Effects** - FOR THE LATEST IN TECHNOLOGY Join TechMall's Custom News And Information Resource Service! Complete listing of past top stories and new product releases. Search Top Tech Stories Get stock quotes, news
http://www.techmall.com/techdocs/TS971112-4.html

9. Star Trek: The Experience - news virtual tour comm center background the team Rhythm & Hues Studios -- Producer (Film) Rhythm & Hues Studios produces live-action commercials as well as **computer-generated** images and **visual** effect
http://www.startrekexp.com/bkgd/rhythm.html

10. VisualFX - Picture this: 100100101 **VisualEffects** by the Numbers by Frank Garcia Clue: Godzilla toys, BC Tel, X-Files and Knowledge Network. If you were playing Jeopardy! responding to the category of Special FX
http://204.191.245.9/Dec94/VisualEffects.html

[699 More Web Sites about **computer generated visual effects + films**]

NEWS ARTICLES [WEB SITES | NEWS ARTICLES]

10 articles were found from a search of the Web's leading news sites

1. NOVA Online | Special **Effects**: Titanic and Beyond | Resources - NOVA Online (click here for NOVA home) Special **Effects** Titanic and Beyond Site Map Resources Links | Books | Magazines | Schools | Job Opportunities/Internships | Credits | Special Thanks Links SIGGRA
More Articles about **computer generated visual effects + films** from pbs.org

2. NOVA Online | Special **Effects**: Titanic and Beyond | Virtual Humans - NOVA Online (click here for NOVA home) Special **Effects** Titanic and Beyond Site Map Virtual Humans By Kelly Tyler After millions of years of natural selection, humans beings have some serious competiti
More Articles about **computer generated visual effects + films** from pbs.org

3. U.S. News: A step closer to creating a wholly digital cinematic human (5/24/99) - U.S. News Online This Week's Highlights News & Views NextCard Internet Visa - Apply Now Urban campuses finally join their neighbors Rubin's sense of timing is exquisite to the end Need a College Loan?
More Articles about **computer generated visual effects + films** from usnews.com

[7 More News Articles about **computer generated visual effects + films**]

Movie magazines Bid on a computer at Lycos Auctions

Again, we've found a great assortment of articles. Here's another that looks interesting.

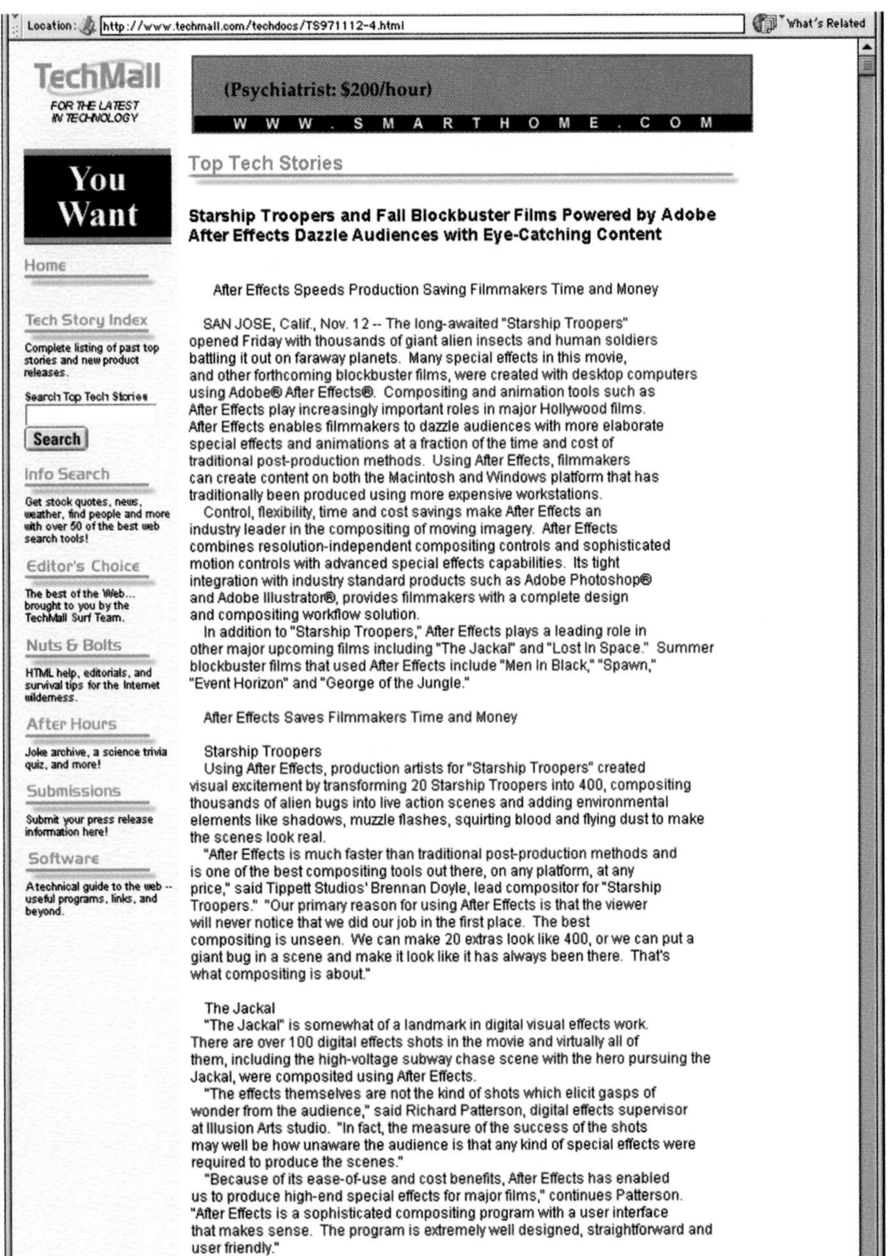
Location: http://www.techmall.com/techdocs/TS971112-4.html

What's Related

TechMall

FOR THE LATEST IN TECHNOLOGY

(Psychiatrist: $200/hour)

WWW.SMARTHOME.COM

You Want

Home

Tech Story Index

Complete listing of past top stories and new product releases.

Search Top Tech Stories

Search

Info Search

Get stock quotes, news, weather, find people and more with over 50 of the best web search tools!

Editor's Choice

The best of the Web... brought to you by the TechMall Surf Team.

Nuts & Bolts

HTML help, editorials, and survival tips for the Internet wilderness.

After Hours

Joke archive, a science trivia quiz, and more!

Submissions

Submit your press release information here!

Software

A technical guide to the web -- useful programs, links, and beyond.

Top Tech Stories

Starship Troopers and Fall Blockbuster Films Powered by Adobe After Effects Dazzle Audiences with Eye-Catching Content

After Effects Speeds Production Saving Filmmakers Time and Money

SAN JOSE, Calif., Nov. 12 -- The long-awaited "Starship Troopers" opened Friday with thousands of giant alien insects and human soldiers battling it out on faraway planets. Many special effects in this movie, and other forthcoming blockbuster films, were created with desktop computers using Adobe® After Effects®. Compositing and animation tools such as After Effects play increasingly important roles in major Hollywood films. After Effects enables filmmakers to dazzle audiences with more elaborate special effects and animations at a fraction of the time and cost of traditional post-production methods. Using After Effects, filmmakers can create content on both the Macintosh and Windows platform that has traditionally been produced using more expensive workstations.

Control, flexibility, time and cost savings make After Effects an industry leader in the compositing of moving imagery. After Effects combines resolution-independent compositing controls and sophisticated motion controls with advanced special effects capabilities. Its tight integration with industry standard products such as Adobe Photoshop® and Adobe Illustrator®, provides filmmakers with a complete design and compositing workflow solution.

In addition to "Starship Troopers," After Effects plays a leading role in other major upcoming films including "The Jackal" and "Lost In Space." Summer blockbuster films that used After Effects include "Men In Black," "Spawn," "Event Horizon" and "George of the Jungle."

After Effects Saves Filmmakers Time and Money

Starship Troopers

Using After Effects, production artists for "Starship Troopers" created visual excitement by transforming 20 Starship Troopers into 400, compositing thousands of alien bugs into live action scenes and adding environmental elements like shadows, muzzle flashes, squirting blood and flying dust to make the scenes look real.

"After Effects is much faster than traditional post-production methods and is one of the best compositing tools out there, on any platform, at any price," said Tippett Studios' Brennan Doyle, lead compositor for "Starship Troopers." "Our primary reason for using After Effects is that the viewer will never notice that we did our job in the first place. The best compositing is unseen. We can make 20 extras look like 400, or we can put a giant bug in a scene and make it look like it has always been there. That's what compositing is about."

The Jackal

"The Jackal" is somewhat of a landmark in digital visual effects work. There are over 100 digital effects shots in the movie and virtually all of them, including the high-voltage subway chase scene with the hero pursuing the Jackal, were composited using After Effects.

"The effects themselves are not the kind of shots which elicit gasps of wonder from the audience," said Richard Patterson, digital effects supervisor at Illusion Arts studio. "In fact, the measure of the success of the shots may well be how unaware the audience is that any kind of special effects were required to produce the scenes."

"Because of its ease-of-use and cost benefits, After Effects has enabled us to produce high-end special effects for major films," continues Patterson. "After Effects is a sophisticated compositing program with a user interface that makes sense. The program is extremely well designed, straightforward and user friendly."

Obviously we could go on and on. The important thing to remember is to use your imagination plus a little deductive reasoning. Just imagine you are a cyberspace detective sniffing out clues on a case!

When doing research on the Internet, never give out your name, address, telephone number, or school name without checking with your teacher and/or your parents. Although most sites are safe, a few sites may not use the information in the way they say they are going to use it.

LANGUAGE

CHAPTER 1

The Sentence

Directions

Write the letter of the term that correctly identifies the underlined word or words in each sentence.

EXAMPLE **1.** Many species of plants are used for medicinal purposes.

1 **A** simple subject
B complete subject
C simple predicate
D complete predicate

ANSWER **1** **B**

1. Last summer my aunt invited me to her farm in New Mexico.
2. One morning I cooked some toast and made some orange juice.
3. I shoved a rack with sliced bread into the oven and burned my finger.
4. Aunt May broke off a piece of a spiny plant on her windowsill.
5. She squeezed a gooey substance from the plant and rubbed it on my burn.
6. In no time my finger felt as good as new.
7. Learned the name of this miraculous plant—aloe.
8. Aloe looks somewhat like a cactus but belongs to the lily family.
9. Many gardeners in the southern and southwestern parts of the United States.
10. Have you ever seen the leaves of an aloe plant?

1 **A** simple subject
B complete subject
C simple predicate
D complete predicate

2 **A** complete subject
B complete predicate
C compound subject
D compound verb

3 **A** simple subject
B complete subject
C complete predicate
D simple predicate

4 **A** complete predicate
B complete subject
C compound subject
D compound verb

5 **A** complete subject
B complete predicate
C compound subject
D compound verb

6 **A** simple subject
B complete subject
C simple predicate
D complete predicate

7 **A** sentence fragment
B inverted order
C simple predicate
D compound subject

8 **A** complete subject
B complete predicate
C compound subject
D simple predicate

9 **A** sentence fragment
B inverted order
C simple predicate
D compound subject

10 **A** sentence fragment
B inverted order
C simple predicate
D compound subject

Jaune Quick-to-See Smith.
Family Tree, 1986.
Pastel on paper, 30 by 22 inches.
Collection of Bernice and Harold Steinbaum. Courtesy of Bernice Steinbaum Gallery, Miami, FL.

Describe What images do you recognize in this drawing? Is one image more striking than the others?

Analyze What ideas do you think the artist wanted to convey? How do the artist's name and the title of the drawing support this message?

Interpret How could a writer express in words the same ideas that Jaune Quick-to-See Smith expresses in images?

Judge Do you think this pastel drawing or the written word would make the more powerful statement about these ideas? Why do you think so?

At the end of this chapter, you will use the artwork to stimulate ideas for writing.

Recognizing Sentences

A sentence is a group of words that expresses a complete thought.

In conversation, people sometimes express their ideas incompletely.

> KIM: Do you want to play a game of football?
> ALLEN: In this weather? No way!

Kim easily understood Allen's reply, even though he used only parts of a sentence to answer her. However, in standard written English, you need to use complete sentences to be sure your message is clear and your reader understands it accurately.

CONNECT TO SPEAKING AND WRITING

When you speak, you convey your ideas not only with your words but also with your facial expression, body language, and tone of voice. When you write, your words alone convey your thoughts and feelings.

The following groups of words are incomplete thoughts:

> The player in the torn jersey.
> Made a touchdown.
> Blocking the defense.
> When the game ended.

A group of words that expresses an incomplete thought is a **sentence fragment.**

To change these fragments into sentences, you need to add the missing information.

> The player in the torn jersey **is the team's best player.**
> **The running back** made a touchdown.
> Blocking the defense **allowed the running back to score.**
> When the game ended, **the team celebrated.**

You can learn more about fragments on pages 257–266.

Practice Your Skills

Check Your Understanding

Recognizing Sentences and Fragments

Contemporary Life

Label each group of words *S* if it is a sentence or *F* if it is a fragment.

1. The fans at the football game cheered wildly.
2. Because the weather turned cold.
3. Brought a blanket to the game.
4. The quarterback for the winning team.
5. My family watched the game from the fifty-yard line.
6. Buying hot chocolate from the concession stand.
7. Since we know the coach of the team.
8. Practices for four hours each day.

Connect to the Writing Process: Revising

Writing Complete Sentences from Fragments

9.–14. **Add information to expand each fragment above into a sentence. When you write your sentences, remember to begin each sentence with a capital letter and end it with a punctuation mark.**

Communicate Your Ideas

APPLY TO WRITING

Friendly Letter: ***Complete Sentences***

Write a letter to your school coach asking to attend a summer sports camp. Decide on the type of sports camp you would like to attend. List the reasons you want to attend. Include the following sentence fragments, written correctly as sentences.

- Is important to me.
- Instruction at camp.
- Practicing for next season.
- My favorite sport.

Subjects and Predicates

A sentence has two main parts: a subject and a predicate.

The **subject** names the person, place, thing, or idea that the sentence is about.

The **predicate** tells something about the subject.

	SUBJECT	PREDICATE
PERSON	Albert Einstein	was a very famous scientist.
PLACE	The United States	became his home.
THING	Many inventions	came from his ideas.
IDEA	His intelligence	made him a celebrity.

Complete and Simple Subjects

A **complete subject** includes all the words used to identify the person, place, thing, or idea that the sentence is about.

To find a complete subject, ask yourself *Whom?* or *What?* the sentence is about.

The tour guide at the science museum told us about atoms.

(Whom is this sentence about? Who told us about atoms? *The tour guide at the science museum* is the complete subject.)

Microscopes with powerful lenses magnify the atoms.

(What is this sentence telling about? What magnifies the atoms? *Microscopes with powerful lenses* is the complete subject.)

Practice Your Skills

Check Your Understanding
Finding Complete Subjects

Science Topic **Write the complete subject in each sentence.**

1. Young Albert Einstein showed an interest in math and science.
2. His grades in other subjects were poor.
3. The future scientist finished high school and technical college in Switzerland.
4. The Swiss patent office hired Einstein in 1902.
5. Scholarly journals gave Einstein a forum for his ideas.
6. A German physics journal published some of his articles.
7. These articles discussed radical theories about the nature of matter.
8. Publication of these articles changed scientists' view of the universe.
9. The theory of relativity was Einstein's most important contribution.
10. The Nobel Prize in physics was awarded to Einstein in 1921.

Simple Subjects

A **simple subject** is the main word in the complete subject.

The simple subject is the one word that directly answers the question *Who?* or *What?*

> **Many immigrants** arrived at Ellis Island in the early part of the twentieth century.
>
> **Officials at the station** processed more than twelve million immigrants.

Sometimes a complete subject and a simple subject are the same.

Albert Einstein came to the United States in 1933.
He became a United States citizen seven years later.

Throughout the rest of this book, the word subject *refers to the simple subject.*

Practice Your Skills

Check Your Understanding
Finding Complete and Simple Subjects

Social Studies Topic

Write the complete subject in each sentence. Then underline each simple subject.

1. New York Harbor is home to the Statue of Liberty.
2. This figure of a woman with a torch stands at the entrance to the harbor.
3. She holds a tablet in her left hand.
4. Seven rays surround her head.
5. Broken chains lie at her feet.
6. The statue weighs 225 tons.
7. The people of France gave the statue to the United States.
8. A formal presentation occurred in 1886.
9. Major repairs were made to the statue in the 1980s.
10. Tourists from around the world visit this famous lady.

Connect to the Writing Process: Drafting
Writing Complete Subjects

Add a complete subject to each of the following sentences.

11. ■ work very hard at their jobs.
12. ■ climb the tall tower.
13. ■ could be considered dangerous.
14. ■ may mean hours of extra work.

15. ■ makes the effort worthwhile.
16. ■ is not finished.
17. ■ will complete the assignment soon.
18. ■ will be admired by many people.
19. ■ should do well in the Olympics.
20. ■ finished the school yearbook.

Communicate Your Ideas

APPLY TO WRITING

Writer's Craft: *Analyzing the Use of Subjects*

Writers often choose words and phrases to create an effect on their audience. In this paragraph from "The Washwoman," Isaac Bashevis Singer writes about an old woman who does laundry for his family. Read the paragraph and then follow the instructions below.

> She would bring the laundry back about two weeks later. My mother had never been so pleased with any washwoman. Every piece of linen sparkled like polished silver. Every piece was neatly ironed. Yet she charged no more than the others. She was a real find. Mother always had her money ready ....
>
> —*Isaac Bashevis Singer,* "The Washwoman"

- Write the complete subject of each sentence and then underline the simple subject.
- Referring to your list of subjects, explain who or what seems to be most important in this paragraph.
- What is the total effect of Singer's choice of subjects on the reader?

Complete and Simple Predicates

A **complete predicate** includes all the words that tell what the subject is doing or that tell something about the subject.

To find a complete predicate, first find the subject. Then ask, *What is the subject doing?* or *What is being said about the subject?*

Wild horses roamed across the prairie.

(The subject is *horses.* What did the horses do? *Roamed across the prairie* is the complete predicate.)

Check Your Understanding
Finding Complete Predicates

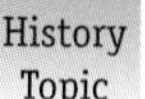

Write the complete predicate in each sentence.

1. Prehistoric humans hunted horses for food.
2. Humans later recognized the value of live horses.
3. The knights of the Middle Ages rode strong horses into battle.
4. The horses wore armor for protection.
5. The Spanish conquistadors brought horses to the New World.
6. Native Americans captured wild horses.
7. They became expert riders.
8. The settlers traveled west in covered wagons.
9. Horses pulled the wagons from Missouri to Oregon.
10. The horse is no longer a principal means of transportation.

Simple Predicates

A simple predicate, or verb, is the main word or phrase in the complete predicate.

In the following examples, the simple predicate, or verb, is underlined:

Everyone in the park **enjoyed the fireworks.**

The Roman candle **burned beautifully in the night sky.**

Sometimes verbs are hard to find because they do not show action; instead, they tell something about a subject. The following common verb forms are used to make a statement about a subject:

am is are was were be being been

Verbs that make a statement are also called linking verbs.

You can learn more about linking verbs on pages L75–L78.

CONNECT TO SPEAKING AND WRITING

When you speak or write, vivid verbs can make your ideas more interesting. Because the predicate conveys action in a sentence, choosing strong verbs can help your audience visualize what is happening. Notice the difference between the verbs in the following sentences.

The noise of the fireworks **affected** the baby.
The noise of the fireworks **frightened** the baby.

PRACTICE YOUR SKILLS

Check Your Understanding

Finding Complete and Simple Predicates

General Interest **Write the complete predicate in each sentence. Then underline the verb.**

1. Millions of Americans watch displays of fireworks on the Fourth of July.

2. Pyrotechnics is another name for fireworks.
3. Fireworks are not a recent invention.
4. The Chinese invented fireworks centuries ago.
5. They used them for celebrations.
6. Fireworks existed before the invention of guns and gunpowder.
7. The Italians manufactured fireworks during the 1500s.
8. Gases propel the fireworks into the air.
9. The fireworks explode in an array of colors.
10. The bright colors of fireworks come from different metallic salts.

Connect to the Writing Process: Revising

Using Vivid Verbs

Write each sentence, replacing each verb with a more vivid verb.

11. The fireworks went into the night sky.
12. The colors of the rockets showed against the dark sky.
13. My sister ran to the edge of the water.
14. The colors appeared on the surface of the lake.
15. The firecrackers popped loudly.

Communicate Your Ideas

APPLY TO WRITING

Description: ***Predicates***

A new student from another country has never been to a Fourth of July celebration. Write a description, telling him about a celebration and fireworks display that you have seen. Include details about the sights, sounds, and smells, using vivid verbs to make your writing come alive.

History Topic **Write the subject and verb in each sentence.**

1. In 1848, a settler discovered gold in northern California's mountains.
2. That discovery transformed San Francisco from a frontier town into a busy city.
3. People on the East Coast heard of the discovery of gold.
4. Thousands of gold prospectors invaded the city on their way to the mountains.
5. Two steamship companies brought an endless stream of people to San Francisco.
6. Other people arrived by stagecoach.
7. The Pony Express brought mail to the population.
8. Soon, telegraph lines provided additional communication to the city.
9. Few prospectors found gold in San Francisco.
10. However, many of them settled there.

Verb Phrases

A **verb phrase** includes the main verb plus any helping, or auxiliary, verbs.

The helping verb or verbs are underlined in the following examples:

> Kerry **is choosing** plants for the garden.
>
> Those seeds **can be planted** next month.
>
> The tulip bulbs **should have been planted** in the fall.

As you can see from the examples above, a verb phrase may include as many as three helping verbs. The following verbs are often used as helping verbs.

COMMON HELPING VERBS	
be	am, is, are, was, were, be, being, been
have	has, have, had
do	do, does, did
Others	may, might, must, can, could, shall, should, will, would

Practice Your Skills

Check Your Understanding
Finding Verb Phrases

Science Topic **Write the verb phrase in each sentence.**

1. Trees are known as the largest of all plants.
2. They have been identified as the oldest living things.
3. Some giant sequoia trees have lived for thousands of years.
4. The fruit of the coconut palm can be eaten.
5. You might bake a tasty pie from the fruit of apple trees.
6. Pine trees will remain green all year long.
7. Broadleaf trees do not lose their leaves in winter.
8. Trees can prevent the loss of topsoil.
9. For a very long time, people have used trees for wood.
10. Malaria is treated with quinine from the bark of the cinchona tree.

Sometimes a verb phrase is *interrupted* by other words.

A bloodhound **can** easily **follow** a day-old scent.
Most household pets **have** never **hunted** for food.

In a question the subject may come in the middle of a verb phrase.

Is Toto **scratching** at the door?

CONNECT TO SPEAKING AND WRITING

The word *not* and its contraction, *n't,* often interrupt verb phrases. Neither is part of the verb.

Health laws **do** not **allow** dogs in grocery stores.
The pet store in the mall **is**n't **selling** fish.

When you are doing a piece of formal writing, you should spell out the word *not.* You should use the contraction *n't* only in speaking and informal writing situations.

Throughout the rest of this book, the word verb *also refers to the verb phrase.*

PRACTICE YOUR SKILLS

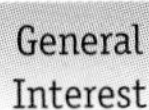

Check Your Understanding
Finding Verbs

General Interest **Write the verb in each sentence. Remember that words that interrupt a verb phrase are not part of the verb.**

1. German shepherds are often trained as guide dogs.
2. Guide dogs are always allowed in public places with their owners.
3. The guide dog must quickly adjust to the leather harness and stiff handle.
4. The dog doesn't obey all commands from its owner.
5. A command could sometimes place an owner in a dangerous situation.
6. A dog will not lead its owner into the middle of a busy street.
7. Labrador retrievers and golden retrievers are also used as guide dogs.

8. Golden retrievers have often been recommended as the best dog for a family.

9. Dogs do not usually live longer than twelve to fifteen years.

10. Have you ever had a dog for a pet?

Connect to the Writing Process: Revising
Using Verb Interrupters

11.–15. Verb interrupters change the meaning of sentences. Add verb interrupters to the following sentence and write five new sentences, each with a different meaning.

Cats have threatened dogs.

Communicate Your Ideas

APPLY TO WRITING

Informal Speech: *Verbs*

Your guidance counselor has written you a note telling you that the local veterinarian is looking for an assistant. She believes that you would be perfect for the job. She wants to meet with you before the end of the day so that you can tell her why the job is one you want or do not want. Write a short speech that you will present to the guidance counselor to explain how you feel about the possibility of working in a veterinarian's office. Use the following verbs, with or without interrupters, in your speech.

- have enjoyed
- am suited for
- is challenging
- would be interested
- was happy

Compound Subjects

A **compound subject** is two or more subjects in one sentence that have the same verb and are joined by a conjunction.

The conjunctions that usually join compound subjects are *and, or,* or *nor.* Pairs of conjunctions, such as *either/or, neither/nor, not only/but also,* and *both/and* may also be used. In the following examples, each subject is underlined once, and the verb is underlined twice. Notice that the conjunction is not part of a compound subject.

> Janice spent the hot day at the beach.
>
> Janice and Kate spent the hot day at the beach.
>
> Janice, Kate, and Sue spent the hot day at the beach.
>
> Either Kate or Sue had brought the food.
>
> Neither Janice nor Kate ate much dessert.
>
> Not only Kate but also Janice went swimming.

Connect to Speaking and Writing

To make your writing smoother and less repetitious, you can combine two or more sentences that have the same verb but different subjects.

> **Jon** has a surfboard.
> **Rick** has a surfboard.
> **Tammy** has a surfboard.
> **Jon, Rick,** and **Tammy** have surfboards.

Sometimes, when you are speaking, you might not want to combine subjects. For example, if you are trying to persuade your parents to let you have a surfboard, you might want to repeat the entire sentence each time.

PRACTICE YOUR SKILLS

Check Your Understanding

Finding Compound Subjects

Contemporary Life **Write the subject in each sentence.**

1. Rick and Tammy brought their surfboards to the beach.
2. Both the wind and the waves were impressive.
3. Jamie and Rob rented jet skis.
4. Their beach towels and sandals were almost swallowed up by the tide.
5. Two baby crabs and a starfish washed up on shore.
6. The sandwiches and fruit in the lunches were a target for the seagulls.
7. Neither Tammy nor Rick stayed up on a surfboard for very long.
8. Thunder and lightning signaled a storm in the distance.
9. The beach patrol and the lifeguards ordered everyone out of the water.
10. Jamie, Rob, Tammy, and Rick quickly gathered up their belongings and headed for the car.

Connect to the Writing Process: Revising

Combining Sentences

Combine each pair of sentences into one sentence with a compound subject. Use *and* or *or* to connect your sentences.

11. Cod feed along the ocean bottom. Flounder feed along the ocean bottom.
12. Clams live on the sea floor. Lobsters live there, too.
13. Manatees stay in the ocean for their entire lives. Whales also stay in the ocean for their entire lives.
14. Sea lions spend time on land. Walruses spend time on land.
15. Winds cause ocean waves. Earthquakes cause ocean waves.

Compound Verbs

A **compound verb** is formed when two or more verbs in one sentence have the same subject and are joined by a conjunction.

Just as some sentences have compound subjects, some sentences may have compound verbs. Conjunctions such as *and, or, nor,* and *but* are used to connect the verbs. In the following examples, each subject is underlined once, and each verb is underlined twice.

Jeff pours the juice into his glass.

Jeff pours the juice into his glass and rinses the bottle.

Jeff pours the juice into his glass, rinses the bottle, and places it in the recycling bin.

Some sentences have both a compound subject and a compound verb.

Nancy and Pete save their newspapers and bring them to the collection center.

PRACTICE YOUR SKILLS

Check Your Understanding

Finding Compound Verbs

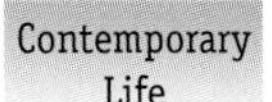

Write the verbs in the following sentences.

1. Many people drink the last sip of soda and throw the can away.

2. You should save your cans and deliver them to a recycling center.

3. An employee will take the cans and give you some money.

4. Trucks collect the old cans and unload them at a recycling plant.
5. Machines at the plant flatten the cans and dump them onto conveyor belts.
6. The cans are then shredded and cleaned.
7. Next, workers load the pieces into a hot furnace and soften them.
8. The soft metal is made into long sheets and cooled.
9. Beverage companies buy the sheets and make new cans out of them.
10. With these new cans, the beverage companies have prevented extra waste and thereby have saved everyone money.

Connect to the Writing Process: Revising
Combining Sentences

Combine each pair of sentences into one sentence with a compound verb. Use *and, or, nor,* or *but* to connect your sentences.

11. Our county has a mandatory recycling program. Our county provides each household with special bins.
12. You can put your cans and bottles in the green bin. You can save your newspapers in the orange bin.
13. The county collects plastic drink containers. The county refuses all other plastic containers.
14. Yard waste is also picked up. Yard waste must be in plastic bags.
15. Tree limbs must be cut up. The limbs must be bundled together with rope or heavy twine.
16. Hazardous materials should not be thrown out with the trash. They should be taken to special collection centers.
17. Batteries are considered hazardous materials. Batteries must never be placed with ordinary trash.

Communicate Your Ideas

APPLY TO WRITING

Writer's Craft: *Combining Sentences*

Writers often combine sentence parts to make their writing less wordy and avoid repetition. Occasionally a writer chooses not to combine sentences. Read the first stanza of this poem by Lilian Moore and then follow the instructions below.

> Three poets see a star.
> One says *how cold.*
> One thinks *how bright.*
> One sighs *how far.*
>
> –*Lilian Moore,* "Each in a Different Voice"

- Write the three sentences that have the same subject. Then combine the sentences into one sentence with a compound verb.
- Read the new sentence. Compare it with the original sentences. Why do you think the writer chose not to combine the sentences? Try to give at least two reasons.

Position of Subjects

When the subject in a sentence comes before the verb, the sentence is in **natural order.**

When the verb or part of a verb phrase comes before the subject, the sentence is in **inverted order.**

To find the subject and verb in a sentence that is in inverted order, put the sentence in its natural order. To do this, first find the verb. Then ask who or what is doing the action. In the following examples, each subject is underlined once, and each verb is underlined twice.

Into the dungeon marched the prisoners.
The prisoners marched into the dungeon.

Questions are often in inverted order. To find the subject in a question, turn the question around so that it makes a statement.

Do you like mystery stories?
You do like mystery stories.

Sentences that begin with *here* or *there* are often in inverted order. To find the subject of this kind of sentence, drop the word *here* or *there.* Then put the rest of the words in their natural order. Remember that *here* or *there* can never be the subject.

Here comes the librarian with my favorite book.
The librarian comes with my favorite book.

There are several mysteries in the book.
Several mysteries are in the book.

CONNECT TO WRITER'S CRAFT

Professional writers use sentences in both natural and inverted order. Changing the normal subject-verb order creates sentence variety and adds interest. Notice the position of the subjects and verbs in Poe's description of some rooms.

> The panes here were scarlet—a deep blood color. Now in no one of the seven apartments was there any lamp or candelabrum, amid the profusion of golden ornaments that lay scattered to and fro or depended from the roof. There was no light of any kind emanating from lamp or candle within the suite of chambers.
>
> *–Edgar Allan Poe,* "The Masque of the Red Death"

You can learn more about sentences in inverted order on pages L392–L393.

Practice Your Skills

Check Your Understanding

Finding Subjects in Sentences in Inverted Order

Literature Topic

Write the subject and verb in each sentence.

1. Do you enjoy Edgar Allan Poe's short stories?
2. From "The Cask of Amontillado" comes a scary scene.
3. There is no happy ending for Fortunato.
4. Behind a wall of Montresor's house lie Fortunato's bones.
5. How did the bones get behind the wall?
6. From the brain of a madman came the plot.
7. There were many wrongs done to Montresor.
8. Had Montresor really been the victim of slights by Fortunato?
9. Did Fortunato deserve his fate?
10. There exists scant evidence against Fortunato.
11. Have you ever read "The Pit and the Pendulum"?
12. In that story are some very macabre events.
13. There is a pendulum with a sharp scythe.
14. For the squeamish reader, there are even some rats.

Connect to the Writing Process: Revising

Varying Sentence Beginnings

15.–19. Add interest to this paragraph by varying five sentence beginnings.

The band marched onto the football field. Two helicopters flew directly overhead. The helicopters hovered over the crowd. The noise from the helicopters was loud. The band could not be heard. The helicopters finally rose higher into the sky. They flew away. The crowd cheered in grateful response.

Communicate Your Ideas

APPLY TO WRITING

News Article: ***Position of Subjects***

Edouard Manet, *The Exposition Universelle in Paris,* 1867.
Oil on canvas, 42 1/8 by 76 1/16 inches. National Gallery, Oslo, Norway.

The year is 1867, and you are a newspaper reporter from the United States. You have just arrived in Paris to cover the World's Fair. This painting shows the scene before you. You decide to write an article about your first impressions for your readers back home. In your article be sure to vary the position of the subjects of your sentences so your readers will not be bored.

Understood Subjects

When the subject of a sentence is not stated, the subject is an ***understood you.***

The subject of a command or a request is an understood *you.*

(You) Meet me in the cafeteria at lunchtime.
(You) Please wait for me.

In the following example, *you* is still the understood subject.

Danielle, (you) please be there also.

Practice Your Skills

Check Your Understanding
Finding Subjects

Contemporary Life **Write the subject and verb in each sentence. If the subject is an understood *you,* write (you).**

1. The lunch line is always long.

2. Hand me a tray, please.

3. Save a place for me at your table.

4. May I have a slice of pizza?

5. Ken, have your money ready.

6. Please pass me some milk.

7. Do the potatoes need some salt?

8. Pile the empty trays by the kitchen window.

9. Take this ticket for your lunch.

10. Maria, try some of this strawberry applesauce.

Connect to the Writing Process: Revising
Using Understood You

Instructions are usually easier to follow when an understood *you* is the subject. Revise these instructions for washing a car, using the understood *you.*

11. First, you should have a bucket with soap and hot water.

12. Then, you wet the car with a hose.

13. You put the sponge in the bucket and soap it well.

14. Next, you wash the car with the sponge.

15. The hose is used to rinse away the soap.

16. Last, you dry the car with a soft cloth.

Communicate Your Ideas

APPLY TO WRITING

Directions: *Understood* You

Do you know how to change a flat tire? Do you know how to make a tasty pizza? Perhaps you know how to make a great-looking holiday decoration. Share what you know with your classmates by writing directions for what you can do well. Use sentences with an understood *you* so that your directions are easy to follow.

Mixed Practice

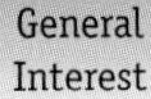

Write the subject and verb in each sentence. If the subject is an understood *you*, write (you).

1. Have you ever been to an automobile museum?
2. Visit one soon.
3. There are cars from every era on display.
4. Do not sit in any of the cars, though.
5. By each car is usually found an information card.
6. Read the card for interesting facts.
7. There was an old Rolls-Royce in the center of the floor.
8. To the right of it was a Model T Ford.
9. Does the crank on that car turn?
10. Please crank it for me.

Sentence Diagraming

Diagraming Subjects and Verbs

A **sentence diagram** is a picture made up of lines and words. It can help you clearly see the different parts of a sentence. These parts make up the structure of your sentences. By varying your sentence structure, you can make your writing more interesting.

Subjects and Verbs All sentence diagrams begin with a baseline. A straight, vertical line then separates the subject (or subjects) on the left from the verb (or verbs) on the right. Notice in the following diagram that the capital letter in the sentence is included, but not the punctuation. Also notice that the whole verb phrase is included on the baseline.

She has remembered.

She | has remembered

Inverted Order A sentence in inverted order, such as a question, is diagramed like a sentence in natural order.

Were you talking?

you | Were talking

Understood Subjects When the subject of a sentence is an understood *you,* put parentheses around it in the subject position. When a name is included with the understood subject, place it on a horizontal line above the understood subject.

Ted, listen.

Compound Subjects and Verbs Place compound subjects and verbs on parallel lines. Put the conjunction connecting them on a broken line between them. Notice in the following example that two conjunctions are placed on either side of the broken line.

Both cameras and computers were displayed.

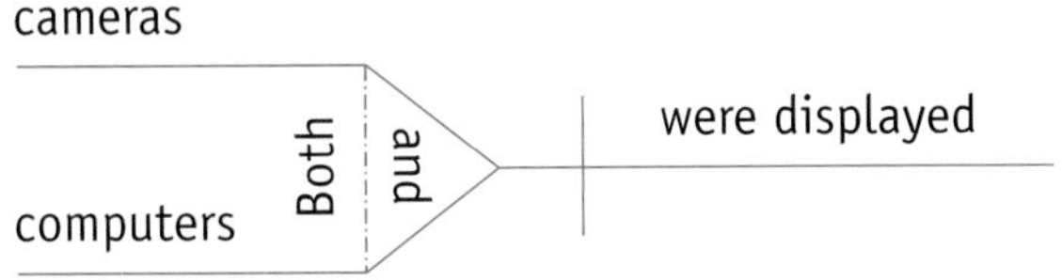

Jan has gone but will return.

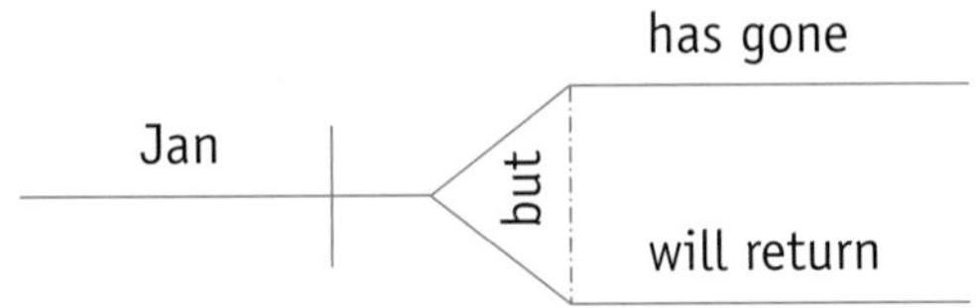

Balloons, hats, and horns were bought but have been lost.

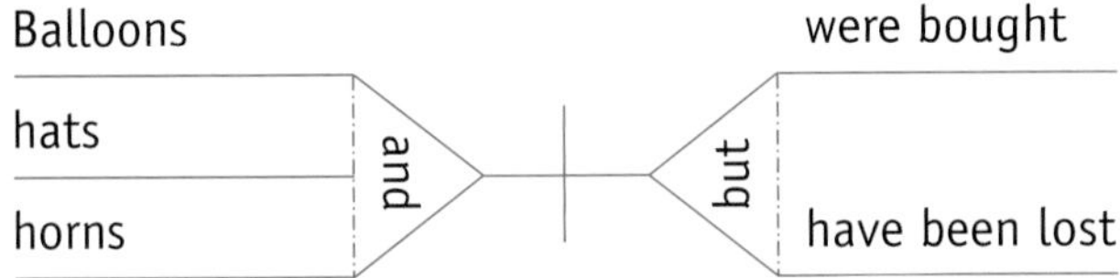

PRACTICE YOUR SKILLS

Diagraming Subjects and Verbs

Diagram the following sentences or copy them. If you copy them, draw one line under each subject and two lines under each verb. If the subject is an understood *you*, write *you* in parentheses.

1. Pigeons are landing.
2. Look!
3. Both males and females are eating.
4. Are you looking?
5. Birds leave but return.
6. Ben and Zach have come and are watching.
7. Zach, listen.
8. Birds are cooing.
9. Do pigeons migrate?
10. They might stay or leave.

CheckPoint

Finding Subjects and Verbs

Write the subjects and verbs in the following sentences. Label each word *S* for subject or *V* for verb.

1. Often volcanoes will remain inactive for centuries.
2. Then they will erupt and blow tops of mountains completely off!
3. Some eruptions have killed tens of thousands of people.
4. A few really powerful volcanoes have buried cities and covered mountains.
5. Here is an incredible fact.
6. The force of a few volcanoes has even changed the world's weather for years!
7. Despite the dangers of molten or hot rock, many people live near volcanoes.
8. Can you guess the reason why?
9. Several kinds of crops and plants grow extremely well in volcanic soil.
10. Many valuable ores and metals are also found in volcanic soil.
11. In A.D. 79, the eruption of Mount Vesuvius buried the Roman city of Pompeii and left a time capsule of Roman life.
12. Centuries later archaeologists found houses and bodies under ten feet of hard ash.
13. Today many scientists and tourists visit this site in Italy each year.
14. Have you ever visited this famous city?
15. There is no other place on Earth like it.

Finding Subjects and Verbs

Write the subjects and verbs in the following sentences. If the subject is an understood *you*, write the word *you* in parentheses.

1. Do you know anything about elephants?
2. Look at this book about elephants.
3. Here are many very interesting facts.
4. Elephants, for example, are the largest land animals in the world.
5. An elephant can run at a rate of twenty-four miles per hour!
6. The trunk of an elephant is longer than the nose of any other animal.
7. There are forty thousand muscles and tendons in the elephant's trunk.
8. With its trunk, an elephant can pick a single flower or carry a huge log.
9. For centuries the elephant has been a good friend to people throughout the world.
10. Read more about elephants on your own.

Writing Sentences

Write five sentences that follow the directions below. (The sentences may come in any order.) Write about one of the following topics or a topic of your choice: an animal in the natural world or an event in nature.

1. Write a sentence with a compound subject.
2. Write a sentence with a compound verb.
3. Write a sentence that starts with the word *there.*
4. Write a question.
5. Write a sentence with an understood *you* as the subject.

Underline each subject once and each verb twice. Remember to add capital letters and end punctuation.

Language and *Self-Expression*

American Indian artist Jaune Quick-to-See Smith uses her art to help others understand her heritage. For example, her great-great-grandmother, great-grandmother, and grandmother were all involved in trading. Her father, who was raised by these women, then became a horse trader. How does the artist show this in *Family Tree*?

Imagine the stories that Jaune Quick-to-See Smith may have heard during her childhood. What stories have you heard about your relatives or ancestors? Which of these have become a part of your family's lore? Write the story in a few paragraphs, using the third person (*Mother, he, she*). Form sentences that express your ideas clearly. Vary your writing by using compound subjects and verbs. Then tape your story and play it for your family members.

Prewriting You may want to create a cluster diagram showing your subject's most interesting characteristics. Then make a Sequence of Events chart detailing the main events in the story.

Drafting Use the Sequence of Events chart to tell the story and the cluster diagram to bring your subject to life. Your first sentence should capture the tone of the story or set the scene. Your concluding sentence should summarize the story or state its main point.

Revising Read aloud your first and last sentences to a classmate. Ask him or her how they relate to each other. Then have your partner read and give you feedback on your story. Make sure that each sentence expresses a complete thought.

Editing Check your story for errors in spelling and punctuation. Be sure that you have capitalized people's names and the names of places.

Publishing Prepare a final copy and use an audiocassette recorder to tape it. If possible, play it for your family.

Another Look

Recognizing Sentences

A **sentence** is a group of words that expresses a complete thought.

A **sentence fragment** is a group of words that expresses an incomplete thought.

Subjects and Predicates

The **subject** names the person, place, thing, or idea that the sentence is about. *(page L7)*

A **complete subject** includes all the words used to identify the person, place, thing, or idea that the sentence is about. *(page L7)*

A **simple subject** is the main word in the complete subject. *(pages L8–L9)*

A **compound subject** is two or more subjects in one sentence that have the same verb and are joined by a conjunction. *(page L18)*

The **predicate** tells something about the subject. *(page L7)*

A **complete predicate** includes all the words that tell what the subject is doing or that tell something about the subject. *(page L11)*

A **simple predicate,** or **verb,** is the main word or phrase in the complete predicate. *(page L12)*

A **verb phrase** includes the main verb plus any helping, or auxiliary, verbs. *(pages L14–L15)*

A **compound verb** is two or more verbs in one sentence that have the same subject and are joined by a conjunction. *(page L20)*

Position of Subjects

When the subject in a sentence comes before the verb, the sentence is in **natural order.** *(page L22)*

When the verb or part of a verb phrase comes before the subject, the sentence is in **inverted order.** *(pages L22–L23)*

When the subject of a sentence is not stated, the subject is an **understood *you*.** *(pages L25–L26)*

Directions

Write the letter of the term that correctly identifies the underlined word or words in each sentence.

EXAMPLE **1.** Scientists have developed new ways to keep food fresh.

1 **A** simple subject
B complete subject
C simple predicate
D complete predicate

ANSWER **1 D**

1. Fruits and vegetables can spoil if they become too ripe.
2. Many foods need to refrigerated so they will be safe for eating.
3. A candy maker in France developed the method of canning in the 1790s.
4. Made it possible for fruits and vegetables to be stored for a long time.
5. He cooked the foods and poured them into clean glass bottles.
6. He sealed and sterilized the bottles by heating them in boiling water.
7. High temperatures will destroy organisms in food.
8. Charles Birdseye, a scientist, developed a way to keep foods fresh.
9. Did he freeze the foods?
10. Today routinely freeze the foods.

1
A complete subject
B complete predicate
C compound subject
D compound verb

2
A simple subject
B complete subject
C simple predicate
D complete predicate

3
A simple subject
B complete subject
C simple predicate
D complete predicate

4
A sentence fragment
B inverted order
C simple predicate
D compound subject

5
A complete subject
B complete predicate
C compound subject
D compound verb

6
A simple subject
B compound subject
C simple predicate
D complete predicate

7
A sentence fragment
B inverted order
C simple predicate
D complete subject

8
A simple subject
B complete predicate
C compound subject
D compound verb

9
A sentence fragment
B inverted order
C simple predicate
D compound subject

10
A sentence fragment
B inverted order
C simple predicate
D compound subject

CHAPTER 2

Nouns and Pronouns

Directions

Write the letter of the term that correctly identifies the underlined word or words in each sentence.

EXAMPLE **1.** Many people learn to cook at the <u>Culinary Institute of America</u>.

1 **A** abstract noun
B common noun
C proper noun
D collective noun

ANSWER **1 C**

1. At the CIA, <u>chefs</u> teach the classes.
2. Each <u>class</u> learns a different kind of cooking.
3. The <u>classrooms</u> are equipped with stoves and refrigerators.
4. The students are responsible for cleaning <u>their</u> workstations.
5. <u>Each</u> must pass an intensive cooking examination to graduate.
6. The students get great <u>satisfaction</u> from learning cooking skills.
7. <u>Those</u> are the skills they will use all their lives.
8. <u>Who</u> will go on to cook professionally?
9. They <u>themselves</u> do not know the answer until after graduation.
10. They must prepare <u>themselves</u> for a difficult job search.

1 **A** common noun
B collective noun
C abstract noun
D proper noun

2 **A** proper noun
B abstract noun
C compound noun
D collective noun

3 **A** abstract noun
B collective noun
C compound noun
D proper noun

4 **A** personal pronoun
B reflexive pronoun
C intensive pronoun
D indefinite pronoun

5 **A** intensive pronoun
B indefinite pronoun
C personal pronoun
D reflexive pronoun

6 **A** compound noun
B proper noun
C abstract noun
D collective noun

7 **A** interrogative pronoun
B indefinite pronoun
C reflexive pronoun
D demonstrative pronoun

8 **A** demonstrative pronoun
B intensive pronoun
C interrogative pronoun
D personal pronoun

9 **A** intensive pronoun
B interrogative pronoun
C indefinite pronoun
D reflexive pronoun

10 **A** indefinite pronoun
B reflexive pronoun
C demonstrative pronoun
D intensive pronoun

Marc Chagall. *I and the Village,* 1911.
Oil on canvas, 75$\frac{5}{8}$ inches by 59$\frac{5}{8}$ inches. The Museum of Modern Art, New York.

Describe What figures do you see in the painting? What do you think they represent?

Analyze What is the center of interest in the painting? How does the painter draw the eye to it?

Interpret What do you think the artist is trying to express about his village? Explain.

Judge How well do you think Chagall's use of color and image conveys a sense of memory? Explain.

At the end of the chapter, you will use this artwork to stimulate ideas for writing.

Nouns

A dictionary lists thousands of words. All these words can be divided into eight groups called the parts of speech. A word's part of speech is determined by the job it does in a sentence.

THE EIGHT PARTS OF SPEECH	
noun (names)	**adverb** (describes, limits)
pronoun (replaces)	**preposition** (relates)
verb (states action or being)	**conjunction** (connects)
adjective (describes, limits)	**interjection** (expresses strong feeling)

In English, there are more nouns than any other part of speech.

A **noun** is the name of a person, place, thing, or idea.

Concrete and Abstract Nouns

Nouns can be divided into **concrete nouns** and **abstract nouns.** You can easily identify concrete nouns because they name people, places, and things you can usually see or touch. Abstract nouns are harder to identify because they name ideas and qualities.

CONCRETE NOUNS	
People	sailor, brother, Mrs. Wong, singers, Heather
Places	forest, mountains, amusement park, Texas, beach, Empire State Building, rooms, Germany
Things	rug, flower, explosion, flu, chipmunk, colors, guitar, slogan, lists

ABSTRACT NOUNS	
Ideas and Qualities	freedom, fun, love, inflation, bravery, anger, honesty, sickness, faith, democracy, thought, honor, belief, hunger

Connect to Speaking and Writing

When you speak or write, the words you use create certain pictures in the minds of your audience. The nouns you choose can make these pictures dull and fuzzy or clear and exact. Vague, general nouns should almost always be replaced with specific nouns to bring your word pictures into sharper focus. Notice the difference between the two sentences that follow.

The **bugs** crawled over the **flower.**

The **ants** crawled over the **daisy.** 

You can learn more about forming plurals of nouns on pages L627–L634. You can learn more about possessive nouns on pages L575–L577.

Practice Your Skills

Check Your Understanding
Finding Nouns

Write the nouns in each sentence.

1. During springtime, flowers bloom.

2. The fragrance of the buds fills the air.

3. Bees are attracted to the perfume of flowers.

4. These insects see color, pattern, and movement.

5. Bees taste blooms with their front legs and antennae.

6. These creatures have short bodies covered with hair.

7. Pollen clings to the hair on the body of the insect.

8. Bees make honey from the nectar of flowers.

9. Humans have harvested honey for many centuries.

10. Our appreciation of this golden liquid continues today.

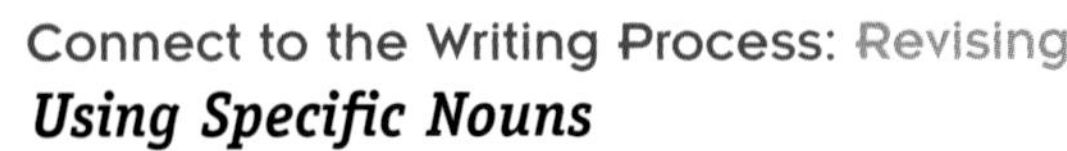

Connect to the Writing Process: Revising

Using Specific Nouns

Rewrite the following sentences, changing the underlined general noun to a specific noun that creates a clearer picture.

11. The tree was covered with insects.

12. Fruit hung from its branches.

13. A bird circled above the building.

14. A cool wind blew across the land.

Communicate Your Ideas

APPLY TO WRITING

Writer's Craft: ***Analyzing the Use of Nouns***

Writers often choose nouns to create a specific picture in the minds of their readers. In this paragraph from "In the Heart of the Heart of the Country," William H. Gass writes about two fruit trees that remind him of his childhood. Read the paragraph, and then follow the instructions below.

> I knew nothing about apples. Why should I? My country came in my childhood, and I dreamed of sitting among the blooms like the bees. I failed to spray the pear tree too. I doubled up under them at first, admiring the sturdy low branches I should have pruned, and later I acclaimed the blossoms. Shortly after the fruit formed there were . . . apples the size of goodish stones which made me wobble on my ankles when I walked about the yard. Sometimes a piece crushed by a heel would cling on the shoe to track the house. . . .
>
> *–William H. Gass,* "In the Heart of the Heart of the Country"

- List the nouns in the passage.
- Underline the nouns that are specific nouns.
- What is the effect of the author's use of specific nouns?

Common and Proper Nouns

A **common noun** names any person, place, or thing.

A **proper noun** names a particular person, place, or thing.

All nouns are either common nouns or proper nouns. Every proper noun begins with a capital letter.

COMMON NOUNS	PROPER NOUNS
woman	Maria Chavez
city	Paris
building	World Trade Center
team	Houston Astros
day	Sunday

A proper noun sometimes includes more than one word. For example, even though *World Trade Center* is three words, it is considered one noun. It is the name of *one* place.

You can learn more about the capitalization of proper nouns on pages L464–L467.

PRACTICE YOUR SKILLS

Check Your Understanding
Finding Common and Proper Nouns

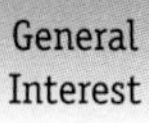

General Interest

Make two columns on your paper. Label the first column *Common Nouns* and the second column *Proper Nouns.* Then, in the appropriate column, write the nouns from the following sentences.

1. In Colombia, ants are sold as snacks by vendors on the street.
2. Fried worms are eaten in Mexico.
3. People in Uganda crush flies and shape them into pancakes.

4. In other parts of Africa, termites are munched like pretzels.
5. Certain spiders are roasted in New Guinea.
6. Some insects taste like nuts.
7. Restaurants in New York City serve ants dipped in chocolate.
8. In recent years the North American Bait Farms have held a cooking contest using worms.
9. In some cookbooks you can find a recipe for peppers stuffed with earthworms.
10. Actually, insects give people necessary protein and vitamins.

Connect to the Writing Process: Editing
Capitalizing Proper Nouns

The following postcard message contains many proper nouns, but the writer forgot to begin them with capital letters. Rewrite the message, capitalizing all the proper nouns.

Dear sandy,

My vacation in europe has been great! I have been eating my way across the continent. After touring the louvre in paris, I dined on escargots. A few days later, I enjoyed spaghetti near the coliseum in rome. Today, I ate feta cheese in greece. Tomorrow I will try borscht after seeing the hermitage in st. petersburg.

On wednesday, I will fly home to denver and begin a diet. See you soon!

Your friend,

josie

Communicate Your Ideas

APPLY TO WRITING

E-Mail Message: ***Proper Nouns***

You have invited a friend to come for dinner. Send her an E-mail message giving her details about the meal. Be sure to include the day and time when the dinner will be held. You should also give her directions to your house. Take special care to capitalize the proper nouns in the message.

Compound and Collective Nouns

A noun that includes more than one word is called a **compound noun.**

Some nouns include more than one word. *Post* is one noun, *office* is one noun, but *post office* is also one noun. *Post office* is an example of a compound noun. It is not always easy to know how to write a particular compound noun. The best way to find out is to check in a dictionary. Compound nouns can take one of three forms.

COMPOUND NOUNS	
Separate Words	living room, home run, peanut butter, ice cream
Hyphenated	break-in, attorney-at-law, bird-watcher, great-grandmother
Combined	birdhouse, headband, flashlight, crosswalk, brainpower

You can learn more about punctuation of compound nouns on page L603.

A **collective noun** names a group of people or things.

COMMON COLLECTIVE NOUNS			
band	crew	flock	nation
committee	crowd	herd	orchestra
colony	family	league	swarm

Practice Your Skills

Check Your Understanding

Finding Compound and Collective Nouns

Contemporary Life

Make two columns on your paper. Label the first column *Compound Nouns* and the second column *Collective Nouns.* Then, in the appropriate column, write each noun.

1. My classmates and I listened to presentations by members of an environmental group.

2. One speaker discussed water pollution and how it affects a species of wild ducks.

3. Another pair of presenters warned of the decline in the population of the grasshopper.

4. According to the organization, a number of animals have recently been declared endangered.

5. Because the group was so interesting, the entire faculty of the high school came to hear them.

Connect to the Writing Process: Editing

Writing Nouns Correctly

Edit the following advertisement copy to eliminate errors in capitalization of proper nouns and misspellings of compound nouns. Write the corrected paragraph.

Let ollie's outdoor expeditions take you to visit mothernature for the day! Join our group as we travel to the st. francis river, where we will spend the day discussing the flora and fauna, as well as the wild-life of the area. Birdwatchers will enjoy viewing the flock of geese that live in the area, while animallovers will appreciate the herd of deer that often come to drink at the river. Children will enjoy building bird houses while their parents become fossilhunters for the day. Stop by ollie's outdoor expeditions at 211 sunnyvale street for more details.

Mixed Practice

General Interest **Write the nouns in each sentence.** (There are 33 nouns.)

1. How did Houdini escape from jails, straitjackets, and strange containers?
2. Sometimes he kept keys in his throat.
3. He used the same method sword-swallowers use.
4. Once, when escaping from a jail in New York, he hid a piece of metal in a callus in the heel of one foot.
5. He attached it to a wire that he had hidden in his hair to make a key.
6. He also designed trick cabinets with locks and hinges in secret places.
7. This magician also had great strength and agility.
8. Like a professional athlete, he kept his body and mind in top shape.
9. Moreover, he could dislocate his joints.
10. His skill mystified audiences throughout the world.

Pronouns

A **pronoun** is a word that takes the place of one or more nouns.

Speaking and writing would be very repetitious if there were no words to take the place of nouns. Pronouns do this job. The second example below reads more smoothly and is easier to understand when pronouns are substituted for two of the nouns.

Holly took Holly's sweater with Holly on the class trip.
Holly took **her** sweater with **her** on the class trip.

Pronoun Antecedents

The noun a pronoun refers to or replaces is called its **antecedent.**

In the following examples, an arrow has been drawn from the pronoun to its antecedent. Notice that the antecedent usually comes before the pronoun.

Dion said that **he** couldn't go to the zoo.

Lynn asked **Sandy,** "Did **we** miss the dolphin show?"

You can learn more about pronouns and antecedents on pages L355–L356.

PRACTICE YOUR SKILLS

Check Your Understanding
Finding Antecedents

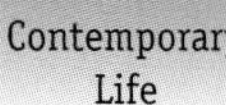

Write the antecedent for each underlined pronoun.

1. Juanita brought her camera on the trip to the zoo.

2. Steve asked Juanita to take a picture of him.

3. Linda said, "I enjoy the reptiles."
4. Gretchen and Margo said they were looking for the penguins.
5. Ms. Jackson told Henry that she liked to watch the monkeys.
6. The monkey cage had a tire swing in it.
7. Jeff asked Ms. Jackson, "Did you bring the monkeys a banana?"
8. Chris and Jesse asked the teacher, "Are we leaving now?"
9. Juanita said that she wanted one more picture of the peacocks.
10. Ms. Jackson's students enjoyed their trip to the zoo.

Connect to the Writing Process: Revising

Replacing Nouns with Pronouns

Rewrite the paragraph, replacing nouns with pronouns where they are needed.

Investigations into the intelligence of gorillas show that gorillas are much smarter than people once thought gorillas were. Gorillas will stack boxes to help gorillas reach bananas that are too high to pick. Gorillas will use sticks as tools to pull food into gorillas' cages. One scientist, Dr. James White, trained a female gorilla named Congo to perform various actions. When the scientist returned some years later, Congo remembered the scientist. Congo also repeated some of the actions the scientist had taught Congo. Congo's behavior in these instances helped convince scientists of gorillas' intelligence.

APPLY TO WRITING

Journal Entry: *Pronouns*

Rosa Bonheur. *The King of the Desert,* 19th century. Oil on canvas, 39⅜ by 37⅝ inches.

The year is 1850, and you are an explorer who has come to Africa. Today, while on safari for the first time, you came face-to-face with a magnificent lion. This painting of "the king of the desert" shows your memory of that moment. It is evening now. As you sit in your tent reflecting calmly on the experience, write a description of the big cat for your travel journal. In your journal entry, be sure to describe the lion's appearance, as well as any sounds you may have heard or feelings you may have had. Use pronouns to prevent your writing from becoming repetitious.

Personal Pronouns

Personal pronouns are the most common type of pronoun. These pronouns can be divided into the following three groups.

PERSONAL PRONOUNS	
FIRST PERSON	(the person speaking)
SINGULAR	I, me, my, mine
PLURAL	we, us, our, ours
SECOND PERSON	(the person spoken to)
SINGULAR	you, your, yours
PLURAL	you, your, yours
THIRD PERSON	(the person or thing spoken about)
SINGULAR	he, him, his, she, her, hers, it, its
PLURAL	they, them, their, theirs

The following sentences use personal pronouns.

FIRST-PERSON PRONOUNS	**I** want to take **my** notebook with **me** to the convention.
	We think **our** plan of political action is best for **us.**
SECOND-PERSON PRONOUNS	Did **you** bring **your** list of questions for the candidate?
	Are these pamphlets **yours** or do they belong to Mary?
THIRD-PERSON PRONOUNS	The reporter took **his** camera and film with **him.**
	They enjoyed **their** new leader's speech to the delegates.

Practice Your Skills

Check Your Understanding

Finding Personal Pronouns

History Topic **Write the personal pronouns in each sentence.**

1. In the United States, Elizabeth Cady Stanton and Susan B. Anthony devoted their lives to women's suffrage.

2. If you are a woman in the United States, you owe many of your legal and political rights to these courageous suffragists.

3. At the time when Anthony began her work, women had few legal rights.

4. When African American men were given the right to vote in 1869, she began a movement to secure the same rights for women.

5. In 1869, the territory of Wyoming was the first area in the U.S. to allow its female citizens to vote.

6. Anthony was president of the American Woman Suffrage Association until she was eighty.

7. Anthony voted in the election of 1872, but she was fined $100 for breaking the law.

8. She refused to pay it.

9. We can see that few people are as devoted to a cause as she.

10. American women did not gain their right to vote until 1920.

11. Elizabeth Cady Stanton studied law in her father's office when he was a Supreme Court justice.

12. In 1848, she helped lead the first convention that demanded women's suffrage.

13. Stanton also wrote articles for a newspaper that she and Anthony ran together.

Reflexive and Intensive Pronouns

Reflexive pronouns and **intensive pronouns** refer to or emphasize another noun or pronoun.

These pronouns are formed by adding *–self* or *–selves* to certain personal pronouns.

REFLEXIVE AND INTENSIVE PRONOUNS	
SINGULAR	myself, yourself, himself, herself, itself
PLURAL	ourselves, yourselves, themselves

Although the reflexive and intensive pronouns are the same words, their function in a sentence differs. A reflexive pronoun reflects back to a noun or a pronoun mentioned earlier in the sentence. An intensive pronoun is used directly after its antecedent to intensify, or emphasize, a statement. A reflexive pronoun is necessary to the meaning of the sentence, but an intensive pronoun is not.

REFLEXIVE Pioneers organized **themselves** into wagon trains before their long journey.

INTENSIVE I **myself** could not have survived the hardships of the westward trek.

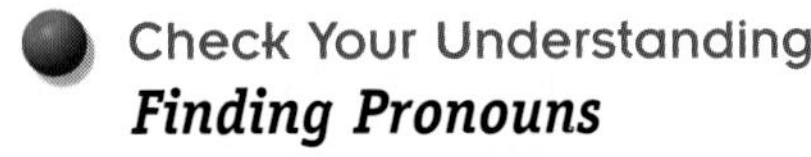

Check Your Understanding

Finding Pronouns

History Topic **Write the personal, reflexive, and intensive pronouns in each sentence and label them *P* for personal, *R* for reflexive, and *I* for intensive.**

1. In the early 1840s, adventurous settlers readied themselves for the overland trip to the West.
2. Life in the Oregon country held new promise for them.

3. The settlers themselves could never have anticipated all the hardships they encountered on the two-thousand-mile Oregon Trail.
4. When it was loaded, a covered wagon often weighed thousands of pounds.
5. It was pulled across various types of terrain by teams of horses, mules, or oxen.
6. The wagons were uncomfortable for the passengers themselves.
7. On many occasions, settlers might walk beside them rather than ride.
8. The journey was hard for the travelers, but many nights they sang by their campfires.
9. The route was mapped in 1804 by Lewis and Clark themselves.
10. Today, we can drive our cars along modern roads beside the historic trail.

Connect to the Writing Process: Revising

Using Intensive Pronouns

Add intensive pronouns to the following sentences to make the statements stronger.

11. On many days, a woman rode alone in the covered wagon.
12. She often drove the long miles and cared for her children at the same time.
13. Sometimes on the trail, disputes arose among the settlers.
14. The wagon master often served as the mediator of these disputes.
15. He knew how dangerous fights among the settlers could be.

Communicate Your Ideas

APPLY TO WRITING

Persuasive Letter: ***Pronouns***

Imagine that you are a settler traveling to Oregon in a covered wagon. Write a letter to a friend back home in the East, encouraging or discouraging him or her to take the same trip. Give at least three reasons to explain your viewpoint. As you write, use pronouns to keep your writing from being repetitive.

 Other Kinds of Pronouns

Three other kinds of pronouns are indefinite pronouns, demonstrative pronouns, and interrogative pronouns.

Indefinite Pronouns

Indefinite pronouns refer to unnamed people, places, things, or ideas.

Indefinite pronouns often do not have definite antecedents as personal pronouns do.

Several have qualified for the contest.
Many collected the newspapers.
I've gathered **everything** now.

COMMON INDEFINITE PRONOUNS	
SINGULAR	another, anybody, anyone, anything, each, either, everybody, everyone, everything, much, neither, nobody, no one, one, somebody, someone, something
PLURAL	both, few, many, others, several
SINGULAR/PLURAL	all, any, most, none, some

Connect to Speaking and Writing

The ten indefinite pronouns in color on the preceding chart may be singular or plural. The other indefinite pronouns are always singular. When you speak or write, remember that a pronoun must agree with its antecedent. If singular indefinite pronouns serve as antecedents to other pronouns, both pronouns must be singular.

Everything was in **its** place.

Everyone at the gym has **his** or **her** own locker.

Each of the girls ate **her** lunch.

Several brought **their** lunches. 

You can learn more about indefinite pronouns as antecedents on pages L357–L358.

Practice Your Skills

Check Your Understanding
Finding Indefinite Pronouns

Contemporary Life **Write the indefinite pronouns in each sentence.**

1. Many feel they cannot help the environment.
2. Some say the problem is too large.
3. However, anyone can recycle.
4. Almost everything has more than one use.
5. Everybody can conserve natural resources.
6. A small action is better than none.
7. We should encourage others in this pursuit.
8. Nothing is wrong with thanking citizens who recycle their trash.
9. Anyone can join the effort.
10. No one should forget to recycle.
11. Each can make a difference.
12. Everyone can learn how to recycle.

13. We should do anything to reduce waste.
14. All have a right to a cleaner environment.
15. Most have access to recycling bins nowadays.

Connect to the Writing Process: Revising

Making Pronouns and Their Antecedents Agree

Change the underlined pronouns in the following sentences so that they agree with their antecedents. Write the new sentences.

16. Either of the girls could have reused their paper scraps in art projects.
17. Both of the boys recycled his cans.
18. Does everyone know where their recycling bin is?
19. Some of the men left his cans on the table.
20. Each of the girls cleaned up their area.
21. Few forget to recycle her newspapers.
22. Neither recycles their glass.
23. Several remembered to label his recycling bins.
24. Many keep her recycling bins handy.
25. Everyone takes their recycling seriously.

Demonstrative Pronouns

Demonstrative pronouns point out a specific person, place, thing, or idea.

DEMONSTRATIVE PRONOUNS			
this	that	these	those

This is Mary's coat on the hanger.
Are **these** John's glasses?

Interrogative Pronouns

Interrogative pronouns are used to ask questions.

INTERROGATIVE PRONOUNS				
what	which	who	whom	whose

What is known about the case?
Who is coming to the party?

You can learn about another type of pronoun, the relative pronoun, on pages L229–L234.

Practice Your Skills

Check Your Understanding

Finding Demonstrative and Interrogative Pronouns

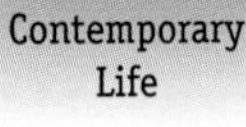

Contemporary Life

Write the demonstrative pronouns and the interrogative pronouns. Use the label *D* for demonstrative and *I* for interrogative.

1. Who is going to the dance on Saturday?
2. That is the most important question on our minds.
3. This is my outfit for the dance.
4. Of all my shoes, these will match my dress best.
5. What is the first song going to be?
6. Those are great tunes for dancing.
7. Which is your favorite?
8. That is a good example of rap.
9. Are those the latest style?
10. Whom did you meet at the last school dance you attended?

Connect to the Writing Process: Drafting

Using Pronouns

Add pronouns to complete the following sentences. Choose personal, indefinite, demonstrative, or interrogative pronouns.

11. The little girl found ■ all alone in the department store.

12. ■ began to cry.

13. ■ in the store turned to look at ■.

14. Suddenly, ■ felt a hand on ■ small shoulder.

15. ■ had found her?

16. ■ mother smiled down at her.

17. "■ was a scary feeling," she told her mother.

18. ■ is why little girls should not wander from ■ mothers.

19. "Well, ■ are safe now," said the mother.

20. "May ■ get two ice cream cones for ■?"asked the little girl.

21. "Should ■ eat lunch first?" asked her mother.

22. "■ should we eat for lunch?" she also asked the girl.

23. "■ good," the girl decided.

Communicate Your Ideas

APPLY TO WRITING

Personal Narrative: ***Nouns and Pronouns***

Write a narrative for your classmates about your first day in ninth grade. Did you feel lost or right at home? Did you know most of the people or did you have to make new friends? Use a variety of nouns and pronouns to make your narrative interesting.

QuickCheck Mixed Practice

Contemporary Life

Write the pronouns in the following sentences. Label each *P* for personal, *Ind* for indefinite, *D* for demonstrative, or *Int* for interrogative.

1. That was the year we built the tree house in our backyard.
2. Whose was it?
3. Who actually helped build it for your younger brothers and sisters?
4. This was the block where we used to live when all of us were in grade school.
5. These are the streets where we played ball with others.
6. Which is the school you and the rest of your family attended?
7. What are the subjects you studied with my older brother?
8. Whom among all of your mathematics teachers did you like the best?
9. Those were the days when no one realized how quickly our lives would change.
10. That used to be fun when we played ball on summer evenings.

CheckPoint

Identifying Nouns and Pronouns

Write each noun and pronoun in the following sentences. Then label each one *N* for noun or *P* for pronoun. Note: A date, such as 1533, is a noun.

1. Born in 1533, Elizabeth I was one of the most famous rulers of England.
2. Her court was well known for its artists and playwrights.
3. When she was a young girl, Elizabeth was locked up in the Tower of London by her half-sister Mary.
4. When Mary died, Elizabeth came to the throne of England and ruled for forty-five years.
5. Born in 1769, Napoleon was a famous ruler of France.
6. He conquered large parts of Europe and made himself emperor over them.
7. He was born on the island of Corsica.
8. Eventually he became the most powerful man in the French army and won many victories throughout Europe.
9. He reorganized France and improved the law, banks, trade, and education.
10. When his enemies in Europe invaded France, Napoleon was exiled to an island off the coast of Italy.
11. He eventually returned to France with his soldiers, but he was finally defeated at the Battle of Waterloo.
12. Whom do you remember from centuries ago?
13. Only a few stand out in our history books for their bravery, great deeds, or incredible lives.
14. In the modern world, however, people instantly become famous because of television, movies, and newspapers.
15. Of course, few of these instant celebrities will be remembered next month.

Recognizing Pronouns and Their Antecedents

Write each personal pronoun and its antecedent in the following sentences.

1. Because Jamie was absent, he missed the field trip.
2. When the twins dress alike, they look identical.
3. An anteater can extend its tongue about two feet.
4. Lisa told Tim, "If you bring your racket, we can play a game."
5. Ken took his raincoat with him to the baseball game.
6. Mr. Ash told Nancy, "You should give your report now."
7. Bill and Ron rode their bicycles to school today.
8. "I didn't see you at the mall," Pam told Terry.
9. Linda said she is making her own dinner tonight.
10. "My friends asked me to visit them," Daniel told his dad.

Using Nouns and Pronouns

Write ten sentences that follow the directions below. (The sentences may include other nouns and pronouns besides those listed, and they may come in any order.) Write about one of the following topics or a topic of your own choice: a famous leader, sports figure, or musician. Write *N* above each noun and *P* above each pronoun.

Write a sentence that . . .

1. includes nouns that name a person, a place, and a thing.
2. includes a noun that names an idea.
3. includes a common noun and a proper noun.
4. includes a collective noun.
5. includes a compound noun.
6. includes several personal pronouns.
7. includes a reflexive pronoun.
8. includes one or two indefinite pronouns.
9. includes a demonstrative pronoun.
10. includes an interrogative pronoun.

Language and *Self-Expression*

Marc Chagall (1887–1985) grew up in Vitebsk, Russia. He left home to study art in St. Petersburg and then moved to Paris. Many of his paintings show people and animals floating across the canvas in a dreamlike state, and others include scenes of his childhood home, Vitebsk.

Think of a scene from your own childhood that stirs fond memories. It can be an actual event or something as simple as the memory of a dinner table, spread with food and surrounded by familiar faces. Write a description of that event or scene. Include as many different kinds of nouns and pronouns as you can.

Prewriting You may wish to make a cluster diagram of your memory of the scene. Include people, places, things, and ideas in your diagram.

Drafting Use the cluster diagram to organize your description as you begin drafting. Tell what people and things are part of your memory and explain how the memory makes you feel.

Revising Read your description to a partner. Ask your partner if you have conveyed the feelings the memory brings you. Make sure all your pronouns have clear antecedents.

Editing Check your description for errors in spelling and punctuation. Be sure you have capitalized all proper names.

Publishing Prepare a final copy. If possible, find a photograph to accompany your description. Place it in a class book of memories.

Another Look

A **noun** is the name of a person, place, thing, or idea.

Classification of Nouns

A **concrete noun** names people, places, or things you can see or touch. *(page L39)*

An **abstract noun** names ideas or qualities. *(pages L39–L40)*

A **common noun** names any person, place, or thing. *(page L42)*

A **proper noun** names a particular person, place, or thing. *(page L42)*

A **compound noun** includes more than one word. *(page L44)*

A **collective noun** names a group of people or things. *(page L45)*

A **pronoun** is a word that takes the place of one or more nouns.

The noun that a pronoun refers to or replaces is called its **antecedent.**

Kinds of Pronouns

Personal pronouns can be divided into several groups. *(page L50)*

Reflexive pronouns and **intensive pronouns** refer back to or emphasize another noun or pronoun. *(page L52)*

Indefinite pronouns refer to unnamed people, places, things, or ideas. *(pages L54–L55)*

Demonstrative pronouns point out specific persons, places, things, or ideas. *(page L56)*

Interrogative pronouns are used to ask questions. *(page L57)*

Posttest

Directions

Write the letter of the term that correctly identifies the underlined word or words in each sentence.

EXAMPLE **1.** For ten months during 1997 and 1998, fires burned in Indonesia.

1 **A** proper noun
B abstract noun
C collective noun
D common noun

ANSWER **1 D**

1. Indonesia had been in the grip of a long drought throughout the year.

2. The rain forests were drier than we remembered them ever being before.

3. They burned with a hot intensity day and night for months.

4. This produced a severe smog over much of the country and surrounding areas.

5. What were the results of this disaster?

6. Everything in the country came to a halt.

7. Farm families were left without livelihoods.

8. Sickness and hunger were rampant.

9. If they stayed outdoors, people found themselves wheezing and fainting.

10. Indonesia itself lost over a billion dollars in farm and other products.

1 A abstract noun
B proper noun
C common noun
D collective noun

2 A compound noun
B proper noun
C collective noun
D abstract noun

3 A reflexive pronoun
B intensive pronoun
C personal pronoun
D demonstrative pronoun

4 A personal pronoun
B demonstrative pronoun
C intensive pronoun
D indefinite pronoun

5 A intensive pronoun
B indefinite pronoun
C interrogative pronoun
D demonstrative pronoun

6 A reflexive pronoun
B demonstrative pronoun
C intensive pronoun
D indefinite pronoun

7 A compound noun
B collective noun
C abstract noun
D proper noun

8 A abstract noun
B compound noun
C proper noun
D collective noun

9 A intensive pronoun
B indefinite pronoun
C reflexive pronoun
D interrogative pronoun

10 A indefinite pronoun
B reflexive pronoun
C intensive pronoun
D demonstrative pronoun

CHAPTER 3

Verbs

Directions

Write the letter of the term that correctly identifies the underlined word or words in each sentence.

EXAMPLE **1.** The class has selected a play.

1 **A** transitive verb
B intransitive verb
C helping verb
D linking verb

ANSWER **1** **A**

1. The students chose William Shakespeare's *Julius Caesar* for their class play.
2. William very much wanted the part of Caesar in the school production.
3. He would have been a great Caesar.
4. Instead, the rest of the class chose Nick for the part of the famous Roman leader.
5. Nick was good in rehearsals.
6. No one could have worked harder.
7. Julia designed the sets for the play.
8. She painted after school every day.
9. Raul and Sally were the costume designers as well as the make-up artists.
10. They must have sewn more than a dozen togas for the actors.

1 A transitive verb
B intransitive verb
C linking verb
D helping verb

2 A linking verb
B transitive verb
C helping verb
D intransitive verb

3 A helping verb
B linking verb
C transitive verb
D intransitive verb

4 A linking verb
B intransitive verb
C helping verb
D transitive verb

5 A intransitive verb
B helping verb
C linking verb
D transitive verb

6 A helping verb
B linking verb
C transitive verb
D intransitive verb

7 A intransitive verb
B helping verb
C linking verb
D transitive verb

8 A helping verb
B intransitive verb
C transitive verb
D linking verb

9 A intransitive verb
B transitive verb
C linking verb
D helping verb

10 A transitive verb
B helping verb
C intransitive verb
D linking verb

Joan Mitchell. *George Went Swimming at Barnes Hole, But It Got Too Cold,* 1957. Oil on canvas, 85¼ by 78¼ inches. Albright-Knox Art Gallery, Buffalo, New York. Gift of Seymour H. Knox, 1958. © Estate of Joan Mitchell.

Describe What colors and patterns do you see in this painting?

Analyze How do the light and dark areas work in the painting? What effect do they have?

Interpret The artist stated that the painting reflected "the memory of a feeling." What feeling do you think she was remembering as she painted?

Judge How do the bold strokes and colors of the painting affect you? Do you feel the artist clearly expresses her ideas in her style? Explain.

At the end of this chapter, you will use the artwork to stimulate ideas for writing.

Action Verbs

An essential part of every sentence is the verb because a verb breathes life into a sentence.

A **verb** is a word that expresses action or a state of being.

One kind of verb, an action verb, gives a subject action and movement.

An **action verb** tells what action a subject is performing.

Most action verbs show physical action.

Marine biologists **observe** the creatures of the sea.

Many fish **swim** in the world's oceans.

Some action verbs show mental action. Others show ownership or possession.

Our class **studied** water mammals.

The teacher **has** a photograph of a killer whale.

You may recall that helping verbs are often used with an action verb to form a verb phrase.

A **verb phrase** includes a main verb plus any helping, or auxiliary, verbs.

The verb phrase may contain more than one helping verb. It may also be interrupted by other words.

The whales **will have migrated** by October.

The students **could** certainly **learn** more about the sea.

Should our class **visit** the ocean?

I **have** never **seen** a killer whale.

Here is a list of the most common helping verbs.

COMMON HELPING VERBS	
be	am, is, are, was, were, am, be, being, been
have	has, have, had
do	do, does, did
OTHERS	may, might, must, can, could, shall, should, will, would

You can learn about regular and irregular verbs on pages L279–L288.

CONNECT TO SPEAKING AND WRITING

When you speak or write, the verbs you use show action in the sentence. You can use these words to make your audience see what is happening. When you choose your verbs carefully, you can also help your audience hear the action in the sentence.

The motorboat **cut** through the water.

The motorboat **whirred** through the water.

Verbs have the power to appeal to all five senses. You can make your writing more interesting by choosing the action words in your sentences carefully.

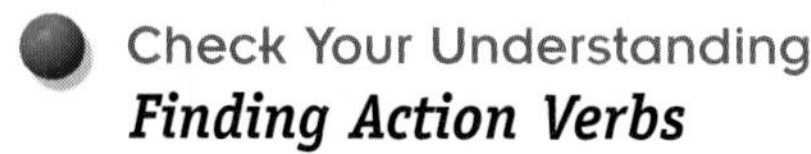

Check Your Understanding
Finding Action Verbs

Science Topic **Write the verb or verb phrase in the following sentences. Remember, words that interrupt a verb phrase are not part of the verb.**

1. Dr. Lilly, a scientist from California, has been experimenting with dolphins for many years.

2. He has made some curious claims about them.

3. Dolphins have larger brains than humans.
4. Their language contains at least fifty thousand words.
5. Their brains can handle four different conversations at one time.
6. They can also judge between right and wrong.
7. Dolphins can remember sounds and series of sounds.
8. They can even communicate among themselves.
9. They use a series of clicks, buzzes, and whistles.
10. Dolphins have discharged some of these sounds at the rate of seven hundred times a second.

Check Your Understanding
Finding Verb Phrases

Science Topic

Write the verb or verb phrase in the following sentences.

11. Humans have been fascinated by the whale for centuries.
12. Whales can be divided into two basic types.
13. They are classified by scientists as either baleen or toothed whales.
14. Some small whales must surface for air several times each hour.
15. The larger creatures can remain underwater for an hour or more.
16. One species of baleen whale, the blue whale, can weigh up to fifteen hundred tons.
17. This species of whale was almost hunted to extinction in the early 1900s.
18. Didn't early whale hunters see their beauty and grace?
19. Some of them may not have realized the consequences of their actions.
20. Today, many wildlife organizations protect whales from hunters.

Connect to the Writing Process: Revising

Replacing Verbs

Change the underlined verbs in the following sentences to help the reader "hear" rather than "see" the action.

21. The waterfall ran over the rocks.

22. Children have been playing in the water throughout the morning.

23. The tugboat moved through the water.

24. The waves rushed against the rocks.

25. The whale blew water from its spout.

Communicate Your Ideas

APPLY TO WRITING

Postcard: ***Action Verbs***

You are vacationing at the seashore. Your younger brother has never been to the beach. Write a postcard to him describing your first day on the beach. Remember to include vivid action verbs to make your writing interesting.

Transitive and Intransitive Verbs

A **transitive verb** is an action verb that passes the action from a doer to a receiver.

An **intransitive verb** expresses action or states something about the subject but does not pass the action from a doer to a receiver.

All action verbs fall within two general classes: transitive or intransitive. You can determine whether a verb is transitive or intransitive by identifying the subject and the verb. Then ask,

What? or *Whom?* A word that answers either question is called an object. An action verb that has an object is transitive. An action verb that does not have an object is intransitive.

TRANSITIVE	Many birds **eat** insects.
	(Birds eat what? *Insects* is the object. Therefore, *eat* is a transitive verb.)
INTRANSITIVE	Most geese **travel** in flocks.
	(Geese travel what? Geese travel whom? Since there is no object, *travel* is an intransitive verb.)

The same verb may be transitive in one sentence and intransitive in another.

TRANSITIVE	We **hung** birdhouses in the trees.
	(We hung what? *Birdhouses* is the object.)
INTRANSITIVE	The birdhouse **hung** from a rope in the oak tree.
	(Birdhouse hung what? There is no object.)

You can learn about object complements, which follow transitive verbs, on pages L149–L150.

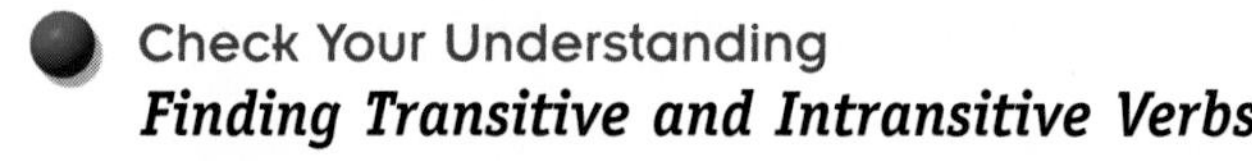

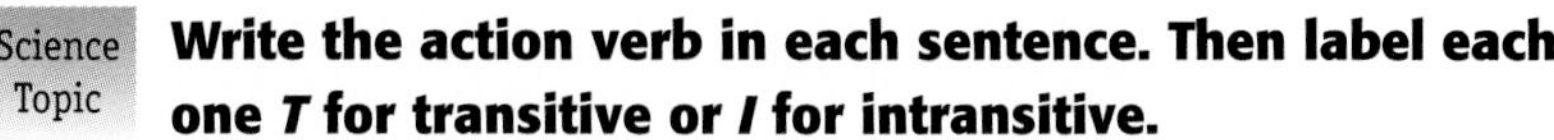

Finding Transitive and Intransitive Verbs

Science Topic **Write the action verb in each sentence. Then label each one *T* for transitive or *I* for intransitive.**

1. Birds live in trees, on the ground, and in the sides of cliffs.
2. Many different birds nest near the seashore.
3. Some owls build their nests in burrows.

4. Eagles keep the same nest throughout their lives.
5. Hummingbirds sometimes fly backward.
6. Snow buntings lose their brown feathers in winter.
7. Lice live on some birds and mammals.
8. Ibises often steal material for their nests from other birds.
9. Robins migrate in winter.
10. Due to population growth, humans pose the greatest danger to the bird population.

Connect to the Writing Process: Editing

Using Action Verbs

Supply an action verb for each of the following sentences. Label each one *T* for transitive or *I* for intransitive.

11. Scientists ■ the migration patterns of birds.
12. During autumn many birds ■ from the north to the south.
13. Most adult birds ■ their young from dangers.
14. In forests you ■ birds' songs all around you.
15. Two cardinals ■ across the wooded path.
16. Falcons ■ down on their prey at speeds of more than 200 miles per hour.
17. Penguins ■ their wings like flippers in the water.
18. Most birds ■ the nest when they are a few months old.
19. A bobwhite can ■ up to 15,000 seeds a day.
20. Many people around the world ■ birds as pets.

Linking Verbs

A **linking verb** links the subject with another word in the sentence. The other word either renames or describes the subject.

The farm **is** my home.

(*Is* links *home* with *farm*. *Home* renames the subject.)

Have you **been** sad lately?

(Turn a question into a statement: *You have been sad lately*. Then you can easily see that *have been* links *sad* and the subject *you*. *Sad* describes the subject.)

Here is a list of common linking verbs. They are all forms of the verb *be*. Any verb phrase ending in *be* or *been* is a form of *be* and can be used as a linking verb.

	COMMON FORMS OF *BE*	
be	shall be	have been
is	will be	has been
am	can be	had been
are	could be	could have been
was	should be	should have been
were	would be	may have been
	may be	might have been
	might be	must have been

The forms of *be* are not always linking verbs. To be a linking verb, a verb must link the subject with another word that renames or describes it. The word that renames or describes the subject is known as the subject complement. In the examples on the next page, the verbs simply make statements and are not linking verbs.

Our farm **is** over that hill.
The cows **will be** in the barn.

You can learn more about subject complements on pages L154–L155.

PRACTICE YOUR SKILLS

Check Your Understanding

Finding Linking Verbs

General Interest **Write the linking verb in each sentence. Then write the two words that the verb links.**

1. My childhood on the farm was great.
2. Childhood memories should be happy for everyone.
3. My mother had been a city girl.
4. My father could have been a doctor.
5. Instead, he was a farmer.
6. Wheat can be a difficult crop.
7. Dad was always lucky with our harvests.
8. In summer our fields were golden.
9. Because of this, gold will always be my favorite color.
10. I could never be happy anywhere else.

Additional Linking Verbs

A few other verbs besides *be* can be linking verbs.

ADDITIONAL LINKING VERBS			
appear	grow	seem	stay
become	look	smell	taste
feel	remain	sound	turn

These verbs also link the subject with a word that describes or renames it.

The air **feels** humid today.
(*Humid* describes the *air.*)

The tornado **remains** a destructive force of nature.
(*Force* renames *tornado.*)

Practice Your Skills

Check Your Understanding
Finding Linking Verbs

General Interest **Write the linking verb in each sentence. Then write the two words that the verb links.**

1. The weather suddenly turned colder.
2. The sky looks dark today.
3. The clouds have grown thicker.
4. The gentle breeze became a strong wind.
5. The raindrops felt cold against my skin.
6. The dog appeared quite upset.
7. The thunder sounded very loud.
8. Does the weather seem scary to you?
9. I remained calm throughout the storm.
10. Afterward, the air smelled fresh.

Connect to the Writing Process: Revising
Changing Questions into Statements

Change the following questions into statements. Underline the linking verb in each of your sentences.

11. Does the rain seem heavier?
12. Are you afraid of storms?
13. Are the windows in your bedroom shut?

14. Do I look pale?

15. Was that the worst storm ever in your town?

Communicate Your Ideas

APPLY TO WRITING

Descriptive Paragraph: *Linking Verbs*

Your town has just experienced a devastating tornado. You are standing in a neighborhood looking at the damage. A radio reporter walks up to you and asks you to describe how the neighborhood looked before the storm. Write a paragraph describing how the neighborhood looked. Underline the linking verbs you use in your description.

Linking Verb or Action Verb?

Most linking verbs can also be action verbs.

Linking Verb	The darkness **felt** oppressive to us.
	(*Oppressive* describes the subject.)
Action Verb	In the darkness my little sister **felt** for my hand.
	(*Felt* shows action. It tells what *sister* did.)

You can decide whether a verb is a linking verb or an action verb by asking two questions: *Does the verb link the subject with a word that renames or describes the subject? Does the verb show action?*

Linking Verb	My little sister **looked** afraid.
Action Verb	My mother **looked** for the candles.

PRACTICE YOUR SKILLS

Check Your Understanding
Distinguishing Between Linking Verbs and Action Verbs

Contemporary Life

Write the verb in each sentence. Then label each one *A* for action or *L* for linking.

1. Suddenly the room grew dark.
2. Did you turn off the light?
3. I looked for the light switch.
4. The night turned darker.
5. The phone rang suddenly.
6. My sister grew afraid in the dark.
7. Tall vines grew outside the window.
8. In the moonlight, they become a prowler.
9. The clock sounded loud in the darkness.
10. We felt better with the lights on.

Connect to the Writing Process: Drafting
Writing Sentences

Write a sentence using each verb as a linking verb. Then use the verb as an action verb. Label each one *A* for action or *L* for linking.

11. taste
12. look
13. smell
14. appear
15. grow
16. sound
17. turn
18. become
19. remain
20. feel

Communicate Your Ideas

APPLY TO WRITING

Personal Narrative: *Action and Linking Verbs*

Have you ever experienced a storm like the one pictured above? Might that be a tornado forming between the streaks of lightning?

Think back to a time when you experienced a bad storm. What happened? Were you caught outside without shelter, or did you watch from the relative safety of a basement window? How did you feel? Write a brief narrative account of the occurrence to share with your classmates. As you write, remember to vary your use of action and linking verbs. Be prepared to identify the verbs in your narrative and to tell whether they are transitive or intransitive.

QuickCheck Mixed Practice

Science Topic

Write the verb or verb phrase in each sentence. Then label the verb *A* for action verb or *L* for linking verb. If the verb is an action verb, label it *T* for transitive or *I* for intransitive.

1. Cryogenics is the study of cold.
2. At very cold temperatures, your breath will turn into a liquid.
3. At colder temperatures, it actually freezes into a solid.
4. Cold steel becomes very soft.
5. A frozen banana can serve as a hammer.
6. Shivers can raise the body temperature seven degrees.
7. People with a low body temperature feel lazy.
8. One should wear layers of clothing for protection from cold.
9. Chipmunks have found a good solution to the cold.
10. They hibernate all winter long!
11. Other animals also appear lifeless during the cold winter months.
12. The heavy coats of bears protect them from the cold during hibernation.

CheckPoint

Identifying Verbs and Verb Phrases

Write each verb or verb phrase in the following sentences. Then label each one *action verb* or *linking verb*.

1. The world is filled with incredible creatures.
2. Facts about these creatures will be equally incredible.
3. A dragonfly is extremely small.
4. Dragonflies, however, have been clocked at fifty miles per hour.
5. The largest animal in the world actually swims in the ocean.
6. The blue whale can weigh more than thirty elephants.
7. Your pet goldfish might live as long as thirty or forty years!
8. Does a goldfish ever look old?
9. The fastest land animal probably would be given a ticket on a highway.
10. The cheetah can actually run faster than sixty miles per hour.
11. Cockroaches are the oldest species on earth.
12. They looked similar more than 320 million years ago.
13. Do baby cockroaches appear beautiful to their mothers?
14. A skunk can hit something twelve feet away with its smell.
15. Have you ever smelled a skunk's scent?
16. The spray of a skunk smells absolutely horrible!
17. The ostrich egg is by far the biggest egg.
18. Some have actually weighed almost four pounds.
19. An ostrich egg must cook for at least two hours.
20. Have you read about any other incredible creatures?

Understanding Transitive and Intransitive Verbs

Write the verb or verb phrase in each sentence. Then label each verb or verb phrase *T* for transitive or *I* for intransitive.

1. Most of the apples fell from the tree during the storm.
2. Spiders have transparent blood.
3. Dad is reading on the porch.
4. Most American car horns beep in the key of F.
5. I usually answer the phone on the second ring.
6. Did you read this book for your book report?
7. Cut the grass tomorrow.
8. The robot will always answer politely.
9. Thomas Jefferson invented the calendar clock.
10. The fire engine rushed through the red light.

Using Verbs

Write ten sentences that follow the directions below. (The sentences may come in any order.) Write about one of the following topics or a topic of your own choice: a pet you have had, a pet you would like to have, a wild animal, or an endangered animal. You also could write about what animal you would like to be and why.

Write a sentence that . . .

1. includes an action verb.
2. includes a linking verb.
3. includes a verb phrase.
4. includes an interrupted verb phrase.
5. includes *taste* as an action verb.
6. includes *taste* as a linking verb.
7. includes *look* as an action verb.
8. includes *look* as a linking verb.
9. includes *appear* as an action verb.
10. includes *appear* as a linking verb.

Underline each verb or verb phrase.

Language and *Self-Expression*

Joan Mitchell paints in a style known as Abstract Expressionism. In this type of painting, techniques such as slashing and sweeping with the brush and dripping, spattering, and pouring paint help artists express their feelings about life.

Think back to a swimming experience you have had that reminds you in some way of the painting. If you prefer, you can imagine such an experience, using the painting as an inspiration. Write a few paragraphs that explain what happened in your experience. Use different kinds of verbs to make the action in your story interesting.

Prewriting Brainstorm some ideas for your story. After you have chosen one of your ideas, you may wish to make a chart showing the sequence of events in your story. Include words such as *first, next, then,* and *finally* to indicate the order of events.

Drafting Use your chart to organize your writing as you draft your story. Choose your verbs carefully to help your readers see, hear, and feel what happens.

Revising Read your story aloud to a classmate. Have your partner tell you if your action verbs are vivid and give life to your work. Replace dull, ordinary verbs with vivid, precise ones.

Editing Check your story for errors in spelling and punctuation. Make any corrections that are necessary. Be sure you spell irregular verbs correctly.

Publishing Make a final copy of your story. Collect it in a volume with classmates' stories. Take the time to read your classmates' stories and think about how the artwork inspired you in different directions.

Another Look

A **verb** is a word used to express an action or a state of being.

Classification of Verbs

An **action verb** tells what action a subject is performing. *(page L69)*

A **helping verb** is used with an action verb or linking verb to form a verb phrase. *(pages L69–L70)*

A **verb phrase** includes a main verb plus any helping verbs. *(page L69)*

COMMON HELPING VERBS	
be	am, is, are, was, were, am, be, being, been
have	has, have, had
do	do, does, did
OTHERS	may, might, must, can, could, shall, should, will, would

A **transitive verb** is an action verb that passes the action from a doer to a receiver. *(pages L72–L73)*

An **intransitive verb** expresses action or states something about the subject, but does not pass the action from a doer to a receiver. *(pages L72–L73)*

A **linking verb** links the subject with another word in the sentence. The other word either renames or describes the subject. Most linking verbs are forms of the verb *be.* *(pages L75–L78)*

Common forms of the verb *be* can be used as linking verbs. *(page L75)*

Other verbs besides *be* can be linking verbs. *(pages L76–L77)*

Most **linking verbs** can also be **action verbs.** *(page L78)*

Directions

Write the letter of the term that correctly identifies the underlined word or words in each sentence.

EXAMPLE **1.** Jesse's family has visited the same cabin in Maine each summer for eight years.

1 **A** transitive verb
B intransitive verb
C helping verb
D linking verb

ANSWER **1 C**

1. Jesse and his father fish for their dinner each day after Jesse comes home from school.
2. They have caught some enormous bass and pickerel that Jesse's father cooks on the grill.
3. Ducks and loons swim on the lake in the pleasant summer evenings.
4. The loon's call sounds eerie.
5. Sometimes the family will hear the loon calls for hours into the night.
6. The water is great for swimming, boating, and skipping stones, too.
7. Jesse's mother can swim for miles.
8. The whole family canoes around the lake in a sturdy craft built by Jesse's grandfather.
9. Sometimes they will paddle the canoe to the small island in the center.
10. There, a huge raven has made a nest.

1 **A** transitive verb
B intransitive verb
C helping verb
D linking verb

2 **A** helping verb
B intransitive verb
C transitive verb
D linking verb

3 **A** linking verb
B helping verb
C transitive verb
D intransitive verb

4 **A** transitive verb
B helping verb
C linking verb
D intransitive verb

5 **A** intransitive verb
B linking verb
C transitive verb
D helping verb

6 **A** linking verb
B transitive verb
C intransitive verb
D helping verb

7 **A** transitive verb
B helping verb
C linking verb
D intransitive verb

8 **A** intransitive verb
B linking verb
C transitive verb
D helping verb

9 **A** linking verb
B transitive verb
C helping verb
D intransitive verb

10 **A** linking verb
B transitive verb
C intransitive verb
D helping verb

CHAPTER 4

Adjectives and Adverbs

Directions

Write the letter of the term that correctly identifies the underlined word in each sentence.

EXAMPLE **1.** The <u>county</u> fair is always fun.

1 **A** adjective
B proper adjective
C adverb
D pronoun

ANSWER **1** **A**

1. There are <u>wild</u> rides in the carnival section.

2. Sometimes young children become <u>nervous</u> or frightened.

3. The food section <u>always</u> features exotic treats from around the world.

4. The <u>deep-dish</u> pizza is a real favorite among the carnivalgoers.

5. Many people enjoy the <u>Greek</u> salads topped with feta cheese.

6. In long barns the <u>farm</u> animals are judged on appearance and merit.

7. The cows and horses behave <u>well</u>.

8. Last year <u>several</u> of the sheep got loose from their pens.

9. The sheep led their owners on a <u>merry</u> chase around the fair.

10. Needless to say, <u>those</u> sheep did not win prizes.

1 **A** adjective
B adverb
C pronoun
D compound adjective

2 **A** adjective
B adverb
C pronoun
D article

3 **A** adjective
B proper adjective
C adverb
D article

4 **A** article
B proper adjective
C adverb
D compound adjective

5 **A** adverb
B compound adjective
C proper adjective
D article

6 **A** article
B adjective
C adverb
D noun

7 **A** adverb
B adjective
C article
D pronoun

8 **A** adverb
B pronoun
C proper adjective
D article

9 **A** article
B compound adjective
C adjective
D pronoun

10 **A** pronoun
B adverb
C article
D adjective

Clara Maria Nauen-von Malachowski. *Little Girl in a Blue Apron,* ca. 1938.
Oil on board, 27 by 19 inches. Stadtische Museum, Monchengladbach.

Describe What colors stand out in the painting? Why do you think the artist used such vivid colors?

Analyze What is unusual about the little girl? What do you think this reveals about her?

Interpret What do you think the artist reveals about herself in this painting?

Judge What sort of person do you think the child in the painting might be? Do you feel the artist has captured her personality in the portrait? Explain your answer.

At the end of the chapter, you will use this artwork to stimulate ideas for writing.

Adjectives

Your sentences would be very short and dull with only nouns and pronouns.

> The girls watched movies.

However, you can use adjectives and adverbs to give color and sharper meaning to a sentence.

> The **teenage** girls **avidly** watched the **classic** movies **yesterday.**

Adjectives modify, or make more precise, the meanings of nouns and pronouns. For example, what is your favorite movie like? Is it *long, short, happy, interesting,* or *scary?* All these possible answers are adjectives because they all make the meaning of the word *movie* more precise.

An adjective is a word that modifies a noun or a pronoun.

To find an adjective, first find each noun and pronoun in a sentence. Then ask yourself, *What kind? Which one(s)? How many?* or *How much?* about each one. The answers will be adjectives.

WHAT KIND?	The **silent** crowd watched the film.
	Do you like **scary** movies?
WHICH ONE(S)?	**That** role was written for the actress.
	I like the **funny** parts.
HOW MANY?	**Thirty** people stood in line to buy a ticket.
	I have seen the movie **many** times.
HOW MUCH?	He deserves **much** praise for his performance.
	Few seats in the theater were empty.

Connect to Speaking and Writing

When you speak and write, adjectives should help your listeners or readers picture what you are describing. Some adjectives, however, are used so often that they lose their meaning. When you are revising something you have written, you can look for fresh adjectives in a thesaurus.

Overused Adjective	I just watched a **great** movie.
Fresh Adjective	I just watched an **extraordinary** movie.

Practice Your Skills

Check Your Understanding

Finding Adjectives

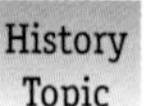

Write the adjectives from the following sentences.

1. For more than 100 years, people have been entertained in dark theaters.
2. Movies have a rich and interesting history.
3. Thomas Edison and a helpful assistant were among the first people to use celluloid film.
4. Early movies amazed most audiences.
5. Because of a sunny climate, California became the home of modern movies.
6. After many years the first permanent studio was built in Los Angeles in 1911.
7. Because early films did not have sound, a pianist would play musical pieces to accompany the action of the silent film.
8. One of the first filmmakers to shoot different angles with a camera was D. W. Griffith.
9. The lavish costumes and elaborate settings of early films cost a lot of money.

10. Even so, most people went to early movies not to see beautiful costumes but to see popular stars of the era.

Connect to the Writing Process: Drafting

Supplying Adjectives

Write an adjective to complete each sentence.

11. The ■ movie will be opening soon.
12. Do you want a ■ seat or one at the back of the room?
13. It was hard to find my friend in the ■ theater.
14. If we are late, there will be ■ seats available.
15. I love to eat the ■ popcorn from the concession stand.

Connect to the Writing Process: Revising

Using Vivid Adjectives

Write each sentence, replacing the underlined adjective with a more vivid one.

16. Training animals to star in movies is a hard job.
17. How do trainers get cute dogs to bark on cue?
18. Big bears are trained to wrestle with actors without hurting them.
19. Chimpanzees make funny faces at the camera.
20. The good trainers are paid well for their services.

Communicate Your Ideas

APPLY TO WRITING

Movie Review: *Adjectives*

You have been asked to write a review of your favorite movie for the school newspaper. Be sure to include the stars' names. Remember to write about the plot, setting, and costumes. Use descriptive details, including vivid adjectives that will compel others to see the movie. Underline all the adjectives you use in your review.

Different Positions of Adjectives

Adjectives can modify different nouns or pronouns, or they can modify the same noun or pronoun.

DIFFERENT NOUNS	Mandy wore a **red** vest with a **white** shirt.
THE SAME NOUN	The vest had **big blue** buttons.

PUNCTUATION WITH TWO ADJECTIVES

Sometimes you will write two adjectives before the noun they describe. If the adjectives are not connected by a conjunction—such as *and* or *or*—you might need to put a comma between them.

To decide whether a comma belongs, read the adjectives and add the word *and* between them.

- If the adjectives make sense, put a comma in to replace the *and.*
- If the adjectives do not make sense with the word *and* between them, do not add a comma.

COMMA NEEDED	The **soft, furry** vest is on the hanger.
NO COMMA NEEDED	The **red corduroy** vest is in the drawer.

You can learn more about placing commas between multiple adjectives that come before nouns on page L508.

Usually an adjective comes before the noun or pronoun it modifies. However, an adjective can also follow a noun or pronoun, or it can follow a linking verb.

BEFORE A NOUN	She wore the **latest** fashion.
AFTER A NOUN	His shirt, **big** and **baggy,** hung down to his knees.
AFTER A LINKING VERB	Ron looks quite **handsome** today.

You can learn more about adjectives that follow linking verbs on pages L75–L78.

Connect to Writer's Craft

Professional writers use a variety of positions for adjectives, placing some of them before the nouns they modify and others after the nouns they modify. This is one of the ways that writers add variety to their descriptions and make their writing more interesting. Notice the position of the underlined adjectives in Bradbury's description of a Martian spaceship. What does Bradbury do with his adjectives that adds to the effect of his description?

> In the blowing moonlight, like metal petals of some ancient flower, like blue plumes, like cobalt butterflies immense and quiet, the old ships turned and moved over the shifting sands, the masks beaming and glittering, until the last shine, the last blue color, was lost among the hills.
>
> –*Ray Bradbury,* The Martian Chronicles 

Practice Your Skills

Check Your Understanding

Finding Adjectives

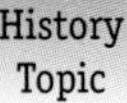

Write the adjectives in each sentence. Then beside each adjective, write the word it modifies.

1. For several centuries men dressed with more color and greater style than women.
2. During the 1600s, men wore lacy collars and fancy jackets with shiny buttons.
3. Their curly long hair reached their shoulders.
4. Men even carried small purses on huge belts.
5. After all, there were no pockets in the warm, colorful tights they wore.
6. By 1850, men's clothing had become drab and conservative.

7. Gone were the elegant white silk shirts, purple vests, lacy cuffs, and stylish black boots.
8. Men's clothing stayed colorless and dreary until the Beatles came along in the 1960s.
9. Their clothes, bright and informal, created a new style for men.
10. Today, people don't follow one style; everyone dresses to suit personal taste.
11. Still, we are all influenced by current trends.
12. Who knows what strange and wonderful clothes we will be wearing in 2050?

Proper Adjectives

You have learned that a proper noun is the name of a particular person, place, or thing—*Mexico* or *Northeast,* for example. A **proper adjective** is an adjective formed from a proper noun—*Mexican* food and *Northeastern* states, for example. Like a proper noun, a proper adjective begins with a capital letter.

PROPER NOUNS	PROPER ADJECTIVES
Greece	**Greek** salad
France	**French** bread
Mexico	**Mexican** fiesta

Some proper adjectives keep the same form as the proper noun.

PROPER NOUNS	PROPER ADJECTIVES
New York	**New York** restaurant
Monday	**Monday** dinner
Thanksgiving	**Thanksgiving** holiday

You can learn more about capitalizing proper adjectives on pages L479–L480.

Compound Adjectives

You have also learned that compound nouns are nouns made up of two or more words. **Compound adjectives** are adjectives that are made up of two or more words.

COMPOUND ADJECTIVES	
rooftop café	**household** word
faraway lands	**record-breaking** sprint

Articles

A, an, and *the* form a special group of adjectives called **articles.** *A* comes before words that begin with consonant sounds and *an* before words that begin with vowel sounds.

A new theater showed **an** old movie.

You will not be asked to list the articles in the exercises in this book.

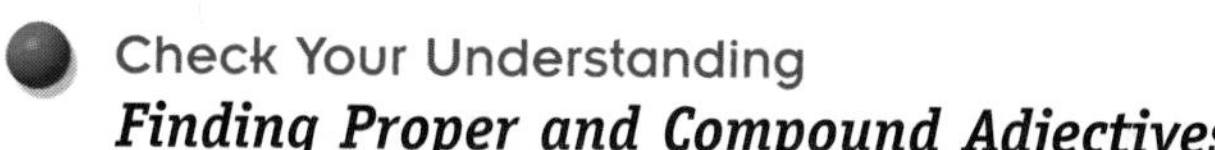

PRACTICE YOUR SKILLS

Check Your Understanding
Finding Proper and Compound Adjectives

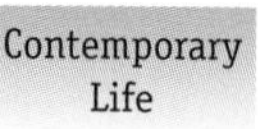

Contemporary Life

Write the proper adjectives and the compound adjectives in each sentence below. Then beside each adjective, write the word it modifies.

1. That seafront restaurant offered a variety of dishes from faraway lands.

2. The straightforward waitress described the European delicacies in simple language.

3. While Caribbean music played, diners enjoyed Russian caviar served with Italian bread.

4. One couple ate a Caesar salad with Greek olives.

5. Some Japanese tourists ate Indian food and drank Turkish coffee.
6. The restaurant recently received a five-star rating in an American travel magazine.
7. Our after-dinner treat was some Hawaiian pineapple.
8. The tuxedo-clad waiter brought a Chinese fortune cookie with our check.
9. When they visit, our Canadian friends and I will probably dine at the award-winning restaurant.
10. Of course, I usually prefer a hamburger with Swiss cheese from a fast-food restaurant.

Connect to the Writing Process: Editing

Capitalizing Proper Adjectives

Find the proper adjective in each sentence and rewrite it with a capital letter.

11. Our european vacation took us to some historic places.
12. The london subway system was quite a marvel.
13. Our english hotel was once a famous poet's home.
14. My favorite activity was visiting ancient roman ruins.
15. We even had the opportunity to ski in the swiss Alps.

Communicate Your Ideas

APPLY TO WRITING

Description: *Adjectives*

You have just returned from a visit to a beautiful place. Write a description of the place for your class. Be sure to include details about where and with whom you went. Write about what you did while you were there. Use at least three proper adjectives and three compound adjectives in your description.

Adjective or Noun?

The same word can be an adjective in one sentence and a noun in another sentence.

ADJECTIVE	I hope to finish my **school** assignment before dinner. (*School* tells what kind of work.)
NOUN	I left my English book at **school.** (*School* is the name of a place.)
ADJECTIVE	While setting the table, I broke a **dinner** plate.
NOUN	My father often cooks **dinner.**

PRACTICE YOUR SKILLS

Check Your Understanding

Distinguishing Between Adjectives and Nouns

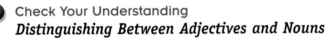

Contemporary Life **Write the underlined word in each sentence. Then label each word *A* for adjective or *N* for noun.**

1. Dad put our dinner in the oven.

2. We sat down to watch a television show.

3. We watched our favorite news program.

4. The reception on our set was bad, so the picture was fuzzy.

5. I put on oven mitts to take the casserole out of the stove.

6. As I brought out the casserole, I dropped the glass dish.

7. My brother and I cleaned up the glass.

8. My mom turned off the television.

9. The news was over.

10. Instead of casserole, we ate sandwiches as we looked out the picture window.

Connect to the Writing Process: Drafting

Writing Sentences Using Adjectives and Nouns

Write two sentences for each of the following words. In the first sentence, use the word as an adjective. In the second sentence, use the word as a noun. Label the use of each one.

11. birthday

12. rose

13. bicycle

14. top

15. paper

16. movie

17. snow

18. road

19. lemon

20. school

Adjective or Pronoun?

The following words can be used as adjectives or pronouns.

WORDS USED AS ADJECTIVES OR PRONOUNS			
Demonstrative	**Interrogative**	**Indefinite**	
this	what	all	many
these	which	another	more
that	whose	any	most
those		both	neither
		each	other
		either	several
		few	some

All these words are adjectives if they come before a noun and if they modify a noun. They are pronouns when they stand alone.

Adjective	I have been to **this** camp before.
Pronoun	Do you like **this?**
Adjective	**What** time is it?
Pronoun	**What** is planned for today?
Adjective	I called you **several** times before we left.
Pronoun	**Several** of the campers got poison ivy.

Sometimes the possessive pronouns *my, your, his, her, its, our,* and *their* are called adjectives because they answer the question *Which one?* Throughout this book, however, these words will be considered pronouns.

Practice Your Skills

Check Your Understanding

Distinguishing Between Adjectives and Pronouns

Contemporary Life **Write the underlined word in each sentence. Then label each word *A* for adjective or *P* for pronoun.**

1. Both of my brothers came to camp with me last summer.
2. Some friends came along as well.
3. I prefer this camp to the one I attended two years ago.
4. These mosquitoes will not stop biting me!
5. Which of the canoes do you want?
6. I dropped both paddles into the water.
7. These are designed to float.
8. After this, let's go horseback riding.
9. Which horse is the most gentle?
10. Some of them are very well trained.

Connect to the Writing Process: Drafting

Writing Sentences Using Adjectives and Pronouns

Write two sentences for each of the following words. In the first sentence, use the word as an adjective. In the second sentence, use the word as a pronoun. Label the use of each one.

11. many

12. each

13. what

14. several

15. that

16. some

17. both

18. which

19. few

20. neither

Communicate Your Ideas

APPLY TO WRITING

Advertisement: ***Adjectives***

You have been hired by an advertising agency to write an ad for a summer camp for teenagers. Decide first what kind of camp you will advertise. Is it a camp in the country, a sports camp, a space camp, or another type of camp? Remember to make the camp appealing to someone like you, but also try to describe a summer experience for which parents would gladly pay. Describe activities, meals, and other aspects of the camp that are enticing. Underline all the adjectives you use in your description.

History Topic **Write each adjective and the word it modifies.**

Nikolai, a Russian athlete, helped the American team win the Olympic ice hockey championship in 1960. The Americans had beaten the Canadian team and the Russian team. Now all they had to do was defeat the Czechs in the final game. After two periods, the Americans were losing. The thin air in the California mountains was slowing them down. Between the second period and the third period, Nikolai visited the weary Americans. Unfortunately he didn't speak any English. Through many gestures, however, he told them to inhale some oxygen. The team immediately felt lively and energetic. For the first time, an American team won the title.

Adverbs

An **adverb** is a word that modifies a verb, an adjective, or another adverb.

Just as adjectives add more information about nouns and pronouns, adverbs make verbs, adjectives, and other adverbs more precise. You probably know that many adverbs end in *-ly*.

> **Recently** my family voted **unanimously** for a vacation in the national forest.
>
> We strolled **casually** through the woods.

Following is a list of common adverbs that do not end in *-ly*.

COMMON ADVERBS			
afterward	far	not (n't)	soon
again	fast	now	still
almost	hard	nowhere	straight
alone	here	often	then
already	just	outside	there
also	late	perhaps	today
always	long	quite	tomorrow
away	low	rather	too
before	more	seldom	very
down	near	so	well
even	never	sometimes	yesterday
ever	next	somewhat	yet

You probably use many contractions in casual conversation. *Not* and its contraction *n't* are always adverbs.

> We could **not** find our binoculars.
> Do**n't** disturb the other campers.

Adverbs That Modify Verbs

Most adverbs modify verbs. To find these adverbs, first find the verb. Then ask yourself, *Where? When? How?* or *To what extent?* about the verb. The answers to these questions will be adverbs. The adverbs in the following examples are in bold type. An arrow points to the verb each adverb modifies.

WHERE?	Look **everywhere** for wildlife.
	Wild animals are **there.**
WHEN?	We **frequently** camp in the forest.
	I **sometimes** sleep in a tent.
HOW?	I **carefully** approached the deer.
	The animal **swiftly** and **surely** jumped over the boulder.
TO WHAT EXTENT?	My sister **completely** enjoys the experience.
	We have **almost** arrived at the waterfall.

An adverb can come before or after the verb or in the middle of a verb phrase.

CONNECT TO SPEAKING AND WRITING

Sentence variety is important in effective writing. You can give your writing added variety by beginning some sentences with an adverb.

The group of hikers **wearily** trudged into camp.
Wearily the group of hikers trudged into camp.

They saw mosquitoes **everywhere.**
Everywhere they saw mosquitoes. 

PRACTICE YOUR SKILLS

Check Your Understanding
Finding Adverbs That Modify Verbs

Science Topic

Write the adverbs in each sentence. Then beside each adverb, write the verb it modifies.

1. Porcupines never shoot their quills.
2. Usually the quills catch on something.
3. Then they fall out.
4. Porcupines always use their quills for protection.
5. Occasionally another animal will greatly disturb a porcupine.
6. The porcupine's quills will immediately stand upright.
7. Often the porcupine will bump the other animal.
8. The quills do not miss.
9. They stick swiftly and securely in the animal's skin.
10. An animal rarely bothers a porcupine twice.

Connect to the Writing Process: Drafting
Using Adverbs for Sentence Variety

Use each of the following adverbs at the beginning of a sentence about a forest.

11. suddenly
12. twice
13. happily
14. soon
15. clumsily
16. surprisingly
17. always
18. narrowly
19. tomorrow
20. totally

Communicate Your Ideas

APPLY TO WRITING

Writer's Craft: *Analyzing the Use of Adverbs*

Writers often use the placement of words to create an effect on their audiences. In this passage from *The Great Gatsby,* F. Scott Fitzgerald describes a tense encounter between two of the main characters. Read the passage and then follow the instructions below.

> The telephone rang inside, startlingly, and as Daisy shook her head decisively at Tom the subject of the stables, in fact all subjects, vanished into air. Among the broken fragments of the last five minutes at table I remember the candles being lit again, pointlessly.
>
> –*F. Scott Fitzgerald,* The Great Gatsby

- Write all of the adverbs in the passage. (You should find five adverbs.)
- What do you notice about Fitzgerald's placement of adverbs?
- What is the total effect of this placement?

Adverbs That Modify Adjectives and Other Adverbs

A few adverbs modify adjectives and other adverbs.

MODIFYING AN ADJECTIVE	Visiting national parks is **always** fun.
MODIFYING AN ADVERB	You should approach wild animals **very** cautiously.

To find adverbs that modify adjectives or other adverbs, first find the adjectives and the adverbs in a sentence. Then ask yourself *To what extent?* about each one. Notice in the preceding examples that the adverbs that modify adjectives or other adverbs usually come before the word they modify.

Practice Your Skills

Check Your Understanding

Finding Adverbs that Modify Adjectives and Other Adverbs

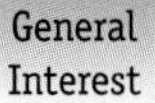

Write each adverb that modifies an adjective or another adverb. Then beside each adverb, write the word it modifies.

1. Yellowstone National Park is an exceptionally beautiful place.
2. The drive through the park can be rather long.
3. As they drive, tourists go very slowly as they attempt to see wildlife.
4. Bison and moose are quite abundant in the park.
5. Bears are almost never seen from the roadways.
6. Geysers are surprisingly common attractions in the park.
7. Old Faithful, a large geyser, is the most famous one in the park.
8. The benches around Old Faithful are extremely full of tourists.
9. Due to minerals in the water, a sulfur smell is very strong throughout the park.
10. If you decide to go, plan your vacation very early in the summer.
11. The park is unusually busy in July.
12. May is most assuredly the best month to visit the park.

Connect to the Writing Process: Revising
Adding Adverbs

Rewrite the following sentences, adding an adverb to modify the underlined adjective or adverb.

13. My trip to Yellowstone this past summer was interesting.
14. I met active people.
15. They were friendly.
16. The park is full of attractive sites.
17. I liked the famous geyser.
18. I camped comfortably in my tent.
19. Often I went fishing for trout and salmon in a rushing stream.
20. The water I stood in was cold.
21. I caught a trout that was lively.
22. I also climbed a nearby rock face.
23. It was a steep climb to the top.
24. I saw that the water in the Morning Glory Pool is clear.
25. The time flew by quickly during that week.
26. Although I enjoyed the trip, I was glad to return to my home.
27. I had missed my familiar friends.
28. It felt good to sleep in a bed again.
29. I missed the wonderful sights and sounds of the natural world, however.
30. I can almost hear the noisy crickets.
31. I still dream of the beautiful trees.
32. I did not miss bumping into other campers at every turn.

Adverb or Adjective?

As you have seen in the previous section, many adverbs end in *-ly*. You should, however, be aware that some adjectives end in *-ly*. In addition, many words can be used as either adverbs or adjectives. Always check to see how a word is used in a sentence before you decide what part of speech it is.

ADVERB	We visit my Aunt Sylvia **yearly.**
ADJECTIVE	Our **yearly** visits to Aunt Sylvia are filled with fun.
ADVERB	My cousin hit the baseball quite **hard.**
ADJECTIVE	The **hard** ball broke Aunt Sylvia's window.

You can learn about the comparison of adverbs and adjectives on pages L413–L421.

PRACTICE YOUR SKILLS

Check Your Understanding

Distinguishing Between Adjectives and Adverbs

Contemporary Life

Write the underlined word in each sentence. Then label each one as *adverb* or *adjective*.

1. My early memories are filled with visits to Aunt Sylvia's house in the country.
2. She had a warm smile and lively eyes.
3. I especially loved her delicious apple pies.
4. Her house was high on a hill overlooking an open field of wildflowers.
5. My cousins and I joyfully roamed the countryside near her home.
6. Sometimes we would swim in the lake.
7. We knew the area very well.
8. We always had a good time.

9. All of Aunt Sylvia's neighbors were friendly to us.
10. We would run loudly through her house.
11. Aunt Sylvia was extremely patient.
12. My cousins would climb to high perches in Aunt Sylvia's trees.
13. After a big supper on the porch, we went to bed early.
14. It was easy for us to fall asleep.
15. We were feeling well the next morning.
16. The rich smell of hot pancakes greeted us.
17. We happily raced to the table.
18. We ate slowly so we could savor the maple syrup she had warmed for us.
19. Those pancakes were the best I have tasted.
20. The sausage Aunt Sylvia served with them was excellent.

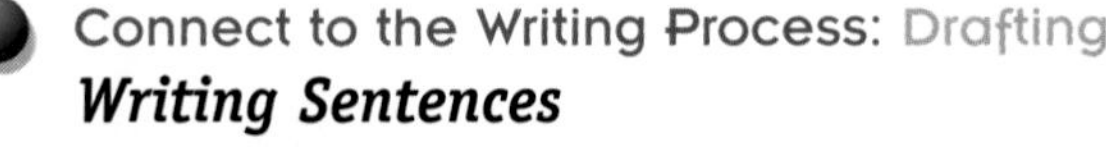

Writing Sentences

Write two sentences for each word. In the first, use the word as an adverb and in the second as an adjective.

21. monthly
22. low
23. closer
24. just
25. kindly
26. late
27. higher
28. farthest
29. daily
30. hard

APPLY TO WRITING

Description: *Adverbs*

Carmen Lomas Garza. *Sandía/Watermelon,* 1986. Gouache painting, 20 by 28 inches. Collection of Dudley D. Brooks and Tomas Ybarra-Frausto, New York. ©1986 Carmen Lomas Garza.

Look carefully at Carmen Lomas Garza's painting *Sandía/Watermelon*. Pretend that you are the boy sitting on the steps. Describe the scene from his point of view, as if he were talking to a friend. What is happening? Remember to include details such as what time of day it is and who the other people are. Use adverbs in your description to make the picture come alive. Underline each adverb you use in your writing.

QuickCheck Mixed Practice

General Interest **Write the adverbs in the following paragraphs. Then beside each adverb, write the word or words it modifies.**

The first pair of roller skates appeared in 1760. They were unsuccessfully worn by Joseph Merlin. Merlin had unexpectedly received an invitation to a very large party. Quite excitedly, he planned a grand entrance. The night finally arrived. Merlin rolled unsteadily into the ballroom on skates as he played a violin. Unfortunately, he couldn't stop. Merlin crashed into an extremely large mirror. The mirror broke into a million pieces. Merlin also smashed his violin and hurt himself severely.

Roller skates were never used again until 1823. Robert Tyers eventually made another attempt. His skates had a single row of five very small wheels. In 1863, James Plimpton finally patented the first pair of four-wheel skates. With these skates, people could keep their balance easily. They could even make very sharp turns. In-line skates would not be reinvented for many years.

Diagraming Adjectives and Adverbs

Adjectives and adverbs are diagramed on slanted lines below the words they modify.

My small brother swam.

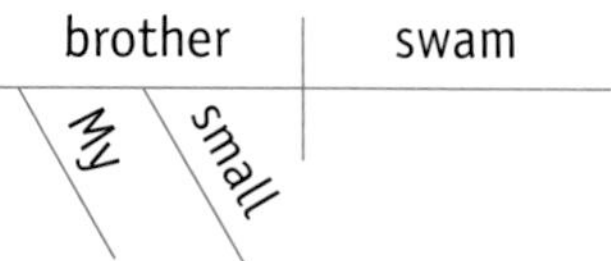

He swam skillfully.

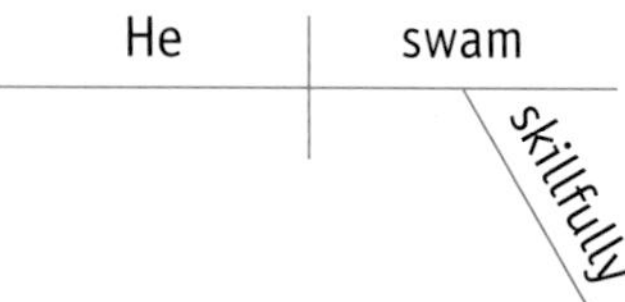

My small but strong brother swam fast and skillfully.

brother | swam

My, but, small, strong, and, fast, skillfully

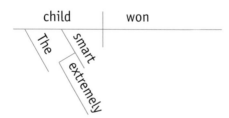

An adverb that modifies an adjective or another adverb is written on a line parallel to the word it modifies.

The extremely smart child won.

child | won

The, smart, extremely

She ate too quickly.

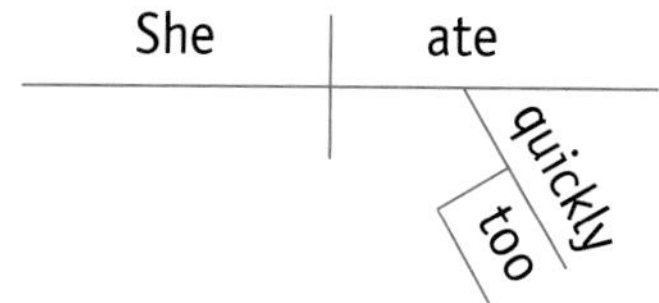

A rather large cat purred very softly.

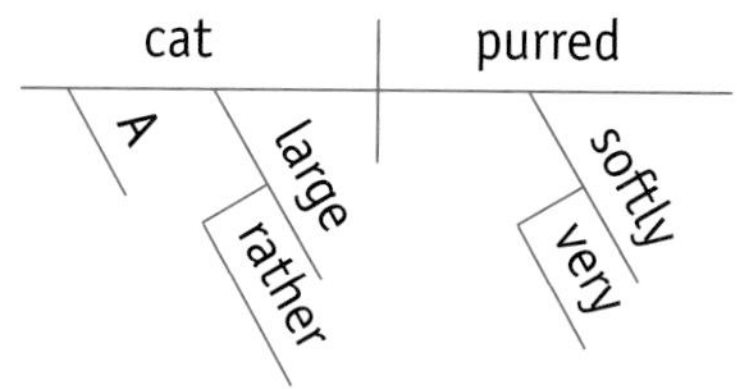

Practice Your Skills

Diagraming Adjectives and Adverbs

Diagram the following sentences or copy them. If you copy them, draw one line under each subject and two lines under each verb. Then label each modifier *adj.* for adjective or *adv.* for adverb.

1. A large octopus appeared.
2. It paused briefly.
3. Octopuses can move very quickly.
4. They also swim forward and backward.
5. The extremely large arms stretched out.
6. Suddenly an inky fluid squirted out.
7. Some small fish were blinded.
8. Others were even poisoned.
9. Then this large but flexible creature turned.
10. Suddenly it swam away forever.

CheckPoint

Identifying Adjectives and Adverbs

For each sentence below, draw a line under each modifier and label each one *adj.* for adjective or *adv.* for adverb. Do not include articles (*a, an,* and *the*).

1. Recently thirty students and several teachers took a bus trip from South Carolina to the Everglades National Park in the southern part of Florida.
2. This national park uniquely combines prairies, swamps, saltwater marshes, and freshwater lakes.
3. The Everglades is actually a river, a very unusual river.
4. It flows from Lake Okeechobee southward to the Gulf of Mexico.
5. Everyone carefully got into canoes for a tour of the Everglades.
6. Initially the landscape seemed somewhat monotonous to these first-time visitors.
7. Then they looked closely and saw hundreds of unusual things.
8. The park is the home to a large variety of animals.
9. Alligators are the most famous occupants of the park.
10. The ranger pointed to the tall, dense grasses.
11. Students immediately and excitedly saw two huge alligators in the grass.
12. Suddenly everyone looked up into the cloudless blue sky.
13. A roseate spoonbill, large and graceful, landed nearby on a park pond. (*Roseate spoonbill* is the whole name of the bird.)
14. The pink color of the bird comes from the many shrimp it eats.
15. Every South Carolina student also saw many different birds, fish, turtles, and snakes.

Distinguishing Among Different Parts of Speech

Write the underlined words in each sentence. Then label each one *N* for noun, *P* for pronoun, *adj.* for adjective, or *adv.* for adverb.

1. Your apple pie tastes much better than this.
2. Both of my brothers went to the play rehearsal.
3. Most drivers couldn't see the street sign.
4. Some of the fawns stood close to their mothers.
5. I have waited a long time to see this play.
6. The car roared down the street.
7. The kindly gentleman offered some good advice.
8. Most of the car dealers are holding sales.
9. Apples were given to both children.
10. She spoke kindly of her close friend.

Using Adjectives and Adverbs

Write ten sentences that follow the directions below. (The sentences may come in any order.) Write about one of the following topics or a topic of your own choice: a place you have visited or a place you would like to visit.

Write a sentence that. . .

1. includes two adjectives before a noun.
2. includes an adjective after a linking verb.
3. includes two adjectives after a noun.
4. includes a proper adjective.
5. includes a compound adjective.
6. includes *that* as an adjective.
7. includes an adverb at the beginning of a sentence.
8. includes the adverb *very*.
9. includes *daily* as an adjective.
10. includes *daily* as an adverb.

Language and Self-Expression

Clara Maria Nauen-von Malachowski was a German painter who worked in the style known as German Expressionism. Expressionists used simple designs and brilliant colors to express feelings, thoughts, and moods. How do you think the artist uses color and design to express a mood in the portrait?

A portrait can tell us a great deal about a person. You can paint a portrait in words, too. Think of someone you know who would make a good subject for a portrait in words. What is special, unusual, or memorable about the person? Write a description of the person, using vivid adjectives and adverbs to paint an effective word portrait.

Prewriting Create a Character-Traits Chart for your subject. In it, briefly describe his or her physical characteristics and personality traits.

Drafting Use the Character-Traits Chart to organize your description. Your sentences should include adjectives and adverbs that tell why your subject is special.

Revising Reread your description. Have you introduced your subject in a way that will grab a reader's attention? Is your word portrait vivid enough? Substitute interesting adjectives and adverbs for less vivid words.

Editing Check your description for errors in spelling and punctuation. Place your adjectives and adverbs in a variety of positions in your sentences. If you use more than one adjective to describe a noun or pronoun, separate the adjectives with a comma if necessary. Capitalize proper adjectives.

Publishing Make a final copy of your description and show it to your subject.

Another Look

An **adjective** is a word that modifies a noun or a pronoun.

Kinds of Adjectives

A **proper adjective** is an adjective that is formed from a proper noun and begins with a capital letter. *(page L96)*

A **compound adjective** is an adjective that is made up of two or more words. *(page L97)*

A, an, and *the* form a special group of adjectives called **articles.** *A* comes before words that begin with consonant sounds and *an* before words that begin with vowel sounds. *(page L97)*

An **adverb** is a word that modifies a verb, an adjective, or another adverb.

To find adverbs that modify verbs, find the verb. Then ask *Where? When, How?* or *To what extent?* about the verb. The answers to these questions will be adverbs. *(page L105)*

To find adverbs that modify adjectives and other adverbs, find the adjectives and adverbs in a sentence. Then ask *To what extent?* about each one. The answers to this question will be adverbs. *(pages L107–L108)*

Many adverbs end in -ly. *(page L104)*

Not and its contraction *n't* are always adverbs. *(page L104)*

Other Information About Adjectives and Adverbs

Using punctuation with two adjectives *(page L94)*

Distinguishing between adjectives and nouns *(page L99)*

Distinguishing between adjectives and pronouns *(pages L100–L101)*

Distinguishing between adverbs and adjectives *(page L110)*

Directions

Read the passage. Write the letter of the answer each underlined adjective or adverb modifies.

EXAMPLE Flying squirrels <u>actually</u> **(1)** glide rather than fly through the air.

1 **A** Flying squirrels
B glide
C fly
D air

ANSWER **1 B**

The wooly flying squirrel is very <u>rare</u> **(1)**. It is found only in <u>the</u> **(2)** Himalayan Mountains of northern Pakistan. It is <u>much</u> **(3)** larger than other flying squirrels and may be the largest squirrel in the world. It sails <u>gracefully</u> **(4)** off cliff ledges and glides to the trees <u>below</u> **(5)**. Skin membranes between its wrists and hind legs allow it to glide <u>long</u> **(6)** distances. It uses its <u>flat</u> **(7)** tail to guide its flight. For <u>many</u> **(8)** years, scientists thought the wooly flying squirrel was extinct. Scientists <u>recently</u> **(9)** rediscovered it, and its <u>high-altitude</u> **(10)** habitat is now being preserved.

1 A the
B flying squirrel
C is
D wooly

2 A Himalayan Mountains
B it
C Pakistan
D only

3 A flying
B other
C larger
D squirrels

4 A cliff
B sails
C it
D glides

5 A glides
B cliff
C sails
D ledges

6 A allow
B it
C distances
D wrists

7 A uses
B tail
C guide
D flight

8 A scientists
B years
C squirrel
D extinct

9 A rediscovered
B scientists
C it
D habitat

10 A its
B scientists
C preserved
D habitat

CHAPTER 5

Other Parts of Speech

Directions

Write the letter of the term that correctly identifies the underlined word in each sentence.

EXAMPLE **1.** Danielle decided to give a dinner party <u>during</u> spring vacation.

1 **A** interjection
B preposition
C adverb
D coordinating conjunction

ANSWER **1 B**

1. Danielle had never cooked a whole dinner before, <u>but</u> she was eager to try.
2. Danielle began <u>at</u> noon.
3. <u>First</u> she baked an apple pie.
4. <u>Not only</u> did she put too much flour in the crust, <u>but</u> she <u>also</u> forgot the sugar.
5. She then placed a large rump roast on a tray <u>in</u> the oven.
6. First she forgot to turn on the oven, <u>and</u> then she turned it on too high.
7. <u>Oh, no!</u> The smoke alarm went off!
8. At the same time, two pots on the stove boiled <u>over</u>.
9. <u>In spite of</u> these disasters, Danielle remained cool and collected.
10. Before the guests could figure out what had happened, Danielle whisked them off <u>to</u> a pizza parlor.

1 **A** coordinating conjunction
B preposition
C correlative conjunction
D adverb

2 **A** coordinating conjunction
B correlative conjunction
C interjection
D preposition

3 **A** preposition
B interjection
C adverb
D adjective

4 **A** coordinating conjunctions
B correlative conjunctions
C prepositions
D adverbs

5 **A** interjection
B coordinating conjunction
C preposition
D adverb

6 **A** adverb
B coordinating conjunction
C correlative conjunction
D preposition

7 **A** interjection
B preposition
C adverb
D adjective

8 **A** interjection
B adjective
C adverb
D preposition

9 **A** coordinating conjunction
B preposition
C correlative conjunction
D interjection

10 **A** adjective
B correlative conjunction
C coordinating conjunction
D preposition

Artist unknown. *Hall of Bulls and Horses,* date unknown.
Montignac, France.

Describe What colors did the artist use? What images do you recognize?

Analyze What do you think the artist intended to represent? What story was he or she telling?

Interpret What information can you infer about the artist from the images in the painting? What might some of his or her hopes and fears have been?

Judge Do you think cave paintings such as this one are important to our understanding of Ice Age peoples? How might they supplement discoveries of tools or other artifacts? Explain.

At the end of the chapter, you will use this artwork to stimulate ideas for writing.

Prepositions

A preposition is a word that shows the relationship between a noun or a pronoun and another word in the sentence.

The three words in **bold** print in the following sentences are prepositions. Each of these prepositions shows a different relationship between Lori and the letter. As a result, changing only the preposition will alter the meaning of the whole sentence.

The letter **to** Lori was lost.

The letter **from** Lori was lost.

The letter **about** Lori was lost.

Following is a list of the most common prepositions.

COMMON PREPOSITIONS				
aboard	before	down	off	till
about	behind	during	on	to
above	below	except	onto	toward
across	beneath	for	opposite	under
after	beside	from	out	underneath
against	besides	in	outside	until
along	between	inside	over	up
among	beyond	into	past	upon
around	but (except)	like	since	with
as	by	near	through	within
at	despite	of	throughout	without

A preposition that is made up of two or more words is called a **compound preposition.**

COMMON COMPOUND PREPOSITIONS		
according to	by means of	instead of
ahead of	in addition to	in view of
apart from	in back of	next to
as of	in front of	on account of
aside from	in place of	out of
because of	in spite of	prior to

PRACTICE YOUR SKILLS

Check Your Understanding
Finding Prepositions

History Topic **Write the prepositions from the following sentences.**

1. The legendary Pony Express rode its way into American history.
2. The riders' trail began at Joseph, Missouri.
3. A weary rider would often reach California in ten days.
4. Wild Bill Cody was one of the riders for this early mail system.
5. In spite of its popularity, the Pony Express lasted only eighteen months.
6. Because of its expense, the Pony Express cost its owners $200,000.
7. Later, dromedary camels were imported from the Middle East.
8. However, the camels were not used for regular mail service.
9. These dromedaries delivered salt between several western towns.
10. Today, the United States mail is transported by airplanes and trucks.

Connect to the Writing Process: Drafting

Supplying Prepositions

Write each sentence twice, using a different preposition to fill each blank.

11. The mail plane flew ■ the storm clouds.

12. The package ■ the chair is mine.

13. Caleb should go ■ the post office.

14. A letter came ■ Christopher.

15. Get the mail ■ the mailbox.

16. ■ that package you will find the tape dispenser.

17. Will you open the box ■ me?

Prepositional Phrases

A **prepositional phrase** begins with a preposition and ends with a noun or a pronoun.

A preposition is always part of a group of words called a prepositional phrase. The noun or pronoun that ends the prepositional phrase is called the **object of the preposition.** Any number of modifiers can come between a preposition and its object.

England is the setting ***of*** **this suspenseful mystery.**

The detective chases the criminal ***through*** **London's streets.**

A sentence can have several prepositional phrases, and the phrases can come anywhere in the sentence.

Without **a moment's hesitation,** the detective leaped ***into*** **the criminal's path.**

Before **the end** ***of*** **books** ***by*** **Agatha Christie,** I usually can identify the criminal.

CONNECT TO SPEAKING AND WRITING

You can create sentence variety by starting some sentences with prepositional phrases.

The true villain is always discovered ***by* the book's end.**
***By* the book's end,** the true villain is always discovered.

I like mysteries ***because of* the suspense.**
***Because of* the suspense,** I like mysteries. 

PRACTICE YOUR SKILLS

Check Your Understanding

Finding Prepositional Phrases

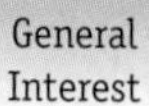

Write the prepositional phrases in the following sentences.

1. A nurse at a London hospital had a young girl in her ward.
2. None of the doctors could find a cure for her.
3. Before work the nurse read a chapter in a mystery by Agatha Christie.
4. After several pages she put the book into her bag and hurried to the hospital.
5. According to the book, someone had taken a rare poison called thallium.
6. The description of the victim's symptoms matched the symptoms of the young girl.
7. The nurse placed the book in front of the doctors.
8. She told them about her suspicions.
9. Within minutes the doctors prescribed a new series of treatments for the girl.
10. Because of a mystery by Agatha Christie, a young girl's life was saved.

Connect to the Writing Process: Drafting

Creating Sentence Variety

Use each preposition below in a sentence. Then rewrite the sentence, changing the position of the prepositional phrase to create a variation on the original sentence.

11. next to
12. through
13. because of
14. beyond
15. in back of
16. around

Communicate Your Ideas

APPLY TO WRITING

Setting: ***Prepositional Phrases***

You are working for a famous movie producer who is looking for a location for a film based on a mystery novel. You come across this building and determine it would be perfect. After realizing your camera is not working, you decide to write a description of the setting. Remember that prepositional phrases will help your producer picture the setting. Underline the prepositional phrases you use.

Preposition or Adverb?

The same word can be used as a preposition in one sentence and an adverb in another sentence. Just remember that a preposition is always part of a prepositional phrase. An adverb stands alone.

PREPOSITION	***Below* the stairs** is the storage area for our new sleds.
ADVERB	The snow fell from the roof to the ground **below.**
PREPOSITION	We raced ***up* the hill**
ADVERB	Pull your sled **up** onto the porch.

You can learn more about prepositional phrases on pages L173–L182.

Check Your Understanding

Distinguishing Between Prepositions and Adverbs

Contemporary Life **Write the underlined word in each sentence. Then label it *P* for preposition or *A* for adverb.**

1. Last week a blizzard raged <u>outside</u> our warm house.
2. Snow accumulated <u>around</u> the town.
3. The flakes drifted <u>off</u> our roof.
4. Today, the weather <u>outside</u> is perfect for sledding.
5. My friends and I looked <u>around</u> for our sleds.
6. I went <u>down</u> the hill before Jaime.
7. <u>Down</u> the hill I raced on my sled.
8. I fell <u>off</u> near the bottom of the hill.
9. Jaime had never been sledding <u>before</u>.
10. He squealed as his sled raced <u>down</u>.
11. It was hard pulling our sleds back <u>up</u> the hill.
12. <u>Behind</u> me Jamie complained loudly.

Connect to the Writing Process: Drafting

Writing Sentences

Write two sentences using each of the words below. In the first sentence, use the word as a preposition. In the second sentence, use it as an adverb.

13. near
14. across
15. out
16. aboard
17. within
18. beneath
19. outside
20. before
21. on
22. over
23. around
24. beyond

Mixed Practice

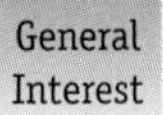

Write the prepositional phrases from the following paragraph.

In the Beartooth Mountains of Montana, there is a most unusual glacier. Within the ice of the glacier are frozen millions of grasshoppers. According to scientists, an immense swarm of grasshoppers made a forced landing on the glacier two centuries ago! They were then quickly frozen by a snowstorm. Today the grasshoppers are still well preserved. During the warm weather, birds and animals throughout the region flock to the glacier for an addition to their normal sources of food. When the ice melts, the grasshoppers provide them with a most unusual meal.

Conjunctions

A **conjunction** connects words or groups of words. One kind of conjunction is the **coordinating conjunction,** a single connecting word.

COORDINATING CONJUNCTIONS						
and	but	for	nor	or	so	yet

SINGLE WORDS	An astronomer observes **stars *and* planets.** (nouns)
	He *or* she watches the night sky. (pronouns)
	They **watch** asteroids ***and* chart** their courses. (verbs)
	The astronomer's job is **difficult *but* interesting.** (adjectives)
	Now *and* then, they discover a new comet. (adverbs)
GROUPS OF WORDS	He looked **through the telescope *and* into space.** (prepositional phrases)
	Earth has one moon, *but* Neptune has eight satellites. (sentences)

Correlative conjunctions are pairs of connecting words.

CORRELATIVE CONJUNCTIONS		
both/and	either/or	neither/nor
not only/but also	whether/or	

Both **Gretta** ***and*** **Emmaline** own telescopes.

You should study ***either*** **comets** ***or*** **asteroids.**

You can learn about the third type of conjunction, a subordinating conjunction, on pages 225–226.

CONNECT TO WRITER'S CRAFT

When you revise your writing, you can often use conjunctions to make your writing more interesting. You can combine sentences or elements of sentences to make your writing less repetitive.

The moon is bright tonight. We can see only see a few stars.
The moon is bright tonight, **so** we can see only a few stars.

Our group can study the moon. We can study the planets.
Our group can study **either** the moon **or** the planets.

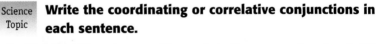

PRACTICE YOUR SKILLS

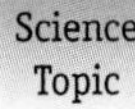

Check Your Understanding

Finding Conjunctions

Science Topic **Write the coordinating or correlative conjunctions in each sentence.**

1. Neither Mercury nor Venus has its own natural satellite.
2. After Mars and before Jupiter, there lies an asteroid belt.
3. Earth rotates on its axis and revolves around the sun.
4. Pluto is the most distant planet, so it was not discovered until 1930.
5. Each planet is classified as either an inner or an outer planet.
6. Ceres is a large asteroid, but most asteroids are relatively small.

7. Both beautiful and mysterious, Saturn's rings can be observed from Earth through binoculars.
8. Slowly but surely, the planets make their way around the sun.
9. A meteor is a rock or a metal fragment that enters Earth's atmosphere.
10. Humans have studied the heavens for centuries, yet many mysteries remain.

Connect to the Writing Process: Revising

Using Conjunctions to Combine Sentences

Combine each pair of sentences into one sentence using coordinating or correlative conjunctions.

11. Carmen wrote a report about black holes. Maria wrote a report about black holes.
12. You can read a book about quasars. You can see a video about quasars.
13. My dad knows nothing about space. My mom took astronomy in college.
14. Tell Jesse about meteors. Tell Jesse about comets.
15. Mercury is my favorite planet. I wrote a play about Mercury.

Communicate Your Ideas

APPLY TO WRITING

Directions: ***Conjunctions***

You are writing directions to your house for a new friend. Write directions that begin at your school and explain the best way to reach your home. Remember to be specific and make the directions easy to follow. Use at least two coordinating conjunctions and one correlative conjunction. After completing your directions, underline the conjunctions you used in your writing.

Interjections

An **interjection** is a word that expresses strong feeling or emotion.

Interjections express feelings such as joy or anger. They usually come at the beginning of a sentence. Since they are not related to the rest of the sentence, they are separated from it by a comma or an exclamation point.

Hurrah! Our team won.

Well, they have worked hard.

Yeah, now they compete for the championship.

Wow! I can't believe it.

PRACTICE YOUR SKILLS

Check Your Understanding
Finding Interjections

Contemporary Life **Write the interjections from the following sentences.**

1. Oh, did you see that pass?
2. Whew! I can't believe Jim caught it.
3. Hurrah, he's running down the field!
4. Great, he made a touchdown!
5. Gee, what a great play that was!
6. Hey, wait for me!
7. Goodness, what a heavy suitcase this is.
8. No! What more can go wrong?
9. Ugh! This is awful.
10. Yeah, I'm on my way.

Connect to the Writing Process: Drafting

Writing Sentences with Interjections

Using the following interjections, write sentences about the hockey game in the picture. Remember to separate the interjection from the rest of the sentence with a comma or an exclamation point.

11. aha

12. ouch

13. well

14. oops

15. wow

16. yes

17. no

18. terrific

19. oh

20. surprise

Parts of Speech Review

How a word is used in a sentence determines its part of speech. For example, the word *near* can be used as four different parts of speech.

VERB	The plant will **near** its full growth soon.
ADJECTIVE	I will plant my flower garden in the **near** future.
ADVERB	The best planting time is drawing **near.**
PREPOSITION	Plant the flowers ***near** the house*.

To find out what part of speech a word is, ask yourself, *What is each word doing in this sentence?*

NOUN	Is the word naming a person, place, thing, or idea? **Nathaniel** bought **plants** at the **nursery.**
PRONOUN	Is the word taking the place of a noun? **This** is **my** favorite flower.
VERB	Is the word showing action? Kiki **planted** the rose bush. Does the word link two words in the sentence? The daisy **is** a simple flower.
ADJECTIVE	Is the word modifying a noun or a pronoun? Does it answer *What kind? Which one(s)? How many?* or *How much?* **Three yellow** tulips bloomed today.
ADVERB	Is the word modifying an adverb, an adjective, or another adverb? Does it answer the question *How? When? Where?* or *To what extent?* The seedling grew **very quickly** in the **extremely** rich soil.

PREPOSITION	Is the word showing a relationship between a noun or pronoun and another word in the sentence? ***Because of* the sunlight,** the plant grew well ***on* the windowsill.**
CONJUNCTION	Is the word connecting words or groups of words? Kiki and I grow **neither** fruits **nor** vegetables. I planted marigolds, **but** they didn't grow.
INTERJECTION	Is the word expressing strong feelings? **Wow!** The petunias in the window box are blooming.

PRACTICE YOUR SKILLS

Check Your Understanding
Determining Parts of Speech

General Interest

Write the underlined words. (There are 25 words.) Then beside each word, write its part of speech, using the following abbreviations:

noun = *n.*	adjective = *adj.*
pronoun = *pron.*	preposition = *prep.*
verb = *v.*	conjunction = *conj.*
adverb = *adv.*	interjection = *interj.*

Caution! Music may wilt your leaves. In 1969, Dorothy Retallack ran some experiments with plants and music. She proved that music affects the growth of plants. In one test, loud rock greatly stunted the growth of corn, squash, and several flowers. In another test, several of the plants grew tall, but their leaves were extremely small. Also, they needed water, and their roots were very short. Within several weeks all the marigolds in one experiment died. Identical healthy flowers, however, bloomed nearby. These flowers had been listening to classical music!

Connect to the Writing Process: Drafting
Writing Sentences

Write two sentences using the underlined word as directed.

26. Use light as a verb and a noun.

27. Use that as a pronoun and an adjective.

28. Use below as a preposition and an adverb.

29. Use these as a pronoun and an adjective.

30. Use secret as an adjective and a noun.

Communicate Your Ideas

APPLY TO WRITING

Informative Writing: *Parts of Speech*

You are a creature from another planet who has been sent to Earth by your government to report on the lives of human beings. Your ship lands near a high school gymnasium. Unseen, you enter the gym and watch a basketball game. Since you have no idea what is going on, you decide that you must write a report to the people of your planet describing this bizarre Earth ritual. Be sure to include details of the things you see around you. Describe them from the point of view of someone who is totally foreign to this world. In your report use each of the parts of speech at least once. Be prepared to point out one or more nouns, pronouns, verbs, adjectives, adverbs, prepositions, conjunctions, and interjections.

CheckPoint

Identifying Prepositions, Conjunctions, Interjections, and Prepositional Phrases

Write each sentence. Then label each of the following parts of speech *preposition, conjunction,* and *interjection.* Finally, underline each prepositional phrase.

1. Wow! You have a really big test ahead of you on Friday.
2. Never wait until the last minute.
3. Start two nights before any test.
4. Review both your material and your notes from class.
5. Yes! Study with a friend or classmate.
6. Not only review old tests throughout your notebook, but also look for certain kinds of familiar questions.
7. During the night before the test, review the most important points and the main topics.
8. Neither study late nor stay up late.
9. According to many studies, your brain will need proper food and rest for the best results.
10. Avoid sweets like doughnuts around the time of the test.

Determining Parts of Speech

Write the underlined words. Then beside each word, write its part of speech using the following abbreviations.

noun = *n.*	pronoun = *pron.*	verb = *v.*
adjective = *adj.*	adverb = *adv.*	preposition = *prep.*
conjunction = *conj.*	interjection = *interj.*	

In 1928, a farmer was planting <u>horseradishes</u> in a field <u>in</u> <u>West Virginia</u>. He noticed a greasy, <u>shiny</u> stone. He picked it <u>up</u> and took <u>it</u> home. <u>Ten</u> years later he made a startling discovery. The stone was a thirty-two-carat diamond. Wow!

Diamonds, however, are not necessarily rare in the United States. The Eagle diamond was found in Wisconsin. Other large stones have also been discovered in Ohio, Illinois, and Indiana.

Determining Parts of Speech

Write the underlined words. Then beside each word, write its part of speech using the following abbreviations.

noun = *n.* pronoun = *pron.* verb = *v.*
adjective = *adj.* adverb = *adv.* preposition = *prep.*
conjunction = *conj.* interjection = *interj.*

1. Steel workers were laid off because demand for steel dropped.
2. Did those horses really eat those?
3. Turn left because a left turn will take you to the park.
4. Will you water the plants with the water in this can?
5. Everyone drew near and sat near the fire.

Completing Sentence Skeletons

Make up ten sentences matching the ten skeletons below. You can use an article (*a, an,* or *the*) for an adjective. Use the following abbreviations: noun (*n.*), pronoun (*pron.*), verb (*v.*), adjective (*adj.*), adverb (*adv.*), preposition (*prep.*), conjunction (*conj.*), or interjection (*interj.*).

EXAMPLE *adj. n. prep. adj. n. v. adj.*
POSSIBLE ANSWER **The winner of the contest was happy.**

1. n. v. adj. adj. n.
2. pron. v. adv.
3. adj. adj. n. prep. adj. n. v. adj.
4. n. conj. n. v. adv.
5. n. v. adj. prep. adj. n.

Language and *Self-Expression*

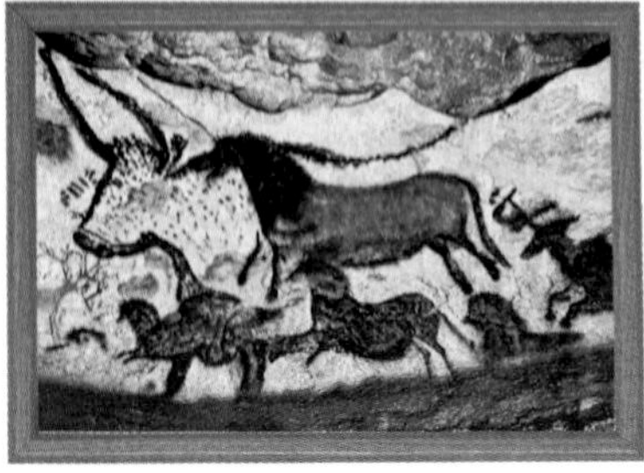

This painting was found in a cave in Lascaux, France, by four boys who were looking for a lost dog. It was done by Cro-Magnon people sometime between 15,000 and 10,000 B.C. The artist or artists used ground-up rocks mixed with animal fat to create the colors in the painting.

Imagine what the four boys experienced when they found this ancient painting. Write the scene in a few paragraphs. Use prepositions, conjunctions, and interjections to add variety. Then read your scene aloud to the class.

Prewriting You may wish to create a plot diagram for your scene. Include information about the characters, setting, rising action, climax, falling action, and resolution in your diagram.

Drafting Use your plot diagram to tell the story of the boys' discovery. Include interjections to show the boys' reactions to what they have found.

Revising Reread your scene carefully. Vary your sentences by placing prepositional phrases in different parts of the sentences. To make your writing less repetitive, combine sentences or elements of sentences with conjunctions.

Editing Check your scene for errors in spelling and punctuation. Be sure you have separated each interjection from the rest of the sentence with a comma or exclamation point.

Publishing Read your scene aloud to the class. When everyone has had a chance to read, discuss how the stories differ. Talk about which ones work best and why.

Another Look

A **preposition** is a word that shows the relationship between a noun or a pronoun and another word in the sentence.

A **prepositional phrase** begins with a preposition and ends with a noun or a pronoun.

A **conjunction** connects words or groups of words.

A **coordinating conjunction** is a single connecting word.

Correlative conjunctions are pairs of connecting words.

An **interjection** is a word that expresses strong feeling or emotion.

Parts of Speech Review

To find out what part of speech a word is, ask yourself these questions:

- Is the word naming a person, place, thing, or idea? It is a **noun.** *(page L137)*
- Is the word taking the place of a noun? It is a **pronoun.** *(page L137)*
- Is the word showing action or linking two words in the sentence? It is a **verb.** *(page L137)*
- Is the word modifying a noun or a pronoun? It is an **adjective.** *(page L137)*
- Is the word modifying a verb, an adjective, or another adverb? It is an **adverb.** *(page L137)*
- Is the word showing a relationship between a noun or pronoun and another word in the sentence? It is a **preposition.** *(page L138)*
- Is the word connecting words or groups of words? It is a **conjunction.** *(page L138)*
- Is the word expressing strong feelings? It is an **interjection.** *(page L138)*

Directions

Read the passage. Write the letter of the term that correctly identifies the underlined word or words in each sentence.

EXAMPLE English royalty (1) has a troubled history.

1 **A** noun
2 **B** verb
3 **C** adjective
4 **D** adverb

ANSWER **1** **A**

For hundreds of years, historians have wondered what happened to the two sons of (1) the English (2) king, Edward IV. When Edward IV died, his eldest son should have become (3) king. However, Edward's brother Richard took the throne and (4) put his nephews in the Tower of London. After (5) July of 1483, no one ever saw the boys again. Either (6) they were killed on Richard's orders, or (6) they were sent away in exile. Richard III's supporters claimed (7) that someone else killed the princes. Well (8), that may be true, but (9) there is no way to prove it. No one but Richard himself will ever (10) know the truth.

1 **A** adverb
B preposition
C verb
D interjection

2 **A** proper adjective
B compound adjective
C preposition
D adverb

3 **A** action verb
B adverb
C linking verb
D adjective

4 **A** interjection
B correlative conjunction
C preposition
D coordinating conjunction

5 **A** verb
B adverb
C preposition
D adjective

6 **A** prepositions
B adverbs
C correlative conjunctions
D interjections

7 **A** verb
B preposition
C adjective
D correlative conjunction

8 **A** adverb
B article
C interjection
D preposition

9 **A** correlative conjunction
B coordinating conjunction
C article
D interjection

10 **A** adjective
B preposition
C coordinating conjunction
D adverb

Complements

Directions

Write the letter of the term that correctly identifies the underlined word in each sentence.

EXAMPLE **1.** The whole Northeast faced a <u>drought</u> that year.

1 **A** predicate adjective
B indirect object
C direct object
D predicate nominative

ANSWER **1** **C**

1. It was the worst <u>drought</u> in decades.

2. Lawns turned <u>brown</u> and died.

3. Town governments sent <u>citizens</u> warnings about the need to conserve water.

4. People could not even wash their <u>cars</u>.

5. They were <u>unhappy</u> but resigned.

6. Some watered their <u>gardens</u> after dark because they were not allowed to do so between certain hours of the day.

7. Police could give <u>them</u> a ticket if they were caught.

8. The weather remained <u>dry</u> for weeks.

9. Radio announcers gave <u>listeners</u> the same report every day.

10. "It will be <u>sunny</u> and in the eighties, with no chance of rain."

1	**A**	direct object	**6**	**A**	indirect object
	B	predicate adjective		**B**	direct object
	C	indirect object		**C**	predicate adjective
	D	predicate nominative		**D**	predicate nominative
2	**A**	predicate adjective	**7**	**A**	predicate adjective
	B	direct object		**B**	predicate nominative
	C	predicate nominative		**C**	direct object
	D	indirect object		**D**	indirect object
3	**A**	direct object	**8**	**A**	predicate nominative
	B	indirect object		**B**	predicate adjective
	C	predicate adjective		**C**	indirect object
	D	predicate nominative		**D**	direct object
4	**A**	indirect object	**9**	**A**	indirect object
	B	predicate nominative		**B**	predicate nominative
	C	direct object		**C**	direct object
	D	predicate adjective		**D**	predicate adjective
5	**A**	predicate adjective	**10**	**A**	direct object
	B	predicate nominative		**B**	indirect object
	C	indirect object		**C**	predicate adjective
	D	direct object		**D**	predicate nominative

Clara McDonald Williamson. *The Old Chisholm Trail,* 1952.
Oil on panel, 24 by 36½ inches. The Roland P. Murdock Collection, Wichita Art Museum, Wichita, Kansas.

Describe	What event does this painting depict? What kind of people does it show? When does it take place?
Analyze	What details in the painting tell you about the job of moving cattle?
Interpret	How do you think the artist uses perspective to give viewers a sense of the cattle drive?
Judge	Do you think the painting gives an effective sense of a real cattle drive? What might be different on a more modern drive? Explain.

At the end of this chapter, you will use the artwork to stimulate ideas for writing.

Kinds of Complements

Sometimes a complete thought can be expressed with just a subject and a verb. At other times a subject and a verb need another word to complete the meaning of the sentence.

Greg likes. Ruth seems.

To complete the meaning of these subjects and verbs, a completer, or complement, must be added.

Greg likes **snakes.** Ruth seems **wary.**

There are four common kinds of complements: direct objects, indirect objects, predicate nominatives, and predicate adjectives. Together, a subject, a verb, and a complement are called the sentence base.

Direct Objects

A direct object is a noun or pronoun that receives the action of the verb.

Direct objects complete the meaning of action verbs. To find a direct object, first find the subject and the action verb in a sentence. Then ask yourself, *What?* or *Whom?* after the verb. The answer to either question will be a direct object. In the following sentences, subjects are underlined once, and verbs are underlined twice.

d.o.
Dylan saw a **snake** in the river.

(Dylan saw what? He saw a snake. *Snake* is the direct object.)

d.o.
He called **Nicole** over to the water.

(He called whom? *Nicole* is the direct object.)

Verbs that show ownership are action verbs and take direct objects.

Anna owns a **python.**

Sometimes two or more direct objects, called a **compound direct object**, will follow a single verb. On the other hand, each part of a compound verb may have its own direct object. The verbs are underlined in the sentences below.

Did you see a **cobra** or a **viper** at the zoo?

I took **pictures** at the zoo and developed the **film** later.

A direct object can never be part of a prepositional phrase.

At the petting zoo, Caroline touched **one** of the snakes.
(*One* is the direct object. *Snakes* is part of the prepositional phrase *of the snakes.*)

Our class walked around the zoo.
(*Zoo* is part of the prepositional phrase *around the zoo.* Even though this sentence has an action verb, it has no direct object.)

You can learn more about transitive verbs, or verbs that take direct objects, on pages L72–L73.

Practice Your Skills

Check Your Understanding

Finding Direct Objects

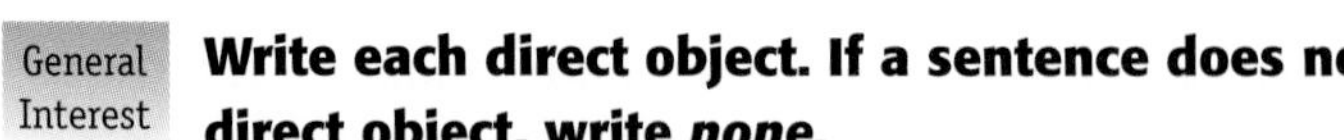

General Interest **Write each direct object. If a sentence does not have a direct object, write *none.***

1. Many people fear snakes because of their slimy appearance and slithery movements.

2. Thousands of people die from venomous snakebites each year.
3. Humans kill many of them each year.
4. However, some snakes serve a useful purpose.
5. Snakes eat rats and other small mammals.
6. Some people buy nonvenomous reptiles and keep them as pets.
7. Snakes are found throughout the world.
8. Boa constrictors suffocate their prey.
9. Rattlesnakes periodically shed their fangs.
10. The rattlesnake gets its name from the noisemaking rattles on its tail.

Connect to the Writing Process: Drafting

Writing Sentences with Direct Objects

Write sentences using each of the words below as a direct object. Remember that a sentence must contain an action verb to have a direct object.

11. cobra
12. mouse
13. teeth
14. teacher
15. zoo
16. tail
17. venom
18. cage
19. food
20. prey

Indirect Objects

An **indirect object** answers the questions *To* or *For whom?* or *To* or *For what?* after an action verb.

If a sentence has a direct object, it also can have another complement, called an indirect object. To find indirect objects, first find the direct object. Then ask yourself, *To whom? For whom? To what?* or *For what?* about each direct object. The answers to these questions will be an indirect object. An indirect object always comes before a direct object in a sentence.

Daniel sent his **friends** (i.o.) invitations (d.o.) to his birthday party.

(*Invitations* is the direct object. Daniel sent invitations to whom? *Friends* is the indirect object.)

Daniel gave his **pets** (i.o.) a bath (d.o.) before the party.

(*Bath* is the direct object. Daniel gave a bath to what? *Pets* is the indirect object.)

A verb in a sentence can have two or more indirect objects called a **compound indirect object**.

Daniel's aunt read **Daniel** (i.o.) and his **friends** (i.o.) a poem (d.o.) about birthdays.

Daniel should not have given his **dog** (i.o.) and **cat** (i.o.) cake (d.o.).

Keep in mind that an indirect object is never part of a prepositional phrase.

Daniel's dad showed **us** (i.o.) a baby picture (d.o.) of Daniel.

(*Us* is the indirect object. It comes between the verb and the direct object, and it is not a part of a prepositional phrase.)

Daniel's dad showed a baby picture (d.o.) of Daniel to us.

(*Us* is not an indirect object. It does not come between the verb and the direct object. It follows the direct object and is part of the prepositional phrase *to us*.)

You cannot have an indirect object without a direct object in a sentence.

Practice Your Skills

Check Your Understanding

Finding Indirect Objects

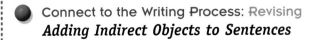

Contemporary Life

Write the indirect objects from the sentences below. If a sentence does not have an indirect object, write *none.*

1. The whole class came to the party.
2. Daniel gave all his friends party favors.
3. Show his mother those beautiful pictures of our recent class trip.
4. I already gave the pictures to his sister.
5. Daniel's mom showed us some home movies.
6. We told his aunt and uncle a story about Daniel and his dog.
7. I handed him my present first.
8. I gave Daniel a collar for his dog.
9. My sister sent him a card.
10. We will visit his family again.

Connect to the Writing Process: Revising

Adding Indirect Objects to Sentences

Add indirect objects to the following sentences by changing each underlined prepositional phrase into an indirect object.

11. Daniel also sent an invitation to our homeroom teacher.
12. Mrs. Jenkins brought some delicious lemon cookies for Daniel.
13. Cindi and Josh taught some great new tricks to Daniel's dog.
14. Will you show the presents to me?
15. We will send a note of thanks to his parents.
16. Have you made a present for Aunt Liz yet?
17. I will mail the present to her.

Communicate Your Ideas

APPLY TO WRITING

Description: ***Direct and Indirect Objects***

Your family is planning a birthday party for you. They are trying to decide what the party's theme should be. They also need to decide what food should be served and who should be invited. For your family, write a description of what you consider to be the perfect birthday party. Whom would you invite? Where would the party take place? What presents would you receive? Be sure to include plenty of detail. Underline three direct objects and two indirect objects that you use in your description.

Predicate Nominatives

A **predicate nominative** is a noun or a pronoun that follows a linking verb and identifies, renames, or explains the subject.

Direct objects and indirect objects follow action verbs. Two other kinds of complements follow linking verbs. They are called **subject complements** because they either rename or describe the subject. One subject complement is a predicate nominative.

To find a predicate nominative, first find the subject and the verb. Check to see if the verb is a linking verb. Then find the noun or the pronoun that identifies, renames, or explains the subject. This word will be a predicate nominative. Notice in the second example that a predicate nominative can be a compound.

> The cat has become America's favorite **pet.** (p.n.)
> (pet = cat)
>
> Two common house cats are the **manx** (p.n.) and the **Burmese.** (p.n.)
> (manx = cats, Burmese = cats)

Following is a list of common linking verbs.

COMMON LINKING VERBS	
***Be* Verbs**	is, am, are, was, were, be, being, been, shall be, will be, can be, should be, would be, may be, might be, has been, have been, had been
Others	appear, become, feel, grow, look, remain, seem, smell, sound, stay, taste, turn

Like a direct object and an indirect object, a predicate nominative cannot be part of a prepositional phrase.

> p.n.
> The Siamese is **one** of the most exotic breeds.
> (*One* is the predicate nominative. *Breeds* is part of the prepositional phrase *of the most exotic breeds.*)

You can learn more about linking verbs on pages L75–L78.

Practice Your Skills

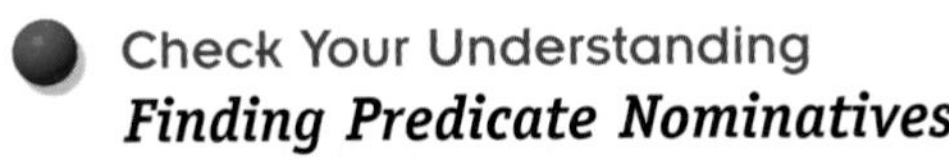

Check Your Understanding

Finding Predicate Nominatives

General Interest **Write the predicate nominatives from the sentences below.**

1. The cat can be an excellent companion.
2. The two classifications of cats are the long-haired Persian cat and the short-haired domestic feline.
3. Cats were sacred creatures to the ancient Egyptians.
4. Until recently, the most popular pet in America was the dog.
5. Some house cats can be rather large animals.
6. The cat's most effective weapon might be its claws.
7. Its claws are excellent tools for defense.

8. Its whiskers can be sense organs of touch.
9. The Siberian tiger is the largest member of the cat family.
10. Is the cheetah the fastest land animal?

Connect to the Writing Process: Drafting
Writing Sentences with Predicate Nominatives

Write a sentence using the words below as predicate nominatives. Remember that a sentence must contain a linking verb to have a predicate nominative.

11. pet
12. fur
13. friends
14. cat
15. lion

Predicate Adjectives

A **predicate adjective** is an adjective that follows a linking verb and modifies the subject.

The second kind of subject complement is a predicate adjective. Notice the difference between a predicate nominative and a predicate adjective in the following examples.

p.n.
The test was a long **one.**

(A predicate nominative renames the subject.)

p.a.
The test was **long.**

(A predicate adjective modifies or describes the subject.)

To find a predicate adjective, first find the subject and the verb. Check to see if the verb is a linking verb. Then find an adjective that follows the verb and describes the subject. This word will be a predicate adjective. Notice in the second example that there is a compound predicate adjective.

> Does our assignment for history seem **easy** to you? (p.a.)
>
> (*Easy* describes the assignment.)
>
> The project for science was **fun** and **interesting.** (p.a., p.a.)
>
> (*Fun* and *interesting* describe the project.)

Do not confuse a regular adjective with a predicate adjective. Remember that a predicate adjective must follow a linking verb and describe the subject of a sentence.

REGULAR ADJECTIVE	Some dinosaurs were **great** hunters.
PREDICATE ADJECTIVE	The dinosaurs were **great** as hunters.

You can learn more about adjectives on pages L91–L103.

PRACTICE YOUR SKILLS

Check Your Understanding

Finding Predicate Adjectives

Contemporary Life **Write each predicate adjective. If the sentence does not have a predicate adjective, write *none.***

1. Today was the first day of school.

2. This year most of my classes will be difficult.

3. I was very nervous.

4. The hallways at my new high school are long and narrow.

5. Most classrooms appeared large.

6. In my science class, the lab tables are high off the floor.

7. For some reason the seniors in the auditorium seemed very tall.

8. The locker room in the gym smelled bad.
9. The cafeteria food tastes delicious.
10. After the first day, I felt better.

Connect to the Writing Process: Drafting
Adding Predicate Adjectives to Sentences

Write the sentences, adding a predicate adjective to each sentence.

11. On the first day of school, my stomach always feels ■.
12. Of all my classes, English has become my ■.
13. The weekends are ■.
14. Our art teacher should be ■.
15. Most of the time, school is ■.
16. Last year's rock concert was ■.
17. Unfortunately, the lead singer was ■.
18. This year's concert will be ■.

Communicate Your Ideas

APPLY TO WRITING

Friendly Letter: ***Subject Complements***

A new girl has just come to your school from another country. Write a friendly letter to this new student welcoming her to your school. Then, in order to make her feel more comfortable, describe what a day is like at your campus. Use your own experience as a basis for your description. What do you do in school? What are your classes? Where do you eat lunch? You may even wish to give her advice about what classes to take or which clubs to join. Be prepared to point out the predicate adjectives and the predicate nominatives in your letter.

General Interest

Write each complement. Then label each one *direct object, indirect object, predicate nominative,* or *predicate adjective.* If there is no complement, write *none.*

1. The 1960s were an interesting decade for entertainment.
2. In 1960, Chubby Checker started a new dance craze.
3. Dancers loved the twist.
4. The Beach Boys were also popular.
5. Their songs filled the heads of young people with dreams of California sun and surf.
6. The most popular rock group was the Beatles.
7. At that time the Beatles' hair was fairly short.
8. By the end of the decade, this band was legendary.
9. Americans watched more and more television.
10. *American Bandstand* was popular with the teenagers of the day.
11. *Sesame Street* taught young children letters and numbers.
12. Other popular television programs were *Captain Video* and *Captain Midnight.*
13. Elephant jokes were the rage in the early 1960s.
14. For example, why do elephants wear green sneakers?
15. Their blue ones are dirty.
16. The miniskirt became the fashion rage.
17. Christiaan Barnard transplanted a human heart.
18. Olympic officials gave Peggy Fleming a gold medal for figure skating.
19. President Kennedy had wanted an astronaut on the moon by the end of the decade.
20. In 1969, humans landed on the moon.

Using Sentence Patterns

The boy ran.
The four-year-old boy ran frantically down the street.

These two sentences are exactly alike in one respect. They both follow the same subject-verb sentence pattern. Even though there are an endless number of sentences that can be written, there are only a few basic sentence patterns.

Pattern 1: S-V (subject-verb)

S V
Everyone cheered.

S V
Everyone at the game cheered wildly.

Pattern 2: S-V-O (subject-verb-direct object)

S V O
Birds eat insects.

S V O
Many birds eat harmful insects.

Pattern 3: S-V-I-O (subject-verb-indirect object-direct object)

S V I O
Grandfather sends me coins.

S V I O
My grandfather from Ohio always sends me coins from foreign countries.

Pattern 4: S-V-N (subject-verb-predicate nominative)

S V N
The chair is an antique.

S V N
The blue velvet chair is an antique from the 1800s.

Pattern 5: S-V-A (subject-verb-predicate adjective)

S V A
The siren sounds scary.

S V A
The siren on the fire truck always sounds very scary.

Practice Your Skills

Check Your Understanding

Write the sentence pattern that each sentence follows.

EXAMPLE The jacket with the hood is the one for me.

ANSWER S-V-N

1. The Japanese have developed a half-inch camera.
2. The action in a hockey game is fast and furious.
3. My radio alarm doesn't work anymore.
4. A guppy is a small tropical fish.
5. At the student assembly, the principal gave the athlete a trophy.
6. The holiday catalog was large and colorful.
7. The scholarship award was a check for five hundred dollars.
8. My grandparents from Iowa travel extensively throughout the United States.
9. Pure radium resembles ordinary table salt.
10. The computer gave us the answer to the question.

Writing a Short Story

If you had to become a piece of food, what would you be—a bunch of grapes, a piece of cheese, a turkey leg? Make a list of your favorite foods and choose one. Then imagine what it would be like to be that piece of food for a day. Write freely for several minutes. Write a story about one day, or one incident, in your life as a piece of food. Write the story from the first-person point of view using the pronouns *I, me,* and *my*.

When you have finished, read over your story. Make sure that your sentences have followed a variety of different sentence patterns. Check your ending. Is it as interesting or unexpected as it could be? Revise your story until it is the best it can be. If you have included any dialogue, edit it for correct punctuation. Then edit the rest of your story for any other errors. Finally, write a clean copy.

Diagraming Complements

Together, a subject, a verb, and a complement are called the **sentence base.** Since complements are part of the sentence base, they are diagramed on or below the baseline.

Direct Objects A direct object is placed on the baseline after the verb. It is separated from the verb by a vertical line that stops at the baseline.

Some sharks have no natural enemies.

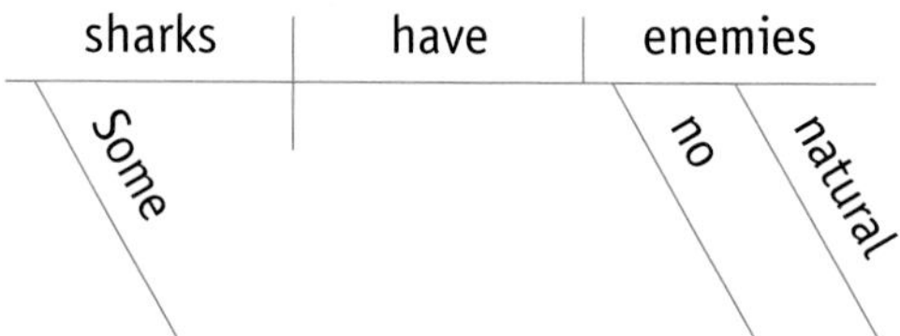

Indirect Objects An indirect object is diagramed on a horizontal line that is connected to the verb.

Phil prepared his friends a big dinner.

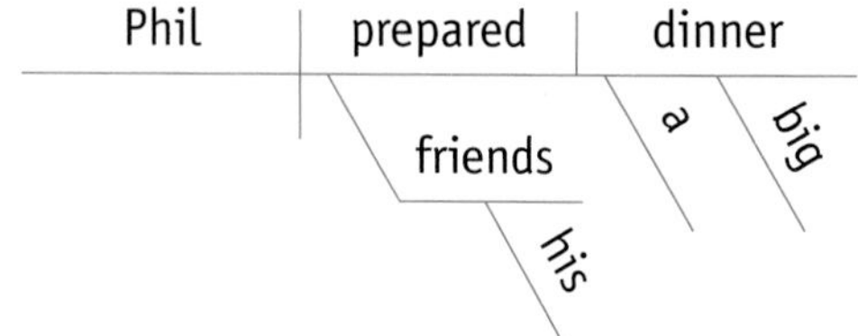

Subject Complements Both subject complements are diagramed in the same way. They are placed on the baseline after the verb. They are separated from the verb by a slanted line that points back toward the subject.

This tree is an oak.

tree | is \ oak
This
an

The painting is very old.

painting | is \ old
The
very

The winners are two freshmen and one senior.

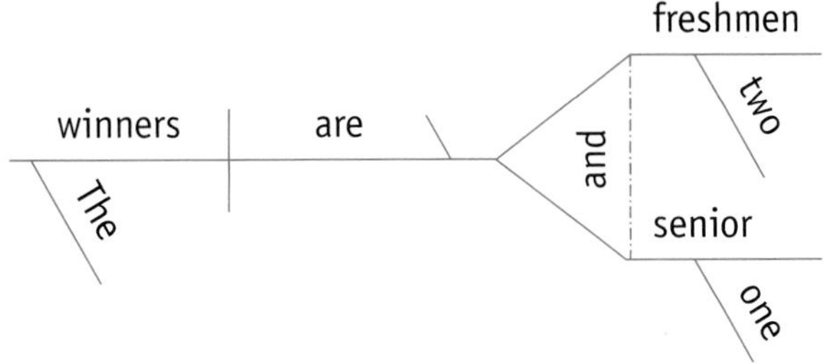

Practice Your Skills

Diagraming Complements

Diagram the following sentences or copy them. If you copy them, draw one line under each subject and two lines under each verb. Then label each complement *d.o.* for direct object, *i.o.* for indirect object, *p.n.* for predicate nominative, or *p.a.* for predicate adjective.

1. My soft sculpture won first prize.

2. Don gave me a new notebook.

3. The director is a wonderful man.

4. I have visited pretty gardens and parks.

5. That flower looks very delicate.

6. Will you show Jan and me your coin collection?

7. Haven't you given him your answer yet?

8. The books were very old and dusty.

9. Sing us another song. (You)

10. My favorite sports are basketball and baseball.

CheckPoint

Identifying Complements

Write each complement. Then label each one, using the following abbreviations.

direct object = *d.o.*
indirect object = *i.o.*
predicate nominative = *p.n.*
predicate adjective = *p.a.*

1. In an average lifetime, a person will walk seventy thousand miles.

2. One out of every twenty people is left-handed.

3. Matt gave me some help with my homework.

4. The loud crash of thunder frightened our dog and cat.

5. The moon looked hazy behind the thick clouds.

6. Bananas are the most popular fruit in the world.

7. The receptionist greeted Matthew and me at the door.

8. Your brain is 80 percent water.

9. Hand me the scissors.

10. Ricardo is president of the Honor Society.

11. Fish have no eyelids.

12. Eric is only one of the contestants in the show.

13. The crowd at City Hall grew loud and angry.

14. Americans eat approximately two billion pounds of cookies a year.

15. Send your grandparents a card for their anniversary.

16. The two most popular items in a grocery store are cereals and sodas.

17. I offered Ben a slice of pizza.

18. An ocean sunfish can lay 300 million eggs in one year.

19. Before the big game, the sky looked cloudy and dark.

20. The benefit concert was a huge success.

Identifying Complements

Write each complement. Then label each one, using the following abbreviations.

direct object = *d.o.* predicate nominative = *p.n.*
indirect object = *i.o.* predicate adjective = *p.a.*

1. I will tell you an unusual story.
2. During World War I, a Canadian pilot was flying a small military plane over Germany.
3. Of course, in those days, military planes were open.
4. Captain J. H. Hedley was the other person in the plane.
5. Suddenly an enemy plane attacked their plane.
6. The pilot took the plane into a nearly vertical dive, and Hedley shot out of his seat and into the air.
7. Several hundred feet lower the plane was finally level again.
8. Then, incredibly, Hedley grabbed the tail of the plane.
9. Apparently the extremely powerful suction of the steep dive had pulled Hedley back to the plane.
10. With tremendous relief, he eventually reached his seat on the plane.

Using Complements

Write five sentences that follow the directions below. (The sentences may come in any order.) Write about one of the following topics or a topic of your choice: the funniest present you ever gave or the funniest present you ever received.

Write a sentence that . . .

1. includes a direct object.
2. includes an indirect object and a direct object.
3. includes a predicate nominative.
4. includes a predicate adjective.
5. includes a compound predicate adjective.

Underline and label each complement.

Language and *Self-Expression*

Clara McDonald Williamson (1875–1976) was from Texas and often painted Texan subjects. The Old Chisholm Trail extended from Texas to Kansas, and cattle were often driven along it to market or to new pastures.

Young boys were sometimes taken on cattle drives to learn cowboy ways. Imagine that you are one of those boys, and that you are keeping a journal of your days on the trail. Write an entry for your journal about one day of your trip. Create variety in your sentences by including direct objects, indirect objects, predicate nominatives, and predicate adjectives.

Prewriting You might wish to create a cluster diagram showing what you would see, hear, smell, taste, and feel on the trail. Include events as well as sense impressions in your diagram.

Drafting Use your cluster diagram to write your journal entry. After you date the entry, describe your experiences on that particular day.

Revising Reread your entry carefully. Be sure your sentences include direct objects, indirect objects, predicate nominatives, and predicate adjectives.

Editing Check your entry for errors in spelling and punctuation. Capitalize all proper nouns and proper adjectives.

Publishing Make a final copy of your journal entry. Then collect it with classmates' entries to make a complete journal of the cattle drive.

Another Look

A **complement** is a word or group of words that completes the meaning of subjects and verbs.

Kinds of Complements

A **direct object** is a noun or pronoun that receives the action of the verb. *(pages L149–L150)*

An **indirect object** answers the question *To* or *for whom?* or *To* or *for what?* after an action verb. *(pages L151–L152)*

A **predicate nominative** is a noun or pronoun that follows a linking verb and identifies, renames, or explains the subject. *(pages L154–L155)*

COMMON LINKING VERBS	
***Be* Verbs**	is, am, are, was, were, be, being, been, shall be, will be, can be, should be, would be, may be, might be, has been, have been, had been
Others	appear, become, feel, grow, look, remain, seem, smell, sound, stay, taste, turn

A **predicate adjective** is an adjective that follows a linking verb and modifies the subject. *(pages L156–L157)*

Directions

Write the letter of the term that correctly identifies the underlined word in each sentence.

EXAMPLE **1.** Honeybees use special <u>dances</u> to find new homes.

1 **A** direct object
B indirect object
C predicate adjective
D predicate nominative

ANSWER **1** **A**

1. In spring, queen bees send worker <u>bees</u> signals to vacate the hive.

2. Half the hive becomes <u>eager</u> to leave.

3. Scout bees search the <u>area</u> for new nest sites.

4. When a scout finds a nest site, it gives the other <u>bees</u> a dance signal.

5. The bees are amazing <u>dancers</u>.

6. The dances tell the <u>bees</u> the location of the new nesting place.

7. The bees investigate many different <u>sites</u> as possible nesting places.

8. They are very picky <u>insects</u>.

9. All the bees must be <u>happy</u> with the site in order to begin the move.

10. Then the worker bees give the <u>swarm</u> directions to the new nest.

1. **A** predicate adjective
   B indirect object
   C direct object
   D predicate nominative

2. **A** indirect object
   B direct object
   C predicate nominative
   D predicate adjective

3. **A** direct object
   B indirect object
   C predicate adjective
   D predicate nominative

4. **A** predicate nominative
   B predicate adjective
   C direct object
   D indirect object

5. **A** predicate adjective
   B direct object
   C predicate nominative
   D indirect object

6. **A** direct object
   B indirect object
   C predicate adjective
   D predicate nominative

7. **A** indirect object
   B predicate nominative
   C predicate adjective
   D direct object

8. **A** predicate adjective
   B predicate nominative
   C direct object
   D indirect object

9. **A** direct object
   B indirect object
   C predicate adjective
   D predicate nominative

10. **A** predicate adjective
    B predicate nominative
    C direct object
    D indirect object

Phrases

Directions

Write the letter of the term that correctly identifies the underlined phrase in each sentence.

EXAMPLE **1.** In the West coyotes have been considered pests for decades.

1 **A** participial
B infinitive
C appositive
D prepositional

ANSWER **1** **D**

1. These animals, the subject of many Native American legends, have spread eastward.
2. There were no coyotes in the East until the twentieth century.
3. Coyotes have managed to spread quickly.
4. Hunters with permits kill hundreds each year.
5. Coyotes have been known to eat cats and small dogs.
6. Yipping loudly is the way the coyote announces its presence.
7. Adapting easily to harsh conditions, the coyote is a survivor.
8. Coyotes could not flourish when there were wolves to compete with them.
9. The wolf, a relative of the coyote, is a better predator.
10. With its fierce instincts, a wolf could kill a coyote.

1 **A** gerund
B appositive
C participial
D prepositional

2 **A** gerund
B participial
C appositive
D prepositional

3 **A** participial
B gerund
C infinitive
D prepositional

4 **A** participial
B prepositional
C appositive
D infinitive

5 **A** infinitive
B prepositional
C appositive
D participial

6 **A** gerund
B infinitive
C participial
D prepositional

7 **A** infinitive
B prepositional
C participial
D gerund

8 **A** prepositional
B gerund
C participial
D infinitive

9 **A** appositive
B gerund
C prepositional
D participial

10 **A** gerund
B appositive
C prepositional
D participial

Fernando Botero. *Dancing in Colombia,* 1980.
Oil on canvas, 74 by 91 inches. The Metropolitan Museum of Art. ©Fernando Botero, courtesy Marlborough Gallery, N.Y.

Describe What instruments are the people playing in this painting? What else are they doing?

Analyze Which figures are the focal point of the painting? Why do you think the artist made them the focal point?

Interpret How do you think the size of the figures affects the meaning of the painting?

Judge Do you think the artist has effectively created an atmosphere of joyous movement? Explain.

At the end of this chapter, you will use the artwork to stimulate ideas for writing.

Prepositional Phrases

A **phrase** is a group of related words that function as a single part of speech. A phrase does not have a subject and a verb.

You know that a prepositional phrase begins with a preposition and ends with a noun or pronoun called the object of the preposition.

> Why don't you go **with Jennifer?**
>
> The man **beneath the tightrope** was a famous person **in New York.**
>
> **On Monday** we will ride **around the stadium** when we get **out of school.**

Following is a list of common prepositions.

COMMON PREPOSITIONS			
about	beneath	inside	over
above	beside	instead of	past
across	between	into	since
after	beyond	near	through
against	by	next to	throughout
ahead of	down	of	to
along	during	off	toward
among	except	on	under
around	for	on account of	until
at	from	onto	up
before	in	out	with
behind	in addition to	out of	within
below	in back of	outside	without

You can learn more about prepositions and prepositional phrases on pages L125–L130.

Practice Your Skills

Check Your Understanding

Finding Prepositional Phrases

General Interest **Write the prepositional phrases in this paragraph.**

In 1859, Charles Blondin walked across Niagara Falls on a tightrope. He was high above the water. Later he crossed with a blindfold over his eyes. Then he crossed on stilts. Finally, he really amazed everyone. Halfway across the falls, he stopped for breakfast. He cooked some eggs, ate them, and continued to the other side!

Adjective Phrases

An **adjective phrase** is a prepositional phrase that is used to modify a noun or a pronoun.

Like a single adjective, an adjective phrase answers the question *Which one(s)?* or *What kind?* about a noun or pronoun.

Which One(s)	The dog **with the short legs** is a dachshund.
What Kind?	Please give me that bag **of dog food.**

An adjective phrase usually modifies the noun or the pronoun directly in front of it. Occasionally, an adjective phrase will modify a noun or a pronoun in another phrase.

The story ***about* the dog *with* a broken leg** was sad.

Two adjective phrases can also modify the same noun or pronoun.

That spaniel ***with* the red collar *on* the porch** is mine.

CONNECT TO WRITER'S CRAFT

To avoid short, choppy sentences in your writing, you can combine sentences by using adjective phrases.

Have you seen that movie? It's about two dogs and a cat.
Have you seen that movie **about two dogs and a cat?**

Combining sentences makes your writing smoother. 

PRACTICE YOUR SKILLS

 Check Your Understanding

Recognizing Adjective Phrases as Modifiers

Contemporary Life **Write each adjective phrase. Then beside each phrase, write the word it modifies.** Some sentences have more than one adjective phrase.

1. Dogs can be great friends to humans.
2. There are many breeds of dogs.
3. The smallest type of canine is the Chihuahua.
4. One of the largest breeds in the American Kennel Club is the Irish wolfhound.
5. Some of these dogs are taller than their owners!
6. The news stories about dogs without homes make me sad.
7. A friend of mine adopted a tiny puppy with little brown spots.
8. The puppy from the shelter was a mix of many different breeds.
9. The size of that tiny puppy changed rapidly.
10. Now the tiny puppy is a huge dog with big, brown spots.
11. My friend is writing a short story about her dog.
12. Another friend across the street just got a Persian kitten.

Connect to the Writing Process: Revising
Using Adjective Phrases to Combine Sentences

Combine each pair of sentences, putting some information into an adjective phrase.

13. Have you read this book? It is about dog training.
14. That dog protects their home. He has a scary bark.
15. A beautiful dog is the collie. The collie has long fur.
16. My cousin lives on a farm. He has many dogs.
17. I took a picture. The photo showed dogs at the shelter.
18. My cousin wrote me a letter. He described his vacation.
19. He helped an elderly couple. He did the farmwork.
20. The barn was new. It sat on the hilltop.

Communicate Your Ideas

APPLY TO WRITING

Persuasive Letter: *Adjective Phrases*

You wish to adopt a puppy from the local shelter. Make a list of some possible objections a parent might have to your owning a dog. Then make a list of positive things about having a dog that might answer your parent's concerns. After that, write a letter to your parent in which you attempt to persuade him or her to let you adopt a dog. Underline four adjective phrases you used in your letter.

Adverb Phrases

An **adverb phrase** is a prepositional phrase that is used to modify a verb, an adjective, or an adverb.

The following examples show how adverb phrases may be used to modify verbs.

Single Adverb	A mosquito buzzed **by.**
Adverb Phrase	A mosquito buzzed **by my ear.**
Single Adverb	Everyone came **here.**
Adverb Phrase	Everyone came **to the picnic.**

Like a single adverb, an adverb phrase answers the question *Where? When? How? To what extent?* or *To what degree?* Most adverb phrases modify the verb. Notice that an adverb phrase modifies the whole verb phrase, just as a single adverb does.

Where?	We should meet **at the park.**
When?	We will meet **by noon.**
How?	We planned the picnic **with excitement.**

Adverb phrases also modify adjectives and adverbs.

Modifying An Adjective	Liz was happy **with her new kite.**
	The picnic blanket was soft **against my skin.**
Modifying An Adverb	The picnic continued late **into the evening.**
	Liz's kite soared high **into the sky.**

An adverb phrase does not necessarily come next to the word it modifies. Also, several adverb phrases can modify the same word.

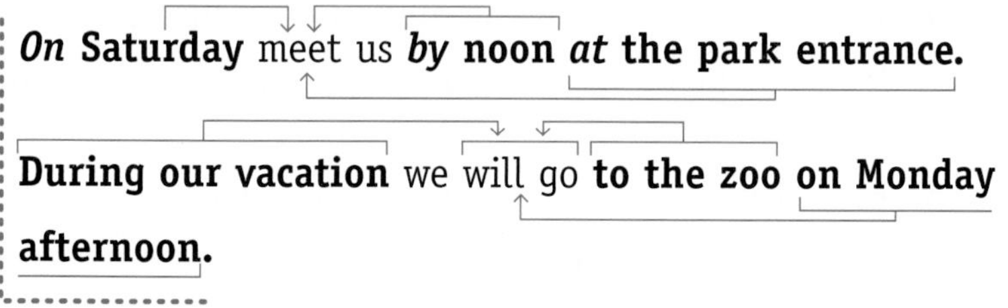

***On* Saturday** meet us ***by* noon *at* the park entrance.**

During our vacation we will go **to the zoo on Monday afternoon.**

PUNCTUATION WITH ADVERB PHRASES	
If a short adverb phrase comes at the beginning of a sentence, usually no comma is needed. You should, however, place a comma after an introductory phrase of four or more words or after several introductory adverb phrases.	
NO COMMA	**At noon** we met at the park.
COMMA	**Because of the heavy traffic,** Dee was late.
	In the shade under the tree, we ate our picnic lunch.

PRACTICE YOUR SKILLS

Check Your Understanding

Recognizing Adverb Phrases as Modifiers

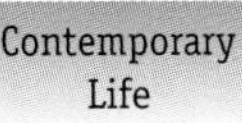

Contemporary Life

Write each adverb phrase. Then beside each phrase, write the word it modifies. Some sentences have more than one adverb phrase.

1. Since Monday we have been planning a picnic.
2. On Saturday I awakened with happy anticipation.
3. My brother drove me across town to the park.
4. I brought sandwiches and cold drinks in a large blue ice chest.
5. Before noon my friends had arrived at the park.
6. We put a blanket on the ground over the rocks.
7. Near our picnic blanket, Amanda tossed a baseball to her little brother.
8. For a while we watched the many joggers.
9. After that Luke and Brittany flew their kites into the wind.
10. After a long day, we put our trash into the garbage cans and left the park.

Connect to the Writing Process: Editing

Punctuating Adverb Phrases

Rewrite the following sentences, placing commas after the introductory phrases, if needed. If a comma is not necessary, write *C* for correct.

11. Because of our love for the outdoors my friends and I helped clean the park.

12. For years the park has been the heart of our city.

13. Within two or three hours we had removed most of the trash from the area.

14. In a recent election the citizens of our city voted for park improvements.

15. During the spring the city will plant more trees.

Communicate Your Ideas

APPLY TO WRITING

Compare and Contrast: *Adverb Phrases*

Susan Merritt. *Picnic Scene,* ca. 1853.
Watercolor and collage on paper, 26 by 36 ½ inches. The Art Institute of Chicago.

Alma Gunter. *Dinner on Grounds,* 1979–80.
Acrylic on canvas, 24 by 18 inches. African American Museum, Dallas, Texas.

Many painters use everyday scenes of life as subjects for their art. Susan Merritt's *Picnic Scene* on the preceding page and Alma Gunter's *Dinner on Grounds* above both show people at a picnic. While the works have a few similarities, the style of these two paintings is different. Write a paper for your teacher, pointing out two similarities and two differences in these paintings. Underline at least four adverb phrases in your writing. Remember, use commas with introductory phrases as needed.

Misplaced Modifiers

Because a prepositional phrase is used as a modifier, it should be placed as close as possible to the word it describes. If a phrase is too far away from the word it modifies, the result may be a **misplaced modifier.** Misplaced modifiers create confusion and misunderstanding for readers.

MISPLACED	On the stage the audience applauded for the performers.
CORRECT	The audience applauded for the performers **on the stage.**
MISPLACED	The actor told us about his career in his dressing room.
CORRECT	**In his dressing room,** the actor told us about his career.

PRACTICE YOUR SKILLS

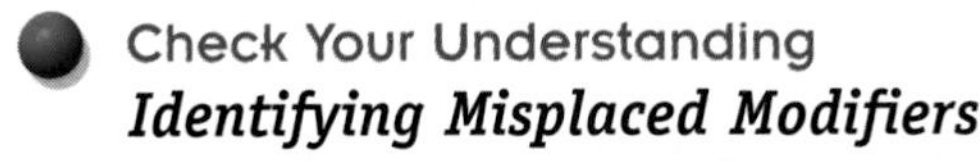

Check Your Understanding

Identifying Misplaced Modifiers

Contemporary Life

Write *MM* for misplaced modifier if the underlined prepositional phrase is too far away from the word it modifies. Write *C* for correct if the underlined prepositional phrase is correctly placed.

1. From the script the actor practiced his lines.
2. Tonight the audience will see the actor's first performance in the play.
3. The cast waited for the start of the play behind the curtain.
4. The character actor heard a strange noise from the back row.
5. The actors bowed to the appreciative audience in their costumes.
6. We looked in the program for the names of the talented cast.
7. From a blue glass, the villain took a long drink.
8. The stage manager directed the entrances of the cast.
9. With a scream the actor fell to the floor.
10. We read about the play in the newspaper.

Connect to the Writing Process: Revising

Correcting Misplaced Modifiers

11.–15. Rewrite correctly the sentences in the preceding exercise that have misplaced modifiers.

QuickCheck Mixed Practice

History Topic

Write each prepositional phrase. Then label each one *adjective* or *adverb*.

1. The Braille family lived in a village near Paris, France.

2. As a boy, Louis Braille played in his father's shop.

3. On one fateful afternoon, young Louis was playing with an awl.

4. His father made holes in leather with the sharp tool.

5. Without any warning the awl accidentally went into Louis's left eye.

6. After several days an infection in this injured eye spread to his good eye.

7. Because of the accident, Louis became totally blind.

8. Louis later entered the school in his neighborhood.

9. He could hear his teachers, but he couldn't learn from books.

10. At ten he entered a school for the blind in Paris.

11. Children at that school were reading from special books.

12. Letters of the alphabet were pressed into thick paper.

13. This pressing created raised outlines on the paper.

14. The students would feel the outlines with their fingers.

15. The books were heavy because of the huge letters.

16. One day a retired captain came to the school with a code.

17. His system of dots and dashes proved too difficult.

18. By the age of fifteen, Braille had developed a new system of only dots.

Appositives and Appositive Phrases

An **appositive** is a noun or a pronoun that identifies or explains another noun or pronoun in the sentence.

Sometimes a noun or a pronoun is followed immediately by another noun or pronoun that identifies or explains it. This identifying noun or pronoun is called an appositive.

> My brother **Pat** returned from his trip.
>
> On vacation he visited his favorite city, **Washington, D.C.**

Most of the time, an appositive is used with modifiers to form an **appositive phrase.**

> The president, **the nation's leader,** lives in the White House.
>
> The nation's capital is named for George Washington, **the first president.**

Notice that a prepositional phrase can be part of an appositive phrase.

> Washington's nickname, **the Father of Our Country,** is familiar to all Americans.

PUNCTUATION WITH APPOSITIVES AND APPOSITIVE PHRASES

If the information in an appositive is essential to the meaning of a sentence, no commas are needed. The information is usually essential if it names a specific person, place, or thing.

A comma is needed before and after an appositive or an appositive phrase if the information is not essential to the meaning of the sentence.

Essential	Last year in American history, we read Lincoln's speech "The Gettysburg Address."
Nonessential	"The Gettysburg Address," a speech by Abraham Lincoln, is read by many students of history.

Practice Your Skills

Check Your Understanding

Finding Appositives and Appositive Phrases

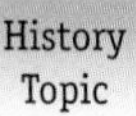

Write the appositive or appositive phrase in each sentence. Then, beside each one, write the word or words it identifies or explains.

1. We know many interesting details about the men of America's highest office, the presidency.
2. Our president Grover Cleveland entered the White House as a bachelor.
3. While in office he married Frances Graves, a beautiful young woman.
4. Thomas Jefferson, the author of the *Declaration of Independence,* was an architect, a writer, and a politician.
5. William Henry Harrison, our ninth president, died after only one month in office.
6. His vice president, John Tyler, succeeded him as president.
7. Woodrow Wilson, a great intellectual, led America through World War I.
8. President Bill Clinton plays the saxophone, a woodwind instrument.
9. Ronald Reagan, a former actor, was elected president in 1980.
10. Theodore Roosevelt, a sickly child, grew up to become a war hero.

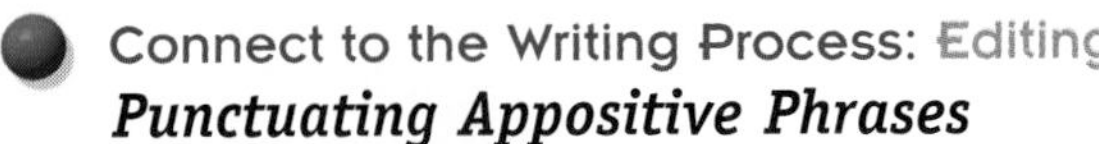
Connect to the Writing Process: Editing

Punctuating Appositive Phrases

Rewrite the following sentences placing commas before and after the appositive or appositive phrase if needed. If commas are not necessary, write *C* for correct.

11. Only one American president Richard Nixon resigned from office.

12. From 1953 to 1961, Nixon served as vice president during the terms of Dwight Eisenhower the thirty-fourth president.

13. Nixon was defeated by a narrow margin in the 1960 presidential election by the young senator from Massachusetts John F. Kennedy.

14. In 1968, Nixon was elected to the nation's highest office the presidency.

15. In 1974, he resigned because of Watergate a political scandal.

16. Nixon's vice president Gerald R. Ford was sworn in as the nation's thirty-eighth president.

Communicate Your Ideas

APPLY TO WRITING

Editorial: ***Appositives***

You are a newspaper reporter who has been asked to write an opinion piece about leadership. Consider the qualities that are important in a leader. What does one need to be effective in that role? Describe three characteristics of a good leader. In your editorial, use specific examples of people from history or people you have known who have been effective leaders. Use at least three appositives or appositive phrases in your editorial.

Verbals and Verbal Phrases

You are already familiar with some of the information you will cover in this section. For example, you already know that the words *exhausted* and *cheering* in the following sentence are used as adjectives.

> The **exhausted** singers bowed before the **cheering** fans.

What you may not know is that they belong to a special group of words called verbals. A **verbal** is a verb form that is used as some other part of speech. In the example above, for instance, *exhausted* and *cheering* look like verbs but are actually used as adjectives.

There are three kinds of verbals: participles, gerunds, and infinitives. All of these verbals are important writing tools. They add variety when placed at the beginning of a sentence, and they add conciseness when they are used to combine two simple sentences.

Participles

A participle is a verb form that is used as an adjective.

The words *exhausted* and *cheering* in the example above are participles. To find a participle, ask the adjective questions *Which one?* or *What kind?* about each noun or pronoun. If a verb form answers one of these questions, it is a participle. The participles in the following examples are in **bold** type. An arrow points to the noun or pronoun each participle modifies.

> The **screaming** fans surrounded the **delighted** vocalists.
>
> Their manager, **surprised** and **frightened**, pulled them away from the **adoring** crowd.

There are two kinds of participles. **Present participles** end in *–ing*. **Past participles** usually end in *–ed,* but some have irregular endings such as *–n, –t,* or *–en.*

PARTICIPLES	
Present Participle	adoring, screaming, cheering
Past Participle	surprised, frightened, torn, bent, fallen

Everyone enjoyed the sound of the **singing** group.

Their voices filled the **hushed** stadium.

Practice Your Skills

Check Your Understanding

Recognizing Participles as Modifiers

Contemporary Life

Write each participle that is used as an adjective. Then, beside each one, write the word it modifies.

1. The rock band stepped into the blinding spotlights.
2. Their fans, standing and applauding, welcomed their entrance.
3. One musician struck a loud, ringing chord on his guitar.
4. The drummer and the bass player joined the screaming melody.
5. After the first song, the dancing crowd yelled for more.
6. The obliging band played another great song.
7. The pleased crowd sang along with the band.
8. After the concert many fans stayed to meet the exhausted band.
9. These loyal fans held up crumpled pieces of paper to the performers.
10. The band members signed the papers and handed them back to the thrilled fans.

Participle or Verb?

Because a participle is a verb form, you must be careful not to confuse it with the verb in a verb phrase. When a participle is used in a verb phrase, it is part of the verb, not an adjective.

PARTICIPLE	The **burning** forest poses a threat to nearby homes.
VERB	The fire **is burning** out of control.
PARTICIPLE	Many **injured** animals escaped the blaze.
VERB	No campers **were injured** by the fire.

Also be careful not to confuse a participle with the main verb. Sometimes the participle form is the same as the past tense verb form.

PARTICIPLE	The **charred** trees were black against the blue sky.
VERB	The fire **charred** many acres of forest.

Check Your Understanding
Distinguishing Between Participles and Verbs

Contemporary Life **Write the underlined word in each sentence. Then label it *P* for participle or *V* for verb.**

1. The firefighter is caring for an injured deer.
2. Caring campers thoroughly douse their campfires.
3. The questioning reporter inquired about the cause of the fire.
4. The police officer was questioning several nearby residents.
5. The paramedic discarded her dirty gloves.
6. A discarded cigarette started the blaze.

7. The man's camping gear was destroyed in the fire.
8. That couple had been camping near the man.
9. A man was talking to the couple in a quiet voice.
10. The talking man was a park ranger.

Connect to the Writing Process: Drafting

Writing Sentences with Participles and Verbs

Use each of the following words in two sentences. In the first sentence, use the word as a participle. In the second sentence, use it as part of a verb phrase.

11. ringing
12. rusted
13. barking
14. organized
15. swinging
16. swimming

Participial Phrases

A **participial phrase** is a participle with its modifiers and complements—all working together as an adjective.

Because a participle is a verb form, it can have modifiers or a complement. A participle plus any modifiers or complements forms a participial phrase. The following examples show three variations of a participial phrase. Notice that a participial phrase can come at the beginning, the middle, or the end of a sentence.

Participle with an Adverb	**Flying low**, the plane circled the airport.
Participle with a Prepositional Phrase	The crowd **standing on the ground** watched the airplane.
Participle with a Complement	A cheer went up for the woman **piloting the small craft.**

PUNCTUATION WITH PARTICIPIAL PHRASES

A participial phrase that comes at the beginning of a sentence is always followed by a comma.

Slowly turning the plane, Amelia Earhart flew away.

Participial phrases that come in the middle or at the end of a sentence may or may not need commas. If the information in the phrase is essential, no commas are needed. Information is essential if it identifies a person, place, or thing in the sentence.

If the information is nonessential, commas are needed to separate it from the rest of the sentence. A participial phrase is nonessential if it can be removed without changing the meaning of the sentence.

Essential	The photograph **hanging on the wall** is of Amelia Earhart.
Nonessential	The picture, **given to me as a gift,** was taken in 1937.

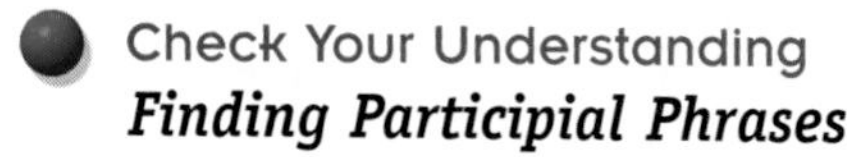

Practice Your Skills

Check Your Understanding

Finding Participial Phrases

History Topic **Write the participial phrase in each sentence. Then underline the participle.**

1. Gaining fame in 1928, Amelia Earhart was the first woman to fly across the Atlantic.
2. She was not the pilot but a passenger riding in that plane.
3. Flying solo, Earhart first soared across the Atlantic Ocean in 1932.
4. Greatly interested in commercial aviation, Earhart worked for an early airline service.
5. Amelia Earhart, flying with navigator Fred Noonan, left Miami, Florida, in June of 1937.

6. Attempting an around-the-world flight, Amelia Earhart flew a twin-engine plane.
7. The mystery surrounding her disappearance is still debated today.
8. Vanishing near Howland Island, the plane was never found.
9. Some historians, suspecting foul play, believe that Earhart and Noonan were forced down and killed by the Japanese.
10. Others, believing a different story, claim that she and Noonan crashed on a Pacific island.

Check Your Understanding
Recognizing Participial Phrases as Modifiers

History Topic **Write the participial phrase in each sentence. Then beside each one, write the word it modifies.**

11. Charles Lindbergh, born in 1902, was raised in Minnesota.
12. Known by the nickname "Lucky Lindy," Lindbergh was a pioneer of aviation.
13. In 1927, he flew solo across the Atlantic in a plane called *Spirit of St. Louis.*
14. Departing from Long Island, the plane flew into a stormy sky.
15. Awaiting Lindbergh in Paris, the crowd grew extremely anxious.
16. Two Frenchmen, attempting the same feat, had recently lost their lives.
17. The enthusiastic crowd cheered the plane landing on the strip.
18. Emerging a hero, Lindbergh waved to the crowd.
19. Marrying Anne Morrow in 1929, Charles Lindbergh gained more than a wife.
20. Flying with Lindbergh, Anne Morrow Lindbergh served as his copilot and navigator on later flights.

Connect to the Writing Process: Drafting

Using Participial Phrases in Sentences

Write a sentence for each of the following participial phrases. Use commas where needed.

21. lost in the Pacific Ocean

22. flying a small airplane

23. stored in the attic

24. using a compass

25. buying a ticket

Communicate Your Ideas

APPLY TO WRITING

The Writer's Craft: ***Analyzing the Use of Participles***

Writers use participles and participial phrases to describe nouns and pronouns throughout their works. Read the following paragraphs by Isaac Asimov from *Science Past—Science Future* and follow the directions at the top of the next page.

> On December 17, 1903, the American gliding enthusiasts Wilber and Orville Wright placed an engine on a glider and successfully flew 120 feet, remaining in the air for 12 seconds. That was the first powered flight of a heavier-than-air machine.
>
> Other "airplanes" were built. In 1905, one of the Wright brothers stayed in the air half an hour and flew 24 miles. In 1909, the French aeronaut Louis Blériot flew from France to England, across the English Channel, in a home-built plane—the first international flight.
>
> As late as 1914, though, airplanes were still little more than engines mounted on gliders, with daredevil stuntmen riding them.
>
> —*Isaac Asimov,* Science Past—Science Future

- Write each participle or participial phrase from the paragraphs. Beside each one, write the word it modifies.
- Could Asimov have placed any of the participial phrases in a different place in the sentence? Why do you think he chose the placement that he did?
- How do participles affect Asimov's description?

Gerunds

A **gerund** is a verb form that is used as a noun.

Both the gerund and the present participle end in *–ing*. A gerund, however, is used as a noun, not as an adjective. A gerund is used in all the ways in which a noun is used.

Subject	**Swimming** is my favorite activity.
Direct Object	Do you enjoy **skiing?**
Indirect Object	I gave **diving** my full attention.
Object of the Preposition	The lifeguard saved her from **drowning.**
Predicate Nominative	My sister's favorite pastime is **boating.**
Appositive	I have a new hobby, **sailing.**

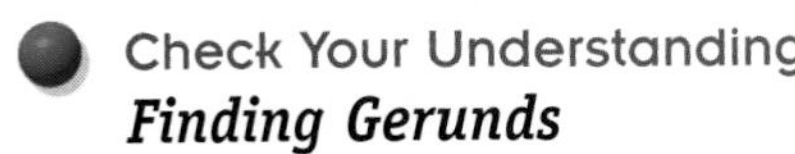

Practice Your Skills

Check Your Understanding

Finding Gerunds

Contemporary Life

Write the gerund in each sentence. Then label it *subject, direct object, indirect object, object of the preposition, predicate nominative,* or *appositive.*

1. In the summer swimming is a great way to stay cool.

2. I just finished a book about sailing.

3. Another enjoyable activity at the lake is water skiing.
4. The hardest part of skiing is balance.
5. Kim has always enjoyed boating.
6. My new exercise, rowing, keeps me fit.
7. The little child gave swimming a try.
8. At first, the sound of laughing came from the water's edge.
9. Suddenly, I heard yelling from that direction.
10. By running, the lifeguard was able to reach the child first.

Gerund or Participle?

It is easy to confuse a gerund and a present participle because they both end in *–ing*. Just remember that a gerund is used as a noun. A participle is used as an adjective.

GERUND	My best friend earns extra money by **sewing.**
	(*Sewing* is the object of the preposition.)
PARTICIPLE	I might take a **sewing** class.
	(*Sewing* modifies *class*.)

PRACTICE YOUR SKILLS

Check Your Understanding

Distinguishing Between Gerunds and Participles

Contemporary Life **Write the underlined word in each sentence. Then label it *G* for gerund or *P* for participle.**

1. Many teenagers start working to make extra money.
2. Others become working people to help out their families.

3. Cooking is another good way to earn some extra money.
4. Meg took a cooking class to improve her culinary skills.
5. Jason's singing helps bring in some cash.
6. People pay him to hear his beautiful singing voice.
7. Can you get paid for reading?
8. There are some reading services for the visually impaired.
9. If you're good at swimming, you could be a lifeguard at the beach.
10. My cousin teaches swimming classes.

Connect to the Writing Process: Drafting

Using Gerunds and Participles in Sentences

Write two sentences for each word. In the first sentence, use the word as a gerund. In the second, use the word as a participle.

11. falling
12. singing
13. laughing
14. talking
15. screaming
16. running

Gerund Phrases

A **gerund phrase** is a gerund with its modifiers and complements—all working together as a noun.

Like a participle, a gerund can be combined with modifiers or a complement to form a **gerund phrase.** At the top of the following page are four variations of a gerund phrase.

Gerund with an Adjective	**His heavy breathing** was due to an intense workout.
Gerund with an Adverb	**Exercising daily** is important for everyone.
Gerund with a Prepositional Phrase	**Jogging in the park** is a pleasant form of exercise.
Gerund with a Complement	**Walking a mile** every day will help keep you healthy.

Be sure to use the possessive form of a noun or pronoun before a gerund. A possessive form before a gerund is considered part of the gerund phrase.

We were not surprised by **Keisha's** winning the marathon.
The family has always encouraged **her** running.

Practice Your Skills

Check Your Understanding

Finding Gerund Phrases

Contemporary Life **Write the gerund phrase in each sentence. Then underline the gerund.**

1. At the mall many people choose riding the escalator.
2. You can stay fit by walking up the stairs.
3. Exercising regularly is not just good for your body.
4. Doing a little workout each day helps fight depression.
5. Most athletes do not go for a day without working their bodies.
6. Lifting weights is a good way to build muscles.
7. Another way is rowing a boat.
8. Many people work out by aerobic dancing.
9. Playing basketball daily helps many people stay fit.
10. Making a daily workout goal will focus your mind on fitness.

Check Your Understanding
Understanding the Uses of Gerund Phrases

General Interest **Write the gerund phrase in each sentence. Then label the use of each one, using the following abbreviations.**

subject = *subj.*	direct object = *d.o.*
indirect object = *i.o.*	object of a preposition = *o.p.*
appositive = *appos.*	predicate nominitive = *p.n.*

11. Every four years the world enjoys watching the Summer Olympics.

12. Breaking records is the goal of many Olympic athletes.

13. One event, long-distance running, captures a great deal of attention.

14. Another exciting event is the jumping of the hurdles.

15. Successful hurdlers win by barely skimming the barrier.

16. Running fast between hurdles also helps a competitor win the race.

17. Throwing the discus takes a very strong arm.

18. An especially difficult event is competing in the two-day decathlon.

19. Data tables are used in this event for comparing the athletes' performances.

20. Competing in the Olympics is the dream of many athletes.

Connect to the Writing Process: Drafting
Using Gerunds in Sentences

Write a sentence for each of the following gerund phrases.

21. driving a car

22. swimming ten laps

23. reading a book

24. writing a story

25. completing my homework

Communicate Your Ideas

APPLY TO WRITING

Informative Article: *Gerunds*

The editor of your school newspaper has asked you to write an informative article about fitness. Interview three classmates, asking them what they do to stay in shape. Write a brief description of each person's method of achieving fitness and why it is important. Underline the gerunds or gerund phrases in your article.

Infinitives

An infinitive is a verb form that usually begins with *to.* It is used as a noun, an adjective, or an adverb.

A third kind of verbal is called the infinitive. It looks different from a participle or a gerund because it usually begins with the word *to.* An infinitive is used in almost all the ways in which a noun is used. It can also be used as an adjective or an adverb.

NOUN	**To succeed** was his only goal in life.
	(subject)
	He wanted **to win** more than anything else.
	(direct object)
ADJECTIVE	That is a difficult goal **to accomplish.**
	(*To accomplish* modifies the noun *goal.*)
	His desire **to win** was very strong.
	(*To win* modifies the noun *desire.*)

ADVERB He was eager **to triumph.**

(*To triumph* modifies the adjective *eager.*)

He worked hard **to succeed.**

(*To succeed* modifies the verb *worked.*)

PRACTICE YOUR SKILLS

Check Your Understanding

Finding Infinitives

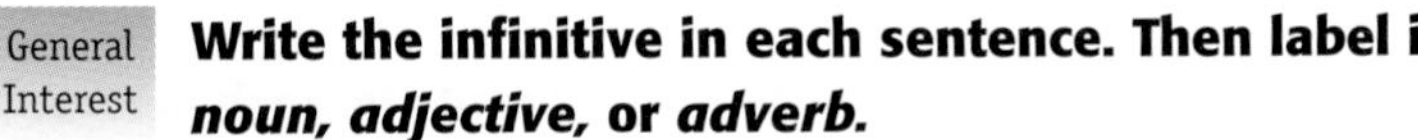

General Interest **Write the infinitive in each sentence. Then label it *noun, adjective,* or *adverb.***

1. In the 1960s and 1970s, Muhammad Ali was the boxer to see.

2. His life is interesting to research.

3. He had one goal, to win.

4. As a young child, he learned to box.

5. For his opponents his punches were too fast to avoid.

6. For several years he was not allowed to compete.

7. When he was drafted by the army, he refused to go.

8. He refused on religious grounds to fight.

9. In 1979, Muhammad Ali decided to retire.

10. Later he came out of retirement to fight again.

Infinitive or Prepositional Phrase?

Because an infinitive usually begins with the word *to,* it is sometimes confused with a prepositional phrase. Just remember that an infinitive is *to* plus a verb form. A prepositional phrase is *to* plus a noun or a pronoun.

INFINITIVE	I am learning **to drive.** (ends with the verb form *drive*)
PREPOSITIONAL PHRASE	My mom drove me **to school.** (ends with the noun *school*)

PRACTICE YOUR SKILLS

Check Your Understanding

Distinguishing Between Infinitives and Prepositional Phrases

Contemporary Life

Write the underlined words in each sentence. Then label them *I* for infinitive or *PP* for prepositional phrase.

1. We need some time to rest.
2. What do you want to do?
3. Now I would like to go.
4. Should I take my bag with me to gym?
5. That bag is too heavy to carry.
6. Give your bag to Dylan.
7. Take my bag to class with you.
8. Let's go to band.
9. I think the drums are the most fun to play.
10. Let's walk to lunch together.

Connect to the Writing Process: Drafting

Using Infinitives in Sentences

Use the following infinitives in complete sentences. Use at least one as a noun, one as an adjective, and one as an adverb.

11. to glow
12. to spin

13. to shriek
14. to see
15. to ride

Infinitive Phrases

An **infinitive phrase** is an infinitive with its modifiers and complements—all working together as a noun, an adjective, or an adverb.

The following examples show three variations of an infinitive phrase.

Infinitive with an Adverb	My friends have learned **to read quickly.**
Infinitive with a Prepositional Phrase	Alexandra and I plan **to go to the library.**
Infinitive with a Complement	Haley went to the library **to get a book.**

Sometimes *to* is omitted when an infinitive follows such verbs as *dare, feel, hear, help, let, need, see,* and *watch*.

Will you and Jesse help me **find** the library's reference section?
(to find)

No one dared **talk** in the quiet reading room.
(to talk)

Molly helped her little sister **read** an illustrated children's book.
(to read)

Will the librarian let you **check out** five books?
(to check out)

CONNECT TO SPEAKING AND WRITING

A **split infinitive** occurs when modifiers are placed between *to* and the verb. Until recently, a split infinitive was considered grammatically incorrect. Although split infinitives are usually acceptable nowadays, you should still avoid them in formal speaking and writing situations.

SPLIT INFINITIVE	The librarian asked us **to quickly move** at the sound of the bell.
BETTER	The librarian asked us **to move quickly** at the sound of the bell.

PRACTICE YOUR SKILLS

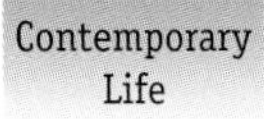

Check Your Understanding

Finding Infinitive Phrases

Contemporary Life

Write the infinitive phrase in each sentence. Then underline the infinitive. Remember that sometimes the word *to* is omitted.

1. I like to spend time at the public library.

2. Sometimes I go to choose a book.

3. To research a topic, I use the reference section.

4. Those reference books help me understand several complex topics.

5. Many go to the library to find rare magazines and academic journals.

6. On Thursday mornings my mom takes my little sister to hear a storyteller.

7. The friendly staff will help us locate specific books.

8. To determine a book's call number, use the computer system or card catalog.

9. Libraries offer books on tape to serve the visually impaired.

10. A quiet library is a great place to study for a test.

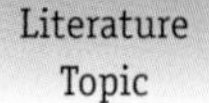

Check Your Understanding

Recognizing Infinitive Phrases as Modifiers

Literature Topic

Write the infinitive phrase in each sentence. Then label it *noun, adjective,* or *adverb.*

11. In English classes many students are asked to read the novels of John Steinbeck.

12. After high school Steinbeck left Salinas to attend Stanford University.

13. He did not stay to earn his degree.

14. To support himself, Steinbeck worked as a laborer.

15. He began to publish novels in 1929.

16. In 1935 with *Tortilla Flat,* he managed to gain critical acclaim.

17. Critics consider his greatest work to be *The Grapes of Wrath*.

18. Steinbeck traveled to North Africa to serve as a war correspondent.

19. Throughout his life he continued to write novels and short stories.

20. In 1962, Steinbeck was honored to win the Nobel Prize for literature.

Connect to the Writing Process: Revising

Correcting Split Infinitives

Rewrite each sentence to avoid using split infinitives.

21. While he was a laborer, Steinbeck continued to diligently write.

22. He managed to daily meet interesting people.

23. Some of his novels, like *Tortilla Flat,* attempt to humorously portray the workers' struggle.

24. Others, like *The Grapes of Wrath,* show characters trying to bravely overcome their circumstances.

25. Modern critics continue to greatly praise his body of work.

Communicate Your Ideas

APPLY TO WRITING

Writer's Craft: ***Analyzing the Use of Infinitives***

Writers often use infinitives in their works. In this passage from *Cannery Row,* John Steinbeck uses infinitives to explain Doc's motivation for walking. Read the passage and then answer the questions that follow.

> Because he loved true things he tried to explain. He said he was nervous and besides he wanted to see the country, smell the ground and look at grass and birds and trees, to savor the country, and there was no other way to do it save on foot. And people didn't like him for telling the truth.
>
> —*John Steinbeck,* Cannery Row

- List the infinitives in the passage.
- In the lengthy second sentence, Steinbeck uses *and* to string together a compound infinitive phrase. How many infinitives does he use? How does this construction affect the reader?
- Why do you think Steinbeck places commas around the infinitive phrase *to savor the country?* What effect is he trying to achieve?

Misplaced and Dangling Modifiers

Participial phrases and infinitive phrases can be used as modifiers. Therefore, they should be placed as close as possible to the word they modify. When they are placed too far from the word they modify, they become **misplaced modifiers.**

MISPLACED	We saw an elk hiking along with our cameras.
CORRECT	**Hiking along with our cameras,** we saw an elk. (The participial phrase modifies *we*.)

Notice that to correct a misplaced modifier, you simply move the verbal phrase closer to the word it modifies.

At other times verbal phrases that should be functioning as modifiers have nothing to describe. These phrases are called **dangling modifiers.**

DANGLING	To go on the camping trip, a permission slip must be signed.
CORRECT	**To go on the camping trip,** you must bring a signed permission slip. (The infinitive phrase modifies *you*.)

Notice that to correct a dangling modifier, you must add words or change the sentence around so that the verbal phrase has a noun or pronoun to modify.

Check Your Understanding

Recognizing Misplaced and Dangling Modifiers

Contemporary Life

Label the underlined verbal phrases in the following sentences *MM* for misplaced modifier or *DM* for dangling modifier. If there is no mistake in the placement of the verbal, write *C* for correct.

1. To avoid last-minute problems, our teacher made plans for the field trip well in advance.

2. We saw a deer riding along on the bus.

3. Studying the plants and wildlife around us, we collected data for a report.
4. We admired the autumn leaves gliding along in our canoe.
5. Weighed down by our packs, the trail seemed endless.
6. Jack noticed two woodpeckers hiking through the woods.
7. Lost on the trail, my compass was a big help.
8. We ate our lunches sitting on the ground.
9. Having hiked for hours, weariness overcame us.
10. Returning from the field trip, we all fell asleep.

Connect to the Writing Process: Revising
Correcting Misplaced and Dangling Participles

11.–17. Rewrite the incorrect sentences above so that the modifiers are used correctly.

Mixed Practice

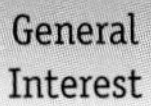

Write each verbal or verbal phrase from the following sentences. Then label it *P* for participle, *G* for gerund, or *I* for infinitive.

1. Weighing over three hundred pounds, Louis Cyr may have been the strongest man in recorded history.
2. Lifting a full barrel of cement with one arm was an easy task for him.
3. One story, known to everyone in Quebec, tells about his pushing a heavy freight car up an incline.
4. To entertain townspeople, Cyr also would lift 588 pounds off the floor by using only one finger!
5. Pitting himself against four horses in 1891 was, however, his greatest feat.

6. Standing before a huge crowd, Cyr was fitted with a special harness.
7. The horses, lined up two on each side, were attached to the harness.
8. Planting his feet wide apart, Cyr stood with his arms on his chest.
9. The signal was given, and the horses began to pull.
10. Moving either arm from his chest would disqualify him.
11. The horses strained hard to dislodge him.
12. The grooms urged the slipping horses to pull harder.
13. Not budging an inch, Louis held on.
14. After minutes of tugging, the winner of the contest was announced.
15. Louis Cyr bowed before the cheering crowd.
16. Another amazing perfomer was Harry Houdini.
17. Known not for his strength but for his escapes, Houdini held the attention of large crowds.
18. His most daring feat was escaping from an airtight tank.
19. The airtight tank, filled with water, could easily have caused the death of Houdini.
20. However, Houdini quickly freed himself from the doom of suffocating or drowning.

Diagraming Phrases

In a diagram a prepositional phrase is connected to the word it modifies. The preposition is placed on a connecting slanted line. The object of a preposition is placed on a horizontal line that is attached to the slanted line.

Adjective Phrase An adjective phrase is connected to the noun or pronoun it modifies. Notice that sometimes a phrase modifies the object of a preposition of another phrase.

The squirrel with the fluffy tail gathered acorns from the ground under the oak tree.

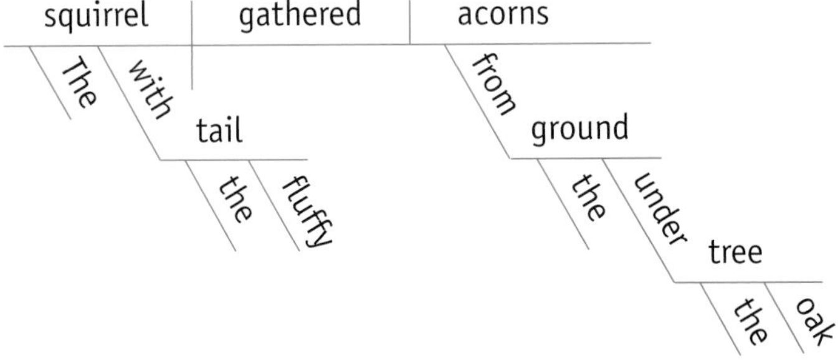

Adverb Phrase An adverb phrase is connected to the verb, adjective, or adverb it modifies.

We drove to the park on Sunday.

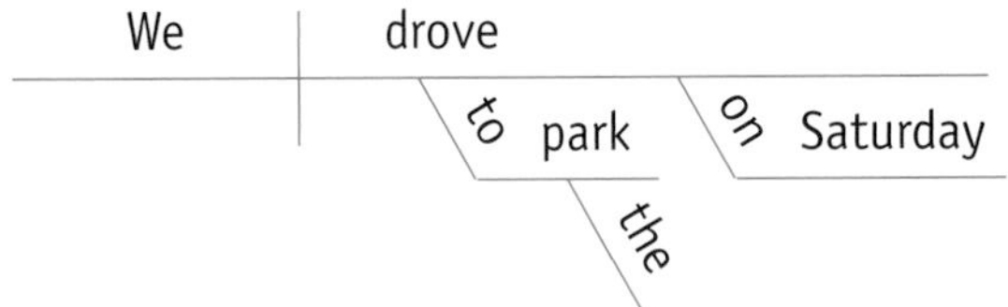

Notice in the next example that an adverb phrase that modifies an adjective or an adverb needs an additional line.

The score was tied early in the inning.

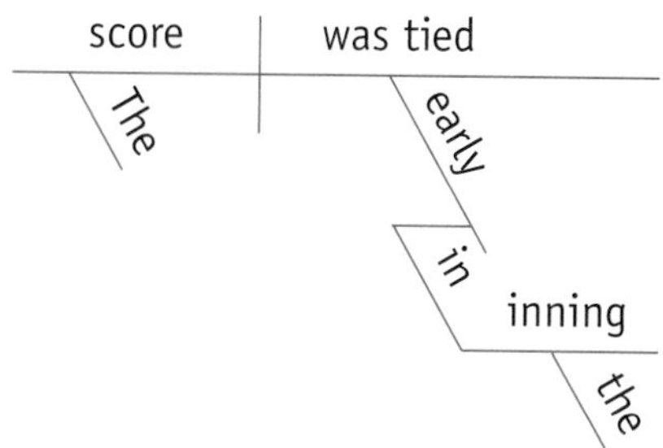

Appositive and Appositive Phrase An appositive is diagramed in parentheses next to the word it identifies or explains.

I bought a new calendar, one with pictures of horses.

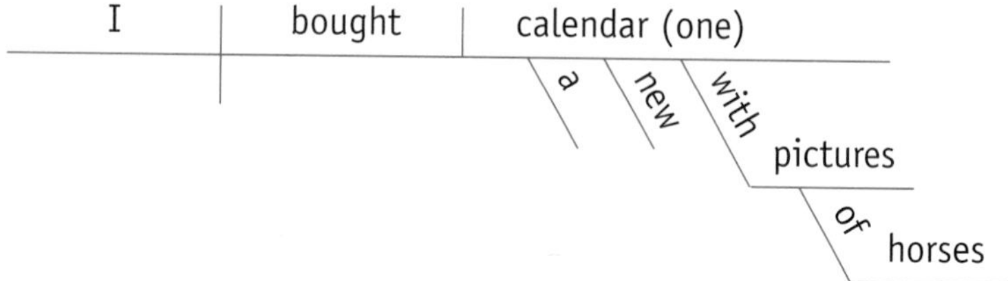

Practice Your Skills

Diagraming Phrases

Diagram the following sentences or copy them. If you copy them, draw one line under each subject and two lines under each verb. Then put parentheses around each phrase and label each one *adj.* for adjective, *adv.* for adverb, or *appos.* for appositive.

1. Many children can swim at an early age.
2. I just bought a new radio, a small portable one.
3. The posters for the dance are beautiful.
4. I went to Mexico with my sisters.
5. My friend Bert collects stamps from foreign countries.
6. The tips of the daffodils showed through the snow.
7. Meg left the store with the groceries.
8. Wendy, my best friend, went to the horse show.
9. At the signal every swimmer dived into the water.
10. The summit of Mount McKinley is always covered with snow.

Diagraming Verbal Phrases

How a verbal phrase is used in a sentence will determine how it is diagramed.

Participial Phrases Because a participial phrase is always used as an adjective, it is diagramed under the word it modifies. The participle, however, is written in a curve.

Hiking through the mountains, we used the trails marked by the rangers.

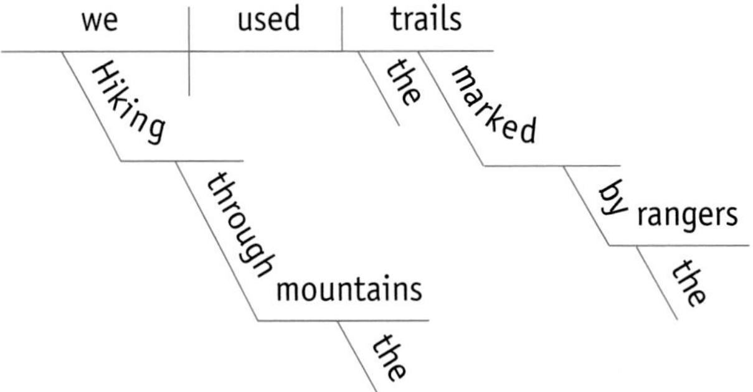

Gerund Phrases Because a gerund phrase is used as a noun, it can be diagramed in any noun position. In the following example, a gerund phrase is used as a direct object. Notice that the complement *plants* and a prepositional phrase are part of the gerund phrase.

José enjoys growing plants in his room.

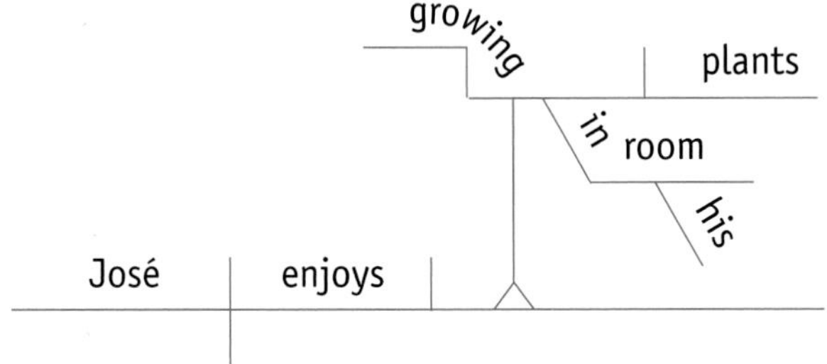

Infinitive Phrases Because an infinitive phrase may be used as an adjective, an adverb, or a noun, it is diagramed in several ways. The following example shows how an infinitive phrase used as an adjective is diagramed.

This is the best place to stop for lunch.

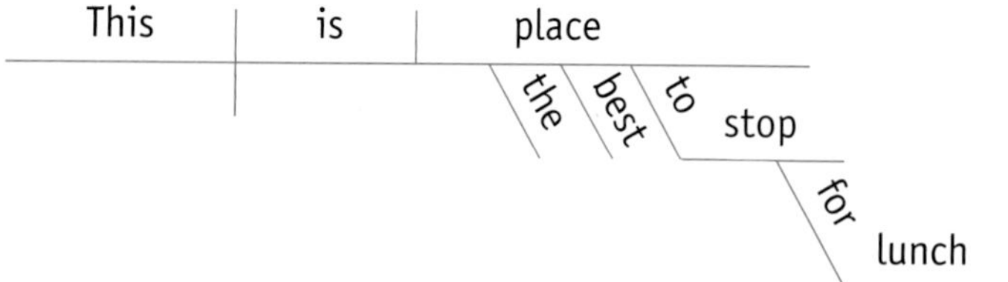

An infinitive phrase used as a noun can be diagramed in any noun position. In the following example, an infinitive phrase is used as the subject of the sentence.

To arrive on time is important.

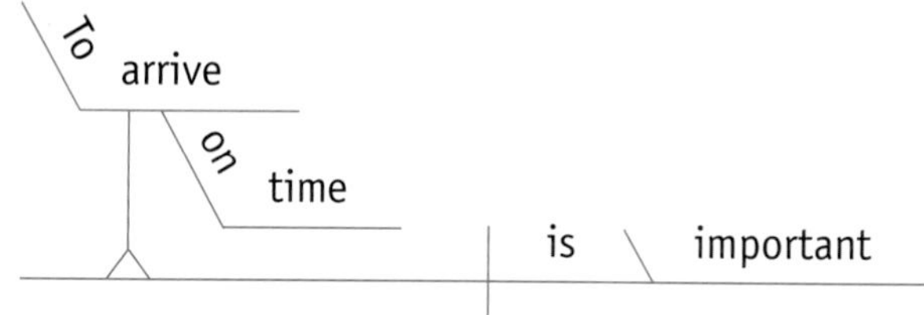

Practice Your Skills

Diagraming Verbal Phrases

Diagram the following sentences or copy them. If you copy them, draw one line under each subject and two lines under each verb. Then put parentheses around each verbal phrase and label each one *part.* for participial, *ger.* for gerund, or *inf.* for infinitive.

1. Sitting on the doorstep, the dog waited for its owner.

2. Spilled by accident, the milk dripped from the counter.

3. No one noticed Sally tiptoeing down the stairs.

4. I enjoy speaking before an audience.

5. The team practiced kicking the football between the goalposts.

6. Eating food in the halls is not permitted.

7. This is the best shovel to use for that job.

8. To rush into a decision is a mistake.

9. The uniform to wear to the banquet is the blue one.

10. We want to watch this movie.

CheckPoint

Identifying Prepositional and Appositive Phrases

Write each prepositional phrase and each appositive phrase. Then label each one *adj.* for adjective, *adv.* for adverb, or *appos.* for appositive.

1. The "Zip" in *Zip Code* stands for *zone improvement plan.*
2. The Abyssinian, a beautiful short-haired feline, developed entirely from the African wildcat.
3. The largest of the python family of snakes grows to a length of twenty-five feet.
4. The center of the earth, a ball of solid iron and nickel, has a temperature of 9,000°F.
5. Lungfish of Africa sleep out of water for an entire summer.
6. A famous art museum in New York City has a collection of 200,000 baseball cards.
7. A completely blind chameleon will still change to the color of its environment.
8. A year is eighty-eight days on Mercury, the planet closest to the sun.
9. A grasshopper's sense of hearing is centered in its front knees.
10. James Naismith, the inventor of basketball, was a YMCA instructor in Massachusetts.

Identifying Verbal Phrases

Write each verbal phrase. Then label each one *participial, gerund,* or *infinitive.*

1. Steam is water expanded sixteen hundred times.
2. The first apples to reach America arrived from England in 1629.

3. A house cat can be expected to live from eight to twenty years.
4. Ancient Egyptian boats were constructed by binding together bundles of papyrus stems.
5. One out of every four human beings living in the world today is Chinese.
6. Pumping blood steadily through our bodies, our hearts never take a rest.
7. Eating honey from a beehive has provided nourishment for lost hikers.
8. It takes approximately ten seconds to slice six cucumbers in a food processor.
9. Long ago doctors used leeches for sucking blood from patients.
10. Polo is the oldest game played with a stick and ball.

Using Phrases

Write five sentences that follow the directions below. (The sentences may come in any order.) Write about one of the following topics or a topic of your own choice: a singer at a concert, a score at a hockey game, or the final lap of a car race.

Write a sentence that . . .

1. includes at least two prepositional phrases.
2. includes an appositive phrase.
3. includes an introductory participial phrase.
4. includes a gerund phrase.
5. includes an infinitive phrase.

Underline and label each phrase. Then check for correct punctuation in each sentence.

Language and *Self-Expression*

Fernando Botero began painting at the age of fourteen. Even then, he used large figures in his work. These figures became rounder and fuller, and Botero called their appearance *plasticity.* In what ways do the figures appear plastic in *Dancing in Colombia?*

Imagine you are a news reporter whose assignment is to write a news story about the social event shown in the painting. Write the article in a few paragraphs. To create sentence variety, include as many different kinds of phrases as you can.

Prewriting You may wish to create an outline using a news reporter's five questions: *Who? When? What? Where?* and *Why?* Jot down answers to your questions.

Drafting Use the outline you have created to write your news story. Include descriptions of the people and their actions in the story. Make your word pictures as vivid as the artist's images.

Revising Reread your news story. Be sure you have answered all the reporter's questions. Correct any misplaced or dangling modifiers and split infinitives.

Editing Check your story for errors in spelling and punctuation. Add commas after long adverb phrases or several phrases in a row. Also add a comma after participial phrases that begin sentences. Set off nonessential appositive phrases with commas.

Publishing Make a final copy of your article. Read it into a tape recorder as if you were a television news reporter. Then play the tape for the class.

Another Look

A **phrase** is a group of related words that function as a single part of speech. A phrase does not have a subject and a verb.

Classification of Phrases

A **prepositional phrase** begins with a preposition and ends with a noun or pronoun called the object of the preposition. *(page L173)*

An **adjective phrase** is a prepositional phrase that is used to modify a noun or a pronoun. *(page L174)*

An **adverb phrase** is a prepositional phrase that is used to modify a verb, an adjective, or an adverb. *(pages L176–L177)*

An **appositive** is a noun or a pronoun that identifies or explains another noun or pronoun in the sentence. An appositive used with modifiers forms an **appositive phrase.**

Verbals and Verb Phrases

A **participle** is a verb form that is used as an adjective. *(pages L186–L187)*

A **participial phrase** is a participle with its modifiers and complements—all working together as an adjective. *(pages L189–L190)*

A **gerund** is a verb form that is used as a noun. *(page L193)*

A **gerund phrase** is a gerund with its modifiers and complements—all working together as a noun. *(pages L195–L196)*

An **infinitive** is a verb form that usually begins with *to.* It is used as a noun, an adjective, or an adverb. *(pages L198–L199)*

An **infinitive phrase** is an infinitive with its modifiers and complements—all working together as a noun, an adjective, or an adverb. *(page L201)*

Other Information About Phrases

Punctuating adverb phrases *(page L178)*

Punctuating appositives and appositive phrases *(pages L525–L526)*

Punctuating participial phrases *(page L513)*

Avoiding misplaced and dangling modifiers *(pages L204–L205)*

Directions

Write the letter of the term that correctly identifies the underlined phrase in each sentence.

EXAMPLE **1.** Some dogs are trained specifically to help disabled people.

1 **A** gerund
B participial
C infinitive
D adjective

ANSWER **1 C**

1. Service dogs are trained to aid people with problems of mobility, strength, or coordination.
2. They help people in many ways in their homes.
3. Dogs help people to get to the bathroom.
4. Using a dog for support, a disabled person can keep his or her balance.
5. Dogs help deaf people recognize important sounds.
6. They alert their owners to the ringing of a phone.
7. Noticing a dog with a person in a wheelchair, people are more likely to be friendly.
8. A well-trained assistant, a service dog, can allow a disabled person to interact with others more fully.
9. Service dogs usually work for eight years before they are replaced.
10. Overlapping with a new dog, the old service dog can help the young one.

1 **A** prepositional
B gerund
C appositive
D infinitive

2 **A** infinitive
B prepositional
C participial
D gerund

3 **A** participial
B infinitive
C gerund
D prepositional

4 **A** gerund
B participial
C prepositional
D infinitive

5 **A** prepositional
B participial
C infinitive
D gerund

6 **A** adjective
B adverb
C participial
D gerund

7 **A** prepositional
B participial
C appositive
D gerund

8 **A** adjective
B adverb
C appositive
D prepositional

9 **A** gerund
B infinitive
C prepositional
D participial

10 **A** participial
B prepositional
C appositive
D gerund

CHAPTER 8

Clauses

Directions

Write the letter of the term that correctly identifies each sentence or underlined part of a sentence.

Example **1** Because I have neat handwriting, Maisie asked me to design the card.

1 **A** simple sentence
B compound sentence
C complex sentence
D compound-complex sentence

Answer **1 C**

1. I used my calligraphy pen and blue ink.

2. Before I made a final version, I practiced on a separate sheet of paper.

3. The card was for a teacher who was leaving in June.

4. She had been there twenty years, and everyone would miss her.

5. Because she was so well-liked, we expected a big turnout, and we were not disappointed.

6. Mrs. Strout was the person <u>who taught me calligraphy</u>.

7. <u>When I first met her</u>, I was just starting middle school.

8. Her art class was harder <u>than I had expected</u>.

9. <u>That I'd had art in the past</u> did not prepare me for Mrs. Strout's class.

10. Her talents, <u>which were many</u>, inspired me.

1 **A** simple sentence
B compound sentence
C complex sentence
D compound-complex sentence

2 **A** simple sentence
B compound sentence
C complex sentence
D compound-complex sentence

3 **A** simple sentence
B compound sentence
C complex sentence
D compound-complex sentence

4 **A** simple sentence
B compound sentence
C complex sentence
D compound-complex sentence

5 **A** simple sentence
B compound sentence
C complex sentence
D compound-complex sentence

6 **A** independent clause
B adverb clause
C adjective clause
D noun clause

7 **A** independent clause
B adverb clause
C adjective clause
D noun clause

8 **A** independent clause
B adverb clause
C adjective clause
D noun clause

9 **A** independent clause
B adverb clause
C adjective clause
D noun clause

10 **A** independent clause
B adverb clause
C adjective clause
D noun clause

Jacob Lawrence. "In a free government, the security of civil rights must be the same as that for religious rights. It consists in the one case in the multiplicity of interest, and in the other, in the multiplicity of sects." (the words of James Madison), 1976.
Opaque watercolor and pencil on paper, mounted on fiberboard 30 X 22⅛ inches. National Museum of American Art, Smithsonian Institution, Washington, D.C.

Describe Who is portrayed in this painting? Where do they seem to be?

Analyze What symbols does the artist use in this painting? Based on the title of the painting, why do you think he included these symbols?

Interpret How might the same quotation inspire a writer of fiction? How might it inspire a writer of nonfiction?

Judge Would you rather look at a political painting or read a political story or essay? Why?

At the end of the chapter, you will use this artwork to stimulate ideas for writing.

Independent and Subordinate Clauses

In the preceding chapter, you learned about a group of words called a phrase that can be used as a noun, an adjective, or an adverb. In this chapter you will learn about another group of words called a clause, which can also be used as a noun, an adjective, or an adverb.

A **clause** is a group of words that has a subject and a verb.

From the definition of a clause, you can easily see the difference between a clause and a phrase. A clause has a subject and a verb, but a phrase does not.

PHRASE I wrote a letter **after dinner.**

After dinner is a prepositional phrase that modifies the verb *wrote.*

CLAUSE I wrote a letter **after dinner was finished.**

(*Dinner* is the subject of the clause; *was finished* is the verb.)

There are two kinds of clauses. One kind is called an independent clause or a main clause.

An **independent (main) clause** can stand alone as a sentence because it expresses a complete thought.

An independent clause is called a sentence when it stands by itself. However, it is called a clause when it appears in a sentence with another clause.

In the following example, each subject is underlined once, and each verb is underlined twice.

I will write a few sentences, and you can analyze my handwriting.

The sentence at the bottom of the preceding page has two independent clauses. Each clause could be a sentence by itself.

I will write a few sentences. You can analyze my handwriting.

The second kind of clause is called a subordinate clause or a dependent clause.

A **subordinate (dependent clause)** cannot stand alone as a sentence because it does not express a complete thought.

The subordinate clause in each of the following examples does not express a complete thought—even though it has a subject and a verb.

subordinate clause / independent clause

If you are interested, you can read about handwriting analysis.

independent clause / subordinate clause

My friends read a book that was about graphology.

CONNECT TO WRITER'S CRAFT

When writers want to persuade an audience to adopt a particular viewpoint, they can acknowledge the opposing point of view by presenting it in a subordinate clause rather than in an independent clause.

Although some argue that art and music classes take valuable time and budget resources away from basic academic subjects, new findings indicate that art and music instruction adds to a student's overall intelligence.

By beginning the statement with a subordinate clause, the writer lets the audience know he or she understands the arguments against retaining art and music in the curriculum but believes these subjects benefit learning in all areas. Putting each viewpoint in its own independent clause would, by contrast, give each position equal weight.

Practice Your Skills

Check Your Understanding

Distinguishing Between Kinds of Clauses

General Interest **Write each underlined clause. Then label each one *I* for independent or *S* for subordinate.**

1. Graphology, which is the study of handwriting, has existed for many years.
2. Many people think that handwriting can reveal personality traits.
3. Because some businesses accept this theory, they analyze job applicants' handwriting.
4. When you apply for a job, watch your handwriting.
5. You can always go back to your old ways after you have been hired.
6. If your writing slants to the right, you are probably friendly and open.
7. If your writing slants to the left, you might very well be a nonconformist.
8. Writing uphill indicates an optimist, and writing downhill suggests a reliable person.
9. Capital letters that are inserted in the middle of a word reveal a creative person.
10. An *i* dotted with a circle shows an artistic nature, and a correctly dotted *i* indicates a careful person.
11. When an *i* is dotted high above the letter, the writer is thought to be a serious thinker.
12. None of this should be taken too seriously, however, since graphology is not a technical science.

Uses of Subordinate Clauses

A subordinate clause can be used in several ways. It can function as an adverb, an adjective, or a noun.

Adverb Clauses

An **adverb clause** is a subordinate clause that is used like an adverb to modify a verb, an adjective, or an adverb.

A subordinate clause can be used like a single adverb or like an adverb phrase. When it functions in one of those ways it is called an adverb clause.

SINGLE ADVERB	Our plane left **early.**
ADVERB PHRASE	Our plane left **at dawn.**
ADVERB CLAUSE	Our plane left **as the sun came up over the horizon.**

An adverb clause answers the adverb question *How? When? Where? How much?* or *To what extent?* An adverb clause also answers the question *Under what condition?* or *Why?*

WHEN?	We will travel **until we have seen all of England.**
UNDER WHAT CONDITION?	**If our flight is late,** the tour guide will wait for us.
WHY?	We took an early flight **because it was less expensive.**

The adverb clauses in the preceding examples all modify verbs. Notice that they modify the whole verb phrase. Adverb clauses also modify adjectives and adverbs.

MODIFYING AN ADJECTIVE	I am happy **whenever I am traveling.**
MODIFYING AN ADVERB	The flight lasted longer **than I had expected.**

Subordinating Conjunctions

All adverb clauses begin with a **subordinating conjunction**. Keep in mind that *after, as, before, since,* and *until* can also be prepositions.

COMMON SUBORDINATING CONJUNCTIONS

after	as soon as	in order that	until
although	as though	since	when
as	because	so that	whenever
as far as	before	than	where
as if	even though	though	wherever
as long as	if	unless	while

Unless you hear from me, I will return at six o'clock.

The flight has not changed **as far as I know.**

PUNCTUATION WITH ADVERB CLAUSES

Always place a comma after an adverb clause that comes at the beginning of a sentence.

Before we visited Ireland, we saw the sights of London.

Sometimes an adverb clause will interrupt an independent clause. If it does, place a comma before and after the adverb clause.

Our schedule, **as far as I can tell,** seems reasonable.

When an adverb clause follows an independent clause, no comma is needed.

We will drive **so that we can see the countryside.**

Practice Your Skills

Check Your Understanding
Finding Subordinating Conjunctions

Contemporary Life

Write the adverb clause in each sentence. Then underline the subordinating conjunction.

1. Because we flew into London, we toured England first.
2. My mother toured a castle while my sister and I watched the changing of the guard.
3. I will remember that trip as long as I live.
4. Although we were interested, we did not see Shakespeare's birthplace.
5. Unless we hurry, we will miss our flight.
6. Tourism in Europe increases when summer comes.
7. We rented a car after we left London.
8. As Mother drove, my sister studied the road map.
9. If we had arranged for a longer vacation, we would have traveled to Scotland as well.
10. We visited Wales even though we were in a hurry.

Check Your Understanding
Recognizing Adverb Clauses as Modifiers

Social Studies

Write the adverb clause in each sentence. Then beside it, write the verb, adjective, or adverb that it modifies.

11. After Theodore Roosevelt visited Yellowstone, he established the country's first national park.

12. In order that the United States would have public lands, the government has created many more national parks.
13. These lands are protected so that all Americans can see the beauty of nature.
14. Campers are happy whenever they sleep under the stars of California's Yosemite National Park.
15. The drive through Glacier National Park takes longer than most tourists realize.
16. The Grand Canyon in Arizona stretches farther than the eye can see.
17. Because it is unusually beautiful, many tourists visit Arches National Park in Utah.
18. When people visit Big Bend National Park in Texas, they are surprised by the Chisos Mountains.
19. If you like mountains, you will love Rocky Mountain National Park in Estes Park, Colorado.
20. Because they belong to all of us, Americans should visit these magnificent places.

Connect to the Writing Process: Editing

Punctuating Adverb Clauses

Rewrite the following sentences adding commas if needed. If no punctuation is necessary, write *C* for correct.

21. All national parks as far as I know charge an entrance fee.
22. You should still go since the fee is more reasonable than other vacation costs.
23. Because most national parks have a museum you can learn a great deal about the area.
24. Whenever you are ready to camp you should look for a park ranger.
25. They will tell you where you can set up a tent for the night.

Connect to the Writing Process: Drafting

Writing Sentences Using Adverb Clauses

Write sentences about taking a trip that follow the directions below. Then underline each adverb clause. Include commas where needed in your sentences.

26. Include an adverb clause that begins with *than.*

27. Include an adverb clause that begins with *even though.*

28. At the beginning of the sentence, include an adverb clause that begins with *because.*

29. Include an adverb clause that begins with *unless* and interrupts an independent clause.

30. At the beginning of the sentence, include an adverb clause that begins with *whenever.*

Communicate Your Ideas

APPLY TO WRITING

Persuasive Letter: *Adverb Clauses*

Your local newspaper is having a contest. The newspaper will send the winner of the contest on a trip anywhere in the world. To enter, contestants must write a letter of one hundred words or less stating what place in the world they would like to visit and what they would like to do there. The newspaper will give the grand prize to the person who writes the most persuasive letter.

- Write a letter for the contest. Remember that your letter must be no more than one hundred words and it must be very persuasive.

- Underline at least three adverb clauses that you use in your letter. Check that you have used commas correctly with all of your adverb clauses.

Adjective Clauses

An **adjective clause** is a subordinate clause that is used like an adjective to modify a noun or a pronoun.

A subordinate clause can be used like a single adjective or an adjective phrase. It is then called an adjective clause.

SINGLE ADJECTIVE	My great-uncle witnessed a **famous** disaster.
ADJECTIVE PHRASE	My great-uncle witnessed a disaster **of air travel.**
ADJECTIVE CLAUSE	My great-uncle witnessed a disaster **that is still remembered today.**

An adjective clause answers the adjective question *Which one?* or *What kind?*

WHICH ONE?	He saw one man **who jumped to the ground.**
WHAT KIND?	The airship, **which was a zeppelin,** came down in flames.

Relative Pronouns

Most adjective clauses begin with a relative pronoun. A **relative pronoun** relates an adjective clause to its antecedent—the noun or pronoun it modifies.

RELATIVE PRONOUNS				
who	whom	whose	which	that

The crash, **which occurred in 1937,** destroyed the *Hindenburg.*

The zeppelin carried a fuel **that was highly flammable.**

Sometimes a word such as *where* or *when* can also introduce an adjective clause.

Frankfurt, Germany, is the place **where the *Hindenburg's* flight originated.**

This was an era **when commercial air travel was just beginning.**

Practice Your Skills

Check Your Understanding
Finding Relative Pronouns

History Topic **Write the adjective clause in each sentence. Then underline the relative pronoun.**

1. The *Hindenburg,* which was a magnificent zeppelin, left Frankfurt, Germany, for a two-day flight to the United States.
2. The passengers who made the journey enjoyed great comfort on the airship.
3. The world was interested in the flight of the *Hindenburg,* which was the largest human-made object ever to fly.
4. The passengers had a glorious view from the windows that lined the zeppelin.
5. In the United States, the people who gathered at the naval airstation awaited the *Hindenburg*'s arrival.
6. The *Hindenburg* was over Lakehurst, New Jersey, which was its destination, when a spark ignited the airship.

7. Some spectators who had family members on board began to scream in horror.
8. The zeppelin was filled with hydrogen, which is a very combustible gas.
9. Another cause for the blaze may have been the flammable material that covered the outside of the airship.
10. About one third of the people who were on board the *Hindenburg* died in the disastrous accident.

Check Your Understanding

Recognizing Adjective Phrases as Modifiers

History Topic **Write the adjective clause in each sentence. Then, beside it, write the noun or pronoun it modifies.**

11. In 1912, the *Titanic* was crossing the North Atlantic, where icebergs were a constant threat.
12. The passengers, who felt secure on this great ship, were enjoying themselves.
13. Several iceberg warnings, which should have been heeded, were ignored by the crew.
14. An iceberg, whose size was tremendous, suddenly appeared in front of the ship.
15. A slight impact, which scarcely disturbed the passengers, had actually struck the ship a fatal blow.
16. At first the passengers, who were unaware of their danger, chatted casually about the accident.
17. The lifeboats that were on board could carry only a fraction of the passengers.
18. Lifeboats that were launched in haste were not filled completely.
19. The panic that overcame the passengers at the end might have been avoided.
20. The disaster, which resulted in the loss of 1,513 lives, will never be forgotten.

Functions of a Relative Pronoun

In addition to introducing an adjective clause, a relative pronoun has another function. It can serve as a subject, a direct object, or an object of a preposition within the adjective clause. It can also show possession.

SUBJECT	The Great Depression, **which began in 1929,** was a bleak time in American history. (*Which* is the subject of *began.*)
DIRECT OBJECT	The economic confidence **that most Americans enjoyed** was shattered. (*That* is the direct object of *enjoyed.*)
OBJECT OF A PREPOSITION	The time period **about which I am writing** lasted for eleven years. (*Which* is the object of the preposition *about.*)
POSSESSION	Few were the Americans **whose lives were unaffected.** (*Whose* shows possession of *lives.*)

Sometimes the relative pronoun *that* is omitted from an adjective clause. Nevertheless, it still has its function within the clause.

The *Grapes of Wrath* is a novel **John Steinbeck wrote about the Depression.**

(*That John Steinbeck wrote about the Depression* is the adjective clause. *That* [understood] is the direct object within the adjective clause.)

PUNCTUATION WITH ADJECTIVE CLAUSES

If an adjective clause contains information that is essential to identifying a person, place, or thing in the sentence, do not set it off with commas from the rest of the sentence.

If a clause is nonessential, do set it off with commas. A clause is nonessential if it can be removed without changing the basic meaning of the sentence.

Essential	Dorothea Lange's photograph **that shows a tired-looking mother with her children** is on display. (No commas are used because the clause is essential to identify which photograph is on display.)
Nonessential	The photograph, **which was taken in 1936,** is striking. (Commas are needed because the clause could be removed from the sentence without changing its meaning.)

It is customary to use the relative pronoun *that* in an essential clause and *which* in a nonessential clause.

The photograph, **which** was taken in 1936, shows an image **that** is striking.

 PRACTICE YOUR SKILLS

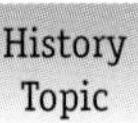

Check Your Understanding

Determining the Function of a Relative Pronoun

History Topic

Write each adjective clause and underline the relative pronoun. Label its use in the adjective clause as *subject, direct object, object of the preposition,* or *possessive.* If *that* is omitted from the clause, write *that* in parentheses.

1. "Black Tuesday" refers to the stock market crash that occurred on Tuesday, October 24, 1929.

2. The Great Depression devastated America's farmers, who were contending with a terrible drought.

3. Many farmers left their homes in states like Oklahoma and Kansas, which were especially hard hit.
4. These states were located in the Great Plains region, which became known as the "Dust Bowl."
5. Farmers headed west to California, which offered many job opportunities.
6. In large cities soup kitchens that fed hungry people had long lines at every meal.
7. Woody Guthrie was an American folksinger who sang about the Depression.
8. One song he wrote is still familiar to almost every American.
9. "This Land Is Your Land" is a song whose words still resonate with Americans.
10. Herbert Hoover, on whom the blame for the economic disaster was placed, was not reelected in 1932.
11. Franklin Roosevelt, whose 1932 election brought him to the presidency, enacted programs to put Americans back to work.
12. Most Americans, for whom finding work was impossible, welcomed Roosevelt's programs.

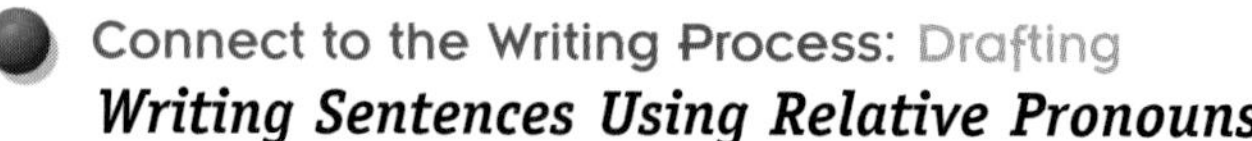

Writing Sentences Using Relative Pronouns

Write a sentence using each adjective clause. Use commas where needed.

13. who is a hero
14. whom we know
15. whose style is charismatic
16. which is important to me
17. that I found most enjoyable
18. to whom we owe a debt
19. for which we need an example
20. whose character is above reproach

APPLY TO WRITING

Friendly Letter: *Adjective Clauses*

Dorothea Lange. *Migrant Mother, Nipomo, California,* 1936. Black-and-white photograph. The Oakland Museum of California.

Look closely at this photograph. The year is 1936, and you are the woman in this photograph. Two days ago, you and your family left your home in Kansas. You are bound for California, where you have heard that jobs are available. Write a letter to your mother, describing your feelings. What are your hopes and desires? What are your concerns? Are you optimistic or pessimistic about your prospects? As you write, remember to include adjective clauses in your letter.

Misplaced Modifiers

Remember to place an adjective clause as near as possible to the word it modifies. A clause that is too far away from the word it modifies is called a **misplaced modifier.**

Misplaced	Mark plays the guitar **who lives down the street.**
Correct	Mark, **who lives down the street,** plays the guitar.

Practice Your Skills

Check Your Understanding
Identifying Misplaced Modifiers

Contemporary Life

Each sentence below contains an adjective clause. If the clause is correctly placed, write *C* for correct. If the clause is too far away from the noun or pronoun it modifies, write *MM* for misplaced modifier.

1. Some kids started a rock band who live in my neighborhood.
2. Heather's garage is very small where they practice each evening.
3. I can hear them from my house, which is way down the street.
4. Shelby plays the bass guitar who is my age.
5. Heather's father works at a factory that makes amplifiers.
6. The neighbors call Heather's unconcerned parents who hate the noise.
7. The songs were written by Mark that their rock band plays.
8. Mark's guitar screams across the neighborhood which is electric.
9. We will have a big party on my sixteenth birthday, which is in June.
10. The band will play at my party, which will really be fun.

Connect to the Writing Process: Editing

Correcting Misplaced Modifiers

11.–16. Correctly rewrite the sentences on the preceding page that contain misplaced modifiers. Remember to use commas where they are needed.

Noun Clauses

A **noun clause** is a subordinate clause that is used like a noun.

A subordinate clause can also be used like a single noun. It is then called a noun clause.

SINGLE NOUN	I just learned an interesting **fact.**
NOUN CLAUSE	I just learned **that Russia was once ruled by tsars.**

A noun clause can be used in all the ways in which a single noun can be used.

SUBJECT	**Whatever you read** is fine with our English teacher.
DIRECT OBJECT	Does anybody know **when Leo Tolstoy was born?**
INDIRECT OBJECT	Give **whoever comes to class** a copy of the reading list.
OBJECT OF A PREPOSITION	I was intrigued by **what our teacher said.**
PREDICATE NOMINATIVE	The literature of Russia is **what interests me most.**

A list of words that often begin noun clauses appears on the following page.

COMMON INTRODUCTORY WORDS FOR NOUN CLAUSES			
how	whatever	which	whomever
if	when	who	whose
that	where	whoever	why
what	whether	whom	

Keep in mind that the words *who, whom, whose, which,* and *that* may also begin an adjective clause. Therefore, do not rely on the introductory words themselves to identify a clause. Instead, decide how a clause is used in a sentence.

NOUN CLAUSE	**That Leo Tolstoy is a great Russian writer** is common knowledge. (used as a subject)
ADJECTIVE CLAUSE	The short story **that I like best** is "The Death of Ivan Ilych." (used to modify story)

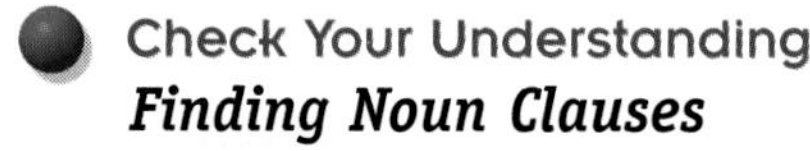

Check Your Understanding

Finding Noun Clauses

Literature Topic **Write the noun clause from each sentence.**

1. That Leo Tolstoy is revered today is a testament to his genius.
2. Many critics believe that *War and Peace* is Tolstoy's greatest novel.
3. The contention of others is that *Anna Karenina* is his greatest work.
4. His works bring great pleasure to whoever reads them.
5. That Tolstoy was a member of the Russian upper class is obvious in his novels.

6. He did, however, write about what the peasants' lives were like.
7. His novels and short stories give whoever reads them a taste of Russian life.
8. Why *Anna Karenina* is known as a psychological novel is easy to explain.
9. The reason for this label is that Tolstoy reveals the thoughts of all the characters in the book.
10. What makes Tolstoy's novels so realistic is their mixture of tragedy and happiness.
11. Most critics agree that Fyodor Dostoyevsky is second only to Tolstoy as Russia's greatest writer.
12. That Dostoyevsky spent four years in a prison in Siberia affected his life profoundly.
13. His early novel *Poor Folks* gives whoever reads it a look at the first Russian social novel.
14. The truth is that Dostoyevsky's great novels are clever murder mysteries on the surface.
15. On a deeper level, they show that humanity is in a constant struggle between good and evil.

Check Your Understanding
Determining the Uses of Noun Clauses

16.–30. Label each noun clause in the preceding sentences as *subject, direct object, indirect object, object of a preposition, or predicate nominative.*

Connect to the Writing Process: Drafting
Writing Sentences with Subordinate Clauses

Finish the subordinate clauses and write complete sentences. Then underline the subordinate clause and label it *adverb, adjective,* or *noun.*

31. What ■ amazed all of the readers.
32. Since ■, we were all late for English.
33. Those are the books that ■.
34. The book review mentioned that ■.

35. The writer who ■ made a speech in our town.

36. Did you know that ■?

37. Because ■, we never finished the book.

38. That some books ■ is certainly true.

39. We were not disappointed even though ■.

40. The character who ■ really made me think.

Communicate Your Ideas

APPLY TO WRITING

The Writer's Craft: ***Analyzing the Use of Subordinate Clauses***

Writers use subordinate clauses to fill their sentences with interesting details. Read the following passage from "Family Happiness" by Leo Tolstoy and follow the directions below.

> It was three days since Sergey Mikhaylych had been to see us; we were expecting him, all the more because our bailiff reported that he had promised to visit the harvest-field. At two o'clock we saw him ride on to the rye-field. With a smile and a glance at me, Katya ordered peaches and cherries, of which he was very fond, to be brought; then she lay down on the bench and began to doze. I tore off a crooked flat lime-tree branch, which made my hand wet with its juicy leaves and juicy bark.
>
> —*Leo Tolstoy,* "Family Happiness"

- Write the subordinate clauses in the passage. Label each one *noun, adjective,* or *adverb.*
- Find the sentence that begins with the words "With a smile." Rewrite the sentence, making the subordinate clause into an independent clause. What happens to the flow of the sentence?

- Why do you think an author might choose to include information in a subordinate clause rather than writing two separate sentences?

Mixed Practice

History Topic

Write each subordinate clause in the following paragraphs and label each one *adverb, adjective,* or *noun.* (There are 14 subordinate clauses.)

The Panama Canal, which connects two oceans, is the greatest constructed waterway in the world. Because it was completed more than eighty-five years ago, few people can remember the tragic problems that occurred during its construction. In 1881, a French firm that was headed by Ferdinand de Lesseps began to dig the canal. Although the work was hard, it was possible. What wasn't possible was finding a way to overcome the mosquitoes that infested the whole area. Within eight years, nearly twenty thousand men had died of malaria as they worked on the canal. The French company that had first built the Suez Canal finally went bankrupt after it had lost $325 million.

After eighteen years, some Americans tried their luck. They first found a plan that wiped out the mosquitoes. Their work then proceeded without the hazard that had doomed the French. The construction, which began at both ends, moved inland through the dense jungle. Finally, after ten billion tons of earth had been removed, the canal was opened in 1914.

Kinds of Sentence Structure

Once you know the difference between independent and subordinate clauses, you can understand the four kinds of sentence structure: simple, compound, complex, and compound-complex.

A simple sentence consists of one independent clause.

The subject and the verb in a simple sentence, however, can be compound. In the following examples, each subject is underlined once and each verb is underlined twice.

> The blueberry pie cooled on the windowsill.
>
> Tyrone and Lili prepared and baked the blueberry pie.

A compound sentence consists of two or more independent clauses.

> independent clause / independent clause
>
> Dad just baked an angel food cake, and I can't wait to taste it.
>
> independent clause / independent clause
>
> Mom and Tyrone set the table; Lili poured the milk and served the food.

CONNECT TO WRITER'S CRAFT

When you write compound sentences, be sure the ideas in each clause are closely related. If two ideas are not related, they should be placed in different sentences. Notice that the clauses in the following sentences are not closely related, so a compound sentence is not a good choice.

> My favorite dish is spaghetti, but the plates are in the cabinet.
>
> My favorite dish is **spaghetti. The** plates are in the cabinet.

PUNCTUATION WITH COMPOUND SENTENCES

You can join independent clauses in a compound sentence with a comma and a conjunction.

The pie had baked for a while, **but** it still was not done.

You can also join independent clauses with a semicolon and no conjunction.

A hot cake is impossible to ice; you must wait for it to cool.

A **complex sentence** consists of one independent clause and one or more subordinate clauses.

subordinate clause | independent clause
Since I learned to cook, I have made dinner each Friday.

subordinate clause | independent clause | subordinate clause
After the game is over, we can go to my house where we can eat dinner.

A **compound-complex sentence** consists of two or more independent clauses and one or more subordinate clauses.

independent clause | independent clause
Baking a cake is easy for me, so I baked three of them

subordinate clause | subordinate clause
so that we could sell them when we had our bake sale.

To punctuate compound-complex sentences, follow the rules for both compound and complex sentences.

CONNECT TO WRITER'S CRAFT

You can often tell an author's intended audience by the complexity of the sentence structure in his or her work. When authors write for children, they generally use simple or compound sentences. Notice the structure of the sentences in the following passage from a book for children.

Spring slipped away and it was summer again. The children helped Father and Robert cut and store the wild hay. Then the three adventurers took their buckets and went out into the woods to harvest the summer berries for their mother.

—*Carol Ryrie Brink,* Caddie Woodlawn

When they write for more mature readers, authors tend to use longer, more complex sentences with more phrases and clauses. Notice the difference in the sentence structure in this passage from a novel written for adults.

The dinner, the dining-room, the dinner-service, the waiting at table, the wine, and the food were not only in keeping with the general air of up-to-date luxury throughout the house, but were, if anything, even more sumptuous and modern. Dolly observed all this luxury, which was novel to her, and, being herself the mistress of a house, she instinctively noted every detail (though she had no hope of introducing anything she saw to her own household—such luxury was far above her means and manner of life), and wondered how it was all done and by whom.

—*Leo Tolstoy,* Anna Karenina 

Practice Your Skills

Check Your Understanding

Classifying Sentences

General Interest **Label each sentence *simple, compound, complex,* or *compound-complex.***

1. The hamburger came from Hamburg, Germany, and the hot dog came from Frankfurt.
2. The idea of placing meat on a bun, however, came from the United States.

3. When the hamburger first arrived in the United States, it was eaten raw.
4. The French still prefer their meat rare, but the Germans eat raw hamburger meat.
5. Hamburgers first became popular among German immigrants who lived in Cincinnati.
6. Hamburger meat wasn't placed on a bun until the twentieth century.
7. Officially, the first hamburger sandwich appeared in 1904 in St. Louis, Missouri, which is also the birthplace of the ice-cream cone.
8. Today the hot dog is not as popular, but the hamburger is on the rise.
9. Chopped meat now accounts for about thirty percent of all meat sales.
10. Because people have become more health conscious, they are eating less meat, so many stores now sell hamburger patties made from soybeans.

Connect to the Writing Process: Drafting
Writing Different Types of Sentences

Write four sentences about food. Make the first a simple sentence, the second a compound sentence, the third a complex sentence, and the fourth a compound-complex sentence. Remember to punctuate the sentences properly.

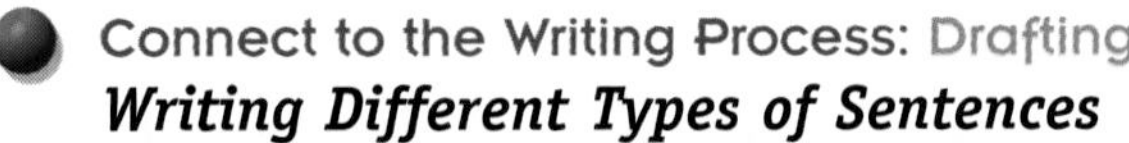

APPLY TO WRITING

Commercial: ***Sentence Structure***

Write a commercial about your favorite food. Give all the reasons why it is better than any other food. As you write your commercial, use variety in your sentence structure. Write at least one simple, one compound, one complex, and one compound-complex sentence. Be prepared to point out these different sentence types.

Diagraming Clauses

The simple sentences that you diagramed earlier in this book had only one baseline. In the diagrams for compound, complex, and compound-complex sentences, each clause has its own baseline.

Compound Sentences These sentences are diagramed like two simple sentences, except that they are joined by a broken line on which the conjunction is placed. The broken line connects the verbs.

Mysteries are interesting, but I prefer biographies.

Mysteries | are \ interesting
but
I | prefer | biographies

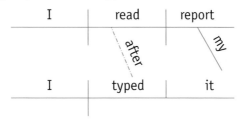

Complex Sentences In a complex sentence, an adverb clause is diagramed beneath the independent clause. The subordinating conjunction goes on a broken line that connects the verb in the adverb clause to the word the clause modifies.

I read my report after I typed it.

I | read | report
after
my
I | typed | it

An adjective clause is also diagramed beneath the independent clause. The relative pronoun is connected by a broken line to the noun or pronoun the clause modifies.

This song is one that I will never forget.

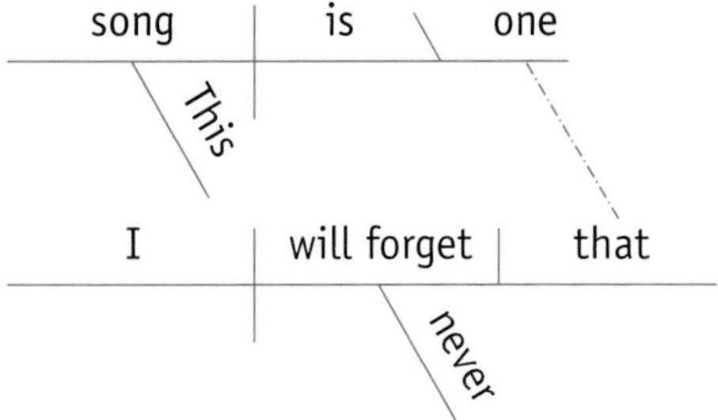

A noun clause is diagramed on a pedestal in the same place a single noun with the same function would be placed. The noun clause in the following diagram is used as the subject.

What the teacher said pleased Jane.

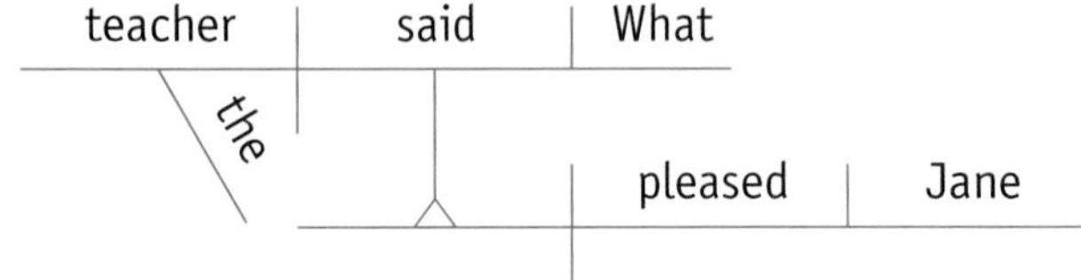

Compound-Complex Sentences To diagram this kind of sentence, apply what you just learned about diagraming compound and complex sentences.

Practice Your Skills

Diagraming Clauses

Diagram the following sentences or copy them. If you copy them, draw one line under each subject and two lines under each verb. Put parentheses around each subordinate clause. Label each clause *adverb, adjective,* or *noun.*

1. *Skylab* orbited the earth in the 1970s, and from *Skylab* astronauts studied the sun.
2. A million planets that are the size of the earth could be squashed inside the sun.
3. If the sun were dark for a few days, most life-forms on Earth would die.
4. Some scientists believe that the sun will grow hotter.
5. Never look at the sun because the light could blind you.

CheckPoint

Identifying Subordinate Clauses

Write the subordinate clause in each sentence. Then label each one *adverb, adjective,* or *noun.*

1. Do you know what metal is used to make most cans?
2. If you can crush a can, it probably was made from aluminum.
3. Aluminum, which makes up nearly eight percent of the earth's crust, is the most common metal in the world.
4. Although aluminum is so abundant, it has been used for only about one hundred years.
5. The problem is that aluminum is found only in combination with other substances in the rocks.
6. In 1886, it was Charles Hall who finally separated the aluminum from these other substances.
7. What he accomplished changed the canning industry forever.
8. Today you see aluminum products wherever you look.
9. Aluminum is useful because it is strong and lightweight.
10. Some aluminum products that you have heard of are pots and pans and parts for airplane and automobile engines.
11. Aluminum is also useful in wiring because it is a good conductor of heat and electricity.
12. Pure aluminum is soft and lacks strength although its alloys have many useful properties.
13. Another good thing about aluminum is that you can recycle it.
14. You should save empty soda cans until you can take them to a recycling center.
15. Did you know that you can earn money by recycling aluminum cans?

Classifying Sentences

Label each sentence *simple, compound, complex,* or *compound-complex.*

1. Does color affect you in any way?
2. Color experts say that different colors make a big difference in people's lives.
3. For example, people won't buy ice cream in a red carton because they associate red with meat.
4. Pink calms people, and yellow makes them nervous.
5. As a result, you should never paint your bedroom yellow.
6. People will eat less from blue plates, but they will eat more from red plates.
7. People who like candy prefer it in pink boxes.
8. Younger children go mainly for colors that are bright, but as teenagers they prefer softer colors.
9. Do you know what is the most popular color?
10. Most Americans pick blue as their favorite color, and red comes next.

Using Sentence Structure

Write five sentences that follow the directions below. (Clauses may come in any order.) Write about one of the following topics or a topic of your choice: your favorite color, your favorite game, or your favorite food.

1. Write a simple sentence.
2. Write a complex sentence with an introductory adverb clause.
3. Write a complex sentence with an adjective clause.
4. Write a compound sentence.
5. Write a complex sentence with a noun clause.

Label each sentence and check its punctuation.

Language and *Self-Expression*

Jacob Lawrence is known for his narrative images of African Americans. This painting is part of the *Great Idea Series.* In the series, Lawrence explores American history as the source of his imagery. The words of James Madison are his inspiration for this painting.

Famous people can inspire writers as well as artists. Choose one of the quotations below, and explain in an essay what you think the speaker meant. Vary your sentences by combining clauses.

"If a nation expects to be ignorant and free, in a state of civilization, it expects what never was and never will be."

–Thomas Jefferson

"If a free society cannot help the many who are poor, it cannot save the few who are rich."

–John F. Kennedy

"Power in defense of freedom is greater than power in behalf of tyranny and oppression."

–Malcolm X

Prewriting Choose one quotation and brainstorm a list of ideas about it. Number them in order of their importance.

Drafting Use your numbered ideas to draft your essay. Include a topic sentence, then follow with details that explain the quotation. Conclude with a sentence summarizing your ideas.

Revising Read your essay critically, looking for ideas that do not flow. Cut and add material as needed.

Editing Correct any errors in grammar, capitalization, punctuation, and spelling.

Publishing Prepare a final copy of your essay. You might publish it by sharing it with your class.

Another Look

A **clause** is a group of words that has a subject and a verb.

Kinds of Clauses

An **independent (or main) clause** can stand alone as a sentence because it expresses a complete thought. *(pages L221–L222)*

A **subordinate (or dependent) clause** cannot stand alone as a sentence because it does not express a complete thought. *(page L222)*

Uses of Subordinate Clauses

An **adverb clause** is a subordinate clause that is used like an adverb to modify a verb, an adjective, or an adverb. *(pages L224–L225)*

All adverb clauses begin with a **subordinating conjunction.** *(page L225)*

An **adjective clause** is a subordinate clause that is used like an adjective to modify a noun or pronoun. *(page L229)*

Most adjective clauses begin with a **relative pronoun.** *(pages L229–L230)*

A **noun clause** is a subordinate clause that is used like a noun. *(pages L237–L238)*

Kinds of Sentence Structure

A **simple sentence** consists of one independent clause. *(page L242)*

A **compound sentence** consists of two or more independent clauses. *(page L242)*

A **complex sentence** consists of one independent clause and one or more subordinate clauses. *(page L243)*

A **compound-complex sentence** consists of two or more independent clauses and one or more subordinate clauses. *(page L243)*

Other Information About Clauses

Recognizing misplaced modifiers *(pages L235–L236)*

Punctuating adverb clauses *(pages L225–L226)*

Determining the function of a relative pronoun *(page L232)*

Punctuating adjective clauses *(pages L232–L233)*

Directions

Write the letter of the term that correctly identifies each sentence or underlined part of a sentence.

Example **1.** The boat left the dock as the clock struck eight.

1 **A** simple sentence
B compound sentence
C complex sentence
D compound-complex sentence

Answer **1 C**

1. The evening dinner cruise was considerably more fun than I had expected.

2. We traveled up the west shore of Seneca Lake.

3. After we had been aboard for half an hour, dinner finally was served.

4. The food was unexciting, but the exotic atmosphere was truly delightful.

5. When dinner was over, we all went downstairs, and a band serenaded us.

6. The man <u>who led the band</u> was really a showman.

7. <u>How he danced around</u> made everyone laugh.

8. <u>As the band took a break</u>, I watched a nearby sailboat.

9. I asked the two women next to me <u>whether they enjoyed sailing</u>.

10. As it turned out, <u>one of them was a sailing instructor</u>.

1 **A** simple sentence
B compound sentence
C complex sentence
D compound-complex sentence

2 **A** simple sentence
B compound sentence
C complex sentence
D compound-complex sentence

3 **A** simple sentence
B compound sentence
C complex sentence
D compound-complex sentence

4 **A** simple sentence
B compound sentence
C complex sentence
D compound-complex sentence

5 **A** simple sentence
B compound sentence
C complex sentence
D compound-complex sentence

6 **A** independent clause
B adverb clause
C adjective clause
D noun clause

7 **A** independent clause
B adverb clause
C adjective clause
D noun clause

8 **A** independent clause
B adverb clause
C adjective clause
D noun clause

9 **A** independent clause
B adverb clause
C adjective clause
D noun clause

10 **A** independent clause
B adverb clause
C adjective clause
D noun clause

Sentence Fragments and Run-ons

Directions

Read the passage. Write the letter of the best way to write each underlined section. If the underlined section contains no error, write D.

EXAMPLE Ancient Greece was a civilization. That (1) produced important thinkers.

1 **A** civilization, and that
B civilization that
C civilization; that
D No error

ANSWER **1** **B**

Pythagoras was a Greek philosopher. Lived (1) in the sixth century B.C. The Pythagoreans, his followers, were skilled mathematicians. They were the first to teach. That the (2) earth rotates daily on its axis. Pythagoras is famous for a theorem. We (3) studied this year. It involves triangles geometry (4) depends on it. According to the theorem, the (5) square of the length of the hypotenuse of a right triangle equals the sum of the squares of the lengths of the other two sides.

1 **A** philosopher. Who lived
B philosopher he lived
C philosopher who lived
D No error

2 **A** teach that the
B teach that. The
C teach, and the
D No error

3 **A** theorem. Which we
B theorem we
C theorem, we
D No error

4 **A** triangles. And geometry
B triangles, and geometry
C triangles, geometry
D No error

5 **A** theorem. The
B theorem; the
C theorem the
D No error

Charles Willson Peale. *The Artist in His Museum,* 1822. Oil on canvas, 103¾ by 79⅞ inches. Courtesy of the Museum of American Art of the Pennsylvania Academy of the Fine Arts, Philadelphia. Gift of Mrs. Sarah Harrison (The Joseph Harrison Jr., Collection).

Describe Who is the focus of this painting? Where is he located? What is in the foreground? What is in the background?

Analyze Considering that the person portrayed is the artist himself, what message does he seem to be sending to the viewer? How does his stance help to convey that message?

Interpret Imagine that Peale chose to write a brochure inviting people to his museum. What words might he use on the cover to convey the same message that he is sending in his painting?

Judge Would a brochure be a better means of inviting people to visit the museum? Why or why not?

At the end of this chapter, you will use the artwork as a visual aid for writing.

Sentence Fragments

A **sentence fragment** is a group of words that does not express a complete thought.

Writers sometimes express an incomplete thought as a sentence. These incomplete thoughts are called sentence fragments. Some sentence fragments are missing either a subject or a verb. These are fragments due to incomplete thoughts.

No Subject	Was running and catching snowflakes on her tongue.
	Skate at the ice rink.
No Verb	Gretchen and her two little sisters.
	The snow shovel next to the snowblower in the garage.

Some sentence fragments are due to incorrect punctuation.

Part of a Compound Verb	Will you wait for us? **Or come back to get us?**
	We rushed to the ice. **And started to skate.**
Items in a Series	We will have to take warm clothes with us. **Coats, wool scarves, and gloves.**
	Rachel brought snacks for us. **Pretzels, chips, and hot chocolate.**

Ways to Correct Sentence Fragments

When you edit your writing, always check specifically for any missing subjects or missing verbs. You can fix these kinds of fragments by adding a subject or verb.

FRAGMENT	Was running and catching snowflakes on her tongue.
SENTENCE	**My little sister** was running and catching snowflakes on her tongue. (A complete subject, *my little sister,* was added.)

FRAGMENT	The snow shovel next to the snowblower in the garage.
SENTENCE	The snow shovel **is** next to the snowblower in the garage. (The verb *is* was added.)

Another way to correct a sentence fragment is to attach it to a related group of words near it. Sometimes you can simply include the information from the fragment into another sentence. Other times you can write two separate sentences.

SENTENCE AND FRAGMENT	Will you wait for the two of us? **Or come back to get us?**
ATTACHED	Will you wait for the two of us **or come back to get us?**
SEPARATE SENTENCES	Will you wait for the two of us? Will you come back to get us?

SENTENCE AND FRAGMENT	Rachel brought snacks for us. **Pretzels, chips, and hot chocolate.**
ATTACHED	Rachel brought pretzels, chips, and hot chocolate for us.
SEPARATE SENTENCES	Rachel brought snacks for us. She brought pretzels, chips, and hot chocolate for us.

You can learn more about complete sentences on page L5.

PRACTICE YOUR SKILLS

Check Your Understanding
Recognizing Fragments

Contemporary Life

Label each group of words *sentence* or *fragment.*

(1) Skating is my favorite winter activity. I usually go with friends from my neighborhood. **(2)** We hurry to the ice. **(3)** And skate as fast as possible. **(4)** Try to catch each other. **(5)** Sometimes I fall down. **(6)** And go sliding across the ice. **(7)** Since we all own them, usually bring our own skates. **(8)** Yesterday, however, Katie had to rent skates. **(9)** Her feet had grown since last winter. **(10)** Her old skates too small.

Connect to the Writing Process: Revising
Correcting Sentence Fragments

11.–15. Rewrite each fragment from the previous exercise as a complete sentence. You may add words or attach the fragment to another sentence.

Communicate Your Ideas

APPLY TO WRITING

E-mail Message: ***Complete Sentences***

Write an E-mail message to two friends. Invite them to join you as you do your favorite winter activity. Decide what you will invite them to do. Then write your message. Tell them the day, time, and place of the activity. Use the following fragments written correctly as sentences in your message.

- Coming with me.
- And drop you off at home.
- You need to bring.
- Hope you can come!

Other Kinds of Sentence Fragments

There are other kinds of sentence fragments. Each one of them is missing one or more essential elements to make it a complete sentence.

Phrase Fragments

Since a phrase does not have a subject and a verb, it can never stand alone as a sentence. When phrases are written alone, they are called **phrase fragments.** Following are examples of different phrase fragments in **bold** type. Notice that they are capitalized and punctuated as if they were sentences.

Prepositional Phrases	Mandy and Grant Saunders vacationed in Africa. **During the winter just after Christmas.**
	Before their trip to Zimbabwe and South Africa. Grant read about the continent.
Appositive Phrases	Mandy was fascinated by the African elephant. **The largest land mammal.**
	Have you seen Grant's books? **The ones about Africa.**
Participial Phrases	**Traveling by canoe on a wild river.** They saw a crocodile.
	Their canoe glided through a river. **Teeming with dangerous animals.**
Infinitive Phrases	Grant and Mandy bought a new camera. **To bring along on the trip.**
	They went to their doctor for vaccinations. **To prevent illness.**

Ways to Correct Phrase Fragments

When you edit your written work, always look for phrase fragments. If you find any, correct them in one of two ways: (1) add words to turn the phrase into a sentence; or (2) attach the phrase to a related group of words that has a subject and a verb.

SENTENCE AND PHRASE FRAGMENT	Mandy and Grant Saunders vacationed in Africa. **During the winter just after Christmas.**
SEPARATE SENTENCES	Mandy and Grant Saunders vacationed in Africa. **Their vacation was during the winter just after Christmas.**
ATTACHED	Mandy and Grant Saunders vacationed in Africa **during the winter just after Christmas.**

SENTENCE AND PHRASE FRAGMENT	Mandy was fascinated by the African elephant. **The largest land mammal.**
SEPARATE SENTENCES	Mandy was fascinated by the African elephant. **The African elephant is the largest land mammal.**
ATTACHED	Mandy was fascinated by the African elephant, **the largest land mammal.**

SENTENCE AND PHRASE FRAGMENT	Their canoe glided through a river. **Teeming with dangerous animals.**
SEPARATE SENTENCES	Their canoe glided through a river. **It was teeming with dangerous animals.**
ATTACHED	Their canoe glided through a river **teeming with dangerous animals.**

SENTENCE AND PHRASE FRAGMENT	They went to their doctor for vaccinations. **To prevent illness.**
SEPARATE SENTENCES	They went to their doctor for vaccinations. **The shots prevent illness.**
ATTACHED	They went to their doctor for vaccinations **to prevent illness.**

Practice Your Skills

Check Your Understanding

Recognizing Phrase Fragments

Science Topic **Label each group of words *S* for sentence or *PF* for phrase fragment.**

1. To learn more about wild animals.
2. Living in bushes and forest areas.
3. Gorillas are herbivores.
4. Scavengers like jackals and hyenas.
5. Lionesses raise their cubs together.
6. Found in Africa on game reserves.
7. One interesting animal in Africa is the zebra.
8. The lemur is found only in Madagascar.
9. On a photographic safari with an African guide.
10. Seeing animals in their natural habitats.
11. The aardvark has short and stumpy legs.
12. To scare away predators.

Connect to the Writing Process: Revising

Correcting Phrase Fragments

13.–19. Rewrite each phrase fragment from the previous exercise as a complete sentence. You may add words or attach the fragment to another sentence.

Communicate Your Ideas

APPLY TO WRITING

Writer's Craft: ***Analyzing the Use of Phrase Fragments***

Rather than use complete sentences, writers often intentionally use phrase fragments to express themselves. Read the following excerpt from *The Woman Warrior* by Maxine Hong Kingston and then follow the directions.

To shut the door at the end of the workday, which does not spill into evening. To throw away books after reading them so they don't have to be dusted. To go through boxes on New Year's Eve and throw out half of what's inside. Sometimes for extravagance to pick a bunch of flowers for the one table. Other women besides me must have this daydream about a carefree life.

–Maxine Hong Kingston, The Woman Warrior

- Write the one complete sentence from the excerpt.
- What kind of phrase fragment does Kingston use again and again in this passage?
- Rewrite two of the phrase fragments to form a complete sentence. Compare your work to Kingston's original. Which do you prefer? Why?
- In the final sentence, Kingston points out that the previous phrases describe daydreams. Why do you think she chose to describe these daydreams in fragments rather than in complete sentences?

Clause Fragments

All clauses have a subject and a verb, but only an independent clause can stand alone as a sentence. As you know, a subordinate clause does not express a complete thought. When a subordinate clause stands alone, it is known as a **clause fragment.**

Following are examples of clause fragments in **bold** type. Notice they are punctuated and capitalized as if they were complete sentences.

ADVERB CLAUSE FRAGMENT	You will miss the exhibit. **If you don't purchase advance tickets.**
ADJECTIVE CLAUSE FRAGMENT	This is a masterpiece. **That Pablo Picasso painted.**

Ways to Correct Clause Fragments

Looking for fragments should always be a part of your editing process. If you find a clause fragment, you can correct it in one of two ways. First, you can add words to make it into a separate sentence. Second, you can attach it to the sentence next to it.

SENTENCE AND CLAUSE FRAGMENT	You will miss the exhibit. **If you don't purchase advance tickets.**
SEPARATE SENTENCES	You will miss the exhibit. **You should purchase advance tickets.**
ATTACHED	You will miss the exhibit **if you don't purchase advance tickets.**

SENTENCE AND CLAUSE FRAGMENT	This is a masterpiece. **That Pablo Picasso painted.**
SEPARATE SENTENCES	This is a masterpiece. **Pablo Picasso painted it.**
ATTACHED	This is a masterpiece **that Pablo Picasso painted.**

Check Your Understanding

Recognizing Clause Fragments

Art Topic **Label each group of words *S* for sentence or *CF* for clause fragment.**

(1) Pablo Picasso who was born in 1881. **(2)** He led the artistic movement against naturalism. **(3)** Which is realism in art. **(4)** His father was an art teacher. **(5)** Who realized very early his son's great talent.

(6) His painting evolved throughout his life. (7) When he was a young man. (8) He painted more realistic works. (9) As he matured, he experimented with line, form, and color. (10) Which allowed him to create amazing pieces of art.

Connect to the Writing Process: Revising
Correcting Clause Fragments

11.-15. Rewrite each clause fragment from the previous exercise as a complete sentence. You may add words or attach the fragment to another sentence.

Communicate Your Ideas

APPLY TO WRITING

Narrative: ***Complete Sentences***

Pablo Picasso. *The Tragedy,* 1903. Wood, 41½ by 27⅛ inches. National Gallery of Art, Washington, D.C.

Imagine that you are the child in this painting by Pablo Picasso. Write a narrative account for your teacher of what has happened to create the scene before you. How do you feel? How has what happened affected these adults? What will happen next? Use the following clause fragments written correctly as sentences in your narrative.

- As we stood barefoot on the sand.
- That they had heard the story.
- Who is such a kind person.

Mixed Practice

History Topic **Rewrite the following paragraphs, correcting all sentence fragments. Add capital letters and punctuation marks where needed.**

When Jesse Owens graduated from East Technical High School in Cleveland, Ohio. He had established three national high school records in track. At Ohio State University, Jesse broke a few more world records. Then in the 1936 Olympic Games at Berlin. He acquired world fame by winning four gold medals!

Owens's performance on May 25, 1935, at the Big Ten Conference championships, however, will always be remembered. Getting up from a sickbed. He ran the 100-yard dash in 9.4 seconds. To tie the world record. Ten minutes later in the broad jump. He leaped 26 feet 8.25 inches on his first try. To beat a world record. When the 220-yard dash was over. Owens had smashed another world record. He then negotiated the hurdles in 22.6 seconds. And shattered another record. Within three quarters of an hour. Jesse Owens had established world records in four events.

Run-on Sentences

A mistake some writers make is to combine several thoughts and write them as one sentence. This results in a run-on sentence.

A **run-on sentence** is two or more sentences that are written together and are separated by a comma or no mark of punctuation at all.

Generally, run-on sentences are written in either of two ways.

WITH A COMMA	The class trip was in April, **we went to Washington D.C.**
WITH NO PUNCTUATION	On the trip we visited four museums **the Smithsonian was the best.**

Ways to Correct Run-on Sentences

To correct a run-on sentence, you can turn it into (1) separate sentences; (2) a compound sentence; or (3) a complex sentence.

RUN-ON SENTENCE	I walked all over the city my feet were very tired at the end of the day.
SEPARATE SENTENCES	I walked all over the city. My feet were very tired at the end of the day. (separated with a period and a capital letter)
COMPOUND SENTENCES	I walked all over the city, so my feet were very tired at the end of the day. (clauses combined with a comma and a conjunction)
	I walked all over the city; my feet were very tired at the end of the day. (clauses combined with a semicolon)
COMPLEX SENTENCE	Because I walked all over the city, my feet were very tired at the end of the day. (clauses combined by changing one of them into a subordinate clause)

Connect to Writer's Craft

Another way to edit for sentence errors is to use two different colored highlighting markers. Highlight your first sentence in one color; highlight your second sentence in another color. Continue alternating. Then you can easily see the length of each sentence. If a group of words looks short, read it carefully to be sure it's a complete sentence. If a sentence looks long, read closely to be sure it is not a run-on.

Practice Your Skills

Check Your Understanding

Recognizing Run-on Sentences

History Topic

Label each group of words *S* for sentence or *RO* for run-on.

(1) George Washington was the first president he was not the first to live in the White House. **(2)** The second president, John Adams, was the first head of state to live in the White House. **(3)** In 1800, John and Abigail Adams moved in the builders had completed only six rooms. **(4)** Still, Abigail Adams was impressed by the place she was glad to live in such a beautiful mansion.

(5) The White House wasn't always white, it started out gray. **(6)** During the War of 1812, British troops invaded Washington they burned the structure on August 24, 1814. **(7)** Only a shell was left standing. **(8)** Under the direction of the original architect, the building was restored. **(9)** The work was completed in 1817. **(10)** "The White House" did not become its official name until 1902, Theodore Roosevelt adopted it.

Connect to the Writing Process: Revising

Correcting Run-on Sentences

11.–16. Correct each run-on sentence from the previous exercise. Add capital letters and punctuation marks where needed.

Communicate Your Ideas

APPLY TO WRITING

Description: ***Complete Sentences***

Your parents have just told you that you can redesign your room. Write a description for your parents of what you consider to be the perfect bedroom. Don't forget to include all the details you've always desired in your living space! After writing your description, read it aloud to a classmate. As you read, listen for any sentence errors that you may have made. Correct any fragments and run-ons.

Mixed Practice

General Interest

Rewrite the following paragraphs, correcting all sentence fragments and run-on sentences. Add capital letters and punctuation marks where needed.

If you owned *Marvel Comics #1* You would be a rich person. In 1939, it cost a dime today it is worth fifteen thousand dollars! No one knows exactly which comic books to save. There are, however, a few things. To look for when you're buying them. Buy the first issue of any comic book. And hold onto it. Origin issues are also valuable, they are the issues in which a character is born or comes into being.

Do you have any old comic books? Lying around the house. You can find out how much they are worth by looking in a book it's called *The Comic Book Price Guide* by Robert Overstreet. It can be found in most public libraries.

CheckPoint

Correcting Sentence Fragments and Run-on Sentences

Write the following sentences, correcting each sentence fragment or run-on sentence. Use capital letters and punctuation marks where needed.

1. A large tree had fallen. At the end of the road leading to the lake.
2. We have three kinds of trees growing in our yard. Oak, maple, and spruce.
3. "Smith" is a very common name. Appearing in over forty languages.
4. In 1946, there were 10,000 television sets in the United States, there were twelve million five years later.
5. Of all the ore dug in a diamond mine. Only one carat in every three tons proves to be a diamond.
6. Yesterday I mowed the lawn. And trimmed the bushes and hedges.
7. If the moon were placed on the surface of the United States. It would extend from California to Ohio.
8. The hardiest of all the world's insects is the mosquito, it can be found in all parts of the world.
9. South American Indians introduced tapioca to the world it comes from the root of a poisonous plant.
10. We must have loaned the snowblower to Uncle Pete I can't find it.

Correcting Sentence Fragments and Run-on Sentences

Rewrite the following paragraph, correcting all sentence fragments and run-on sentences. Be sure to correct the errors in a variety of ways. Add capital letters and punctuation where needed.

According to a common superstition. The groundhog is supposed to come out of its underground home on February 2. National Groundhog Day. If the animal sees its shadow. It hurries back to its snug bed. For another six weeks. This means that there will be six more weeks of winter, people should not put their winter coats away. Of course, if the little critter stays out of its burrow, spring will soon begin. Should you believe this superstition? The National Geographic Service says that the groundhog. Has been right only 28 percent of the time that's not a very good record. Still, next February 2, hundreds of reporters will be waiting. To see if the groundhog will see its shadow.

Writing Sentences

Write five sentences that follow the directions below. Beware of sentence fragments and run-ons. Write about your favorite holiday or about a topic of your choice.

1. Write a sentence that contains only a subject and a verb.
2. Write a sentence that consists of a simple sentence with an attached phrase.
3. Write a sentence that consists of a simple sentence with an attached dependent clause.
4. Write a compound sentence containing the word *and.*
5. Write a compound sentence with a semicolon.

Language and *Self-Expression*

Charles Willson Peale is known for his portraits of colonial Americans, including a very famous portrait of George Washington. Peale also founded a natural history museum. This self-portrait shows the artist inviting the viewer into his museum.

A descriptive paragraph in spatial order is a paragraph that is organized—not step-by-step over time—but step-by-step from one place to another. Use the painting by Charles Willson Peale as a visual aid to imagine that you are standing in the artist's place in the foreground of the painting. Now imagine that you walk slowly along the corridor to the end. What do you see? Tell a visitor to the museum about it in spatial order, moving from the foreground to the background of the painting. Use your imagination to picture what is on the shelves of the natural history museum.

Prewriting Make a list of the objects you might see in Peale's museum. Number these in the order a visitor might see them as he or she walks down the corridor.

Drafting Begin with a sentence that states the main idea of your paragraph. Use your notes and the painting to add details in the order in which a visitor would see them.

Revising Reread your paragraph and add descriptive words that give specific details. If you find any sentence fragments or run-ons, correct them. Make sure that your paragraph uses spatial order.

Editing Review your paragraph, looking for errors in grammar, capitalization, punctuation, and spelling. Make any corrections that are necessary.

Publishing Prepare a final copy of your paragraph. Share your paragraph with a classmate to see how you differed in your imaginative descriptions of Peale's museum.

Another Look

A **sentence fragment** is a group of words that does not express a complete thought.

Kinds of Fragments

Because a phrase does not have a subject and verb, it cannot stand alone. If it does, it is called a **phrase fragment.** *(page L260)*

KINDS OF PHRASE FRAGMENTS	
Prepositional Phrase	After the storm.
Appositive Phrase	The worst storm of all.
Participial Phrase	Blowing up a storm.
Infinitive Phrase	To clean up the storm's debris.

All clauses have a subject and verb, but only an independent clause can stand alone. If a subordinate clause stands alone, it is called a **clause fragment.** *(page L263)*

KINDS OF CLAUSE FRAGMENTS	
Adverb Clause	If you don't watch out.
Adjective Clause	That I ever saw.
Noun Clause	Whatever happened to the survivors.

A **run-on sentence** is two or more sentences that are written as one sentence and are separated by a comma or no mark of punctuation at all.

Other Information About Fragments and Run-ons

Correcting phrase fragments *(page L261)*
Correcting clause fragments *(page L264)*
Correcting run-on sentences *(page L267)*

Directions

Read the passage. Write the letter of the best way to write each underlined section. If the underlined section contains no error, write *D*.

EXAMPLE

I just finished a very interesting book. About (1) a mountain climbing expedition.

1 **A** book about
B book, about
C book its about
D No error

ANSWER **1 A**

At its peak the (1) Incan empire controlled the entire Andean mountain region. Despite the rough terrain, the Incas were able to grow crops. They did this by terracing the ground. And they (2) irrigated extensively. The Incas raised llamas and alpacas. With (3) their heavy coats. These unusual (4) animals are well suited to the mountain climate. The Incan civilization was quite advanced. The Incas built extraordinary structures and their artwork (5) is still admired today.

1 **A** At, its peak the

B At its peak. The

C At its peak of the

D No error

2 **A** ground and they irrigated

B ground and irrigating

C ground and, they irrigated

D No error

3 **A** alpacas, with their

B alpacas with their

C alpacas and with their

D No error

4 **A** coats, these unusual

B coats these, unusual

C coats and these unusual

D No error

5 **A** structures. And their artwork

B structures, and their artwork

C structures and, their artwork

D No error

Using Verbs

Pretest

Directions

Read the passage and choose the word or group of words that belongs in each underlined space. Write the letter of the correct answer.

EXAMPLE Every July and August many people __(1)__ to new homes.

1 **A** move
B had been moving
C will move
D had moved

ANSWER **1 A**

Moving day __(1)__ at last! Yesterday I __(2)__ all my belongings into boxes. Later, when my friend Jason arrives, I __(3)__ them into the back of a rental truck. He __(4)__ his help. I __(5)__ him at the door now. Jason __(6)__ used to moving because he moves to a new apartment every other year. He __(7)__ some old blankets for us to use today. Before Jason arrived, I __(8)__ to protect my furniture with towels. He __(9)__ some blankets over the piano, and we are ready to go. I feel a little sad to leave because I __(10)__ in this apartment a long time.

1 A will have been coming
B had been coming
C has been coming
D has come

2 A packed
B pack
C will pack
D am packing

3 A had loaded
B loaded
C will load
D have loaded

4 A will have offered
B has offered
C will have been offering
D offers

5 A will hear
B hear
C had heard
D will have heard

6 A will be
B will have been
C is being
D is

7 A has been bringing
B has brought
C will have brought
D had been bringing

8 A will try
B try
C had been trying
D will have tried

9 A lays
B will lay
C had laid
D will have laid

10 A live
B will live
C have lived
D will have lived

Ant Farm (Charles L. Lord, Hudson Marquez, Doug Michels).
Cadillac Ranch, 1974. © Ant Farm (Lord, Marquez, and Michels).

Describe How would you describe this sculpture to someone who hasn't seen it?

Analyze What does the artwork make you think of? What, in the artwork, causes you to make that connection?

Interpret What techniques do you think a writer of a short story could use to evoke similar thoughts?

Judge Would you rather view a sculpture or read a short story about this subject? Explain why you feel as you do.

At the end of this chapter, you will use the artwork to stimulate ideas for writing.

The Principal Parts of a Verb

This chapter begins the section of the book on usage. You will learn how to use the various elements of grammar covered in Chapters 1–9.

In this chapter you will look more closely at verbs. Because verbs have so many forms, people often make mistakes when they use them in writing and in speaking. Even though verbs can be the most informative—and most powerful—words in the English language, they can also be difficult to master. This chapter will help you learn more about the various forms of the verbs you use every day. The chapter will also show you how the tense of a verb is used to express time when you are writing a story. The different tenses of a verb are based on its four basic forms, called principal parts.

The **principal parts of a verb** are the present, the present participle, the past, and the past participle.

The principal parts of the verb *jog* are used in the following examples. Notice that the present participle and the past participle must have a helping verb when they are used as verbs.

Present	I **jog** two miles every day.
Present Participle	I *am* **jogging** to the lake and back.
Past	Today I **jogged** with Ashley.
Past Participle	I *have* **jogged** every day for a year.

Regular Verbs

A **regular verb** forms its past and past participle by adding *–ed* or *–d* to the present.

The following chart shows the principal parts of the regular verbs *paint, share, stop,* and *trim*. Notice that the present participle is formed by adding *–ing* to the present form and the past participle is formed by adding *–ed* or *–d* to the present form.

REGULAR VERBS

PRESENT	PRESENT PARTICIPLE	PAST	PAST PARTICIPLE
paint	(is) painting	painted	(have) painted
share	(is) sharing	shared	(have) shared
stop	(is) stopping	stopped	(have) stopped
trim	(is) trimming	trimmed	(have) trimmed

Notice that when endings such as *–ing* and *–ed* are added to some verbs, such as *share, stop,* and *trim,* the spelling changes. If you are unsure of the spelling of a verb form, look it up in the dictionary.

PRACTICE YOUR SKILLS

Check Your Understanding

Determining the Principal Parts of a Verb

Make four columns on your paper. Label them *Present, Present Participle, Past,* and *Past Participle.* Then, using all four columns, write the four principal parts of each of the following regular verbs.

1. ask **2.** use **3.** hop **4.** row **5.** share **6.** climb **7.** wrap **8.** jump **9.** taste **10.** weigh **11.** shout **12.** stare **13.** check **14.** drop **15.** cook **16.** gaze **17.** call **18.** talk **19.** shop **20.** look

Irregular Verbs

An **irregular verb** does not form its past and past participle by adding *–ed* or *–d* to the present form.

The irregular verbs have been divided into six groups, according to the way they form their past and past participle. Remember, though, that the word *is* is not part of the present participle and the word *have* is not part of the past participle. They have been added to the lists of irregular verbs, however, to remind you that all the present and past participles must have a form of one of these helping verbs when they are used as a verb in a sentence.

CONNECT TO SPEAKING AND WRITING

It is sometimes easier to hear a verb used incorrectly when you are reading aloud than it is to see a mistake when you are reading silently. When you edit your work, you can find errors of many kinds if you simply read the piece aloud.

Group 1 These irregular verbs have the same form for the present, the past, and the past participle.

GROUP 1			
Present	**Present Participle**	**Past**	**Past Participle**
burst	(is) bursting	burst	(have) burst
cost	(is) costing	cost	(have) cost
hit	(is) hitting	hit	(have) hit
hurt	(is) hurting	hurt	(have) hurt
let	(is) letting	let	(have) let
put	(is) putting	put	(have) put
set	(is) setting	set	(have) set

Group 2 These irregular verbs have the same form for the past and past participle.

GROUP 2			
Present	**Present Participle**	**Past**	**Past Participle**
bring	(is) bringing	brought	(have) brought
buy	(is) buying	bought	(have) bought
catch	(is) catching	caught	(have) caught
feel	(is) feeling	felt	(have) felt
find	(is) finding	found	(have) found
get	(is) getting	got	(have) got or gotten
hold	(is) holding	held	(have) held
keep	(is) keeping	kept	(have) kept
lead	(is) leading	led	(have) led
leave	(is) leaving	left	(have) left
lose	(is) losing	lost	(have) lost
make	(is) making	made	(have) made
say	(is) saying	said	(have) said
sell	(is) selling	sold	(have) sold
send	(is) sending	sent	(have) sent
teach	(is) teaching	taught	(have) taught
tell	(is) telling	told	(have) told
win	(is) winning	won	(have) won

Practice Your Skills

Check Your Understanding

Using the Correct Verb Form

Contemporary Life

Write the past or past participle of each verb in parentheses.

1. The left fielder has (hit) his second long, high fly ball.
2. Dee (win) the prize for most valuable player.
3. She (put) the trophy on her bookshelf at home.
4. Our coach (tell) us about good sportsmanship.
5. I (find) my lucky bat in the coach's bag.
6. Amanda has (leave) our baseball team.
7. The batter blew a bubble that (burst) all over his face.
8. The concession stand has always (sell) the players bubble gum for half price.
9. Our coach (lead) us to five straight victories.
10. Vince (keep) striking out player after player.
11. My dad has (bring) our team ice and water.
12. Having Dee on our team has not (hurt) our chances to win the championship.
13. Dee has (make) many home runs this season.
14. My mother has (keep) my baseball picture on her desk.
15. The team (hold) their breath when Dee came up to bat.

Connect to the Writing Process: Editing

Correcting Improperly Used Verbs

Write each sentence, correcting the underlined verb. If the verb in the sentence is correct, write C.

16. Our coach has let us choose our team mascot.
17. We buyed socks to match our uniforms.
18. The players had say the Pledge of Allegiance before the game.
19. Has Val catched a pop fly during this game?
20. Our coach teached us to bunt the ball.

21. I feeled so happy after my home run!

22. The catcher's error costed their team the game.

23. My dad send a letter to the newspaper praising our coach.

24. We all got a trophy.

25. We have losed only two games in two years.

Connect to Speaking: Making an Announcement

Correcting Improperly Used Verbs

Read the following intercom announcement aloud to a classmate or your teacher. As you read, correct any verb errors you find.

Attention all students: We are hold tryouts for next year's baseball teams on Tuesday. If you have ever catch a ball or hitted a home run, you should put your name on the tryout list. Many old players have leave the team, so there are many positions available. All students interested in playing should letted the coaches know by four o'clock today.

Group 3 These irregular verbs form their past participle by adding *-n* to the past form.

GROUP 3			
Present	**Present Participle**	**Past**	**Past Participle**
break	(is) breaking	broke	(have) broken
choose	(is) choosing	chose	(have) chosen
freeze	(is) freezing	froze	(have) frozen
speak	(is) speaking	spoke	(have) spoken
steal	(is) stealing	stole	(have) stolen

Group 4 These irregular verbs form their past participle by adding *–n* to the present.

GROUP 4			
PRESENT	**PRESENT PARTICIPLE**	**PAST**	**PAST PARTICIPLE**
blow	(is) blowing	blew	(have) blown
draw	(is) drawing	drew	(have) drawn
drive	(is) driving	drove	(have) driven
fly	(is) flying	flew	(have) flown
give	(is) giving	gave	(have) given
grow	(is) growing	grew	(have) grown
know	(is) knowing	knew	(have) known
see	(is) seeing	saw	(have) seen
take	(is) taking	took	(have) taken
throw	(is) throwing	threw	(have) thrown

PRACTICE YOUR SKILLS

Check Your Understanding

Determining the Correct Verb Form

Contemporary Life **Write the correct verb form for each sentence.**

1. I have just (chose, chosen) the seeds for our garden.
2. Last year I planted too early, so the seedlings (froze, frozen).
3. Tomatoes have always (grew, grown) well in this soil.
4. By the end of last season, I had (gave, given) many vegetables to our neighbors.
5. The wind (blew, blown) very hard last night!
6. It (broke, broken) some of my small tomato plants.

7. Last summer rabbits (stole, stolen) carrots from my garden.
8. They (took, taken) the carrots before they were mature.
9. I have never (saw, seen) them in the act.
10. I (knew, known) that rabbits were the culprits because of their tracks.

Check Your Understanding
Using the Correct Verb Form

Contemporary Life **Write the past or past participle of each verb in parentheses.**

11. Mr. Foster has (grow) vegetables for more than fifteen years.
12. He (speak) to me about my rabbit problem.
13. He (drive) rabbits away from his garden by playing a portable radio in the garden at night.
14. Then he (draw) them away from his yard by putting vegetable scraps on the other side of his fence.
15. He said that many farmers have (throw) a party after ridding themselves of rabbits.

Connect to the Writing Process: Editing
Correcting Improperly Used Verbs

Rewrite the sentences, using the correct verb form. If the verb form is correct, write C.

16. I am glad that Mr. Foster had chose not to hurt the rabbits.
17. Since I have used Mr. Foster's technique, no rabbits have stole carrots this year.
18. I took an organic gardening class last fall.
19. Because of that class, I have chose not to use pesticides this year.
20. I am driving the pests from my garden by natural methods.

Connect to Speaking: Making a Radio Announcement
Correcting Improperly Used Verbs

Read the following radio announcement aloud to a classmate or your teacher, correcting any verb errors you find.

Have you ever drove your car on an icy driveway? Have you ever threw salt on your sidewalk to make ice melt? Well, those days are over. We are introducing new Bye-Ice. Bye-Ice will broke up ice like nothing you've ever saw! Just sprinkle some on icy sidewalks or driveways. It clears any cement or asphalt that has froze over. Don't believe it until you have saw for yourself. Buy Bye-Ice today!

Group 5 These irregular verbs form their past and past participles by changing a vowel.

GROUP 5

PRESENT	PRESENT PARTICIPLE	PAST	PAST PARTICIPLE
begin	(is) beginning	began	(have) begun
drink	(is) drinking	drank	(have) drunk
fling	(is) flinging	flung	(have) flung
ring	(is) ringing	rang	(have) rung
shrink	(is) shrinking	shrank	(have) shrunk
sing	(is) singing	sang	(have) sung
sink	(is) sinking	sank	(have) sunk
sting	(is) stinging	stung	(have) stung
swim	(is) swimming	swam	(have) swum

Group 6 These irregular verbs form the past and the past participle in other ways.

GROUP 6			
PRESENT	PRESENT PARTICIPLE	PAST	PAST PARTICIPLE
come	(is) coming	came	(have) come
do	(is) doing	did	(have) done
eat	(is) eating	ate	(have) eaten
fall	(is) falling	fell	(have) fallen
go	(is) going	went	(have) gone
ride	(is) riding	rode	(have) ridden
run	(is) running	ran	(have) run
tear	(is) tearing	tore	(have) torn
wear	(is) wearing	wore	(have) worn
write	(is) writing	wrote	(have) written

PRACTICE YOUR SKILLS

Check Your Understanding

Determining the Correct Verb Form

Contemporary Life **Write the correct verb form for each sentence.**

1. My friends and I have (went, gone) to the lake every weekend this year.

2. Juan (swam, swum) from the boat to the pier.

3. Mindy has (wrote, written) for a sample of that new sunscreen lotion.

4. I always (wear, worn) a hat to shade my eyes from the sun.

5. My hat has (fell, fallen) in the lake before.

6. Lesli has (sank, sunk) her brother's boat!
7. Cali (rode, ridden) on the inner tube behind the ski boat.
8. Our water polo match has not (began, begun) yet.
9. On the dock my cell phone (rang, rung) so loudly that everyone stared at me.
10. I dropped my phone, and it (sank, sunk) to the bottom of the lake.

Check Your Understanding
Using the Correct Verb Form

General Interest **Write the past or past participle of each verb in parentheses.**

11. Each spring in Austin, Texas, the Mexican free-tail bats have (come) to the Congress Avenue Bridge to make their homes underneath.
12. Long ago many people feared that bats (drink) human blood.
13. The Austin bats are welcomed by this city, where they have (eat) large numbers of pesky mosquitoes.
14. They have also (do) another helpful thing.
15. Tourists have (begin) to come to see the bats, which constitute the largest urban bat colony in the United States.
16. Many joggers have (run) under the bridge to see the bats.
17. Local musicians have (sing) songs about the flying mammals.
18. For years the bats have (tear) across the darkening sky at sunset.
19. Throughout the summers Austinites have (come) down to watch the spectacle.
20. In the fall disappointed tourists find that the bat population has (shrink) due to the bats' migration to Mexico.

Check Your Understanding
Finding Principal Parts in a Dictionary

Make four columns on your paper. Label them *present, present participle, past,* and *past participle.* Then look up each of the following irregular verbs in a dictionary. Write the principal parts of each one in the appropriate columns.

21. swing
22. strive
23. swear
24. spin
25. shake
26. become
27. arise
28. weave
29. build
30. sleep
31. bend
32. forget
33. lend
34. meet
35. fight
36. pay
37. mean
38. creep
39. hold
40. sweep

Connect to the Writing Process: Drafting
Writing Sentences Using Irregular Verbs

Write sentences using the indicated form of the verb. Use your list from the above exercise to help you.

41. present form of *swing*
42. present participle form of *pay*
43. past form of *shake*
44. past participle form of *become*
45. present form of *build*
46. present participle form of *forget*
47. past form of *meet*
48. past participle form of *arise*
49. past form of *creep*
50. past participle form of *sweep*

Communicate Your Ideas

APPLY TO WRITING

Announcement: *Verb Forms*

Your teacher has asked you to write a short announcement to be read over the school intercom, inviting students to a meeting of the school's new book club. Remember, a good announcement should give information about the club and the location of the meeting. Use the following forms of the verbs listed as you write your announcement.

- Present participle of *come*
- Past participle of *grow*
- Past participle of *speak*
- Present form of *make*
- Past participle of *put*

Mixed Practice

General Interest **Write the past or past participle of each verb in parentheses.**

1. In first-century Rome, Nero had snow (bring) from the nearby mountains.
2. With the snow he (make) the first frozen dessert.
3. He (experiment) with snow, honey, and fruit.
4. Until the thirteenth century, no one in Europe had (see) a frozen milk dessert.
5. Marco Polo (introduce) a version of ice cream to Europe.
6. Improvements on this dessert (lead) to the creation of ice cream in the sixteenth century.
7. Ice cream, however, (remain) a treat for the rich only.
8. For years the great chefs (keep) the secret of ice cream to themselves.
9. After a French café (begin) serving ice cream, it (become) everyone's favorite.
10. Only a few Americans had (eat) ice cream before 1700.

Six Problem Verbs

In addition to learning the principal parts of irregular verbs, it is sometimes necessary to look closely at the meanings of certain pairs of verbs because they are easily confused with each other. The following six verbs often cause problems in speaking and writing.

lie and *lay*

Lie means "to rest or recline." *Lie* is never followed by a direct object. *Lay* means "to put or set (something) down." *Lay* is usually followed by a direct object.

You can learn about direct objects on pages L149–L151.

PRESENT	PRESENT PARTICIPLE	PAST	PAST PARTICIPLE
lie	(is) lying	lay	(have) lain
lay	(is) laying	laid	(have) laid

LIE Our puppies always **lie** near the fireplace in the living room.

They **are lying** there now.

They **lay** there all last night.

They **have lain** there in that same spot for an hour.

LAY **Lay** the puppies' mats on the floor.
(You lay what? *Mats* is the direct object.)

Jon **is laying** the puppies' mats on the floor.

My sister **laid** the mats on the floor last night.

Usually I **have laid** the mats on the floor.

rise and *raise*

Rise means "to move upward" or "to get up." *Rise* is never followed by a direct object. *Raise* means "to lift (something) up," "to increase," or "to grow something." *Raise* is usually followed by a direct object.

PRESENT	PRESENT PARTICIPLE	PAST	PAST PARTICIPLE
rise	(is) rising	rose	(have) risen
raise	(is) raising	raised	(have) raised

RISE **Rise** out of that bed!

The sick puppy **is rising** off the mat.

He **rose** and went to the kitchen.

He **has risen** early every morning since we took him to the veterinarian.

RAISE **Raise** the litter of puppies carefully.

(You raise what? *Litter* is the direct object.)

Benjamin **is raising** a litter of puppies at the kennel.

Benjamin **raised** a litter of puppies last year, too.

Benjamin **has raised** litters of puppies for thirteen years now.

sit and *set*

Sit means "to rest in an upright position." *Sit* is never followed by a direct object. *Set* usually means "to put or place (something)." *Set* is usually followed by a direct object.

Present	Present Participle	Past	Past Participle
sit	(is) sitting	sat	(have) sat
set	(is) setting	set	(have) set

Sit — **Sit** down by the fire and get warm.

My puppy **is sitting** near the fire.

Her puppy **sat** there for almost an hour.

The dogs **have** never **sat** there before.

Set — **Set** the dogs' dishes on the kennel floor. (You set what? *Dishes* is the direct object.)

He **is setting** the dishes on the kennel floor.

She **set** the dishes on the kennel floor yesterday.

He **has set** the dishes on the kennel floor many times before.

You can learn more about other problem verbs on pages L281–L288.

Practice Your Skills

Check Your Understanding

Using the Correct Verb

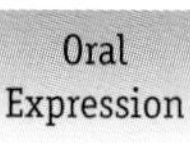

Read the following sentences aloud to practice saying the underlined verbs and hearing them used correctly. Be prepared to explain why each verb is correct.

1. My dogs always get excited before I set their food dishes down.
2. One morning Rover actually sat still when I came in with his food.

3. When Rover is sick, he lies on my bed.
4. I had laid Rover's medicine on my nightstand the night before.
5. For a whole day, Rover never raised his head.
6. The next day he felt stronger, but he still lay there.
7. Finally, on the third day, he rose to his feet.
8. He drank the water I had set on the floor for him.
9. I sat and watched as he ate a little food.
10. Then he laid his head on my lap and went to sleep again.

Check Your Understanding

Using the Correct Verb

Contemporary Life **Write the correct verb for each sentence.**

11. Mom asked me to (sit, set) the dishes on the table for a special dinner.
12. I was (sitting, setting) comfortably in front of the fireplace.
13. I (rose, raised) from my chair and went into the dining room.
14. I (lay, laid) placemats on the table.
15. I decided to use the good china, which had (lain, laid) in the cabinet for months.
16. As I (rose, raised) a china plate to the table, it slipped from my hand.
17. The dish (laid, lay) in shattered pieces all over our tile floor.
18. I (set, sat) down the other plate carefully and started cleaning up the mess.
19. (Raising, Rising) from the floor with the broken dish, I felt bad about the accident.
20. I decided I would (sit, set) aside some of my allowance to buy a new dish.

Connect to the Writing Process: Editing

Correcting Verb Usage

Write each sentence, correcting the underlined verb. If the verb in the sentence is correct, write C.

21. Most hens lay at least one egg each day.

22. They set on the eggs in order to keep them warm enough to hatch.

23. They raise from their nests to eat but return to the eggs as soon as possible.

24. The eggs lay in the nest waiting for the hen's speedy return.

25. If the eggs have been fertilized, the hen will soon be rising baby chicks.

26. Chicks usually are risen on farms.

27. Some farmers also rise cows.

28. Baby calves do not lie in a nest as baby chicks do.

29. Some ranchers will sit hay in a field for their cows to eat.

30. When farmers are not working, you might find them as they set in the shade.

Communicate Your Ideas

APPLY TO WRITING

Informative Paragraph: *Problem Verbs*

Your health teacher has asked you to write about fire safety. Write an informative paragraph that tells your classmates the proper way to react if their clothes catch on fire. Be sure to consult a reliable source for appropriate safety rules. In your paragraph properly use at least one form of the six problem verbs: *lie, lay, sit, set, rise,* and *raise.*

Mixed Practice

Contemporary Life

Write the correct form of the verbs in parentheses.

1. The magician (raised, rose) from a deep bow to the audience.
2. He (sat, set) a tall top hat on the table at the front of the stage.
3. His lovely assistant (lay, laid) a feather inside the hat on the table.
4. Then she (set, sat) a blue, silk handkerchief over the hat.
5. The magician (rose, raised) his wand over the hat three times.
6. The hat that was (lying, laying) on the table began to shake violently.
7. The top hat tumbled from the table on which it had (set, sat).
8. As the hat fell, a beautiful dove (rose, raised) from inside it.
9. The audience could not (set, sit) still at the sight of the graceful dove.
10. They (rose, raised) from their seats, applauding the magnificent magician.

Verb Tense

The six tenses of a verb are the present, past, future, present perfect, past perfect, and future perfect.

The time expressed by a verb is called the **tense** of a verb.

In the following examples, the six tenses of *run* are used to express action at different times.

PRESENT	I **run** a mile every day.
PAST	I **ran** a mile yesterday
FUTURE	I **will run** a mile tomorrow.
PRESENT PERFECT	I **have run** a mile every day since June.
PAST PERFECT	I **had** not **run** that much before.
FUTURE PERFECT	I **will have run** almost two hundred miles before the end of the year.

Uses of Tenses

As the previous examples show, verbs in the English language have six basic tenses: three simple tenses and three perfect tenses. All these tenses can be formed from the four principal parts of a verb and the helping verbs *have, has, had, will,* and *shall.*

Present tense is the first of the three simple tenses. It is used to express an action that is going on now. To form the present tense, use the present form (the first principal part of the verb) or add *–s* or *–es* to the present form.

PRESENT TENSE	I **watch** music videos
	Megan **sings** along with the videos.
	Even her parents **enjoy** some of the videos.

Past tense expresses an action that has already taken place or was completed in the past. To form the past tense of a verb, add *–ed* or *–d* to the present form. To form the past of an irregular verb, check a dictionary for the past form or look for it on pages L281–L288.

PAST TENSE	I **watched** the music awards program on television.
	Megan **sang** beautifully at the concert last night.
	Her parents **enjoyed** the concert.

Future tense is used to express an action that will take place in the future. To form the future tense, use the helping verb *shall* or *will* with the present form.

FUTURE TENSE	I **shall watch** the awards program again this year.
	Megan **will sing** at the concert tomorrow night.
	Her parents probably **will enjoy** the concert.

In formal English, *shall* is used with *I* and *we,* and *will* is used with *you, he, she, it,* or *they*. In informal speech, however, *shall* and *will* are used interchangeably with *I* and *we* except for questions, which still use *shall*.

You can learn more about shall *and* will *on page L447.*

Present perfect tense is the first of the three perfect tenses. The present perfect tense expresses an action that was completed at some indefinite time in the past. It also expresses an action that started in the past and is still going on. To form the present perfect tense, add *has* or *have* to the past participle.

Present Perfect Tense	I **have watched** the award program for several years now. Megan **has sung** here before now. Her parents **have enjoyed** watching her perform.

Past perfect tense expresses an action that took place before some other action in the past. To form the past perfect tense, add *had* to the past participle.

Past Perfect Tense	I **had watched** my video before I watched yours. Megan **had sung** the national anthem before the concert. Her parents **had enjoyed** listening to her rehearse.

Future perfect tense expresses an action that will take place before another future action or time. To form the future perfect tense, add *shall have* or *will have* to the past participle.

Future Perfect Tense	I **shall have watched** more than ten videos by Friday. By Saturday Megan **will have sung** at the concert. By Saturday Megan's parents **will have enjoyed** listening to all the music.

Verb Conjugation

One way to see or study all the tenses of a particular verb is to look at a conjugation of that verb. A **conjugation** is a list of all the singular and plural forms of a verb in its various tenses.

Regular verbs are conjugated like irregular verbs. The only variations result from the differences in the principal parts of the verbs themselves. Following is a conjugation of the irregular verb *ride,* whose four principal parts are *ride, riding, rode,* and *ridden*.

SIMPLE TENSES OF THE VERB *RIDE*

Singular	Plural
Present	
I ride	we ride
you ride	you ride
he, she, it rides	they ride
Past	
I rode	we rode
you rode	you rode
he, she, it rode	they rode
Future	
I shall/will ride	we shall/will ride
you will ride	you will ride
he, she, it will ride	they will ride

PERFECT TENSES OF THE VERB *RIDE*

Singular	Plural
Present Perfect Tense	
I have ridden	we have ridden
you have ridden	you have ridden
he, she, it has ridden	they have ridden
Past Perfect Tense	
I had ridden	we had ridden
you had ridden	you had ridden
he, she, it had ridden	they had ridden

Future Perfect Tense	
Singular	**Plural**
I shall/will have ridden	we shall/will have ridden
you will have ridden	you will have ridden
he, she, it will have ridden	they will have ridden

The present participle is used to conjugate only the progressive forms of a verb. You can learn more about those verbs on pages 307–308.

Since the principal parts of the verb *be* are highly irregular, the conjugation of that verb is different from other irregular verbs. Following is the conjugation of the verb *be,* whose four principal parts are *am, being, was,* and *been.*

SIMPLE TENSES OF THE VERB *BE*	
Present	
Singular	**Plural**
I am	we are
you are	you are
he, she, it is	they are
Past	
Singular	**Plural**
I was	we were
you were	you were
he, she, it was	they were
Future	
Singular	**Plural**
I shall/will be	we shall/will be
you will be	you will be
he, she, it will be	they will be

PERFECT TENSES OF THE VERB *BE*	
Present Perfect Tense	
SINGULAR	**PLURAL**
I have been	we have been
you have been	you have been
he, she, it has been	they have been
Past Perfect Tense	
SINGULAR	**PLURAL**
I had been	we had been
you had been	you had been
he, she, it had been	they had been
Future Perfect Tense	
SINGULAR	**PLURAL**
I shall/will have been	we shall/will have been
you will have been	you will have been
he, she, it will have been	they will have been

CONNECT TO WRITER'S CRAFT

You have probably noticed that most folk literature is written in the past tense, as is this excerpt from "Hansel and Gretel."

> Hard by a great forest dwelt a poor wood-cutter with his wife and his two children. The boy was called Hansel and the girl Gretel. He had little to bite and to break, and once when great dearth fell on the land, he could no longer procure even daily bread.
>
> —*Grimm Brothers,* "Hansel and Gretel"

When you write about the literature you read, however, it is proper to write about it in the present tense. For example, if you were to write about the passage above, you might say:

The story of "Hansel and Gretel" opens with a description of the sad state of the children's family. Hansel and Gretel live with their father and his wife in a great forest. They barely ever have enough food, and it soon becomes impossible for the wood-cutter to get any food at all to feed his family.

Practice Your Skills

Check Your Understanding
Identifying Verb Tense

General Interest **Write the tense of each underlined verb.**

1. Today popular bands make videos for each of their hit songs.
2. Prior to 1980, filming music videos was rare.
3. Before that year musicians had recorded only audio albums.
4. Even today many bands have never produced any professional recordings of their music.
5. Recording an album in a music studio costs a great deal of money.
6. Writers have composed many songs for other musicians to play.
7. Most people will probably never hear these songs on the radio.
8. Famous singers and bands earn a considerable amount of money.
9. By age eighteen, you will have seen many music videos on television.
10. You will likely watch even more after that.

Check Your Understanding
Using Tenses of the Verb Be

History Topic **For each blank, write the tense of the verb *be* that is indicated in parentheses.**

11. The history of the monarchy in England ■ (present) truly interesting.

12. Many scholars ■ (present) experts in this area of British history.

13. Many men and women ■ (past perfect) rulers of England.

14. King John always ■ (future) famous as the signer of the Magna Carta.

15. Lady Jane Grey ■ (past) queen of England for only nine days.

16. Henry VIII's son Edward ■ (past perfect) ruler before her.

17. Mary ■ (past) queen of England before her half-sister Elizabeth I.

18. King James I ■ (present) famous for the English version of the Bible begun during his reign.

19. In the year 2003, Elizabeth I ■ (future perfect) dead for four hundred years.

20. Who ■ (future) the next monarch of Britain?

Connect to the Writing Process: Drafting
Using Verb Tense

Write sentences, using the tense of the verb indicated.

21. Present tense of *share*

22. Past tense of *sell*

23. Future tense of *speak*

24. Present perfect tense of *know*

25. Past perfect tense of *drink*

26. Future perfect tense of *run*

27. Future tense of *wear*

28. Present perfect tense of *lay*

29. Past perfect tense of *rise*

30. Future perfect tense of *set*

Communicate Your Ideas

APPLY TO WRITING

Friendly Letter: ***Verb Tenses***

Artist unknown. (Detail) *Queen Tiy, from the Tomb of Userhat,* 18th dynasty. Limestone relief, 16¾ by 15½ inches. Courtesy Musées Royaux d'Art et d'Histoire, Brussels, Belgium.

Imagine that you are the Egyptian queen whose face is carved in the pharaoh's tomb. Write a letter to your sister, who will be coming to visit you soon. Describe for her what a typical day is like at your palace. What do you do to occupy your time? What will you and your sister do when she comes to visit you? Use your imagination to make the letter seem realistic. After you have written your letter, underline seven verbs you have used. Above each verb, label its tense.

Progressive Verb Forms

Each of the six verb tenses has a progressive form. The **progressive form** is used to express continuing or ongoing action. To form the progressive, add a form of the *be* verb to the present participle. Notice in the following examples that all the progressive forms end in *–ing*.

Present Progressive	I am riding.
Past Progressive	I was riding.
Future Progressive	I will (shall) be riding.
Present Perfect Progressive	I have been riding.
Past Perfect Progressive	I had been riding.
Future Perfect Progressive	I will (shall) have been riding.

The **present progressive form** shows an ongoing action that is taking place now.

I **am eating** very hot soup.

Occasionally the present progressive can be used to show action in the future when the sentence contains an adverb or a phrase that indicates the future—such as *tomorrow* or *next month.*

I **am eating** at a restaurant tomorrow night.

The **past progressive form** shows an ongoing action that took place in the past.

I **was eating** hot French onion soup when I burned my tongue.

The **future progressive form** shows an ongoing action that will take place in the future.

> By six o'clock tonight, I **will be eating** Grandma's delicious soup.

The **present perfect progressive form** shows an ongoing action that is continuing in the present.

> I **have been eating** Grandma's soup my whole life.

The **past perfect progressive form** shows an ongoing action in the past that was interrupted by another past action.

> I **had been eating** Grandma's soup when the doorbell rang.

The **future perfect progressive form** shows a future ongoing action that will have taken place by a stated future time.

> I **will have been eating** Grandma's soup for at least twenty-one years by the time I graduate from college.

Practice Your Skills

Check Your Understanding
Identifying Progressive Verb Forms

Contemporary Life **Write the verbs in the following sentences. Then write which progressive form of the verb is used.**

1. Grandma has been cooking famous dishes for more than forty years.
2. She was serving a variety of great soups and stews before my mother's birth.
3. Until recently, her neighbors had been begging her for the recipes.
4. Now I am helping Grandma with her latest project.
5. We have been writing down all her recipes.

6. Next year a local company will be publishing her recipes in a cookbook.
7. By then Grandma will have been serving her soups for a half century.
8. We are hoping the cookbook will sell well.
9. Grandma has been dreaming of a trip to Paris.
10. My entire family will be joining her on the trip.

Connect to the Writing Process: Drafting
Writing Sentences

Write sentences, using the indicated progressive form of the verb.

11. Past progressive of *go*
12. Future progressive of *swim*
13. Present perfect progressive of *give*
14. Past perfect progressive of *freeze*
15. Future perfect progressive of *lose*

Communicate Your Ideas

APPLY TO WRITING

Writer's Craft: ***Analyzing the Use of the Past Progressive Form***

Writers often use the past progressive form in their writing. In this paragraph from *The Liar's Club*, Mary Karr describes an incident at the beach when her sister Lecia was stung by a jellyfish. Read the paragraph and then follow the directions.

> The guy in the camouflage pants had dragged Lecia out of the water while I was fetching my parents. He was kneeling beside her with his pink grandma gloves on when we came up. Lecia sat on the sand with her legs straight out in front of her like some drugstore doll. She had stopped squealing. In fact, she had a glassy look, as

if the leg with the man-of-war fastened to it belonged to some other girl. She wasn't even crying, though every now and then she sucked in air through her teeth like she hurt. The camouflaged guy with the pink gloves was trying to peel the tentacles off her, but it was clumsy work. Mother was looking at Daddy and saying what should they do. She said this over and over, and Daddy didn't appear to be listening.

—*Mary Karr,* The Liar's Club

- Write all the progressive verbs from the passage. Be careful not to confuse gerunds (verb forms used as nouns) with progressive verbs.
- In the first sentence, how does the verb "had dragged" function with "was fetching," which appears later in the sentence?
- How does Karr's use of progressive verb forms work to make the action seem more vivid?

Shifts in Tense

When you write, it is important to keep your tenses consistent. For example, if you are telling a story that took place in the past, use the past tense of verbs. If you suddenly shift to the present, you will confuse your readers.

Avoid unnecessary shifts in tense within a sentence or with related sentences.

INCORRECT	I **opened** (past) the front door, and something **flies** (present) past me.
CORRECT	I **opened** (past) the front door, and something **flew** (past) past me.
CORRECT	I **open** (present) the front door, and something **flies** (present) past me.

INCORRECT When the excitement **had passed,** I **looked** (past) around in the hallway. I **find** (present) a baseball on the floor.

CORRECT When the excitement **had passed,** (past perfect) I **looked** (past) around in the hallway. I **found** (past) a baseball on the floor.

Notice that there is a change of tense here, from *had passed* (past perfect) to *looked* and *found* (simple past). Sometimes more than one tense is needed to show a sequence of events.

PRACTICE YOUR SKILLS

Check Your Understanding

Identifying Shifts in Tense

Sports Topic

If the sentence contains a shift in tense, change the second verb to the correct tense. If a sentence is correct, write *C*.

1. Babe Ruth was born in 1895, and his birth name is George Herman Ruth.
2. Ruth learned to play baseball in school, and a priest helps him get his first job with the Baltimore Orioles.
3. When Ruth started his professional career, he earned six hundred dollars for his first season.
4. Babe Ruth began his career as a pitcher, but he is later shifted to the outfield.
5. Because he was such an amazing hitter, the manager wants him to play every game.
6. The Orioles sold him to the Boston Red Sox, who later sell him to the New York Yankees.
7. He had his best year in 1927, when he knocks in a season record of sixty home runs.

8. Even though he was famous and popular on the field, Babe Ruth has problems off the field.
9. He got in trouble, and in 1925 he is suspended for his behavior off the field.
10. In 1935, he joined the Boston Braves, but before the end of that season, he has quit playing the game.
11. Today baseball is still the popular sport it has been in the past.
12. Each year thousands of fans have flocked to stadiums across the country.
13. Fans always eagerly await the playoffs because the games were so intense.
14. Do you hope the team you watched last year also will have won this year?
15. Whichever team wins the World Series will have had an excellent year.

Connect to the Writing Process: Revising

Correcting Shifts in Tense

History Topic **Rewrite the following paragraph, correcting shifts in tense.**

Modern baseball was once named town ball. It first become popular in the United States in the 1830s. Wooden stakes are the bases, and the playing field is square. A pitcher is called a feeder, and a batter was called a striker. After a batter hits the ball, he ran clockwise. After a fielder catches the ball, he gets a runner out by hitting him with the ball. In the early days of baseball, balls are soft and are made by winding yarn around a piece of rubber.

Communicate Your Ideas

APPLY TO WRITING

Persuasive Article: ***Verb Tenses***

What is your favorite sport? Why do you like it? A sports magazine has asked its readers to write a short article to persuade other people to watch their favorite sport. Write a short article for the magazine, persuading others to enjoy your favorite sport. As you write, be careful to avoid inappropriate shifts in verb tense. Read your article aloud to a classmate, having him or her listen for shifts in tense. Correct any errors and submit a final copy to your teacher.

Mixed Practice

Music Topic

Rewrite the paragraph below, correcting any incorrect verb forms or shifts in tense.

Mozart's father play in a string quartet. One day the quartet had planned to practice at his home. When the second violinist did not appear, Mozart takes his place. Even though he had never saw the music before, Mozart plays it perfectly. Mozart was only five years old at the time! Three years later Mozart written his first complete symphony. No one has ever doubted that Mozart is the greatest musical genius of his time.

Active and Passive Voice

In addition to tense, a verb has voice. A verb is used in either the active voice or the passive voice.

The **active voice** indicates that the subject is performing the action.

The **passive voice** indicates that the action of the verb is being performed upon the subject.

In the following examples, the same verb is used in the active voice in one sentence and the passive voice in the other. The verb in the active voice has a direct object. The verb in the passive voice does not have a direct object.

Active Voice	Our world history class **studied** the history of Chile.
	(*History* is the direct object.)
Passive Voice	The history of Chile **was studied** by our world history class.
	(There is no direct object.)

You can learn more about direct objects on pages L149–L151.

Use of the Active and Passive Voice

Only **transitive verbs**—verbs that take direct objects—can be used in the passive voice. When an active verb is changed to passive, the direct object of the active verb becomes the subject of the passive verb. The subject of the active verb can be used in a prepositional phrase.

ACTIVE VOICE	Pedro de Valdivia founded **Santiago, Chile,** (direct object) in 1541.
PASSIVE VOICE	**Santiago, Chile,** (subject) was founded by Pedro de Valdivia in 1541.

A verb in the passive voice consists of a form of the verb *be* plus a past participle.

Early explorers **were startled** by Chile's unfamiliar animals.

Llamas **are** still **used** as beasts of burden in South America.

Use the active voice as much as possible. It adds greater directness and forcefulness to your writing. However, you should use the passive voice when the doer of the action is unknown or unimportant. Also use it when you want to emphasize the receiver of the action.

Notebooks of the early Spanish explorers **will be displayed** at our local museum.
(The doer is unknown.)

Grand descriptions of llamas and other animals **were recorded** by early explorers.
(Emphasis is on the receiver, *descriptions*.)

PRACTICE YOUR SKILLS

Check Your Understanding

Recognizing Active and Passive Voice

Literature Topic **Write the verb in each sentence and label it *A* for active or *P* for passive.**

1. Literature is respected by Chileans.
2. Many poems were written by Chile's most famous poet, Pablo Neruda.
3. He continued his education in Santiago.

4. His life was devoted to writing poetry.
5. Neruda also served the government of Chile as a diplomat.
6. He accepted the Lenin Peace Prize in 1953.
7. His collection *Spain in the Heart* was written during the Spanish Civil War.
8. Neruda is remembered for such poems as "General Song."
9. Many critics consider that poem to be his greatest work.
10. Pablo Neruda was awarded the prestigious Nobel Prize in 1971.

Connect to the Writing Process: Revising
Changing Verbs to Active Voice

History Topic **Rewrite the following paragraph, changing passive-voice verbs to active voice, if appropriate.**

In 1814, the small South American country of Chile was ruled by Spain. However, the freedom of Chile was being fought for by Bernardo O'Higgins and a small band of Chilean patriots. For a while all seemed lost for them. Then an unusual idea came to O'Higgins. A large herd of sheep, mules, goats, and dogs was rounded up by O'Higgins's men. When the Chileans startled the animals, they charged off toward the Spaniards. The Spaniards, of course, got out of their way, and right behind the animals were the patriots. After the battle the Chileans reorganized in the hills. Eventually the Spaniards were defeated by them.

Communicate Your Ideas

APPLY TO WRITING

Movie Review: *Active and Passive Voice*

Your class is putting together a booklet for ninth graders about the best movies of all time. Write a review of your personal all-time favorite movie. It may be a recent film or something you saw when you were much younger. Use active-voice verbs to make your writing lively. If you use any passive-voice verbs, be prepared to explain why they are appropriate.

QuickCheck Mixed Practice

Science Topic

Rewrite the paragraph below, correcting any incorrect verb forms, shifts in tense, or inappropriate use of the passive voice.

The seafloor is littered by shipwrecks. Many of these sunken ships will contain treasures made of glass that have been perfectly preserved in the salty water. While the water protects the glass objects, they shrink and become brittle after they are bring to the surface. A way has been discovered by scientists to preserve these artifacts. The objects are submerged in silicone polymers, which invade the pores of the glass. Then the glass is covered in a thin layer of polymers that strengthened the glass and kept it from breaking. This technique has save many artifacts, including glass jars from a sixteenth-century sunken pirate hideout in Jamaica.

CheckPoint

Using the Correct Verb Form

Write the past or past participle form of each verb in parentheses.

1. Ten minutes after the downpour, the sun (come) out.
2. How long have you (know) about the party?
3. The sun (rise) at 5:36 yesterday.
4. Lake Erie has never (freeze) over completely.
5. My sister has (sing) twice on television.
6. Have you (write) your history report yet?
7. Who (write) the screenplay for that movie?
8. The telephone hasn't (ring) all day.
9. You should have (go) to the dance last night.
10. Dana has already (take) those books back to the library.
11. Before World War II, the United States had (give) the Philippines a guarantee of independence.
12. I should have (do) my homework earlier.
13. Until 1875, no one had ever successfully (swam) the English Channel.
14. My wallet hadn't been (steal) after all.
15. Who (choose) brown as the color for this room?
16. Tom (fall) off his skateboard yesterday, but fortunately he was wearing a helmet.
17. Have you ever (wear) those hiking boots on a hike of more than two miles?
18. Who (draw) that picture of Mr. Turner's barn?
19. Lately I have (grow) more confident using the laptop computer.
20. Waiting on the windy corner, we nearly (freeze).

Understanding Tenses

Write the tense of each underlined verb.

1. I am going to the library.
2. Lenny has seen Sarah somewhere before.
3. On Monday Mrs. Saunders will announce the names of the new class officers.
4. Tim was enthusiastic about the project.
5. I have been practicing for my recital every night for a month.
6. Next year will be the third year he will have played for the soccer team.
7. Laura discovered that she had left the tickets at home.
8. Pilar knows that we will be working together on the dance committee.
9. Marie has been happy ever since she won the CD player.
10. Susan and Greg were riding the bus when they first met.

Writing Sentences

Write ten sentences that follow the directions below. Write about a pet or a topic of your choice.

Write a sentence that...

1. includes the past tense of *choose.*
2. includes the past perfect tense of *become.*
3. includes the future tense of *take.*
4. includes the present perfect tense of *lie.*
5. includes the past tense of *lay.*
6. includes the present progressive tense of *rise.*
7. includes the future progressive tense of *set.*
8. includes the present tense of *be.*
9. includes any verb in the active voice.
10. includes any verb in the passive voice.

Language and *Self-Expression*

This sculpture shows the tail fins of ten cars buried hood-down in a field in Texas. When its artists visited the field for the first time, they were greeted by an expanse of gently blowing wheat. The rippling waves reminded one artist of an ocean. When he visualized dolphins leaping gracefully from its surface, the idea for the sculpture was born.

A dazzling sight in nature ignited the creativity behind *Cadillac Ranch.* What scenes in nature have inspired your creativity? Think of such a sight—perhaps a vividly colored shell, an imposing mountain, or shadows in a forest. Write a personal narrative that describes what you saw and what it inspired—a poem, a rap song, a photographic collage, or a special conversation, for example. Select verb forms and tenses that will tell your story. Also use the active voice as much as possible. Share your narrative with a small group of classmates.

Prewriting Begin by freewriting about the object or scene that inspired you. Then plan a beginning, middle, and end for your narrative. The beginning will describe what you saw; the middle will describe what it inspired; the end will summarize these details.

Drafting Write your narrative, using ideas from your freewriting and plan. Choose active verbs whenever possible.

Revising Read your narrative aloud, marking places that need work. After you have made changes, ask a classmate to read your story. Ask whether the sequence of your story is easy to follow.

Editing Check your story for errors in spelling and punctuation and check for consistency of tenses.

Publishing Prepare a final copy of your narrative. Read it to a group of classmates.

Another Look

The **principal parts of a verb** are the *present,* the *present participle,* the *past,* and the *past participle.*

Regular and Irregular Verbs

A **regular verb** forms its past and past participle by adding *-ed* or *-d* to the present form. *(pages L279–L280)*

An **irregular verb** does not form its past and past participle by adding *-ed* or *-d* to the present form. *(pages L281–L288)*

Verb Tense

The time expressed by a verb is called the **tense** of a verb. The six tenses of a verb are the *present, past, future, present perfect, past perfect,* and *future perfect.* *(pages L298–L300)*

Progressive Verb Forms

Each of the six verb tenses has a **progressive form.** The progressive forms are used to express continuing or ongoing action. To form the progressive, add a form of the *be* verb to the present participle. All progressive forms end in *–ing.*

The progressive forms of a verb are the *present progressive, past progressive, future progressive, present perfect progressive, past perfect progressive,* and the *future perfect progressive.* *(pages L307–L308)*

Active and Passive Voice

The **active voice** indicates that the subject is performing the action. *(pages L314–L315)*

The **passive voice** indicates that the action of the verb is being performed upon the subject. *(pages L314–L315)*

Other Information About Verbs

Using consistent verb tenses *(pages L310–L311)*

Distinguishing among problem verbs *(pages L292–L294)*

Directions

Read the passage and choose the word or group of words that belongs in each underlined space. Write the letter of the correct answer.

EXAMPLE For the past few summers, action films __(1)__ the list of popular movies.

1 **A** top
B will top
C are topping
D have topped

ANSWER **1** **D**

Yesterday my sister and I __(1)__ the movie *A Wild Ride.* The story __(2)__ on an actual event. Joe, the main character, __(3)__ money from his boss for years until he was caught. My sister __(4)__ the movie three times already. She probably __(5)__ to the same movie again! She __(6)__ to one movie a week since last June. My favorite scene __(7)__ at the end of the movie. Three police officers __(8)__ Joe in a dense forest after he had made his break from prison. He __(9)__ to escape through a secret tunnel before they made their move. Since yesterday I __(10)__ to tell everyone I know how the movie ends.

1 **A** see
B saw
C will see
D will be seeing

2 **A** is basing
B was basing
C will be based
D is based

3 **A** steals
B is stealing
C had been stealing
D will steal

4 **A** sees
B will see
C has been seeing
D has seen

5 **A** goes
B will go
C will have been going
D went

6 **A** is going
B has gone
C will go
D will be going

7 **A** has happened
B will have happened
C happened
D is happening

8 **A** will surround
B will have surrounded
C surrounded
D will be surrounding

9 **A** was hoping
B hopes
C will hope
D is hoping

10 **A** will want
B have been wanting
C am wanting
D will have been wanting

CHAPTER 11

Using Pronouns

Directions

Read the passage and choose the pronoun that belongs in each underlined space. Write the letter of the correct answer.

EXAMPLE Ms. Key, __(1)__ teaches algebra, always gives difficult tests.

1 **A** whose
B whoever
C who
D whom

ANSWER **1** **C**

The students in Ms. Key's class knew that __(1)__ would have to study hard for the test. Jan and Marisa asked Jeff, __(2)__ they always called for help, to study with __(3)__. __(4)__ all agreed to meet at Jan's house that afternoon. Both Marisa and Jeff brought __(5)__ review notes. Marisa gave __(6)__ to Jan to look over. Jan, __(7)__ notes were messy, was relieved that her friend took better notes. Jan was also glad to study with Jeff, __(8)__ knew more about solving equations than __(9)__. However, neither Jeff nor Marisa could match __(10)__ skill at graphing.

1 **A** they
B it
C them
D he

2 **A** he
B whose
C whom
D who

3 **A** they
B them
C she
D her

4 **A** He
B She
C They
D Them

5 **A** them
B their
C her
D our

6 **A** her
B his
C them
D hers

7 **A** whose
B who
C whom
D whomever

8 **A** him
B he
C who
D she

9 **A** her
B hers
C she
D him

10 **A** they
B their
C her
D hers

William H. Johnson. *Jitterbugs I,* ca. 1940–1941. Oil on plywood, 39¾ by 31¼ inches. National Museum of American Art, Washington, D.C./ Art Resource, New York.

Describe Describe the man and woman in the painting. What are they wearing? What colors and patterns does the artist use?

Analyze What kind of music do you imagine is playing in this room? Why do you think so?

Interpret How do you think a writer of a descriptive paragraph helps his or her audience "hear" music?

Judge Do you feel that this painting or a written description would be more effective in capturing the mood and sound of lively music? Why do you think so?

At the end of this chapter, you will use the artwork to stimulate ideas for writing.

The Cases of Personal Pronouns

In German, words change their form depending upon how they are used in a sentence. You say *kinder* if *children* is the subject, but *kindern* if *children* is the indirect object. This is because all nouns and pronouns have case.

Case is the form of a noun or a pronoun that indicates its use in a sentence.

There are three cases in English: the nominative case, the objective case, and the possessive case. Unlike nouns in German, nouns in English change form only in the possessive case. For example, *Mary* is the nominative form and is used as a subject. *Mary* is also the objective form and is used as an object. *Mary's,* though, is the possessive form and is used to show that Mary has or owns something. Unlike nouns, pronouns usually change form for each of the three cases.

NOMINATIVE CASE	
(Used for subjects and predicate nominatives)	
SINGULAR	I, you, he, she, it
PLURAL	we, you, they
OBJECTIVE CASE	
(Used for direct objects, indirect objects, and the objects of a preposition)	
SINGULAR	me, you, him, her, it
PLURAL	us, you, them
POSSESSIVE CASE	
(Used to show ownership or possession)	
SINGULAR	my, mine, your, yours, his, her, hers, its
PLURAL	our, ours, your, yours, their, theirs

Practice Your Skills

Check Your Understanding

Determining Case

Contemporary Life

Write the pronouns in each sentence. Then identify the case of each pronoun, using *N* for nominative, *O* for objective, and *P* for possessive.

1. Why wasn't he invited to Anila's party?
2. I hope Anila left me directions to her house.
3. My sister will pick us up after Anila's party.
4. Did my brother go with them to the party?
5. We don't know whether the present they left in the chair is his or hers.
6. They often speak of their respect for Anila.
7. Our friends like to go to your parties rather than ours.
8. You should speak to them about the awful music they play.
9. She knew that the best present was mine.
10. Are the decorations yours or theirs?
11. A professional planned my mother's last party.
12. That party was more successful than our other parties have been.
13. My mother's friends said they were very impressed.
14. When the party ended, we thanked them for coming.
15. The party took a large amount of work, but it was a complete success.
16. Businesses often have their summer parties in June.
17. We went to a summer party last year, and it was fun.
18. I ate watermelon and went swimming.
19. Our friends were there enjoying the fun with us.
20. We would like her to go with us to the next party scheduled.

Nominative Case

The personal pronouns in the nominative case are *I, you, he, she, it, we,* and *they*.

The **nominative case** is used for subjects and predicate nominatives.

Pronouns Used As Subjects

Pronoun subjects are always in the nominative case.

SUBJECTS If **they** are late, **we** will keep the food warm for at least an hour.

She and **I** are chopping the vegetables.

Choosing the right case for a single subject does not usually present any problem. Errors occur more often, however, when the subject is compound, but there is a test that will help you check your choice.

Eric and (she, her) are cooking dinner tonight for twenty-seven guests.

To find the correct answer, say each choice separately as if it were a single subject.

She is cooking dinner tonight for twenty-seven guests.
Her is cooking dinner tonight for twenty-seven guests.

Separating the choices makes it easier to see and hear which pronoun is correct. The nominative case *she* is the correct form to use.

Eric and **she** are cooking tonight for twenty-seven guests.

You can learn more about compound subjects on page 18.

You can also use this test when both parts of a compound subject are pronouns.

(He, Him) and (she, her) planned the menu.
(She, Her) and (I, me) enjoyed the food.

Try each choice alone as the subject of the sentence.

He planned the menu.
Him planned the menu.
She planned the menu.
Her planned the menu.

She enjoyed the food.
Her enjoyed the food.
I enjoyed the food.
Me enjoyed the food.

You can see that the correct choices are *he* and *she* in the first sentence, and *she* and *I* in the second.

He and **she** planned the menu.
She and **I** enjoyed the food.

A pronoun that is used as a subject can also have a noun appositive. An **appositive** is a word that comes right after the pronoun and identifies or renames it. The appositive in each of the following sentences is underlined.

We siblings worked together to cook dinner.

I, the assistant chef, worked hard.

An appositive, however, will never affect the case of a pronoun. In fact, you can check whether you have used the correct pronoun by dropping the appositive.

We worked together to cook dinner.
I worked hard.

You can learn more about appositives on pages L183–L185.

PRACTICE YOUR SKILLS

Check Your Understanding

Using Nominative Pronouns as Subjects

Contemporary Life **Write the correct form of the pronoun in parentheses.**

1. My brother Chris and (I, me) love to cook together.
2. (Him, He) can cook great Italian specialties.
3. (They, Them) are his most delicious dishes.
4. When our mom works late, (us, we) prepare the meals.
5. When (he, him) cooks, our neighbor always calls.
6. (Her, She) can smell Chris's lasagna baking.
7. (We, Us) all learned how to cook from our mom.
8. (She, Her) felt that both boys and girls should have this skill.
9. When (we, us) were tall enough to reach the counter, (her, she) put us to work in the kitchen.
10. Before my little brother could walk, (he, him) was tossing salads.
11. Before my dad met my mom, (him, he) had never touched a stove.
12. When Mom married Dad, (her, she) taught him to cook better, too.
13. (She, Her) and (he, him) like to cook spicy dishes.
14. Although (us, we) are all good cooks, Chris is the best.
15. Now (he, him) needs to learn to clean up the kitchen when (he, him) finishes cooking!
16. (I, me) am usually the one who gets to wash the dishes.
17. Sometimes Chris helps, but (he, him) is not very good at it.
18. (We, Us) all joke about Chris's sloppiness.
19. Even (he, him) sees the humor in it.
20. Mom says that (she, her) thinks Chris is a comedian.

Pronouns Used as Predicate Nominatives

A **predicate nominative** is a noun or a pronoun that follows a linking verb and identifies or renames the subject.

PREDICATE NOMINATIVE — The best speller on the team was **he.**

(speller = he)

The finalists were **she** and Greg.

(finalists = she and Greg)

Sometimes using a pronoun as a predicate nominative sounds awkward even though the pronoun is correct. When you write, you can avoid awkwardness if you reword a sentence, making the predicate nominative the subject.

AWKWARD — The team captain last year was **she.**

The last person to join the team was **he.**

NATURAL — **She** was the team captain last year.

He was the last person to join the team.

A pronoun that is used as a predicate nominative can also have a noun appositive. The appositives in the following sentences are underlined.

The biggest supporters of the team are **we** <u>freshmen</u>.

The most enthusiastic fan of all is **I**, <u>Lisa</u>.

An appositive, however, will never affect the case of a pronoun. In fact, you can check whether you have used the correct pronoun by dropping the appositive and making the predicate nominative the subject.

We are the biggest supporters of the team.

I am the most enthusiastic fan of all.

Connect to Speaking and Writing

In everyday conversation, people do not always use the nominative case for predicate nominatives. It is common to hear someone say, "It's ***me***" instead of "It is ***I,***" or "That's ***him***" instead of "That is ***he.***" While this usage is common in conversation, you should avoid it when you write.

You can find a list of linking verbs on page L75. You can find out more about predicate nominatives on pages L154–L155.

Practice Your Skills

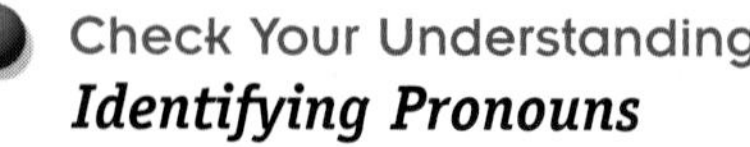

Check Your Understanding
Identifying Pronouns

Oral Expression **Read the sentence aloud, saying each pronoun separately. Decide which pronoun is correct. Try turning each sentence around, making the predicate nominative the subject.**

1. The coach of the spelling team is (he, him).
2. Our toughest opponents are (them, they).
3. The winners of the championship will be (we, us).
4. Our most enthusiastic supporters are Robert and (she, her).
5. The team's best spellers are (we, us) girls.

Check Your Understanding
Pronouns as Predicate Nominatives

Contemporary Life **Write the correct form of the pronoun in parentheses.**

6. Action movies are great, and my favorite films are (they, them).
7. My favorite actor in these movies is (he, him).
8. By far the most exciting films are (they, them).

9. When a new action movie is showing, the first people in line are (us, we).
10. Two other big fans of these movies are Kassidy and (he, him).
11. The best actress to watch is (her, she).
12. I love the parts with special effects; my favorite scenes are (them, they).
13. The finest director of action movies is (he, him).
14. The most realistic movies of the genre are (they, them).
15. The fittest stars in Hollywood are (them, they) who star in these movies.

Check Your Understanding
Supplying Pronouns in the Nominative Case

Contemporary Life

Complete each sentence by writing an appropriate pronoun in the nominative case.

16. Do not make a decision about transferring to another school until ■ have voted.
17. The only people voting will be ■ students in the ninth grade.
18. The person who ran for class president was ■.
19. ■ had to wait in line to vote.
20. The two most popular candidates for vice president were Fallon and ■.
21. Neither Antoine nor ■ ran for an office.
22. No one can predict whether ■ will be elected.
23. If ■ are patient, we will know the answer soon.
24. The votes have been counted, and the new class president is ■.
25. ■ students are all glad that we voted.
26. Now the new president must prove that ■ is up to the job.
27. Many students think that ■ should run for office next year.

Connect to the Writing Process: Editing

Using Nominative Case Pronouns

Rewrite the sentences, correcting any errors in pronoun usage. If the sentence is correct, write *C*.

28. Us girls decided to start a neighborhood swim team.

29. Our weakest swimmer is either Sammi or she.

30. We will practice hard before our first meet.

31. The best teams in the league are that group of boys and them.

32. The other teams and us will work hard to win the tournament.

APPLY TO WRITING

Friendly Letter: ***Nominative Case Pronouns***

Your friend has just suffered a great disappointment. Perhaps he or she lost an election or an important game. Write a letter to your friend, giving him or her advice about dealing with this outcome. Tell your friend about someone you've known or read about who dealt with a similar situation. As you write your letter, include at least four nominative pronouns. Use two of these pronouns as predicate nominatives. After you write, underline all of the nominative pronouns you used.

Objective Case

The personal pronouns in the objective case are *me, you, him, her, it, us,* and *them.*

The **objective case** is used for direct objects, indirect objects, and objects of a preposition.

Pronouns Used as Direct and Indirect Objects

A **direct object** answers the question *What?* or *Whom?* after an action verb. If a sentence has a direct object, it also can have an indirect object. An **indirect object** answers the questions *To or For Whom?* or *To or For What?*

DIRECT OBJECT — Carlos will join **us** when he returns. (Carlos will join whom? *Us* is the direct object.)

Mom took **him** to the dentist.

INDIRECT OBJECT — Dr. Garcia showed **him** X-rays of his teeth. (*X-rays* is the direct object. Dr. Garcia showed the X-rays to whom? *Him* is the indirect object.)

Please give **me** a new toothbrush.

Use the same test you used for compound subjects to find the correct pronoun in a compound direct or indirect object.

Please take Carlos and (he, him) with you.
Please take **he** with you.
Please take **him** with you.

Once more, it is easy to both see and hear that the objective case pronoun *him* is correct. Pronouns in the objective case can also have appositives.

Dr. Garcia's explanations really helped **us** patients.

PRACTICE YOUR SKILLS

Check Your Understanding
Using Pronouns as Direct and Indirect Objects

Contemporary Life — **Write the correct form of the pronoun in parentheses.**

1. Mom told (us, we) that it was time for our dental appointments.

2. Dr. Garcia, our dentist, always tells (I, me) jokes.
3. It helps (me, I) so that I relax.
4. He gives (we, us) new toothbrushes and dental floss.
5. Dr. Garcia also offers my brother and (I, me) good advice about cavity prevention.
6. My dad knew (him, he) in college.
7. My mother met (they, them) both when she visited their college campus.
8. Mom and Dad always tell (us, we) stories about Dr. Garcia in college.
9. My brother Carlos, who wants to be a dentist, especially admires (he, him).
10. Dr. Garcia lets Carlos watch (him, he) as he works.

Pronouns Used as Objects of Prepositions

An **object of a preposition** is always a part of a prepositional phrase.

OBJECTS OF PREPOSITIONS	That song was written for Pat and **me.** (*For Pat and me* is a prepositional phrase. *Pat* and *me* are the objects of the preposition *for*.)
	Singers like **her** are very rare.

If an object of a preposition is compound, use the same test you used for other compound objects. Say each pronoun separately.

Isn't Marta going with Jeff and (I, me) to the concert?
Isn't Marta going with **I** to the concert?
Isn't Marta going with **me** to the concert?

Again, it is easy to see and hear that the objective form *me* is the correct form to use.

You can find a list of commonly used prepositions on page L125.

CONNECT TO SPEAKING AND WRITING

A common mistake occurs with the preposition *between.* In trying to sound formal or correct, people will often use nominative-case pronouns after *between.* However, all pronouns used as objects of a preposition should be in the objective case. In this case, the more common-sounding expression is correct.

INCORRECT	The agreement is between he and I.
CORRECT	The agreement is between **him** and **me.** 

PRACTICE YOUR SKILLS

Check Your Understanding

Identifying Pronouns

Oral Expression

Read the sentence aloud, saying each pronoun carefully. Decide which pronoun is correct. If the object is compound, try saying each pronoun separately.

1. Hand the guitar to (she, her) or (he, him).
2. Between you and (I, me), she is a better guitar player than he is.
3. Brittany gave the microphone to (they, them) when she finished.
4. They sang a ballad for (we, us).
5. The audience offered a round of applause for all of (they, them).

Check Your Understanding

Using Pronouns as Objects of Prepositions

Contemporary Life

Write the correct form of the pronoun in parentheses.

6. For help there is no one like Madison or (he, him).
7. They have been very helpful to my friends and (I, me).

8. Madison and Will are leaders in our class and role models for (we, us).
9. Our class sponsors divide many of the class's duties between (they, them).
10. People like (she, her) are fun to have around.
11. Madison comes to every game and gives her support to Will and (I, me).
12. The rest of the team also looks to (she, her) for support.
13. No other freshman can come close to (she, her) in school spirit.
14. The students in our class should do something to recognize the efforts of (he, him) and (she, her).
15. When we are seniors, I hope that scholarships will be presented to (they, them).

Check Your Understanding

Supplying Pronouns in the Objective Case

Complete each sentence by writing an appropriate pronoun in the objective case. (Do not use *you* or *it*.) Then indicate how each pronoun is used by writing *D* for direct object, *I* for indirect object, or *O* for object of the preposition.

16. Aunt Laura gave ■ good advice.
17. Her point of view always comes as a big surprise to ■.
18. Uncle Fred usually agrees with ■.
19. After our visit he drove ■ back home.
20. He took ■ with us.
21. Did we send ■ a thank-you note for their hospitality?
22. Aunt Laura always gives ■ lots of attention.
23. Our family respects ■ immensely.
24. We wanted to do something special for ■.
25. He and I are throwing ■ a big birthday party next month.

Connect to the Writing Process: Drafting
Writing Sentences

Write ten sentences that use the expressions correctly.

26. Corey and I
27. us students
28. him and me
29. she and Jan
30. Don and he
31. you and me
32. we players
33. Mom, Dad, and I
34. she and I
35. Alex or her

Communicate Your Ideas

APPLY TO WRITING

Journal Entry: ***Nominative and Objective Case Pronouns***

Miguel Vivancos. *Village Feast,* 1951. Oil on canvas, approximately 22½ by 29¼ inches. Musée National d'Art Moderne, Centre Georges Pompidou, Paris.

Imagine you are a young child from the country, and you have come to the village on the special feast day depicted in this painting. At the day's end, you return home and sit down with your journal to record the exciting events at the feast. Write a vivid account of your day. After writing your journal entry, underline all the nominative and objective case personal pronouns you used. Write *N* above the nominative pronouns and *O* above the objective pronouns.

Mixed Practice

Contemporary Life

Write each pronoun that is in the wrong case. Then write each pronoun correctly. If a sentence is correct, write *C*.

1. Without you and I, the trip would have been boring.
2. We told Aaron and she funny stories as we drove.
3. During that trip we friends visited the city's boardwalk.
4. You and me rode the big, wooden roller coaster.
5. We bought saltwater taffy and had some shipped to our cousins and they.
6. Aaron invited we three for a picnic on the beach.
7. Our group ate a picnic lunch packed by Julie and he.
8. We shared a bag of chips among Aaron, you, and me.
9. I divided the leftover melon between Aaron and she.
10. Her and me are planning another trip for next summer.

Possessive Case

The **possessive case** is used to show ownership or possession.

The personal pronouns in the possessive case are *my, mine, your, yours, his, her, hers, its, our, ours, their,* and *theirs*. Some possessive pronouns can be used to show possession before a noun or a gerund. Others can be used by themselves.

BEFORE A NOUN	Kylie shared **her** latest set of poems with Alyssa.
BEFORE A GERUND	Ryan takes **his** writing seriously.
BY THEMSELVES	This pencil could be **mine.**

Personal possessive pronouns are not written with an apostrophe. Sometimes an apostrophe is incorrectly included because possessive nouns are written with an apostrophe.

POSSESSIVE NOUN	**Alyssa's** journal is on the table.
POSSESSIVE PRONOUN	The notebook is **hers.** (not her's)

Also, do not confuse a contraction with a possessive pronoun. *Its, your, their,* and *theirs* are possessive pronouns. *It's, you're, they're,* and *there's* are contractions.

POSSESSIVE PRONOUN	I like the story because of **its** characters.
CONTRACTION	**It's** (It is) time to share our ideas.

CONNECT TO SPEAKING AND WRITING

When you use an apostrophe with a pronoun, you can check whether you have written a contraction or a possessive pronoun. You can do this by removing the apostrophe and adding the letter that it replaced back into the word. Then read the sentence to see if the contraction was used properly or if you really needed to use a possessive pronoun.

CORRECT	You're such a good writer. (You are such a good writer.)
INCORRECT	I am you're writing partner. ("I am you are writing partner" does not make sense.)
CORRECT	It's his turn to walk the dogs. (It is his turn to walk the dogs.)
INCORRECT	We cannot find it's leash. ("We cannot find it is leash" does not make sense.)

Practice Your Skills

Check Your Understanding
Possessive Pronoun or Contraction?

Oral Expression

Read the following sentences aloud, saying the word with the apostrophe as two words. Then tell whether the form is correct.

1. It's a beautiful poem.

2. Are all of you're poems like this one?

3. You're going to keep writing.

4. Is you're story finished?

5. When did you send you're manuscript to them?

Check Your Understanding
Using Pronouns in the Possessive Case

Contemporary Life

Write the correct word in parentheses.

6. Are (their, they're) poems well written?

7. (Your, You're) article is due tomorrow.

8. That box of old writings is (hers, her's).

9. Joining the writers' group has improved (me, my) writing.

10. The poem that Ryan wrote doesn't fit (its, it's) title.

Check Your Understanding
Supplying Pronouns in All Cases

Contemporary Life

Complete the sentence by writing appropriate pronouns. (Do not use *you* or *it*.)

11. Read ■ and ■ your poem.

12. ■ listened to ■ and Alyssa read.

13. ■ helped ■ with new ideas for a story.

14. ■ thanked Ryan and ■.

15. Kylie showed ■ and ■ the new literary magazine.

16. ■ was writing with Alyssa and ■.

17. ■ went to the library with ■ for books about poets and playwrights.

Connect to the Writing Process: Drafting

Using Possessive Pronouns and Contractions

Write sentences using the following words correctly.

18. your
19. they're
20. its
21. ours
22. their
23. it's
24. hers
25. we're
26. his
27. theirs

Communicate Your Ideas

APPLY TO WRITING

Personal Narrative: ***Personal Pronouns***

Imagine that you are one of the people in the picture. You are playing a game of golf with some of your friends; you might even be on vacation. Write a personal narrative about the golf game. Before you begin, think about these questions:

- Who are the people in the picture and where was the picture taken?
- What particularly interesting thing happened while you were playing? Remember that you are more apt to hold a reader's interest with an unusual incident than with a chronological account of the game.

Then write your narrative. When you have finished, check that you have used pronouns correctly.

Mixed Practice

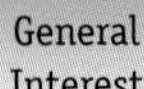

Write the correct word in parentheses.

1. Both wild and domesticated animals are very protective of (their, they're) young.
2. You should cautiously approach (your, you're) pet if (she, her) is a new parent.
3. (She, Her) is likely to act differently toward you and (your, you're) family.
4. You should give (she, her) a comfortable, secluded place to care for (her, hers) newborns.
5. A wild animal is even more likely to attack humans who come near (its, it's) young.
6. Each spring hikers are mauled by female bears protecting (their, they're) cubs.
7. The bear is just following (she, her) natural instincts.
8. The one to blame for such attacks is not (she, her).
9. (We, Us) hikers endanger ourselves when (we, us) come between a cub and (its, it's) mother.
10. Careful hikers make lots of noise to warn bears of (their, they're) presence when (they, them) walk through the wilderness.

Pronoun Problems

Pronoun choice can be a problem. Should you say, "Who is calling?" or "Whom is calling?" Should you say, "Is Jim taller than I?" or "Is Jim taller than me?" This section will cover these and other common pronoun problems.

Who or Whom?

The correct case of *who* is determined by how the pronoun is used in a question or a clause.

Who is a pronoun that changes its form depending on how it is used in a sentence.

	WHO* OR *WHOM?
NOMINATIVE CASE	who, whoever
OBJECTIVE CASE	whom, whomever
POSSESSIVE CASE	whose

Who and its related pronouns are used in questions and in subordinate clauses.

In Questions

Forms of *who* are often used in questions. The form you choose depends upon how the pronoun is used.

NOMINATIVE CASE — **Who** planned the school dance? (subject)

OBJECTIVE CASE — **Whom** did you call for that information? (direct object)

To whom is the invitation addressed? (object of the preposition *to*)

When deciding which form to use, turn a question around to its natural order.

QUESTION	**Whom** did you ask?
NATURAL ORDER	You did ask **whom.**

CONNECT TO SPEAKING AND WRITING

While *whom* is not used as much today in everyday speaking and writing, it is important to know its proper use. When you write formal papers and letters or prepare speeches and debates, be sure to use *whom* instead of *who* whenever appropriate.

PRACTICE YOUR SKILLS

Check Your Understanding

Using Forms of* Who *in Questions

Contemporary Life

Write the correct form of the pronoun in parentheses. Then indicate how each pronoun is used by writing *S* for subject, *D* for direct object, and *O* for object of the preposition.

1. (Who, Whom) is on the telephone?
2. (Who, Whom) told you that Ashley was going with me to the dance?
3. With (who, whom) did Paige say she was going?
4. (Who, Whom) will play the music at the dance?
5. From (who, whom) did you get an invitation to the dance?
6. (Who, Whom) sent you that note about the dance?
7. (Who, Whom) will you take to the dance?
8. (Who, Whom) is the best dancer in the ninth grade?
9. (Who, Whom) is designing the decorations?
10. With (who, whom) did you go to the dance last year?

In Clauses

Forms of *who* can be used in both adjective clauses and noun clauses. The form you use depends on how the pronoun is used within the clause—not on any word outside the clause. The following examples show how *who* and *whom* are used in adjective clauses.

NOMINATIVE CASE	Dr. Rush is the woman **who will serve as marshal of the parade.** (*Who* is the subject of *will serve.*)
OBJECTIVE CASE	She is the woman **whom you met yesterday.** (You met whom yesterday. *Whom* is the direct object of *met.*)
	Have you met Mr. Keats, **from whom we got our idea for the freshman float?** (We got our idea from whom. *Whom* is the object of the preposition *from.*)

The following examples show how forms of *who* are used in noun clauses.

NOMINATIVE CASE	The prize winners will be **whoever builds the best float**. (The entire noun clause is the predicate nominative of the sentence. *Whoever* is the subject of the noun clause.)
	Do you know **who organizes the homecoming parade?** (The entire noun clause is the direct object of the sentence. *Who* is the subject of the noun clause).
OBJECTIVE CASE	I don't know **by whom the parade is organized.** (The entire noun clause is the direct object. *Whom* is the object of the preposition *by.*

Invite **whomever you want to the homecoming game.** (The entire noun clause is the direct object of the sentence. *Whomever* is the direct object of *want.*)

PRACTICE YOUR SKILLS

Check Your Understanding
Using Forms of Who *in Clauses*

Contemporary Life

Write the correct form of the pronoun in parentheses. Then, using the following abbreviations, write how each pronoun is used in the clause.

subject = *subj.*
object of the preposition = *o.p.*
direct object = *d.o.*

1. Bailey doesn't know (who, whom) will lead the parade.
2. The organizers of the parade accept (whoever, whomever) they wish.
3. They couldn't tell to (who, whom) the entry form belonged.
4. (Whoever, Whomever) wins the title of homecoming queen will ride on the big float.
5. The person (who, whom) the most students vote for will win the title.
6. Does Shelly know (who, whom) will judge the competition for best float?
7. I spoke with the committee (who, whom) organized the parade.
8. They want all (who, whom) are participating in the parade to be lined up by three o'clock.
9. The people to (who, whom) I spoke informed me that the parade route had changed.
10. The parade will be led by two drum majors (who, whom) will be dressed in gold and white.

Connect to the Writing Process: Drafting

Writing Sentences Using Forms of Who

Write a sentence using the correct form of *who* or *whom* in the indicated construction.

11. as the object of a preposition

12. as the subject of a sentence

13. as the predicate nominative in a sentence

14. as the direct object of the verb in a noun clause

15. as the subject in an adjective clause

Communicate Your Ideas

APPLY TO WRITING

Explanation: *Forms of* Who

Your history teacher has asked you to write a 150-word essay titled "The Greatest Person Who Ever Lived." Choose a person—living or dead, famous or obscure—whom you feel deserves this designation. Write a short essay for your teacher, explaining why you feel that this person is important. As you write, use the following forms of *who* correctly at least once: *who, whom, whoever, whomever.*

Mixed Practice

General Interest **Write the correct form of the pronoun in parentheses.**

1. (Who, Whom) was the first president of the United States?

2. There are few Americans (who, whom) could not answer that question.

3. George Washington, (who, whom) is known as "the father of his country," was the first president.
4. He is a person about (who, whom) much history has been written.
5. Even in his own day, Washington did not fail to impress (whoever, whomever) he met.
6. Legend tells us it was George Washington (who, whom) could not lie to his father about chopping down a cherry tree.
7. History tells us that Washington led the Continental Army, against (who, whom) the British and their loyalists fought.
8. (Who, Whom) was the first vice president of the United States?
9. Few Americans know to (who, whom) this distinction belongs.
10. John Adams, (who, whom) was America's second president, was the nation's first vice president.

Pronouns in Comparisons

Over the years writers have introduced shortcuts into the language. One such shortcut, an **elliptical clause,** is a subordinate clause in which words are omitted but are understood to be there. Elliptical clauses begin with *than* or *as.*

Delisa takes more classes **than I.**
Noah takes as many classes **as she.**

In an elliptical clause, use the form of the pronoun you would use if the clause were completed.

In the examples at the top of the following page, both expressions in bold type are elliptical clauses. Both are also correct because they have two different meanings.

Delisa studies with us more **than he.**
Delisa studies with us more **than him.**

He is correct in the first example because it is used as the subject of the elliptical clause.

Delisa studies with us more **than *he* studies with us.**

Him is correct in the second example because it is used as an object of a preposition.

Delisa studies with us more **than she studies with *him*.**

Because the meaning of a sentence with an elliptical clause sometimes depends upon the case of a pronoun, be careful to choose the correct case. One way to do this is to complete the elliptical clause mentally before you say it or write it. Then choose the form of the pronoun that expresses the meaning you want.

Noah helps her as much as (I, me).
Noah helps her as much **as *I* help her.**
Noah helps her as much **as he helps *me*.**

In the previous example, decide which meaning you want. Then choose either *I* or *me.*

PRACTICE YOUR SKILLS

Check Your Understanding
Completing Elliptical Clauses

Oral Expression **Read the sentence aloud, completing the elliptical clause.**

1. Delisa is a better student than he.

2. She spends more time on her homework than I.

3. Jesse knows her better than we.

4. They study together more than we.

5. Jesse and Noah make better grades than we.
6. We work just as hard as they.
7. Noah likes math better than you.
8. Jesse and Delisa have won just as many awards as I.
9. I am just as pleased about my grades as they.
10. Noah will do just as well in school this semester as we.
11. Jessie is as good at science as I.
12. I study more than she.
13. Delisa made better grades this time than we.
14. Noah was not as happy about his grades as she.
15. He still made higher grades than I.

Check Your Understanding

Using Pronouns in Elliptical Clauses

Contemporary Life

Write each sentence, completing the elliptical clause. Then underline the pronoun you chose.

16. Noah spends more time at the library and in the computer lab than (I, me).
17. Our teacher didn't review the test with us as much as (they, them).
18. I studied longer and harder than (they, them).
19. The topic we covered sounds more exciting to them than (we, us).
20. Did you answer as many questions on the math test as (they, them)?
21. No one was more prepared than (I, me) for the last history quiz.
22. The professor from the university talked to us longer than (them, they).
23. That grade means more to Noah than (she, her).
24. Everyone should be as studious as (he, him).
25. I think Jesse is a better test taker than (I, me).

Connect to the Writing Process: Drafting
Writing Sentences with Elliptical Clauses

Write sentences that follow the instructions. Each sentence should contain an elliptical clause.

26. Compare a history class with a math class.

27. Compare two basketball players.

28. Compare two sports.

29. Compare two foods.

30. Compare two television shows.

31. Compare two Hollywood superstars.

32. Compare a summer vacation you had with an ideal winter vacation.

33. Compare your two favorite bands.

34. Compare two kinds of animals as pets.

35. Compare board games with video games.

Communicate Your Ideas

APPLY TO WRITING

Paragraph of Comparison: *Elliptical Clauses*

Your parents cannot understand why you like the music you do. They constantly ask you to turn down the volume on your stereo. Write a paragraph for your parents in which you compare and contrast your music to the music of their generation. Depending on their age and tastes, groups they may have listened to include the Rolling Stones, the Who, the Commodores, or the Bee Gees. Be sure to use elliptical clauses that begin with *than* or *as* to explain the differences and similarities between your music and that of your parents.

Pronouns and Their Antecedents

In Chapter 2 you learned that a pronoun takes the place of a noun. That noun is called the pronoun's antecedent. In the first example below, *Duke Ellington* is the antecedent of *his.* In the second example, *orchestra* is the antecedent of *its*.

> **Duke Ellington** left **his** mark on American music.
>
> Ellington's **orchestra** had **its** own sound.

A pronoun must agree in number and gender with its antecedent.

Number is the term used to indicate whether a noun or pronoun is singular or plural. **Singular** indicates one, and **plural** indicates more than one. **Gender** is the term used to indicate whether a noun or a pronoun is masculine, feminine, or neuter. Remember that the forms of *I, you,* and *they* do not show gender because they can be either masculine or feminine.

GENDER			
Masculine	he	him	his
Feminine	she	her	hers
Neuter	it	its	

If the antecedent of a pronoun is one word, there usually is no problem with agreement.

> The **man** playing the trumpet lowered **his** horn.
>
> The **listeners** showed **their** appreciation of the music.

If the antecedent of a pronoun is more than one word, there are two rules you should remember.

If two or more singular antecedents are joined by *or, nor, either/or,* or *neither/nor,* use a singular pronoun to refer to them.

These conjunctions indicate a choice. In the following example, Maria will play her long clarinet solo or Lacey will play her long clarinet solo.

> Either **Maria** or **Lacey** will play **her** long clarinet solo next.

If two or more singular antecedents are joined by *and* or *both/and,* use a plural pronoun to refer to them.

These conjunctions always indicate more than one. In the following example, Maria and Lacey—together—volunteered their help with the musical project.

> Both **Maria** and **Lacey** volunteered **their** help with the musical project.

Sometimes you will not know whether an antecedent is masculine or feminine. Standard written English solves this problem by using *his or her* to refer to such vague antecedents.

> Each orchestra **member** will donate two hours of **his or her** time to help with the project.
>
> Each **violinist** must practice **his or her** solo many times before the opening performance.

You can avoid this problem completely if you rewrite such sentences, using plural forms.

> All orchestra **members** will donate two hours of **their** time to help with the project.
>
> The **violinists** must practice **their** solos many times before the opening performance.

PRACTICE YOUR SKILLS

Check Your Understanding
Making Pronouns and Antecedents Agree

Contemporary Life

Write the pronoun that correctly completes each sentence. Make sure that the pronoun agrees in both number and gender with its antecedent.

1. Either Felix or Jason left ■ trombone on the stage after practice.
2. All the orchestra members should wear ■ best outfits to the show.
3. Tricia and Max will sing ■ songs while the orchestra accompanies them.
4. Neither Aura nor Tricia remembered to take ■ music stand.
5. Felix took three music stands with ■ on our orchestra's tour.
6. Each player is responsible for ■ own instrument.
7. After the orchestra members left the stage, ■ went to the bus.
8. Jason carried his trombone and put ■ on the bus for the trip home.
9. Either Jane or Tricia will play ■ own song tomorrow night.
10. The trumpet was placed carefully in ■ case after the performance.

Indefinite Pronouns as Antecedents

Sometimes an indefinite pronoun is the antecedent of a personal pronoun. Making the personal pronoun and the indefinite pronoun agree can be confusing because some singular indefinite pronouns suggest a plural meaning. Other indefinite pronouns can be either singular or plural. The following lists break common indefinite pronouns into three groups.

SINGULAR INDEFINITE PRONOUNS			
anybody	either	neither	one
anyone	everybody	nobody	somebody
each	everyone	no one	someone

One of the girls left **her** bike unlocked.

Sometimes the gender of a singular indefinite pronoun is not indicated. You can solve this problem by using *his or her.*

Everyone must keep **his or her** bike locked up.

When you use several instances of *he or she, his or her,* or *him or her* in a short piece of writing, awkwardness may result. You can often eliminate this problem by rewriting the sentences in the plural form.

All students must keep **their** bikes locked up.

PLURAL INDEFINITE PRONOUNS			
both	few	many	several

Many of the younger children have **their** own bikes.

SINGULAR OR PLURAL INDEFINITE PRONOUNS				
all	any	most	none	some

Agreement with one of these indefinite pronouns depends upon the number and gender of the object of the preposition that follows it.

Some of the **chrome** on Stevie's bike has lost **its** shine.

Most of his **friends** keep **their** bikes out of the sun.

PRACTICE YOUR SKILLS

Check Your Understanding

Making Personal Pronouns Agree with Indefinite Pronouns

Contemporary Life

Write the pronoun that correctly completes each sentence.

1. All of the little boys in my apartment complex received a bicycle for ■ birthdays.
2. Each of them had ■ bike painted a different color.
3. Not one of the boys in the apartment complex painted ■ bike red.
4. Many of the neighbors near our complex let the boys ride in ■ driveways.
5. One of our local organizations put up fliers about ■ bicycle races.
6. All of the boys decided ■ would enter.
7. Some of us in the complex gave them ■ encouragement to enter the race.
8. Someone in the boys' group had ■ bike stolen.
9. One of the winners of the race bought the unfortunate boy a new bike with ■ prize money.
10. All of the younger boys were glad ■ friend had a bike again.

Connect to the Writing Process: Revising

Correcting Pronoun Agreement Errors

Rewrite the following sentences, correcting any problems with pronoun agreement. If a sentence is correct, write *C*.

11. Each of the girls won their softball letter.
12. No one on the girls' team liked her uniform.
13. Neither of the boys received their trophy for baseball.
14. Both of the Randall sisters practice batting in their backyard.
15. One of the girls lost their baseball glove.

Communicate Your Ideas

APPLY TO WRITING

Analysis: *Comparing Poems*

Many poets have written poems about parents. In "Taught Me Purple," Evelyn Tooley Hunt writes from a daughter's point of view about her mother. In "Mother to Son," Langston Hughes writes from the mother's point of view in giving advice to her son. Read the two passages below and then follow the directions.

> My mother taught me purple
> Although she never wore it.
> Wash-gray was her circle,
> The tenement her orbit.
>
> My mother taught me golden
> And held me up to see it,
> Above the broken molding,
> Beyond the filthy street.
>
> —*Evelyn Tooley Hunt,* "Taught Me Purple"

> Well, Son, I'll tell you
> Life for me ain't been no crystal stair.
> It's had tacks in it,
> And splinters,
> And boards torn up,
> And places with no carpets on the floor,
>
> Bare.
> But all the time
> I'se been climbin' on
> And reachin' landin's
> And turnin' corners. . . .
>
> —*Langston Hughes,* "Mother to Son"

- Write a short essay for your English teacher in which you compare these two passages. What do they have in common? How are they different?
- As you write, correctly use the following pairs of words in your essay: *both/their, each/its, several/their.*

QuickCheck Mixed Practice

Contemporary Life

Write the pronoun that correctly completes each sentence.

1. The high school band prepared for (their, its) first performance.
2. (All, Each) of the band members were a little nervous, but they were ready.
3. Alicia was the only one (who, whom) did not seem prepared.
4. Consuela helped (her, his) friend get ready.
5. Consuela was more prepared than (I, me).
6. Our director, Mrs. Chandler, gave us (their, our) usual pre-game instructions.
7. After her speech, (each, all) in the band gave a cheer and the crowd joined in.
8. Because we had practiced so hard, (we, us) in the band thought we would do our best.
9. As we walked onto the field, the crowd cheered (us, them).
10. That night the band played (its, their) best performance.

Unclear, Missing, or Confusing Antecedents

The object of writing and speaking most often is to communicate with someone else. Sometimes that communication gets cloudy or confused if pronouns have no clear antecedent.

Every personal pronoun should clearly refer to a specific antecedent.

UNCLEAR	We tried to call the employment agency, but **it** was busy. (The antecedent of *it* is not clear, but the context of the sentence suggests that the pronoun *it* refers to the telephone.)
CLEAR	We tried to call the employment agency, but **its telephone** was busy.
UNCLEAR	I checked the Internet for job listings because **you** can always get good information there. (*You* is incorrectly used because it does not refer to the person being spoken to. Instead, it refers to the speaker.)
CLEAR	I checked the Internet for job listings because **I** can always get good information there.
MISSING	In the newspaper **it** lists the requirements for every job. (What does *it* refer to in this sentence? The antecedent in this sentence is missing.)
CLEAR	The **newspaper** lists the requirements for every job.
MISSING	**It** had many job listings for entry-level computer positions. (*It* is unclear. The antecedent is missing.)
CLEAR	The **employment section of the newspaper** had many job listings for entry-level computer positions.

CONFUSING	My mother drove Liza to the interview, but **she** didn't go into the office. (Who didn't go into the office, the mother or Liza?)
CLEAR	My mother drove Liza to the interview, but **my mother** didn't go into the office.
CONFUSING	Liza put the business card into her purse, but now she can't find **it.** (Does *it* refer to the business card or the purse?)
CLEAR	Liza put the business card into her purse, but now she can't find **the business card.**

PRACTICE YOUR SKILLS

Check Your Understanding
Identifying Antecedent Problems

Contemporary Life

Label the antecedent problems in the sentences below as *unclear, missing,* or *confusing* and rewrite the sentences correctly. If the sentence is written correctly, write *C*.

1. Almost all teenagers can find a job if you try hard enough.

2. My dad helped Elizabeth get a job, but she didn't like it very much.

3. So she could choose a date for the interview, Marybeth asked her mother where her calendar was.

4. Almost everyone I know likes to work if it is interesting.

5. I like dog walking because you get lots of outdoor exercise.

6. The employment agent stared at the boy, but he said nothing.

7. To earn a little extra money, Jenni and Michael took the rugs off the floor and cleaned them.

8. Sarah wants to work at a veterinarian's office because you could learn a lot about animals.
9. My sister told Jenni about the job, and then she applied for it.
10. I saw the job listing in the newspaper earlier today, but now I cannot find it.
11. As soon as Elizabeth and Sarah returned home, I asked her to tell me about her job.
12. Sarah said it was a lot of fun.
13. Elizabeth was not as enthusiastic about it.
14. The veterinarian's office was so close that Sarah could walk to it.
15. Our mother had to drive Elizabeth to her job.

Connect to the Writing Process: Revising

Correcting Pronoun References

Rewrite the following letter, correcting unclear, missing, or confusing pronoun references.

Dear Ms. Gonzalez:

I am writing in response to your classified advertisement in Sunday's newspaper. In the paper it said you wanted someone to work at your day-care center. I have always wanted to work with children because you can help them learn.

Please read the attached résumé and call me if you think I am qualified for it. Although I have never worked with preschool children, I would be good at that.

Sincerely,
Tiffany Washington

Communicate Your Ideas

APPLY TO WRITING

Response Letter: ***Pronoun References***

You have found a job listing in your local newspaper that interests you. Write a response letter to the contact person whose name appears in the advertisement. Remember to indicate what position you are interested in, why you are interested, and what your qualifications are. Be sure to use correct pronoun references.

Mixed Practice

Contemporary Life

Each sentence below contains an error in pronoun usage. Rewrite the sentence, correcting the error.

1. During the national election, many of the citizens cast his or her votes early.
2. According to the polls, they said the incumbent president will win.
3. Several of the candidates gave his or her speeches.
4. I read the newspaper articles about the candidates, because you can learn a lot.
5. Neither of my parents has cast their vote yet.
6. My parents went to vote, and it was crowded.
7. During the town meeting, all of our neighbors asked the candidates their questions.
8. My mom took Granny to the debate, but she didn't listen to the candidates.
9. All of the candidates were responsible for raising his or her own campaign money.
10. Depending upon who wins the mayoral election, Ms. Sands or Mr. Stone will try their hand at running our city.

Checkpoint

Using Pronouns Correctly

Write the correct form of the pronoun in parentheses.

1. Neither Sue nor Rebecca has had (her, their) turn at bat.
2. One of the girls left (her, their) tennis shoes in the gym.
3. Please explain to (we, us) students how to get a pass.
4. To (who, whom) should I send the invitation?
5. Do other students study as hard as (we, us)?
6. (They, Them) made a delicious dinner for us.
7. Sandra went to the movies with David and (I, me).
8. Both Raul and Ted forgot (his, their) skates.
9. Our debaters will be Jorge and (he, him).
10. It was (she, her) who won the local marathon.
11. Jessica and (he, him) went to the game with us.
12. (Whoever, Whomever) draws the best picture will win a prize.
13. That was quick thinking for an inexperienced quarterback like (he, him).
14. No one types as fast as (she, her) on a word processor.
15. Between you and (I, me), we're never going to get there on time.
16. She is the only person (who, whom) arrived early.
17. (We, us) joggers need to pay special attention to the traffic lights.
18. I think that's (she, her) in the blue coat.
19. Yes, I think she dives as well as (I, me).
20. I think Mr. Pentose is someone (who, whom) we met in Florida last year.

Making Personal Pronouns Agree with Their Antecedents

Write the personal pronoun that correctly completes each sentence.

1. Either Mary or Suzanne will bring ■ guitar.
2. One of my brothers just received ■ diploma.
3. Both Heidi and John turned in ■ reports early.
4. The tire has lost most of ■ air.
5. All of the students will be assigned to ■ homerooms.
6. Several of my friends want to add biology to ■ schedules.
7. Both of the girls think that ■ will compete in the race.
8. Sam or Ernesto should drive ■ car to the game.
9. After we painted the posters, we hung ■ in the halls.
10. None of the silver pieces had lost ■ shine.
11. Either of the boys will share ■ lunch.
12. Several of the tourists lost ■ way.
13. That tree is beginning to lose ■ leaves.
14. Neither Mindy nor Sue can finish ■ picture.
15. Either Claire or Erica will have ■ camera at the game.

Writing Sentences

Rewrite these sentences so there is a clear antecedent for each pronoun.

1. Rita tried to call her friend, but she did not feel like talking.
2. Rita drove to Lisa's house and listened to her new CD.
3. Then Rita drove her sister to the library, but she forgot her library card.
4. Rita put her book in a bag, but she left it on the counter at the library.
5. Rita's book fell on the floor, and it was damaged.

Language and *Self-Expression*

In this painting a man and a woman are dancing the jitterbug, a dance form that originated in the African American community and then became popular during the swing era of the 1930s and 1940s. The jitterbug can include slow steps or energetic moves including lifts, swings, and turns.

The artist uses bold colors and patterns of lines and shape to show a dance that is associated with a certain period in history. How could you use words to capture the movements of a dance or sport that is popular today? Choose a dance or sporting event at your school or on television. Watch the event and take notes. Then write a two-minute radio announcement describing it for a listening audience. Be sure to use pronouns with clear antecedents. Record your announcement and play it for your class.

Prewriting List action verbs that describe the movements of the people you watched in the event. Chart sequences of movements you want to describe.

Drafting Write your announcement using ideas from your list and chart. Use pronouns to make your writing concise.

Revising Read your announcement, marking places that need work. After you have made the changes, read the announcement aloud. Do your words help a person "see" the event?

Editing Check your story for errors in spelling and punctuation. Be sure you have used pronouns correctly.

Publishing Prepare a final copy and use an audiocassette recorder to tape it. Play the tape for your classmates.

Another Look

Case is the form of a noun or a pronoun that indicates its use in a sentence.

Kinds of Cases

The **nominative case** is used for subjects and predicate nominatives. *(pages L329–L335)*

The **objective case** is used for direct objects, indirect objects, and objects of prepositions. *(pages L335–L341)*

The **possessive case** is used to show ownership or possession. *(pages L341–L345)*

Using the Correct Case of *Who*

The correct case of *who* is determined by how the pronoun is used in a question or a clause. *(pages L346–L351)*

Nominative Case	who, whoever
Objective Case	whom, whomever
Possessive Case	whose

Pronouns in Comparisons

In an elliptical clause, use the form of the pronoun you would use if the clause were completed. *(pages L351–L354)*

Pronouns and Their Antecedents

A pronoun must agree in number and gender with its antecedent. *(page L355)*

If two or more singular antecedents are joined by *or, nor, either/or,* or *neither/nor,* use a singular pronoun to refer to them. *(page L356)*

If two or more singular antecedents are joined by *and* or *both/and,* use a plural pronoun to refer to them. *(page L356)*

Every personal pronoun should clearly refer to a specific antecedent. *(page L362)*

Directions

Read the passage and choose the pronoun that belongs in each underlined space. Write the letter of the correct answer.

EXAMPLE As Jerome walked onto the stage, __(1)__ knees were shaking.

1 **A** his
B him
C my
D mine

ANSWER **1** **A**

It was the big night of the talent show. Everybody in school watched as Jerome approached the microphone. __(1)__ singing partner Juan, __(2)__ was already on the stage, handed __(3)__ the guitar. Jerome immediately felt calmer. He began to strum the guitar strings, and __(4)__ began to sing. "__(5)__ have chosen a ballad for __(6)__ first selection," Juan said as Jerome continued to play the guitar. When they finished the song, all of the students clapped and cheered loudly. Mr. Watkins, the principal, went to the microphone. "__(7)__ knew that __(8)__ had such talent right here under __(9)__ noses?" __(10)__ asked.

1 A His
B Our
C Him
D Their

2 A whoever
B whom
C who
D whomever

3 A him
B he
C who
D whom

4 A they
B its
C his
D their

5 A Us
B We
C Our
D Ours

6 A my
B we
C us
D our

7 A Whom
B Whose
C Who
D Whomever

8 A we
B us
C our
D ours

9 A us
B our
C ours
D we

10 A his
B him
C he
D them

CHAPTER 12

Subject and Verb Agreement

Directions

Read the passage. Write the letter of the answer that shows the correct way to rewrite each underlined word or group of words. If the underlined part contains no error, write *D*.

EXAMPLE Scientists who study rocks is called (1) geologists.

1 A has been called
B is calling
C are called
D No error

ANSWER 1 C

All geologists categorizes (1) rocks according to origin. Sometimes magma move (2) up through cracks in the earth's crust and cools (3). This action creates igneous rocks. Sedimentary rocks is made (4) from pieces of rocks, sand, and other material. These sediments is washed (5) into oceans, and they settle (6) to the bottom. Then the layers of sediment is pressed (7) together to create rocks. The third group are (8) metamorphic rocks. Heat and pressure creates (9) these rocks from igneous and sedimentary rocks. Both of these sometimes becomes (10) metamorphic rocks.

1 **A** is categorizing
B categorize
C has categorized
D No error

2 **A** moves
B is moving
C have moved
D No error

3 **A** cool
B is cooling
C have cooled
D No error

4 **A** is being made
B was made
C are made
D No error

5 **A** is washing
B are washed
C washes
D No error

6 **A** settles
B are settles
C is settled
D No error

7 **A** are pressed
B is pressing
C has been pressed
D No error

8 **A** is
B is being
C are being
D No error

9 **A** has created
B create
C is creating
D No error

10 **A** become
B has become
C is becoming
D No error

Melissa Miller. *Flood,* 1983.
Oil on linen, 59 by 95 inches. Collection, Museum of Fine Arts, Houston. © 1983 Melissa Miller.

Describe Moving from left to right, describe the subjects in the painting.

Analyze What statement do you think the artist wanted to make? What elements in the painting support this message?

Interpret Read the title of the painting. What feelings do you associate with this word? What kind of writing might create the same mood?

Judge Do you think it is possible for a writer to elicit from an audience feelings that are as intense as those generated by this artist? Explain your ideas.

At the end of this chapter, you will use the artwork as a visual aid for writing.

Agreement of Subjects and Verbs

Language is very much like a jigsaw puzzle. You must put all the pieces of a jigsaw puzzle together correctly to end up with a complete picture. You must also fit all the parts of a sentence together correctly in order to communicate clearly. For example, some subjects and verbs fit together, while others may seem to fit together but actually do not. In the English language, when a subject and a verb fit together, they are said to be in **agreement.**

This chapter will show you how to make subjects and verbs agree so that your speaking and writing will communicate a complete, clear picture to your listener or reader. One basic rule applies to this entire chapter.

A verb must agree in number with its subject.

Number

In the last chapter, you learned that **number** refers to whether a noun or a pronoun is singular or plural. You know that singular indicates one and that plural indicates more than one. In this chapter you will learn that verbs also have number and that the number of a verb must agree with the number of its subject.

The Number of Nouns and Pronouns

In English the plural of most nouns is formed by adding *–s* or *–es* to the singular form. However, some nouns form their plurals in other ways. You should always check a dictionary to see whether a noun has an irregular plural.

NUMBER			
SINGULAR	floor	tax	child
PLURAL	floors	taxes	children

In the last chapter, you also learned that pronouns have singular and plural forms. For example, *I, he, she,* and *it* are singular, and *we* and *they* are plural.

You can find a list of pronoun forms on page L327.

Practice Your Skills

Check Your Understanding

Determining the Number of Nouns and Pronouns

Write each word and label it *S* for singular or *P* for plural.

1. Jessica
2. everyone
3. children
4. several
5. schools
6. hats
7. mice
8. rakes
9. anyone
10. lights
11. they
12. both
13. women
14. cap
15. we
16. bike
17. he
18. Jamison
19. it
20. radio

The Number of Verbs

The singular and plural forms of nouns and pronouns are fairly easy to recognize. You can easily see, for example, that *eagle* and *it* refer to only one, while *eagles* and *they* refer to more than one.

The number of verbs, however, is not so easy to recognize. Only the form of the verb indicates its number. Most verbs form their singulars and plurals in exactly the opposite way that nouns form their singulars and plurals. Most verbs in the present tense add *–s* or *–es* to form the singular. Plural forms of verbs in the present tense drop the *–s* or *–es*.

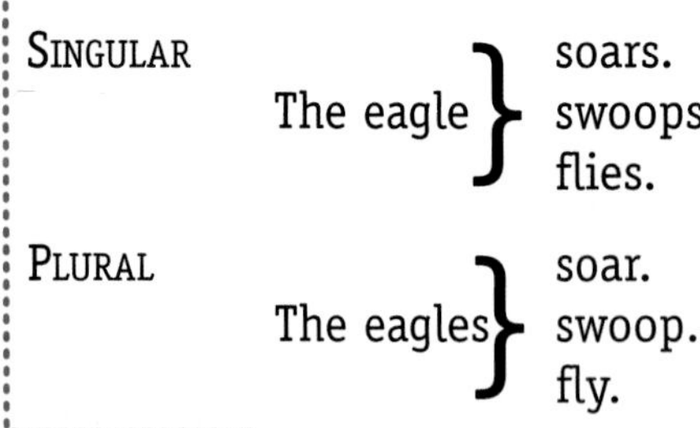

SINGULAR
The eagle
soars.
swoops.
flies.
PLURAL
The eagles
soar.
swoop.
fly.

Most verbs have the same form for both singular and plural when the verbs are used in the past tense.

SINGULAR	The eagle **soared.**
PLURAL	The eagles **soared.**

The irregular verb *be* indicates number differently from other verbs. The singular is not formed by adding *–s* or *–es*.

FORMS OF *BE*			
SINGULAR FORMS	am/is	was	has been
PLURAL FORMS	are	were	have been

SINGULAR	The eagle **is** a majestic bird.
PLURAL	Eagles **are** majestic birds.

PRACTICE YOUR SKILLS

Check Your Understanding
Determining a Verb's Number

Write each verb and label it *S* for singular or *P* for plural.

1. breaks
2. freezes
3. are
4. have been
5. keep
6. works
7. was
8. reads
9. am
10. has
11. is
12. tear
13. look
14. sings
15. walk
16. swim
17. see
18. speak
19. were
20. barks

Singular and Plural Subjects

Because a verb must agree in number with its subject, you need to remember two rules.

A singular subject takes a singular verb.

A plural subject takes a plural verb.

To make a verb agree with its subject, ask yourself two questions: *What is the subject?* and *Is the subject singular or plural?* Then choose the correct verb form.

SINGULAR	A **geologist studies** rocks and minerals.
PLURAL	**Geologists study** rocks and minerals.
SINGULAR	**She examines** layers of the earth.
PLURAL	**They examine** layers of the earth.
SINGULAR	The **emerald is** a beautiful gemstone.
PLURAL	**Emeralds are** beautiful gemstones.

The pronouns *you* and *I* are the only exceptions to these agreement rules. The pronoun *you,* whether singular or plural, always takes a plural verb.

SINGULAR	**You use** a shovel.	**You are** a geologist.
PLURAL	**You** two **use** shovels.	**You are** scientists.

The pronoun *I* also takes a plural verb—except when it is used with a form of *be.*

SINGULAR	**I am** a researcher.	**I was** her assistant.
PLURAL	**I like** minerals and gems.	**I have** some rock samples.

Connect to Speaking and Writing

Many errors in subject and verb agreement occur when writers do not edit their work. Never turn in a first draft without reading through your work and correcting errors. Reading a piece aloud to yourself or to a friend can help you find errors more easily than reading your work silently.

Practice Your Skills

Check Your Understanding

Making Subjects and Verbs Agree

Science Topic **Write the subject in each sentence. Next to each, write the form of the verb in parentheses that agrees with the subject.**

1. Jewelers (place, places) a high value on emeralds of good quality.
2. Emeralds (is, are) a rarer find than diamonds.
3. An emerald (is, are) a special type of the mineral beryl.
4. Geologists (know, knows) the exact minerals that make up all precious stones.
5. Geology also (involve, involves) the study of Earth's landforms and surface features.
6. You (see, sees) these features wherever you look in nature.
7. A volcano (interest, interests) some specialized geologists.
8. Magma (is, are) molten rock contained within the earth.
9. When it comes to the surface, magma (become, becomes) lava.
10. I (study, studies) stones and minerals more than land formations.

Connect to the Writing Process: Editing

Correcting Errors in Subject and Verb Agreement

Write the verbs that do not agree with their subjects. Then write the verbs correctly. If a sentence is correct, write *C*.

11. Diamonds is the world's favorite gem.

12. You finds them in most countries of the world.

13. South Africa exports the most diamonds.

14. A diamond's brilliance determine its value.

15. Most diamonds have color.

16. Blue and pink stones is the most valuable.

17. When found, these precious stones resembles glass.

18. It take a diamond to cut a diamond and other hard surfaces.

19. Gem cutters use diamonds to shape other diamonds and gems.

20. Some factories has tools covered with diamonds to cut metal surfaces.

Agreement with Verb Phrases

If a sentence contains a verb phrase, make the first helping verb agree with the subject.

The first helping verb must agree in number with the subject.

In the following sentences, each subject is underlined once and each verb is underlined twice.

Kristy **was** writing a poem.

(*Kristy* is singular, and *was* is singular.)

They **have** been writing all afternoon.

(*They* is plural, and *have* is plural.)

The following chart shows the singular and plural forms of common helping verbs.

	COMMON HELPING VERBS
Singular	am, is, was, has, does
Plural	are, were, have, do

In the following sentences, each subject is underlined once and each verb is underlined twice.

Singular	Kristy **is** writing a sonnet.
	The teacher **does** not have a dictionary of rhymes.
Plural	The poetry books **are** located in this section of the library.
	Our poems **have** been published in the local newspaper.

Check Your Understanding

Making Subjects and Verb Phrases Agree

Literature Topic

Write the subject in each sentence. Next to each, write the form of the verb in parentheses that agrees with the subject.

1. Sonnets (is, are) written according to certain rules.
2. A new poet (is, are) often intimidated by the sonnet's rigid structure.
3. This particular poetic form (was, were) made popular by Petrarch in the 1300s.
4. His mystery woman Laura (has, have) become immortal through Petrarch's sonnets.

5. Sonnets (was, were) also written by William Shakespeare.
6. Other poets (do, does) attempt this type of verse.
7. They (has, have) tried to write sonnets of Shakespeare's quality.
8. However, Shakespeare's sonnets (is, are) considered to be the finest collection by a single person.
9. I (was, were) awed when I read Shakespeare's sonnets.
10. When you read them aloud, you (do, does) hear the beauty in his words.

Connect to the Writing Process: Revising
Correcting Errors in Agreement

Rewrite correctly the sentences in which the verb phrases do not agree with their subjects. If a sentence is correct, write *C*.

11. You was really missed at the poetry reading.
12. They has finished sharing their poems.
13. The poem do sound familiar to me.
14. She have read it to us before.
15. Kevin have submitted three sonnets for publication.
16. His poems is often chosen as our group's best.
17. I were just reading one of his poems.
18. The college coffeehouse does have poetry readings.
19. We has attended several times.
20. I am going next Tuesday.

Agreement and Interrupting Words

If the subject is separated from the verb by a phrase or a clause, it is easy to make a mistake in agreement. The reason is that either the object of a prepositional phrase or some other word is closer to the verb than the subject is. Agreement of the verb may then be incorrectly made with that word—rather than with the subject.

The agreement of a verb with its subject is not changed by any interrupting words.

In the following examples, notice that the subjects and verbs agree in number—despite the words that come between them. Each subject is underlined once, and each verb is underlined twice.

> A bouquet of roses **was** given to the skater.
>
> (*Was* agrees with the singular subject *bouquet.* The verb does not agree with *roses,* the object of the prepositional phrase, even though *roses* is closer to the verb.)
>
> The skaters who won medals at the competition **were** invited to the White House.
>
> (*Were* agrees with the subject *skaters*—not with *competition,* the object of the prepositional phrase.)

Compound prepositions, such as *in addition to, as well as,* and *along with,* often begin interrupting phrases.

> The gold medal winner, along with her teammates, **was** called back to the ice.
>
> (*Was* agrees with the subject *winner*—not with *teammates,* the object of the compound preposition *along with.*)

PRACTICE YOUR SKILLS

Check Your Understanding

Making Interrupted Subjects and Verbs Agree

Sports Topic

Write the subject in each sentence. Next to each, write the form of the verb in parentheses that agrees with the subject.

1. The blades on a pair of ice skates (is, are) called runners.
2. The runners on the earliest ice skates (was, were) probably made of bone.
3. The original purpose of ice skates (was, were) for travel.

4. Competition lovers in Scotland (is, are) credited with turning ice skating into a sport.
5. The invention of roller skates (was, were) probably the work of ice skaters who wanted to skate year round.
6. Today skaters from around the world (compete, competes) on the ice before adoring fans.
7. Figure skating at the modern Olympic Games (is, are) one of the most popular attractions.
8. In 1998, Tara Lipinski, together with her teammates, (was, were) a delight to Olympic audiences.
9. Ice dancing in pairs (has, have) been an Olympic sport since 1976.
10. Speed skating by men and women also (draw, draws) a large Olympic audience.

Connect to the Writing Process: Editing

Correcting Errors in Subject and Verb Agreement

Write the verbs that do not agree with their subjects. Then write the verbs correctly. If a sentence is correct, write *C*.

11. The best athletes in the world competes at the Olympic Games.
12. A team of athletes is sent to the Games by almost every country.
13. The modern spectacle of competing athletes were named for contests held in ancient Greece.
14. The original Olympic Games in Greece was banned in A.D. 394.
15. The modern international competition of amateur athletes was revived in 1896.
16. Winter sports like figure skating and skiing have been a part of the Olympics since 1924.
17. The summer sports of this worldwide competition includes boxing, gymnastics, soccer, and yachting.
18. In the summer, track and field events including the decathlon attract large crowds.

19. The popularity of the winter games have made figure skaters into celebrities.

20. The countries of the world comes together to honor their best athletes.

Communicate Your Ideas

APPLY TO WRITING

Persuasive Letter: ***Subject and Verb Agreement***

Imagine that the Olympic Committee has decided to remove basketball from the list of Olympic sports. Write a letter to the committee either supporting or challenging the committee's decision. Be sure to list at least three strong reasons you feel basketball should or should not be an Olympic sport. After completing your letter to the Olympic Committee, read through your work, correcting any errors in subject and verb agreement.

Contemporary Life

Write the verbs that do not agree with their subjects. Then write the verbs correctly. If a sentence is correct, write *C*.

1. My dog Muscles chases squirrels in our backyard.

2. You has to see him!

3. I watches Muscles and laugh at him.

4. Muscles crouches on his haunches and barks at the squirrels.

5. The location of the trees in our backyard are fairly far from the house.

6. The squirrels in that oak tree jumps across to that far elm.

7. Right now, one squirrel on the back steps are chattering at Muscles.

8. The squirrel seem to tease him.

9. Muscles, like most dogs, hate to be teased.

10. Muscles starts toward the squirrel.

11. Squirrels, aware of the danger, always jumps quickly to a nearby tree.

12. Muscles, standing at the bottom of the tree, bark angrily at the intruders.

13. The squirrel, now safe in the branches, resume his chattering.

14. Everyday Muscles wait for his chance to catch a squirrel.

15. The frustrated canine never give up his quest.

Common Agreement Problems

When you edit your written work, look for agreement problems. They are often the result of quickly written first drafts. Compound subjects and subjects in inverted order, for example, can pose problems.

 Compound Subjects

Agreement between a verb and a compound subject can sometimes be confusing. The following rules will help you avoid errors of agreement.

When subjects are joined by *or, nor, either/or,* or *neither/nor,* the verb agrees with the subject that is closer to it.

This rule applies even when one subject is singular and the other subject is plural.

Either rain showers or sleet **is** expected tomorrow.

(The helping verb is singular because the subject closer to it is singular.)

Wind or rising temperatures dispel fog.

(The verb is plural because the subject closer to it is plural.)

Neither my brother nor my parents like to drive in wet weather.

(The verb is plural because the subject closer to it is plural—even though the other subject, *brother,* is singular.)

When subjects are joined by *and* or *both/and,* the verb is plural.

With *and* or *both/and,* the verb should be plural—whether the subjects are singular, plural, or a combination of singular and plural.

Both hail and high wind accompany many storms.

(Two things—*hail* and *wind*—accompany storms. The verb must be plural to agree.)

My brother and his roommates **were** not injured in the storm.

(Even though one subject is singular, the verb is still plural because *brother* and *roommates*—together—are more than one.)

There are two exceptions to the second rule. Sometimes two subjects that are joined by *and* refer to only one person or thing. Then a singular verb must be used.

My family's weather expert and storm lover **is** my sister.

(one person)

Thunder and lightning **is** music to her.

(considered one thing)

The other exception occurs when the word *every* or *each* comes before a compound subject whose parts are joined by *and.* Since each subject is being considered separately in these sentences, a singular verb is called for.

Every thunderclap and lightning bolt **delights** my sister exceedingly.

(*Thunderclap* and *lightning bolt* are considered separately. The verb must be singular to agree.)

Each fall and spring **brings** the increased possibility of severe weather.

(*Fall* and *spring* are considered separately. The verb must be singular to agree.)

PRACTICE YOUR SKILLS

Check Your Understanding

Making Verbs Agree with Compound Subjects

Science Topic **Write the correct form of the verb in parentheses.**

1. Weather and other natural phenomena (is, are) interesting to study.

2. Neither meteorologists nor other scientists (has, have) been able to develop systems for controlling weather.

3. Radar and computer technology (help, helps) them predict and understand the patterns of weather.

4. Climate conditions and soil types (combine, combines) to affect vegetation.

5. Every animal and plant (react, reacts) to the surrounding environment.

6. For instance, moisture and warm air (is, are) needed to make orchids grow.

7. A tropical plant or flower (do, does) not grow in the desert.

8. Due to their white pelts, polar bears and arctic hares (thrive, thrives) in snowy climates.

9. Today great ice caps and glaciers (cover, covers) one tenth of the earth's surface.

10. Dark clouds and high winds (alert, alerts) people to changing weather.

11. The air currents and weather patterns (change, changes) constantly.

12. Neither a lightning strike nor a tornado (is, are) easy to predict.

13. Snow or showers (is, are) easier to forecast.

14. A typhoon or hurricane (has, have) been known to cause mass destruction.

15. Dull sunsets and hot, humid air (signal, signals) the approach of a hurricane.

16. Wind and water (combine, combines) to wear down rocks and create canyons.

17. Both intensive training and a thorough knowledge of climate (is, are) required to be a meteorologist.

18. Every dark cloud and cyclone warning (is, are) taken seriously in tornado-prone areas.

19. Cirrocumulus clouds and humid air (mean, means) rain is certain.

20. Every year, hurricanes and tornadoes (cause, causes) billions of dollars in property damage.

Connect to the Writing Process: Editing

Correcting Errors in Agreement

Write the verbs that do not agree with their subjects. Then write the verbs correctly. If a sentence is correct, write *C*.

21. Earthquakes and volcanoes has caused cities to sink beneath the sea.

22. Broken dams or volcanic activity sometimes follows earthquakes.

23. Often fires or flood is caused by earthquakes.

24. Each collapsed building or damaged home presents a danger after a quake.

25. Tsunamis at coastal areas and landslides in mountainous regions is also associated with earthquakes.

26. Both Japan and Indonesia has been the site of disastrous tsunamis.

27. In Alaska in 1958, ice and rock was broken off a glacier by the jolt of an earthquake.

28. The force and fury of the resulting splash cause a tsunami.

29. Buildings and other structures is now being designed to withstand earthquakes.

30. Neither humans nor property are safe from the threat of earthquakes.

Indefinite Pronouns as Subjects

In the last chapter, you learned that not all indefinite pronouns have the same number.

COMMON INDEFINITE PRONOUNS	
SINGULAR	anybody, anyone, each, either, everybody, everyone, neither, nobody, no one, one, somebody, someone
PLURAL	both, few, many, several
SINGULAR/PLURAL	all, any, most, none, some

A verb must agree in number with an indefinite pronoun used as a subject.

SINGULAR Everyone in the room owns a dog.

PLURAL Many of the dogs are poodles.

The number of an indefinite pronoun in the last group in the box is determined by the object of the prepositional phrase that follows the pronoun.

SINGULAR OR PLURAL

Most of the training **has** been effective.
(Since *training,* the object of the prepositional phrase, is singular, *has* is also singular.)

Most of the dogs **have** learned a lot in obedience school.
(Since *dogs,* the object of the prepositional phrase, is plural, *have* is also plural.)

None of the dog owners **were** unhappy with the program.
(Since *owners,* the object of the prepositional phrase, is plural, *were* is also plural.)

Practice Your Skills

Check Your Understanding
Making Verbs Agree with Indefinite Pronouns

Contemporary Life

Write the subject in each sentence. Next to each, write the correct form of the verb in parentheses that agrees with the subject.

1. Several of her dogs (is, are) collies.
2. Each of you (is, are) needed to train the dogs.
3. Some of the new leashes (is, are) in the closet.
4. One of the dogs in the class (was, were) a beagle.
5. Many of the dogs (has, have) been adopted at the shelter.
6. None of the owners (was, were) disappointed in the class.
7. Nobody (want, wants) a badly behaved dog.
8. Both of her puppies (walk, walks) on a leash together.
9. Most of the dogs (was, were) fast learners.
10. Either of these classes (is, are) a good one to take next.

Connect to the Writing Process: Drafting
Writing Sentences

Write ten sentences, each using one of the phrases below as a beginning.

11. Both of the dogs
12. Anybody at the shelter
13. Few of the older dogs
14. All of the kittens
15. None of the volunteers
16. Each of the cages
17. No one at the desk
18. Several of the stores
19. Some of the pets
20. Neither of the cats

Subjects in Inverted Order

A verb must agree in number with the subject, regardless of whether the subject comes before or after the verb.

The subject and the verb of an inverted sentence must agree in number.

There are several types of inverted sentences. To find the subject in an inverted sentence, turn the sentence around to its natural order, placing the subject first.

INVERTED ORDER	At the bottom of the trunk were my great uncle's medals.
	(My great uncle's medals were at the bottom of the trunk.)
QUESTIONS	Are the medals from World War II?
	(The medals are from World War II.)
SENTENCES BEGINNING WITH *HERE* OR *THERE*	There were many letters also in the trunk.
	(Many letters were also in the trunk. The word *there* is dropped from the sentence.)

You can learn more about inverted sentences on pages L22–L23.

PRACTICE YOUR SKILLS

Check Your Understanding

Making Subjects and Verbs in Inverted Order Agree

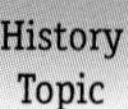

History Topic **Write the subject in each sentence. Next to each, write the form of the verb in parentheses that agrees with the subject.**

1. There (was, were) many countries involved in World War II.
2. In Europe (was, were) the locations of many of the battles.
3. (Do, Does) any war have only one cause?
4. At the core of the fighting (was, were) many factors.

5. There (was, were) much tension remaining in Europe after World War I.
6. In the numerous battles of the war (was, were) men from all countries.
7. (Was, Were) anyone able to predict that Hitler would gain such power?
8. (Have, Has) the world learned anything from these world wars?
9. At the end of World War II (was, were) a new struggle for political power in Europe.
10. (Is, Are) there any good results that come from such wars?

Connect to the Writing Process: Drafting
Writing Sentences

Write five sentences, each using one of the phrases below as a beginning. Be sure that the verb you choose agrees with the subject.

11. There are
12. In the newspaper was
13. At the top of the page were
14. There is
15. On the front page are

Communicate Your Ideas

APPLY TO WRITING

The Writer's Craft: ***Analyzing the Use of Inverted Order***

Writers mix sentences in inverted order with sentences in natural order to vary their sentence structure and make their writing interesting. Read the following passage by Pearl Buck.

But not all the copper pence did Wang Lung spend on food. He kept back all he was able to buy mats to build a shed for them when they reached the south. There were men and women in the firewagon who had been south in other years; some went each year to the rich cities of the south to work and to beg and thus save the price of food.

–Pearl Buck, The Good Earth

- List the subject and verb in each sentence. Be sure to list the subject and verb from the last independent clause, which follows the semicolon.
- Arrange the first sentence in natural order.
- Do you prefer Buck's original sentence or your rewritten one? Explain your answer.
- Why do you think Pearl Buck wrote the first and third sentences in inverted order?

Mixed Practice

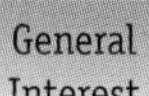

Find each verb that does not agree with its subject. Then write the correct form of the verb and its subject.

Everyone have read folktales about cunning wolves. Movies and television has shown wolves attacking people. Is all of these stories about wolves really true? According to Boye Rensberger, they isn't. He says that wolves doesn't like to fight. In fact, wolves often go out of their way to avoid harming humans. Rensberger goes on to say that wolf packs is tightly knit families. Both the mother wolf and the father wolf raises the young. When both of the parents goes out to hunt, another wolf baby-sit the pups.

Other Agreement Problems

A few special situations also may cause agreement problems. Look for the following problems when you edit your written work.

Doesn't or *Don't?*

Doesn't, don't, and other contractions often present agreement problems. When you write a contraction, always say the two words that make up the contraction. Then check for agreement with the subject.

The verb part of a contraction must agree in number with the subject.

Doesn't, isn't, wasn't, and *hasn't* are singular and agree with singular subjects. *Don't, aren't, weren't,* and *haven't* are plural and agree with plural subjects.

> He **does**n't know any musicians.
>
> (He *does* not know)
>
> **Do**n't they know anyone?
>
> (They *do* not know)

Collective Nouns

In Chapter 2 you learned that a collective noun names a group of people or things.

COMMON COLLECTIVE NOUNS			
band	congregation	flock	orchestra
class	crew	gang	swarm
colony	crowd	herd	team
committee	family	league	tribe

How a collective noun is used will determine its agreement with the verb.

Use a singular verb with a collective noun subject that is thought of as a unit. Use a plural verb with a collective noun subject that is thought of as individuals.

The committee **is** planning to hire a band for the big event.

(The committee is working as a single unit. Therefore, the verb is singular.)

The committee **are** unable to agree on the band for the big event.

(The individuals on the committee are acting separately. Therefore, the verb is plural.)

Words Expressing Amounts

Words that express amounts of time or money or that express measurements or weights are usually considered singular.

A subject that expresses an amount, a measurement, a weight, or a time is usually considered singular and takes a singular verb.

Subjects expressing amounts can be confusing because they are sometimes plural in form.

Amounts	Five dollars is the price of admission to the dance. (one sum of money)
Time	Nine tenths of Adriana's spare time **has** been spent planning the dance. (one part of time)

Once in a while, an amount is thought of as individual parts. When this happens, a plural verb must be used.

Three quarters **were** left in the cash box.

Practice Your Skills

Check Your Understanding
Making Subjects and Verbs Agree

Contemporary Life

Write the subject in each sentence. Next to each, write the form of the verb in parentheses that agrees with the subject.

1. (Aren't, Isn't) you going to the dance?
2. A group (has, have) been chosen to perform.
3. Those singers (is, are) a big hit now.
4. The swim team (has, have) a meet on the same night as the dance.
5. Invitations to join the dance committee (was, were) extended to them.
6. Three fourths of the refreshment table (was, were) covered with plates of cookies.
7. Thirty dollars (was, were) donated to our class to purchase decorations.
8. Three days (was, were) spent looking for a purple banner for the wall.
9. They (wasn't, weren't) interested in hiring Daria's band for the dance.
10. One result of their choice of bands (is, are) that her feelings were hurt.
11. Eight feet of purple ribbon (was, were) used to make a bow for the stage.
12. Three gallons of lime sherbet (was, were) mixed into ginger ale to make the punch.
13. (Doesn't, Don't) your mother make tropical punch exactly like that?
14. The freshman class (was, were) asked to line up for a picture.
15. Each time they pose, the group (argue, argues) about how to line up for pictures.

Connect to the Writing Process: Drafting

Writing Sentences

Add to the following phrases to make complete sentences. Be sure that your subjects and verbs agree.

16. The pack of wolves ■.

17. Seventy-five percent of the forest ■.

18. Three fifty-dollar bills ■.

19. The Sierra Club ■.

20. Three tablespoons of sugar ■.

Singular Nouns That Have Plural Forms

Words like *measles, mathematics, economics,* and *news* each end in *–s;* but they name single things, such as one disease or one area of knowledge.

Use a singular verb with certain subjects that are plural in form but singular in meaning.

In middle school, mathematics **was** Felicia's best subject.
The news **is** that she now likes English better.

Subjects with Linking Verbs

Sometimes a sentence will have a subject and a predicate nominative that do not agree in number.

A verb agrees with the subject of a sentence, not with the predicate nominative.

In the following examples, the number of the predicate nominative does not affect the number of the verb.

Felicia's topic of discussion **was** the novels of Jane Austen.

The novels of the Victorian period **are** Felicia's passion.

Titles

Titles may have many words, and some of those words may be plural. Nevertheless, a title is the name of only one book or work of art.

A title takes a singular verb.

Wuthering Heights by Emily Brontë **is** her favorite Victorian novel.

Van Gogh's *Irises* **hangs** next to the bookshelf in her living room.

Practice Your Skills

Check Your Understanding
Making Subjects and Verbs Agree

General Interest **Write the subject in each sentence. Next to each, write the form of the verb in parentheses that agrees with the subject.**

1. *Sense and Sensibility* (was, were) much easier to read than I had expected it to be.
2. One challenge in reading the book (is, are) that many words are unfamiliar to us.
3. The news that we would read the book (was, were) not welcomed by the class.
4. Manners in Jane Austen's time (is, are) a fascinating topic.
5. The main focus of our discussion (was, were) the characters in the novel.
6. One result of our discussions (was, were) our reading more of Austen's novels.
7. Picasso's *Three Musicians* (is, are) our next discussion topic.

8. *The Martian Chronicles* by Ray Bradbury (follow, follows) the work by Picasso.
9. The early blues by B. B. King (is, are) also one of her interests.
10. Topics in Mrs. Smith's class (is, are) one thing you can never predict!

Connect to the Writing Process: Editing

Correcting Errors in Agreement

Write the verbs that do not agree with their subjects. Then write the verbs correctly. If a sentence is correct, write *C*.

11. Economics are my hardest class this semester.
12. One problem in the class are lots of homework.
13. The news of a stock market crash were exciting to discuss.
14. Problems in the stock market is a common phenomenon.
15. *Investing Dollars with Sense* are the title of our economics textbook.
16. There is many trading simulation games on the Internet.
17. Blue chip stocks usually has the highest money value.
18. Prices usually rise in a bull market.
19. A bear market generally mean declining prices.
20. A bear market is probably better for a buyer.
21. The economy vary from month to month.
22. Most consumers does not like bear markets.
23. Our professor of economics were a stockbroker.
24. The tests he gives is usually difficult.
25. My grades this semester will be higher than they usually is.

Communicate Your Ideas

APPLY TO WRITING

Art Review: *Subject and Verb Agreement*

Jacob Lawrence. *Self-Portrait,* 1977.
Gouache, 22⅛ by 30 inches. Collection of the National Academy of Design, New York, NY.

Look carefully at *Self-Portrait* by Jacob Lawrence. You have been asked by the editor of the school newspaper to write a review of this painting, which is currently on display in a local museum. Begin your review by describing the painting. Then tell readers why they should or should not go to see this work at the museum. After you write your review, read it to make sure that your subjects and verbs agree. Correct any errors before you turn it in.

QuickCheck Mixed Practice

General Interest

Write the verbs that do not agree with their subjects. Then write the verbs correctly. If a sentence is correct, write *C*.

1. The groundhog for years have been used to predict the arrival of spring.
2. The fuzz on wooly caterpillars are used to determine how hard a winter will be.
3. Neither a groundhog nor caterpillars is really dependable for forecasting, though.
4. Many of the predictions are wrong.
5. There are reports that some kinds of animals can sense earthquakes.
6. Ten catfish in a research laboratory was observed for two years.
7. During that time twenty earthquakes was experienced in the area.
8. Most of the earthquakes was inaccurately forecast by humans.
9. Seventeen of the quakes, nevertheless, were sensed early by the fish.
10. Catfish does not talk, of course, but they wiggled their whiskers just before the quakes struck.

CheckPoint

Making Subjects and Verbs Agree

For each sentence write the subject and the verb that agrees with it.

1. (Isn't, Aren't) these four loaves of bread enough?
2. There (is, are) still horse ranches within the city limits of San Diego.
3. Neither of the loudspeakers (was, were) working by the end of the concert.
4. Two members of the golf team (was, were) able to finish the course at five under par.
5. Off the coast of Maine (is, are) many rocky islands.
6. Ten dollars (was, were) a fair price for the used tennis racket.
7. My height and weight (is, are) average for my age.
8. (Doesn't, Don't) you think we can win?
9. The team (was, were) fighting among themselves over the choice of a new captain.
10. *Incredible Athletic Feats* (is, are) an interesting book by Jim Benagh.
11. Every student and teacher (was, were) at the dedication ceremony.
12. Both Ellen's sister and my sister (is, are) at the University of Wisconsin.
13. One fourth of the world's population (lives, live) on less than two thousand dollars a year.
14. (Wasn't, Weren't) you able to solve the math problem?
15. One of our best pitchers (was, were) unable to play in the county championships.

Subject and Verb Agreement

Find the verbs that do not agree with their subjects and write them correctly. If a sentence is correct, write *C*.

1. Was you with Les in the crowd after the game?
2. In the picnic basket were sandwiches for everyone.
3. Fifty dollars were contributed by my friends and me.
4. Crackers and cheese are my favorite snack.
5. Either red or green looks good on you.
6. Every actor and dancer were dressed in a colorful costume.
7. Don't that dripping faucet bother you?
8. There are few poisonous snakes in northern regions.
9. Each of the members are assigned to a committee.
10. Is your father and mother at home this evening?

Writing Sentences

Write ten sentences that follow the directions below. The verb in each sentence should be in the present tense.

Write a sentence that...

1. includes *dogs in the park* as the subject.
2. includes *a game of dominoes* as the subject.
3. includes *Mom and Dad* as the subject.
4. includes *neither bats nor balls* as the subject.
5. includes *don't* at the beginning of a sentence.
6. includes *here* at the beginning of a sentence.
7. includes *many* as the subject.
8. includes *team* as the subject.
9. includes *three fourths* as the subject.
10. includes *Romeo and Juliet,* the title of the play, as the subject.

Language and *Self-Expression*

In this painting two tigers are trapped by the tumultuous waters of a flood. Their beautiful markings contrast with the devastation around them. In the painting the artist uses color, line, and shape to depict the physical characteristics of these animals.

How could you use words to describe the characteristics of tigers? Imagine that this pair of tigers is part of a temporary exhibition for a zoo in your area. Write an informative paragraph for a sign that could be placed near the display. Include information that will interest visitors as they view the animals. Use active verbs wherever possible and be sure that your subjects and verbs agree.

Prewriting As you read about tigers, take notes on the information you learn. Highlight the most interesting facts.

Drafting Create an opening sentence that will grab the reader's attention. Then write several sentences that describe the tigers. Your final sentence should summarize the information in the paragraph or leave the reader with an interesting fact.

Revising Invite a classmate to review your paragraph and suggest changes.

Editing Check your story for errors in spelling and punctuation. Do the subjects and verbs in your sentences agree in number?

Publishing Share your paragraph with a group of classmates. You may want to choose a few selections from the class to post on a classroom Website.

Agreement of Subjects and Verbs

A verb must agree with its subject in number. *(page L375)*

A singular subject takes a singular verb. *(page L378)*

A plural subject takes a plural verb. *(page L378)*

The first helping verb must agree in number with the subject. *(page L380)*

The agreement of a verb with its subject is not changed by any interrupting words. *(pages L382–L383)*

A verb must agree in number with an indefinite pronoun used as a subject. *(page L391)*

The subject and the verb of an inverted sentence must agree in number. *(pages L392–L393)*

Common Agreement Problems

When subjects are joined by *or, nor, either/or,* or *neither/nor,* the verb agrees with the closer subject. *(page L387)*

When subjects are joined by *and* or *both/and,* the verb is plural. *(pages L387–L388)*

The verb part of a contraction must agree in number with the subject. *(page L396)*

Use a singular verb with a collective noun subject that is thought of as a unit. Use a plural verb with a collective noun subject that is thought of as individuals. *(page L397)*

A subject that expresses an amount, a measurement, a weight, or a time is usually considered singular and takes a singular verb. *(page L397)*

Use a singular verb with certain subjects that are plural in form but singular in meaning. *(page L399)*

A verb must agree with the subject of a sentence, not with the predicate nominative. *(page L399)*

A title takes a singular verb. *(page L400)*

Directions

Read the passage. Write the letter of the answer that shows the correct way to rewrite each underlined word or group of words. If the underlined part contains no error, write *D*.

EXAMPLE What <u>is</u> (1) some signs of an impending earthquake?

1 **A** be
B are
C is being
D No error

ANSWER **1 B**

According to the United States Geological Survey, there really <u>is</u> (1) no surefire ways to predict an earthquake. Seismologists, nevertheless, <u>is continuing</u> (2) to work on this problem. For example, some people <u>have observed</u> (3) unusual animal behavior before a quake: a pet dog or rabbit sometimes <u>become</u> (4) strangely agitated; a swarm of bees <u>have been seen</u> (5) evacuating its hive in a panic; catfish in a lake <u>has leaped</u> (6) out of the water onto dry land. Many earthquake researchers throughout the world <u>is seeking</u> (7) a scientific explanation for these events. Fluctuations in the earth's magnetic field, for example, <u>occurs</u> (8) at the epicenter of an earthquake, and certain animals <u>is</u> (9) sensitive to electromagnetic changes. Some seismologists studying this problem <u>hopes</u> (10) to develop similarly sensitive geophysical instruments for detecting earthquakes.

1 **A** has been
B are
C be
D No error

2 **A** are continuing
B continues
C has continued
D No error

3 **A** observes
B is observing
C has observed
D No error

4 **A** is becoming
B are becoming
C becomes
D No error

5 **A** has been seen
B are seen
C are being seen
D No error

6 **A** have leaped
B is leaping
C leaps
D No error

7 **A** are seeking
B has been seeking
C seeks
D No error

8 **A** occur
B is occurring
C has occurred
D No error

9 **A** has been
B are
C is being
D No error

10 **A** hope
B is hoping
C has hoped
D No error

CHAPTER 13

Using Adjectives and Adverbs

Directions

Read the passage and choose the word or group of words that belongs in each underlined space. Write the letter of the correct answer.

EXAMPLE The concert was the __(1)__ one in years.

1 **A** best
B better
C good
D well

ANSWER **1 A**

The __(1)__ audience in the history of the performance hall filled the auditorium. Robyn and Alison's seats were __(2)__ than the ones they had had the year before. However, the man in front of Alison was __(3)__ than she. Luckily, the girls found empty seats that were __(4)__ to the front.

The six musicians wore hats with the __(5)__ colors Robyn had ever seen. The __(6)__ one was the guitarist with a purple and pink top hat. The __(7)__ hat had sequined antlers and belonged to the drummer.

Robyn said, "I've never been __(8)__ than I am right now!" She pointed out that the drummer seemed __(9)__ than the lead guitarist. The girls decided that, as the leader of the band, the guitarist had to be __(10)__.

1 **A** largest
B larger
C most large
D large

2 **A** good
B more good
C better
D gooder

3 **A** tall
B taller
C more tall
D most tall

4 **A** more close
B close
C closest
D closer

5 **A** brightest
B most bright
C more bright
D bright

6 **A** more interesting
B interestingest
C most interesting
D interestinger

7 **A** most funny
B funniest
C funnier
D more funny

8 **A** most excited
B excited
C more excited
D exciteder

9 **A** most animated
B more animated
C animateder
D animated

10 **A** more serious
B seriouser
C most serious
D seriousest

Nam June Paik. *Video Flag Z,* 1985.
Television sets, videocassette players, videotapes, Plexiglas modular cabinet, 74½ by 138¾ by 18 inches. Los Angeles County Museum of Art.

Describe Describe the artwork and the materials the artist used to create it.

Analyze How is this flag like a real flag of the United States? How is it different?

Interpret Many viewers may compare this artwork to a real flag and attempt to interpret the symbolism of each. How could a writer use words to help an audience interpret an important symbol of the United States?

Judge Do you think a visual or a verbal medium helps an audience more easily interpret the meaning of a national symbol such as a flag? Explain your answer.

At the end of this chapter, you will use the artwork to stimulate ideas for writing.

Comparison of Adjectives and Adverbs

Before you buy a bicycle, you should do some comparison shopping. You might find out, for example, that one make of bicycle is a *good* buy. A second make, however, is a *better* buy, and a third make is the *best* buy of all. This example shows that different forms of a modifier are used to show comparison.

Most adjectives and adverbs have three forms: the positive, the comparative, and the superlative. These forms are used to show differences in degree or extent.

Most modifiers show degrees of comparison by changing form.

The **positive degree** is the basic form of an adjective or an adverb. It is used when no comparison is being made.

This is a **hot** summer.
Carla is **mature.**
Eric is a **tall** basketball player.

The **comparative degree** is used when two people, things, or actions are being compared.

This summer is **hotter** than last summer.
Carla is **more mature** than her sister.
Eric is **taller** than Josh.

The **superlative degree** is used when more than two people, things, or actions are being compared.

This is the **hottest** summer of the past three years.
Carla is the **most mature** of all her sisters.
Eric is the **tallest** player on the team.

Following are additional examples of the three degrees of comparison.

POSITIVE	Today's game is a **big** one. Josh practices **often.**
COMPARATIVE	Today's game is **bigger** than last week's game. Josh practices **more often** than Eric.
SUPERLATIVE	Tomorrow's game will be the **biggest** game of the year. Josh practices the **most often** of all the team members.

Some adverbs, such as too, somewhere, very, *and* never, *cannot be compared. If you want to review how adjectives and adverbs are used in a sentence, go to pages L91–L113.*

PRACTICE YOUR SKILLS

Check Your Understanding
Determining Degrees of Comparison

Contemporary Life

Write the underlined modifier in each sentence. Then label its degree of comparison *P* for positive, *C* for comparative, or *S* for superlative.

1. Mario ran hurriedly to the locker room with his uniform in hand.
2. The team was dressing for the most important game of the season.
3. This week's game will be more difficult than last week's game.
4. The coach sent in his fastest runners, and Mario led them out.
5. A player on the other team sauntered lazily down the court.
6. Mario, who was quicker than that player, took the ball from him.
7. Eric worked harder than Josh to defend Mario as he dribbled down the court.

8. Josh, however, was the most helpful member of the team.
9. He played a wonderful game.
10. He had fewer chances to score than Mario, but he played great defense.
11. Ming Ho is more serious than the coach is about his game performance.
12. The audience is the loudest one I have ever heard at a school game.
13. John is slower than the other players.
14. The referee jumped clumsily out of the way.
15. In another two months, this team will be better than their opponents.

 Regular Comparison

The number of syllables in a modifier determines how it forms its comparative and superlative degrees.

Add *–er* to form the comparative degree and *–est* to form the superlative degree of one-syllable modifiers.

POSITIVE	COMPARATIVE	SUPERLATIVE
brave	braver	bravest
kind	kinder	kindest
soon	sooner	soonest

The comparative and superlative degrees of many two-syllable modifiers are formed the same way. However, some two-syllable modifiers sound awkward when *–er* or *–est* is added. For these modifiers, *more* or *most* should be used to form the comparative and superlative degrees. (*More* and *most* are always used with adverbs that end in *–ly*.)

Use *–er* or *more* to form the comparative degree and *–est* or *most* to form the superlative degree of two-syllable modifiers.

POSITIVE	COMPARATIVE	SUPERLATIVE
happy	happier	happiest
helpful	more helpful	most helpful
quickly	more quickly	most quickly

When deciding whether to add *er/est* or to use *more/most* with a two-syllable modifier, let your ear be your guide. If adding *–er* or *–est* makes a word awkward or difficult to pronounce, use *more* or *most* instead. Your ear tells you to avoid awkward comparisons such as "helpfuler" and "faithfuler" or "helpfulest" and "faithfulest."

Use *more* to form the comparative degree and *most* to form the superlative degree of modifiers with three or more syllables.

POSITIVE	COMPARATIVE	SUPERLATIVE
trivial	more trivial	most trivial
serious	more serious	most serious
vigorously	more vigorously	most vigorously

Because *less* and *least* mean the opposite of *more* and *most,* use these words to form negative comparisons.

	NEGATIVE COMPARISONS	
trivial	less trivial	least trivial
serious	less serious	least serious
vigorously	less vigorously	least vigorously

Practice Your Skills

Check Your Understanding
Forming the Comparison of Modifiers

Write each modifier. Then write its comparative and superlative forms.

1. difficult
2. colorful
3. eagerly
4. swiftly
5. abrupt
6. quick
7. sure
8. muddy
9. hastily
10. heavy
11. safe
12. high
13. lively
14. loudly
15. fast
16. slow
17. seasick
18. dark
19. easily
20. frisky

Check Your Understanding
Forming the Negative Comparison of Modifiers

21.–25. Write the first five modifiers in the previous exercise. Then write the negative comparative and superlative forms, using *less* and *least*.

Connect to the Writing Process: Drafting
Writing Sentences with Comparisons

Write sentences using the indicated form of the words below.

26. positive form of *high*
27. comparative form of *low*
28. superlative form of *eagerly*
29. positive form of *definite*
30. comparative form of *hasty*
31. superlative form of *close*
32. positive form of *serious*
33. comparative form of *sunny*

34. superlative form of *swiftly*
35. positive form of *leisurely*

Irregular Comparison

The following adjectives and adverbs are compared irregularly. The comparative and superlative forms of these modifiers should be memorized.

POSITIVE	COMPARATIVE	SUPERLATIVE
bad	worse	worst
badly	worse	worst
ill	worse	worst
good	better	best
well	better	best
little	less	least
many	more	most
much	more	most

Do not add regular comparison endings to the comparative and superlative degrees of these irregular modifiers. For example, *worse* is the comparative form of *bad*. You should never use "worser."

Connect to Speaking and Writing

As writers work, they usually have a good dictionary on hand to use as a reference. When you write comparisons, use the dictionary if you are unsure of the comparative or superlative form of an adjective or adverb. The dictionary will list the various forms of adjectives and adverbs if they are irregular. The dictionary also shows if the addition of *–er* or *–est* changes the spelling of the base word in any way. A good collegiate dictionary can be a writer's best friend.

PRACTICE YOUR SKILLS

Check Your Understanding
Forming the Comparison of Irregular Modifiers

Contemporary Life **Write the comparative and superlative forms of the underlined modifier.**

1. That movie was really bad.
It was ■ than the movie we saw last week.
In fact, it was the ■ movie I have ever seen in my entire life.

2. Felipe showed much concern about the poor quality of the movie.
Belinda showed even ■ concern than Felipe.
Amazingly, Juana showed the ■ concern of all.

3. Many movies are filmed in Texas.
■ movies are filmed in New York.
The ■ movies are filmed in California.

4. The movie we rented this morning was good.
The movie we rented yesterday was ■.
The movie we rented last month was the ■ I had ever seen.

5. I have little interest in watching another movie this week.
I have ■ interest in watching television.
I have the ■ interest in listening to music.

Check Your Understanding
Finding Forms of Comparison in a Dictionary

Write each modifier below. Then write its comparative and superlative forms. (If you are unsure of the form or its spelling, look up the word in a dictionary.)

6. mad
7. lovely
8. timely
9. far
10. hot
11. fun
12. easy
13. homey
14. lonely
15. malevolent

Connect to the Writing Process: Editing
Using Forms of Comparison

Write each incorrect modifier and then write it correctly. If a sentence is correct, write *C*.

16. I have the baddest cold I have ever had.

17. One morning I felt a little run down, but by the afternoon I was iller.

18. I wanted to get better in the littlest amount of time possible.

19. My sister called the doctor, who gave me many instructions.

20. In fact, it was the manyest instructions I had ever received from a doctor.

21. He told me to drink mucher water than usual.

22. He also recommended a good night's sleep.

23. The next day I felt gooder than I had the day before.

24. Of all the instructions he gave, I was glad about the recommendation for sleep.

25. I hope I never have a bad cold like that one again.

Communicate Your Ideas

APPLY TO WRITING

Tall Tale: ***Comparison with Adjectives and Adverbs***

Tall tales are a part of American legends. Paul Bunyan and Pecos Bill are two heroes of tall tales. Make up a Paul Bunyan–like character and write a tall tale about him or her. Remember that these characters are always strong and powerful, and their actions are often used to explain natural formations like the Grand Canyon or the Great Lakes. After you have finished, underline the adjectives and adverbs you used in your tall tale. Label each modifier *P* if it is the positive form, *C* if it is the comparative form, or *S* if it is the superlative form.

QuickCheck Mixed Practice

Contemporary Life

Write each incorrect modifier and then write it correctly. If the modifier in a sentence is correct, write *C*.

1. Spending the day at an amusement park is the more enjoyable thing to do.
2. Amusement parks are one of the better places on Earth!
3. The more exciting ride of all is the roller coaster.
4. When the car drops down from the tallest hill on the ride, the car almost flies.
5. Roller coasters seem quickest than sports cars.
6. A most crowded place than the roller coaster is the midway.
7. Kids love to try to win the bigger stuffed animals at the ring-toss booth.
8. Of course, children rush most quickly to this booth than their parents do.
9. Their parents know the games are most difficult than they look.
10. Most parents think that the midway is the worse place to spend money in the entire amusement park.
11. Everyone in our family likes the water rides more than the roller coasters.
12. One water ride is scariest than a roller coaster.
13. This summer was lesser enjoyable than last summer.
14. We enjoy the amusement park the mostest of all the parks in town.
15. The worse part about going to the amusement park is having to leave.

Problems with Comparisons

The following special problems may arise when you compare people and things.

Double Comparisons

Use only one method of forming the comparative and superlative degree of a modifier.

Do not use both *–er* and *more* to form the comparative degree, or both *–est* and *most* to form the superlative degree.

DOUBLE COMPARISON	Our city is more larger than most.
CORRECT	Our city is **larger** than most.
DOUBLE COMPARISON	I have the most accuratest map of the city.
CORRECT	I have the **most accurate** map of the city.

Illogical Comparisons

Only similar things should be compared. If you compare different things, you end up with an illogical comparison, a comparison that does not make sense.

Compare only items of a similar kind.

ILLOGICAL COMPARISON	This building's roof is steeper than the bank. (A roof is being compared to a bank.)
LOGICAL COMPARISON	This building's roof is steeper than the bank's. (A roof is being compared with another roof.)

ILLOGICAL COMPARISON	The tour guide's description of the building's history was better than the girls. (The description is being compared to girls.)
LOGICAL COMPARISON	The tour guide's description of the building's history was better than the girls' description. (The description is being compared to a description.)

You can learn about the use of an apostrophe with possessive nouns on pages L575–L577.

Other and *Else* in Comparison

Be sure that you do not make the mistake of comparing one thing with itself when it is part of a group. You can avoid this by adding *other* or *else* to your comparison.

Add *other* and *else* when comparing a member of a group with the rest of the group.

In the first example that follows, the bank building is supposedly being compared with the *other* structures in the city. However, without the word *other,* the building is also being compared with itself. It is a structure in the city.

INCORRECT	The bank building is taller than any structure in the city.
CORRECT	The bank building is taller than any **other** structure in the city.
INCORRECT	The bank president delivers more speeches than anyone in the company. (Since the bank president works in the company, he or she is being compared with himself or herself.)
CORRECT	The bank president delivers more speeches than anyone **else** in the company. (With the addition of the word *else*, the bank president no longer is being compared to himself or herself.)

Practice Your Skills

Check Your Understanding
Making Comparisons

Contemporary Life

Write *I* if the comparison in the sentence is incorrect. Write *C* if it is correct.

1. Our map of the downtown area made locations more clearer for my visiting uncle.
2. Our city has a more interesting history than any city in the state.
3. Our city is more picturesque than most other cities its size and age.
4. The architecture of the bank is more interesting than the city hall.
5. The sidewalks were constructed of the most beautiful cobblestones.
6. The town hall is more farther south than any building except the old courthouse at the end of Alexandria Street.
7. To make it across town in time for the lecture, we will have to walk more faster than we have been walking so far.
8. Mrs. Little, the mayor of our city, knows more about the city's history than any other citizen has ever known or recorded.
9. I think that was the most interestingest lecture I have ever heard.
10. The mayor's lecture lasted longer than the police officer.

Connect to the Writing Process: Revising
Correcting Mistakes in Comparisons

11.–18. Rewrite the sentences above that contain errors in comparison.

APPLY TO WRITING

Comparing and Contrasting: *Adjectives and Adverbs*

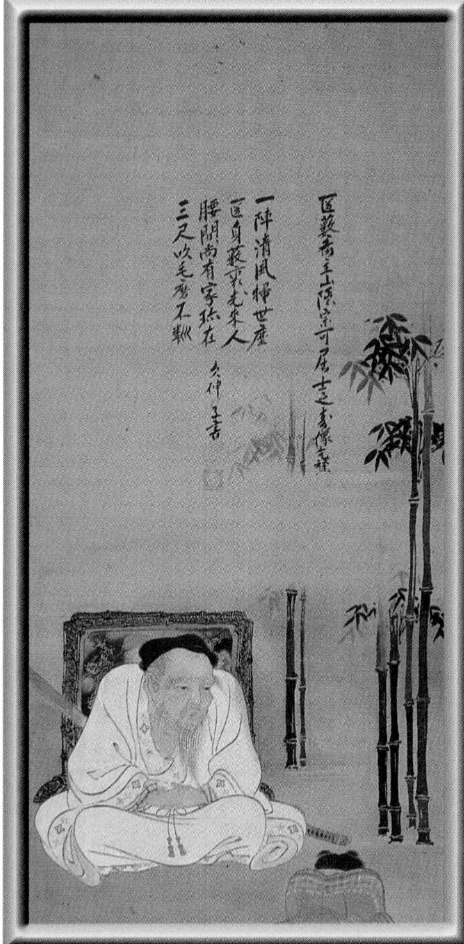

Rembrandt van Rijn.
Self-Portrait, 1659.
Oil on canvas, $33\frac{1}{4}$ by 26 inches.
National Gallery of Art, Washington, DC.

Kano Tan'yu. (Detail) *Sakuma Shogen,*
Edo period, ca. 1636.
Ink and color on silk, $25\frac{1}{8}$ by $11\frac{1}{8}$ inches. ©Shinju-an Temple, Kyoto, Japan.

Both of these works of art are portraits, artworks that show likenesses of people. Look carefully at each of the works. What is similar about them? How do they differ? Write a short essay for your classmates in which you compare and contrast these two portraits. Be sure to use the correct form of comparison of adjectives and adverbs.

General Interest **Write each incorrect modifier and then write it correctly. If a sentence is correct, write *C*.**

1. Norman Rockwell was one of America's best known illustrators.
2. Of these two pictures, I enjoyed this one the most.
3. The painting with the boy and the Santa Claus suit is the most cutest picture I have ever seen.
4. The most versatile artist in our class is Roberta.
5. She is the youngest of the two Compton sisters.
6. In our class the person with the less interest in art is Anthony.
7. His painting is messier than any painting in the class.
8. Sherry's sketch is better than anyone in the show.
9. My class this year is more difficult than last year.
10. I have worked more harder this year than ever before.
11. The museum's exhibit this month is more interestinger than last month.
12. These paintings are more abstracter than other paintings.
13. Charlene likes Picasso's works most than other painters.
14. We enjoyed this exhibit the most of all the exhibits that we visited.
15. Carlos thinks painting with oils is hardest than painting with watercolors.

Problems with Modifiers

Most words that end in *–ly* are adverbs. However, some adjectives such as *friendly* and *lovely* also have this ending. It is important to know whether a word is an adjective or an adverb in order to form the comparisons correctly.

Good or *Well?*

Good is an adjective that follows a linking verb. *Well* is an adverb that often follows an action verb. However, when *well* means "in good health" or "satisfactory," it is used as an adjective.

That baking bread smells **good.** (adjective)

I like **good**, homemade bread! (adjective)

Jocelyn cooks **well.** (adverb)

I feel quite **well** since I have eaten. (adjective meaning "in good health")

Double Negatives

Words such as *but* (when it means "only"), *hardly, never, no, nobody, not* (and its contraction *n't*), *nothing, only,* and *scarcely* are all negatives. Two negatives should not be used to express one negative meaning.

Avoid using a double negative.

A double negative often cancels itself out, leaving a positive statement. For example, if you say, "There isn't no more time," you are really saying, "There is more time."

DOUBLE NEGATIVE	Don't never cook while Mom is gone.
CORRECT	Do**n't** cook while Mom is gone.
CORRECT	**Never** cook while Mom is gone.

PRACTICE YOUR SKILLS

Check Your Understanding
Comparing with Problem Modifiers

Contemporary Life

Write *I* if the comparison in the sentence is incorrect. Write *C* if it is correct.

1. I didn't go nowhere near the stove today.
2. We had a well selection of chips and sandwiches, so I ate that instead of cooking.
3. I can hardly wait until Mom returns from her business trip today.
4. I haven't done nothing about preparing our meals since she has been gone.
5. I would have cooked, but I wasn't feeling good.
6. I didn't tell my mom because I didn't never want to worry her.
7. Mom's business trip went good, but she was glad to be home.
8. She cooks very well, and I enjoyed the chicken soup she made me.
9. I'm a good cook, and I don't mind cooking.
10. When I feel well, there is not nothing I'd rather do than cook.

Connect to the Writing Process: Revising
Using Modifiers Correctly

11.–17. Rewrite correctly the preceding sentences that contain errors in comparison.

Communicate Your Ideas

APPLY TO WRITING

Persuasive Speech: *Modifiers*

Your school board has proposed ending physical education courses at your high school. At the next meeting of the board, you will have five minutes to explain why you agree or disagree with the proposal. Think about your position on this matter. List reasons and examples that support your position, being as specific as possible. Then arrange your notes in logical order and write the first draft of your speech. Edit your work, paying special attention to comparative and superlative forms of any modifiers. Then write a final draft and practice reading your speech aloud.

Mixed Practice

Sports Topic **Rewrite the following paragraph, correcting each mistake in the use of comparisons.**

The Olympic decathlon is held in greater esteem than any event in sports. The champion of this event is generally considered the most greatest athlete in the world. The performances in the decathlon are watched more than those in any Olympic event. The athletes competing in this event must be well at several different activities. They can't hardly go even one day without running or practicing their sport. A decathlon performer must be able to jump the highest, run the fastest, and throw the javelin the most farthest. The winner must be the bestest.

CheckPoint

Using Modifiers Correctly

Write the following sentences, correcting each error. If a sentence is correct, write *C*.

1. For its size the honeybee is much more stronger than a person.
2. Paul hasn't done nothing yet about the garden.
3. Rainbow Bridge in Utah is larger than any other natural arch.
4. Woodworking is the bestest class I have this year.
5. Sean hasn't never seen *Star Wars*.
6. English contains more words than any language.
7. There isn't no more hamburger for the picnic.
8. The Great Dane is among the most largest of all dogs.
9. I think Molly is smarter than anyone in her class.
10. The copies seem brightest than the originals.
11. Which is hardest, ice-skating or roller-skating?
12. Do people in the United States have a higher standard of living than anyone in the world?
13. Nobody knew nothing about the defective fuse.
14. The flood last week was the worst yet.
15. That was the less expensive gift I could find.
16. Even an expert could hardly tell the difference between the real and the counterfeit bill.
17. Lee plays the drums better than anyone in his band.
18. Of Sarah's parents, her dad is most easygoing.
19. Tulips haven't never done well on that side of the house.
20. Of the two finalists, Carl has the best chance of winning.

Writing with Modifiers

Write the correct form of each modifier below.

1. the comparative of *quickly*
2. the comparative of *wide*
3. the superlative of *good*
4. the superlative of *generous*
5. the comparative of *little*
6. the superlative of *bright*
7. the comparative of *carefully*
8. the superlative of *bad*
9. the comparative of *brave*
10. the comparative of *many*
11. the superlative of *angry*
12. the superlative of *evenly*
13. the comparative of *zany*
14. the negative superlative of *courageous*
15. the comparative of *nervous*
16. the comparative of *easily*
17. the comparative of *swiftly*
18. the superlative of *heavy*
19. the negative comparative of *abrupt*
20. the superlative of *surely*
21. the superlative of *thin*
22. the negative comparative of *seasick*
23. the comparative of *ill*
24. the superlative of *much*
25. the comparative of *fast*

Writing Sentences

Write a paragraph that compares three pets or three desserts. Use modifiers in the positive, comparative, and superlative degrees.

Language and *Self-Expression*

To create this "moving painting," the artist placed a series of televisions and videocassette players side by side. The resulting wall of video represents the flag of the United States. As viewers compare the artwork to a real flag, they often experience a variety of feelings, such as national pride or anxiety about the future effects of technology.

Words can also help people experience a variety of feelings. Write a poem that compares a national symbol with a feeling or a concept. In your poem include at least two modifiers that use the comparative or superlative degree. Post your poem on a classroom bulletin board for your classmates to read. You may also want to share your writing with an American history class.

Prewriting Create a Venn diagram comparing the symbol and the feeling or concept you selected. Your diagram should show how these things are alike and how they are different.

Drafting Write either a rhyming or a free verse poem. Write the first draft quickly, letting your words and ideas flow. Use a variety of adjectives and adverbs to add interest to your writing.

Revising Read your poem aloud to a partner. Ask your partner to listen for the rhythm and flow of the poem. Do transitional words guide him or her from the beginning to the end of the poem?

Editing Read your work again. Check your poem for errors in spelling and punctuation. Be sure that you used the comparative and superlative forms of modifiers correctly.

Publishing Prepare a final copy of your poem and post it in the classroom.

Another Look

The **positive degree** is the basic form of an adjective or an adverb. It is used when no comparison is being made.

The **comparative degree** is used when two people, things, or actions are being compared.

The **superlative degree** is used when more than two people, things, or actions are being compared.

Regular and Irregular Comparison

Add *-er* to form the comparative degree and *-est* to form the superlative degree of one-syllable modifiers. *(page L415)*

Add *-er* or *more* to form the comparative degree and *-est* or *most* to form the superlative degree of two-syllable modifiers. *(page L416)*

Use *more* to form the comparative degree and *most* to form the superlative degree of modifiers with three or more syllables. *(page L416)*

Use *less* and *least* to form negative comparisons of modifiers. *(page L416)*

The comparative and superlative forms of some modifiers must be memorized. These modifiers include: *bad, badly, ill, good, well, little, many, much.* *(page L418)*

Problems with Comparisons

Do not use both *-er* and *more* to form the comparative degree, or both *-est* and *most* to form the superlative degree. *(page L422)*

Compare only items of a similar kind. *(pages L422–L423)*

Add *other* and *else* when comparing a member of a group with the rest of the group. *(page L423)*

Problems with Modifiers

Good is an adjective that follows a linking verb. *Well* is an adverb that often follows an action word. However, when *well* means "in good health" or "satisfactory," it is used as an adjective. *(page L427)*

Avoid using double negatives. *(pages L427–L428)*

Directions

Read the passage and choose the word or group of words that belongs in each underlined space. Write the letter of the correct answer.

EXAMPLE Jim saw the __(1)__ car he had ever seen in the showroom window.

1 **A** sleekest
B sleeker
C most sleek
D more sleek

ANSWER **1 A**

The new car was __(1)__ than Jim's old car. With four-wheel drive, it also had __(2)__ brakes for his trips to the mountains. However, it was __(3)__ than what Jim could afford.

Later Jim went to the mall. He saw two jackets. One was __(4)__ than the other. The __(5)__ jacket had __(6)__ buttons. Although they were both blue, the more formal one was a __(7)__ shade. The more formal jacket also had the __(8)__ sleeves. Jim decided to buy the __(9)__ jacket. "Buying a jacket is certainly __(10)__ than buying a car," he thought.

1 **A** powerful
B more powerful
C most powerful
D powerfulest

2 **A** better
B good
C more good
D best

3 **A** expensive
B more expensive
C most expensive
D more expensiver

4 **A** formaler
B most formal
C more formal
D formal

5 **A** least formal
B less formal
C unformal
D formal

6 **A** more fewer
B fewest
C fewer
D most fewer

7 **A** more deeper
B most deep
C deepest
D deeper

8 **A** most wide
B more wide
C widest
D wider

9 **A** lightest
B lighter
C more lighter
D most lightest

10 **A** affordable
B affordabler
C most affordable
D more affordable

A Writer's Glossary of Usage

In the last four chapters, you covered the fundamental elements of usage. A Writer's Glossary of Usage presents some specific areas that might give you difficulty. Before you use the glossary, though, there are some terms that you should know.

You will notice references in the glossary to various levels of language. Two of these levels of language are standard English and nonstandard English. **Standard English** refers to the rules and the conventions of usage that are accepted and used most widely by English-speaking people throughout the world. **Nonstandard English** has many variations because it is influenced by regional differences and dialects, as well as by current slang. Remember that *nonstandard* does not mean that the language is wrong but that the language may be inappropriate in certain situations. Because nonstandard English lacks uniformity, you should use standard English when you write.

You will also notice references to formal and informal English. **Formal English** is used for written work because it follows the conventional rules of grammar, usage, and mechanics. Examples of the use of formal English can usually be found in business letters, technical reports, and well-written compositions. **Informal English,** on the other hand, follows the conventions of standard English but might include words and phrases that would seem out of place in a formal piece of writing. Informal English is often used in magazine articles, newspaper stories, and fiction writing.

The items in this glossary have been arranged alphabetically so that you can use this section as a reference tool.

a, an Use *a* before words beginning with consonant sounds and *an* before words beginning with vowel sounds.

> Did you buy **a** new CD?
> No, it was given to me as **an** early birthday gift.

accept, except *Accept* is a verb that means "to receive with consent." *Except* is usually a preposition that means "but" or "other than."

> Everyone **except** Bernie **accepted** the news calmly.

advice, advise *Advice* is a noun that means "a recommendation." *Advise* is a verb that means "to recommend."

> I usually follow my doctor's **advice.**
> He **advised** me to exercise more often.

affect, effect *Affect* is a verb that means "to influence" or "to act upon." *Effect* is usually a noun that means "a result" or "an influence." As a verb, *effect* means "to accomplish" or "to produce."

> Does the weather **affect** your mood?
> No, it has no **effect** on me.
> The medicine **effected** a change in my disposition.

Connect to Speaking and Writing

Professional writers sometimes use *ain't* to enhance a dialect and create a humorous effect. Notice the effectiveness of this device in Mark Twain's writing.

> Tom's most well now, and got his bullet around his neck on a watch-guard for a watch, and is always seeing what time it is, and so there **ain't** nothing more to write about, and I am rotten glad of it, because if I'd 'a' knowed what a trouble it was to make a book I wouldn't 'a' tackled it, and **ain't** a-going to no more.
>
> –*Mark Twain,* The Adventures of Huckleberry Finn

ain't This contraction is nonstandard English. Avoid it in your writing.

NONSTANDARD	Ken **ain't** here yet.
STANDARD	Ken **isn't** here yet.

all ready, already *All ready* means "completely ready." *Already* means "previously."

We were **all ready** to go by seven o'clock.
I had **already** told my parents that we were going to the movies.

all together, altogether *All together* means "in a group." *Altogether* means "wholly" or "thoroughly."

Let's try to sing **all together** for a change.
The traditional song will sound **altogether** different if we do.

a lot People very often write these two words incorrectly as one. There is no such word as "alot." *A lot,* however, even when it is written as two words, should be avoided in formal writing.

INFORMAL	Famous movie stars receive **a lot** of fan mail.
FORMAL	Famous movie stars usually receive **a large quantity** of fan mail.

among, between These words are both prepositions. *Among* is used when referring to three or more people or things. *Between* is used when referring to two people or things.

Put your present **among** the others.
Then come and sit **between** Judith and me.

amount, number *Amount* refers to a singular word. *Number* refers to a plural word.

Although there were a **number** of rainy days this month, the total **amount** of rain was less than usual.

Connect to Speaking and Writing

To avoid confusion in usage between *amount* and *number* when speaking and writing, remember that *amount* refers to things in bulk or mass that cannot be counted, whereas *number* refers to things that can be counted.

I was surprised at the **amount** of coffee he drank.
(Coffee cannot be counted.)

He put a large **number** of coffee beans into the machine.
(Coffee beans can be counted.) 

anywhere, everywhere, nowhere, somewhere Do not add *-s* to any of these words.

I looked **everywhere** but could not find my keys.

at Do not use *at* after *where.*

NONSTANDARD	Do you know **where** we're **at?**
STANDARD	Do you know **where** we are?

a while, awhile *A while* is made up of an article and a noun; together, they are mainly used after a preposition. *Awhile* is an adverb that stands alone and means "for a short period of time."

We can stay on the job for **a while.**
After we work **awhile,** we can take a break.

Practice Your Skills

Check Your Understanding
Finding the Correct Word

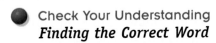

Contemporary Life **Write the word in parentheses that correctly completes each sentence.**

1. The junior varsity team has (all ready, already) started football practice.

2. (Accept, Except) for a few players, the team is in excellent condition.

3. This year's team has (a, an) difficult schedule.
4. Their coaches offer the players useful (advice, advise) (everywhere, everywheres) the team plays.
5. In addition, they teach the eager squad a large (amount, number) of plays.
6. Loyalty (among, between) the members of the football team is encouraged.
7. (A lot, A large amount) of time is spent in daily practice.
8. Players arriving late (affect, effect) the practice schedule.
9. The players meet (all together, altogether) before and after practice (a while, awhile) for a pep talk.
10. It (ain't, isn't) long before the first game will be played.

Connect to the Writing Process: Revising
Recognizing Correct Usage

Add interest to this paragraph by replacing the term *a lot* with a more precise word or phrase. As you rewrite the paragraph, use a different word or phrase each time.

A lot of students waited eagerly for the first football game. When the day arrived, a lot of the ninth grade class met for a pep rally. The teachers advised the students not to wander around a lot. After cheering and applauding a lot, they returned to class, a lot satisfied with their class spirit.

bad, badly *Bad* is an adjective and often follows a linking verb. *Badly* is used as an adverb. In the first two examples, *felt* is a linking verb.

Nonstandard	Luke felt **badly** all day.
Standard	Luke felt **bad** all day.
Standard	Luke **badly** needs a haircut.

bring, take *Bring* indicates motion toward the speaker. *Take* indicates motion away from the speaker.

> **Bring** me the stamps.
> Now, please **take** this letter to the post office.

can, may *Can* expresses ability. *May* expresses possibility or permission.

> I **can** baby-sit for you tonight.
> **May** I watch TV after Kenny is asleep?

doesn't, don't *Doesn't* is singular and must agree with a singular subject. *Don't* is plural and must agree with a plural subject, except when used with the singular pronouns *I* and *you.*

> This article **doesn't** make sense to me. (singular subject)
>
> These articles **don't** make sense to me. (plural subject)

double negative Words such as *barely, but* (when it means "only"), *hardly, never, no, none, no one, barely, nobody, not* (and its contraction *n't*), *nothing, nowhere, only,* and *scarcely* are all negatives. Do not use two negatives to express one negative meaning.

NONSTANDARD	I **hardly never** see you anymore.
STANDARD	I **hardly** see you anymore.
STANDARD	I **never** see you anymore.

etc. *Etc.* is an abbreviation for the Latin phrase *et cetera,* which means "and other things." Never use the word *and* with *etc.* If you do, what you are really saying is "and and other things." You should not use this abbreviation at all in formal writing.

INFORMAL	Before moving, we had to pack our clothes, books, records, **etc.**
FORMAL	Before moving, we had to pack our clothes, books, records, **and other belongings.**

fewer, less *Fewer* is plural and refers to things that can be counted. *Less* is singular and refers to quantities and qualities that cannot be counted.

> There seem to be **fewer** hours in the day.
> I seem to have **less** time to get my homework done.

good, well *Good* is an adjective and often follows a linking verb. *Well* is an adverb and often follows an action verb. However, when *well* means "in good health" or "satisfactory," it is used as an adjective.

> The biscuits smell **good.** (adjective)
>
> Janice cooks **well.** (adverb)
>
> I feel quite **well** after eating the chicken soup. (adjective meaning "in good health")

have, of Never substitute *of* for the verb *have.* When speaking, many people make a contraction of *have.* For example, they might say, "We should've gone." Because *'ve* may sound like *of, of* is often mistakenly substituted for *have* in writing.

NONSTANDARD	We should **of** started earlier.
STANDARD	We should **have** started earlier.

hear, here *Hear* is a verb that means "to perceive by listening." *Here* is an adverb that means "in this place."

> I can't **hear** the music from **here**.

hole, whole A *hole* is an opening. *Whole* means "complete" or "entire."

> Have you noticed the **hole** in your coat?
> Did you leave your coat on for the **whole** movie?

in, into Use *in* when you are referring to a stationary place. Use *into* when you want to express motion from one place to another.

> Is the money **in** your coat pocket?
> Why don't you transfer it **into** your wallet?

its, it's *Its* is a possessive pronoun and means "belonging to it." *It's* is a contraction for *it is.*

> The dog returned home to **its** owner.
> **It's** fun to watch **its** happy expression.

PRACTICE YOUR SKILLS

Check Your Understanding
Finding the Correct Word

Literature Topic **Write the word in parentheses that correctly completes each sentence.**

1. Who (doesn't, don't) enjoy an interesting detective story?
2. It (can, may) also be referred to as a mystery story or whodunit.
3. Some writers use (fewer, less) clues than others, but all detective stories contain clues designed to solve a crime.
4. The detective story made (its, it's) first appearance in Edgar Allan Poe's writings.
5. Poe also wrote essays, poems, short stories, (etc., and other works).
6. His fictional detective, C. Auguste Dupin, (may have, may of) been based on a real-life detective.
7. Poe wrote a (hole, whole) group of stories that featured Detective Dupin.
8. Detective Dupin first appeared (in, into) Poe's "The Murders in the Rue Morgue."
9. (Its, It's) a known fact that Sir Arthur Conan Doyle, a British writer, later used Dupin as a model for Sherlock Holmes.
10. Would Doyle feel (bad, badly) if he knew that the name Sherlock Holmes is better known today than his?

Connect to the Writing Process: Revising

Recognizing Correct Usage

Rewrite the following paragraph, changing the words that are used incorrectly.

In fiction an author don't often leave readers in suspense. Usually the hole case is carefully tied together into a neat package. Hardly ever is a crime left unsolved in a fictional detective story. In real life, however, its often not what we hear about. On television, for example, news programs sometimes bring us to the scene of a unsolved mystery and try to recreate it. Some shows present the facts good while others present them bad. Regardless of the way the program is presented, the crime don't have a final resolution as fictional detective stories do.

Communicate Your Ideas

APPLY TO WRITING

Explanatory Writing: ***Adjectives and Adverbs***

You have been asked to tutor a student who is experiencing difficulty with the following terms: *bad/badly* and *good/well.* In your own words, write an explanation to offer the student for the choice(s) underlined in each of the following sentences.

1. Interest in a detective story often depends on whether the plot is bad or good.
2. Clues that are presented well prevent the reader from solving the crime too quickly.
3. If the description of a possible suspect is presented badly, it detracts from the story.
4. A writer might present a suspect as being in bad health to gain sympathy from the reader for that particular character.
5. Most people feel good at the end of a detective story because justice has been served.

knew, new *Knew,* the past tense of the verb *know,* means "was acquainted with." *New* is an adjective that means "recently made" or "just found."

Michael's sneakers looked so clean and white that I **knew** they were **new.**

learn, teach *Learn* means "to gain knowledge." *Teach* means "to instruct" or "to show how."

I just **learned** how to use that computer program that Mom bought for us.

Now I can **teach** you how to use it.

leave, let *Leave* means "to depart" or "to go away from." *Let* means "to allow" or "to permit."

NONSTANDARD	**Leave** me help you carry those packages into the house.
STANDARD	**Let** me help you carry those packages into the house.
STANDARD	Don't **leave** before you help me carry in my packages.

lie, lay *Lie* means "to rest or recline." *Lie* is never followed by a direct object. Its principal parts are *lie, lying, lay,* and *lain. Lay* means "to put or set (something) down." *Lay* is usually followed by a direct object. Its principal parts are *lay, laying, laid,* and *laid.*

LIE	Our kittens always **lie** on the sofa. They are **lying** there now. They **lay** there all morning. They have **lain** there for a long time.
LAY	**Lay** their food dish on the floor. (*Dish* is the direct object.)
	Jill is **laying** the dish on the floor. Molly **laid** the dish on the floor yesterday. Until recently Gary always has **laid** the dish on the floor.

You can learn more about using the verbs lie *and* lay *on pages L291–L292.*

like, as *Like* is a preposition that introduces a prepositional phrase. *As* is usually a subordinating conjunction that introduces an adverb clause.

STANDARD	Betty should read stories **like** these. (prepositional phrase)
NONSTANDARD	Betty usually does **like** she is told. (clause)
STANDARD	Betty usually does **as** she is told.

passed, past *Passed* is the past tense of the verb *pass.* As a noun *past* means "a time gone by." As an adjective *past* means "just gone" or "elapsed." As a preposition *past* means "beyond."

In the **past** I have **passed** all math tests.
(*past* as a noun)

I have walked **past** my math class for the **past** few days, hoping to see my final grade posted.
(*past* as a preposition and then as an adjective)

rise, raise *Rise* means "to move upward" or "to get up." *Rise* is never followed by a direct object. Its principal parts are *rise, rising, rose,* and *risen. Raise* means "to lift (something) up," "to increase," or "to grow something." *Raise* is usually followed by a direct object. Its principal parts are *raise, raising, raised,* and *raised.*

> Dad will **rise** at 7:00 A.M.
> At that time, he will **raise** the shades.
> (*Shades* is the direct object.)

You can learn more about using the verbs rise *and* raise *on pages L292–L293.*

shall, will Formal English uses *shall* with first-person pronouns and *will* with second- and third-person pronouns. Today, *shall* and *will* are used interchangeably with *I* and *we,* except that *shall* should be used with *I* and *we* for questions.

> **Shall** I invite her to join the club?
> I **will** ask her tonight.

sit, set *Sit* means "to rest in an upright position." *Sit* is never followed by a direct object. Its principal parts are *sit, sitting, sat,* and *sat. Set* means "to put or place (something)." *Set* is usually followed by a direct object. Its principal parts are *set, setting, set* and *set.*

> After Mom has **set** the timer, we will **sit** and wait thirty minutes for dinner.
> (*Timer* is the direct object of *set.*]

You can learn more about using the verbs sit *and* set *on pages L293–L294.*

than, then *Than* is a subordinating conjunction and is used for comparisons. *Then* is an adverb and means "at that time" or "next."

NONSTANDARD	Jupiter is much larger **then** Saturn.
STANDARD	After learning that Jupiter is much larger **than** Saturn, we **then** learned some other interesting facts about our solar system.

that, which, who All three words are relative pronouns. *That* refers to people, animals, or things; *which* refers to animals or things; and *who* refers to people.

> The airline tickets **that** I bought for the trip were expensive.
> From the air we saw the cows, **which** looked like little dots.
> The flight attendant **who** was on our plane gave instructions.

Practice Your Skills

Check Your Understanding
Finding the Correct Word

Contemporary Life **Write the word in parentheses that correctly completes each sentence.**

1. The family (shall, will) go on their annual family picnic tomorrow.
2. Leslie and David (knew, new) they could each invite one friend.
3. They invited the twins (which, who) live in the house down the road.
4. The family members will (raise, rise) early and pack the car.
5. Leslie (lain, laid) out the tablecloth and the paper plates the night before the picnic.
6. Their parents always (leave, let) them help prepare food for the picnic basket and decide on the sporting equipment to use at the picnic.
7. David first wanted to (learn, teach) how to make deviled eggs.
8. His cooking (passed, past) inspection after the family sampled the eggs.
9. Leslie declared that they tasted exactly (like, as) the ones from the deli.

10. (Than, Then) she began baking brownies.
11. Later they took out the sporting equipment, (which, who) was in the garage.
12. Leslie and David (sit, set) a variety of sporting equipment next to the car.
13. David remembered to include his (new, knew) baseball and glove.
14. Leslie and David decided to (teach, learn) the twins how to play volleyball.
15. The whole family agreed they would have a better time (than, then) last year.

Connect to the Writing Process: Drafting

Writing Correct Forms of Verbs

Rewrite the following paragraph, changing the words that are used incorrectly.

On the day of the picnic, Leslie had sat her alarm for 7:00 A.M. After the alarm rang, she set up on the side of the bed. Next, she slowly raised the blinds to see if the sun had raised. Deciding to rest another few minutes, she lied down on the bed again, carefully laying her head on the pillow. When the alarm sounded, she went downstairs to help sit the picnic items inside the basket. Before sitting down to eat, she called David. David came to the table and set down. He watched Leslie rise the blinds so that they could watch the sunrise while they ate. After breakfast, David lay an old blanket on the floor and quickly folded it before the dog could lay down on it.

Communicate Your Ideas

APPLY TO WRITING

Description: *Verbs*

Pretend you have arrived at the beach or park for a family picnic. Write a well-developed paragraph in which you describe the day's events. Use the scene in the picture to help you get started. In your description, include at least four of the phrases listed below, making sure you use the correct principal parts of the verbs in parentheses.

- on the blanket *(lie, lay)*
- the golden sun *(sit, set)*
- food to the picnic area *(bring, take)*
- the volleyball net *(sit, set)*
- the picnic basket to the car *(bring, take)*
- at the picnic bench *(sit, set)*

their, there, they're *Their* is a possessive pronoun. *There* is usually an adverb, but sometimes it begins an inverted sentence. *They're* is a contraction for *they are.*

Tell them to take **their** time.
There will be many reporters gathered in the hall.
They're meeting at seven o'clock for the press conference.

theirs, there's *Theirs* is a possessive pronoun. *There's* is a contraction for *there is*.

These messages are ours; those messages are **theirs.**
There's a message for you in the office.

them, those Never use *them* as a subject or as an adjective.

NONSTANDARD	**Them** are freshly picked tomatoes. (subject)
STANDARD	**Those** are freshly picked tomatoes.
NONSTANDARD	Did you like **them** tomatoes? (adjective)
STANDARD	Did you like **those** tomatoes?

this here, that there Avoid using *here* or *there* in addition to *this* or *that.*

NONSTANDARD	**That there** chair is very comfortable.
STANDARD	**That** chair is very comfortable.
NONSTANDARD	**This here** sofa matches your chair.
STANDARD	**This sofa** matches your chair.

threw, through *Threw* is the past tense of the verb *throw. Through* is a preposition that means "in one side and out the other."

Denny **threw** the ball over the fence.

He's lucky that it didn't go **through** the window of the house.

to, too, two *To* is a preposition. *To* also begins an infinitive. *Too* is an adverb that modifies a verb, an adjective, or another adverb. *Two* is a number.

> Keith went **to** the gym **to** practice.
>
> **Two** members of the team arrived **too** late.
>
> Only one was asked **to** play in the game, but the other played **too.**

use to, used to Be sure to add the *d* to *use*.

NONSTANDARD	I **use to** have three cats, but now I have one.
STANDARD	I **used to** have three cats, but now I have one.

way, ways Do not substitute *ways* for *way* when referring to a distance.

NONSTANDARD	We have gone a long **ways** since noon.
STANDARD	We have gone a long **way** since noon.

when, where Do not use *when* or *where* directly after a linking verb in a definition.

NONSTANDARD	A *presbyope* is **when** a person is farsighted.
STANDARD	A *presbyope* is a farsighted person.
NONSTANDARD	A *domicile* is **where** people live.
STANDARD	A *domicile* is a place **where** people live.

where Do not substitute *where* for *that*.

NONSTANDARD	I heard **where** crime rates are going down.
STANDARD	I heard **that** crime rates are going down.

who, whom *Who,* a pronoun in the nominative case, is used as either a subject or a predicate nominative. *Whom,* a pronoun in the objective case, is used as a direct object, an indirect object, or an object of a preposition.

> **Who** is coming to your party? (subject)
>
> **Whom** did you choose? (direct object)

You can learn more about using who *and* whom *on pages 346–347.*

whose, who's *Whose* is a possessive pronoun. *Who's* is a contraction for *who is.*

> **Whose** is the bicycle that you borrowed?
> **Who's** going to ride with you?

your, you're *Your* is a possessive pronoun. *You're* is a contraction for *you are.*

> Are these **your** campaign posters?
> **You're** the one we want for president of the class.

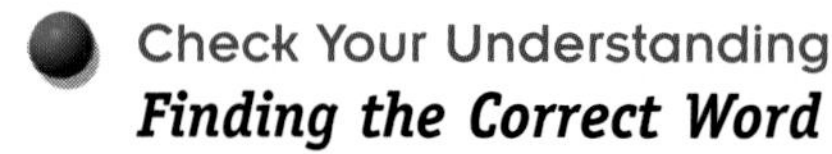

Practice Your Skills

Check Your Understanding

Finding the Correct Word

Social Studies **Write the word in parentheses that correctly completes each sentence.**

1. Edward J. Smith, (who, whom) was called the "Millionaire's Captain" by some, commanded the *Titanic* on its fateful journey.
2. Captain Smith, (whose, who's) reputation for experience and safety were excellent, planned to retire after this voyage.
3. (Their, There) have been many accounts written about the sinking of the *Titanic.*
4. Most people believed the ship (to, too) be unsinkable.

5. Regulations never (use to, used to) require lifeboat space for every person.
6. The *Titanic* had traveled a long (way, ways) from Southampton, England, when it struck an iceberg.
7. Some hours later, passengers were instructed to put on (their, there) life jackets.
8. There were sixteen wooden lifeboats; at first, only women and children were allowed on (them, those) lifeboats.
9. Hundreds of passengers (threw, through) themselves into the freezing water.
10. Today the ship's (too, two) main sections lie on the ocean floor.

Connect to the Writing Process: Revising

Recognizing Correct Usage

Rewrite the following paragraph, changing the words that are used incorrectly.

Imagine the excitement on that day in 1912 when the *Titanic* left port. On shore their would have been many who bid they're farewells by waving, while others through flowers and kisses too their loved ones. Many passengers were used to traveling on large ships. Few, however, could imagine those lavish staterooms that awaited them when they walked threw the corridors. One such passenger, who's name was well known, was John Jacob Astor, a fur trader and American millionaire. This idyllic scene tragically changed on the night of the sinking of the *Titanic*. Astor was among the approximately fifteen hundred passengers to who death came that fateful night.

Mixed Practice

History Topic **Write the word in parentheses that best completes each sentence.**

1. The *Titanic* tragedy was difficult to (accept, except) because of the ship's "unsinkable" reputation.

2. Everyone (who, whom) had helped design and build the *Titanic* believed it to be unsinkable.

3. In spite of the (advice, advise) of the original designer, however, only sixteen wooden lifeboats were on board.

4. The (amount, number) of other luxury features onboard impressed even those in first class.

5. (There, Their, They're) was even a kennel for the dogs of first-class passengers.

6. First-class passengers could walk (in, into) a gymnasium for a workout or exercise on the tennis court.

7. The ship featured a swimming pool (that, which, who) was filled with seawater.

8. (A lot of, A great many) features on the *Titanic* were inspired by the French.

9. (Among, Between) the ship's many remarkable features was its spectacular Grand Staircase.

10. Even second-class and third-class accommodations were better (than, then) those on other ships.

11. None of the passengers (knew, new) that iceberg alerts had been received on several occasions during the voyage.

12. Even after the *Titanic* had hit an iceberg, passengers throughout the (hole, whole) ship believed themselves to be safe.

13. Many of the passengers boarded the lifeboats (like, as) they were told, but others refused to leave their families.

14. As the water was (raising, rising), the band courageously continued to play.

15. (Fewer, Less) than fifteen people were saved from the freezing water, and only about seven hundred of the more than two thousand aboard the ship survived.

CHAPTER 14

Capital Letters

Directions

For each sentence, choose the word or words that should be capitalized. Write the letter of your answer. If the sentence contains no error, write *D*.

EXAMPLE **1.** i took a poetry class at the community center last summer.

1 **A** I, Poetry
B I
C I, Community Center
D No error

ANSWER **1** **B**

1. The class was called poetry I.
2. It was taught by a real poet, winifred smith.
3. She is the author of *down time*.
4. Though she is american, she spoke with a foreign accent.
5. I think she grew up in france.
6. Now she teaches during the year at hampshire college.
7. She read us poems from different eras; I especially liked the ones from the renaissance.
8. I love hearing ms. smith read her poems with her french accent.
9. My favorite poem begins, "did i miss something?/my back was turned for just a moment...."
10. My friend anita and i wrote a lot of poetry for the class.

1 **A** Class, Poetry
B Class
C Poetry
D No error

2 **A** Poet, Winifred Smith
B Poet, Smith
C Winifred Smith
D No error

3 **A** Author
B *Down Time*
C Author, *Down Time*
D No error

4 **A** American, Foreign
B Foreign
C American
D No error

5 **A** France
B She
C Up
D No error

6 **A** Hampshire
B College
C Hampshire College
D No error

7 **A** Renaissance
B Eras, Renaissance
C Eras
D No error

8 **A** Ms. Smith
B French
C Ms. Smith, French
D No error

9 **A** Did
B Did, I, My
C I
D No error

10 **A** Anita
B Poetry
C Anita, I
D No error

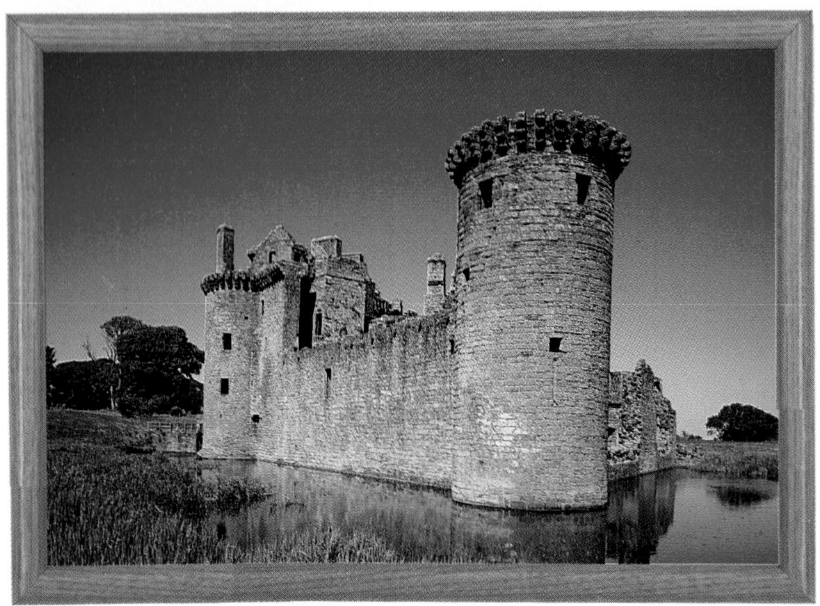

Architect unknown. *Caerlaverock Castle,* ca. A.D. 1270. Dumfries, Scotland.

Describe What material is this castle made of? Describe its location.

Analyze Notice the high walls, small windows, and strong towers of Caerlaverock Castle. Also notice the *crenations,* or curved and scalloped edges, which appear around the top of each tower. What do you think the main function of the castle was?

Interpret What do you think the main concerns of the people who lived in the castle were? Explain.

Judge This castle is more than 700 years old. What impression does the castle give? Why does it give you that impression?

At the end of this chapter, you will use the photograph as a visual aid for writing.

Capitalization

Written English is a bit like a detective story. It is filled with many clues that help readers understand the writer's message. Capitalization and punctuation are two such clues. If some of the clues are missing or misused, the message can easily become confused and misleading.

By now you probably know most of the rules for capitalization. This chapter, however, can serve as a review—especially since capital letters provide important clues to the meaning of your writing.

First Words and the Pronoun *I*

A capital letter signals the beginning of a new idea, whether it is in the form of a sentence, a line of poetry, or a formal outline.

Sentences and Poetry

Capitalize the first word of a sentence and of a line of poetry.

SENTENCES	**A** lone rose stood in the vase. **C**rystal vases are beautiful. **R**oses have a special fragrance.
LINES OF POETRY	**S**he went as quiet as the dew **F**rom a familiar flower. **N**ot like the dew did she return **A**t the accustomed hour! *–Emily Dickinson*

CONNECT TO WRITER'S CRAFT

Modern poets often deliberately misuse or eliminate capital letters. Notice the lack of capitalization at the beginning of lines in this excerpt.

> Dead daisies, shriveled lilies, withered bodies
> of dried chrysanthemums. Among these, and waste
> leaves
> of yellow and brown fronds of palm and fern,
> I came, and found
> a rose
> left for dead, heaped with the hopeless dead,
> its petals still supple.
>
> —*Li-Young Lee,* "Always a Rose"

When you are quoting lines of poetry, copy them exactly as the poet has written them, including any nonstandard capitalization or punctuation.

You can learn about capitalizing quotations on pages L553–L554.

Parts of Letters

Capitalize the first word in the greeting of a letter and the first word in the closing of a letter.

SALUTATIONS AND CLOSINGS		
Salutations	**T**o whom it may concern:	**D**ear Ashley,
	Dear Sir or Madam:	**D**ear boys and girls,
Closings	**Y**ours truly,	**T**hank you,
	With love,	**S**incerely,

Outlines

Capitalize the first word of each item in an outline and the letters that begin major subsections of the outline.

Wildflowers

- I. **S**tonecrop family
  - **A.** **P**igmyweed
  - **B.** **S**tonecrop
    - 1. **R**ose-flowered sedum
    - 2. **Y**ellow stonecrop
  - **C.** **E**cheveria
    - 1. **S**avior flower
    - 2. **B**luff weed
- II. **S**axifrage family
  - **A.** **S**axifrage
    - 1. **M**ountain lettuce
    - 2. **T**ufted saxifrage
  - **B.** **S**ullivantia
  - **C.** **B**oykinia
- III. **F**ireweed family
  - **A.** **P**urple-leaved willowherb
  - **B.** **P**ink fireweed
  - **C.** **O**range paintbrush

The Pronoun *I*

Capitalize the pronoun *I*, both alone and in contractions.

I hope **I**'ve picked enough greenery for the flower arrangement.

I know **I**'ll enjoy seeing those flowers bloom when spring arrives.

Last spring **I** planted daisies, but this year **I**'m going to plant bluebonnets.

I'd like to grow roses, but they require a great deal of care.

Practice Your Skills

Check Your Understanding

Using Capital Letters

Contemporary Life **Rewrite the following items, correcting the errors in capitalization.**

1. dear Mr. Shakespeare,

2. shall i compare thee to a summer's day?
thou art more lovely and more temperate: . . .

—*William Shakespeare,* Sonnet XVIII

3. i went to the play, and i really enjoyed it.

4. Types of Poems
  I. rhyming
    A. Limerick
    B. Sonnet
      1. petrarchan
      2. shakespearean
    C. Ballad

5. the poems of other Elizabethan writers also interest me.

Connect to the Writing Process: Editing

Correcting Errors in Capitalization

Rewrite the following letter, correcting the errors in capitalization.

dear Mrs. Wallace,

i really enjoyed your recent Lecture on the sonnets of Shakespeare. i am interested in finding a copy of one of his sonnets, but i'm not sure what number it is. the first two lines are as follows:

When in disgrace with fortune and men's eyes,
i all alone beweep my outcast state. . . .

would you please let me know which of Shakespeare's sonnets this is? you may write me back at the address i've enclosed.

thank You,
Mikayla Simpson

Communicate Your Ideas

APPLY TO WRITING

Writer's Craft: *Analyzing the Use of Capitalization*

When writing poetry, the American poet E. E. Cummings ignored the rules of capitalization and punctuation. He even signed his name using lowercase letters. Read the following excerpt and then follow the directions.

> somewhere i have never travelled, gladly beyond
> any experience, your eyes have their silence:
> in your most frail gesture are things which enclose me,
> or which i cannot touch because they are too near
>
> your slightest look easily will unclose me
> though i have closed myself as fingers. . . .
>
> —*E. E. Cummings,* "somewhere i have never travelled"

- How does the lack of capitalization in this poem affect you as a reader?
- Rewrite the lines of poetry, capitalizing the words that, according to convention, you should capitalize.
- Compare your new version with Cummings's original. How does adding capitalization change the poem?
- Why do you think a poet might choose to leave out capital letters or punctuation?

Proper Nouns

Capitalize proper nouns and their abbreviations.

Names of persons and animals should be capitalized. Also capitalize initials that stand for people's names.

NAMES OF PERSONS AND ANIMALS	
PERSONS	**J**osh, **T**iffany **S**heryl **J**ohnson, **S**usan **B.** **A**nthony, **G**rant **L**awrence, **T. H.** **M**urphy, **J**r., **C**hris
ANIMALS	**S**pot, **M**uffin, **R**over, **S**cout, **B**uttercup

You can learn about the capitalization of titles of persons on pages L481–L482.

Geographical names, including particular places and bodies of water, should be capitalized.

GEOGRAPHICAL NAMES	
STREETS, HIGHWAYS	**M**aple **A**venue (**A**ve.), the **P**ennsylvania **T**urnpike (**T**pk.), **R**oute (**R**t.) 30, **F**orty-second **S**treet (**S**t.) (The second part of a hyphenated numbered street is not capitalized.)
TOWNS, CITIES	**S**an **F**rancisco, **C**hicago, **M**inneapolis, **C**heyenne, **P**hoenix, **A**tlanta, **M**iami, **A**ustin, **S**anta **F**e
COUNTIES, PARISHES, TOWNSHIPS	**D**ade **C**ounty, **I**beria **P**arish, **O**range **C**ounty, **T**ownship 531, **H**idalgo **C**ounty
STATES	**T**exas (**TX**), **M**aine (**ME**), **W**yoming (**WY**), **N**ew **M**exico (**NM**), **K**ansas (**KS**), **N**ew **H**ampshire (**NH**)
COUNTRIES	**C**anada, the **U**nited **S**tates (**US**), **F**rance

Sections of a Country	the **M**idwest, **N**ew **E**ngland, the **S**unbelt, the **E**ast, the **S**outhwest (Compass directions do not begin with capital letters: *Go east on Route 4.*)
Continents	**A**frica, **S**outh **A**merica, **A**ntarctica, **A**sia
World Regions	**N**orthern **H**emisphere, **S**outh **P**ole, **S**candinavia, the **M**iddle **E**ast
Islands	the **H**awaiian **I**slands, **L**ong **I**sland, the **G**alapagos **I**slands
Mountains	the **H**imalayas, the **R**ocky **M**ountains, **M**ount **E**verest, **M**ount **S**t. **H**elens, the **A**ndes **M**ountains
Parks	**S**erengeti **N**ational **P**ark, **G**rand **C**anyon **N**ational **P**ark, **Y**ellowstone **N**ational **P**ark, **G**lacier **N**ational **P**ark
Bodies of Water	the **N**ile **R**iver, the **I**ndian **O**cean, the **B**lack **S**ea, the **G**reat **L**akes, **V**ictoria **F**alls

Words like *street, lake, ocean,* and *mountain* are capitalized only when they are part of a proper noun.

Which is the smallest **l**ake of the **G**reat **L**akes?
Mount **M**cKinley is the tallest **m**ountain in North America.

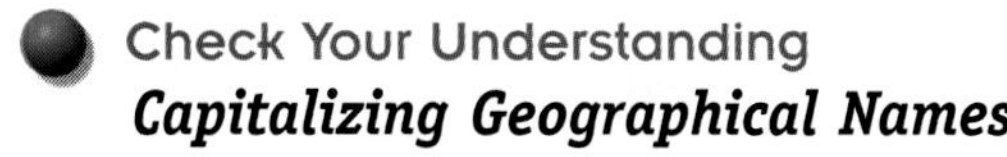

Check Your Understanding

Capitalizing Geographical Names

Write *a* or *b* to indicate the item that is correctly capitalized in each of the following pairs.

1. **a.** New delhi, india
b. New Delhi, India

2. **a.** Munroe falls
b. Munroe Falls

3. a. Thirty-third Street
   b. Thirty-Third Street

4. a. Great smokey mountains
   b. Great Smokey Mountains

5. a. lake Michigan
   b. Lake Michigan

6. a. a river in Georgia
   b. a River in Georgia

7. a. Ft. Lauderdale
   b. Ft. lauderdale

8. a. north Dakota
   b. North Dakota

9. a. the South
   b. the south

10. a. antarctica
    b. Antarctica

11. a. south America
    b. South America

12. a. Central Park
    b. Central park

13. a. north on Route 20
    b. North on Route 20

14. a. el paso, Texas
    b. El Paso, Texas

15. a. Dawson County
    b. Dawson county

16. a. the Indian Ocean
    b. the indian ocean

17. a. Saudi arabia
    b. Saudi Arabia

18. a. Catalina island
    b. Catalina Island

19. a. Mount Rushmore
    b. mount rushmore

20. a. the Memorial highway
    b. the Memorial Highway

Check Your Understanding

Using Capital Letters

Geographic Topic **Identify the words in each sentence that should be capitalized and write them correctly.**

21. here are some facts about the western hemisphere.
22. did you know that quito is the capital of ecuador?
23. lake titicaca in south america is the highest large lake above sea level.
24. on one of his voyages for spain, christopher columbus discovered the virgin islands.
25. brazil, the largest country in south america, is also the most populous country in latin america.
26. la salle, an early explorer, discovered the mouth of the mississippi river.

27. in order to fly to antarctica, a plane usually leaves from chile.
28. charles darwin studied bird species after visiting the galapagos islands.
29. nova scotia lies off the coast of canada.
30. william henry seward purchased alaska for the united states from russia in 1867.

Connect to the Writing Process: Editing
Correcting Errors in Capitalization

Rewrite the following paragraphs, correcting the errors in capitalization.

high in the lofty, snow-covered andes mountains, the amazon river begins. it runs eastward across the continent of south america, flowing through the jungles of brazil. finally it empties into the atlantic ocean.

the mighty amazon river has more water flowing through it than the mississippi river, the nile river, and the yangtze river—all put together! the reason for this amazing fact is that the drainage basin of this giant river lies in one of the rainiest regions of the world.

Communicate Your Ideas

APPLY TO WRITING

E-mail Message: ***Capitalization***

You have invited a new friend to your home. Since he has never been to your house before, you must give him directions. Beginning at your school, write the directions to your house. Remember to be very specific so that your friend does not get lost. Include the names of streets and landmarks. After you have written your directions, check to make sure that you have used capital letters correctly.

Nouns of historical importance, such as historical events, periods, and documents, should be capitalized.

HISTORIC NAMES	
EVENTS	**W**orld **W**ar II (**WWII**), the **B**attle of **B**ull **R**un
PERIODS	the **R**enaissance, the **M**iddle **A**ges, the **S**hang **D**ynasty, the **I**ndustrial **R**evolution
DOCUMENTS	the **M**agna **C**arta, the **D**eclaration of **I**ndependence, the **T**reaty of **V**ersailles

Prepositions that are part of a proper noun are not usually capitalized.

Names of groups, such as organizations, businesses, institutions, government bodies, teams, and political parties, should be capitalized.

NAMES OF GROUPS	
ORGANIZATIONS	the **A**merican **R**ed **C**ross, the **U**nited **N**ations (**UN**), the **G**irl **S**couts of **A**merica (**GSA**)
BUSINESSES	the **D**ahl **M**otor **C**ompany (**C**o.), the **L**eed **C**orporation (**C**orp.), **L**exington **L**umber
INSTITUTIONS	the **U**niversity of **C**hicago (**U** of **C**), **E**merson **H**igh **S**chool, **M**emorial **H**ospital (Words such as *high school* and *hospital* are not capitalized unless they are a part of a proper noun: *The nearest* ***h****ospital is Mercy General* ***H****ospital.*)
GOVERNMENT BODIES/AGENCIES	**C**ongress, the **S**tate **D**epartment, the **B**ureau of **L**and **M**anagement

TEAMS	the **B**oston **R**ed **S**ox, the **L**os **A**ngeles **L**akers, the **L**ake **B**randon **H**igh **S**chool **P**atriots
POLITICAL PARTIES	the **R**epublican **P**arty, the **L**abor **P**arty, a **R**epublican, a **D**emocrat

Specific time periods and events, including the days of the week, the months of the year, civil and religious holidays, and special events, should be capitalized.

TIME PERIODS AND EVENTS	
DAYS, MONTHS	**T**uesday (**T**ues.), **F**riday (**F**ri.), **F**ebruary (**F**eb.), **O**ctober (**O**ct.)
HOLIDAYS	**V**alentine's **D**ay, **K**wanzaa, the **F**ourth of **J**uly, **V**eteran's **D**ay
SPECIAL EVENTS	the **R**ose **B**owl **P**arade, the **B**oston **M**arathon, the **J**unior **P**rom
TIME ABBREVIATIONS	**B.C./A.D., A.M./P.M.**

However, do not capitalize a season of the year unless it is part of a proper noun.

I like **w**inter best.
Did you go to the **W**inter **F**air?

PRACTICE YOUR SKILLS

Check Your Understanding
Capitalizing Proper Nouns

Write *a* or *b* to indicate the item that is correctly capitalized in each of the following pairs.

1. a. World War I
b. world war I

2. a. Thanksgiving day
b. Thanksgiving Day

3. a. summer
   b. Summer

4. a. the Orlando Magic
   b. the Orlando magic

5. a. the U.S. senate
   b. the U.S. Senate

6. a. december
   b. December

7. a. the Stone Age
   b. the stone age

8. a. Veterans day
   b. Veterans Day

9. a. monday
   b. Monday

10. a. the united way
    b. the United Way

11. a. a hospital in New Jersey
    b. a Hospital in New Jersey

12. a. a Fourth of July parade
    b. a fourth of july parade

13. a. Acme brick company
    b. Acme Brick Company

14. a. the Rock Island Railroad
    b. the rock island railroad

15. a. a high school in Detroit
    b. a High School in Detroit

16. a. the Monroe doctrine
    b. the Monroe Doctrine

17. a. the Defense Department
    b. the defense department

18. a. the library of Congress
    b. the Library of Congress

19. a. the treaty of paris
    b. the Treaty of Paris

20. a. the Republican party
    b. the Republican Party

Check Your Understanding
Using Capital Letters

History Topic **Identify each word that should begin with a capital letter and then rewrite the words correctly.**

21. Signed in july of 1776, the declaration of independence is an important document in the history of the united states.

22. The treaty of paris ended the american revolution.

23. Written several years after the american revolution, the constitution of the united states is a vital document.

24. The signing of a treaty, such as the treaty of neuilly, is an important event.

25. In the winter of 1918, woodrow wilson, a president representing the democratic party, announced his fourteen points as the basis for the peace settlement of world war I.

26. Wilson was warmly received in paris, where he traveled to sign the treaty of versailles after world war I.

27. Wilson helped establish the league of nations, the precursor of the modern united nations.

28. The republican party controlled congress, and wilson's political enemies refused to allow the united states to enter the league of nations.

29. They even refused to ratify the treaty of versailles.

30. In 1920, whether the united states should join the league of nations became a major issue in the presidential election between candidates from the republican and democratic parties.

Connect to the Writing Process: Editing

Correcting Errors in Capitalization

Rewrite the following paragraphs, correcting the errors in capitalization.

winning the greatest battle in baseball, the world series, is the goal of every professional baseball player. the first game of the modern world series was played in 1903. in that series the boston pilgrims, who would later become known as the red sox, defeated the pittsburgh pirates.

the first player to be named Most Valuable Player was johnny podres of the brooklyn dodgers in 1955. that was the first world championship for the dodgers, who defeated their rivals from across the city, the new york yankees.

just two years later, the dodgers would disappoint their brooklyn fans by moving the team out of new york to los angeles, california.

Communicate Your Ideas

APPLY TO WRITING

Business Letter: *Capital Letters*

You are writing a report on a European country, focusing on two of its major cities. You must include information about the history, culture, and major attractions of the cities. Write a letter to a local travel agent, requesting information. After you have written your letter, check that you have capitalized all the proper nouns correctly.

Names of nationalities, races, and languages should be capitalized.

NATIONALITIES, RACES, AND LANGUAGES	
Nationalities	an **A**merican, a **G**erman, **C**anadians
Races	**C**aucasian, **A**sian, **H**ispanic
Languages	**S**panish, **E**nglish, **M**andarin, **R**ussian
Computer Languages	**J**ava, **C**obol, **C**++, **V**isual **B**asic

Religions, religious holidays, and religious references, such as the names referring to the Deity, the Bible, and divisions of the Bible, should be capitalized. Also, capitalize pronouns that refer to the Deity.

RELIGIOUS NAMES	
Religions	**C**hristianity, **B**uddhism, **J**udaism, **I**slam
Religious Holidays	**H**anukkah, **C**hristmas, **R**amadan, **E**piphany, **P**urim, **P**assover, **P**otlatch, **E**aster
Religious References	**G**od, the **L**ord, **G**od and **H**is children, the **B**ible, **E**xodus, the **S**criptures, the **K**oran, **A**llah, **B**uddha

Notice that the word god is not capitalized when it refers to gods in polytheistic religions.

> Neptune, who was also called Poseidon, was the **g**od of the sea.

Names of stars, planets, and constellations are capitalized.

ASTRONOMICAL NAMES	
Stars	the **D**og **S**tar, **C**anopus, the **N**orth **S**tar

PLANETS	**M**ars, **S**aturn, **V**enus, **P**luto, **J**upiter
CONSTELLATIONS	the **B**ig **D**ipper, **O**rion's **B**elt, the **M**ilky **W**ay

The words sun *and* moon *are not capitalized.* Earth *is not capitalized if it is preceded by the word* the.

Other proper nouns should also begin with capital letters.

OTHER PROPER NOUNS	
AIRCRAFT, SPACECRAFT	the ***C****oncorde,* ***T****itan* ***II****,* ***A****pollo 13*
AWARDS	the **N**obel **P**rize, the **H**eisman **T**rophy
BRAND NAMES	**N**ew **F**oam soap, **S**ilkie shampoo, **C**runchies cat food
TECHNOLOGICAL TERMS	**E**-mail, **I**nternet, **W**eb, **W**orld **W**ide **W**eb, **W**ebsite, **W**eb **A**rt, **W**eb **P**age
BRIDGES AND BUILDINGS	the **G**olden **G**ate **B**ridge, the **E**mpire **S**tate **B**uilding, the **E**iffel **T**ower
MEMORIALS, MUSEUMS, MONUMENTS	the **L**incoln **M**emorial, the **H**olocaust **M**useum, the **S**tatue of **L**iberty
SHIPS, TRAINS, PLANES	the ***M****ayflower,* the ***W****abash* ***C****annonball,* the ***S****pirit of* ***S****t.* ***L****ouis*
NAMES OF COURSES	**E**nglish **I**, **H**istory **IA**, **A**rt **II**, **L**atin **III**

Do not capitalize the name of an unnumbered course, such as *history, math,* or *biology,* unless it is the name of a language.

Last year I studied **h**istory, **a**rt, and **J**apanese.

CONNECT TO WRITER'S CRAFT

When you are unsure whether to capitalize a word, use a reference source. A good dictionary will include most proper nouns. Many dictionaries contain specific sections with geographical and biographical information where you can find the correct spelling and capitalization of the names of famous people and places. An encyclopedia will also give you such information. A professional writer always has good reference sources available.

PRACTICE YOUR SKILLS

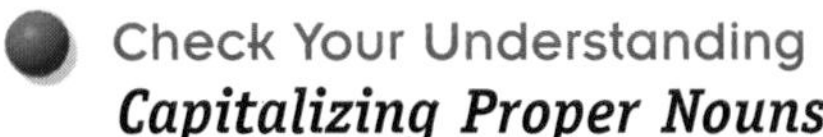

Check Your Understanding

Capitalizing Proper Nouns

Write *a* or *b* to indicate the item that is correctly capitalized in each of the following pairs.

1. **a.** geometry and Spanish
   b. geometry and spanish
2. **a.** Mello cheese
   b. mello cheese
3. **a.** the New Testament
   b. the new testament
4. **a.** satin fur cat food
   b. Satin Fur cat food
5. **a.** god and his kingdom
   b. God and His kingdom
6. **a.** the Vietnam Memorial
   b. the Vietnam memorial
7. **a.** advanced algebra I
   b. Advanced Algebra I
8. **a.** the Pulitzer prize
   b. the Pulitzer Prize
9. **a.** judaism
   b. Judaism
10. **a.** *Spirit of St. Louis*
    b. *spirit of st. louis*
11. **a.** the Sun and Mars
    b. the sun and Mars
12. **a.** Polish and Russian
    b. polish and russian
13. **a.** a presbyterian
    b. a Presbyterian
14. **a.** the *Lusitania*
    b. the *lusitania*
15. **a.** an african
    b. an African
16. **a.** the Statue of Liberty
    b. the statue of liberty
17. **a.** a hindu
    b. a Hindu
18. **a.** the war of 1812
    b. the War of 1812
19. **a.** the world trade center
    b. the World Trade Center
20. **a.** Sirius and other Stars
    b. Sirius and other stars

Check Your Understanding

Using Capital Letters

History Topic **Identify each word that should begin with a capital letter and then rewrite the words correctly.**

21. The middle ages was a historical period in western europe that lasted from about a.d. 400 to a.d. 1400.

22. During the dark ages and middle ages, common people worked only 260 days per year.

23. They did not work on religious holidays such as easter and christmas.

24. On december 6, people would celebrate st. nicholas's day, a children's holiday.

25. On most days between 9 a.m. and noon, people living in a castle would eat dinner, a very large meal.

Connect to the Writing Process: Editing

Correcting Errors in Capitalization

Rewrite the following paragraph, correcting the errors in capitalization.

every few years a city in a major country like canada, japan, france, or the united states hosts a world's fair. the united states has hosted fairs in major cities like new york, chicago, and st. louis. one of the earliest fairs, however, was held in london, england, in 1851. that was during the early reign of queen victoria. the queen hired joseph paxton, an english architect, to design the exhibition hall in london's hyde park. he created the largest glass building ever made. it contained 3,300 columns to support its three stories. after the exhibition, it was taken down and moved to a different part of london. there it became known as the crystal palace. unfortunately, it was destroyed by a fire in 1936.

Communicate Your Ideas

APPLY TO WRITING

Advertisement: *Capital Letters*

You are the owner of the first intergalactic travel agency to take people on tours of the planets and outer space. Write an advertisement for an upcoming tour of one of the planets. Inform prospective clients as to the travel accommodations, such as the comfort and safety of your spacecraft, the sites they will see, the cost of space travel, and the activities they might enjoy. In your advertisement, be sure to give your company a name. After you have finished writing your ad, check to make sure that you have used proper capitalization.

QuickCheck Mixed Practice

General Interest

In each of the following trivia questions, find the words that should be capitalized and write the words correctly. Then see if you can answer the questions!

1. was william sherman a general in the civil war or the american revolution?
2. who wrote the declaration of independence?
3. who carried the message that the british were coming through massachusetts?
4. is andrew wyeth a painter or a united states senator?
5. who were the two explorers who led an expedition from st. louis, missouri, to the pacific ocean in 1804?
6. was george c. scott a composer or the winner of an oscar?
7. who was the couple that tried to rule the roman empire from egypt?
8. what famous person's address is 1600 pennsylvania avenue, washington, d.c.?
9. is hillary clinton a winner in the olympics or a public figure?
10. did captain james kirk or captain bligh command the starship *enterprise*?
11. who joined the boston bruins at age eighteen and led the team to win the stanley cup?
12. who was the first american to set foot on the moon?
13. who flew across the atlantic ocean in the *spirit of st. louis?*
14. who paid for the statue of liberty in new york by giving donations: the french or the americans?
15. did thomas edison or george eastman invent the first camera?

16. who delivered the gettysburg address during the civil war?

17. who painted the ceiling of the sistine chapel?

18. washington, jefferson, lincoln, and who else are shown on the mount rushmore national memorial?

19. who was the fictitious character who lived on baker street in london, england?

20. who led his troops across the delaware river to attack the british during the american revolution?

21. did tara lipinski win a gold medal for ice skating or for gymnastics?

22. which president's last name is the name of a state in the northwest?

23. in 1848, was gold found in california or in colorado?

24. which is the capital of the state of new york, albany or new york city?

25. which highway goes from maine to florida, interstate 95 or route 66?

Proper Adjectives

Proper adjectives are formed from proper nouns. Like proper nouns, proper adjectives begin with capital letters.

Capitalize most proper adjectives.

PROPER NOUNS	PROPER ADJECTIVES
France	**F**rench doors
Rome	**R**oman numerals
Alaska	**A**laskan cruise
Boston	**B**oston baked beans

Some adjectives that originated from proper nouns are so common that they are no longer capitalized.

Be careful not to drop the **c**hina plate.

Practice Your Skills

Check Your Understanding
Capitalizing Proper Adjectives

Write the following items, adding capital letters where needed.

1. a chinese restaurant
2. a british naval officer
3. a former french colony
4. an ancient egyptian tomb
5. irish stew
6. new england weather
7. a german clock
8. a turkish towel
9. maine lobster
10. a swedish ship

Connect to the Writing Process: Editing
Correcting Errors in Capitalization

Rewrite the following paragraph, correcting the errors in capitalization.

my sister took a european vacation recently. she brought back more stories and souvenirs than i've ever seen! while visiting madrid, she saw an actual spanish flamenco dance. then she traveled to great britain for a tour of the english countryside. after buying my mother some beautiful irish linen, she flew to france and toured notre dame in paris. she skied in the swiss alps and then toured tuscany. she has promised to take me on her next trip.

Titles

Capital letters indicate the importance of titles of people, written works, and other works of art.

Capitalize certain titles.

Titles Used with Names of Persons

Capitalize a title showing office, rank, or profession when it comes directly before a person's name.

BEFORE A NAME	Have you met **D**r. Anna Richman?
AFTER A NAME	Jennifer Kemp is also a **d**octor.
BEFORE A NAME	Dr. Richman voted for **G**overnor Harper.
AFTER A NAME	Did you think Jennifer Kemp would be elected **g**overnor?

Titles Used Alone

Capitalize a title that is used alone when the title is being substituted for a person's name in direct address.

USED AS A NAME	Please, **G**overnor, may I speak with you?
	I didn't see the sign, **O**fficer.

Titles of high government officials, such as the *President, Vice President, Chief Justice,* and *Queen of England,* are almost always capitalized when they stand alone.

I have come to see the **Q**ueen of England.
The **P**resident visited Governor Harper.

President *and* vice president *are capitalized when they stand alone only if they refer to the current president or vice president.*

Titles Showing Family Relationships

Capitalize a title showing a family relationship when it comes directly before a person's name. When the title is used as a name, or when the title is substituted for a person's name in direct address, it is also capitalized.

BEFORE A NAME	I am going to see **A**unt **L**ori.
USED AS A NAME	I told **M**om that I would vacuum my room tomorrow.
SUBSTITUTED FOR A PERSON'S NAME IN DIRECT ADDRESS	May I borrow the car for just a few hours, **D**ad?
	Will you come, **G**randpa, to my game on Saturday?

Do not capitalize titles showing family relationships when they are preceded by possessive nouns or pronouns—unless the titles are considered part of someone's name.

Have you met Kristen's **a**unt?
Have you met Kristen's **A**unt Diane?

PRACTICE YOUR SKILLS

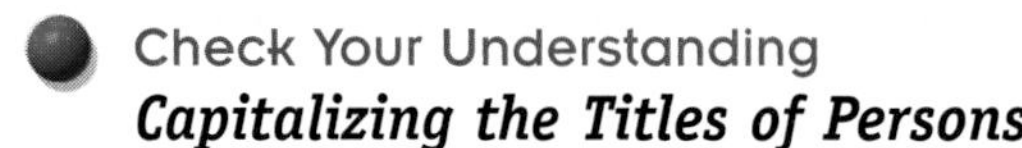

Check Your Understanding

Capitalizing the Titles of Persons

Write *a* or *b* to indicate the correctly capitalized title in each of the following pairs.

1. **a.** our family doctor
b. our family Doctor

2. **a.** Senator Barrientos
b. senator Barrientos

3. **a.** aunt Ruthie
b. Aunt Ruthie

4. **a.** a Governor
b. a governor

5. **a.** Granny Taylor
b. granny Taylor

6. **a.** my uncle
b. my Uncle

7. **a.** a state senator
   b. a state Senator

8. **a.** a president of Egypt
   b. a President of Egypt

9. **a.** Mayor Wilson
   b. mayor Wilson

10. **a.** president Nixon
    b. President Nixon

Connect to the Writing Process: Editing

Correcting Errors in Capitalization

Rewrite the following letter, correcting the errors in capitalization.

dear grandma hazel,

i hope you are doing well. i heard from aunt linda that you had been ill. did you go to the doctor? i enjoyed meeting dr. williams when i visited you last summer. i'm sure she would take good care of you if you would make an appointment.

well, i'd better close this letter. i promised mom and uncle denny that i would take out the trash before the president's state of the union address on television tonight.

love always,

samantha

Titles of Written Works and Other Works of Art

Capitalize the first word, the last word, and all important words in the titles of books, newspapers, periodicals, stories, poems, movies, plays, musical compositions, and other works of art. However, do not capitalize a preposition, a conjunction, or an article (*a, an,* and *the*) unless it is the first word of a title.

BOOKS AND CHAPTER TITLES	I finished reading a chapter called "**T**he **M**an on the **T**or" in the book ***T**he **H**ound of the **B**askervilles.*
SHORT STORIES	I enjoyed Truman Capote's story "**C**hildren on **T**heir **B**irthdays."
POEMS	My favorite poems are "**F**rom **B**lossoms" and "**T**he **W**eight of **S**weetness" by Li-Young Lee.
NEWSPAPERS AND NEWSPAPER ARTICLES	I read an article called "**L**ocal **W**riter **H**as **N**ovel **P**ublished" in today's issue of the ***N**ew **Y**ork **T**imes.*
	(Generally, do not capitalize *the* as the first word of a newspaper or magazine title.)
MAGAZINES AND MAGAZINE ARTICLES	I read "**I**nterview with the **N**ew **T**alent" about that author in ***P**eople* magazine last week.
TELEVISION SERIES	Two popular British television comedy series are ***K**eeping **U**p **A**ppearances* and ***A**s **T**ime **G**oes **B**y.*

You can learn more about the punctuation of titles on pages L544–L548.

PRACTICE YOUR SKILLS

Check Your Understanding

Capitalizing Titles of Written Works and Other Works of Art

Write *a* or *b* to indicate the correctly capitalized title in each of the following pairs.

1. **a.** *the last supper*
b. *The Last Supper*

2. **a.** "The Raven"
b. "the Raven"

3. **a.** "amazing grace"
b. "Amazing Grace"

4. **a.** *seventeen* magazine
b. *Seventeen* magazine

5. a. *American Gothic*
   b. *american gothic*

6. a. *The return of the Jedi*
   b. *The Return of the Jedi*

7. a. *The Great Gatsby*
   b. *The great gatsby*

8. a. "The Lottery"
   b. "the lottery"

9. a. *the Dallas Morning News*
   b. *the Dallas morning news*

10. a. *Singin' in the Rain*
    b. *Singin' in the rain*

11. a. *The Count of Monte Cristo*
    b. *The count of monte Cristo*

12. a. *War and peace*
    b. *War and Peace*

13. a. "The Listeners"
    b. "the Listeners"

14. a. *It Happened One Night*
    b. *It happened one night*

15. a. *Life* Magazine
    b. *Life* magazine

Connect to the Writing Process: Editing

Correcting Errors in Capitalization

Rewrite the following paragraph, correcting the errors in capitalization.

the 1950s was an interesting time in the history of entertainment. In music, rock 'n' roll was born. elvis presley recorded hit songs like "hound dog" and "that's all right." he also made a historic appearance on *the ed sullivan show.* other popular television shows at that time included the comedy *i love lucy* and *the twilight zone.* suspense was popular in the movies and TV shows of alfred hitchcock. two of Hitchcock's most famous movies of the 1950s were *Strangers on a train* and *rear window.* in literature, a new generation of writers was heralded by jack kerouac and allen ginsberg. kerouac's *on the road* tells stories of crossing and recrossing the highways of the united states, far outside the mainstream 1950s culture.

Communicate Your Ideas

APPLY TO WRITING

Friendly Letter: *Capital Letters*

You have a new pen pal who lives across the country from you. Write a letter of introduction to him or her. Tell your pen pal all about yourself, including your school's name, the subjects you're studying, and your favorite book, magazine, song, and television show. After you have written your letter, check to make sure that you have used capital letters correctly.

Mixed Practice

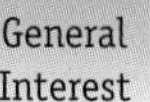

In each of the following trivia questions, find the words that should be capitalized and write the words correctly. Then see if you can answer the questions!

1. what are the names of the stars in the classic comedies *duck soup* and *a night at the opera?*
2. what are the seven roman numerals?
3. what god in greek mythology held the world on his shoulders?
4. an old form of which sport takes place in the story "rip van winkle"?
5. what is the name of a fictional reporter who worked on the *daily planet* in the city of metropolis?

6. what is the name of the movie in which fay wray, the empire state building, and a giant ape are featured?

7. what is the name of the captain of the *nautilus* in the book *20,000 leagues under the sea?*

8. what is the motto of the boy scouts of america?

9. what does the initial stand for in president john f. kennedy's name?

10. is the name of the football team in dallas, texas, the cowboys or the broncos?

11. what was the name of the president of the confederacy during the civil war?

12. what are the chief ingredients in english muffins?

13. what group recorded "i want to hold your hand"?

14. which television series has run longer: *meet the press* or *days of our lives?*

15. who is the author of *the red badge of courage?*

16. in the united states, what is the first monday in september called?

17. which sea separates the scandinavian countries from the rest of europe: the baltic or the mediterranean?

18. in what art museum does the *mona lisa* hang?

19. what is the name of the first united states writer to win a nobel prize?

20. in what book is captain ahab a character: *two years before the mast* or *moby dick?*

CheckPoint

Using Capital Letters Correctly

Correctly write each word that should begin with a capital letter.

1. let's turn back the clock to the year 1900 and look at the united states at the turn of that century.
2. the population had reached nearly seventy-six million, and the center of the population was near columbus, indiana.
3. the united states had about ten miles of concrete pavement and fewer than eight thousand automobiles.
4. the first well-organized automobile race was held at springfield, long island, on april 15.
5. in the presidential election, president william mckinley was re-elected for a second term.
6. r. a. fessenden, an american scientist, became the first person to transmit human speech through radio waves.
7. the united states and england inaugurated a tennis competition for the davis cup.
8. casey jones, the famous engineer in song and legend, died on april 30 at the throttle of his locomotive, the *cannonball,* trying to save his passengers' lives.
9. the wright brothers, wilbur and orville, built their first full-scale glider and flew it at kitty hawk, nc.
10. among rising young novelists of the day were such writers as zane grey, edgar rice burroughs, and theodore dreiser.
11. irving bacheller wrote the novel *eben holden*, a best-seller.
12. ray c. ewry won eight olympic gold medals.
13. a notable painter of the time was albert pinkham ryder, whose famous painting, *toilers of the sea,* is a ghostly sea scene.
14. famous archeologist arthur clark discovered artifacts from the minoan culture in his excavations in crete.
15. the largest railroad was the new york central.

Editing for the Correct Use of Capital Letters

Write each sentence using capital letters correctly.

1. the world's largest church is st. peter's in rome.
2. the *voyager* missions studied jupiter and saturn.
3. required courses for juniors are english, math II, biology, and american history.
4. in his novel *the grapes of wrath,* john steinbeck tells about the problems of the poor in oklahoma.
5. the houston oaks hotel is in the southwest.
6. did michigan ever beat nebraska in the cotton bowl?
7. yes, senator parks will speak at logan high school.
8. the west indies form an island arc in the atlantic ocean.
9. the irish potato orginated in south america.
10. the snake river flows from wyoming to washington.

Writing Sentences

At the library, find a fact that pertains to each of the following topics. Each fact should include a proper noun, a proper adjective, or a title.

1. geography
2. political parties
3. the presidency
4. astronomy
5. art
6. literature
7. holidays
8. history
9. space exploration
10. languages

Language and *Self-Expression*

Caerlaverock Castle was built in Scotland in the late 1200s. The castle is surrounded by a moat and built of impregnable rock because, in the Middle Ages, wars often broke out among kings and other wealthy landowners. These nobles built fort-like castles, which served as both home and defense. Windows were small and narrow because rooms were heated only with fireplaces and because knights shot arrows from the windows if the castle was attacked.

Caerlaverock Castle was often attacked. Its moat and thick walls helped keep its inhabitants safe. Imagine what it might be like for those inhabitants during an attack. Write a scene set in Caerlaverock during a battle. Use capitalization for proper nouns and other appropriate words.

Prewriting Create a plot diagram for your scene. Include information about characters and setting in your diagram and describe the rising action, climax, falling action, and resolution of your plot.

Drafting Use your plot diagram as the basis for writing your first draft. Specific details will help capture your readers' interest.

Revising Reread what you have written. Have you created an atmosphere of danger in your story? Does it give readers a sense of life in the Middle Ages? Make any changes you need to help make your action more gripping and realistic.

Editing Correct any errors in grammar, spelling, and punctuation. Be sure the first word of each sentence and all proper nouns and adjectives are capitalized.

Publishing Make a final copy of your scene. Read classmates' scenes and see if you can combine any scenes to make a full story of the battle at Caerlaverock Castle.

Another Look

Capitalizing First Words and the Pronoun *I*

Capitalize the first word of a sentence and of a line of poetry. *(page L459)*
Capitalize the first word in the greeting of a letter and the first word in the closing of a letter. *(page L460)*
Capitalize the first word of each item in an outline and the letters that begin major subsections of the outline. *(page L461)*
Capitalize the pronoun *I*, both alone and in contractions. *(page L461)*

Capitalizing Proper Nouns and Adjectives

Capitalize the following kinds of proper nouns:
Names of persons and animals *(page L464)*
Geographical names *(pages L464–L465)*
Names of historical importance *(page L468)*
Names of groups *(pages L468–L469)*
Specific time periods and events *(page L469)*
Names of nationalities, races, and languages *(page L473)*
Religions, religious holidays, and religious references *(page L473)*
Names of stars, planets, and constellations *(pages L473–L474)*
Aircraft, spacecraft, awards, brand names, bridges, technological terms, buildings, memorials, museums, ships, trains, and names of courses *(page L474)*
Capitalize most proper adjectives. *(pages L479–L480)*

Capitalizing Titles

Capitalize titles showing office, rank, or profession when used directly before a person's name. *(page L481)*
Capitalize titles used alone when substituted for a person's name in direct address. *(page L481)*
Capitalize titles of current high government officials when they stand alone. *(page L481)*
Capitalize titles showing family relationships when directly before a person's name, part of a name, or in place of a name. *(page L482)*
Capitalize the first word, the last word, and all important words in titles of books, newspapers, periodicals, stories, poems, movies, plays, musical compositions, and other works of art. *(pages L483–L484)*

Directions

For each sentence, choose the word or words that should be capitalized. Write the letter of your answer. If the sentence contains no error, write *D*.

EXAMPLE **1.** I have a pen pal from belgium.

1 **A** Pen Pal
B Belgium
C Pal, Belgium
D No error

ANSWER **1** **B**

1. My friend speaks flemish most of the time at her home near the city of bruges.
2. She also knows the english language well enough to write great letters.
3. Her name is helen.
4. She told me that belgium became a country only in modern times.
5. Long ago during the renaissance, the part of the country where she lives was known as flanders.
6. Some great painters such as hans memling lived there.
7. I've seen one of his paintings, *adoration of the magi*, which now hangs in a museum within a hospital in bruges.
8. almost every month i get a letter from helen.
9. She begins them all, "dear American friend."
10. I write back to her, "Dear belgian friend."

1 **A** Flemish, Bruges
B Home
C Flemish, Home
D No error

2 **A** English
B Language
C English Language
D No error

3 **A** Name
B Helen
C Name, Helen
D No error

4 **A** Modern Times
B Belgium, Modern
C Belgium
D No error

5 **A** Renaissance
B Renaissance, Flanders
C Flanders
D No error

6 **A** Memling
B Hans Memling
C Hans
D No error

7 **A** *Adoration*
B *Adoration, Of, Magi*
C *Adoration, Magi,* Bruges
D No error

8 **A** Almost, I
B Helen
C Almost, I, Helen
D No error

9 **A** Dear
B Dear, Friend
C Friend
D No error

10 **A** Belgian, Friend
B Belgian
C Friend
D No error

CHAPTER 15

End Marks and Commas

Directions

Write the letter of the term that correctly identifies each type of sentence.

EXAMPLE **1.** A hurricane hit our town this September.

1 A declarative
B imperative
C interrogative
D exclamatory

ANSWER **1 A**

1. The winds started rising during the night.
2. They were incredibly strong!
3. The police and other emergency workers patrolled the streets and made loudspeaker announcements.
4. "Prepare to evacuate the island!"
5. Would we suffer a direct hit?
6. The island could be completely submerged under water!
7. By midday most people had packed up and left the island.
8. We were packed and ready to go, but my sister couldn't find her cat.
9. Where was he hiding?
10. My father ordered her to get into the car.

1 A declarative
B imperative
C interrogative
D exclamatory

2 A declarative
B imperative
C interrogative
D exclamatory

3 A declarative
B imperative
C interrogative
D exclamatory

4 A declarative
B imperative
C interrogative
D exclamatory

5 A declarative
B imperative
C interrogative
D exclamatory

6 A declarative
B imperative
C interrogative
D exclamatory

7 A declarative
B imperative
C interrogative
D exclamatory

8 A declarative
B imperative
C interrogative
D exclamatory

9 A declarative
B imperative
C interrogative
D exclamatory

10 A declarative
B imperative
C interrogative
D exclamatory

Claude Monet. *Arrival of the Normandy Train, Gare Saint-Lazare,* 1877.
Oil on canvas, 23¼ by 31¼ inches. The Art Institute of Chicago.

Describe What does the painting show? What colors does the artist use to create light and shadow?

Analyze Notice the blurry quality of the artist's brushstrokes. What effect do you think the blurred lines of the painting have on its atmosphere? How does Monet convey a real sense of the interior of the train shed?

Interpret Why do you think the artist chose not to show precise details in this painting?

Judge How does this style of painting affect you? Do you have a clear impression of place and time?

At the end of this chapter, you will use the artwork to stimulate ideas for writing.

Kinds of Sentences and End Marks

Imagine New York City without any traffic lights or stop signs. There would be utter confusion. The result of writing without end marks or commas would be very much the same.

In this chapter you will review the three different end marks as well as the four different types of sentences to which those end marks are added. In addition, you will review the use of the period with abbreviations and the uses of the comma.

A sentence may have one of four different purposes or functions. The purpose of a sentence determines the punctuation mark that goes at the end. A sentence may be declarative, imperative, interrogative, or exclamatory.

One purpose of a sentence is to make a statement or to express an opinion.

A **declarative sentence** makes a statement or expresses an opinion and ends with a period.

The following examples are declarative sentences. Notice that the second sentence makes a statement, even though it contains an indirect question.

> My brothers were going to the tennis courts**.**
>
> I asked them what time they were leaving home**.**
> (A direct question would be *What time are they leaving home?*)

A second purpose of a sentence is to give directions, make requests, or give commands. The subject of these kinds of sentences is usually an understood *you*.

An **imperative sentence** gives a direction, makes a request, or gives a command. It ends with either a period or an exclamation point.

Although all of the following examples are imperative, two are followed by a period, and one is followed by an exclamation point.

> Turn left when you see the tennis courts**.**
>
> Please take me with you**.**
>
> Call the police**!**
>
> (This command would be stated with great excitement or emphasis.)

A third purpose of a sentence is to ask a question.

An **interrogative sentence** asks a question and ends with a question mark.

The following examples are interrogative sentences. Notice that the second example is phrased as a statement but is intended as a question.

> Where is my tennis racket**?**
>
> You have played tennis eight times this weekend**?**

Some questions are not expressed completely; nevertheless, they are followed by a question mark.

> You have decided not to play tennis. Why**?**

A fourth purpose of a sentence is to express a feeling—such as excitement, joy, anger, fear, or surprise.

An **exclamatory sentence** expresses strong feeling or emotion and ends with an exclamation point.

The following examples are exclamatory sentences. Notice they express strong feeling.

> I beat my brother at tennis**!**
>
> I feel fabulous**!**

Use exclamatory sentences sparingly when you write. They lose their impact when they are used too often. Remember that an exclamation point also follows an interjection.

> Wow**!** That was my best match ever.

You can learn more about interjections on pages L135–L136.

Practice Your Skills

Check Your Understanding
Classifying Sentences

Contemporary Life

Label each sentence *declarative, imperative, interrogative,* or *exclamatory* according to the meaning of the sentence.

1. I love to play tennis!
2. Please bring me my racket.
3. Are you ready to play?
4. You have never played before?
5. I began playing tennis when I was eight years old.
6. Stand behind the baseline to serve.
7. You have a powerful arm!
8. Drive the ball diagonally across the net.
9. The game is challenging and fun.
10. Would you like to play again?

Connect to the Writing Process: Editing
Correcting End Punctuation

Write the correct end punctuation for each sentence. Then label each sentence *declarative, imperative, interrogative,* or *exclamatory.*

11. Have you heard of the "Battle of the Sexes"
12. In 1973, Bobby Riggs challenged female tennis player Billie Jean King to a winner-take-all match

13. America watched the amazing match with great excitement
14. Riggs had declared that there was no way a woman could beat a man
15. Wow, King showed him in no uncertain terms how wrong he was
16. King defeated Riggs in each match to handily win the set
17. Look at any magazine of the time
18. You will see how this tennis match captured America's attention
19. Can you imagine how this victory affected the future of women's tennis
20. Find out more about this event by looking at old newspapers

Communicate Your Ideas

APPLY TO WRITING

Instructions: ***Sentence Variety***

You have been asked by your coach to explain the rules of your favorite sport to someone who has never played the game before. Write a paragraph in which you explain the basics that everyone beginning the sport should know. Try to give thorough directions while conveying just how much fun the sport is. Use at least one of each type of sentence—declarative, interrogative, exclamatory, and imperative—as you write.

Other Uses of Periods

Periods are also used in places other than at the ends of sentences.

With Abbreviations

ABBREVIATIONS					
Titles with Names	Mr. Mrs.	Ms. Dr.	Rev. Gen.	Sgt. Lt.	Jr. Sr.
Initials for Names	R. L. Rosen, Sarah E. Campbell, J. J. Jackson, K. Petra Beck				
Times with Numbers	A.M. (*ante meridiem*—before noon) P.M. (*post meridiem*—after noon) B.C. (before Christ) A.D. (*anno Domini*—in the year of the Lord)				
Addresses	Ave.	St.	Blvd.	Rt.	Dept.
Organizations and Companies	Co.	Inc.	Corp.	Assn.	

Some organizations and companies are known by abbreviations that stand for their full name. The majority of these abbreviations do not use periods. A few other common abbreviations also do not include periods.

> FAA = Federal Aviation Administration
> UN = United Nations
> CIA = Central Intelligence Agency
> IQ = intelligence quotient
> km = kilometer

If an abbreviation is the last word of a statement, only one period is used. Two marks are needed when a sentence ends with an abbreviation and a question mark or exclamation point.

> I would like to introduce you to Ronald Franklin, Jr**.**
> Should I meet you at 10:00 P.M.**?**

Today almost everyone uses the U.S. Postal Service's two-letter state abbreviations. These abbreviations do not include periods.

A list of these abbreviations can be found in the front of most telephone books. The following are a few examples.

AK = Alaska
AL = Alabama
CT = Connecticut
HI = Hawaii
MD = Maryland
ME = Maine
MI = Michigan
NV = Nevada
NY = New York
OH = Ohio
TX = Texas
UT = Utah

CONNECT TO WRITER'S CRAFT

If you are unsure of the spelling or punctuation of an abbreviation, look it up in the dictionary. You can usually find the abbreviation in the entry for the word that you are trying to shorten. Most dictionaries also have a separate section on abbreviations at the back.

With Outlines

Use a period after each number or letter that shows a division in an outline.

I. Guitars
    A. Electric
        1. Hollow body
        2. Solid body
    B. Acoustic

II. Drums
    A. Hand
    B. Zylo

Practice Your Skills

Check Your Understanding
Using End Marks

Write the abbreviations that stand for the following items. Be sure to end them with a period whenever appropriate. If you are not sure of the abbreviation, use a dictionary.

1. dozen
2. major
3. ounce
4. latitude
5. mountain
6. Fahrenheit
7. Rhode Island
8. television
9. association
10. boulevard
11. incorporated
12. before Christ
13. Bachelor of Arts
14. miles per hour
15. post meridiem

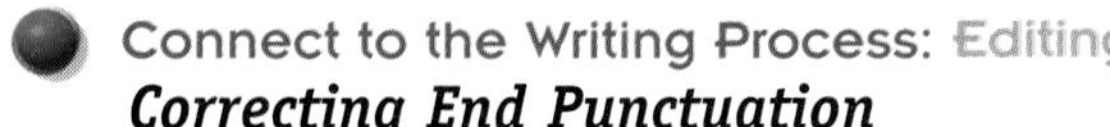

Connect to the Writing Process: Editing
Correcting End Punctuation

Rewrite the following outline, adding periods where needed.

I Types of Businesses
  A Corp
  B Co
  C Inc

II States
  A Eastern
    1 NY
    2 VT
    3 MA
  B Western
    1 CA
    2 OR
    3 WA

III Organizations
  A FBI
  B NATO
  C UN

Communicate Your Ideas

APPLY TO WRITING

Outline: ***Using Periods***

Write an outline of what you ate yesterday. Use a separate Roman numeral for each meal and snack. Be sure to list all the food you had at each meal. As you make your outline, be sure that you place periods appropriately throughout.

Contemporary Life

Rewrite the following sentences, adding end punctuation and periods to abbreviations if needed. Then label each sentence declarative, imperative, interrogative, or exclamatory.

1. Have you called Dr Wilson
2. Dr Barry Wilson, Jr has been our family physician for years
3. Please get the phone book
4. Call him right this minute
5. Mrs Smith, the school nurse, thinks that my right arm is broken
6. Ouch, it hurts
7. I fell off the auditorium stage during Mr Miller's drama class
8. When did it happen
9. It happened just after class started at 2:00 P M
10. What a relief it will be to see Dr Wilson

Commas That Separate

Commas are used to prevent confusion and to keep items from running into one another. The following are specific rules for commas that are used to separate items.

Items in a Series

Three or more similar items—words, phrases, or clauses—that are placed together form a series.

Use commas to separate items in a series.

WORDS	**Blackberries, raspberries,** and **strawberries** are all members of the rose family. (nouns)
	We **picked, washed,** and **ate** as many fresh berries as we could. (verbs)
	At the end of the day**,** we were **tired, dirty,** and **full.** (adjectives)
PHRASES	The buckets for the berries could be **in the garage, in the pantry,** or **on the porch.**
	Are they going **to the picnic, to the park,** or **to the campground?**
CLAUSES	We know **where the berries are, if they are ripe,** and **when they should be picked.**
	She told us **where to go, how to get there,** and **what to wear.**

When a conjunction connects the last two items in a series, some writers omit the last comma. Although this is acceptable, it can be confusing. Therefore, it is better to get into the habit of including the comma before the conjunctions.

CONFUSING	We fixed sandwiches, glasses of juice and cookies.
CLEAR	We fixed sandwiches, glasses of juice, and cookies.

When conjunctions connect all items in a series, no commas are needed.

We ate **and** rested **and** ate some more.

Some pairs of words, such as *bacon and eggs,* are thought of as a single item. If one of these pairs of words appears in a series, consider it one item.

For dinner you can have a burger and fries**,** fish and chips**,** or pork and sauerkraut.

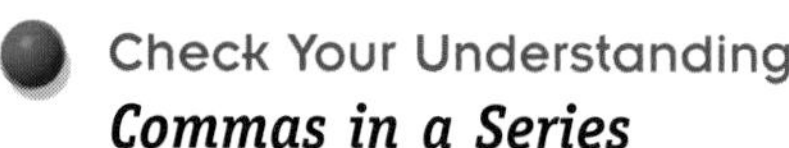

PRACTICE YOUR SKILLS

Check Your Understanding

Commas in a Series

Contemporary Life

Write *I,* for incorrect, if the sentence is missing one or more commas, and *C* if the sentence is correct. Then, for each incorrect sentence, write the words, phrases, or clauses in a series and add commas.

1. Combine flour shortening pecans and cold water to make a tasty pie crust.

2. Preheat the oven oil the pan and prepare the crust.

3. Shall we bake raisin and nut or apple and cinnamon or butter and oatmeal muffins?

4. Whipped cream ice cream and cheddar cheese make excellent toppings for apple pie.

5. Please mix the batter pour it into a pan, and place it in the oven.
6. Use soap and hot water and a fresh towel to clean your hands before cooking.
7. I enjoy a glass of milk or a small dessert or a piece of fruit after lunch.
8. The best cakes are made with fresh butter and milk powdered sugar and cinnamon and brown eggs.
9. We will bake the dessert cook the steaks, and toss the salad when the guests arrive.
10. Shawna and Jennifer and the twins are all coming to eat with us.

Connect to the Writing Process: Drafting

Writing Sentences

Finish each sentence with a series of three or more appropriate items. Add commas where needed.

11. When I make a hamburger, I like to add ■.
12. This year in school I am studying ■.
13. When we have a holiday dinner, my favorite foods are ■.
14. I ■ to stay in shape.
15. Before leaving for school each morning, I usually like to ■.
16. Three places in the United States I would like to visit are ■.
17. ■ are the friends whom I trust the most to help me in difficult situations.
18. I enjoy watching ■.
19. I enjoy playing ■.
20. After I graduate from high school, I would like to ■.

Adjectives Before a Noun

If a conjunction is missing between two adjectives that come before a noun, a comma is sometimes used to take its place.

> The rabbits disappeared into the tall, thick grass of the Nebraska plain.
>
> That is the oldest, most beautiful tree in the redwood forest.
>
> Several delicate, fragrant flowers blossomed from the desert cactus.

A comma is sometimes needed to separate two adjectives that precede a noun and are not joined by a conjunction.

A useful test can help you decide whether a comma is needed between two adjectives. If the sentence reads sensibly with the word *and* between the adjectives, a comma is needed.

COMMA NEEDED	Mississippi is a damp, lush place.
	(*A damp and lush place* reads well.)
COMMA NOT NEEDED	Today was a damp spring day.
	(*A damp and spring day* does not read well.)

Usually no comma is needed after a number or after an adjective that refers to size, shape, or age. For example, no commas are needed in the following expressions.

ADJECTIVE EXPRESSIONS
six oak trees
a large green meadow
one hundred beautiful butterflies
his old brown guitar
the ancient oral saga

Practice Your Skills

Check Your Understanding

Using Commas with Adjectives

Geography Topic

Read the sentences below. Write *C* if the sentence is punctuated correctly. Write *I* if it is punctuated incorrectly.

1. America is a land of diverse colorful regions.

2. Prickly cactus produces beautiful delicate flowers in the harsh deserts of Arizona.

3. Some parts of California are famous for sturdy redwood trees.

4. The golden wheat fields of Kansas are a glorious sight to behold.

5. The city of Chicago offers many great vistas of Lake Michigan.

6. The lovely quaint villages of New England attract many tourists.

7. Florida has large sandy beaches along both the Atlantic Ocean and the Gulf of Mexico.

8. Central Texas contains dark rich farmland and a good supply of water.

9. Its numerous active volcanoes make Hawaii like no other state.

10. Minnesota is famous for its ten thousand fresh lakes.

11. Austin, Texas, is well known for its rolling green hills.

12. New Mexico is a mixture of hot dry desert lands and snow-topped mountains.

Connect to the Writing Process: Editing

Correcting Comma Errors

13.–17. Rewrite the incorrectly punctuated sentences from the exercise above, adding commas where needed.

Communicate Your Ideas

APPLY TO WRITING

Postcard: ***Using Commas***

Henry Moore. (Detail) *Family Group,* 1951. Bronze, 59¼ by 26½ inches.

You are on vacation at a very beautiful place. You have been wandering through a park when you come upon this sculpture. Write a postcard to your best friend and describe this sculpture. In your message use one example of items in a series and another of two adjectives before a noun that require a comma to separate them. Underline these in your writing.

Compound Sentences

A comma is usually used to separate the independent clauses in a compound sentence.

Use a comma to separate the independent clauses of a compound sentence if the clauses are joined by a conjunction.

A coordinating conjunction most often combines the independent clauses in a compound sentence.

COORDINATING CONJUNCTIONS						
and	but	for	nor	or	so	yet

Notice in the following examples that the comma comes before the conjunction.

I play the flute**,** and my sister plays the guitar.
Pick up my guitar**,** or it might get left behind.

A comma is not needed in a very short compound sentence.

Lisa played and I sang.

Do not confuse a compound sentence with a sentence that has a compound verb. No comma comes between the parts of a compound verb unless there are three or more verbs.

Compound Sentence	We waited for twenty minutes, but Lisa never appeared on stage.
Compound Verb	We waited for twenty minutes and then left.

A compound sentence can also be joined by a semicolon. You can learn more about compound sentences on pages L242–L243.

Practice Your Skills

Check Your Understanding
Using Commas with Compound Sentences

Music Topic **Read the sentences below. Write *C* if the sentence is punctuated correctly. Write *I* if it is punctuated incorrectly.**

1. Musicologists study the history of music and analyze its meaning to society.

2. The history of rap music is interesting and so many musicologists are beginning to examine it.

3. In 1979, Sugar Hill Gang recorded "Rappers' Delight" and this song changed the music world.

4. The song "Rappers' Delight" was a breakthrough and its lyrics provided the term *hip hop*.

5. Hip hop is related to rap music but they are different in some ways.

6. Rap is the spoken words of the song and hip hop refers to the background music.

7. Rappers speak the words of their songs rapidly and accent some phrases more than others.

8. In 1982, the first rap song with a political message was recorded and this song gave a social conscience to rap.

9. Sampling pieces of other songs began in 1986 and opened rap music to many lawsuits.

10. In 1986, rap videos began to appear on TV and attracted a new audience.

Connect to the Writing Process: Editing

Correcting Comma Errors

11.–16. Rewrite the incorrectly punctuated sentences from the exercise above. Add or remove commas where needed.

Connect to the Writing Process: Drafting

Writing Compound Sentences

Write one compound sentence for each of the following subjects. Make sure the clauses in each compound sentence are related. Add commas where needed.

17. music

18. hobbies

19. friends

20. sports

Introductory Elements

Some words, phrases, and clauses at the beginning of a sentence need to be separated from the rest of the sentence by a comma.

Use a comma after certain introductory elements.

The following are examples of introductory elements that should be followed by a comma.

WORDS	**No,** I have not heard about the earthquake. **Yes,** it was a bad one. (Other words include *now, oh, well,* and *why*—except when they are part of the sentence. *Why didn't you tell me?*)
PREPOSITIONAL PHRASE	**After the earthquake in San Francisco,** neighbors joined together to help one another. **In just a few seconds,** people's lives changed dramatically. (A comma comes after two or more prepositional phrases or a single phrase of four or more words.)
PARTICIPIAL PHRASE	**Feeling the ground begin to rumble,** residents ran nervously from their homes and offices into the street.
ADVERB CLAUSE	**As one man exited his home,** the roof caved in.

Notice on the following page that the punctuation of shorter phrases varies. Also, never place a comma after a phrase or phrases followed by a verb.

OTHERS **In Room 37,** 19 students were injured.

(A comma is usually used after an introductory phrase that ends in a number.)

In the road, blocks of wood were a hazard.

(The commas prevent confusion.)

On the floor of a destroyed home lay a child's teddy bear.

(The phrases are followed by the verb.)

PRACTICE YOUR SKILLS

Check Your Understanding

Using Commas with Introductory Elements

History Topic

Read the sentences below. Write *C* if the sentence is punctuated correctly. Write *I* if it is punctuated incorrectly.

1. Because of its proximity to the San Andreas Fault San Francisco experiences frequent earthquakes.

2. Although not all are violent, several have devastated the city.

3. Yes the 1906 quake was especially destructive.

4. In that earthquake a total of 450 or more people perished.

5. Throughout the city for three long days fires ravaged homes and buildings.

6. Coming together to help one another, the citizens rebuilt their devastated city.

7. From the rubble and ashes of the earthquake and fires, rose a city determined to host the Panama-Pacific International Exhibition in 1915.

8. In 1989 60,000 baseball fans were shaken in Candlestick Park when the city's next severe earthquake occurred.

9. Caving in parts of the Bay Bridge and causing gas mains to rupture the earthquake measured 7.1 on the Richter scale.

10. Because the earthquake occurred at rush hour, many commuters were on the Bay Area's streets and highways.

Connect to the Writing Process: Editing

Correcting Comma Errors

11.–16. Rewrite the incorrectly punctuated sentences from the exercise above. Add or remove commas where needed.

Connect to the Writing Process: Drafting

Writing Sentences

Write a sentence using each of the following introductory words or phrases. Add commas where needed.

17. After the long thunderstorm
18. As the sky began to clear
19. Well
20. Hearing the raindrops on our roof
21. In Room 206
22. When the sounds stopped
23. Because the lights went out
24. Hiding under her desk
25. In the heat of the day

Commonly Used Commas

When you tie your shoelaces, you do not have to think about how to do it as you did when you were little. You do it automatically. There are some comma rules you have been using for so many years that they probably have also become automatic. The following is a brief review of those rules for using commas.

With Dates and Addresses

For clarity, commas are used to separate the various elements in a date or an address from one another.

Use commas to separate the elements in dates and addresses.

Notice in the following examples that a comma is also used to separate a date or an address from the rest of the sentence.

DATE	On Tuesday, February 2, 1941, my grandmother was born.
ADDRESS	Her parents lived at 29 Bank Street, Long Beach, California, at the time.

A comma is not used to separate the state and the ZIP code.

Send your request for information to Genealogy Research, 500 West 52nd Street, New York, NY 10019.

In Letters

Use a comma after the salutation of a friendly letter and after the closing of all letters.

SALUTATIONS AND CLOSINGS	
SALUTATIONS	Dear Uncle Joe, Dear Emily, Dearest Grandmother,
CLOSINGS	Love, Yours truly, Sincerely, Thank you, Regards,

Connect to Speaking and Writing

Often the use of too many commas is as confusing as not using enough commas. Use commas only where a rule indicates they are needed. In other words, use commas only where they make the meaning of your writing clearer. If you cannot find a rule that says you need a comma, follow this saying: "When in doubt, leave it out."

Practice Your Skills

Check Your Understanding

Using Commas

Write *a* or *b* to indicate which sentence in each pair shows the correct use of commas.

1. a. Dear Felipe,
b. Dear Felipe

2. a. Wednesday, June 2, 1999
b. Wednesday June 2, 1999

3. a. Roslyn Donovan, 510 Houghton Street, Marlin, Texas 76661
b. Roslyn Donovan, 510 Houghton Street, Marlin, Texas, 76661

4. a. With love,
b. With love

5. a. Tampa Florida
b. Tampa, Florida

6. a. Thursday, October 3, 1960
b. Thursday, October 3 1960

7. a. Dr. Tonya Jackson 21 Jewel Road Park City Idaho 92714
b. Dr. Tonya Jackson, 21 Jewel Road, Park City, Idaho 92714

8. a. Thank you

b. Thank you,

9. a. Dear Darla,

b. Dear, Darla

10. a. December 7, 1941

b. December 7 1941

11. a. El Paso, Texas

b. El Paso Texas,

Connect to the Writing Process: Revising

Correcting Comma Errors

Rewrite the following letter, adding commas where needed.

27 Duvall Road
Austin, Texas 78702
May 2, 2000

Dear Grandma

I am trying to get some information for a family-tree project that I have to do for social studies. I know that your father was born on March 26 1919. His place of birth was his aunt's home on 26 Lasso Lane Bozeman Montana. What can you tell me about your father's parents?

Please send a response to me at my school address, which is Lake Travis High School 3322 Ranch Road Austin, Texas 78734.

Love
Jake

Communicate Your Ideas

APPLY TO WRITING

Informative Note: *Commas*

You are applying for a job as a counselor in training for a summer camp. Your prospective employer, Ms. Smythe, has requested that you send her a note that contains all the following information:

- your full name
- your date of birth
- your current address
- your previous work experience
- the date on which you can begin work

Because Ms. Smythe is a prospective employer, you want to make a good impression. Be sure to write in complete sentences and then check your work for the proper use of commas.

Mixed Practice

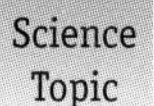

Read the paragraphs below. Write each word that should be followed by a comma.

Pinnipeds are fin-footed mammals with limbs that are used as paddles or flippers. The three main kinds of pinnipeds are the walrus the sea lion and the seal. All pinnipeds are meat eaters and they all live in the water. Most pinnipeds live in the cold waters of the Arctic and the Antarctic oceans but several forms live in fresh water. Since pinnipeds spend most of their lives in the water they have become well adapted to this kind of existence. Their tapered streamlined bodies make them excellent swimmers. Their thick layer of blubber gives them added buoyancy and helps keep them warm.

Searching for food pinnipeds can dive two or three hundred feet below the water's surface. When they are underwater their nostrils close. Most pinnipeds have sharp backward-pointing teeth. This feature makes it possible for a pinniped to seize prey and direct it down its throat. Because pinnipeds are sociable animals they live together in large herds.

The walrus is one type of pinniped. Some scientists classify the walrus as a type of large seal. Having tusks to defend itself the walrus can protect itself from the threat of the much larger polar bear. When walruses climb onto ice they can also use their tusks as hooks.

The sea lion lives in the northern Pacific Ocean and parts of the Southern Hemisphere. Using all four flippers sea lions can walk on land. Their thick blubbery layers keep them warm.

The harbor seal and elephant seal are two kinds of earless seals. Without ear flaps but with ears these seals have excellent hearing. They cannot use their rear flippers for walking but they move along on their bellies.

Commas That Enclose

Some expressions interrupt the flow of a sentence. These expressions generally add information that is not needed to understand the main idea of the sentence. If one of these interrupters comes in the middle of a sentence, a comma is placed before and after the expression to set it off.

The movie**, to tell the truth,** was boring.

Sometimes an interrupting expression comes at the beginning or the end of a sentence. When an interrupter appears in one of these places, only one comma is needed to separate it from the rest of the sentence.

To tell the truth, the movie was boring.
The movie was boring**, to tell the truth.**

Direct Address

Names, titles, or words that are used to address someone are set off by commas. These expressions are called nouns of **direct address.**

Use commas to enclose nouns of direct address.

Shelli, what is your opinion?
Your explanation**, Marc,** was excellent.
Did you like the movie**, Maria**?

CONNECT TO WRITER'S CRAFT

Writers often use commas when writing dialogue to indicate pauses in their characters' words. What do the pauses in the following dialogue tell you about what is happening?

"What in the world happened here?" our father asked in disbelief.

"Well, uh, we were just, uh, playing." 

Practice Your Skills

Check Your Understanding
Using Commas with Direct Address

Contemporary Life

Read the sentences below. Write *C* if the sentence is punctuated correctly. Write *I* if it is punctuated incorrectly.

1. As our drama teacher, Mrs. Washburn, will you explain that movie to us?
2. Certainly Shelli but the explanation is lengthy.
3. We thought the movie was boring Mrs. Washburn.
4. The plot was complicated, class.
5. Marc, would you like to explain it to the class?
6. The plot, Mrs. Washburn was actually one big story with two smaller subplots.
7. Yes, Marc, that is very true.
8. Mrs. Washburn why did the director make the movie so hard to understand?
9. The movie is not all that difficult to understand if you pay attention, Shelli.
10. Class it is important that you pay attention to all the little details in this film.

Connect to the Writing Process: Editing
Correcting Comma Errors

11.–15. Rewrite the incorrectly punctuated sentences from the exercise above. Add commas where needed.

Connect to the Writing Process: Drafting
Writing Sentences

Write sentences using the following nouns in direct address. Add commas where needed.

16. Mr. Green
17. Abby

18. Officer
19. President Smith
20. Sir
21. Dr. Gonzalez
22. Travis
23. Ms. Dalton
24. Mom
25. Erin

 Parenthetical Expressions

A parenthetical expression provides additional or related ideas. It is related only loosely to the rest of the sentence. The parenthetical expression could be removed without changing the meaning of the sentence.

Use commas to enclose parenthetical expressions.

COMMON PARENTHETICAL EXPRESSIONS	
after all	in fact
at any rate	in my opinion
by the way	of course
consequently	on the contrary
however	on the other hand
for example	moreover
for instance	nevertheless
generally speaking	to tell the truth
I believe (guess, hope, expect)	

By the way, did you bring your binoculars?

The indigo bunting**, in my opinion,** is a beautiful bird.

We can watch the birds a little longer**, I guess.**

Nicole**, on the other hand,** has to leave.

After all, she has been here for two hours.

We**, however,** just arrived.

Other expressions, as well, can be used as parenthetical expressions.

The roseate spoonbill**, although it looks like a flamingo,** is a different bird.

According to my book, puffins are not found in Florida.

Birds**, it is known,** communicate with one another.

Contrasting expressions, which usually begin with *not,* are also considered parenthetical expressions.

The mockingbird**, not the cardinal,** is the state bird of Texas.

The seagull is found inland**, not just by the ocean.**

My sister**, not I,** is the family bird expert.

PRACTICE YOUR SKILLS

Check Your Understanding

Using Commas with Parenthetical Expressions

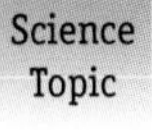

Read the sentences below. Write *C* if the sentence is punctuated correctly. Write *I* if it is punctuated incorrectly.

1. Generally speaking birds are animals that have wings and fly.

2. Not all birds however fit this description.

3. In fact, many birds are unable to fly but have wings.
4. Consequently, scientists classify birds as animals with both wings and feathers.
5. It is not, in fact, the ability to fly that sets them apart.
6. Nevertheless birds are among nature's most interesting creatures.
7. Burrowing owls for example are ingenious birds.
8. After all, they nest in the ground, often in prairie dog towns.
9. Other birds, however, make their homes far off the ground in steep cliff walls.
10. These cliffs of course afford them great safety from predators.

Connect to the Writing Process: Editing
Correcting Comma Errors

11.–15. Rewrite the incorrectly punctuated sentences from the preceding exercise, adding commas where needed.

Connect to the Writing Process: Drafting
Writing Sentences with Parenthetical Expressions

Write sentences using the parenthetical expression below in the part of the sentence indicated. Add commas where needed.

16. *I know* in the middle of a sentence
17. *by the way* at the beginning of a sentence
18. *to tell the truth* at the end of a sentence
19. *in fact* at the beginning of a sentence
20. *for instance* in the middle of a sentence

Appositives

An appositive with its modifiers identifies or explains a noun or a pronoun in the sentence. Notice in the example at the top of the next page that an appositive is enclosed in commas.

The Greenville firehouse**, a town landmark,** has finally been restored.

Use commas to enclose most appositives and their modifiers.

Notice in the following examples that an appositive can come in the middle of a sentence or at the end of a sentence. If an appositive comes in the middle of a sentence, two commas are needed to enclose it.

Greenville**, an old Western town,** is an interesting place to visit.

Hannah bought me a beautiful gift**, some Greenville turquoise.**

Titles and degrees that follow a person's name are a type of appositive. As such, they should also be set off by commas.

Rose Watts**, Ph.D.,** is a well-known expert on the history of Greenville.

Harry Jackson**, Jr.,** was the first sheriff in Greenville.

Mr. Smith**, CEO,** joined the Greenville Historical Society in 1999.

Commas are not used if an appositive identifies a person or thing by telling which one or ones when there is more than one possibility. Usually these appositives are names and have no modifiers.

My friend **Greta** will travel to Greenville with us.

The book ***Western History*** devotes two pages to a description of the town.

We **students** studied the Old West last year.

You can learn more about appositives on pages L183–L184.

Practice Your Skills

Check Your Understanding
Using Commas with Appositives

History Topic **Read the sentences below. Write *C* if the sentence is punctuated correctly. Write *I* if it is punctuated incorrectly.**

1. Manifest Destiny the belief that it was America's mission to expand westward inspired many explorers and settlers in the 1800s.

2. The explorers Lewis and Clark set out to cross the unmapped continent in 1804.

3. The third president Thomas Jefferson had purchased a large portion of that land from France.

4. Jefferson secured $2,500 a grant from the Congress to support the Lewis and Clark expedition.

5. The Native American guide Sacajawea helped the party cross the unfamiliar terrain.

6. Lewis and Clark also hired Sacajawea's husband, Toussaint Charbonneau to guide them.

7. Sacajawea, a Shoshone, was fluent in many native languages.

8. The explorer Meriwether Lewis was familiar with many Indian tribes.

9. We Americans have mythologized Lewis and Clark's adventures.

10. In 1996, Stephen E. Ambrose Ph.D. published the book *Undaunted Courage* an account of the Lewis and Clark expedition.

Connect to the Writing Process: Editing
Correcting Sentences with Appositives

11.–15. Rewrite the incorrectly punctuated sentences from the exercise above. Add commas where needed.

Connect to the Writing Process: Drafting

Writing Sentences with Appositives

Write sentences using the phrases below as appositives. Add commas where needed.

16. my favorite animal

17. the best pet

18. a famous dog

19. the most beautiful bird

20. a furry creature

Mixed Practice

General Interest **Rewrite the paragraph below, adding commas where needed.**

A man who lived in California constructed a musical robot. The amazing thing about this achievement however is that the man made it in 1940! The robot by the way looked like a woman. Sitting on a couch the robot would play the zither. The zither a musical instrument has thirty to forty strings. Anyone who was within a twelve-foot radius could ask it to play any of about three thousand tunes. A person's voice not a switch touched off it controls. The machinery inside it included 1,187 wheels and 370 electromagnets. No one has discovered in spite of extensive research whatever happened to Isis the world's first robot musician.

Nonessential and Essential Elements

Sometimes a particular phrase or a clause is not essential to the meaning of a sentence.

Use commas to set off nonessential participial phrases and nonessential clauses.

A participial phrase or a clause is nonessential if it provides extra information that is not essential to the meaning of the sentence.

NONESSENTIAL	Dallas**, lying in the eastern part of Texas,** receives quite a bit of rain. (participial phrase)
NONESSENTIAL	Carol**, wearing a raincoat but no hat,** likes the rain. (participial phrase)
NONESSENTIAL	Three inches is the annual rainfall in Yuma, Arizona**, which is in the southwestern part of the state.** (clause)

If the nonessential phrase and clause in the preceding examples were dropped, the main idea of the sentences would not be changed in any way.

Dallas receives quite a bit of rain.

Carol likes the rain.

Three inches is the annual rainfall in Yuma, Arizona.

If a participial phrase or a clause is essential to the meaning of a sentence, no commas are used. Essential phrases and clauses usually identify a person or thing and answer the question *Which one?* when there might be confusion otherwise. Adjective clauses that begin with *that* are usually essential whereas those that begin with *which* are often nonessential.

ESSENTIAL	We enjoyed the program **presented by station's meteorologists.**
	(participial phrase)
ESSENTIAL	The speaker **who closed the program** is my father.
	(clause)
ESSENTIAL	His prediction **that the summer would be very dry** proved accurate.
	(clause)

If the essential phrases and clauses in the preceding examples were dropped, necessary information would be missing. The main idea of the sentence would be incomplete.

We enjoyed the program.
(*Which* program?)

The speaker is my father.
(*Which* speaker?)

His prediction proved accurate.
(*Which* prediction?)

Nonessential and essential elements are sometimes called nonrestrictive *and* restrictive *elements.*

PRACTICE YOUR SKILLS

Check Your Understanding

Using Commas with Nonessential Elements

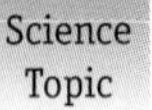

Write *C* if the sentence is punctuated correctly. Write *I* if it is punctuated incorrectly.

1. Lightning that strikes in dry forests can cause forest fires.
2. Often thunderstorms produce lightning that ignites wet areas.

3. Lightning which occurs all over the world is an amazing phenomenon.
4. Thunder which can be quite loud follows a lightning flash.
5. Lightning which is caused by streams of electricity also strikes humans quite frequently.
6. A bolt of lightning striking a person usually causes very serious injury or death.
7. The phenomenon of lightning bolts traveling between two clouds is quite common.
8. Animals alarmed by the loud noises usually find cover during thunderstorms.
9. Lightning that strikes an airplane can cause severe damage.
10. Lightning which can strike telephone and electrical lines has ruined many televisions and computers not guarded by surge protectors.

Connect to the Writing Process: Editing
Adding Commas to Sentences

11.–15. Rewrite the incorrectly punctuated sentence from the exercise above. Add commas where needed.

Connect to the Writing Process: Drafting
Writing Sentences

Write sentences using the following groups of words as nonessential elements. Add commas where needed.

16. which is my favorite desert
17. used as a topping
18. which was a great restaurant
19. who used to visit often
20. located in the mall
21. which is always crowded
22. who prefers to shop closer to home

23. that is on the upper level
24. which has received awards
25. eating at a five-star restaurant

Communicate Your Ideas

APPLY TO WRITING

Writer's Craft: *Analyzing the Use of Commas*

Professional writers often use commas to make their work easier to read. The following passage is from *Across the Wide Missouri,* a nonfiction book by Bernard DeVoto, who won the Pulitzer Prize in 1947 for his realistic portrayal of Western expansion in America. In the passage below, DeVoto discusses mapmaking of the early 1800s. Read this passage, noticing the author's use of commas. Then follow the directions.

> Tanner's and Burr's bulge at about the Bitterroot Mountains and Tanner's not-so-often imitated Platte were about the only advances over William Clark that had been made by the time we deal with. In fact, apart from Clark's map, they were about the only advances over A. Arrowsmith and L. Lewis, *A New and Elegant General Atlas,* an English work published the year when Lewis and Clark started up the Missouri.
>
> –*Bernard DeVoto,* Across the Wide Missouri

- Reread the sentences that contain commas. Which rules does DeVoto follow in placing those commas?
- Rewrite the second sentence eliminating the commas. Which is easier to read, the new version or DeVoto's original one? Why?
- If you were the editor of DeVoto's book, would you have changed anything he did? Explain your answer.

Science Topic **Rewrite the paragraphs below, adding commas where needed.**

The bald eagle of course is not bald. It was named at a time when *bald* meant "white." Because it has white feathers on its head the adult eagle has its present name. In contrast to its white head and tail the bald eagle's body and wings are brown. Its eyes beak and feet are yellow. An eagle can be over three feet long and its wingspan may be over seven feet. Its toes end in talons which are strong claws.

An eagle is a hunter. It feeds mainly on dead or dying fish but sometimes will eat small animals. It swoops down picks up its prey in its talons and flies off. An eagle that weighs eight to twelve pounds is able to carry an animal weighing as much as seventeen pounds!

Even though the bald eagle is the national emblem it had become an endangered species by the 1960s. After years of federal action and nationwide attention this magnificent bird was declared out of danger in 1999.

CheckPoint

Understanding Kinds of Sentences and End Marks

Write each sentence and its appropriate end mark. Then label each one *D* for declarative, *IM* for imperative, *IN* for interrogative, or *E* for exclamatory.

1. Listen to these interesting facts about your body
2. No one else in the whole world has the same fingerprints or voiceprint as you do
3. If it takes fourteen muscles to smile, how many muscles does it take to frown
4. The answer is twenty, which means that it's easier to smile than to frown
5. Wait until you hear this next fact
6. Particles in a sneeze can travel at speeds of over one hundred miles per hour
7. Did you ever cry when you cut an onion
8. A cut onion releases a gas that irritates your eyes
9. Then your tears automatically come to your eyes to wash away the gas—like windshield wipers
10. There are 206 bones in the human body
11. Do you know the name of the longest bone
12. The longest is the femur, or the thigh bone
13. Take care of your bones by drinking plenty of milk
14. What have we learned from these facts
15. Without a doubt, the workings of the human body are extraordinarily amazing

Using Commas Correctly

Write each sentence, adding a comma or commas where needed. If a sentence needs no commas, write *C*.

1. Pablo is your birthday on Tuesday March 6?
2. Gazelles and prairie dogs seldom drink water.
3. The Marianas Trench in the Pacific the lowest point on Earth is 36,198 feet below sea level.
4. Jennifer is only one day older than her cousin.
5. An old farmhouse owned by Ito stands near a meadow.
6. On Monday my brother will enter the Army at Fort Dix New Jersey.
7. Before locking up the custodian turned off the lights.
8. In Switzerland official notices are printed in French German Italian and Romansch.
9. Generally speaking a worker bee may live for six months but a queen bee may live for six years.
10. No Leslie doesn't live in Louisville Kentucky anymore.

Writing Sentences

Write ten sentences that follow the directions below.

Write a sentence that...

1. includes a series of nouns.
2. includes two adjectives before a noun.
3. has two independent clauses joined by a coordinating conjunction.
4. includes an introductory participial phrase.
5. includes an introductory adverbial clause.
6. includes direct address.
7. includes a parenthetical expression.
8. includes an appositive.
9. includes a nonessential adjective clause.
10. includes a street number and name, city, and state.

Language and *Self-Expression*

Claude Monet was a founder of the Impressionist Movement of the late 1800s. The Impressionists were French painters who painted or drew their impressions of moments of everyday life. Impressionists painted with hundreds of strokes and dabs to reveal the way light changed their subjects.

Arrival of the Normandy Train, Gare Saint-Lazare captures a moment in time as Monet saw it. What other sensory impressions can you imagine from this painting? Write a description of the scene, including the sounds, smells, tastes, sights, and textures of the *gare* (station).

Prewriting Create a sensory details web for your description. Include circles labeled "Sights," "Sounds," "Smells," "Tastes," and "Feels." Use your imagination to think of sense impressions that reflect what you see in the painting.

Drafting Use your details web to write a first draft of your description. Try to create a strong mental image of the train station for your readers.

Revising Read your description to a classmate. Ask if you have successfully captured the feeling of the train station as it is depicted in the painting. Add any details necessary to make your description evocative and complete.

Editing Go over your description, checking for errors in grammar, spelling, and punctuation. Be sure your sentences end with appropriate punctuation and include commas wherever necessary.

Publishing Make a final copy of your description. Read classmates' descriptions, and see who has best captured in writing the sensory impression made by the painting.

Recognizing Sentences

A **declarative sentence** makes a statement or expresses an opinion and ends with a period (.).

An **imperative sentence** gives a direction, makes a request, or gives a command. It ends with either a period or an exclamation point (. or !).

An **interrogative sentence** asks a question and ends with a question mark (?).

An **exclamatory sentence** expresses strong feeling or emotion and ends with an exclamation point (!).

Other Uses of Periods

Periods are used in places other than at the ends of sentences. *(page L501)*
In titles with names (Dr., Ms.)
With initials for names (R. D. Stein)
In times with numbers (P.M., A.D.)
In addresses (St., Dept.)
In organizations and companies (Co., Inc.)
Use a period after each number or letter in an outline. *(page L502)*

Commas that Separate

Use commas to separate items in a series. *(pages L505–L506)*
Use a comma sometimes to separate two adjectives that precede a noun and are not joined by a conjunction. *(page L508)*
Use a comma to separate the independent clauses of a compound sentence if the clauses are joined by a conjunction. *(pages L510–L511)*
Use a comma after certain introductory elements. *(pages L513–L514)*
Use commas to separate the elements in dates and addresses. *(page L516)*
Use commas in the salutations and closings of letters. *(page L516)*

Commas that Enclose

Use commas to enclose nouns of direct address. *(page L521)*
Use commas to enclose parenthetical expressions. *(pages L523–L524)*
Use commas to enclose nonessential appositives and their modifiers, and to set off nonessential phrases and clauses. *(pages L526–L530)*

Directions

Write the letter of the mark of punctuation that correctly completes each sentence. If the sentence contains no error, write *D.*

EXAMPLE **1** Shopping for school is always a huge production for the Alistair family of Cincinnati Ohio.

1 **A** period
B comma
C question mark
D No error

ANSWER **1** **B**

1. The Alistairs have ten children, whose ages range from fifteen years to six months.

2. How do they manage a shopping trip

3. They load the kids into two vans and they drive to a large shopping mall.

4. Then the fun begins

5. Each older wiser kid takes charge of a younger one.

6. The Alistairs go to clothing stores shoe stores, and stationery stores.

7. Don't lose anyone

8. By the end of the day everyone is exhausted and ready to go home.

9. They meet in a pizza restaurant inside the mall.

10. With a little bit of luck all of the children and their parents will have accomplished their shopping on time.

1 A period
B comma
C question mark
D No error

2 A period
B comma
C question mark
D No error

3 A period
B comma
C exclamation point
D No error

4 A exclamation point
B comma
C question mark
D No error

5 A period
B comma
C question mark
D No error

6 A period
B comma
C question mark
D No error

7 A exclamation point
B comma
C question mark
D No error

8 A period
B comma
C question mark
D No error

9 A period
B comma
C question mark
D No error

10 A period
B comma
C question mark
D No error

CHAPTER 16

Italics and Quotation Marks

Directions

Read the passage and write the letter of the answer that correctly punctuates each underlined part. If the underlined part contains no error, write *D*.

EXAMPLE Ellie looked forward to reading Beowulf and works by Chaucer (1) in her English class.

1 **A** Beowulf and works by *Chaucer*
B *Beowulf* and "works by Chaucer"
C *Beowulf* and works by Chaucer
D No error

ANSWER **1 C**

"Are you taking advanced English, Jay" Ellie asked? (1)

"No," Jay replied, "math is what interests me." (2)

Ellie said, "I hope we do some of Emily Dickinson's poems, such as 'I Am Nobody.'" (3) I read in a magazine that our English classes don't feature enough women writers."

"We have to write five papers"! Anthony exclaimed. (4)

Ellie couldn't believe her ears. Did she just hear him say, "We have to write five papers"? (5)

1 **A** "Are you taking advanced English, Jay"? Ellie asked.
B "Are you taking advanced English, Jay?" Ellie asked.
C "Are you taking advanced English, Jay Ellie asked"?
D No error

2 **A** "No." Jay replied, "Math is what interests me."
B "No." Jay replied. "Math is what interests me."
C "No," Jay replied. "Math is what interests me."
D No error

3 **A** Ellie said, "I hope we do some of Emily Dickinson's poems, such as 'I Am Nobody.'
B Ellie said, "I hope we do some of Emily Dickinson's poems, such as *I Am Nobody*.
C Ellie said, "I hope we do some of Emily Dickinson's poems, such as '*I Am Nobody.*'
D No error

4 **A** "We have to write five papers" Anthony exclaimed!
B "We have to write five papers." Anthony exclaimed.
C "We have to write five papers!" Anthony exclaimed.
D No error

5 **A** 'We have to write five papers'?
B 'We have to write five papers?'
C "We have to write five papers?"
D No error

"It's just the architect's model, but I'm very excited."

Leo Cullum. "It's just the architect's model, but I'm very excited." 1997. Ink, 4 by 5 inches.

Describe What is the setting of this cartoon? What are the characters doing?

Analyze Cartoons are meant to entertain and amuse, and they often mean something different to each person. Think of your favorite cartoon and ask yourself how it expresses humor. How do you think the details and exaggeration of Cullum's cartoon make it funny?

Interpret What does the title of the cartoon mean to you? Why is it funny?

Judge What other things might the dogs say that would be funny?

At the end of this chapter, you will use the artwork to stimulate ideas for writing.

Italics (Underlining)

This chapter will cover the various uses of italics as well as the uses of quotation marks with titles and direct quotations.

As you probably already know, italics are printed letters that slant to the right. If you are using a computer, you need to highlight what should be italicized and then use the command for italics. If you are writing by hand, you need to underline whatever should be italicized.

ITALICS	My mom read *Charlie and the Chocolate Factory* to my little sister.
UNDERLINING	My mom read <u>Charlie and the Chocolate Factory</u> to my little sister.

Certain letters, numbers, and words should be italicized (underlined).

Italicize (underline) letters, numbers, and words when they are used to represent themselves. Also italicize (underline) foreign words that are not generally used in the English language.

When you use the computer, you should italicize. When you write, you should underline. Do not do both.

LETTERS	My little sister has trouble writing *5*s and *B*s.
	or
	My little sister has trouble writing <u>5</u>s and <u>B</u>s.
WORDS, PHRASES	She cannot pronounce the word *teeth*.
	or
	She cannot pronounce the word <u>teeth</u>.

FOREIGN WORDS	We call our German grandmother *Oma*. or We call our German grandmother Oma.

Notice in the example on the preceding page that only the 5 and B are italicized (underlined)—not the *s*.

Italicize (underline) the titles of long written or musical works that are published as a single unit. Also italicize (underline) the titles of periodicals, movies, radio and television series, paintings and sculptures, and the names of vehicles.

TITLES	
BOOKS	*Jane Eyre* White Fang
NEWSPAPERS	*Chicago Tribune* Sacramento Bee
PERIODICALS	*Seventeen,* the Reader's Digest (In general, do not underline *the,* which often appears before newspaper or periodical titles.)
PLAYS, MOVIES	*Romeo and Juliet* The Wizard of Oz
BOOK-LENGTH POEMS	*Evangeline* Odyssey
RADIO AND TELEVISION SERIES	*The Shadow* The Wonder Years
LONG MUSICAL WORKS	*Faust* La Traviata
WORKS OF ART	*Mona Lisa* Venus de Milo

Ships, Planes, Other Crafts	*Titanic* Spirit of St. Louis *Voyager 2* Discovery

You can learn about capitalization of titles on pages L483–L487.

Practice Your Skills

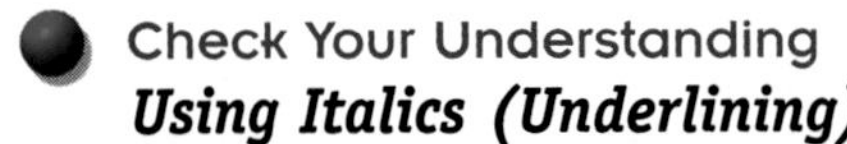

Check Your Understanding

Using Italics (Underlining)

Write *a* or *b* to indicate which item in each pair shows the correct use of underlining.

1. **a.** the aircraft carrier USS Enterprise
   b. The Aircraft Carrier USS Enterprise
2. **a.** the novel The Mill on the Floss
   b. the novel The Mill on the Floss
3. **a.** the opera The Barber of Seville
   b. the opera The Barber of Seville
4. **a.** the magazine Boy's Life
   b. The Magazine Boy's Life
5. **a.** the novel The Red Badge of Courage
   b. the novel The Red Badge of Courage
6. **a.** the book Mathematics for All Ages
   b. the book Mathematics for All Ages
7. **a.** the play Our Town
   b. the play Our Town
8. **a.** the Los Angeles Times
   b. the Los Angeles Times

9. **a.** the painting The Last Supper
   b. the painting The Last Supper

10. **a.** The Musical The Phantom of the Opera
    b. the musical The Phantom of the Opera

11. **a.** The Poetry Collection Field: A Haiku Circle
    b. the poetry collection Field: A Haiku Circle

12. **a.** the film Citizen Kane
    b. The Film Citizen Kane

13. **a.** Shakespeare's play Twelfth Night
    b. Shakespeare's play Twelfth Night

14. **a.** the television show The X-Files
    b. the television show The X-Files

15 **a.** The Shuttle Atlantis
   b. the shuttle Atlantis

Connect to the Writing Process: Editing

Using Underlining

Rewrite the following sentences, underlining the words that should be italicized.

16. I love adventure books like 20,000 Leagues Under the Sea by Jules Verne.
17. I can imagine myself on a submarine like the Nautilus.
18. Of course, this book was written before transportation innovations like the Concorde.
19. In The Wonderful Wizard of Oz, published in 1900, tornadoes, horses, and hot-air balloons are all used for transportation.
20. In 1912, the allegedly unsinkable ship Titanic sank after striking an iceberg.
21. The word titanic actually means "colossal."

22. It is derived from the Greek word titanikos, which relates to the mythological Titans.
23. Other famous vehicles that suffered a tragic end include the zeppelin Hindenburg and the ocean liner Lusitania.
24. The history of steamships, such as the Queen Mary and the Queen Elizabeth, is rich.
25. Magazines like Aviation History and Collectible Automobile regularly feature stories about the history of transportation.

Communicate Your Ideas

APPLY TO WRITING

E-mail: *Titles*

Your English class is exchanging E-mail messages with students from another country. Write a message to another teenager telling him or her about yourself. Recommend two good books and some of your favorite movies. Before you begin writing, look over these questions and jot down some ideas.

- How will you introduce yourself to the other student?
- What is one interesting thing about yourself that you would like to share with the student?
- What do you like to do in your free time?
- What two books will you recommend?
- What two movies will you recommend?
- What reasons will you give for your recommendations?

Then write your message. When you have finished, check to make sure that you have punctuated the titles correctly.

Quotation Marks

When you use quotation marks, always remember that they come in pairs. They are placed at the beginning and at the end of certain titles and uninterrupted quotations.

Quotation Marks with Titles

You have learned that titles of long works are italicized (underlined). Most long works are made up of smaller parts. For example, books are composed of chapters, and magazines contain many articles. The titles of these smaller parts should be enclosed in quotation marks.

Use quotation marks to enclose the titles of chapters, articles, stories, one-act plays, short poems, and songs.

CHAPTERS	Read "I Am Born," the first chapter in my favorite book, <u>David Copperfield</u>. (The chapter in the book is in quotation marks, but the title of the book is underlined.)
ARTICLES	Have you seen the article "Charles Dickens's England" in <u>Newsweek</u>?
STORIES	I read "Everyday Use" by Alice Walker yesterday.
ONE-ACT PLAYS	Sherry is going to be in the school's performance of "Drama Club."
SHORT POEMS	My favorite poem in the book <u>Famous Twentieth Century Poetry</u> is "Sea Lullaby."
SONGS	When I was younger, I used to love to sing "Puff, the Magic Dragon."

You will learn more about other punctuation, such as commas and periods, with quotation marks later in this chapter.

PRACTICE YOUR SKILLS

Check Your Understanding
Punctuating Titles

Write *a* or *b* to indicate which title in each pair is correctly punctuated.

1. a. The Lottery (short story)
b. "The Lottery" (short story)
2. a. The Elegance of Memory (poem)
b. "The Elegance of Memory" (poem)
3. a. "Somewhere Over the Rainbow" (song)
b. Somewhere Over the Rainbow (song)
4. a. "The Washwoman" (short story)
b. The "Washwoman" (short story)
5. a. The Romantic Poets (chapter)
b. "The Romantic Poets" (chapter)
6. a. Twinkle, Twinkle Little Star (song)
b. "Twinkle, Twinkle Little Star" (song)
7. a. "The Road Not Taken" (poem)
b. The "Road Not Taken" (poem)
8. a. "The Rocking-Horse Winner" (short story)
b. The Rocking-Horse Winner (short story)
9. a. The Art of Georgia O'Keeffe (chapter)
b. "The Art of Georgia O'Keeffe" (chapter)
10. a. "Frozen" (song)
b. Frozen (song)

Connect to the Writing Process: Drafting
Writing Titles in Sentences

Write sentences that include a title of each type of work indicated. Add quotation marks where needed.

11. short story
12. chapter of a book
13. article
14. one-act play

Communicate Your Ideas

APPLY TO WRITING

Persuasive Letter: *Quotation Marks with Titles*

Your music teacher is considering which songs the choir will sing in an upcoming performance. Write a letter to your teacher suggesting two songs that should be included in the choir performance. They can be hymns, recent popular songs, or any songs that you like from opera or musicals. Give her convincing reasons why you think the choir should choose these two songs. After you have finished your letter, check that you have punctuated the titles of the songs appropriately.

Mixed Practice

Contemporary Life

Write each sentence, adding quotation marks or underlining where needed.

1. The Roots of Old Verse is the lead article in the Atlantic Literary Journal.
2. The familiar lullaby Rock-a-Bye Baby dates from the Elizabethan period.
3. Ring Around the Roses is an old rhyme from the Middle Ages.
4. Did you read the chapter called Early Children's Poetry in the book English Poems and Commentary?
5. No, I read Mending Wall in the book Selected Poems of Robert Frost.
6. I read an article about him called Frost's New England in Newsweek.
7. Two of Robert Frost's most famous poems are Birches and Stopping by Woods on a Snowy Evening.

8. Do you know the song I Can't Choose by John Knight?
9. It is based on The Road Not Taken, which was also written by Frost.
10. There is a great paragraph about his works in the chapter called American Poets in the book Writers to Remember.

Quotation Marks with Direct Quotations

The most important thing to remember when writing direct quotations is that quotation marks enclose only the *exact words* of a speaker. In other words, quotation marks are used only with a **direct quotation.**

Use quotation marks to enclose a person's exact words.

"I just finished my homework," Zoe said.

Will said, "I'll be glad to check it for you."

Sometimes, when you write, you may paraphrase what someone has said—without using his or her exact words. When you paraphrase, you are indirectly quoting a person. Do not use quotation marks with **indirect quotations.**

Zoe said that she had just finished her homework.

Will said he would check it for her.

In the first example above, the word *that* signals the indirect quotation. In the second example, *that* is understood.

A one-sentence direct quotation can be written in several ways. It can be placed before or after a speaker tag, such as *she said* or *Mr. Billings asked.* In both cases quotation marks enclose the person's exact words—from beginning to end.

"Yesterday I left my homework in my locker," Zoe added.

Zoe added, "Yesterday I left my homework in my locker."

For variety or emphasis, a quotation can also be interrupted by a speaker tag. When this interruption occurs, you need two pairs of quotation marks because quotation marks enclose only a person's exact words, not the speaker tag.

> "Yesterday," Zoe added, "I left my homework in my locker."

To quote more than one sentence, put quotation marks at the beginning and at the end of the entire quotation. Do not put quotation marks around each sentence within a quotation—unless a speaker tag interrupts.

> Zoe added, "Yesterday I left my homework in my locker. Mrs. Cash was very nice about it. She wrote a hall pass so that I could retrieve it."
>
> "Yesterday I left my homework in my locker," Zoe said. "Luckily, Mrs. Cash wrote a hall pass so I could retrieve it."

Notice in the above examples that the comma or period that follows the quotation is placed *inside* the closing quotation marks. Of course, if the sentence ends with the speaker tag, then the period follows the speaker tag.

> "I got my homework and returned to class," said Zoe.

CONNECT TO SPEAKING AND WRITING

When you write speaker tags in direct quotations, it is important not to repeat the word *said* too often. Try to convey to your reader the tone or mood of the speaker by using vivid speaker tags. You can do this by using a different word for *said* or by adding an adverb showing how the speaker spoke his or her words.

> "You're finally here," **laughed** Jennifer.
>
> "You're finally here," **whined** Jennifer.
>
> "You're finally here," **snapped** Jennifer **impatiently**.

How many other ways can you think of to say *said?* 

Practice Your Skills

Check Your Understanding
Using Quotation Marks with Direct Quotations

Contemporary Life

Write *I* if a sentence is punctuated incorrectly. Write *C* if a sentence is punctuated correctly.

1. Joey told Mrs. Cash that the dog ate his homework.
2. That's the oldest excuse there is, said Mrs. Cash.
3. Mrs. Cash asked us to get out our math books.
4. "I wonder what our topic is today," said Zoe.
5. Today, Mrs. Cash said, we'll be discussing real-life math.
6. She said that we were going to discuss how to count a customer's change back to him or her.
7. Our teacher continued, We will also talk about how to determine sales tax.
8. "Mrs. Cash, Will said, most cash registers tell a clerk how much change to give a customer."
9. Mrs. Cash reminded the class that it's still important to know how to do some mental math.
10. Joey said, Even my dog can do some mental math."

Connect to the Writing Process: Editing
Adding Quotation Marks to Direct Quotations

11.–15. Rewrite the incorrect sentences from the preceding exercise, adding quotation marks where needed. When a comma or a period follows a quotation, don't forget to place it *inside* the closing quotation marks.

Capital Letters with Direct Quotations

Begin each sentence of a direct quotation with a capital letter.

"**U**sually, bees swarm in the spring," my teacher said.

My teacher said, "**U**sually, bees swarm in the spring."

If a single-sentence quotation is interrupted by a speaker tag, use only one capital letter—at the beginning of the sentence.

"**U**sually," my teacher said, "bees swarm in the spring."

Practice Your Skills

Check Your Understanding

Using Capital Letters with Direct Quotations

Contemporary Life

Read the sentences below. Write *I* if the sentence is capitalized incorrectly. Write *C* if the sentence is capitalized correctly.

1. "When honey bees swarm," said Mr. Johnson, "They are usually engorged with honey."

2. Maya asked, "Will they sting people then?"

3. "Yes, they might," replied the teacher, "But they are less likely to sting than at other times."

4. "Bees are not native to America," Mr. Johnson said.

5. Greg said, "in a magazine I read an article that said they were brought here from Europe."

6. "Mr. Johnson, what's the difference between a regular bee and a killer bee?" asked Maya.

7. The teacher answered, "well, they're not actually killers."

8. "The African honey bee is a more aggressive bee suited to tropical climates," He explained.

9. Greg asked, "How did they get to the United States?"

10. "They escaped," said Mr. Johnson, "From an apiary in Brazil in 1957."

Connect to the Writing Process: Editing

Capitalizing Direct Quotations

11.–16. Rewrite each incorrect sentence from the preceding exercise, adding capital letters where needed.

Commas with Direct Quotations

When you are reading quoted material aloud, your voice naturally pauses between the speaker tag and the direct quotation. In written material these pauses are indicated by commas.

Use a comma to separate a direct quotation from a speaker tag. Place the comma inside the closing quotation marks.

> "The ice cream isn't frozen yet**,**" Jordan cautioned.
>
> Jordan cautioned**,** "The ice cream isn't frozen yet."
>
> "The ice cream**,**" Jordan cautioned**,** "isn't frozen yet."

In the second and third examples above, note that the comma before the opening quotation marks is placed after the speaker tag, outside the opening quotation marks.

PRACTICE YOUR SKILLS

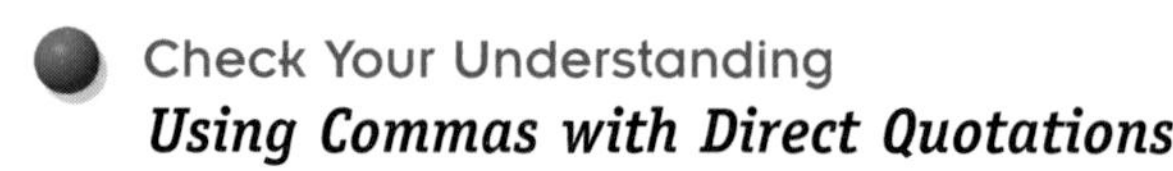

Check Your Understanding

Using Commas with Direct Quotations

Contemporary Life **If the use of commas in the sentence is incorrect, write *I*. If the use of commas is correct, write *C*.**

1. "I love making homemade ice cream", said Jordan.

2. Lori admitted, "I've never done that before."

3. "It's not hard," said Jordan "as long as you have an ice cream maker."

4. "My grandfather has one of the old ones," said Lori, "with a crank."

5. "Ours is electric", said Jordan "but either one will do."

6. "Let's use my grandfather's ice cream maker with the crank", suggested Lori.

7. "It'll give us a good workout," said Jordan.

8. "Mix the ingredients listed on page twenty-four of that cookbook," said Jordan.

9. "Add ice and rock salt to the outside area" said Jordan, "and then turn the crank for about thirty minutes."

10. "This is the best ice cream", said Lori.

Connect to the Writing Process: Editing

Using Commas in Direct Quotations

11.–16. Rewrite each incorrect sentence from the preceeding exercise, adding commas where needed.

End Marks with Direct Quotations

End marks come at the end of a quoted sentence, just as they do in a sentence that is not a quotation.

Place a period inside the closing quotation marks when the end of the quotation comes at the end of the sentence.

Carlos said, "This afternoon we'll hike in Grand Canyon**.**"

"This afternoon," Carlos said, "we'll hike in Grand Canyon**.**"

If a quotation comes at the beginning of a sentence, the period follows the speaker tag.

"This afternoon we'll hike in Grand Canyon," Carlos said**.**

A period comes at the end of each sentence within a quotation that has more than one sentence.

"This afternoon we'll hike in Grand Canyon," Carlos said**.** "Tomorrow we'll visit an archaeological dig**.** The next day we'll go home**.**"

Sometimes you may want to quote a question someone has asked or a sentence someone has said with strong feeling.

Place a question mark or an exclamation point inside the closing quotation marks when it is part of the quotation.

Madison asked, "Is the canyon close or will we drive there**?**"

"Is the canyon close," Madison asked, "or will we drive there**?**"

"Is the canyon close or will we drive there**?**" Madison asked.

Dani screamed, "Watch out for that snake**!**"

"Watch out for that snake**!**" Dani screamed.

A question mark or an exclamation point is placed inside the closing quotation marks when it is part of the quotation. When either of these punctuation marks is part of the whole sentence, however, it is place *outside* the closing quotation marks.

Did I hear the guide say, "That snake is not harmful"**?**

(The whole sentence—not the quotation—is the question.)

It was the happiest moment of my life when Carlos said, "It's time for a break"**!**

(The whole sentence is exclamatory, not the quotation.)

Notice that in the preceding examples, the end marks for the quotations themselves are omitted.

Practice Your Skills

Check Your Understanding

Using End Marks with Direct Quotations

Contemporary Life

Write *I* if the end mark in the sentence is incorrect. Write *C* if the sentence is correct.

1. "Hiking the Grand Canyon can be fun," said Carlos. "However, you have to be careful."

2. "Going down is much easier than coming up," exclaimed Madison!

3. Carlos said, "It's also much hotter down by the river than at the canyon rim".
4. "Bring plenty of water," warned the guide. "It's also important to wear proper shoes or hiking boots."
5. Did you hear that ranger say, "Some trails are closed?"
6. "Maybe we should stop every fifteen minutes" suggested Tim. "We could go back to the top if one of us is too tired."
7. The guide shouted, "Don't get too close to the edge!"
8. From a few feet down the path, our friends shouted, "Wait until you see this!".
9. I was very excited when the guide said, "There is an Indian Reservation in the canyon"!
10. "Can we make it all the way to the river today," asked Madison?

Connect to the Writing Process: Editing
Punctuating Direct Quotations

11.–16. Rewrite each incorrect sentence from the preceding exercise, placing the end punctuation properly.

Communicate Your Ideas

APPLY TO WRITING

Editorial: *Quotations*

What is love? Why do people fall in love? Nikki Giovanni once said, "We love because it's the only true adventure." Also on the subject of love, Frances Ellen Watkins Harper said, "Intense love is often akin to suffering."

Collect two quotations about love from two people you know. Then using all four quotations, the preceding two and the two you collect, write an editorial about the meaning of love. Your local paper wants to run a special Valentine's section with your article featured in it. After you write your article, read it to correct any errors. Don't forget to punctuate the quotations properly.

Mixed Practice

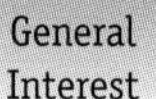

Write each sentence, adding capital letters, quotation marks, and other punctuation marks where needed.

1. a cat has absolute honesty Ernest Hemingway noted
2. someone once said it's nice for children to have pets—until the pets start having children
3. if things went by merit Mark Twain announced you would stay out and your dog would go in
4. young gorillas are friendly Will Cuppy said
5. Samuel Butler said the hen is an egg's way of producing another egg
6. if ants ever take over the world he mused I hope they remember that I invited them to all my picnics
7. all animals are equal said George Orwell but some are more equal than others
8. money will buy a pretty good dog commented Josh Billings but it won't buy the wag of its tail
9. what modest claim do kittens make David Irvine asked they claim the ownership of humans
10. animals are such agreeable friends George Eliot stated they ask no questions and pass no criticisms
11. it amuses me to talk to animals George Bernard Shaw said
12. He added the intellectual content of our conversations may to some extent escape them
13. can one love animals or children too much Jean-Paul Sartre once asked

14. a cat can be trusted to purr when she is pleased said William Inge which is more than can be said for humans
15. it is odd Frederick Goodyear once said that few animals are more unsteady on their feet than centipedes
16. William Lyon Phelps asked what is a dog's ideal in a life That's easy. it is a life of active uselessness.
17. of this I am sure someone once said that nothing is sure
18. Emily Dickinson said my ideal cat always has a huge rat in its mouth
19. The caribou seem to have no idea whatever of personal comfort William Parker Greenough noted
20. to me someone once said the noblest of dogs is the hot dog it feeds that hand that bites it

Other Uses of Quotation Marks

Once you know how to punctuate a direct quotation correctly, you will be able to apply what you know to the following situations.

Dialogue

Dialogue means "a conversation between two or more persons." In writing, dialogue is treated in a special way so that a reader always knows who is speaking, even if there are no speaker tags such as "he said" or "she asked."

When writing dialogue, begin a new paragraph each time the speaker changes.

In the following excerpt from *Oliver Twist* by Charles Dickens, each sentence follows the rules that you have just studied for direct quotations. Notice, however, that a new paragraph begins each time the housekeeper or Oliver speaks. They are discussing a painting of a beautiful woman that has been taken from the wall.

> "Ah!" said the housekeeper, watching the direction of Oliver's eyes. "It is gone, you see."
>
> "I see it is, ma'am," replied Oliver. "Why have they taken it away?"
>
> "It has been taken down, child, because Mr. Brownlow said, that as it seemed to worry you, perhaps it might prevent your getting well, you know," rejoined the old lady.
>
> "Oh, no, indeed. It didn't worry me, ma'am," said Oliver. "I liked to see it. I quite loved it."
>
> —*Charles Dickens,* Oliver Twist

CONNECT TO WRITER'S CRAFT

One writer who chooses not to add the conventional punctuation to his dialogue is Cormac McCarthy. While he does begin a new paragraph when the speaker changes, McCarthy provides readers with no quotation marks, so dialogue blends with the speaker tags and the narrative uninterrupted. McCarthy eliminates some apostrophes, as well. The following excerpt is a conversation between two characters.

> She pushed the tray forward between them. Please, she said. Help yourself.
>
> I better not. I'll have crazy dreams eatin this late.
>
> She smiled. She unfolded a small linen napkin from off the tray.
>
> I've always had strange dreams. But I'm afraid they are quite independent of my dining habits.
>
> Yes mam.
>
> —*Cormac McCarthy,* All the Pretty Horses 

Long Passages

When you write a report and want to support a point, you may want to quote more than one paragraph from a book. If this is the case, you use quotation marks in a slightly different manner.

When quoting a passage of more than one paragraph, place quotation marks at the beginning of each paragraph—but at the end of only the last paragraph.

Closing quotation marks are omitted at the end of each paragraph, except the last one, to indicate to a reader that the quotation is continuing.

> "Charles Dickens wrote some of the most popular books of the nineteenth century. He was one artist who enjoyed as much fame during his lifetime as after his death.
>
> (no closing quotation marks)
>
> "The characters created by Dickens still resonate with modern readers of all ages. From the rags-to-riches-to-rags Pip of *Great Expectations* to the tragic Sydney Carton of *A Tale of Two Cities,* Dickens wrote remarkable accounts of the human condition.
>
> (no closing quotation marks)
>
> "Known after his first novel *The Pickwick Papers* as a writer of humor, Dickens turned to the darker side of orphanages and the Victorian workhouse in *Oliver Twist,* his second book. Through Oliver's eyes, readers experience the ugliness of poverty and the cruelty of adults to children."
>
> (closing quotation marks)

Another way to quote a long passage is to set it off from the rest of the text by indenting both left and right margins. If you are using a computer, you also could set the passage in a smaller type size. When you use this method of quoting a long passage, no quotation marks are needed.

Quotations Within Quotations

A quotation within a quotation follows all the rules covered previously in this chapter. However, to avoid confusion, use single quotation marks to make a distinction between the two quotations.

To distinguish a quotation within a quotation, use single quotation marks to enclose the inside quotation.

"Is the song 'Food, Glorious Food' from the musical *Oliver!* by Lionel Bart?" Li asked.

Mr. Sanders said, "The most famous of Oliver Twist's lines in Dickens's book and Bart's musical is 'Please, Sir, I want some more.' "

Notice in the second example above that the closing single quotation mark and the closing double quotation marks come together.

Practice Your Skills

Check Your Understanding

Using Quotation Marks Correctly

Literature Topic

Write *I* if the quotation marks in a sentence are used incorrectly. Write *C* if the quotation marks in a sentence are used correctly.

1. Mr. Sanders explained, "Charles Dickens's works have now become a part of our everyday language."
2. He continued, "Few educated people do not recognize these opening lines from *A Tale of Two Cities*. It was the best of times; it was the worst of times."
3. "Mr. Sanders," Li interrupted, "who is your favorite character from *Great Expectations?*"
4. "That's hard to say," answered Mr. Sanders, "but I do love the blacksmith Joe."

5. "I like it when he calls Miss Haversham Miss A," laughed Steve.
6. Cindi said, "I love it when Sydney Carton says, It is a far, far better thing I do than I have ever done."
7. "Yes, that's the beginning of the last sentence in *A Tale of Two Cities*," said Mr. Sanders.
8. "Why does Mr. Grimwig keep saying I'll eat my head in *Oliver Twist*?" asked Cindi.
9. Li said, "I think that's his way of saying, I'll do anything to prove I'm right."
10. Mr. Sanders finished the discussion by saying, "Yes, Dickens liked his eccentric characters!"

Connect to the Writing Process: Editing
Using Quotation Marks

11.–15. Rewrite each incorrect sentence from the preceding exercise, correcting the use of single and double quotation marks.

Communicate Your Ideas

APPLY TO WRITING

Short Story: *Dialogue*

Think about the word *trunk*. Then write freely for several minutes, jotting down anything your mind associates with that word. When you are finished, choose one of the ideas as the basis for a short story. (Limit your characters to two or three.)

Write the first draft of your short story in which a trunk has some part. Be sure to include dialogue between the main characters of your story. As you edit, correct any punctuation errors in the dialogue. Make a final copy and read your story to a classmate.

Contemporary Life

Rewrite each sentence, adding quotation marks, end punctuation, capital letters, commas, and underlining where needed.

1. Where asked Leesha did you find that book of short stories
2. I got it at the library said Sarah I don't own a copy of it
3. The cover says true stories for dog lovers said Leesha
4. Yes, but the title said Sarah is James Herriot's Dog Stories
5. Who said dogs are a man's best friend
6. My favorite chapter in the book is Shep's Hobby said Leesha
7. What other books do you like asked Grant I'm looking for some good poetry
8. I don't know about Sarah said Leesha I like the book Modern and Contemporary Afro-American Poetry
9. There are many poems by Langston Hughes in that book stated Sarah
10. My two favorite poems said Leesha are Mother to Son and The Weary Blues
11. Did you see asked Grant the article about Langston Hughes in Newsweek?
12. No said Sarah was it interesting
13. Yes, it was answered Grant the writer discussed Hughes's book of verse called Shakespeare in Harlem
14. When was that published inquired Leesha
15. In 1942 said Grant five years before his book Fields of Wonder

CheckPoint

Punctuating Quotations Correctly

Write each sentence, adding capital letters, quotations marks, and other punctuation marks where needed.

1. Abigail Adams once wrote to her husband we have many high sounding words, and too few actions that correspond to them
2. trees are swayed by winds, but men are swayed by words wrote the author Joan Aiken
3. she went on to say words are like spices too many is worse than too few
4. in the book Little Women, the character Jo said I like good strong words that mean something
5. look was Pa's favorite word it meant admire, wonder, goggle at the beauty and excitement all around us said Lucy in the book The Ballad of Lucy Whipple
6. Scrooge said bah! humbug! in Charles Dickens's A Christmas Carol
7. words can destroy said Jeane Kirkpatrick what we call each other ultimately becomes what we think of each other, and it matters
8. the ballpoint pen said Noah in the book The View from Saturday has been the biggest single factor in the decline of Western Civilization it makes the written word cheap, fast, and totally without character
9. the famous artist Georgia O'Keeffe once said I found I could say with color and shapes what I couldn't say in any other way
10. polite words open iron gates says a Serbo-Croatian proverb

Punctuating Quotations Correctly

Write each sentence, adding underlining, capital letters, quotation marks, and other punctuation marks where needed.

1. where asked Ina did you find those incredible, fluorescent earrings?
2. A hairstylist's sign on Bradbury St. read we curl up and dye for you.
3. I just read Oliver Twist, Jan said it was better than any movie version I have ever seen.
4. News Ben Bradlee once said is the first rough draft of history.
5. Have you ever read the Christian Science Monitor Dan asked.
6. Cathleen asked is the ocean rough today
7. Ken declared I'm going to be the new class president
8. Please don't break us apart the sign over the bananas read
9. Arlene remarked we grew up together
10. That was an incredible pass exclaimed Dave
11. Work is the best escape from boredom Eleanor Dean once said
12. Who said little things affect little minds
13. Defeat is not the worst of failures said G. E. Woodberry not to have tried is the true failure
14. We saw a production of the Shakespearean play As You Like It at the Lyric State Cheryl announced
15. Life shrinks or expands in proportion to one's courage Anaïs Nin commented

Writing Sentences

Follow the directions below.

1. Write a dialogue between you and a fictional person: a superhero, a character in a book, a cartoon character, or someone created in your imagination. Punctuate the dialogue correctly.
2. After an introductory paragraph, quote a long passage.

Language and *Self-Expression*

"It's just the architect's model, but I'm very excited."

Leo Cullum creates cartoons for periodicals such as the *New Yorker* and the *Harvard Business Review.* When he is not drawing, he works as a pilot for a commercial airline.

This cartoon is particularly funny because the cartoonist places dogs in a human situation. Many people think of their pets as nearly human and have conversations with them, making them a part of the family. Imagine what dogs think of their owners, though. Create a dialogue that two dogs might have if they could talk. What do they think of a particular aspect of their owners' behavior?

Prewriting Freewrite a description of the dogs, their humans, and the behavior that the dogs are commenting on. Include as many details as you can imagine.

Drafting Use your freewriting details to write a first draft of your dialogue. Try to picture the humans' behavior from the dogs' point of view. Include details the dogs might find bewildering or comical.

Revising Read your dialogue aloud with a partner. Ask your partner to comment on your interpretation of the dogs' eye view of life with humans. Make any changes necessary to sharpen your dialogue and make it more amusing.

Editing Check your dialogue to be sure you have used quotation marks, punctuation, and capitalization correctly. Ensure that when each new speaker talks, you begin a new paragraph.

Publishing With your partner, read your dialogue aloud to the class. Encourage listeners to comment on your version of the dogs' dialogue.

Another Look

Italics (Underlining)

Italicize (underline) letters, numbers, and words when they are used to represent themselves. Also italicize (underline) foreign words that are not generally used in English. *(pages L543–L544)*

Italicize (underline) the titles of long written or musical works that are published as a single unit. Also italicize (underline) titles of paintings and sculptures and the names of vehicles. *(pages L544–L545)*

Quotation Marks

Use quotation marks to enclose the titles of chapters, articles, stories, one-act plays, short poems, and songs. *(page L548)*

Use quotation marks to enclose a person's exact words. *(pages L551–L552)*

Begin each sentence of a direct quotation with a capital letter. *(pages L553–L554)*

Use a comma to separate a direct quotation from a speaker tag. Place the comma inside the closing quotation marks. *(page L555)*

Place a period inside the closing quotation marks when the end of the quotation comes at the end of the sentence. If a quotation comes at the beginning of a sentence, the period follows the speaker tag. A period comes at the end of each sentence within a quotation that has more than one sentence. *(page L556)*

Place a question mark or exclamation point inside the closing quotation marks when it is part of the quotation. *(pages L556–L557)*

Other Uses of Quotation Marks

When writing dialogue, begin a new paragraph each time the speaker changes. *(pages L560–L561)*

When quoting a passage of more than one paragraph, place quotation marks at the beginning of each paragraph—but at the end of only the last paragraph. *(page L562)*

To distinguish a quotation within a quotation, use single quotation marks to enclose the inside quotation. *(page L563)*

Directions

Read the passage and write the letter of the answer that correctly punctuates each underlined part. If the underlined part contains no error, mark *D*.

EXAMPLE Kayla got a part in the television series

A Day in the Life
(1)

1 A "A Day in the Life"
B *A Day in the Life.*
C "A Day in the Life."
D No error

ANSWER **1 B**

The show got a favorable review in our newspaper, the Enquirer. (1) In the first show, Kayla's only line was, "Coming, Mother"! (2)

Kayla was also interviewed in our newspaper.

"How," the reporter asked, "did you get this part"? (3)

Kayla answered, "In my tryout, I read from the poem The Lake Isle of Innisfree. (4) The director told me that his favorite poet is Yeats!"

"Really, it was just luck, then," the reporter said.

"Oh, no," Kayla protested, "he really liked my work." (5)

1 **A** newspaper, the "Enquirer."

B newspaper, the *Enquirer.*

C newspaper, the *"Enquirer."*

D No error

2 **A** "Coming, Mother!"

B "Coming, *Mother"!*

C *"Coming, Mother"*

D No error

3 **A** "How," the reporter asked, "did you get this part?"

B "How?" the reporter asked, "did you get this part?"

C "How," the reporter asked? "did you get this part?"

D No error

4 **A** "In my tryout, I read from the poem "The Lake Isle of Innisfree."

B "In my tryout, I read from the poem *The Lake Isle of Innisfree.*

C "In my tryout, I read from the poem 'The Lake Isle of Innisfree.'

D No error

5 **A** "He really liked my work."

B he really liked my work."

C He really liked my work."

D No error

CHAPTER 17

Other Punctuation

Directions

Write the letter of the answer that correctly punctuates the underlined part in each sentence. If the underlined part contains no error, write *D*.

EXAMPLE **1** I was in charge of a group of third grade kids at a summer camp.

1 **A** third grade kids'
B third-grade kids
C third-grade kids'
D No error

ANSWER **1 B**

1. This summer was the camps first year.
2. The counselors were all nervous many of us had never worked with kids before.
3. Our day began at 930 A.M.
4. The kids at least most of them were eager to play.
5. In my group one girl was incredibly self assured.
6. She organized groups for games helped me hand out lunches, snacks, and drinks; and soothed nervous kids.
7. She was the camp directors niece, so I shouldn't have been surprised at her maturity.
8. I couldnt have done my job without Anna's help.
9. I like to think that it was Annas and my work that made the third-grade group do so well.
10. The Matthews family were new to the area and had seven children in the camp.

1 **A** camp's first year
B camps' first year
C camp's first-year
D No error

2 **A** nervous; many of us
B nervous: many of us
C nervous (many of us)
D No error

3 **A** 9:30 (AM).
B 93:0 A.M.
C 9:30 A.M.
D No error

4 **A** kids—at least most of them—
B kids—at least most of them
C kids: at least most of them
D No error

5 **A** self; assured
B self-assured
C selfassured
D No error

6 **A** games; helped me
B games: helped me
C games—helped me
D No error

7 **A** camp directors—niece
B camp directors-niece
C camp director's niece
D No error

8 **A** I couldn't have
B I could'nt have
C I couldnt' have
D No error

9 **A** Annas, and my work
B Annas' and my work
C Anna's and my work
D No error

10 **A** Matthews family,
B Matthew's family
C Matthews' family
D No error

Honoré Daumier. *The Third-Class Carriage,* ca. 1863.
Oil on canvas, 25¾ by 35½ inches. The Metropolitan Museum of Art.

Describe In this painting the artist Honoré Daumier gives us a glimpse into a railway compartment of the 1860s. What does this scene show? What are the people in the carriage doing? Describe their facial expressions.

Analyze What do you think the title of the painting means?

Interpret What message do you think the artist is trying to convey in the painting? How might a writer convey the same message?

Judge How would you feel if you were a passenger on this train? Explain.

At the end of this chapter, you will use the artwork to stimulate ideas for writing.

Apostrophes

The most costly punctuation error of all time occurred in 1962. A hyphen was omitted from a set of directions sent to the rocket powering the *Venus* space probe. As a result of the omission, the rocket self-destructed. Most errors that are made in punctuation do not have such disastrous results. Nevertheless, correct punctuation is necessary for clear communication—right here on Earth.

Omitting a tiny apostrophe, for example, can make a big difference in a sentence. In fact, including apostrophes in certain words is as important as spelling those words correctly. Without an apostrophe, the first sentence in the following examples does not make any sense. With an apostrophe, however, the meaning of the sentence instantly becomes clear.

> Well go with you to the game tonight.
>
> We'll go with you to the game tonight.

In addition to being used in contractions, apostrophes are commonly used with nouns and some pronouns to show ownership or relationship.

Apostrophes to Show Possession

One of the most common uses of an apostrophe is to show that someone or something owns something else.

> Lani's softball = the softball of Lani
>
> a woman's house = the house of a woman
>
> the Spensers' garage = the garage of the Spensers

As you can see from these examples, nouns have a special form to show possession. An apostrophe or an apostrophe and an *s* are added to the noun.

Possessive Forms of Singular Nouns

To form the possessive of a noun, first decide whether the noun is singular or plural.

Add *'s* to form the possessive of a singular noun.

Remember that you do not need to add or omit a letter. Just write the word and put *'s* at the end.

baby + 's = baby's	Give me the baby**'s** blanket.
Joey + 's = Joey's	That is Joey**'s** little sister.
boss + 's = boss's	Joey is my boss**'s** best worker.

The *'s* is added to the last word of compound words and the names of most businesses and organizations.

The passerby**'s** gaze fell on the cute child.
The baby broke the jack-in-the box**'s** spring.
The YMCA**'s** advertisements appeal to young families.

Connect to Speaking and Writing

Occasionally a singular noun will end in *s*. When the noun—especially a name—is two or three syllables long, it may be awkward to pronounce with *'s*. In such cases, add only an apostrophe.

The **Prentiss's** house is on the corner.

The **Prentiss'** house is on the corner. 

Check Your Understanding
Forming Possessive Singular Nouns

Write the possessive form of each noun.

1. apple
2. Pep Club
3. starfish
4. Georgia
5. cat
6. mother-in-law

7. brother
8. Mike
9. sailor
10. Bess
11. girl
12. Reese Company
13. Hope College
14. maid-of-honor
15. Mr. Rogers

Writing Sentences

16.–20. Use five of the singular possessive nouns from the preceding exercise in sentences of your own.

Possessive Forms of Plural Nouns

There are two rules to follow to form the possessive of plural nouns.

Add only an apostrophe to form the possessive of a plural noun that ends in *s.*

Add *'s* to form the possessive of a plural noun that does not end in *s.*

Deciding which rule to follow is simple if you take two steps. First, write the plural of the noun. Second, look at the ending of the word. If the word ends in *s,* add only an apostrophe. If it does not end in *s,* add an apostrophe and an *s.*

POSSESSIVE FORMS OF PLURAL NOUNS				
Plural	**Ending**	**Add**		**Possessive**
babies	s	'	=	babies'
foxes	s	'	=	foxes'
mice	no *s*	**'s**	=	mice**'s**
children	no *s*	**'s**	=	children**'s**
sheep	no *s*	**'s**	=	sheep**'s**

Practice Your Skills

Check Your Understanding
Forming Possessive Plural Nouns

Write the plural form of each noun. Then make it possessive.

1. friend	**6.** wolf	**11.** book	**16.** man
2. box	**7.** tomato	**12.** goose	**17.** Smith
3. house	**8.** girl	**13.** store	**18.** woman
4. deer	**9.** Lutz	**14.** cloud	**19.** paper
5. boy	**10.** city	**15.** album	**20.** Ryan

Check Your Understanding
Forming Possessive Nouns

Contemporary Life **Write the possessive form, singular or plural, of each underlined word.**

21. We went to the hospital to see my sister-in-law new baby.
22. My brother first child is a girl.
23. My parents excitement was obvious as they gazed at their first grandchild.
24. The hospital policy allowed the newborn to sleep in her mother room.
25. The infant cries were certainly loud for such a small baby.
26. I helped my sister-in-law write comments in the baby book pages.
27. Several nurses comments were complimentary.
28. My new niece name is Sabrina.
29. Sabrina crib was surrounded by flowers.
30. My brother had balanced a teddy bear on the crib edge.

Connect to the Writing Process: Editing
Using Possessive Nouns

If the underlined possessive form is incorrect, write it correctly. If the possessive form is correct as is, write *C*.

31. Many people were astonished by scientists' discoveries in the twentieth century.

32. In 1903, the Wright brother's accomplishment led to an explosion of transportation possibilities.

33. Alternative energy sources had to be developed to satisfy peoples' need for electrical power.

34. In 1900, most Americans' homes did not have electricity.

35. By the year 2000, very few places in the United States were without electricitys' effects.

36. Marconi's invention of the radio revolutionized mass communication.

37. The telephone's development throughout the century was truly remarkable.

38. The Soviet Union's achievement in launching the first manned satellite into space challenged the U.S. space program.

39. America's success in sending the first humans to the moon sparked the nation's imagination.

40. The future promises more evidence of sciences' advancements.

Possessive Forms of Pronouns

Unlike nouns, personal pronouns do not use an apostrophe to show possession. Instead, they change form: *my, mine, your, yours, his, her, hers, its, our, ours, their,* and *theirs.*

Do not add an apostrophe to form the possessive of a personal pronoun.

The camera is **hers.**

The dog wagged **its** tail for the photographer.

Indefinite pronouns, however, form the possessive the same way singular nouns do—by adding *'s.*

Add *'s* to form the possessive of an indefinite pronoun.

> This seems to be everyone**'s** favorite photo.
> Someone**'s** film cartridge was left under the seat.

You can find a list of common indefinite pronouns on page L54.

Practice Your Skills

Check Your Understanding
Using the Possessive of Pronouns

Contemporary Life **Write the correct form of the pronoun in parentheses.**

1. Are these photographs (yours, your's)?
2. (Anyone's, Anyones') photos may be entered in the contest.
3. The album is beautiful with (its, it's) photos of the Rocky Mountains.
4. They looked at my portfolio, but Heather hasn't submitted (hers, her's) yet.
5. (No one's, No ones') photographs were chosen for the prize.
6. I hope (everybody's, everybodys') photos are published.
7. Those cameras are (ours, our's).
8. Has (everyones, everyone's) film been developed?
9. It was (nobody's, nobodys') fault that the film was ruined.
10. The best photographs are (their's, theirs).

Connect to the Writing Process: Revising
Using Possessive Pronouns

Rewrite the following sentences, using possessive personal or indefinite pronouns.

11. Does that photograph album belong to him?
12. The cover of it has gold lettering.

13. The snapshots of everyone are in that box.
14. The puppy belongs to her.
15. Did the entry of anyone make it to the finals?

Apostrophes to Show Joint and Separate Ownership

Sometimes it is necessary to show that something belongs to more than one person.

To show joint ownership, make only the last word possessive in form.

These are Nan and Faron**'s** compact discs.

(The compact discs belong to both Nan and Faron.)

The only exception to this rule occurs when one word showing joint ownership is a possessive pronoun. In such cases the noun must also show possession.

This is Hannah**'s** and **my** stereo.

Separate ownership is shown in a different way from joint ownership.

To show separate ownership, make each word possessive in form.

These are Nan**'s** and Faron**'s** compact discs.

(Each girl has her own compact discs.)

Apostrophes with Nouns Expressing Time or Amount

When you use a noun that expresses time or amount as an adjective, write it in the possessive form.

Use an apostrophe with the possessive form of a noun that expresses time or amount.

That compact disc player cost Nan two week**s'** salary.
Nan really got her money**'s** worth.

Other words that express time include such words as *minute, hour, day, month,* and *year.* Other words that express amount include such words as *dollar, quarter, dime, nickel,* and *penny.*

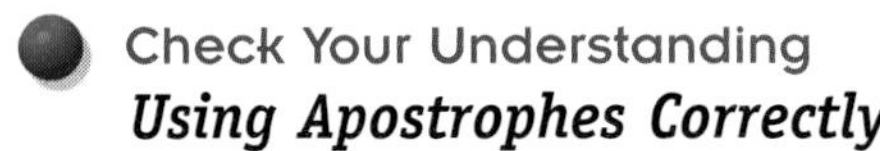

Check Your Understanding
Using Apostrophes Correctly

Contemporary Life **Add an apostrophe and *s,* if needed, to each underlined word to make it possessive. If the word is correct as is, write *C.***

1. The woman and man's voices on that compact disc sound great together.
2. The woman on the recording was Nan and my music teacher.
3. I picked up two more compact discs for Jason and Dad's birthdays.
4. Dawn and Tiffany's song was recorded by a professional group.
5. My family spent a week vacation watching them record in the studio.
6. The band we watched earns a month rent in one night at a concert.
7. The crew brought in the guitarist and the drummer's instruments.
8. Nan and my excitement was very high!
9. My father and brother's opinions of the band were very different.
10. Watching the recording session increased Faron and my interest in becoming singers.

Connect to the Writing Process: Editing
Using Possessive Forms Correctly

Write the possessive forms that are used incorrectly in the following sentences. Then write the correct possessive forms. If a sentence does not contain any errors in the use of possessives, write *C*.

11. My uncles ranch is a days drive from the town of Rock Springs.

12. On almost all ranches, there are many workers.

13. During our visit my brothers and I stayed in the workers bunkhouse.

14. Everyone's is coming to my uncles' ranch for a big dance tonight.

15. Dad's and Mom's suggestions for party decorations were immediately accepted.

16. Have you seen Uncle Ryan's new hat?

17. My efforts at learning to square dance were finally rewarded.

18. Her's were not.

19. I spent a months allowance on a new pair of beautiful red boots.

20. The times we have at Uncle Ryan's ranch are always the best.

Connect to the Writing Process: Drafting
Writing Sentences

Write sentences using the following possessives correctly.

21. any possessive personal pronoun

22. any possessive indefinite pronoun

23. two proper nouns showing joint ownership

24. two proper nouns showing separate ownership

25. a proper noun and a personal pronoun showing joint ownership

Communicate Your Ideas

APPLY TO WRITING

Dialogue: *Possessive Nouns and Pronouns*

Horace Pippin. *Domino Players,* 1943.
Oil on composition board, 12 3/4 by 22 inches. ©The Phillips Collection, Washington, D.C.

Imagine that you are listening to the conversation taking place around this domino table. What is the topic? What are they saying? Write a brief dialogue using the subjects in this painting as the speakers. In your dialogue use at least three possessive nouns and three possessive pronouns. Underline the nouns and pronouns you used.

QuickCheck Mixed Practice

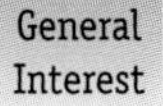

General Interest **Write the following paragraph, correcting any errors in the use of possessives.**

One of the most popular childrens books of all times is L. Frank Baum *The Wonderful Wizard of Oz,* published in 1900.

While many people have read the book, most are more familiar with Metro-Goldwyn Mayer 1939 movie version, *The Wizard of Oz.*

Both the book and the movie feature Dorothy Gayle and friends of her—the Scarecrow, the Tin Woodsman, and the Cowardly Lion. Everybody favorite little dog Toto is also in both versions. The makers of the movie were true to Baum book in many other ways.

One major change in the movie version is the color of Dorothy shoes. In the movie they are ruby red. In the book they are silver. Technicolor was new to Hollywoods studios in 1939. While silver didn't show up well on the big screen, red looked dazzling. The filmmakers decision changed forever how many people would remember Baum work.

 Other Uses of Apostrophes

Apostrophes have other uses besides showing the possessive of nouns and some pronouns.

Apostrophes with Contractions

A contraction is a shortcut. It usually combines two words into one. An apostrophe is added to take the place of one or more missing letters.

Use an apostrophe in a contraction to show where one or more letters have been omitted.

These examples show how some contractions are formed.

CONTRACTIONS	
do ~~not~~ = don't	there ~~is~~ = there's
we ~~are~~ = we're	who ~~is~~ = who's
of ~~the~~ clock = o'clock	let ~~us~~ = let's

In most contractions, no letters are added or changed around. There is one common exception: *will* + *not* = *won't.*

Do not confuse the contractions *it's, you're, they're, there's,* and *who's* with the possessive pronouns *its, your, their, theirs,* and *whose.*

Practice Your Skills

Check Your Understanding
Using Apostrophes with Contractions

Write the contraction for each pair of words.

1. are not
2. will not
3. did not
4. has not
5. you are
6. do not
7. is not
8. let us
9. I have
10. we have
11. we will
12. that is
13. I would
14. does not
15. have not
16. were not
17. they are
18. there is
19. I am
20. who is

Check Your Understanding
Distinguishing Between Contractions and Possessive Pronouns

Contemporary Life

Write the correct word in parentheses to complete each sentence.

21. If (were, we're) going to breakfast, (its, it's) now or never.

22. Please tell the server how you would like (your, you're) eggs.

23. I don't know if (their, they're) joining us or not.

24. If (theirs, there's) anything you need, let the server know.

25. (Whose, Who's) going to pay for this meal?

26. Do you know if (your, you're) going to order pancakes?

27. This bill must be (theirs, there's).

28. (Whose, Who's) orange juice is this?

29. (Its, It's) mine.

30. Did you speak to (their, they're) server?

Apostrophes with Certain Plurals

To prevent confusion, certain items form their plurals by adding *'s.*

Add *'s* to form the plural of lowercase letters, some capital letters, and some words that are used as words.

Sue's *i***'s** and *e***'s** look similar.
Jon's report card has two *A***'s.**

The plurals of most other letters, symbols, numerals, and other words used as words can be formed by adding *s*.

My little sister writes *3***s** for *E***s.**
Why did you put two *!***s** after that sentence?
This composition has too many *and***s.**

Notice the number *3*, the letter *E,* the exclamation point, and the word *and* are italicized. However, the *s* or the apostrophe and *s* with them are *not* italicized.

Some writers prefer to add 's, instead of just s, *to form the plural of all letters, symbols, numerals, and words used as words.*

Apostrophes with Certain Dates

An apostrophe is also used when numbers are dropped from a date.

Use an apostrophe to show that numbers were omitted in a date.

We moved here in ‘01. (2001)
My grandfather joined the army in ‘41. (1941)

Practice Your Skills

Check Your Understanding
Using Apostrophes

Contemporary Life

If a sentence is missing one or more apostrophes, write *I* for incorrect. If a sentence is correct, write *C*.

1. Have you ever tried to read documents from early America?

2. Many times the *s*s look like *f*s.

3. The numbers can also be hard to read.

4. The *1*s, *9*s, and *6*s all look different than ours today.

5. When the years are written without the first digits, such as *04* or *76,* it’s hard to know in what year the document was produced.

6. Take a look at an original draft of the Declaration of Independence.

7. Some of Jefferson’s letters look very strange to our modern eyes.

8. His cursive *t*s and *r*s are formed differently than ours.

9. If you look at an earlier document like the Magna Carta, which was written in 1215, you can recognize some letters, such as *a*s, *n*s, and *c*s.

10. However, it’s difficult for modern Americans to read the original Magna Carta because it’s written in Latin!

Connect to the Writing Process: Editing
Correcting Possessive Forms

11.–14. Rewrite the incorrect sentences from the preceding exercise, adding apostrophes where needed.

Communicate Your Ideas

APPLY TO WRITING

Friendly Letter: *Apostrophes*

A young child you know is having difficulty learning to write his or her letters and numbers. Can you remember the challenges you faced when you learned to write? Write a short letter to this child encouraging him or her to keep trying. Share your experiences learning to write. What letters and numbers did you have difficulty with? As you write, use as least two plural letters, two plural numbers, and two contractions. Be sure to punctuate them properly.

Mixed Practice

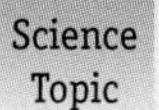

Write correctly the words that need an apostrophe.

Has a moth ever turned one of your favorite sweaters into a tasty meal for itself? If so, you might be able to prevent future feasts by knowing the difference between a moth and a butterfly. Listen carefully. Recognizing the difference wont be easy. First, look at the insects feelers. If theyre thin, they belong to a butterfly. A moths feelers are usually broad and feathery. Next, observe the insect in question when its resting. Butterflies wings are folded in an upright position, with the wings undersides facing toward you. A moth sits holding its wings horizontally, with only the upper sides of the wings showing. If this information doesnt help, youd better buy a summers supply of mothballs!

Semicolons

Independent clauses in a compound sentence can be joined by a conjunction and a comma.

Josh's favorite animal is the tiger, **but** mine is the bear.

The clauses in a compound sentence can also be joined by a semicolon.

Josh's favorite animal is the tiger**;** mine is the bear.

Use a semicolon between the clauses of a compound sentence that are not joined by a conjunction.

Use a semicolon only if the clauses are closely related.

INCORRECT	Eagles usually nest in pairs**;** wolves hunt for prey.
CORRECT	Eagles usually nest in pairs**;** wolves travel in packs.

You can find out more about independent clauses on pages L221–L222.

Semicolons with Conjunctive Adverbs and Transitional Words and Phrases

The following list contains conjunctive adverbs and transitional words and phrases that, with a semicolon, can be used to combine the clauses of a compound sentence.

COMMON CONJUNCTIVE ADVERBS		
accordingly	besides	finally
also	consequently	furthermore

hence	nevertheless	still
however	otherwise	therefore
instead	similarly	thus

COMMON TRANSITIONAL WORDS		
as a result	in addition	in other words
for example	in fact	on the other hand

Use a semicolon between clauses in a compound sentence that are joined by certain conjunctive adverbs or transitional words.

Notice in the following examples that the conjunctive adverb *nevertheless* and the transitional words *as a result* are preceded by a semicolon and followed by a comma.

> Giraffes are not hunters**; nevertheless,** they manage to get plenty of food.
>
> Giraffes can close their nostrils**; thus,** they can keep out sand and dust.
>
> Their necks are very long**; as a result,** they can reach the leaves of very tall trees.

Some of the conjunctive adverbs and transitional words listed in the preceding boxes can also be used as parenthetical expressions within a single clause.

Joining Clauses	The hippopotamus is related to the hog**; however,** it looks very different.
Within a Clause	The hippopotamus**, however,** has a huge mouth.

You can learn more about parenthetical expressions on pages L523–L524.

PRACTICE YOUR SKILLS

Check Your Understanding
Using Semicolons with Compound Sentences

General Interest **Write *a* or *b* to indicate the letter of the correctly punctuated sentence in each of the following pairs.**

1. a. An ailurophile loves cats, an ailurophobe dislikes cats.
b. An ailurophile loves cats; an ailurophobe dislikes cats.

2. a. Elephants are found in both Africa and Asia, however, the two species differ in some ways.
b. Elephants are found in both Africa and Asia; however, the two species differ in some ways.

3. a. African bull elephants, for example, may weigh six to eight tons.
b. African bull elephants; for example, may weigh six to eight tons.

4. a. A male kangaroo is called a boomer, a female kangaroo is called a flyer.
b. A male kangaroo is called a boomer; a female kangaroo is called a flyer.

5. a. The emu is an unusual species of bird; for example, it is the male that cares for the young.
b. The emu is an unusual species of bird, for example, it is the male that cares for the young.

6. a. Parrots are a large family of birds; and different species of parrots include the parakeet and the cockatiel.
b. Parrots are a large family of birds, and different species of parrots include the parakeet and the cockatiel.

7. a. A polecat is not a cat at all; the term actually designates a skunk.
b. A polecat is not a cat at all, the term actually designates a skunk.

8. a. The ostrich is unable to fly, therefore, it runs at great speeds to escape predators.
b. The ostrich is unable to fly; therefore, it runs at great speeds to escape predators.

9. **a.** A crocodile cannot move its tongue; it is rooted to the base of its mouth.
   b. A crocodile cannot move its tongue, it is rooted to the base of its mouth.

10. **a.** The giant panda of western China resembles a bear; however, it is more closely related to the raccoon.
    b. The giant panda of western China resembles a bear, however, it is more closely related to the raccoon.

Check Your Understanding

Using Semicolons and Commas with Compound Sentences

Science Topic **Write *C* if a sentence is punctuated correctly. Write *I* if a sentence is punctuated incorrectly.**

11. Many plants are good for humans and animals, and some have no effect at all.
12. Plants are necessary to life on earth, however, many of these plants are harmful to us.
13. Some plants will simply make a person sick, others can kill humans and animals.
14. The precatory pea has a beautiful red berry, but just a single seed of this plant can kill an adult human.
15. A plant known as fiddleneck is fatal to horses, it can also kill cows and pigs.
16. In small doses St. John's wort is safe for humans, however, it can kill rabbits and cause sheep to lose their wool.
17. Wisteria is a beautiful flowering plant, still it can cause abdominal pain and nausea if ingested by humans.
18. You should always know therefore about a plant before you eat it.

Connect to the Writing Process: Editing

Correcting Punctuation Errors

19.–24. Rewrite the incorrect sentences from the previous exercise, adding commas or semicolons where needed.

Semicolons to Avoid Confusion

Sometimes a semicolon is used to take the place of a comma between the clauses of a compound sentence.

Use a semicolon, instead of a comma, between the clauses of a compound sentence connected with a coordinating conjunction if there are commas within a clause.

> To get to Maine from New York, we travel through Connecticut, Massachusetts, and New Hampshire**;** but the trip takes us only four hours.

A semicolon takes the place of a comma in another situation as well.

Use a semicolon instead of a comma between the items in a series if the items themselves contain commas.

> I have relatives in Hartford, Connecticut**;** in Boston, Massachusetts**;** and in Portsmouth, New Hampshire.

You can find out more about using commas on pages L505–L533.

PRACTICE YOUR SKILLS

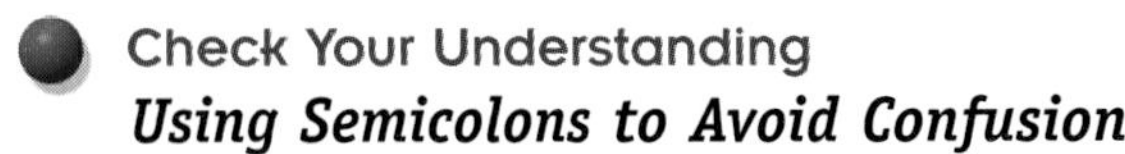

Check Your Understanding

Using Semicolons to Avoid Confusion

Geography Topic **Write *C* if a sentence is punctuated correctly. Write *I* if a sentence is punctuated incorrectly.**

1. Popular tourist attractions around the world include Parliament in London, England, the Eiffel Tower in Paris, France, and the Coliseum in Rome, Italy.

2. The white marble exterior of the Taj Mahal in Agra, India, is inlaid with semiprecious stones, floral designs, and arabesques.

3. Three sites in the United States that many Europeans like to visit are the Grand Canyon in Arizona, Las Vegas, Nevada, and San Francisco, California.
4. Most travelers make the choice of flying, driving, or taking a train, but some people still choose to travel by ship.
5. Other favorite world sites are the Great Wall of China and Red Square in Moscow, Russia.
6. Copenhagen is a major port, cultural center, and the capital of Denmark, and so it is a popular place to visit.
7. During World War II, Copenhagen was occupied by the German army, and this occupation lasted for almost five years.
8. Many tours of Scandinavia include stops in Copenhagen, Rotterdam, and Stockholm.
9. A popular tourist destination in New York, New York, is the United Nations headquarters.
10. Former Secretaries General of the United Nations include Dag Hammarskjold of Sweden, Kurt Waldheim of Austria; and Boutros Boutros-Ghali of Egypt.

Connect to the Writing Process: Editing
Correcting Errors in Punctuation

11.–16. Rewrite the incorrect sentences from the preceding exercise, using the correct punctuation.

Communicate Your Ideas

APPLY TO WRITING

Persuasion: *Semicolons*

Your family has won a two-week vacation. All of you must decide where you will go. Your mom has asked you to choose three places, anywhere in the world, that you would like to visit.

Write a paragraph about each of the destinations you have chosen, emphasizing why your family should visit there. Order your paragraphs so that you write about your least favorite choice first and your most favorite choice last. Use semicolons at least three times in your writing.

QuickCheck Mixed Practice

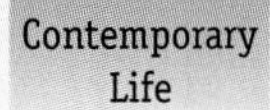

Contemporary Life

Write the following sentences, adding commas and semicolons where needed.

1. I love spending summers at my Aunt Betty's farm she is so much fun.
2. For breakfast she cooks bacon eggs and sausage squeezes fresh orange juice and serves strawberries fresh from the garden.
3. Aunt Betty grew up on a ranch therefore she loves having lots of animals around.
4. She keeps three horses in her stable moreover I'm allowed to ride them whenever I want.
5. She taught me how to tie a lasso mend a saddle and brush a horse and so she expects me to help out when I visit.
6. It is hard work nevertheless I enjoy doing it.
7. I could spend all day brushing the horses for example.
8. My sister and I feed the hogs they even seem to recognize us.
9. Aunt Betty says pigs are smarter than dogs furthermore they are easier to train.
10. She has in fact trained one pig to fetch a ball!

Colons

A colon (**:**) is used most often to introduce a list of items. Commas should separate the items in the list.

Use a colon before most lists of items, especially when the list comes after the expression *the following.*

All students will need the following**:** a pen, a sheet of paper, and a dictionary.

There are five stages in the writing process**:** prewriting, drafting, revising, editing, and publishing.

Three common prewriting strategies are these**:** lists, outlines, and graphic organizers.

Never use a colon directly after a verb or a preposition.

INCORRECT	My three favorite authors are**:** Charles Dickens, Jane Austen, and Thomas Hardy.
CORRECT	My three favorite authors are Charles Dickens, Jane Austen, and Thomas Hardy.
CORRECT	These are my three favorite authors**:** Charles Dickens, Jane Austen, and Thomas Hardy.

Colons are also used in a few other situations.

Use a colon to introduce a long, formal quotation.

Catherine Drinker Bowen once had this to say about writing: "Writing, I think, is not apart from living. Writing is a kind of double living. The writer experiences everything twice. Once in reality and once in that mirror which waits always before or behind."

You can learn more about writing long quotations on page L562.

Use a colon in certain special situations.

COLON USAGE	
Hours and Minutes	5:30 a.m.
Biblical Chapters and Verses	John 3:16
Salutations in Business Letters	Dear Sir or Madam:

Practice Your Skills

Check Your Understanding

Using Colons

Literature Topic

Write *I* for incorrect if the sentence contains an error in the use of a colon. Write *C* if the sentence is correct.

1. My three favorite books by Dickens are: *A Christmas Carol, Great Expectations,* and *A Tale of Two Cities.*

2. In *A Christmas Carol,* the spirit of Jacob Marly warns Scrooge that a ghost will visit him at 1;00 A.M.

3. Through the ghosts' visits, Scrooge learns the kind of love Paul wrote about in I Corinthians 13:13.

4. In *Oliver Twist* the two most evil characters are: Fagin and Bill Sikes.

5. Thomas Hardy wrote many controversial novels, including his masterpieces *Jude the Obscure* and *Tess of the d'Urbervilles.*

6. He also wrote *The Dynasts:* an epic historical drama in verse.

7. Three of Hardy's most memorable characters are the following Bathsheba Everdene, Gabriel Oak, and Michael Henchard.

8. My favorite books of this period are: *Northanger Abbey, The Mayor of Castorbridge,* and *Nicholas Nickleby.*

9. The four novels of Jane Austen published before her death did not have her name on the title page.

10. These novels included: *Sense and Sensibility, Pride and Prejudice, Mansfield Park,* and *Emma.*

Connect to the Writing Process: Editing

Using Colons Correctly

11.–17. Rewrite the incorrect sentences from the preceding exercise, adding or deleting colons or other punctuation where needed.

Communicate Your Ideas

APPLY TO WRITING

Informative Article: ***Colons***

You have been asked to write an article about the local animal shelter for your town's newspaper. What kind of animals does the shelter house? How many animals does it get in a day? What kinds of donations does it need? As you write your article, use three colons in your work. Be sure that you can explain the reason for each one.

Mixed Practice

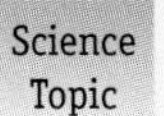

Write the following paragraph, adding apostrophes, semicolons, and colons where needed.

Whos the worlds champion jumper? If youre thinking of a person, youre wrong. The kangaroo lays claim to this title. This curious-looking Australian mammal cannot walk however, it certainly can jump. It can easily hop over a parked car it can also travel over thirty-nine miles per hour.

The kangaroo has some quite unusual physical characteristics a small head, large pointed ears, very short front limbs, and hindquarters the size of a mules. Its feet sometimes measure ten inches from the heel to the longest toe. The kangaroos thick tail is so strong that it can use the tail as a stool. The kangaroo is strictly a vegetarian it will not eat another animal.

There are five groups of large kangaroos the eastern grey kangaroo, the western grey kangaroo, the red kangaroo, the wallaroo, and the antilopine wallaroo. You would have to travel far to see one of these kangaroos in its native home in fact, you would have to travel to Australia.

Hyphens

The principal use of a hyphen (-) is to divide a word at the end of a line. Whenever possible, avoid dividing words in your writing. Sometimes, however, it is necessary to divide words in order to keep the right-hand margin of a composition or story fairly even.

Use a hyphen to divide a word at the end of a line.

GUIDELINES FOR DIVIDING WORDS

Using the following six guidelines will help you divide words correctly.

1. **Divide words only between syllables.**

   gym-nastics or gymnas-tics

2. **Never divide a one-syllable word.**

   myth rhyme strength

3. **Never separate a one-letter syllable from the rest of the word.**

   Do Not Break e-vent, sleep-y, o-boe, i-tem.

4. **A two-letter word ending should not be carried over to the next line.**

   Do Not Break cred-it, hang-er, part-ly.

5. **Divide hyphenated words only after the hyphens.**

   mother-in-law maid-of-honor attorney-at-law

6. **Do not divide a proper noun or a proper adjective.**

   Beckerman Memphis Atlantic Indian

If you are unsure how to divide a word, you can always check a dictionary.

Practice Your Skills

Check Your Understanding
Using Hyphens to Divide Words

Write each word, adding a hyphen or hyphens to show where the word can be correctly divided. If a word should not be divided, write *no.*

1. event
2. hamster
3. growth
4. invoice
5. son-in-law
6. amazement
7. action
8. jury
9. syllable
10. Cairo
11. gathering
12. Timothy
13. forgery
14. flip-flop
15. avoid

Connect to the Writing Process: Drafting
Writing Sentences

Write sentences using the words below. Place a hyphen where the word could break if it needed to be divided.

16. science
17. mathematics
18. history
19. economics
20. athletic

Other Uses of Hyphens

In addition to dividing words, hyphens have other important uses.

Hyphens with Numbers Hyphens are needed with certain numbers.

Use a hyphen when writing out the numbers *twenty-one* through *ninety-nine.*

There are thirty-one students in this class.
Our teacher asked us to find twenty-five soil samples for the experiment.

Hyphens with Compound Nouns Some compound nouns need one or more hyphens.

Use one or more hyphens to separate the parts of some compound nouns.

Our teacher is my great-uncle.
His son-in-law is my favorite relative.

Hyphens with Certain Adjectives Hyphens are needed with fractions used as adjectives and with some compound adjectives.

Use a hyphen when writing out a fraction used as an adjective. Also use one or more hyphens between words that make up a compound adjective in front of a noun.

COMPOUND ADJECTIVE	I found some **dark-brown** soil in our backyard.
	It was **foul-smelling** dirt.

A hyphen is used only when a fraction is used as an adjective, not when it is used as a noun.

FRACTION USED AS AN ADJECTIVE	Our teacher said our soil samples should measure at least **one-quarter** cup.
FRACTION USED AS A NOUN	We put **one half** of the soil sample in the beaker.

A hyphen is used only when a compound adjective comes before a noun, not when it follows a linking verb and comes after the noun it describes.

ADJECTIVE BEFORE A NOUN	Our science teacher insists on **well-written** lab reports.
ADJECTIVE AFTER A NOUN	I always try to make sure that my lab reports are **well written**.

Hyphens with Prefixes

Use a hyphen after certain prefixes and before the suffix *-elect.*

HYPHENS USED WITH PREFIXES AND SUFFIXES		
Use hyphens in the following situations:		
1. between a prefix and a proper noun or proper adjective.		
all-American	mid-Atlantic	pre-Columbian
2. after the prefix *self-*		
self-righteous	self-satisfied	
3. after the prefix *ex-* when it means "former" or "formerly"		
ex-mayor	ex-governor	ex-senator
4. after a person's title when it is followed by the suffix *-elect*		
president-elect	mayor-elect	

PRACTICE YOUR SKILLS

Check Your Understanding
Using Hyphens

Write *a* or *b* to indicate the letter of the correctly written words in each of the following pairs.

1. **a.** seventy seven
b. seventy-seven

2. **a.** self-assured
b. self assured

3. **a.** governor elect
b. governor-elect

4. **a.** four-teen
b. fourteen

5. **a.** ex-husband
   b. exhusband

6. **a.** mid-Pacific
   b. mid Pacific

7. **a.** one-quarter teaspoon
   b. one quarter teaspoon

8. **a.** mother in law
   b. mother-in-law

9. **a.** jack in the box
   b. jack-in-the-box

10. **a.** one quarter of the pie
    b. one-quarter of the pie

Connect to the Writing Process: Editing

Using Hyphens

Correctly write each word that should be hyphenated. If none of the words in a sentence needs a hyphen, write *C* for correct.

11. I will enjoy having a new sister in law when my brother finally marries.
12. My brother is going to marry my friend's step sister in June.
13. She is twentyseven years old.
14. Her mother, May Meriwether, is the mayor elect of our city.
15. She beat the ex mayor by the narrow margin of only ninety two votes.
16. My brother and his fiancée have invited seventyfive people to the wedding.
17. One half of the guests are our relatives.
18. I will serve as the bride's maid of honor.
19. The bride, who is very self reliant, will bake her own wedding cake.
20. I believe that the new mayor will like having my brother as her son in law.

Communicate Your Ideas

APPLY TO WRITING

The Writer's Craft: ***Analyzing the Use of Hyphens***

Writers of poetry and prose often use hyphenated adjectives before nouns. Read the following excerpt from Li-Young Lee's poem "Furious Versions" and answer the questions that follow.

> It was a tropical night.
>
> It was a half a year of sweat and fatal memory.
>
> It was one year of fire
>
> out of the world's diary of fires,
>
> flesh-laced, mid-century fire,
>
> teeth and hair infested,
>
> napalm-dressed and skull-hung fire,
>
> and imminent fire, an elected
>
> fire come to rob me
>
> of my own death, my damp bed
>
> in the noisy earth,
>
> my rocking toward a hymn-like night.
>
> –*Li-Young Lee,* "Furious Versions"

- List all the hyphenated words in the excerpt.
- Why are these words hyphenated?
- How does Lee's use of these hyphenated words affect the rhythm of the poem?
- Would the poem have the same effect without the hyphenated words? Explain your answer.

Dashes and Parentheses

A dash (—) and parentheses ( ) are used like commas in some situations because they separate certain words or groups of words from the rest of the sentence. There are, of course, some distinctions among the uses of these three marks of punctuation.

Dashes

Dashes indicate a greater pause between words than commas do. They can be used in the following situations.

Use dashes to set off an abrupt change in thought.

Mr. Becker—at least I think that's his name—is the drivers' education teacher.

"Where's the —?" Dana began and then hesitated when she saw the car.

The Drivers' Ed car—it's old and dented—is parked in the next lot.

Use dashes to set off an appositive that is introduced by words such as *that is, for example,* or *for instance.*

Certain traffic laws—for instance, making a right turn on a red light—vary from state to state.

Use dashes to set off a parenthetical expression or an appositive that includes commas.

Driving a car—like taking a test, performing in a play, or singing a song—requires concentration.

If you do not know how to make a dash on the computer, you can use two hyphens together. Do not leave a space before or after a dash.

You can find out more about appositives on pages L183–L184.

You can find out more about parenthetical expressions on pages L523–L524.

Parentheses

Always remember that parentheses come in pairs.

Use parentheses to enclose information that is not related closely to the meaning of the sentence.

To decide whether or not you should use parentheses, read the sentence without the parenthetical material. If the meaning and structure of the sentence are not changed, then add parentheses. Just keep in mind that parenthetical additions to sentences slow readers down and interrupt their train of thought. As a result, you should always limit the amount of parenthetical material that you add to any one piece of writing.

> During the late teen years (16–19), many drivers pay higher rates for car insurance.

When the closing parenthesis comes at the end of a sentence, the end mark usually goes outside the parenthesis. However, occasionally the end mark goes inside the parenthesis if the end mark actually belongs with the parenthetical material.

END MARK WITHIN PARENTHESES	Take your written driver's exam in pencil. (Be sure to use a number 2 pencil.)
END MARK OUTSIDE PARENTHESES	To earn your driver's license, you must pass both tests (with a score of 70 or better).

PRACTICE YOUR SKILLS

Check Your Understanding
Using Dashes and Parentheses

General Interest

Write *I* for incorrect if the commas in a sentence should be dashes or parentheses. If a sentence is correct as is, write *C*.

1. Three rules of the road, courtesy to others, respect of pedestrians' right of way, and careful driving should always be followed.

2. Motor vehicles, such as cars and trucks, can be difficult to control on icy streets.

3. Certain privileges, like driving at night, should not be granted to novice drivers.

4. Use your blinker, located on the steering column by your right hand, to signal a turn.

5. Certain states, like Texas, will take away a teenager's license if he or she commits a crime.

6. During the first days of automobiles, the early twentieth century, drivers weren't required to be licensed.

7. In cities like New York and Boston, many people use public transportation rather than drive a car.

8. Certain innovations, like automatic transmission and power steering, have made cars easier to drive.

9. Driving while intoxicated, a very serious offense, is severely punished in most states.

10. Georgia has three stages of graduated licensing, supervised learner, intermediate, and full-privilege, for beginning drivers.

Connect to the Writing Process: Editing
Using Dashes and Parentheses

11.–16. Rewrite the incorrect sentences from the preceding exercises, adding dashes or parentheses where needed.

Communicate Your Ideas

APPLY TO WRITING

The Writer's Craft: *Analyzing the Use of Dashes*

Emily Dickinson is one poet who made liberal use of dashes in her poetry. Read the following poem by Emily Dickinson and then follow the directions.

He ate and drank the precious Words—

His spirit grew robust—

He knew no more that he was poor,

Nor that his frame was Dust—

He danced along the dingy Days

And this Bequest of Wings

Was but a Book—What Liberty

A loosened spirit brings—

–Emily Dickinson

- Read the poem aloud, ignoring all the punctuation marks.
- Next, read the poem aloud, making long pauses only where the dashes are. You should pause briefly at the comma.
- How did your readings of the poem differ?
- Would any other punctuation marks have served the purpose of these dashes? If so, which ones? Explain your answer.
- Why do you think Dickinson chose to use dashes?

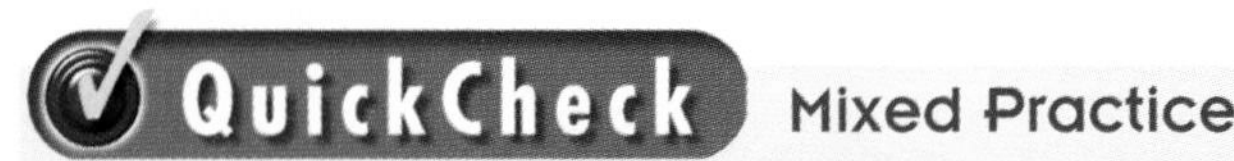

General Interest **Rewrite the following paragraph, adding hyphens, dashes, and parentheses where needed.**

Humphrey Bogart 1899–1957 was voted the greatest screen legend male screen legend, that is, by the American Film Institute AFI in 1999. Bogart who is my favorite movie star was a stage actor at the beginning of his career. His movie credits include *The Maltese Falcon* 1941 and *Casablanca* 1942. In 1951, he won an Oscar for his role in *The African Queen.* In this award winning role, he played opposite Katherine Hepburn who, by the way, was the AFI pick for the greatest female screen legend.

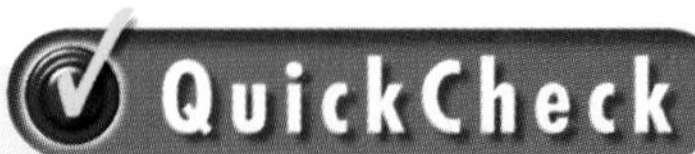

History Topic **Rewrite the following paragraphs, adding apostrophes, semicolons, colons, and hyphens where needed.**

The Mayas occupied much North American land in pre Spanish times. There was quite a variety of land mountains, rain forests, plains, and coastal areas. Today, this area covers many of the Mexican states the current countries of Guatemala, Belize, El Salvador, and parts of Honduras also were homes to the Mayas.

The Mayas religion was perhaps the most important part of their lives. Some of their gods included *Chaac,* god of rain and lightning *Ik,* god of the wind and *Ah Puch,* god of death.

CheckPoint

Using Punctuation Correctly

Write each sentence, adding punctuation where needed. If a sentence is punctuated correctly write *C*.

1. Rattlesnakes don't lay eggs they bear live young.
2. The worlds largest gem is a 596 pound topaz.
3. The soybean is a versatile vegetable for example, forty different products can be made from it.
4. Greg wont be satisfied until hes totally self sufficient.
5. The following famous people had red hair George Washington, Thomas Jefferson, and Mark Twain.
6. Lenny Burns received a two thirds majority vote in this years mayoral election.
7. When Snuffys leash broke, he jumped the neighbors fence and dove into their pool.
8. The official name of India is not *India* it is *Bharat.*
9. My brother in law is president elect of the club.
10. Salt is found in the earth in three basic forms salt water, brine deposits, and rock salt crystal.
11. The rarely seen Indian sea snake is the most poisonous snake in the world.
12. The poet H.D.s real name is Hilda Doolittle.
13. The people on the panel included Terry Hayden, an editorial writer Thelma Casey, a fashion consultant and Judith Howe, a high school teacher.
14. Today, there are more than seven thousand varieties of apples nevertheless only twenty varieties are widely grown.
15. Twenty two people how could we have invited so many! are supposed to arrive for dinner at 630 P.M.

Editing for Correct Punctuation

Write the paragraph, adding apostrophes, semicolons, colons, and hyphens where needed.

Everyone has heard of the Nobel Prizes but most people havent heard about Alfred Nobel, the man who established the prizes. He was born in Sweden in 1833. Thirty three years later, he invented dynamite. This invention made him very rich it also made him feel very guilty later on. As a result, his will set up a trust fund that annually awards prizes to people throughout the world who excel in the following categories literature, physics, chemistry, medicine, and peace. Now, every December 10, the anniversary of Nobels death, each winner receives up to $959,070.

Writing Sentences

Write ten sentences that follow the directions below.

Write a sentence that . . .

1. includes the possessive form of the nouns *uncle* and *dollars.*
2. includes the possessive form of the pronouns *it* and *no one.*
3. includes the joint ownership of something.
4. includes the plural of *no.*
5. includes the word *nevertheless* between two independent clauses in a compound sentence.
6. includes a series of dates.
7. includes a specific time.
8. includes *three fourths* as an adjective.
9. includes a dash.
10. includes parentheses.

Language and *Self-Expression*

Honoré Daumier was a nineteenth-century French artist who focused on social and political problems in his art. Much of his work depicted poor people in anonymous surroundings. In *The Third-Class Carriage,* Daumier shows a group of travelers who are unable to afford first-class tickets on a train.

In 1861, the time the painting was done, France was gripped by high unemployment and great poverty. The clothing, body language, and facial expressions of the travelers reveal much about them. Imagine how the travelers might have lived, and write a brief biography of one of the figures in the third-class carriage. Explain in detail his or her experiences and expectations. Include various kinds of punctuation in the sentences you write.

Prewriting Make a time line for the figure you have chosen to write about. Note the subject's date of birth and other events important in his or her life. Include details about births and deaths of family members.

Drafting Use your time line to help you write a first draft of your biography. Include any events you imagine had an impact on your subject's life.

Revising Reread your biography. Be sure you have included information about your subject's home, work, and family. Also include details that reveal how your subject views his or her life.

Editing Check your biography for errors in grammar, spelling, and punctuation. Be sure you have used apostrophes, semicolons, colons, hyphens, dashes, and parentheses correctly.

Publishing Read your biography aloud to the class. Ask classmates to guess which figure in the painting you have chosen as a subject.

Another Look

Using Apostrophes

To show joint ownership, make only the last word possessive in form. *(page L581)*

To show separate ownership, make each word possessive in form. *(page L581)*

Use an apostrophe with the possessive form of a noun that expresses time or amount. *(pages L581–L582)*

Use an apostrophe in a contraction to show where one or more letters in a word or numbers in a date have been omitted. *(pages L585–L588)*

Using Semicolons and Colons

Use a semicolon between the clauses of a compound sentence that are not joined by a conjunction. *(page L590)*

Use a semicolon, instead of a comma, between the clauses of a compound sentence if there are commas within a clause. *(page L594)*

Use a semicolon, instead of a comma, between the items in a series if the items themselves contain commas. *(page L594)*

Use a colon before most lists of items, especially when the list comes after the expression *the following.* *(page L597)*

Use a colon to introduce a long, formal quotation. *(page L597)*

Use a colon in certain special situations:
- Between hours and minutes
- Between Biblical chapters and verses
- After salutations in business letters *(page L598)*

Using Hyphens

Use a hyphen to divide a word at the end of a line. *(page L601)*

Use a hyphen when writing out the numbers *twenty-one* through *ninety-nine.* *(page L602)*

Use one or more hyphens to separate the parts of some compound nouns or to separate words of a compound adjective in front of a noun. *(page L603)*

Use a hyphen when writing out a fraction that is used as an adjective. *(page L603)*

Use a hyphen after certain prefixes and before the suffix *-elect.* *(page L604)*

Using Dashes and Parentheses

Use dashes to set off an abrupt change in thought. *(page L607)*

Use dashes to set off a parenthetical expression or an appositive that includes commas. *(page L607)*

Use parentheses to enclose information. *(page L608)*

Directions

Write the letter of the answer that correctly punctuates the underlined part in each sentence. If the underlined part contains no error, write *D*.

EXAMPLE **1.** According to a study by American Sports Data, Inc., the treadmill is the most popular kind of exercise equipment.

1 A American Sports Data—Inc.
B American Sports Data Inc.
C American Sports' Data, Inc.
D No error

ANSWER **1 C**

1. There has been a huge increase in the number of treadmill users in fact, while only 4.4 million used treadmills in 1987, 37.1 million used them in 1998.

2. The second most popular machine is the stair climber.

3. There are several reasons for the treadmill's popularity it keeps you fit, it is easy to use, and it is safe and reliable.

4. The treadmill is a home exercisers dream.

5. When it rains outside, you can still exercise there is no excuse for slacking off.

6. For some people those who love exercise that is reason enough to own a treadmill.

7. Some people dont like the treadmill because they find it boring.

8. For them, its difficult to stay motivated.

9. Even the self motivated can get bored doing the same exercise day after day.

10. One answer (though it's not for everyone) is to place the treadmill in front of a television.

1 **A** users—in fact
B users; in fact,
C users: in fact
D No error

2 **A** the stair, climber
B (the stair climber)
C the stair-climber
D No error

3 **A** popularity: it keeps
B popularity; it keeps
C popularity—it keeps
D No error

4 **A** home-exerciser's dream
B home-exercisers' dream
C home exercisers' dream
D No error

5 **A** still exercise: there
B still exercise—there
C still exercise; there
D No error

6 **A** (those who love exercise)
B those who love exercise;
C those who love exercise:
D No error

7 **A** dont' like the treadmill
B don't like the treadmill
C do'nt like the treadmill
D No error

8 **A** it's difficult
B its' difficult
C its: difficult
D No error

9 **A** (self motivated)
B self; motivated
C self-motivated
D No error

10 **A** answer, though, it's not
B answer: though it's not
C answer; though it's not
D No error

A Writer's Guide to Citing Sources

When you use someone else's words or ideas in your own report—even if you only paraphrase—you must give that person proper credit. One way to do this is to follow the guidelines of the Modern Language Association (MLA), which credits the source in parentheses.

Parenthetical citations give readers just enough information to identify the source of the material you have borrowed. The complete source information will appear on the works-cited page at the end of your report. The following examples will help you use parenthetical citations.

Book by One Author	Give author's last name and page number(s): (McKluskie 68–72).
Book by More Than One Author	Give both authors' names and page number(s): (Geller and Eaton 79).
Article with Author Named	Give author's last name and page number(s): (Natale 4).
Article with Author Unnamed	Give a shortened form of the title (unless full title is already short) and page number(s): ("Gimme That Sinking Feeling" 11).
Article in a Reference Work; Author Unnamed	Give title (full or shortened) and page number(s); if the article is a single page from an encyclopedia, no page number is needed: ("Titanic").

Parenthetical citations should be close to the words or ideas being credited. Therefore, place them at the end of a phrase, clause, or sentence. If a parenthetical citation falls at the end of a sentence, place it before the period. With a quotation, place it after the closing quotation mark and before the period.

You may prefer to use **footnotes** or **endnotes** to identify sources. For either type of note, place a small number halfway above the line immediately after the borrowed material. This number matches that of the complete citation at the bottom of the page—the footnote—or at the end of the report—the endnote.

[1]Tom McKluskie, Anatomy of the Titanic. (San Diego: Thunder Bay, 1998) 120.

A **works-cited page** is the alphabetical list, by author, of sources in a research paper. If an author is unknown, the source is alphabetized by title. In the following examples, note the order of the sources, the indentation, and the punctuation.

General Reference Works	Marcus, Geoffrey J. "Titanic." Encyclopedia Americana. 1999 ed.
Books by One Author	McKluskie, Tom. Anatomy of the Titanic. San Diego: Thunder Bay Press, 1998.
Books by Two or More Authors	Geller, Judith B. and John P. Eaton. Titanic: Women and Children First. New York: W. W. Norton & Co., 1998.
Articles in Magazines; Author Named	Koretz, Gene. "How the Titanic Hit Wall Street." Business Week 7 Dec. 1998:22.
Articles in Magazines; Author Unnamed	"Gimme That Sinking Feeling." People Weekly 18 Jan. 1999: 11.
Articles in Newspapers	Natale, Richard. "Box-Office Showing Good, If Not 'Titanic.'" Los Angeles Times 7 May 1999, sec. C: 4.
Reviews	Biel, Steven. Rev. of Titanic, dir. James Cameron. Journal of American History Dec. 1998: 1177-1179.
Article from a CD-ROM	"Titanic Disaster." Encarta 1998. CD-ROM. Redmond: Microsoft, 1998.
Article from an Online Database with a Print Version	Maslin, Janet. Rev. of Titanic, dir. James Cameron. The New York Times on the Web. 19 Dec. 1997. 7 Sept. 1999 <http://www.nytimes.com/library/film/archive main-t.html>.
Article from an Online Database Without a Print Version	Gilbert, John. MSN Online Tonight with James Cameron. 21 Jan. 1999. 7 Sept. 1999 <http://onlinetonight.msn.co.uk/titanic/transcript.htm>.

Spelling Correctly

Pretest

Directions

Read the passage. Write the letter of the choice that correctly spells each underlined word. If the word contains no error, write *D*.

EXAMPLE The preperation (1) for their cross-country trip was long and painstaking.

1 **A** preperration
B preparation
C prepareation
D No error

ANSWER **1 B**

In history class we read some correspondance (1) between pioneers and their familys (2) back home. As they proceded (3) on their journies (4), these pioneers often stopped at trading posts. There they were ocasionally (5) able to post letters to relatives. These tales of inconceivable (6) hardship and couragous (7) actions teach us today. Reading the actual words of our ancestors helps us relate to the lonelyness (8), terrors, and everyday joys of pioneer life. We delight in their innocent beleif (9) in a better life, and we recall that heros (10) start out as ordinary people.

1 **A** corespondance
B correspondence
C correspondants
D No error

2 **A** familyes
B familes
C families
D No error

3 **A** proceeded
B proseded
C preceeded
D No error

4 **A** journys
B journeys
C journeyses
D No error

5 **A** ocasionaly
B occasionally
C occassionally
D No error

6 **A** inconcievable
B inconceiveable
C inconcevable
D No error

7 **A** courageous
B couragious
C couraggous
D No error

8 **A** lonlyness
B lonelynes
C loneliness
D No error

9 **A** belief
B beleef
C beleiv
D No error

10 **A** heroses
B hero
C heroes
D No error

Strategies for Learning to Spell

Learning to spell involves a variety of senses. You use your senses of hearing, sight, and touch to spell a word correctly. Here is a five-step strategy that many people have used successfully as they learned to spell unfamiliar words.

1 Auditory

Say the word aloud. Answer these questions.

- Where have I heard or read this word before?
- What was the context in which I heard or read the word?

2 Visual

Look at the word. Answer these questions.

- Does this word divide into parts? Is it a compound word? Does it have a prefix or a suffix?
- Does this word look like any other word I know? Could it be part of a word family I would recognize?

3 Auditory

Spell the word to yourself. Answer these questions.

- How is each sound spelled?
- Are there any surprises? Does the word follow spelling rules I know, or does it break the rules?

4 Visual/Kinesthetic

Write the word as you look at it. Answer these questions.

- Have I written the word clearly?
- Are my letters formed correctly?

5 Visual/Kinesthetic

Cover up the word. Visualize it. Write it. Answer this question.

- Did I write the word correctly?
- If the answer is no, return to step 1.

Spelling Strategies

Spelling is easier for some people than it is for others, but everyone needs to make an effort to spell correctly. Misspellings are distracting for the reader, and they make writing hard to read. Here are some strategies you can use to improve your spelling.

STRATEGY **Use a dictionary.** If you are not sure how to spell a word, or if a word you have written doesn't "look right," check the word in a dictionary.

STRATEGY **Proofread your writing carefully.** Be on the lookout for misspellings and for words you are not sure you spelled correctly. One way to proofread your writing for misspellings is to start at the end of your paper and read backward. That way misspellings should pop out at you.

PRACTICE YOUR SKILLS

Check Your Understanding
Recognizing Misspelled Words

Write the letter of the misspelled word in each line. Then write the word correctly.

1. (a) abbreviation (b) boulevard (c) extream
2. (a) burea (b) confer (c) forgery
3. (a) fasinating (b) guarantee (c) illustrate
4. (a) irritate (b) luxury (c) mischeif
5. (a) authentic (b) brillance (c) disguise
6. (a) mysterious (b) ocasionally (c) prestige
7. (a) legislasure (b) merchandise (c) notch
8. (a) punctual (b) resign (c) resterant

9. (a) ridicilous (b) sizable (c) thesaurus

10. (a) coupon (b) chrystal (c) dissatisfied

STRATEGY **Be sure you are pronouncing words correctly.** "Swallowing" syllables or adding extra syllables can cause you to misspell a word.

Practice Your Skills

Check Your Understanding
Pronouncing Words

Oral Expression **Practice saying each syllable in the following words to help you spell the words correctly.**

1. mis•chie•vous
2. lit•er•a•ture
3. pros•per•ous
4. tem•per•a•ture
5. light•ning
6. ath•lete
7. li•brar•y
8. es•cape
9. sim•i•lar
10. prob•a•bly
11. fi•er•y
12. qui•et

STRATEGY **Make up mnemonic devices.** A phrase like "My niece is nice" can help you remember to put *i* before *e* in *niece.* A device like "2 *m*'s, 2 *t*'s, 2 *e*'s" can help you remember how to spell *committee.*

STRATEGY **Keep a spelling journal.** Use it to record the words that you have had trouble spelling. Here are some suggestions for organizing your spelling journal.

- Write the word correctly.
- Write the word again, underlining or circling the part of the word that gave you trouble.
- Write a tip to help you remember how to spell the word.

weird *weird* *Weird is weird. It doesn't follow the i before e rule.*

Spelling Generalizations

Knowing common spelling generalizations can help you to spell hundreds of words. Some of these generalizations are based on spelling patterns, such as the choice between *ie* and *ei*. Other generalizations deal with forming plurals, writing numbers as numerals or as words, and adding prefixes and suffixes to words.

Spelling Patterns

Understanding certain common word patterns can help take the guesswork out of spelling many new words.

Words with *ie* and *ei*

When you spell words with *ie* or *ei*, *i* comes before *e* except when the letters follow *c* or when they stand for the long *a* sound.

IE AND *EI*				
EXAMPLES	**ie**	bel**ie**ve	f**ie**ld	
	ei after **c**	c**ei**ling	rec**ei**ve	
	sounds like **a**	n**ei**ghbor	w**ei**gh	
EXCEPTIONS	anc**ie**nt	effic**ie**nt	n**ei**ther	s**ei**ze
	consc**ie**nce	spec**ie**s	h**ei**ght	w**ei**rd
	suffic**ie**nt	**ei**ther	l**ei**sure	for**ei**gn

The generalization about *ie* and *ei* applies only when the letters occur in the same syllable and spell just one vowel sound. It does not apply when *i* and *e* appear in different syllables.

IE AND *EI* IN DIFFERENT SYLLABLES			
b**e** **i**ng	r**e** **i**mburse	sc**i** **e**nce	soc**i** **e**ty

Word Alert

The words *siege* and *seize* are sometimes confused. Be sure you use the word that suits your meaning.

siege—[noun] the surrounding of an area by military forces trying to stage a takeover; a steady try to get something

The rebel forces planned a *siege* of the capital.

seize—[verb] to snatch or grab suddenly; to capture

The security guard *seized* the photographer's camera.

Words ending in *–sede, –ceed,* and *–cede*

Words ending with a syllable that sounds like "seed" are usually spelled with *–cede.* Only one word in English is spelled with *–sede,* and only three words are spelled with *–ceed.*

–SEDE, –CEED, AND *–CEDE*				
EXAMPLES	con**cede**	pre**cede**	re**cede**	se**cede**
EXCEPTIONS	super**sede**	ex**ceed**	pro**ceed**	suc**ceed**

PRACTICE YOUR SKILLS

Check Your Understanding
Using Spelling Patterns

Write each word correctly, adding *ie* or *ei.*

1. th ■ f
2. n ■ ce
3. y ■ ld
4. w ■ gh
5. h ■ ght
6. bel ■ f
7. c ■ ling
8. rec ■ pt
9. gr ■ ve
10. ■ ght
11. p ■ ce
12. r ■ ns
13. n ■ ther
14. dec ■ ve
15. rel ■ ve
16. br ■ f
17. rec ■ ve
18. retr ■ ve
19. n ■ ghbor
20. l ■ sure

Write each word correctly, adding *–sede, –ceed,* or *–cede.*

21. re ■
22. ex ■
23. ac ■
24. se ■
25. suc ■
26. con ■
27. pre ■
28. pro ■
29. super ■
30. inter ■

Connect to the Writing Process: Editing
Using Spelling Patterns

History Topic **Rewrite this paragraph, correcting any spelling errors.**

For the state of Kentucky, the War Between the States was truly a civil war. Kentucky did not sesede from the Union, as did the nieghboring states of Tennessee and Virginia. Officially Kentucky supported niether the Union nor the Confederacy. Kentucky proceded to declare neutrality on May 16, 1851, but Kentuckians did not succeed in staying out of the conflict. The number of Kentuckians who fought for the Confederacy exceded 30,000, and twice that number joined the Union Army. Neighbors, freinds, and families were greivously divided in thier loyalties. President Lincoln concedeed that Kentucky was one of the country's "troubling stepchildren" because its location bordered Union states, but many residents supported the Confederacy.

Plurals

You know that many nouns form their plural form by adding *s* or *es* to the singular form. Some nouns form their plurals in other ways, though. Forming the plural of a noun becomes easier when you remember to use the following generalizations.

Regular Nouns

To form the plural of most nouns, simply add *s.*

MOST NOUNS				
SINGULAR	artist	symbol	maze	sardine
PLURAL	artist**s**	symbol**s**	maze**s**	sardine**s**

If a noun ends with *s, ch, sh, x,* or *z,* add *es* to form the plural.

S, CH, SH, X, AND *Z*				
SINGULAR	loss	chur**ch**	di**sh**	fo**x**
PLURAL	loss**es**	church**es**	dish**es**	fox**es**

Nouns Ending in *y*

Add *s* to form the plural of a noun ending with a vowel and *y.*

VOWELS AND *Y*				
SINGULAR	d**ay**	displ**ay**	journ**ey**	t**oy**
PLURAL	day**s**	display**s**	journey**s**	toy**s**

Change the *y* to *i* and add *es* to a noun ending in a consonant and *y.*

CONSONANTS AND *Y*				
SINGULAR	memo**ry**	trop**hy**	la**dy**	socie**ty**
PLURAL	memor**ies**	troph**ies**	lad**ies**	societ**ies**

Practice Your Skills

Check Your Understanding
Forming Plurals

Write the plural form of each noun.

1. theme
2. valley
3. crash
4. comedy
5. virus
6. reflex
7. theory
8. tomboy
9. waltz
10. image
11. ability
12. stitch
13. holiday
14. apology
15. trapeze
16. galaxy
17. effect
18. trolley
19. issue
20. vacancy

Connect to the Writing Process: Editing
Spelling Plural Nouns

General Interest **Rewrite these sentences, changing singular nouns to plural nouns as needed.**

21. Television set as we know them today were invented in the 1930s.

22. World War II interrupted the development and manufacturing of all consumer product.

23. In 1947, when the war was over, factory started making product for consumer again.

24. The period from 1947 to 1957 is regarded as the "Golden Year" of television.

25. During this time popular radio program became television show, and radio listener became TV watcher.

26. "I Love Lucy," which premiered in 1951, was one of the few early situation comedy that did not start out as a radio program.

27. It began the practice of filming show in front of live audience using three camera.

28. In those day all performance were live.

29. If actor and actress forgot their lines, they had to make up something.

30. When you watch those early show, you can sometimes notice the blunder and glitch.

Nouns Ending with *o*

Add *s* to form the plural of a noun ending with a vowel and *o.*

VOWELS AND *O*				
SINGULAR	rat**io**	stud**io**	rod**eo**	igl**oo**
PLURAL	ratio**s**	studio**s**	rodeo**s**	igloo**s**

Add *s* to form the plural of musical terms ending in *o.*

MUSICAL TERMS WITH *O*				
SINGULAR	alt**o**	du**o**	pian**o**	cell**o**
PLURAL	alto**s**	duo**s**	piano**s**	cello**s**

The plurals of nouns ending in a consonant and *o* do not follow a regular pattern.

CONSONANTS AND *O*				
SINGULAR	ec**ho**	ve**to**	si**lo**	e**go**
PLURAL	echo**es**	veto**es**	silo**s**	ego**s**

When you are not sure how to form the plural of a word that ends in *o,* consult a dictionary. If the dictionary does not give a plural form, the plural is usually formed by adding *s.*

Nouns Ending in *f* or *fe*

To form the plural of some nouns ending in *f* or *fe,* just add *s.*

F AND *FE*				
SINGULAR	belie**f**	gul**f**	che**f**	fi**fe**
PLURAL	belief**s**	gulf**s**	chef**s**	fife**s**

For some nouns ending in *f* or *fe,* change the *f* to *v* and add *es* or *s.*

F AND *FE* TO *V*				
SINGULAR	hal**f**	shel**f**	lea**f**	kni**fe**
PLURAL	hal**ves**	shel**ves**	lea**ves**	kni**ves**

Consult a dictionary to check the plural form of a word that ends with *f* or *fe.*

PRACTICE YOUR SKILLS

Check Your Understanding
Forming Plurals

Write the plural form of each noun. Check a dictionary to be sure you have formed the plural correctly.

1. radio
2. stereo
3. shampoo
4. solo
5. potato
6. taco
7. yo-yo
8. roof
9. tariff
10. elf
11. calf
12. self

Connect to the Writing Process: Editing
Spelling Plural Nouns

Music Topic **Rewrite this paragraph, correcting any spelling errors.**

Most high schools do not have room or funds for music studioes. However, music teachers themselfs continue to teach the fundamentals of reading music to interested students. The notes for music are positioned on a set of lines and spaces called a staff. Two stafves always appear together, one above the other. Each one is marked with a clef. The clefs tell what notes the lines and spaces stand for. The high notes played by piccoloes or sung by sopranos are on the top staff. The low notes played by celloes and sung by basses are on the bottom staff.

Compound Nouns

Most compound nouns are made plural in the same way as other nouns. The letter *s* or *es* is added to the end of the word. But when the main word in a compound noun appears first, that word becomes plural.

COMPOUND NOUNS			
EXAMPLES	snowflake snowflake**s**	lunchbox lunchbox**es**	hallway hallway**s**
EXCEPTIONS	passerby passer**s**by	editor-in-chief editor**s**-in-chief	mother-in-law mother**s**-in-law

Numerals, Letters, Symbols, and Words as Words

To form the plurals of numerals, letters, symbols, and words used as words, add an *s.* To prevent confusion, it is best to use an apostrophe and *s* with lowercase letters, some capital letters, and some words used as words.

EXAMPLES
Those *G*s look like *6*s.
Swing dancing from the 1940s is back.
Use *s to mark footnotes.
Don't give me any *if*s, *and*s, or *but*s.

EXCEPTIONS
There are four *i*'s and four *s*'s in *Mississippi.*
Name five foods that are shaped like *O*'s.
We need an equal number of *he*'s and *she*'s.

Practice Your Skills

Check Your Understanding
Forming Plurals

Write the plural form of each item.

1. attorney-at-law
2. bystander
3. ‘90
4. sergeant-at-arms
5. hummingbird
6. *?*
7. sister-in-law
8. *z*
9. *&*
10. mousetrap
11. toothache
12. runner-up
13. *S*
14. pen pal
15. 1900
16. maid of honor
17. *in* and *out*
18. classroom
19. *X* and *O*
20. *ABC*

Connect to the Writing Process: Editing
Spelling Plural Nouns

Science Topic **Write each sentence, changing the underlined items from singular to plural.**

21. In the 1960, the alligator was classified as an endangered species.
22. Before the end of the '70, however, alligators made a comeback, and they were reclassified as threatened.
23. There are two *l* in the word *alligator.*
24. Write about the animals in your observation log, and put *?* beside spellings you are unsure of.
25. Hummingbird are always seen in flight because their weak feet cannot support them on flat surfaces.
26. Man-o'-war bird can soar motionless for hours, but they are awkward on land and their feathers get waterlogged in the water.
27. People used to use lily of the valley as a heart medicine.
28. The dried roots of the butterfly bush have been used as a medicine to prevent spasms.
29. The fuzzy brown spikes are actually the fruits of cattail.
30. Some kinds of firefly lay eggs that glow just as the adult insects do.

Other Plural Forms

Irregular plurals are not formed by adding *s* or *es*.

IRREGULAR PLURALS					
Singular	tooth	foot	mouse	child	woman
	goose	ox	man	die	
Plural	t**ee**th	f**ee**t	m**ice**	child**ren**	wom**en**
	g**ee**se	ox**en**	m**e**n	d**ice**	

Some nouns have the same form for singular and plural.

SAME SINGULAR AND PLURAL			
Vietnamese	Sioux	salmon	headquarters
Japanese	deer	species	measles
Swiss	moose	scissors	politics

Words from Latin and Greek

Some nouns from Latin and Greek have plurals that are formed as they are in the original language. For a few Latin and Greek words, there are two ways to form the plural.

FOREIGN WORDS				
Examples	alumnus	memorandum	crisis	thesis
	alumn**i**	memorand**a**	cris**es**	thes**es**
Exceptions	hippopotamus			
	hippopotam**uses** or hippopot**ami**			
	formula			
	formula**s** or formul**ae**			

Check a dictionary when forming the plural of words from Latin and Greek. When two forms are given, the first one is preferred.

Practice Your Skills

Check Your Understanding
Forming Plurals

Write the plural form of each noun. Check a dictionary if you are not sure of the preferred form.

1. mouse
2. child
3. tooth
4. foot
5. louse
6. woman
7. synopsis
8. octopus
9. stylus
10. vacuum
11. hypothesis
12. appendix
13. spectrum
14. analysis
15. salmon
16. deer
17. Swiss
18. pliers
19. corps
20. trout

Connect to the Writing Process: Editing
Forming Plurals

General Interest **Decide if the underlined plurals are formed correctly. If any are incorrect, write the correct form.**

Deer and Canadian gooses have become a serious nuisance in many communities, according to the news mediums. Various hypothesises have been put forth, but apparently a major cause of the problem is demographicses. According to the latest analyses, people are living in areas that used to be wilderness. Places that in the 1940s were home to many specieses of wild animals are suburban neighborhoods now. Deers, with no other place to forage, devour gardens and shrubbery and ruin lawns with their sharp, pointed feet. Geese foul lawns and parks and can turn aggressive toward men, womans, and childs who try to shoo them away.

Communicate Your Ideas

APPLY TO WRITING

Opinion Paragraph: *Plurals*

Some people look at land like this and see something that should be kept exactly as it is. Other people look at land like this and see endless possibilities for developing it and turning it into something different. What do you see? Answer that question by writing a paragraph to share with your classmates. Use at least ten plural nouns in your paragraph. Before writing, brainstorm answers to the following questions.

- What are the beautiful characteristics of this land?
- Where is the nearest city or town?
- What would happen to the water and trees if the land were developed?
- How would the people of the area benefit from leaving the land as it is?
- Should the land remain as it is? Explain why or why not.

 Mixed Practice

Write the plural form of each word. Use a dictionary whenever necessary.

1. antenna	**6.** hero	**11.** belief	**16.** lamb
2. synopsis	**7.** hoof	**12.** 100	**17.** appendix
3. scissors	**8.** echo	**13.** opus	**18.** stadium
4. ox	**9.** 1980	**14.** *X*	**19.** lexicon
5. cello	**10.** buffalo	**15.** valley	**20.** *why*

Spelling Numbers

When you are writing something that includes numbers, you may be unsure whether you should write the number in words or use a numeral or numerals. Use the following generalizations to help guide you.

Numerals or Number Words

Spell out numbers that can be written in one or two words. Use numerals for other numbers. Always spell out a number that begins a sentence.

The election was held **ten** days ago.
The final vote was **563** for and **1,067** against.
Six hundred thirty people came out to vote.

When you have a series of numbers, and some are just one or two words while others are more, use numerals for them all.

In the "Favorite Ice Cream Flavor Poll," **347** young people said chocolate was their favorite flavor; **158** liked brownie fudge; **121** liked chocolate chip; and **40** liked vanilla best.

Ordinal Numbers

Always spell out numbers used to tell the order.

He promised to be here **first** thing in the morning.
Andrea wanted to finish **first,** but she came in **third.**

Numbers in Dates

Use a numeral for a date when you include the name of the month. Always use numerals for the year.

EXAMPLES	Dr. Seuss's birthday is March 2. He was born in 1904.
EXCEPTION	Do you know anyone whose birthday is the twenty-ninth of February? (Always spell out ordinal numbers.)

PRACTICE YOUR SKILLS

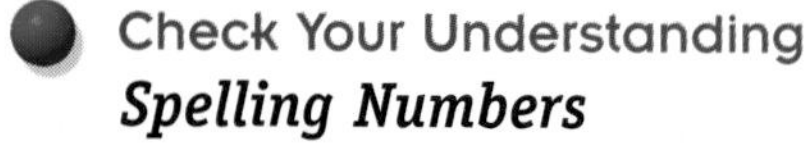

Check Your Understanding
Spelling Numbers

Write the correct form of the number given in parentheses to complete each sentence.

1. (9) This year's marathon was scheduled for October ■.

2. (2) The deadline for entering the race was ■ weeks before, on September 17.

3. (15th) On the ■ of September, organizers were disappointed by the lack of interest.

4. (58) Only ■ people had signed up for the race.

5. (1996) That was very different from the first marathon the town had in ■.

6. (590) ■ people had signed up for that race just days after it had been announced.

7. (3) Now, just ■ days before the deadline, very few people seemed interested.

8. (48) But in ■ hours, everything changed.

9. (768) By the deadline, a total of ■ runners had entered.

10. (2,000) That was amazing, considering that the entire population of the town was only ■.

11. (18) The marathon was open to runners ■ and older.

12. (50) Among the entrants, there were 410 college-age runners, 308 adults, and ■ seniors.

13. (12) Runners ran the length of the town and then ran to the next town, which was ■ miles away, and back again.

14. (1st) No one knew who would finish ■.

15. (26) Very few runners actually ran the entire ■ miles.

Connect to the Writing Process: Editing
Writing Numbers Correctly

History Topic **Rewrite this paragraph, correcting any mistakes in writing numbers.**

The marathon race was first included in the Olympic games in Athens in 1896. Just 1 year later, in 1897, the very first Boston Marathon was run. Originally called the American Marathon Race, the Boston Marathon has been held every year, except 1918, for more than 100 years. The very first winner of the race was John J. McDermott of New York City, who finished the race in two hours, 55 minutes, and ten seconds. For finishing 1st, McDermott received a laurel wreath and a pot of beef stew.

Prefixes and Suffixes

A **prefix** is one or more syllables placed in front of a base word to form a new word. When you add a prefix, the spelling of the base word does not change.

PREFIXES	
in + accurate = **in**accurate	**re** + tell = **re**tell
pre + arrange = **pre**arrange	**over** + do = **over**do
dis + satisfied = **dis**satisfied	**mis** + use = **mis**use
re + evaluate = **re**evaluate	**un** + able = **un**able
ir + regular = **ir**regular	**il** + legal = **il**legal

A **suffix** is one or more syllables placed after a base word to change its part of speech and possibly also its meaning.

Suffixes *–ness* and *–ly*

The suffixes *–ness* and *–ly* are added to most base words without any spelling changes.

–NESS AND *–LY*	
open + **ness** = open**ness**	cruel + **ly** = cruel**ly**
plain + **ness** = plain**ness**	real + **ly** = real**ly**

Words Ending in *e*

Drop the final *e* in the base word when adding a suffix that begins with a vowel.

SUFFIXES WITH VOWELS	
EXAMPLES	drive + **ing** = driv**ing** isolate + **ion** = isolat**ion** sane + **ity** = san**ity**
EXCEPTIONS	courage + **ous** = courage**ous** pronounce + **able** = pronounce**able**

Keep the final *e* when adding a suffix that begins with a consonant.

SUFFIXES WITH CONSONANTS	
EXAMPLES	care + **ful** = care**ful**
	price + **less** = price**less**
	like + **ness** = like**ness**
	state + **ment** = state**ment**
EXCEPTIONS	argue + **ment** = argu**ment**
	true + **ly** = tru**ly**

Word Alert

If you are adding *–ly* to a word to make the word an adverb, be sure you add the suffix to the correct word. Two adverbs that are often confused are *respectively* and *respectfully*.

respectively—[respective + ly] in the order given

The postal abbreviations for Nebraska and Nevada are *respectively* NE and NV.

respectfully—[respectful + ly] in a polite or courteous manner

He answered his grandmother's curious questions *respectfully*.

Check Your Understanding

Adding Suffixes

Combine the base words and suffixes. Remember to make any necessary spelling changes.

1. lone + some
2. move + ment
3. like + ness
4. note + able
5. notice + able
6. guide + ance
7. peace + ful
8. pure + ity
9. create + ion
10. sure + ly
11. one + ness
12. outrage + ous
13. love + ly
14. close + est
15. hope + ful

Connect to the Writing Process: Editing
Spelling Words with Prefixes and Suffixes

Science Topic **Find the words in this paragraph that have prefixes or suffixes, and correct those that are spelled incorrectly.**

The continueous movment of air in the troposphere is the cause of all our weather. This air is not only restless, but it is full of water vapor. If all the water in the air were suddenly released, it would actualy cover the earth completly with three feet of water. The air moves constantly because the sun warms the earth unnevenly. In warmer places, the air rises, causing updrafts and the createion of clouds. In colder places, the air sinks. When masses of warm air and cold air meet, unpleaseant weather is the predictable effect.

Words Ending with *y*

To add a suffix to most words ending with a vowel and *y*, keep the *y*.

SUFFIXES WITH VOWELS AND *Y*		
Examples	enjoy + **able** = enjoy**able**	joy + **ful** = joy**ful**
Exceptions	day + **ly** = dai**ly**	gay + **ly** = gai**ly**

To add a suffix to most words ending in a consonant and *y*, change the *y* to *i* before adding the suffix.

SUFFIXES WITH CONSONANTS AND *Y*		
Examples	easy + **ly** = easi**ly**	worry + **ed** = worri**ed**
Exceptions	shy + **ness** = shy**ness**	study + **ing** = study**ing**

Doubling the Final Consonant

Sometimes the final consonant in a word is doubled before a suffix is added. This happens when the suffix begins with a vowel and the base word satisfies both these conditions: (1) It has only one syllable or is stressed on the final syllable, and (2) it ends in one consonant preceded by one vowel.

DOUBLE CONSONANTS	
One-Syllable Words	hop + ing = ho**pp**ing grin + ed = gri**nn**ed red + est = re**dd**est
Final Syllable Stressed	refer + al = refe**rr**al begin + er = begi**nn**er refer + ing = refe**rr**ing remit + ed = remi**tt**ed

Practice Your Skills

Check Your Understanding
Adding Suffixes

Combine the base words and suffixes. Remember to make any necessary spelling changes.

1. regret + able
2. play + ful
3. repel + ent
4. rely + able
5. mercy + less
6. slug + ish
7. grumpy + ly
8. deter + ent
9. sly + ness
10. defy + ant
11. coy + ly
12. pig + ish

Connect to the Writing Process: Editing
Adding Suffixes

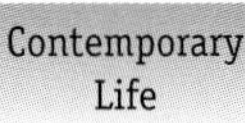

Rewrite this dialogue, correcting the words with suffixes that are spelled incorrectly.

"Mine is not an envyable duty," Inspector Fields began, struggling to overcome his shyness, "but I must ask you,

Lady Penelope, where you were when this regretable crime was commited?"

"It was midnight," Lady Penelope said huffyly. "I was where I ordinarily am at that hour—asleep in bed."

"What would you say if I told you that a relyable witness has testified that he saw you in the garden?"

"I would be compeled to question your witness's vision," Lady Penelope replyed with icy haughtyness.

Communicate Your Ideas

APPLY TO WRITING

Dialogue: *Suffixes*

Continue the dialogue between Inspector Fields and Lady Penelope to share with your classmates. You can decide what the regrettable crime was and what, if anything, Lady Penelope had to do with it. Use five words with suffixes in your dialogue.

Mixed Practice

Add the prefix or suffix to each base word, and write the new word.

1. pre + determine

2. move + able

3. prepare + ation

4. gay + ly

5. open + ness

6. true + ly

7. timid + ity

8. il + logical

9. create + ive
10. like + ly
11. play + ful
12. full + ly
13. believe + able
14. shake + ly
15. worry + ed
16. lonely + ness
17. pre + occupied
18. likely + hood
19. outrage + ous
20. begin + er
21. rebel + ed
22. spin + ing

WORDS TO MASTER

Make it your goal to learn to spell these fifty words this year. Use them in your writing and practice writing them until spelling them correctly comes automatically.

ach**ie**vement
a**ckn**owled**gm**ent
actua**ll**y
arg**um**ent
begi**nn**ing
bel**ie**ve
ch**ie**f
conc**ei**vable
contin**uo**us
co**rr**espond**en**ce
courag**eo**us
cur**ios**ity
eighth
ex**ceed**ingly
exce**ll**ent
exci**ta**ble
glor**io**us
gra**cio**us
happ**i**ness
ignor**a**nce
indispen**sa**ble
insur**a**nce
in**ter**esting
jud**gm**ent
l**ei**sure
lon**eli**ness
ma**rri**age
mil**ea**ge
natura**ll**y
n**ie**ce
notic**ea**ble
o**cc**asiona**ll**y
o**ccurr**ence
pre**cede**
prefe**rr**ed
prepa**ra**tion
pro**ceed**
read**ily**
reaso**na**bly
remo**va**l
requir**em**ent
resist**an**ce
ridicu**lo**us
sep**ar**ate
su**cceed**
su**cc**essful
tr**uly**
unfortunat**ely**
u**nn**eces**s**ary
w**ei**rd

CheckPoint

Applying Spelling Rules

Write the letter of the misspelled word in each group. Then write the word, spelling it correctly.

1.	(a) niece	(b) ratios	(c) happyness
2.	(a) intercede	(b) foriegn	(c) innumerable
3.	(a) embarass	(b) seize	(c) engagement
4.	(a) offered	(b) criticize	(c) atheletics
5.	(a) conceit	(b) branches	(c) niether
6.	(a) accidentally	(b) thinness	(c) payed
7.	(a) peaceful	(b) immediatly	(c) misstep
8.	(a) twentieth	(b) rideing	(c) argument
9.	(a) journies	(b) rained	(c) proceed
10.	(a) trapped	(b) knives	(c) permited
11.	(a) mispell	(b) relieve	(c) patios
12.	(a) immobile	(b) occuring	(c) betrayal
13.	(a) forcible	(b) spying	(c) mathmatics
14.	(a) surprised	(b) reign	(c) ridiculeous
15.	(a) realy	(b) stepping	(c) valleys
16.	(a) passersby	(b) leafs	(c) holidays
17.	(a) caring	(b) decieve	(c) studying
18.	(a) receipt	(b) beliefs	(c) easyly
19.	(a) echos	(b) misguided	(c) geese
20.	(a) joyful	(b) seperate	(c) interfere
21.	(a) biggest	(b) delaying	(c) liesure
22.	(a) generaly	(b) boxes	(c) roofs
23.	(a) pettiness	(b) disatisfied	(c) writer
24.	(a) anonymous	(b) likeness	(c) dayly
25.	(a) editors-in-chief	(b) grammer	(c) eighth

Another Look

Spelling Patterns *(pages L625–L626)*

When you spell words with *ie* or *ei, i* comes before *e* except when the letters follow *c* or when they stand for the long *a* sound.

Words that end in a syllable that sounds like "seed" are usually spelled with *-cede.* Only one word in English is spelled with *-sede,* and only three words are spelled with *-ceed.*

Plurals *(pages L627–L634)*

If a noun ends with *s, ch, sh, x,* or *z,* add *es* to form the plural.

Add *s* to form the plural of a noun ending with a vowel and *y.*

Change the *y* to *i* and add *es* to a noun ending in a consonant and *y.*

Add *s* to form the plural of a noun ending with a vowel and *o.*

The plurals of nouns ending in a consonant and *o* do not follow a regular pattern.

To form the plural of some nouns ending in *f* or *fe,* just add *s.*

For some nouns ending in *f* or *fe,* change the *f* to *v* and add *es* or *s.*

Most compound nouns are made plural in the same way as other nouns. The letters *s* or *es* are added to the end of the word. However, when the main word in a compound word appears first, that word becomes plural.

Spelling Numbers *(pages L637–L638)*

Spell out numbers that can be written in one or two words. Always spell out a number that begins a sentence.

Always spell out numbers used to tell order, or ordinal numbers.

Use a numeral for a date when you include the name of the month. Always use numerals for the year.

Prefixes and Suffixes *(pages L640–L643)*

The suffixes *-ness* and *-ly* are added to most base words without any spelling changes.

Drop the final *e* in a base word when adding a suffix that begins with a vowel.

Keep the final *e* when adding a suffix that begins with a consonant.

To add a suffix to most words ending with a vowel and *y,* keep the *y.*

To add a suffix to most words ending in a consonant and *y,* change the *y* to *i* before adding the suffix.

To add *-ing* or *-ed* to most words ending in a consonant, double the final consonant.

Directions

Read the passage. Write the letter of the choice that correctly spells each underlined word. If the word contains no error, write *D.*

EXAMPLE Whatever else you might say about P. T. Barnum, he was an exellent (1) salesman.

1 **A** excellent
B excellant
C excelent
D No error

ANSWER **1** **A**

P. T. Barnum began his life of odd acheivements (1) with the opening of his American Museum in 1842. When passersby (2) were treated to advertisements promising "The Eigth (3) Wonder of the World" and the like, it is little wonder that curiousity (4) brought the public in by the 1000s (5). Barnum went on to manage the outragously (6) successfull (7) tour of Swedish singer Jenny Lind. In 1871, he opened "The Greatest Show on Earth," designed to put all other circusses (8) to shame. Featureing (9) everything from men swallowing knifes (10) to the best of European acrobats, the circus merged with its major competitor in 1881 and was subsequently known as "Barnum & Bailey."

1 **A** achevements
B achievements
C achiefments
D No error

2 **A** passerbys
B passerbyes
C passers by
D No error

3 **A** 8th
B Eight
C Eighth
D No error

4 **A** curiosity
B curiusity
C curiousty
D No error

5 **A** 1000's
B 1000
C thousands
D No error

6 **A** outrageously
B outragousally
C outragely
D No error

7 **A** successful
B sucesfull
C succesful
D No error

8 **A** circusies
B circi
C circuses
D No error

9 **A** Featurring
B Featuring
C Featureng
D No error

10 **A** kniffes
B knives
C knife
D No error

A Study Guide for Academic Success

To succeed academically, you should be not only familiar with the material but also aware that there are various test-taking strategies. In some ways, preparing for a test is like learning to play chess. You can't simply sit across from an opponent and announce, "Checkmate." You must first learn the rules of the game, the ways the pieces can move, and the strategies for attacking and defending. If you learn the strategies and apply helpful tips and pointers, for example, you can become both a better chess player and a better test taker. Also, the more practice you have, the better prepared you will be to play a difficult match or take an important test.

In the following chapter, you will become familiar with the various questions used in standardized tests. Pay close attention to the "rules" for each kind of question and the strategies used to master them. These lessons and practice exercises will help you develop your test-taking strengths.

Keep in mind that many of the abilities you acquire in this chapter will carry over into homework and daily classroom assignments and beyond. Learning how to read different kinds of information and developing strategies for approaching different types of questions will help you sharpen the critical thinking skills you use when you do homework, play sports, and make important decisions.

Learning Study Skills

Applying good study habits helps you in taking tests as well as in completing daily classroom assignments. Begin to improve your study habits by using the following strategies.

Strategies for Effective Studying

- Choose an area that is well lighted and quiet.
- Equip your study area with everything you need for reading and writing, including a dictionary and a thesaurus.
- Keep an assignment book for recording due dates.
- Allow plenty of time. Begin your assignments early.
- Adjust your reading rate to suit your purpose.

Adjusting Reading Rate to Purpose

Your reading rate is the speed at which you read. Depending on your purpose in reading certain material, you may decide to read quickly or slowly. If your purpose is to get a general impression of the material, you may quickly read only parts of a page. If your purpose is to find the main point of a selection, you read more thoroughly. When you are reading to learn specific information, you slow your reading rate considerably to allow for close attention to facts and details.

Scanning

Read the title, headings, subheadings, picture captions, words and phrases in boldface or italics, and any focus questions. You can quickly determine what the material is about and what questions to keep in mind. **Scanning** is reading to get a general impression and to prepare for learning about a subject.

Skimming

After scanning a chapter, section, or article, quickly read the introduction, the topic sentence and summary sentence of each paragraph, and the conclusion. **Skimming** is reading quickly to identify the purpose, thesis, main ideas, and supporting ideas of a selection. Skimming is useful for reading supplementary material and for reviewing material previously read.

Close Reading

After scanning a selection, read it more slowly, word for word. **Close reading** is for locating specific information, following the logic of an argument, or comprehending the meaning or significance of information. Most of your assignments for school will require close reading.

Taking Notes

Taking notes helps you to identify and remember the essential information in a textbook or lecture. Three methods of taking notes are the informal outline, the graphic organizer, and the summary.

In an **informal outline,** you use words and phrases to record main ideas and important details. This method is especially useful when you are studying for a multiple-choice test because it allows you to see the most important facts.

In a **graphic organizer,** words and phrases are arranged in a visual pattern to indicate the relationships between main ideas and supporting details. This is an excellent tool for studying information for an objective test, for an open-ended assessment, or for writing an essay. The visual organizer allows you, instantly, to see important information and its relationship to other ideas.

In a **summary** you use sentences to express important ideas in your own words. A good summary should do more than restate the information. It should express relationships among the ideas and draw conclusions. For this reason, summarizing is a good way to prepare for an essay test.

Whether you are taking notes in modified outline form or in summary form, include only the main ideas and important details. In the following passage from a science textbook, the essential information is underlined.

MODEL: Essential Information

Characteristics of Fish

All fish have certain characteristics in common. For example, all fish have backbones and are cold-blooded. In addition, most fish breathe through gills. The gills, which are found on either side of a fish's head, take up oxygen that is dissolved in water. As a fish opens its mouth, water enters and passes over the gills, where oxygen molecules diffuse from the water into the fish's blood. At the same time, carbon dioxide passes out of its blood into the water.

Other characteristics of most fish include scales, which cover and protect their bodies, and fins, which aid fish in swimming. Certain fins act as steering guides, while others help a fish keep its balance in the water. Another aid in swimming that most fish have is a streamlined body, one in which the head and tail are smaller and more pointed than the middle part of the body. This streamlined shape helps fish swim by making it easier for them to push water aside as they propel themselves through the water.

INFORMAL OUTLINE:

Characteristics of Fish

1. Have backbones and are cold-blooded (all)
2. Breathe through gills (most)
3. Have scales, fins, and streamlined bodies (most)

GRAPHIC ORGANIZER:

Characteristics of Fish

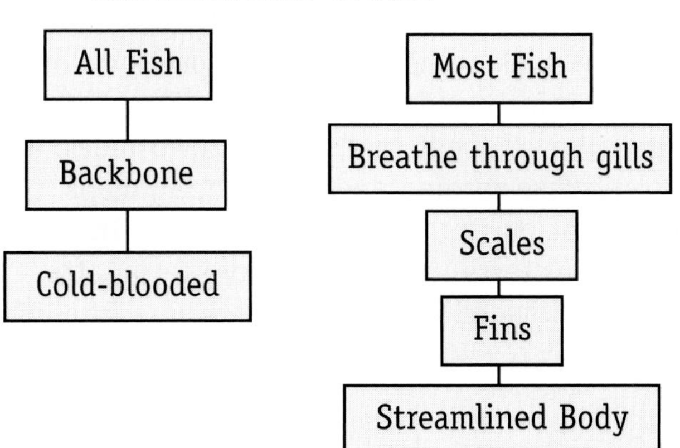

Characteristics of Fish

SUMMARY: All fish share two common characteristics: backbones and cold-bloodedness. Most fish breathe through gills and have scales for protection. Most fish also have fins and streamlined bodies for efficient swimming.

No matter which note-taking method you use, the following strategies will help make your notes clear and useful.

Strategies for Taking Notes

- Label your notes with the title and page numbers of the chapter or the topic and date of the lecture.
- Record only the main ideas and important details, using key words and phrases.
- Use the titles, subtitles, and words in special type to help you select the most important information.
- Use your own words; do not copy word for word.
- Use as few words as possible.

Preparing Subject-Area Assignments

The strategies you have learned in this chapter for reading textbooks and taking notes can be applied to assignments in any subject area.

Mathematics and science textbooks often list rules, formulas, equations, or models. In these subjects, you should focus on applying the rules or models to solve problems or show the truth of scientific principles.

History, government, and economics courses, on the other hand, emphasize reading and interpreting maps, charts, graphs, time lines, documents, and statistical data. In preparing for these assignments or tests, you should pay special attention to information provided in those formats.

Taking Standardized Tests

Standardized tests measure your skills, progress, and achievement in such a way that the results can be compared with those of other students in the same grade. Standardized tests that measure your verbal or language skills are divided into two broad categories: analogy tests and tests of reading and writing ability.

Strategies for Taking Standardized Tests

- Read the test directions carefully. Answer sample questions to be sure you are following the instructions.
- Try to relax. You can expect to be a little nervous, but concentrate on doing your best.
- Skim the entire section to get an overview of the kinds of questions you will be asked.
- Plan your time carefully. Be aware of how much time you are allotted for each part of the test.
- Answer first the questions you find easiest. Skip questions you find too difficult, but come back to them later.
- Read all the choices before selecting the best answer. If you are not sure of an answer, eliminate choices that are obviously incorrect. Educated guessing often helps.
- If you have time, check your answers. Be sure you have correctly marked your answer sheet.

Analogies

Analogy questions test your skill at figuring out relationships between words. The first step is to determine how the two words are related. The second step is to decide which other pair has the same relationship as the words in capital letters.

The punctuation in an analogy question stands for the words *is to* and *as.*

CLOCK : TIME :: thermometer : temperature

The example reads, "A *clock* is to *time* as a *thermometer* is to *temperature.*" That is, a clock has the same relationship to time as a thermometer has to temperature. A clock measures time as a thermometer measures temperature.

Try to explain to yourself in one sentence the relationship between the two words in capital letters. In the following example, you might say, "Handlebars are part of a bicycle."

HANDLEBARS : BICYCLE ::
(A) moose : antlers
(B) tire : fender
(C) carpenter : hammer
(D) steering wheel : automobile
(E) golf : sport

(The answer is *(D) steering wheel : automobile* because the relationship between these two words is that of part to whole; a steering wheel is part of an automobile.

Remember that the words in the answer must be in the same order as the words in the given analogy. If the given pair of words in the analogy expresses a cause-to-effect relationship, the words in the correct answer should also be in order of cause to effect.

Rain is to *flood* as *virus* is to ■.
(A) computer (B) drought (C) illness (D) energy
(E) nurse

(The first two italicized words are a cause and an effect: rain causes flood. Therefore, the correct answer is *(C) illness,* an effect of a virus.)

Knowing some of the common types of analogies, like those in the following chart, will help you figure out word relationships.

COMMON TYPES OF ANALOGIES

Analogy	Example
word : synonym	plain : simple
part : whole	lens : camera
cause : effect	burn : pain
worker : tool	gardener : shovel
item : purpose	pencil : write

Practice Your Skills

Check Your Understanding

Recognizing Analogies

Write the letter of the word pair that has the same relationship as the word pair in capital letters.

1. DENTIST : DRILL ::
(A) calendar : date
(B) sculptor : chisel
(C) lumberjack : forest
(D) eyeglasses : sight
(E) hammer : carpenter

2. HASTEN : HURRY ::
(A) laugh : talk
(B) trust : doubt
(C) stammer : whisper
(D) attempt : try
(E) explain : understand

Check Your Understanding

Completing Analogies

Complete the analogy by writing the letter of the word that best completes the sentence.

3. *Carelessness* is to *error* as *exploration* is to ■.
(A) invention
(B) bravery
(C) sailing
(D) artifacts
(E) discovery

4. *Page* is to *book* as *card* is to ■.
(A) king
(B) clubs
(C) deck
(D) suit
(E) joker

Sentence-Completion Tests

Sentence-completion tests measure your ability to comprehend what you read and to use context correctly. Each item consists of a sentence with one or more words missing. First read the entire sentence. Then read the answer choices and select the one that completes the sentence in a way that makes sense.

The town of Odessa, Delaware, now has a population of only five hundred, but it was once a ■ seaport.
(A) fascinating
(B) tiny
(C) Pacific
(D) bustling
(E) sleepy

(The answer is *(D) bustling*. The sentence contrasts the small size of the town today with its previous size.)

Some sentence-completion questions have two blanks in the same sentence, with each answer choice including two words.

Even today, the ■ of the soldiers who bravely fought in World War II is remembered with ■.

(A) fear . . . scorn
(B) courage . . . horror
(C) honor . . . indifference
(D) story . . . anger
(E) heroism . . . pride

(The answer is *(E) heroism . . . pride*. None of the other choices fit the idea of remembering brave soldiers.)

Practice Your Skills

Check Your Understanding

Completing Sentences

Write the letter of the word that best completes each of the following sentences.

1. Sharks do not have good eyesight, but their sense of smell is ■.
(A) poor
(B) keen
(C) decisive
(D) huge
(E) inferior

2. After ten to fourteen days in its chrysalis, the monarch caterpillar ■ as a beautiful monarch butterfly.
(A) transforms
(B) becomes
(C) emerges
(D) looms
(E) struggles

Check Your Understanding

Completing Sentences with Two Blanks

Write the letter of the words that best complete each of the following sentences.

3. The ■ empire fell shortly after a series of ■ battles with an invading army.
(A) new . . . successful
(B) Roman . . . victorious
(C) mighty . . . easy
(D) crumbling . . . ruinous
(E) old . . . jubilant

4. The abandoned warehouse was an eyesore with its windows ■, its paint ■, and its roof sagging.
(A) gleaming . . . shining
(B) sparking . . . fading
(C) open . . . bright
(D) cracked . . . peeling
(E) broken . . . vivid

Reading Comprehension Tests

Reading comprehension tests assess your ability to understand and analyze written passages. The information you need to answer the test questions may be either directly stated or implied in the passage. You must study, analyze, and interpret a passage in order to answer the questions that follow it. The following strategies will help you answer questions on reading tests.

Strategies for Answering Reading Questions

- Begin by skimming the questions that follow the passage.
- Read the passage carefully and closely. Notice the main ideas, organization, style, and key words.
- Study all possible answers. Avoid choosing one answer the moment you think it is a reasonable choice.
- Use only the information in the passage when you answer the questions. Do not rely on your own knowledge or ideas on this kind of test.

Most reading questions will focus on one or more of the following characteristics of a written passage.

- **Main idea** At least one question will usually focus on the central idea of the passage. Remember that the main idea of a passage covers all sections of the passage—not just one section or paragraph.
- **Supporting details** Questions about supporting details test your ability to identify the statements in the passage that back up the main idea.
- **Implied meanings** In some passages not all information is directly stated. Some questions ask you to interpret information that the author has merely implied.
- **Purpose and Tone** Questions on purpose and tone require that you interpret or analyze the author's attitude toward his or her subject and purpose for writing.

Practice Your Skills

Check Your Understanding
Reading for Comprehension

Read the following passage and write the letter of each correct answer.

KIDNAPPED BY UFO ALIENS. You have seen countless newspaper headlines or television stories like this. Although such tales are common today, hoaxes and rumors about space creatures go back many years. One famous example, the "*Sun* moon story," dates to 1835. In August of that year, the *New York Sun* announced that a distinguished British astronomer had made some wondrous discoveries while using a new telescope. The newspaper printed a series of articles describing the plants, animals, and winged men that lived on the moon. The stories helped make the *Sun* the best-selling daily newspaper in the world. Eventually reporter Richard Adams Locke admitted making up the articles. After the truth was discovered, Edgar Allan Poe abandoned a story he had begun about a man who flies to the moon in a balloon. He claimed to have been "outdone" by the newspaper's tales.

While readers of the *Sun* enjoyed the fantastic descriptions of life on the moon, listeners of another great hoax were terrified. Orson Welles's 1938 broadcast of "War of the Worlds" caused alarm all across the United States. In 1898, when the story was actually written, Mars was in close proximity to Earth. People could easily observe it and speculate about possible life on the planet. The writer, H. G. Wells, created a tale of Martian invaders with powerful new weapons resembling the atomic, nuclear, and biological weapons known to us today. When the story was broadcast over the radio in 1938, World War I was a recent event and World War II was fast approaching. Most listeners were panic-stricken; few recognized the program as fiction. Today, we are less afraid of an alien invasion, but we are just as fascinated by the idea of meeting life from outer space.

1. The "*Sun* moon story" met with
   (A) contempt from the scientific community.
   (B) enthusiasm from readers worldwide.
   (C) skepticism from the public.
   (D) fear about an alien invasion.
   (E) jealousy from other American writers.
2. The passage indicates that space creature hoaxes
   (A) are always believed.
   (B) are usually treated as harmless practical jokes.
   (C) often involve little green men.
   (D) have existed for over a hundred years.
   (E) began in the 1930s.
3. This passage would most likely appear in
   (A) a science fiction novel.
   (B) a textbook on the solar system.
   (C) a history of American newspapers.
   (D) an article on the rise of NASA.
   (E) a book on public fascination with life in outer space.

The Double Passage

You may also be asked to read a pair of passages and answer questions about each passage individually and about the way the two passages relate to each other. The two passages may present similar or opposing views or may complement each other in other ways. A brief introduction preceding the passages may help you anticipate the relationship between them.

Practice Your Skills

Check Your Understanding

Reading for Double-Passage Comprehension

These passages present two descriptions of tropical islands. The first passage is from an article called "An Aloha State of Mind" by William Ecenbarger. The second is from *In the South Seas* by Robert Louis Stevenson. Read each passage and answer the questions that follow.

Passage 1

Hot golden sunshine covers everything along Maui's southern coast, as though someone has spilled it. On the beaches, children, sugared in sand, whittle away at their parents' patience, while honeymooners stroll by, hand in hand, through the white lace left by the retreating surf. Coppery sunbathers stretch out like cookies on a baking sheet. . . .

Not far inland, Haleakala volcano begins its steep, 10,000-foot ascent, and about halfway up, there are thin layers of drifting clouds. It's twenty degrees cooler here, and the air is redolent with eucalyptus, woodsmoke, and the odors of earth and cattle. Looking down the slope you can see the beach five miles away. The sea appears as an immense blue fabric, rumpled and creased, and ends with the scrawling signature of the shore.

Passage 2

I have watched the morning break in many quarters of the world; it has been certainly one of the chief joys of my existence, and the dawn that I saw with the most emotion shone upon the Bay of Anaho. The mountains abruptly overhang the port with every variety of surface and of inclination, lawn, and cliff, and forest. Not one of these but wore its proper tint of saffron, of sulphur, of the clove, and of the rose. The lustre was like that of satin; on the lighter hues there seemed to float an efflorescence; a solemn bloom appeared on the more dark. The light itself was the ordinary light of morning, colourless and clean; and on this ground of jewels, pencilled out the least detail of drawing. Meanwhile, around the hamlet, under the palms, where the blue shadow lingered, the red coals of cocoa husk and the light trails of smoke betrayed the awakening business of the day . . . .

1. The tone of Passage 1 is
(A) humorous
(B) poetic
(C) sarcastic
(D) objective
(E) ironic

2. The author of Passage 1 probably wrote the passage to
(A) encourage people to visit Maui.
(B) warn people about the dangers of sunbathing.
(C) inform people about the volcanoes of Hawaii.
(D) describe the tourists who visit the islands.
(E) persuade people to write for travel magazines.

3. Which of the following best describes the author's purpose in Passage 2?
(A) to argue for conservation of tropical islands
(B) to persuade other travelers to visit the Bay of Anaho
(C) to describe a beautiful morning scene
(D) to show off his writing skills
(E) to inform people what life is like for the people of the South Seas.

4. Both authors would probably agree with which of the following statements?
(A) The Bay of Anaho is a beautiful site.
(B) Maui is a popular destination for tourists.
(C) The richest colors on earth exist in the sunrise.
(D) Too much sun is bad for your skin.
(E) Tropical islands are wonderful to visit.

Tests of Standard Written English

Objective tests of standard written English assess your knowledge of the language skills used for writing. They contain sentences with underlined words, phrases, and punctuation. The underlined parts will contain errors in grammar, usage, mechanics, vocabulary, and spelling. You are asked to find the error in each sentence, or, on some tests, to identify the best way to revise a sentence or passage.

Error Recognition

The most familiar way to test grammar, usage, capitalization, punctuation, word choice, and spelling is through an error-recognition sentence. A typical test item of this kind is a sentence with five underlined choices. Four of the choices suggest possible errors. The fifth choice, *E,* states that there is no error.

> Some scientists believe (A) that the first dog's (B) were (C) tamed over (D) 10,000 years ago.
>
> (The answer is *B*. The word *dogs* should not have an apostrophe because it is plural, not possessive.)

Some sentences have no errors. Before you choose *E (No error),* however, be sure that you have carefully studied every part of the sentence. The errors are often hard to notice.

Remember that the parts of a sentence not underlined are presumed to be correct. You can use clues in the correct parts of the sentence to help you search for errors in the underlined parts.

PRACTICE YOUR SKILLS

Check Your Understanding

Recognizing Errors in Writing

Write the letter that is below the underlined word or punctuation mark that is incorrect. If the sentence contains no error, write *E*.

(1) Temperatures on summer nights are (A) often cooler (B) in the suburbs then (C) in (D) the city. **(2)** One reason for the difference is (A) that (B) suburbs have less (C) buildings than (D) the city has. **(3)** During the day city streets, sidewalks, (A) and buildings (B) absorb (C) the Summer (D) heat. **(4)** At night the suburbs cool (A) down, (B) but, (C) the city does (D) not. **(5)** Buildings and streets release (A) the heat absorbed during the day, (B) this heat keeps (C) the city warmer throughout the night. (D) **(6)** The suburbs have (A) more trees (B) and grass that hold (C) rainwater (D) near the surface. **(7)** The water evaporates (A) in the heat, (B) and cools (C) down the temperature. (D) **(8)** Furthermore, the trees, (A) like (B) a fan, (C) keeps (D) a breeze blowing. **(9)** Tall and unbending, (A) the buildings in the city retain (B) the warm air as (C) an oven does. (D) **(10)** Its (A) easy to understand why people (B) often try (C) to leave the city to visit the countryside on a hot July (D) weekend.

Sentence-Correction Questions

Sentence-correction questions assess your ability to recognize appropriate phrasing. Instead of locating an error in a sentence, you must select the most appropriate way to write the sentence.

In this kind of question, a part of the sentence is underlined. The sentence is then followed by five different ways of writing the underlined part. The first way shown, (A), simply repeats the original underlined portion. The other four give alternative ways of writing the underlined part. The choices may involve grammar, usage, capitalization, punctuation, or word choice. Be sure that the answer you choose does not change the meaning of the original sentence.

Many colleges and universities in the United States, such as The College of William and Mary in Virginia, is named after historical figures.

(A) Virginia, is named after historical figures.
(B) Virginia. Is named after historical figures.
(C) Virginia is named after historical figures.
(D) Virginia, are named after historical figures.
(E) Virginia are named after historical figures.

(The answer is *(D)*. The verb *is* must be changed to agree with the subject *colleges and universities.* Choices *(A)*, *(B)*, and *(C)* do not correct the subject-verb agreement problem. Choice *(E)* adds an error by removing the comma.)

Practice Your Skills

Check Your Understanding
Correcting Sentences

Write the letter of the correct way, or the best way, of phrasing the underlined part of each sentence.

1. Is it true that Betsy Ross probably didn't never sew the first American flag?
(A) didn't never sew the first American flag?
(B) didn't ever sew the first american flag?
(C) didn't never sewed the first American flag?
(D) didn't sew the first American flag?
(E) did not never sew the first american flag?

2. There is shiny white and gold fish in the pool in my grandmother's garden.
(A) There is shiny white and gold fish
(B) There is shiny white, and gold fish
(C) There are shiny white and gold fish
(D) There are shiny white, and gold fish
(E) Here is shiny white and gold fish

Revision-in-Context

Another type of multiple-choice question that appears on some standardized tests is called revision-in-context. The questions following the reading ask you to choose the best revision of a sentence, a group of sentences, or the essay as a whole or to clearly identify the writer's intention.

Practice Your Skills

Check Your Understanding
Correcting Sentences

Carefully read the passage, which is the beginning of an essay about *The Jungle Book.* Answer the questions that follow.

(1) Rudyard Kipling's collection of stories known as *The Jungle Book* features tales about animals and people living in India. **(2)** One story is about a mongoose named Rikki-Tikki-Tavi. **(3)** It is his job to protect his adopted family from two cobras. **(4)** The cobras are called Nag and Nagaina. **(5)** Threatening the other animals in the garden and the family in the house are the large and powerful cobras. **(6)** Despite the odds against him, the little mongoose must find a way to defeat the deadly cobras.

1. In relation to the rest of the passage, which of the following best describes the writer's intention in sentence 6?
   (A) to restate the opening sentence
   (B) to propose an analysis of the story
   (C) to explain a metaphor
   (D) to interest the reader in the outcome of the story
   (E) to summarize the paragraph

2. Which best combines sentences 2, 3, and 4?
   (A) One story is about Rikki-Tikki-Tavi, a mongoose who must protect his adopted family from the cobras Nag and Nagaina.
   (B) One story is about Rikki-Tikki-Tavi, who must protect his adopted family from two cobras.
   (C) One story is about a mongoose who must protect his adopted family from Nag and Nagaina.
   (D) One story is about Rikki-Tikki-Tavi, who must protect his adopted family from Nag and Nagaina.
   (E) Protecting his adopted family from the cobras Nag and Nagaina is the mongoose Rikki-Tikki-Tavi.

Taking Essay Tests

Essay tests are designed to assess both your understanding of important ideas and your ability to see connections, or relationships, between these ideas. You must be able to organize your thoughts quickly and express them logically and clearly.

Kinds of Essay Questions

Always begin an essay test by reading the instructions for all the questions. Then, as you reread the instructions for your first question, look for key words, such as those in the box.

KINDS OF ESSAY QUESTIONS	
ANALYZE	Separate into parts and examine each part.
COMPARE	Point out similarities.
CONTRAST	Point out differences.
DEFINE	Clarify meaning.
DISCUSS	Examine in detail.
EVALUATE	Give your opinion
EXPLAIN	Tell how, what, or why.
ILLUSTRATE	Give examples.
SUMMARIZE	Briefly review main points.
TRACE	Show development or progress.

As you read the instructions, jot down what is required in your answer or circle key words and underline key phrases.

> Evaluate the contributions of Louis Pasteur to the world of science in a short essay of three paragraphs. Use specific examples. Be sure to include his "germ theory of disease," which states that most infectious diseases are caused by germs.

Writing an Effective Essay Answer

Writing an essay for a test is basically the same as writing any essay. Therefore, you should recall and apply all you have learned about using the writing process to write an essay. The major difference is that you will have a very strict time limit.

Prewriting — Writing Process

Because of the limited time in a test situation, you must carefully plan your essay. You should first brainstorm for ideas and organize your answer by writing a simple informal outline or constructing a graphic organizer. This plan will give structure to your essay and help you avoid omitting important points.

OUTLINE: **Louis Pasteur's Contributions to Science**

(thesis statement)

1. Contribution 1: "germ theory of disease"

2. Contribution 2: immunization

3. Contribution 3: pasteurization

(conclusion)

Your next step is to write a thesis statement. It is often possible to reword the test question into a thesis statement.

ESSAY QUESTION: Evaluate the contributions of Louis Pasteur to the world of science in a short essay. Use specific examples. Be sure to include his "germ theory of disease," which states that most infectious diseases are caused by germs.

THESIS STATEMENT: Louis Pasteur was a great scientist whose contributions, including the "germ theory of disease," revolutionized the world of science.

Drafting — Writing Process

As you write your essay, keep the following strategies in mind.

Strategies for Writing an Essay Answer

- Write an introduction that includes the thesis statement.
- Follow the order of your outline, writing one paragraph for each main point.

- Provide adequate support for each main point—using specific facts, examples, and/or other supporting details.
- Use transitions to connect your ideas and/or examples.
- End with a strong concluding statement that summarizes the main idea of the essay.
- Write clearly and legibly.

Model: Essay Test Answer

THESIS STATEMENT:

Louis Pasteur was a great scientist whose contributions, including the "germ theory of disease," revolutionized the world of science. Before Pasteur proposed the "germ theory of disease," the causes of infectious diseases were unknown. After Pasteur discovered that tiny microbes passed from person to person, infecting each with disease, he argued for cleaner hospital practices. The germs of one patient were no longer passed to another through nonsterile instruments, dirty bed linens, and shared air.

Pasteur's research also led him to immunization. Although another scientist first created the vaccine for smallpox, Pasteur took the idea and applied it to other diseases, including rabies. He discovered that by using a weaker form of the virus that causes rabies, he could protect dogs from contracting the stronger form of the virus. Also, he was able to develop a cure for humans who had been bitten by rabid animals.

Pasteur's reputation as a great scientist led the Emperor Napoleon III to request his help with another problem. The French economy was suffering because French wine was diseased and unsellable. After some investigation, Pasteur discovered that the wine could be heated so that the germs were killed, but the wine remained

CONCLUSION: unaffected. This process is now called pasteurization and is applied to many perishable foods, including beer and milk. Pasteur's research and discoveries have led to healthier lives all over the world.

Always leave a few minutes to revise and edit your essay answer. As you revise, think of the following questions.

- Did you thoroughly follow the instructions?
- Did you begin with a thesis statement?
- Did you include facts, examples, and other details?
- Did you use transitions to connect ideas and examples?
- Did you end with a strong concluding statement that summarizes your essay?
- Did you stick to the topic?

Once you have made revisions, quickly read your essay for mistakes in spelling, usage, or punctuation. Use proofreading symbols to make changes. As you edit, check for the following:

- agreement between subjects and verbs *(chapter 12)*
- agreement of antecedents and pronouns *(pages L355–L358)*
- avoidance of tense shift *(pages L310–L311)*
- correct capitalization of proper nouns and proper adjectives *(pages L464–L480)*
- correct use of apostrophes *(pages L575–L588)*

Timed Writing

Throughout your school years, you will be tested on your ability to organize your thoughts quickly and to express them in a limited time. Time limits can vary from twenty to sixty to ninety minutes, depending upon the task. For a twenty-minute essay, you might consider organizing your time in the following way:

5 minutes: Brainstorm and organize ideas.
12 minutes: Write a draft.
3 minutes: Revise your work and edit it for mistakes.
12
1
2
3
4
5
6
7
8
9
10
11

The more you practice writing under time constraints, the better prepared you will be for tests.

Communicate Your Ideas

APPLY TO WRITING

Prewriting, Drafting, Revising, Editing: *Timed Writing*

You will have twenty minutes to write a complete essay on the following topic.

- Discuss an important issue facing people of your age today. Explain why this issue is important and how you think people should respond to it.

Plan time for each stage of the writing process, set a timer, and begin your response.

GLOSSARY

A

Abbreviation shortened form of a word.

Abstract summary of points of writing, presented in skeletal form.

Action verb word that tells what action a subject is performing.

Active voice the voice a verb is in when it expresses that the subject is performing the action.

Adequate development quality of good writing in which sufficient supporting details develop the main idea.

Adjective word that modifies a noun or a pronoun.

Adjective clause subordinate clause that is used like an adjective to modify a noun or a pronoun.

Adjective phrase prepositional phrase that is used to modify a noun or a pronoun.

Adverb word that modifies a verb, an adjective, or another adverb.

Adverb clause subordinate clause that is used like an adverb to modify a verb, an adjective, or an adverb.

Adverb phrase prepositional phrase that is used like an adverb to modify a verb, an adjective, or an adverb.

Alliteration repetition of a consonant sound at the beginning of a series of words.

Analogies logical relationships between pairs of words.

Antecedent word or group of words that a pronoun replaces or refers to.

Antonym word that means the opposite of another word.

Appositive noun or a pronoun that identifies or explains another noun or pronoun in a sentence.

Article the special adjectives *a, an, the.*

Audience person or persons who will read your work or hear your speech.

B

Body one or more paragraphs comprised of details, facts, and examples that support the main idea.

Brainstorming prewriting technique of writing down everything that comes to mind about a subject.

Business letter writing form that uses formal language and contains six parts: heading, inside address, salutation, body, closing, and signature.

C

Case form of a noun or a pronoun that indicates its use in a sentence. In English there are three cases: the nominative case, the objective case, and the possessive case.

Cause and effect method of development in which details are grouped according to what happens and why it happens.

Characterization variety of techniques used by writers to show the personality of a character.

Chronological order the order in which events occur.

Clarity the quality of being clear.

Classics literary works that withstand the test of time and appeal to readers from generation to generation and from century to century.

Classification method of development in which details are grouped into categories.

Clause group of words that has a subject and verb and is used as part of a sentence.

Clause fragment subordinate clause standing alone.

Cliché overused expression that is no longer fresh or interesting to the reader.

Clustering a visual form of brainstorming that is a technique used for developing supporting details.

Coherence logical and smooth flow of ideas connected with clear transitions.

Colloquialism informal phrase or colorful expression appropriate for conversation but not for formal writing.

Comparison and contrast method of development in which details are grouped according to similarities and differences.

Complement word that completes the meaning of an action verb.

Complete predicate all the words that tell what the subject is doing or that tell something about the subject.

Complete subject all the words used to identify the person, place, thing, or idea that the sentence is about.

Complex sentence one independent clause and one or more subordinate clauses.

Composition writing form that presents and develops one main idea in three or more paragraphs.

Compound-complex sentence two or more independent clauses and one or more subordinate clauses.

Compound noun word made up of two smaller words that can be separated, hyphenated, or combined.

Compound sentence two or more independent clauses in one sentence.

Compound subject two or more subjects in one sentence that have the same verb and are joined by a conjunction.

Compound verb two or more verbs that have the same subject and are joined by a conjunction.

Concluding sentence a strong ending added to a paragraph that summarizes the major points, refers to the main idea, or adds an insight.

Conclusion paragraph that completes an essay and reinforces its main idea.

Conflict struggle between opposing forces around which the action of a work of literature revolves.

Conjunction word that joins together sentences, clauses, phrases, or other words.

Connotation the meaning that comes from attitudes attached to a word.

Context clue clue to a word's meaning provided by the sentence, the surrounding words, or the situation in which the word occurs.

Contraction word that combines two words into one. It uses an apostrophe to replace one or more missing letters.

Cooperative learning strategy in which a group works together to achieve a common goal or accomplish a single task.

Coordinating conjunction single connecting word used to join words or groups of words.

Correlative conjunction pairs of conjunctions used to connect compound subjects, compound verbs, and compound sentences.

Creative writing writing style in which the writer creates characters, events, and images within stories, plays, or poems to express feelings, perceptions, and points of view.

D

Dangling modifier phrase that has nothing to describe in a sentence.

Declarative sentence a statement or expression of an opinion. It ends with a period.

Definition method of development in which the nature and characteristics of a word, object, concept, or phenomenon are explained.

Demonstrative pronoun word that substitutes for a noun and points out a person or a thing.

Denotation the literal meaning of a word.

Descriptive writing writing that creates a vivid picture of a person, an object, or a scene by stimulating the reader's senses.

Dewey decimal system system by which nonfiction books are arranged on shelves in numerical order according to ten general subject categories.

Dialect regional variation of a language distinguished by distinctive pronunciation and some differences in word meanings.

Dialogue a conversation between two or more persons.

Direct object noun or pronoun that receives the action of a verb.

Direct quotation passage, sentence, or words written or spoken exactly as a person wrote or said them.

Double negative use of two negative words to express an idea when only one is needed.

Drafting stage of the writer's process in which he or she draws together ideas on paper.

E

Editing stage of the writing process in which the writer polishes his or her work by correcting errors in grammar, usage, mechanics, and spelling.

Elaboration addition of explanatory or descriptive information, such as supporting details, facts, and examples, to an essay.

Electronic publishing various ways to present information through the use of technology. It includes desktop publishing (creating printed documents on a computer), audio and video recordings, and online publishing (creating a Website).

Elliptical clause subordinate clause in which words are omitted but understood to be there.

E-mail electronic mail that can be sent all over the world from one computer to another.

Emoticons symbols used by E-mail users to convey emotions.

Encyclopedia reference that contains general information about a variety of subjects.

Endnote complete citation of the source of borrowed material at the end of a research report.

Essay composition that presents and develops one main idea in three or more paragraphs.

Essential phrase or clause group of words essential to the meaning of a sentence; therefore, not set off with commas.

Etymology history of a word, from its earliest recorded use to its present use.

Exclamatory sentence expression of strong feeling. It ends with an exclamation point.

F

Fact statement that can be proved.

Fiction prose works of literature, such as short stories and novels, which are partly or totally imaginary.

Figurative language imaginative, nonliteral use of language.

Footnote complete citation of the source of borrowed material at the bottom of a page in a research report.

Free verse poetry without meter or a regular, patterned beat.

Freewriting prewriting technique of writing freely about ideas as they come to mind.

Friendly letter writing form that may use informal language and contains a heading, salutation, body, closing, and signature.

G

Gerund a verb form ending in *–ing* that is used as a noun.

Glittering generality word or phrase that most people associate with virtue and goodness that is used to trick people into feeling positively about a subject.

H

Helping verb auxiliary verb that helps to make up a verb phrase.

I

Idiom phrase or expression that has a meaning different from what the words suggest in their usual meanings.

Imperative sentence a direction, a request, or a command. It ends with either a period or an exclamation point.

Indefinite pronoun word that substitutes for a noun and refers to an unnamed person or thing.

Independent clause group of words that stands alone as a sentence because it expresses a complete thought.

Indirect object noun or a pronoun that answers the question *to* or *from whom?* or *to* or *for what?* after an action verb.

Infinitive verb form that usually begins with *to* and is used as a noun, an adjective, or an adverb.

Informative writing writing that provides information or explains a process.

Inquiring prewriting technique in which the writer asks questions such as *Who? What? Where? Why?* and *When?*

Interjection a word that expresses strong feeling.

Internet a worldwide network of computers (see also *Basic Internet Terminology* in *a Writer's Guide to Using the Internet*).

Interrogative pronoun used to ask a question.

Interrogative sentence a question. It ends with a question mark.

Intransitive verb action verb that does not pass the action from a doer to a receiver.

Introduction paragraph in an essay that introduces a subject, states or implies a purpose, and presents a main idea.

Irregular verb verb that does not form its past and past participle by adding *–ed* to the present form.

J

Jargon specialized vocabulary used in particular professions.

Journal a daily notebook in which a writer records personal thoughts and feelings.

L

Linking verb verb that links the subject with another word in the sentence. This other word either renames or describes the subject.

Listening the process of comprehending, evaluating, organizing, and remembering information presented orally.

Literary analysis interpretation of a work of literature supported by appropriate responses, details, and quotations.

Loaded words subjective words that are interjected into a seemingly objective context to emotionally sway the audience without the audience knowing it.

M

Metaphor figure of speech that compares by implying one thing is another.

Meter rhythm of a specific beat of stressed and unstressed syllables found in many poems.

Misplaced modifier phrase or clause that is placed too far away from the word it modifies, thus creating an unclear sentence.

Mood overall atmosphere or feeling created by a work of literature.

N

Narrative writing writing that tells a real or an imaginary story.

Nonessential phrase or clause group of words that is not essential to the meaning of a sentence and is therefore set off with commas.

Nonfiction prose writing that contains facts about real people and real events.

Noun word that names a person, a place, a thing, or an idea. A common noun gives a general name. A proper noun names a specific person, place, or thing and always begins with a capital letter. A collective noun names a group of people or things.

Noun clause subordinate clause that is used like a noun.

Novel long work of narrative fiction.

O

Observing prewriting technique that helps a writer use the powers of observation to gather details.

Occasion motivation for composing; the factor that prompts communication.

Onomatopoeia use of words whose sounds suggest their meaning.

Opinion belief or judgment that cannot be proved.

Oral interpretation performance or expressive reading of a literary work.

Order of importance order in which supporting evidence is arranged from least to most (or most to least) important.

Outline information about a subject organized into main topics and subtopics.

P

Paragraph group of related sentences that present and develop one main idea.

Parallelism one or more ideas linked with coordinate or correlative conjunctions and expressed in the same grammatical form.

Parenthetical citation credit for a source of information within or at the end of a sentence; cites source and page number.

Participial phrase participle with its modifiers and complements—all working together as an adjective.

Participle verb form that is used as an adjective.

Passive voice the voice a verb is in when it expresses that the action is being performed upon its subject.

Peer conference meeting with one's peers, such as other students, to share ideas and offer suggestions for revision.

Personal pronoun type of pronoun that can be categorized into one of three groups, dependent on the speaker position: first person (*I*), second person (*you*), and third person (*she/he*).

Personal writing writing that expresses the writer's personal point of view on a subject drawn from the writer's own experience.

Personification comparison in which human qualities are given to an animal, an object, or an idea.

Persuasive writing writing that expresses an opinion on a subject and uses facts, examples, and reasons to convince readers.

Phrase group of related words that functions as a single part of speech and does not have a subject and a verb.

Plagiarism act of using another person's words, pictures, or ideas without giving proper credit.

Play composition written for dramatic performance on the stage.

Plot sequence of events leading to the outcome or point of the story.

Poem highly structured composition that expresses powerful feeling with condensed, vivid language, figures of speech, and often the use of meter and rhyme.

Point of view vantage point from which a writer tells a story or describes a subject.

Portfolio collection of work representing various types of writing and the progress made on them.

Possessive pronoun pronoun used to show ownership or possession.

Predicate part of a sentence that gives information about the subject.

Predicate adjective adjective that follows a linking verb and modifies the subject.

Predicate nominative noun or pronoun that follows a linking verb and identifies, renames, or explains the subject.

Prefix one or more syllables placed in front of a root or base word to modify the meaning of the root or base word or to form a new word.

Preposition word that shows the relationship between a noun or a pronoun and another word in the sentence.

Prepositional phrase group of words that has no subject or verb and that modifies, or describes, other words in a sentence.

Prewriting invention stage in the writing process in which the writer plans for drafting based on the subject, occasion, audience, and purpose for writing.

Principal parts of a verb the *present*, the *past*, and the *past participle*. The principal parts help form the tenses of verbs.

Progressive verb form verbs used to express continuing or ongoing action. Each of the six verb tenses has a progressive form.

Pronoun word that takes the place of one or more nouns.

Proofreading carefully rereading and making corrections in grammar, usage, spelling, and mechanics in a piece of writing.

Proofreading symbols kind of shorthand that writers use to correct their mistakes while editing.

Propaganda effort to persuade by distorting and misrepresenting information or by disguising opinions as facts.

Proper adjective adjective formed from a proper noun.

Publishing stage of a writer's process in which the writer may choose to share the work with an audience or make the work "public."

Purpose reason for writing or speaking.

Q

Quatrain four-line stanza in a poem.

R

Readers' Guide to Periodical Literature print or online index of magazine and journal articles.

Reflecting act of thinking quietly and calmly about an experience.

Reflexive pronoun pronoun that is formed by adding *–self* or *–selves* to a personal pronoun. It is used to reflect back to the subject of the sentence.

Regular verb verb that forms its past and past participle by adding *–ed* to the present.

Relative pronoun pronoun that relates an adjective clause to the modified noun or pronoun.

Research paper a composition of three or more paragraphs that uses information drawn from books, periodicals, media sources, and interviews with experts.

Revising stage of a writer's process in which the writer rethinks what is written and reworks it to increase its clarity, smoothness, and power.

Rhyme scheme regular pattern of rhyming in a poem.

Rhythm sense of flow produced by the rise and fall of accented and unaccented syllables.

Root part of a word that carries the basic meaning.

Run-on sentence two or more sentences that are written together and are separated by a comma or have no mark of punctuation at all.

S

Sensory details details that appeal to one of the five senses: seeing, hearing, touching, tasting, and smelling.

Sentence group of words that expresses a complete thought.

Sentence base a subject, a verb, and a complement.

Sentence combining method of combining short sentences into longer, more fluent sentences by using phrases and clauses.

Sentence fragment group of words that does not express a complete thought.

Sequential order the order in which details are arranged according to when they take place or where they are done.

Setting environment (location and time) in which the action takes place.

Short story short work of narrative fiction.

Simile figure of speech comparing two objects using the words *like* or *as*.

Simple predicate main word or phrase in the complete predicate.

Simple sentence one independent clause.

Simple subject main word in a complete subject.

Slang nonstandard expressions developed and used by particular groups.

Sound devices ways to use sounds in poetry to achieve certain effects.

Spatial order order in which details are arranged according to their location.

Speech oral composition presented by a speaker to an audience.

Stanza group of lines in a poem that the poet decides to set together.

Style visual or verbal expression that is distinctive to an artist or writer.

Subject word or group of words that names the person, place, thing, or idea that the sentence is about; topic of a composition.

Subject complement renames or describes the subject and follows a linking verb. The two kinds are predicate nominatives and predicate adjectives.

Subordinate clause group of words that cannot stand alone as a sentence because they do not express a complete thought.

Subordinating conjunction single connecting word used in a complex sentence to introduce an adverb clause.

Suffix one or more syllables placed after a root or base word to change the word's part of speech and possibly also its meaning.

Summary information written in a condensed, concise form, touching only on the main ideas.

Supporting sentences specific details, facts, examples, or reasons that explain or prove a topic sentence.

Symbol object, event, or character that stands for a universal idea or quality.

Synonym word that has nearly the same meaning as another word.

T

Tense form a verb takes to show time. The six tenses are the *present*, *past*, *future*, *present perfect*, *past perfect*, and *future perfect*.

Theme underlying idea, message, or meaning of a work of literature.

Thesaurus specialized print or online dictionary of synonyms.

Thesis statement statement of the main idea that makes the writing purpose clear.

Tired word word that has been so overused that it has been drained of meaning.

Tone writer's attitude toward the subject and audience of a composition (closely related to the writer's *voice*).

Topic sentence statement of the main idea of the paragraph.

Transitions words and phrases that show how ideas are related.

Transitive verb action verb that passes the action from a doer to a receiver.

U

Understood subject unstated subject that is understood.

Unity combination or ordering of parts in a composition so that all the sentences or paragraphs work together as a whole to support one main idea.

V

Verb word that expresses action or a state of being.

Verbal verb form used as some other part of speech.

Verb phrase main verb plus any helping, or auxiliary, verbs.

Voice particular sound and rhythm of language that the writer uses (closely related to *tone*).

W

World Wide Web network of computers within the Internet, capable of delivering multimedia content and text over communication lines into personal computers all over the globe.

Wordiness use of words and expressions that add nothing to the meaning of a sentence.

Working thesis statement that expresses the possible main idea of a composition or research report.

Works cited page an alphabetical listing of sources cited in a research paper.

Writing process recursive stages that a writer proceeds through in his or her own way when developing ideas and discovering the best way to express them.

Note: Italic page numbers indicate skill sets.

Note: Italic page numbers indicate skill sets.

Note: Italic page numbers indicate skill sets.

Note: Italic page numbers indicate skill sets.

INDEX

Note: Italic page numbers indicate skill sets.

Note: Italic page numbers indicate skill sets.

Note: Italic page numbers indicate skill sets.

Note: Italic page numbers indicate skill sets.

INDEX

Note: Italic page numbers indicate skill sets.

INDEX

Note: Italic page numbers indicate skill sets.

Note: Italic page numbers indicate skill sets.

Note: Italic page numbers indicate skill sets.

Note: Italic page numbers indicate skill sets.

INDEX

Note: Italic page numbers indicate skill sets.

Note: Italic page numbers indicate skill sets.

Note: Italic page numbers indicate skill sets.

Note: Italic page numbers indicate skill sets.

INDEX

Note: Italic page numbers indicate skill sets.

Note: Italic page numbers indicate skill sets.

INDEX

Note: Italic page numbers indicate skill sets.

Barrett Kendall Publishing has made every effort to trace the ownership of all copyrighted selections in this book and to make full acknowledgment of their use. Grateful acknowledgment is made to the following authors, publishers, agents, and individuals for their permission to reprint copyrighted material.

Composition

C3: Copyright © 1987 by Sandra Cisneros. First published in *The Texas Observer,* September 1987. Reprinted by permission of Susan Bergholz Literary Services, New York. All rights reserved. **C57:** From *I Know Why The Caged Bird Sings* by Maya Angelou. Copyright © 1969 and renewed 1997 by Maya Angelou. Reprinted by permission of Random House, Inc. **C91:** Copyright © 1958 by *Harper's* magazine. All rights reserved. Reproduced from the October issue by special permission. **C165:** Copyright © 1976 by Paxton Davis. Excerpt from *A Flag At The Pole,* published by Atheneum. Reprinted by permission of Curtis Brown, Ltd. **C217:** From *When Heaven and Earth Changed Places* by Le Ly Hayslip. Copyright © 1989 by Le Ly Hayslip and Charles Jay Wurts. Used by permission of Doubleday, a division of Random House, Inc. **C251:** From *Barrio Boy* by Ernesto Galarza. Copyright © 1971 by University of Notre Dame Press. Reprinted by permission of the publisher. **C285:** Copyright © 1982 by Annie Dillard. Reprinted by permission of HarperCollins Publishers, Inc. **C293:** Reprinted by permission of International Creative Management, Inc. Copyright © 2000 Joanna Greenfield **C299, C301:** Reprinted by permission of Sterling Lord Literistic, Inc. Copyright 1978 by Barry Holstun Lopez. **C325:** Reprinted by permission of International Creative Management, Inc. Copyright © 1999 Arthur Miller. **C332:** Reprinted with permission of Scribner, a Division of Simon & Schuster, from *Winner Take Nothing* by Ernest Hemingway. Copyright 1933 by Charles Scribner's Sons. Copyright renewed © 1961 by Mary Hemingway. **C360:** Reprinted by permission of International Creative Management, Inc. Copyright © 1999 Arthur Miller. **C372:** From *The Poetry of Robert Frost,* edited by Edward Connery Lathem. Copyright 1923, © 1969 by Henry Holt and Company, LLC. Copyright © 1951 by Robert Frost. Reprinted by permission of Henry Holt and Company, LLC. **C373:** *House of Light: Poems by Mary Oliver.* © 1990 by Mary Oliver. Beacon Press. **C385:** From *A History of US: All the People,* Volume 10 by Joy Hakim. Copyright © 1995 by Joy Hakim. Used by permission of Oxford University Press, Inc. **C433:** Courtesy of Gary Kimble, and the Cleveland Indians. **C471:** From "Say It with Flowers" by Toshio Mori. Reprinted by permission of Caxton Press. **C521:** From "Rancho Buena Vista: It's a Way of Life and Traditions" by Fermina Guerra, from *Texan Stomping Ground,* by J. Frank Dobie. Publications of the Texas Folklore Society, No. XVII, 1941. **C587:** National Space Society. **C623:** Copyright © 1999 by the New York Times Co. Reprinted by permission. **C631:** Reprinted by arrangement with The Heirs to the Estate of Martin Luther King, Jr., c/o Writers House, Inc. as agent for the proprietor. Copyright 1963 by Martin Luther King, Jr., copyright renewed 1991 by Coretta Scott King.

Language

L10: Excerpt from "The Washwoman" from *A Day of Pleasure* by Isaac Bashevis Singer. Copyright © 1969 by Isaac Bashevis Singer. Copyright renewed © 1997 by the Estate of Isaac Bashevis Singer. Reprinted by permission of Farrar, Straus and Giroux, LLC. **L22:** Copyright 1975 Lilian Moore. Used by permission of Marian Reiner for the author. **L41:** Excerpt from *In the Heart of the Country* by William Gass. Copyright © 1968 by William Gass. Reprinted by permission of the author. **L360:** "Taught Me Purple" courtesy of *Negro Digest* magazine. **L360:** From *The Collected Poems* by Langston Hughes. Copyright © 1994 by the Estate of Langston Hughes. Reprinted by permission of Alfred A. Knopf, Inc. **L459:** Reprinted by permission of the publishers and the Trustees of Amherst College from *The Poems of Emily Dickinson,* Ralph W. Franklin ed., Cambridge, Mass. The Belknap Press of Harvard University Press, copyright © 1998 by the President and Fellows of Harvard College. Copyright 1951, 1955, 1979 by the President and Fellows of Harvard College. **L460:** Excerpt from "Always a Rose," copyright © 1986 by Li-Young Lee. Reprinted from *Rose* by Li-Young Lee with the permission of BOA Editions, Ltd. **L463:** The lines from "somewhere i have never travelled, gladly beyond." Copyright 1931, © 1959, 1991 by the Trustees for the E.E. Cummings Trust. Copyright © 1979 by George James Firmage, from *Complete Poems: 1904–1962* by E.E. Cummings, edited by George J. Firmage. Used by permission of Liveright Publishing Corporation. **L606:** Excerpt from "Furious Versions" copyright © 1990 by Li-Young Lee. Reprinted from *The City in Which I Love You,* by Li-Young Lee, with permission of BOA Editions, Ltd. **L610:** Reprinted by permission of the publishers and the Trustees of Amherst College from *The Poems of Emily Dickinson,* Ralph W. Franklin ed., Cambridge, Mass. The Belknap Press of Harvard University Press, copyright © 1998 by the President and Fellows of Harvard College. Copyright 1951, 1955, 1979 by the President and Fellows of Harvard College.

PHOTO CREDITS

Key: (t) top, (c) center, (b) bottom, (l) left, (r) right.

Composition and Language title pages: (cl) *Patiently Waiting* by Michael Mortimer Robinson. Michael Mortimer Robinson/SuperStock

Composition

C3: © Burke Triolo/FoodPix/PictureQuest. **C8:** Michael T. Sedam/Corbis. **C27:** © Jonathan Blair/Corbis. **C62:** © John Biggers. Photograph by Earlie Hudnall. **C87:** © Karl Weatherly/Corbis. **C91:** © John Cancalosi/ Stock Boston/PictureQuest. **C96: (t)** © John Cancalosi/ Stock Boston/PNI; **(b)** © Tim Davis/Allstock/PNI. **C149:** © Burke Triolo/FoodPix/PictureQuest. **C171:** Scott Polar Research Institute. **C198:** © John Noble/Corbis. **C217:** © Wolfgang Kaehler/Corbis. **C220:** © Ric Ergenbright/ Corbis. **C285:** © Judd Cooney/Phototake/PictureQuest. **C290:** The Minneapolis Institute of Arts, the Kate and Hall J. Peterson Fund. **C325:** S. Krulwich/NYT Pictures. **C385:** David Sams/Stock Boston/Picture Quest. **C390:** © Archive Photos/PNI. **C457:** © Perry Conway/Corbis. **C502:** © Mike Kelly. **C525:** © Corbis. **C576:** © Raymond

Gehman/Corbis. **C595: (l)** © American Lung Association; **(r)** © American Lung Association. **C659: (t)** © PhotoSphere/PictureQuest; **(b)** © Asian Art & Archaeology, Inc./Corbis. **C660:** © Wolfgang Kaehler/Corbis.

Language

L4, L22: © Jaune Quick-to-See Smith. Courtesy of Bernice Steinbaum Gallery, Miami, FL. **L25:** National Gallery, Oslo, Norway/Bridgeman Art Library. **L265:** © 1996 Board of Trustees, National Gallery of Art, Washington, D.C. Chester Dale Collection. © 2000 Estate of Pablo Picasso/Artists Rights Society (ARS), New York. **L38, L62:** The Museum of Modern Art, New York, Mrs. Simon R. Guggenheim Fund. Photograph © 2001, The Museum of Modern Art, New York. © 2001 Artists Rights Society (ARS), New York/ADAGP, Paris. **L49:** © 1999, Sotheby's, Inc. **L68, L84:** Albright-Knox Art Gallery, Buffalo, New York. Gift of Seymour H. Knox, 1958. © Estate of Joan Mitchell. **L80:** © VCG/FPG International. **L90, L118:** © 2001 Artists Rights Society (ARS), New York/VG Bild-Kunst, Bonn. Photograph by Wolfgang von Contzen. **L112:** Photograph by Wolfgang Dietze, courtesy of Carmen Lomas Garza. **L124, L142:** © FPG International. **L148, L166:** The Roland P. Murdock Collection, Wichita Art Museum, Wichita, Kansas. **L172, L214:** The Metropolitan Museum of Art. Anonymous gift, 1983 (1983.251). Photograph © 1983 The Metropolitan Museum of Art. © Fernando Botero, *Dancing in Colombia,* 1980. Courtesy Marborough Gallery, NY. **L179:** The Art Institute of Chicago. Gift of Elizabeth R. Vaughan. Photograph © 1996, The Art Institute of Chicago. 1950.1846. All rights reserved. **L180:** Billy R. Allen Folk Art Collection. African American Museum, Dallas, Texas. Gift of Mr. and Mrs. Robert Decherd. **L220, L250:** Gift of the Container Corporation of America, National Museum of American Art, Smithsonian Institution, Washington, D.C./Art Resource, New York. Courtesy of the artist and Francine Seders Gallery, Seattle, Washington. **L235:** Copyright the Dorothea Lange Collection, The Oakland Museum of California, The City of Oakland. Gift of Paul S. Taylor. **L256, L272:** Courtesy of the Pennsylvania Academy of the Fine Arts, Philadelphia. Gift of Mrs. Sarah Harrison (The Joseph Harrison, Jr., Collection). **L278, L320:** Photograph by C. Lord. **L326, L368:** National Museum of American Art, Washington, D.C./Art Resource, New York. **L344:** © Bob Daemmrich. **L380, L412:** Photograph by Bill Kennedy. **L385:** LPI/M. Yada/FPG International. **L418, L438:** Copyright © 1996 Museum Associates, Los Angeles County Museum of Art. Gift of the Art Museum Council. **L425: (l)** Photograph courtesy Kyoto National Museum; **(r)** Andrew W. Mellon Collection. © 1996 Board of Trustees, National Gallery of Art, Washington, D.C. Photograph by Richard Carafelli. **L444:** Corbis. **L450:** © Charles Schneider/FPG International. **L458, L461:** Manley/SuperStock. **L477:** Barry Blackman/SuperStock. **L502, L542:** The Art Institute of Chicago, Mr. and Mrs. Martin A. Ryerson Collection, 1933.1158. Photograph © 1998 The Art Institute of Chicago. All rights reserved. **L510:** © Boltin Picture Library, Croton-on-Hudson, New York. **L574, L614:** The Metropolitan Museum of Art, H.O. Havemeyer Collection, bequest of Mrs. H.O. Havemeyer, 1929 (29.100.129). Photograph by Schecter Lee, © 1986 The Metropolitan Museum of Art. **L532, L569:** © The New Yorker Collection 1997 Leo Cullum from cartoonbank.com. All rights reserved.
L584: © The Phillips Collection, Washington, D.C.
L599: Zigy Kaluzny/Tony Stone Images.
L636: Roine Magnusson/Tony Stone Images.